Alan Rogers

t[illegible]t campsites

2010 EDITION

in France

Compiled by: Alan Rogers Guides Ltd

Designed by: Paul Effenberg, Vine Design Ltd

Additional photography: T Lambelin, www.lambelin.com
Maps created by Customised Mapping (01769 540044)
contain background data provided by GisDATA Ltd
Maps are © Alan Rogers Guides and GisDATA Ltd 2010

Published by: Alan Rogers Guides Ltd,
Spelmonden Old Oast, Goudhurst, Kent TN17 1HE
www.alanrogers.com Tel: 01580 214000

British Library Cataloguing-in-Publication Data:
A catalogue record for this book is available
from the British Library.

ISBN 978-1-906215-24-8

Print managed in Great Britain by DPI Print & Production Ltd
and printed by Stephens & George Print Group

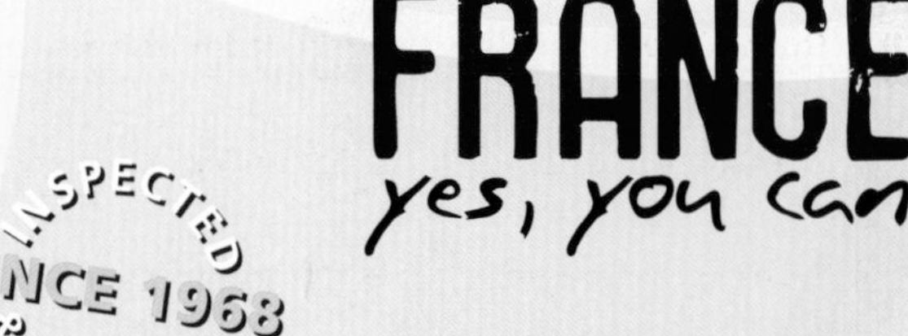

Contents

Alan Rogers

Alan Rogers – in search of 'the best'

Alan Rogers Guides were first published over 40 years ago. Since Alan Rogers published the first campsite guide that bore his name, the range has expanded and now covers 27 countries in five separate guides. No fewer than 20 of the campsites selected by Alan for the first guide are still featured in our 2010 editions.

There are over 11,000 campsites in France of varying quality: this guide contains impartially written reports on almost 1,000, including many of the very finest, each being individually inspected and selected. We aim to provide you with a selection of the best, rather than information on all – in short, a more selective, qualitative approach. New, improved maps and indexes are also included, designed to help you find the choice of campsite that's right for you. We hope you enjoy some happy and safe travels – and some pleasurable 'armchair touring' in the meantime!

Alan Rogers
the best campsites in France
2010 EDITION
INSPECTED SINCE 1968 & SELECTED
OVER 800 independent reviews

How do we find the best?

The criteria we use when inspecting and selecting sites are numerous, but the most important by far is the question of good quality. People want different things from their choice of campsite so we try to include a range of campsite 'styles' to cater for a wide variety of preferences: from those seeking a small peaceful campsite in the heart of the countryside, to visitors looking for an 'all singing, all dancing' site in a popular seaside resort. Those with more specific interests, such as sporting facilities, cultural events or historical attractions, are also catered for.

The size of the site, whether it's part of a chain or privately owned, makes no difference in terms of it being required to meet our exacting standards in respect of its quality and it being 'fit for purpose'. In other words, irrespective of the size of the site, or the number of facilities it offers, we consider and evaluate the welcome, the pitches, the sanitary facilities, the cleanliness, the general maintenance and even the location.

ALAN ROGERS' selected sites for caravanning and camping in Europe 1968

"...the campsites included in this book have been chosen entirely on merit, and no payment of any sort is made by them for their inclusion."

Alan Rogers, 1968

INSPECTED SINCE 1968 & SELECTED

Expert opinions

We rely on our dedicated team of Site Assessors, all of whom are experienced campers, caravanners or motorcaravanners, to visit and recommend campsites. Each year they travel some 100,000 miles around Europe inspecting new campsites for the guide and re-inspecting the existing ones. Our thanks are due to them for their enthusiastic efforts, their diligence and integrity.

We also appreciate the feedback we receive from many of our readers and we always make a point of following up complaints, suggestions or recommendations for possible new campsites. Of course we get a few grumbles too – but it really is a few, and those we do receive usually relate to overcrowding or to poor maintenance during the peak school holiday period. Please bear in mind that, although we are interested to hear about any complaints, we have no contractual relationship with the campsites featured in our guides and are therefore not in a position to intervene in any dispute between a reader and a campsite.

Independent and honest

Whilst the content and scope of the Alan Rogers guides have expanded considerably since the early editions, our selection of campsites still employs exactly the same philosophy and criteria as defined by Alan Rogers in 1968.

'telling it how it is'

Firstly, and most importantly, our selection is based entirely on our own rigorous and independent inspection and selection process. Campsites cannot buy their way into our guides – indeed the extensive Site Report which is written by us, not by the site owner, is provided free of charge so we are free to say what we think and to provide an honest, 'warts and all' description. This is written in plain English and without the use of confusing icons or symbols.

Looking for the best?

HIGHLY RESPECTED BY SITE OWNERS AND READERS ALIKE, THERE IS NO BETTER GUIDE WHEN IT COMES TO FORMING AN INDEPENDENT VIEW OF A CAMPSITE'S QUALITY. WHEN YOU NEED TO BE CONFIDENT IN YOUR CHOICE OF CAMPSITE, YOU NEED THE ALAN ROGERS GUIDE.

- SITES ONLY INCLUDED ON MERIT
- SITES CANNOT PAY TO BE INCLUDED
- INDEPENDENTLY INSPECTED, RIGOROUSLY ASSESSED
- IMPARTIAL REVIEWS
- OVER 40 YEARS OF EXPERTISE

Welcome to the 2010 Edition

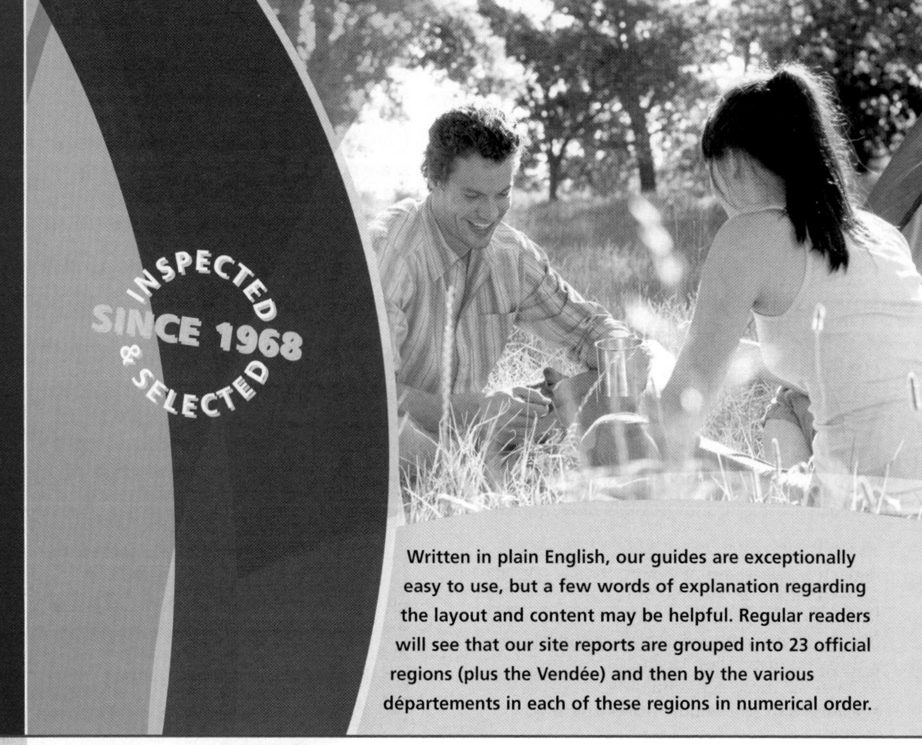

Written in plain English, our guides are exceptionally easy to use, but a few words of explanation regarding the layout and content may be helpful. Regular readers will see that our site reports are grouped into 23 official regions (plus the Vendée) and then by the various départements in each of these regions in numerical order.

Region

The Reports – *Example of an entry*

Index town

Site name

Postal address (including département) T: **telephone number**. E: **email address**
alanrogers.com web address (including Alan Rogers reference number)

A description of the site in which we try to give an idea of its general features – its size, its situation, its strengths and its weaknesses. This section should provide a picture of the site itself with reference to the facilities that are provided and if they impact on its appearance or character. We include details on pitch numbers, electricity (with amperage), hardstandings etc. in this section, as pitch design, planning and terracing affect the site's overall appearance. Similarly we include reference to pitches used for caravan holiday homes, chalets, and the like. Importantly at the end of this column we indicate if there are any restrictions, e.g. no tents, no children, naturist sites.

Facilities

Lists more specific information on the site's facilities and amenities and, where available, the dates when these facilities are open (if not for the whole season).

Off site: here we give distances to various local amenities, for example, local shops, the nearest beach, plus our featured activities (bicycle hire, fishing, horse riding, boat launching). Where we have space we list suggestions for activities and local tourist attractions.

Open: Site opening dates.

Directions

Separated from the main text in order that they may be read and assimilated more easily by a navigator en-route. Bear in mind that road improvement schemes can result in road numbers being altered.

GPS: references are provided as we obtain them for satellite navigation systems (in degrees and minutes).

Charges 2010 (or a general guide).

Maps, campsite listings and indexes

For this 2010 guide we have changed the way in which we list our campsites and also the way in which we help you locate the sites within each region.

We now include a map immediately after our Introduction to that region. These maps show the towns near which one or more of our featured campsites are located.

Within each regional section of the guide, we list these towns and the site(s) in that vicinity in alphabetical order.

You will certainly need more detailed maps for navigation, for example the Michelin atlas. We provide GPS coordinates for each site to assist you. Our three indexes will also help you to find a site by its reference number and name, by region and site name, or by the town where the site is situated.

Regions and départements

For administrative purposes France is divided into 23 official regions covering the 95 départements (similar to our counties). The départements included in each region are stated in our introductions, together with their official number (eg. the département of Manche is number 50). We use these département numbers as the first two digits of our campsite reference numbers, so any campsite in the Manche département will start with the number 50, prefixed with FR.

Facilities

Toilet blocks

We assume that toilet blocks will be equipped with a reasonable amount of British style WCs, washbasins with hot and cold water and hot showers with dividers or curtains, and will have all necessary shelves, hooks, plugs and mirrors. We also assume that there will be an identified chemical toilet disposal point, and that the campsite will provide water and waste water drainage points and bin areas. If not the case, we comment. We do mention certain features that some readers find important: washbasins in cubicles, facilities for babies, facilities for those with disabilities and motorcaravan service points. Readers with disabilities are advised to contact the site of their choice to ensure that facilities are appropriate to their needs.

Shop

Basic or fully supplied, and opening dates.

Bars, restaurants, takeaway facilities and entertainment

We try hard to supply opening and closing dates (if other than the campsite opening dates) and to identify if there are discos or other entertainment.

Children's play areas

Fenced and with safety surface (e.g. sand, bark or pea-gravel).

Swimming pools

If particularly special, we cover in detail in our main campsite description but reference is always included under our Facilities listings. We will also indicate the existence of water slides, sunbathing areas and other features. Opening dates, charges and levels of supervision are provided where we have been notified. There is a regulation whereby Bermuda shorts may not be worn in swimming pools (for health and hygiene reasons). It is worth ensuring that you do take 'proper' swimming trunks with you.

Leisure facilities

For example, playing fields, bicycle hire, organised activities and entertainment.

Dogs

If dogs are not accepted or restrictions apply, we state it here. Check the quick reference list at the back of the guide.

Off site

This briefly covers leisure facilities, tourist attractions, restaurants etc. nearby.

Charges

These are the latest provided to us by the sites. In those cases where 2010 prices have not been provided to us by the sites, we try to give a general guide.

Reservations

Necessary for high season (roughly mid-July to mid-August) in popular holiday areas (i.e. beach resorts). You can reserve many sites via our own Alan Rogers Travel Service or through other tour operators. Or be wholly independent and contact the campsite(s) of your choice direct, using the phone or e-mail numbers shown in the site reports, but please bear in mind that many sites are closed all winter.

Telephone numbers

All numbers assume that you are phoning from within France. To phone France from outside that country, prefix the number shown with the relevant International Code (00 33) and drop the first 0, shown as (0) in the numbers indicated.

Opening dates

Are those advised to us during the early autumn of the previous year – sites can, and sometimes do, alter these dates before the start of the following season, often for good reasons. If you intend to visit shortly after a published opening date, or shortly before the closing date, it is wise to check that it will actually be open at the time required. Similarly some sites operate a restricted service during the low season, only opening some of their facilities (e.g. swimming pools) during the main season; where we know about this, and have the relevant dates, we indicate it – again if you are at all doubtful it is wise to check.

Alan Rogers

Sometimes, campsite amenities may be dependent on there being enough customers on site to justify their opening and, for this reason, actual opening dates may vary from those indicated.

Some French site owners are very relaxed when it comes to opening and closing dates. They may not be fully ready by their stated opening dates – grass and hedges may not all be cut or perhaps only limited sanitary facilities open. At the end of the season they also tend to close down some facilities and generally wind down prior to the closing date. Bear this in mind if you are travelling early or late in the season – it is worth phoning ahead.

The Camping Cheque low season touring system goes some way to addressing this in that many participating campsites will have all key facilities open and running by the opening date and these will remain fully operational until the closing date.

476 Our Accommodation Section

Over recent years, more and more campsites have added high quality mobile home and chalet accommodation. In response to feedback from many of our readers, and to reflect this evolution in campsites, we have now decided to include a separate section on mobile homes and chalets. If a site offers this accommodation, it is indicated above the site report with a page reference where full details are given. We have chosen a number of sites offering some of the best accommodation available and have included full details of one or two accommodation types at these sites. Please note however that many other campsites listed in this guide may also have a selection of accommodation for rent.

Whether you're an 'old hand' in terms of camping and caravanning or are contemplating your first trip, a regular reader of our Guides or a new 'convert', we wish you well in your travels and hope we have been able to help in some way. We are, of course, also out and about ourselves, visiting sites, talking to owners and readers, and generally checking on standards and new developments.

We wish all our readers thoroughly enjoyable Camping and Caravanning in 2010 – favoured by good weather of course!

THE ALAN ROGERS TEAM

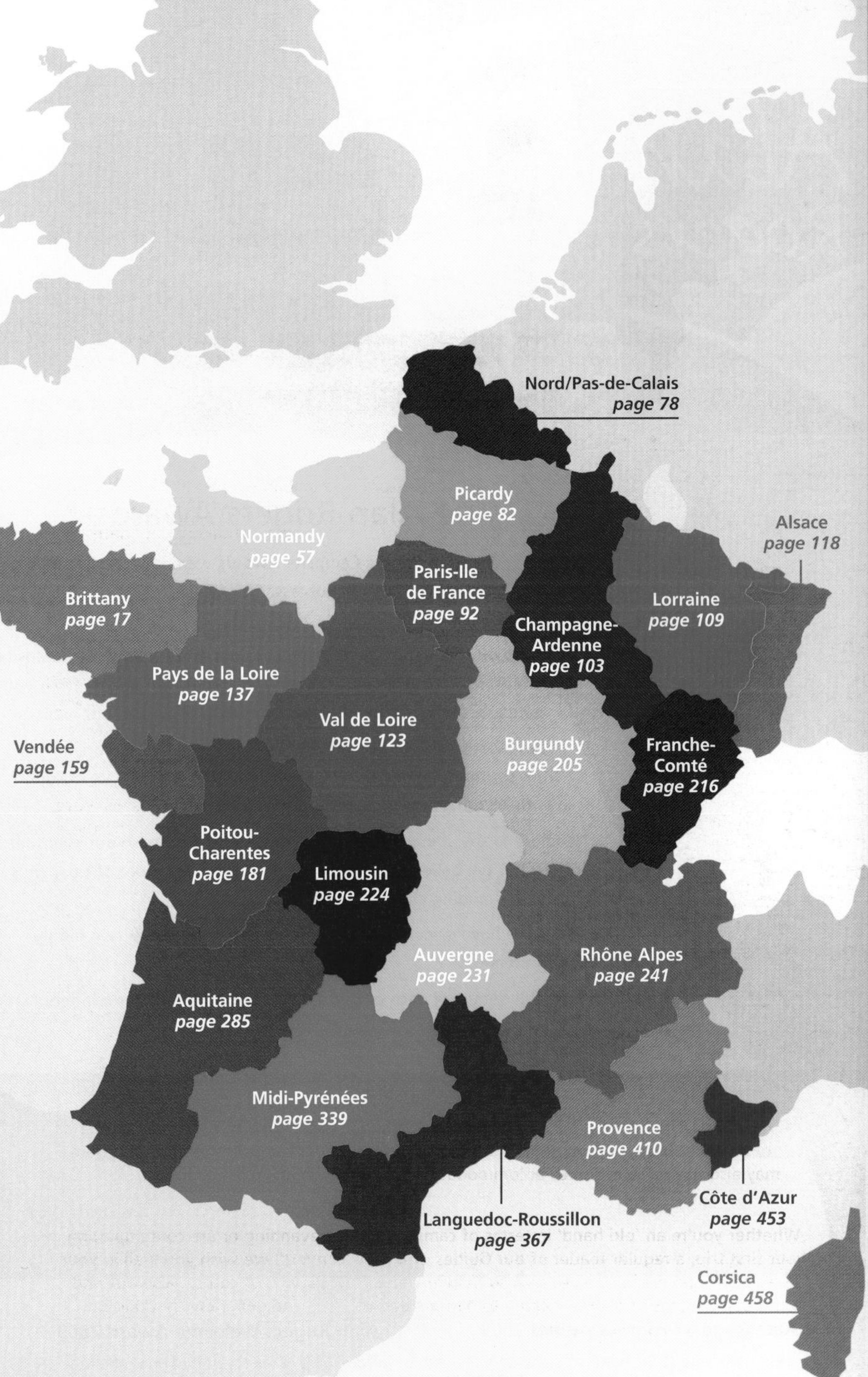
Nord/Pas-de-Calais
page 78
Picardy
page 82
Normandy
page 57
Alsace
page 118
Brittany
page 17
Paris-Ile
de France
page 92
Lorraine
page 109
Champagne-
Ardenne
page 103
Pays de la Loire
page 137
Val de Loire
page 123
Vendée
page 159
Burgundy
page 205
Franche-
Comté
page 216
Poitou-
Charentes
page 181
Limousin
page 224
Auvergne
page 231
Rhône Alpes
page 241
Aquitaine
page 285
Midi-Pyrénées
page 339
Provence
page 410
Côte d'Azur
page 453
Languedoc-Roussillon
page 367
Corsica
page 458

The Alan Rogers Awards

The Alan Rogers Campsite Awards were launched in 2004 and have proved a great success.

Our awards have a broad scope and before committing to our winners, we carefully consider more than 2,000 campsites featured in our guides, taking into account comments from our site assessors, our head office team and, of course, our readers.

Our award winners come from the four corners of Europe, from southern Portugal to Slovenia, and this year we are making awards to campsites in 13 different countries.

Needless to say, it's an extremely difficult task to choose our eventual winners, but we believe that we have identified a number of campsites with truly outstanding characteristics.

In each case, we have selected an outright winner, along with two highly commended runners-up.

Listed below are full details of each of our award categories and our winners for 2009.

Our warmest congratulations to all our award winners and our commiserations to all those not having won an award on this occasion.

THE ALAN ROGERS TEAM

Alan Rogers Progress Award 2009

This award reflects the hard work and commitment undertaken by particular site owners to improve and upgrade their site.

WINNER

FR40180 Le Vieux Port, France

RUNNERS-UP

FR29050 L'Orangerie de Lanniron, France

AU0265 Park Grubhof, Austria

Alan Rogers Welcome Award 2009

This award takes account of sites offering a particularly friendly welcome and maintaining a friendly ambience throughout reader's holidays.

WINNER

FR71070 Domaine de l'Eperviere, France

RUNNERS-UP

NL6970 't Weergors, Netherlands

UK0805 Woodovis, England

Alan Rogers Active Holiday Award 2009

This award reflects sites in outstanding locations which are ideally suited for active holidays, notably walking or cycling, but which could extend to include such activities as winter sports or water sports

WINNER

SV4200 Bled, Slovenia

RUNNERS-UP

FR29010 Ty Nadan, France

CZ4720 Frymburk, Czech Republic

Alan Rogers Motorhome Award 2009

Motorhome sales are increasing and this award acknowledges sites which, in our opinion, have made outstanding efforts to welcome motorhome clients.

WINNER

DE3003 Wulfener Hals, Germany

RUNNERS-UP

NL5675 Vliegenbos, Netherlands

DE3833 LuxOase, Germany

Alan Rogers 4 Seasons Award 2009

This award is made to outstanding sites with extended opening dates and which welcome clients to a uniformly high standard throughout the year.

WINNER

ES87420 La Marina, Spain

RUNNERS-UP

FR74230 Le Giffre, France

ES89650 Picos de Europa, Spain

Alan Rogers Seaside Award 2009

This award is made for sites which we feel are outstandingly suitable for a really excellent seaside holiday.

WINNER

IT68200 Baia Domizia, Italy

RUNNERS-UP

CR6765 Kovacine, Croatia

NL6870 De Lakens, Netherlands

Alan Rogers Country Award 2009

This award contrasts with our former award and acknowledges sites which are attractively located in delightful, rural locations.

WINNER

NL6285 Wildhoeve, Netherlands

RUNNERS-UP

FR85260 La Guyonniere, France

UK2030 Wareham Forest, England

Alan Rogers Rented Accommodation Award 2009

Given the increasing importance of rented accommodation on many campsites, we feel that it is important to acknowledge sites which have made a particular effort in creating a high quality 'rented accommodation' park.

WINNER

FR34110 Yelloh! Village Le Club Farret, France

RUNNERS-UP

SV4210 Sobec, Slovenia

DK2010 Hvidbjerg Strand, Denmark

Alan Rogers Unique Site Award 2009

This award acknowledges sites with unique, outstanding features – something which simply cannot be found elsewhere and which is an important attraction of the site.

WINNER

IT60370 International Jesolo, Italy

RUNNERS-UP

AU0525 Fisching 50+, Austria

PO8030 Rio Alto, Portugal

Alan Rogers Family Site Award 2009

Many sites claim to be child friendly but this award acknowledges the sites we feel to be the very best in this respect.

WINNER

IT60200 Union Lido, Italy

RUNNERS-UP

FR83020 Esterel Caravaning, France

HU5370 Napfeny, Hungary

Alan Rogers Readers' Award 2009

We believe our Readers' Award to be the most important. We simply invite our readers (by means of an on-line poll at **www.alanrogers.com**) to nominate the site they enjoyed most.

The outright winner for 2009 is:

WINNER

ES83900 Vilanova Park, Spain

FREE 2010 Brochure

call 01580 214000

Over 100 French campsites hand picked for you

www.**alanrogers.com/travel**

Book with us

For the best holidays on the best campsites

The Alan Rogers Travel Service was originally set up to provide a low cost booking service for readers. We pride ourselves on being able to put together a bespoke holiday, taking advantage of our experience, knowledge and contacts. Our experience is second to none and our prices are extremely competitive

Unbeatable ferry deals

At the Alan Rogers Travel Service we're always keen to find the best deals and keenest prices. There are always great savings on offer, and we're constantly negotiating new ferry rates and money-saving offers, so just call us on

01580 214000

and ask about the latest deals.

or visit www.**alanrogers.com/travel**

When you book with us, you will be allocated an experienced Personal Travel Consultant to provide you with personal advice and manage every stage of your booking. Our Personal Travel Consultants have first-hand experience of many of our campsites and access to a wealth of information. They can check availability, provide a competitive price and tailor your holiday arrangements to your specific needs.

- Discuss your holiday plans with a friendly person with first-hand experience
- Let us reassure you that your holiday arrangements really are taken care of
- Tell us about your special requests and allow us to pass these on
- Benefit from advice which will save you money – the latest ferry deals and more
- Remember, our offices are in Kent not overseas and we do NOT operate a queuing system!

The aims of the Travel Service are simple

- To provide convenience - a one-stop shop to make life easier.
- To provide peace of mind - when you need it most.
- To provide a friendly, knowledgeable, efficient service – when this can be hard to find.
- To provide a low cost means of organising your holiday – when prices can be so complicated.

HOW IT WORKS

Choose your campsite(s) – we can book around 500 across Europe. Look for the yellow coloured campsite entries in this book. You'll find more info and images at www.alanrogers.com/travel

Please note: the list of campsites we can book for you varies from time to time.

Then just call us for an instant quote

01580 214000

or visit

www.alanrogers.com/travel

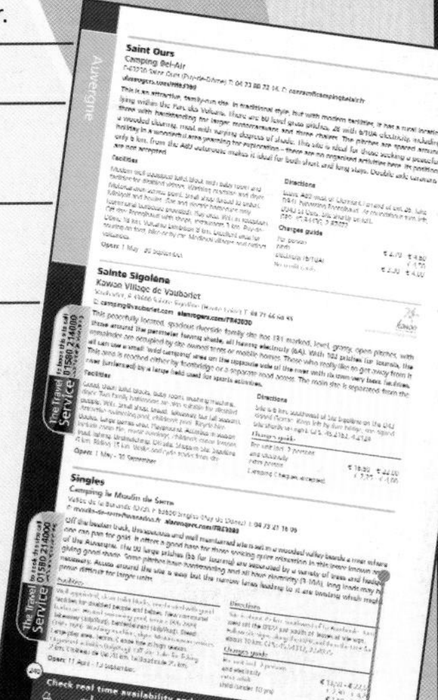

Auvergne

Saint Ours

Camping Bel-Air

Sainte Sigolène

Kawan Village de Vaubarlet

Singles

Camping le Moulin de Serre

Check real time availability and at-the-gate prices...

www.alanrogers.com

LOOK FOR A CAMPSITE ENTRY LIKE THIS TO INDICATE WHICH CAMPSITES WE CAN BOOK FOR YOU.

THE LIST IS GROWING SO PLEASE CALL FOR UP TO THE MINUTE INFORMATION.

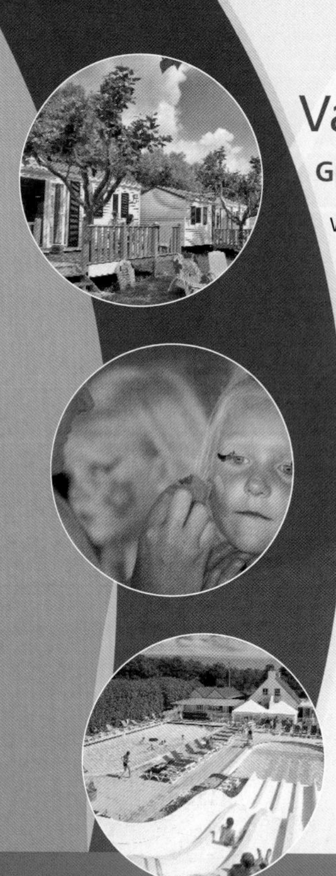

Value, Value, Value

Great Savings AND Complete Service

We work hard to offer quality and choice at remarkably low prices. And we pride ourselves on providing a friendly, personal service coupled with the in-depth knowledge of a specialist tour operator. We are not a large company and your holiday is important to us.

Our prices are based on the campsite's 'at-the-gate' prices. The campsite's own booking fees are not charged but are replaced by a standard Travel Service fee of just £45 per booking (not per site). Please bear in mind campsites typically charge a booking fee of around 30€ (perhaps £25) to customers booking direct - you will avoid this by booking with our Travel Service.

What's more, a campsite's own booking fee is charged at each campsite you visit. Our booking fee applies only once.

Our in-house travel team handles all aspects of your booking, for your peace of mind.

- **FREE** child places on most campsites – exclusive to the Travel Service
- Payment in sterling with no risk of exchange rate fluctuations
- Secure bookings – all campsite fees and deposits are paid in advance* with all ferry-inclusive holidays fully protected by our ABTA bond
- We have long-standing relationships with all campsites and Special Requests are passed on – details that can make a real difference
- Low cost ferries – special fares only available when booking a ferry-inclusive holiday
- **FREE** European Campsites sat nav disk (retails at £13.95) - directions to over 4,000 campsites
- A one-stop-shop for all your travel plans – campsite booking, overnight stops, low cost ferries and travel insurance – all in one place

** excluding any nominal local tourist taxes, payable locally*

Already Booked Your Ferry?

We're confident that our ferry inclusive booking service offers unbeatable value. However, if you have already booked your ferry then we can still make a pitch-only reservation for you (minimum 5 nights). Since our prices are based on our ferry inclusive service, you need to be aware that a non-ferry booking may result in slightly higher prices than if you were to book direct with the site.

It's all on-line

www.alanrogers.com/travel is a website designed to give you everything you need to know when it comes to booking your Alan Rogers inspected and selected campsite, and your low cost ferry.

Our friendly, expert team of travel consultants is always happy to help on

01580 214000 – but they do go home sometimes!

Campsite Information

- ✓ Details of all Travel Service campsites - **instantly**
- ✓ Find latest special offers on campsites - **instantly**
- ✓ Check campsite availability - **instantly**

Ferry Information

- ✓ Check ferry availability - **instantly**
- ✓ Find latest ferry deals - **instantly**
- ✓ Book your ferry online - **instantly**
- ✓ Save money - **instantly**

Alan Rogers

Crossing the Channel

One of the great advantages of booking your ferry-inclusive holiday with the Alan Rogers Travel Service is the tremendous value we offer. Our money-saving Ferry Deals have become legendary. As agents for all major cross-Channel operators we can book all your travel arrangements with the minimum of fuss and at the best possible rates.

Just call us for an instant quote

01580 214000

or visit

www.**alanrogers.com/travel**

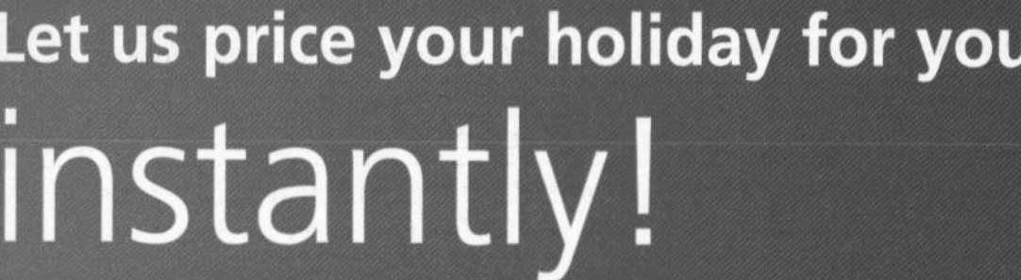

Let us price your holiday for you

instantly!

The quickest and easiest way is to call us for advice and an instant quote. We can take details of your vehicle and party and, using our direct computer link to all the operators' reservations systems, can give you an instant price. We can even check availability for you and book a crossing while you're on the phone!

Please note we can only book ferry crossings in conjunction with a campsite holiday reservation.

Rolling sandy beaches, hidden coves, pretty villages and a picturesque coastline all combine to make Brittany a very popular holiday destination. Full of Celtic culture steeped in myths and legends, Brittany is one of the most distinctive regions of France.

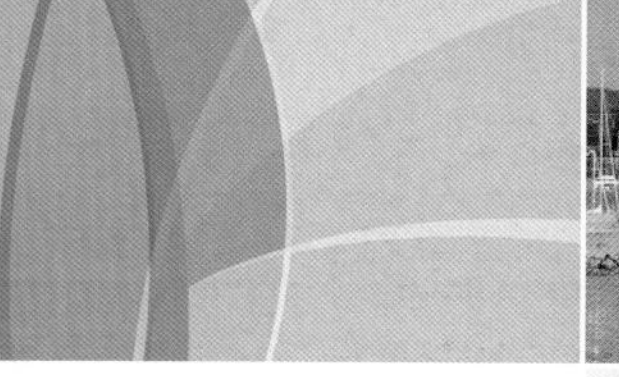

DÉPARTEMENTS: 22 CÔTES D'ARMOR, 29 FINISTÈRE, 35 ILLE-ET-VILAINE, 56 MORBIHAN

MAJOR CITIES: RENNES AND BREST

Brittany's 800 miles of rocky coastline offers numerous bays, busy little fishing villages and broad sandy beaches dotted with charming seaside resorts. The coastline to the north of Brittany is rugged with a maze of rocky coves, while to the south, the shore is flatter with long sandy beaches. Inland you'll find wooded valleys, rolling fields, moors and giant granite boulders, but most impressive is the wealth of prehistoric sites, notably the Carnac standing stones.

Breton culture offers a rich history of menhirs, crosses, cathedrals and castles. Strong Celtic roots provide this region with its own distinctive traditions, evident in the local Breton costume and music, traditional religious festivals and the cuisine, featuring crêpes and cider. Many castles and manor houses, countless chapels and old towns and villages provide evidence of Brittany's eventful history and wealth of traditions. The abbey fortress of Mont St Michel on the north coast (in Normandy) should not be missed and Concarneau in the south is a lovely walled town enclosed by granite rocks.

Places of interest

Cancale: small fishing port famous for oysters.

Carnac: 3,000 standing stones (menhirs).

Concarneau: fishing port, old walled town.

Dinan: historic walled town.

Perros-Guirec: leading resort of the 'Pink Granite Coast'.

Quiberon: boat service to three islands: Belle Ile (largest of the Breton islands), Houat, Hoedic.

Rennes: capital of Brittany, medieval streets, half-timbered houses; Brittany Museum.

St Malo: historic walled city, fishing port.

Cuisine of the region

Fish and shellfish are commonplace; traditional *crêperies* abound and welcome visitors with a cup of local cider.

Agneau de pré-salé: leg of lamb from animals pastured in the salt marshes and meadows.

Beurre blanc: sauce for fish dishes made with shallots, wine vinegar and butter.

Cotriade: fish soup with potatoes, onions, garlic and butter.

Crêpes Bretonnes: the thinnest of pancakes with a variety of sweet fillings.

Galette: can be a biscuit, cake or pancake; with sweet or savoury fillings.

Gâteau Breton: rich cake.

Poulet blanc Breton: free-range, quality, white Breton chicken.

www.brittanytourism.com
tourism-crtb@tourismebretagne.com
(0)2 99 28 44 30

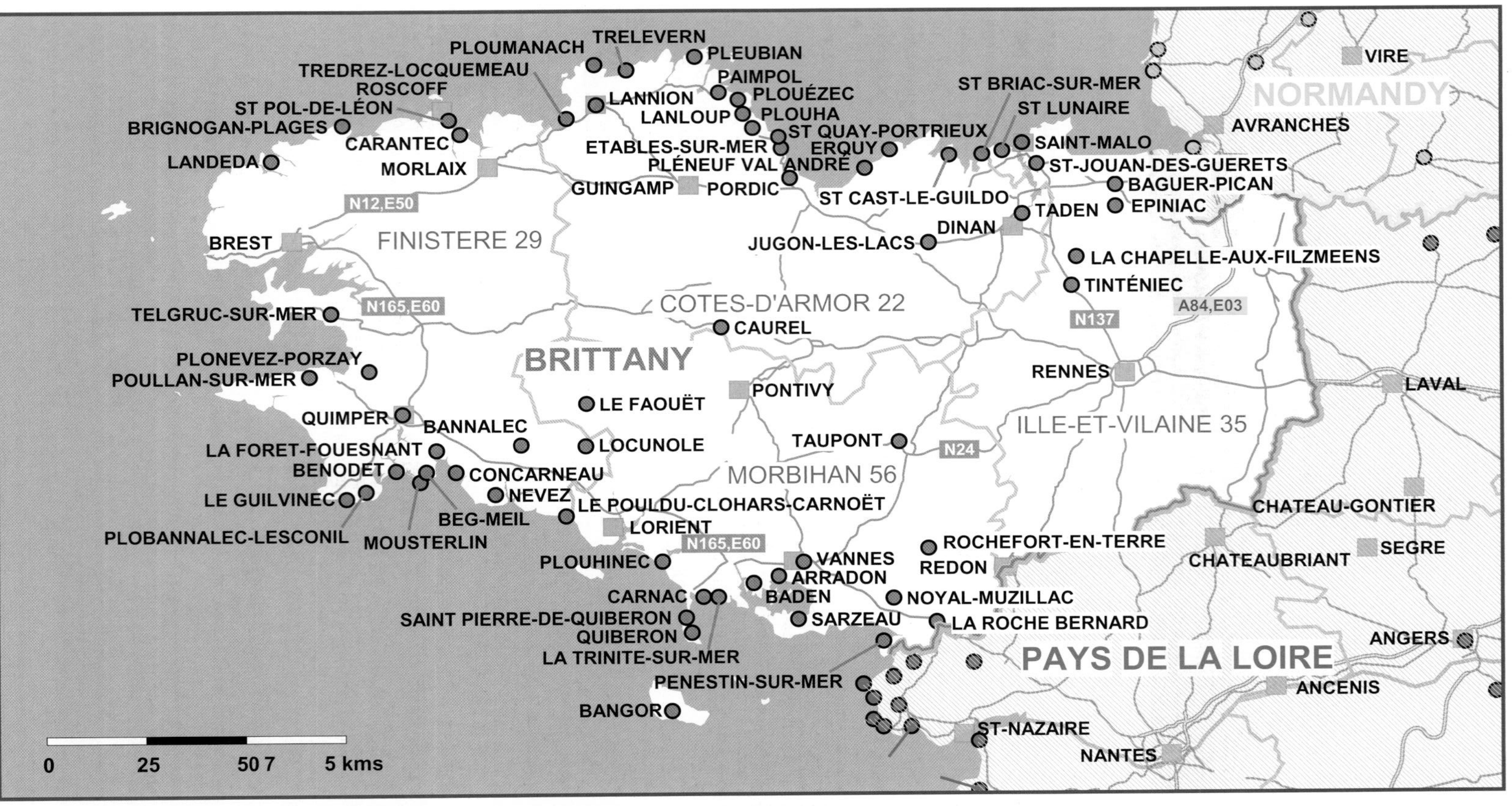

PLOUMANACH
TRELEVERN
PLEUBIAN
TREDREZ-LOCQUEMEAU
PAIMPOL
ROSCOFF
PLOUÉZEC
ST BRIAC-SUR-MER
VIRE
NORMANDY
ST POL-DE-LÉON
LANNION
LANLOUP
PLOUHA
ST LUNAIRE
AVRANCHES
BRIGNOGAN-PLAGES
CARANTEC
ST QUAY-PORTRIEUX
SAINT-MALO
ETABLES-SUR-MER
ERQUY
LANDEDA
MORLAIX
PLÉNEUF VAL ANDRÉ
ST-JOUAN-DES-GUERETS
GUINGAMP
PORDIC
BAGUER-PICAN
ST CAST-LE-GUILDO
N12,E50
TADEN
EPINIAC
BREST
FINISTERE 29
DINAN
JUGON-LES-LACS
LA CHAPELLE-AUX-FILZMEENS
TINTÉNIEC
TELGRUC-SUR-MER
N165,E60
COTES-D'ARMOR 22
A84,E03
N137
CAUREL
PLONEVEZ-PORZAY
BRITTANY
POULLAN-SUR-MER
RENNES
LAVAL
PONTIVY
LE FAOUËT
QUIMPER
BANNALEC
ILLE-ET-VILAINE 35
TAUPONT
LA FORET-FOUESNANT
LOCUNOLE
N24
BENODET
CONCARNEAU
MORBIHAN 56
NEVEZ
LE GUILVINEC
LE POULDU-CLOHARS-CARNOËT
CHATEAU-GONTIER
BEG-MEIL
LORIENT
PLOBANNALEC-LESCONIL
MOUSTERLIN
ROCHEFORT-EN-TERRE
N165,E60
SEGRE
PLOUHINEC
VANNES
REDON
CHATEAUBRIANT
ARRADON
CARNAC
BADEN
NOYAL-MUZILLAC
SAINT PIERRE-DE-QUIBERON
SARZEAU
LA ROCHE BERNARD
QUIBERON
ANGERS
LA TRINITE-SUR-MER
PAYS DE LA LOIRE
PENESTIN-SUR-MER
ANCENIS
BANGOR
ST-NAZAIRE
0
25
50 7
5 kms
NANTES

Arradon

Camping de Penboch

9 chemin de Penboch, F-56610 Arradon (Morbihan) T: **02 97 44 71 29**. E: **camping.penboch@wanadoo.fr**
alanrogers.com/FR56040

Penboch is 200 metres by footpath from the shores of the Golfe du Morbihan with its many islands, and plenty to do including watersports, fishing and boat trips. The site, in a peaceful, rural area, is divided into two – the main part, on open ground, with hedges and young trees, the other across a minor road in woodland with lots of shade. Penboch offers 175 pitches on flat grass, 105 are for touring and they are mostly divided into groups. Electricity (6/10A) is available on all pitches and most also have water and drainage. A 'Sites et Paysages' member.

Facilities

Three toilet blocks, two on the main part (one heated) and one in the annex, include washbasins in cabins. There are new washing facilities including family cabins. Laundry facilities. Motorcaravan service point. Bar with snacks and takeaway. Shop (all 13/5-10/9). Heated pool with slide and paddling pool (1/5-19/9). Indoor pool (all season) with relaxation area, jacuzzi and massage tables. Good playground. Games room. Caravan storage. American motorhomes accepted in low season. Off site: Beach, fishing 200 m. Sailing, windsurfing 2 km. Bicycle hire 2 km. Golf and riding 6 km.

Open: 3 April - 25 September.

Directions

From N165 at Auray or Vannes, take D101 along northern shores of the Golfe du Morbihan; or leave N165 at D127 signed Ploeren and Arradon. Take turn to Arradon and site is signed.
GPS: 47.62206, -2.8007

Charges 2010

Per unit incl. 2 persons and electricity	€ 19,40 - € 39,30
extra person	€ 4,00 - € 6,20
child (2-7 yrs)	€ 3,00 - € 4,50
dog	€ 1,50 - € 3,50

The Travel Service to book this site call 01580 214000 ...we'll arrange everything

Baden

Camping Mané Guernehué

52 rue Mané er Groez, F-56870 Baden (Morbihan) T: **02 97 57 02 06**. E: **mane-guernehue@wanadoo.fr**
alanrogers.com/FR56130

Located close to the Morbihan Gulf, Mané Guernehué is a smart, modern site with excellent amenities and a variety of pitches. Some are terraced beneath pine trees, others in a former orchard with delightful views of the surrounding countryside. The 377 pitches are generally large, 200 being occupied by mobile homes and chalets. Most pitches have 10A electricity and a few also have water and drainage. Many are level but a few, particularly in the centre of the site, slope to varying degrees. An impressive new indoor pool complex has been added to the existing complex of outdoor pools.

Facilities

Three modern toilet blocks include washbasins in cabins. The maintenance of the blocks does seem to be under some pressure. Facilities for disabled visitors. Washing machines and dryers. Small shop, bar and takeaway. Heated outdoor swimming pool (1/5-1/9) new heated indoor pool (all season), water slide, jacuzzi and gym. Fishing. Minigolf. Pony trekking. Teenagers' room with games and TV. Play area. Tree top adventure area. Varied entertainment programme in high season, based around a large purpose built hall. Off site: Beach, golf 3 km.

Open: 1 April - 1 November.

Directions

From Auray or Vannes use the D101 to Baden and watch for signs to site. GPS: 47.61419, -2.92596

Charges 2010

Per unit incl. 2 persons and electricity	€ 19,70 - € 41,70

Camping Cheques accepted.

The Travel Service to book this site call 01580 214000 ...we'll arrange everything

Baguer-Pican

Camping le Vieux Chêne

Baguer-Pican, F-35120 Dol-de-Bretagne (Ille-et-Vilaine) T: **02 99 48 09 55**. E: **vieux.chene@wanadoo.fr**
alanrogers.com/FR35000

This attractive, family owned site is situated between Saint Malo and Mont Saint-Michel. Developed in the grounds of a country farmhouse dating from 1638, its young and enthusiastic owner has created a really pleasant, traditional atmosphere. In spacious, rural surroundings it offers 199 good sized pitches on gently sloping grass, most with 10A electricity, water tap and light. They are separated by bushes and flowers, with mature trees for shade. A very attractive tenting area (without electricity) is in the orchard. The site is used by a Dutch tour operator (20 pitches). There are three lakes in the grounds and centrally located leisure facilities include a restaurant with a terrace overlooking an attractive pool complex. Some entertainment is provided in high season, which is free for children. A 'Sites et Paysages' member.

Facilities

Three very good, unisex toilet blocks, which can be heated, include washbasins in cabins, a baby room and facilities for disabled people. Small laundry. Motorcaravan services. Shop, takeaway and restaurant (15/5-15/9). Heated swimming pool, paddling pool, slides (15/5-15/9; lifeguard July/Aug). TV room (satellite). Games room. Tennis. Minigolf. Giant chess. Play area. Riding in July/Aug. Fishing.
Off site: Dol 3 km. Golf 12 km. Beach 20 km.

Open: 31 March - 22 September.

Directions

Site is by the D576 Dol-de-Bretagne - Pontorson road, just east of Baguer-Pican. It can be reached from the new N176 taking exit for Dol-Est and Baguer-Pican.
GPS: 48.54924, -1.684

Charges guide

Per person	€ 4,50 - € 5,75
child (under 13 yrs)	free - € 3,90
pitch incl. electricity	€ 10,00 - € 21,50
dog	€ 1,50

Bangor

Flower Camping le Kernest

Bangor, F-56360 Belle Ile-en-Mer (Morbihan) T: **02 97 31 56 26**. E: **info@camping-kernest.com**
alanrogers.com/FR56460

Belle Ile is a large island lying around 14 km. off the Quiberon peninsula. Access to the island can be made by ferry from either Quiberon, Vannes or Lorient (reservation is recommended in high season). Le Kernest is a family site and a member of the Flower group. It is located around 800 m. from a sandy beach with direct access by footpath. There are 100 pitches here, some of which are occupied by wooden chalets. Touring pitches are grassy and well shaded, and all have electrical connections. Leisure facilities on site include a tennis court and multisports terrain, as well as a snack bar. Numerous cycle tracks cross the island, including one around the perimeter.

Facilities

Shop. Snack bar. Takeaway. Tennis. Multisports terrain. Play area. TV room. Activity and entertainment programme. Chalets for rent. Off site: Nearest beach 800 m. (direct path). Riding. Fishing. Cycle tracks.

Open: 1 June - 30 September.

Directions

Upon arrival at Le Palais, follow signs to Bangor on D90 and then to Kernest. Site is well signed from here. GPS: 47.31479, -3.18912

Charges guide

Per unit incl. 2 persons and electricity	€ 13,90 - € 21,90
extra person	€ 3,50 - € 5,00
child (2-7 yrs)	€ 2,20 - € 3,50
dog	€ 2,50 - € 3,00

Bannalec

Camping les Genets d'Or

Kermerour, Pont Kereon, F-29380 Bannalec (Finistère) T: **02 98 39 54 35**. E: **Enquiries@holidaybrittany.com**
alanrogers.com/FR29160

A jewel of a small site, Les Genets d'Or is situated in a tiny country hamlet at the end of a road from Bannalec, 12 km. from Pont-Aven in Finistère. The spacious surroundings offer a safe haven for young children and a rural, tranquil environment for adults. The gently sloping, grassy site is edged with mature trees and divided into hedged glades with the odd apple tree providing shade. There are only 52 pitches (42 for touring units), all of a good size – some of over 100 sq.m. – and most pitches have electricity, each glade having a water point.

Facilities

The good quality toilet block provides all the necessary amenities and washing facilities, including a shower for disabled campers. Washing machine and dryer. Shop (15/6-30/9). Bar area. Bread delivered in season. Ice pack service. Indoor games room. Bicycle hire. Play and picnic area. Caravan storage. Off site: Riding 3 km. Beach 12 km. The village is 15 minutes walk with bars, shop, baker, etc.

Open: Easter/1 April - 30 September.

Directions

Take exit D4 from N165 towards Bannalec. In Bannalec turn right into Rue Lorec (signed Quimperlé) and follow site signs for 1 km. GPS: 47.92167, -3.68667

Charges 2010

Per unit incl. 2 persons and electricity	€ 16,00
extra person	€ 2,50 - € 3,50
electricity (6A)	€ 3,00

Less 10% for over 7 nights.

Beg-Meil

Camping de la Piscine

B.P.12 Kerleya, Beg-Meil, F-29170 Fouesnant (Finistère) T: **02 98 56 56 06**
E: **contact@campingdelapiscine.com** **alanrogers.com/FR29170**

There are many campsites in this area but La Piscine is notable for the care and attention to detail that contribute to the well-being of its visitors. Created by the Caradec family from an apple orchard, the 185 level, grass pitches are of generous size and are separated by an interesting variety of hedges and trees. Water, drainage and electricity points are provided, normally one stand between two pitches. A quiet site, set back from the sea, La Piscine will appeal to families looking for good quality without too many on-site activities.

Facilities

Two refurbished toilet units include British and Turkish style toilets and washbasins in cabins. Facilities for disabled people. Laundry facilities. Motorcaravan service point. Shop. Takeaway (high season). Pool complex with three slides, waterfall and jacuzzi. Sauna and solarium. Play area. BMX track. Half-court tennis. TV room. Entertainment organised in high season. Off site: Beach 1 km. Bicycle hire, fishing and riding within 4 km. Golf 7 km.

Open: 13 May - 12 September.

Directions

Site is 5 km. south of Fouesnant. Turn off the N165 expressway at Coat Conq signed Concarneau and Fouesnant. At Fouesnant join D45 signed Beg Meil and shortly turn left on D145 signed Mousterlin. In 1 km. turn left and follow signs to site. GPS: 47.86568, -4.01553

Charges 2010

Per unit incl. 2 persons and electricity	€ 20,00 - € 30,60
extra person	€ 2,00 - € 6,30

Bénodet

Camping de la Plage

20 rue du Poulquer, F-29950 Bénodet (Finistère) T: **02 98 57 00 55**. E: **info@campingdelaplagebenodet.com**
alanrogers.com/FR29500

This is a large well organised site that has a rural feel, although it is only 300 m. from the beach and 800 m. from the popular seaside town of Bénodet. It has a very short season for touring. There is a great variety of shrubs and trees offering ample shade and privacy for the 300 grassy pitches. There are 190 for touring (electricity 6/10A), all attractively and informally laid out on one side of the site. Access for large units may be difficult. A further 100 pitches are used for mobile homes to rent over a longer season. A splendid pool complex has a retractable cover, flumes, a toboggan and a jacuzzi.

Facilities

Four large adequate toilet blocks with facilities for campers with disabilities although access is not easy. Motorcaravan services. Shop (1/7-31/8). Bar with TV and takeaway (1/7-31/8). Heated swimming and paddling pools (one can be covered), flumes, toboggan, jacuzzi (1/5-30/9). Multisport court. Boules. Exercise bikes. Good play areas. Games room. Internet access. Miniclub and entertainment (July/Aug). Bicycle hire. Mobile homes and chalets for rent (26/4-30/9). Off site: Beach 300 m. Seaside resort of Bénodet, bars, restaurants, shop, cinema 800 m. Boat trips. Fishing, golf, riding and bicycle hire 1 km.

Open: 15 June - 15 September.

Directions

From Fouesnant take D44 west towards Bénodet. After 10 km. take Le Letty road south. Site is well signed. GPS: 47.86768, -4.09626

Charges guide

Per unit incl. 2 persons and electricity	€ 20,90 - € 14,10
extra person	€ 6,20
child (2-10 yrs)	€ 3,30
dog	€ 2,60

Bénodet

Camping du Letty

F-29950 Bénodet (Finistère) T: **02 98 57 04 69**. E: **reception@campingduletty.com**

alanrogers.com/FR29030

The Guyader family have ensured that this excellent and attractive site has plenty to offer for all the family. With a charming ambience, the site on the outskirts of the popular resort of Bénodet spreads over 22 acres with 493 pitches, all for touring units. Groups of four to eight pitches are set in cul-de-sacs with mature hedging and trees to divide each group. Most pitches have electricity, water and drainage. Although there is no swimming pool here, the site has direct access to a small sandy beach and has provided a floating pontoon (safe bathing depends on the tides). At the attractive floral entrance, former farm buildings provide a host of facilities including an extensively equipped fitness room and new 'wellness' rooms for massage and jacuzzis. There is also a modern, purpose-built nightclub and bar providing high quality live entertainment most evenings (situated well away from most pitches to avoid disturbance).

Facilities

Six well placed toilet blocks are of good quality and include mixed style WCs, washbasins in large cabins and controllable hot showers (charged). One block includes a separate laundry and dog washing enclosures. Baby rooms. Separate facility for disabled visitors. Launderette. Hairdressing room. Motorcaravan service points. Well stocked shop. Extensive snack bar and takeaway. Bar with games room and night club. Library/reading room with four computer stations. Entertainment room with satellite TV. Fitness centre (no charge). Saunas, jacuzzi and solarium (all on payment). Tennis and squash (charged). Boules. Archery. Well equipped play area. Entertainment and activities (July/Aug). WiFi in reception. Off site: Sailing, fishing, riding and golf all nearby. Benodet and Quimper.

Open: 15 June - 6 September.

Directions

From N165 take D70 Concarneau exit. At first roundabout take D44 to Fouesnant. Turn right at T-junction. After 2 km. turn left to Fouesnant (still D44). Continue through La Forêt Fouesnant and Fouesnant, picking up signs for Bénodet. Shortly before Bénodet at roundabout turn left (signed Le Letty). Turn right at next mini-roundabout and site is 500 m. on left. GPS: 47.86700, -4.08783

Charges guide

Per person	€ 4,00 - € 6,50
child (1-6 yrs)	€ 2,00 - € 3,25
pitch incl. vehicle and electricity	€ 12,50 - € 15,00
dog	€ 2,30

Bénodet

Yelloh! Village Port de Plaisance

7 route de Quimper, F-29950 Bénodet (Finistère) T: **02 98 57 02 38**. E: **info@campingbenodet.fr**
alanrogers.com/FR29380

Sometimes larger campsites can lack ambiance, but it is not so with Port de Plaisance. This is a delightful, family run site with 340 pitches of which 77 are for touring campers, all with electric (6A). The pitches are mostly in two areas, where they are hedged and positioned in small groups amongst the many mature trees and flowering shrubs. Although there are five holiday tour operators on site, their presence is unobtrusive because of careful positioning amongst the trees. This is truly a campsite with something for everybody, with a wide range of entertainment and activities provided over a long season. The restaurant that overlooks the pool complex boasts a very good menu. There is entertainment for all ages, from up-to-date films to taster aquadiving lessons in the covered, heated pool. The marina at the mouth of the Odet river is 500 m. away, and from here you can enjoy a boat trip up to Quimper. The large seaside town of Bénodet, with all the shops, bars and restaurants that you could wish for is just 1 km.

Facilities

Three toilet blocks, older and simple in style, include British style toilets, showers and washing cubicles. Baby room. Facilities for disabled visitors. Laundry room. Shop, bar and restaurant (all season) and takeaway (15/5-15/9). Swimming pool complex with flumes and toboggan. Games room. Programme of entertainment. Multisport court. Bicycle hire. Large indoor pool complex with spa and toboggan. Off site: Bénodet 1 km. Fishing 1 km. Riding 2 km. Golf 3 km. Beach 1 km.

Open: 2 April - 19 September.

Directions

Take the D34 south from Quimper. Site is on the left just as you enter Bénodet.
GPS: 47.882065, -4.103282

Charges 2010

Per unit incl. 2 persons and electricity (6A)	€ 15,00 - € 39,00
extra person	€ 4,00 - € 7,00
child (0-7 yrs)	free - € 4,00
dog	€ 4,00

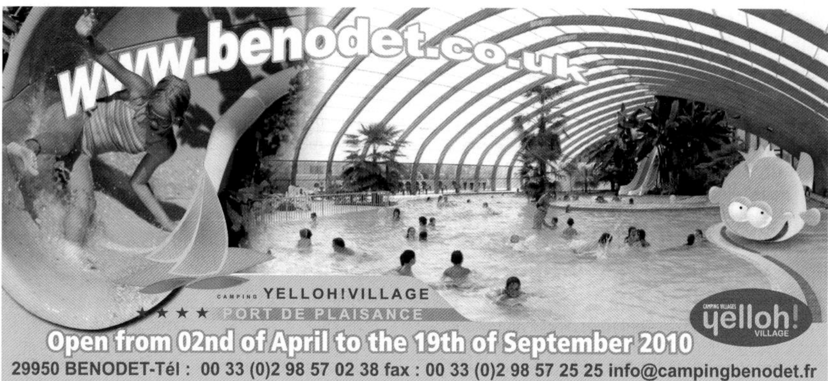

www.benodet.co.uk
CAMPING YELLOH!VILLAGE
PORT DE PLAISANCE
yelloh! VILLAGE
Open from 02nd of April to the 19th of September 2010
29950 BENODET-Tél : 00 33 (0)2 98 57 02 38 fax : 00 33 (0)2 98 57 25 25 info@campingbenodet.fr

Brignogan-Plages

Camping de la Côte des Légendes

B.P. 36 Keravezan, F-29890 Brignogan-Plages (Finistère) T: **02 98 83 41 65**
E: **camping-cote-des-legendes@wanadoo.fr** **alanrogers.com/FR29340**

With direct access to a safe, sandy beach on the Baie de Brignogan and adjacent to a Centre Nautique (sailing, windsurfing, kayaking), this site could be ideal for a family seaside holiday in high season. It is very quiet in low season. There are 102 level touring pitches arranged in rows and protected by hedges, together with 31 privately-owned mobile homes and 14 for rent. A shop, bar and takeaway are open in July and August when activities are arranged for adults and children by the helpful manager Manuelle; she and her assistant Pierre both speak good English.

Facilities

Main toilet facilities (open only in July and August) are at the rear of the site in a large block that provides washbasins in cubicles, laundry room, baby baths and facilities for disabled visitors. The upper floor provides a games room with views of the sea. At other times the only facilities are in the snack bar building and are fairly basic. Motorcaravan service point. Bar, small shop and takeaway (July/Aug). Playground and playing field. WiFi available in most areas. Off site: Watersports centre adjacent. Village services 700 m. Bicycle hire 1 km. Riding 6 km. Golf 35 km.

Open: Easter - 1 November.

Directions

Brignonan-Plages is 35 km. west of Roscoff. From ferry terminal take the D58 towards Morlaix and after 6 km. turn right on the D10 towards Plouescat and then Plouguerneau. Turn right on the D770 to Brignogan-Plages. At top of main street bear left following signs (NOT satnav!) for site and Club Nautique. GPS: 48.67278, -4.32929

Charges guide

Per unit incl. 2 persons	€ 11,90 - € 13,90
extra person	€ 2,35 - € 4,20
electricity (5/10A)	€ 2,50 - € 3,50

Carantec

Yelloh! Village les Mouettes

50 route de La Grande Grève, F-29660 Carantec (Finistère) T: **02 98 67 02 46**. E: **camping@les-mouettes.com**
alanrogers.com/FR29000

Les Mouettes is a sheltered site on the edge of an attractive bay with access to the sea at the front of the site. In a wooded setting with many attractive trees and shrubs, the 434 pitches include just 112 for touring units, all with electricity, water and drainage. The remainder are taken by tour operators and by around 172 mobile homes and chalets for rent. At the centre of the 'village' are shops, bar, restaurant, entertainment stage, sports facilities and an impressive heated pool complex with swimming, paddling and water slide pools, plus a 'tropical river', jacuzzi and sauna.

Facilities

Three clean sanitary blocks include controllable showers, washbasins in cabins and mainly British toilets. In the main block there are showers with washbasins and rooms for children and babies. Facilities for disabled visitors. Laundry. Motorcaravan services. Shop. Takeaway. Bar with TV. Crêperie/pizzeria/grill. Pool complex. Beauty Salon. Games rooms. Play area. Half-court tennis. Minigolf. Entertainment in main season. Large units should phone first. No dogs after 26/6. WiFi in central area (free). Off site: Fishing 1 km. Beach and golf 2 km. Riding 6 km. Bicycle hire, 10 km.

Open: 16 May - 6 September.

Directions

Carantec is 15 km. northwest of Morlaix and 15 km. by road from Roscoff. From D58 Roscoff - Morlaix road, turn east to Carantec on D173. In 4 km. site is signed to the left at roundabout just after passing supermarket on right. GPS: 48.65807, -3.92833

Charges guide

Per unit incl. 2 persons, electricity and water	€ 14,00 - € 44,00
extra person	€ 5,00 - € 7,00
dog	€ 3,00 - € 5,00

Carnac

Camping les Menhirs

Allée Saint-Michel, F-56340 Carnac (Morbihan) T: **02 97 52 94 67**. E: **contad@lesmenhirs.com**
alanrogers.com/FR56270

Although located within the built-up area of the popular resort of Carnac, and only 300 m. from the beach, this campsite feels much more rural. Catering for all ages, this is a friendly site and lively in high season with plenty of activities including evening entertainment and a club for children. There are 350 pitches; 154 touring pitches and the remainder used for mobile homes and chalets, of which the majority are used by tour operators. The touring pitches are in groups and are large, level and hedged. All have electricity (10A), water and drainage, and 14 have hardstanding. The central complex containing the pools and games areas, all overlooked by the bar and its terrace, makes a convivial focal point. The town and seafront can be explored on foot and the Brittany coast and the Gulf of Morbihan are within easy reach by car or bicycle.

Facilities

Three spotless, modern, light toilet blocks with washbasins in cabins, facilities for children, babies and disabled people. A further en-suite unit for disabled people is by the pool complex. Laundry. Shop. Comfortable bar with satellite TV and takeaway (13/5-16/9). Heated indoor and outdoor swimming pools, the latter with slides (all season). Fitness complex with massage, multi-gym, jacuzzi, sauna and solarium. Multisport pitch. Tennis. Boules. Riding (1/7-31/8). Play areas. Children's club and evening entertainment (July/Aug). Off site: Beach 300 m. Bicycle hire 500 m. Golf 800 m. Sailing 1 km. Town centre 1 km. Bars and restaurants within easy walking distance.

Open: 1 May - 26 September.

Directions

From Auray take D786 to Carnac and Quiberon. After 5 km. turn south on D119 towards Carnac at roundabout. 600 m. beyond next roundabout fork left, signed La Trinité-sur-Mer and Plages. Keep straight on at lights. Fork left at first roundabout. Turn left at next roundabout (T-junction) and site is signed at 250 m. on left. GPS: 47.57653, -3.06890

Charges guide

Per person	€ 3,92 - € 7,83
child (0-6 yrs)	€ 2,92 - € 5,81
pitch with electricity, water and drainage	€ 18,14 - € 32,62

Carnac

Castel Camping la Grande Métairie

Route des Alignements de Kermario, B.P. 85, F-56342 Carnac (Morbihan) T: **02 97 52 24 01**
E: **info@lagrandemetairie.com** **alanrogers.com/FR56010**

La Grande Métairie is a good quality site situated a little back from the sea, close to the impressive rows of the famous Carnac 'menhirs' (giant prehistoric standing stones). The site has 575 individual pitches (108 for touring units), surrounded by hedges and trees. All have electricity (some need long leads). The site is well known and popular and has many British visitors with 314 pitches taken by tour operators. It is ideal for families with children of all ages, but probably not suitable for those who find walking difficult. The site has a great deal to offer and is lively and busy over a long season. Musical evenings, barbecues and other organised events including occasional dances are held in an outdoor amphitheatre (pitches near these facilities may be noisy late at night – the bar closes at midnight). Paddocks with ponds are home for ducks, goats and ponies to watch and feed. There are also pony rides around the site. A super pool complex comprises heated indoor and outdoor pools, water slides and toboggans and a jacuzzi. A local market takes place at Carnac on Wednesdays and Sundays.

Facilities

Three large well maintained toilet blocks, with washbasins in cabins. Facilities for babies and disabled people. Laundry facilities. Motorcaravan service points. Shops (from 22/5). Bar lounge and terrace, restaurant and takeaway (all from 22/5). TV and games rooms. Swimming pool complex with bar. Playgrounds and playing field. Tennis. Minigolf. BMX track. Bicycle hire. Fishing. Zip-wire. Paintball. Helicopter rides (July/Aug). Amphitheatre. Organised events and entertainment. American motorhomes accepted up to 27 ft. Off site: Riding 1 km. Beach 3 km. Golf 12 km.

Open: 3 April - 11 September (all services from 22/5).

Directions

From N165 take Quiberon/Carnac exit onto the D768. After 5 km. turn south onto D119 towards Carnac. At roundabout and after 4 km. turn left (northeast) onto D196 to the site. GPS: 47.5973, -3.0607

Charges guide

Per unit incl. 2 persons and electricity	€ 18,00 - € 43,40
extra person	€ 4,00 - € 7,70
child (4-7 yrs)	€ 3,50 - € 5,40

Less 20% 22/5-29/6 and after 1/9.

Carnac

Kawan Village le Moustoir

Route du Moustoir, F-56340 Carnac (Morbihan) T: **02 97 52 16 18**
E: **info@lemoustoir.com** **alanrogers.com/FR56110**

Camping le Moustoir is a friendly, family run site situated about three kilometres inland from the many beaches of the area and close to the famous 'alignments' of standing stones. Pitches are grassy and separated by shrubs and hedges, with several shaded by tall pine trees. There is a popular pool area with slides, swimming pool and a paddling pool with 'mushroom' fountain and a second covered pool complex. The bar and terrace become the social centre of the site in the evenings. A high season entertainment programme includes a daily 'Kids' Club' attracting children of several nationalities.

Facilities

The substantial, traditional style toilet block is well maintained (outside peak season some sections may be closed). Motorcaravan service facilities. Shop, bar, restaurant and takeaway (all season). Heated swimming pool (21 x 8 m), water slides, and paddling pool (from 1/5). Heated indoor swimming pool (all season) added in 2008. Adventure playground. Tennis. Boules. Volleyball, football and basketball. Table tennis and pool. 'Kids' Club'. Barrier deposit € 20. Off site: Watersports at Carnac Plage. Fishing, bicycle hire, riding 2 km. Beach 3 km. Golf 10 km.

Open: 1 April - 30 September.

Directions

From N165, take exit to D768 (Carnac and Quiberon). At second crossroads after 5 km. turn left (D119) towards Carnac. After 3 km. turn left (oblique turning) after a hotel. Site is 500 m. on left.
GPS: 47.60825, -3.06587

Charges guide

Per unit incl. 2 persons and electricity	€ 19,60 - € 31,60
extra person	€ 4,90
child (2-7 yrs)	free - € 4,90

Camping Cheques accepted.

Caurel

Camping Nautic International

Route de Beau-Rivage, F-22530 Caurel (Côtes d'Armor) T: **02 96 28 57 94**. E: **contact@campingnautic.fr**
alanrogers.com/FR22030

This friendly family site is on the northern shore of the Lac de Guerledan. The lake is popular for all manner of watersports and there are some pleasant walks around the shores and through the surrounding Breton countryside and forests. The site is terraced down to the lake shore and offers 100 large pitches, all with electrical connections. A number of 'super pitches' (160-200 sq.m) are also available. There is an imaginatively designed swimming pool and smaller children's pool, both heated by a woodburning stove. Small boats can be launched from the site, and other boating activities are available on the lake. A member of 'Sites et Paysages'.

Facilities

The two toilet blocks provide adequate facilities and are well placed on the site. The slopes probably make the site unsuitable for disabled people. Washing and drying machines. Small shop and takeaway (10/7-31/8). Swimming pools (15/5-25/9). Gym. Giant chess. Play area. Fishing. Tennis. Games room. Mobile homes for rent.
Off site: Restaurants nearby. Watersports. Sailing school. Riding. Canal from Nantes to Brest. Sea 50 minutes by car.

Open: 15 May - 25 September.

Directions

From N164 Rennes - Brest road, turn off between Mur-de-Bretagne and Gouarec to the village of Caurel. Site is well signed from there. GPS: 48.20853, -3.051

Charges 2010

Per unit incl. 2 persons and electricity	€ 20,00 - € 27,60
extra person	€ 3,80 - € 6,00
child (0-7 yrs)	€ 1,90 - € 3,30
dog	€ 1,80

Concarneau

Camping le Cabellou Plage

Avenue du Cabellou, F-29185 Concarneau (Finistère) T: **02 98 97 37 41**. E: **info@le-cabellou-plage.com**
alanrogers.com/FR29520

Le Cabellou Plage is a recently developed site located close to Concarneau. The newly grassed pitches are divided by young hedges, all have 10A electricity and some also have water and drainage. Many have fine views across the estuary to the old walled town. The enthusiastic owner has tastefully landscaped many areas of the site with shrubs and flowers. A large swimming pool on site is overlooked by a terrace and bar and the beach is just 25 m. away. La Cabellou is ideally situated for those wishing to visit Concarneau with its twice-weekly market, Pont Aven and the cathedral city of Quimper.

Facilities

One modern toilet block is bright and cheerful and provides mainly open style washbasins and preset showers. Baby room. Facilities for disabled visitors. Laundry room. Shop. Bar with television and internet access. Swimming pool. Scuba lessons and water gymnastics. Bicycle hire.
Off site: Bus stop outside site. Supermarkets, shops and restaurants in Concarneau 4 km. Tennis 3 km. Riding 7 km. Golf 10 km.

Open: 3 April - 18 September.

Directions

Site is just south of Concarneau. Take the D783 towards Tregunc. Turn right onto Avenue Cabellou. Site is well signed from here.
GPS: 47.85516, -3.90521

Charges guide

Per unit incl. 2 persons and electricity	€ 13,00 - € 22,00
with water and drainage	€ 15,00 - € 28,00
extra person	€ 3,00 - € 6,00
pet	€ 3,00

Concarneau

Camping les Sables Blancs

Avenue Le Dorlett, F-29900 Concarneau (Finistère) T: **02 98 97 16 44**
E: **camping.les-sablesblancs@libertysurf.fr** **alanrogers.com/FR29150**

This is a steeply terraced site overlooking the sea on the outskirts of Concarneau. Most of the 113 touring pitches are shaded by large mature trees and shrubs. All with 10A electricity, they are level but tend to be small and access to some could prove difficult for large units. A traditionally styled bar and restaurant opens out onto a new terrace with swimming pool overlooking the bay of De La Forêt. The climb from the bottom of the site to the top is via some very steep steps, so those with walking difficulties would be advised to choose one of the higher pitches. The site is run by young owners who work very hard and make you feel welcome. An advantage of the site's position is its close proximity to Concarneau, which is said to be the second largest fishing port in France.

Facilities

One new modern toilet block provides very good facilities including washbasins (both open and in cubicles) and showers. Facilities for babies and disabled visitors. New laundry facilities. Bar (1/6-1/9). Restaurant in bar (1/7-1/9). Heated outdoor swimming pool (12/5-15/9). Play area. Evening entertainment (July/Aug). Billiard room.
Off site: Concarneau with shops, bars and restaurants. Beach 150 m. Riding 1 km. Bicycle hire, boat launching 1.5 km. Golf 6 km.

Open: 3 April - 30 October.

Directions

Leave the N165 for Concarneau on D70. The site is situated on the northern edge of town on the coast road. Well signed. GPS: 47.88195, -3.92915

Charges guide

Per unit incl. 2 persons	€ 12,00 - € 17,00
extra person	€ 4,00 - € 5,50
child	€ 1,00 - € 3,20
electricity (10A)	€ 3,50

Concarneau

Camping les Prés Verts

B.P. 612, Kernous-Plage, F-29186 Concarneau Cedex (Finistère) T: **02 98 97 09 74**. E: **info@presverts.com**

alanrogers.com/FR29190

What sets this family site apart from the many others in this region are its more unusual features – its stylish pool complex with Romanesque style columns and statue, and its plants and flower tubs. The 150 pitches are mostly arranged on long, open, grassy areas either side of main access roads. Specimen trees, shrubs or hedges divide the site into smaller areas. There is an area towards the rear of the site where the pitches have sea views. There is direct access to the sandy beach with no roads to cross (300 m). Concarneau is just 2.5 km. A 'Sites et Paysages' member.

Facilities

Two toilet blocks provide unisex WCs, but separate washing facilities for ladies and men. Preset hot showers and washbasins in cabins for ladies, both closed 21.00-08.00 hrs. Some child-size toilets. Laundry facilities. Shop (1/7-25/8). Pizza service twice weekly. Heated swimming pool (1/6-31/8) and paddling pool. Playground (0-5 yrs). Minigolf (charged). Off site: Path to sandy/rocky beach 300 m. Riding 1 km. Bicycle hire 1.5 km. Supermarket 2 km.

Open: 1 May - 22 September.

Directions

Turn off C7 road, 2.5 km. north of Concarneau, where site is signed. Take third left after Hotel de l'Océan. GPS: 47.89616, -3.95433

Charges guide

Per unit incl. 2 persons	€ 16,00 - € 20,00
extra person	€ 4,80 - € 6,00
child (2-7 yrs)	€ 3,20 - € 4,00
electricity (2-10A)	€ 3,20 - € 7,00

Epiniac

Castel Camping le Domaine des Ormes

Epiniac, F-35120 Dol-de-Bretagne (Ille-et-Vilaine) T: **02 99 73 53 00**. E: **info@lesormes.com**

alanrogers.com/FR35020

This impressive site, in the grounds of the Château des Ormes is in the north east part of Brittany, about 30 km. from the old town and ferry port of Saint-Malo. In an estate of wooded parkland and lakes, it has a pleasant atmosphere, busy in high season but peaceful at other times, with an impressive range of facilities. Of the 800 pitches only 160 are for tourers (120 with 6A electricity). They are of varying sizes and there is a choice of terrain – flat or gently sloping, wooded or open. The rest are occupied by tour operators (550) and by mobile homes (50 to rent).

Facilities

The toilet blocks are of fair standard, one refurbished but still cramped, including washbasins in cabins and facilities for disabled visitors. A new more spacious block has family cubicles (shower and washbasin). Motorcaravan services. Supermarket, bar, restaurant, pizzeria and takeaway. Games room, bar and disco. Indoor and outdoor pools. Adventure play area. Golf. Bicycle hire. Fishing. Equestrian centre. Minigolf. Tennis. Sports ground. Paintball. Archery. Cricket club. WiFi in bar area. Off site: Beaches 25 km. Historic Saint-Malo, Dinan, and fashionable Dinard are all nearby.

Open: 16 May - 5 September, with all services.

Directions

Site is off D795 8 km. south of Dol-de-Bretagne, 11 km north of Combourg. GPS: 48.49030, -1.72787

Charges guide

Per person	€ 4,20 - € 7,50
pitch incl. electricity (6A)	€ 18,60 - € 29,60
drainage	€ 1,70 - € 2,00
dog	€ 1,70 - € 2,00

Erquy

Camping le Vieux Moulin

14 rue des Moulins, F-22430 Erquy (Côtes d'Armor) T: **02 96 72 34 23**. E: **camp.vieux.moulin@wanadoo.fr**

alanrogers.com/FR22050

Le Vieux Moulin is a family run site, just 2 km. from the little fishing port of Erquy on Brittany's Emerald Coast on the edge of a pine forest and nature reserve. It is about 900 m. from a beach of sand and shingle. Taking its name from the old mill opposite, the site has 173 pitches all with electricity (6/9A) and some with electricity, water and drainage. One section of 39 pitches is arranged around a pond. Most pitches are of a fair size in square boxes with trees giving shade. Evening entertainment is organised and there is a friendly pizzeria.

Facilities

Two good quality toilet blocks have mostly British style toilets and individual washbasins, facilities for disabled people and babies. A further small block provides toilets and dishwashing only. Washing machines and dryer. Motorcaravan service point. Shop. Pizzeria and takeaway. Bar and terrace. Heated, covered pool complex with jacuzzi and paddling pool. Play areas. Tennis. Fitness gym. TV room and games room. Bicycle hire. No electric barbecues. Off site: Beach 900 m. Fishing 1.2 km. Golf and riding 7 km.

Open: 24 April - 4 September.

Directions

Site is 2 km. east of Erquy. Take minor road towards Les Hôpitaux and site is signed from junction of the D786 and D34 roads. GPS: 48.63858, -2.44189

Charges guide

Per unit incl. 2 persons and electricity	€ 35,00 - € 44,30
extra person	€ 3,50 - € 6,10

No credit cards.

Erquy

Yelloh! Village les Pins

Route du Guen, le Guen, F-22430 Erquy (Côtes d'Armor) T: **04 66 73 97 39**
E: **info@yellohvillage-les-pins.com** **alanrogers.com/FR22360**

Erquy is a pretty holiday resort nestling between two promontories. There are plenty of great sandy beaches around here, and one of the best is just 900 m. from this wooded site. Les Pins is a long-established site with many of the original facilities still in use. There are 235 touring pitches here and a further 148 pitches are occupied by mobile homes and chalets. The site boasts some impressive amenities including a top class swimming pool complex extending over 600 sq.m. with water slides, lazy river and various other water features.

Facilities

Four very old toilet blocks, with mostly Turkish style toilets and other poor facilities. New facilities at the pools. Shop. Bar. Restaurant. Snack bar and takeaway (from 15/6). Large swimming pool complex. Children's pool. Fitness centre. Sauna. Tennis. Play area. Activity and entertainment programme. Off site: Nearest beach 900 m. Walking and cycle trails. Fishing 900 m. Sailing. Sand yachting. Sea kayaking. Golf, riding and bicycle hire 2.5 km. Casino.

Open: 26 April - 13 September.

Directions

From St Brieuc, take the northbound D786 to Erquy. Continue through the town following signs to Cap d'Erquy and the site is well indicated.
GPS: 48.63841, -2.45565

Charges guide

Per unit incl. 2 persons and electricity	€ 17,00 - € 34,00
extra person (over 1 yr)	€ 4,00 - € 5,00

Erquy

Camping Bellevue

Route de la libération, F-22430 Erquy (Côtes d'Armor) T: **02 96 72 33 04**. E: **campingbellevue@yahoo.fr**
alanrogers.com/FR22210

Situated a mile from the beaches between Erquy and Pléneuf Val-André, Camping Bellevue offers a quiet country retreat with easy access to the cliffs of Cap Fréhel, Sables d'Or and Saint Cast. There are 140 pitches of which 120 are available for touring units, most with electricity (6/10A) and 15 with water and drainage. The site also has 20 mobile homes and tents to rent. Children are well catered for at this campsite – there are heated swimming and paddling pools, three play areas and minigolf, pétanque and volleyball. A 'Sites et Paysages' member.

Facilities

Two modern, unisex toilet blocks are of a high standard. Some washbasins in cubicles. Facilities for disabled visitors. Laundry facilities. Shop and bar (15/6-10/9). Restaurant and takeaway (12/6-30/9). Swimming and paddling pools (April - Sept). Play areas. Games room and library. Minigolf. Pétanque. Entertainment and organised activities in high season. Multisport area. Off site: Beach and fishing 2 km. Golf 3 km. Bicycle hire 5 km. Riding 6 km.

Open: 4 April - 30 September.

Directions

From St Brieuc road take D786 towards Erquy. Site is adjacent to the D786 at St Pabu and is well signed.
GPS: 48.59426, -2.48475

Charges guide

Per unit incl. 2 persons and electricity	€ 22,00 - € 25,30
extra person	€ 4,00 - € 5,00
child (0-12 yrs)	free - € 4,40

Etables-sur-Mer

Camping l'Abri Côtier

Ville Es Rouxel, F-22680 Etables-sur-Mer (Côtes d'Armor) T: **02 96 70 61 57**
E: **camping.abricotier@wanadoo.fr** **alanrogers.com/FR22100**

L'Abri Côtier is a well cared for, family-run site 500 m. from a sandy beach. Small and tranquil, it is arranged in two sections separated by a lane. The pitches are marked out on part level, part sloping grass, divided by mature trees and shrubs with some in a charming walled area. The second section has an orchard type setting. There are 120 touring pitches, all with electrical connections (long leads useful) and 60 are fully serviced. Tim and Pierrette Lee are busy with ideas for this very popular, friendly site.

Facilities

Good clean sanitary facilities include some washbasins in cabins and pushbutton showers. Facilities for disabled visitors. Baby bath/shower. Laundry room. Well stocked shop. Bar providing a simple takeaway service (plus set menu in high season). Covered terrace and games area. Sheltered, heated swimming pool with paddling pool and outdoor jacuzzi. Small play area. Some entertainment in peak season. WiFi in bar (charged). Off site: Beach and sailing 500 m. Restaurants and indoor pool in the village. Riding 1 km. Fishing and boat launching 2 km. Bicycle hire 4 km. Golf 10 km.

Open: 7 May - 14 September.

Directions

Etables-sur-Mer is 20 km north of Saint Brieuc, roughly half-way between Roscoff and Saint Malo. From N12 (Saint Brieuc bypass) take D786 towards St Quay Portrieux. After 12 km. ignore signs to Etables, pass Aire de la Chapelle on the right and take second left towards Etables-sur-Mer (site signed). Take second right at top of hill to site at crossroads in 100 m.
GPS: 48.63559, -2.83546

Charges guide

Per unit incl. 2 persons and electricity	€ 18,60 - € 22,60
extra person	€ 3,00 - € 4,90

La Forêt-Fouesnant

Domaine du Saint-Laurent

Kerleven, F-29940 La Forêt-Fouesnant (Finistère) T: **02 98 56 97 65**. E: **info@camping-du-saint-laurent.fr**
alanrogers.com/FR29020

Saint-Laurent is a well established site, situated on a sheltered wooded slope bordering one of the many attractive little inlets that typify the Brittany coastline. The site is on the coastal footpath that leads from Kerleven to Concarneau. The 260 pitches are on level terraces, under tall trees. All are of average size (100 sq.m) and divided by hedges and partly shaded, all with electricity connections. Around 60% of the pitches are occupied by site owned mobile homes. Touring pitches with the best sea views tend to be adjacent to the cliff edge and may not be suitable for families with young children. Access to some touring pitches can be a little difficult. The outdoor swimming pool (complete with paddling pool and two water slides) is overlooked by the bar terrace and adjacent to this is a covered pool. With organised activities and entertainment in high season, this site is ideal for a lively family holiday, particularly for older children. There is direct access from the site to two small sandy bays, which empty at low tide to reveal numerous rock pools (ideal for children to explore)..

Facilities

Two sanitary blocks provide combined shower and washbasin cubicles, separate washbasin cubicles, baby changing and facilities for disabled people. Washing machines, dryers and ironing. Small shop at reception (all season). Bar, snack bar and takeaway (1/7-31/8). Swimming pools. Gym and sauna. Canoe and boat hire. Two tennis courts (free). Play area. Entertainment in July/Aug. for adults and children (in English and French) with discos in the bar each evening. Bicycle hire. Internet access.

Open: 5 April - 29 September.

Directions

From N165 take the D70 Concarneau exit. At first roundabout take first exit D44 (Fouesnant). After 2.5 km. turn right at T-junction, follow for 2.5 km, then turn left (Port La Forêt). Continue to roundabout, straight ahead and after 1 km. turn left (site signed). In 400 m. left turn to site. GPS: 47.8961, -3.9551

Charges guide

Per unit incl. 2 persons and electricity	€ 15,00 - € 33,00
extra person	€ 2,60 - € 7,00

La Forêt-Fouesnant

Camping de Kéranterec

Route de Port la Forêt, F-29940 La Forêt-Fouesnant (Finistère) T: **02 98 56 98 11**
E: **info@camping-keranterec.com** **alanrogers.com/FR29240**

A well established family run site with a very French ambience, Keranterec has 265 grassy pitches in two distinct areas. The upper part of the site is more open and has little shade, and is also largely taken up by private mobile homes. The lower and more mature area is predominantly for tourers, with terraced pitches set in a former orchard. Spacious and divided by mature hedging, all pitches have electrical connections (25 m. cable advised) and most also offer water and drainage. Some pitches have shade from the many trees on the lower part of the site, and some also overlook a little cove.

Facilities

Two modern, fully equipped toilet blocks kept very clean include washbasins in cubicles, baby baths and facilities for disabled visitors. Laundry facilities. Small shop and bar (15/6-10/9) and takeaway (1/7-31/8). TV room with satellite. Heated outdoor swimming pool (1/6-10/9) with paddling pool, jacuzzi and three slides and a covered, heated pool. Tennis. Boules. Play area. In July/August organised events and activities for all the family, and a free children's club. Free WiFi. Off site: Attractive sandy beach of Kerleven 10 minutes walk. Golf 0.8 km. Riding 2 km.

Open: 5 April - 21 September.

Directions

From N165 take the D70 Concarneau exit. At first roundabout take D44 signed Fouesnant. After 2.5 km. turn right at T-junction, and follow for 2.5 km. and turn left (Port La Forêt). Continue to roundabout and take second exit (straight ahead), signed Port La Forêt. After 1 km. turn left (site signed), then in 400 m. turn left to site on left. GPS: 47.8991, -3.95198

Charges guide

Per person	€ 7,00 - € 8,50
child (1-7 yrs)	€ 3,00 - € 4,00
pitch incl. electricity	€ 13,00 - € 17,00

Jugon-les-Lacs

Camping Au Bocage du Lac

Rue du Bocage, F-22270 Jugon-les-Lacs (Côtes d'Armor) T: **02 96 31 60 16**. E: **contact@campingjugon.com**
alanrogers.com/FR22200

This well kept former municipal site has been updated over the past few years by the current owners M. and Mme. Rivière. It is on the edge of the village beside a lake, 25 km. from the sea. It offers 181 good size pitches, all with electrical connections, set on gently sloping grass and divided by shrubs and bushes, with mature trees providing shade. Some 40 wooden chalets and mobile homes are intermingled with the touring pitches. On-site facilities include a good pool with children's section and sunbathing patio. There is also a small animal park.

Facilities

Two main sanitary blocks include facilities for disabled visitors. British and Turkish style WCs and some washbasins in cabins. Washing machine. Small shop. Bar. Swimming pool (15/6-10/9). Tennis. Football. Play area. Activity programmes July/Aug. Fishing. Bicycle hire.
Off site: Supermarket in village 1 km. River 1 km.

Open: 1 April - 31 October.

Directions

From N176 (E401) Lamballe - Dinan road, about 15 km. from Lamballe take turning for Jugon-les-Lacs. Site is signed shortly after. GPS: 48.40120, -2.31736

Charges guide

Per person	€ 3,70 - € 4,70
child (under 7 yrs)	€ 2,70 - € 3,20
pitch	€ 13,10 - € 17,40
electricity (5A)	€ 3,00

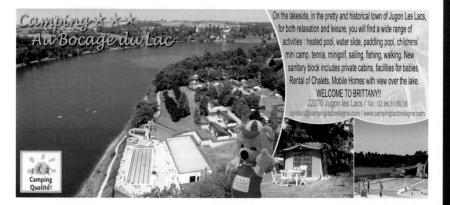

La Chapelle-aux-Filtzmeens

Domaine du Logis

Le Logis, F-35190 La Chapelle-aux-Filtzmeens (Ille-et-Vilaine) T: **02 99 45 25 45**
E: **domainedulogis@wanadoo.fr** **alanrogers.com/FR35080**

This is an attractive rural site, set in the grounds of an old château. The site's facilities are housed in converted barns and farm buildings, which although old, are well maintained and equipped. There are a total of 180 pitches, 83 of which are for touring. The grass pitches are level, of a generous size and divided by mature hedges and trees. All have 10A electricity connections. This site would appeal to most age groups with plenty to offer the active including a new fitness room with a good range of modern equipment or for those who prefer to relax, perhaps a quiet days fishing beside the lake. The site is well placed for excursions to Mont Saint-Michel, Dinard and Dinan..

Facilities

One comfortable toilet block with washbasins and showers. Toilet and shower for disabled visitors. Laundry facilities. Bar with Sky TV (1/4-7/11). Restaurant and takeaway (1/7-29/8). Outdoor swimming pool (from 1/5). Fitness and games rooms. BMX circuit. Bicycle hire (€ 5 for half a day, € 9 per day). Unfenced play areas. Children's club (high season). Free Wifi-Internet access. Lake fishing. Off site: Boating on the canal. Riding 10 km.

Open: 1 April - 7 November.

Directions

Turn south off N176 onto D795 signed Dol-de-Bretagne. Continue to Combourg and then take D13 to La Chapelle-aux-Filtzmeens. Continue for 2 km. to site on right. GPS: 48.37716, -1.83705

Charges 2010

Per unit incl. 2 persons and electricity	€ 20,40 - € 27,40
extra person	€ 4,00 - € 4,50
child (2-12 yrs)	€ 2,50
dog	€ 2,00

Camping Cheques accepted.

La Roche Bernard

Camping Municipal le Pâtis

3 chemin du Pâtis, F-56130 La Roche Bernard (Morbihan) T: **02 99 90 60 13**. E: **camping-info@wanadoo.fr**
alanrogers.com/FR56080

This is another of those excellent municipal sites one comes across in France. Situated beside the River Vilaine, a five-minute walk from the centre of the very attractive old town of La Roche Bernard and beside the port and marina, it provides 69 level grass, part-hedged pitches in bays of four, with 7A electricity and water. 18 special pitches for motorcaravans have been created at the entrance. Next door is a sailing school, boats to hire, fishing, tennis, archery, etc. A restaurant and bar are on the quayside, with others uphill in the town.

Facilities

There are two fully equipped sanitary blocks, one new and very modern, the other fully refurbished. Laundry room behind reception with washing machine and dryer. Small play area. Bicycle hire. Off site: Fishing 500 m. Riding 5 km. Golf 15 km.

Open: April - 30 September.

Directions

Go into town centre and follow signs for the Port around a one-way system and then a sharp turn down hill. GPS: 47.51817, -2.30317

Charges guide

Per unit incl. 2 persons and electricity	€ 13,00
extra person	€ 3,00
child (under 9 yrs)	€ 1,50
animal	€ 1,00

La Trinité-sur-Mer

Camping de la Plage

Plage de Kervilaine, F-56470 La Trinité-sur-Mer (Morbihan) T: **02 97 55 73 28**
E: **camping@camping-plage.com** **alanrogers.com/FR56020**

The Carnac/La Trinité area of Brittany is popular with British holidaymakers. Camping de la Plage is one of two sites, close to each other and owned by members of the same family, with direct access to the safe sandy beach of Kervilaine Plage. There are 198 grass pitches of which 112 are for touring (58 are used by tour operators). All are hedged and have electricity (6/10A), water and drainage. The site has a pronounced slope and some pitches reflect this. With narrow roads and sharp bends, it is not suitable for large units.

Facilities

Toilet blocks have washbasins in cubicles and facilities for disabled people and small children. Laundry facilities. Small swimming pool with water slides. Play areas including ball pool. Tennis. TV. Entertainment programme in high season for all ages. Bicycle hire. Beach. Guided tours. Internet access. Communal barbecue areas (gas or electric only on pitches). Off site: Fishing 50 m. Shop with bakery. Bar, restaurant, crêperie, takeaway (all 200 m). Sailing 1.5 km. Riding 3.5 km. Golf 13 km.

Open: 7 May - 19 September.

Directions

From N165 at Auray take D28 (La Trinité-sur-Mer). On through town following signs to Carnac-Plage on D186. Site signed off this road to the south. Take care to take road signed to Kervilaine Plage where it forks. At seafront turn right. Site is 300 m. on right.
GPS: 47.57563, -3.02890

Charges 2010

Per unit incl. 2 persons and electricity	€ 20,00 - € 40,00
extra person	€ 2,00 - € 5,20

La Trinité-sur-Mer

Camping de la Baie

Plage de Kervillen, F-56470 La Trinité-sur-Mer (Morbihan) T: **02 97 55 73 42**
E: **contact@campingdelabaie.com** **alanrogers.com/FR56030**

This site is one of two owned by members of the same family. It is situated on the coast overlooking the safe, sandy beach of Kervilaine Plage, with its little rocky outcrops providing a naturally enclosed swimming area. This is a very friendly site, which is ideal for quiet or family holidays in an area with lots of local interest. There are 170 pitches, of which 60 are used by tour operators. The 91 touring pitches are all of good size, hedged and all have electricity (6/10A) water and drainage. Some shade is provided by mature and maturing trees.

Facilities

Two modern, very clean toilet blocks include well equipped baby rooms and full en-suite facilities for disabled visitors. Laundry facilities. Bar, restaurant and takeaway (open to the public all season). Well stocked shop (all season). Small (12 m.) swimming pool with slide. Play areas. Multi-sport pitches. TV room. Indoor games room. Bicycle hire. Internet access. Off site: Beach, fishing and boat ramp 50 m. Tennis and minigolf 200 m. (shared with Camping de la Plage). Riding 3 km. Sailing school 1.5 km. Golf 5 km.

Open: 17 May - 14 September.

Directions

From N165 at Auray take D28 signed La Trinité-sur-Mer. Keep on through the town following signs to Carnac Plage on D186. Site is well signed off this road to the south. Be careful to take the road signed to Kervilaine Plage where it forks.
GPS: 47.57364, -3.02758

Charges guide

Per unit incl. 2 persons and electricity	€ 16,10 - € 35,00
extra person (over 2 yrs)	€ 2,50 - € 3,50

La Trinité-sur-Mer

Camping de Kervilor

F-56470 La Trinité-sur-Mer (Morbihan) T: **02 97 55 76 75**. E: **ebideau@camping-kervilor.com**
alanrogers.com/FR56050

Kervilor may be a good alternative for those who find the beach-side sites in La Trinité too busy and lively. In a village on the outskirts of the town, it has 230 pitches on flat grass and is attractively landscaped with trees (silver birch) and flowers giving a sense of spaciousness. The pitches are in groups divided by hedges, separated by shrubs and trees and all have electricity (6/10A). Around 116 are used for touring units. Used by tour operators (10 pitches). The site has an inviting, well designed pool complex with swimming and paddling pools, slides and fountains.

Facilities

Two modern toilet blocks of a good standard with further facilities in an older block. They include many washbasins in cabins, facilities for disabled people and babies. Small laundry. Small shop and takeaway. Bar with terrace. Pool complex. Play area. Minigolf, pétanque, tennis and volleyball. Bicycle hire. Only charcoal barbecues are allowed. WiFi in bar area. Off site: Town facilities 1.5 km. Sandy beach, fishing or riding 2 km. Golf 12 km.

Open: 1 May - 14 September.

Directions

Site is north of La Trinité-sur-Mer and is signed in the town centre. From Auray take D186 Quiberon road; turn left at site sign at Kergroix on D186 to La Trinité -sur-Mer, and left again at outskirts of town.
GPS: 47.60213, -3.03672

Charges guide

Per unit incl. 2 persons and electricity	€ 24,40 - € 31,80
extra person	€ 2,55 - € 5,15

Landéda

Camping des Abers

Dunes de Sainte Marguerite, F-29870 Landéda (Finistère) T: **02 98 04 93 35**
E: **camping-des-abers@wanadoo.fr** **alanrogers.com/FR29130**

This delightful 12-acre site is in a beautiful location almost at the tip of the Presqu'île Sainte Marguerite on the northwestern shores of Brittany. The peninsula lies between the mouths (abers) of two rivers, Aber Wrac'h and Aber Benoît. Camping des Abers is set just back from a wonderful sandy beach with rocky outcrops and islands you can walk to at low tide. There are 180 pitches, landscaped and terraced, some with amazing views, others sheltered by mature hedges, trees and flowering shrubs. Vera and Hubert le Cuff make you very welcome and speak excellent English.

Facilities

Three clean toilet blocks, all recently refurbished, provide washbasins in cubicles and roomy showers (token € 0.65-€0.85). Good facilities for disabled visitors and babies. Laundry. Motorcaravan service point. Shop with basics (25/5-22/9). Simple takeaway dishes (1/7-31/8). Good play area. Games room. Hairdresser. Massage. Breton music and dancing, cooking classes. Splendid beach with good bathing and watersports. Long leads needed in places. Torch useful. Free internet and WiFi. Off site: Pizzeria next door. Tennis nearby. Sailing club 3 km. Riding 7 km.

Open: 28 April - 30 September.

Directions

Landéda is 55 km. west of Roscoff via D10 to Plougerneau then D13 crossing river bridge (Aber Wrac'h) and turning west to Lannilis. From N12 Morlaix-Brest road turn north on D59 to Lannilis. Continue through town taking road to Landéda and from there follow signs for Dunes de Ste Marguerite, 'camping' and des Abers. GPS: 48.59306, -4.60305

Charges guide

Per person	€ 2,72 - € 3,40
child (1-7 yrs)	€ 1,52 - € 1,90
pitch incl. electricity	€ 6,80 - € 8,50

Lanloup

Camping le Neptune

Ker Guistin, F-22580 Lanloup (Côtes d'Armor) T: **02 96 22 33 35**. E: **contact@leneptune.com**
alanrogers.com/FR22160

Situated on the Côte de Goëlo at Lanloup, Le Neptune offers a peaceful, rural retreat for families. The friendly owners, François and Marie Jo Camard, keep the site neat and tidy and there is a regular programme of renovation. There are 84 level, grass pitches (65 for touring units) separated by trimmed hedges providing privacy. All have electricity. There are also 21 mobile homes to rent. Within walking distance is the local village, with a restaurant and shop, and sandy beaches are a short drive away.

Facilities

The modern toilet block is of a good standard and provides washbasins in cubicles and pushbutton showers. It is clean and well maintained and will be heated for the 2010 season. Facilities for disabled visitors. Laundry room. Motorcaravan services. No restaurant but good takeaway. Small well-stocked shop. Bar with indoor and outdoor seating. Heated swimming pool with retractable roof (Easter-end Oct). Pétanque. Play area. Entertainment and children's activities in high season. Off site: Tennis 300 m. Fishing and beach 2 km. Golf 4 km. Riding 8 km.

Open: 1 April - 31 October.

Directions

Lanloup is 30 km. north west of Saint Brieuc. From N12 Saint Brieuc by-pass take D786 Paimpol (par la Côte). After 28 km. on approaching Lanloup, site is well signed, turning right at crossroads by café. GPS: 48.71212, -2.96704

Charges guide

Per person	€ 4,00 - € 5,30
child (under 7 yrs)	€ 2,50 - € 3,40
pitch incl. electricity (10A)	€ 10,30 - € 12,40

Camping Cheques accepted.

Lannion

Kawan Village les Alizés

Route de Trébeurden, F-22300 Lannion (Côtes d'Armor) T: **02 96 47 28 58**
E: **info@camping-perros.com** **alanrogers.com/FR22430**

Les Alizés is located between Lannion and Trébeurden, close to some of the finest sandy beaches of the Trégor region. The site boasts an excellent new pool complex (including a covered pool) and a good range of other amenities, including a sauna and Turkish bath. A small shop stocks a selection of basic provisions. Other shops are available close to the site. The pitches here are of a good size and grassy, most being equipped with electricity. A number are occupied by mobile homes (available for rent). Off site, there is an excellent footpath leading through the stunning Côte du Granit Rose. Nearby, Perros Guirec is a stylish resort and its harbour is the departure point for excursions to the archipelago of Les Sept Iles, part of which is a bird sanctuary. This dramatic section of coast is also popular for sub-aqua diving and a dive centre, as well as a sailing school, is located at nearby Trébeurden.

Facilities

Small shop. Swimming pool. Children's pool. Covered pool. Sauna. Turkish bath. Games room. Play area. Tourist information. Mobile homes for rent. Off site: Nearest beach 3.5 km. Walking and cycle track. Sub-aqua diving. Excursions to Les Sept Iles.

Open: 1 April - 31 December.

Directions

From Lannion head northwest on tje D85 towards Trébeurden. The site can be found shortly after passing the village of Servel. GPS: 48.751, -3.506

Charges guide

Per unit incl. 2 persons and electricity	€ 13,00 - € 18,00

Le Faouët

Camping Municipal Beg Er Roch

Route de Lorient, F-56320 Le Faouët (Morbihan) T: **02 97 23 15 11**. E: **camping.lefaouet@wanadoo.fr**
alanrogers.com/FR56310

Like many of today's municipal campsites this one is immaculate and offers excellent value. There are 52 well kept grassy pitches with electricity (10A) available. There are also a few furnished tents and mobile homes for rent. For those campers that are anglers a river at the bottom of the site (fenced) provides salmon and trout fishing at a supplement. For the more energetic, the manager can provide details and maps of local walks. For shops and other amenities the town of Le Faouët is only 2 km. away.

Facilities

A single toilet block provides toilets, washbasins and showers. Facilities for campers with disabilities. Washing machine and dryer. Play area. Minigolf. Boules. Fishing. Large games room with TV and bar billiards.

Open: 15 March - 30 September.

Directions

Take the D769 north from Lorient to Le Faouet. Site is well signed from this road. GPS: 48.01823, -3.47009

Charges guide

Per unit incl. 2 persons and electricity	€ 10,90 - € 13,85

Le Pouldu-Clohars-Carnoët

479

Camping les Embruns

Rue du Philosophe Alain, le Pouldu, F-29360 Clohars-Carnoët (Finistère) T: **02 98 39 91 07**
E: **camping-les-embruns@wanadoo.fr** **alanrogers.com/FR29180**

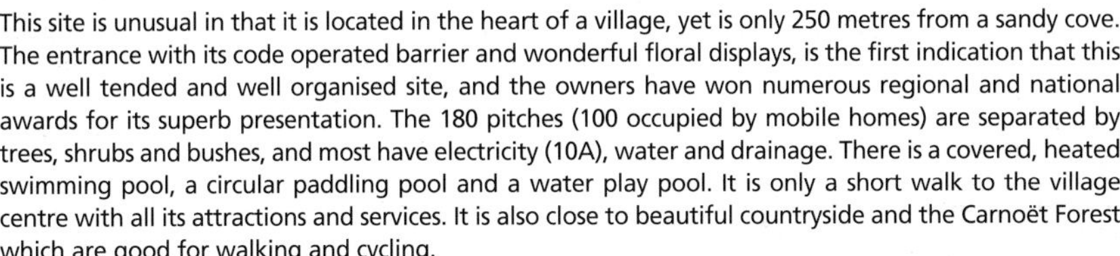

This site is unusual in that it is located in the heart of a village, yet is only 250 metres from a sandy cove. The entrance with its code operated barrier and wonderful floral displays, is the first indication that this is a well tended and well organised site, and the owners have won numerous regional and national awards for its superb presentation. The 180 pitches (100 occupied by mobile homes) are separated by trees, shrubs and bushes, and most have electricity (10A), water and drainage. There is a covered, heated swimming pool, a circular paddling pool and a water play pool. It is only a short walk to the village centre with all its attractions and services. It is also close to beautiful countryside and the Carnoët Forest which are good for walking and cycling.

Facilities

Two modern sanitary blocks, recently completely renewed and heated in winter, include some washbasins in cubicles, baby baths and good facilities for disabled visitors. Family bathrooms. Laundry facilities. Motorcaravan services (€ 4). Shop and restaurant by entrance. Bar and terrace (1/7-31/8). Takeaway (20/6-5/9). Covered, heated swimming and paddling pools. Large games hall. Play area. Football field. Minigolf. Communal barbecue area. Daily activities for children and adults organised in July/Aug. Bicycle hire. WiFi in reception area (charged). Off site: Nearby sea and river fishing and watersports. Beach 250 m. Riding 2 km.

Open: 3 April - 19 September.

Directions

From N165 take either 'Kervidanou, Quimperlé Ouest' exit or 'Kergostiou, Quimperlé Centre, Clohars Carnoët' exit and follow D16 to Clohars Carnoët. Then take D24 for Le Pouldu and follow site signs in village. GPS: 47.76852, -3.54494

Charges guide

Per unit incl. 2 persons and electricity	€ 14,50 - € 33,90
extra person	€ 3,95 - € 5,50
child (under 7 yrs)	€ 2,60 - € 3,50
animal	€ 2,00 - € 2,50

Le Guilvinec

Yelloh! Village la Plage

F-29730 Le Guilvinec (Finistère) T: **02 98 58 61 90**. E: **info@yellohvillage-la-plage.com**
alanrogers.com/FR29110

La Plage is a spacious site located beside a long sandy beach between the fishing town of Le Guilvinec and the watersports beaches of Penmarc'h on the southwest tip of Brittany. It is surrounded by tall trees which provide shelter and is made up of several flat, sandy meadows. The 410 pitches (100 for touring units) are arranged on either side of sandy access roads, mostly not separated but all numbered. There is less shade in the newer areas. Electricity is available on most pitches. Like all beach-side sites, the facilities receive heavy use. There is plenty to occupy one at this friendly site but the bustling fishing harbour at Le Guilvinec and the watersports of Penmarc'h and Pointe de la Torche are within easy travelling distance.

Facilities

Four sanitary blocks are of differing designs but all provide modern, bright facilities including washbasins in cabins, good facilities for children and disabled people. Laundry facilities. Motorcaravan service point. Shop with gas supplies. Bright, airy well furnished bar, crêperie and takeaway (all open all season). Covered heated swimming pool with paddling pool and slide. Sauna and fitness complex. Play area. TV room. Tennis. Minigolf. Pétanque. Giant chess/draughts. Bicycle hire. Beach. Multisport and football fields. Entertainment all season. Off site: Fishing and watersports near. Riding 5 km. Golf 20 km.

Open: 2 April - 12 September.

Directions

Site is west of Guilvinec. From Pont l'Abbé, take the D785 road towards Penmarc'h. In Plomeur, turn left on D57 signed Guilvinec. On entering Guilvinec fork right signed Port and camping. Follow road along coast to site on left. GPS: 47.8025, -4.3072

Charges guide

Per unit incl. 2 persons and 6A electricity	€ 15,00 - € 40,00
extra person	€ 5,00 - € 7,00
child (under 10 yrs)	free - € 5,00
electricity (10A)	€ 1,00
dog	€ 4,00

Locunolé

479

Runner up Alan Rogers Awards 2009

Castel Camping le Ty-Nadan

Route d'Arzano, F-29310 Locunolé (Finistère) T: **02 98 71 75 47**. E: **infos@camping-ty-nadan.fr**

alanrogers.com/FR29010

Ty-Nadan is a well organised site set amongst wooded countryside along the bank of the River Elle. The 183 pitches for touring units are grassy, many with shade and 99 are fully serviced. The pool complex with slides and paddling pool is very popular as are the large indoor pool complex and indoor games area with a climbing wall. There is also an adventure play park and a 'Minikids' park for five to eight year olds, not to mention tennis courts, table tennis, pool tables, archery and trampolines. This is a wonderful site for families with children. Several tour operators use the site. An exciting and varied programme of activities is offered throughout the season – canoe and sea kayaking expeditions, rock climbing, mountain biking, aqua-gym, paintball, horse riding or walking – all supervised by qualified staff. A full programme of entertainment for all ages is provided in high season including concerts, Breton evenings with pig roasts, dancing, etc. (be warned, you will be actively encouraged to join in!).

Facilities

Two older, split-level toilet blocks are of fair quality and include washbasins in cabins and baby rooms. A newer block provides easier access for disabled people. Washing machines and dryers. Restaurant, takeaway, bar and well stocked shop. Heated outdoor pool (17 x 8 m). Indoor pool. Small river beach (unfenced). Indoor badminton and rock climbing facility. Activity and entertainment programmes (all season).Horse riding centre. Bicycle hire. Boat hire. Canoe trips. Fishing. Internet access and WiFi (charged). Off site: Beaches 20 minutes by car. Golf 12 km.

Open: 27 March - 2 September.

Directions

Make for Arzano which is northeast of Quimperlé on the Pontivy road and turn off D22 just west of village at site sign. Site is about 3 km.
GPS: 47.90468, -3.47477

Charges guide

Per unit incl. 2 persons and electricity	€ 20,80 - € 47,80
extra person	€ 4,50 - € 9,10
child (2-6 yrs)	€ 1,90 - € 5,60
dog	€ 1,90 - € 6,00

Less 15-20% outside July/Aug.
Camping Cheques accepted.

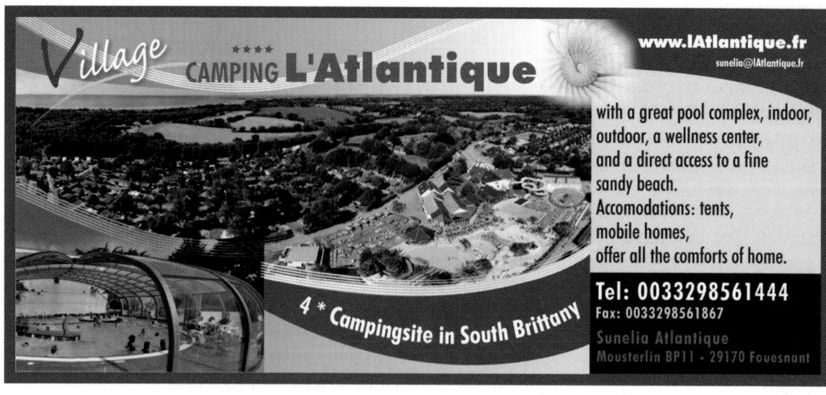

Village
CAMPING L'Atlantique
www.lAtlantique.fr
sunelia@lAtlantique.fr
with a great pool complex, indoor, outdoor, a wellness center, and a direct access to a fine sandy beach.
Accomodations: tents, mobile homes, offer all the comforts of home.
Tel: 0033298561444
Fax: 0033298561867
Sunelia Atlantique
Mousterlin BP11 - 29170 Fouesnant
4 * Campingsite in South Brittany

Mousterlin

Camping le Grand Large

48 route du Grand Large, Mousterlin, F-29170 Fouesnant (Finistère) T: **02 98 56 04 06**
E: **grandlarge@franceloc.fr** **alanrogers.com/FR29290**

Le Grand Large is a beach-side site situated on the Pointe de Mousterlin in natural surroundings. The site is separated from the beach by the road that follows the coast around the point. It is also protected from the wind by an earth bank with trees and a fence. There are 260 pitches with just 51 places used for tourers. Electricity is available everywhere (long leads useful) and some pitches have drainage. A small river runs through the site but it is fenced. The ground is rather sandy in places with some shrubs and mature trees. Benodet (7 km.) and Fouesnant (5 km.) are near in different directions and the sandy beach is just up the steps and across the road. A family site, Le Grand Large would also suit nature lovers in low season as it is next to a large tract of protected land, Marais de Mousterlin, ideal for walking, cycling and birdwatching. The beach itself looks over the bay towards the Isles de Glénan.

Facilities

Two neat toilet blocks, the largest only opened in high season, include plenty of washbasins in cabins. Facilities for children in the larger block, for disabled people in both. Laundry facilities. Shop. Bar overlooking the sea with attractive terrace. Grill restaurant including takeaway. Swimming pool with paddling pool, water slides in separate pool. Tennis. Multisport court. Small play area. TV and games rooms. Bicycle hire. Off site: Beach, fishing 100 m. Golf and riding 5 km.

Open: 3 April - 12 September.

Directions

Site is 7 km. south of Fouesnant. Turn off N165 expressway at Coat Conq, signed Concarneau and Fouesnant. At Fouesnant take A45 signed Beg Meil, then follow signs to Mousterlin. In Mousterlin turn left and follow camping signs. GPS: 47.84200, -4.03533

Charges guide

Per unit incl. 2 persons and electricity	€ 15,00 - € 34,70
extra person	€ 4,70 - € 7,00
child (under 10 yrs)	€ 2,60 - € 4,50

CAMPINGS
FranceLoc
BRETAGNE
Domaine du grand Large****
At the Mousterlin promontory in exceptionnal surrounding s, Le Grand Large, is located at the heart of the first Finistere resort. Relax by the aquatic area, where water and vegetation coexist in a peaceful atmosphere.
Domaine du Grand Large ****
F - 29170 Mousterlin Fouesnant
Tel : +33 (0) 2 98 56 04 06 - Email : grandlarge@franceloc.fr
www.campings-franceloc.fr

Mousterlin

Sunêlia l'Atlantique

Mousterlin, BP 11, F-29170 Fouesnant (Finistère) T: **02 98 56 14 44**. E: **sunelia@latlantique.fr**

alanrogers.com/FR29350

L'Atlantique is quietly situated just outside Beg-Meil. The 432 pitches are predominantly used by tour operators with about 60 for independent visitors. Level and grassy, all with electricity, they are separated by low shrubs, with apple orchards used for cider production also on the site. All the facilities are grouped together in the centre including an innovative play area and pool complex with water slides and a paddling pool. The sandy beach faces the Glénan Islands and is a pleasant 400 m. walk away through a nature reserve. Coastal paths await exploration and Concarneau, Pont-Aven and La Pointe du Raz are all nearby.

Facilities

Fully equipped toilet blocks (cleaned three times a day) include facilities for disabled visitors. Shop, bar, snack bar with takeaway meals and pizza (all 1/5-12/9). Heated outdoor and indoor pools, water complex with slides (all 1/5-12/9). Tennis. TV room. Billiards. Minigolf. Sports ground. Play area. Children's club (4-12 yrs) and evening entertainment in July/Aug. Bicycle hire. Off site: Fishing 300 m. Windsurf hire 1 km. Boat hire 3 or 5 km. Riding 3 km. Golf 8 km.

Open: 25 April - 12 September.

Directions

From Fouesnant follow directions for Mousterlin for 2 km, then follow Chapelle de Kerbader. Site is signed. GPS: 47.856564, -4.020658

Charges 2010

Per unit incl. 2 persons and electricity	€ 22,00 - € 39,00
extra person	€ 3,00 - € 7,00
child (0-10 yrs)	€ 2,00 - € 4,00

Camping Cheques accepted.

Névez

479

Camping le Raguenès-Plage

19 rue des Iles, F-29920 Névez (Finistère) T: **02 98 06 80 69**. E: **info@camping-le-raguenes-plage.com**

alanrogers.com/FR29090

Mme. Guyader and her family will ensure you receive a warm welcome on arrival at this well kept and pleasant site. Le Raguenès-Plage is an attractive and well laid out campsite with many shrubs and trees. The 287 pitches are a good size, flat and grassy, separated by trees and hedges. All have electricity, water and drainage. The site is used by two tour operator (81 pitches), and has 49 mobile homes of its own. A pool complex complete with water toboggan is a key feature and is close to the friendly bar, restaurant, shop and takeaway. From the far end of the campsite a delightful five minutes' walk along a path and through a cornfield takes you down to a pleasant, sandy beach looking out towards the Ile Verte and the Presqu'île de Raguenès.

Facilities

Two clean, well maintained sanitary blocks include mixed style toilets, washbasins in cabins, baby baths and facilities for disabled visitors. Laundry room. Motorcaravan service point. Small shop (from 15/5). Bar and restaurant (from 1/6) with outside terrace and takeaway. Reading and TV room, internet access point. Heated pool with sun terrace and paddling pool. Sauna (charged). Play areas. Games room. Various activities are organised in July/Aug. WiFi (charged). Off site: Beach, fishing and watersports 300 m. Supermarket 3 km. Riding 4 km.

Open: 1 April - 30 September.

Directions

From N165 take D24 Kerampaou exit. After 3 km. turn right towards Nizon and bear right at church in village following signs to Névez (D77). Continue through Névez, following signs to Raguenès. Continue for 3 km. to site entrance on left (entrance is quite small and easy to miss). GPS: 47.79337, -3.80049

Charges 2010

Per unit incl. 2 persons and electricity	€ 20,00 - € 36,80
extra person	€ 4,40 - € 5,90
child (under 7 yrs)	€ 2,20 - € 3,70
dog	€ 1,50 - € 3,20

The Travel Service
to book this site call 01580 214000
...we'll arrange everything

Névez

Camping les Deux Fontaines

Feunteun Vilian, Raguenèz, F-29920 Névez (Finistère) T: **02 98 06 81 91**. E: **info@les2fontaines.fr**
alanrogers.com/FR29470

Les Deux Fontaines is a large site with 288 pitches. Of these 115 are for touring, 118 are used by tour operators, and the remainder for mobile homes. The well cared for pitches are on grass, level and well laid out amongst mature trees and shrubs. All have 6/10A electricity connections. Trees have been carefully planted creating one area with silver birch, one with apple trees and another with palms and tropical plants. The pool complex is an excellent feature complete with chutes, flumes and waterfalls. There are numerous daytime activities for all the family to enjoy and a variety of entertainment in the evening. A short drive away you can experience some of the most scenic coastline of Brittany.

Facilities

Two modern toilet blocks are of good quality and provide washbasins in cabins and pre-set showers. Separate facilities for disabled visitors. Laundry facilities. Well stocked shop. Bar. Restaurant (1/7-31/8). Takeaway (1/6-31/8). Basic motorcaravan services. Large swimming pool complex. Fitness and pamper room. Play area. Skateboard park. 6-hole golf course. Driving range. Rollerblade hire. Off site: Fishing 1 km. Bicycle hire, riding 5 km.

Open: 15 May - 6 September.

Directions

Travel south from Nevez on D1. The site is on the left after 3 km. and is well signed.
GPS: 47.79937, -3.79017

Charges guide

Per unit incl. 2 persons	€ 17,50 - € 30,40
extra person	€ 3,70 - € 5,80
child (2-7 yrs)	free - € 3,90
electricity (6A)	€ 3,50

Noyal-Muzillac

Camping Moulin de Cadillac

Route de Berric, F-56190 Noyal-Muzillac (Morbihan) T: **02 97 67 03 47**. E: **infos@moulin-cadillac.com**
alanrogers.com/FR56430

Le Moulin de Cadillac is a riverside site located 15 minutes by car from the beaches of the Morbihan. Set in the heart of rural Brittany, this attractive site has 192 pitches, 139 of which are for touring. Pitches are generous (100-150 sq.m) although access to some is tight and may not be suitable for larger units. They are well laid out on grass and a profusion of trees and shrubs provide both shade and privacy. Electricity is available to all, but water supply may mean a short walk to one of the three sanitary blocks.

Facilities

Three well appointed toilet blocks include facilities for children and disabled visitors. No shop but some basics are kept in reception. Bar (July/Aug). Swimming pool with slides (heated July/Aug) and paddling pool. Games room. TV room. All weather sports pitch. Tennis. Minigolf. Three play areas. Two fishing lakes. Children's zoo. Some entertainment in high season. Mobile homes and chalets for rent. Off site: Muzillac 8 km. Nearest beaches 10 km. Riding and bicycle hire 10 km. Golf 15 km.

Open: 30 May - 30 September.

Directions

From Vannes travel south east on the N165. Exit on D140 in the direction of Berric. After 3 km. at Lauzach, site is well signed on the right. Continue for a further 4 km. GPS: 47.61310, -2.50140

Charges guide

Per person	€ 3,50 - € 4,70
child (under 7 yrs)	€ 2,00 - € 2,80
pitch	€ 4,50 - € 7,00
electricity (10A)	€ 3,20

Paimpol

Camping Municipal de Cruckin

Rue de Cruckin, Kérity, F-22500 Paimpol (Côtes d'Armor) T: **02 96 20 78 47**
E: **contact@camping-paimpol.com** **alanrogers.com/FR22250**

A neat and well managed municipal site situated close to the historical fishing port of Cité des Islandais and within easy reach of the Ile de Bréhat. This is an ideal location for many interesting walks. The site has 130 well maintained, mostly level pitches set in both wooded and open areas and all have electricity connections (5-12A). A very large area has been provided for sports, a play area and picnic tables. Although the site does not have its own swimming pool, the beach is just a short walk away.

Facilities

One modern and heated toilet block (a second block is planned). Washbasins in cabins and showers. Facilities for babies and disabled visitors. Laundry facilities. Bread and milk (high season). Snack bar/takeaway (July/Aug). Motorcaravan service point. Large field for football. Petanque. Fenced play area. Internet access on request. Bicycle hire. Fishing. Off site: Beach. Kérity village with shops, restaurants and cafés. Riding 2 km. Golf 10 km.

Open: 1 April - 10 October.

Directions

From N12 St Brieuc bypass, take D786 north towards Paimpol. Village of Kérity is 3 km. south of Paimpol. Site is signed. GPS: 48.76966, -3.02209

Charges guide

Per person	€ 2,90 - € 3,30
child (under 7 yrs)	€ 1,50 - € 2,10
pitch	€ 5,60 - € 7,10
electricity	€ 3,10 - € 3,05
dog	€ 1,10 - € 1,50

Pénestin-sur-Mer

Camping le Cénic

F-56760 Pénestin-sur-Mer (Morbihan) T: **02 99 90 33 14**. E: **info@lecenic.com**

alanrogers.com/FR56180

Le Cénic is attractively set amidst trees and flowers, providing activities for all tastes. An attractive covered aquatic complex has water slides, bridges, rivers and a jacuzzi, whilst the outdoor pool comes complete with water slide, 'mushroom' fountain and sunbathing areas. You may fish in the lake or use inflatables, watched by the peacock, the geese and turkeys. There is a hall for table tennis and a range of indoor games. There are 310 pitches, 160 of which are for touring. Of these, 90 have electricity (6A), but long leads will be required. The area has much to offer from the beaches of La Mine d'Or, the harbour at Trébiguier-Pénestin, the Golf du Morbihan with its numerous islands, La Baule with its magnificent beach and the medieval city of Guérande to the unique Brière nature reserve..

Facilities

Good new toilet block includes washbasins in cabins, facilities for disabled visitors, baby room and laundry and dishwashing sinks. Separate laundry. Bar and shop (1/7 -31/8). TV and games rooms (1/7-31/8). Indoor (15/4-15/9) and outdoor (1/7-31/8) swimming pools. Play area. Fishing. Off site: Riding 500 m. Bicycle hire 1 km. Sailing 2 km. Pénestin town 2 km. Sandy beaches 2.5 km. Golf 30 km.

Open: 1 May - 30 September.

Directions

From D34 (La Roche-Bernard), at roundabout just after entering Pénestin take D201 south (Assérac). After 100 m. take first turning on left. After 800 m. turn left and campsite is 300 m. on right down a narrow winding lane. GPS: 47.47910, -2.45643

Charges 2010

Per unit incl. 2 persons and electricity	€ 18,00 - € 31,00

Pénestin-sur-Mer

Camping des Iles

La Pointe du Bile, B.P. 4, F-56760 Pénestin-sur-Mer (Morbihan) T: **02 99 90 30 24**

E: **contact@camping-des-iles.fr** **alanrogers.com/FR56120**

You will receive a warm, friendly welcome at this family run campsite. The owner, Madame Communal, encourages everyone to make the most of this beautiful region. Of the 184 pitches, 103 are for touring. Most are flat, hedged and of a reasonable size (larger caravans and American motorhomes are advised to book) and all have electricity. Some pitches have sea views and overlook the beach. There is direct access to cliff-top walks and local beaches (you can even walk to small off-shore islands at low tide).

Facilities

The new large central toilet block is spotlessly clean with washbasins in cabins and showers. Laundry facilities. Facilities for disabled people and baby room. Shop (all season). Bar and restaurant with takeaway (15/5-15/9). Pool complex (1/5-30/9). Bicycle hire. Riding. Activities and entertainment in July/Aug. Across the road in Parc des Iles (mobile home section of site): TV room, multisport pitch, tennis court and motorcaravan service point.
Off site: Windsurfing 500 m. Sailing 3 km. Golf 20 km.

Open: 2 April - 17 October.

Directions

From D34 (La Roche-Bernard), at roundabout just after entering Pénestin take D201 south (Assérac). Take right fork to Pointe-du-Bile after 2 km. Turn right at crossroads just before beach. Site is on left.
GPS: 47.44543, -2.48396

Charges 2010

Per unit incl. 2 persons and electricity	€ 19,50 - € 39,50
extra person (over 7 yrs)	€ 2,30 - € 5,80
child (2-7 yrs)	€ 1,30 - € 3,26
dog	€ 4,00

Camping Cheques accepted.

Pénestin-sur-Mer

Yelloh! Village Domaine d'Inly

Route de Couarne, B.P. 24, F-56760 Pénestin-sur-Mer (Morbihan) T: **02 99 90 35 09**
E: **info@yellohvillage-domaine-inly.com** **alanrogers.com/FR56240**

This very large site is mainly taken up with mobile homes and cottages, some belonging to the site owner, some private and some belonging to tour operators. Most pitches are arranged in groups of 10 to 14 around a central stone circle with a water point in the middle. Of the 500 pitches, 100 are for touring units and all are large (150-200 sq.m) with 10A electrical connections (Europlug). Most are sloping. There is an attractive lake at the bottom of the site where one can fish or canoe, and next to it the riding school.

Facilities

Two toilet blocks with facilities for disabled visitors and a baby room. Laundry. Shop, comfortable bar, with large screen satellite TV, attractive restaurant and takeaway (all season). Heated swimming pool complex with slide (outdoor 15/5-15/9, indoor all season). Games room. Play areas. Football pitch (weekly games organised in July/Aug). Lake for fishing/canoeing. Riding.
Off site: Pénestin town centre 2 km. Supermarket 1 km. Golf 25 km. Sailing and boat ramp 2.5 km. Beach 2 km.

Open: 3 April - 20 September.

Directions

From D34 from La Roche-Bernard, at roundabout just after entering Pénestin take D201 south, signed Assérac. After 100 m. take first turning on left (site signed) opposite Intermarché supermarket. After 650 m. turn right, again signed, and campsite is 400 m. on left. GPS: 47.471483, -2.467267

Charges guide

Per unit incl. 2 persons and electricity	€ 15,00 - € 39,00
extra person	€ 5,00 - € 6,00
child (3-7 yrs)	free - € 6,00
dog	€ 4,00

Pléneuf Val André

Campéole les Monts Colleux

26, rue Jean Lebrun, F-22370 Pléneuf Val André (Côtes d'Armor) T: **02 96 72 95 10**
E: **cplmontscolleux@atciat.com** **alanrogers.com/FR22380**

Les Monts Colleux is a member of the Campéole group with an unusual town centre location in Le Val André. The site, however, has a hilltop setting and some pitches have fine views of the sea. This was formerly a municipal site and is well managed with well kept hedges and pitches. The reception area and shop have been added recently, although the toilet blocks are older. Pitches are generally flat, although, given its hillside location, there are some sloping pitches. The 125 pitches all have electrical connections (10A). Although there is no swimming pool on site, there is a large covered municipal pool adjacent with limited free access for campers. Around 70 pitches are occupied by mobile homes, chalets and fully equipped bungalow tents (available for rent). The nearest beach is close – just 300 m, and boats can be launched nearby. An attractive golf course is 1 km. distant. Val André is an attractive resort and the town centre is just 300 m. from the site. There are many activities during the high season, including weekly free jazz concerts.

Facilities

Shop. Snack bar. Takeaway meals. Play area and bouncy castle. Games/TV room. Activity and entertainment programme. Tourist information. Mobile homes and chalets for rent. Off site: Municipal covered swimming pool adjacent. Val André centre 300 m. Golf 1km. Nearest beach 300 m. Fishing.

Open: 1 April - 30 September.

Directions

Approaching from the east (St Malo and Dinard) on the D786, bypass Erquy and continue to Pléneuf Val André and then to Le Val André. Follow signs to 'Piscine Municipale' – the site is adjacent.
GPS: 48.5894, -2.5508

Charges guide

Per pitch incl. electricity	€ 7,55 - € 10,75

Pleubian

Camping de Port la Chaine

F-22610 Pleubian (Côtes d'Armor) T: **02 96 22 92 38**. E: **info@portlachaine.com**

alanrogers.com/FR22140

Michelle and Thierry Suquet offer a warm welcome to this comfortable, quiet, family site. In a beautiful location on the Presqu'île Sauvage between Paimpol and Perros-Guirec, attractive trees and shrubs provide a balance of sun and shade for the 200 pitches. Of these, 140 are for touring, all with electricity (long leads may be needed in places) and some also have water and drainage. Pitches are on grassy terraces on the gradual descent towards the bay and the sea (a sandy bay with rocks). Most terraces have a slight slope, so those with motorcaravans will need to choose their pitch carefully.

Facilities

Two traditional style toilet blocks are comfortable and fully equipped, both now completely renovated. Washbasins in cabins, British and Turkish style toilets. Cabins for families or disabled visitors. Washing machines and dryer. Bar/restaurant with terrace and takeaway (1/7-25/8). Heated swimming pool (13/6-5/9). Play area. Games room. Pétanque. Children's entertainer in July/Aug. Beach, fishing and sailing. WiFi in reception area. Off site: Bus 1 km. Village 2 km. for tennis, market, shops and restaurants. Good fishing and diving. Boat launching 1 km. Bicycle hire 2 km. Riding 6 km. Golf 18 km.

Open: 4 April - 20 September.

Directions

Pleubian is 37 km. north of Guingamp and 87 km. by road east of Roscoff. From D786 Lannion - Paimpol road, east of Tréguier turn north on D20 to Pleubian and on for 2 km. towards l'Armor Pleubian. Site signed to left. GPS: 48.8555, -3.1327

Charges guide

Per person	€ 3,50 - € 5,70
child (2-7 yrs)	€ 3,00 - € 3,70
pitch with electricity	€ 9,00 - € 14,10
dog	€ 2,90

The Travel Service to book this site call 01580 214000 ...we'll arrange everything

Plonevez-Porzay

Domaine de Kervel

Kervel, F-29550 Plonevez-Porzay (Finistère) T: **02 98 92 51 54**. E: **camping.kervel@wanadoo.fr**

alanrogers.com/FR29480

This is a large, well maintained site with many mature trees providing shade and colourful landscaping with shrubs and flowers. Marked by faint lines on the ground, the grassy pitches are level and well kept. Arranged in enclosures of five to six units, each group is surrounded by trees. The excellent pool complex provides indoor and outdoor pools, sunbathing terraces, paddling pools and a slide. Nearby are a comfortable bar and separate restaurant and for youngsters on a rainy day, a large, well equipped games room. The beach of Douarnenez Bay is 1 km. and is wide, safe and popular with sail-boarders. Douarnenez itself is 15 minutes by car and offers shops, bars and restaurants. There is a variety of accommodation for rent.

Facilities

One large and one small toilet block provide toilets, showers and washbasins in cabins. Baby room. Washing machines and dryers (at the large block). Bar. Restaurant. Snack bar. Shop. Swimming pools, indoor and outdoor. Games room. Multisport court. Minigolf. Off site: Beach 1 km. Douarnenez 15 minutes by car.

Open: 31 March - 30 September.

Directions

From Plonevez-Porzay travel southwest on the D107 for about 3 km. Turn west on CD107 signed Kervel and site is signed from here. GPS: 48.11605, -4.26737

Charges guide

Per person	€ 4,00 - € 5,50
child (2-7 yrs)	€ 2,50 - € 3,00
pitch	€ 7,50 - € 12,50
electricity (10A)	€ 3,50

Plobannalec-Lesconil

Yelloh! Village le Manoir de Kerlut

F-29740 Plobannalec-Lesconil (Finistère) T: **02 98 82 23 89**. E: **info@yellohvillage-manoir-de-kerlut.com**
alanrogers.com/FR29120

Le Manoir de Kerlut is a comfortable site in the grounds of a manor house on a river estuary near Pont l'Abbé. The campsite itself has neat, modern buildings and is laid out on flat grass providing 240 pitches (90 for touring units). All have electricity connections, some also have water and drainage and around ten pitches have hardstanding. One area is rather open with separating hedges planted, the other part being amongst more mature bushes and some trees which provide shade. Site amenities are of good quality. The old 'Manoir' is still open to the public and is used during the high season as a crêperie.

Facilities

Toilet facilities in two good blocks (each with several rooms, not all open outside July/Aug), include washbasins all in cabins, and facilities for babies and disabled people. Laundry. Small shop. Takeaway. Large modern bar with TV (satellite) and entertainment all season. Two swimming pools (one covered and heated), paddling pool and water slide. Sauna, solarium and small gym. Fitness and sauna centre. Play area. Tennis. Petanque. Games room. Bicycle hire. Off site: Beach 2 km. Fishing 2 km. Riding 5 km. Golf 15 km.

Open: 7 May - 19 September, with all services.

Directions

From Pont l'Abbé, on D785, take D102 road towards Lesconil. Site is signed on the left, shortly after the village of Plobannalec. GPS: 47.81234, -4.22105

Charges 2010

Per unit incl. 2 persons and electricity	€ 15,00 - € 39,00
extra person	€ 5,00 - € 7,00
child (under 10 yrs)	free
dog	€ 4,00

See advertisement on page 36

Plouézec

Camping le Cap Horn

Port Lazo, F-22470 Plouézec (Côtes d'Armor) T: **02 96 20 64 28**. E: **lecaphorn@hotmail.com**
alanrogers.com/FR22320

Le Cap Horn is in a magnificent setting with exceptional views of the Bay of Paimpol and the Ile de Bréhat. The enthusiastic owners are keen to make visitors welcome at their site which is well positioned for exploring the Goëlo Coast, Paimpol and the Pink Granite Coast. The campsite is in two sections and slopes down to the beach. The upper section is mostly devoted to mobile homes and is reached by a road or a series of steep steps, the lower section is for tourers. There are 149 pitches with 115 good sized grass pitches for touring (90 with 6A electricity).

Facilities

Two toilet blocks including facilities for campers with disabilities but site not ideal for those with walking difficulties. Small shop. Bar, restaurant with takeaway and terrace with views over the bay (July/Aug). Heated swimming pool, paddling pool (1/6-15/9). Play area. Boules. Fishing. Watersports. Sports area. Bicycle hire, Organised activities (July/Aug). Internet access. Off site: Beach 100 m. Boat ramp 300 m. Riding 6 km. Golf 12 km. Shops, bars restaurant at Plouézec and Paimpol.

Open: 7 April - 30 September.

Directions

From Saint Brieuc take D786 north to Paimpol (par la Côte). Site is at Plouézec, south of Paimpol, well signed from D786. GPS: 48.759792, -2.962795

Charges guide

Per unit incl. 2 persons	€ 14,00 - € 21,00
incl. electricity (6A)	€ 17,00 - € 25,00
extra person	€ 4,00 - € 5,50
child (under 7 yrs)	€ 3,00 - € 5,00

Plouha

Castel Camping Domaine de Keravel

La Trinité, F-22580 Plouha (Côtes d'Armor) T: **02 96 22 49 13**. E: **renseignement@keravel.com**
alanrogers.com/FR22400

This site is in the grounds of a manor house that has a rather faded grandeur. The setting is spectacular, the site being on the tree-clad slopes below the house from where there are glimpses of the sea in the distance. However, when we visited at the very start of their season, the site had not opened on schedule and the pitches had not been prepared. There are 112 grass pitches among the trees, all with electricity and 50 with water and a drain. Agnes and Gilles Pierre have plans to improve the site and we wish them well. There is a good beach nearby and this is an excellent area for walking and cycling enthusiasts.

Facilities

Large but rather drably-furnished toilet block with washbasins in cubicles and controllable showers. Baby room. Facilities for disabled visitors. Laundry room with washing machine and dryer. Motorcaravan service point. Heated swimming pool. Tennis court. There will be a shop, restaurant (with drinks licence) and takeaway, but no bar. Off site: Beach1 km. Bicycle hire 2 km. Riding, sailing and boat launching all 3 km. Golf 4 km. Village 2 km.

Open: 15 May - 30 September.

Directions

Plouha is 100 km. from both Roscoff and Saint Malo. From N12 Saint Brieuc by-pass take D786 Paimpol (par la Côte). On reaching Plouha turn east at second roundabout to town centre and follow signs to campsite in 2 km. GPS: 48.68968, -2.90848

Charges guide

Per unit incl. 2 persons and electricity	€ 27,90
extra person	€ 6,60
child (0-7 yrs)	€ 3,60

Plouhinec

Camping Moténo

Route du Magouër, F-56680 Plouhinec (Morbihan) T: **02 97 36 76 63**. E: **camping-moteno@wanadoo.fr**
alanrogers.com/FR56440

This site is situated on the east side of the river d'Etel just before it enters the sea. The grass pitches are of average size, hedged and shaded by large trees. Of the 256 pitches, 181 are occupied by mobile homes, mostly for rent. The new aqua park complex with covered and open areas is superb and includes slides, flumes and various pools. The beach is easily accessible, just 800 m. as is the little port facing Etel which can be reached by a regular ferry service. Plouhinec, the nearest town, is 5 km. by road where you will find shops and restaurants.

Facilities

Three toilet blocks (only one open when we visited in June) are old and poorly maintained. Washing machines and dryer. Shop and bar (July/Aug). New aqua complex. Multisport court. Gym. Bicycle hire. Play area. Entertainment (July/Aug). Off site: Beach 800 m. Ferry to Etel for bars and shopping.

Open: 5 April - 13 September.

Directions

From Plouhinec, southeast of Lorient, take the D781 in the direction of Carnac. Site is signed on right in 4 km. Follow signs for Plage. GPS: 47.66457, -3.22098

Charges guide

Per unit incl. 2 persons and electricity € 18,20 - € 26,00
extra person € 3,60 - € 6,00

Ploumanach

Yelloh! Village le Ranolien

Ploumanach, F-22700 Perros-Guirec (Côtes d'Armor) T: **02 96 91 65 65**
E: **info@yellohvillage-ranolien.com** **alanrogers.com/FR22080**

Le Ranolien has been attractively developed around a former Breton farm – everything here is either made from, or placed on or around the often massive pink rocks. Of the 520 pitches only 110 are for touring, mostly large and flat, but some quite small and all with electricity and some with water and drainage. The rest of the site is taken up with mobile homes and chalets for hire and several tour operators. The site is on the coast, with beaches and coves within walking distance and there are spectacular views from some pitches.

Facilities

The main toilet block is heated in cool weather and has washbasins in cabins, mostly British style WCs and good showers, some spacious and with washbasins. Facilities for disabled visitors. Laundry. Motorcaravan service point. Supermarket and gift shop. Restaurant, crêperie and bar (all open all season). Indoor and outdoor swimming pool complex. Wellness centre. Disco in high season. Minigolf. Games room. Play area. Cinema. Gym and steam room. Mobile homes for hire, including new 'gypsy caravans' and luxury chalets. Internet and free WiFi. Off site: Beach 150 m. Bicycle hire 1 km. Riding 3 km. Golf 10 km.

Open: 4 April - 13 September.

Directions

Perros-Guirec is 12 km. north of Lannion and 80 km. by road northeast of Roscoff. From Lannion take D788 to Perros-Guirec. Follow signs to 'Centre Ville' past main harbour area and then turn right along coast road (signed Centre Ville par la Corniche and Trégastel). Continue through north of town and on to village of La Clarté. After a sharp left hand bend site is immediately on the right. GPS: 48.82798, -3.47623

Charges guide

Per unit incl. 2 persons and electricity € 12,00 - € 40,00
extra person € 5,00 - € 8,00

Pordic

Camping les Madières

Le Vau Madec, F-22590 Pordic (Côtes d'Armor) T: **02 96 79 02 48**. E: **campinglesmadieres@wanadoo.fr**
alanrogers.com/FR22110

Les Madières is well placed for exploring the Goëlo coast with its seaside resorts of St Quay-Portrieux, Binic and Etables-sur-Mer, ports used in the past by fishing schooners and now a haven for pleasure boats though a few coastal fishing boats remain. Laurence and Thierry Dumand, the young and enthusiastic owners are always on hand to ensure the smooth running of this quiet, friendly campsite. The 93 pitches (11 with mobile homes for rent) are mainly set among trees and separated by hedges. An open area without electrical connections is available for campers.

Facilities

Two traditional heated toilet blocks include washbasins in cubicles and pushbutton showers. Facilities for disabled visitors. Laundry facilities. Motorcaravan services. Simple shop (all season). Bar, restaurant and takeaway (all season). Swimming pool (1/6-20/9). Games room. Play area. Some entertainment (high season). Off site: Bus service 400 m. Beach 800 m. Shops, bars and restaurants in village 2 km. Riding 2.5 km. Sailing 3 km. Bicycle hire 4 km.

Open: 1 April - 30 October.

Directions

Pordic is 10 km. north west of Saint Brieuc and 80 km. west of Saint Malo. From Saint Brieuc ring-road (N12), turn north on D786 signed Paimpol (par la côte). In 3 km. follow 'campings' signs through Pordic. Site is 2 km. north east of village (well signed).
GPS: 48.58240, -2.80480

Charges guide

Per person € 5,00
pitch incl. electricity (10A) € 11,00
Discounts outside July and August.

Poullan-sur-Mer

Flower Camping Caravaning le Pil-Koad

Route de Douarnenez, F-29100 Poullan-sur-Mer (Finistère) T: **02 98 74 26 39**
E: **info@pil-koad.com** **alanrogers.com/FR29060**

Pil-Koad is an attractive, family run site just back from the sea near Douarnenez in Finistère. It has 190 pitches on fairly flat ground, marked out by separating hedges and of quite good quality, though varying in size and shape. With 88 pitches used for touring units, the site also has a number of mobile homes and chalets. All pitches have electrical connections and the original trees provide shade in some areas. A large room, the 'Woodpecker Bar', is used for entertainment with discos and cabaret in July and August, when weekly outings and clubs for children are also organised.

Facilities

Two main toilet blocks in modern style include washbasins mostly in cabins and facilities for disabled visitors. Laundry facilities. Motorcaravan service point. Gas supplies. Small shop for basics (1/4-30/9). Bar, new restaurant and takeaway (all 1/6-31/8). Heated swimming and paddling pools (1/4-30/9, no Bermuda-style shorts). Tennis. Minigolf. Fishing. Bicycle hire. Playground. Off site: Restaurants in village 500 m. Riding 4 km. Nearest sandy beach 5 km. Douarnenez 6 km.

Open: 4 April - 27 September.

Directions

Site is 500 m. east from the centre of Poullan on D7 road towards Douarnenez. From Douarnenez take circular bypass route towards Audierne; if you see road for Poullan sign at roundabout, take it, otherwise there is a camping sign at turning to Poullan from the D765 road. GPS: 48.0824, -4.40805

Charges guide

Per unit incl. 2 persons and electricity	€ 16,00 - € 30,80
extra person	€ 3,60 - € 5,10
child (2-7 yrs)	€ 2,30 - € 3,40
dog	€ 2,80 - € 3,50

Quiberon

Camping Do Mi Si La Mi

31 rue de la Vierge, Saint Julien-Plage, F-56170 Quiberon (Morbihan) T: **02 97 50 22 52**
E: **camping@domisilami.com** **alanrogers.com/FR56360**

Occupying a five hectare site on the Quiberon Peninsula just 100 metres from the sandy beaches, this campsite has plenty to offer. Of the 350 pitches, 194 are for touring and are set amongst high mature hedges giving plenty of shade and privacy; some have sea views. Long leads are required on a few pitches as hook-ups can be shared between three or four pitches. The excellent facilities for children are in a well fenced area and include climbing frames, bouncy castles and multisport courts. Treasure hunts and other activities are organised daily. Staff at the well managed reception gave us excellent customer service and we enjoyed our stay on this site which is ideally situated for exploring this fascinating area.

Facilities

Seven sanitary blocks, with good hot showers. Separate laundry. Shop. Bar. TV room. Bouncy castles. Multisport courts. Children's club. Off site: Bar, restaurant, supermarket 50 m. Beaches 100 m. Bicycle hire 100 m. Town centre 2 km. Golf, riding 3 km.

Open: 1 April - 31 October.

Directions

From the N165 Vannes-Lorient dual carriageway south of Auray, take the exit for Carnac/Ploemel. Continue southwest on D768 through the town of Plouharmel following signs for Quiberon. About 25 km. from the N165 but before reaching the town of Quiberon, the site is signed to the left at St Julien-Plage. GPS: 47.49974, -3.12026

Charges guide

Per person	€ 3,00 - € 4,10
child (under 7 yrs)	€ 1,80 - € 2,70
pitch	€ 7,80 - € 12,00
electricity (3/10A)	€ 2,70 - € 4,10

480

Runner up Alan Rogers Awards 2009

Quimper

Castel Camping l'Orangerie de Lanniron

Château de Lanniron, F-29336 Quimper (Finistère) T: **02 98 90 62 02**. E: **camping@lanniron.com**

alanrogers.com/FR29050

L'Orangerie is a beautiful and peaceful family site set in 10 acres of a 17th-century, 42-acre country estate on the banks of the Odet river, formerly the home of the Bishops of Quimper. The site has 199 grassy pitches (156 for touring units) of three types varying in size and services. They are on flat ground laid out in rows alongside access roads with shrubs and bushes providing pleasant pitches. All have electricity and 88 have three services. The original outbuildings have been attractively converted around a walled courtyard. Used by tour operators (30 pitches). With lovely walks within the grounds, the restaurant and the gardens are both open to the public and in spring the rhododendrons and azaleas are magnificent. The site is just to the south of Quimper and about 15 km. from the sea and beaches at Bénodet. The restoration of the park, including the original canal, fountains, ornamental 'Bassin de Neptune', the boathouse and the gardens is now complete. Recent additions include a nine-hole golf course and driving range, and a new aqua-park with balneo, spa, and water chutes, slides and geysers.

Facilities

Excellent heated block in the courtyard and second modern block serving the top areas of the site. Facilities for disabled people and babies. Washing machines and dryers. Motorcaravan services. Shop (15/5-9/9). Gas supplies. Bar, snacks and takeaway. New restaurant (open daily). Swimming and paddling pools. New aqua-park with balneo, spa and water slides. Small play area. Tennis. Minigolf. Golf course and driving range. Fishing. Archery. Bicycle hire. General reading, games and billiards rooms. TV/video room. Karaoke. Outdoor activities. Large room for indoor activities. Pony rides and tree climbing (high season). Internet access and WiFi. Off site: Two hypermarkets 1 km. Historic town of Quimper under 3 km. Local activities include golf, cycling, fishing, canoeing, surfing and sailing. Beach 15 km.

Open: 15 May - 15 September.

Directions

From Quimper follow Quimper Sud signs, then 'Toutes Directions' and general camping signs, finally signs for Lanniron. GPS: 47.97685, -4.11102

Charges guide

Per person	€ 4,25 - € 7,10
child (2-9 yrs)	€ 2,75 - € 4,50
pitch (100 sq.m)	€ 10,25 - € 17,70
incl. electricity (10A)	€ 13,25 - € 22,20
special pitch (120/150 sq.m) incl. water and electricity	€ 17,00 - € 27,70

Camping Cheques accepted.

Rochefort-en-Terre

Camping de Moulin Neuf

Chemin de Bogeais, F-56220 Rochefort-en-Terre (Morbihan) T: **02 97 43 37 52**
alanrogers.com/FR56100

This quiet family site is in wooded countryside, 600 m. from the town. Ian and Norma Hetherington have worked hard to develop Moulin Neuf into a neat, tidy and organised site. There are 72 pitches (60 for tourers, 44 with 10A electricity) of good size (120 sq.m.) on neat grass, with two levels. The top level, with a limited number of electrical hook-ups, is flat and pitches are divided by young shrubs. The entrance is here and reception is located just beyond the security gate. The lower level is partly sloping with mature trees, shade and electricity on all pitches.

Facilities

The modern heated sanitary block is kept very clean and includes large, comfortable showers, cabins with washbasins and British and Turkish style WCs. Provision for disabled people. Baby room. Laundry facilities with washing lines. Bread delivered each morning. Heated swimming pool (1/6-31/8). Tennis. Two play areas. Off site: Lake 500 m. with watersports. Shop 600 m. Riding and golf.

Open: 15 May - 16 September.

Directions

From Redon take D775 Vannes road west for 25 km. Branch north on D774 signed Rochefort-en-Terre. Follow road past the lake on left, in 800 m. Turn left and follow sign to site. GPS: 47.69515, -2.34913

Charges 2010

Per unit incl. 2 persons	€ 16,60 - € 19,00
incl. electricity	€ 21,10 - € 23,50
extra person	€ 3,10 - € 5,50

Saint Cast-le-Guildo

Camping le Châtelet

Rue des Nouettes, F-22380 Saint Cast-le-Guildo (Côtes d'Armor) T: **02 96 41 96 33**. E: **chateletcp@aol.com**
alanrogers.com/FR22040

Carefully developed over the years from a former quarry, Le Châtelet is pleasantly and quietly situated with lovely views over the estuary from many pitches. It is well laid out, mainly in terraces with fairly narrow access roads. There are 216 good-sized pitches separated by hedges, all with electricity and 112 with water and drainage. Some pitches are around a little lake (unfenced) which can be used for fishing. Used by three different tour operators (73 pitches). A 'green' walking area is a nice feature around the lower edge of the site and a path leads from the site directly down to a beach (about 200 m. but including steps).

Facilities

Four toilet blocks with access at different levels include washbasins in cabins and facilities for children. Three small toilet blocks on the lower terraces. Some facilities are closed outside July/Aug. Motorcaravan services. Heated swimming and paddling pools. Shop for basics, takeaway, bar lounge and general room with satellite TV and pool table. Games room. Play area. Organised games and activities in season. Off site: Beach 200 m. Bicycle hire, riding and golf 1.5 km.

Open: 24 April - 10 September.

Directions

Best approach is to turn off D786 road at Matignon towards St Cast; just inside St Cast limits turn left at sign for 'campings' and follow camp signs on C90. GPS: 48.63723, -2.26934

Charges 2010

Per unit incl. 2 persons and electricity	€ 22,00 - € 42,00
extra person	€ 3,00 - € 7,00

Saint Cast-le-Guildo

Castel Camping le Château de Galinée

La Galinée, F-22380 Saint Cast-le-Guildo (Côtes d'Armor) T: **02 96 41 10 56**. E: **chateaugalinee@wanadoo.fr**
alanrogers.com/FR22090

Situated a few kilometres back from Saint Cast and owned and managed by the Vervel family, Galinée is in a parkland setting on level grass with numerous and varied mature trees. It has 273 pitches, all with electricity, water and drainage and separated by many mature shrubs and bushes. The top section is mostly for mobile homes. An attractive outdoor pool complex has swimming and paddling pools and two pools with a water slide and a 'magic stream'. A new indoor complex has now also been added and includes a swimming pool, bar, restaurant and large entertainment hall.

Facilities

The large modern sanitary block includes washbasins in private cabins, facilities for babies and a good unit for disabled people. Laundry room. Shop for basics, bar and excellent takeaway menu (all 21/5-5/9). Attractive heated pool complex (indoor 11/4 and outdoor 8/5-11/9) with swimming and paddling pools. New covered complex with heated swimming pool, bar, restaurant, entertainment hall and internet access. Outside terrace with large play area. Tennis. Fishing. Field for ball games. Off site: Beach and golf 3.5 km. Riding 6 km.

Open: 8 May - 11 September.

Directions

From D168 Ploubalay - Plancoet road turn onto D786 towards Matignon and St Cast. Site is very well signed 1 km. after leaving Notre Dame de Guildo. GPS: 48.58475, -2.25656

Charges 2010

Per unit incl. 2 persons and electricity	€ 21,50 - € 37,00
extra person	€ 4,00 - € 6,50
child (under 7 yrs)	€ 2,50 - € 4,50
dog	€ 3,50

Camping Cheques accepted.

Saint Jouan-des-Guerets

Camping le P'tit Bois

Saint Malo, F-35430 Saint Jouan-des-Guerets (Ille-et-Vilaine) T: **02 99 21 14 30**
E: **camping.ptitbois@wanadoo.fr** **alanrogers.com/FR35040**

On the outskirts of Saint Malo, this neat, family-oriented site is very popular with British visitors, being ideal for one night stops or for longer stays in this interesting area. Le P'tit Bois provides 274 large level pitches with 114 for touring units. In two main areas, either side of the entrance lane, these are divided into groups by mature hedges and trees, separated by shrubs and flowers and with access from tarmac roads. Nearly all have electrical hook-ups and over half have water taps. There are site-owned mobile homes and chalets, consequently the facilities are open over a long season (if only for limited hours).

Facilities

Two fully equipped toilet blocks, include washbasins in cabins. Baby baths. Laundry facilities. Simple facilities for disabled people. Motorcaravan service point. Small shop, bar (with entertainment in July/Aug), snack bar with stakeaway (open all season). TV room. Games rooms. Heated swimming pool, paddling pool and two water slides (heated from 1/5). Heated indoor pool with Turkish baths and Jacuzzi (all season). Playground. Multisport court. Tennis. Minigolf. Bicycle hire. Electric barbecues not permitted. Off site: Beach 4.5 km. Fishing 1.5 km. Buses 2 km. Riding 5 km. Golf 15 km.

Open: 11 April - 12 September.

Directions

Saint Jouan is west off the St Malo - Rennes road (N137) just outside St Malo. Site is signed from the N137 (take second exit for Saint Jouan on the D4). GPS: 48.60993, -1.98665

Charges 2010

Per unit incl. 2 persons and electricity	€ 22,00 - € 40,00
extra person	€ 5,00 - € 8,00
child (1-6 yrs)	€ 3,00 - € 6,00
dog	€ 4,00 - € 6,00

Saint Lunaire

Camping la Touesse

171 rue Ville Gehan, F-35800 Saint Lunaire (Ille-et-Vilaine) T: **02 99 46 61 13**
E: **camping.la.touesse@wanadoo.fr** **alanrogers.com/FR35060**

This family campsite was purpose built and has been developed since 1987 by Alain Clément who is keen to welcome more British visitors. Set just back from the coast road, 300 metres from a sandy beach, it is in a semi-residential area. It is, nevertheless, a pleasant, sheltered site with a range of trees and shrubs. Of the 141 level, grass pitches in bays, 90 are for touring units, all with electricity. The plus factor of this site, besides its proximity to Dinard, is the fine sandy beach which is sheltered – so useful in early season – and safe for children. The owners speak English.

Facilities

The central toilet block is well maintained, heated in low season with all modern facilities. Part of it may not be open outside July/Aug. Baby bath. Toilet for disabled people. Laundry facilities. Motorcaravan service point. Shop for basics (1/4-20/9). Pleasant bar/restaurant with TV. Video games for children. Sauna. Internet access in reception and WiFi planned in bar area. Off site: Buses 100 m. Sandy beach, fishing 300 m. Saling 400 m. Riding 500 m. Bicycle hire 1.5 km. Golf 3 km. Shops, bars and restaurants nearby.

Open: 1 April - 30 September.

Directions

Saint Lunaire is 5 km. west of Dinard and 13 km. from Saint Malo by road. From ferry terminal follow signs for Dinard. From other directions take D976/N176 and follow signs for Dinard. Turn west onto D168, then north west onto D64 towards St Lunaire. Follow signs to campsite at La Fourberie east of town. GPS: 48.63084, -2.08418

Charges guide

Per unit incl. 2 persons and electricity	€ 19,40 - € 24,60
extra person	€ 4,20 - € 5,20
child (under 7 yrs)	€ 2,40 - € 2,90
dog	€ 1,50

No credit cards.

Saint Malo

Domaine de la Ville Huchet

Route de la Passagère, Quelmer, F-35400 Saint Malo (Ille-et-Vilaine) T: **02 99 81 11 83**
E: **info@villehuchet.com** **alanrogers.com/FR35050**

Domaine de la Ville Huchet was taken over a few years ago by the owners of Camping Les Ormes (FR35020). It has been transformed into a superb site with modern facilities and lots of character. The pitches are well laid out and of generous size, most with 6A electricity and some with shade. They are set around an old manor house (disused) at the centre of the site. A splendid pool complex with its slides and pirate theme is particularly exciting for children. A range of entertainment for young and old takes place in the spacious bar area and a new creperie provides a range of food. This is a useful site, positioned on the edge of St Malo with easy access to the ferry terminal, old town and beaches. A bus service to take you into the town is 400 m. away.

Facilities

The sanitary blocks are modern and clean. Facilities for disabled visitors. Shop. Bar, crêperie and snack bar. Aqua park with water slides. Bicycle hire. Play area. Entertainment programme in peak season (including live bands).
Off site: Aquarium 700 m. St Malo (beaches, ferry terminal and old town) 4 km.

Open: 19 April - 13 September.

Directions

From St Malo take D301 heading south. Join D165 signed Quelmer and the site is well signed (2 km).
GPS: 48.61507, -1.98782

Charges guide

Per person	€ 3,65 - € 5,50
child (2-13 yrs)	€ 2,45 - € 3,30
pitch	€ 9,45 - € 13,15
electricity (6A)	€ 3,85 - € 4,65
dog	€ 1,60

Saint Pierre-de-Quiberon

Flower Camping l'Océan

16 avenue de Groix, BP 18 Kerhostin, F-56510 Saint Pierre-de-Quiberon (Morbihan)
T: **02 97 30 91 29**. E: **info@relaisdelocean.com** **alanrogers.com/FR56470**

L'Océan is a member of the Flower group and can be found just 100 m. from the nearest beach, halfway down the Quiberon peninsula. The site forms a part of a holiday complex that was established in 1925 and which also includes a hotel. There are 275 pitches which are generally well shaded, although some sunnier pitches are also available. A selection of mobile homes and fully equipped tents are for rent. In peak season, a varied entertainment programme is on offer, including traditional Celtic folk evenings and magic shows, as well as discos and concerts. The site's bar/restaurant 'Ty Mouss' is the focal point and specializes in pizzas and crêpes, as well as other light meals.

Facilities

Sanitary facilities provide hot showers. Facilities for disabled visitors. Laundry facilities. Motorcaravan services. Shop, bar/restaurant and takeaway (all July/Aug). Multisports terrain. Fishing. Bicycle hire. Tennis. Bicycle hire. Canoe hire. Play area. TV/games room. Activity and entertainment programme. Mobile homes and equipped tents for rent. Internet access and WiFi (charged). Off site: Nearest beach 100 m. Riding 3 km. Golf 15 km. Cycle tracks. Prehistoric stones at Carnac.

Open: April - November.

Directions

Leave the N165 at the Quiberon exit and head south on the D768. Continue towards St Pierre-de-Quiberon, passing through Plouharnel. Site is located at Kerhostin and is signed to the right, before St Pierre.
GPS: 47.534327, -3.139558

Charges guide

Per unit incl. 2 persons and electricity	€ 14,50 - € 21,90
extra person	€ 3,50 - € 5,00
child (2-7 yrs)	€ 2,20 - € 3,50
dog	€ 2,50 - € 3,00

Saint Pol-de-Léon

Camping Ar Kleguer

Plage Sainte Anne, F-29250 Saint Pol-de-Léon (Finistère) T: **02 98 69 18 81**. E: **info@camping-ar-kleguer.com**
alanrogers.com/FR29040

Ar Kleguer is less than 20 minutes from the Roscoff ferry terminal in the heart of the Pays du Léon in north Finistère. One section of the site (used in high season) has a 'country' feel and incorporates a small domestic animal park. The main section is divided into several areas, some on terraces at the edge of the sea with spectacular views overlooking the Bay of Morlaix. There are 173 large and well kept pitches, 125 for touring units, all with 10A electricity connections. Of these, 125 are for touring units. This neat site is decorated with attractive flowers, shrubs and trees. There is direct, but steep, access to a creek, and two grassy, rock-clad hillocks provide excellent and peaceful view points. This site would suit for long or short stays and is immaculately kept by the Kerbrat family. However, the real plus here is the beautiful surroundings, with the sea and beaches right on the doorstep. The friendly and helpful owners will advise on how best to enjoy this peaceful part of Brittany and suggest activities in the local area that might include walking, cycling and riding, or watersports, diving and sand-yachting.

Facilities

Three modern, tiled toilet blocks are well maintained and kept clean. Facilities for babies, children and disabled visitors. Laundry room. Shop, bar and takeaway (July/Aug). Good heated pool complex with paddling pools and slide (20/6-5/9). Pool table. Tennis. Bicycle hire. Animal park. Play area. Activities for children and some entertainment in high season. Beach adjacent with fishing and sailing. Free WiFi. Off site: Restaurant at site entrance. Sailing and boat launching 1 km. Riding 4 km. Golf 7 km.

Open: Easter - 30 September.

Directions

Saint-Pol is 18 km. northwest of Morlaix just off the D58 Morlaix-Roscoff road. Site is best approached from south, leaving D58 on the D769 signed Saint-Pol Littoral. Turn right at Cemetery following signs for 'Plages et Port' and Campsites. Turn left along seafront to site at end. GPS: 48.69151, -3.96717

Charges guide

Per person	€ 4,00 - € 5,35
child (2-7 yrs)	€ 2,40 - € 3,65
pitch incl. electricity	€ 9,00 - € 10,00
dog	€ 2,10 - € 2,60
car	€ 2,10 - € 2,80

Saint Quay-Portrieux

Camping Bellevue

68 boulevard du Littoral, F-22410 Saint Quay-Portrieux (Côtes d'Armor) T: **02 96 70 41 84**
E: **campingbellevue22@orange.fr** **alanrogers.com/FR22230**

With magnificent coastal views, this attractive and well cared for site lives up to its name. Family owned for many years, it is situated on the outskirts of the popular seaside resort of St Quay-Portrieux and you will be made to feel most welcome by the owners. The 173 numbered touring pitches vary in size and 140 have 6A electricity. Some are separated by hedges, whilst others are in groups of four. Entertainment on site is limited but there is plenty to do and see around the area and a great opportunity for exploring the Goëlo coast.

Facilities

Two clean sanitary blocks provide both open and cubicled washbasins and controllable showers. Facilities for disabled visitors and babies. Laundry facilities. Motorcaravan service point. Shop for basics. Simple snack bar (1/7-31/8). Outdoor pool (1/6-18/9; no Bermuda shorts). Paddling pool. Volleyball. Boules. Play area. Off site: Within walking distance of St Quay-Portrieux with shops, bars, restaurants and casino. Bicycle hire 1 km. Riding 8 km. Golf 10 km.

Open: 30 April - 18 September.

Directions

From N12 St Brieuc by-pass, take D786 north towards Paimpol. Site is well signed northwest of St Quay-Portrieux, 13 km. from the bypass.
GPS: 48.66277, -2.84443

Charges 2010

Per unit incl. 2 persons and electricity	€ 21,50
extra person (over 7 yrs)	€ 4,00 - € 5,20
child	€ 3,00 - € 3,30
dog	€ 1,50

Saint Briac-sur-Mer

Camping Emeraude

7 chemin de la Souris, F-35800 Saint Briac-sur-Mer (Ille-et-Vilaine) T: **02 99 88 34 55**
E: **camping.emeraude@wanadoo.fr** **alanrogers.com/FR35100**

M. et Mme. Giroux have, over the past ten years, created a pleasant site with a French feel and some surprising features for such a compact site. Notably these include an attractive heated leisure pool with water slides, whirlpool and a paddling pool, safely separated from the main pool and with its own little slide. There are 71 level pitches for touring, separated by hedges or shrubs and all with electricity connection adjacent (6A). Beyond these are 121 mobile homes and chalets (65 for rent). Although in an urban setting, the sandy beaches of the attractive Côte Eméraude are only a short drive away.

Facilities

Large toilet block with washbasins in cubicles and controllable showers. Facilities for disabled visitors. Baby room. Washing machine and dryer. Motorcaravan service points. Swimming pool (8/5-10/9). Shop and takeaway (all season). Bar (July/Aug). Games room. Excellent play area. Minigolf. Bicycle hire. Children's activities and evening entertainment for families (July/Aug). Gas barbecues only (available for hire). No twin-axle caravans or motorhomes. Off site: Beach, fishing, sailing and boat-launching 900 m. Golf 3 km. Shops, bars and restaurants nearby.

Open: 3 April - 19 September.

Directions

Saint Briac is 7 km. west of Dinard and 14 km. from Saint Malo by road. From ferry terminal follow signs for Dinard. Turn west onto D168. Keep west onto D603 and follow signs for 'Camping Eméraude par la côte' (avoids town centre); site is well signed from there. From other directions take D976/N176 and follow signs for Dinard. GPS: 48.62776, -2.130865

Charges 2010

Per unit incl. 2 persons and electricity € 22,80 - € 29,60

Sarzeau

Camping la Ferme de Lann-Hoëdic

Rue Jean de la Fontaine, F-56370 Sarzeau (Morbihan) T: **02 97 48 01 73**. E: **contact@camping-lannhoedic.fr**
alanrogers.com/FR56200

Camping la Ferme is an attractively landscaped site with many flowering shrubs and trees. The 108 touring pitches, all with electricity (10A), are large and mostly level, with maturing trees which are beginning to offer some shade. The 20 pitches with mobile homes are in a separate area. The working farm produces cereal crops and the summer months are an interesting time for children to see the harvest in progress. Mireille and Tim, the owners, go out of their way to make this a welcoming and happy place to stay. Located in the countryside on the Rhuys Peninsula, Golfe du Morbihan, it is an ideal base for cycling, walking and water based activities.

Facilities

Two new, high quality toilet blocks with facilities for disabled people and babies. Washing machines and dryers. Bread delivery. Ice creams and soft drinks available at reception. Takeaway meals and traditional Breton 'soirées' (high season). Bicycle hire. Playground with modern well designed equipment. Pétanque. Off site: Beach, fishing and boating 800 m. Sarzeau 2 km. Riding 2 km. Golf 6 km.

Open: 1 April - 31 October.

Directions

East of Vannes on the N165, join the D780 in the direction of Sarzeau. Exit D780 at the 'Super U'; roundabout south of Sarzeau, following signs for Le Roaliguen. Campsite is signed.
GPS: 47.50745, -2.76092

Charges 2010

Per unit incl. 2 persons and electricity € 15,60 - € 19,90

No credit cards.
Camping Cheques accepted.

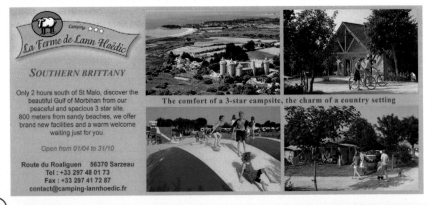

Sarzeau

Camping Manoir de Ker An Poul

Lieu-dit Penvins, F-56370 Sarzeau (Morbihan) T: **02 97 67 33 30**. E: **info@manoirdekeranpoul.com**
alanrogers.com/FR56450

Le Manoir de Ker an Poul has an attractive location, close to the sea (700 m.) in the southern Morbihan region. The old manor house is charming and the site has been developed in the grounds. This is quite a large site with around 350 pitches, around half of which are occupied by mobile homes and chalets. There is a large pool and aquagym is organized in peak season. Scuba diving lessons are available for children. Many other activities are on offer in high season, including evening entertainment and a children's club.

Facilities

Sanitary facilities include hot showers, washbasins in cabins and facilities for disabled visitors. Laundry facilities. Shop, bar and snack bar (all 1/7-31/8). Swimming and paddling pools. Games room. Tennis. Multisports pitch. Play area. Bicycle hire. Activity and entertainment programme. Mobile homes and chalets for rent. Off site: Nearest beach 700 m. Sarzeau 7 km. Cycle and walking tracks. Fishing.

Open: 5 April - 27 September.

Directions

From Vannes, head south on D780 towards Sarzeau. At St Armel join the D199 (Route de Menez) to Penvins and site is clearly signed.
GPS: 47.50542, -2.68325

Charges guide

Per unit incl. 2 persons and electricity	€ 23,00 - € 29,00
extra person	€ 2,70 - € 5,50

Taden

Camping Municipal la Hallerais

4 rue de la Robardais, F-22100 Taden (Côtes d'Armor) T: **02 96 39 15 93**
E: **camping.la.hallerais@wanadoo.fr** **alanrogers.com/FR22060**

La Hallerais has a lot more to offer than most municipal sites. It is ideally located for exploring this fascinating area and is quite a short run from Saint-Malo and from the resorts of the Côte d'Armor. It is just outside the attractive old medieval town of Dinan, beyond and above the little harbour on the Rance estuary. There is a pleasant riverside walk to the port and up into the town. Of the 226 pitches, 107 are for touring, all with electricity (6A), water and drainage, and are mainly on level, shallow terraces, with trees and hedges giving a park-like atmosphere.

Facilities

Two toilet blocks, one recently refurbished to a high standard, are of good quality and heated in cool weather. Unit for disabled visitors. Launderette. Shop. Attractive bar/restaurant with outside terrace and good-value takeaway (all season). Swimming and paddling pools (15/5 -30/9). Tennis. Minigolf. Games room with TV room above. Play area. Fishing. Mobile homes for rent. Free internet and WiFi. Off site: Riding 2 km. Bicycle hire 5 km. Beach, sailing and boat launching 15 km. Dinan 4 km. by road.

Open: 14 March - 15 November.

Directions

Dinan is due south of Saint-Malo (32 km by road). From N176 (Avranches/Saint-Brieuc) take Taden exit north of Dinan, turn towards Taden and follow blue signs to site. GPS: 48.47148, -2.02284

Charges guide

Per person	€ 3,25 - € 3,85
child (under 7 yrs)	€ 1,37 - € 1,67
pitch incl. electricity	€ 7,00 - € 12,10

Taupont

Camping la Vallée du Ninian

Le Rocher, F-56800 Taupont (Morbihan) T: **02 97 93 53 01**. E: **info@camping-ninian.com**
alanrogers.com/FR56160

M. and Mme. Joubaud have developed this peaceful family run site in central Brittany from a former farm and they continue to make improvements to ensure that their visitors have an enjoyable holiday. The level site falls into the three areas – the orchard with 100 large, hedged pitches with electricity, the wood with about 13 pitches more suited to tents, and the meadow by the river providing a further 35 pitches delineated by small trees and shrubs, with electricity. The bar has as its centre-piece; a working cider press with which M. Joubaud makes his own 'potion magique'.

Facilities

A central building houses unisex toilet facilities including washbasins in cubicles, large cubicle with facilities for disabled visitors and laundry area with washing machines, dryer and ironing board. Shop (July/Aug) selling bread. Small (7 x 12 m) heated swimming pool and children's pool with slide and fountain. Swings, slides and large trampoline. Trout fishing (permits from office). Off site: Riding 2 km. Bicycle hire, golf 7 km.

Open: 15 April - 15 September.

Directions

From Ploërmel follow signs to Taupont north on N8. Continue through Taupont and turn left (east) signed Vallée du Ninian. Follow road for 3 km. to site on left. From Josselin follow signs for Hellean. Through village, sharp right after river Ninian bridge. Site is 400 m. on right. GPS: 47.96931, -2.47014

Charges guide

Per unit incl. 2 persons and electricity (6A)	€ 14,70 - € 17,50
extra person	€ 3,20 - € 4,00

Credit cards accepted in July/Aug. only.

Telgruc-sur-Mer

480

Camping le Panoramic

Route de la Plage-Penker, F-29560 Telgruc-sur-Mer (Finistère) T: **02 98 27 78 41**

E: **info@camping-panoramic.com** **alanrogers.com/FR29080**

This medium sized traditional site is situated on quite a steep, ten-acre hillside with fine views. It is personally run by M. Jacq and his family who all speak good English. The 200 pitches are arranged on flat, shady terraces, in small groups with hedges and flowering shrubs and 20 pitches have services for motorcaravans. Divided into two parts, the main upper site is where most of the facilities are located, with the swimming pool, its terrace and a playground located with the lower pitches across the road. Some up-and-down walking is therefore necessary, but this is a small price to pay for such pleasant and comfortable surroundings. This area provides lovely coastal footpaths. A 'Sites et Paysages' member.

Facilities

The main site has two well kept toilet blocks with another very good block opened for main season across the road. All three include British and Turkish style WCs, washbasins in cubicles, facilities for disabled people, baby baths, plus laundry facilities. Motorcaravan services. Small shop (1/7-31/8). Refurbished bar/restaurant with takeaway (1/7-31/8). Barbecue area. Heated pool, paddling pool and jacuzzi (1/6-15/9). Playground. Games and TV rooms. Tennis. Bicycle hire. WiFi. Off site: Beach and fishing 700 m. Riding 6 km. Golf 14 km. Sailing school nearby.

Open: 1 May - 15 September.

Directions

Site is just south of Telgruc-sur-Mer. On D887 pass through Ste Marie du Ménez Horn. Turn left on D208 signed Telgruc-sur-Mer. Continue straight on through town and site is on right within 1 km. GPS: 48.22409, -4.37186

Charges 2010

Per unit incl. 2 persons and electricity	€ 25,10 - € 26,50
extra person	€ 5,00
child (under 7 yrs)	€ 3,00
dog	€ 2,00

Less 20% outside July/Aug.

Tinténiác

Camping Les Peupliers

F-35190 Tinténiác (Ille-et-Vilaine) T: **02 99 45 49 75**. E: **camping.les.peupliers@wanadoo.fr**

alanrogers.com/FR35110

In the grounds of La Domaine de Besnelais, this little site has a very French feel. It is in a quiet area with wonderful opportunities for walking and cycling, with a flight of eleven locks on the attractive canal nearby. Of the 100 level, grassy pitches separated by hedges and bushes, 40 are for touring, all with electricity (10A). There are a couple of small fishing lakes. The site is close to the D137 Saint Malo - Rennes expressway and could be used as a peaceful base from which to visit Dinan and Dinard, Mont Saint-Michel and the bustling city of Rennes.

Facilities

The traditional toilet block is kept very clean and has mainly British style toilets, controllable showers and some washbasins in cubicles. Laundry room. Swimming and paddling pools (15/5-30/9, heated 15/6-15/9). Bar with terrace (limited hours in low season). Weekly themed evening and some children's activities in high season. Takeaway food (to order in low season). Friterie (July/Aug). Basic supplies in reception. Tennis. Minigolf. Putting green. Boules. Fishing. Bicycle hire. Internet and free Wifi. Some mobile homes to rent (1/3-31/10). Off site: Riding 200 m. Boat launching 2 km. Restaurants and bars just down the road. Golf 25 km. Beaches and sailing 30 km.

Open: 1 April - 30 September.

Directions

Tinténiác is 43 km. south of Saint Malo and 30 km. north of Rennes. Site is 2.5 km. south of village and is signed. From D137, leave at exit for Hédé and turn east then north towards Tinténiac. Site is 1.5 km. GPS: 48.310016, -1.821075

Charges guide

Per unit incl. 2 persons and electricity	€ 19,40 - € 21,10

Tredrez-Locquémeau

Camping les Capucines

Kervourdon, F-22300 Tredrez-Locquémeau (Côtes d'Armor) T: **02 96 35 72 28**. E: **les.capucines@wanadoo.fr**
alanrogers.com/FR22010

A warm welcome awaits at Les Capucines which is quietly situated about a kilometre from the village of Saint Michel with its good, sandy beach and also very near Locquémeau, a pretty fishing village. This attractive, family run site has 100 pitches on flat or slightly sloping ground. All are well marked out by hedges, with mature trees and with more recently planted. There are 70 pitches with electricity, water and drainage, including ten for larger units. A good value restaurant/crêperie can be found at Trédrez; others at Saint Michel. A 'Sites et Paysages' member.

Facilities

Two modern toilet blocks, clean and very well kept, include washbasins mainly in cabins, facilities for babies and disabled people. Laundry with washing machines and dryer. Small shop for essentials (bread to order). Takeaway, bar with TV and games room. New covered, heated swimming pool. Paddling pool. Playground. Tennis. Minigolf. New multisport area. Chalets and mobile homes to rent. WiFi. Off site: Beach 1 km. Fishing 1 km. Riding 2 km. Golf 15 km.

Open: 1 April - 30 September.

Directions

Turn off main D786 road northeast of St Michel where site is signed, and 1 km. to site.
GPS: 48.69274, -3.55663

Charges 2010

Per unit incl. 2 persons	€ 14,40 - € 20,30
incl. electiricty (7A), water and drainage	€ 18,00 - € 27,00

Trélévern

Camping de Port l'Epine

Venelle de Pors Garo, F-22660 Trélévern (Côtes d'Armor) T: **02 96 23 71 94**
E: **camping-de-port-lepine@wanadoo.fr** **alanrogers.com/FR22130**

Port l'Epine is a pretty little site in a unique situation on a promontory with direct access to the sea, and views across the attractive bay to Perros Guirec. There are 160 grass pitches, 101 for touring, all with electricity (16A) and some fully serviced. They are separated by attractive hedging and trees. The rest are used for mobile homes. This site is ideal for families with young children, though not for teenagers looking for lots to do! On the north side is a little port facing an archipelago of seven small islands.

Facilities

The original toilet block is well equipped and a second block has been refurbished in modern style with thermostatically controllable showers and washbasin in cubicles. Baby room. Facilities for disabled visitors. Modern launderette. Shop and bar (all season) restaurant with takeaway (1/7-31/8). Small heated swimming pool and paddling pool (May-Sept). Fenced play area near the bar/restaurant. Video games. Bicycle hire. Fishing and boat launching. Internet and WiFi in bar. Off site: Riding 2 km. Sailing 5 km. Golf 15 km. Useful small supermarket up hill from site. Many coastal paths to enjoy. Boat trips from Perros Guirec 10 km.

Open: Mid May - 11 September.

Directions

Trélévern is 14 km. northeast of Lannion and 70 km. by road east of Roscoff. From roundabout south of Perros Guirec take D6 towards Tréguier. After passing through Louannec, turn left at crossroads for Trélévern. Go through village following camping signs - Port l'Epine is then clearly marked as distinct from the municipal site. GPS: 48.81311, -3.38598

Charges guide

Per unit incl. 2 persons and electricity	€ 14,50 - € 33,00
extra person	€ 5,00 - € 7,00
child (2-11 yrs)	€ 3,00 - € 5,00

Vannes-Meucon-Monterblanc

Camping du Haras

Aérodrome Vannes-Meucon, Kersimon, F-56250 Vannes-Meucon-Monterblanc (Morbihan)
T: **02 97 44 66 06**. E: **camping-vannes@wanadoo.fr** **alanrogers.com/FR56150**

Close to Vannes and the Golfe du Morbihan in southern Brittany, Le Haras is a small, family run, rural site that is open all year. There are 140 pitches, in a variety of settings, both open and wooded, the pitches are well kept and of a good size, all with electricity (4-10A) and most with water and drainage. Whilst M. Danard intends keeping the site quiet and in keeping with its rural setting, he provides plenty of activities for lively youngsters, including some organised games and evening parties.

Facilities

The two modern toilet blocks (heated in winter) provide a few washbasins in cabins and controllable showers. Facilities for babies and disabled visitors. Laundry facilities. No shop but basics are kept in the bar. Bar with snacks (May-Oct). Takeaway (July/Aug). Swimming pool with waves and slide (1/5-31/10). Play area. Animal park. Trampoline. Minigolf. Bicycle hire. Organised activities (high season). Off site: Riding 400 m. Fishing 3 km. Beach 15 km.

Open: All year.

Directions

From Vannes on N165 take exit signed Pontivy and airport on the D767. Follow signs for airport and Meucon. Turn right on the D778, follow airport and yellow campsite signs. GPS: 47.730477, -2.72801

Charges guide

Per unit incl. 2 persons and electricity (10A)	€ 19,00 - € 25,00
extra person	€ 4,00 - € 5,00
child (0-7 yrs)	€ 2,00 - € 3,00

A striking area whose beauty lies not only in the landscape. Famed for its seafood and Celtic tradition, certain areas of Normandy remain untouched and wonderfully old fashioned.

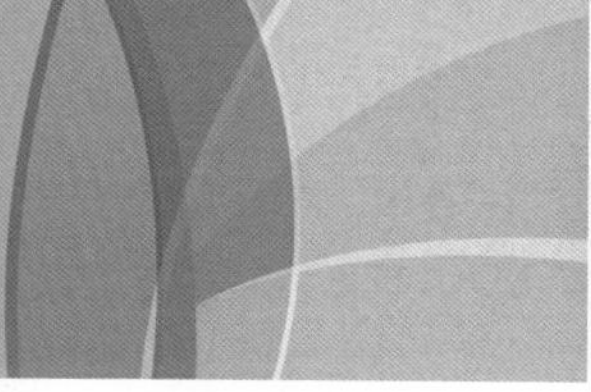

DÉPARTEMENTS: 14 CALVADOS, 27 EURE, 50 MANCHE, 61 ORNE, 76 SEINE MARITIME

MAJOR CITIES: CAEN AND ROUEN

Normandy has a rich landscape full of variety. From the wild craggy granite coastline of the northern Cotentin to the long sandy beaches and chalk cliffs of the south. It also boasts a superb coastline including the Cotentin Peninsula, cliffs of the Côte d'Albâtre and the fine beaches and fashionable resorts of the Côte Fleurie. Plus a wealth of quiet villages and unspoilt countryside for leisurely exploration.

The history of Normandy is closely linked with our own. The famous Bayeux Tapestry chronicles the exploits of the Battle of Hastings and there are many museums, exhibitions, sites and monuments, including the Caen Memorial Museum, which commemorate operations that took place during the D-Day Landings of 1944.

Known as the dairy of France you'll also find plenty of fresh fish, rich cream, butter, and fine cheeses such as Camembert and Pont l'Evêque. The many apple orchards are used in producing cider and the well known Calvados, Normandy's apple brandy.

Places of interest

Bayeux: home to the famous tapestry; 15th-18th-century houses, cathedral, museums.

Caen: feudal castle, Museum of Normandy, Museum for Peace.

Omaha Beach: D-Day beaches, Landing site monuments, American Cemetery.

Deauville: seaside resort, horse racing centre.

Giverny: home of impressionist painter Claude Monet, Monet Museum.

Honfleur: picturesque port city with old town.

Lisieux: pilgrimage site, shrine of Ste Thérèse.

Mont St-Michel: world famous abbey on island.

Rouen: Joan of Arc Museum; Gothic churches, cathedrals, abbey, clock tower.

Cuisine of the region

Andouillette de Vire: small chitterling (tripe) sausage.

Barbue au cidre: brill cooked in cider and Calvados.

Douillons de pommes à la Normande: baked apples in pastry.

Escalope (Vallée d'Auge): veal sautéed and flamed in Calvados with cream and apples.

Ficelle Normande: pancake with ham, mushrooms and cheese.

Tripes à la Mode de Caen: stewed beef tripe with onions, carrots, leeks, garlic, cider and Calvados.

www.normandy-tourism.travel
info@normandie-tourisme.org
(0)2 32 33 79 00

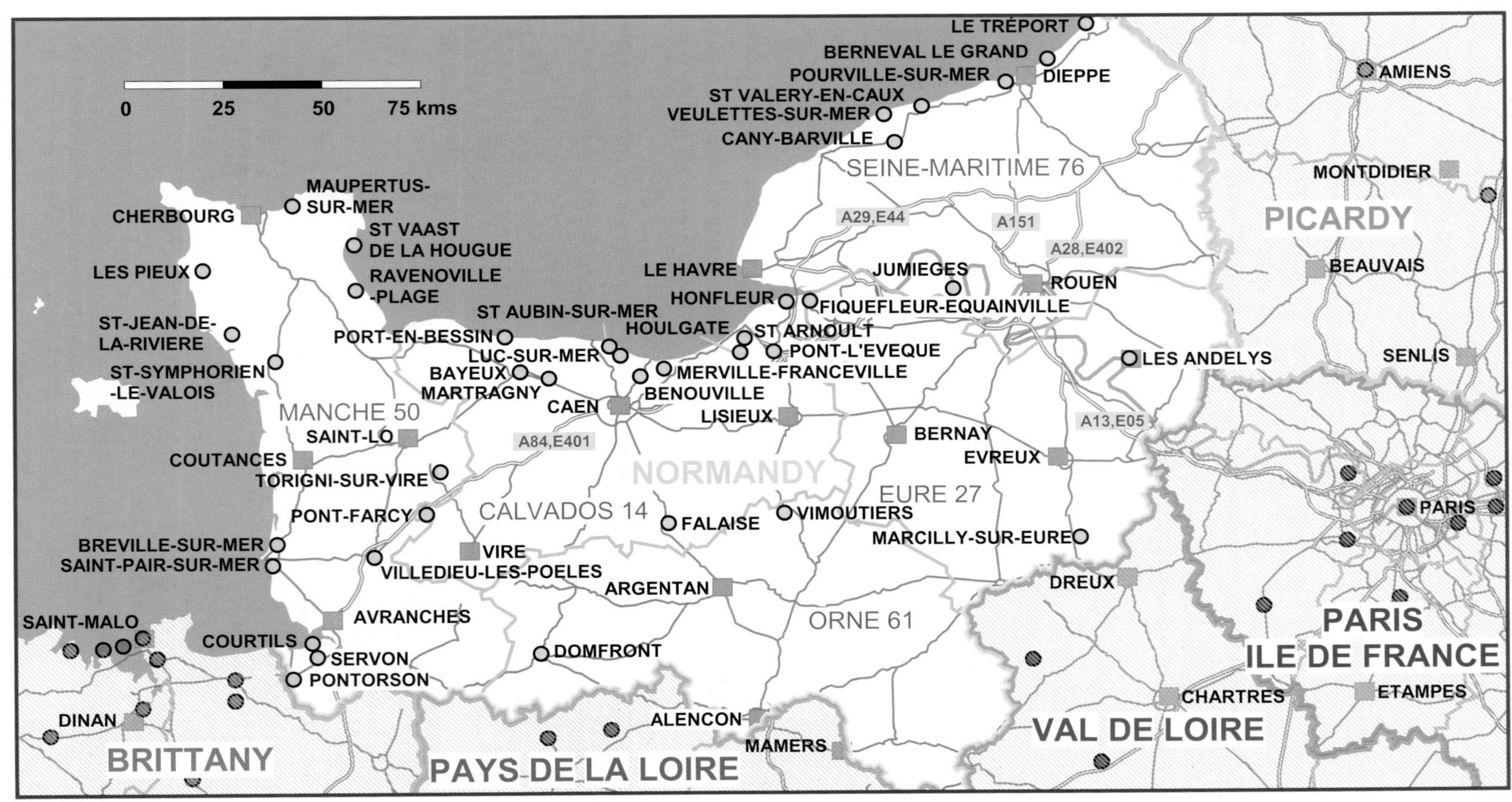

0
25
50
75 kms
LE TRÉPORT
BERNEVAL LE GRAND
POURVILLE-SUR-MER
DIEPPE
ST VALERY-EN-CAUX
VEULETTES-SUR-MER
CANY-BARVILLE
AMIENS
SEINE-MARITIME 76
MONTDIDIER
PICARDY
MAUPERTUS-SUR-MER
CHERBOURG
ST VAAST DE LA HOUGUE
LES PIEUX
RAVENOVILLE-PLAGE
A29,E44
A151
A28,E402
LE HAVRE
JUMIEGES
ROUEN
BEAUVAIS
HONFLEUR
FIQUEFLEUR-EQUAINVILLE
ST AUBIN-SUR-MER
HOULGATE
ST ARNOULT
ST-JEAN-DE-LA-RIVIERE
PORT-EN-BESSIN
LUC-SUR-MER
PONT-L'EVEQUE
LES ANDELYS
SENLIS
ST-SYMPHORIEN-LE-VALOIS
BAYEUX
MERVILLE-FRANCEVILLE
MARTRAGNY
BENOUVILLE
CAEN
MANCHE 50
LISIEUX
A13,E05
SAINT-LO
A84,E401
BERNAY
COUTANCES
EVREUX
TORIGNI-SUR-VIRE
NORMANDY
EURE 27
CALVADOS 14
PONT-FARCY
VIMOUTIERS
PARIS
FALAISE
MARCILLY-SUR-EURE
BREVILLE-SUR-MER
VIRE
SAINT-PAIR-SUR-MER
VILLEDIEU-LES-POELES
ARGENTAN
DREUX
SAINT-MALO
AVRANCHES
ORNE 61
PARIS
ILE DE FRANCE
COURTILS
SERVON
DOMFRONT
PONTORSON
CHARTRES
ETAMPES
DINAN
ALENCON
VAL DE LOIRE
MAMERS
BRITTANY
PAYS DE LA LOIRE

Andelys

Camping de l'île des Trois Rois

1 rue Gilles Nicolle, F-27700 Andelys (Eure) T: **02 32 54 23 79**. E: **campingtroisrois@aol.com**
alanrogers.com/FR27070

One hour from Paris and 30 minutes from Rouen, L'île des Trois Rois has an attractive setting on the banks of the Seine, with a private fishing lake and is a haven of peace. It is overlooked by the impressive remains of the Château-Gaillard and would be ideal as an overnight stop or for longer. The site has been owned by the Français Family for the past four years and they live on site. Within walking distance of the town and shops, the site has 100 spacious and partly-shaded grass pitches, all with electricity (long leads may be required for some). Water taps are rather scarce. There are also five mobile homes for rent and 60 pitches occupied by private mobile homes/seasonal units. Medieval Festival in Les Andelys – last weekend in June. Bread and cakes are available 24 hrs from a vending machine.

Facilities

Four small, unheated toilet blocks have British style toilets (no seats), showers and washbasins all in cubicles, dishwashing and laundry sinks. One has facilities for disabled people and another has a laundry facility. Motorcaravan service point. Two heated swimming pools (15/5-15/9). Fishing in the Seine or in the private lake. Fenced play area. Entertainment. Bar and restaurant, evening entertainment (4/7-30/8). Bicycles and barbecues for hire. Internet access and satellite TV. Off site: Day trips to Paris and Rouen. Cycling and walking trails. Riding 5 km. Golf 9 km.

Open: 15 March - 15 November.

Directions

From the A13 motorway, take exit 17 and join the D316 to Les Andelys. In Les Andelys follow signs to Evreux, and the campsite is located just off the island before passing the bridge over the Seine.
GPS: 49.23592, 1.40064

Charges guide

Per unit incl. 2 persons	€ 17,00
extra person	€ 5,00
child (under 3 yrs)	free
dog	€ 2,00

Bayeux

Camping Municipal du Bayeux

Boulevard Eindhoven, F-14400 Bayeux (Calvados) T: **02 31 92 08 43**
alanrogers.com/FR14020

Only a few kilometres from the coast and the landing beaches this site makes a very useful night stop on the way to or from Cherbourg, whether or not you want to see the tapestry. The 140 pitches are in two areas (many on hardstanding), well marked and generally of good size with electricity. The site is busy over a long season – early arrival is advised as reservations are not taken. There is a full-time warden from 15/6-15/9, otherwise reception is open from 08.00-10.00 and 17.00-19.00 hrs. There may be some road noise on one side of the site. Pleasantly laid out with grassy lawns and bushes, its neat, cared for appearance makes a good impression.

Facilities

The two good quality toilet blocks have British and Turkish style WCs, washbasins in cabins in main block, and units for disabled people. Motorcaravan service point. Laundry room. Takeaway food and snacks. Two playgrounds. Reading room with TV. Games room. Off site: Large public indoor swimming pool adjoins site with children's pool and jacuzzi. Supermarket nearby (closes 8 pm). Bicycle hire 1 km. Riding 5 km. Beach, golf or fishing 8 km.

Open: 1 May - 30 September.

Directions

Site is on the south side of northern ring road (D613) to town, and just west of the junction with the D516 to autoroute. GPS: 49.2839, -0.6976

Charges guide

Per unit incl. 2 persons and electricity	€ 14,20
extra person	€ 3,35
child (under 7 yrs)	€ 1,75

Less 10% for stay over 5 days.

Bénouville

Camping les Hautes Coutures

Route de Ouistreham, F-14970 Bénouville (Calvados) T: **02 31 44 73 08**
E: **info@campinghautescoutures.com** **alanrogers.com/FR14060**

Les Hautes Coutures is a pleasant site whose new owner has made considerable improvements to the leisure facilities so that it is now not only an ideal site for overnight stops (being just 4 km. from the Caen – Portsmouth ferry terminal) but also well worth considering for a longer stay. There are 120 good-sized grass touring pitches separated by mature hedges, all with electrical connections (4-10A). An area close to the canal has large, unmarked pitches. There are also around 150 mobile homes, 30 available to rent. The site is beside the Caen ship canal and a short walk along the footpath takes you to Pegasus Bridge and the Pegasus Memorial museum. In the other direction the path (and cycle track) goes to Ouistreham.

Facilities

Two toilet blocks include showers, washbasins in cabins (warm water). Facilities can be under pressure at peak times with variable hot water supply. Laundry facilities. Motorcaravan service point. Small shop, restaurant and takeaway (July/Aug) Bar (May - Sept). Attractive new pool complex with water slides and an outdoor pool linked to another with retractable roof (May - Sept). Small lounge/TV area and games room. Impressive new play area, trampoline and outdoor fitness equipment. Multisport court. Fishing. Minigolf. Boules. Off site: Pegasus Bridge and Memorial Museum short walk along canal path. Beach, sailing, boat launching, water-skiing and riding all 2-3 km. Golf 4 km.

Open: 1 April - 30 October.

Directions

Bénouville is 10 km. north east of Caen. From northern ring road (N 814) at exit 3, take D515 towards Ouistreham (or follow car ferry signs from other points). After Bénouville (now the D514) take first exit and site entrance is ahead. From ferry take D514 towards Caen; in 4 km. take slip road for Bénouville and at T-junction turn left to site. (Owner awaits arrivals from evening ferry).
GPS: 49.24948, -0.27217

Charges 2010

Per unit incl. 2 persons and electricity	€ 34,10 - € 34,60
extra person	€ 9,40
child (under 7 yrs)	€ 5,50

Berneval Le Grand

Camping Municipal Le Val Boise

Avenue du Capitaine Portheous, F-76370 Berneval Le Grand (Seine-Maritime) T: **02 35 85 29 18**
E: **camping-berneval@wanadoo.fr** **alanrogers.com/FR76020**

This pleasant, well run municipal site is located in a wooded valley running down from the village to the sea. The reception and a group of 14 larger pitches, a few occupied by seasonal caravans, are situated next to the road leading down to the sand and shingle beaches. There are also six attractive wooden chalets for hire. The remaining 16 touring pitches are on wooded terraces. All pitches have 16A electricity but only a few have shade. Val Boisé is ideal for those seeking a simple, inexpensive site close to Dieppe, from which to explore this stretch of coast.

Facilities

Two well maintained toilet blocks provide free hot showers (pushbutton) and some washbasins in cubicles. Facilities for disabled visitors. Washing machine and dryer. Motorcaravan service point. Activities room. Small play area for younger children. Large field for kite flying and ball games. Children's activities and tournaments (July/Aug). Free internet access in reception, plus free WiFi (also on adjacent pitches).
Off site: Beach and sea fishing 600 m. Boat launching 3 km. Riding, sailing and bicycle hire 10 km. Golf 12 km. Fishing 15 km. Buses from outside site to Dieppe and Le Tréport.

Open: 1 April - 1 November.

Directions

Berneval is 10 km. east of Dieppe. From A29 take N27 to Dieppe, turn east on ring road to join D925 towards Le Tréport. From ferry: after 2 km. turn east on D925. In about 5 km. turn north on D54 to Berneval le Grand and in village follow site signs.
GPS: 49.96203, 1.19362

Charges guide

Per unit incl. 2 persons and electricity	€ 11,50 - € 12,55
extra person	€ 0,80 - € 2,10
dog	€ 0,75 - € 0,80

Breville-sur-Mer

Kawan Village la Route Blanche

F-50290 Breville-sur-Mer (Manche) T: **02 33 50 23 31**

E: **larouteblanche@camping-breville.com** **alanrogers.com/FR50150**

La Route Blanche has a bright and cheerful atmosphere and Philippe and Corinne, the owners, are working continually to make an excellent site even better. The 140 pitches for touring are generous and numbered on well-cut grass and divided by young conifers. There are many shrubs and flowers and mature trees give shade to some areas. 67 pitches have 6/10A electricity and long leads may be necessary for some. Although the site does not have its own restaurant, there are five to choose from within a short distance and the beaches of Breville-sur-Mer are within a ten minute walk.

Facilities

Well maintained sanitary facilities with British style toilets, washbasins in cabins and showers. Good provision for disabled visitors. Laundry and dishwashing facilities. Bread available all season. Bar and takeaway (July/Aug). New large swimming pool complex with flumes, toboggan and bubble pool. Play area. Multisports court. Entertainment in high season. Off site: Golf (opposite). Fishing 500 m. Riding 1 km.

Open: 1 April - 31 October.

Directions

Take D971 that runs between Granville and Coutance. Then one of the roads west to Breville-sur-Mer. Site is well signed. GPS: 48.8696, -1.5627

Charges 2010

Per unit incl. 2 persons and electricity	€ 22,00 - € 33,00
extra person	€ 4,50 - € 6,00
child (2-7 yrs)	free - € 4,80
dog	€ 2,50 - € 3,00

Camping Cheques accepted.

Courtils

Camping Saint-Michel

35 route du Mont Saint-Michel, F-50220 Courtils (Manche) T: **02 33 70 96 90**

E: **infos@campingsaintmichel.com** **alanrogers.com/FR50110**

This delightful site is owned and run by an enthusiastic young couple, the Duchesnes. It is located in a peaceful, rural setting, yet is only 8 km. from the busy tourist attraction of Mont St-Michel. The site has 100 pitches which include 36 for touring units and 30 for mobile homes to rent. Electricity connections (6A) are available to all pitches and many trees and shrubs provide a good amount of shade. From the restaurant and its terrace overlooking the pool, the site slopes gently down to a small enclosure of farm animals kept to entertain children and adults alike. Meet Nestor and Napoléon, the donkeys and Linotte the mare, as well as miniature goats, sheep, chickens and ducks. It is the intention of M. and Mme. Duschesne to maintain a quiet and peaceful site, hence there are no discos or organised clubs.

Facilities

Two small, well maintained toilet blocks have washbasins in cubicles and pushbutton showers. Separate laundry. Baby room.En-suite facilities for disabled visitors. Motorcaravan service point. Shop and bar (15/3-15/10). Restaurant and takeaway (4/6-13/9). Heated swimming pool (1/5-30/9). Animal farm. Play area. Games room. Bicycle hire. Internet access and WiFi in reception area. Off site: Fishing (sea) 2 km, (river) 6 km. Riding 9 km. Sailing 25 km. Beach 2 km or (for swimming) 30 km.

Open: 6 February - 4 November.

Directions

Courtils is 8 km. east of Mont Saint-Michel. From the south on A84 and from north on A84/N175 leave at junction 33/34 and follow signs for Mont Saint Michel (N175/D43) and Courtils. From St Malo take the D137 south and join N176 east to Pontorson where it becomes N175. In 12 km. turn northwest on D43 signed Courtils. Site is through village on the left. GPS: 48.627616, -1.416

Charges guide

Per person	€ 4,50 - € 6,50
child (0-7 yrs)	€ 2,00 - € 2,80
pitch incl. car	€ 5,00 - € 6,50
electricity (6A)	€ 3,00 - € 3,50
dog	€ 1,00

Cany-Barville

Camping Municipal Cany-Barville

Route de Barville, F-76450 Cany-Barville (Seine-Maritime) T: **02 35 97 70 37**

E: **camping-canybarville@orange.fr** **alanrogers.com/FR76100**

This good quality site, first opened in 1997 next to the municipal sports stadium, has a floral entrance and tarmac roads. There are 100 individual hedged pitches available for tourists. There are around 40 concrete hardstandings (awnings can be a problem) and the remainder are on grass: 75 are fully serviced with water, drainage and electric hook-ups (10A). Shade from new specimen trees is still very limited. Cany-Barville is a bustling small town with a traditional Normandy market on Monday mornings.

Facilities

The modern, centrally located, sanitary unit can be heated and has British style toilets, controllable showers and washbasins in cubicles. Laundry facilities. Copious hot water. Separate suites for disabled people. Drive-over motorcaravan service point. Boules. Games room. Off site: Bakery, restaurants 600 m. Supermarket 1 km. Sailing and windsurfing centre 2 km. Beach 10 km.

Open: 1 April - 1 October.

Directions

Cany-Barville is 20 km. east of Fécamp on D925 to Dieppe. From traffic lights on east of town turn south on D268 towards Yvetot. Go under railway. Site is 600 m. from town on right, after stadium. GPS: 49.7831, 0.6424

Charges guide

Per unit incl. 2 persons and electricity	€ 14,10
extra person	€ 3,15
child (under 14 yrs)	€ 1,30
dog	€ 1,20

Domfront

Camping Municipal du Champ Passais

F-61700 Domfront (Orne) T: **02 33 37 37 66**. E: **mairie@domfront.com**
alanrogers.com/FR61040

Situated on the edge of the fascinating fortified town of Domfront, this small site has 34 individual pitches on a series of level terraces and a separate open grassy area for tents. The nine pitches nearest the entrance are all hardstandings separated by grass and with 10A electricity. Grass pitches on the lower levels, divided by shrubs and hedges, have 5A electricity and most have water and waste water points. The site is cared for by a lady warden who keeps everything immaculate and is justifiably proud of the entries in her visitors' book.

Facilities

Excellent sanitary facilities include British style toilets and some washbasins in cubicles. Facilities for disabled people. Washing machine. Motorcaravan service point outside gate (small charge). No separate chemical disposal point, but a notice tells visitors where to empty toilet cassettes. TV. Boules. Play area. Double axle caravans not accepted under any circumstances; American RVs can be accommodated. Off site: Sports centre adjacent. Supermarket 800 m. Fishing and bicycle hire 1 km. Riding 15 km.

Open: 1 April - 30 September.

Directions

Domfront is on the N176 Alençon - Mont St Michel road and site is just off this to the south of town; signed to the right up the hill towards town centre – or the left as you leave town heading west.
GPS: 48.5915, -0.6524

Charges guide

Per unit incl. 2 persons	€ 5,70
extra person	€ 2,65
electricity (10A)	€ 4,00

No credit cards.

Falaise

Camping Municipal du Château

3 rue du Val d'Ante, F-14700 Falaise (Calvados) T: **02 31 90 16 55**. E: **camping@falaise.fr**
alanrogers.com/FR14100

The location of this site is really quite spectacular, lying in the shadow of the Château of William the Conqueror, within walking distance of the historic town of Falaise in the 'coeur de Normandie'. The site itself is small, with only 66 pitches (most with electricity) either beside the little river, on a terrace above or on gently sloping ground. With trees and hedges providing some shade as well as open grassed areas, this site has a rather intimate 'up-market' feel about it, different from the average municipal site. Charges are reasonable and the reception friendly.

Facilities

Although the sanitary facilities are dated, they are of good quality and kept clean. Free hot water to showers, washbasins in cubicles for the ladies (all closed overnight). Unit for disabled visitors (shower room and separate WC). Motorcaravan service point. Excellent new play area for younger children. New tennis courts and boules pitch. TV room. Fishing. Free WiFi access. Off site: Bicycle hire 300 m. Riding 500 m. Kayak club 19 km.

Open: 1 May - 30 September.

Directions

Falaise is 35 km. southeast of Caen. Site on western side of town, well signed from ring road. From N158 heading south take first roundabout into Falaise and follow site signs through residential suburb to site.
GPS: 48.89556, -0.20468

Charges guide

Per person	€ 3,30
pitch	€ 4,00
electricity (5A)	€ 2,50

Fiquefleur-Equainville

Camping du Domaine Catinière

Route de Honfleur, F-27210 Fiquefleur-Equainville (Eure) T: **02 32 57 63 51**. E: **info@camping-catiniere.com**
alanrogers.com/FR27020

A peaceful, friendly site, close to the Normandy coast, in the countryside yet in the middle of a very long village, this site is steadily achieving a modern look, whilst retaining its original French flavour. In addition to 19 rental and 24 privately owned mobile homes, there are 87 pitches for touring units, plus a large open field for tents and units not needing electricity. Caravan pitches are separated, some with shade, others are more open and all have electricity hook-ups. The site is divided by well fenced streams, popular with young anglers. The site is a good base for visiting this part of Normandy.

Facilities

Toilet facilities include mostly British style WCs, some washbasins in cubicles, and facilities for disabled visitors and babies. Washing machine and dryer. Reception with shop. Small bar/restaurant. Heated swimming pool with slides and flume (1/6-15/9). Two playgrounds. Trampoline. Children's farm. Boules. Off site: Large supermarket close to southern end of the bridge. Smaller supermarket in Beuzeville 7 km. Beach 7 km. Golf 15 km.

Open: 10 April - 21 September.

Directions

From the Pont de Normandie (toll bridge). Take first exit on leaving bridge (exit 3, A29) signed Honfleur. At roundabout turn left under motorway in direction of Le Mans and Alencon on D180. Take second exit on right after 2.5 km, onto D22 towards Beuzeville. Site is on right after 1 km. GPS: 49.40090, 0.30608

Charges guide

Per unit incl. 2 persons	€ 20,00 - € 27,00

Credit cards accepted (minimum of € 70).

Honfleur

Camping la Briquerie

Equemauville, F-14600 Honfleur (Calvados) T: **02 31 89 28 32**. E: **info@campinglabriquerie.com**
alanrogers.com/FR14180

La Briquerie is a large, neat municipal site on the outskirts of the attractive and popular harbour town of Honfleur. Very well cared for and efficiently run by a family team, the site has 420 pitches, many of which are let on a seasonal basis. There are also 130 medium to large, hedged touring pitches. All have electricity (5/10A), water and drainage. One of the main attractions here is the close proximity to Honfleur where one can watch the fishing boats from the quay or browse the work of the artists who display their work in the galleries around the town.

Facilities

Two toilet blocks with washbasins in cubicles and showers. Good facilities for disabled visitors. Laundry room. Large restaurant (July/Aug). Takeaway (1/6-15/9). Bar (1/6-30/9). Small shop (July/Aug). Large pool complex (15/5-15/9). Sauna. Jacuzzi. Fitness room. Boules. Minigolf. TV and internet access. Off site: Supermarket adjacent. Beach 2 km.

Open: 1 April - 30 September.

Directions

Site is well signed from Honfleur on the D579, beside the Intermarché on the D62. GPS: 49.39735, 0.20849

Charges guide

Per unit incl. 2 persons, electricity, water and drainage	€ 20,80 - € 26,80
extra person	€ 3,00 - € 7,40

Houlgate

Camping de la Vallée

88 rue de la Vallée, F-14510 Houlgate (Calvados) T: **02 31 24 40 69**. E: **camping.lavallee@wanadoo.fr**
alanrogers.com/FR14070

Camping de la Vallée is an attractive site with good, well-maintained facilities, situated on the rolling hillside above the seaside resort of Houlgate. The original farmhouse building has been converted to house a bar/brasserie and a comfortable TV lounge and billiards room overlooking the pool. The site has 373 pitches with 98 for touring units. Large, open and separated by hedges, all the pitches have 4A or 6A electricity and some also have water and drainage. Part of the site is sloping, the rest level, with gravel or tarmac roads. Shade is provided by a variety of well kept trees and shrubs.

Facilities

Three good toilet blocks include washbasins in cabins, mainly British style toilets, facilities for disabled visitors and baby bathrooms. Laundry facilities. Motorcaravan services. Shop (from 1/5). Bar. Snack bar with takeaway in season (from 15/5). Heated pool (1/5-30/9; no shorts). Playground. Bicycle hire. Tennis. Entertainment in Jul/Aug. Internet access. Only one dog per pitch. Off site: Beach, town, fishing 1 km. Golf 2 km.

Open: 1 April - 30 September.

Directions

From A13 take exit for Cabourg and follow D400 to Dives-sur-Mer, then D513 (Houlgate) until the sea front. After 1 km. at lights turn right and follow site signs to site in 1 km. GPS: 49.2940, -0.0683

Charges guide

Per unit incl. 2 persons	€ 21,00 - € 30,00
electricity (6A)	€ 2,00

Camping Cheques accepted.

Jumièges

Kawan Village de la Forêt

Rue Mainberthe, F-76480 Jumièges (Seine-Maritime) T: **02 35 37 93 43**
E: **info@campinglaforet.com** **alanrogers.com/FR76130**

This is a pretty family site with a friendly, relaxed atmosphere. It is located just 10 km. from the A13 Paris – Caen autoroute. Cars and smaller motorcaravans can approach by ferry across the River Seine (not caravans). Formerly a municipal site, it has recently been over by the Hoste family. The 111 grassy pitches (84 for tourers) are attractively located in woodland. Many pitches have some shade and all have 10A electrical connections. There is a separate area for tents. The site organises some activities in high season and these include treasure hunts and guided walks. Jumièges is just 600 m. The great abbey at Jumièges was founded in 654 by St Philibert, rebuilt by the Normans and consecrated in the presence of William the Conqueror – well worth a visit! A range of shops, cafes, restaurants can also be found here.

Facilities

Two toilet blocks, both of modern construction and maintained to a good standard with British toilets, some basins in cubicles and preset showers. Baby room. Facilities for disabled visitors. Laundry facilities. Motorcaravan service point. Shop. Baker calls daily. Pizzas on Friday and Saturday evenings 18.30 hrs. Small swimming pool and paddling pool (heated 1/6-15/9). Playground. Boules. Games room with TV. Bicycle hire. Chalets and mobile homes to let. Off site: Bar/restaurant 600 m. Rouen 20 km. Riding and golf 8 km.

Open: 11 April - 25 October.

Directions

From A29, junction 8, follow Yvetot - Pon de Brotonne. Before bridge, turn left and follow Le Trait and Jumièges. Site clearly signed.
GPS: 49.43487, 0.82897

Charges guide

Per unit incl. 2 persons and electricity	€ 21,00 - € 23,50
extra person	€ 4,50
child (under 7 yrs)	€ 2,00 - € 2,50

Camping Cheques accepted.

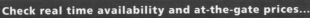

Les Pieux

Kawan Village le Grand Large

F-50340 Les Pieux (Manche) T: **02 33 52 40 75**. E: **info@legrandlarge.com**

alanrogers.com/FR50060

Kawan VILLAGES www.kawan-villages.com

Le Grand Large is a well-established, quality family site with direct access to a long sandy beach and within a 20 km. drive of Cherbourg. It is a neat and tidy site with 147 touring pitches divided and separated by hedging giving an orderly, well laid out appearance. A separate area has 40 mobile homes for rent. The reception area is at the entrance (with a security barrier) and the forecourt is decorated with flower beds. To the rear of the site and laid out in the sandhills is an excellent play area with swings, slides and climbing frame. Not surprisingly the sandy beach is the big attraction. Roads around the site are tarmac and there are pleasant views across the bay to the tip of the Cherbourg peninsula.

Facilities

Two well maintained toilet blocks. The main one is modern and includes washbasins in cubicles and some family rooms. WCs are mostly to the outside of the building. Provision for disabled people. Baby bathroom. Laundry area. Motorcaravan services. Shop for basics, bar (all season). Restaurant and takeaway (3/7-28/8). WiFi. Swimming and paddling pools (24/4-19/9). Play area. Tennis. Boules. Fishing. TV room. Entertainment (July/Aug). Off site: Bicycle hire and riding 5 km. Golf 15 km.

Open: 10 April - 19 September.

Directions

From Cherbourg port take N13 south for about 2 km. Branch right on D650 (previously D904) signed Cartaret. Continue for 18 km. to Les Pieux. Take the D4 in town and turn left just after the 'Super U' supermarket. Follow site signs via the D117/517.
GPS: 49.49452, -1.84246

Charges 2010

Per unit incl. 2 persons and electricity	€ 21,00 - € 35,00
extra person	€ 4,50 - € 7,00
child (under 18 yrs)	€ 3,00 - € 4,00

Camping Cheques accepted.

The Travel Service to book this site call 01580 214000 ...we'll arrange everything

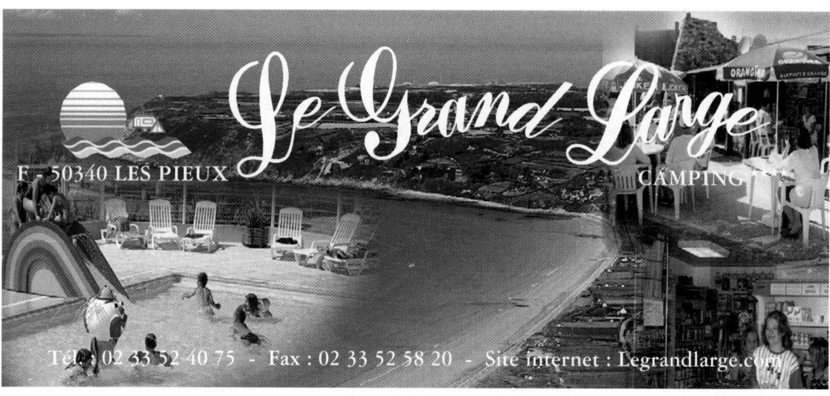

Le Grand Large
CAMPING
F - 50340 LES PIEUX
Tél : 02 33 52 40 75 - Fax : 02 33 52 58 20 - Site internet : Legrandlarge.com

Le Tréport

Camping Municipal les Boucaniers

Rue Pierre Mendès France, F-76470 Le Tréport (Seine-Maritime) T: **02 35 86 35 47**
E: **camping@ville-le-treport.fr** **alanrogers.com/FR76110**

This is a large, good quality, municipal site which has undergone redevelopment. It has an attractive entrance and some floral displays, tarmac roads and site lighting. The 260 pitches are on level grass, some with dividing hedges, and trees to provide a little shade. There are 22 good quality wooden chalets for rent, and some privately owned mobile homes, which leaves around 215 pitches for tourists, all with electric hook-ups (6A; some long leads are needed). A small unit acts as shop, bar and takeaway all season, the baker calls daily in high season, and every day except Monday in low season.

Facilities

Three well equipped sanitary blocks (one can be heated) provide mainly British style WCs, washbasins in cubicles, preset hot showers, with new facilities for small children and disabled persons in one block. Multisport court. Minigolf. Boules. Off site: Tennis, football and gymnasium nearby. Fishing, golf and beach 2 km. Riding 3 km. Markets at Le Tréport (Mon and Sat) and at Eu (Fri).

Open: 1 April - 30 September.

Directions

From D925 Abbeville - Dieppe road take the D1915 towards Le Tréport centre. At new roundabout take first exit to right and site entrance is 150 m. on right in rue Pierre Mendès-France. GPS: 50.05772, 1.38870

Charges guide

Per person	€ 3,20
child (2-12 yrs)	€ 2,30
pitch	€ 3,00
incl. electricity	€ 7,30

Luc-sur-Mer

Camping la Capricieuse

2 rue Brummel, F-14530 Luc-sur-Mer (Calvados) T: **02 31 97 34 43**. E: **info@campinglacapricieuse.com**
alanrogers.com/FR14170

La Capricieuse is situated on the edge of the delightful small seaside town of Luc-sur-Mer. It is an ideal location for those looking for a superb municipal site just a few minutes drive from the Ouistreham car ferry. This immaculate site has 204 touring pitches of varying size, on level grass with hedges and a variety of trees give some shade. 105 have electricity and 52 also have water and drainage. Although the site does not have its own shop, bar or restaurant, these can be found within walking distance in Luc-sur-Mer.

Facilities

Three modern toilet blocks with washbasins in cubicles and showers are kept very clean. Fully equipped facilities for disabled visitors. Laundry and dishwashing facilities. Motorcaravan service point. Large TV room. Games room. Adventure playground (unfenced). Tennis. Boules.
Off site: Fishing and bicycle hire nearby. Riding 3 km. Golf 30 km.

Open: 1 April - 30 September.

Directions

Take the D514 from Ouistreham car ferry and head west to Luc-sur-Mer. Campsite is well signed from the western end of St Luc. GPS: 49.31797, -0.35780

Charges guide

Per unit incl. 2 persons and electricity	€ 15,90 - € 20,35
extra person	€ 3,60 - € 4,50
child (0-7 yrs)	€ 1,92 - € 2,40

Marcilly-sur-Eure

501

Domaine de Marcilly

Route de Saint-Andre-de-l'Eure, F-27810 Marcilly-sur-Eure (Eure) T: **02 37 48 45 42**
E: **domainedemarcilly@wanadoo.fr** **alanrogers.com/FR27060**

The pitches at this campsite are used exclusively for mobile home accommodation. For full details please see our PRL section starting on page 501.

Martragny

Castel Camping le Château de Martragny

F-14740 Martragny (Calvados) T: **02 31 80 21 40**. E: **chateau.martragny@wanadoo.fr**
alanrogers.com/FR14030

Martragny is an attractive site in a parkland setting adjoining the château. Close to D-Day beaches, it is also convenient for the ports of Caen and Cherbourg, and has the facilities and charm to encourage both long stays and stopovers. The pleasant lawns surrounding and approaching the château take 160 units, with electricity connections for 140. Most pitches are divided by either a small hedge or a few trees. Bed and breakfast (en-suite) accommodation is available in the château all year (reservation essential). Madame de Chassey takes great pride in the site and takes care that peace and quiet is preserved.

Facilities

Three modernised sanitary blocks include washbasins in cabins, sinks for dishes and clothes and two baby baths. Disabled people are well catered for. Good laundry. Shop (all season). Takeaway food and bar (24/5-10/9). Swimming pool (20 x 6 m.) and paddling pool heated in poor weather. Play areas. Tennis. Minigolf. Games and TV room. Fishing. Bicycle and buggy hire. Off site: Riding 1 km. Beach 15 km. Golf 20 km.

Open: 1 May - 10 September.

Directions

Site is off the N13, 8 km. southeast of Bayeux. Take Martragny exit from dual carriageway.
GPS: 49.24941, -0.60237

Charges 2010

Per unit incl. 2 persons and electricity	€ 26,50 - € 32,00
extra person	€ 3,00 - € 7,00

Camping Cheques accepted.

Maupertus-sur-Mer

Castel Camping Caravaning l'Anse du Brick

Route du Val de Saire, F-50330 Maupertus-sur-Mer (Manche) T: **02 33 54 33 57**
E: **welcome@anse-du-brick.com** **alanrogers.com/FR50070**

A friendly, family site, l'Anse du Brick overlooks a picturesque bay on the northern tip of the Cotentin peninsula, eight kilometres east of Cherbourg port. This quality site makes a pleasant night halt or an ideal longer stay destination for those not wishing to travel too far. Its pleasing location offers direct access to a small sandy beach and a woodland walk. This is a mature, terraced site with magnificent views from certain pitches. Tarmac roads lead to the 117 touring pitches (all with 10A electricity) which are level, separated and mostly well shaded by many trees, bushes and shrubs.

Facilities

New sanitary facilities are kept spotlessly clean and are well maintained. British style toilets, washbasins mainly in cubicles and pushbutton showers. Provision for disabled visitors. Laundry area. Motorcaravan service point. Shop (1/4-30/9). Restaurant and bar/pizzeria (1/5-10/9). Heated swimming pool (1/5-15/9). Tennis. Play area. Organised entertainment in season. Miniclub (6-12 yrs). Bicycle and kayak hire. Off site: Fishing 100 m. Riding 4 km. Golf 10 km.

Open: 1 April - 30 September.

Directions

From Cherbourg port follow signs for Caen and Rennes. After third roundabout, take slip road to right, under road towards Bretteville-en-Saire (D116). From southeast on N13 at first (Auchan) roundabout, take slip road to right towards Tourlaville (N13 car ferry), ahead at next roundabout, right at third lights on D116 to Bretteville. Continue for 7 km. Site signed to right. GPS: 49.66715, -1.48704

Charges 2010

Per unit incl. 2 persons	€ 19,60 - € 36,00
extra person	€ 3,20 - € 7,20

Merville-Franceville

Camping les Peupliers

Allée des Pins, F-14810 Merville-Franceville (Calvados) T: **02 31 24 05 07**. E: **asl-mondeville@wanadoo.fr**
alanrogers.com/FR14190

Les Peupliers is run by friendly, family managers who keep this site attractive and tidy. It is just 300 metres from a long, wide, sandy beach. The touring pitches, of which there are 85, are on level open ground, all with 10A electricity. Those in the newest part are hedged but, with just a few trees on the edge of the site, there is little shade. The campsite amenities are near the entrance, housed in neat modern buildings. An entertainment programme for children and various activities are organised in high season. This site is ideally located for visiting Caen, Bayeux and the seaside towns of Deauville and Trouville.

Facilities

Two excellent heated toilet blocks with washbasins in cabins and showers. Good facilities for disabled visitors and for babies. Laundry room. Small shop, bar with terrace and takeaway (all July/Aug). Heated swimming pool and paddling pool (May-Sept). Play area. Games room. Entertainment in high season. Off site: Fishing, riding and golf all within 1 km. Bicycle hire 2 km.

Open: 1 April - 30 October.

Directions

From Ouistreham take the D514 to Merville -Franceville. Site is well signed off Allée des Pins. From Rouen on A13 (exit 29B), take D400 to Cabourg then the D514 to Merville-Franceville.
GPS: 49.28326, -0.17053

Charges 2010

Per unit incl. 2 persons and electricity	€ 21,70 - € 27,10
extra person	€ 5,55 - € 6,90

Merville-Franceville

Camping Point du Jour

Route de Cabourg, F-14810 Merville-Franceville (Calvados) T: **02 31 24 23 34**
E: **camp.lepointdujour@wanadoo.fr** **alanrogers.com/FR14210**

This former municipal site has a very French flavour and is an ideal location for family holidays as it has direct access to a fine sandy beach. There are 142 pitches bordered by shrubs and hedging, including 18 occupied by mobile homes and chalets (12 for hire). Although there are quite a few seasonal units, most have to be removed for high season. All touring pitches have 10A electricity, including those on the sea-dyke looking down onto the beach. Facilities are simple, but there is a smart new heated pool with retractable roof.

Facilities

Two toilet blocks (one heated) provide washbasins in cubicles, pushbutton showers, and fairly basic facilities for babies and for disabled visitors. Laundry facilities. Motorcaravan service points. All-purpose room with small bar, projector for films and football matches, pool table and exercise machines. Children's play area. Bicycle hire. Bread delivery. Entertainment and activity programme in high season. Internet access and WiFi in reception area.
Off site: Fishing 0.5 km. Golf, riding, boat launching, sailing, shops, bars and restaurants all within 2 km.

Open: 1 March - 15 November.

Directions

From A13 motorway at exit 29 take D400 towards Dives-sur-Mer and bear left on D400a to Cabourg. Follow signs for Merville-Franceville along D514. Site is on right in 2 km. From Ouistreham Car Ferry (16 km) follow signs for Caen and turn east on D514 over Pegasus Bridge and through Merville to site on left. GPS: 49.28319, -0.19098

Charges guide

Per unit incl. 2 persons and electricity	€ 20,00 - € 24,60
extra person	€ 2,30 - € 6,20

Pont-Farcy

Camping Municipal Pont Farcy

F-14380 Pont-Farcy (Calvados) T: **02 31 68 32 06**
alanrogers.com/FR14140

This well tended, riverside site is in a tranquil location within easy walking distance of the small village. Just off the A84 motorway it is within easy driving distance of Cherbourg or Caen. A warden lives on site. The 60 numbered pitches are on grass, some separated by small hedges, with electricity (10A) available to all (long leads may be needed). Activities either on-site or at the adjacent 'base plein air' include tennis, minigolf, volleyball, pétanque, canoe/kayak, pedalo and cycle hire, walking and fishing. Swimming is not permitted and the river is well fenced with access gates for anglers.

Facilities

A stylish modern building houses all the facilities, including some washbasins in cubicles and a suite for disabled campers. First floor 'salle' with dining tables, table tennis and games (ask the warden). A lift from the ground floor. Adventure-style playground (5-12 yrs). Off site: Village garage with a small shop, bakery, butcher, post office. Bar/hotel. Nearby attractions include Gorges de la Vire.

Open: 1 April - 30 September.

Directions

Pont-Farcy is about 25 km. due south of St Lô. From A84, exit 39, take D21 south for 1 km. Site is on left at entrance to village. GPS: 48.93992, -1.03533

Charges guide

Per unit incl. 1 or 2 persons	€ 9,00
extra person	€ 1,00 - € 2,15
electricity	€ 1,85

No credit cards.

Le Brévedent

Castel Camping du Brévedent

Le Brévedent, F-14130 Pont-l'Evêque (Calvados) T: **02 31 64 72 88**. E: **contact@campinglebrevedent.com**
alanrogers.com/FR14090

Le Brévedent is a well established, traditional site with 144 pitches (109 for tourists, 31 used by tour operators) set in the grounds of an elegant 18th century hunting pavilion. Pitches are either around the fishing lake, in the lower gardens (level), or in the old orchard (gently sloping). Most have electricity. It is an excellent holiday destination within easy reach of the Channel ports and its peaceful, friendly environment makes it ideal for mature campers or families with younger children (note: the lake is unfenced). Reception provides vast tourist information and English is spoken.

Facilities

Three toilet blocks with washbasins in cubicles and facilities for disabled visitors. One refurbished with en-suite cubicles. Laundry facilities. Motorcaravan service point. Shop Bar. Restaurant (24/5-19/9). Takeaway (1/5-25/9). Internet access. TV and library. Heated swimming and paddling pools (1/5-25/9). Playground. Minigolf. Boules. Games room. Fishing. Rowing. Bicycle and buggy hire. Organised excursions. Entertainment and children's club (high season). Dogs are not accepted. Off site: Riding 1 km. Tennis. Golf, boat launching and river swimming 12 km. Beach 25 km.

Open: 28 April - 23 September.

Directions

Pont-l'Evêque is due south of Le Havre. Le Brévedent is 13 km south east from Pont-l'Evêque: take D579 toward Lisieux for 4 km. then D51 towards Moyaux. At Blangy le Château continue ahead on D51 to Le Brévedent. GPS: 49.22525, 0.30438

Charges guide

Per person	€ 5,20 - € 6,70
child (1-12 yrs)	€ 2,20 - € 4,50
pitch	€ 7,00 - € 9,00
electricity	€ 2,45 - € 3,20

Pontorson

Kawan Village Haliotis

Chemin des Soupirs, F-50170 Pontorson (Manche) T: **02 33 68 11 59**
E: **camping.haliotis@wanadoo.fr** **alanrogers.com/FR50080**

kawan VILLAGES www.kawan-villages.com

Philippe and Cathérine Duchesne have achieved a remarkable transformation of this former municipal site and offer a warm welcome to visitors. Situated on the edge of the little town of Pontorson, the site has 152 pitches, including 118 for touring units. Most have electricity (16A) and 34 really large ones also have water and drainage. Excellent private sanitary facilities are available on 12 'luxury' pitches. The comfortable reception area incorporates a pleasant bar, opening onto the swimming pool terrace. This site is attractively laid out and includes a Japanese garden. Haliotis (which takes its name from a large shell) is next to the river Couesnon and it is possible to walk, cycle or canoe along the river to Mont Saint -Michel, 9 km. away. An auberge at half-distance could provide a welcome break! A good bus service is available from close to the site entrance to all major towns in the area.

Facilities

Well equipped heated toilet block with controllable showers and washbasins in cubicles. Good facilities for disabled visitors incorporating baby room. Laundry facilities. Bar where breakfast is served. Bread to order. Heated swimming pool with jacuzzi and separate paddling pool. Sauna and solarium. Good fenced play areas. Trampoline. Pétanque. Archery. Games room. Tennis court. Golf practice range. Multisport court. Outdoor fitness equipment. Bicycle hire. Fishing in the River Couesnon. Japanese garden and animal park. Club for children. Internet access in bar and WiFi throughout (both free). Off site: Local services including large supermarket, bars, restaurants and takeaways in Pontorson within easy walking distance. Riding 5 km. Bay 10 km. Beach, sailing and golf all 30 km.

Open: 1 April - 5 November.

Directions

Pontorson is 22 km. south west of Avranches and is by-passed by the N176 which links with D137 from Saint Malo to the west and (via N175) with A84 (Caen - Rennes) to the east. Site is 300 m. north of the town centre and is well signed. NB. Entrance is on rue du Général Patton. Satnav users should follow signs! GPS: 48.55836, -1.51429

Charges 2010

Per unit incl. 2 persons and electricity	€ 18,50 - € 22,00
with private sanitary facility	€ 22,50 - € 26,00
extra person	€ 5,00 - € 6,00
child (under 12 yrs)	€ 2,00 - € 3,50

Camping Cheques accepted.

The Travel Service to book this site call 01580 214000 ...we'll arrange everything

Port-en-Bessin

Sunelia Port'land

Chemin du Castel, F-14520 Port-en-Bessin (Calvados) T: **02 31 51 07 06**. E: **campingportland@wanadoo.fr**
alanrogers.com/FR14150

The Gerardin family will make you most welcome at Port'land, now a mature site lying 700 m. to the east of the little resort of Port-en-Bessin, one of Normandy's busiest fishing ports. The 300 pitches are large and grassy with 202 available for touring units, including 128 with 15A electricity. There is a separate area for tents without electricity. The camping area has been imaginatively divided into zones, some overlooking small fishing ponds and another radiating out from a central barbecue area. An attractive modern building houses reception and the good amenities which include a shop and a bar/restaurant with fine views over the Normandy coastline. A member of the 'Sunelia' group.

Facilities

The two sanitary blocks are modern and well maintained. Special disabled facilities. Heated swimming pool (covered in low season) and paddling pool. Bar, restaurant, takeaway. TV and games room. Multisports pitch. Fishing. Play area. WiFi access. Off site: Nearest beach 4 km. Golf course adjacent. Fishing 600 m. Bicycle hire and riding 10 km.

Open: 29 March - 5 November.

Directions

Site is clearly signed off the D514, 4 km. west of Port-en-Bessin. GPS: 49.3463, -0.7732

Charges guide

Per unit incl. 2 persons and electricity	€ 25,00 - € 37,00
extra person	€ 4,80 - € 7,30
child (2-10 yrs)	€ 2,80 - € 4,20

The Travel Service to book this site call 01580 214000 ...we'll arrange everything

Pourville sur Mer

Camping le Marqueval

1210, rue de la Mer, F-76550 Pourville sur Mer (Seine-Maritime) T: **02 35 82 66 46**
E: **contact@campinglemarqueval.com** **alanrogers.com/FR76010**

Le Marqueval is a well-established, family site of 290 pitches, located close to the seaside town of Hautot-sur-Mer, just west of Dieppe. The site has been developed around three small lakes (one unfenced, suitable for fishing). There are 50 grass pitches for touring units, all of a good size, separated by hedges and with electrical connections (6A). The majority of the pitches here are used for privately-owned mobile homes. Leisure amenities include a swimming pool and smaller children's pools. The site's bar also functions as a snack bar and during the high season evening entertainment is occasionally organized here. The site's owners will be happy to recommend places of interest in the area and these include Dieppe, with its old town, and the stylish resort of Le Tréport. This stretch of the Normandy coastline is well known for its towering white cliffs and fine sandy beaches. There are some superb coastal walks along the clifftops and quiet lanes, ideal for exploration by cycle. The nearby château at Miromesnil, birthplace of Maupassant, is well worth a visit and has magnificent gardens.

Facilities

The single toilet block is at the entrance to the site. Motorcaravan service point (charge). Snack bar. Swimming pool. Fishing (charged). Playground. Entertainment and activity programme. Mobile homes for rent. Off site: Nearest beach 1.2 km. Riding 1.5 km. Tennis. Cycle and walking tracks. Dieppe 5 km. St Valery-en-Caux (fishing port). Supermarket in Dieppe.

Open: 17 March - 15 October.

Directions

Head west from Dieppe on the D925 as far as Hautot-sur-Mer. Then turn right onto the D153 towards Pourville. Site is well signed from here.
GPS: 49.9088, 1.0406

Charges 2010

Per unit incl. 2 persons and electricity € 15,50 - € 23,00

Ravenoville-Plage

Kawan Village le Cormoran

Ravenoville-Plage, F-50480 Sainte Mère-Eglise (Manche) T: **02 33 41 33 94**
E: **lecormoran@wanadoo.fr** **alanrogers.com/FR50050**

kawan VILLAGES
www.kawan-villages.com

This welcoming, family-run site, close to Cherbourg (45 km) and Caen (95 km), is just across the road from a long sandy beach. It is also close to Utah beach and is ideally located for those wishing to visit the many museums, landing beaches and remembrance gardens of WW2. On flat, quite open ground, the site has 100 good size pitches on level grass, all with 6A electricity. Some extra large pitches are available. The well kept pitches are separated by mature hedges and the site is decorated with flowering shrubs. A covered pool, a sauna and a gym were among improvements in 2009. These facilities, plus a shop, comfortable bar and takeaway are open all season. This modern, clean and fresh looking campsite caters for both families and couples and would be ideal for a holiday in this interesting area of France. The country roads provide opportunities for exploring on foot or by bike. There are many small towns in the area and in early June, you may find historical groups re-enacting battles and the events of 1944-1945.

Facilities

Four toilet blocks, one heated, are of varying styles and ages but all are maintained to a good standard. Laundry. New kitchen facilities. Shop. Bar and terrace. Snacks and takeaway. Outdoor pool (1/6-15/9, unsupervised). New covered pool, sauna and gym (all season). Play areas. Tennis. Boules. Entertainment, TV and games room. Bicycle and shrimp net hire. Riding (July/Aug). Communal barbecues. Off site: Beach 20 m. Sand yachting. Golf (9 holes) 3 km.

Open: 3 April - 26 September.

Directions

From N13 take Ste Mère-Eglise exit and in centre of town take road to Ravenoville (6 km), then Ravenoville-Plage (3 km). Just before beach turn right and site is 500 m. GPS: 49.46643, -1.23533

Charges 2010

Per unit incl. 1 or 2 persons and electricity	€ 20,00 - € 32,00
extra person	€ 4,00 - € 7,50
child (5-10 yrs)	€ 2,00 - € 3,00
dog	€ 3,00

Camping Cheques accepted.

Saint Arnoult

Camping la Vallée de Deauville

Avenue de la Vallée, F-14800 Saint Arnoult (Calvados) T: **02 31 88 58 17**. E: **contact@camping-deauville.com**
alanrogers.com/FR14200

Close to the traditional seaside resorts of Deauville and Trouville, this large, modern site is owned and run by a delightful Belgian couple. With a total of 450 pitches, there are many mobile homes, both for rent and privately owned, and 150 used for touring units. These pitches are level, of a reasonable size and mostly hedged, and 60 have 10A electricity connections. A brand new pool complex complete with flumes, lazy river, jacuzzi and fun pool makes an attractive focal point near the entrance and there is a large fishing lake. The bar and restaurant are large and comfortable and there is a very good shop on the site. The wide sandy beaches of this coast are 3 km. With the various new developments at this site, it promises to be a good choice in the Deauville and Caen area.

Facilities

Two new heated toilet blocks with showers and washbasins in cubicles. Good facilities for babies and disabled visitors. Laundry facilities. Small shop, bar and restaurant (high season). Takeaway (all season). New swimming pool complex. Good play area and play room. Entertainment in high season. Off site: Beach 3 km. Golf and riding 2 km. Bicycle hire 3 km.

Open: 1 April - 31 October.

Directions

From the north, take the A29, then the A13 at Pont l'Eveque. Join the N177 (Deauville/Trouville) and after 9 km. take the D27 signed St Arnoult. Site is well signed on edge of village. GPS: 49.32864, 0.086

Charges guide

Per unit incl. 2 persons and electricity	€ 20,40 - € 34,00
extra person	€ 3,00 - € 9,00

Saint Aubin-sur-Mer

Yelloh! Village la Côte de Nacre

Rue du Général Moulton, F-14750 Saint Aubin-sur-Mer (Calvados) T: **02 31 97 14 45**
E: **info@yellohvillage-cote-de-nacre.com** **alanrogers.com/FR14010**

La Côte de Nacre is a large, commercial site with many facilities, all of a high standard. This could be an ideal holiday location for families with older children and teenagers. Two thirds of the site is given over to mobile homes and there are four tour operators on the site. The touring pitches are reasonable, both in size and condition. With pleasant, well cared for flowerbeds, there is some hedging to the pitches, but not much, and a few trees, so little shade. There is a 'state of the art' pool complex which includes a covered pool (with lifeguards in attendance).

Facilities

One open toilet block has showers and washbasins in cubicles. New block (completed in 2007). Laundry room. Bar, restaurant and takeaway. Pool complex with outdoor and indoor pools, slides, etc. Play area. Library. Games room. Children's club. Multisports area. Iceskating.
Off site: Town 1 km.

Open: 2 April - 26 September.

Directions

Travel west from Ouistreham on D514 to St Aubin-sur-Mer. Site is well signed, just off the main road in a residential area. GPS: 49.322333, -0.387333

Charges 2010

Per unit incl. 2 persons and electricity	€ 20,00 - € 44,00
extra person	€ 5,00 - € 8,00
child (3-7 yrs)	free - € 5,00

Saint Jean-de-la-Riviere

Yelloh! Village les Vikings

4 rue des Vikings, Saint Jean-de-la-Riviere, F-50270 Barneville-Carteret (Manche) T: **04 66 73 97 39**
E: **info@yellohvillage-lesvikings.com** **alanrogers.com/FR50200**

Les Vikings is located close to the attractive resort of Barneville-Carteret on the western side of the Cherbourg peninsula. The site is just 400 m. from a sandy beach. There are 250 pitches of which around 70 are reserved for touring, the rest being occupied by mobile homes and chalets, some of which are for rent. Pitches are grassy and of a reasonable size. Most of the site's amenities are grouped around the entrance, including a swimming pool (covered and heated), a restaurant/pizzeria and bar and a grocery shop. During the whole season, various activities are organized including discos and karaoke evenings.

Facilities

Shop. Bar. Restaurant, snack bar and takeaway. Swimming pool. Games room. Play area. Activity and entertainment programme. Mobile homes for rent. Off site: Supermarket. Trips to the Channel Islands and D-day beaches. Mont St-Michel.

Open: 27 March - 4 October.

Directions

From Cherbourg, head southwest on the D650 to Barneville-Carteret. Site is at St Jean-de-la-Rivière, just to the south of the town and clearly signed.
GPS: 49.3641, -1.75347

Charges 2010

Per unit incl. 2 persons and electricity	€ 15,00 - € 39,00
extra person	€ 5,00 - € 7,00
child (3-7 yrs)	free - € 5,00

Saint Pair-sur-Mer

Castel Camping le Château de lez Eaux

Saint Aubin-des-Préaux, F-50380 Saint Pair-sur-Mer (Manche) T: **02 33 51 66 09**. E: **bonjour@lez-eaux.com**
alanrogers.com/FR50030

Set in the spacious grounds of a château, Lez Eaux lies in a rural situation just off the main route south, under two hours from Cherbourg. There are 229 pitches of which 113 are for touring, all with electricity (5/10A) and 70 fully serviced. Most of the pitches are of a very good size, partly separated by trees and shrubs on either flat or very slightly sloping, grassy ground overlooking Normandy farmland or beside a small lake (with carp and other fish). There is a considerable tour operator presence, but these units by no means dominate, being generally tucked away in their own areas.

Facilities

Three modern clean toilet blocks include hot showers and washbasins in cabins, facilities for children and babies, and for disabled people. Shop, small bar, snacks and takeaway (all from 1/5). Small heated swimming pool and indoor tropical-style fun pool (from 1/5, no T-shirts or Bermuda-style shorts). Play area. Tennis. Games and TV rooms. Bicycle hire. Lake fishing. Torches useful. Only one dog per pitch. Off site: Beach 4 km. Riding 5 km. Golf 7 km.

Open: 1 April - 15 September.

Directions

Lez Eaux is just to the west of the D973 about 17 km. northwest of Avranches and 7 km. southeast of Granville. Site is between the two turnings east to St Aubin-des-Préaux and well signed.
GPS: 48.79778, -1.52498

Charges guide

Per unit incl. 2 persons	€ 14,00 - € 30,00
extra person	€ 8,50
child (under 7 yrs)	€ 6,50
electricity (5A)	€ 7,00
all services	€ 10,00

Saint Symphorien-le-Valois

Camping l'Etang des Haizes

43 rue Cauticotte, F-50250 Saint Symphorien-le-Valois (Manche) T: **02 33 46 01 16**

E: **info@campingetangdeshaizes.com** **alanrogers.com/FR50000**

This is an attractive and very friendly site with a swimming pool complex with four-lane slides, jacuzzi and a paddling pool. L'Etang des Haizes has 160 good size pitches, of which 100 are for touring units, on fairly level ground and all with electricity (10A). They are set in a mixture of conifers, orchard and shrubbery, with some very attractive, slightly smaller pitches overlooking the lake and 60 mobile homes inconspicuously sited. The fenced lake has a small beach (swimming is permitted), ducks and pedaloes, and offers good coarse fishing for huge carp (we are told)! Believe it or not, a turtle can sometimes be seen on a fine day! Just one kilometre away is La Haye-du-Puits with two supermarkets, good restaurants and a market on Wednesdays. A good sandy beach is within 10 km. and the Normandy landing beaches are 25 km.

Facilities

Two well kept and modern unisex toilet blocks have British style toilets, washbasins in cabins, units for disabled people and two family cabins. Small laundry. Motorcaravan services. Milk, bread and takeaway snacks available (no gas). Snack bar/bar with TV and terrace. Swimming pool complex (all amenities 20/5-10/9). Play areas. Bicycle hire. Pétanque. Organised activities including treasure hunts, archery and food tasting (5/7-25/8). Off site: Beach 10 km.

Open: 1 April - 15 October.

Directions

Site is just north of La Haye-du-Puits on the primary route from Cherbourg to Mont St-Michel, St Malo and Rennes. It is 24 km. south of N13 at Valognes and 29 km. north of Coutances: leave D900 at roundabout at northern end of bypass (towards town). Site signed on right. GPS: 49.2954, -1.55494

Charges guide

Per unit incl. 2 persons and electricity	€ 16,00 - € 36,00
person (over 4 yrs)	€ 5,00 - € 6,50
dog	€ 1,00 - € 2,00

Camping Cheques accepted.

Saint Vaast-la-Hougue

Camping la Gallouette

F-50550 Saint Vaast-la-Hougue (Manche) T: **02 33 54 20 57**. E: **contact@camping-lagallouette.fr**
alanrogers.com/FR50010

Claudine and Jean Luc Boblin will give you a warm welcome at their seaside campsite which is ideally placed for visiting Barfleur, Sainte Mère-Eglise and the Normandy landing beaches. There are 183 level pitches in total, 119 of which are for touring and all have 6/10A electricity. Some are separated by hedges and there are many colourful flower beds, shrubs and trees but little shade. A light and airy bar faces onto a terrace and swimming pool and there is also a state-of-the-art multisport court.

Facilities

Three modern sanitary blocks, one open and two enclosed, have British style toilets, showers and washbasins (some in cabins). Area for disabled visitors and for babies. Laundry facilities. Small shop. Snack bar. Bar with terrace. Swimming pool. Multisports court. Play area. Pétanque. Fishing. Internet access. Entertainment in high season. Off site: Beach 300 m. Shops and restaurant in St Vaast. Riding 5 km. Golf 12 km.

Open: 1 April - 30 September.

Directions

The D902 runs between Barfleur and Valognes on the eastern side of the Cherbourg peninsula. About half way along at Quettehou take the D1 to St Vaast. Site signed on right on entering town.
GPS: 49.58400, -1.26783

Charges 2010

Per unit incl. 2 persons and electricity	€ 25,70 - € 37,20
extra person	€ 4,60 - € 6,00
child (1-10 yrs)	€ 2,90 - € 3,60
animal	€ 1,80

Saint Valery-en-Caux

Camping Municipal d'Etennemare

Hameau d'Etennemare, F-76460 Saint Valery-en-Caux (Seine-Maritime) T: **02 35 97 15 79**
alanrogers.com/FR76090

This comfortable, neat municipal site is two kilometres from the harbour and town, 30 km. west of Dieppe. Quietly located, it has 116 pitches of which 49 are available for touring units. The grassy pitches are all on a slight slope, all with electricity (6A), water and drain, but there is very little shade. Reception is open all day in July and August, but in low season is closed 12.00-15.00 hrs daily and all day Wednesday: there is a card-operated security barrier.

Facilities

Two modern, clean and well maintained sanitary buildings are side by side, one containing showers and the other, more recently refitted, has toilets, both open and cubicled washbasins and facilities for disabled people. Both blocks can be heated in winter. Dishwashing and laundry sinks. Washing machines. Small shop (July/Aug). Playground. Table tennis. Off site: Hypermarket 1.5 km. Harbour and beach (pebbles) 2 km.

Open: All year.

Directions

From Dieppe keep to D925 Fécamp road (not through town). At third roundabout turn right on D925E towards hypermarket. From Fécamp turn left on D925E as before. Take first right (site signed) to site on left in 1 km. GPS: 49.8585, 0.7046

Charges guide

Per unit incl. 2 persons and electricity	€ 13,40
extra person	€ 2,75
child (under 10 yrs)	€ 1,75

Servon

Campéole

Campéole Saint Grégoire

F-50170 Servon (Manche) T: **02 33 60 26 03**. E: **nadine.ferran@atciat.com**
alanrogers.com/FR50190

This small rural site is simple and well cared for. Modestly sized pitches are in groups of three or four with very little indication of pitch boundaries. Shrubs and well trimmed hedges are planted throughout. Half of the 85 pitches are occupied by chalets and mobile homes. One building houses all of the facilities which are modern, bright and of a high standard. A reasonable car journey will take you to Mont Saint-Michel, Saint Malo or Avranches.

Facilities

One modern sanitary block has washbasins in cabins and controllable showers. Baby room. Very good facilities for disabled visitors. Washing machine. Takeaway (July/Aug). Small swimming pool. Boules. Play area (3-8 yrs). Torches required. Off site: Several beaches can be reached by car. Mont St-Michel. St Malo. Avranches.

Open: 1 April - 30 September.

Directions

On the RN175 from Avranches towards St Malo, take exit for Servon on the right. Site is on the right in 200 m. GPS: 48.59703, -1.41316

Charges guide

Per unit incl. 2 persons	€ 11,00 - € 15,40
extra person	€ 4,00 - € 6,60
child (2-6 yrs)	free - € 3,70
electricity	€ 4,00

Torigni-sur-Vire

Camping le Lac des Charmilles

Route de Vire, F-50160 Torigni-sur-Vire (Manche) T: **02 33 56 91 74**
E: **contact@camping-lacdescharmilles.com** **alanrogers.com/FR50170**

The very friendly new owners have recently acquired this former municipal site and have already made some outstanding changes. Situated next to a lake on the outskirts of Torigni-sur-Vire (1 km) and surrounded by farmers' fields the 39 touring pitches are divided by mature hedges giving plenty of privacy. Additions have included an exceptional new bar and restaurant with an attractive wooden terrace, a new sanitary block providing the most modern facilities and a multisport court along with trampolines and bouncy castle. So, although still lacking some facilities, the first-class additions already installed make this a great choice if visiting this area. There are plans to increase the number of pitches and with so much unused land much more may be achieved over the coming months and years.

Facilities

Two sanitary blocks including one new central block with excellent facilities including those for disabled visitors. Bar/restaurant with full menu and takeaway. Outdoor swimming pool (heated 15/6-15/9). TV, table tennis, go-karts, pétanque, multisport court, trampoline, bouncy castle. Motorhome service point. Large units accepted. Off site: Fishing 200 m. Village with shops, bars, banks etc. 1 km. Canoes 5 km. Riding 13 km. Golf 30 km. Beaches of Normandy 45 mins.

Open: 1 April - 15 October.

Directions

Exit the A84 Caen - Rennes motorway at junction 40 and head north on the N174 towards St Lô. The campsite is on your right just before you enter the town of Torigni-sur-Vire. GPS: 49.02851, -0.97190

Charges guide

Per unit incl. 2 persons and electricity	€ 17,80 - € 20,80
extra person	€ 3,90
child (0-6 yrs)	€ 2,90
dog	€ 1,50

Camping Cheques accepted.

Veulettes-sur-Mer

Camping Municipal Veulettes-sur-Mer

8 rue de Greenock, F-76450 Veulettes-sur-Mer (Seine-Maritime) T: **02 35 97 53 44**
E: **campingmunicipal-veulettes-sur-mer@orange.fr** **alanrogers.com/FR76120**

A good value, well kept municipal site in an attractive little coastal town, just 500 m. from the beach and all town services. There are 116 marked pitches on open level grass, 40 of which are seasonal pitches, which leaves 76 pitches for touring units, all with electric hook-ups, water and waste water drain. Reception keeps soft drinks and ices during July/August. Also on site is an attractive 'salle' (open all day in July/August) with a library and TV, a games area, table tennis, babyfoot and further toilet facilities. There is a traffic free cycle path to the next village 4 km. away.

Facilities

Three good modern sanitary units in traditional style buildings are of varying ages (one can be heated). These provide preset hot showers, washbasins in cubicles, and facilities for disabled people in the smallest unit on the far side of the site. Laundry room. Playground. Boules. TV and library. Off site: Public park with tennis courts and large playground, beach (pebble), watersports centre and all shops and services are within 500 m. Golf 200 m. Fishing 1 km. Beach 500 m.

Open: 1 April - 31 October.

Directions

Veulettes-sur-Mer is on the coast about 45 km. west of Dieppe. Site is central in town, lying about 500 m. back from the main promenade (signed). GPS: 49.84945, 0.59652

Charges guide

Per person	€ 2,75
child (4-10 yrs)	€ 1,39
pitch	€ 2,40
electricity (10A)	€ 2,75
car	€ 1,13

Villedieu-les-Poêles

Flower Camping les Chevaliers

2 impasse Pré de la Rose, F-50800 Villedieu-les-Poêles (Manche) T: **02 33 61 02 44**
E: **contact@camping-deschevaliers.com** **alanrogers.com/FR50180**

This pleasant site is situated less than five minutes' walk from the attractive and interesting town of Villedieu-les-Poêles with its history of metalwork shops and foundries. There are five museums to visit, three of which are close by. This former municipal site is undergoing many modernisations and so far the sanitary facilities have been renovated and a heated (15/6-15/9) outdoor swimming pool added. The 84 touring pitches are separated by low hedges the mature trees give plenty of shade. There are plenty of electrical hook-ups (6A). A small river runs alongside the site which is safely fenced with gate access.

Facilities

Two sanitary blocks provide adequate facilities. One main block situated behind reception has all modern facilities, the other centrally located with toilets and sinks only. Shop. Bar and restaurant with terrace. Takeaway snacks and pizzas. Multisport court. Purpose-built skateboard park. Playground with trampoline and bouncy castle. Go-karts and bicycle hire. Fishing. Off site: Shops, bars, restaurants in town 500 m.

Open: 1 April - 15 October.

See advertisement on page 74

Directions

From the A84 Rennes - Caen motorway, take exit 37 and head east on the D524 to Villedieu-les-Poêles. Follow signs for the Office de Tourisme and continue on, keeping the Office and Post Office on left. The campsite is 200 m. on left. GPS: 48.83665, -1.21697

Charges guide

Per unit incl. 2 persons and electricity	€ 19,80 - € 22,80
extra person	€ 2,90 - € 3,90

Vimoutiers

Camping Municipal la Campière

Boulevard du Docteur Dentu, F-61120 Vimoutiers (Orne) T: **02 33 39 18 86**
E: **mairie.vimoutiers@wanadoo.fr** **alanrogers.com/FR61010**

This small, well kept site is situated in a valley to the north of the town, which is on both the Normandy Cheese and Cider routes. Indeed the town is famous for its cheese and has a Camembert Museum, five minutes walk away in the town centre. The 40 pitches here are flat and grassy, separated by laurel hedging and laid out amongst attractive and well maintained flower and shrub beds. There is some shade around the perimeter and all pitches have electricity.

Facilities

The single central sanitary block is clean and heated, providing open washbasins, good sized, well designed showers, children's toilets and a bathroom for disabled visitors. Dishwashing and laundry facilities under cover. Off site: No shop but a large supermarket is 300 m. Tennis courts and a park are adjacent. Restaurant, water sports facilities or riding 2 km.

Open: May - October.

Directions

Site is on northern edge of town, signed from main Lisieux - Argentan road next to large sports complex. GPS: 48.9265, 0.1967

Charges guide

Per unit incl. 2 persons and electricity	€ 12,95 - € 13,40
extra person	€ 2,59 - € 3,10
child (-10)	€ 1,55 - € 1,85
dog	€ 1,13 - € 1,35

Reductions for 7th and subsequent days.

Nord/Pas-de-Calais,
with its lush countrys
and market towns, is
much more than just
a stop off en-route to or
from the ports. The peaceful
rural unspoilt charms of the regi
provide a real breath of fresh air
Alan Rogers

DÉPARTEMENTS: 59 NORD, 62 PAS-DE-CALAIS

MAJOR CITY: LILLE

It is most likely that you will both arrive and leave France via this region through the ports of Calais or Boulogne, whether by ferry or via the Tunnel. Centuries of invaders from the north as well as from Britain have influenced the development of the area and from a more recent age, the region around Flanders and the Somme is imprinted with the battles of two Great Wars.

The area however is predominately rural. Inland and south are long vistas of rolling farmland broken by little rivers and well scattered with pockets of forest woodland. The coastline is characterised by sandy beaches, shifting dunes and ports. It is a quiet and sparsely populated area with peaceful villages and churches that provide evidence of the glorious achievements of French Gothic architecture. Boulogne is home to Nausicaa, the world's largest sea-life centre and from Cap Griz-Nez you may be able to see the White Cliffs of Dover. There are also many huge hypermarkets where you may stock up on wine, beer and cheese.

Places of interest

Arras: on the river Scarpe, has beautiful 13th- and 14th-century houses and the lovely Abbey of Saint Waast.

Boulogne: best entered by way of the lower town with the 13th-century rampar of the upper town in the background. Th castle next to the Basilica of Notre Dame is impressive.

Calais: the port of Calais was of strategic importance in the Middle Ages and is tod noted for the manufacture of tuille and la as well as being a busy cross-channel port

Le Touquet: pleasant, all year round, coas resort town with six miles of sandy beach

Cuisine of the region

The further north one goes, the more bee is drunk and used in the kitchen, especial in soups and ragouts. There are also many herring dishes.

Caudière (Chaudière, Caudrée): versions o fish and potato soup.

Croquelots or Bouffis: lightly salted and smoked herring.

Gris de Lille: a really salty square of chees with a strong smell.

Hochepot: a thick Flemish soup with virtu everything in it but the kitchen sink.

Waterzooï: a cross between soup and ste usually of fish or chicken.

www.northernfrance-tourism.com
contact@crt-nordpasdecalais.fr
(0)3 20 14 57 57

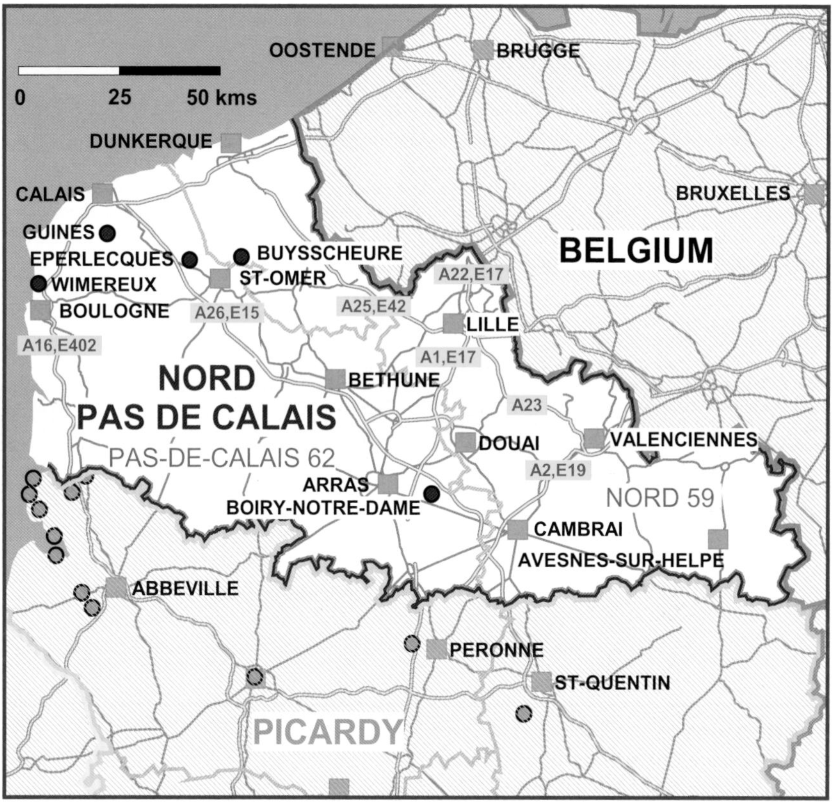

Boiry-Notre-Dame

Camping la Paille Haute

145 rue de Sailly, F-62156 Boiry-Notre-Dame (Pas-de-Calais) T: **03 21 48 15 40**. E: **la-paillehaute@wanadoo.fr**
alanrogers.com/FR62080

Quietly situated in a small village overlooking beautiful countryside and easily accessed from the A1 and A26 autoroutes, this site makes an ideal overnight stop, whilst at the same time being a good base from which to explore the city of Arras and its surroundings. There are 100 pitches here, 65 for touring and all with 6/10A electricity. Some pitches are on open, level grass with lovely views over the countryside, and others are by the site's small fishing lake. You can be sure of a warm welcome here from the friendly owner, who is working hard still developing areas of the site.

Facilities

One modern, basic toilet block, unisex. Extra toilets by pool. One toilet/shower room for disabled visitors. Washing machine and dryer under canopy. Motorcaravan service point. Bar and snacks. Swimming pool (15/6-15/9). Poolside bar and pizza oven. TV in bar. Fishing pond. Playground. Boules. Internet access. Entertainment.
Off site: Supermarket 500 m. City of Arras with Flemish architecture, and network of cellars and tunnels spreading beneath the town centre. WW1 Canadian memorial at Vimy Ridge.

Open: 1 April - 31 October.

Directions

From A1 take exit 15 and D939 southeast. Follow signs for Boiry-Notre-Dame. From A26 take exit 8 and D939 northwest following signs for Boiry-Notre-Dame. From village follow camping signs to site.
GPS: 50.273533, 2.948667

Charges guide

Per unit incl. 2 persons	€ 15,00 - € 18,00
extra person	€ 3,00 - € 3,50
child (under 7 yrs)	€ 2,00 - € 2,50
electricity (6A)	€ 3,00

Buysscheure

Camping Caravaning la Chaumière

529 Langhemast Straete, F-59285 Buysscheure (Nord) T: **03 28 43 03 57**
E: **camping.LaChaumiere@wanadoo.fr** **alanrogers.com/FR59010**

This is a very friendly, pleasant site, in the département du Nord with a strong Flanders influence, There is a real welcome here. Set just behind the village of Buysscheure, the site has 29 touring pitches separated by trees and bushes. Each pair shares a light, electricity connections, water points and rubbish container. Access from narrow site roads can be difficult. A small, fenced fishing lake contains some large carp (seen!) A bonus is that Bernadette works for the local vet and can arrange all the documentation for British visitors' pets. English is spoken.

Facilities

Modern unisex toilet facilities are simple and small in number, with two WCs, one shower and one washbasin cabin. Facilities for disabled visitors may also be used (a toilet and separate washbasin/shower room). Dishwashing and laundry facilities. Motorcaravan services. Basic chemical disposal. Bar (daily) and restaurant (weekends only, all day, in season). Dog exercise area. Heated outdoor pools. Play area. Minigolf. Archery. Off site: Local market (Monday) at Bergues. St Omer. Beach 30 km. Lille 60 km.

Open: 1 April - 30 September.

Directions

From Calais take N43 (St Omer) for 25 km. Just beyond Nordausques take D221 left (Watten). In Watten turn left for centre, then right on D26 (Cassel). Soon after Lederzeele site signed to right. On reaching Buysscheure turn left, then right, site signed. Single track road (1 km.) with bend.
GPS: 50.80152, 2.33924

Charges guide

Per unit incl. 2 persons and electricity	€ 18,00
extra person	€ 7,00
child (under 7 yrs)	€ 3,50
dog	€ 1,00

No credit cards.

Eperlecques

Kawan Village Château du Gandspette

kawan VILLAGES
www.kawan-villages.com

133 Rue de Gandspette, F-62910 Eperlecques (Pas-de-Calais) T: **03 21 93 43 93**
E: **contact@chateau-gandspette.com** **alanrogers.com/FR62030**

This spacious, family-run site, in the grounds of a 19th-century château, conveniently situated for the Channel ports and tunnel, provides overnight accommodation together with a range of facilities for longer stays. There are 100 touring pitches, all with electric hook-ups, intermingled with 50 French-owned mobile homes and caravans, and a further 18 for hire. Pitches are delineated by trees and hedging. Mature trees form the perimeter of the site, through which there is access to woodland walks.

Facilities

Two sanitary blocks with a mixture of open and cubicled washbasins. Good facilities for disabled people and babies. Laundry facilities. Motorcaravan service point. Shop (all season). Bar, grill restaurant and takeaway (all 15/5-15/9). Swimming pools (15/5-30/9). Playground and playing field. Tennis. Pétanque. Children's room. Entertainment in season. Off site: Supermarket 1 km. Fishing 3 km. Riding, golf 5 km. Beach 30 km.

Open: 1 April - 30 September.

Directions

From Calais follow D943 (St Omer) for 25 km. Southeast of Nordausques take D221 (east). Follow site signs for 5-6 km. From St Omer follow D943 to roundabout at junction with D300. Turn right on D300 (Dunkirk). After 5 km. turn left on D221. Site is 1.5 km. on right. GPS: 50.81924, 2.17753

Charges 2010

Per unit incl. 2 persons and electricity	€ 17,00 - € 27,00
extra person (over 6 yrs)	€ 5,00 - € 6,00
child (3-6 yrs)	€ 3,00 - € 4,00
dog	€ 1,00

Camping Cheques accepted.

Guînes

Castel Camping Caravaning la Bien-Assise

D231, F-62340 Guînes (Pas-de-Calais) T: **03 21 35 20 77**. E: **castels@bien-assise.com**

alanrogers.com/FR62010

A mature and well developed site, the history of La Bien-Assise goes back to the 1500s. There are 198 grass pitches mainly set among mature trees with others on a newer field. Connected by gravel roads and of a good size (up to 300 sq.m), shrubs and bushes divide most of the pitches. Being close to Calais, the Channel Tunnel exit and Boulogne, makes it a good stopping point en-route, but it is well worth a longer stay. The site can have heavy usage at times (when maintenance can be variable). Used by tour operators (40 pitches).

Facilities

Three well equipped toilet blocks provide many washbasins in cabins, mostly British style WCs and provision for babies, laundry and dishwashing. The main block is in four sections, two unisex. Motorcaravan service point. Shop. Restaurant. Bar/grill and takeaway (evenings from 1/5). TV room. Pool complex (1/5-20/9) with toboggan, covered paddling pool and outdoor pool. Play areas. Minigolf. Tennis. Bicycle hire. Off site: Fishing 8 km. Beach 9 km. Riding 10 km.

Open: 25 April - 20 September.

Directions

From ferry or tunnel follow signs for A16 Boulogne. Take exit 11 (Frethun, Gare TGV) and RD215 (Frethun). At first roundabout take third exit (Guines). Pass under the TGV. In Frethun take RD246 towards Guines and St Tricat and at roundabout take exit for Guines. Pass through St Tricat and Hames Boucres, and in Guines follow site signs. GPS: 50.86632, 1.85698

Charges 2010

Per unit incl. 2 persons and electricity	€ 17,50 - € 28,50
extra person	€ 3,00 - € 5,00
child (under 13 yrs)	€ 3,00 - € 4,00

Less 10% in low seasons

Wimereux

Camping l'Eté Indien

Hameau Honvault, F-62930 Wimereux (Pas-de-Calais) T: **03 21 30 23 50**. E: **ete.indien@wanadoo.fr**

alanrogers.com/FR62120

L'Eté Indien is a new site located near the resort of Wimereux, a little to the north of Boulogne. It offers a quiet and tranquil environment in which to enjoy your holiday – apart from some train noise (every 30 minutes, daytime only). Pitches for touring and camping are furthest from the entrance and vary in size. All have electrical connections (10A). In keeping with its Wild West theme, there is a small village of four Indian 'teepees' for rent, as well as more conventional mobile homes and chalets. The swimming pool and children's pool are a fair distance from the touring pitches.

Facilities

Two toilet blocks include facilities for babies and disabled people. Laundry. Small shop. Bar. Snack bar and takeaway. Motorcaravan services. Swimming pool. Children's pool. Play area with trampoline. Boules. Games room. Internet access and WiFi. Bicycle hire. Fishing pond. Off site: Wimereux, Le Touquet, Boulogne and the Nausicaa museum. Cité de l'Europe shopping complex at Calais. Beach 1 km. Riding adjacent. Golf 1.5 km.

Open: All year.

Directions

From the A16 take exit 32 (Wimereux) and follow signs to Wimereux (D96 and D940). After 1.5 km. turn right. Site is well signed from here and is located on the left, close to a riding centre. Approach is rather narrow, with speed ramps and is poorly surfaced. GPS: 50.75142, 1.60728

Charges guide

Per unit incl. 2 persons and electricity	€ 15,50 - € 20,00
extra person	€ 3,20 - € 4,00
child (under 13 yrs)	€ 2,00 - € 2,50
dog	€ 1,50 - € 2,00

The birthplace of Got
architecture in France
with no less than six
cathedrals, the region
still predominately rural
with deep river valleys, for
of mature beech and oak, peacef
lakes and sandy beaches providi
plenty of contrast.

DÉPARTEMENTS: 02 AISNE, 60 OISE, 80 SOMME

MAJOR CITY: AMIENS

France itself was born in this northern province located between the Marne and the Somme rivers, for it was here that the Franks – ancestors of the French – first settled. Picardy tends to be a region that most people travel through and this was the invaders route. Evidence of this is visible in the 17th-century defensive citadels designed by Vauban at the end of a long period of conquests by English kings and Burgundian dukes. From a more recent age, acres of immaculately tended war graves are a sobering reminder of two Great Wars. At Vimy Ridge near Arras, World War One trenches have been preserved intact, a most poignant sight. Elsewhere, almost every village between Arras and Amiens has its memorial.

Picardy's coastline is the least urbanised in all France with miles upon miles of beautiful sandy beaches and dunes – great for windsurfing, land yachting, sailing, swimming and building castles. Do not miss the magnificent 'Baie de Somme' or the largest bird park in Europe, the Marquenterre.

Places of interest

Abbéville: church of St Vulfran, Bagatelle Château, Baie de Somme nature reserve.

Amiens: Notre Dame cathedral, impressiv for its size and richly sculpted façade and the stone carvings of the choir; monumer to the 1918 Battle of the Somme; remarkable 'hortillonnages' (water garder and interlocking canals.

Aisne: surrounded by 60 fortified churche

Chantilly: Château of Chantilly with a 17t century stable with a 'live' Horse Museum

Compiègne: Seven miles east of the town Clairière de l'Armistice. The railway coach here is a replica of the one in which the 1918 Armistice was signed and in which Hitler received the French surrender in 19

Laon: 12th-century cathedral, WW1 trenches, Vauclair Abbey.

Marquenterre: one of Europe's most important bird sanctuaries.

Cuisine of the region

Fresh fish and seafood is popular, as is chicory flavoured coffee.

Carbonnade de Boeuf à la Flamande: braised beef with beer, onions and bacon

Caudière (Chaudière, Caudrée): versions of fish and potato soup.

Ficelles Picardes: ham pancakes with mushroom sauce.

Flamiche aux poireaux: puff pastry tart with cream and leeks.

Soupe courquignoise: soup with white w fish, moules, leeks and Gruyère cheese.

www.picardietourisme.com/en
documentation@picardietourisme.c
(0)3 22 22 33 63

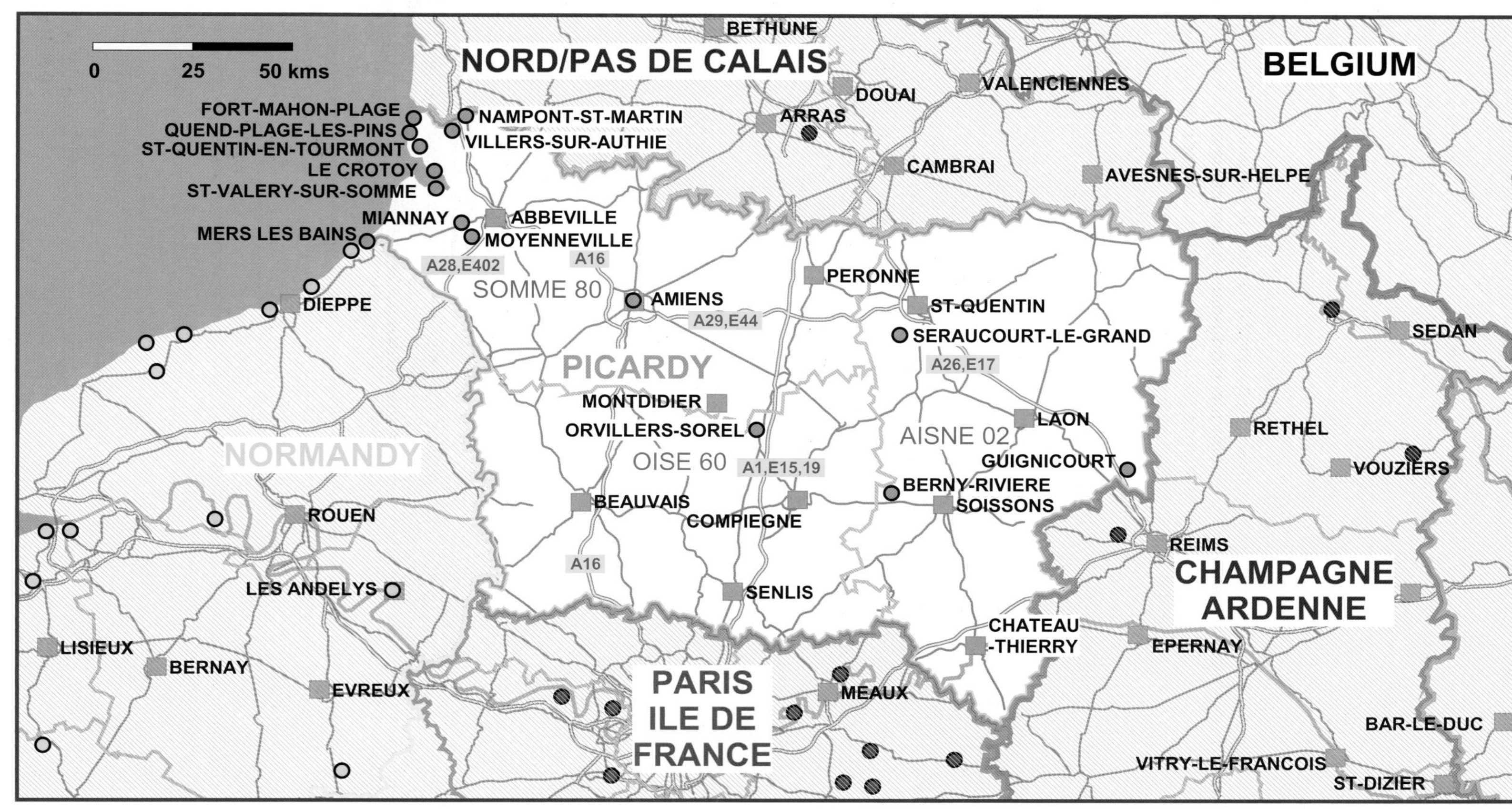
0 25 50 kms
NORD/PAS DE CALAIS
BELGIUM
BETHUNE
DOUAI
VALENCIENNES
ARRAS
CAMBRAI
AVESNES-SUR-HELPE
FORT-MAHON-PLAGE
QUEND-PLAGE-LES-PINS
ST-QUENTIN-EN-TOURMONT
LE CROTOY
ST-VALERY-SUR-SOMME
NAMPONT-ST-MARTIN
VILLERS-SUR-AUTHIE
MIANNAY
ABBEVILLE
MERS LES BAINS
MOYENNEVILLE
A16
A28,E402
SOMME 80
AMIENS
A29,E44
DIEPPE
PERONNE
ST-QUENTIN
SERAUCOURT-LE-GRAND
A26,E17
SEDAN
PICARDY
MONTDIDIER
ORVILLERS-SOREL
LAON
AISNE 02
RETHEL
NORMANDY
OISE 60
A1,E15,19
GUIGNICOURT
VOUZIERS
BERNY-RIVIERE
SOISSONS
BEAUVAIS
COMPIEGNE
ROUEN
REIMS
CHAMPAGNE
ARDENNE
A16
LES ANDELYS
SENLIS
CHATEAU
-THIERRY
LISIEUX
BERNAY
EPERNAY
EVREUX
PARIS
ILE DE
FRANCE
MEAUX
BAR-LE-DUC
VITRY-LE-FRANCOIS
ST-DIZIER

Amiens

Camping Parc des Cygnes

111 avenue des Cygnes, F-80080 Amiens (Somme) T: **03 22 43 29 28**. E: **camping.amiens@wanadoo.fr**

alanrogers.com/FR80100

Formerly Camping de l'Ecluse, this 3.2-hectare site has been completely levelled and attractively landscaped. Bushes and shrubs divide the site into areas and some 20 mature trees are planned to provide some shade. The 145 pitches are for touring, with plans for a handful of mobile homes for rent. All pitches are grassed with plenty of space on the tarmac roads in front of them for motorcaravans to park in wet conditions. There are 81 pitches with electricity (6-16A), of which 37 also have water and drainage and further water points throughout the rest of the site. The site is just a few minutes from the N1, the A16 Paris - Calais motorway and the A29/A26 route to Rouen and the south, so it is useful as a stopover being about 50 km. from the ports. Amiens itself is an attractive cathedral city where you can eat out on the waterfront of the 'Venice of the North' or take a boat trip around the 'floating gardens' of 'Les Hortillonnages'. A 'Sites et Paysages' member.

Facilities

Two toilet blocks (one open only when site is busy) with separate toilet facilities but unisex shower and washbasin area. Baby bath. Facilities for disabled people. Reception building also has toilets, showers and washbasins (heated when necessary). Laundry facilities. Shop (open on request all season), bar and takeaway (7/5-14/9; weekends only in low season). Games and TV room. Bicycle hire. Fishing. Off site: Golf and riding 5 km. Beaches 70 km.

Open: 1 April - 14 October.

Directions

From A16, leave at exit 20. Take the Rocade Nord (northern bypass) to exit 40, follow signs for Amiens Longpré. At roundabout take second exit to Parc de Loisirs, then right to site (signs all the way).
GPS: 49.920916, 2.258833

Charges 2010

Per unit incl. 2 persons and electricity	€ 14,60 - € 20,30
extra person	€ 6,00
child (4-12 yrs)	€ 5,00
dog	€ 2,10

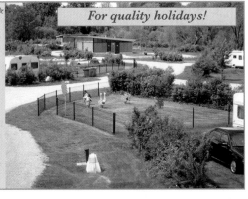

Berny-Riviere

Caravaning la Croix du Vieux Pont

F-02290 Berny-Riviere (Aisne) T: **03 23 55 50 02**. E: **info@la-croix-du-vieux-pont.com**

alanrogers.com/FR02030

Located on the banks of the River Aisne, la Croix du Vieux Pont is a very smart, modern 34-hectare site offering a high standard of facilities. Many pitches are occupied by mobile homes and tour operator tents, but there are 60 pleasant touring pitches, some on the banks of the Aisne. Maintained to a high standard, the excellent amenities include four heated swimming pools, one indoors with a waterslide and jacuzzi. At the heart of the site is a well stocked fishing lake which is also used for pedaloes and canoes. There are two tennis courts, an amusement arcade and volleyball court.

Facilities

The six toilet blocks are modern and kept very clean, with washbasins in cabins and free hot showers. Laundry facilities. Facilities for disabled visitors. Large supermarket. Bar, takeaway and good value restaurant (most amenities 1/4-30/9). Swimming pool complex (covered pool 1/4-30/10, outdoor 1/5-30/9). Play area. Fishing. Bicycle hire. Apartments to let. Off site: Riding 100 m. Golf 30 km.

Open: 8 April - 31 October.

Directions

From Compiegne take N31 towards Soissons. At Vic-sur-Aisne turn right, towards Berny-Riviere and site is on right after 400 m. GPS: 49.40487, 3.12840

Charges guide

Per unit incl. 2 persons and electricity	€ 21,50 - € 24,00
incl. 4 persons	€ 30,50 - € 33,00

Camping Cheques accepted.

Fort-Mahon-Plage

Camping le Royon

1271 route de Quend, F-80120 Fort-Mahon-Plage (Somme) T: **03 22 23 40 30**. E: **info@campingleroyon.com**
alanrogers.com/FR80040

This busy site, some two kilometres from the sea, has 397 pitches of which 116 are used for touring units. Most are near the entrance, some are set amongst the mobile homes. They are of either 95 or 120 sq.m, marked, numbered and divided by hedges and are arranged either side of access roads. Electricity (6A) and water points are available to all. The remaining 281 pitches are used for mobile homes. The site is well lit, fenced and guarded at night (€ 30 deposit for barrier card). Entertainment is organised for adults and children in July/Aug when it will be very full.

Facilities

Four toilet blocks provide unisex facilities with British and Turkish style WCs and washbasins in cubicles. Units for disabled people. Baby baths. Laundry facilities. Shop. Gas supplies. Mobile takeaway calls evenings in July/Aug. Clubroom and bar. Heated, open air and covered pools. Open air children's pool and sun terrace. Play area. Games room with TV. Multicourt. Tennis. Boules. Bicycle hire. Internet access and WiFi. Off site: Fishing, riding, golf and watersports centre within 1 km. Public transport nearby.

Open: 15 March - 1 November.

Directions

From A16 exit 24, take D32 around Rue (road becomes D940 for a while) then continues as D32 (Fort-Mahon-Plage). Site is on right after 19 km. GPS: 50.33229, 1.5796

Charges guide

Per unit incl. up to 3 persons and electricity	€ 17,50 - € 29,00
extra person (over 1 yr)	€ 7,00
dog	€ 3,00

Guignicourt

Camping Municipal Guignicourt

14 bis rue des Godins, F-02190 Guignicourt (Aisne) T: **03 23 79 74 58**. E: **mairie-guignicourt@wanadoo.fr**
alanrogers.com/FR02060

This very pleasant little municipal site has 100 pitches, 20 for long stay units and 80 for touring units. These two sections are separated by the main facilities on a higher terrace. Pitches are generally large and level, although you might need an extra long electricity lead for some, but there are few dividing hedges. Pitches along the river bank have most shade, with a few specimen trees providing a little shade to some of the more open pitches. On a quiet evening you are likely to hear the site's nightingales. The town is quite attractive and is worthy of an evening stroll.

Facilities

The modern sanitary unit has British and Turkish style toilets, washbasins (cold only except for the one in a cubicle), pushbutton hot showers, dishwashing and laundry sinks. Playground. Boules. Fishing. Off site: The town has all services including a supermarket and bank. Golf 3 km. Beach 15 km. Good train service into Reims with its spectacular cathedral.

Open: 1 April - 30 September.

Directions

Guignicourt is about 20 km. north of Reims, just east of the A26, junction 14. The site is well signed from D925 in the village. GPS: 49.4320, 3.9704

Charges guide

Per person	€ 2,20
child (under 12 yrs)	€ 1,50 - € 1,50
pitch incl. electricity	€ 11,10 - € 13,20
animal	€ 1,50

Le Crotoy

Kawan Village le Ridin

kawan VILLAGES www.kawan-villages.com

Lieu-dit Mayocq, F-80550 Le Crotoy (Somme) T: **03 22 27 03 22**
E: **contact@campingleridin.com** **alanrogers.com/FR80110**

Le Ridin is a popular family site in the countryside just 2 km. from Le Crotoy with its beaches and marina, and 6 km. from the famous bird reserve of Le Marquenterre. The site has 162 pitches, including 40 for touring, the remainder occupied by mobile homes and chalets (for rent). There is some shade. The pitches and roads are unsuitable for large units. The site amenities are housed in beautifully converted barns across the road and these include a heated pool, fitness centre, bar/restaurant and bicycles for hire. Reception staff are helpful and will advise on local excursions.

Facilities

Toilet blocks are heated in cool weather and provide good showers and special facilities for children. Restaurant/bar. Small shop. Swimming and paddling pools. Fitness centre. Games room. Play area. TV room. Bicycle hire. Entertainment and activity programme. Off site: Golf 2 km. Fishing and riding 3 km. Birdwatching 6 km.

Open: 1 April - 7 November.

Directions

From A16 (Calais - Abbéville) take exit 24 and follow signs to Le Crotoy. At roundabout on arrival at Le Crotoy turn towards St Férmin, then second road on right. GPS: 50.23905, 1.63182

Charges 2010

Per unit incl. 2 persons and electricity	€ 19,50 - € 30,00
extra person	€ 5,30 - € 5,80
child (0-7 yrs)	€ 4,30 - € 4,80

Camping Cheques accepted.

Le Crotoy

Camping les Aubépines

Saint Firmin, F-80550 Le Crotoy (Somme) T: **03 22 27 01 34**. E: **contact@camping-lesaubepines.com**
alanrogers.com/FR80120

This peaceful, family-run site is on the edge of the Parc Ornithologique du Marquenterre and is just 1 km. from a beach on the Baie de Somme, a river estuary famous for its resident population of seals. There are 196 pitches, although around 100 are occupied by privately-owned mobile homes with a few available for rent. Consequently there are just 71 touring pitches scattered throughout the site. All on level ground, they are of a reasonable to good size, separated by hedges and trees and with water taps and electricity (3-10A) close by.

Facilities

Two unisex toilet blocks, fairly basic but clean and in good order. British style toilets (seatless), washbasins in cubicles, push button showers and some larger cubicles with shower and basin. Baby bath and toilet. Facilities for disabled visitors are minimal (no grab rails). Laundry room. Shop. Indoor games. Small play area. Bicycle hire. Off site: Riding adjacent. Beaches: 1 km. and 10 km. Fishing 2 km. Bird sanctuary, tennis 3 km. Golf 10 km.

Open: 1 April - 1 November.

Directions

Le Crotoy is on the D940 Berck - Le Tréport road. At roundabout for town, take D4 to St Firmin, turn right at next roundabout. After village sign, turn left to site (signed) on right in about 500 m.
GPS: 50.24976, 1.61196

Charges guide

Per unit incl. 2 persons	€ 19,00 - € 29,00
extra person	€ 5,00 - € 5,20
child (under 7 yrs)	€ 4,00 - € 4,20

Mers-les-Bains

Flower Camping le Rompval

Lieu dit Blengues, F-80350 Mers-les-Bains (Somme) T: **02 35 86 25 40**
alanrogers.com/FR80220

Le Rompval is a former municipal site located in the pleasant seaside resort of Mers-les-Bains, around 25 km. west of Abbéville, at the mouth of the River Bresle. There are 135 pitches here and these are grassy and of a good size. Most are equipped with electricity (8/13A). Around 10 pitches are occupied by chalets (available for rent). The site boasts some interesting architecture and a number of amenities including a small shop and takeaway food service. The nearest beach is 1.5 km. distant. This is a great sweep of sand, ideal for sand yachting and windsurfing.

Facilities

Shop. Takeaway. Tourist information. Play area. Activity programme (high season). Chalets for rent. Off site: Nearest beach 1.5 km. Mers-les-Bains (attractive seaside resort with Belle Epoque villas). Cliff top walks. Supermarket. Windsurfing and sand yachting.

Open: 1 April - 31 October.

Directions

Approaching from the north, leave the A16 motorway at exit 23 (Abbéville Nord). Briefly join the southbound A28 and then take D925 to Eu. Here, head west on D1015 to Mers-les-Bains and follow signs to the site.
GPS: 50.077262, 1.414474

Charges guide

Per unit incl. 2 persons and electricity	€ 20,00 - € 24,00

Miannay

Camping le Clos Cacheleux

Route de Bouillancourt, F-80132 Miannay (Somme) T: **03 22 19 17 47**
E: **raphael@camping-lecloscacheleux.fr** **alanrogers.com/FR80210**

Le Clos Cacheleux is a well situated campsite of six hectares bordering woodland in the park of the Château Bouillancourt which dares from the 18th century. The site was first opened in July 2008. It is 11 km. from the Bay of the Somme, regarded as being amongst the most beautiful bays in France. There are 100 very large, grassy pitches (200 sq.m) and all have electricity hook-ups and water points. The aim of the owners is to make your stay as enjoyable as possible by providing high quality services and activities. Visitors have access to the swimming pool, bar and children's club at the sister site – Le Val de Trie (20 m). A 'Sites et Paysages' member.

Facilities

The single sanitary block is clean and well maintained. Facilities for disabled visitors. Baby room. Laundry room with washing machine and dryer. Motorcaravan service point. At the sister site: shop, bar with terrace (1/4-15/10), library and TV room, restaurant and takeaway (26/4-4/9). Covered pool (15/4-30/9). Play area. Boules. Picnic tables. Freezer for ice packs. Barbecue hire. Bicycle hire. Fishing pond. Caravan storage. Off site: Village 1 km. Hypermarket in Abbéville. Riding 4 km. Sandy beaches of the Picardy coast 12 km. Golf 9 km. Riding 14 km.

Open: 15 March - 15 October.

Directions

From the A28 at Abbéville take the D925 towards Eu and Le Tréport; do not go towards Moyenville. Turn left in Miannay village on the D86 towards Toeufles. The road to Bouillancourt-sous-Miannay is on the left after 2 km. and site is signed in the village.
GPS: 50.08352, 1.71343

Charges guide

Per unit incl. 2 persons and electricity	€ 18,50 - € 24,80
extra person	€ 3,10 - € 5,10

The Travel Service to book this site call 01580 214000 ...we'll arrange everything

Moyenneville

481

Camping le Val de Trie

Rue des Sources, Bouillancourt-sous-Miannay, F-80870 Moyenneville (Somme) T: **03 22 31 48 88**
E: **raphael@camping-levaldetrie.fr** **alanrogers.com/FR80060**

Le Val de Trie is a natural countryside site in woodland, near a small village. The 100 numbered, grassy pitches are of a good size, divided by hedges and shrubs with mature trees providing good shade in most areas, and all have electricity (6A) and water. Access roads are gravel (site is possibly not suitable for the largest motorcaravans). It can be very quiet in April, June, September and October. If there is no-one on site, just choose a pitch or call at farm to book in. There are five Dutch tour operator tents. This is maturing into a well managed site with modern facilities and a friendly, relaxed atmosphere. There are good walks around the area and a notice board keeps campers up to date with local market, shopping and activity news. English is spoken. The owners of Le Val de Trie have recently opened a new campsite nearby, Le Clos Cacheleux (FR80210).

Facilities

Two clean sanitary buildings include washbasins in cubicles, units for disabled people, babies and children. Laundry facilities. Motorcaravan services. Shop (from1/4), bread to order and butcher visits in season. Bar with TV (1/4-15/10), snack bar with takeaway (23/4-4/9). Room above bar for children. Covered heated swimming pool (15/4-30/9).
Off site: Riding 14 km. Golf 10 km. Beach 12 km.

Open: 1 April - 15 October.

Directions

From A28 take exit 2 near Abbéville and the D925 to Miannay. Turn left on the D86 to Bouillancourt-sous-Miannay: site is signed in village.
GPS: 50.08539, 1.71499

Charges 2010

Per unit incl. 2 persons and electricity	€ 18,50 - € 24,80
extra person	€ 3,10 - € 5,10
child (under 7 yrs)	€ 1,90 - € 3,10
dog	€ 1,00 - € 1,50

Camping Cheques accepted.

Nampont-Saint Martin

Kawan Village la Ferme des Aulnes

1 rue du Marais, Fresne-sur-Authie, F-80120 Nampont-Saint Martin (Somme)
T: **03 22 29 22 69**. E: **contact@fermedesaulnes.com** **alanrogers.com/FR80070**

This peaceful site, with 120 pitches, has been developed on the meadows of a small, 17th-century farm on the edge of Fresne and is lovingly cared for by its enthusiastic owner and his hard-working team. Restored outbuildings house reception and the facilities, around a central courtyard that boasts a fine heated swimming pool. A new development outside, facing the main gate, has 20 large, level grass pitches for touring. There is also an area for tents. In the centre, a warden lives above a new facility building. The remaining 22 touring pitches are in the main complex, hedged and fairly level. Activities are organised for children and there are indoor facilities for poor weather. From here you can visit Crécy, Agincourt, St Valéry and Montreuil (where Victor Hugo wrote Les Misérables). The nearby Bay of the Somme has wonderful sandy beaches and many watersports.

Facilities

Both sanitary areas are heated and include washbasins in cubicles with a large cubicle for disabled people. Dishwashing and laundry sinks. Shop. Piano bar and restaurant. Motorcaravan service point. TV room. Swimming pool (16 x 9 m; heated and with cover for cooler weather). Jacuzzi and sauna. Fitness room. Aquagym and balneotherapy. Playground. Boules. Archery. Rooms with Play Stations and videos. Internet café. WiFi (free). Shuttle service to stations and airports. Off site: Private lake fishing (free) 2 minutes away. River fishing 100 m. Golf 1 km. Riding 8 km.

Open: 1 April - 1 November.

Directions

From Calais, take A16 to exit 25 and turn for Arras for 2 km. and then towards Abbeville on N1. At Nampont-St Martin turn west on D485 and site will be found in 2 km. GPS: 50.33645, 1.71285

Charges guide

Per unit incl. 2 persons and electricity	€ 28,00 - € 33,00
extra person	€ 7,00
child (under 7 yrs)	€ 4,00
dog	€ 4,00

Camping Cheques accepted.

Orvillers-Sorel

Aestiva Camping de Sorel

Rue Saint-Claude, F-60490 Orvillers-Sorel (Oise) T: **03 44 85 02 74**. E: **contact@aestiva.fr**
alanrogers.com/FR60020

Aestiva Camping de Sorel is located north of Compiègne, close to the A1 motorway and is ideal as an overnight stop. The site has 80 large grassy pitches, of which 50 are available for touring, all with electrical connections (three with water and waste water). The original farm buildings have been carefully converted to house the site's amenities including a bar, TV room and the toilet facilities. The site is open for a long season but most amenities are only open from April to September. The site is, however, close to the village of Sorel with its shops and restaurants. There are four mobile homes for rent. Compiègne lies 15 km to the south and its château is well worth a visit and houses a number of interesting museums. There is an important golf course in the town. Closer to the site, the GR123 long distance footpath runs through Sorel, and also offers the opportunity to explore the surrounding countryside on foot.

Facilities

Toilet block with facilities for children and disabled visitors. Motorcaravan service point. Small shop. Bar, snack bar and takeaway (15/5-15/10). TV room. Play area. Boules. Hairdressing service. Bicycle hire. WiFi. Off site: Tennis. Riding 5 km. Fishing 2 km. Golf 7 km. Compiègne 15 km.

Open: 1 February - 14 December.

Directions

Take exit 11 from the A1 motorway (Lille - Paris) and join the northbound N17. Site is signed to the right on reaching village of Sorel after around 8 km.
GPS: 49.56688, 2.70841

Charges 2010

Per unit incl. 2 persons and electricity	€ 16,50 - € 18,00
extra person	€ 6,00
child (under 4-7 yrs)	€ 5,00

Camping Cheques accepted.

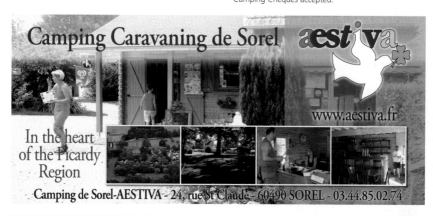

Quend-Plage-les-Pins

Flower Camping les Vertes Feuilles

25 route de la Plage Monchaux, F-80120 Quend Plage les Pins (Somme) T: **03 22 23 55 12**
E: **contact@lesvertesfeuilles.com** **alanrogers.com/FR80130**

Situated on the Picardy coast, three kilometres from the beach, this 1.5 hectare site provides 46 touring pitches out of a total of 106. The remainder contain a mix of mobile homes and semi-residential caravans. It is a charming campsite where a pleasant welcome awaits you. The site roads are slightly narrow, so larger units cannot be accommodated. This whole area is bustling in high season with many campsites and holiday villages but this makes for a wonderful French style seaside holiday. Don't forget to visit the nearby Aquaclub, the Abbey and Gardens of Valloires and the bird reserve of Le Marquenterre.

Facilities

One large toilet block, old but renovated, has unisex showers, washbasins in cubicles and 3 family rooms. Ramped facilities for disabled visitors. Snack bar in season. Covered heated swimming pool (2/4-30/09). Play areas. Bicycle hire. Off site: Beach 4 km. Fishing 3 km. Golf 2 km. Riding 5 km. Local markets.

Open: 1 April - 1 November.

Directions

From A16 Rue exit, take D32 around Rue, when road becomes D940 for a while, then continues again as D32 towards Fort-Mahon-Plage. After left turn for Quend Plage, site on left. GPS: 50.31950, 1.60583

Charges 2010

Per unit incl. 2 persons and electricity	€ 16,50 - € 30,40
extra person	€ 4,50 - € 5,50
child (2-7 yrs)	€ 3,00 - € 4,50

No credit cards.

Saint Quentin-en-Tourmont

Camping Caravaning le Champ Neuf

Rue du Champ Neuf, F-80120 Saint Quentin-en-Tourmont (Somme) T: **03 22 25 07 94**
E: **contact@camping-lechampneuf.com** **alanrogers.com/FR80020**

Part of a large farm, the campsite was started in 1995 and all the charming family are now involved (although Maman is firmly in charge). There are 157 pitches with 59 for touring, of which 30 are in a new field with the remainder scattered amongst more permanent mobile homes and caravans. All pitches are on level grass with 3 or 6A electricity. The site is only 75 minutes from Calais, 18 km. off the motorway. This is a quiet site with home cooking and soirées, and with the famous Marquenterre bird reserve next door, bird-watching enthusiasts will appreciate the dawn chorus and migrating birds.

Facilities

Two toilet blocks have British style toilets, washbasins in cubicles, family cubicles and facilities for disabled visitors. Laundry facilities. Motorcaravan service point. Bar, entertainment area and snack bar. Games room. Tennis. Covered, heated pool area has been added. Off site: Shops, restaurants, bars in Rue 7 km.

Open: 1 April - 1 November.

Directions

From A16 exit 24, take D32 towards and around Rue. At second roundabout take second exit on D940, then left on D4 for 1.5 km. before turning right on D204 to Le Bout des Crocs. Site is signed to the left. GPS: 50.26895, 1.60263

Charges guide

Per unit incl. 2 persons and electricity	€ 19,00 - € 24,00
extra person	€ 4,50 - € 6,00

Saint Valery-sur-Somme

481

Camping Airotel Le Walric

Route d'Eu, F-80230 Saint Valery-sur-Somme (Somme) T: **03 22 26 81 97**. E: **info@campinglewalric.com**
alanrogers.com/FR80150

A clean, well-kept and managed site, Le Walric is about 75 minutes from Calais. A former municipal site, it has been completely updated with a new bar and snack bar, a pool complex, two play areas and entertainment in high season. There are 263 well laid out, large and level grass pitches. Of these, 47 with electricity connections are for touring with the remainder used for a mix of new mobile homes and semi-residential caravans. The site's situation on the outskirts of the town make it an ideal holiday location. Medieval Saint Valéry is renowned for its association with William the Conqueror.

Facilities

Two toilet blocks include British style WCs, washbasins in cubicles and showers. Facilities for disabled visitors. Laundry room with baby changing. Motorcaravan service point. Bar with snacks and TV (1/4-1/11). Heated outdoor pool (1/5-15/9). Off site: Shops, restaurants, bars in St Valéry. Bicycle hire and beach 2 km.

Open: 1 April - 1 November.

Directions

From the A16 exit 24, followthe D32 across the N1. At roundabout take D235 to Morlay; turn left on D940 and continue around Saint Valéry until second roundabout where take first exit on D3 to site on right. GPS: 50.1838, 1.61791

Charges guide

Per unit incl. 3 persons and electricity	€ 17,50 - € 29,00
extra person	€ 7,00
dog	€ 3,00

Saint Valéry-sur-Somme

Castel Camping le Château de Drancourt

B.P. 80022, F-80230 Saint Valéry-sur-Somme (Somme) T: **03 22 26 93 45**. E: **chateau.drancourt@wanadoo.fr**
alanrogers.com/FR80010

This is a popular, busy and lively site within easy distance of the Channel ports, between Boulogne and Dieppe. There are 356 pitches in total, of which 220 are occupied by several tour operators; 30 units for rent, and 26 privately owned. The 80 touring pitches are on level grass, of good size, some in shade and others in the open, all with electricity. Fully-serviced pitches are available on reservation. The site is well landscaped and, in spite of the numbers in high season, does not feel overcrowded. It can be dusty around the reception buildings and the château in dry weather.

Facilities

Three toilet blocks include washbasins in cubicles, family bathrooms and facilities for disabled visitors. Laundry facilities. Drainage difficulties can cause occasional problems. Shop, restaurant and takeaway. Several bars. TV rooms, one for children. Games room. Heated pools, one indoor, one outside and paddling pool. Tennis. Golf practise range. Minigolf. Bicycle hire. Fishing. Off site: Beach 14 km.

Open: Easter - 5 November.

Directions

Site is 2.5 km. south of St Valéry and signed from the D940 Berck - Le Tréport road. Turn south on D48 Estreboeuf road. Turn immediately left to Drancourt and site. GPS: 50.15281, 1.63614

Charges guide

Per unit incl. 2 persons	€ 12,00 - € 30,00
extra person	€ 5,00 - € 6,70
child (under 5 yrs)	€ 2,00 - € 4,70

The Travel Service to book this site call 01580 214000 ...we'll arrange everything

Seraucourt-le-Grand

Camping Caravaning du Vivier aux Carpes

10 rue Charles Voyeux, F-02790 Seraucourt-le-Grand (Aisne) T: **03 23 60 50 10**
E: **camping.du.vivier@wanadoo.fr** **alanrogers.com/FR02000**

Vivier aux Carpes is a small quiet site, close to the A26, two hours from Calais, so is an ideal overnight stop but is also worthy of a longer stay. The 59 well spaced pitches, are at least 100 sq.m. on flat grass with dividing hedges. The 40 for touring units all have electricity (6A), some also with water points, and there are special pitches for motorcaravans. This is a neat, purpose designed site imaginatively set out with a comfortable feel. The enthusiastic owners and manager speak excellent English and are keen to welcome British visitors.

Facilities

The spacious, clean toilet block has separate, heated facilities for disabled visitors, made available to other campers in the winter. Laundry facilities. Motorcaravan service point (fresh water for large vans is charged). Large TV/games room. Small play area. Bicycle hire. Pétanque. Fishing (about € 5.50 p/day). Gates close 22.00 hrs, office open 09.00-21.30. Rallies welcome. WiFi (free). Off site: Village has post office, doctor, chemist and small supermarket in village. Large supermarket in Gauchy 6 km. Markets in St Quentin and Gauchy. Riding 500 m. Golf 12 km.

Open: 1 March - 30 October.

Directions

Leave the A26 (Calais - Reims) at exit 11. Take D1 left towards Soissons for 4 km. Take D8, on entering Essigny-le-Grand (4 km.) turn sharp right on the D72 signed Seraucourt-le-Grand (5 km). Site signed. GPS: 49.78217, 3.21403

Charges guide

Per unit incl. 2 persons and electricity	€ 18,50
extra person	€ 3,70
child (under 10 yrs)	€ 2,70
pet	€ 1,00

Monthly, weekly or weekend rates available. Discounts for students with tents. No credit cards.

Villers-sur-Authie

Kawan Village Caravaning le Val d'Authie

20 route de Vercourt, F-80120 Villers-sur-Authie (Somme) T: **03 22 29 92 47**
E: **camping@valdauthie.fr** **alanrogers.com/FR80090**

In a village location, this well organised site is fairly close to several beaches, but also has its own excellent pool complex, small restaurant and bar. The owner has carefully controlled the size of the site, leaving space for a leisure area with an indoor pool complex. There are 170 pitches in total, but with many holiday homes and chalets, there are only 60 for touring units. These are on grass, some are divided by small hedges, with 6/10A electric hook-ups, and ten have full services.

Facilities

Good toilet facilities include some shower and washbasin units, washbasins in cubicles, and limited facilities for disabled people and babies. Facilities may be under pressure in high season and cleaning variable. Shop (not October). Bar/restaurant (4/4-12/10; hours vary). Swimming and paddling pools with lifeguards in July/Aug). Playground, club room with TV. Weekend entertainment in season (discos may be noisy until midnight, once weekly). Multicourt, beach volleyball, football, boules and tennis court. Internet room. Fitness room including sauna (charged).

Open: 29 March - 12 October.

Directions

Villers-sur-Authie is 25 km. NNW of Abbéville. From A16 junction 24 take N1 to Vron, then left on D175 to Villers-sur-Authie. Or use D85 from Rue, or D485 from Nampont St Martin. Site is at southern end of village at road junction. GPS: 50.31357, 1.69488

Charges guide

Per unit incl. 2 persons	€ 19,00 - € 25,00
extra person	€ 6,00
child (2-6 yrs)	€ 3,00
electricity (6/10A)	€ 5,00 - € 8,00

Camping Cheques accepted.

With its tree lined boulevards, museums art galleries, the Arc Triomphe and of cour the famous Eiffel Towe this cosmopolitan city ha plenty to offer. Less than 30 r from the heart of the capital, a fun-packed trip to Disneyland Paris is also within reach.

DÉPARTEMENTS: 75 PARIS, 77 SEINE-ET-MARNE, 78 YVELINES, 91 ESSONE, 92 HAUTS-DE-SEINE, 93 SEINE-ST-DENIS, 94 VAL DE MARNE, 95 VAL D'OISE

MAJOR CITIES: PARIS, VERSAILLES, IVRY, MELUN, NANTERRE, BOBIGNY, CRETEIL AND PONTOISE

One of the most chic and culturally rewarding cities in the world, Paris has something for everyone. The list of things to do is virtually endless and could easily fill many holidays - window shopping, the Eiffel Tower, Notre Dame, Montmartre, trips on the Seine, pavement cafés and the Moulin Rouge, the list goes on.

As a peaceful retreat, you can relax and enjoy the lush scenery of surrounding hills and secret woodlands of the Ile de France. Square bell towers in gentle valleys, white silos on endless plains of wheat; soft and harmonious landscapes painted and praised by La Fontaine, Corot and all the landscape painters. Paris is surrounded by forests, Fontainebleau, Compiègne, Saint-Germain-en-Laye and majestic châteaux such as Fontainbleau and Vaux-le-Vicomte.

Disneyland Resort Paris provides a great day out for all the family with two fantastic theme parks with over 70 attractions and shows to choose from. On the outskirts of Paris is Parc Astérix. with one of Europe's most impressive roller-coasters.

Places of interest

Fontainebleau: château and national museum, history of Napoléon from 1804-1815.

Malmaison: château and national museur

Meaux: agricultural centre, Gothic cathec chapter house and palace.

Paris: obviously! The list of places is too extensive to include here.

St Germain-en-Laye: château, Gallo-roma and Merovingian archeological museum.

Sèvres: ceramics museum.

Thoiry: château and Parc Zoologique, 450-hectare park with gardens and Africa reserve containing 800 animals.

Versailles: Royal Castle, Royal Apartments Hall of Mirrors, Royal Opera and French History Museum.

Cuisine of the region

Although without a specific cuisine of its own, Paris and Ile de France offer a wide selection of dishes from all the regions of France. Paris also has a wide choice of foreign restaurants, such as Vietnamese and North African.

www.new-paris-idf.com
info@nouveau-paris-idf.com
(0)1 44 50 19 98

BEAUVAIS
COMPIEGNE
SOISSONS
NORMANDY
PICARDY
SENLIS
CHATEAU -THIERRY
VARREDDES
A4,E50
A3,E15
VERNEUIL-SUR-SEINE
MAISONS-LAFFITTE
VILLEVAUDE
MEAUX
JABLINES
A13,E05
LA FERTE-GAUCHER
PARIS
POMMEUSE
CHAMPAGNE-ARDENNE
VERSAILLES
CREVECOEUR -EN BRIE
TOUQUIN
YVELINES 78
DREUX
VILLIERS-SUR-ORGE
LOUAN
RAMBOUILLET
SEINE-ET-MARNE 77
A10,E05,50
PARIS ILE DE FRANCE
MELUN
PROVINS
NOGENT SUR-SEINE
A5,E54
CHARTRES
ETAMPES
A6,E15
VENEUX-LES-SABLONS
VAL DE LOIRE
SENS
PITHIVIERS
BURGUNDY
CHATEAUDUN
0 25 50 kms

Crèvecoeur-en-Brie

Caravaning des 4 Vents

Rue de Beauregard, F-77610 Crèvecoeur-en-Brie (Seine-et-Marne) T: **01 64 07 41 11**. E: **f.george@free.fr**
alanrogers.com/FR77040

This peaceful, pleasant site has been owned and run by the same family for over 35 years. There are around 200 pitches, with many permanent or seasonal units, however, there are 130 spacious grassy pitches for tourists, well separated by good hedges, all with 6A electricity and a water tap shared between two pitches. The whole site is well landscaped with flowers and trees everywhere. This is a great family site with pool and games facilities at the top end of the site so that campers are not disturbed.

Facilities

Three modern sanitary units (heated in cooler weather) provide British style WCs, washbasins (mainly in cubicles) and pushbutton showers. Facilities for disabled people. Laundry facilities. Motorcaravan service point. In high season (July/Aug) a mobile snack bar and pizzeria (open 16.00-23.00), and a baker (07.30-11.00). Well fenced, circular swimming pool (16 m. diameter; June - Sept). Playground, games room, volleyball court, billiard hall and boules court. Riding (high season). Off site: La Houssaye 1 km. Fontenay Tresigny 5 km.

Open: 1 March - 1 November.

Directions

Crèvecoeur is just off the D231 between A4 exit 13 and Provins. From north, pass obelisk and turn right onto the C3 in 3 km. From south 19 km. after junction with N4, turn left at signs to village. Follow site signs. GPS: 48.75063, 2.89708

Charges 2010

Per unit incl. 2 persons and electricity	€ 27,00
extra person (over 5 yrs)	€ 6,00

Jablines

Camping International de Jablines

Base de Loisirs, F-77450 Jablines (Seine-et-Marne) T: **01 60 26 09 37**. E: **welcome@camping-jablines.com**
alanrogers.com/FR77030

Jablines is a modern site which, with the leisure facilities of the adjacent 'Espace Loisirs', offers an interesting, if a little impersonal, alternative to other sites in the region. Man-made lakes provide opportunities for many water-based activities. The Grand Lac is said to have the largest beach on the Ile-de-France. The site itself has 150 pitches, of which 141 are for touring units. Most are of a good size, often slightly sloping, with gravel hardstanding and grass, accessed by tarmac roads and marked by fencing panels and shrubs. All have 10A electrical connections, 60 with water and waste connections also. The whole complex close to the Marne has been developed around old gravel workings. Whilst staying on the campsite admission to the Base de Loisirs is free. Water activities include catamaran sailing, windsurfing, water boarding, canoeing, fishing and supervised bathing, plus a large equestrian centre, an orienteering course, a multisport court and mountain-bike trails. In high season, activities at the leisure complex are supplemented by a bar/restaurant and a range of French-style group activities.

Facilities

The two toilet blocks, heated in cool weather, include pushbutton showers, some washbasins in cubicles. Dishwashing and laundry facilities. Motorcaravan service point (charged). Shop. Play area. Internet point in reception. Ticket sales for Disneyland and Parc Astérix. Mobile homes for rent. Off site: Bar/restaurant adjacent (500 m) at Base de Loisirs with watersports, riding, tennis and minigolf. Golf 15 km.

Open: 28 March - 25 October.

Directions

From A4 Paris - Rouen turn north on A104. Take exit 8 on D404 Meaux/Base de Loisirs Jablines. From A1 going south, follow signs for Marne-la-Vallée using A104. Take exit 6A Clay-Souilly on N3 (Meaux). After 6 km. turn south on D404 and follow signs. At park entry keep left for campsite. GPS: 48.91378, 2.73451

Charges guide

Per unit incl. 2 persons	€ 22,00 - € 27,00
extra person	€ 4,00 - € 7,00

Camping Cheques accepted.

La Ferté Gaucher

Flower Camping la Ferté Gaucher

flower campings

Route de St Martin des Champs, F-77320 La Ferté Gaucher (Seine-et-Marne) T: **01 64 20 20 40**
E: **info@flowercampings-la-ferte-gaucher.com** **alanrogers.com/FR77150**

La Ferté Gaucher is an attractive town in the valley of the Grand Morin, a tributary of the Marne. The site is a member of the Flower group and extends over four hectares of parkland. There are 199 grassy pitches with 149 available for touring, all of a good size and with electrical connections. The river runs through the site but is well fenced. The bar/restaurant has an imaginative menu, with barbecues in fine weather and during the peak season, occasional evening entertainment is organised. Shops, bars and restaurants are withing walking distance.

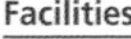

Facilities

Two very traditional sanitary blocks (desperately in need of renovation) provide basic facilities including pushbutton showers, some washbasins in cubicles and a mix of British and Turkish-style WCs. Facilities for disabled visitors. Motorcaravan service point. Good little bar/restaurant with takeaway (all season). Fishing. Play area. Occasional entertainment. Mobile homes for rent. Off site: Tennis and swimming pool adjacent. Bicycle hire 600 m. Riding 12 km. Golf 30 km. Disneyland 55 km. Central Paris 80 km.

Open: 1 March - 30 November.

Directions

From the A4 autoroute, leave at exit 16 (Crécy-la-Chapelle). Take D934 southeast through Coulommiers to la Ferté Gaucher. In town centre look for signs for 'Camping Municipal' or 'Ensemble Sportif'. Site is on the D14 towards St Martin des Champs.
GPS: 48.78232, 3.31205

Charges guide

Per unit incl. 2 persons and electricity	€ 15,00 - € 26,00
extra person	€ 2,00 - € 4,00

Louan

Yelloh! Village Paris/Ile-de-France

Route de Montaiguillon, F-77560 Louan (Seine-et-Marne) T: **04 66 73 97 39**
E: **info@yellohvillage-paris-iledefrance.com** **alanrogers.com/FR77140**

Formerly known as La Cerclière, this Yelloh! Village site to the east of Paris lies at the heart of the Montaiguillon forest, around 50 km. from Disneyland Paris and 80 km. from the city itself. This 11-hectare site contains 220 pitches, of which 40 are currently for touring units and 72 for mobile homes and chalets of which 20 are privately owned. The owners plan to bring more touring pitches into use during 2009. The current pitches are well shaded, although some are rather small and only a few have electricity. The site boasts some impressive amenities including a swimming pool with water slides, as well as a balnéotherapy pool.

Facilities

Six toilet blocks, but when we visited only three were in use with quite a walk from some pitches. Provision was fairly basic and facilities for disabled visitors, motorcaravans and chemical disposal were very limited. Shop. Bar. Restaurant. Takeaway. Swimming pool complex with slides. Balneotherapy pool. Bicycle hire. Tennis. Fishing. Pony rides (charged). Activity and entertainment programme. Play area. Internet access and WiFi (charged). Off site: Disneyland Paris 50 km. Paris centre 80 km. Walking and cycle trails.

Open: 26 April - 6 September.

Directions

Take exit 16 from the A4 (Paris - Metz) and join the N34. Continue on this road as far as La Ferté Gaucher and then turn right to join the southbound D204. At the N4 turn left and then right on to the D15 to Villiers St Georges. Continue on D60 to Louan Villegruis Fontaine from where site is well signed as Camping la Cercliere. GPS: 48.63095, 3.49193

Charges guide

Per unit incl. 2 persons	€ 14,00 - € 35,00
extra person (over 3 yrs)	€ 5,00 - € 7,00

Maisons-Laffitte

Camping Caravaning International

1 rue Johnson, F-78600 Maisons-Laffitte (Yvelines) T: **01 39 12 21 91**. E: **ci.mlaffitte@wanadoo.fr**
alanrogers.com/FR78010

This site on the banks of the Seine is consistently busy, has multilingual, friendly reception staff and occupies a grassy, tree covered area bordering the river. There are 351 pitches, 57 occupied by mobile homes and 70 used by tour operators, plus two areas dedicated to tents. Most pitches are separated by hedges, are of a good size with some overlooking the Seine (unfenced access), and all 195 touring pitches have electricity hook-ups (6A). The roads leading to the site are a little narrow so large vehicles need to take care. Train noise can be expected.

Facilities

Three sanitary blocks, two insulated for winter use and one more open (only used in July/Aug). Facilities are clean with constant supervision necessary, due to volume of visitors. Provision for people with disabilities. Laundry and dishwashing areas. Motorcaravan service point. Self-service shop. Restaurant/bar. Takeaway food and pizzeria (all open all season).TV in restaurant, table tennis, football area. Internet point. Off site: Sports complex adjoining. Riding 500 m. Bicycle hire 5 km.

Open: 27 March - 31 October.

Directions

Best approached from A13 or A15 autoroute. From A13 take exit 7 (Poissy) and follow D153 (Poissy), the D308 (Maisons-Laffitte), then site signs on right before town centre. From A15 exit 7 take D184 towards St Germain, after 11 km. turn left on D308 (Maisons-Laffitte). Follow site signs. GPS: 48.9399, 2.14589

Charges guide

Per unit incl. 2 persons and electricity	€ 25,30 - € 31,20
extra person	€ 2,60 - € 6,40

Paris

Camping du Bois de Boulogne

2 allée du bord de l'eau, F-75016 Paris (Paris) T: **01 45 24 30 00**. E: **camping-boulogne@stereau.fr**
alanrogers.com/FR75020

A busy site and the nearest to the city, set in a wooded area between the Seine and the Bois de Boulogne. The site is quite extensive but nevertheless becomes very full with many international visitors. There are 510 pitches (including mobile homes and a few chalets) of which 280 are marked, with electricity (10A), water, drainage and TV aerial connections. The site has undergone a huge improvement and development programme including the refurbishment of all toilet blocks. Reservations are made for pitches – if not booked, arrive early in season (mornings).

Facilities

Toilet blocks have British style WCs, washbasins in cubicles and showers with divider and seat (hot water throughout). All these facilities suffer from heavy use in season. Laundry facilities. Five motorcaravan service points. Shop. Bar and restaurant (1/4-15/10). Bar open 07.00-24.00 most times and until 02.00 hrs in peak season. Pizza bar and takeaway. Playground. Off site: Fishing 1 km. Bicycle hire 2 km.

Open: All year.

Directions

Site is on east side of Seine between the river and the Bois de Boulogne, just north of the Pont de Suresnes. Easiest approach is from Port Maillot. Traffic lights at site entrance. Follow signs closely and use a good map. GPS: 48.86829, 2.23545

Charges guide

Per unit incl. 2 persons	€ 11,00 - € 35,70
extra person	€ 2,40 - € 6,50

Melun

Kawan Village la Belle Etoile

Quai Joffre, la Rochette, F-77000 Melun (Seine-et-Marne) T: **01 64 39 48 12**
E: **info@campinglabelleetoile.com** **alanrogers.com/FR77070**

Alongside the River Seine, this site has an overall mature and neat appearance, although the approach road is somewhat off-putting with several industrial plants. However, you will discover that La Belle Etoile enjoys a pleasant position with pitches to the fore of the site within view of the barges which continually pass by. The 170 touring pitches, 130 with 6A electricity connections, are on grass and laid out between the many shrubs and trees. There are ten units for hire. A friendly, family-run site with pleasant and helpful English speaking owners, it is ideally situated for visiting Fontainebleau and Paris.

Facilities

The toilet blocks are not new but they are kept very clean and the water is very hot. Laundry room. Baby bath. Facilities for disabled visitors (shower, washbasin and WC). Motorcaravan service point. Small bar, snacks, shop and takeaway (all 1/7-29/8). Heated outdoor swimming pool (1/5-15/9). Play area. Bicycle hire. Tickets for Disney and Vaux le Vicomte are sold by the site. Off site: Fontainebleau and Paris. Golf 15 km. Bus to connect with trains 100 m. Fishing 100 m.

Open: 27 March - 17 October.

Directions

Travelling north on RD606 Fontainebleau - Melun road, on entering La Rochette, pass petrol station on left. Turn immediately right into Ave de la Seine. At end of road turn left at river, site on left in 500 m. GPS: 48.52502, 2.66940

Charges 2010

Per unit incl. 2 persons and electricity	€ 20,00 - € 23,00
extra person	€ 5,40 - € 6,40
child (3-11 yrs)	€ 3,50 - € 4,50
dog	€ 1,50

Camping Cheques accepted.

Pommeuse

482

Camping le Chêne Gris

24 place de la Gare de Faremoutiers, F-77515 Pommeuse (Seine-et-Marne) T: **01 64 04 21 80**
E: **info@lechenegris.com** **alanrogers.com/FR77020**

This site is being progressively developed by a Dutch holiday company. A principal building houses reception on the ground floor and also an airy restaurant/bar plus a takeaway. Of the 198 pitches, 65 are for touring, many of which are on aggregate stone, the rest (higher up the hill on which the site is built) being occupied by over 100 mobile homes and 25 tents belonging to a Dutch tour operator. Terraces look out onto the heated leisure pool complex and an adventure-type play area for over-fives, whilst the play area for under-fives is at the side of the bar with picture windows overlooking it. The site is next to a railway station with trains to Paris (45 minutes). Disneyland is 20 km. The site is next to a railway station with trains to Paris (45 minutes). Disneyland is 20 km.

Facilities

One toilet block with pushbutton showers, washbasins in cubicles and a laundry area. At busy times these facilities may be under pressure. A second block is to be added. Facilities for disabled visitors. Bar, restaurant and takeaway. Pool complex (all season). Off site: Shops, bars and restaurants nearby. Fishing and riding 2 km.

Open: 1 April - 8 November.

Directions

From A4 at exit 16 take N34 towards Coulommiers. In 10 km. turn south for 2 km. on D25 to Pommeuse; site on right. GPS: 48.808213, 2.993935

Charges guide

Per unit incl. 2 persons	€ 24,00 - € 37,00
extra person	€ 2,00 - € 3,75

Camping Cheques accepted.

Rambouillet

HUTTOPIA

Huttopia Rambouillet

Rue du Château d'Eau, F-78120 Rambouillet (Yvelines) T: **01 30 41 07 34**. E: **rambouillet@huttopia.com**
alanrogers.com/FR78040

Huttopia Rambouillet is in a peaceful forest location beside a lake, with good tarmac access roads and site lighting. The 190 touring pitches, 150 with electrical connections, are set among the trees and in clearings. As a result, shade is plentiful and grass sparse. The main area is traffic-free but there is a section for motorcaravans and those who needto have their car with them. The result is a safe, child-friendly site. There is an 'espace nature' with 40 huge pitches for campers. As Huttopia have built a 'Natural Swimming Pool' as part of their efforts to be environmentally friendly. The water is filtered by reeds and it was used for the first time in 2008 passing the strict tests of France's Ministry of Health. The opening date each year will vary according to how quickly the reeds do their work. From your pitch, you can stroll out into the forest and there are many good cycle routes and footpaths in the area. It is possible to visit Paris by rail (30-minutes) and the Mobilis 'transport package' ticket is available from the railway station.

Facilities

The brand new sanitary block has controllable showers, some washbasins in cubicles and a number of spacious 'family' cubicles. Facilities for disabled visitors. Laundry facilities. Three outlying 'rondavels' each with two family rooms. Motorcaravan service point. Small shop selling basics plus bar/restaurant with terrace (July/Aug and weekends). Games room with TV. Free internet and WiFi. Play area. 'Natural' swimming pool (June - Sept, earlier if possible). Bicycle hire. Fishing. Children's and family activities (July/Aug). No American motorhomes or twin-axle caravans. Off site: Riding 5 km. Lake with beach 10 km. Golf 15 km.

Open: 4 April - 5 November.

Directions

Rambouillet is 52 km. south west of Paris. Site is south east of town: from N10 southbound take Rambouillet/Les Eveuses exit, northbound take Rambouillet centre exit, loop round (site signed) and rejoin N10 southbound, taking next exit. Pass under N10, following signs to site in 1.7 km.
GPS: 48.62638, 1.84375

Charges guide

Per unit incl. 2 persons and electricity	€ 22,00 - € 41,80
extra person	€ 3,00 - € 6,80

The Travel Service to book this site call 01580 214000 ...we'll arrange everything

Touquin

Camping les Etangs Fleuris

Route Couture, F-77131 Touquin (Seine-et-Marne) T: **01 64 04 16 36**. E: **contact@etangs-fleuris.com**
alanrogers.com/FR77090

This is a pleasant, peaceful site which has a very French feel despite the presence of a fair number of mobile homes, since these occupy their own areas round the periphery. The 80 touring pitches are grouped on the level ground around the attractive lakes, all with electricity (10A) and water, separated by hedges and with shade from mature trees. The life of the site centres round a smart bar/function room which doubles as reception and a shop, as well as the lakes and an attractive, irregularly shaped pool. The lakes are home to some sizeable carp as well as being restocked daily with trout (fishing € 5 for half a day). The site is near enough to both Paris (50 km) and Disneyland (23 km) to provide a practical alternative to the busier sites nearer the centre.

Facilities

A fairly simple, heated toilet block has pushbutton showers and open washbasins (with dividers and hooks) for men but mainly in cubicles for ladies. No facilities for disabled visitors. Another heated block is only opened when site is very busy. Laundry facilities. Motorcaravan service area. Shop for basics in bar. Heated pool with paddling section (15/4-15/9). Takeaway meals and snacks (15/5-10/9). Internet access and WiFi. Multisports pitch. Minigolf. Trampoline.
Off site: Riding 5 km. Golf 15 km. Zoo 5 km.

Open: 15 April - 15 September.

Directions

Touquin is off the D231, 21 km. from exit 13 of A4 motorway and 30 km. northeast of Provins. From D231 follow signs for Touquin, then Etangs Fleuris. Site is 2.5 km. west of village.
GPS: 48.733054, 3.046978

Charges 2010

Per unit incl. 2 persons and electricity	€ 19,00
extra person	€ 9,00
child (2-10 yrs)	€ 4,00
dog	€ 1,50

Varreddes

Le Village Parisien

Route de Congis (D121), F-77910 Varreddes (Seine-et-Marne) T: **01 64 34 80 80**
E: **contact@villageparisien.com** **alanrogers.com/FR77050**

If you are intending to visit Disneyland, this site is ideally situated 12 km. away. Tickets can be purchased at the site and taxi travel can be arranged. The site has 224 pitches and is reasonably well cared for with mature hedges dividing the pitches. There are about 50 used for touring units and these vary both in size and quality. Access on some could be difficult for larger units. Le Village Parisien is unfortunately rather dominated by the large number of seasonal pitches (80%). The three toilet blocks are old and only just adequate. There is a reasonably large swimming pool (unheated). The opening of the facilities, such as the bar and shop are somewhat erratic and depends on the numbers on the site and whether it is a school or public holiday.

Facilities

Three toilet blocks (old and in need of refurbishment). Dishwashing and laundry facilities. Small shop and takeaway. Bar with entertainment and TV. Swimming and paddling pools (unheated). Tennis. Play area. Fishing. Bicycle hire. Tickets and taxis for Disneyland. Off site: Golf 10 km.

Open: 15 March - 1 November.

Directions

Heading south on the A1 towards Paris, turn southeast on N330 at Senlis. Head towards Meaux, then turn left on D405 for Varreddes. Site is well signed from here (about 2 km).
GPS: 49.002938, 2.941412

Charges guide

Per unit incl. 2 persons and electricity	€ 19,00 - € 29,00
extra person (over 4 yrs)	€ 4,00
dog	free

Camping Cheques accepted.

Veneux-les-Sablons

Camping les Courtilles du Lido

Les Courtilles du Lido, Chemin du Passeur, F-77250 Veneux-les-Sablons (Seine-et-Marne) T: **01 60 70 46 05**
E: **lescourtilles-dulido@wanadoo.fr** **alanrogers.com/FR77130**

Les Courtilles du Lido is a well established, family run site located just outside the 14th-century village of Moret-sur-Loing on the edge of the Forêt de Fontainebleau. There are 180 well shaded grassy pitches with 10A electricity, dispersed throughout the five-hectare terrain. A good range of amenities includes a pool and an 18-hole minigolf course, as well as a pizzeria and bar. There are 17 mobile homes for rent. Paris lies 55 km. to the north and can be accessed by either the A5 or A6 motorways or by rail from the local station (within walking distance). Some train noise can be heard from the site.

Facilities

A single toilet block provides adequate facilites. No facilities for children and disabled people. Shop, pizzeria, bar and takeaway (all season). Outdoor swimming pool (15/5-22/9). Play area. Games room. Motorcaravan services. Minigolf. Short tennis. Boules. Internet access and free WiFi.
Off site: Moret-sur-Loing (an attractive Gallo-Roman village) 2 km. Fishing 500 m. Canoeing. Golf 10 km and horse riding 15 km. Fontainebleau 5 km. River cruises 5 km. Paris 55 km.

Open: 3 April - 20 September.

Directions

Site is close to the point where the Loing joins the Seine. From Fontainebleau take the southbound N6 (towards Sens). Upon arrival at Veneux les Sablons follow signs for Moret-sur-Loing and then St Mammès. Final approach is through a tunnel. Site is well signed. GPS: 48.38321, 2.80303

Charges guide

Per unit incl. 2 persons and electricity	€ 16,00 - € 22,00
extra person	€ 4,00
child (under 10 yrs)	€ 3,00 - € 8,50
dog	€ 1,50

Verneuil-sur-Seine

Camping le Val de Seine

Base de Loisirs, chemin du Rouillard, F-78480 Verneuil-sur-Seine (Yvelines) T: **01 39 28 16 20**
E: **vds78@orange.fr** **alanrogers.com/FR78050**

This is an excellent little site, completely refurbished to high standards and located in a large leisure and country park on the western outskirts of Paris. Campers have free access to the huge country park (800 m. from site) with its three large lakes, one with a beach for swimming, others for sailing and pedalo hire. The site has 87 pitches in two sections, one end for campers (mainly groups) with its own toilet block, the other for caravans and tents. Here there are 37 level pitches, all but four with electricity (6A), water and drainage. There is some aircraft and train noise.

Facilities

Two modern toilet blocks have controllable showers and some washbasins in cubicles. Facilities for disabled visitors (touring area). Dishwashing provision. Small block for children plus baby room (camping area). Laundry facilities. Motorcaravan service point. Reception sells bread (to order) and basics. Country park with lakes, fishing, sailing, many other sports facilities, a self-service restaurant and brasserie. Tennis courts, 18-hole minigolf. Communal barbecue in camping area. Off site: Riding adjacent. Golf 7 km. Paris 20 mins by train and 30 mins by car.

Open: 15 April - 30 September.

Directions

From A13 take exit 8 (Meulan-les Mureaux). Follow signs for 'Base de Loisirs du Val de Seine'. Go through Les Mureaux and bear right on D154 towards Verneuil. At roundabout turn left (signed 'Base de Loisirs') to site. GPS: 48.99643, 1.9601

Charges 2010

Per person (4 yrs and over)	€ 3,25 - € 3,75
pitch	€ 3,20 - € 5,30
electricity	€ 4,30

Versailles

HUTTOPIA

Huttopia Versailles

31 rue Berthelot, F-78000 Versailles (Yvelines) T: **01 39 51 23 61**. E: **versailles@huttopia.com**
alanrogers.com/FR78060

This Huttopia site is rather different. When the French owners visited Canada and experienced 'back to nature' camping, they were so impressed that they decided to introduce the idea to France. This is probably a little like camping as it used to be, but with some big differences. Gone are the formal pitches with neatly trimmed hedges and instead there are 145 places of ample size arranged informally amongst the trees. The terrain is as nature intended with very little grass and much of it steep and rugged (there are plans to introduce some terracing). Long electricity leads are required and be prepared to use blocks and corner steadies on many pitches. Most pitches have good shade. All the site buildings are designed and built to fit into the natural concept. Attractive wooden huts, tents and gypsy style caravans can be rented. This is a different but popular site that will suit campers who, while still wanting their creature comforts, would like to be in more natural surroundings.

Facilities

Three well designed toilet blocks (wood cabin style) are evenly dispersed around the site and provide basic facilities. Special bivouacs set up for cooking and washing up. Restaurant with takeaway food (30/4-27/9 and weekends). Bar. Games room. Simple swimming and paddling pools (May - Sept). Playground. Bicycle hire. Children's club. Off site: Versailles and its château (tickets can be purchased at the site). Hiking. Cycling trails. Fishing 1 km. Golf 3 km. Riding 5 km. Paris 20 minutes by RER express train from Versailles.

Open: 19 December - 5 November.

Directions

From the front of the château of Versailles take the Avenue de Paris and the site is signed after 2 km. GPS: 48.78967, 2.15633

Charges guide

Per unit incl. 2 persons and electricity	€ 27,30 - € 41,80
extra person	€ 6,20 - € 8,50
child (2-7 yrs)	€ 3,00 - € 4,30
dog	€ 4,00

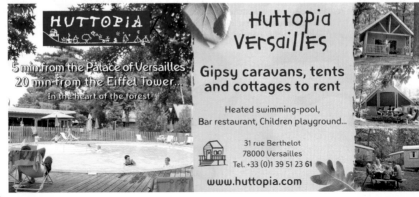

Villevaudé

Camping Club le Parc de Paris

Rue Adèle Claret, Montjay la Tour, F-77410 Villevaudé (Seine-et-Marne) T: **01 60 26 20 79**
E: **info@campingleparc.fr** **alanrogers.com/FR77110**

This rural, sloping site (open all year) is conveniently situated as an overnight stop or for a visit to Disneyland or to Paris. The 200 largely level, grassy touring pitches all have access to 4A electricity, though some areas have yet to be fully prepared for use. There are 100 mobile homes for rent. The new owners have ongoing plans for improving the site. A ten-minute drive takes you to a station on a Metro (RER) line to Paris and there is free parking. Disneyland and Parc Astérix are easily reached via the motorways. The Base de Loisirs with its man-made lakes at nearby Jablines (7 km) provides great opportunities for water-based and other leisure activities and it has the largest beach in the Ile-de-France region. There is a small shop in the nearby village of Villaudé and a bar/restaurant in the next hamlet.

Facilities

The three toilet blocks have some washbasins in cabins, mainly British-style toilets and pushbutton showers. Facilities for young children and disabled visitors. Laundry. Motorcaravan service point. Bar, snack bar and takeaway. Play area. Games area. TV room. Internet access in reception and WiFi throughout (charged). Off site: Fishing and riding both 5 km. Base de Loisirs with sailing and other water-sports, fishing, swimming, tennis, mountain-bike hire and a riding centre 7 km. Golf 14 km. Paris 20 km. Disneyland 20 km. Astérix Park 40 km.

Open: All year.

Directions

From the north: A1 Paris, join A104 Marne la Vallée and leave at exit 6B onto N3. After Claye-Souilly turn right on D404 towards Villevaudé and follow signs to site on left. From the south: A4 Reims, Metz, Nancy, join A104 Lille and take exit 8 to join D404 towards Claye-Souilly and Villevaudé then follow signs to site on right after village. GPS: 48.91282, 2.67465

Charges guide

Per unit incl. 2 persons and electricity	€ 23,00 - € 29,00
extra person	€ 4,00 - € 7,00

Villiers-sur-Orge

Camping Caravaning le Beau Village

1 voie des Prés, F-91700 Villiers-sur-Orge (Essonne) T: **01 60 16 17 86**. E: **le-beau-village@wanadoo.fr**
alanrogers.com/FR91010

This is a pleasant, typically French campsite just 25 km. south of Paris and conveniently located at the centre of a triangle formed by the A6 motorway, the N20/A10 to Orleans and the N104 east/west link road 'La Francilienne'. Half of its 100 pitches are occupied on a seasonal basis by Parisians or by mobile homes to rent; the remainder are touring pitches, all hedged and with 10A electricity. Trees provide some shade. Reception, in a traditionally-styled building, also has a pleasant little bar, a games room and an attractive terrace with wooden tables, benches, thatched canopies and a stone-built barbecue.

Facilities

Three toilet blocks, heated as necessary, have controllable showers and some washbasins in cabins. The main block has been refurbished and has a baby changing room and laundry facilities. A second (older) block has adequate facilities for disabled visitors, the third is in a Portacabin with some additional washbasins outside in a very tired row of cubicles. Small bar (open high season and on demand). WiFi in reception area (free sessions). Adventure play area. Free loan of canoes. Boules. Off site: Trains to Paris (20 mins) 700 m. Shops and restaurants nearby. Golf, riding 2 km. River beach and sailing 3 km. Boat launching 4 km.

Open: All year.

Directions

From A6 leave at exit 6 (Savigny-sur-Orge). Turn south west, follow signs for Quartier Latin on D25 then right at roundabout on D35 to Villiers-sur-Orge. Turn left immediately after river on Voie des Prés along river bank to site on left. From A10 turn east on N104. From N104 take N20 north. From N20 at Ballainvillers take exit for La Ville du Bois on D35 south east to Villiers-sur-Orge. In village (foot of hill), turn right, then as above. GPS: 48.65527, 2.30409

Charges guide

Per unit incl. 2 persons and electricity	€ 16,00
extra person	€ 2,25 - € 4,50

Champagne & Ardenne TOURISME

[Ethnology]
STRANGE AQUATIC TRIBES

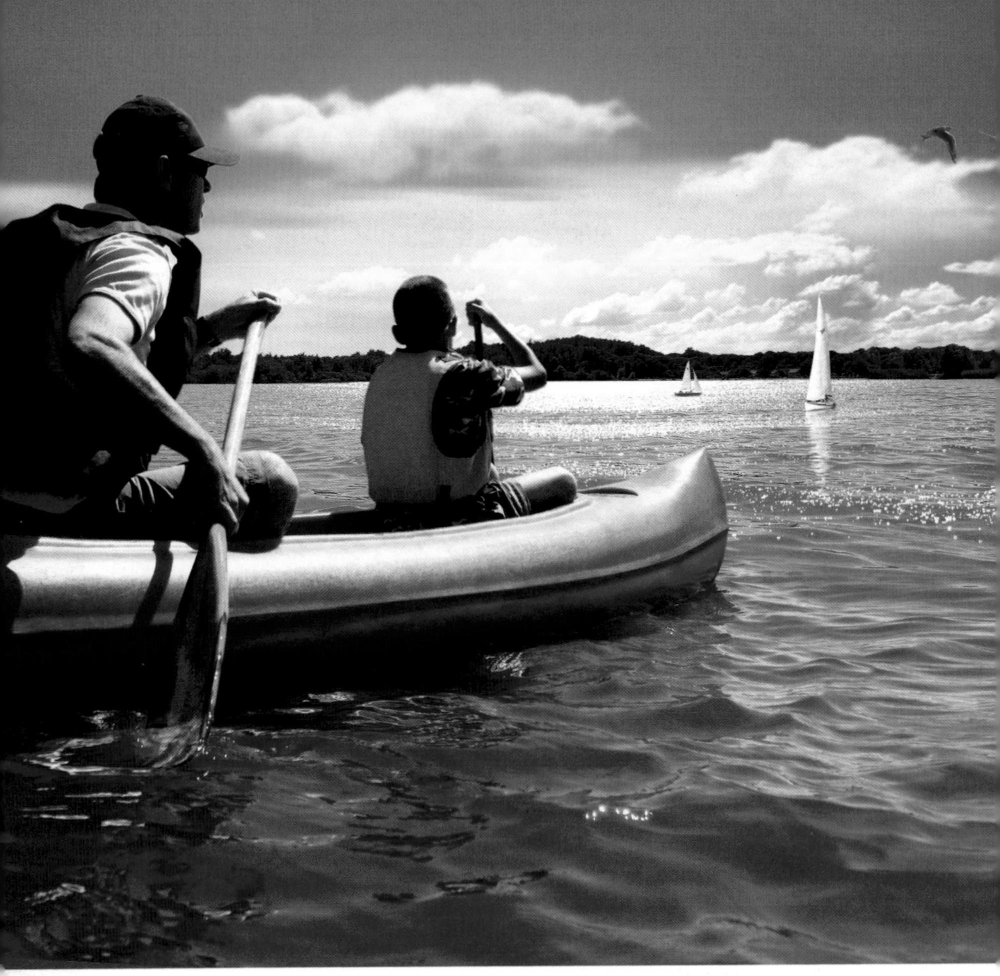

Playful nature,
Explore the diversity of the vegetation and natural landscapes of Champagne-Ardenne, France's most floral region.

Gourmet delights,
Treat yourself in Champagne-Ardenne to a selection of local produce which will set your taste buds dancing!

Fan of novel adventures,
Champagne-Ardenne frees your traveller's soul. On land, on water and in the air, whether calm or exciting, the adventure can begin!

Lover of eloquent stories,
Attentive observer or gentle rambler, Champagne-Ardenne transports you, beyond the centuries, through the wealth of its heritage.

You'll see, Champagne-Ardenne will be your next conquest!

Your next conquest

www.tourisme-champagne-ardenne.com

CHAMPAGNE ARDEN
TOURISME

The varied landscapes of Champagne-Ardenne include dense forests, vineyards and winding rivers. The whole area is dotted with fascinating ancient churches and castles, towns and villages.

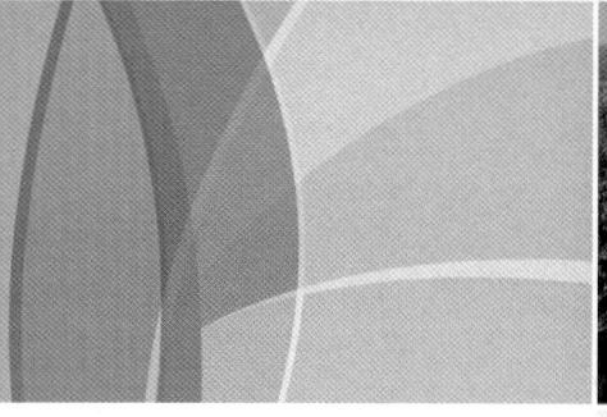

DÉPARTEMENTS: 08 ARDENNES, 51 MARNE, 10 AUBE, 52 HAUTE-MARNE

MAJOR CITY: REIMS

Situated on the flatlands of Champagne are the most northerly vineyards in France where special processing turns the light, dry wine into 'le Champagne'. Nowhere else in the world are you allowed to make sparkling wine and call it Champagne. Reims and Epernay are the centres for the wine trade. It is not the names of the vineyards that have become famous but those of the shippers, such as Moet Chandon and Veuve Clicquot.

This is essentially a place of rural peace, with chalky rolling fields, although there is some heavy industry in the north. This north-eastern slice of France has seen many European battles and the hilly terrain and deep forests of the Ardennes gave some advantage to the Resistance fighters of the last war when Ardennes was annexed to Germany. Its main city of Charleville-Mezieres was two distinct towns lying on either side of the Meuse river until their amalgamation in 1966 and each retains its individuality.

Places of interest

Charleville-Mezieres: arcaded Palace Ducale, similar in style to the Place des Vosges in Paris. Birthplace of the poet Arthur Rimbaud.

Chalons-sur-Marne: perfect Gothic style cathedral with 12th century tower.

Épernay: home of Champagne production. There are 72 miles of underground galleries in the chalk beneath the city to store the wine for the delicate operations required to make the champagne.

Reims: 13th-century Gothic cathedral. In 406, Clovis the first king of France was baptised here and the kings of France from Louis V11 to Charles X were crowned here.

Troyes: ancient capital of the Champagne region with a beautifully preserved city centre with a Gothic cathedral, dozens of churches and 15th century houses. A system of boulevards shaped like a champagne cork. Musée d'Art Moderne including works by Degas and Gaugin.

Cuisine of the region

Flamiche aux poixeaux: puff pastry tart with cream and leeks.

Madeleine de Commercy: small, shell-shaped, buttery pastries with orange flavouring.

Flamiche aux Maroilles/Goyere: a hot creamy tart based on local cheese.

Tarte (aux mirabelles): golden plum tart. Also made with other fruits.

www.tourisme-champagne-ardenne.com
contact@tourisme-champagen-ardenne.com
(0)3 26 21 85 80

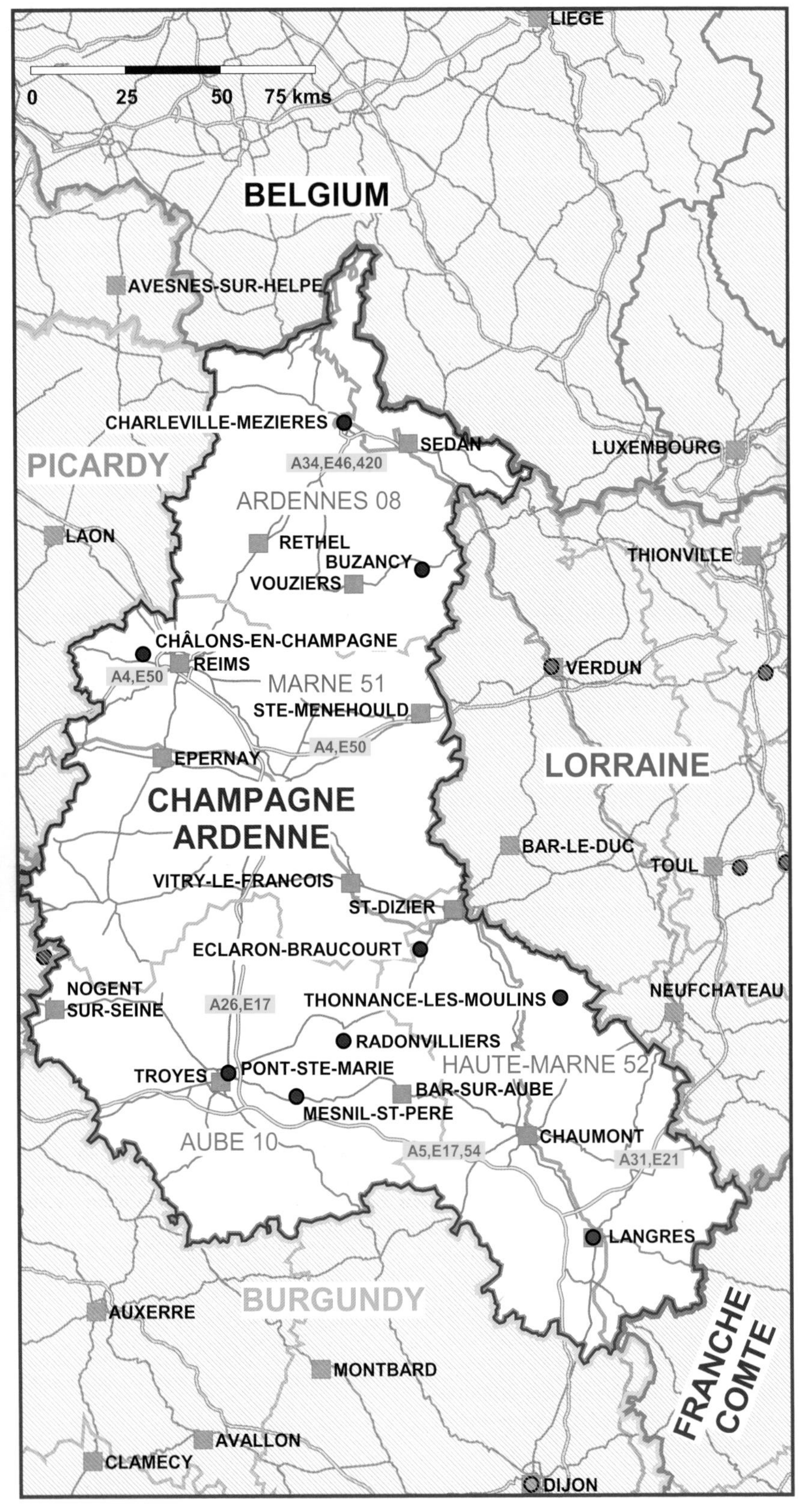
0 25 50 75 kms
LIEGE
BELGIUM
AVESNES-SUR-HELPE
CHARLEVILLE-MEZIERES
SEDAN
LUXEMBOURG
PICARDY
A34,E46,420
ARDENNES 08
LAON
RETHEL
BUZANCY
THIONVILLE
VOUZIERS
CHÂLONS-EN-CHAMPAGNE
REIMS
VERDUN
A4,E50
MARNE 51
STE-MENEHOULD
A4,E50
EPERNAY
LORRAINE
CHAMPAGNE
ARDENNE
BAR-LE-DUC
TOUL
VITRY-LE-FRANCOIS
ST-DIZIER
ECLARON-BRAUCOURT
NOGENT
SUR-SEINE
A26,E17
THONNANCE-LES-MOULINS
NEUFCHATEAU
RADONVILLIERS
HAUTE-MARNE 52
TROYES
PONT-STE-MARIE
BAR-SUR-AUBE
MESNIL-ST-PERE
CHAUMONT
AUBE 10
A5,E17,54
A31,E21
LANGRES
BURGUNDY
AUXERRE
FRANCHE
COMTE
MONTBARD
AVALLON
CLAMECY
DIJON

Buzancy

Camping la Samaritaine

Rue des Etangs, F-08240 Buzancy (Ardennes) T: **03 24 30 08 88**. E: **info@campinglasamaritaine.com**
alanrogers.com/FR08040

A delightful new site in the heart of the Ardennes. It is peacefully situated just outside the village beside a stream. There may be some high season noise from a nearby lake where you can swim or fish. Flowers decorate the entrance and bushes and saplings separate the pitches. The 101 numbered touring pitches all have electricity (10A) and are on level grass off hard access roads. They vary in size up to 130 sq.m. 55 have water and drain, and there are small wooden containers for waste. There are also ten mobile homes and nine chalets for rent.

Facilities

Sanitary facilities provide private cabins. Baby bath. Facilities for disabled visitors. Laundry facilities. Motorcaravan service point. Bread delivered daily. A few essentials are kept in reception. Snack bar/takeaway (20/6-31/8). Large recreation room with games and tables. Play area. Boules. Accompanied walks and entertainment programme (high season). Off site: Restaurant in village.

Open: 1 May - 20 September.

Directions

Buzancy is about 22 km. east of Vouziers on the RD947 towards Stenay and Montmédy. Site is just over 1.5 km. from centre of village down a small road. Well signed. GPS: 49.42640, 4.94010

Charges guide

Per unit with 2 persons and electricity	€ 16,50 - € 18,50
extra person	€ 2,00 - € 3,50

No credit cards.

Châlons-en-Champagne

Camping Municipal Châlons-en-Champagne

Rue de Plaisance, F-51000 Châlons-en-Champagne (Marne) T: **03 26 68 38 00**
E: **camping.mairie.chalons@wanadoo.fr** **alanrogers.com/FR51020**

The location of Châlons, south of Reims and near the A4 and A26 autoroutes, about 200 miles from Calais and Boulogne, makes this an ideal stopover. This site on the southern edge of town is an example of a good municipal site. The wide entrance with its neatly mown grass and flower beds sets the tone for the rest of the site; 96 of the 148 pitches, accessed from tarmac roads, are on a gravel base with the rest on grass. All have electricity (10A). The generously sized gravel pitches are separated by hedges. The newest area of pitches overlooks the small lake.

Facilities

Two toilet blocks (one can be heated) include washbasins in cabins, baby room and hairdressing station. Facilities for disabled visitors. Laundry and dishwashing facilities. Refuse bins. Bread to order. Bar, snack bar and takeaway (20/5-31/9 evenings, lunchtime July/Aug). Gas supplies. Games and TV rooms. Playground. Minigolf, tennis, volleyball, boules, minifootball. Motorcaravan service point. Off site: Bus stop. Fishing.

Open: 1 April - 31 October.

Directions

From north on A4, take La Veuve exit (27) onto N44 which by-passes town. Leave at last exit (St Memmie), follow camping signs. From south on A26, take exit 18 on N77 and towards town. Site well signed 'Camping', (south of town on D60).
GPS: 48.9359, 4.3832

Charges guide

Per person	€ 4,80
child (under 7 yrs)	€ 1,85
pitch incl. electricity	€ 8,00
vehicle	€ 3,20

Charleville-Mezieres

Camping Municipal du Mont Olympe

Rue des Paquis, F-08000 Charleville-Mezieres (Ardennes) T: **03 24 33 23 60**
E: **camping-charlevillemezieres@wanadoo.fr** **alanrogers.com/FR08010**

Attractively situated alongside the Meuse River, within easy walking distance across a footbridge to the centre of the pleasant large town, this site was completely rebuilt in 2002. It now offers excellent facilities, with 129 grass pitches, all with electricity (10A), water and waste water connections. There are 66 from 108 to 219 sq.m. in size, 49 up to 106 sq.m. and seven hardstandings for motorcaravans.

Facilities

Two heated buildings provide first class showers, private cabins, baby rooms and facilities for disabled visitors. Well equipped laundry room. Motorcaravan service point. Shop (July/Aug). Play area. TV and games room. Barbecues allowed at communal area only. Off site: Municipal pool next door. Boat trips on the river. Attractive town centre close by. Bicycle hire 1 km. Golf 20 km.

Open: 1 April - 1 October.

Directions

Site is north of Charleville on the island of Montcy-St Pierre. From north D988/D1 follow river, over bridge, then immediately left. From southeast (A203/N51/N43) take 'centre' exit, head for 'Gare' then follow Avenue Forest north and sharp left after bridge. Site is 150 m. GPS: 49.7790, 4.7207

Charges guide

Per unit incl. 2 persons and electricity	€ 15,31 - € 17,61
extra person	€ 1,70 - € 3,35
electricity (10A)	€ 3,90

Eclaron

Yelloh! Village en Champagne

F-52290 Eclaron (Haute-Marne) T: **04 66 73 97 39**. E: **info@yellohvillage-en-champagne.com**

alanrogers.com/FR52050

Formerly known as Les Sources du Lac, this Yelloh! Village site is located close to the village of Eclaron and has direct access to the Lac du Der. This is a very large lake with 77 km. of shoreline and is home to over 270 species of birds. Part of the lake is an ornithological reserve but a wide range of water based activities are on offer in other areas. These include including fishing, windsurfing and sailing, and a separate area is reserved for motor boats. There are just 30 touring pitches at this site and around 120 mobile homes and chalets for rent.

Facilities

Two toilet blocks include facilities for babies. The facilities may be under pressure at busy times. Shop (July/Aug). Bar. Restaurant. Takeaway. Swimming pool. Paddling pool. Direct access to the lake and beach. Play area. Bicycle hire. Fishing. Ornithological activities. Activity and entertainment programme. Off site: Riding 10 km. Walking and cycle trails. Fishing. The 'Champagne route'. Grange aux Abeilles (bee barn) at Giffaumont Champaubert.

Open: 1 May - 30 September.

Directions

Take the southbound N44 from Chalons-en-Champagne as far as Vitry-le François and then join the eastbound N4 as far as St Dizier. From the St Dizier ring road take the D384 towards Montier-en-Der and upon reaching Eclaron-Braucourt follow signs to the site. GPS: 48.57213, 4.84891

Charges guide

Per unit incl. 2 persons	€ 15,00 - € 30,00
extra person	€ 4,00 - € 5,00
child (3-7 yrs)	free - € 5,00

Eclaron-Braucourt

Flower la Presqu'ile de Champaubert

F-52290 Eclaron-Braucourt (Haute-Marne) T: **03 25 04 13 20**. E: **ilechampaubert@free.fr**

alanrogers.com/FR52010

This is a good municipal site of the type found all over France. It is situated beside what is said to be the largest man-made inland lake in Europe (4,800 ha), the Lac du Der Chantecoq. This provides superb facilities for windsurfing, sailing, etc. and even for swimming from a 100 m. beach alongside the site (lifeguard in main season). There is also a swimming pool on site. The site itself is situated on the shores of the lake, with 195 fairly level grassy pitches of a good size, 70 for tourers, all with electrical connections (10A). They are separated by hedges and trees that also provide a fair amount of shade. The general appearance and the views across the lake are very attractive.

Facilities

Toilet facilities in two modern blocks are fully equipped and of a good standard with individual small buildings for WCs. Washbasins are in private cabins. Laundry facilities. Motorcaravan service point. Small shop for essentials in the reception area. Bar/restaurant. Swimming pool. Playground. Fishing. Mobile homes for rent. Off site: Miles of walking and cycle tracks. Ornithology. Sailing and windsurfing on Lac de Der (200m).

Open: 3 April - 11 November.

Directions

From St Dizier, take D384 past Eclaron to Braucourt and follow signs to the site (3 km). GPS: 48.55425, 4.79235

Charges 2010

Per unit incl. 2 persons and electricity	€ 13,00 - € 31,00
extra person	€ 4,00 - € 5,00
child (3-7 yrs)	free - € 5,00

Langres

Kawan Village Lac de la Liez

Peigney, F-52200 Langres (Haute-Marne) T: **03 25 90 27 79**. E: **campingliez@free.fr**

alanrogers.com/FR52030

Managed by the enthusiastic Baude family, this excellent lakeside site is near the city of Langres. Only ten minutes from the A5, Camping Lac de la Liez provides an ideal spot for an overnight stop en route to the south of France. There is also a lot on offer for a longer stay. The site provides 131 fully serviced pitches, some with panoramic views of the 250 hectare lake with its sandy beach and small harbour where boats and pedalos may be hired. Ideal for swimming and watersports, access to the lake is down steps and across quite a fast road (in total 150 m).

Facilities

Two toilet blocks have all facilities in cabins (only one is open in low season). Facilities for disabled people and babies. Laundry facilities. Motorcaravan services. Shop, bar and restaurant (with takeaway food). Indoor pool complex with spa and sauna. Heated outdoor pool (15/6-15/9). Games room. Playground. Games area. Tennis (free in low season). WiFi. Off site: Lake with beach. Boat and bicycle hire. Cycle tracks around lake. Fishing 100 m. Riding 5 km.

Open: 1 April - 15 October.

Directions

From Langres take the N19 towards Vesoul. After 3 km. turn right, straight after the large river bridge, then follow site signs. GPS: 47.87022, 5.37627

Charges guide

Per unit incl. 2 persons and electricity	€ 22,00 - € 31,00
extra person	€ 6,00 - € 8,00
child (2-12 yrs)	€ 3,00 - € 4,50

Camping Cheques accepted.

Langres

Camping Navarre

9 boulevard Maréchal de Lattre de Tassigny, F-52200 Langres (Haute-Marne) T: **03 25 87 37 92**
E: **campingnavarre@free.fr** **alanrogers.com/FR52060**

Camping Navarre is a small municipal site of 66 pitches, with the advantage of being located in a unique position within the town of Langres. The pitches here are grassy, well shaded and of a good size, mostly with electrical connections. The site's toilet block has all the usual facilities and is a new building of architectural merit. Although there are few amenities on site, the town centre is just a short walk away with a wide selection of shops, cafés and restaurants. Langres, with its 3.5 km. of ancient ramparts and imposing towers, is classified as one of the 50 most beautiful towns in France and makes a popular overnight stop. For those choosing to spend longer in the Haute-Marne, the surrounding countryside, Lac de la Liez (resulting from the construction of the Marne - Saône canal) and the Marne valley are well worth exploration. The Liez sailing school offers opportunities for windsurfing, sailing, and canoe and pedalo hire.

Facilities

Modern, heated toilet block with facilities for disabled visitors. Washing machines. Play area. WiFi (free, near reception). Off site: Langres centre. Lac de la Liez 5 km. Fishing (river) 3 km. Cycle and walking tracks.

Open: 15 March - 31 October.

Directions

Langres is close to the intersection of the A5 and A31 motorways. Leave either motorway and head for the town centre. Site is well signed.
GPS: 47.86085, 5.33029

Charges guide

Per unit incl. 2 persons and electricity	€ 12,10 - € 14,10
extra person	€ 1,20 - € 2,70

Mesnil-Saint Père

Kawan Resort Lac d'Orient

kawan VILLAGES www.kawan-villages.com

Rue du Lac, F-10140 Mesnil Saint Père (Aube) T: **03 25 40 61 85**
E: **info@camping-lacdorient.com** **alanrogers.com/FR10020**

Le Lac d'Orient opened in 2009 and is one of the first Kawan Resorts, a new group of campsites in attractive rural locations and equipped with a good range of leisure amenities. The site can be found at the centre of the large Forêt d'Orient natural park and is just 100 m. from the Lac d'Orient which is ideal for all manner of watersports. Previously, a small municipal site, Kawan Resort Lac d'Orient has been rebuilt and offers a new takeaway and bar, as well as indoor and outdoor heated swimming pools, all in one complex with the reception. The pitches here are large and are semi-shaded with mature trees.

Facilities

One new, purpose built toilet block and one totally refurbished, both of a high standard. Facilities for disabled visitors. Laundry facilities. Motorcaravan services (outside site). Bar and takeaway. Shop. Indoor and outdoor swimming pools. Paddling pool. Sauna and spa bath. TV room. Play area. Multisport court. Off site: Troyes centre 20 km. Lac de l'Orient 100 m. Windsurfing and sailing. Canoe and pedalo hire. Fishing. Cycle and walking tracks.

Open: 15 May - 30 September.

Directions

Mesnil-Saint Père is close to the intersection of the A5 and A26 motorways, 20 km. east of Troyes. From the north, leave the A26 at exit 23 and join the eastbound D619, signed Lac d'Orient. Turn left on D43 following signs to Mesnil-Saint Père and then site. From the south on the A5 take exit 22, the D443 to Vendeuvre then D619 towards Troyes. After 9 km. turn right to Mesnil-St Père and signs to site.
GPS: 48.254856, 4.341359

Charges guide

Per unit incl. 2 persons and electricity	€ 21,50 - € 28,00
extra person	€ 2,50 - € 6,00

Camping Cheques accepted.

Pont-Sainte Marie

Camping Municipal de Troyes

7 rue Roger Salengro, F-10150 Pont-Sainte-Marie (Aube) T: **03 25 81 02 64**. E: **info@troyescamping.net**
alanrogers.com/FR10010

This municipal campsite, within the Troyes city boundary and about 2 km. from the centre, has been taken over by two young enthusiastic managers who are turning it into an attractive place to stay. Their plans include adding a heated pool for 2010. There are 110 level grassy pitches (six with hardstanding), all for tourers, about equally shaded and open. Electricity connections and water points are to be improved for the 2010 season. Being on one of the main routes from Luxembourg to the southwest of France, and on the main route from Calais to the Mediterranean, Troyes makes a good night stop.

Facilities

Two modern toilet blocks contain British style WCs, washbasins and preset showers. Facilities for disabled people. Motorcaravan services. Washing machines and dryer. Shop for basics. Gas supplies. Restaurant, snack bar and takeaway (15/5-15/9). TV room. Games room. Playground. Minigolf. Boules. Bicycle hire. Off site: Bus to Troyes centre 100 m. Supermarket 100 m. Other shops, restaurants, bars, ATM 300 m. Riding 8 km.

Open: 1 April - 15 October.

Directions

From all routes follow signs for Troyes and Pont Sainte-Marie (just north of the old city centre), then signs for Camping Municipal. Site is on the Chalons road no. 77. GPS: 48.31124, 4.09683

Charges guide

Per person	€ 4,80
child (2-11 yrs)	€ 3,35
pitch	€ 7,00
electricity (5A)	€ 2,80

Radonvilliers

Flower Camping Lac d'Orient

Rue des Anciens Combattants, F-10500 Radonvilliers (Aube) T: **03 25 92 21 46**.
alanrogers.com/FR10050

This is a new member of the Flower group, and formerly a municipal site known as Le Garillon. The site is located on the northeastern side of the large Lac d'Orient, close to the village of Radonvilliers. There are just 55 pitches here, of which around 38 are available for touring. These are of a good size and mostly equipped with electricity. Other pitches are occupied by mobile homes or fully equipped tents (for rent). The lake is around 2 km. distant and offers a wide range of watersports.There are few amenities on site, but a selection of shops, restaurants and a supermarket are available within a 5 km. radius.

Facilities

Play area. Tourist information. Fully equipped mobile homes and tents for rent. Off site: Supermarket 5 km. Restaurant 5 km. Fishing 3 km. Sailing 15 km. Riding 3 km. Golf 15 km.

Open: 1 May - 15 September.

Directions

Leave A26 autoroute at exit 21 and follow D441 to Lesmont. Then follow D960 to Brienne. On the south side of the village follow D11b to Radonvilliers and then signs to the site. GPS: 48.358602, 4.501889

Charges 2010

Contact the campsite.

Thonnance-les-Moulins

Castel Camping la Forge de Sainte-Marie

F-52230 Thonnance-les-Moulins (Haute-Marne) T: **03 25 94 42 00**. E: **info@laforgedesaintemarie.com**
alanrogers.com/FR52020

This most attractive campsite, entered through an arched gateway, was created in 1995 by careful conservation of original forge buildings to create modern facilities in this secluded valley. A picturesque bridge links the upper part with a lower road to the section near the river. Another old building has been converted into gîtes for letting. Grass pitches, 165 for touring units, are of a very generous size on terraces amongst trees or in more open areas. Electricity (6A) and water are available and 120 pitches are fully serviced. There are also 30 mobile homes and chalets, and 22 tour operator units.

Facilities

Two sanitary blocks (under pressure at peak times). Additional facilities at reception or pool complex. Shop, restaurant and bar with terrace. Pizzeria in high season. Heated indoor pool and one for children (28/4-12/9). Play areas. Bicycle hire. Fishing on payment. Games room. Internet terminal. Organized games for children (high season). Programme for adults including farm visit with barbecue, music, dancing and excursions. Riding.
Off site: Golf 45 km.

Open: 25 April - 11 September.

Directions

Site is 12 km. southeast of Joinville between Poissons and Germay on road D427. The site entrance may be a little tight for large units. GPS: 48.406449, 5.271093

Charges guide

Per unit incl. 2 persons and electricity	€ 18,70 - € 29,90
extra person	€ 3,60 - € 7,20
child (2-9 yrs)	€ 1,80 - € 3,60
animal	€ 1,50

Camping Cheques accepted.

For centuries, Lorraine has been a major European crossroads, resulting in a rich mixture of cultural influences. Today, it is an idyllic setting for holidays with a diverse historical and cultural heritage, plus endless forests, lakes, rivers and mountains to explore.

DÉPARTEMENTS: 54 MEURTHE-ET-MOSELLE, 55 MEUSE, 57 MOSELLE, 88 VOSGES

MAJOR CITIES: NANCY, METZ

Along with Alsace, Lorraine has suffered as a tract of Europe over which nations have incessantly waged war. Lorraine became part of France in the late 18th century, after which there was a further period of German rule from 1872-1918, followed by a temporary re-annexation under Hitler. In the north and the east of the region, architecture, cuisine and language show Germanic influence, yet the people consider themselves thoroughly French.

From Nancy north to the border is a region of outstanding beauty with dense woodlands the haunt of deer and boar. South of Nancy are spa towns and villages such as Vittel, Bains-les-Bains and Plombières, and the birthplace of St Joan of Arc at Domrémy. The Vosges crests formed part of the battle front in World War One and military requirements led to the building of the road now known as the Route des Cretes which runs near to the highest peaks. It goes past more WWI sites than vineyards, and more 'ballons' (the highest peaks are so-called because they are round and bald) than villages but the view from the top is utterly breathtaking.

Places of interest

Epinal: picturesque town and capital of the Vosges.

Fermont: underground fort at Longuyon, 50 km. north of Verdun.

Metz: a Gallo-Roman city, situated in a strategic defensive position and as a crossroads of trade routes. Some medieval walls and arches, but pride of place goes to the 13th-century cathedral of St Etienne.

Nancy: at the confluence of the Meurthe and Moselle rivers, owes many of its architectural attractions to Duke Stanislas, an exiled king of Poland. Influenced by Louis XV (his son-in-law, he modelled the town on the mode favoured by the court at that time – elaborate facades, imaginative gardens and fountains and vanities such as the Arc de Triomphe of Place Stanislas.

Verdun: hill forts such as Fort de Vaux and Fort de Douaumont, large military cemetery at Douaumont.

Cuisine of the region

The cooking is peppery and hearty and quite unlike any other region.

Bar-le-Duc ('Lorraine caviar'): redcurrant jam de-seeded with a goose quill.

Quiche Lorraine: made only in the classical manner with cream, eggs and bacon.

Vittel and Contrexeville: famous as the sources of mineral waters.

Eaux-de-vie: a strong, white alcohol liqueur distilled from fermented fruit juices, including mirabelles (small yellow plums), cherries and pears.

www.tourism-lorraine.com
contact@tourisme-lorraine.fr
(0)3 83 80 01 80

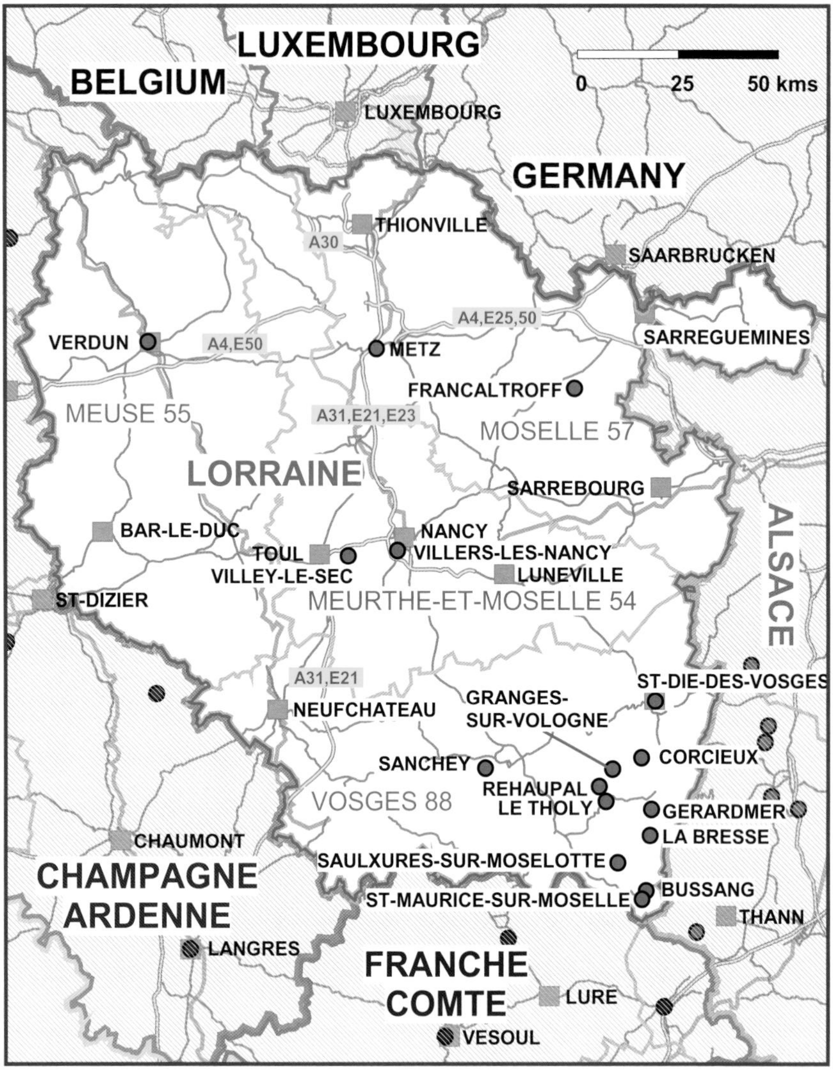

LUXEMBOURG
BELGIUM
0 25 50 kms
LUXEMBOURG
GERMANY
THIONVILLE
A30
SAARBRUCKEN
A4,E25,50
SARREGUEMINES
VERDUN
A4,E50
METZ
FRANCALTROFF
MEUSE 55
A31,E21,E23
MOSELLE 57
LORRAINE
SARREBOURG
ALSACE
BAR-LE-DUC
NANCY
TOUL
VILLERS-LES-NANCY
VILLEY-LE-SEC
LUNEVILLE
ST-DIZIER
MEURTHE-ET-MOSELLE 54
A31,E21
ST-DIE-DES-VOSGES
GRANGES-SUR-VOLOGNE
NEUFCHATEAU
CORCIEUX
SANCHEY
REHAUPAL
LE THOLY
VOSGES 88
GERARDMER
LA BRESSE
CHAUMONT
SAULXURES-SUR-MOSELOTTE
CHAMPAGNE ARDENNE
BUSSANG
ST-MAURICE-SUR-MOSELLE
THANN
LANGRES
FRANCHE COMTE
LURE
VESOUL

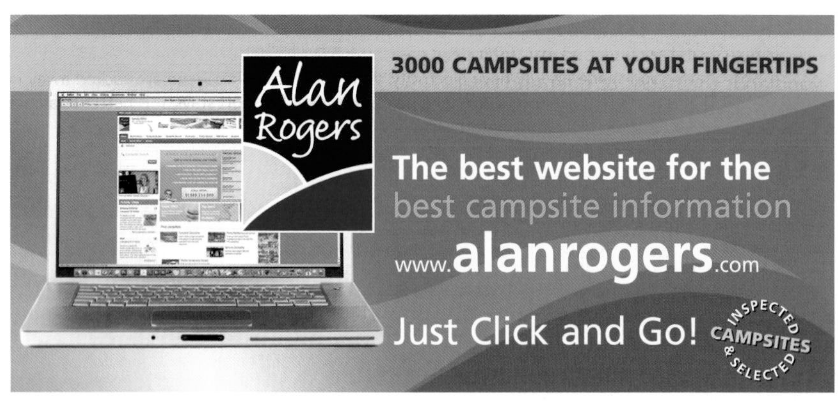

Bussang

Kawan Village Domaine de Champé

14 rue des Champs-Navés, F-88540 Bussang (Vosges) T: **03 29 61 61 51**
E: **info@domaine-de-champe.com** **alanrogers.com/FR88050**

Bordered by the Moselle river and located just off the town square, this site is open all year making it a good base from which to explore in summer, and ideal for skiing in winter, when you might be tempted to rent one of the 12 chalets. Domaine de Champé is a level site with 110 touring pitches, all with electricity (4-12A), spread over a fairly large area on both sides of a tributary stream, so some are a quite a distance from the facilities. Recent additions include a good sized, heated, outdoor pool and a new leisure centre with a sauna, steam room, jacuzzi and massage. This is an improving site where you will receive a hospitable welcome.

Facilities

Two sanitary units, one behind reception, with a smaller one in a more central position, are adequate rather than luxurious. Facilities for disabled campers. Motorcaravan services. Bar (all year). Restaurant and takeaway (weekends only in low season). Swimming pool (1/5-30/9). Sauna, steam room, jacuzzi and massage. Tennis. Small play area. Fishing. Internet access and WiFi. Off site: Shops and all other services in town. Lake fishing 3.5 km. Riding 4 km. Skiing 3 km.

Open: All year.

Directions

Bussang is about midway between Remiremont and Mulhouse on N66, almost due north of Belfort. Site is signed from town centre. GPS: 47.888617, 6.85715

Charges guide

Per person	€ 4,60 - € 6,00
child (4-10 yrs)	€ 2,40 - € 3,20
pitch	€ 5,20 - € 7,10
electricity (4A)	€ 3,40 - € 4,50

The Travel Service to book this site call 01580 214000 ...we'll arrange everything

Corcieux

yelloh! VILLAGE

Yelloh! en Vosges Domaine des Bans

Rue James Wiese, F-88430 Corcieux (Vosges) T: **03 29 51 64 67**. E: **info@yellohvillage-domaine-des-bans.com**
alanrogers.com/FR88080

Domaine des Bans is a large, busy holiday village with plenty of opportunities to be busy and open all year. There is a very high percentage of static and tour operator units, but still room for about 80 touring units. These pitches are numbered, vary in size and are scattered around the campsite with some on low terraces. Most have good shade and all have electricity, water and drainage. Some are tucked away in quiet areas with others nearer where activities take place. Not ideal for short stays, it is better as a base for exploring the varied and interesting countryside.

Facilities

Three functional toilet blocks provide all necessary facilities including for disabled visitors and babies. Shop and bar (30/5-15/9). Restaurant (1/5-15/9). Takeaway (30/4-15/9). Large swimming pool complex (outdoor 1/6-15/9, indoor 1/5-15/9). Playground and area for ball games. Tennis. Minigolf. Archery. Bicycle hire. Riding. Three lakes for fishing and boating. High season entertainment including discos (soundproof room), theatre performances and live music. 'Goats' Castle' with about two dozen goats. Internet access. WiFi. Off site: Restaurant outside site. Shops, bars, restaurant, Monday market in Corcieux 500 m. Several marked walks and cycle tracks in the area.

Open: 26 April - 6 September.

Directions

Corcieux is about 25 km. south of St Dié. From the St Dié - Gérardmer road (N415, then D8), turn west on the D60 just north of Gerbépal to Corcieux. Site is signed and is just south of the town.
GPS: 48.16903, 6.88028

Charges guide

Per unit incl. 2 persons and electricity	€ 15,00 - € 39,00
extra person	€ 5,00 - € 7,00
child (3-7 yrs)	free - € 7,00

Corcieux

Camping Au Clos de la Chaume

21 rue d'Alsace, F-88430 Corcieux (Vosges) T: **03 29 50 76 76**. E: **info@camping-closdelachaume.com**

alanrogers.com/FR88120

This pleasant site is within walking distance of the town, on level ground with a small stream adjacent. The friendly family owners live on site and do their best to ensure campers have an enjoyable relaxing stay. There are 100 level grassy pitches of varying sizes, with some holiday homes (private and rental) leaving 70 pitches for tourists. All have electricity hook-ups (6/10A) and some are divided by shrubs and trees. Access roads are sandy and large units or American RVs should telephone first to check pitch availability. A 'Sites et Paysages' member.

Facilities

Two units provide well maintained facilities including a laundry with washing machines and dryers, a dual-purpose room for families and disabled visitors. Motorcaravan service point. Reception keeps basic supplies (July/Aug). Swimming pool (13 x 7 m; June - Sept). Games room. Boules. Off site: Bicycle hire 800 m. Riding 2 km. Fishing 3 km. Golf 30 km. Corcieux market (Mondays).

Open: 4 April - 26 September.

Directions

Corcieux is 17 km. southwest of St Dié des Vosges. Site is on D60, east of town centre, by the town boundary sign. GPS: 48.16826, 6.89025

Charges guide

Per unit incl. 2 persons and electricity	€ 16,00 - € 19,60
extra person	€ 4,50
child (0-7 yrs)	€ 2,80

Francaltroff

Parc Résidentiel de la Tensch

501

F-57670 Francaltroff (Moselle) T: **03 87 01 79 04**. E: **tensch@tensch.com**

alanrogers.com/FR57090

The pitches at this campsite are used exclusively for mobile home accommodation. For full details please see our PRL section starting on page 501.

Gérardmer

Camping de Ramberchamp

21 chemin du Tour du Lac, F-88150 Gérardmer (Vosges) T: **03 29 63 03 82**. E: **boespflug.helene@wanadoo.fr**

alanrogers.com/FR88150

A long established, family run site in a beautiful location on the southern side of Lake Gérardmer, de Ramberchamp is very peaceful. It benefits from a bar and restaurant adjacent to reception, which is on one side of the D69, with mostly long stay units on the pitches around it. Most of the 200 touring pitches are on the opposite side of the road by the lakeside, with the larger sanitary building. Pitches here vary in size, larger ones being further from the lake, all with electricity (4A) and quite level. Those by the lakeside are mostly on gravel and are very popular.

Facilities

The main sanitary unit is fairly central and has been refurbished with modern fittings, whilst retaining its old French style and character. Baby room. Unit for disabled campers. Laundry. Motorcaravan service point. A second smaller older unit serves pitches on the other side of the road. Bar/restaurant with takeaway (15/4-15/9). Small play area. Max length of unit 8.5 m. Off site: Fishing, riding and bicycle hire 500 m. Town centre with shops, banks, buses and railway station 1.5 km.

Open: 15 April - 15 September.

Directions

Site is west of Gérardmer, on D69 on southern side of the lake. Best approached from N417 towards Le Tholy, turning on D69, passing Lido. Site reception on right hand side, site entrance opposite. GPS: 48.064333, 6.8537

Charges guide

Per unit incl. 2 persons	€ 16,00
extra person	€ 5,00
child (4-7 yrs)	€ 3,00
electricity (4A)	€ 3,50

No credit cards.

Granges-sur-Vologne

Camping la Sténiole

1 le Haut Rain, F-88640 Granges-sur-Vologne (Vosges) T: **03 29 51 43 75**. E: **steniole@wanadoo.fr**
alanrogers.com/FR88110

Set in a lovely rural area in the heart of the Vosges massif, this attractive site is run by a dedicated young couple who are constantly improving the site and its facilities. There are 70 pitches, either separated by hedges or beside the water. A small river has been used to form a small lake for fishing and swimming and a series of separate ponds (water quality is checked regularly). An atmosphere of relaxation is encouraged and the whole family can have a good time here. At an altitude of 720 m. there is easy access to 160 km. of paths and tracks for walking and cycling.

Facilities

A new toilet block now supplements the original, together with further facilities in the main building provide all necessities including 4 private cabins. Washing machines and dryers. Bar. Restaurant (July/Aug). Takeaway (1/6-30/8). Internet access on the terrace. Lake swimming. Fishing. Games room with TV and library. Play area. Tennis. Apartments and mobile homes to rent. Off site: Walking and cycling. Riding 5 km. Bicycle hire 10 km. Golf 30 km.

Open: 1 May - 30 September.

Directions

Take the N420 from Epinal to Gérardmer then the D423 to Granges. There are two sites not far away from each other. GPS: 48.1217, 6.8284

Charges 2010

Per unit incl. 2 persons and electricity	€ 15,20
extra person	€ 3,00
child (under 8 yrs)	€ 2,00
dog	€ 1,00

No credit cards.

La Bresse

Domaine du Haut des Bluches

5 route des Planches, F-88250 La Bresse (Vosges) T: **03 29 25 6480**. E: **hautdesbluches@labresse.fr**
alanrogers.com/FR88210

Le Haut des Bluches is attractively located in the rolling hills of the Vosges and is close to the ski resorts of Gérardmer and Xonrupt-Longemer. The site is open most of the year with skiing possible in winter and it is a good base for nature lovers in summer. There are 140 slightly uneven and sloping grass/gravel pitches informally laid out in groups on terraces. These include 108 for touring, all with electricity (4/8/13A), long leads and rock pegs advised. Special areas of hardstanding for motorcaravans include some electricity hook-ups. Although there is little organised on the site, La Bresse (4 km) has a wide range of activities on offer.

Facilities

Two well appointed, modern, heated toilet blocks include cabins with WC, basin and shower. Facilities for babies and campers with disabilities. Motorcaravan services. Small shop (bread to order) and bar (all year). Restaurant and takeaway (high season and weekends in low season). Games/TV room. Play area. Multisport court. Boules. Internet.
Off site: Several ski resorts, 5-8 km. La Bresse with shops, bars, restaurants, museums and market 4 km.

Open: mid December - 31 October.

Directions

La Bresse is 25 km. south of Gérardmer on the D486. At the eastern end of the town turn south on Route des Planches. Site is signed, entrance in 350 m.
GPS: 47.998986, 6.918324

Charges 2010

Per unit incl. 2 persons and electricity	€ 12,40 - € 17,70

Le Tholy

Camping de Noirrupt

5 chemin de l'Etang, F-88530 Le Tholy (Vosges) T: **03 29 61 81 27**. E: **info@jpvacances.com**
alanrogers.com/FR88030

An attractive, modern, family-run site, Camping de Noirrupt has a commanding mountainside position with some magnificent views especially from the upper terraces. This is a very comfortable and high quality site and one that is sure to please. The tarmac site road winds up through the site with pitches being terraced and cars parked in separate small car parks close by. The 70 lawn-like touring pitches are generally spacious, and the whole site is beautifully landscaped and divided up with many attractive shrubs, flower beds, decking and trees. Paved paths and steps take more direct routes between levels.

Facilities

Two very modern buildings at different levels, plus a small unit behind reception, all immaculate with modern fittings. Washbasins in cubicles, facilities for babies, children and disabled campers. Washing machines and dryer. Shop. Bar, snack bar and takeaway (4/7-20/8). Swimming pool (15 x 10 m. 1/6-15/9). TV room (1/6-15/9). Tennis. Entertainment in season. No double axle caravans or American RVs. Off site: Riding 300 m. Fishing 2 or 5 km. Golf 30 km. Le Tholy 2 km. Gérardmer 10 km.

Open: 15 April - 15 October.

Directions

From Gérardmer take the D417 west towards Remiremont. In Le Tholy turn right on D11, continue up hill for 2 km., and site is signed to your left.
GPS: 48.0889, 6.728483

Charges 2010

Per unit incl. 2 persons and electricity	€ 23,70 - € 25,70
extra person	€ 5,80
child (under 7 yrs)	€ 3,30
dog	€ 1,50

Metz

Camping Municipal de Metz-Plage

Allée de Metz-Plage, F-57000 Metz (Moselle) T: **03 87 68 26 48**. E: **campingmetz@mairie-metz.fr**
alanrogers.com/FR57050

As this site is just a short way from the autoroute exit and within easy walking distance for the city centre, it could make a useful night stop if travelling from Luxembourg to Nancy or for a longer stay if exploring the area. By the Moselle river, the 151 pitches are on fairly level grass and most are under shade from tall trees. 65 pitches are fully serviced and 84 have electricity (10A). Tent pitches have a separate place beside the river.

Facilities

The two sanitary blocks, one newer than the other, are acceptable if not luxurious. Facilities for disabled visitors. Baby room. Laundry and dishwashing facilities. Motorcaravan service point. Shop. Bar, restaurant and takeaway. Hardstanding pitches for over night stops for motorcaravans without electricity. WiFi (free). Bicycle hire. Fishing (permits for sale). Off site: Indoor pool adjacent (free entry). Riding 5 km. Golf 8 km.

Open: 24 April - 5 October.

Directions

From autoroute take Metz-Nord - Pontiffray exit 33 and follow site signs. GPS: 49.12402, 6.16917

Charges guide

Per unit incl. 2 persons and electricity	€ 14,00 - € 14,50
extra person	€ 3,00
child (4-10 yrs)	€ 1,50
dog	€ 0,50

Rehaupal

Camping du Barba

45 le village, F-88640 Rehaupal (Vosges) T: **03 29 66 35 57**. E: **barba@campingdubarba.com**
alanrogers.com/FR88100

Located in the refreshing and beautiful Haute-Vosges region, this small, very pleasant campsite is owned and run by a dedicated couple. There is room for 50 units on well tended, unmarked grass where you pitch where you like. This creates a very relaxed, natural environment with hedges and mature trees providing shelter and shade. The site is in the heart of the village with an auberge next door for fine wines and good food, including local specialties. The surrounding hills offer 150 km. of marked walking and bike trails. Gérardmer and the Valley of the Lakes are just 15 minutes away.

Facilities

The single toilet block, built in chalet style, is of a high standard and should be sufficient. Washing machine and dryer. Bread delivered. Auberge next door for meals and takeaway (to order) and small shop. Off site: Supermarket 5 km. Walking, cycling, skiing and fishing. Riding 6 km.

Open: 1 May - 1 October.

Directions

From Gérardmer follow signs to Rehaupal. Site is very well signed. GPS: 48.11892, 6.73130

Charges 2010

Per unit incl. 2 persons and electricity	€ 14,80 - € 17,50
extra person	€ 3,60
child (under 7 yrs)	€ 2,00
dog	€ 1,00

Saint Dié-des-Vosges

Kawan Village Vanne de Pierre

5 rue du camping, F-88100 Saint Dié-des-Vosges (Vosges) T: **03 29 56 23 56**
E: **vannedepierre@orange.fr** **alanrogers.com/FR88130**

La Vanne de Pierre is a neat and attractive site with 118 pitches, many of which are individual with good well trimmed hedges giving plenty of privacy. There are 13 chalets and mobile homes (for rent) and a few seasonal units, leaving around 101 tourist pitches, all multi-serviced with water, drainage and electricity hook-up (6/10A). The reception building has been recently refitted and provides a well stocked small shop plus a restaurant/bar with a takeaway facility (all year but opening hours may vary).

Facilities

Main unit is heated with good facilities including washbasins in cubicles. Three family rooms each with WC, basin, and shower and two similar units fully equipped for disabled campers. Dishwashing and laundry rooms. A second, older unit (opened July/Aug). Bar/restaurant and takeaway. Shop. Swimming pool (1/4-30/9, weather permitting). Internet access. Gas supplies. Bicycle hire. Nordic walking is organised. Off site: Golf, tennis, archery and riding all 1 km. Fishing. Supermarkets.

Open: All year.

Directions

St Dié is southeast of Nancy. Site is east of town on north bank of river Meurthe and south of D82 to Nayemont les Fosses. Site is well signed.
GPS: 48.2858, 6.96898

Charges guide

Per unit incl. 2 persons and electricity	€ 22,00 - € 31,00
extra person	€ 5,00 - € 8,00
child (4-10 yrs)	free - € 5,00
dog	free - € 3,00

Camping Cheques accepted.

Saint Maurice-sur-Moselle

Camping les Deux Ballons

17 rue du Stade, F-88560 Saint Maurice-sur-Moselle (Vosges) T: **03 29 25 17 14**
E: **stan@camping-deux-ballons.fr** **alanrogers.com/FR88010**

St Maurice-sur-Moselle is in a narrow valley 7 km. from the source of the River Moselle in the massif of Haute-Vosges, on the main N66 which leads to the Col de Bussang. This is a pleasant leafy area for winter skiing and summer outdoor activities. Les Deux Ballons lies in a small valley surrounded by mountains with a stream running through the site and a cover of trees giving deep shade in most parts. The 180 pitches are on stony ground with sparse grass under the firs or on two terraces, and all have electrical connections (4A). Some long leads may be required. Torches are recommended.

Facilities

Unisex sanitary facilities in four units of varying ages (only two open in low season). Washbasins and some showers are rather small. Facilities for disabled people and babies. Laundry facilities. Motorcaravan service point. Shop. Gas supplies. Bar (30/6-25/8). Snack bar and takeaway (1/7-27/8). Large heated swimming pool with slide and children's pool (15/6-31/8). Walks, fishing, bowls, riding, paragliding (high season). TV. Internet point and WiFi. Tennis. Fishing. Off site: Bicycle hire 5 km.

Open: 10 April - 15 September.

Directions

Site is on main N66 Le Thillot - Bussang road on western edge of St Maurice behind Avia filling station (entrance partly obscured - keep a look out).
GPS: 47.85517, 6.81108

Charges guide

Per caravan or tent incl. 2 persons	€ 15,55 - € 25,90
extra person	€ 5,10 - € 5,35
child (2-7 yrs)	€ 3,80 - € 3,90
electricity (4/15A)	€ 4,25 - € 5,35
dog	€ 2,80 - € 3,35

No credit cards (except for on-line bookings).

Sanchey

Kawan Village Lac de Bouzey

19 rue du Lac, F-88390 Sanchey (Vosges) T: **03 29 82 49 41**. E: **lacdebouzey@orange.fr**
alanrogers.com/FR88040

Open all year, Camping Lac de Bouzey is 8 km. west of Épinal, at the start of the Vosges Massif. The 160 reasonably level grass pitches are separated by very tall trees and some hedging giving varying amounts of shade. There are 121 for touring, all with electricity (6-10A) and 100 fully serviced. They are on a gently sloping hillside above the lake and a view have views over the lake and its sandy beaches. In high season there is entertainment for all ages, especially teenagers and in high season the site will be very lively. English is spoken.

Facilities

The refurbished toilet block includes a baby room and one for disabled people (there is up and down hill walking). Small, heated section in the main building with toilet, washbasin and shower is used in winter. Laundry facilities. Motorcaravan service point. Shop, bar, restaurant and takeaway (all season). Heated pool (1/5-30/9). Fishing. Riding. Games room. Archery. Bicycle hire. Internet access. Soundproof room for cinema and discos (high season). Lake beach, bathing and boating. Off site: Golf 8 km.

Open: All year.

Directions

Site is 8 km. west of Épinal on the D460. From Épinal follow signs for Lac de Bouzey and Sanchey. At western end of Sanchey turn south, site signed.
GPS: 48.16692, 6.35990

Charges guide

Per unit incl. 2 persons and electricity	€ 22,00 - € 33,00
extra person	€ 6,00 - € 9,00
child (4-10 yrs)	free - € 7,00
dog	free - € 3,00

Camping Cheques accepted.

Saulxures-sur-Moselotte

Base de Loisirs du Lac de la Moselotte

Les Amias B.P. 34, F-88290 Saulxures-sur-Moselotte (Vosges) T: **03 29 24 56 56**
E: **lac-moselotte@ville-saulxures-mtte.fr** **alanrogers.com/FR88090**

This neat, well-run, spacious lakeside site, part of a leisure village complex, has 105 grassy pitches with 72 for touring. All have electricity (10A) and 25 of these also have water and drainage. They are individually hedged and a variety of young trees give only a little shade. The site is fully fenced with a security barrier with a key used for the gates to the lakeside. The adjacent 'Base de Loisirs' has a wide variety of activities on offer and the area is very good for walking and cycling. This is a good base for both summer and winter.

Facilities

The heated toilet block has key entry, controllable hot showers, some washbasins in cubicles and good facilities for babies and disabled campers. Laundry facilities. Shop (July/Aug). Bread to order. Bar/snack bar and terrace (all year). Bicycle hire. Play area. Outdoor skittle alley. Entertainment programme (July/Aug). 'Base de Loisirs' adjacent with lake (swimming supervised July/Aug), sandy beach, play area, climbing wall, fishing, archery and hire of pedaloes, canoes and kayaks. 30 chalets for rent. Off site: Saulxures-sur-Moselotte 1.5 km. with shops, bars and restaurants. Riding 2 km. Golf 15 km. Skiing 15 km.

Open: All year.

Directions

Saulxures-sur-Moselotte is 20 km. east of Remiremont. From Remiremont take D417 east (St Amé), then right (southeast) on D43 towards La Bresse for 10.5 km. Turn left into Saulxures (site signed), entrance on right by lake after 700 m. GPS: 47.95273, 6.75212

Charges guide

Per unit incl. 2 persons	€ 12,00 - € 15,00
extra person	€ 4,00 - € 5,00
child (4-10 yrs)	€ 2,40 - € 3,00
electricity (10A)	€ 5,00 - € 6,00
animal	€ 1,00

Verdun

Camping les Breuils

Allée des Breuils, F-55100 Verdun (Meuse) T: **03 29 86 15 31**. E: **contact@camping-lesbreuils.com**
alanrogers.com/FR55010

Thousands of soldiers of many nations are buried in the cemeteries around this famous town and the city is justly proud of its determined First World War resistance. Les Breuils is a neat, attractive site beside a small fishing lake and close to the town and Citadel. It provides 166 flat pitches of varying sizes on two levels (144 for touring units), many with shade. Separated by trees or hedges, they are beside the lake and 120 offer electricity (6A) – long leads will be necessary for some. The 'Citadelle Souterraine' is well worth a visit and is within walking distance of the site.

Facilities

Two sanitary blocks are a mixture of old and new, including washbasins in cabins for ladies. Laundry facilities. Facilities for disabled visitors and babies. Cleaning can be variable. Motorcaravan services. Shop (1/5-30/9). Guide books on sale at reception (1/5-31/8). Restaurant (1/6-20/8), bar (evenings 1/5-30/9). Swimming pool (200 sq.m) and children's pool (1/6-31/8). Fenced gravel play area. Multisports complex. Off site: Bicycle hire, town 1 km. Riding 5 km.

Open: 1 April - 30 September.

Directions

The RN3 forms a sort of ring road round the north of the town. Site is signed from this on the west side of the town (500 m. to site). GPS: 49.15404, 5.36573

Charges guide

Per person	€ 4,20 - € 5,80
child (2-10 yrs)	€ 3,00 - € 3,70
pitch	€ 3,00 - € 5,00
electricity (6A)	€ 4,00
dog	€ 1,60 - € 1,80

Discounts for low season and longer stays.
Credit cards accepted for minimum of € 15.

Villers-les-Nancy

Campéole

Campéole le Brabois

Avenue Paul Muller, F-54600 Villers-les-Nancy (Meurthe-et-Moselle) T: **03 83 27 18 28**
E: **nadine.ferran@atciat.com** **alanrogers.com/FR54000**

This former municipal site is within the Nancy city boundary and 5 km. from the centre. Situated within a forest area, there is shade in most parts and, although the site is on a slight slope, the 185 good-sized, numbered and separated pitches are level. Of these, 160 pitches have electrical connections (5/15A) and 30 also have water and drainage. Being on one of the main routes from Luxembourg to the south of France, Le Brabois makes a good night stop. However, Nancy is a delightful city in the heart of Lorraine and well worth a longer stay. There are many attractions in the area including the interesting 18th-century Place Stanislas (pedestrianised) and 11th-century city centre. The British manager has a wide range of tourist literature, publishes a monthly English newsletter and is pleased to help plan visits and day trips. Horse racing takes place every two weeks at the Nancy race track next to the campsite, and good wine is produced nearby.

Facilities

Six sanitary blocks (old and due for refurbishment over the next few years) with a mix of British and Turkish style WCs and some washbasins in cubicles. One can be heated in cool weather. Units for disabled visitors. Laundry facilities. Motorcaravan service point. Shop. Bread to order. Restaurant with bar and small shop (15/6-31/8). Library. Playground. Off site: Restaurants, shops 1 km. Walking and cycling. Regular buses to Nancy.

Open: 1 April - 15 October.

Directions

From autoroute A33 take exit 2b for Brabois and continue for 500 m. to 'Quick' restaurant on left. Turn left, pass racetrack to T-junction, turn right and after 400 m. turn right on to site entrance road.
GPS: 48.66440, 6.14330

Charges guide

Per unit incl. 2 persons and electricity	€ 15,00 - € 18,20
extra person	€ 4,00 - € 5,50
electricity	€ 4,00

Credit cards minimum € 15.

Villey-le-Sec

Camping de Villey-le-Sec

34 rue de la Gare, F-54840 Villey-le-Sec (Meurthe-et-Moselle) T: **03 83 63 64 28**
E: **info@campingvilleylesec.com** **alanrogers.com/FR54010**

This neat campsite is a popular overnight stop, but the area is worth a longer stay. Villey-le-Sec has its own fortifications, part of the defensive system built along France's frontiers after the 1870 war, and a long cycle track passes near the site. On a bank of the Moselle river, there are 75 level grassy marked touring pitches, with electricity (6A) and plenty of water taps. There are also individual water taps and waste water drainage for eight of these pitches. Another area without electricity accommodates 11 tents. Just outside the site is an overnight stopping place for motorcaravans.

Facilities

Two modern toilet blocks (one heated) contain British style WCs, washbasins in cabins and controllable showers. Facilities for disabled people and babies. Motorcaravan services. Washing machine and dryer. Gas supplies. Shop. Bar/restaurant. Snack bar and takeaway. Games room. Playground. Playing field. Table tennis. Boules. Fishing. Off site: Riding 2 km. Rock climbing 4 km. Golf 15 km.

Open: 1 April - 30 September.

Directions

Villey-le-Sec is 7 km. east of Toul. Leave A31 west of Nancy at exit 15 and after 1 km. at roundabout (Leclerc supermarket) take D909 to Villey-le-Sec. In village follow signs 'Camping, Base de Loisirs' to the right. At bottom of hill turn left to site in 300 m.
GPS: 48.65281, 5.99151

Charges guide

Per person	€ 3,00
child (0-7 yrs)	€ 1,90
pitch	€ 2,30 - € 3,60
electricity (6-10A)	€ 3,50 - € 4,50

Lying between the Rhine and the Vosge mountains, to the no and east Alsace shares a border with Germany, the south with German-spea Switzerland and to the west wit Lorraine and Franche Comté.

DÉPARTMENTS: 67 BAS-RHIN, 68 HAUT-RHIN

MAJOR CITY: STRASBOURG

Historically speaking, Alsace was part of the German-speaking area of central Europe and to this day a large proportion of the population, of all generations, speak or understand Alsacian, a dialectal form of German closely resembling the German spoken in Switzerland. In the last two centuries, Alsace has passed back and forth between Germany and France and back and back again; consequently, it is a region that was not part of France at the time of the makings of the modern-day nation, and has held on to a number of institutional differences, particularly concerning religious affairs. For example, Good Friday is a public holiday in Alsace, but not in the rest of France.

In architectural terms, Alsace is definitely Germanic. Descend from the Vosges mountains into the Alsace vineyards and the fairy-tale wine villages and towns which fringe the broad Rhine Valley with the Grand Canal d'Alsace running parallel. Follow the well signed tourist route, the 'Route des Vins' and look in on the most picturesque towns – Obernai, Riquewihr and Ribeauville. Strasbourg is the capital, a busy city with a wide industrial girdle and an exquisite medieval centre, now the home of the European Parliament.

Places of interest

Colmar: interesting for its 16th-century timber houses. Musée d'Unterlinden.

Kayserberg: small town, birthplace of Alb Schweitzer. Special Christmas market.

Le Linge: a football pitch-sized hilltop wh in 1915, 17,000 French and German soldi lost their lives. The opposing trenches including rusty barbed wire have been le as they were as a reminder of the pain ar futility of war.

Mulhouse: famous for the Musée Nation de l'Automobile and the Musée Francais Chemin de Fer.

Riquewihr: almost untouched since the 1 century (whilst almost every other village was decimated by war) with 13/14th-century fortifications and medieval house

Cuisine of the region

Beckenoffe (Baeckeoffe): a hotpot of potatoes, lamb, beef, pork and onions, cooked in local wine.

Choucroute: sauerkraut with peppercorn boiled ham, pork, Strasbourg sausages a boiled potatoes.

Chou farci: stuffed cabbage.

Foie gras: goose liver.

Tarte a l'oignon Alsacienne: onion and cream tart.

www.tourisme-alsace.com
crt@tourisme-alsace.com
(0)3 89 24 73 50

GERMANY
SAARBRUCKEN
KARLSRUHE
SARREGUEMINES
WISSEMBOURG
A35
HAGUENAU
A4,E25
BAS-RHIN 67
SARREBOURG
WASSELONNE
LORRAINE
STRASBOURG
MOLSHEIM
A35
ALSACE
RHINAU
BASSEMBERG
SELESTAT
SAINT-DIE
GERMANY
A35,E25
RIBEAUVILLE
RIQUEWIHR
COLMAR
EGUISHEIM
FREIBURG
SAINTE-CROIX-EN-PLAINE
HAUT-RHIN 68
GUEBWILLER
THANN
MASEVAUX
MULHOUSE
A36
E54/60
A35
E25/60
LURE
ALTKIRCH
BASEL
MONTBELIARD
SWITZERLAND
FRANCHE
-COMTE
0 10 20 30 40 kms

Bassemberg

Campéole

Campéole le Giessen

Route de Villé, F-67220 Bassemberg (Bas-Rhin) T: **03 88 58 98 14**. E: **nadine.ferran@atciat.com**

alanrogers.com/FR67070

Le Giessen is a member of the Campéole group and can be found at the foot of the Vosges mountains, with easy access to many of the best loved sights in Alsace. Although there is no pool on site, a large complex, comprising an indoor and outdoor pool with a water slide, can be found adjacent to the site, with free admission for all campers. Pitches here are grassy and of a good size, mostly with electrical connections. A number of mobile homes and fully equipped tents are available for rent. Various activities are organised in high season including a children's club and disco evenings. Nearby places of interest include the magnificent fortified castle of Haut-Koenigsbourg, as well as the great cities of Strasbourg and Colmar. This is a good base for exploring the Vosges and the 'Route du Vin' (bicycle hire in the village). The site's friendly managers will be pleased to recommend possible itineraries.

Facilities

Multisport court. Bar. Children's play area. Activities and entertainment. Tourist information. Mobile homes and equipped tents for rent. Off site: Swimming pool complex adjacent. Tennis. Rollerblading rink. Hiking and mountain biking. Bicycle hire. Riding. Strasbourg 50km.

Open: 21 March - 21 September.

Directions

Leave the A35 autoroute at exit 13 (Zellwiller) and head west on D203 and D253 to Villé. Continue south on D39 to Bassemberg from where the site is well indicated. GPS: 48.33722, 7.28862

Charges 2010

Per unit incl. 2 persons and electricity	€ 15,10 - € 24,50

Eguisheim

Camping Municipal les Trois Châteaux

10 rue du Bassin, F-68420 Eguisheim (Haut-Rhin) T: **03 89 23 19 39**. E: **camping.eguisheim@wanadoo.fr**

alanrogers.com/FR68040

The village of Eguisheim is on the Alsace 'Rue du Vin' to the west of Colmar. The three châteaux from which the site gets its name are clearly visible on the distant hills. Being close to the village, Les Trois Châteaux is busy and popular. Flowers, shrubs and trees, and well tended grass areas make this a very pleasant place. The 121 pitches, 115 with electricity (6/10A), are either on a slight slope or a terrace, and are marked and numbered, most with good shade. Around 80% of pitches have some gravel hardstandings, most of irregular shape and size.

Facilities

The single sanitary block in the centre of the site has hot showers and warm water only to washbasins. Some washbasins in cubicles and facilities for disabled people. Motorcaravan service point. Playground. Bicycle hire. Off site: Fishing 3 km. Golf, riding 10 km.

Open: 1 April - 8 October.

Directions

Eguisheim is just off the N83 and the site is well signed in the village. GPS: 48.04255, 7.29989

Charges guide

Per unit incl. 2 persons	€ 11,50 - € 13,00
extra person	€ 3,50 - € 4,00
child (0-12 yrs)	€ 0,10 - € 2,50
electricity (6/10A)	€ 3,00 - € 5,00
dog	€ 1,50 - € 2,00

Masevaux

Camping de Masevaux

3 rue du Stade, F-68290 Masevaux (Haut-Rhin) T: **03 89 82 42 29**. E: **camping-masevaux@tv-com.net**
alanrogers.com/FR68030

Masevaux is a pleasant little town in the Haut-Rhin département of Alsace, just north of the A36 Belfort - Mulhouse motorway. The neatly mown 120 pitches for tourists are on level grass, of reasonable size, marked by trees and hedges, and all have electricity (3/6A). Most are well shaded with good views of the surrounding hills. The pleasant and helpful Scottish managers, who take pride in the site, would like to welcome more British visitors. A good choice for one night or a longer stay to explore this interesting region, and an ideal destination for serious walkers.

Facilities

A modern, well designed and well equipped sanitary block has most washbasins in private cabins. Baby room. Laundry. Café/bar serving snacks. Baker calls in high season. Ice-creams and soft drinks from reception. TV room, small library. Boules. Play area. Tennis (extra charge). Fishing. Off site: Supermarket, restaurants and indoor pool. Market in Masavaux Wednesdays. Bicycle hire 300 m. Golf 7 km. Riding 10 km.

Open: All year.

Directions

From D466 in Masevaux follow signs for Belfort then 'Camping Complexe Sportif'. GPS: 47.7782, 6.9909

Charges 2010

Per unit incl. 2 persons and electricity	€ 15,50
extra person	€ 3,80
child (2-12 yrs)	€ 1,50
dog	€ 0,50 - € 3,80

Rhinau

Camping la Ferme des Tuileries

1 rue des Tuileries, F-67860 Rhinau (Bas-Rhin) T: **03 88 74 60 45**. E: **camping.fermetuileries@neuf.fr**
alanrogers.com/FR67040

Close to the German border, this ten-hectare, family-run site has 150 large open pitches, hardstanding for 15 motorcaravans and room for 50 seasonal caravans. The site buildings have a traditional external appearance but all have modern interiors. Welcoming reception staff will provide information about the site and the local area. A small lake with two water slides is used for swimming, fishing and boating (split into two areas) and there is also a small unsupervised swimming pool (hats compulsory). A newly-built restaurant and bar are at the lakeside. A ferry crosses the Rhine river into Germany from 1 km. away.

Facilities

Three modern, bright and cheerful blocks with the normal facilities. Two washing machines and two dryers. Controllable showers. Family bathroom at no extra charge. Fully equipped facilities for disabled visitors (no key, no coins). Motorcaravan services. Newly built restaurant and bar. Small lake for swimming, fishing, boating, two water slides. Swimming pool (unguarded) open July/Aug. Tennis. Pétanque. Minigolf. Off site: Supermarket 500 m. Ferry across the Rhine. Good level region for cycling.

Open: 1 April - 30 September.

Directions

Coming from Colmar (A35) take exit 14 (Kogenheim-Benfeld-Erstein) then the N83 to exit for Benfeld-Rhinau, following site signs. From Strasbourg on A35 take exit 7 (Erstein-Fegersheim) then the N83. GPS: 48.321, 7.698

Charges 2010

Per unit incl. 2 persons and electricity	€ 11,90 - € 13,70
extra person	€ 1,50 - € 3,50

No credit cards or cheques.

Ribeauvillé

Camping Municipal Pierre de Coubertin

23 rue de Landau, F-68150 Ribeauvillé (Haut-Rhin) T: **03 89 73 66 71**. E: **camping.ribeauville@wanadoo.fr**
alanrogers.com/FR68050

The fascinating medieval town of Ribeauvillé on the Alsace Wine Route is within walking distance of this attractive, quietly located site. Popular and well run, it has 226 touring pitches, all with 16A electricity and some separated by shrubs or railings. There are tarmac or gravel access roads. This is a site solely for touring units – there are no mobile homes or seasonal units here. The small shop is open daily for most of the season (hours vary) providing bread, basic supplies and some wines. Only breathable ground-sheets are permitted.

Facilities

Large, heated block provides modern facilities with washbasins in cubicles. Baby facilities. Large laundry and dishwashing rooms. A smaller unit at the far end of the site is opened for July/Aug. Very good facilities for disabled campers at both units. Shop (Easter - Oct). Excellent adventure-style play area with rubber base. Tennis. Boules. TV room. Off site: Outdoor pool (June - Aug). Bicycle hire 200 m. Fishing 500 m. Golf 12 km.

Open: 15 March - 15 November.

Directions

Ribeauvillé is 13 km. southwest of Sèlestat and site is well signed. Turn north off the D106 at traffic lights by large car park, east of the town centre.
GPS: 48.19482, 7.33654

Charges 2010

Per unit incl. 2 persons and electricity	€ 15,50 - € 16,50
extra person	€ 4,00
child (0-7 yrs)	€ 2,00
dog	€ 1,00

Riquewihr

Camping Intercommunal Riquewihr

Route des Vins, F-68340 Riquewihr (Haut-Rhin) T: **03 89 47 90 08**. E: **camping.riquewihr@tiscali.fr**
alanrogers.com/FR68060

Surrounded by vineyards and minutes from the delightful village of Riquewihr, this is a well run site which has earned its good reputation. Situated in the heart of the Alsace wine region the site covers three hectares with views across the open countryside. To the right of the security barrier stands a modern, part-timbered building housing reception. Close by is a small summer house and both are heavily garlanded with flowers. The 161 spacious individual pitches, many with shade and divided by hedging, have electrical connections (6/10A). Most of the pitches are on grass but there are also a few with hardstandings. Wine caves are just 200 m. away.

Facilities

Three sanitary blocks, one of a more modern design (not all open in low season). Facilities include private cabins with basins, good nursery room with baby bath, child's WC and changing mat, and excellent facilities for disabled people. Laundry areas. Motorcaravan service point. Campers' room with tables and chairs. Shop for basic necessities, drinks and papers (1/7-31/8). TV room. Playground. Off site: Ball games area and sports field nearby. Fishing 3 km. Swimming pool 4 km. Bicycle hire 5 km.

Open: Easter - 31 December.

Directions

From N83 north of Colmar take D4 westwards (Bennwihr). Turn north on D1bis for 2 km. towards Ribeauvillé. Site signed off roundabout at southern end of Riquewihr bypass. Do not enter village.
GPS: 48.16218, 7.31690

Charges guide

Per person	€ 3,25 - € 3,60
child (under 7 yrs)	€ 1,55 - € 1,70
pitch incl. electricity	€ 7,10 - € 8,00
dog	€ 1,10 - € 1,20

Saint Croix-en-Plaine

Camping Clair Vacances

Route de Herrlisheim, F-68127 Saint Croix-en-Plaine (Haut-Rhin) T: **03 89 49 27 28**
E: **clairvacances@wanadoo.fr** **alanrogers.com/FR68080**

Clair Vacances is a very neat, tidy and pretty site with 130 level pitches of generous size which are numbered and most are separated by trees and shrubs. All have electricity connections (8-13A) and ten are fully serviced with water and drainage. The site has been imaginatively laid out with the pitches reached from hard access roads. This is a quiet family site. The friendly couple who own and run it will be pleased to advise on the attractions of the area. The site is 1 km. from the A35 exit, not far from Colmar in the region of Alsace, a popular and picturesque area.

Facilities

Two excellent, modern toilet blocks include washbasins in cabins, well equipped baby rooms and good facilities for disabled visitors. Laundry facilities. Shop with limited supplies. Swimming and paddling pools (heated) with large sunbathing area (15/6-15/9). Playground. Community room. Archery in high season. Camping Gaz. Dogs are not accepted. No barbecues or football. American motorhomes and twin axle caravans are not accepted. Off site: Colmar with restaurants and shops is not far away.

Open: Week before Easter - 15 October.

Directions

Site is signed from exit 27 of the A35 south of Colmar on the Herrlisheim road (D1). GPS: 48.01606, 7.35016

Charges guide

Per unit incl. 2 persons and electricity	€ 15,50 - € 25,00
extra person	€ 5,00 - € 7,00
child (0-7 yrs)	€ 0,20 - € 3,00
child (8-12 yrs)	€ 4,00 - € 6,00

Wasselonne

Camping Municipal Wasselonne

Route de Romanswiller, F-67310 Wasselonne (Bas-Rhin) T: **03 88 87 00 08**
E: **camping-wasselonne@wanadoo.fr** **alanrogers.com/FR67050**

A good quality municipal site with a resident warden, facilities here include a well stocked small shop, a crêperie in season and the added bonus of free admission to the superb indoor heated swimming pool adjacent to the site. There are 80 tourist pitches and around 20 seasonal units, on grass with a slight slope, all with electricity hook-ups (10A). Four new rental chalets are in a separate fenced area and there are six new private chalets. This could be an excellent base from which to visit Strasbourg.

Facilities

The single, large, and well maintained sanitary unit has unisex facilities with ample sized showers and washbasins in cubicles. Laundry facilities and covered dishwashing sinks. No specific facilities for disabled visitors but the rooms are spacious and should be accessible to many. Excellent drive-over motorcaravan service point. Off site: Heated pool, hotel with restaurant, tennis courts, plus athletics stadium all adjacent. Supermarket 500 m. Fitness trail, riding 1 km.

Open: 15 April - 15 October.

Directions

Wasselonne is 25 km. west of Strasbourg. Site lies southwest of town centre on D224 towards Romanswiller, and is well signed.
GPS: 48.6377, 7.4318

Charges guide

Per unit incl. 1 person	€ 7,30 - € 7,70
extra person	€ 3,40 - € 3,60
child (0-10 yrs)	€ 1,80 - € 1,90
electricity	€ 3,00

With over one hundred of France's finest châteaux, this is a region to inspire the imagination. The Loire valley is a charming region of lush countryside, fields of sunflowers, rolling vineyards and of course the great river itself.

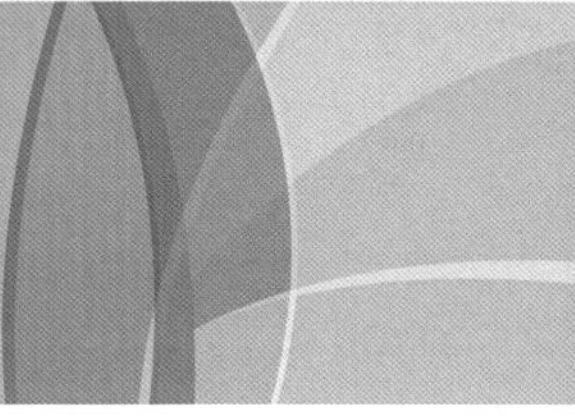

DÉPARTEMENTS: 18 CHER, 28 EURE-ET-LOIR, 36 INDRE, 37 INDRE-ET-LOIRE, 41 LOIR-ET-CHER, 45 LOIRET

MAJOR CITIES: ORLÉANS, TOURS

For centuries the Loire valley was frequented by French royalty and the great river winds its way past some of France's most magnificent châteaux: Amboise, Azay-le-Rideau, Chenonceau, with its famous arches that span the river and appear to 'float' on the water, and the fairytale Ussé with myriad magical turrets are just some of the highlights.

Known as the Garden of France, the Loire's mild climate and fertile landscape of soft green valleys, lush vineyards and fields of flowers makes it a favourite with the visitors. Renowned for its wines, with hundreds to choose from, all are produced from vineyards stretching along the main course of the River Loire. Imposing abbeys, troglodyte caves, tiny Romanesque churches, woodland areas such as the Sologne and sleepy, picturesque villages reward exploration. Cities like Blois and Tours are elegant with fine architecture and museums, and Paris is only one hour by TGV.

Places of interest

Amboise: château, Leonardo da Vinci museum.

Beauregard: château with Delft tiled floors.

Blois: château with architecture from Middle Ages to Neo-Classical periods.

Chambord: Renaissance château.

Chartres: cathedral with stained glass windows.

Chinon: old town, Joan of Arc museum

Loches: old town, château and its fortifications.

Orléans: Holy Cross cathedral, house of Joan of Arc.

Tours: Renaissance and Neo-Classical mansions, cathedral of St Gatien.

Vendôme: Tour St Martin, La Trinité.

Villandry: famous Renaissance gardens.

Cuisine of the region

Wild duck, pheasant, hare, deer, and quail are classics, and fresh water fish such as salmon, perch and trout are favourites. Specialities include rillettes, andouillettes, tripes, mushrooms and the regional cheeses of Trappiste d'Entrammes and Cremet d'Angers, Petit Sable and Ardoises d'Angers cookies.

Bourdaines: baked apples stuffed with jam.

Tarte a la citrouille: pumpkin tart.

Tarte Tatin: upside-down tart of caramelised apples and pastry.

www.visaloire.com
crtcentre@visaloire.com
(0)2 38 79 95 28

MONTDIDIER
LE HAVRE
COMPIEGNE
BEAUVAIS
ROUEN
SOISSONS
PICARDY
LES ANDELYS
SENLIS
LISIEUX
BERNAY
EVREUX
MEAUX
NORMANDY
ARGENTAN
DREUX
PARIS
PROVINS
ILE DE FRANCE
SENONCHES
CHARTRES
ETAMPES
ALENCON
EURE-ET-LOIR 28
MAMERS
SENS
ILLIERS-COMBRAY
A11,E50
PITHIVIERS
CHATEAUDUN
VAL DE LOIRE
MONTARGIS
COMBREUX
LE MANS
LOIR-ET-CHER 41
ORLEANS
A77
PAYS DE LA LOIRE
LOIRET 45
ST-PERE-SUR-LORIE
VENDOME
MUIDES-SUR-LOIRE
POILLY-LEZ-GIEN
GIEN
SUEVRES
BLOIS
LA FLECHE
CHÂTILLON SUR LOIRE
MESLAND
PIERREFITTE-SUR-SAULDRE
SONZAY
CHEVERNY
AUBIGNY-SUR-NERE
CANDE-SUR-BEUVRON
RILLE
A10,E05,60
TOURS
BALLAN-MIRE
FRANCUEIL-CHENONCEAU
VIERZON
INDRE-ET-LOIRE 37
A71,E11
CHINON
LOCHES-EN-TOURAINE
BOURGES
TROGUES
STE-MAURE-DE-TOURAINE
CHER 18
CHATELLERAULT
CHATEAUROUX
INDRE 36
A20,E09
POITIERS
AUVERGNE
MONTMORILLON
GUERET
POITOU CHARENTES
BELLAC
LIMOUSIN
AUBUSSON
0
25
50
75 kms
LIMOGES

Aubigny sur Nère

Flower Camping les Etangs

Route de Sancerre, F-18700 Aubigny-sur-Nère (Cher) T: **02 48 58 02 37**
E: **camping.aubigny@orange.fr** **alanrogers.com/FR18010**

Les Etangs is a site of 100 pitches, close to the Sancerre vineyards and the lakes of the Sologne. A member of the Flower group, this site extends over two hectares and borders a small lake (suitable for fishing). Pitches are large and grassy (most have electrical connections). There are chalets available for rent. The town of Aubigny-sur-Nère is very close (1 km.) and has a close attachment with Scotland, thanks to the 'Auld Alliance'. The town is the only one in France to celebrate French – Scottish friendship on Bastille Day. Bring your bicycle hireas there are many tracks running through the surrounding forests.

Facilities

Two heated toilet blocks are a good provision and are well located. Small shop. Bar (high season). Snack bar. Takeaway. Play area. Bicycle hire. Fishing (permit required). Activity and entertainment programme. WiFi (free). Chalets and tents for rent. Off site: Aubigny-sur-Nère 1 km. Walking and cycle tracks. Swimming pool 50 m. (with aquagym). Riding 20 km. Sancerre vineyards.

Open: 1 April - 30 September.

Directions

Aubigny is southeast of Orléans. Approaching from the north (Orléans) on the A71 autoroute take exit 4 for Salbris and head east on D724 and D924 until Aubigny. Take the D923 towards Sancerre and site is 1 km. GPS: 47.48435, 2.45703

Charges guide

Per unit incl. 2 persons and electricity	€ 13,90 - € 17,80
extra person	€ 2,60 - € 4,00
child (2-7 yrs)	€ 2,00 - € 2,50
dog	free

The Travel Service to book this site call **01580 214000** ...we'll arrange everything

Ballan-Miré

Camping de la Mignardière

22 avenue des Aubépines, F-37510 Ballan-Miré (Indre-et-Loire) T: **02 47 73 31 00**. E: **info@mignardiere.com**
alanrogers.com/FR37010

Southwest of the city of Tours, this site is within easy reach of several of the Loire châteaux, notably Azay-le-Rideau. There are also many varied sports amenities on the site or very close by. The site has 177 numbered pitches of which 139 are for touring units, all with electricity (6/10A) and 37 with drainage and water. Pitches are of a good size on rather uneven grass with limestone gravel paths (which are rather 'sticky' when wet). The barrier gates (coded access) are closed 22.30 - 07.30 hrs. Reservation is essential for most of July/August.

Facilities

Three toilet blocks include washbasins in private cabins, a unit for disabled people, baby bath and laundry facilities. Motorcaravan service point. Shop. Takeaway. Two large, heated swimming pools (one covered). Paddling pool. Tennis. Bicycle hire. Off site: Attractive lake 300 m. Family fitness run. Fishing 500 m. Riding 1 km. Golf 3 km. Tours centre 8 km.

Open: 1 April - 25 September.

Directions

From A10 autoroute take exit 24 and D751 towards Chinon. Turn right after 5 km. at Campanile Hotel following signs to site. From Tours take D751 towards Chinon. GPS: 47.35509, 0.63408

Charges guide

Per unit incl. 2 persons	€ 14,00 - € 21,00
incl. electricity, water and drainage	€ 20,00 - € 29,00
extra person	€ 4,00 - € 5,30
child (2-10 yrs)	€ 2,60 - € 3,20

Camping Cheques accepted.

The Travel Service to book this site call **01580 214000** ...we'll arrange everything

Candé-sur-Beuvron

Kawan Village la Grande Tortue

3 route de Pontlevoy, F-41120 Candé-sur-Beuvron (Loir-et-Cher) T: **02 54 44 15 20**.
E: **grandetortue@wanadoo.fr** **alanrogers.com/FR41070**

In the region that the Kings of France chose to build their most beautiful residences, this pleasant, shady site has been developed in the surroundings of an old 800-hectare forest, just 1 km. from the banks of the Loire river. For those seeking a relaxing holiday, it provides 169 touring pitches (the majority of more than 100 sq.m), 150 with 10A electricity and the remainder fully serviced. The friendly family owners continue to develop the site with a new multisport court and an attractive swimming pool complex. During July and August, they organise a programme of trips including canoeing and horse riding excursions, as well as twice weekly concerts and shows. La Grande Tortue is very well placed for visiting the châteaux of the Loire or the cities of Orléans and Tours. It is located on the long distance 'Loire à Vélo' cycle track and this leads from the site to Chaumont, Blois and Chambord, with over 300 km. of marked cycle tracks in the surrounding area. There are a number of good restaurants close at hand, although the site restaurant is also recommended with a range of good-value meals in a pleasant environment.

Facilities

Three sanitary blocks offer British style WCs, washbasins in cabins and pushbutton showers. Facilities for disabled visitors in one block. Laundry facilities. Motorcaravan service point. Shop. Terraced bar and restaurant with reasonably priced food and drink (15/4-15/9). Takeaway. Swimming pool and two shallower pools for children (1/5-30/9). Trampolines, a ball crawl with slide and climbing wall, two bouncy inflatables. Club for children (July/Aug). Multisport court. Off site: Walking and cycling. Bicycle hire 1 km. Fishing 500 m. Golf 10 km. Riding 12 km. Châteaux at Blois 10 km, Chambord 20 km, Chenonceau 20 km.

Open: 9 April - 30 September.

Directions

The site is just outside Candé-sur-Beuvron on D751, between Amboise and Blois. From Amboise, turn right just before Candé, then left into the site.
GPS: 47.48982, 1.25858

Charges guide

Per unit incl. 2 persons and electricity	€ 21,00 - € 31,50
extra person	€ 6,00 - € 8,50
child (3-9 yrs)	€ 3,50 - € 5,50
dog	€ 3,70

Camping Cheques accepted.

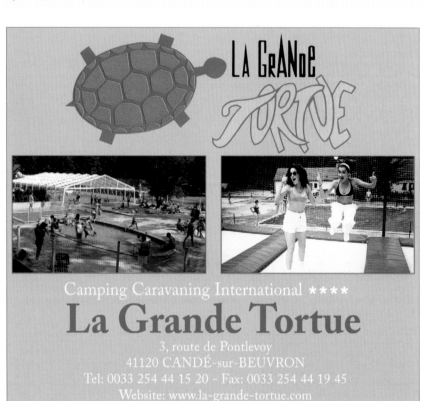

Châtillon-sur-Loire

Camping Hortus, l'Ecluse des Combes

Chemin de Loire, Briare, F-45 250 Châtillon-sur-Loire (Loiret) T: **02 38 31 42 92**
E: **info@camping-hortus.com** **alanrogers.com/FR45060**

The site gets its name from the canal close to which it stands. The home of the manager and also the site office, were once the old Lock Keeper's house. The campsite is split into three sections, one for tents (no electricity), one for touring units bordering the Loire (electricity and water) and one for seasonal pitches. The site is ex-municipal and has recently been taken over by the owner of FR45040. He has many plans to develop the site during the next few years. There is a restaurant on the opposite side of the road and a large municipal play area and two floating restaurants on the opposite banks of the Loire.

Facilities

A rather dated small toilet block, not heated, is equipped with showers and washbasins in cabins. Separate cubicles for disabled visitors. Baby bath. Simple motorcaravan service point. No washing machines. Play area. Fishing. Trigano type tents (3) to rent. Off site: Restaurants nearby. Town with bank, pharmacy, baker, bar and restaurant 1 km. Supermarket 2 km. Golf 2 km. Riding 4 km.

Open: 1 April - 31 October.

Directions

From the A77, take the N7 south and after 4 km. turn right on the D50 towards Chattillon-sur-Loire. Just before river bridge, turn right into site road. The site has a narrow entrance. GPS: 47.597482, 2.765851

Charges guide

Per unit incl. 2 persons and electricity	€ 12,00 - € 14,00
extra person	€ 2,50 - € 3,00
child (7-12 yrs)	€ 1,90 - € 2,30
dog	€ 1,50

Cheverny

Camping les Saules

Route de Contres (D102), F-41700 Cheverny (Loir-et-Cher) T: **02 54 79 90 01**
E: **contact@camping-cheverny.com** **alanrogers.com/FR41100**

Set in the heart of the châteaux region, has recently been revitalised and re-opened by a local family. The tastefully renovated traditional reception buildings in their lakeside setting give a very pleasant welcome. There are 166 good size, level pitches with 149 available for touring units. All have shade from the many trees on the site, 150 have electrical connections (a few will require leads longer than 25 m), and there are ample water taps. Cheverny is considered to have the best interior and furnishings of all the châteaux in the Loire region, and many others are within easy reach. A 'Sites et Paysages' member.

Facilities

Two sanitary blocks with toilets, showers, washbasins in cubicles and facilities for disabled visitors. Laundry facilities. Motorcaravan service point. Gas supplies. Shop. Restaurant (July/Aug). Bar. Snack bar and takeaway. Swimming and paddling pools. TV/social room with toys, board games, books. Two play areas. Large grass area for ball games. Minigolf (free). Fishing. Bicycle hire. Internet and WiFi. Off site: Golf 3 km. Riding 3 km.

Open: 1 April - 30 September.

Directions

From Cheverny take D102 south towards Contres. Site is on the right after about 2 km.
GPS: 47.50000, 1.46113

Charges guide

Per unit incl. 2 persons, car and electricity	€ 19,50 - € 29,00
extra person	€ 4,50
child (4-10 yrs)	€ 2,00
dog	€ 2,00

Val de Loire

The Travel Service to book this site call 01580 214000 ...we'll arrange everything

Chinon

Camping de l'Ile Auger

Quai Danton, F-37500 Chinon (Indre-et-Loire) T: **02 47 93 08 35**. E: **communaute.r.c.sb@wanadoo.fr**
alanrogers.com/FR37070

This traditional municipal-style site is well placed for exploring the old medieval town of Chinon and lies alongside the River Vienne opposite the impressive castle which was once the home of England's Henry II and includes a museum to Joan of Arc. A five-minute walk over the bridge takes you to the town centre. The 277 level pitches are numbered but not separated and trees provide some shade. All have electricity (long leads needed in places). Nearby are châteaux at Azay le Rideau and Villandry and the abbey at Fontevraud.

Facilities

Hot water is provided to showers and basins in two blocks near the entrance and in a small block at the far end of the site. WCs here are mainly British style. Three small blocks around the rest of the site, provide additional WCs (many Turkish style) and basins with cold water. Motorcaravan service point. Laundry facilities. Playground. Boules court. Fishing. Canoes. Barrier locked 22.00-07.00 hrs. A warden lives on site. Off site: Town with shops, bars and restaurants 500 m. Tennis. Indoor and outdoor swimming pools nearby. Bicycle hire, boat launching 0.1 km. River beach (no swimming) 1 km. Riding 10 km.

Open: 1 April - 31 October.

Directions

Chinon is 45 km. south west of Tours. From A85 at exit 9 (Chinon) follow D749 for 10 km. and turn south on D751 for 3 km. Turn east on D751E then north towards town centre. Follow one-way system, cross traffic coming out of town at bridge and continue ahead to campsite entrance on right. From A10 exit 25 take D760 to Chinon, then as above.
GPS: 47.16433, 0.23327

Charges guide

Per unit incl. 2 persons and electricity € 10,45 - € 11,85

Combreux

Camping Hortus, l'Etang de la Vallée

Vitry aux Loges, F-45530 Combreux (Loiret) T: **02 38 36 35 94**. E: **info@camping-hortus.com**
alanrogers.com/FR45070

Etang de la Vallée is a member of the new Hortus group and can be found deep within the massive Forêt d'Orléans, and close to the very large Etang de la Vallée. There are 180 pitches here and a small number of mobile homes. A bar/restaurant are opposite the site, as well as a large sandy beach (lifeguard in high season). Rowing boats and canoes may be hired there, as well as bicycles to explore the many miles of cycle trails through the woods. Pitches here are large and well shaded, and most have electricity. Orléans is easily accessible for a day trip. Fishing is popular in the lake and fishing lessons are available. The city of Its cathedral is a magnificent mix of the late Renaissance and early Louis XIV style. Although started during the reign of Henri IV it is one of France's most recent! This is still a prosperous city, located little over an hour from the capital. There are some fine châteaux to visit east of Orléans, if less well known, such as Chamerolle and Châteauneuf sur Loire.

Facilities

Bar/restaurant (opposite site). Play area. Sandy beach with canoes, boat and bicycle hire (opposite site). Tourist information. Mobile homes for rent. Off site: Walking and cycle tracks through the forest. Fishing. Beach volleyball. Orléans.

Open: 1 April - 1 October.

Directions

Approaching from Orléans, use N60 and leave at the Châteauneuf-sur Loire exit. Take the northbound D10 to Vitry-aux-Loges and then follow signs to Etang de la Vallée and the campsite.
GPS: 47.958555, 2.281557

Charges guide

Per unit incl. 2 persons and electricity € 15,40

Francueil-Chenonceau

Camping le Moulin Fort

F-37150 Francueil-Chenonceau (Indre-et-Loire) T: **02 47 23 86 22**. E: **lemoulinfort@wanadoo.fr**

alanrogers.com/FR37030

Camping Le Moulin Fort is a tranquil, riverside site with British owners, John and Sarah Scarratt. The 137 pitches are enhanced by trees and shrubs offering plenty of shade and 110 pitches have electricity (6A). From the snack bar terrace adjacent to the restored mill building a timber walkway over the mill race leads to the unheated swimming pool and paddling pools. The site is ideal for couples and families with young children, although the river is unfenced. There is occasional noise from trains passing on the opposite bank of the river. All over the campsite, visitors will find little information boards about local nature (birds, fish, trees and shrubs), about the history of the mill and fascinating facts about recycling. The owners are keen to encourage recycling on the site. The picturesque Château of Chenonceau is little more than 1 km. along the Cher riverbank and many of the Loire châteaux are within easy reach, particularly Amboise and its famous Leonardo de Vinci museum.

Facilities

Two toilet blocks with all the usual amenities of a good standard, include washbasins in cubicles, baby baths and facilities for disabled visitors. Motorcaravan service point. Shop, bar (limited hours), restaurant and takeaway (all 22/5-18/9). Swimming pool (22/5-18/9). Excellent play area. Minigolf. Pétanque. Games room and TV. Library. Fishing. Bicycle and canoe hire. In high season regular family entertainment including wine tasting, quiz evenings, activities for children, light-hearted games tournaments and live music events. WiFi in bar area. Off site: Boat launching 2 km. River beach 4 km. Riding 12 km. Golf 20 km. Trains to Tours 1.5 km.

Open: 1 April - 30 September.

Directions

Site is 35 km. east of Tours off the D976 Vierzon road. From A85 at exit 11 take D31 towards Bléré and turn east on D976 (Vierzon) for 7 km. then turn north on D80 (Chenonceau) to site. From north bank of Cher (D140/D40) turn south on D80 to cross river between Chenonceau and Chisseaux. Site on left just after bridge. GPS: 47.32735, 1.08936

Charges guide

Per unit incl. 2 persons and electricity	€ 13,00 - € 26,00
extra person	€ 3,00 - € 5,00
child (4-12 yrs)	€ 2,00 - € 4,00
dog	€ 2,00 - € 3,00

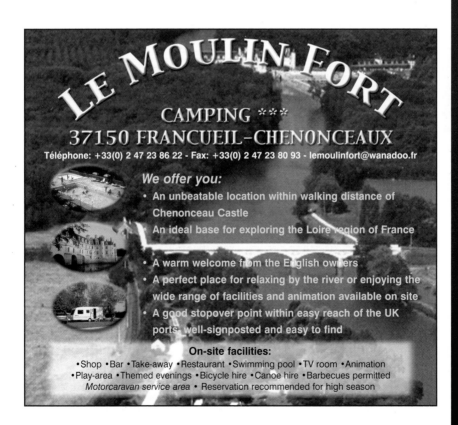

Gien

Kawan Village les Bois du Bardelet

kawan VILLAGES www.kawan-villages.com

Route de Bourges, Le Petit Bardelet, F-45500 Gien (Loiret) T: **02 38 67 47 39**
E: **contact@bardelet.com** **alanrogers.com/FR45010**

This attractive, lively site, ideal for families with young childrem, is in a rural setting and well situated for exploring the less well known eastern part of the Loire Valley. Two lakes (one for boating, one for fishing) and a pool complex have been attractively landscaped in 12 hectares of former farmland, blending old and new with natural wooded areas and more open field areas with rural views. Bois du Bardelet provides 260 pitches with around 130 for touring units. All are larger than 100 sq.m. and have electrical connections, with some new, luxury pitches of 200 sq.m. with water and waste water.

Facilities

Two sanitary blocks (only one open outside 15/6-31/8) include washbasins in cabins. Facilities for disabled visitors and babies. Washing machines. Shop (1/4-30/9). Bar. Snack bar, takeaway, restaurant (all 1/4-14/9) and pizzeria (8/7-21/8). Outside pool (1/5-31/8). Indoor children's pool. Indoor pool, heated (with purchased club card). Aquagym, fitness and jacuzzi room. Games area. Archery. Canoeing and fishing. Tennis. Minigolf. Bicycle hire. Playground. Internet access. Off site: Supermarket 5 km. Riding 7 km.

Open: 1 April - 30 September.

Directions

From Gien take D940 (Bourges). After 5 km. turn right and right again to cross road and follow site signs. From Argent sur Sauldre take D940 (Gien). Site signed to right after 15 km. GPS: 47.64152, 2.61528

Charges 2010

Per unit incl. 2 persons and electricity	€ 19,20 - € 32,00
extra person (over 2 yrs)	€ 4,90 - € 6,50

Camping Cheques accepted.

The Travel Service to book this site call 01580 214000 ...we'll arrange everything

Illiers-Combray

Flower Camping le Bois Fleuri

Route de Brou, F-28120 Illiers-Combray (Eure-et-Loir) T: **02 37 24 03 04**
E: **infos@camping-chartres.com** **alanrogers.com/FR28100**

The elegant city of Chartres is, of course, best known for its sublime cathedral, widely considered to be the finest Gothic cathedral in France, and included on the UNESCO list of World Heritage sites. Le Bois Fleuri is a small, wooded site, 20 km. from Chartres, open for an extended season. There are 89 pitches here as well as a number of mobile homes available for rent. Pitches range from 'Nature' (without electricity) to 'Grand Confort' (large pitches with electricity). In the adjacent park there is an attractive swimming pool and various other amenities. On the site there is bicycle hire and a playground.

Facilities

The toilet block is heated and fully tiled, with some washbasins in cabins and the usual under cover laundry and dishwashing sinks. Very small bar and shop (July/Aug). Fishing. Bicycle hire. Play area. Off site: Swimming pool in adjacent park. Fishing. Golf. Chartres 20 km. Illiers Combray 2 km. Riding. Cycle routes.

Open: 1 April - 31 October.

Directions

Leave the A11 at exit 3 (Thivars) and take the N10 towards Chartres, then shortly left onto the D114 and then finally the D921 to Illiers Combray. Site is well signed from the town. GPS: 48.286106, 1.227422

Charges guide

Per unit incl. 2 persons	€ 13,90 - € 19,90

No credit cards. Camping Cheques accepted.

Loches-en-Touraine

Kawan Village la Citadelle

Avenue Aristide Briand, F-37600 Loches-en-Touraine (Indre-et-Loire)
T: **02 47 59 05 91**. E: **camping@lacitadelle.com** **alanrogers.com/FR37050**

A pleasant, well maintained site, La Citadelle's best feature is probably that it is within walking distance of Loches, noted for its perfect architecture and its glorious history, yet at the same time the site has a rural atmosphere. The 86 standard touring pitches are all level, of a good size and with 10A electricity. Numerous trees offer varying degrees of shade. The 30 larger serviced pitches have 16A electricity but little shade. Mobile homes (28 for hire) occupy the other 48 pitches. Loches with its château and dungeons, is a gentle 500 m. walk along the river.

Facilities

Three sanitary blocks provide mainly British style WCs, washbasins and controllable showers. The block at the 'shady' end could be under pressure in high season. Laundry facilities. Motorcaravan service point. Two baby units and provision for disabled visitors (both in need of attention). Heated swimming pool (May-Sept). Paddling pool and play area (adult supervision strongly recommended). Small bar and snack bar (15/6-15/9). Boules, volleyball and games room. Internet access and TV. Off site: Bicycle hire 50 m. Riding 5 km.

Open: 19 March - 10 October.

Directions

Loches is 45 km. southeast of Tours. Site is well signed from most directions. Do not enter town centre. Approach from roundabout by supermarket at the southern end of bypass (D943). Site signed towards town centre and is on right in 800 m.
GPS: 47.12303, 1.00223

Charges guide

Per unit incl. 2 persons	€ 14,80 - € 24,20
incl. electricity, water and drainage	€ 20,20 - € 31,50
extra person	€ 4,30 - € 6,10

Camping Cheques accepted.

Mesland

yelloh! VILLAGE

Camping Village Parc du Val de Loire

155 route de Fleuray, F-41150 Mesland (Loir-et-Cher) T: **02 54 70 27 18**

E: **parcduvaldeloire@wanadoo.fr** **alanrogers.com/FR41010**

Between Blois and Amboise, quietly situated among vineyards away from the main roads and towns, this site is nevertheless centrally placed for visits to the châteaux; Chaumont, Amboise and Blois (21 km) are the nearest in that order. There are 185 touring pitches of reasonable size, either in light woodland marked by trees or on open meadow with separators. All the pitches have electricity (10A) and 100 of them also have water and drainage. Sports and competitions are organised in July/August with a weekly disco and dance for adults and opportunities for wine tasting are arranged weekly.

Facilities

Three original toilet blocks of varying ages are barely acceptable. One unit is very old and only open in July/Aug. Units for disabled visitors and babies. Laundry facilities. Motorcaravan services. Shop with bakery (July/Aug). Bar, restaurant, snacks, pizzeria and takeaway (all 15/5-1/9). TV and recreation rooms. Three swimming pools, one heated and covered (May - mid Sept). Balneo. Tennis. Three playgrounds, one adventure type. Bicycle hire. Minigolf. Off site: Fishing 2 km. Golf 4 km. Riding 10 km.

Open: 31 March - 29 September.

Directions

From A10 exit 18 (Château-Renault, Amboise) take D31 south to Autrèche (2 km). Turn left on D55 for 3.5 km. In Darne-Marie Les Bois turn left and then right onto D43 to Mesland. Follow site signs. Or, from south, site signed from Onzain.
GPS: 47.51002, 1.10481

Charges guide

Per unit incl. 2 persons	€ 14,00 - € 24,00
large pitch with services	€ 22,00 - € 32,00
extra person	€ 3,50 - € 7,00

Muides-sur-Loire

Camping Château des Marais

27 rue de Chambord, F-41500 Muides-sur-Loire (Loir-et-Cher) T: **02 54 87 05 42**

E: **chateau.des.marais@wanadoo.fr** **alanrogers.com/FR41040**

The Château des Marais campsite is well situated to visit the chateau at Chambord (its park is impressive) and the other châteaux in the 'Vallée des Rois'. The site, providing 133 large touring pitches, all with electricity (6/10A), water and drainage and with ample shade, is situated in the oak and hornbeam woods of its own small château. An excellent swimming complex offers pools with two slides, two flumes and a lazy river. A new 'wellness' centre is a recent addition. English is spoken and the reception from the enthusiastic owners and the staff is very welcoming. Used by tour operators (90 pitches).

Facilities

Four modern sanitary blocks have good facilities including some large showers and washbasins en-suite which would also be suitable for visitors with disabilities. Washing machines and dryers. Motorcaravan service point. Shop and takeaway. Bar/restaurant with large terrace. Swimming complex with heated and unheated pools, slide and cover for cooler weather. Wellness spa centre. Bicycle and go-kart hire. Games room. Fishing pond. Excursions to Paris, an entertainment programme and canoe trips organised in high season. Internet access (free). Off site: Riding 5 km.

Open: 8 May - 15 September.

Directions

From A10 autoroute take exit 16 to Mer. Turn left off the N152 to cross the Loire. Turn right to join the D951. Opposite car park in centre of Muides-sur-Loire, turn left onto D103. Site is signed off the D103 to the southwest of the village, 600 m. from junction with D112. GPS: 47.66580, 1.52877

Charges guide

Per unit incl. 2 persons	€ 30,00 - € 42,00
extra person	€ 8,00
child	free - € 7,00

Credit cards accepted over € 80.

Pierrefitte-sur-Sauldre

Leading Camping les Alicourts

Domaine des Alicourts, F-41300 Pierrefitte-sur-Sauldre (Loir-et-Cher) T: **02 54 88 63 34**

E: **info@lesalicourts.com** **alanrogers.com/FR41030**

A secluded holiday village set in the heart of the forest and with many sporting facilities and a super spa centre, Parc des Alicourts is midway between Orléans and Bourges, to the east of the A71. There are 490 pitches, 150 for touring and the remainder occupied by mobile homes and chalets. All pitches have electricity connections (6A) and good provision for water, and most are 150 sq.m. (min. 100 sq.m). Locations vary from wooded to more open areas, thus giving a choice of amount of shade. All facilities are open all season and the leisure amenities are exceptional. A member of 'Leading Campings Group'.

Facilities

Three modern sanitary blocks include some washbasins in cabins and baby bathrooms. Laundry facilities. Facilities for disabled visitors. Motorcaravan services. Shop. Restaurant. Takeaway in bar with terrace. Pool complex. Spa centre. 7 hectare lake (fishing, bathing, canoes, pedaloes). 9-hole golf course. Adventure play area. Tennis. Minigolf. Boules. Bicycle hire. Internet access and WiFi (charged).

Open: 29 April - 9 September.

Directions

From A71, take Lamotte Beuvron exit (no 3) or from N20 Orléans to Vierzon turn left on to D923 towards Aubigny. After 14 km. turn right at camping sign on to D24E. Site signed in 4 km. GPS: 47.54398, 2.19193

Charges guide

Per unit incl. 2 persons	€ 19,00 - € 42,00
extra person	€ 7,00 - € 10,00
child (1-17 yrs)	free - € 8,00

Poilly-lez-Gien

Camping Touristique de Gien

Rue des Iris, F-45500 Poilly-lez-Gien (Loiret) T: **02 38 67 12 50**. E: **camping-gien@wanadoo.fr**
alanrogers.com/FR45030

This open, attractive site lies immediately across the river from Gien on the opposite bank of the Loire with views of the château and town. It has a long river frontage, which includes a good expanse of sandy beach. There are 150 well-sized, level, grassed touring pitches. All have electricity (4/10A), 18 have water and drainage (between two). Some are shaded by mature trees. The bar and restaurant, with a large outdoor area, are open to the public and provide a sociable gathering point. Soirées with different themes are held at least weekly in July and August. The town, with its château, is within a kilometre across the bridge. The site makes an excellent base for exploring the eastern end of the Loire valley, and the town of Gien itself is of interest. The festival celebrating the heritage of this part of the Loire at Ascensiontide is well worth a visit.

Facilities

Three toilet blocks (no seats in toilets, some Turkish), one heated, and one new with an en-suite unit for disabled people. Laundry. Bar and restaurant (1/4-30/9), both open to the public. Shop 20 m. outside gates (all year). Swimming pool paddling pools (15/6-15/9). Play area and grassed games area. Minigolf. Bicycle hire. Canoe hire. Fishing. Off site: Town centre less than 1 km. Hypermarket 1 km. Riding 2 km. Golf 25 km.

Open: 1 March - 7 November.

Directions

North of the river, from north (A77 and RN7) take D940 to Gien; from southeast (A77 and RN7) and from west take D952 to Gien. Follow signs to Centre Ville and turn south over bridge. At traffic lights turn west on D951 towards Pouilly-lez-Gien. Site is signed 300 m. on right. If south of the river, from D940 turn west onto D951 and site is 300 m. on right.
GPS: 47.68229, 2.62315

Charges guide

Per unit incl. 2 persons and electricity	€ 19,50 - € 23,00
extra person	€ 4,00 - € 6,00

Rillé

HUTTOPIA

Huttopia Rillé

Lac de Rillé, F-37340 Rillé (Indre-et-Loire) T: **02 47 24 62 97**. E: **rille@huttopia.com**
alanrogers.com/FR37140

This site in a forest by a lake has plenty of potential. It has recently been acquired by the Huttopia group which aims to provide a traffic-free environment. Cars are to be left in a carpark outside the barrier (allowed on site to unload and load). New arrivals must park outside and gain an entry code from reception. There are 137 pitches of which 42 are occupied by rental accommodation and 24 are for motorcaravans in a separate area. The touring pitches are numbered in groups amongst the trees but are not marked; they vary in size and cost.

Facilities

The central toilet block has family rooms (with showers and basins), washbasins in cubicles and facilities for disabled visitors (shower/basin plus separate toilet) but there are no ramps and access for wheelchairs is very difficult. Another smaller block has separate showers, washbasins and slightly better facilities for disabled visitors. Motorcaravan service point. Heated swimming pool with paddling area (May -Sept). Play area. Fishing. Canoes on lake. Communal barbecue areas. Off site: Riding 6 km. Golf 15 km.

Open: 30 April - 2 November.

Directions

Rillé is 40 km. west of Tours. From D766 Angers - Blois road at Château la Vallière take D749 southwest. From N152 Tours - Angers road go northwest at Langeais on D57. In Rillé turn west on D49. Site on right in a short distance. GPS: 47.45811, 0.2192

Charges guide

Per unit incl. 2 persons and electricity	€ 19,20 - € 37,00
extra person	€ 3,10 - € 6,80

Saint Père-sur-Loire

Camping Hortus, Le Jardin de Sully

1 route d'Orléans (D60), Sully-sur-Loire, F-45600 Saint Père-sur-Loire (Loiret) T: **02 38 36 35 94**
E: **info@camping-hortus.com** **alanrogers.com/FR45040**

Across the river from Sully-sur-Loire with its imposing château, this site makes a comfortable base for exploring this part of the Loire valley. The present owners acquired it from the local authority in 2005 and their drive and initiative have turned it into an attractive site with many facilities. There are 80 well-sized touring pitches, all with electricity, water and drainage, on level grass and divided into groups of four by hedges. There is also an area for tents between the main pitches and the river. Trees provide a degree of shade. New swimming pools, bar and (open air) restaurant make this an ideal site for a quiet family holiday. A 'Sites et Paysages' member.

Facilities

Two modern toilet blocks, one heated, are well equipped: some washbasins in cabins; separate suite for disabled visitors. Small shop for essentials. Bar and open-air restaurant (1/5-30/9). Heated, covered swimming pool (12 x 8 m) and separate paddling pool (both 1/5-30/9). Fishing. Bicycle hire. Minigolf. Play areas. Off site: Town and Château 1.5 km. Two supermarkets 2 km. Golf 2 km. Riding 4 km.

Open: All year.

Directions

From Orléans take N60 then the D952 towards Gien. Turn south on D948 for Sully-sur-Loire. In St Père-sur-Loire, at roundabout just before river bridge, turn west on D60 signed St Benoit-sur-Loire. Site is 300 m. on left. GPS: 47.77106, 2.36214

Charges guide

Per unit incl. 2 persons and electricity	€ 16,50 - € 20,50
extra person	€ 3,70 - € 5,50
child (3-12 yrs)	free - € 3,50
dog	€ 2,00

Sainte Maure-de-Touraine

Castel Camping Parc de Fierbois

Sainte Catherine de Fierbois, F-37800 Sainte Maure-de-Touraine (Indre-et-Loire) T: **02 47 65 43 35**
E: **parc.fierbois@wanadoo.fr** **alanrogers.com/FR37120**

Parc de Fierbois has an impressive entrance and a tree lined driveway and is set among 250 acres of lakes and forest in the heart of the Loire Valley. In all, there are 320 pitches including 100 for touring units, the remainder being used by tour operators and for chalets and mobile homes. There are 80 touring pitches, mostly level and separated by low hedging or small trees, with water, drainage and electricity hook-ups (2-8A). The other pitches are small or medium in size, many unmarked and some sloping and in the shade. This is a lively family holiday site.

Facilities

Three toilet blocks provide British style WCs, hot showers and washbasins in cubicles. Baby room. Dishwashing and laundry facilities. Motorcaravan service point. Shop. Bar. Restaurant. Takeaway. Water park complex (pools, slides, paddling pool, sunbathing areas). Indoor heated pool. Indoor entertainment and games bar. Tennis. Pétanque. Minigolf. Bicycle hire. Go-karts and electric cars. TV/video room. Gym. Fishing. Pedaloes, canoeing and entertainment programme (July/Aug). Off site: Riding 10 km. Golf 30 km.

Open: 18 May - 11 September.

Directions

Travelling south on N10 from Tours, go through Montbazon and on towards Sainte Maure and Chatellerault. Site signed 16 km. outside Montbazon near Sainte Catherine. Turn off main road. Follow site signs. From A10 autoroute use the Sainte Maure exit and turn north up N10. GPS: 47.1487, 0.6548

Charges guide

Per unit incl. 2 persons	€ 16,00 - € 42,00
extra person	€ 6,00 - € 8,00
electricity	€ 4,50

Senonches

HUTTOPIA

Huttopia Senonches

Etang de Badouleau, avenue de Badouleau, F-28250 Senonches (Eure-et-Loir) T: **04 37 64 22 35**
E: **senonches@huttopia.com** **alanrogers.com/FR28140**

Senonches is the latest addition to the Huttopia group and will now be opening for the 2010 season. This site is hidden away in the huge Forêt Dominiale de Senonches and, in keeping with other Huttopia sites, combines a high standard of comfort with a real sense of backwoods camping. There are 126 pitches here, some with electrical connections (6/10A). The pitches are very large ranging from 100 sq.m. to no less than 300 sq.m. There are also ten Canadian style log cabins and tents available for rent. A good range of on-site amenities includes a shop and a bar/restaurant. The swimming pool overlooks a lake and is open from early July until September. The forest can be explored on foot or by cycle (rental available on site) and beyond the forest, the great city of Chartres is easily visited, with its stunning Gothic cathedral, widely considered to be the finest in France.

Facilities

The toilet blocks are modern and are heated in low season, with special facilities for disabled visitors. Shop. Bar. Snack bar. Takeaway. Swimming pool. Fishing. Play area. Bicycle hire. Entertainment and activity programme. Tents and chalets for rent. Off site: Riding 4 km. Senonches (good selection of shops, bars and restaurants). Cycle and walking tracks. Chartres.

Open: 24 April - 5 November.

Directions

Approaching from Chartres, use the ringroad (N154) and then take the D24 in a north westerly direction. Drive through Digny and continue to Senonches, from where the site is well signed. GPS: 48.5533, 1.04146

Charges guide

Per person	€ 5,10 - € 5,90
child (2-7 yrs)	€ 1,90 - € 2,50
pitch	€ 4,20 - € 10,20
electricity	€ 5,00

Sonzay

Kawan Village l'Arada Parc

Rue de la Baratière, F-37360 Sonzay (Indre-et-Loire) T: **02 47 24 72 69**
E: **info@laradaparc.com** **alanrogers.com/FR37060**

A good, well maintained site in a quiet location, easy to find from the motorway and popular as an overnight stop. Camping l'Arada Parc is an attractive family site nestling in the heart of the Touranelle countryside between the Loire and Loir valleys. The 74 grass touring pitches all have electricity and 35 have water and drainage. The clearly marked pitches, some slightly sloping, are separated by trees and shrubs some of which are now providing a degree of shade. An attractive, heated pool is on a pleasant terrace beside the restaurant. Entertainment, themed evenings and activities for children are organised in July and August. This is a new site with modern facilities which include a superb new covered pool and fitness room. The campsite is situated in the heart of 'châteaux country' so you will have the opportunity to visit Villandry, Azay-le-Rideau and Langeaux. Why not try the vineyards too? Chinon, Vouvray, Touraine and Amboise – you'll be spoilt for choice!

Facilities

Two modern toilet blocks provide unisex toilets, showers and washbasins in cubicles. Baby room. Facilities for disabled visitors (wheelchair users may find the gravel access difficult). Laundry facilities. Shop, bar, restaurant and takeaway (all season). Motorcaravan service point. Outdoor swimming pool (no Bermuda-style shorts; 1/5-13/9). Heated, covered pool (all season). Fitness room. Small play area. Games area. Boules. TV room. Bicycle hire. Internet access. WiFi throughout site. Footpath to village.
Off site: Tennis 200 m. Fishing 500 m. Golf 12 km. Riding 14 km.

Open: 27 March - 30 October.

Directions

Sonzay is northwest of Tours. From the new A28 north of Tours take the exit to Neuillé-Pont-Pierre which is on the N138 Le Mans - Tours road. Then take D766 towards Château la Vallière and turn southwest to Sonzay. Follow campsite signs.
GPS: 47.52812, 0.45300

Charges guide

Per unit incl. 2 persons and electricity (10A)	€ 18,60 - € 25,70
extra person	€ 4,00 - € 5,10
child (2-10 yrs)	€ 3,50
dog	€ 1,50 - € 2,00

Camping Cheques accepted.

Suèvres

483

Castel Camping Château de la Grenouillère

RN152, F-41500 Suèvres (Loir-et-Cher) T: **02 54 87 80 37**. E: **la.grenouillere@wanadoo.fr**
alanrogers.com/FR41020

Château de la Grenouillère is a comfortable site with good amenities. It is set in a 28-acre park and the 275 pitches are in three distinct areas. The majority are in a wooded area, with about 60 in the old orchard and the remainder in open meadow, although all pitches are separated by hedges. There is one water point for every four pitches and all have electric hook-up (10A). Additionally, there are 14 fully serviced pitches with a separate sanitary block in the outbuildings of the château.

Facilities

Three sanitary blocks are modern and well appointed, including some washbasins in cabins. Laundry facilities. Shop. Bar. Pizzeria and pizza takeaway. Restaurant and grill takeaway. Swimming complex of four pools (one covered) and slide. Spa and wellness. Whirlpool, jacuzzi, sauna, massage). Tennis. Games room. Internet point. Bicycle and canoe hire (July/Aug). Fishing. Off site: Suèvres 3 km. Riding, and watersports 5 km. Golf 10 km.

Open: 17 April - 11 September.

Directions

Site is between Suèvres and Mer on the north side of the N152 and is well signed. GPS: 47.68557, 1.48686

Charges guide

Per unit incl. 2 persons and electricity	€ 26,00 - € 39,00
incl. full services	€ 30,00 - € 45,00
extra person	€ 5,00 - € 8,00
child (under 7 yrs)	€ 3,00 - € 6,00
dog	€ 4,00

Trogues

Camping du Château de la Rolandière

F-37220 Trogues (Indre-et-Loire) T: **02 47 58 53 71**. E: **contact@larolandiere.com**

alanrogers.com/FR37090

This is a charming site set in the grounds of a château. The owners, Ghislain and Sabine Toulemonde, offer a very warm welcome. There are 50 medium sized, flat or gently sloping pitches, separated by hedges. Most have 6A electricity and water taps nearby and parkland trees give shade. There is a large chalet for hire and the château and adjoining buildings contain rooms to let. The site has a pleasant swimming pool with a sunny terrace and paddling pool, minigolf and an area for ball games, swings and slides. The site is close to both the A10 and the N10, so is convenient for an overnight break. However it certainly merits a longer stay as it is a delightfully peaceful spot from which to visit the châteaux at Chinon, Loches, Villandry or Azay-le-Rideau and the villages of Richelieu and Crissay-sur-Manse. There are interesting excursions to gardens and grottos, and in nearby Azay-le-Rideau, to the wicker craftsmen's workshops. A 'Sites et Paysages' member.

Facilities

The toilet block is older in style but has been refurbished to provide good facilities with modern showers, washbasin and laundry areas around central British style WCs. Provision for disabled visitors. Small shop for basics. Bar with terrace. Snacks and takeaway (July/Aug). Swimming pool (15/5-30/9). Minigolf. Play area. Fitness room. TV lounge. WiFi. Off site: Fishing 1 km. on River Vienne. River beach and boat launching 4 km. Golf 15 km. Bicycle hire 25 km. Restaurant 4 km. St Maure 7 km.

Open: 15 April - 30 September.

Directions

Trogues is 40 km. south-west of Tours on the D760 Loches - Chinon road. Site is east of village, 5 km. west from exit 25 on A10 at St Maure-de-Touraine. Entrance is signed and marked by a model of the château. GPS: 47.10767, 0.51052

Charges guide

Per person	€ 4,50 - € 6,00
child (under 10 yrs)	€ 2,50 - € 3,50
pitch	€ 7,50 - € 11,50
animal	€ 2,00 - € 3,00
electricity	€ 4,00

No credit cards.

The Pays de la Loire covers the area of Western France to the south of Brittany and Normandy. It lies along the lower stretches of the river Loire, the longest river in France, downstream from the châteaux of the Val de Loire region.

DÉPARTEMENTS: 44 LOIRE-ATLANTIQUE, 49 MAINE-ET-LOIRE, 53 MAYENNE, 72 SARTHE

Strictly speaking, the department of 85 Vendée is also part of this region. Because of its importance as a holiday destination for British people, we have featured it separately in this guide.

MAJOR CITIES: ANGERS, NANTES

Pays de la Loire is one of the regions created in the late 20th century to serve as an administrative zone of influence for its capital, Nantes. Whilst the great Loire châteaux lie in the Val de Loire region, the Pays de la Loire is home to many great monuments, such as the castles of Angers, Laval and Mayenne and the Château des Ducs de Bretagne at Nantes, the Royal Fontevraud Abbey and the old city of Le Mans. It also contains many natural parks including the Brière and the Poitou marshes.

The region has become very popular with British visitors involving no more than a day's drive from the Channel ports. It includes 300 km. of Atlantic coastline that offers long, sandy beaches and islands such as the Ile de Noirmoutier and the Ile d'Yeu, contrasting with the lush green countryside through which flows the River Loire.

At the region's heart lies Angers, the capital of the historic province of Anjou, home to the feudal warlords and the Plantagenet kings of England. To the southeast, the Vendée, is a peaceful holiday area very popular with summer visitors.

Places of interest

Angers: art town, medieval castle and tapestries, cathedral.

Brissac: 15th-century castle.

Le Croisic: small fishing port, Naval Museum.

Fontevraud: 11th-century Royal abbey.

Laval: castle, 'Douanier Rousseau' art gallery, boat trips on the Mayenne.

La Baule: holiday resort with lovely sandy bay.

Le Mans: the annual 24-hour car race attracting visitors from all over the world; car museum, old town, cathedral.

Le Puy de Fou: 15-16th-century castle, sound and light show involving over 700 participants.

Les Sables d'Olonne: fishing port and seaside resort.

Noirmoutier: linked to the mainland by a three mile bridge.

Saumer: 13th-century castle, Cadre Noir National School of Horse Riding, wine cellars and Mushroom Museum.

Cuisine of the region

Beure blanc: a buttery sauce that goes well with fish.

Rillauds d'Anjou: muscadet sausages.

Curé Nantais and Port-Salut: local cheeses.

Pâté aux prunes: A specialty of the Angers region and found in all good local bakers in July and August, this sugary pastry is filled with plums.

www.paysdelaloire.co.uk
infotourisme@sem-paysdelaloire.fr
(0)2 40 48 24 20

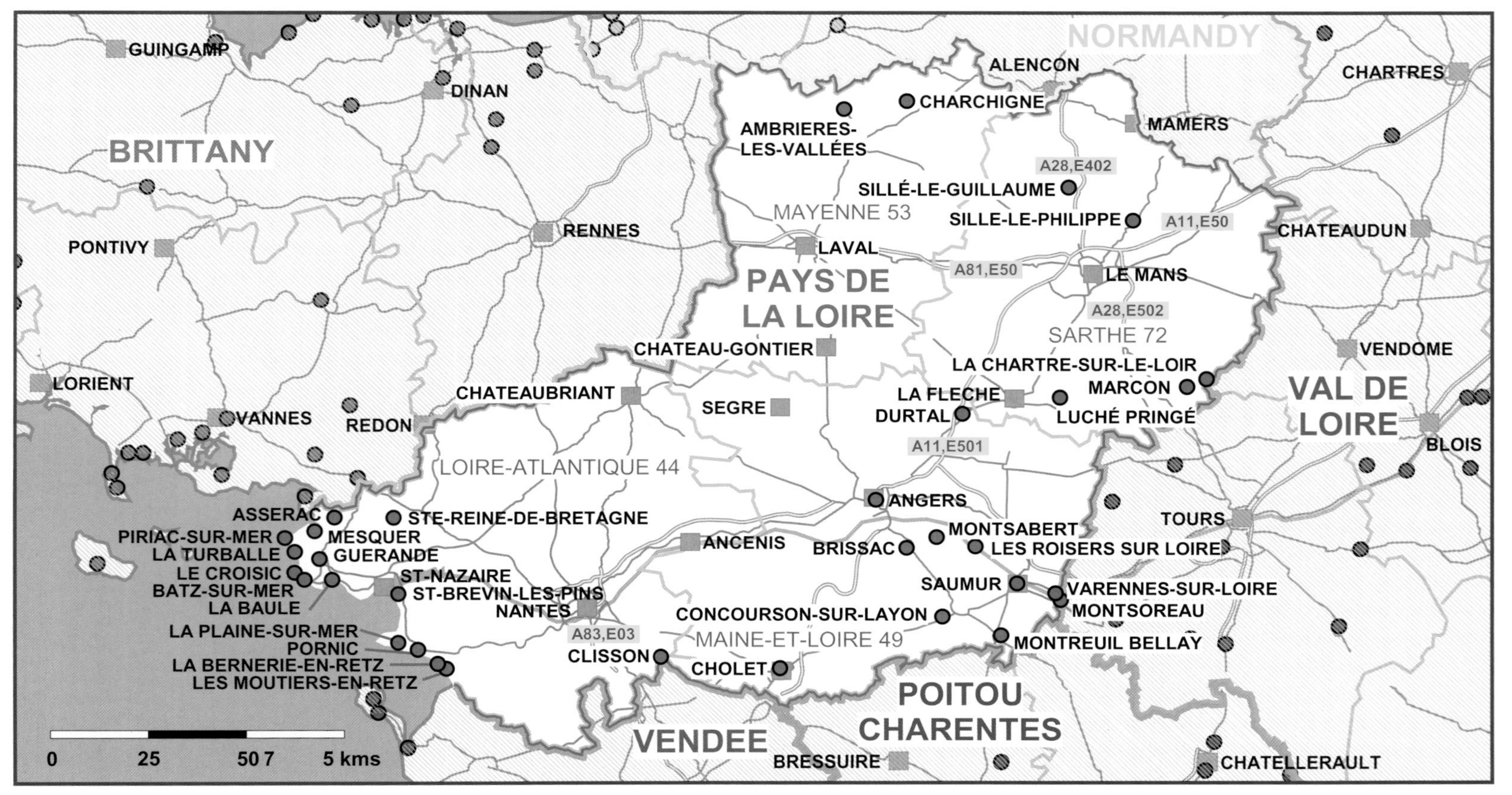

GUINGAMP
DINAN
NORMANDY
ALENCON
CHARTRES
CHARCHIGNE
MAMERS
AMBRIERES-LES-VALLÉES
BRITTANY
A28,E402
SILLÉ-LE-GUILLAUME
MAYENNE 53
SILLE-LE-PHILIPPE
A11,E50
CHATEAUDUN
RENNES
PONTIVY
LAVAL
A81,E50
LE MANS
PAYS DE LA LOIRE
A28,E502
SARTHE 72
CHATEAU-GONTIER
VENDOME
LA CHARTRE-SUR-LE-LOIR
LORIENT
MARCON
VAL DE LOIRE
CHATEAUBRIANT
LA FLECHE
SEGRE
DURTAL
LUCHÉ PRINGÉ
VANNES
REDON
BLOIS
A11,E501
LOIRE-ATLANTIQUE 44
ANGERS
TOURS
ASSERAC
STE-REINE-DE-BRETAGNE
MONTSABERT
PIRIAC-SUR-MER
MESQUER
ANCENIS
BRISSAC
LES ROISERS SUR LOIRE
LA TURBALLE
GUERANDE
LE CROISIC
ST-NAZAIRE
SAUMUR
BATZ-SUR-MER
ST-BREVIN-LES-PINS
VARENNES-SUR-LOIRE
LA BAULE
NANTES
CONCOURSON-SUR-LAYON
MONTSOREAU
A83,E03
LA PLAINE-SUR-MER
MAINE-ET-LOIRE 49
PORNIC
MONTREUIL BELLAY
LA BERNERIE-EN-RETZ
CLISSON
CHOLET
LES MOUTIERS-EN-RETZ
POITOU CHARENTES
VENDEE
0
25
50 7
5 kms
BRESSUIRE
CHATELLERAULT

Ambrières-les-Vallées

Camping Parc de Vaux

35, rue des Colverts, F-53300 Ambrières-les-Vallées (Mayenne) T: **02 43 04 90 25**
E: **parcdevaux@camp-in-ouest.com** **alanrogers.com/FR53010**

Parc de Vaux is an ex-municipal site which has recently been acquired by the owners of FR72080. This is a small site with just 31 touring pitches (a number of other pitches are occupied by mobile homes, available for rent). Pitches are generally grassy and well sized (mostly with electricity). The site is located in the pretty village of Ambrières-les-Vallées, 12 km. north of Mayenne, and may prove a convenient en-route stop. There is a swimming pool (with water slide) and the site also has access to a lake. Amenities here include tennis, mini-golf and archery. Parc de Vaux is adjacent to the River Varenne which runs into the Mayenne. This river was the region's most important transport artery for many years, dating back to the times of Charlemagne. It is now an important tourist feature with a great many pleasure craft in the summer. Ambrières-les-Vallées is now an attractive riverside resort with many cafes and restaurants, as well as its interesting Musée des Tisserands.

Facilities

Swimming pool. Sports field. Fishing. Games room. Children's play area. Tourist information. Mobile homes for rent. Vlakbij: Ambrières-les-Vallées (shops and restaurants). Boating on the River Mayenne. Walking and cycle tracks.

Open: 2 April - 1 November.

Directions

From Mayenne head north on D23 to Ambrières-les-Vallées. The site is clearly signed from here.
GPS: 48.391908, -0.61709

Charges guide

Per unit incl. 2 persons	€ 5,50 - € 9,20
extra person	€ 1,80 - € 2,30
child (under 10 yrs)	€ 0,90 - € 1,10
electricity	€ 2,20 - € 0,00
animal	free

Asserac

Flower Camping Domaine du Pont Mahé

Pont Mahé, F-44410 Asserac (Loire-Atlantique) T: **02 40 01 74 98**. E: **contact@pont-mahe.com**
alanrogers.com/FR44400

La Grande Brière is a vast area of marshland to the north of the Loire estuary. This is an area rich in flora and fauna, arguably best explored using the traditional punts (chalands). Domaine du Pont Mahé is a seaside site to the north of the Brière. Of the 81 pitches, 36 are for touring and the remainder are occupied by mobile homes (27 for rent). Pitches are generally well shaded and of a good size. The site's covered swimming pool is a focal point and is attractively surrounded by a terrace with straw parasols. Bicycle hire is on offer and a number of cycle tracks run close to the site.

Facilities

Sanitary facilities include hot showers and washbasins in cabins. Facilities for disabled visitors. Laundry facilities. Shop. Bar. Takeaway. Covered swimming pool. Children's pool. Play area. Games room. Bicycle and canoe hire. Activity and entertainment programme. Mobile homes and equipped tents for rent. Off site: Nearest beach 250 m. Grande Brière natural park. Fishing. Cycle tracks. La Baule (18 km).

Open: 1 April - 31 October.

Directions

Leave the N165 at Arzal exit and head south on the D139 (which becomes the D83) as far as Assérac. Head west here on D82 to Pont Mahé and site is well signed. GPS: 47.44737, -2.45043

Charges guide

Per unit incl. 2 persons and electricity	€ 14,00 - € 25,00
extra person	€ 3,00 - € 4,00
child (2-7 yrs)	€ 2,00 - € 3,00
dog	€ 3,00

Angers

Camping du Lac de Maine

Avenue du Lac de Maine, F-49000 Angers (Maine-et-Loire) T: **02 41 73 05 03**. E: **camping@lacdemaine.fr**

alanrogers.com/FR49000

The Lac de Maine campsite is situated in the heart of the Anjou region. Most of the 141 level touring pitches are part grass and part gravel hardstanding, with the remainder all gravel. All have water, a drain and electricity (6/10A). The main entrance has a height restriction of 3.2 m, although there is an alternative gate for higher vehicles. This is a useful site, open for a long season and only five minutes from the centre of Angers. With wide access roads, it is also suitable for American RVs. This site has the advantage of being at the southern end of the Parc de Loisirs du Lac de Maine. The adjacent 100-acre lake has a sandy beach for swimmers, windsurfing, sailing and pedaloes available, while the parkland provides tennis courts and a nature reserve.

Facilities

Two sanitary blocks, one which can be heated and includes some washbasins in cubicles. British style WCs (no seats). Facilities for babies and visitors with disabilities. Dishwashing and laundry facilities. Motorcaravan service point. Reception stocks gas. Restaurant/bar (both 15/6-15/9). Heated L-shaped swimming pool (1/6-15/9). Spa. Volleyball. Petanque. Bicycle hire. Internet point. Barrier card deposit € 20. Off site: Lake beach 500 m. Fishing 1 km. Riding 3 km. Golf 5 km.

Open: 25 March - 10 October.

Directions

Site is just west of Angers near the N23 (Angers - Nantes road). Turn south at signs for Quartier de Maine and Lac de Maine. Follow signs for Pruniers and Bouchemaine. Site on D111 and signed. GPS: 47.45434, -0.59619

Charges guide

Per unit incl. 2 persons	€ 11,85 - € 17,00
extra person	€ 3,00
child (under 13 yrs)	€ 2,00
electricity (10A)	€ 3,40

Camping Cheques accepted.

Batz sur Mer

Campéole

Campéole les Paludiers

Rue Nicolas Appert, F-44740 Batz-sur-Mer (Loire-Atlantique) T: **02 40 23 85 84**. E: **paludiers@campeole.com**

alanrogers.com/FR44360

Les Paludiers, part of the Campéole group, is pleasantly situated at Batz-sur-Mer, a typical Breton village between La Baule and the fortified town of Guérande. The site has 300 pitches, with 150 used for touring units on sandy ground, marked and divided by shrubs. There are 70 with 10A electricity. The remainder of the pitches are occupied by mobile homes and canvas bungalows. At the rear of the modern reception building there is a bar and games room. Outside a patio area overlooks a small heated pool and a play area for children. Entertainment is provided for both children and adults in the high season. This site is ideal for families with young children, with a good pool and a safe environment for play. The added bonus here is the close proximity of a lovely sandy beach – just five minutes walk. The drive along the Côte Sauvage to Le Croisic is quite spectacular.

Facilities

Three modern toilet bocks each with good facilities for disabled visitors and a baby room. Laundry facilities, Shop with limited but essential stocks. Bar and snacks (1/7-31/8). Swimming and paddling pools (15/5-15/9). Play area. Games room. Barbecues are only permitted in a dedicated area. Off site: Beach 100 m. Fishing 500 m. Golf, bicycle hire and riding 1 km. Town centre 800 m. Salt marshes and coastal walking paths.

Open: 5 April - 23 September.

Directions

From Nantes take the N171 to St Nazaire and then the D213 towards Guérande. At the D774 follow signs to Batz-sur-Mer, continue through village and take exit from the roundabout into rue Nicolas Appert. Site entrance is on the left. GPS: 47.2788, -2.4913

Charges guide

Per unit incl. 1-3 persons	€ 13,00 - € 21,30

Brissac

Camping de l'Etang

Route de Saint-Mathurin, F-49320 Brissac (Maine-et-Loire) T: **02 41 91 70 61**. E: **info@campingetang.com**

alanrogers.com/FR49040

At Camping de l'Etang many of the 124 level touring pitches have pleasant views across the countryside. Separated and numbered, some have a little shade and all have electricity with water and drainage nearby; 21 are fully serviced. A small bridge crosses the river Aubance which runs through the site (well fenced) and there are two lakes where fisherman can enjoy free fishing. The site has its own vineyard and the wine produced can be purchased on the campsite. The adjacent Parc de Loisirs is a paradise for young children with many activities (reduced entry for campers).

Facilities

Three well maintained toilet blocks provide all the usual facilities. Laundry facilities. Baby room. Disabled visitors are well catered for. Motorcaravan service point. The farmhouse houses reception, small shop and takeaway snacks when bar is closed. A bar/restaurant serves crêpes, salads, etc. (evenings 15/6-31/8). Swimming pool (heated and covered) and paddling pool. Fishing. Play area. Bicycle hire. Wide variety of evening entertainment in high season. WiFi. No electric barbecues. Off site: Golf and riding 10 km. Sailing 25 km.

Open: 15 May - 15 September.

Directions

Brissac-Quincé is 17 km. southeast of Angers on the D748 towards Poitiers. Do not enter the town but turn north on D55 (site signed) in direction of St Mathurin. GPS: 47.3611, -0.4353

Charges guide

Per unit incl. 2 persons	€ 15,00 - € 29,00
extra person	€ 5,00 - € 7,00
child (0-10 yrs)	free - € 4,00
electricity	free - € 3,00
dog	€ 3,00 - € 4,00

Charchigne

Camping le Malidor

F-53250 Charchigne (Mayenne) T: **02 43 03 99 88**. E: **le-malidor@orange.fr**

alanrogers.com/FR53020

This attractive, small, rural site is surrounded by farmland and it provides a real taste of the French countryside. The three private lakes provide great fishing and only a short walk away the path leads to the village. There are 17 pitches, all for touring, all with 10A electricity. They are terraced and divided by mature hedges. The beautiful surrounding countryside is well worth exploring and this site is a perfect place from which to do so. Large units are accepted. Fishing gear and bait are available.

Facilities

One sanitary block provides good facilities but none for campers with disabilities. Bar and restaurant. Play area, paddling pool. Boules. Darts, pool table, hall for groups up to 80. Fishing with three lakes. Minigolf. Bicycle hire. Walks and painting courses. Off site: Village with bar/restaurant and shop 500 m. Beaches 20 km.

Open: Said to be all year, but check before visiting.

Directions

From A81 (Rennes - Le Mans) take exit 3 for Laval. Head northeast on N162 to Mayenne. Then takethe N12 in the same direction towards Alençon for 20 km. Just before Javron turn left on D33 to Cherchigne. Then follow signs to site just before Cherghigné. GPS: 48.41857, -0.40141

Charges 2010

Per unit incl. 2 persons and electricity	€ 15,00
extra person	€ 2,00

Cholet

Centre Touristique Lac de Ribou

Allée Léon Mandin, F-49300 Cholet (Maine-et-Loire) T: **02 41 49 74 30**. E: **info@lacderibou.com**
alanrogers.com/FR49120

Situated just 58 km. southeast of Nantes and a similar distance from the River Loire at Angers and Saumur, this could be a useful place to break a journey or to spend a few days relaxing. Camping Lac de Ribou, with the adjacent 'Village Vacances', forms a holiday complex in pleasant parkland next to an extensive lake on the outskirts of the busy market town of Cholet. 162 touring pitches are on undulating land (some are sloping), divided by hedges and with mature trees proving shade on many; most have electricity (10A) and 115 also have individual water tap and drainage.

Facilities

Two sanitary blocks provide preset showers and washbasins in cabins. Facilities for disabled visitors. Motorcaravan service points. Small shop (July/Aug). Bar and 'snackerie' with takeaway (July/Aug). Large heated swimming pool plus smaller pool with slide and a paddling pool (1/6-30/9). Play area. Very full programme of activities for all ages (July/Aug) including archery, art workshop for children, sub-aqua, aquagym. Professional standard cabaret evenings.
Off site: Fishing and small beach (no swimming) 500 m. Sailing 1 km. Supermarket 2 km. Riding 5 km. Golf 7 km.

Open: 1 April - 30 September.

Directions

From Cholet ringroad east of town, turn east on the D20 towards Maulévrier and Mauléon. At roundabout by Leclerc supermarket, take first exit signed to site which is signed 'Parc de Loisirs de Ribou' all around the town. GPS: 47.036367, -0.843733

Charges guide

Per unit incl. 1 or 2 persons	€ 9,45 - € 17,90
extra person	€ 3,00 - € 4,45
electricity (10A)	€ 3,75 - € 5,20
dog	€ 1,40 - € 2,05

No credit cards.

Clisson

Camping Municipal du Moulin

Route de Nantes, F-44190 Clisson (Loire-Atlantique) T: **02 40 54 44 48**
alanrogers.com/FR44020

This good value, small site is conveniently located on one of the main north - south routes on the edge of the interesting old town of Clisson. A typical municipal site, it is useful for short stays. There are 45 good sized, marked and level pitches with electricity and divided by hedges and trees giving a good degree of privacy and some shade. There is also an unmarked area for small tents. A barbecue and camp fire area is to the rear of the site above the river where one can fish or canoe (via a steep path).

Facilities

The fully equipped toilet block, cleaned each afternoon, includes some washbasins in cabins and others in a separate large room, with hot and cold water. Unit for disabled visitors. Dishwashing and laundry facilities. Bread delivered daily. Table tennis, volleyball, and small playground.
No double axle or commercial vehicles accepted.
Off site: Supermarket with cheap fuel just across the road. Bicycle hire, riding 5 km. Sailing 15 km. Golf 30 km.

Open: mid April - mid October.

Directions

From N249 Nantes - Cholet road, take exit for Vallet and Clisson and D763 south for 7 km. then fork right towards Clisson town centre. At roundabout after passing Leclerc supermarket on your right take second exit (into site). GPS: 47.09594, -1.28271

Charges guide

Per unit incl. 1 person, electricity	€ 7,77 - € 8,20
extra person	€ 2,42 - € 2,55
child (0-7 yrs)	€ 1,61 - € 1,70

No credit cards.

Concourson-sur-Layon

Camping Caravaning la Vallée des Vignes

La Croix Patron, F-49700 Concourson-sur-Layon (Maine-et-Loire) T: **02 41 59 86 35**
E: **Campingvdv@wanadoo.fr** **alanrogers.com/FR49070**

The enthusiasm of the English owners here comes across instantly in the warm welcome received by their guests. Bordering the Layon river, the 50 good sized touring pitches are reasonably level and fully serviced (10A electricity, water tap and drain). Five pitches have a hardstanding for cars. Attractions include an enclosed bar and restaurant, a generously sized sun terrace surrounding the pool and high season activities for children and adults. These include wine tasting, competitions and treasure hunts. An ideal base for visiting the châteaux of the Loire and the many caves and vineyards.

Facilities

The toilet block includes washbasins in cabins, and dishwashing facilities at either end. Baby room. Facilities for disabled visitors. Laundry facilities. Bar (from 15/5 or on request) serving meals, snacks and takeaway (from 15/5). Swimming and paddling pools (from 15/5). Playground, games area and football pitch. Minigolf. Internet access. Fishing. Caravan storage. Pets corner. Off site: Zoo and rose gardens at Doué-la-Fontaine. Grand Parc Puy du Fou.

Open: 15 April - 30 September.

Directions

Site signed off D960 Doué - Vihiers road, just west of Concourson-sur-Layon. GPS: 47.17431, -0.34730

Charges guide

Per unit incl. 2 persons and electricity	€ 21,50 - € 27,00
extra person	€ 5,00 - € 9,00
child (2-12 yrs)	€ 3,00 - € 4,00

Special offers available.

Durtal

Camping les Portes de l'Anjou

9 rue du Camping, F-49340 Durtal (Maine-et-Loire) T: **02 41 76 31 80**
E: **lesportesdelanjou@camp-in-ouest.com** **alanrogers.com/FR49160**

Les Portes de l'Anjou is an ex-municipal site which has recently been acquired by the owners of FR72080. The site can be found at Durtal, an attractive town around 30 km. north of Angers. There are 122 pitches here, all of which are surrounded by hedges and are of a good size (with 6A electricity). A number of mobile homes are available for rent. The town centre is around 500 m. away and a good range of shops and restaurants can be found there. The site enjoys direct access to the Loir and fishing is said to be good here. Various activities are organized on site in the peak season, including special barbecues, pony rides and a children's clubs. The site has canoes for hire and also organizes accompanied cycle tours of the region. The history of Durtal's fine château can be traced back to the 11th century and it is now one of the region's most imposing sights. In complete contrast, the zoo at La Flèche is France's oldest private zoo, and with over 1,200 animals, is now one of the country's largest.

Facilities

Three modern sanitary blocks have British style toilets, washbasins in cubicles, preset showers and separate facilities for disabled visitors. Bar/snack bar. Swimming pool. Fishing. Games room. Canoe hire. Play area. Entertainment and activity programme. Direct river access. Mobile homes for rent. Off site: Durtal (shops, restaurants and château). Walking and cycle tracks. Zoo at La Flèche. Aerial adventure park in the forest of Ecouflant (near Angers).

Open: 1 April - 1 November.

Directions

Durtal is located close to exit 11 of the A11. From there head for the town centre and then follow signs to the site. GPS: 47.671269, -0.235991

Charges guide

Per unit incl. 2 persons and electricity	€ 12,40 - € 14,70

Guérande

484

Camping Parc de Léveno

Route de Sandun, F-44350 Guérande (Loire-Atlantique) T: **02 40 24 79 30**. E: **domaine.leveno@wanadoo.fr**
alanrogers.com/FR44220

There have been many changes to this extensive site over the past three years and considerable investment has been made to provide some excellent new facilities. The number of mobile homes and chalets has increased considerably, leaving just 47 touring pitches. However, these are mainly grouped at the far end of the site where there is more the feel of a real French campsite. Pitches are divided by hedges and trees which offer a good deal of shade and all have electricity (10A). Access is tricky to some and the site is not recommended for larger units. Twin axle caravans and American motorhomes are not accepted.

Facilities

Main refurbished toilet block offers preset showers, washbasins in cubicles and facilities for disabled visitors. Laundry facilities. Small shop selling basics and takeaway snacks. Restaurant, bar with TV and games (all April - Sept). Indoor pool. Heated outdoor pool complex with water slides and a flume, paddling pool (15/5-30/9). Aquatic centre. Fitness room. Excellent, safe play area. Multisport court. Extensive programme of activities and events (high season). Off site: Large hypermarket 1 km. Fishing 2 km. Beach, golf and riding all 5 km.

Open: 4 April - 30 September.

Directions

Site is less than 3 km. from the centre of Guérande. From D774 and from D99/N171 take D99E Guérande by-pass. Turn east following signs for Villejames and Leclerc hypermarket and continue on D247 to site on right. GPS: 47.33352, -2.3906

Charges guide

Per unit incl. 2 persons, electricity and water	€ 18,00 - € 35,00
extra person	€ 4,00 - € 7,00
child (under 7 yrs)	€ 3,00 - € 5,00

See advertisement on page 154

La Baule

Camping les Ajoncs d'Or

Chemin du Rocher, F-44500 La Baule (Loire-Atlantique) T: **02 40 60 33 29**. E: **contact@ajoncs.com**
alanrogers.com/FR44170

This site is situated in pine woods, 1.5 km. on the inland side of La Baule and its beautiful bay. A well maintained, natural woodland setting provides a wide variety of pitch types (just over 200), some level and bordered with hedges and tall trees to provide shade and many others that maintain the natural characteristics of the woodland. Most pitches have electricity and water nearby and are usually of a larger size. A central building provides a shop and open friendly bar that serve snacks and takeaways. The English speaking Bazillails family (the owners) who live on site will welcome you to their campsite.

Facilities

Two good quality sanitary blocks are clean and well maintained. Baby room. Laundry facilities. Shop and bar (July/Aug). Snack bar (July/Aug). Swimming pool and paddling pool (1/6-5/9). Sports and play areas. Bicycle hire. Reception with security barrier (closed 22.30-07.30).
Off site: Beach, fishing and riding 1.5 km. Golf 3 km.

Open: 1 April - 30 September.

Directions

From N171 take exit for La Baule les Pins. Follow signs for 'La Baule Centre', then left at roundabout in front of Carrefour supermarket and follow site signs.
GPS: 47.28950, -2.37367

Charges guide

Per unit incl. 2 persons and electricity	€ 23,00
extra person	€ 3,00 - € 6,00

La Bernerie-en-Retz

Camping les Ecureuils

24 avenue Gilbert Burlot, F-44760 La Bernerie-en-Retz (Loire-Atlantique) T: **02 40 82 76 95**
E: **camping.les-ecureuils@wanadoo.fr** **alanrogers.com/FR44050**

Just 350 metres from both the sea and the centre of the little town of La Bernerie, Les Ecureuils is a family run site. The sandy beach here is great for children; swimming is restricted to high tide, since the sea goes out a long way although at low tide a shallow lagoon remains which is perfect for young children. The site has 167 touring pitches, all with electricity (10A) close by and 19 with their own water tap and drain. There are also 80 mobile homes and chalets for rent and a further 70 privately owned. The site prides itself in its pool complex with heated leisure, swimming and paddling pools including three water slides and a flume. The fishing port of Pornic is worth a visit, as is the Ile de Noirmoutier, just 35 kilometres south.

Facilities

Four toilet blocks are in traditional French style; some have controllable showers and washbasins in cubicles. Facilities for disabled visitors are not all easily accessible. Very basic baby room. All was kept clean on our last visit. Bar with terrace (15/6-31/8), also selling bread (1/7-31/8). Snack bar and takeaway (July/Aug). Swimming pools (15/5-15/9). Playground. Off site: Shops, restaurants and bars 350 m. Also beach, fishing, sailing and boat launching. Golf, riding and bicycle hire 6 km.

Open: 1 May - 15 September.

Directions

La Bernerie-en-Retz is 5 km. south of Pornic and 26 km. south of the Saint Nazaire bridge. From the D213/D13 (St Nazaire - Noirmoutier) turn west on D66 to La Bernerie. Site is signed to right by railway station before reaching town. GPS: 47.0845, -2.036667

Charges 2010

Per unit incl. 2 persons and electricity	€ 18,00 - € 34,00
extra person	€ 4,00 - € 6,50
child (0-2 yrs)	free
child (2-10 yrs)	€ 3,00 - € 5,00

La Chartre-sur-le-Loir

Camping du Vieux Moulin

Chemin des Bergivaux, F-72340 La Chartre-sur-le-Loir (Sarthe) T: **02 43 44 41 18**. E: **camping@lachartre.com**
alanrogers.com/FR72070

Le Vieux Moulin is a pleasant family site, located on the banks of the Loir, close to the pretty town of La Chartre-sur-le-Loir, to the south east of Le Mans. Pitches here are grassy and of a good size. There are also a number of mobile homes and fully equipped tents available for rent. On-site amenities include a heated swimming pool, a paddling pool and a sports field. Canoeing is popular here and canoes can be rented on site. The site becomes livelier in peak season with a limited entertainment and activity programme, including a children's club and occasional karaoke evenings. The Loir Valley may be less well known than its similarly named counterpart to the south, but it has very much to recommend it. It is also a wine-producing region with vineyards and cellars to visit. La Chartre is an interesting town with its fine parish church of St Vincent and curious Tour Jeanne d'Arc. This is a great region to be explored by cycle (hire available on site) and the nearby Forêt de Bercé has more than 300 km. of marked routes.

Facilities

Traditional sanitary block provides pushbutton showers and some washbasins in cubicles. Facilities for disabled visitors. Washing machine and dryer. Motorcaravan service point. Small shop selling basics, restaurant and takeaway with licence (weekends and July/Aug). Swimming and paddling pools (1/6-20/9). Fishing. Canoeing. Bicycle hire. Large sports field. Play area. Tourist information. Mobile homes and equipped tents for rent. Internet access and free WiFi. Occasional excursions are organised during peak season. Off site: Village with shops, bars and restaurants 1 km. Lake with swimming, sailing and watersports 4 km. Cycle and walking tracks in Forêt de Bercé 10 km. Golf 40 km.

Open: 1 May - 20 September.

Directions

La Chartre-sur-le-Loir is 47 km. south east of Le Mans and 44 km. north of Tours. From A28 exit 26, head east to Château du Loir, turn south on the D938/D338 (Caen - Tours road) and cross the Loir. Then head north east on the D305 to La Chartre sur le Loir. After one-way system follow signs to the site, turning left immediately after crossing river.
GPS: 47.7324, 0.57095

Charges guide

Per unit incl. 2 persons and electricity	€ 11,90 - € 18,20
extra person	€ 2,70 - € 3,60
child (under 13 yrs)	€ 1,80 - € 2,20
dog	€ 1,20 - € 1,50

La Plaine-sur-Mer

Camping la Tabardière

F-44770 La Plaine-sur-Mer (Loire-Atlantique) T: **02 40 21 58 83**. E: **info@camping-la-tabardiere.com**

alanrogers.com/FR44150

Owned and managed by the Barré family, this campsite is pleasant, peaceful and immaculate. It will suit those who want to enjoy the local coast and towns but return to an 'oasis' for relaxation. However, it still provides activities and fun for those with energy remaining. The pitches are mostly terraced and care needs to be taken in manoeuvring caravans into position – although the effort is well worth it. The pitches have access to electricity and water taps are conveniently situated nearby. The site is probably not suitable for people using wheelchairs. Whilst this is a rural site, its amenities are excellent with a covered swimming pool, paddling pool and water slide, tennis, boules and a very challenging 18 hole minigolf to keep you occupied, plus a friendly bar. The beautiful beaches are 3 km. with the fishing harbour town of Pornic some 5 km. away, ideal for its cafés, restaurants and the evening strolls. A 'Sites et Paysages' member.

Facilities

Two good, clean toilet blocks are well equipped and include laundry facilities. Motorcaravan service point. Shop, bar, snacks and takeaway (high season). Good sized covered swimming pool, paddling pool and slides (supervised). Playground. Minigolf. Volleyball and basketball. Half size tennis courts. Boules. Fitness programme. Overnight area for motorcaravans (€ 13 per night). Off site: Beach 3 km. Sea fishing 3 km. Golf, riding and bicycle hire all 5 km.

Open: 4 April - 27 September.

Directions

Site is well signed, situated inland off the D13 Pornic - La Plaine-sur-Mer road. GPS: 47.140767, -2.15052

Charges guide

Per unit incl. 2 persons	€ 15,00 - € 26,70
extra person	€ 3,70 - € 6,40
child (2-9 yrs)	€ 2,75 - € 4,35
dog	€ 3,20
electricity (3/8A)	€ 3,30 - € 4,80

Camping Cheques accepted.

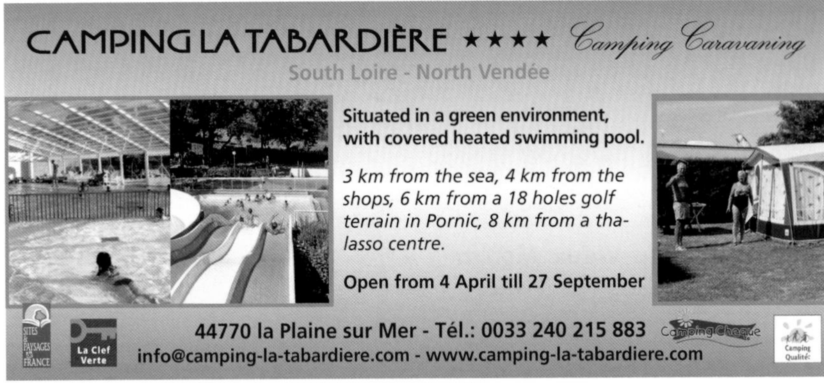

La Plaine-sur-Mer

Camping le Ranch

Les Hautes Raillères, F-44770 La Plaine-sur-Mer (Loire-Atlantique) T: **02 40 21 52 62**
E: **info@camping-le-ranch.com** **alanrogers.com/FR44240**

This is a pleasant, family-run campsite with a friendly atmosphere, close to the beaches of the Jade Coast between Pornic and St Brévin-les-Pins, yet not right on the seashore. The 94 touring pitches all have access to electricity (6A) although on some a long cable may be required; these occupy the central part of the site, with the fringe areas taken up by mobile homes and chalets, 18 for rent and 74 privately owned (although 30 of these are also available for rent in high season). The rows of pitches are separated by well-kept hedges, and small trees mark the corners of most plots. In high season there is a very lively atmosphere and it might seem a little crowded on some pitches; at less busy times it is almost certainly a very peaceful site. A pleasant bar and terrace overlook the attractive pool complex with a swimming pool and paddling pool, together with water slides and a flume. Linked to the bar is a large barn with stage and dance floor which at other times is a games room and an indoor volleyball court.

Facilities

The central sanitary block has preset showers and washbasins in cubicles. Facilities for disabled visitors. Fairly basic baby room. Further small toilet block. Swimming pool (1/5-30/9, heated 15/6-15/9). Bar has small shop selling bread, basics and camping gaz. Good takeaway (July/Aug). Activities for children and entertainment and sports events for families in high season. Off site: Beach 800 m. Bicycle hire 1.5 km. Boat launching 3 km. Fishing 5 km. Sailing 3 km. Riding 4 km. Golf 6 km.

Open: 1 April - 30 September.

Directions

La Plaine-sur-Mer is 16 km. south of the St Nazaire bridge. Site is on D96 5 km. northeast of the town. From D213 (Route Bleue) just south of St Michel-Chef-Chef turn southwest on D96 towards La Plaine. Site on left in about 2 km. GPS: 47.155216, -2.1649

Charges guide

Per unit incl. 2 persons and electricity	€ 16,20 - € 27,30
extra person	€ 3,00 - € 5,00
child (under 7 yrs)	€ 2,00 - € 3,30
dog	€ 2,00 - € 2,50

Camping ★★★
Le Ranch
Friendly summer holiday, near the sea in the south of Brittany
Camping Qualité
www.camping-le-ranch.com
Chemin des Hautes Raillères - 44770 LA PLAINE SUR MER - Tél. 02 40 21 52 62 - info@camping-le-ranch.com

La Turballe

Camping le Parc Sainte-Brigitte

Domaine de Bréhet, chemin des Routes, F-44420 La Turballe (Loire-Atlantique) T: **02 40 24 88 91**
E: **saintebrigitte@wanadoo.fr** **alanrogers.com/FR44040**

Le Parc Sainte-Brigitte is a well established site in the attractive grounds of a manor house, three kilometres from the beaches. It is a spacious site with 150 good pitches, 110 with electricity, water and drainage. Some are arranged in a circular, park-like setting near the entrance, others are in wooded areas under tall trees and the remainder are on more open grass in an unmarked area near the pool. This is a quiet place to stay outside the main season. In high season it can become very busy, mainly with families and its full share of British visitors. One can walk around many of the areas of the estate not used for camping; there are farm animals to see and a fishing lake is very popular.

Facilities

The main toilet block, supplemented by a second block, is of good quality. They include washbasins in cabins and two bathrooms. Laundry facilities and lines provided. Motorcaravan services. Small shop. Pleasant restaurant/bar with takeaway (both 15/5-15/9). Heated swimming pool with retractable roof and paddling pool. Playground. Bicycle hire. Boules. TV room and traditional 'salle de réunion'. Fishing. Off site: Riding 2 km. Nearest beach 2.5 km. Golf 15 km.

Open: 1 April - 1 October.

Directions

Entrance is off the busy La Turballe - Guérande D99 road, 3 km. east of La Turballe. A one-way system operates - in one lane, out via another. GPS: 47.34253, -2.47168

Charges 2010

Per unit incl. 2 persons, water, waste water and electricity	€ 29,80
extra person	€ 5,00 - € 6,30

No credit cards.

Pays de la Loire

La Turballe

Camping la Falaise

1 boulevard de Belmont, F-44420 La Turballe (Loire-Atlantique) T: **02 40 23 32 53**
E: **info@camping-de-la-falaise.com** **alanrogers.com/FR44340**

La Falaise is a simple site enjoying direct access to a wide sandy beach. There are 150 pitches of which 67 are available to tourers with water and electricity. Other pitches are occupied by mobile homes or chalets (some to rent). The pitches are of a reasonable size but are unshaded and tend to be very sandy. This is a quiet site in low season becoming much livelier in July and August. There are relatively few amenities on site but nearby La Turballe has a good selection of shops and restaurants. In high season, a takeaway food service is available. There is one main building housing reception and washing and toilet facilities. La Turballe is a bustling fishing port and nearby Guérande, on the edge of the Grande Brière natural park, merits a visit with its excellent market.

Facilities

Central toilet block (predominantly Turkish style toilets). Bar, restaurant and takeaway (1/6-15/9). Play area (unfenced). Mobile homes and chalets for rent. Direct access to the beach. Off site: Shops 300 m. Fishing. Boat launching 500 m. Golf 2 km. Riding 10 km. Walking and cycle trails. Shops and restaurants in La Turballe 2 km.

Open: 25 March - 5 November.

Directions

Take the D99 from Guérande to La Turballe and then continue towards Piriac sur Mer. Bypass La Turballe and the site is on this road after a further kilometre. GPS: 47.353833, -2.517333

Charges guide

Per unit incl. 2 persons, electricity and water	€ 20,10 - € 30,65
extra person (over 4 yrs)	€ 4,25 - € 4,90

Le Croisic

484

Camping de l'Océan

15 route de la Maison Rouge, F-44490 Le Croisic (Loire-Atlantique) T: **02 40 23 07 69**
E: **camping-ocean@wanadoo.fr** **alanrogers.com/FR44210**

Camping de l'Océan is situated on the Le Croisic peninsula, an attractive part of the Brittany coastline. Out of a total of 400 pitches, 80 are available for tourers with the remainder being taken by mobile homes either privately owned or for rent. The pitches are level and 80-100 sq.m. in size (they were rather worn when we visited). The leisure facilities, which include a restaurant, bar and pool complex, are of an excellent standard. This site, probably more suitable for families with young teenagers, can be very lively in high season with a wealth of activities and entertainment for all ages. Sports are well catered for and there are tournaments in high season. After an excellent meal in the restaurant you can enjoy different entertainment on most evenings in July and August. The site is within walking distance of the Atlantic Ocean and white sandy beaches just 150 m. away.

Facilities

Five adequate toilet blocks include facilities for disabled visitors. Washing machines and dryers. Good restaurant and bar. Takeaway. Shop. Motorcaravan service point. Swimming pool complex comprising an indoor pool, outdoor pool and paddling pool. Volleyball. Football. Basketball. Tennis.
Off site: Market (most days). Le Croisic for shops, bars and restaurants. Sailing, riding and golf.

Open: 5 April - 30 September.

See advertisement on page 154

Directions

From Le Pouliguen, travel west on N171 to Le Croisic. Site is well signed from here and found in about 1.5 km. GPS: 47.29752, -2.53593

Charges guide

Per unit incl. 2 persons and electricity (6A)	€ 20,50 - € 49,00
extra person	€ 4,00 - € 8,00
child (2-7 yrs)	€ 2,00 - € 6,50
dog	€ 2,00 - € 6,50

Les Moutiers-en-Retz

Flower Camping les Brillas

Le Bois des Tréans, F-44760 Les Moutiers-en-Retz (Loire-Atlantique) T: **02 40 82 79 78**
E: **info@campinglesbrillas.com** **alanrogers.com/FR44310**

You are assured of a warm welcome from M. and Mme. Perret, the owners of this site. The small number of touring pitches are on grass, hedged and small. The larger pitches are being taken up by mobile homes of which there is a much higher ratio compared to touring pitches. This could be a useful base for visiting Pornic and St Nazaire where there are many tourist attractions. The reception, bar and restaurant are housed in the same modern building as the sanitary facilities. Care should be taken on the approach road to the site which is a long narrow lane with no passing places.

Facilities

The toilet block is clean but basic and includes a mix of English and Turkish style toilets and preset showers. Facilities for disabled visitors. Laundry facilities. Bar and restaurant (limited menu). Shop in bar. Games area. Small unfenced play area. Basic swimming pool. Bicycle hire. Entertainment (July/Aug). Off site: Fishing and sailing 3 km. Riding 5 km.

Open: 1 April - 30 October.

Directions

Site is 1.5 km. from Les Moutiers. Heading northwest from Les Moutiers on D97 turn right onto Route du Bois des Treans. Site signed. GPS: 47.07166, -2.00433

Charges guide

Per unit incl. 2 persons, electricity	€ 13,00 - € 22,50
extra person	€ 2,50 - € 5,50

Les Roisers-sur-Loire

Flower Camping Val de Loire

6 rue Sainte Baudruehe, F-49350 Les Roisers-sur-Loire (Maine-et-Loire) T: **02 41 51 94 33**
E: **contact@camping-valdeloire.com** **alanrogers.com/FR49180**

This former municipal site on the outskirts of a village on the River Loire between Saumur and Angers has 84 touring pitches, all with electricity, individual water taps and waste water drainage. A further 28 pitches are used for mobile homes, mostly for hire. Recent additions include a pleasant bar with a terrace and a marquee for games and entertainment. There are two new heated swimming pools, one covered, the other surrounded by sunbathing terraces and with a large paddling pool. When we visited in late June, everything was very quiet, but in July/August there is a busy programme of activities.

Facilities

The main sanitary block is modern if rather drab, with controllable showers and washbasins in cubicles. Two older blocks and a new 'portacabin' unit provide additional facilities. Facilities for disabled visitors. Laundry room. Bar with TV serves snacks and fresh bread to order (July/Aug). Covered pool (1/4-30/9). Outdoor pool (1/5-15/9). Children's activities, events and outings, and evening entertainment in season. Play area. Games room. Minigolf. Tennis. Bicycle hire. Off site: Shops, bar and restaurant 800 m. Fishing 800 m. Boat launching 1 km. Riding 2 km. Golf 15 km.

Open: 1 April - 30 September.

Directions

Les Rosiers is 17 km northwest of Saumur. From A85 motorway at exit 1 take southbound D144 to Beaufort-en-Vallée, then continue south on D59. Site is signed to right on approach to village. From D952 Saumur-Angers road turn north in village to site on left in 800 m. GPS: 47.35877, -0.22604

Charges guide

Per unit incl. 2 persons	€ 14,00 - € 20,00
extra person	€ 3,00 - € 5,00
electricity (5/10A)	€ 4,00

Luché-Pringé

Camping La Chabotière

Place des Tilleuils, F-72800 Luché-Pringé (Sarthe) T: **02 43 45 10 00**. E: **contact@lachatbotiere.com**
alanrogers.com/FR72100

This is a delightful little municipal site on the River Loir, just a few steps from the main square of an interesting village classed as a 'Petite Cité de Caractère'. There are 85 pitches, 65 for touring and all with access to electricity and the remainder used for wooden chalets and canvas 'bungalows' for rent. The main part of the site down by the river is kept vehicle free in July and August, ensuring a safer and quieter environment. A child-proof gate leads out onto the river bank and footpath. There are many opportunities for walking, cycling and sightseeing in the area.

Facilities

The traditional toilet block is well maintained and kept clean; it has pushbutton showers and some washbasins in cubicles. Baby room and washbasins for children. Facilities for disabled visitors. Laundry facilities. Motorcaravan service point. Quiet room. Free internet access (adults only). Free Wifi in reception area. Adventure play area. Sports field. Bicycle hire. Fishing. Activities for children and in the evening. Chalets for rent. Off site: 'Espace de Loisirs' (July/Aug) at entrance with free access from site. Shops, bar and restaurants in village. Boat launching 500 m. Lake with beach 7 km. Riding 10 km. Sailing 14 km. Golf 30 km.

Open: 1 April - 15 October.

Directions

Luché-Pringé is 40 km. south of Le Mans. From the A11 between Le Mans and Angers, leave at exits 10 or 11 and head eastwards to La Flèche, then north on D323 towards Le Mans. At Clermont-Créans turn east on D13 to Luché-Pringé. In main square (ignore earlier campsite sign) turn sharp right then left, signed 'Minigolf' then site. GPS: 47.70252, 0.07364

Charges guide

Per unit incl. 2 persons and electricity (10A)	€ 10,10 - € 12,30
extra person	€ 2,20 - € 3,30

Marcon

Camping Lac des Varennes

Saint Lezin, route de Port-Gauthier, F-72340 Marcon (Sarthe) T: **02 43 44 13 72**
E: **contact@lacdesvarennes.com** **alanrogers.com/FR72080**

This extensive site is located near the massive forest of Bercé in the Vallée du Loir and is on the shore of the lake from which it takes its name. There are 250 pitches here, with 175 for tourers, all grassy and with electrical connections (10A). Many also have lake views. The site has its own sandy beach (with a beach volleyball court) and canoes are available for rent. In high season, various activities are organised including a club for children and riding. Mobile homes are available for rent. A gate gives free access to the Base de Loisirs which offers a variety of water and land-based activities. The area is a paradise for walkers and cyclists, with more than 300 km. of tracks through the Forêt de Bercé; the site owners will be pleased to recommend routes. Nearby are the vineyards of Côteaux de Loir whilst the nearest point on the River Loire is just 50 km. to the south, so visits to some of its famous châteaux are possible.

Facilities

Three traditional sanitary blocks are kept clean and provide pushbutton showers, some washbasins in cubicles and a mix of British and Turkish-style toilets. Laundry facilities. Basic facilities for disabled visitors. Motorcaravan service point. Shop, snack bar and takeaway (July/Aug). Simple bar with games and TV. Play area. Entertainment (July/Aug). Direct access to lake with fishing and swimming.
Off site: Base de Loisirs with sailing, boat launching, water slide, carp fishing, tennis, multisport court plus (weekends and July/Aug) minigolf, pedaloes and archery. Riding 5 km. Walking and cycling in the forest 8 km. Golf 38 km.

Open: 26 March - 14 November.

Directions

Marçon is 50 km. southeast of Le Mans and 47 km. north west of Tours. From A28 exit 26, head east to Château du Loir, turn south on the D938/D338 (Caen - Tours road) and cross the Loir. Then head north east on the D305 to Marçon, and turn west in village centre to Base de Loisirs. Site on right in 1 km. GPS: 47.7125, 0.4993

Charges guide

Per unit incl. 2 persons and electricity	€ 13,60 - € 17,10
extra person	€ 3,50 - € 4,70
child (under 13 yrs)	€ 1,70 - € 2,30

Mesquer

Camping le Château du Petit Bois

1820 route de Kerlagadec, F-44420 Mesquer (Loire-Atlantique) T: **02 40 42 68 77**
E: **info@campingdupetitbois.com** **alanrogers.com/FR44270**

This pleasant campsite is located in the wooded grounds of a small château. The 125 good-sized touring pitches, all with electricity (3/6A) have varying degrees of shade and a few are in the open for those who like a sunny plot. Reception is housed in a wooden chalet and is welcoming and informative. The Marin family and their staff are friendly and helpful and the site is very well run. On site there is an attractive swimming pool complex: a heated main pool and paddling pool, and a separate pool with two good water slides which is only open when the pool is supervised. The sea is just over a kilometre away, as is the village of Mesquer and nearby are the salt marshes which produce the famous Sel de Guérande.

Facilities

The main sanitary block has preset showers and open style washbasins together with some cubicles with controllable shower and a washbasin. Dishwashing and laundry facilities. Facilities for disabled visitors. Combined bar, snack bar and takeaway. Small shop selling bread and basics (July/Aug). Pool complex with heated main pool, paddling pool and pool with water slides (only open when supervised). Programme of activities (all July/Aug). Off site: Fishing, bicycle hire, riding and sailing all nearby. Golf 12 km.

Open: 1 April - 30 October.

Directions

Mesquer is 80 km. northwest of Nantes and 16 km. north of La Baule. From N165 Nantes - Vannes road, leave at exit 15 towards La Roche Bernard, turn left to join D774 towards La Baule. 8 km. after Herbignac, turn right on D52 to St Molt and Mesquer. Site is on D52 just west of village (do not go into village). GPS: 47.399016, -2.471316

Charges guide

Per unit incl. 2 persons	€ 15,40 - € 19,20
extra person	€ 4,90 - € 6,10
electricity (3/6A)	€ 4,30 - € 5,40

Montreuil-Bellay

Camping le Thouet

Le Côteaux du Chalet, route Bron, F-49260 Montreuil-Bellay (Maine-et-Loire) T: **02 41 38 74 17**
E: **contact@campinglethouet.com** **alanrogers.com/FR49150**

Open all year, this countryside site occupies a grassy, tree-lined area with the River Thouet running along the far side from the reception and terrace. The site covers an area of 20 acres occupied in part by 37 good sized, unmarked pitches, 32 for touring and all with 10A electricity. Reception is part of an old farmhouse, the home of the owners who, in winter, provide a warm bathroom for the use of the campers. The owner is English and his wife is multilingual. Beside the swimming pool is an attractive sun terrace together with a bar and restaurant. There is a large hardstanding area, with electricity and water, ideal for winter visitors. This is a peaceful and quiet campsite with families and couples in separate areas. It is a good base for touring the famous châteaux of the Loire. It is a good site for birdwatching (the RSPB has recorded 90 species of birds). Booking is advisable in high season.

Facilities

Two modern toilet blocks including facilities for campers with disabilities and baby room. Bread and much more available by request. Outdoor pool, no paddling pool (1/5-30/9) surrounded by terrace, bar/restaurant (1/4-15/10). Wine tasting. Bicycle hire. Boules. Fishing. Large play area. Boat launching, Birdwatching. Off site: Golf and canoeing 5 km. Riding 10 km. beautiful village of Montreuil Bellay, shops, restaurants etc. (5 minutes drive). Fontevraud with its interesting Abbey (15 minutes drive).

Open: All year.

Directions

From Saumur take N147 towards Poitiers. About 6 km. after Le Coudray Macouard turn left, signed Montreuil Belley Centre Ville. Immediately turn left again. Site well signed in under 2 km. GPS: 47.13151, -0.15924

Charges guide

Per unit incl. 2 persons and electricity (10A)	€ 20,00
extra person	€ 4,00

Montsabert

Yelloh! Village Parc de Montsabert

Montsabert, F-49320 Coutures (Maine-et-Loire) T: **02 41 57 91 63**

E: **info@yellohvillage-parcdemontsabert.com** **alanrogers.com/FR49060**

This extensive site has recently been taken over by a friendly French couple who already have plans for improvements. It has a rural atmosphere in the shadow of Montsabert château, from where visiting peacocks happily roam in the spacious surroundings. The main features are the heated swimming pool and the adjoining refurbished restaurant. There are 111 large, well marked touring pitches, divided by hedges and all with water tap, drain and electricity. Picnic tables are provided. The site is used by several small tour operators (12 pitches). Partially wooded by trees, this site offers the peace of the countryside.

Facilities

The main toilet block can be heated and has washbasins and bidets in cabins and a baby room. Laundry facilities. A second block serves the pool and another provides more WCs. Shop, bar and takeaway. Restaurant. Heated pool (no Bermuda style shorts) and paddling pool. Sports hall. Minigolf. Tennis. Play area. Bicycle hire. Entertainment (high season). Archery. Riding. Off site: Canoeing nearby. Fishing 5 km. Golf 8 km.

Open: 10 April - 12 September.

Directions

Coutures is 25 km. southeast of Angers on the D751 to Saumur. From A11 take exit 14 and follow signs for Cholet/Poitiers, then Poitiers on D748. At Brissac-Quincé turn northeast on D55 and in 5 km. turn right to Coutures. Montsabert is north of village. GPS: 47.3744, -0.3469

Charges 2010

Per unit incl. 2 persons and electricity	€ 15,00 - € 29,00
extra person	€ 4,00 - € 5,00

Montsoreau

Kawan Village l'Isle Verte

Avenue de la Loire, F-49730 Montsoreau (Maine-et-Loire) T: **02 41 51 76 60**

E: **isleverte@cvtloisirs.fr** **alanrogers.com/FR49090**

www.kawan-villages.com

This friendly, natural site, with pitches overlooking the Loire, is just 200 m. from the nearest shop, bar and restaurant in Montsoreau, and is an ideal base from which to explore the western Loire area. Most of the 90 shaded, level and good-sized tourist pitches are separated by low hedges but grass tends to be rather sparse during dry spells. All have electricity (16A). Excellent English is spoken in the reception and bar/restaurant. Attractions within walking distance include the château, troglodyte caves (used for traditional mushroom production) and restaurant, wine tasting in the cellars nearby, and a Sunday market in the town. Fishermen are particularly well catered for at Isle verte, there being an area to store equipment and live bait (permits are available in Saumur). Cyclists and walkers could also well be in their element here. For the less energetic, there is a bus service into Saumur with its château and other historic buildings, and all its shops, bars and restaurants. Trains or buses available in Saumur will take you on to other towns along the Vallée de la Loire. Just 5 km. south of Montsoreau is the fascinating 12th-century Abbaye Royale de Fontévraud.

Facilities

A single building provides separate male and female toilets. Washbasins, some in cabins, and showers are unisex. Separate facilities for disabled campers. Baby room. Laundry facilities. Motorcaravan service point. Bar and restaurant (1/5-30/9). Swimming and paddling pools (15/5-30/9). Play area. Table tennis, volleyball and boules. Fishing. Boat launching. WiFi (charged). Off site: Beach on river 300 m. Bicycle hire and sailing 1 km. Golf and riding both 7 km.

Open: 1 April - 30 September.

Directions

Montsoreau is 12 km. southeast of Saumur on the D947 towards Chinon. Site is clearly signed on left along the road into town. GPS: 47.21820, 0.05265

Charges guide

Per unit incl. 2 persons, electricity	€ 17,50 - € 21,50
extra person	€ 3,00 - € 4,00
child (5-10 yrs)	€ 2,00 - € 2,50
animal	€ 1,50

Camping Cheques accepted.

Piriac-sur-Mer

484

Camping Parc du Guibel

Route de Kerdrien, F-44420 Piriac-sur-Mer (Loire-Atlantique) T: **02 40 23 52 67**
E: **camping@parcduguibel.com** **alanrogers.com/FR44070**

This very large site, situated in an extensive wood, describes itself as 'un Hôtel de Plein Air' and prides itself on its spaciousness and its trees. A keen birdwatcher told the owner that he had seen 50 different species of birds. There are 450 pitches of which 307 are for touring scattered among the 14 hectares of woodland, mainly shaded but some in clearings. One section at the top of the site across a minor road is always quiet and peaceful. 110 pitches have electricity (3, 6 or 10A) of which 67 also have water tap and drainage. There are also 134 mobile homes and chalets for rent. A long room houses the bar, snack bar with takeaway and a small restaurant together with an area with electronic games. A small shop sells bread and a few basics. A new pool complex should be open including a slide and paddling pool. Activities and entertainment for children and adults are organised in high season. The sea is just over a kilometre away and nearby are the salt-marshes producing the famous 'Sel de Guérande'.

Facilities

Five sanitary blocks: the newest is smart and well equipped, with controllable showers and washbasins. Two others have been partially refurbished to the same standards. The others are rather old-fashioned, with preset showers and washbasins in cubicles. Facilities for disabled visitors. Baby room. Laundry facilities. Motorcaravan service point. New swimming pool complex (1/5-15/9). Bar, snack bar, takeaway and restaurant (July/Aug). Off site: Riding 400 m. Fishing 1 km. Beach 1.2 km. Sailing 3.5 km. Golf 18 km.

Open: 1 April - 30 September.

Directions

Piriac-sur-Mer is 18 km. northwest of La Baule. On the N165 from Vannes, leave at exit 15 towards La Roche Bernard, turn left to join D774 towards La Baule. 8 km. after Herbignac, turn right on D52 to St Molt and Mesquer towards Piriac. Do not take the coast road but turn left on D52. Site signed in 3 km.
GPS: 47.38616, -2.51029

Charges guide

Per person	€ 3,00 - € 4,95
child (under 7 yrs)	€ 2,00 - € 3,30
pitch	€ 3,00 - € 4,95
electricity (3-10A)	€ 2,85 - € 4,25

camping caravaning ★★★★
Parc du Guibel
New water park in 2009
Rental of mobile homes and chalets, 450 pitches,
In an exceptional green area.
route de Kerdrien,
44420 Piriac sur Mer
Tél : 02 40 23 52 67 Fax : 02 40 15 50 24
Email : camping@parcduguibel.com
www.parcduguibel.com

Pornic

Camping le Patisseau

29 rue du Patisseau, F-44210 Pornic (Loire-Atlantique) T: **02 40 82 10 39**. E: **contact@lepatisseau.com**
alanrogers.com/FR44100

Le Patisseau is situated in the countryside just a short drive from the fishing village of Pornic. It is a relaxed site with a large number of mobile homes and chalets, and popular with young families and teenagers. The 120 touring pitches, all with electrical connections (6A), are divided between the attractive 'forest' area with plenty of shade from mature trees and the more open 'prairie' area. Some are on a slight slope and access to others might be tricky for larger units. A railway runs along the bottom half of the site with trains several times a day, (but none overnight) and the noise is minimal. The Morice family work very hard to maintain a friendly atmosphere.

Facilities

The modern heated toilet block is very spacious and well fitted. Good facilities for disabled visitors and babies. Laundry rooms. Shop and takeaway (1/7-3/9). Bar and restaurant (3/4-11/11). Indoor heated pool with sauna, jacuzzi and spa (all season). Small heated outdoor pools and water slides (1/6-3/9). Play area. Multisport court. Bicycle hire. Off site: Fishing and beach 2.5 km. Riding, golf, sailing and boat launching all 5 km.

Open: 3 April - 11 November.

Directions

Access to site is at junction of D751 Nantes - Pornic road with the D213 St Nazaire - Noirmoutier 'Route Bleue'. From north take exit for D751 Nantes. From south follow D751 Clion-sur-Mer. Avoid Pornic town centre. GPS: 47.118833, -2.072833

Charges guide

Per unit incl. 2 persons and electricity (6A)	€ 25,00 - € 39,00
extra person	€ 3,00 - € 7,00

Pornic

Camping de la Boutinardière

Rue de la Plage de la Boutinardière 23, F-44210 Pornic (Loire-Atlantique) T: **02 40 82 05 68**
E: **info@laboutinardiere.com** **alanrogers.com/FR44180**

This is truly a holiday site to suit all the family whatever their ages, just 200 m. from the beach. It has 250 individual good sized pitches, 100-120 sq.m. in size, many bordered by three-metre-high, well-maintained hedges for shade and privacy. All pitches have electricity available. It is a family owned site and English is spoken by the helpful, obliging reception staff. Beside reception is the excellent site shop and across the road is a complex of indoor and outdoor pools, paddling pool and a twin toboggan water slide. On site there are sports and entertainment areas. Facing the water complex, the bar, restaurant and terraces are new and serve excellent food, be it a snack or restaurant meal or perhaps a takeaway all season. This site is difficult to better in the South Brittany, Loire-Atlantique area. This campsite has it all – 2 km. from the beautiful harbour town of Pornic and 200 m. from the sea, together with the very best of amenities and facilities.

Facilities

Toilet facilities are in three good blocks, one large and centrally situated and two supporting blocks. Washbasins are in cabins. Laundry facilities. Shop. New complex of bar, restaurant, terraces. Three heated swimming pools, one indoor (all season), a paddling pool and water slides (15/5-22/9). Games room. Sports and activity area. Playground. Minigolf. Fitness equipment and sauna.
Off site: Sandy cove 200 m. Golf, riding, sea fishing, restaurants, cafés, fishing harbour, boat trips, sailing and windsurfing, all within 5 km.

Open: 3 April - 28 September.

Directions

From north or south on D213, take Nantes D751 exit. At roundabout (with McDonalds) take D13 signed Bemarie-en-Retz. After 4 km. site is signed to right. Note: do NOT exit from D213 at Pomic Ouest or Centre. GPS: 47.09150, -2.05133

Charges 2010

Per unit incl. 2 persons and electricity	€ 20,00 - € 43,00
extra person	€ 3,50 - € 8,00
child (under 8 yrs)	€ 2,50 - € 6,00
dog	€ 3,00 - € 5,00

Saint Brévin-les-Pins

485

Camping le Fief

57 chemin du Fief, F-44250 Saint Brévin-les-Pins (Loire-Atlantique) T: **02 40 27 23 86**

E: **camping@lefief.com** **alanrogers.com/FR44190**

If you are a family with young children or lively teenagers, this could be the campsite for you. Le Fief is a well established site only 800 m. from sandy beaches on the southern Brittany coast. It has a magnificent 'aqua park' with outdoor and covered swimming pools, paddling pools, slides, river rapids, fountains, jets and more. The site has 220 pitches for touring units (out of 413). Whilst these all have 5A electricity, they vary in size and many are worn and may be untidy. There are also 143 mobile homes and chalets to rent and 55 privately owned units. This is a lively site in high season with a variety of entertainment and organised activity for all ages. This ranges from a miniclub for 5-12 year olds, to 'Tonic Days' with aquagym, jogging and sports competitions, and to evening events which include karaoke, themed dinners and cabaret. There are plenty of sporting facilities for active youngsters.

Facilities

One excellent new toilet block and three others of a lower standard. Laundry facilities. Shop (15/5-15/9). Bar, restaurant and takeaway (15/4-15/9) with terrace overlooking the pool complex. Outdoor pools, etc. (15/5-15/9). Covered pool (all season). Play area. Tennis. Pétanque. Archery. Games room. Internet access. Organised entertainment and activities (July/Aug). Off site: Beach 800 m. Bicycle hire 800 m. Bus stop 1 km. Riding 1 km. Golf 15 km. Planète Sauvage safari park.

Open: 3 April - 3 October.

Directions

From the St Nazaire bridge take the fourth exit from the D213 signed St Brévin-l'Océan. Continue over first roundabout and bear right at the second to join Chemin du Fief. The site is on the right, well signed. GPS: 47.23486, -2.16757

Charges guide

Per unit incl. 2 persons and electricity	€ 22,00 - € 43,00
extra person	€ 5,00 - € 9,00
child (0-7 yrs)	€ 2,50 - € 4,50
dog	€ 2,00 - € 5,00

The Travel Service to book this site call 01580 214000 ...we'll arrange everything

Sainte Reine-de-Bretagne

Kawan Village du Deffay

B.P. 18 Le Deffay, Sainte Reine-de-Bretagne, F-44160 Pontchâteau (Loire-Atlantique)
T: **02 40 88 00 57** E: **campingdudeffay@wanadoo.fr** **alanrogers.com/FR44090**

A family managed site, Château du Deffay is a refreshing departure from the usual formula in that it is not over organised or supervised and has no tour operator units. The 142 good sized, fairly level pitches have pleasant views and are either on open grass, on shallow terraces divided by hedges, or informally arranged in a central, slightly sloping wooded area. Most have electricity. The facilities are located within the old courtyard area of the smaller château that dates from before 1400. A significant attraction of the site is the large, unfenced lake, well stocked for fishermen and with free pedaloes for children. The landscape is wonderfully natural and the site blends well with the rural environment of the estate, lake and farmland which surround it. Alpine type chalets overlook the lake and fit in well environmentally and the larger château (built 1880 and which now offers B&B) stands slightly away from the camping area but provides a wonderful backdrop for an evening stroll. The site is close to the Brière Regional Park, the Guérande Peninsula, and La Baule and is just 20 minutes drive from the nearest beach.

Facilities

The main toilet block is well maintained, if a little dated and is well equipped including washbasins in cabins, provision for disabled people and a baby bathroom. Laundry facilities. Shop, bar, small restaurant with takeaway (1/5-20/9). Covered and heated swimming pool (at 28 degrees when we visited) and paddling pool (all season). Play area. TV. Animation in season including miniclub. Torches useful. Off site: Golf 7 km and horse riding 10 km. Beach 25 km.

Open: 1 May - 30 September.

Directions

Site is signed from D33 Pontchâteau - Herbignac road near Sainte Reine. Also signed from the D773 and the N165-E60 (exit 13). GPS: 47.44106, -2.15981

Charges 2010

Per unit incl. 2 persons and electricity	€ 18,10 - € 27,80
extra person	€ 3,30 - € 5,50
child (2-12 yrs)	€ 2,30 - € 3,80

Camping Cheques accepted.

Saumur

Camping de Chantepie

Saint Hilaire-Saint Florent, F-49400 Saumur (Maine-et-Loire) T: **02 41 67 95 34**
E: **info@campingchantepie.com** **alanrogers.com/FR49020**

On arriving at Camping de Chantepie with its colourful, floral entrance, a friendly greeting awaits at reception, set beside a restored farmhouse. The site is owned by a charitable organisation which provides employment for local disabled people. Linked by gravel roads (which can be dusty), the 150 grass touring pitches are level and spacious, with some new larger ones (200 sq.m. at extra cost – state preference when booking). All pitches have electricity (6/10A) and are separated by low hedges of flowers and trees which offer some shade. This is a good site for families. A 'Sites et Paysages' member.

Facilities

The toilet block is clean and facilities are good with washbasins in cubicles, new showers (men and women separately) and facilities for disabled visitors. Laundry facilities. Baby area. Shop, bar, terraced café and takeaway (all 15/6-31/8). Covered and heated pool, outdoor pool and paddling pool. Play area with apparatus. Terraced minigolf, TV. Video games. Pony rides. Bicycle hire. Internet access. WiFi. Off site: Fishing 500 m. Golf, riding 2 km.

Open: 15 May - 15 September.

Directions

St Hilaire-St Florent is 2 km. west of Saumur. Take D751 (Gennes). Right at roundabout in St Hilaire-St Florent and on until Le Poitrineau and campsite sign, then turn left. Continue for 3 km. then turn right into site road. GPS: 47.29381, -0.14264

Charges guide

Per unit incl. 2 persons	€ 15,00 - € 29,00
extra person	€ 5,00 - € 7,00
electricity	€ 3,00

Saumur

Kawan Village Ile d'Offard

kawan VILLAGES www.kawan-villages.com

Rue de Verden, Ile d'Offard, F-49400 Saumur (Maine-et-Loire) T: **02 41 40 30 00**
E: **iledoffard@cvtloisirs.fr** **alanrogers.com/FR49080**

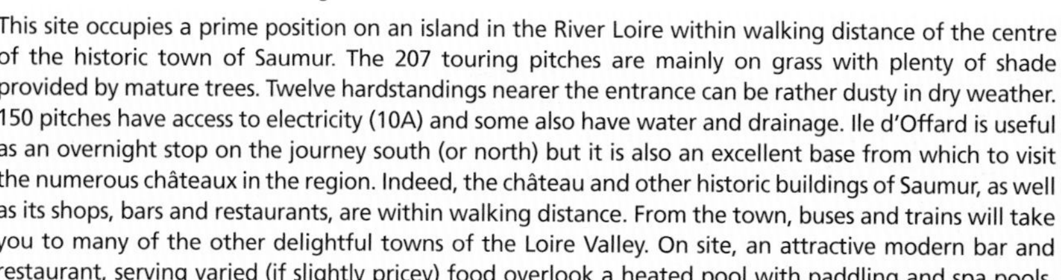

This site occupies a prime position on an island in the River Loire within walking distance of the centre of the historic town of Saumur. The 207 touring pitches are mainly on grass with plenty of shade provided by mature trees. Twelve hardstandings nearer the entrance can be rather dusty in dry weather. 150 pitches have access to electricity (10A) and some also have water and drainage. Ile d'Offard is useful as an overnight stop on the journey south (or north) but it is also an excellent base from which to visit the numerous châteaux in the region. Indeed, the château and other historic buildings of Saumur, as well as its shops, bars and restaurants, are within walking distance. From the town, buses and trains will take you to many of the other delightful towns of the Loire Valley. On site, an attractive modern bar and restaurant, serving varied (if slightly pricey) food overlook a heated pool with paddling and spa pools. Fishing is possible in the Loire and there is direct access from the site (permits are available from Saumur).

Facilities

Three unisex sanitary blocks, one heated in winter, include provision for disabled visitors. Block one has a well equipped laundry. The other blocks are only open in high season. These facilities are generally kept reasonably clean, but are fairly basic and lack finesse. Motorcaravan services. Restaurant and bar (1/5-30/9) with takeaway. Heated swimming, paddling and spa pools (15/4-30/9). Internet access and WiFi (charged). Play area. Some activities and a children's club, wine tastings, etc. in high season.
Off site: Thursday market 500 m. Saturday morning market 2 km. Beach on river, sailing and bicycle hire all 1 km. Golf and riding both 10 km.

Open: 1 March - 15 November.

Directions

From north and A85 exit 3, take D347 south (Saumur). After 2.5 km. go left at roundabout signed 'Saumur touristique'. Follow old road towards river and town. Cross bridge onto island and immediately go left at roundabout. Site is ahead in 1 km.
GPS: 47.25762, -0.06100

Charges guide

Per unit incl. 2 persons and electricity	€ 20,00 - € 30,50
extra person	€ 4,00 - € 5,00
child (5-10 yrs)	€ 2,00 - € 2,50

Camping Cheques accepted.

Sillé-le-Guillaume

Camping Indigo les Molières

Sillé Plage, F-72140 Sillé le Guillaume (Sarthe) T: **02 43 20 16 12**
E: **molieres@camping-indigo.com** **alanrogers.com/FR72040**

Les Molières is an attractive recent addition to the Indigo group. It can be found close to Sillé-le-Guillaume, around 30 km. north of Le Mans. There are 120 large shady pitches here. Most are equipped with electrical connections (10A). A large lake of 32 hectares is ideal for sailing and windsurfing, and the forested surrounds of the Parc Naturel Régional provide an excellent environment for cycling or walking. Swimming is popular from the large sandy beach. The Maison du Lac et de la Forêt is an interesting centre with a wealth of information about the area. In high season a little train trundles around the lake.

Facilities

Direct access to lake. Sailing. Fishing. Bicycle hire. Children's play area. Tourist information. Off site: Walking and cycling tracks. Le Mans 30 km.

Open: 30 April - 26 September.

Directions

From Le Mans head north on D338 and then D304 to Sillé-le-Guillaume. Then follow signs to the Parc Naturel Régional and site. GPS: 48.203383, 0.127667

Charges guide

Per unit incl. 2 persons and electricity	€ 11,50 - € 13,30
extra person	€ 2,00 - € 3,20

Camping Cheques accepted.

Sillé-le-Philippe

Castel Camping le Château de Chanteloup

F-72460 Sillé-le-Philippe (Sarthe) T: **02 43 27 51 07**. E: **chanteloup.souffront@wanadoo.fr**
alanrogers.com/FR72030

An attractive and peaceful site close to Le Mans, Chanteloup is situated in the park of a 19th century château in the heart of the Sarthe countryside. There are 100 pitches all with 6A electricity although long leads will be required in some places. Some are in the woods, many are around the edges of the lawns and completely open, and a few overlook the lake, so there are differing degrees of shade throughout the site. This lack of regimentation enhances the atmosphere and feeling of spaciousness in the grounds surrounding the old château.

Facilities

All sanitary facilities are in the château outbuildings and are well maintained and kept very clean. Washbasins are in cabins. Dishwashing and laundry facilities. Small shop, takeaway and restaurant with covered outdoor seating (all 5/7-24/8). Bar (all season). Swimming pool (all season). Play area (parental supervision essential). Games room, volleyball, table tennis. Mountain bike hire. Organised activities (high season). WiFi. Off site: Riding 7 km. Golf 10 km. Tennis club in Le Mans.

Open: 1 June - 31 August.

Directions

From the autoroute take exit 23, follow signs for Le Mans and Tours, then Le Mans and Savigné l'Evèque. Site is to the east just off main road and signed on southern edge of Sillé. GPS: 48.10586, 0.34108

Charges 2010

Per unit incl. 2 persons and electricity	€ 25,70 - € 39,90
extra person	€ 6,00 - € 10,30
child (under 7 yrs)	€ 3,80

Varennes-sur-Loire

Castel Camping l'Etang de la Brèche

5 impasse de la Breche (RN152), F-49730 Varennes-sur-Loire (Maine-et-Loire) T: **02 41 51 22 92**
E: **mail@etang-breche.com** **alanrogers.com/FR49010**

The Saint Cast family have developed l'Etang de la Brèche with care and attention. The site provides 116 large, level touring pitches with shade from trees and bushes. Less shaded areas are used for recreation. There are electrical connections to all pitches (some long cable may be required), with water and drainage on 63 of them. The restaurant, bar and terrace, also open to the public, provides a social base and is popular with British visitors. The pool complex includes one with a removable cover, one outdoor, and one for toddlers. The site is situated on a 25-hectare estate 4 km. northeast of Saumur on the edge of the Loire behind the dykes.

Facilities

Three toilet blocks, modernised to good standards, include facilities for babies with two units for people with disabilities. Washing up sinks and laundry. Shop and epicerie. Restaurant, pizzeria and takeaway. Heated swimming pools. Tennis. Multisport pitch. Go-karts. Minigolf. Bicycle hire. General room, games and TV rooms. Internet point. Varied sporting and entertainment programme (10/7-25/8). Pony riding. Child minding is arranged in afternoons. Torch useful. Off site: Golf 7 km.

Open: 30 April - 15 September.

Directions

Site is 100 m. north off the main N152, about 4 km. northeast of Saumur on the north bank of the Loire. GPS: 47.24731, -0.00048

Charges guide

Per unit incl. 2 persons and electricity	€ 16,00 - € 39,00
extra person	€ 5,00 - € 8,00
child (4-10 yrs)	€ 3,00 - € 4,00

7th night free in low season.

It's not only the fine beaches that make this holiday region so appealing – sleepy fishing harbours, historic ports and charming towns all create a great holiday atmosphere.

DÉPARTEMENT: VENDÉE

MAJOR CITY: LA ROCHE-SUR-YONNE

Because of its importance as a holiday destination for British visitors to France we have decided in this guide to list the Vendée department as a region in its own right. Administratively the department lies in the region of Pays de la Loire.

With a sunshine record to rival the south of France, the Vendée is among the most popular areas in France. Visitors flock to the region to enjoy the exceptionally mild climate and 160 km. stretch of gently shelving, mostly sandy beaches. Popular resorts in the Vendée include Les Sables d'Ollone, La Tranche-sur-Mer, and St Jean-de-Monts. Explore the coasts for traditional fishing villages or head inland for fields of sunflowers and unspoilt rural villages.

The Vendée was the centre of the counter-revolutionary movement between 1793 and 1799 and a 'son et lumière' held at Le Puy-du-Fou tells the whole story. Les Sables d'Olonne is its main resort renowned for its excellent sandy beach. The area between the Vendée and Charente, the Marais Poitevin, is one of the most unusual in France – a vast tract of marshland with a thousand or more tree-lined canals and slow moving streams.

Places of interest

L'Aiguillon-sur-Mer: The Vendéan mussel-growing capital, famous for its shellfish, marsh, and sea.

Apremont: picturesque village which seems to cling to the rocky sides of the valley of Vie; Renaissance castle and a lake (largest lake in the Vendée) with a sandy beach.

Île-d'Yeu: an hour by boat off the coast where time is believed to have stood still. Colourful shops and bars line the main town. Bicycles and cars for hire.

Jard-sur-Mer: Abbey of Lieu-Dieu (financed by Richard the Lionheart), seaside with attractive, colourful houses.

Le Puy-du-Fou: 15-16th-century castle, sound-and-light show involving over 700 participants.

Les Sables-d'Olonne: the start and finish line of the grand Vendée Globe; arts and crafts shops.

Cuisine of the region

Locally-produced meat and poultry include Charolais beef, salt-marsh lamb, duck from Challans and foie gras. Seafood includes sole sablaise, cooked with lemon, barbecued sardines from Saint Gilles Croix-de-Vie, baked white tuna or mussels from the Baie de l'Aiguillon cooked in white wine.

Samphire: a herb that grows on the edges of the salt marshes.

Bonnottes: potatoes with the taste of hazelnuts, served for a few days each year in France's best restaurants.

www.vendee-toursime.com/en
info@vendee-tourisme.com
(0)2 51 47 88 20

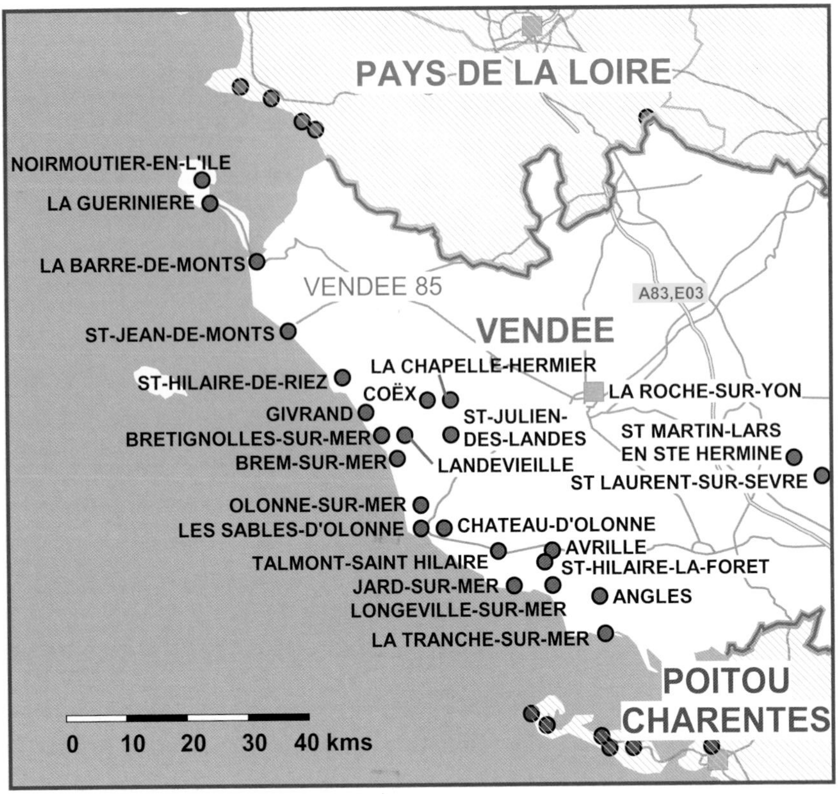

PAYS DE LA LOIRE
NOIRMOUTIER-EN-L'ILE
LA GUERINIERE
LA BARRE-DE-MONTS
VENDEE 85
A83,E03
VENDEE
ST-JEAN-DE-MONTS
LA CHAPELLE-HERMIER
ST-HILAIRE-DE-RIEZ
COËX
LA ROCHE-SUR-YON
GIVRAND
ST-JULIEN-DES-LANDES
ST MARTIN-LARS EN STE HERMINE
BRETIGNOLLES-SUR-MER
BREM-SUR-MER
LANDEVIEILLE
ST LAURENT-SUR-SEVRE
OLONNE-SUR-MER
LES SABLES-D'OLONNE
CHATEAU-D'OLONNE
AVRILLE
TALMONT-SAINT HILAIRE
ST-HILAIRE-LA-FORET
JARD-SUR-MER
ANGLES
LONGEVILLE-SUR-MER
LA TRANCHE-SUR-MER
POITOU CHARENTES
0 10 20 30 40 kms

Angles

Camping le Clos Cottet

Route de la Tranche-sur-Mer, F-85750 Angles (Vendée) T: **02 51 28 90 72**
E: **contact@camping-clos-cottet.com** **alanrogers.com/FR85950**

Le Clos Cottet is an attractive family site, based around an old Vendéen farm. There are 196 pitches here, all of which have reasonable shade. Many of them are occupied by mobile homes and chalets. During the high season (July and August) a free shuttle bus service runs to the nearest beach (6 km). On site, however, there is a fine swimming pool complex with a large outdoor pool with water slides, as well as a heated indoor pool. This complex also contains a sauna and Turkish bath, and a popular aquagym.

Facilities

Shop. Bar. Snack bar. Pool complex with outdoor and covered pools. Water slides. Children's pool. Sauna. Play area. Sports field. Activity and entertainment programme. Mobile homes and chalets for rent. Off site: Angles village centre 1.5 km. Nearest beach 6 km. Les Sables d'Olonne. Cycle and walking tracks.

Open: 4 April - 19 September.

Directions

Leave La Roche-sur-Yon on D747 (towards La Tranche-sur-Mer). Pass Moutiers-les-Mauxfaits then continue to Angles. Site is well signed from the village.
GPS: 46.39239, -1.40365

Charges guide

Per unit incl. 2 persons and electricity	€ 16,00 - € 28,00
extra person	€ 2,50 - € 5,00

Avrillé

Castel Camping Domaine des Forges

Rue des Forges, F-85440 Avrillé (Vendée) T: **02 51 22 38 85**. E: **contact@campingdomainedesforges.com**
alanrogers.com/FR85930

Le Domaine des Forges has recently been acquired by Cathy and Thierry Pacteau. They already have experience in owning a caravan site and it is their intention to create a prestige site with the highest quality of services. Arranged in the beautiful grounds of a 16th-century manor house, the pitches are generous in size (170-300 sq.m) and fully serviced including 32A electricity, internet access and cable TV. At present 140 pitches are ready with a further 155 to be developed over the next few years. The owners' aim is to eventually develop a residential site and there are already mobile homes and chalets on site for viewing. Plans for the future include an indoor pool, gym, bar and games room. An area of hardstanding pitches for motorcaravans is also planned.

Facilities

Two toilet blocks with facilities for disabled visitors and babies. Laundry facilities. Takeaway (1/7-31/8). Outdoor pool (heated 1/7-31/8). Tennis. Minigolf. Fishing lake.
Off site: Village 400 m. Les Sables d'Olonne 25 km. Vendée beaches 8 km.

Open: All year.

Directions

Travel south from La Roche-sur-Yon on the D747 for about 21 km. At the D19, turn right for Avrille (about 6 km). At junction with the D949 turn right and first right again into rue des Forges. Site at the end of the road. GPS: 46.47609, -1.49454

Charges guide

Per unit incl. 2 persons, electricity, water and drainage	€ 16,00 - € 26,00
extra person	€ 2,00 - € 6,00
child (2-6 yrs)	free - € 4,00
animal	€ 3,00

Brem-sur-Mer

Camping l'Océan

Rue des Gabelous, F-85470 Brem-sur-Mer (Vendée) T: **02 51 90 59 16**. E: **contact@campingdelocean.fr**
alanrogers.com/FR85110

Set amongst grapevines and fir trees, Camping l'Océan is situated between the fishing port of St Gilles Croix-de-Ville and Brem-sur-Mer, only 600 metres (15 minutes' walk) from beautiful sandy beaches and the clear Atlantic Ocean. The campsite is family managed (Helen is English) and a very warm welcome awaits at the reception area which is well stocked with local information. The touring pitches are an average of 100 sq.m. in size and have 6A French style electric hook-ups (some require long leads). They are divided by hedges and are centrally located in the campsite with mobile homes to rent on either side.

Facilities

Three old style but very clean unisex toilet blocks have free preset showers, British style WCs, and washbasins in cubicles. Separate toilet and shower for people with disabilities. Shop (July/Aug). Bar and restaurant (weekends only May, June, Sept). Swimming pool (heated 15/6-30/8) with slide. Indoor pool (15/4-30/9). Fitness room. Bicycle hire. Playground in two areas (ages 2-6 yrs and 6-12yrs). Organised activities. Children's club. Off site: Brem-sur-Mer 15 minutes' walk. Supermarket 5 minute drive. Fishing 1 km. Riding 9 km. Golf 15 km.

Open: 1 April - 15 October.

Directions

Take N160 from La Roche-sur-Yon towards Les Sables d'Olonne. Take exit for La Mothe-Achard and Bretignolles-sur-Mer. Follow D54 to Brem-sur-Mer then D38 Bretignolles-sur-Mer. Site is signed on left before Activity Centre. GPS: 40.601654, -1.84404

Charges guide

Per unit incl. 2 persons	€ 13,20 - € 19,00
incl. electricity (6A)	€ 15,80 - € 22,00
extra person	€ 3,50 - € 4,50
child (0-7 yrs)	€ 2,30 - € 2,90

Brem-sur-Mer

Camping Caravaning le Chaponnet

Rue du Chaponnet (N16), F-85470 Brem-sur-Mer (Vendée) T: **02 51 90 55 56**
E: **campingchaponnet@wanadoo.fr** **alanrogers.com/FR85480**

This well established family run site is within five minutes' walk of Brem village and 1.5 km. from a sandy beach. The 80 touring pitches are level with varying amounts of grass, some with shade from mature trees. Pitches are separated by tall hedges and serviced by tarmac or gravel roads and have frequent water and electricity points (long leads may be required). Tour operators have mobile homes and tents on 70 pitches and there are 55 privately-owned mobile homes and chalets. The swimming pool complex also has a jacuzzi, slides and a children's pool, together with a sauna and fitness centre. It is overlooked by the spacious bar and snack bar. Entertainment is provided for all ages by day and three or four musical evenings a week provide family fun rather than teenage activities.

Facilities

The five sanitary blocks are well maintained with washbasins in cubicles, some showers and basins have controllable water temperature. Facilities for babies and disabled people. Laundry facilities. Bar, snack bar and takeaway (all 1/6-31/8). Indoor (heated) and outdoor pools. Waterslide, jacuzzi and sauna. Play area with space for ball games. Tennis. Bicycle hire. Indoor games room. Off site: Shops 200 m. Beach 1.5 km. Fishing 2 km. Golf 12 km. Riding 10 km.

Open: 1 May - 30 September.

Directions

Brem is on the D38 St Gilles - Les Sables d'Olonne road. Site is clearly signed, just off the one-way system in centre of village. GPS: 46.60433, -1.83244

Charges 2010

Per unit incl. 2 persons and electricity	€ 21,10 - € 29,70
extra person	€ 4,60 - € 6,20
child (under 5 yrs)	€ 2,70 - € 3,80
dog	€ 5,00

Bretignolles-sur-Mer

Chadotel Camping la Trévillière

Rue de Bellevue, F-85470 Bretignolles-sur-Mer (Vendée) T: **02 51 90 09 65**. E: **info@chadotel.com**
alanrogers.com/FR85310

A member of the Chadotel group, La Trévillière has a pleasant semi-rural setting on the edge of the little resort town of Bretignolles. After an extension, there are now 200 pitches (90 for tourers with electricity 6/10A)), all with easy access to electricity and water. The original area provides either level or slightly sloping pitches separated by hedges or low bushes either with shade or more open. The new area has no shade as yet. Although just 2 km. from the nearest beach and less than 5 km. from the Plage des Dunes (one of southern Vendée's best beaches), La Trévillière has a more 'laid-back' feel than many other sites in the area, particularly in low season.

Facilities

Three modern, clean toilet blocks include washbasins in cubicles, a unit for disabled people and baby room with bath, shower and toilet. Washing machines and dryers. Bar (limited opening in low season). Small shop and snack bar with takeaway (1/6-10/9). Restaurant. Covered pool with slide and paddling pool. Play area. Minigolf. No charcoal barbecues. Off site: Bus service town. Beach 2 km. Fishing 3 km. Riding 5 km. Golf 10 km.

Open: 3 April - 25 September.

Directions

From north, after St Gilles go through Bretignolles-La Sauzaie (left fork) and before reaching Bretignolles turn left on sharp right hand bend, heading for water tower. Site on right in 800 m. From south, after Bretignolles, turn right (sign Ecoles), then left. Site signed to left after stadium. GPS: 46.63632, -1.85844

Charges 2010

Per unit incl. 2 persons and electricity	€ 15,40 - € 29,50

Château-d'Olonne

Camping les Fosses Rouges

8 rue des Fosses Rouges, F-85180 Château-d'Olonne (Vendée) T: **02 51 95 17 95**
E: **info@camping-lesfossesrouges.com** **alanrogers.com/FR85860**

A family run site, Les Fosses Rouges was created in 1968 on the fields owned by the present owner's grandfather. Since it was built, the site has been surrounded by urban development, but nevertheless it is still a good value and well presented, if compact, site. There are 205 well hedged pitches of small to average size, most with some shade and electricity (10A). Some 45 are used for mobile homes, both private and to rent. There are also some seasonal or long stay tourers. There is a good swimming pool and a separate sports and games area. The site offers some low key entertainment in the main season. Nearby are the zoo and seashell museum at Les Sables d'Olonne, the fascinating salt pans and the museum of modern art at the Abbaye Sainte-Croix.

Facilities

Four colourful toilet blocks in traditional style are evenly distributed around the site. Washbasins in cubicles for ladies, push button showers. Facilities for disabled people. Washing machine at two blocks. Bar and takeaway (1/7-31/8). Shop (15/5-30/9). Motorcaravan service point. Swimming pool (heated, open all season and covered when necessary). Playground. Tennis. Minigolf. Open air stage for animation. Internet access (July/Aug). Communal barbecue areas. Off site: ATM at supermarket 1 km. Fishing 1 km. Golf and riding 4 km. Boat launching 5 km.

Open: 8 April - 30 September.

Directions

Site is southeast of Les Sables d'Olonne between the D949 and the sea. From large roundabout by supermarket on D949 turn towards sea on Avenue Dugay Trouin (signed La Pironnière). Continue straight on at mini-roundabout and in 150 m. turn left into rue des Fosses Rouges to site in 500 m.
GPS: 46.47932, -1.74123

Charges guide

Per unit incl. 2 persons and electricity	€ 16,00 - € 19,60
extra person	€ 2,80 - € 3,60
child (under 7 yrs)	€ 1,40 - € 1,80
dog	free - € 1,60

Château d'Olonne

Camping le Bel Air

6 chemin de Bel Air, F-85180 Château d'Olonne (Vendée) T: **02 51 22 09 67**. E: **camping.belair@wanadoo.fr**
alanrogers.com/FR85710

Le Bel Air is a well established site close to the Vendée's largest resort, Les Sables d'Olonne. This is a very well equipped site with a new and impressive pool complex being the focal point. This complex comprises a large covered pool and separate outdoor pool. Both have water slides and the indoor complex also has a sauna, lazy river, spa bath and a fully equipped gym, amongst other features. There are 305 pitches here of which around 70 are available for touring units. The rest are occupied by mobile homes and chalets (available for rent). Pitches are grassy and all have electrical connections.

Facilities

Bar. Snack bar. Takeaway. Shop. TV room. Swimming pool complex. Indoor pool. Multisports terrain. Playground. Mobile homes and chalets for rent. Off site: Nearest beach 2.5 km. Les Sables d'Olonne 2 km. (shops, cafés and restaurants). Motor museum at Talmont-St Hilaire.

Open: 15 March - 15 November.

Directions

Approaching from the north (D160), follow signs to Les Sables d'Olonne and then Talmont-St Hilaire on D949. Site is well signed when you reach Château d'Olonne. GPS: 46.47207, -1.72646

Charges guide

Per unit incl. 2 persons and electricity	€ 18,00 - € 29,00
extra person	€ 2,50 - € 4,50

Coëx

RCN Camping la Ferme du Latois

F-85220 Coëx (Vendée) T: **02 51 54 67 30**. E: **info@rcn-lafermedulatois.fr**
alanrogers.com/FR85770

Until recently a simple 'Camping à la ferme', this site is being developed by RCN, the Dutch organisation that now owns it, into an extensive and very well equipped campsite. Naturally a very high proportion of its clientele is Dutch, but the owners are keen to attract more British visitors. Located on the far side of two attractive fishing lakes, the original, very spacious pitches are attractively laid out with plenty of grass, hedges and mature trees. The new ones on the near side of the lakes are equally spacious but here the grass, bushes and trees have yet to start growing.

Facilities

Two modern sanitary blocks built in traditional style have excellent toilets, showers and washbasins in cubicles. Good facilities for disabled visitors. Attractively tiled areas for babies and children, with special toilets, basins and showers. Laundry room ('buanderie'). Small shop. Bar counter with terrace. All facilities available all season. Play area. Bicycle hire. Fishing. Off site: Golf and riding 3 km. Beach, sailing, boat launching 12 km.

Open: 14 April - 6 October.

Directions

Coëx is 29 km. west of La Roche-sur-Yon via the D938 to Aizenay, then the D6 St Gilles Croix-de-Vie road. Site is south of the village just off the D40 (La Chaize-Giraud - Brem-sur-Mer) and is clearly signed. GPS: 46.677033, -1.76885

Charges guide

Per unit incl. 2 persons, electricity and water	€ 18,00 - € 45,50
incl. 6 persons	€ 39,20 - € 51,00

Givrand

Camping les Dauphins Bleus

16 rue du Rocher, F-85800 Givrand (Vendée) T: **02 51 55 59 34**. E: **dauphins-bleus@franceloc.fr**
alanrogers.com/FR85810

In a rural setting on the edge of the village and only 2 km. from the sea, this large site has 320 pitches, most taken by mobile homes and chalets for rent. There are just 12 level, grassy, touring pitches, generally small and of odd shapes, and suitable only for small units, tents and camper vans. These are scattered around the site between the rental units. The site is served by two large toilet blocks, one centrally located the other at one end of site and nearest to most of the entertainment and sports areas. The site offers an excellent pool complex and many sporting opportunities.

Facilities

Two modern toilet blocks with washbasins in cubicles, and compact showers. Facilities for babies. Units for campers with disabilities. Launderette with washing machines and dryers. Shop. Bar with TV (April-Sept) and takeaway (May-Sept). Heated pool (May-Sept). Indoor pool (April-Sept). Gym. Tennis. Pétanque. Multisport court. Playground. Bicycle hire. 'Pluto Club' for children, organised activities and evening entertainment July/Aug. Only gas barbecues permitted. Off site: Beach 2 km. Supermarket, ATM 2 km.

Open: 31 March - 29 September.

Directions

From D38 south of St Gilles Croix-de-Vie, turn east on D42 to Givrand where site is well signed to the left. GPS: 46.67299, -1.89494

Charges guide

Per unit incl. 2 persons	€ 11,00 - € 21,00
extra person	€ 5,00 - € 6,00
child (2-7 yrs)	€ 3,50 - € 4,50
electricity (6A)	€ 3,70

Jard-sur-Mer

Camping les Ecureuils

Route des Goffineaux, F-85520 Jard-sur-Mer (Vendée) T: **02 51 33 42 74**. E: **contact@camping-ecureuils.com**
alanrogers.com/FR85210

Les Ecureuils is a wooded site in a quieter part of the southern Vendée. It is undoubtedly one of the prettiest sites on this stretch of coast, with an elegant reception area, attractive vegetation and large pitches separated by low hedges with plenty of shade. Of the 261 pitches, some 128 are for touring units, each with water and drainage, as well as easy access to 10A electricity. This site is popular with tour operators (54 pitches). Jard is rated among the most pleasant and least hectic of Vendée towns. The harbour is home to some fishing boats and rather more pleasure craft.

Facilities

Two toilet blocks, well equipped and kept very clean, include baby baths, and laundry rooms. Small shop (bread baked on site). Snack bar and takeaway (1/6-15/9). Bar with snacks and ice creams. Good sized L-shaped swimming pool and separate paddling pool (30/5-15/9). Indoor pool and fitness centre (all season). Two play areas for different age groups. Minigolf. Club for children (5-10 yrs, July/Aug). Bicycle hire. Internet access. Only gas barbecues are allowed. Dogs are not accepted. Off site: Beach, fishing 400 m. Marina and town.

Open: 4 April - 26 September.

Directions

From Les Sables d'Olonne take the N949 towards Talmont-St Hilaire. Keep right in the centre (D21 towards Jard). From la Roche-sur-Yon follow the D474 and the D49 towards Jard-sur-Mer. From the village follow the signs 'Autre campings' or Camping les Ecureuils. Site is on the left. GPS: 46.4113, -1.5896

Charges guide

Per unit incl. 2 persons, electricity, water and drainage	€ 23,00 - € 30,00
extra person	€ 5,00 - € 6,90
child (0-9 yrs)	€ 1,50 - € 4,00

Jard-sur-Mer

Chadotel Camping l'Océano d'Or

58 rue Georges Clémenceau, B.P. 12, F-85520 Jard-sur-Mer (Vendée) T: **02 51 33 05 05**
E: **info@chadotel.com** **alanrogers.com/FR85270**

This site should appeal to families with children of all ages. It is very lively in high season but appears to be well managed, with a full programme of activities (it can therefore be noisy, sometimes late at night). The site is only 1 km. from the excellent beach. There are 430 flat, grass and sand pitches of which 40% are occupied by tour operators and mobile homes. The 260 for touring units, all with 6A electricity, are quite large (about 100 sq.m). Some are separated by high hedges, others are more open with low bushes between them.

Facilities

Four rather dated, unisex toilet blocks include washbasins all in cabins (cleaning variable). Dishwashing and laundry facilities. Shop (1/6-10/9). Bar and snack bar (1/6-10/9). Swimming pool (heated 20/5-20/9). Walled (three sides) play area.Tennis. Pétanque. Minigolf. Electric barbecues are not allowed. Off site: Excellent beach within walking distance. Golf, riding and karting within 15 km.

Open: 3 April - 25 September.

Directions

Site is on the D21 Talmont-St Hilaire - Longeville-sur-Mer, just east of the turning to the town centre. GPS: 46.42075, -1.5694

Charges 2010

Per unit incl. 2 persons and electricity	€ 15,40 - € 29,90

La Barre-de-Monts

Campéole

Campéole la Grande Côte

Route de la Grande Côte, F-85550 La Barre-de-Monts (Vendée) T: **02 51 68 51 89**
E: **nadine.ferran@atciat.com** **alanrogers.com/FR85840**

A site that lives up to its name, this one is very large, with 727 pitches. However, 245 are occupied by Bengali tents to rent, 60 by private caravans and 29 by tour operators. There are still 394 numbered touring pitches in rows, all with 10A electricity and spread over undulating sand dunes with sparse grass under pine trees. The site is served by eight fairly modern and fairly well maintained toilet blocks around the site. Some of the terraced pitches at the rear of the site have views of the impressive bridge onto the Ile de Noirmoutier, and there is direct access to a sandy beach via a gate. Also on site is an outdoor heated swimming pool. In July and August, the site offers clubs for children of all ages whilst adults can enjoy themed tapas, karaoke, cabaret and aquagym. In high season this site is very busy, but in low season it is quiet with only the pool and the playground open. Footpaths lead from the site to Fromentine where there are shops and services plus the historic 19th-century Estacade and an old lighthouse. You can also buy oysters and other seafood.

Facilities

Eight toilet blocks, all of a similar design, include some washbasins in cubicles, seatless toilets, baby bath, and a good unit for disabled campers. One laundry room. Outdoor swimming pool (15/5-30/9). Shop for bread and basics. Bar and takeaway (1/7- 31/8). Playgrounds, trampoline and bouncy castle. Entertainment and clubs for children (1/7-31/8). Multisports court. Boules. Bicycle hire. No charcoal barbecues. Supplement for double-axle caravans. Off site: Fishing, sailing 50 m. Golf 15 km. Riding 2 km. Boat launching 25 km. Ecomuseum du Oaviaud.

Open: 31 March - 16 September.

Directions

From the north via Bourgneuf-en-Retz take D758 to Beauvoir-sur-Mer, then D22 to La Barre-de-Monts. Continue ignoring road to Fromentine. At town boundary turn right on D38, signed Île de Noirmoutier. In 500 m, straight on at roundabout for 1 km. then right signed Grand Côte and Fromentine. Take next left for 1 km. to site. GPS: 46.8858, -2.1477

Charges guide

Per unit incl. 2 persons	€ 13,00 - € 20,30
extra person	€ 4,50 - € 6,40
electricity (10A)	€ 4,00

La Chapelle-Hermier

Camping le Pin Parasol

Lac du Jaunay, F-85220 La Chapelle-Hermier (Vendée) T: **02 51 34 64 72**. E: **contact@campingpinparasol.fr**
alanrogers.com/FR85680

Tucked away in the Vendée countryside yet just 15 minutes' drive from the beach, the site enjoys a pleasant rural setting above the Lac du Jaunay, well away from the bustle of the coast. There are 284 good sized touring pitches, all with electricity (6A) and 22 with water tap and drainage. The established pitches have some shade, others are in the open with hedges and trees yet to mature. The enthusiastic family owners are very hands-on and the facilities are of a high standard, most notably the pool area with its well constructed new indoor pool, jacuzzi, steam room and fitness suite.

Facilities

Four fully equipped toilet blocks include facilities for babies and disabled visitors. Block in new area can be under some pressure at busy times but you can always walk to the next block! Washing machines and dryers. Shop. Restaurant and bar with terrace. Takeaway. (July/Aug). Heated outdoor pool with paddling pool and slides (15/6-15/9). Indoor pool. Play area. Multisport pitch. Boules. Bicycle hire. Fishing. Tennis. Internet boxes for hire. Off site: Beaches and sailing, 12 km.

Open: 24 April - 26 September.

Directions

La Chapelle-Hermier is 26 km. west of La Roche-sur-Yon. Site is to the south of the D42 La Chapelle-Hermier - l'Aiguillon-sur-Vie road, 2 km. east of the junction with the D40 Co'x-La Chaize - Giraud road and is well signed. GPS: 46.66622, -1.75528

Charges guide

Per unit incl. 2 persons and electricity	€ 12,50 - € 28,00
extra person	€3,00 - € 6,50

La Guérinière

Camping le Caravan'ile

B.P. 4, la Guérinière, F-85680 Ile de Noirmoutier (Vendée) T: **02 51 39 50 29**. E: **contact@caravanile.com**
alanrogers.com/FR85620

This well-appointed, family-run site on the island of Noirmoutier has direct access to the dunes and an extensive sandy beach. It offers heated indoor and outdoor swimming pools with a paddling pool and flume, a sauna, steam room, jacuzzi and mini gym and a variety of entertainment in high season. Most of the 103 level touring pitches are near the beach (shielded by the dune). All have electricity (5A) and are separated by bushes and occasional maturing trees providing a little shade. The site has a very French ambience, with no tour operators, although there are 90 mobile homes for rent and many more privately owned.

Facilities

Three very clean sanitary blocks, each with showers, some washbasins in cabins and facilities for disabled people (showers are closed overnight). Laundry. Small supermarket at entrance (1/4-15/9). Bar, snack bar and takeaway (1/4-15/9). Indoor pool (all season) and outdoor pools (15/5-15/9; heated July/Aug). Games and sports area. Games room. Off site: Restaurant, bicycle hire, boat launching and minigolf all close by. Sailing 2 km. Riding 5 km. Golf 20 km.

Open: 1 March - 15 November.

Directions

The Ile de Noirmoutier is 70 km. southwest of Nantes. Take D38 road from the mainland, cross bridge to island and continue to fourth roundabout. Take exit for La Guérinière and immediately turn left to site. GPS: 46.96633, -2.21743

Charges guide

Per unit incl. 2 persons	€ 11,80 - € 18,70
incl. 5A electricity	€ 13,80 - € 22,00
extra person	€ 2,00 - € 4,60

La Tranche-sur-Mer

Camping Baie d'Aunis

10 rue du Pertuis Breton, F-85360 La Tranche-sur-Mer (Vendée) T: **02 51 27 47 36**
E: **info@camping-baiedaunis.com** **alanrogers.com/FR85870**

This very popular site has direct access to a sandy beach through a pedestrian gate (with key code) and across a car park. The town centre is also only 500 m. away. Shady and level, there are 150 individual pitches, all with electricity (10A). A good number of pitches are on a gravel base and a few are suitable only for smaller units. There are chalets and mobile homes (19) to rent. On site amenities include a heated swimming pool and a good restaurant and bar. This is a popular seaside resort with 13 km. of good quality sandy beaches. All have first aid posts, lifeguards in season and dogs are forbidden on the sands. From the pier by the Centre Nautique, just 50 m. from the site's rear pedestrian gate, you can catch ferries to the islands of Aix and Ré and to the larger resort of La Rochelle across the bay. You can also learn to fly or take pleasure flights from the aerodrome behind the town.

Facilities

The main sanitary unit is large, good quality and very well appointed. A smaller simpler unit is at the far end of the site. British style WCs, washbasins in cubicles, provision for babies and disabled campers. Laundry room at each block. Motorcaravan service point. Bar/restaurant and takeaway (1/5-10/9, w/ends only in low season). Outdoor swimming pool (10 x 20 m; heated May - Sept). Playground. TV room. Dogs and other animals are not accepted July/Aug.
Off site: La Tranche is a major sailboarding centre, with teaching facilities in a special lagoon, plus a surf school. Beach, bicycle hire, sea fishing all within 50 m. Town centre 500 m. Golf 38 km. Riding 12 km. Boat launching 100 m.

Open: 30 April - 19 September.

Directions

La Tranche-sur-Mer is 35 km. south of La Roche-sur-Yon. From La Roche-sur-Yon take 0747 to La Tranche. At roundabout (D747 and D1046) carry straight on to next roundabout and turn right towards town centre. At next (new) roundabout continue straight on to site on left (well signed). GPS: 46.34638, -1.43184

Charges guide

Per unit incl. 2 persons and electricity	€ 23,30 - € 31,00
extra person	€ 5,35 - € 6,35
child (under 5 yrs)	€ 3,25 - € 3,55
dog (not 1/7-31/8)	€ 2,20

La Tranche-sur-Mer

Camping du Jard

123 Mal de Lattre de Tassigny, F-85360 La Tranche-sur-Mer (Vendée) T: **02 51 27 43 79**
E: **info@campingdujard.fr** **alanrogers.com/FR85020**

Camping du Jard is a well maintained site between La Rochelle and Les Sables d'Olonne. First impressions are good, with a friendly welcome from M. Marton or his staff. The 242 touring pitches are level and grassy, hedged on two sides by bushes. The smallest are 100 sq.m. (the majority larger) and most are equipped with electricity, half with water and drainage. It is a comparatively new site, but the large variety of trees are beginning to provide a little shade. An impressive pool complex has a toboggan, paddling pool and an indoor pool with jacuzzi. The site is 700 m. from a sandy beach with many shops and restaurants nearby.

Facilities

Three toilet blocks with facilities for babies and disabled people and most washbasins are in cabins. Laundry facilities. Shop (1/6-10/9), restaurant and bar (25/5-10/9). Heated pool with toboggan and paddling pool, plus heated indoor pool with jacuzzi (no Bermuda-style shorts in pools). Sauna, solarium and fitness room. Tennis. Minigolf. Bicycle hire. Play area, games and TV rooms. Internet access. American motorhomes are not accepted. Pets not accepted.

Open: 26 April - 15 September.

Directions

Site is east of La Tranche-sur-Mer on D46. From D747 (La Roche-sur-Yon - La Tranche) follow signs (La Faute-sur-Mer) along bypass. Take exit for La Grière and then turn east to site. GPS: 46.34836, -1.38738

Charges 2010

Per unit incl. 2 persons and electricity	€ 22,40 - € 31,00
extra person	€ 3,00 - € 5,50

Landevieille

Camping Pong

Rue du Stade, F-85220 Landevieille (Vendée) T: **02 51 22 92 63**. E: **info@lepong.com**
alanrogers.com/FR85130

A comfortable family run site, in a rural situation 12 km. southeast of St Gilles Croix-de-Vie, and 5 km. from the coast at Brétignolles. It has 229 pitches with 187 used for touring units, the remainder for mobile homes and chalets. All have electricity connections (4/6A) and are of a good size. The bar, restaurant, function room, games room, gym and shop have all recently been rebuilt. The original part of the site around the small, lightly fenced fishing lake (there are warning signs) has mature trees, whereas, in the newer areas trees and shrubs are developing well.

Facilities

Four modern, unisex sanitary blocks provide toilets of mixed styles and some washbasins in cabins. Facilities for disabled people, baby room, dishwashing and laundry room. Shop, takeaway, bar and restaurant (15/6-15/9). Swimming pools including heated pool with jacuzzi, toboggan and paddling pool (from 15/5). Gym, TV lounge and games room. Bicycle hire. Fishing. Fenced play area and children's club. Off site: Tennis 200 m. Lac du Jaunay 2.5 km. Beach, golf, riding 5 km.

Open: 1 April - 15 September.

Directions

Site is on the edge of Landevieille and is signed from the D32 (Challans - Les Sables d'Olonne) and D12 (La Mothe Achard - St Gilles Croix-de-Vie).
GPS: 46.64231, -1.79935

Charges guide

Per unit incl. 2 persons and electricity	€ 15,00 - € 24,00
extra person	€ 2,50 - € 4,90
water and drainage	€ 1,70
dog	€ 1,80 - € 2,50

Les Sables-d'Olonne

Chadotel Camping les Roses

Rue des Roses, F-85100 Les Sables-d'Olonne (Vendée) T: **02 51 33 05 05**. E: **info@chadotel.com**
alanrogers.com/FR85450

Les Roses has an urban location, with the town centre and lovely beach just a short walk away. It has an informal air with the 200 pitches arranged interestingly on a knoll. Mature trees give good shade to some areas. There are 100 touring pitches of varying size, many being more suitable for tents than caravans. All pitches have access to electricity (10A) and water (long cables may be needed). In high season caravanners might find site access tricky at times due to overloaded town centre traffic systems. The site has 100 mobile homes and chalets, but no tour operators.

Facilities

Three well maintained toilet blocks have washbasins in cubicles, unit for disabled visitors, baby room, washing machines and dryers. Simple bar and takeaway (15/5-15/9). Simple shop. Small, attractively laid out, heated, outdoor pool with water slide and paddling pool (1/5-30/9). Play area. Volleyball, basketball, pétanque and table tennis. Bicycle hire. Electric barbecues are not permitted.
Off site: Beach 500 m. Golf, riding, fishing all within 5 km.

Open: 3 April - 7 November.

Directions

Site is signed from D949 Les Sables to La Rochelle road, north of the 'Géant Casino' roundabout. Turn south at minor junction. GPS: 46.49167, -1.76517

Charges 2010

Per unit incl. 2 persons and electricity	€ 18,50 - € 31,00

Longeville-sur-Mer

Camping le Petit Rocher

1250 avenue de Docteur Mathevet, F-85560 Longeville-sur-Mer (Vendée) T: **02 51 90 31 57**

E: **rocher85@free.fr** **alanrogers.com/FR85000**

A former municipal site, Le Petit Rocher is now under the same management (M. Guignard) as another local campsite, Les Brunelles. With its seaside location set in a pine forest, there is an air of peace and tranquillity. Although the area is undulating, the 150 good size touring pitches are flat and arranged in terraces throughout the wooded area. Electricity hook-ups are available (Euro style plugs) and there are adequate water points. A grassy play area for children is thoughtfully situated in a hollow, but has limited equipment. A fun pool was added in 2008.

Facilities

Three new, spacious sanitary blocks are clean and well maintained with showers, British style WCs. Facilities for people with disabilities. Washing machine and dryer. Bar, restaurant and takeaway (July/Aug). Tennis court. New heated outdoor pool (8/5-11/9). Off site: Beach 200 m. Bars, restaurant, and small shops nearby. Riding and bicycle hire 2 km. Boat launching 11 km. Fishing 15 km. Golf 20 km.

Open: 8 May - 11 September.

Directions

From Longeville-sur-Mer follow signs for Le Rocher towards La Tranche-sur-Mer. Turn right at first roundabout, following campsite signs to site on right. GPS: 46.403767, -1.507183

Charges guide

Per unit with 2 persons and electricity	€ 16,00 - € 24,00
extra person	€ 3,00 - € 5,00
child (0-4 yrs)	free - € 3,00
dog	€ 3,00

Longeville-sur-Mer

Camping le Zagarella

Route de La Tranche, F-85560 Longeville-sur-Mer (Vendée) T: **02 51 33 30 60**

E: **contact@campingzagarella.com** **alanrogers.com/FR85010**

This pleasant campsite is set in a wooded, six-hectare area, a 900-metre walk from the beach (or 1.5 km. by road). As well as 100 chalets to rent, there are 45 small touring pitches (the site is probably unsuitable for units over six metres). On well drained grass and shaded, the pitches are hedged and all have water and 10A electricity (French connections). Access around the site is by tarmac roads. The site has a landscaped pool complex including slides and a covered pool. An area for sports and games including tennis is across the road via an underpass.

Facilities

Two well maintained toilet blocks of traditional design include British style WCs, washbasins in cubicles and free preset showers. Separate baby room and facilities for people with disabilities. Washing machines. Shop (25/5-5/9). Bar (20/5-5/9). Restaurant and takeaway (1/5-30/9). Swimming pool (1/6-30/9) and indoor pool (heated 1/4-30/9). Playground. Tennis. Bicycle hire. Gas barbecues permitted (available for rent). Off site: Beach 900 m. Riding 1 km. Golf 30 km.

Open: 1 April - 30 September.

Directions

From Longeville-sur-Mer take road to Tranche-sur-Mer and site is on the left (follow green camping signs). GPS: 46.40390, -1.48810

Charges guide

Per unit incl. 2 persons	€ 16,00 - € 28,00
extra person	€ 5,00 - € 6,00
child (0-7 yrs)	€ 3,50 - € 4,00
dog	€ 4,30

Longeville-sur-Mer

Camping les Brunelles

Le Bouil, F-85560 Longeville-sur-Mer (Vendée) T: **02 51 33 50 75**. E: **camping@les-brunelles.com**
alanrogers.com/FR85440

This is a well-managed site with good facilities and a varied programme of high season entertainment for all the family. A busy site in high season, there are plenty of activities to keep children happy and occupied. In 2007 Les Brunelles was combined with an adjacent campsite to provide 600 pitches of which 200 are for tourers; all have electricity (10A) and 20 of the new touring pitches also have water and waste. All are over 100 sq.m. to allow easier access for larger units. On the original Les Brunelles site, the touring pitches are level on sandy grass and separated by hedges, away from most of the mobile homes.

Facilities

Four old, but well maintained and modernised toilet blocks have British and Turkish style toilets and washbasins, both open style and in cabins. Laundry facilities. Shop, takeaway and large modern, airy bar (all season). Covered pool with jacuzzi (all season). Outdoor pool with slides and paddling pools (15/5-18/9). Tennis. Bicycle hire. Off site: Riding 3 km and golf 20 km. Good supervised sandy beach 900 m. St Vincent-sur-Jard 2 km.

Open: 3 April - 18 September.

Directions

From D21 (Talmont - Longueville), between St Vincent and Longueville, site signed south from main road towards coast. Turn left in Le Bouil (site signed). Site is 800 m. on left. GPS: 46.41330, -1.52313

Charges guide

Per unit incl. 2 persons and electricity	€ 21,00 - € 35,00
extra person	€ 5,00 - € 8,00

Camping Cheques accepted.

Noirmoutier-en-l'Île

Camping Indigo Noirmoutier

23 allée des Sableaux, Bois de la Chaize, F-85330 Noirmoutier-en-l'Île (Vendée) T: **02 51 39 06 24**
E: **noirmoutier@camping-indigo.com** **alanrogers.com/FR85720**

Located in woodland and on dunes along a two-kilometre stretch of sandy beach just east of the attractive little town of Noirmoutier on the island of the same name, this could be paradise for those who enjoy a simple campsite in a natural setting. On land belonging to the ONF (France's forestry commission), this site is operated by Huttopia whose aim is to adapt to the environment rather than take it over. The 500 touring pitches, all with electricity, are situated among the pine trees and accessed along tracks. Those on the sand dunes have fantastic views across the Bay of Bourgneuf to Pornic and the Jade Coast. They cost a few euros extra – if you are lucky enough to get one! Cars are only allowed in these areas on arrival and departure and it is planned eventually to provide more car parking at strategic points so that this rule can apply to the whole site. There are no mobile homes, just ten large, traditional, but well equipped tents for rent. Nearby are salt marshes, an aquarium and a water theme park and there are opportunities to walk, cycle, sail and windsurf.

Facilities

Five sanitary blocks currently provide basic facilities including preset showers and some washbasins in cubicles. The central one is larger and more modern, the others have been refurbished. All are kept clean and have facilities for disabled visitors. Washing machines and dryers. Motorcaravan services point. Playground and play field. Bicycle hire. WiFi (reception, bar, pool). Off site: Riding 4 km. Golf 25 km.

Open: 2 April - 3 October.

Directions

The Île de Noirmoutier is 70 km. southwest of Nantes. Take D38 road from the mainland, cross bridge to island and continue to Noirmoutier en l'Île. Go through town past three sets of traffic lights and at roundabout turn right following signs to 'Campings'. GPS: 46.9969, -2.2201

Charges guide

Per unit incl. 2 persons and electricity	€ 16,90 - € 28,50
extra person	€ 1,50 - € 4,60

Camping Cheques accepted.

Olonne-sur-Mer

Camping la Loubine

1 route de la Mer, F-85340 Olonne-sur-Mer (Vendée) T: **02 51 33 12 92**. E: **camping.la.loubine@wanadoo.fr**
alanrogers.com/FR85030

Situated on the edge of a forest, this campsite is just 1.8 kilometres from a sandy beach and five minutes from Les Sables d'Olonne. The 60 grass touring pitches are mostly shaded, all with 6A electricity connections and adequate water points. Only a limited number of pitches is available for large units (over 7 m) because of difficulties with manoeuvring. It is best to confirm availability and book in advance. The focal point of the site is an excellent bar and entertainment area for karaoke and discos with a patio overlooking the splendid pool complex with its water slides. There are many chalets and mobile homes on the site, both privately owned and to rent.

Facilities

Toilet blocks are clean with British style WCs, washbasins in cubicles and controllable showers. Shop. Bar and restaurant (15/5-15/9). Indoor pool (all season). Outdoor swimming pools (15/5-15/9). Tennis. Fitness room. Minigolf. Play area. Bicycle hire. Dogs are not allowed in July and August.
Off site: Beach 2 km. Fishing and boat launching 6 km. Golf 4 km. Riding 1 km. Boat launching 6.5 km. Restaurant, shop, bar within1.5 km.

Open: 5 April - September.

Directions

Site is west of Olonne beside the D80 road. Turn towards the coast at roundabout, signed La Forêt d'Olonne and site (75 m). GPS: 46.54626, -1.80556

Charges guide

Per unit incl. 2 persons	€ 15,50 - € 27,00
extra person	€ 3,25 - € 5,00
child (under 6 yrs)	free - € 2,95
electricity (6A)	€ 3,65

Saint Hilaire-de-Riez

Hotellerie de Plein Air la Puerta del Sol

Les Borderies, chemin de Hommeaux, F-85270 Saint Hilaire-de-Riez (Vendée) T: **02 51 49 10 10**
E: **info@campinglapuertadelsol.com** **alanrogers.com/FR85080**

La Puerta del Sol is a good quality campsite a short distance away from the busy coast. It is suitable not only for families with teenage children to entertain, but also for those seeking a more peaceful and relaxing holiday. There are 216 pitches, of which 102 are used for touring units. Pitches are level with dividing hedges and many receive shade from the mature trees on the site. Each pitch is fully serviced with water, waste water point and electricity. There is one small French tour operator on site (20 pitches). A self-service restaurant and takeaway with reasonably priced food overlooks the pool and terrace.

Facilities

Three heated toilet blocks have a mix of Turkish and British style WCs, washbasins in cabins and baby baths. Dishwashing and laundry facilities. Facilities for disabled visitors. Shop (1/5-31/8). Bar (1/5-15/9). Self-service restaurant and takeaway (1/5-31/8). Swimming pool, slide and paddling pool (1/5-30/9; no Bermuda- style shorts). Play area. Tennis. Bicycle hire. Games room. American motorhomes accepted with reservation. Off site: Beach, riding, fishing and golf 5 km. St Jean-de-Monts 7 km.

Open: 1 April - 30 September.

Directions

From Le Pissot (7 km. north of St Gilles-Croix-de-Vie on D38) take D59 (Le Perrier). Site is 2 km. along this road on the right down a short side road. Site signed. GPS: 46.7645, -1.9572

Charges guide

Per unit incl. 2 persons and services	€ 19,00 - € 29,00
extra person	€ 5,00 - € 6,50
child (under 7 yrs)	€ 2,50 - € 4,50
animal	€ 4,00

Saint Hilaire-de-Riez

Camping les Ecureuils

100 avenue de la Pège, F-85270 Saint Hilaire-de-Riez (Vendée) T: **02 51 54 33 71**
E: **info@camping-aux-ecureuils.com** **alanrogers.com/FR85230**

Of the seaside sites on the Vendée, Les Ecureuils has to be one of the best, run by a friendly and most helpful family. Just 300 m. from a superb beach, the site is ideally situated for exploring from Les Sables d'Olonne to Noirmoutier. Developed on what was originally a farm, there are 215 pitches (42 for touring units). On sandy grass, all have electricity (6A, Euro adaptors avalable), water and drainage. Well kept hedges and mature trees give shade and privacy, although some more open pitches are also available for sun lovers. The site is popular with British tour operators (60%).

Facilities

The two main sanitary blocks are spacious, and include some washbasins in cubicles, and facilities for babies and disabled people. Laundry and dishwashing facilities. Small shop (1/5-4/9). Restaurant. Large, airy bar with screened terrace. Pool complex including pool for small children with its own 'mini aqua park', large heated pool, and water slide with separate splash pool. Indoor pool, paddling pool and jacuzzi. Off site: Beach 300 m. Bicycle hire 200 m. Fishing 4 km. Riding 5 km. Golf and sailing 6 km.

Open: 1 May - 11 September.

Directions

Driving south D38 (St Jean-de-Monts - St Gilles), turn right at L'Oasis hotel/restaurant in Orouet (6 km. outside St Jean-de-Monts), signed Les Mouettes. After 1.5 km. at roundabout turn left (St Hilaire-de-Riez). Site is 500 m. on left. GPS: 46.7361, -2.0095

Charges guide

Per unit incl. 2 persons and electricity	€ 26,60 - € 36,00
extra person	€ 5,00 - € 6,25
child (under 5 yrs)	€ 3,00 - € 4,00

Saint Hilaire-de-Riez

Camping Caravaning la Ningle

Chemin des Roselières 66, F-85270 Saint Hilaire-de-Riez (Vendée) T: **02 51 54 07 11**
E: **campingdelaningle@wanadoo.fr** **alanrogers.com/FR85350**

At Camping La Ningle you are guaranteed to receive a warm welcome from M. et Mme. Guibert, who have established a very pleasant campsite with a friendly, family atmosphere. There are 155 pitches, 60 available for touring units. All have electricity (6A) and all are fully serviced (electricity, water and drainage). Pitches are spacious with dividing hedges and all have some shade. The nearest beach is a 600 m. walk through a pine forest, but there are also three small heated swimming pools on site.

Facilities

Two clean toilet blocks include some washbasins in cubicles. Toilet/shower room for disabled people and large family shower room. Laundry facilities. Bread (July/Aug). Takeaway three evenings per week. Bar (July/Aug). Main swimming pool, larger children's pool, paddling pool and slide. Fitness suite. Tennis court. Games field. Games room. Fishing lake. Children's activities (July/Aug), and regular pétanque and tennis competitions. WiFi in bar area. Off site: Small supermarket and takeaway 200 m.

Open: 20 May - 10 September.

Directions

Driving south on D38 (St Jean-de-Monts - St Gilles), turn right at L'Oasis hotel/restaurant in Orouet, signed Les Mouettes. After 1.5 km. at roundabout, turn left (St Hilaire-de-Riez). Pass two campsites, then next left, signed La Ningle. GPS: 46.7447, -2.0044

Charges guide

Per unit incl. 2 persons and electricity	€ 17,50 - € 29,80
extra person	€ 3,10 - € 4,60
child (under 7 yrs)	€ 1,65 - € 2,90

Saint Hilaire-la-Forêt

Camping la Grand Métairie

8 rue de la Vineuse en Plaine, F-85440 Saint Hilaire-la-Forêt (Vendée) T: **02 51 33 32 38**
E: **info@camping-grandmetairie.com** **alanrogers.com/FR85300**

Just five kilometres from the super sandy beach at Jard-sur-Mer, La Grand' Métairie offers many of the amenities of its seaside counterparts, but with the important advantage of being on the edge of a delightful, sleepy village otherwise untouched by tourism. It is a busy well run site with a programme of lively entertainment in high season. The site has 174 pitches (52 touring pitches), all with electricity. The pitches have good shade, are separated by mature trees and hedges and are reasonable in size.

Facilities

Two modern toilet blocks are very clean and include washbasins mainly in cabins. Units for disabled people. Washing machines and dryers. Fridge hire. Safety deposit boxes. Shop (all season). Smart bar/restaurant and takeaway (all 1/5-28/8). Attractive, heated outdoor pool and paddling pool (1/5-11/9). Indoor pool (all season). Sauna, jacuzzi. Gym. Tennis, minigolf (both free in low season). Visiting hairdressing salon. Internet access. Children's club. Off site: Village shop 100 m. Riding and fishing 5 km. Golf 15 km.

Open: 3 April - 11 September.

Directions

From Les Sables d'Olonne take D949 (La Rochelle) towards Talmont-St Hilaire and Luçon; 7 km. after Talmont turn right on D70 to St Hilaire-la-Forêt. Site is on left before village centre. GPS: 46.44862, -1.52626

Charges guide

Per unit incl. 2 persons and electricity	€ 17,00 - € 27,00
extra person	€ 5,00 - € 8,00
child (2-5 yrs)	€ 3,00 - € 4,00
dog	€ 3,00 - € 4,00

Min. stay 7 nights 13/7-17/8.

Saint Hilaire-la-Forêt

Camping des Batardières

F-85440 Saint Hilaire-la-Forêt (Vendée) T: **02 51 33 33 85**

alanrogers.com/FR85390

Camping des Batardières is a haven of tranquility on the edge of an unspoilt village, yet just 5 km. from the sea. It is an attractive, unsophisticated little site, lovingly maintained by its owners for more than 25 years. Many visitors return year after year. There are 75 good-sized pitches (a few up to 130 sq.m) and all are available for touring units (there are no mobile homes and no tour operators!) All have easy access to water and electricity (6A, or 2A for tents). Otherwise there are few facilities on site.

Facilities

The sanitary block is kept very clean and visitors are asked to keep it that way (no shoes in the shower cubicles, for instance). Some washbasin and shower combination cubicles. Laundry facilities. Tennis court. Play area and field for games, kite-flying etc. Not suitable for American motorhomes or twin-axle caravans. Off site: Village shop and bar 200 m. Jard-sur-Mer 5 km. Bicycle hire 3 km. Fishing 5 km. Golf 16 km.

Open: 27 June - 2 September.

Directions

From Les Sables d'Olonne take D949 (la Rochelle) towards Talmont-St Hilaire and Luçon. 7 km. after Talmont turn right on D70 to St Hilaire-la-Forêt. Site signed to the right approaching village.
GPS: 46.4486, -1.5286

Charges 2010

Per unit incl. 2 persons	€ 20,00
electricity	€ 3,50
extra person	€ 3,00

No credit cards.

Saint Jean-de-Monts

Campéole

Campéole le Dornier

Route de la Tonnelle, F-85160 Saint Jean-de-Monts (Vendée) T: **02 51 58 81 16**. E: **nadine.ferran@atciat.com**

alanrogers.com/FR85960

Le Dornier is a well equipped member of the Campéole group, located on land belonging to the French forestry commission and close to the popular resort of St Jean-de-Monts. The site has direct access to a superb sandy beach and also has a good sized swimming pool with waterfalls. Pitches are mostly sandy and of a reasonable size. Most are equipped with electrical connections. A range of chalets, fully equipped bungalow tents and mobile homes are available for rent including some models specially adapted for the disabled. On-site amenities include a multi-sports terrain and archery. There is a snack bar and shops are available within easy access. The site can become quite lively in high season with a daily children's club and a wide range of evening entertainment, including concerts and discos. A number of cycle tracks pass through the woods close to the site (bicycle hire on site). St Jean is a well equipped resort with dozens of restaurants, cafes and other attractions. The island of Noirmoutier is to the north and can be reached either by a toll bridge or causeway at low tide.

Facilities

Snack bar. Swimming pool. Bicycle hire. Archery. Multisports terrain. Bouncy castle. Play area. Entertainment and activities programme. Tourist information. Direct beach access. Mobile homes, equipped tents and chalets for rent. Off site: St Jean-de-Monts (large resort with shops, cafes and restaurants). Walking and cycle tracks. Fishing. Ile de Noirmoutier.

Open: 4 April - 13 September.

Directions

The site is north of St Jean-de-Monts. Approaching from Challans, head west on D753 to St Jean-de-Monts and then north on D38 towards Notre Dame-de-Monts. Turn left at the roundabout at Les Tonnelles after 6 km. and from here follow signs to the site.
GPS: 46.8094, -2.1208

Charges year

Per unit incl. 2 persons and electricity	€ 17,10 - € 26,60

Saint Jean-de-Monts

Campéole

Campéole les Sirènes

Avenue des Demoiselles, F-85164 Saint Jean-de-Monts (Vendée) T: **02 51 58 01 31**
E: **nadine.ferran@atciat.com** **alanrogers.com/FR85970**

Les Sirènes is a well equipped campsite and a member of the Campéole group. The site can be found in the forest behind the popular resort of St Jean-de-Monts. The nearest beach is just 700 m. away and can be accessed by cycle (hire service on site) using the tracks through the forest and across the sand dunes. The beach is long and sandy, shelving very gradually into the sea. Pitches here are of a good size and well shaded by tall pines. Most have electrical connections. A number of equipped tents and mobile homes (including specially adapted models for disabled people) are available for rent. On-site amenities include a swimming pool and separate children's pool, a multisport pitch and archery. This is a lively site in high season with plenty going on, including a daily children's club and regular discos and karaoke evenings. Les Sirènes has a good location with easy pedestrian access to the beach, shops, restaurants and a daily market. A little further afield, the islands of Yeu and Noirmoutier (accessible by bridge or causeway) are both popular excursions.

Facilities

Restaurant at site entrance. Swimming pool. Children's pool. Multisport pitch. Bicycle hire. Bouncy castle. Archery. Play area. Activities and entertainment programme. Tourist information. Mobile homes and equipped tents for rent. Off site: St Jean-de-Monts (shops, market and restaurants). Nearest beach 700 m. Minigolf. Fishing. Water sports.

Open: 3 April - 14 September.

Directions

From Challans head west on D753 to St Jean-de-Monts. Upon arrival in St Jean follow directions for La Plage and Palais des Congrès. At the roundabout on Avenue de la Forêt, turn left into Avenue des Demoiselles and the site can be found after 500 m. on the left. GPS: 46.780083, -2.055881

Charges year

Per unit incl. 2 persons and electricity	€ 17,10 - € 26,60

Saint Jean-de-Monts

Camping l'Abri des Pins

Route de Notre-Dame-de-Monts, F-85160 Saint Jean-de-Monts (Vendée) T: **02 51 58 83 86**
E: **contact@abridespins.com** **alanrogers.com/FR85090**

L'Abri des Pins is situated on the outskirts of St Jean-de-Monts and is separated from the sea and long sandy beach by a strip of pinewood. The site has 218 pitches, 78 of which are for touring units with 30 larger than average, with electricity, water and drainage. Electricity is also available for the other pitches which are around 100 sq.m, fully marked out with dividing hedges and shade. Many pitches are occupied by privately owned mobile homes, but there are no tour operators on the site. From the site, it is a pleasant 15-minute walk to the beach.

Facilities

The two sanitary blocks include washbasins in cabins, laundry and dishwashing sinks. Good small shop (1/7-31/8) and bar/restaurant provides good quality, value for money meals, both to eat in and take away. Outdoor, heated swimming pool and water slide, plus small pool for children, with decked sunbathing area (open all season; no Bermuda-style shorts). Daily children's club, football, pétanque, aquarobics. Off site: Supermarket. Restaurants. Beach 700 m. Walking, cycling and fishing 1 km. Riding 2 km. Golf 5 km.

Open: 15 June - 16 September.

Directions

Site is 4 km. from town centre on St Jean-de-Monts - Notre-Dame-de Monts/Noirmoutiers road (D38), on left heading north, just after Camping les Amiaux. GPS: 46.8093, -2.109

Charges guide

Per unit incl. 3 persons and electricity	€ 22,50 - € 33,70
extra person	€ 3,60 - € 6,10
child (under 5 yrs)	€ 2,55 - € 4,10
dog	free - € 3,50

Deposit required for armband for access to pool and site (high season only).

Saint Jean-de-Monts

486

Camping la Yole

Chemin des Bosses, Orouet, F-85160 Saint Jean-de-Monts (Vendée) T: **02 51 58 67 17**
E: **contact@la-yole.com** **alanrogers.com/FR85150**

La Yole is an attractive and well run site, two kilometres from a sandy beach. It offers 356 pitches, the majority of which are occupied by tour operators and mobile homes to rent. There are 150 touring pitches, most with shade and separated by bushes and trees. A newer area at the rear of the site is more open. All the pitches are of at least 100 sq.m. and have electricity (10A), water and drainage. The pool complex includes an outdoor pool, a paddling pool, slide and an indoor heated pool with jacuzzi. Entertainment is organised in high season. This is a clean and tidy site, ideal for families with children and you will receive a helpful and friendly welcome.

Facilities

Two toilet blocks include washbasins in cabins and facilities for disabled people and babies. A third block has a baby room. Laundry facilities. Shop (15/5-5/9). Bar (8/5-5/9) plus restaurant and takeaway (15/5-5/9). Outdoor pool and paddling pool. Indoor heated pool with jacuzzi. Play area. Club room. Tennis. Games room. Entertainment in high season. WiFi. Gas barbecues only. Off site: Beach, bus service, bicycle hire 2 km. Riding 3 km. Fishing, golf and watersports 6 km.

Open: 2 April - 24 September.

Directions

Site is signed off the D38, 6 km. south of St Jean-de-Monts in the village of Orouet. Coming from St Jean-de-Monts turn right at l'Oasis restaurant towards Mouette and follow signs to site.
GPS: 46.75659, -2.00792

Charges guide

Per unit incl. 2 persons and electricity	€ 16,00 - € 30,00
extra person	€ 3,70 - € 6,50
child (2-9 yrs)	€ 2,15 - € 5,00
dog	€ 4,00 - € 5,00

Camping Cheques accepted.

Saint Jean-de-Monts

Camping les Places Dorées

Route de Notre-Dame-de-Monts, F-85160 Saint Jean-de-Monts (Vendée) T: **02 51 59 02 93**
E: **contact@placesdorees.com** **alanrogers.com/FR85280**

Les Places Dorées is owned by the same family as Abri des Pins (FR85090) just across the road. It is a newer site with maturing trees beginning to offer some shade. There are 245 grassy pitches, the quietest being towards the back of the site. Each one is separated, all have 10A electricity and some are also equipped with water and drainage. In low season the site is quiet but it can be noisy in high season with the bar and disco closing late. Recently added are a relaxation area with a heated covered pool, spa facilities (balnéo, hammam and weekly massage), a fitness room and a games room for children.

Facilities

Three modern toilet blocks include washbasins in cubicles. Facilities for disabled visitors. Laundry facilities. Bread to order. Bar, snack bar and takeaway. Outdoor pool complex with slides, jacuzzi and waterfall (no Bermuda-style shorts). Covered, heated pool, spa facilities, gym. Games room. High season entertainment and children's club at L'Abri des Pins, also adult activities (pétanque tournaments, aqua aerobics). Facilities at L'Abri des Pins may be used.
Off site: Fishing 500 m. Beach 700 m. Riding 2 km. Golf 5 km.

Open: 1 June - 1 September.

Directions

Site is 4 km. north of St Jean-de-Monts on the D38 St Jean-de-Monts - Notre Dames-de-Monts road on the right hand side, almost opposite L'Abri des Pins. GPS: 46.80993, -2.10992

Charges guide

Per unit incl. 3 persons and electricity	€ 23,00 - € 34,40
extra person	€ 3,70 - € 6,20
child (under 5 yrs)	€ 2,60 - € 4,20

No credit cards.

Saint Jean-de-Monts

Camping Caravaning le Bois Joly

46 route de Notre-Dame-de-Monts, B.P. 507, F-85165 Saint Jean-de-Monts (Vendée) T: **02 51 59 11 63**
E: **campingboisjoly@wanadoo.fr** **alanrogers.com/FR85780**

This is an attractive, family run holiday site with indoor and outdoor pool complexes and 385 pitches, most of which are fully serviced. Of these 202 are taken by mobile homes or chalets, leaving 183 good sized, hedged pitches with 10A electric hook-ups for tourists. Grassy and level, these are served by tarmac roads and four fresh, clean, modern, toilet blocks. A good family holiday location, there are lots of activities and entertainment in July and August. The indoor pool is open all season, the L-shaped outdoor pool complex has a 'menhirs' theme and attractive flower beds. There are four toboggans, a paddling pool and a raised solarium deck. On site there are several small playgrounds for younger children, plus a very large and comprehensive adventure playground. The river behind the site offers opportunities for fishing or canoeing.

Facilities

Four modern toilet blocks with controllable showers, washbasins in cubicles. Facilities for babies and disabled persons. Laundry facilities. One block is heated for low season. Bar and snack bar. Takeaway (July/Aug). Indoor pool (7/4-26/9). Outdoor pools (15/6-15/9). Sauna, solarium and gym. Playgrounds. Multisport court. Pétanque. TV room. Games room. Events, entertainment and canoeing on site in July/Aug. River fishing. Drive-over motorcaravan service point. Safety deposit boxes. No charcoal barbecues allowed. No double axle caravans accepted. Off site: Golf 2 km. Riding and tennis 500 m. Bicycle hire 1.5 km.

Open: 3 April - 26 September.

Directions

Site is at the northern end of St Jean-de-Monts, on the eastern side of the D38, about 300 m. north of junction (roundabout) with the D51.
GPS: 46.79915, -2.0744

Charges guide

Per unit incl. 2 persons and electricity	€ 17,00 - € 30,00
extra person	€ 2,00 - € 5,00
child (under 7 yrs)	€ 1,00 - € 2,50
dog	€ 1,50 - € 3,00

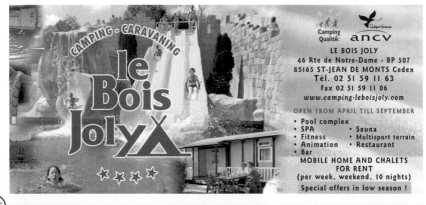

Saint Jean-de-Monts

Camping la Forêt

190 chemin de la Rive, F-85160 Saint Jean-de-Monts (Vendée) T: **02 51 58 84 63**
E: **camping-la-foret@wanadoo.fr** **alanrogers.com/FR85360**

Camping La Forêt is owned by M. and Mme. Jolivet and they work hard to provide a small, quality site. Well run and attractive, with a friendly, family atmosphere, it provides just 63 pitches with 50 for touring units. At 100 sq.m. in size, the pitches are surrounded by mature hedges and have water and electricity. Over 50 species of trees are planted, providing shade to every pitch. There is one tour operator on site (13 pitches), but their presence is not intrusive and the site has a quiet and relaxed atmosphere, ideal for couples or families with young children.

Facilities

The central toilet block includes washbasins in cubicles. Laundry and dishwashing facilities. Baby bath. Facilities for disabled people. Motorcaravan waste tanks can be emptied on request. Basic provisions sold in reception, including fresh bread. Takeaway. Small heated swimming pool (15/5-15/9). Play area. Bicycle hire. Only gas and electric barbecues allowed, communal barbecue in centre of site. Not suitable for American motorhomes. Off site: Beach 400 m. Network of cycle paths through the forest and local marshland.

Open: 1 May - 28 September.

Directions

Follow D38 out of St Jean-de-Monts, towards Notre-Dame-de-Monts. After 5.5 km. turn left at sign for site and Plage de Pont d'Yeu. Follow road and site is on left in about 100 m. GPS: 46.80807, -2.11384

Charges guide

Per unit incl. 2 persons	€ 17,00 - € 27,00
extra person	€ 3,50 - € 5,00
child (under 7 yrs)	€ 3,50 - € 3,90
dog	€ 2,50
electricity (6A)	€ 3,80

Saint Jean-de-Monts

Camping Zagarella

Route des Sables, F-85160 Saint Jean-de-Monts (Vendée) T: **02 51 58 19 82**. E: **zagarella@zagarella.fr**
alanrogers.com/FR85940

Camping Zagarella is an ideal site for happy family holidays, with many facilities for children of all ages. A family run site, the management and staff are very friendly and do all they can to ensure everyone has a good time. There are 278 pitches with 77 used for touring units. These vary in size and shape but are mainly level and grassy, and divided by shrubs. Some areas of the site are heavily wooded but there are more open parts for sun lovers. There are two tour operators here which lead to a nice mix of nationalities. The site has both indoor and outdoor heated swimming pools with a water chute and slides, and the play areas provided for younger children are very well equipped. Children's clubs and family entertainment are organised in high season.

Facilities

Two modern, unheated toilet blocks are clean and well maintained. Both contain good facilities for disabled visitors and baby baths. Laundry. Motorcaravan service point. Small shop, bar and takeaway (21/5-29/8). Indoor pool (all season). Outdoor pool (21/5-13/9). Tennis. Multisport court. Bicycle hire. Gym. Only gas barbecues are permitted. WiFi in bar. Off site: Beach 3 km. Riding 1 km. Golf 3 km.

Open: 4 April - 28 September.

Directions

Travelling south on the D38 St Jean-de-Monts - St Gilles road. About 4 km. south of St Jean keep a sharp look-out for a blue site sign on the right. GPS: 46.781389, -2.018056

Charges guide

Per unit incl. up to 3 persons and electricity	€ 13,80 - € 38,30
extra person	€ 4,50 - € 5,20
child (under 3 yrs)	€ 3,00 - € 3,70
dog	€ 2,70 - € 3,40

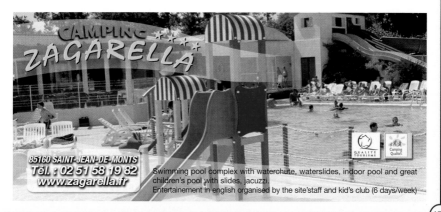

Saint Jean-de-Monts

Camping Aux Coeurs Vendéens

251 route de Notre-Dame-de-Monts, F-85160 Saint Jean-de-Monts (Vendée) T: **02 51 58 84 91**
E: **info@coeursvendeens.com** **alanrogers.com/FR85740**

This is a delightful little site, a real find for those wishing to enjoy the beaches and life-style of this stretch of coastline without the razzmatazz of some of the neighbouring sites. It is family run and everywhere there is attention to detail: flower tubs beside the road as you drive in, whitewashed stones for the pitch numbers, engraved designs on the washbasin mirrors, even plugs for the dishwashing sinks! There are 50 touring pitches, all with electricity available (10A), and a further 67 with mobile homes and chalets, all but seven are available to rent.

Facilities

Two sanitary blocks are bright and cheerful and kept very clean. Controllable showers, washbasins in cubicles, two pleasant baby rooms. En-suite facilities for disabled visitors (wheelchair users might have minor difficulties accessing this). Internet access. Washing machines and dryer. Small shop with takeaway. Swimming pools (7/5-10/9). TV and games rooms. Playgrounds. Trampoline. Minigolf. Bicycle hire. Off site: Beach, sea fishing and boat launching 700 m. Riding 2 km. Sailing 3 km. Golf 4 km. Fresh water fishing 7 km.

Open: 3 April - 18 September.

Directions

Site is on the D38 just over 3 km. north of St Jean-de-Monts, roughly halfway between St Jean-de-Monts and Notre Dame-de-Monts, on the western side of the road. GPS: 46.809133, -2.110167

Charges 2010

Per unit incl. 2 persons and electricity	€ 15,00 - € 29,30
extra person	€ 2,50 - € 4,90
child (under 5 yrs)	free - € 3,30
dog	€ 1,70 - € 3,00

Saint Julien-des-Landes

Flower Camping la Bretonnière

F-85150 Saint Julien-des-Landes (Vendée) T: **02 51 46 62 44**
E: **camp.la-bretonniere@wanadoo.fr** **alanrogers.com/FR85850**

An attractive, modern site on a family farm surrounded by beautiful peaceful countryside, this site is sure to please. With 150 pitches in an area of six hectares, there is plenty of space for everyone. There are 105 touring pitches, 28 tour operator tents and eight alpine-style chalets, spread around several fields, some quite open, others with some shade from perimeter hedges. The grassy pitches are all of a really generous size with electricity (12/16A). Two swimming pools, one covered, the other outdoor, are surrounded by a pleasant terrace, with the bar and reception close by. Also on site is a lovely large fishing lake (unfenced) with a pleasant walk all around. The bar and takeaway operate in July/August, ices and basic tinned food items are available from reception and there is a really good motorcaravan service point. The village of Saint Julien-des-Landes is 2.5 km. and the larger town of La Mothe-Achard is 7 km.

Facilities

Five modern, clean and well appointed toilet blocks are spread evenly around the site, with baby rooms and facilities for disabled people at two blocks. Motorcaravan service point. Bar, snack bar and takeaway (July/Aug). Covered swimming pool (15.5 x 7 m) and outdoor pool (11 x 5 m) open June - Sept. WiFi around bar and reception. Playgrounds. Games/TV room. Tennis. Boules. Fishing lake. Caravan storage. Off site: Village 2.5 km. La Mothe-Achard 7 km. Golf 12 km. Riding 2 km. Boat launching 4 km.

Open: 1 April - 15 October.

Directions

St Julien-des-Landes is 18 km. northeast of Les Sables d'Olonne and 5 km. northwest of La Mothe-Achard. From La Mothe-Achard take D12 west towards Bretignolles-sur-Mer, pass through St Julien and after 2 km. take first turn right (site signed). Site is 500 m. GPS: 46.64463, -1.73328

Charges 2010

Per unit incl. 2 persons and electricity	€ 13,50 - € 24,50
extra person	€ 3,50 - € 4,50
child (2-7 yrs)	€ 2,50 - € 3,50
dog	€ 2,00

Saint Julien-des-Landes

Village de la Guyonnière

Runner up Alan Rogers Awards 2009

La Guyonnière, F-85150 Saint Julien-des-Landes (Vendée) T: **02 51 46 62 59**
E: **info@laguyonniere.com** **alanrogers.com/FR85260**

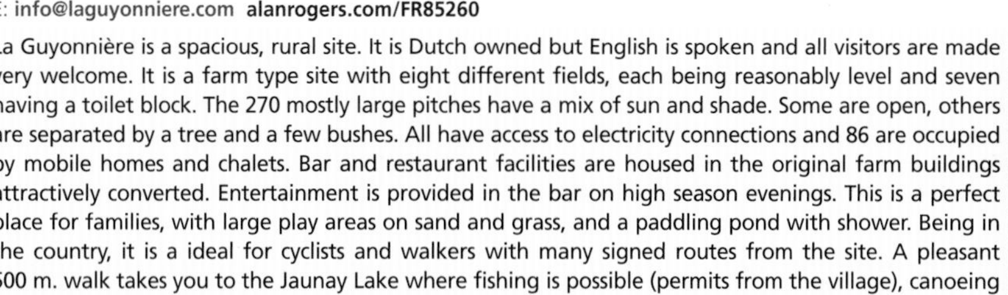

La Guyonnière is a spacious, rural site. It is Dutch owned but English is spoken and all visitors are made very welcome. It is a farm type site with eight different fields, each being reasonably level and seven having a toilet block. The 270 mostly large pitches have a mix of sun and shade. Some are open, others are separated by a tree and a few bushes. All have access to electricity connections and 86 are occupied by mobile homes and chalets. Bar and restaurant facilities are housed in the original farm buildings attractively converted. Entertainment is provided in the bar on high season evenings. This is a perfect place for families, with large play areas on sand and grass, and a paddling pond with shower. Being in the country, it is a ideal for cyclists and walkers with many signed routes from the site. A pleasant 500 m. walk takes you to the Jaunay Lake where fishing is possible (permits from the village), canoeing (life jackets from reception) and pedaloes to hire. There are no tour operators and, needless to say, no road noise. It is popular for many reasons, the main one being the free-and-easy atmosphere.

The Travel Service to book this site call 01580 214000 ...we'll arrange everything

Facilities

Modern toilet blocks. Most cubicles are quite small. Washbasins are in cubicles. Limited provision for babies and disabled visitors. Dishwashing and laundry sinks. Shop. Bar with TV and pool table (both 1/5-15/9). Restaurant (15/6-15/9). Pizzeria with takeaway (1/5-29/9). Small pool and heated pool with jacuzzi and slide. Paddling pool. Play areas, sand pit. Tennis. Bicycle hire. Car wash. WiFi.
Off site: Riding 3 km. Golf 8 km. Beaches 10 km.

Open: 25 April - 25 September.

Directions

Site is signed off the D12 road (La Mothe Achard - St Gilles Croix-de-Vie), about 4 km. west of St Julien-des-Landes, down a lane about 1 km. from the main road. GPS: 46.65273, -1.74987

Charges 2010

Per unit incl. 2 persons and electricity	€ 18,00 - € 36,90
extra person	€ 4,90 - € 6,00
child (3-9 yrs)	€ 3,30 - € 3,90
animal	€ 3,50

Less 10-20% outside high season.

Saint Julien-des-Landes

Castel Camping Caravaning la Garangeoire

F-85150 Saint Julien-des-Landes (Vendée) T: **02 51 46 65 39**. E: **info@garangeoire.com**

alanrogers.com/FR85040

La Garangeoire is a stunning campsite, situated some 15 km. inland near the village of St Julien-des-Landes. Set in 200 ha. of parkland surrounding the small château of La Garangeoire of which there is an outstanding view as you approach through the gates. With a spacious, relaxed atmosphere, the main camping areas are on either side of the old road which is edged with mature trees. The 360 pitches, all named after birds, are individually hedged, some with shade. They are well spaced and are especially large (most 150-200 sq.m), most with electricity (8A) and some with water and drainage also.

Facilities

First class sanitary facilities with washbasins in cabins. Facilities for babies and disabled people. Laundry facilities. Motorcaravan service point. Shop, full restaurant and takeaway (10/5-22/9) with bars and terrace. Pool complex with water slides, fountains and a children's pool. Play field with equipment. Games room. Tennis courts. Bicycle hire. Minigolf. Archery. Riding (July/Aug). Fishing and boating. Bouncy castle. Six Trampolines. Quadricycles (on payment). Off site: Golf 10 km. Beaches 15 km.

Open: 24 April - 25 September.

Directions

Site is signed from St Julien; entrance is to the east off the D21 road, 2.5 km. north of St Julien-des-Landes. GPS: 46.66387, -1.71346

Charges 2010

Per unit incl. 2 persons	
and electricity	€ 17,50 - € 36,50
incl. services	€ 19,50 - € 39,00
extra person	€ 2,50 - € 7,80

Camping Cheques accepted.

Saint Laurent-sur-Sèvre

Camping le Rouge-Gorge

F-85290 Saint Laurent-sur-Sèvre (Vendée) T: **02 51 67 86 39**. E: **campinglerougegorge@wanadoo.fr**

alanrogers.com/FR85890

A family run site, Le Rouge-Gorge is open all year. There are 72 touring pitches, plus some units for rent and privately owned caravans and chalets. The site does accept a small number of workers' units. Slightly sloping and undulating pitches are on grass in a garden-like setting and a small wildlife pond (fenced) is in the centre of the site. It would make a suitable base from which to visit the spectacles of Puy de Fou and the steam railway which runs from Mortagne-sur-Sèvre to Les Herbiers. This is also an excellent stop-over for those heading to and from southern France and Spain, or the ski-resorts.

Facilities

Two toilet blocks, one can be heated, with washbasins in cubicles and facilities for disabled campers and babies. Laundry with washing machine and dryer. Motorcaravan service point. Bread and basic provisions stocked (15/6 -15/9). Swimming pool (1/6-30/9). Some low key family entertainment in high season. Boules. Charcoal barbecues are not permitted. TV room. WiFi. Off site: Fishing 500 m. Riding 2 km. Mortagne - Les Herbiers steam railway passes close to site.

Open: All year.

Directions

Saint Laurent-sur-Sèvre is about 10 km. due south of Cholet, just south of the N149. Site is on D111 west of town towards la Verrie, entrance at top of hill on right. GPS: 46.95809, -0.90341

Charges guide

Per unit incl. 2 persons	€ 17,00 - € 26,00
extra person	€ 3,90
child (under 10 yrs)	€ 2,05

Camping Cheques accepted.

Talmont-Saint Hilaire

yelloh! VILLAGE

Yelloh! Village le Littoral

Le Porteau, F-85440 Talmont-Saint Hilaire (Vendée) T: **02 51 22 04 64**. E: **info@yellohvillage-le-littoral.com**

alanrogers.com/FR85250

One hundred metres from the sea, five minutes from Les Sables d'Olonne, Le Littoral is situated on the South Vendée coast. It has been fully modernised over recent years by the Boursin family. Although the site's 483 pitches are mainly used for mobile homes and chalets for hire, there are 67 touring pitches which are hedged and of a good size. All have water, electricity and drainage. The site has a heated outdoor pool complex together with an indoor heated pool. The minimarket, bar and restaurant are open all season (2/4-12/9) with frequent themed evenings.

Facilities

Three sanitary blocks with British and Turkish style WCs, showers and washbasins in cubicles. Baby rooms. Facilities for disabled visitors. Laundry facilities. Fridge hire. Shop, Bar, restaurant and takeaway. Pizzeria and crêperie. Indoor pool Outdoor pool complex with slides (17/5-10/9). Bicycle hire. Multisport pitches. Tennis. Play area. Games room. Activities, entertainment and excursions. Minibus to beach. New chalets. Off site: Bus. Sea fishing 200 m. Riding 500 m. Golf 1.5 km. Beach 3 km.

Open: 2 April - 12 September.

Directions

From D949 Les Sables - Talmont, take the D4 south to Port Bourgenay. Turn onto the D129 westward and site is on left in 300 m. GPS: 46.451633, -1.702017

Charges guide

Per unit incl. 2 persons	
and electricity	€ 15,00 - € 40,00
extra person	€ 5,00 - € 6,00
child (1-7 yrs)	free - € 6,00
animal	€ 4,00

The Travel Service to book this site call 01580 214000 ...we'll arrange everything

On the Atlantic coast, between the châteaux of the Loire Valley and the Bordeaux vineyards, lies Poitou-Charentes, one of the sunniest parts of the French western coast. Its mild climate – 2,250 hours of sunshine per year – makes it popular with visitors from early spring to late autumn.

DÉPARTEMENTS: 16 CHARENTE, 17 CHARENTE-MARITIME, 79 DEUX SÈVRES, 86 VIENNE

MAJOR CITIES: POITIERS, LA ROCHELLE, COGNAC

Three hundred miles of coastline with fine sandy beaches backed by fragrant pine forests, lively resorts such as La Rochelle and Royan, and the islands of Oléron, Aix and Ré attract many holiday makers, particularly the French themselves. The scenery inland is in marked contrast: vast horizons and wooded valleys, the vineyards of Cognac, the Poitou fens and Marais Poitevin, the soothing tranquility of canals, the valley of Vienne and the foothills of Charente.

Farming is important to the economy; wheat, corn and cattle are raised. Industries produce machinery, chemicals and dairy products. The region is renowned as the home of Cognac – such famous names as Martell, Hennessy and Rémy Martin line the river Charente around the towns of Cognac and Jarnac where the spirit is distilled.

The capital of the region and capital of the Vienne département, is the city of Poitier. Situated on high ground at the confluence of the Clain and Boivre rivers, the city commands the so-called gate of Poitou, a gap 44 miles (71 km) wide between the mountains south of the Loire River and the Massif Central that serves as the connecting link between northern and southern France.

Places of interest

Angoulême: hilltop town surrounded by ramparts, cathedral, Renaissance château.

Cognac: the most celebrated 'eau de vie' in the world, cellars, Valois castle.

Marais Poitevin: marshes also known as the 'Green Venice'.

Poitiers: Palais de Justice, Notre Dame la Grande Romanesque church, old city.

La Rochelle: port, Porte de la Grosse Horloge (clock gate), Museum of the New World.

Saint Savin: 17th-century abbey, mural painting.

Cuisine of the region

Fish predominates, both fresh water (eel, trout, pike) and sea water (shrimps, mussels, oysters).

Bouilliture (bouilleture): eel stew with shallots and prunes in Sauvignon white wine.

Boulaigou: thick sweet or savoury pancake.

Bréjaude: cabbage, leek and bacon soup.

Cagouilles: snails from Charente.

Casserons en matelote: squid in red wine sauce with garlic and shallots.

Farcidure: a dumpling (poached or sautéed).

Farci Poitevin: paté of cabbage, spinach and sorrel, encased in cabbage leaves.

Mouclade: mussels cooked in wine, egg yolks and cream, served with Pineau des Charentes.

www.visit-poitou-charentes.com
crt@poitou-charentes-vacances.com
(0)5 49 50 10 50

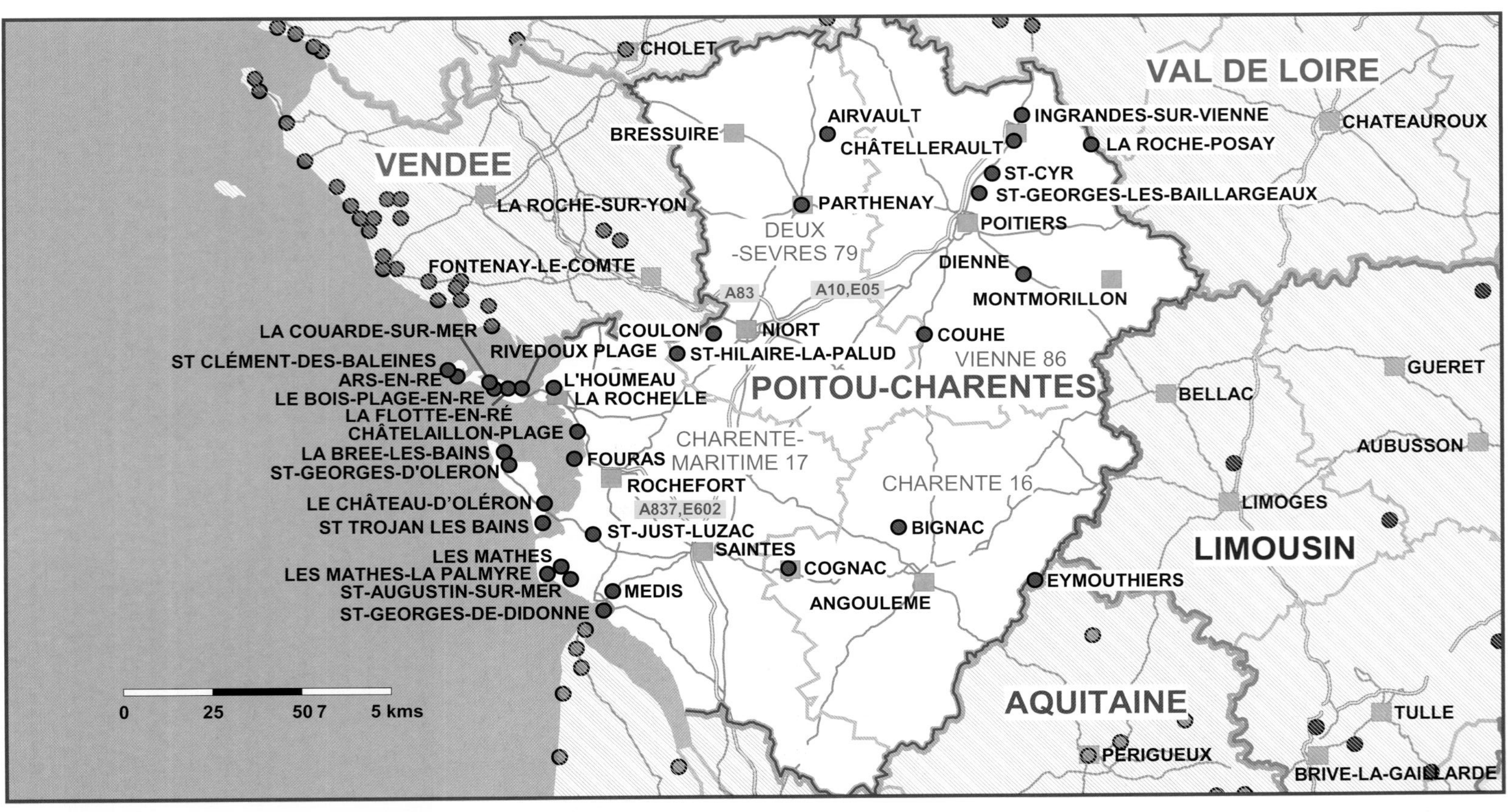
VAL DE LOIRE
VENDEE
POITOU-CHARENTES
LIMOUSIN
AQUITAINE
DEUX -SEVRES 79
VIENNE 86
CHARENTE-MARITIME 17
CHARENTE 16
CHOLET
BRESSUIRE
AIRVAULT
CHÂTELLERAULT
INGRANDES-SUR-VIENNE
LA ROCHE-POSAY
CHATEAUROUX
ST-CYR
ST-GEORGES-LES-BAILLARGEAUX
LA ROCHE-SUR-YON
PARTHENAY
POITIERS
FONTENAY-LE-COMTE
DIENNE
MONTMORILLON
A83
A10,E05
LA COUARDE-SUR-MER
COULON
NIORT
COUHE
RIVEDOUX PLAGE
ST-HILAIRE-LA-PALUD
ST CLÉMENT-DES-BALEINES
ARS-EN-RE
L'HOUMEAU
LE BOIS-PLAGE-EN-RE
LA ROCHELLE
LA FLOTTE-EN-RÉ
GUERET
BELLAC
CHÂTELAILLON-PLAGE
LA BREE-LES-BAINS
FOURAS
ST-GEORGES-D'OLERON
ROCHEFORT
AUBUSSON
A837,E602
LE CHÂTEAU-D'OLÉRON
LIMOGES
ST TROJAN LES BAINS
ST-JUST-LUZAC
BIGNAC
SAINTES
LES MATHES
COGNAC
LES MATHES-LA PALMYRE
EYMOUTHIERS
ST-AUGUSTIN-SUR-MER
MEDIS
ANGOULEME
ST-GEORGES-DE-DIDONNE
0
25
50 7
5 kms
TULLE
PERIGUEUX
BRIVE-LA-GAILLARDE

Ars-en-Ré

Camping le Cormoran

Route de Radia, Ars-en-Ré, F-17590 Ile de Ré (Charente-Maritime) T: **05 46 29 46 04**. E: **info@cormoran.com**
alanrogers.com/FR17260

On the outskirts of Ars-en-Re, Le Cormoran offers a quiet rural holiday. Touring pitches vary in size and are a mixture of sand and grass. Large units may be advised to call ahead. There are 33 pitches for touring units (all with 10A electricity) and the clean sanitary facilities are a mix of modern and traditional. A small comfortable bar and restaurant are located next to the pleasant pool. Being close to the local oyster beds and with numerous cycle paths which include routes through a nature reserve this campsite is popular with families of all ages. Although rural, the campsite is only 500 m. from the sea. During July and August, children's clubs and evening entertainment are organised. The village of Ars-en-Ré is only 800 m. away and a local market is held regularly during the season.

Facilities

One traditional toilet block and one modern unit provide good facilities. Washbasins are mainly in cabins. Provision for disabled visitors. Laundry. Motorcaravan services. Bar, restaurant and takeaway meals (4/4-15/9). Swimming pool (unheated). Fitness centre. Tennis. Games room. Play area. Entertainment programme in high season. Bicycle hire. WiFi. Off site: Nearest beach 500 m. Ars-en-Ré 800 m. Fishing 500 m. Boat launching 1 km. Riding 3 km. Golf 10 km.

Open: 4 April - 26 September.

Directions

Cross the toll bridge from La Rochelle onto the Ile de Ré and continue on D735 to Ars-en-Ré from where site is well signed. GPS: 46.21121, -1.5298

Charges guide

Per unit incl. 2 persons and electricity	€ 23,00 - € 48,70
extra person	€ 5,50 - € 12,25
child (1-9 yrs)	€ 3,50 - € 12,25
dog	€ 2,80 - € 5,70

Airvault

Camping de Courte Vallée

8 rue de Courte Vallée, F-79600 Airvault (Deux-Sèvres) T: **05 49 64 70 65**
E: **camping@caravanningfrance.com** **alanrogers.com/FR79020**

This small and beautifully landscaped site is family run. Set in 10 acres of parkland close to the Thouet river, it is within walking distance of Airvault (the birthplace of Voltaire). In the heart of rural France and off the main tourist tracks, the site offers tranquility and a warm and friendly atmosphere in surroundings maintained to the highest standards. There are 64 grass pitches, many with electricity, water and drainage which makes the site ideal for a long stay to explore the area. Nearby are Puy du Fou, Fontevraud Abbey, Doué la Fontaine zoo and the châteaux of Saumur and Oiron.

Facilities

A modern unisex block has spacious cubicles for showers and washbasins, and shower and WC cubicles for disabled visitors, all kept to a very high standard of cleanliness. Dishwashing area under cover. Washing machine and dryers. Reception sells 'frites', snacks, a selection of beers and wine and ice cream. Internet access. Swimming pool. Boules. Play area. Caravan storage. Wine tasting events and barbecues. Coffee bar. Off site: Airvault (birthplace of Voltaire) is a15-minute walk. Fishing 300 m. Riding 8 km.

Open: 15 March - 31 October.

Directions

From D938 (Parthenay-Thouars) take D725 Airvault. On approaching village turn left over bridge. At T-junction turn sharp left, second exit at roundabout, left at junction to site on left. Note: caravans are not allowed in village. GPS: 46.833056, -0.148333

Charges 2010

Per unit incl. 2 persons and electricity	€ 29,00 - € 33,00
extra person	€ 7,00 - € 8,00
child (under 11 yrs)	€ 3,00 - € 5,00
dog	€ 1,50

No credit cards.

Bignac

Camping Marco de Bignac

Lieu-dit les Sablons, F-16170 Bignac (Charente) T: **05 45 21 78 41**. E: **info@marcodebignac.com**
alanrogers.com/FR16060

The small village of Bignac is set in peaceful countryside not too far from the N10 road, north of Angoulême. This mature, British owned site is arranged alongside an attractive lake. Mature trees fringe the lake which is home to some impressive fish, including carp (fishing is free for guests). In the camping area, the trees are arranged formally to mark 82 touring pitches and two for mobile homes to rent. The pitches are level and offer a mixture of shade with a minimum size of 100 sq.m. Most have 6A electricity. This site is popular with British visitors and is a peaceful, relaxing location for couples or young families.

Facilities

Two traditional style toilet blocks have functional facilities. Washing machine. Bar and restaurant (April - Oct). Small shop. Swimming pool (June - Sept, unsupervised). Football, badminton, tennis, pedaloes, minigolf, boules, fishing, all free. Library. Play area. Pets' corner. Organised activities in high season. A torch may be useful. Off site: Local markets. Cognac Houses. Riding 5 km. Golf 25 km.

Open: 1 March - 30 November.

Directions

From N10 south of Poitiers, 14 km. north of Angoulême, take D11 west to Vars and Basse. Turn right onto D117 to Bignac. Site is signed at several junctions and in village (Camping Bignac). GPS: 45.79761, 0.06284

Charges guide

Per unit incl. 2 persons	€ 16,00 - € 24,00
extra person	€ 3,00 - € 5,00
child (2-7 yrs)	€ 1,50 - € 2,50
electricity (3/6A)	€ 2,00 - € 3,00

Châtelaillon-Plage

Camping Port-Punay

Allée Bernard Moreau, les Boucholeurs, F-17340 Châtelaillon-Plage (Charente-Maritime) T: **05 46 56 01 53**
E: **contact@camping-port-punay.com** **alanrogers.com/FR17340**

Port-Punay is a friendly, well-run site just 200 m. from the beach and 3 km. from the centre of the resort of Châtelaillon-Plage. There are 166 touring pitches laid out on well-trimmed grass, with many mature poplars and low shrubs. The site has a well stocked shop, open all season and a small bar and restaurant only open in high season. A heated swimming pool has a separate gated area for paddling. There is a good range of activities available and in high season some entertainment is arranged. This is a family run site (Famille Moreau) and the son of the family speaks excellent English, as does his Dutch wife. Rochefort to the south and La Rochelle to the north are worth a visit (buses outside the site), as is the nearby town of Châtelaillon-Plage, with its all-year covered market and, in summer, a daily street market Port-Punay has just one large toilet block, centrally positioned on the site, with very good facilities.

Facilities

One large toilet block with good facilities including washbasins in cubicles and large shower cubicles. Facilities for disabled visitors and babies. Washing machines. Shop. Bar, restaurant and takeaway (15/6-15/9). Swimming pool (heated May - Sept). Games area. Play area. Bicycle hire. Internet access. WiFi. Off site: Beach 200 m. Châtelaillon-Plage 3 km. by road, 1.5 km. along the seafront on foot or bike. Buses to Rochefort and La Rochelle from outside site. Riding 2 km. Golf 10 km.

Open: 1 April - 28 September.

Directions

From N137 (La Rochelle - Rochefort) take exit for Châtelaillon-Plage. At first roundabout follow sign for town centre. At 2nd roundabout turn left. Follow signs to site at seaside hamlet of Les Boucholeurs. Here drive to sea-wall then turn left through village to site. GPS: 46.05480, -1.08340

Charges guide

Per unit incl. 2 persons	€ 14,90 - € 22,00
extra person	€ 4,20 - € 5,50
electricity (10A)	€ 4,00 - € 5,00

Châtellerault

Camping le Relais du Miel

Route d'Antran, F-86100 Châtellerault (Vienne) T: **06 07 52 04 74**. E: **camping@lerelaisdumiel.com**
alanrogers.com/FR86030

This is a good site situated halfway between Poiters and Tours and with very easy access to the A10 and N10 roads. The site is set in the 10 acre grounds of a grand house dating from Napoleonic times, beside the River Vienne. Divided by trees and bushes that provide plenty of shade, there are 80 level pitches with 10A electricity and 13 also with water and drainage. One of the two old barns which form the sides of the courtyard behind the house has been converted to provide 19 apartments and these provide additional accommodation to rent. The other barn has been converted to provide a reception area together with a bar and a snack bar. A cycle path leads into the centre of the town 2.5 km. away. Access round the site is good and large motorhomes are accepted. There is a convivial atmosphere and the site is ideal for families with young children and couples of all ages. The airport at Poitiers is only 25 km. and the exciting park of Futuroscope is a lesser distance.

Facilities

Excellent toilet facilities include washbasins in cabins. Facilities for disabled visitors. Laundry facilities. Shop with basic essentials (July/Aug). Bar (all season) and restaurant (July/Aug). Pizzas (from local pizzeria). Takeaway. Snack bar (evenings July/Aug). Swimming and paddling pools with terrace. Playground. Tennis. Bicycle hire. Boules. Games room. Fishing. Internet access. Torch useful. Off site: Supermarket 400 m. Riding 5 km. Golf 11 km.

Open: 15 May - 2 September.

Directions

Châtellerault is between Tours and Poitiers. Site is north of town close to A10 autoroute. Take exit 26 (Châtellerault-Nord) and site is signed just off roundabout. From N10 follow signs for motorway (Tours - Péage) and at roundabout take exit for Antran. GPS: 46.83858, 0.53441

Charges guide

Per unit incl. 2 persons	€ 20,00 - € 25,00
extra person over 5 yrs	€ 3,00 - € 5,00

Cognac

Camping de Cognac

Boulevard de Châtenay, route de Sainte-Sévère, F-16100 Cognac (Charente) T: **05 45 32 13 32**
E: **info@campingdecognac.com** **alanrogers.com/FR16050**

Situated close to the historic town of Cognac, this municipal site is set in a rural area next to the Charente river. It has 168 pitches, 160 for touring caravans and eight mobile homes, which are all available for rent. All have 6A electricity and a water tap but no drain. The pitches are separated by shrubs and hedging, and access for large units on this site is good with tarmac or gravel roads all around. This area is naturally very suitable for people who enjoy brandy, with all the famous Cognac houses offering tours for visitors to see how the drink is made and learn of its history.

Facilities

Two well equipped, fairly modern toilet blocks (access by steps) include children's toilets and washing machines. Separate ground level facilities for disabled visitors. Motorcaravan services. Small swimming pool on site (municipal pool nearby). Shop. Snack bar and takeaway. Fishing. Play area on grass. Minigolf. Double axle caravans not accepted. Off site: Bicycle hire 2 km. Riverside walks. Restaurants, bars and shops in the town (2.3 km). Golf 5 km. Riding 6 km.

Open: 26 April - 30 September.

Directions

Site is to the north of the town beside the river on the D24 to St Sévère. GPS: 45.70916, -0.31289

Charges guide

Per unit incl. 2 persons and electricity	€ 13,00 - € 20,00
extra person	€ 4,00 - € 5,50
child (2-12 yrs)	€ 3,50 - € 4,00
animal	€ 1,50

Couhé

Camping Caravaning les Peupliers

F-86700 Couhé (Vienne) T: **05 49 59 21 16**. E: **info@lespeupliers.fr**
alanrogers.com/FR86080

Les Peupliers is situated in a valley just 25 km. south of Poitiers and close to the N10 motorway. The site has been family owned and run since 1968, and continually updated to provide good facilities. The camping area is divided in the middle by a small river river (unfenced), with crossing points at intervals. There are 180 pitches, 36 of which are for mobile homes available to rent. The 144 level touring pitches are on grass and separated by trees and shrubs. All have 10/16A electricity and 40 are fully serviced. The site enjoys a rural position within this region and tends to benefit from long hours of sunshine.

Facilities

Three sanitary blocks also provide facilities for babies and disabled visitors. Laundry facilities. Motorcaravan service point. TV and fridge rental. Shop. Restaurant, bar and snack bar (July/Aug). Pool complex. Playgrounds. Fishing lake. Minigolf. Multisport court. Entertainment in high season. WiFi. Off site: Tennis 800 m. Bicycle hire 1 km. Riding 5 km. Golf 30 km.

Open: 2 May - 30 September.

Directions

Couhé is 30 km. south of Poitiers on N10. From north, follow signs (Couhé town centre) and campsite (a short distance from slip road on right). From south, take 2nd Couhé exit from N10. Site entrance is opposite end of slip road. GPS: 46.31177, 0.17783

Charges 2010

Per unit incl. 2 persons	€ 30,00
extra person	€ 4,50 - € 7,00

Camping Cheques accepted.

Coulon

Camping de la Venise Verte

178 route des Bords de Sèvre, F-79510 Coulon (Deux-Sèvres) T: **05 49 35 90 36**
E: **accueil@camping-laveniseverte.fr** **alanrogers.com/FR79040**

This family run site on the edge of the Sevre Nortaise and the Marais Poitevin is ideal for short or long stays. With canoe and cycle hire on site you have no excuse for not exploring the local area. In the Deux-Sèvres, the 'department of discovery', so named because it has two rivers named Sevre, the Noirtaise and Nantaise, the Venise Verte provides an excellent site. There are 140 flat pitches here with 100 used for touring units, the remainder occupied by mobile homes. The pitches are of a good size, all with 10A electricity, water and drainage and with some shade. A 'Sites et Paysages' member.

Facilities

Modern, heated toilet facilities are of a high standard with free showers. Washing machine and dryer. Motorcaravan services. Restaurant/bar. Takeaway on request. Swimming pool (1/7-31/8). Play area. Bicycle and canoe hire. Boules area. Barbecues are not permitted. Off site: Coulon 1.0 km. and boat trips in the Marais. Ideal for walking, fishing, cycling or canoeing. Fishing 200 m. Golf and riding 15 km.

Open: 1 April - 30 October.

Directions

From Niort take N11 towards La Rochelle. Turn on the D3 towards Sansais and then north on D1 (Coulon). At traffic lights head towards 'centre ville' (Coulon) at mini-roundabout turn slightly right. Follow Sevre Noirtaise for 1.5 km. to site right.
GPS: 46.31492, -0.60835

Charges 2010

Per unit incl. 2 persons and electricity	€ 18,00 - € 29,00
extra person	€ 2,00 - € 6,00

Dienné

Castel Camping Domaine de Dienné

F-86410 Dienné (Vienne) T: **05 49 45 87 63**. E: **info@domaine-de-dienne.fr**
alanrogers.com/FR86120

This is a wonderful site and unique in what it offers. It concentrates on your 'well being' and provides all the facilities you could wish for in achieving that aim. The site extends over 47 hectares but there are just 30 pitches for touring units and these are on generous plots of 250 sq.m. All have their own water supply, drainage and 10A electricity, and access for the largest of units will not cause a problem. The accommodation to rent includes gypsy-style caravans, tree houses, yurts, a gite and cottages, which are all of superb quality and on large plots. Domaine de Dienné will impress from the moment you arrive.

Facilities

Restaurant. Heated swimming pools. Health and fitness centre. Hairdressing salon. Horse riding centre. Mountain biking. Adventure Park. Climbing tower. Children's games. Walking trails. Fishing. Cooking lessons. WiFi.
Off site: Poitiers airport 25 km. Futuroscope. Crocodile Planet. Monkey Park. Historical sites and castles.

Open: All year.

Directions

From Poitiers take N147 towards Limoges. After the village of Fleure the site is well signed.
GPS: 46.445028, 0.559294

Charges guide

Per unit incl. 2 persons and electricity	€ 25,00 - € 43,00

Eymouthiers

Castel Camping les Gorges du Chambon

Eymouthiers, F-16220 Montbron (Charente) T: **05 45 70 71 70**. E: **info@gorgesduchambon.fr**
alanrogers.com/FR16020

This is a wonderful Castels site with 28 hectares of protected natural environment to be enjoyed in the rolling Perigord Vert countryside. The 90 pitches are extremely generous in size (150 sq.m), mostly level and enjoy a mixture of sunshine and shade. There are 85 with water and 10A electricity, the remaining 5 are fully serviced. The spaciousness is immense, with fine walks through the woodlands and around the grounds. Flora, fauna and wildlife are as nature intended. Here you can feel at peace and enjoy precious moments of quiet. There has been much work done with the ecology association. The songs of the birds can be heard against the backdrop of water flowing gently down a small river on one side of the campsite. The different types of birds that can be found here are numerous. Guided walks are a feature. Les Gorges du Chambon is arranged around a restored Charentaise farmhouse and its outbuildings. A converted barn provides space for the restaurant and bar and the food is excellent, at a reasonable price. There is a pleasant swimming pool together with a paddling pool. There is also a sand beach area along the river and canoes can be hired on the site. The site owners are friendly and very helpful and want you to enjoy your time at their site.

Facilities

Traditional style blocks include facilities for disabled people. Washing machine, dryer. Basic shop. Bar, restaurant (all season). Takeaway (all season). Swimming pool, children's pool. Play area. Games room, TV and library with English books. Tennis. Archery. Minigolf. Bicycle and canoe hire. Organised activities July/Aug, children's club, youth disco, teenagers' corner. Internet access. Dogs are not accepted.
Off site: Private fishing (free) 6 km, with licence 200 m. Golf 6 km. Riding 6 km. Sailing 20 km. Visits are organised to local producers and day trips (low season).

Open: 19 April - 20 September
(rented accommodation 1 May - 31 October).

Directions

From N141 Angoulême - Limoges road at Rochefoucauld take D6 to Montbron village. Follow D6 in direction of Piegut-Pluviers and site is signed to the north on D163 on entering La Tricherie.
GPS: 45.65968, 0.55843

Charges 2010

Per unit incl. 2 persons and electricity	€ 18,30 - € 30,85
extra person	€ 4,30 - € 8,25
child (1-7 yrs)	€ 1,75 - € 5,50

Camping Cheques accepted.

Fouras

Domaine des Charmilles

Saint Laurent de la Prée, F-17450 Fouras (Charente-Maritime) T: **08 20 20 23 27**
E: **charmilles17@wanadoo.fr** **alanrogers.com/FR17170**

Les Charmilles is an impressive, quality site which is maintained to a very high standard. Of the 300 large pitches, 55 are for touring. All pitches have electricity (10A) and many also have water and drainage. There is an attractive restaurant and bar and an extensive entertainment programme in high season. A plan is in place for continual improvements to the site. This is one of the very few sites in France to have all its facilities especially adapted for disabled guests, including 10 of the chalets and the swimming pools. The friendly owner wishes to ensure that all of his visitors have a great holiday.

Facilities

The modern toilet blocks are conveniently placed. Excellent facilities for babies and disabled people. Laundry facilities. Shop, bar, takeaway and restaurant (all May - Sept). Heated swimming pools (one covered), water slides, paddling pool, aquagym and sunbathing terrace (all May - Sept). Massage (two days per week). Playground. Multisports court. Bicycle hire. Minibus service to beach in July/Aug. No charcoal barbecues. Off site: Fishing 3 km. Golf 5 km. Sailing 10 km. Riding 15 km.

Open: 7 April - 22 September.

Directions

Leave N137 at exit for Fouras and St Laurent de la Prée, joining D937 towards Fouras. Site is on left in about 800 m. GPS: 45.9873, -1.0511

Charges guide

Per unit incl. 2 persons	€ 15,00 - € 30,00
extra person	€ 6,00
child (under 5 yrs)	€ 4,00
electricity	€ 4,00

Ingrandes-sur-Vienne

Castel Camping le Petit Trianon

Saint Ustre, 1 rue du Moulin de St Ustre, F-86220 Ingrandes-sur-Vienne (Vienne) T: **05 49 02 61 47**
E: **chateau@petit-trianon.fr** **alanrogers.com/FR86010**

A family-owned site for many years, Le Petit Trianon is situated halfway between Tours and Poitiers. It enjoys a countryside position within the lovely grounds of an 18th-century château. Visitors to the site often return several times after their first visit for the calm and tranquil atmosphere here. There are 99 pitches all with electricity (10A), set in seven hectares which gives a real sense of spaciousness. Plants are well tended and shade is provided in parts by the many attractive trees. Access around the site is good and large units are accepted by prior arrangement.

Facilities

The sanitary facilities include washbasins in cabins, some washbasin and shower units, baby baths, washing machines and dryer. Facilities for disabled visitors. Motorcaravan service point. Shop. Snack bar. Takeaway. Heated swimming pool and paddling pool. Playground. Minigolf. Badminton, croquet, volleyball and boules. Satellite TV. Reading room. Bicycle hire. Bread making. Internet access. WiFi. Caravan storage. Off site: Restaurant 50 m. Tennis 2 km. Fishing 3 km. Riding 15 km. Local markets. Futuroscope.

Open: 20 May - 20 September.

Directions

Take the N10 to Ingrandes sur Vienne and take the D75 in the direction of Oyre. Follow D121 to St Ustre (1.5 km) and site is then well signed. GPS: 46.885533, 0.586133

Charges guide

Per person	€ 7,00
child (3-6 yrs)	€ 3,50
pitch incl. electricity (5/10A)	€ 12,40 - € 12,80
dog	€ 2,10

L'Houmeau

Camping Au Petit Port de l'Houmeau

Rue des Sartieres, F-17137 L'Houmeau (Charente-Maritime) T: **05 46 50 90 82**. E: **info@aupetitport.com**
alanrogers.com/FR17300

Au Petit Port de l'Houmeau is a pretty, quiet and rural site on the edge of the small seaside village of l'Houmeau. The friendly English speaking owners ensure high standards of maintenance. There are 94 pitches (clustered in groups of eight) and of a good size. Most are equipped with 5/10A electricity and virtually all offer some degree of shade. Larger motorcaravans may have difficulty finding a suitable pitch during busy periods. There are relatively few amenities here, but the village shops, bars and a good restaurant are close by. A good base for exploring the Charente Maritime coast, the site' proximity to the fascinating town of La Rochelle and within cycling distance of the Ile de Ré is a bonus.

Facilities

Two well maintained toilet blocks. Washing machines and dryers. Snack bar (July/Aug). Internet point. Bicycle hire. Play area. 'Moules/frites' evenings in high season. Mobile homes and chalets for rent (all year). Off site: Beach 200 m. Hourly bus to La Rochelle from village centre. Shops, bars, restaurant.

Open: 1 April - 30 September.

Directions

From the north take the D137. Join N11/E601 towards La Rochelle then the N237 towards Ile de Ré. Exit onto the D104 to Lagord and follow signs to l'Houmeau from where site is signed. GPS: 46.19568, -1.18789

Charges guide

Per unit incl. 2 persons	€ 13,00 - € 16,00
extra person	€ 3,50 - € 4,50
child (0-13 yrs)	€ 1,80 - € 2,50
electricity (5/10A)	€ 3,50 - € 4,20

La Bree les Bains

Camping Antioche d'Oléron

Route de Proires, F-17840 La Bree les Bains (Charente-Maritime) T: **05 46 47 92 00**
E: **info@camping-antiochedoleron.com** **alanrogers.com/FR17570**

Situated to the northeast of the island, Camping Antioche is quietly located within a five minute walk to the beach. There are 130 pitches, of which 73 are occupied by mobile homes and 57 are for touring units. The pitches are set amongst attractive shrubs and palm trees and all have electricity (10A), water and a drain. A new pool area which comprises two swimming pools (heated), two jacuzzi, two paddling pools and a raised sunbathing deck, is beautifully landscaped with palms and flowers. A small bar, restaurant and takeaway offer reasonably priced food and drinks. The site becomes livelier in season with regular evening entertainment and activities for all the family.

Facilities

The single sanitary block is of a good standard and is kept clean and fresh. Facilities for disabled visitors. Laundry. Motorcaravan services. Bar, restaurant and snack bar (weekends only May and June, daily July/Aug). Swimming and paddling pools. Games room. Play area. WiFi. Bicycle hire (July/Aug). Off site: Beach 150 m. Fishing 150 m. Riding 1.5 km.Golf 7 km.

Open: 1 April - 30 September.

Directions

Cross the bridge on the D26 and join the D734. After St Georges turn right onto the D273E1 towards La Bree-les-Baines. At T-junction turn left from where the campsite is signed. GPS: 46.02007, -1.35764

Charges guide

Per unit incl. 2 persons and electricity	€ 21,15 - € 35,15
extra person	€ 7,10
child (1-14 yrs)	€ 3,70

La Couarde-sur-Mer

Camping l'Océan

La Passe, la Couarde-sur-Mer, F-17670 Ile-de-Ré (Charente-Maritime) T: **05 46 29 87 70**
E: **campingdelocean@wanadoo.fr** **alanrogers.com/FR17230**

L'Océan lies close to the centre of the Ile de Ré, just 50 m. from a sandy beach. There are 338 pitches here with 161 for touring units, the remainder occupied by mobile homes and chalets. The camping area is well shaded and pitches are of a reasonable size, all with electricity (10A). A pleasant bar/restaurant overlooks the large heated swimming pool which is surrounded by an attractive sunbathing terrace. Bicycle hire is popular here as the island offers over 100 km. of interesting cycle routes. A bus goes to La Rochelle from 300 metres outside the site.

Facilities

The new toilet blocks are modern and well maintained with facilities for disabled visitors. Motorcaravan services. Shop. Bar/restaurant and takeaway. Swimming pool. Riding. Bicycle hire. Tennis. Fishing pond adjacent. Play area. Minigolf (free). Helicopter rides, sub-aqua diving and pony riding (high season). Entertainment in high season. No charcoal barbecues. Internet access. Off site: Beach 50 m. La Couarde 2.5 km. Golf 5 km.

Open: 5 May - 28 September.

Directions

After toll bridge, join D735 which runs along the north side of the island until you pass La Couarde. The site is 2.5 km. beyond village (in the direction of Ars-en-Ré). GPS: 46.20433, -1.46767

Charges guide

Per unit incl. 1-2 persons	€ 14,95 - € 38,20
extra person	€ 4,35 - € 9,65
electricity	€ 5,20

Camping Cheques accepted.

La Flotte-en-Ré

Camping les Peupliers

RD735, F-17630 La Flotte-en-Ré (Charente-Maritime) T: **05 46 09 62 35**. E: **camping@les-peupliers.com**
alanrogers.com/FR17290

On the Ile de Ré, you are never far from the sea and the location of this campsite is no exception. It is just 800 metres from the sea with sea views from some of the pitches. English is spoken at reception and the staff go out of their way to make your stay enjoyable. The 21 level touring pitches are in a separate area from 143 chalets for rent, in a wooded area. There are few water points. The trees provide some shade, but the very low hedges provide little privacy as the width and length of the pitches vary.

Facilities

Two new but traditionally designed sanitary blocks are clean and well maintained. Both have unisex facilities including showers and vanity type units in cabins. Separate facilities for people with disabilities. Laundry facilities. Shop, restaurant, takeaway and bar with TV. Heated outdoor swimming pool (15/5-18/9). Play area. Children's club and entertainment (high season). Fridge hire. Bicycle hire.
Off site: Riding 500 m. Beach, boat launching and sailing 800 m. Fishing 800 m. Golf 20 km.

Open: 3 April - 18 September.

Directions

Over the toll bridge and turn left at second roundabout. Site is well signed.
GPS: 46.182816, -1.30083

Charges guide

Per unit incl. 2 persons and electricity	€ 21,00 - € 33,00
extra person	€ 5,00 - € 8,00
child (0-5 yrs)	free - € 5,00
dog	€ 5,00

Camping Cheques accepted.

La Flotte-en-Ré

486

Camping la Grainetière

Route de Saint Martin, F-17630 La Flotte-en-Ré (Charente-Maritime) T: **05 46 09 68 86**
E: **la-grainetiere@orange.fr** **alanrogers.com/FR17280**

A truly friendly welcome awaits you from the owners, Isabelle and Eric, at La Grainetière. It is a peaceful campsite set in almost three hectares of pine trees which provide some shade for the 65 touring pitches of various shapes and sizes. There are also 50 well-spaced chalets for rent. Some pitches are suitable for units up to seven metres (book in advance). There are no hedges for privacy and the pitches are sandy with some grass. Ample new water points and electricity (10A) hook-ups (Euro plugs) serve the camping area. The site is well lit.

Facilities

The unisex sanitary block is first class, with washbasins in cubicles, showers, British style WCs, facilities for children and people with disabilities. Shop, takeaway, swimming pool (heated all season). Bicycle hire. Fridge hire. TV room. Charcoal barbecues are not permitted. New aquatic park and jacuzzi. Off site: Beach and sailing 2 km. Bar and restaurant 2 km. Fishing and boat launching 2 km. Riding 3 km. Golf 10 km.

Open: 1 April - 30 September.

Directions

Follow camping signs from La Flotte, 1 km. from the village. GPS: 46.18755, -1.344933

Charges guide

Per unit incl. 2 persons and electricity	€ 19,00 - € 30,00
extra person	€ 5,00 - € 7,50
child (0-7 yrs)	€ 2,50 - € 3,50
dog	€ 2,50 - € 3,00

La Roche-Posay

Camping le Riveau

Route de Lesigny, F-86270 La Roche-Posay (Vienne) T: **05 49 86 21 23**. E: **info@camping-le-riveau.com**
alanrogers.com/FR86050

Camping Le Riveau is set in eight hectares and has direct access to the Creuse river on which fishing and canoes are popular. There are 200 pitches, of which 30 are used for mobile homes to rent. The touring pitches include 19 with hardstanding, ideal for motorcaravans and with services nearby. Access around the site is good for larger units. The pitches are all large and 16A electricity is available. This is a good, well run site in very natural surroundings. There is a sense of spaciousness at this site where you can relax in a convivial atmosphere.

Facilities

Two fully equipped, heated toilet blocks, one in each section. Excellent facilities for disabled visitors and children. Bar and snackbar. Swimming and paddling pools. Play area. Games room. Fishing. Canoes. Boules. Barbecues are not permitted. Entertainment in high season. Off site: Shops, restaurants, etc. 1 km. Golf 3 km. Riding 500 m.

Open: 28 March - 18 October.

Directions

Site is signed from the D725 town bypass, turning north at roundabout onto D5 towards Lesigny. Site is 50 m. on right. GPS: 46.8001, 0.8085

Charges guide

Per unit incl. 2 persons and electricity	€ 16,50 - € 20,90
extra person	€ 4,00 - € 5,00
child (under 10 yrs)	€ 1,00 - € 3,00
dog	€ 1,00 - € 1,50

No credit cards.

Le Bois-Plage-en-Ré

Sunêlia Interlude

8 route de Gros Jonc, F-17580 Le Bois-Plage-en-Ré (Charente-Maritime) T: **05 46 09 18 22**
E: **infos@interlude.fr** **alanrogers.com/FR17210**

Camping Interlude enjoys a pleasant location with access to an excellent beach. A popular site even in low season (it may become noisy, crowded and overstretched in high season), it has 151 mobile homes for rent and 136 touring pitches. The pitches vary in size and are mostly divided by hedges on part undulating, sandy terrain. Many are to the left of the site in a pine forest setting, others mingle with the tour operators and new mobile homes. All have 6/10 electricity. Units over 7 m. in length are no longer accepted due to the tight roadways and many trees. Facilities are open all season.

Facilities

Two modern, clean and well equipped sanitary blocks provide the usual facilities and some shower units suitable for families with twin washbasins. Baby room, children's toilets. En-suite facilities for disabled visitors. Laundry facilities. Motorcaravan service point. Large restaurant/bar and shop. Swimming pools, one outdoor and one inside. Play area. Boules. Organised events and entertainment. Games/TV room. Tennis. Bicycle hire. Communal barbecues. Multisports area. Internet access and WiFi.

Open: 4 April - 27 September.

Directions

After toll bridge to the Ile de Ré follow sign (Le Bois-Plage). Turn left at first roundabout, straight on at next two, then left at fourth roundabout. Site signed.
GPS: 46.17383, -1.37383

Charges guide

Per unit incl. 2 persons and electricity	€ 23,00 - € 40,00
incl. water and waste	€ 26,00 - € 44,00
extra person (over 4 yrs)	€ 5,00 - € 10,00
dog (max. 1)	€ 4,00 - € 8,00

Le Château-d'Oléron

Airotel Oléron

Domaine de Montravail, F-17480 Le Château-d'Oléron (Charente-Maritime) T: **05 46 47 61 82**
E: **info@camping-airotel-oleron.com** **alanrogers.com/FR17060**

This family-run site on the outskirts of Le Château d'Oléron has very good facilities, including a superb equestrian centre, a full range of sporting activites and an attractive heated pool complex. This is a mature site with about 270 pitches of a good size, with varying degrees of shade provided by trees and shrubs. It is well laid out with 133 touring pitches and the remainder for mobile homes of which 30 are for rent. Most touring pitches have electricity (10A) and four have their own water and drainage. A full entertainment programme is provided in high season and one can enjoy the exploration of the island with its fine sandy beaches on the Atlantic coast and the miles of flat tracks for walking, cycling or horse riding. The equestrian centre offers courses up to a week in length for riders ranging from novice to experienced.

Facilities

Two modern toilet blocks with facilities for disabled visitors and babies. Washing machine and dryer. Motorcaravan services. Shop. Bar, restaurant and takeaway (15/6-15/9). Heated swimming and paddling pools. Equestrian centre. Playground. Multisport court. Tennis. Minigolf. Fishing. Canoe hire. Bicycle hire. TV and games room. Internet access. WiFi. Off site: Supermarket. Local markets. Zoo. Aquarium.

Open: Easter - 30 September.

Directions

Cross the bridge onto the island and continue on D26. At second roundabout turn right, marked Dolus and Le Château. Proceed 500 m. and take first right, marked Campings. Site is 1 km. on the right.
GPS: 45.88207, -1.20648

Charges guide

Per unit incl. 2 persons	€ 13,50 - € 22,00
extra person	€ 4,00 - € 6,50
electricity (8A)	€ 3,90
dog	€ 2,50

The Travel Service
to book this site call 01580 214000
...we'll arrange everything

Le Château-d'Oléron

Camping la Brande

Route des Huitres, F-17480 Le Château-d'Oléron (Charente-Maritime) T: **05 46 47 62 37**
E: **info@camping-labrande.com** **alanrogers.com/FR17220**

A quality environmentally-friendly site, run and maintained to the highest standard, La Brande offers an ideal holiday environment on the delightful Ile d'Oléron, famed for its oysters. La Brande is situated on the oyster route and close to a sandy beach. Pitches here are generous and mostly separated by hedges and trees, the greater number for touring outfits. All are on level grassy terrain and have electricity hook-ups, some are fully serviced. The many activities in high season, plus the natural surroundings, make this an ideal choice for families. A feature of this site is the heated indoor pool (28°) open all season. The Barcat family ensures that their visitors not only enjoy quality facilities, but Gerard Barcat offers guided bicycle tours and canoe trips. This way you discover the nature, oyster farming, vineyards and history of Oléron, which is joined to the mainland by a 3 km. bridge.

Facilities

Three heated, clean sanitary blocks have spacious, well equipped showers and washbasins. Baby facilities. Excellent facilities for people with disabilities. Laundry rooms. Motorcaravan service point. Superb restaurant/takeaway and bar (July/Aug). Shop (July/Aug). Heated indoor swimming pool. Jacuzzi. Sauna. Well equipped playground. Games room. Football field, tennis, minigolf, fishing and archery. Bicycle hire. Canoe hire. Free WiFi. New building for children. Off site: Beach 300 m. Sailing 2 km. Riding 6 km.

Open: 20 March - 14 November.

Directions

After crossing bridge to L'Ile d'Oléron turn right towards Le Château d'Oléron. Continue through village and follow sign for Route des Huitres. Site is on left after 2.5 km. GPS: 45.90415, -1.21525

Charges guide

Per unit incl. 2 persons and electricity	€ 20,00 - € 42,00
extra person	€ 5,00 - € 8,00

Camping Cheques accepted.

Les Mathes

Camping l'Orée du Bois

225 route de la Bouverie, la Fouasse, F-17570 Les Mathes (Charente-Maritime) T: **05 46 22 42 43**
E: **info@camping-oree-du-bois.fr** **alanrogers.com/FR17050**

L'Orée du Bois has 388 pitches of about 100 sq.m. in a very spacious, pinewood setting. There are 150 for touring units, mainly scattered amongst the permanent chalets and tents. They include 40 large pitches with hardstanding and individual sanitary facilities (in blocks of four with shower, toilet, washbasin and dishwashing sink). Pitches are on flat, fairly sandy ground, separated by trees, shrubs and hedges and all have electrical connections (6A). The forest pines offer some shade. Used by several tour operators. A lively site in high season which can be noisy but is tranquil in low season.

Facilities

Four main toilet blocks include some washbasins in cabins. Three have a laundry and facilities for disabled people. Shop. Excellent bar, restaurant, crêperie and takeaway service (1/5-13/9). Heated swimming pools (1/5-13/9), water slide and paddling pool (trunks, not shorts). Play areas. Tennis court, boules, football and basketball. Games room and TV lounge. Bicycle hire. Discos. Entertainment in July/Aug. Internet access. Barbecues in special areas only. WiFi. Off site: Riding 300 m. Fishing 4 km. Golf 5 km.

Open: 1 May - 13 September.

Directions

From north follow D14 La Tremblade. At roundabout before Arvert turn on D268 (Les Mathes and La Palmyre). Site on right in Fouasse. From south, at Royan take D25 (La Palmyre). In town turn north to Les Mathes. At first roundabout in Les Mathes follow sign (Fouasse and La Tremblade). Site on left after 2 km. GPS: 45.7326, -1.1785

Charges 2010

Per unit incl. 2 persons and electricity	€ 18,00 - € 40,00
incl. private sanitary facility	€ 26,50 - € 50,50
extra person	€ 6,00 - € 8,00

Camping Cheques accepted.

Les Mathes-La Palmyre

Camping la Clé des Champs

1188 route de la Fouasse, F-17570 Les Mathes-La Palmyre (Charente-Maritime) T: **05 46 22 40 53**
E: **contact@cledeschamps.com** **alanrogers.com/FR17540**

Situated on the edge of the large Forêt de la Coubre and around 1.5 km. from the village of Les Mathes, La Clé des Champs has 152 good size, grass touring pitches. Set amongst avenues of small trees, most have electricity (6/10A). This quiet campsite is flat, with 143, mostly private, mobile homes which are well positioned at the top end of the site. The two old rather drab sanitary blocks have basic facilities and are reasonably maintained. The swimming pool can be covered by a polythene stucture in low season and a bar and shop are open from mid-June to September. Various cycle tracks lead through the forest to the beaches of the Côte Sauvage (bicycle hire is available on site). These stretch for 70 km. and sandy beaches alternate with rocky coves. The nearby zoo at La Palmyre, with over 1,600 animals, is France's second largest. La Palmyre is a stylish resort with cafes and restaurants, as well as a fine sandy beach.

Facilities

Two old, traditional sanitary blocks with basic facilities. Wahing machine. Shop. Bar. Snack bar and takeaway (mid-June - Sept). Swimming pool. Paddling pool. Games room. Play area. Bicycle hire. Activity and entertainment programme (July/Aug). WiFi. Mobile homes for rent.
Off site: Nearest beach 4 km. Les Mathes village 1.5 km. (good range of shops and restaurants). Riding centre nearby. Minigolf 800 m.

Open: 28 March - 31 October.

Directions

From Saujon take the D14 heading north west towards La Tremblade. At Arvert head south on the D141 to Les Mathes. Beyond the village, head right on the Route de la Fouasse and the site is on the right after a further 500 m. GPS: 45.72098, -1.17149

Charges guide

Per unit incl. 2 persons and electricity	€ 14,30 - € 24,00
extra person	€ 2,50 - € 4,50

Les Mathes-La Palmyre

Camping Caravaning Monplaisir

26 avenue de la Palmyre, F-17570 Les Mathes-La Palmyre (Charente-Maritime) T: **05 46 22 50 31**
E: **campmonplaisir@aol.com** **alanrogers.com/FR17110**

Monplaisir provides a small, quiet haven in an area with some very hectic campsites. It is ideal for couples or families with young children. Quite close to the town and set back from the road, the entrance leads through an avenue of trees, past the owners' home to a well kept, garden-like site with many trees and shrubs. There are 114 level, marked pitches and all but a few have electrical connections (6A); long leads may be required. On 14 there are caravans for rent and a modern building provides flats and studios for rent. Larger units would find this site difficult to navigate.

Facilities

The toilet block has some washbasins in cabins and facilities for disabled visitors. Laundry and dishwashing facilities. Ice pack service in reception. Bread delivered daily. TV, games room and library. Heated swimming pool and paddling pool (early May-30/9). Small play area. Winter caravan storage.
Off site: Supermarket short walk. Minigolf adjacent (owned by the site). Fishing 500 m. Riding 1 km. Golf 5 km.

Open: Easter - 1 October.

Directions

Follow D25 to La Palmyre. In town, turn north to Les Mathes. At roundabout turn right to town centre. Site on left. From north on D14 (La Tremblade) turn onto D268 (Les Mathes and La Palmyre) at roundabout just before Arvert. Keep straight on to Les Mathes, road becomes D141 and turn left (north) at roundabout. Site is 600 m. on left. GPS: 45.71384, -1.15939

Charges guide

Per unit incl. 2 persons	€ 17,00
incl. 3 persons	€ 19,50
extra person	€ 5,00
child	€ 2,50 - € 5,00
electricity	€ 3,00

Less 20% outside July/Aug.

Les Mathes-La Palmyre

Siblu Camping Bonne Anse Plage

La Palmyre, F-17570 Les Mathes-La Palmyre (Charente-Maritime) T: **05 46 22 40 90**
E: **bonneanseplage@siblu.fr** **alanrogers.com/FR17040**

On the edge of the Forêt de la Coubre, just beyond La Palmyre, Bonne Anse Plage is attractively set amongst pines, just a short stroll from a tidal inlet, and just 600 m. from the mouth of the Gironde estuary. This is a spacious, gently undulating site, and is now owned by the Siblu group. There are 850 level, marked pitches, of which around half are for touring units (all with electricity). Most are well shaded, the ones nearer the sea less so and are rather sandier. The reception, restaurant and bar with a spacious outdoor terrace and an impressive pool complex form the social focus. The pool complex also features several giant water slides. A shopping centre which is open all season includes a supermarket, delicatessen and takeaway, bistro, shops for bread and pastries, holiday goods and papers. There is plenty going on in high season with clubs for children of all ages, including Siblu Soccer tournaments throughout the season. Evening entertainment, including children's shows, takes place on the bar's outdoor terrace.

Facilities

Seven well maintained toilet blocks include facilities for disabled visitors and babies. Motorcaravan service point. Shopping centre. Restaurant and bar. Takeaway food. Large pool complex with water slides (including a junior chute). Playground. Video games room. TV. Minigolf. Football. Trampolines. Bicycle hire. Climbing wall. Entertainment and activities in high season. Internet access. Gas barbecues only. Off site: Supervised, safe beaches 500 m. Fishing, riding 1 km. Zoo 1 km. Golf 5 km. Watersports and tennis. Fitness track.

Open: 1 May - 17 September.

Directions

Leave A10 autoroute at Saintes. Head for Royan (N150). In Royan take signs for La Palmyre (D25). At La Palmyre roundabout follow signs for Ronce-les-Bains. Site is 1 km. on left. GPS: 45.69810, -1.19976

Charges guide

Per unit incl. 3 persons and electricity	€ 37,60 - € 44,80
extra person (over 1 yr)	€ 7,60 - € 9,20

Médis

Camping le Clos Fleuri

8 impasse du Clos Fleuri, F-17600 Médis (Charente-Maritime) T: **05 46 05 62 17**. E: **clos-fleuri@wanadoo.fr**
alanrogers.com/FR17160

Camping Le Clos Fleuri really does live up to its name. The profusion of different trees and the lawns and flower beds give this small site a very rural atmosphere. There is always a warm welcome from the Devais family who created this pretty site in 1974. The 123 touring pitches are mostly of generous size (a little uneven in places). They vary from being in full sun to well shaded and 100 have electrical connections. The bar/restaurant is a converted barn providing a cool haven on hot days and a very convivial venue for evening gatherings and entertainment. There is occasional noise from light aircraft. The surrounding countryside is very pleasant with crops of sunflowers, wheat and maize, while beaches of all sorts are within easy reach. All in all the Clos Fleuri combines a great deal of charm, beauty and friendliness with a location from which the attractions of the Charente-Maritime may be discovered.

Facilities

Toilet facilities are kept clean. One block is segregated male and female, the other is unisex with each unit in its own cubicle. Facility for disabled visitors. Baby baths. Laundry facilities. Small pool and paddling pool. Sauna. Shop (5/7-15/9). Restaurant (11/7-31/8) and bar (5/7-15/9). In high season there are twice weekly 'soirées' and boules and archery competitions. Minigolf. WiFi. Large units should call in high season to check there is space. Off site: Médis 2 km.

Open: 1 June - 18 September.

Directions

Médis is on the N150 from Saintes, halfway between Saujon and Royan. Drive into village. Site signed to south at various points in Médis and is about 2 km. outside village. GPS: 45.63011, -0.9458

Charges guide

Per unit incl. 2 persons	€ 18,90 - € 28,00
extra person	€ 6,00 - € 8,00
child (2-7 yrs)	€ 4,00 - € 5,50
electricity (5/10A)	€ 3,00 - € 6,00
dog	€ 2,50 - € 3,30

Parthenay

Kawan Village du Bois Vert

kawan VILLAGES www.kawan-villages.com

14 rue Boisseau, le Tallud, F-79200 Parthenay (Deux-Sèvres) T: **05 49 64 78 43**
E: **bois-vert@wanadoo.fr** **alanrogers.com/FR79050**

This former municipal site is now operated by a campsite group although so far it has changed little. There are 88 pitches of which 74 are for touring, all with electricity (10A) and 30 also with water and drainage. There are 15 mobile homes to rent. Pitches are separated by hedges and there are mature trees providing some shade. The site is on the River Thouet and although there is a secure fence, there is a steep drop to the river bank. Pleasant walkways along both sides and a footbridge close by enable you to walk into the old walled town.

Facilities

Two very traditional sanitary blocks both in need of attention. One has unisex toilets (a few British-style but seatless), showers and washbasins in cubicles. Primitive dishwashing and laundry sinks. The second is slightly better. Facilities for disabled visitors, incl. new mobile homes. Bar with snackbar and takeaway (1/5-30/9). Bread can be ordered. New heated swimming pool. TV. Table tennis and boules. Small play area. Tickets available for Futuroscope and Puy du Fou. Off site: Motorcaravan service point adjacent. Fishing 100 m. Base de Loisirs nearby. Riding and golf 15 km.

Open: 1 April - 30 September.

Directions

Parthenay is 50 km. west of Poitiers (and the A10) via the N149 to Bressuire and Nantes. Site is southwest of the town at Le Tallud on the D949 La Roche sur Yon road. Take ring road and site is on right as you join D949. GPS: 46.6414, -0.2672

Charges guide

Per unit incl. 2 persons	€ 14,50 - € 17,50
incl. electricity	€ 16,50 - € 19,50
extra person	€ 4,00 - € 5,00
child (2-10 yrs)	€ 2,00

Camping Cheques accepted.

Rivedoux Plage

Campéole le Platin

125 avenue Gustave Perreau, F-17940 Rivedoux Plage (Charente-Maritime) T: **05 46 09 84 10**
E: **platin@campeole.com** **alanrogers.com/FR17560**

Located at the gateway to the Ile de Ré, Le Platin is just a short walk from the pleasant village of Rivedoux Plage where there are several good restaurants and shops. In high season a small market is held every morning in the village square. A long, narrow site, the beach is on one side and the main road on the other. It is divided into small avenues with around 20 pitches in each. All have 10A electricity and most are shaded, although the pitches nearest the beach have little shade (but the best views). Of the 200 pitches, 50 are used for canvas bungalows for hire, the rest are seasonal and for touring. Popular with motorcaravanners, Le Platin has a short stay area outside the barrier, and a bus stop 100 m. away makes it easy to explore the island and also to visit La Rochelle on the mainland. A cycle track runs alongside the site. Direct access onto the beach makes it an ideal spot for families, and sea fishing is a popular activity here. The beach is a hive of activity at low tide when the oyster beds are exposed.

Facilities

The toilet facilities here are a little below standard, although one block has good showers and an en-suite bathroom for disabled visitors. This is only the second year Campéole have been here, and there are plans for improvements. A swimming pool complex is due for completion in June. Small bar. Entertainment in high season. Off site: Bicycle hire 200 m.

Open: 1 April - 30 September.

Directions

After crossing the toll bridge from La Rochelle, continue on the D735 into Rivedoux Plage. Site is well signed on the right. GPS: 46.1588, -1.2708

Charges 2010

Per unit incl. 2 persons and electricity	€ 19,10 - € 23,60
extra person	€ 4,10 - € 6,10

Saint Augustin-sur-Mer

Le Logis du Breuil

F-17570 Saint Augustin-sur-Mer (Charente-Maritime) T: **05 46 23 23 45**
E: **camping.Logis-du-Breuil@wanadoo.fr** **alanrogers.com/FR17190**

The first impression on arrival at this impressive campsite is space. The camping area is a 200 m. expanse of farm pasture where (on different areas) cattle graze and children play. The camping areas are set among rows of mature and shady trees giving a dappled effect to the tents, caravans and grassy pitches. The 320 pitches (250 with 3/10A electricity) are very large and have direct access to wide, unpaved alleys, which lead on to the few tarmac roads around the site. The amenities are centred around the reception area and pool complex. The area around the site is very pleasant agricultural land and the beaches of the Atlantic coast are nearby, as are the oyster and the mussel beds of Marennes and La Tremblade. The Gagnard family started the campsite about 25 years ago and obviously take great pride in what it has now become: a peaceful, friendly and very pleasant site from which to explore a delightful holiday area.

Facilities

Four well maintained toilet blocks are spaced around the camping area. Laundry facilities. Excellent shop, bar, restaurant and takeaway. Swimming pools (26/5-15/9). No evening entertainment. Play area. Indoor games area. Bicycle hire. Tennis. Excursions organised. WiFi. Gites, mobile homes and chalets to rent. Off site: Beach 50 minute walk near St Palais-sur-Mer, another to the 'Cote Sauvage'.

Open: 1 May - 30 September.

Directions

From A10 exit 35, take the N150 to Saujon and continue on the N150 to Royan. Take the D25 towards La Palmyre (Zoo), then turn right onto the D145 towards Saint Augustin. Site is signed and is 2 km. on the left. GPS: 45.67555, -1.094817

Charges guide

Per unit incl. 2 persons and electricity	€ 18,25 - € 25,00
extra person	€ 3,95 - € 6,50
child (under 7 yrs)	€ 3,40 - € 4,80

Saint Clément-des-Baleines

Camping la Plage

408 rue du Chaume, F-17590 Saint Clément-des-Baleines (Charente-Maritime) T: **05 46 29 42 62**
E: **info@la-plage.com** **alanrogers.com/FR17590**

This campsite, a member of the Airotel group, can be found at the western end of the Ile de Ré, very close to the imposing Phare des Baleines and just 100 m. from a sandy beach. Pitches are generally spacious and most are equipped with 10A electricity. Good selections of mobile homes are available for rent. Leisure facilities here include an attractive pool with a wide sunbathing terrace, and a multisport terrain. The bar/restaurant is the focal point for the site and a range of activities and entertainment take place there throughout the high season, including a daily children's club.

Facilities

Bar. Restaurant. Takeaway food. Shop. Swimming pool. Children's pool. Mulitsport terrain Play area. Entertainment and activity programme. Mobile homes to rent.
Off site: Sandy beach 100 m. Phare des Baleines. Ars-en-Ré. Riding. Cycle and walking tracks. Fishing.

Open: 4 April - 26 September.

See advertisement on page 183

Directions

From La Rochelle cross the toll bridge to the Ile de Ré. Continue on the D735 to Ars en Ré and then to St Clement des Baleines and the Phare des Baleines. The site is well signed from here.
GPS: 46.241186, -1.55345

Charges 2010

Per unit incl. 3 persons and electricity	€ 40,90 - € 48,70
1 or 2 persons (low season)	€ 23,00 - € 31,00
child (0-10 yrs)	€ 3,50 - € 12,25
dog	€ 2,80 - € 5,70

Saint Cyr

Flower Camping du Lac de Saint-Cyr

F-86130 Saint Cyr (Vienne) T: **05 49 62 57 22**. E: **contact@lacdesaintcyr.com**
alanrogers.com/FR86090

This well organised, 5 hectare campsite is part of a 300 hectare leisure park, based around a large lake with sailing and associated sports, and an area for swimming (supervised July/Aug). Land-based activities include tennis, two half-courts, table tennis, fishing, badminton, pétanque, beach volleyball, TV room, and a well equipped fitness suite, all of which are free of charge. The campsite has around 185 touring pitches, ten mobile homes and three 'yurts' (canvas and wooden tents) for rent. The marked and generally separated pitches are all fully serviced with electricity (10A), water and drainage. Spacious and very natural, this is a tanquil setting. In high season there are extra free activities.

Facilities

The main toilet block is modern and supplemented for peak season by a second unit, although they do attract some use by day-trippers to the leisure facilities. They include washbasins in cubicles, laundry facilities, and facilities for babies and disabled persons. Shop, restaurant and takeaway (April - Sept). Playground on beach. Bicycle hire. Barrier locked 22.00-07.00 hrs (€ 10 deposit for card).
Off site: Riding 200 m. Golf 800 m. Watersports and numerous other leisure activities around the lake.

Open: 1 April - 30 September.

Directions

Saint Cyr is about midway between Châtellerault and Poitiers. Site signed to east of N10 at Beaumont along D82 towards Bonneuil-Matours, and is part of the Parc de Loisirs de Saint Cyr. GPS: 46.71972, 0.46018

Charges guide

Per unit incl. 2 persons and electricity	€ 14,50 - € 27,00
extra person	€ 3,00 - € 5,00
child (2-7 yrs)	€ 2,00 - € 3,00
animal	€ 1,50

Saint Georges-d'Oléron

Camping les Gros Joncs

850 route de Ponthezieres, les Sables Vignier B.P. 17, F-17190 Saint Georges-d'Oléron (Charente-Maritime)
T: **05 46 76 52 29**. E: **info@les-gros-joncs.fr** **alanrogers.com/FR17070**

Situated on the west coast of the island of Ile d'Oléron, Les Gros Joncs is owned and run by the Cavel family who strive to keep the site up to date and of high quality. There are 50 or so touring pitches of a good size (some extra large) with tall pine trees providing a choice between full sun and varying degrees of shade. All have water and electricity (10A) to hand. The main building not only houses a light and airy reception, but also a modern, beautifully presented bar and restaurant, a fully stocked and competitively priced shop, a luxurious indoor swimming pool and a magnificent spa. The indoor pool, with water jets and jacuzzi, has glass sides which in good weather open out onto an outdoor pool area where there are also water slides, a paddling area and plenty of sunbathing terrace. Both pools are heated. The spa offers hydrotherapy and beauty treatments, sauna, and a comprehensive fitness room. Much attention has been given to the needs of disabled visitors here, including chalets where space and equipment are specially adapted. All the amenities are of a standard unusual on a campsite.

Facilities

Traditional style toilet facilities are kept to a high standrd. A new block is planned. Laundry facilities. Motorcaravan services. Well stocked shop with bakery (1/4-15/9). Bar, restaurant and takeaway (all year). Indoor pool with spa and wellness centre (all year). Outdoor pool (heated, 1/4-15/9). Bicycle hire. Children's clubs (1/7-15/9). Internet access and WiFi. ATM. Barbecues are not permitted. Off site: Beach 200 or 400 m. Bus service from Chéray. Fishing 2 km. Riding 6 km. Golf 8 km.

Open: All year.

Directions

Cross the viaduct onto the Ile d'Oléron. Take the D734 (St Georges d'Oléron). At traffic lights in Chéray turn left. Follow signs for camping and Sable Vignier. Soon signs indicate directions to Les Gros Joncs. GPS: 45.95356, -1.37979

Charges guide

Per unit incl. 2 persons and electricity	€ 18,50 - € 45,50
extra person	€ 6,00 - € 11,80
child (0-7 yrs)	€ 2,70 - € 7,30

Saint Georges-d'Oléron

Camping l'Anse des Pins

Chemin du Râteau-Domino, F-17190 Saint Georges-d'Oléron (Charente-Maritime) T: **05 46 76 55 97**
E: **camping-apv@wanadoo.fr** **alanrogers.com/FR17270**

Rock pools, sand dunes and spectacular sunsets, with sea views from many of the pitches, help to make this site attractive to those seeking an away from it all holiday in a quiet part of the island of the Ile d'Oléron. The campsite is arranged in three areas, some areas with good shade, others in full sun. There are 350 pitches including 137 for touring units, the remainder used for mobile homes. All pitches have electricity (3-10A) and 22 also have water and drainage. Across the road are the leisure facilities which include a complex of outdoor pools (unheated) with a toboggan and flume, and an indoor pool.

Facilities

Two main toilet blocks (plus two small blocks for high season use) with mainly British style toilets. Showers and washbasins in cabins. Laundry facilities. Gas supplies. Bar. Shop with limited takeaway and snack bar. Indoor pool (all season) and outdoor swimming and paddling pools (April-Sept). Play area. Activities in high season (1/7-31/8). Tennis. Boules. Bicycle hire. WiFi. Barbecues only permitted in a communal area. Off site: Beach 50 m. Bicycle hire 1 km. Riding 10 km. St Georges 5 km.

Open: April - October.

Directions

Cross the bridge onto Ile d'Oléron and follow D734 (St Dennis). In Chéray, turn left at traffic lights (signed Camping). Stay on this road to Domino (avoid side roads). Follow green signs to Rex and l'Anse des Pins Camping. Narrow roads. GPS: 45.97059, -1.3864

Charges guide

Per unit incl. 2 persons and electricity	€ 21,30 - € 35,20
extra person	€ 3,70 - € 8,00

Saint Georges-les-Baillargeaux

Kawan Village le Futuriste

F-86130 Saint Georges-les-Baillargeaux (Vienne) T: **05 49 52 47 52**

E: **camping-le-futuriste@wanadoo.fr** **alanrogers.com/FR86040**

Le Futuriste is a neat, modern site, open all year and close to Futuroscope. Its location is very convenient for the A10 and N10 motorway network. There are 112 individual, level, grassy pitches of a generous size and divided by flowering hedges. All pitches have electricity (6A) and 30 also have water and waste water connections. Pitches are mostly open although some do have the benefit of shade from trees. All are accessed via tarmac roads. There are lovely panoramic views from this site and the popular attraction of Futuroscope can be clearly seen. Large units are accepted by prior arrangement. There is a pleasant restaurant on site offering good food at reasonable prices. Entertainment takes place in the daytime rather than in the evenings. This site is ideal for a short stay to visit Futuroscope which is only two kilometres away but it is equally good for longer stays to see the region.

Facilities

Excellent, clean sanitary facilities in two heated blocks. Good facilities for disabled visitors and babies. Laundry facilities. Shop (bread to order), bar/restaurant (all 1/5-30/9). Snack bar and takeaway (1/7-31/8). Two heated outdoor pools, one with slide and paddling pool (1/5-30/9). Games room. TV. Boules. Multisport area. Lake fishing. Daily activities in season. Youth groups are not accepted.
Off site: Bicycle hire 500 m. Hypermarket 600 m. Futuroscope 2 km. Golf 5 km. Riding 10 km.

Open: All year.

Directions

From either A10 autoroute or N10, take Futuroscope exit. Site is east of both roads, off D20 (St Georges-les-Baillargeaux). Follow signs to St Georges. Site on hill; turn by water tower and site is on left.
GPS: 46.6644, 0.39463

Charges guide

Per unit incl. 1-3 persons and electricity	€ 19,00 - € 25,70
extra person	€ 2,20 - € 3,00
animal	€ 2,10

Camping Cheques accepted.

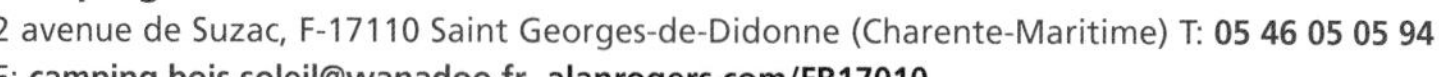

Saint Georges-de-Didonne

486

Camping Bois Soleil

2 avenue de Suzac, F-17110 Saint Georges-de-Didonne (Charente-Maritime) T: **05 46 05 05 94**
E: **camping.bois.soleil@wanadoo.fr** **alanrogers.com/FR17010**

Close to the sea, Bois Soleil is a large site in three parts, with 165 serviced pitches for touring units and a few for tents. All the touring pitches are hedged, and have electricity, with water and drainage between two. The main part, Les Pins, is attractive with trees and shrubs providing shade. Opposite is La Mer with direct access to the beach, some areas with less shade and an area for tents. The third part, La Forêt, is for static holiday homes. It is best to book your preferred area as it can be full mid June - late August. Excellent private sanitary facilities are available to rent, either on your pitch or at a block (subject to availability). There are a few pitches with lockable gates. The areas are well tended and are cleared and raked between visitors. This lively site offers something for everyone, whether it be a beach-side spot or a traditional pitch, plenty of activities or the quiet life. The wide sandy beach is popular with children and provides a pleasant walk to the pretty town of Saint Georges-de-Didonne.

Facilities

Each area has one large and one small sanitary block. Heated block near reception. Cleaned twice daily, they include facilities for disabled people and babies. Launderette. Supermarket, bakery, beach shop (all 4/4-15/9). Restaurant, bar and takeaway (all 4/4-15/9). Swimming pool (heated 15/6-15/9). Steam room. Tennis. Bicycle hire. Play area. TV room and library. Internet terminal and WiFi. Charcoal barbecues not permitted. Dogs are not accepted 23/6-25/8. Off site: Fishing, riding 500 m. Golf 20 km.

Open: 4 April - 2 November.

Directions

From Royan centre take coast road (D25) along the seafront of St Georges-de-Didonne towards Meschers. Site is signed at roundabout at end of the main beach. GPS: 45.583583, -0.986533

Charges guide

Per unit incl. 2 persons and 6A electricity	€ 24,00 - € 39,00
tent incl. 2 persons	€ 18,00 - € 35,00
extra person	€ 3,00 - € 8,00
child (3-7 yrs)	free - € 6,00
dog (not 23/6-25/8)	€ 3,50

Less 20% outside July/Aug.
Camping Cheques accepted.

Saint Just-Luzac

Castel Camping Séquoia Parc

La Josephtrie, F-17320 Saint Just-Luzac (Charente-Maritime) T: **05 46 85 55 55**. E: **info@sequoiaparc.com**
alanrogers.com/FR17140

This is definitely a site not to be missed. Approached by an avenue of flowers, shrubs and trees, Séquoia Parc is a Castel site set in the grounds of La Josephtrie, a striking château with beautifully restored outbuildings and courtyard area with a bar and restaurant. Most of the 426 pitches are 140 sq.m. with 6A electricity connections and separated by mature shrubs providing plenty of privacy. The site has 300 mobile homes and chalets, with 126 used by tour operators. This is a popular site with a children's club and entertainment throughout the season and reservation is necessary in high season. A member of 'Leading Campings Group'.

Facilities

Three spotlessly clean luxurious toilet blocks, include units with washbasin and shower and facilities for disabled visitors and children. Dishwashing sinks. Large laundry. Motorcaravan service point. Gas supplies. Large supermarket. Boutique. Restaurant/bar and takeaway. Impressive swimming pool complex with water slides and large paddling pool. Massage parlour (July/Aug). Multisports pitch. Tennis. Games and TV rooms. Bicycle hire. Pony trekking. Organised entertainment/excursions all season. Children's farm. WiFi in reception area (charged). Off site: Supermarket and bank 5 km. Fishing 5 km. Golf 15 km. Flying trips. Ile d'Oleron. La Rochelle.

Open: 16 May - 6 September, with all services.

Directions

Site is 5 km. southeast of Marennes. From Rochefort take D733 south for 12 km. Turn west on D123 to Ile d'Oléron. Continue for 12 km. Turn southeast on D728 (Saintes). Site signed, in 1 km. on left. From A10 at Saintes take D728 and leave this road by turning right shortly after St Just. Site signed. GPS: 45.81095, -1.06109

Charges guide

Per unit incl. 2 persons and electricity	€ 19,00 - € 44,00
extra person	€ 7,00 - € 9,00
child (3-12 yrs)	€ 3,00 - € 5,00
dog	€ 5,00

ʙois Soleil

Camping ★★★★

Charente-Maritime

ʀounded by pine trees and a sandy beach on the ɪntic Coast, with one direct access to the beach, Bois ɪil proposes to you many attractions like tennis, etennis, children playgrounds and entertainment. ps, take-away and snack-bar with big TV screen.

Spring and Summer

2, avenue de Suzac - 17110 ST GEORGES DE DIDONNE
Tel: 0033 546 05 05 94 - Fax: 0033 546 06 27 43
ww.bois-soleil.com / e-mail: camping.bois.soleil@wanadoo.fr

Saint Hilaire-la-Palud

Camping Indigo Le Lidon

F-79210 Saint Hilaire-la-Palud (Deux-Sèvres) T: **05 49 35 33 64**. E: **le-lidon@camping-indigo.com**
alanrogers.com/FR79060

Le Lidon is a member of the Indigo group of campsites. It is located within the Marais Poitevin, an enchanting region of over 400 km. of rivers, canals and fens lying to the west of Niort. This site has 132 grassy pitches scattered across three hectares. The site's selection of rented accommodation includes fully equipped, Canadian style tents and chalets. The Marais Poitevin is undeniably best explored by canoe or punt and it is possible to rent these on site. During high season, an activity and entertainment programme is organised including a children's club and various family activities. The site bar/restaurant is open in July and August and specializes in local cuisine. The Marais Mouillé makes up around a third of the Marais Poitevin, but it is the best known part, and is otherwise known as La Venise Verte (Green Venice), with miles of conches (channels) and drainage ditches overshadowed by ash and poplars. This is an angler's paradise with eel, pike and perch hiding beneath the green carpet of duckweed which covers much of the water's surface.

Facilities

Shop, bar, snack bar (all season). Heated swimming pool (15/6-31/8). Play area. Direct access to river. Fishing. Canoe hire. Entertainment and activity programme. Tents and chalets for rent. Off site: St Hilaire-La-Palud with a good selection of shops and cafes, as well as an open air cinema. Fishing (river). La Maison des Oiseaux (ornithological centre). Vendee beaches 50 km. Cycle and walking tracks. Riding 15 km. Golf 25 km.

Open: 3 April - 30 September.

Directions

St Hilaire-la-Palud lies midway between Niort and La Rochelle. Approaching from the north (Niort) leave A10 autoroute at exit 33 and head west on the N248 as far as Epannes. Head north here on the D1 to Sansais and then west on the D3 to St Hilaire-la-Palud. Site is well signed to the right just after the village.
GPS: 46.2838, -0.74345

Charges 2010

Per unit incl. 2 persons and electricity	€ 17,80 - € 26,00
extra person	€ 5,20 - € 6,00
child (2-7 yrs)	€ 2,00 - € 2,60

Camping Cheques accepted.

Saint Trojan-les-Bains

Camping Indigo Oléron

11 avenue des Bris, F-17370 Saint Trojan-les-Bains (Charente-Maritime) T: **05 46 76 02 39**
E: **oleron@camping-indigo.com** **alanrogers.com/FR17580**

This site is an attractive new addition to the Indigo group. It can be found close to the popular seaside resort of St Trojan-les-Bains on the south side of the island. There are 200 good sized pitches here, most of which have electrical connections. Indigo Oléron enjoys an attractive forest setting just 1 km. from the nearest sandy beach. The island is popular with cyclists and a track leads from the site to the village centre. In high season, a snack bar service is available as well as a small shop. The nearest supermarket is just 200 m. away.

Facilities

Snack bar. Small shop (mainly bread). Motorcaravan services. Bicycle hire. Play area. Activity and entertainment programme. Tourist information. Off site: Nearest beach and fishing 500 m. Tourist train at St Trojan. Walking and cycling tracks. Riding 1 km. Supermarket 200 m.

Open: 18 June - 3 October.

Directions

From Marennes, cross the bridge to the Ile d'Oléron (D26) and then follow signs to St Trojan on D126. The site is well indicated from the village.
GPS: 45.83152, -1.213882

Charges year

Contact the site.

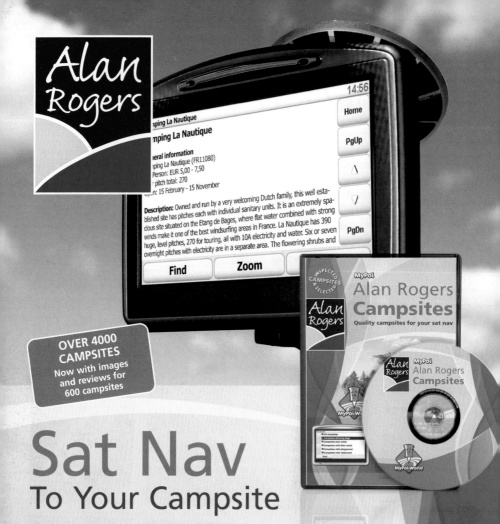

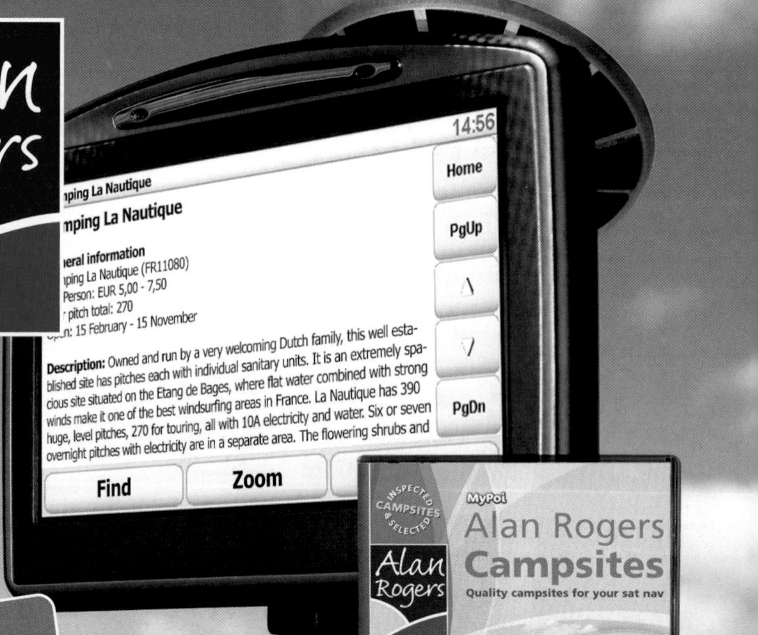

Burgundy is a wonderfully evocative region offering breathtaking châteaux and cathedrals, rolling hills and heady mountain views, vineyards and superlative cuisine, not to mention of course, a wide variety of world-renowned wines.

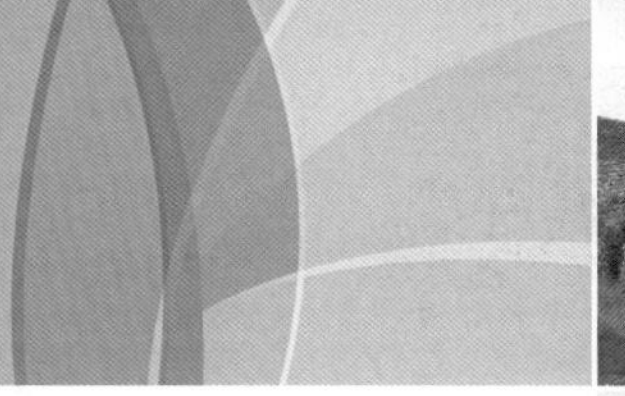

DÉPARTEMENTS: 21 CÔTE D'OR, 58 NIÈVRE, 71 SAÔNE-ET-LOIRE, 89 YONNE

MAJOR CITY: DIJON

In the rich heartland of France, Burgundy was once a powerful independent state and important religious centre. Its golden age is reflected in the area's magnificent art and architecture: the grand palaces and art collections of Dijon, the great pilgrimage church of Vézelay, the Cistercian Abbaye de Fontenay and the evocative abbey remains at Cluny, once the most powerful monastery in Europe.

However, Burgundy is best known for its wine, including some of the world's finest, notably from the great vineyards of the Côte d'Or and Chablis, and also for its sublime cuisine.You'll also notice how driving through the country villages is like reading a wine merchant's list with plenty of opportunities for tasting and choosing your wine.

The area is criss-crossed by navigable waterways and includes the Parc Régional du Morvan; good walking country amidst lush, rolling wooded landscape.

Places of interest

Autun: 12th-century St Lazare cathedral.

Beaune: medieval town; Museum of Burgundy Wine.

Cluny: Europe's largest Benedictine abbey.

Dijon: Palace of the Dukes, Fine Arts Museum, Burgundian Folklore Museum.

Fontenay: Fontenay Abbey and Cloister.

Joigny: medieval town.

Mâcon: Maison des Vins (wine centre).

Paray-le-Monial: Romanesque basilica, pilgrimage centre.

Sens: historic buildings, museum with fine Gallo-Roman collections.

Vézelay: fortified medieval hillside.

Cuisine of the region

Many dishes are wine based, including *Poulet au Meursault* and *Coq au Chambertin*. Dijon is known for its *pain d'épice* (spiced honey cake) and spicy mustard.

Boeuf Bourguignon: braised beef simmered in a red wine-based sauce.

Garbure: heavy soup, a mixture of pork, cabbage, beans and sausages.

Gougère: cheese pastry based on Gruyère.

Jambon persillé: parsley-flavoured ham, served cold in jelly.

Matelote: fresh-water fish soup, usually based on a red wine sauce.

Meurette: red wine-based sauce with small onions, used with fish or poached egg dishes.

www.burgundy-tourism.com
documentation@crt-bougogne.fr
(0)3 80 28 02 80

MEAUX
BAR-LE-DUC
VITRY-LE-FRANCOIS
ST-DIZIER
PARIS ILE DE FRANCE
CHAMPAGNE-ARDENNE
PROVINS
NOGENT SUR-SEINE
NEUFCHATEAU
TROYES
BAR-SUR-AUBE
A5,E54,E511
SENS
CHAUMONT
LANGRES
YONNE 89
AUXERRE
A6,E15,E60
MONTBARD
FRANCHE-COMTE
PAYS DE LA LOIRE
AVALLON
COTE-D'OR 21
A31,E17,E21
CLAMECY
BURGUNDY
A38
DIJON
AUXONNE
VANDENESSE-EN-AUXOIS
A31,E17
ARNAY-LE-DUC
A77
NIEVRE 58
SAVIGNY-LES-BEAUNE
A36,E60
BEAUNE
ST-PEREUSE EN MORVAN
MEURSAULT
AUTUN
NEVERS
ST-HONORE-LES-BAINS
A6,E15
CHALON-SUR-SAONE
LUZY
TAZILLY
LOUHANS
GIGNY-SUR-SAONE
ISSY-L'EVEQUE
SAINT-BOIL
LAIVES
SAONE-ET-LOIRE 71
TOURNUS
PALINGES
MOULINS
DIGOIN
CLUNY
MÂCON
GIBLES
MONTLUCON
AUVERGNE
BOURG-EN-BRESSE
VICHY
RHONE ALPES
ROANNE
VILLEFRANCHE-SUR-SAONE
RIOM
THIERS
LYON
CLERMONT-FERRAND
MONTBRISON
VIENNE
ISSOIRE
AMBERT
ST-ETIENNE
0
25
50
75 kms

Arnay le Duc

Camping de l'Etang de Fouché

Rue du 8 Mai 1945, F-21230 Arnay le Duc (Côte d'Or) T: **03 80 90 02 23**. E: **info@campingfouche.com**
alanrogers.com/FR21040

Useful as a stop en route to or from the Mediterranean or indeed for longer stays. This quite large but peaceful, lakeside site with its new bar/restaurant and swimming pool complex, can be very busy during the school holidays, and is probably better visited outside the main season. There are 190 good-sized pitches, on fairly level grass and all with 10A electricity (some with water). Many are hedged and offer a choice of shade or more open aspect. In July/August there are regular activities for children and adults. A 2 km. stroll around the lake is very pleasant.

Facilities

Two new toilet blocks and third one (totally refurbished) provide all the necessary modern facilities (male and female are separate). Facilities for disabled visitors. Baby room. Washing machines and dishwashing under cover. Shop, bar, restaurant, takeaway (all 15/5-15/9). TV/games room. New small heated outdoor swimming pool. Boules. Playground. Off site: Town centre 800 m. Lakeside beach with playground, water slides, pedaloes, canoes.

Open: 16 April - 16 October.

See advertisement on page 263

Directions

From A6 (exit 24) take the D981, 16 km. to the town. Turn left on D906 for about 400 m. and site is signed to left. GPS: 47.13411, 4.49840

Charges guide

Per unit incl. 2 persons and electricity	€ 18,40 - € 22,50
extra person	€ 4,30 - € 5,40
child (2-10 yrs)	€ 2,20 - € 2,90
animal	€ 2,00

Auxonne

Camping de l'Arquebuse

Route d'Athée, F-21130 Auxonne (Côte d'Or) T: **03 80 31 06 89**. E: **camping.arquebuse@wanadoo.fr**
alanrogers.com/FR21090

This is an all year round site located in the Northern Jura with a riverside setting on the Saône. L'Arquebuse has 100 level, unmarked pitches on grass, of which ten are occupied by mobile homes and chalets. All have 10A electricity and a variety of trees gove shade to some pitches. Auxonne is close to both the A36 and A39 motorways and this site may prove a useful overnight stop. The site has bar/restaurant, Le Pinocchio, and the adjacent 'base nautique' offers a good range of leisure activities, including canoeing, windsurfing, mountain biking as well as a large swimming pool. Auxonne is an attractive town, fortified by Vauban, and is renowned as the capital of the Saone valley. The town's most famous former occupant is Napoleon and he spent two years at the Auxonne military academy. Not surprisingly there are several monuments celebrating his time here!

Facilities

Basic toilet block, heated in winter, provides mostly Turkish style toilets and open washbasins. Washing machine. Small shop (1/5-31/10). Restaurant/bar (1/1-15/12). Pizzeria. Takeaway meals. Play area. TV room. WiFi. Chalets for rent. Off site: Swimming pool, windsurfing, canoeing, boat trips and fishing. Motorcaravan services. Fortified town of Auxonne with shops, bars and restaurants 1 km. Dijon 34 km.

Open: All year.

Directions

From the A39 autoroute take exit 5 and the N5 for about 6 km. to Auxonne. Site is signed to the left just before crossing the bridge over the Saône. Site is a few hundred metres. GPS: 47.19941, 5.38365

Charges guide

Per unit incl. 2 persons and electricity	€ 16,00 - € 17,90
extra person	€ 3,60
child (under 7 yrs)	€ 2,10
dog	€ 1,80

Beaune

Camping Municipal les Cent Vignes

10 rue Auguste Dubois, F-21200 Beaune (Côte d'Or) T: **03 80 22 03 91**
E: **campinglescentvignes@mairie-beaune.fr** **alanrogers.com/FR21020**

Les Cent Vignes is a very well kept site offering 116 individual pitches of good size, separated from each other by neat beech hedges high enough to keep a fair amount of privacy. Over half of the pitches are on grass, ostensibly for tents, the remainder on hardstandings with electricity for caravans. A popular site, within walking distance of the town centre, Les Cent Vignes becomes full mid June to early September but with many short-stay campers there are departures each day and reservations can be made. The Côte de Beaune, situated southeast of the Côte d'Or, produces some of the very best French wines. Beaune is also a city of art and has a charm all of its own and there are several 'caves' in the town just waiting to be visited.

Facilities

Two modern, fully equipped and well constructed sanitary blocks, one of which can be heated, should be large enough. Nearly all washbasins are in cabins. Laundry facilities. Shop, restaurant with takeaway (all 1/4-15/10). Playground. Sports area with tennis, basketball, volleyball and boules. TV room. Barbecue area. Off site: Centre of Beaune 1 km. Bicycle hire 1 km. Fishing and golf 4 km.

Open: 15 March - 31 October.

Directions

From autoroute exit 24 follow signs for Beaune centre on D2 road, camping signs to site in about 1 km. Well signed from other routes. GPS: 47.03304, 4.83911

Charges guide

Per unit incl. 2 persons and electricity	€ 16,60
extra person	€ 3,70
child (under 7 yrs)	€ 1,85

Châlon-sur-Saône

Camping du Pont de Bourgogne

Rue Julien Leneveu, Saint-Marcel, F-71380 Châlon-sur-Saône (Saône-et-Loire) T: **03 85 48 26 86**
E: **campingchalon71@wanadoo.fr** **alanrogers.com/FR71140**

This is a well presented site, useful for an overnight stop or for a few days if exploring the local area and you want a simple site without the frills. It does get crowded in the third week of July during the Châlon street theatre festival. There are 93 pitches (90 sq. m) all with 6A electricity, 10 with a gravel surface. The new owners of the site plan to replace or improve the facilities in the near future, but when we visited there was a bar/restaurant with an outdoor terrace and serving a good selection of simple, inexpensive meals. Although alongside the Saône river, the site is well fenced. The staff are friendly and helpful.

Facilities

Three toilet blocks, two centrally located amongst the pitches and traditional in style and fittings. The third is a superb modern and brand new sanitary facilities include special childrens bathroom, disabled bathroom and family shower. Motorcaravan servicing point already in place. Dishwashing facilities but no laundry. No shop but essentials kept in the bar (bread to order). Modern bar/restaurant. Simple play area. Bicycle hire arranged. Off site: Municipal swimming pool 300 m. Golf 1 km. Riding 10 km.

Open: 1 April - 30 September.

See advertisement on page 211

Directions

From A6 exit 26 (Châlon-Sud) bear right to roundabout and take N80 (Dole) straight on to roundabout at St Marcel. Turn left (fourth exit) and fork right into Les Chavannes. At central traffic lights turn right and under modern river bridge to site entrance. GPS: 46.78448, 4.87295

Charges 2010

Per unit incl. 2 persons and electricity	€ 19,40 - € 24,20
extra person	€ 4,70 - € 5,90
child (under 7 yrs)	€ 3,30 - € 4,50
dog	€ 2,00 - € 2,50

Cluny

Camping Municipal Saint-Vital

Rue des Griottons, F-71250 Cluny (Saône-et-Loire) T: **03 85 59 08 34**. E: **cluny-camping@wanadoo.fr**
alanrogers.com/FR71030

Close to this attractive small town (a 300 m. walk) with its magnificent abbey (the largest in Christendom) and next to the municipal swimming pool (free for campers), this site has 174 pitches. On gently sloping grass, with some small hedges and shade in parts, electricity is available (long leads may be needed). Some rail noise is noticeable during the day but we are assured that trains do not run 23.30 - 07.00 hrs. In high season, on Friday evenings, there is a presentation of local produce in the 'salle de réunion'.

Facilities

Two sanitary buildings provide British and Turkish style WCs, some washbasins in cubicles and controllable showers. Dishwashing and laundry sinks. Washing machine, dryer and ironing board. Chemical toilet disposal. Shop.
Off site: Fishing and bicycle hire 100 m. Riding 1 km. Wine routes, châteaux, churches. The excellent traffic free cycle path from Cluny to Givry is highly recommended.

Open: 1 May - 30 September.

Directions

Site is east of town, by the D15 road towards Azé and Blanot. GPS: 46.43196, 4.66755

Charges guide

Per unit incl. 2 persons and electricity	€ 13,95
extra person	€ 6,90
child (under 7 yrs)	€ 2,25

Digoin

Camping de la Chevrette

Rue de la Chevrette, F-71160 Digoin (Saône-et-Loire) T: **03 85 53 11 49**. E: **info@lachevrette.com**
alanrogers.com/FR71180

This pretty town site has been leased from the municipality for the last few years by an enthusiastic couple. There are 100 neat and tidy pitches which are delineated by hedges (even the pitches for tents) and flowers decorate the site. The level pitches include 75 with electricity (10A) for touring units, 23 for tents and two for caravan holiday homes for rent. At the far end of the site there is direct access to the Loire river and it is this aspect that attracts campers with canoes. The adjacent town swimming pool complex is free for campers. It incorporates a second large pool totally devoted to the sport of water jousting – seven in a boat!

Facilities

Four small toilet blocks, one with cold water only, each provide separate facilities for men and women and some washbasins in cabins. Washing machine and dryer in one block. Facilities for disabled visitors. Small restaurant/snack bar (1/7-31/8). Club room with TV for bad weather. WiFi. Off site: Supermarkets, restaurants and bars in the town. Cycle paths along the canals. Nevers and its cathedral. Riding 3 km. Bicycle hire 15 km.

Open: 15 March - 15 October.

Directions

Digion lies off the N79 and site is well signed from all directions. GPS: 46.47973, 3.96755

Charges guide

Per person	€ 3,20 - € 4,00
child (under 13 yrs)	€ 1,90 - € 2,20
pitch	€ 6,10 - € 6,50
electricity	€ 3,40

Double axle units are charged much more.

Dijon

Camping Dijon Lac Kir

3 boulevard du Chanoine Kir, F-21000 Dijon (Côte d'Or) T: **03 80 43 54 72**. E: **info@camping-dijon.com**
alanrogers.com/FR21100

The great city of Dijon, former capital of the Dukes of Burgundy, is a popular choice for an en route stop and this site, a member of the Via-camp group, is a convenient location. There are 111 pitches, all grassy and with an average size of 100 sq.m. Hardstandings are available. A further 8 pitches are occupied by mobile homes (available for rent). Lac Kir (named after a former mayor of the city) is a delightful haven for swans and duck, extending over 37 hectares and has a large, attractive beach. The lake is within easy walking distance and has a large beach. On-site amenities include a bar/snack bar and shop.

Facilities

Snack bar. Takeaway food. Shop. Tourist information. Motorcaravan services. Play area. Fully equipped mobile homes for rent. Off site: Lac Kir (beach, canoes, windsurfing and other watersports). Supermarket. Restaurants. Fishing. Sailing.

Open: 1 April - 12 October.

See advertisement on page 263

Directions

The site is west of the city. Approaching on the A38, continue to the end of the motorway and then follow D905 towards the city centre passing alongside Lac Kir. At the end of the lake, after crossing the railway, turn right onto Boulevard du Chanoine Kir and the site is on the left. GPS: 47.321312, 5.01079

Charges guide

Per unit incl. 2 persons and electricity	€ 12,50 - € 15,90

Gibles

Camping Caravaning Château de Montrouant

F-71800 Gibles (Saône-et-Loire) T: **03 85 84 51 13**. E: **campingdemontrouant@wanadoo.fr**
alanrogers.com/FR71060

A small, pretty site beside a lake in the grounds of an imposing château, in a steep valley in the Charolais hills. There is shade from mature trees and the 45 pitches (12 used by Dutch tour operators) are on reasonably flat grassy terraces, separated by hedges. Some pitches overlook the lake and some are next to a field. This site is best for smaller units as the approach roads are narrow. It quickly becomes full mid July - mid August and access becomes difficult with extra traffic. Motorcaravan owners should always check in advance as there may not be a suitable pitch. Units are towed off site if required.

Facilities

The sanitary facilities, not too well designed and with variable maintenance, are housed in a part of the château. They include washbasins in cabins. Dishwashing and laundry facilities. Basic supplies available at reception. Small open-air bar/restaurant/takeaway for evening barbecues (only open certain evenings). Swimming pool with secluded sunbathing area. Half-court tennis. Fishing. Torches useful. Off site: The village of Gibles 2 km. Riding 10 km.

Open: 1 June - 4 September.

Directions

Site is west of Mâcon and can be reached from the A6 (Jn 29) via the N79 to Charolles (50 km). Take D25 southeast for 20 km. to Gibles. The last few kilometers are quite narrow and just before village, following signs, there is a very sharp turn to the left, then continue with signs. GPS: 46.3366, 4.382

Charges guide

Per person	€ 6,00
child (under 7 yrs)	€ 3,80
pitch incl. electricity	€ 10,50 - € 16,00

Camping Cheques accepted.

Gigny-sur-Saône

Kawan Village Château de l'Epervière

F-71240 Gigny-sur-Saône (Saône-et-Loire) T: **03 85 94 16 90**
E: **domaine-de-leperviere@wanadoo.fr** **alanrogers.com/FR71070**

This site is peacefully situated in the wooded grounds of the 16th-century Château, near the village of Gigny-sur-Saône, and within walking distance of the river where you can watch the river cruise boats on their way to and from Châlon-sur-Saône. There are 160 pitches in total, of which 45 are occupied by tour operators and five units are for rent. The 110 touring pitches, all with 10A electricity (30 fully serviced) are in two distinct areas. The original part, close to the Château and fishing lake, has semi-hedged pitches on level ground with shade from mature trees. The centre of the second area has a more open aspect. Here there are large hedged pitches and mature trees offering shade around the periphery – birdwatchers will love this area. A partly fenced road across the lake connects the two areas. The château's main restaurant serves regional dishes. Gert-Jan, François and their team enthusiastically organise many activities for visitors including wine tasting in the cellars of the château. Don't forget, you are in the Maconnais and Châlonnaise wine areas and so close to the A6.

Facilities

Two well equipped toilet blocks include washbasins in cabins, showers, baby rooms, facilities for disabled visitors. Washing machine and dryer. Basic shop (24/4-30/9). Second restaurant with basic menu and takeaway (1/4-30/9). Converted barn housing attractive bar, large TV and games room. Unheated outdoor swimming pool (24/4-30/9) partly enclosed by old stone walls. Smaller indoor heated pool, jacuzzi, sauna, paddling pool (1/4-30/9. Play area. Outdoor paddling pool. Fishing. Bicycle hire. Off site: Riding 15 km. Golf 20 km. Historic towns of Châlon and Tournus, both 20 km. The Monday market of Louhans, to see the famous Bresse chickens 26 km.

Open: 1 April - 30 September.

Directions

From the north, A6 exit Châlon-Sud, or Tournus from the south. Take N6 to Sennecey-le-Grand, turn east on D18 and follow site signs for 6.5 km.
GPS: 46.65485, 4.94463

Charges 2010

Per unit incl. 2 persons and electricity	€ 23,40 - € 33,50
extra person	€ 5,70 - € 8,10
child (under 7 yrs)	€ 3,50 - € 5,40
dog	€ 2,40 - € 3,00

Camping Cheques accepted.

Issy-l'Évêque

Flower Camping de l'Etang Neuf

L'Etang Neuf, F-71760 Issy-l'Évêque (Saône-et-Loire) T: **03 85 24 96 05**. E: **info@issy-camping.com**
alanrogers.com/FR71080

This well tended, tranquil campsite overlooking a lake, with views of a forest and the 19th-century Château de Montrifaut, is a real countryside haven for relaxation. The birdsong includes nightingales and golden orioles. The 61 marked, grass pitches have 6A electricity, a small hardstanding area for a car and are separated by a variety of maturing trees giving some shade. There is a separate area nearer the lake for tents. There is no organised entertainment but a play area and a fenced area of the lake, with beach for swimming and paddling plus plenty of space, will keep children happily amused.

Facilities

Two very clean sanitary blocks include washbasins in cabins. Dishwashing and laundry sinks. Washing machine, ironing board and baby room. Separate shower and toilet rooms for disabled people are in the lower block. Motorcaravan services. Bar/restaurant. Bread and croissants to order. Boules. TV/games room. Internet access (WiFi).
Off site: Minigolf just outside the site entrance. Riding or tennis 500 m. Nearest shops 1.2 km. in Issy-l'Évêque. 120 km. of marked footpaths in the area.

Open: 1 May - 30 September.

Directions

From N81 (Autun - Bourbon-Lancy) turn left onto D27/D25 just west of Luzy and continue for about 11 km. Turn right, D42 in centre of Issy-l'Évêque, signed to campsite. The road narrows slightly, entrance on the right. GPS: 46.70773, 3.96018

Charges guide

Per unit incl. 2 persons	€ 13,00 - € 17,50
incl. electricity (6A)	€ 16,50 - € 21,00
extra person	€ 3,50 - € 5,00
child (under 14 yrs)	€ 2,00 - € 3,00

Laives

Camping la Heronnière

Lac de Laives, F-71240 Laives (Saône-et-Loire) T: **03 85 44 98 85**. E: **contact@camping-laheronniere.com**

alanrogers.com/FR71120

Camping la Heronnière is a quiet relaxing site on the edge of a leisure lake in pleasant rolling woodland countryside. The 90 touring pitches are good sized, grassy and level. About half have shade, with electrical connections for 88 and there are plenty of water points. The site is within easy reach of Chalon-sur-Saône, Tournus and the Chalonnais vineyards and wine route. Cluny and the former industrial towns of Le Creusot and Montceau-les-Mines are each about 40 km. away.

Facilities

Well equipped modern sanitary block includes facilities for campers with disabilities. Snack bar (June-Aug). Covered area outside reception, with bread, drinks, ice cream, basic provisions and French breakfast. Heated outdoor pool. Boules. Bicycle hire. Fishing. Marquee with TV, board games. Playground. Off site: Lake swimming, beach, bar and restaurant 300 m. Exercise circuit, canoeing, windsurfing, pedaloes. Riding 10 km. Golf 15 km. Cluny, Chalon, Le Creusot and Montceau-les-Mines. Shops at Laives 4 km.

Open: 1 May - 15 September.

Directions

Leave N6 (Chalon-sur-Saône - Mâcon) at Sennecy-le-Grand (about 18 km. south of the centre of Chalon), taking D18 west to Laives (4 km). In centre of village, take right fork and continue along D18, 4 km. to the northwest. GPS: 46.67198, 4.8333

Charges 2010

Per unit incl. 2 persons and electricity	€ 15,40 - € 23,90

Mâcon

Camping Municipal Mâcon

RN6, F-71000 Mâcon (Saône-et-Loire) T: **03 85 38 16 22**. E: **camping@ville-macon.fr**

alanrogers.com/FR71010

Always useful and well cared for, this site is worth considering as a stopover or for longer stays as it is close to the main route south. The 250 good sized pitches, 190 with 6A electricity and 60 with fresh and waste water points, are on mown, flat grass, accessed by tarmac roads. The gates are closed 10.00 - 06.30, but large units note – the security barrier has a 3.8 m. height restriction so watch those top boxes! This is a pleasant site, remarkably quiet considering its location, and with a generally bright and cheerful ambience. The bar/restaurant is open all year and is a favourite haunt for the locals at lunchtime.

Facilities

Sanitary facilities in three well maintained units, are fully equipped with British and Turkish style WCs, and washbasins in cubicles. A fourth block is modern. Facilities for disabled visitors. Washing machine and dryer. Excellent motorcaravan service point (with Fiamma couplings). Bar. Shop/tabac. Takeaway and restaurant (Le Tipi) open midday and evenings. Heated swimming and paddling pools (campers only, 15/5-15/9). Good TV lounge. Playground. Off site: Supermarket nearby. Centre of Mâcon 3 km.

Open: 15 March - 31 October.

Directions

Site is on northern outskirts of Mâcon on the main N6, 3 km. from the town centre (just south of the A40 autoroute junction). GPS: 46.3021, 4.8325

Charges guide

Per unit incl. 2 persons	€ 11,30 - € 12,50
with electricity (5A)	€ 14,00 - € 15,40

Nevers

Camping de Nevers

Rue de la Jonction, F-58000 Nevers (Nièvre) T: **06 84 98 69 79**. E: **info@campingnevers.com**

alanrogers.com/FR58100

On the banks of the Loire in Nevers, facing the cathedral and the Palace of the Dukes across the river, this small site has 73 grass pitches. Of these, only two are used for caravan holiday homes. Half of the site is for tents and the other half are touring pitches with electricity (6/10A). This site would provide a good base for a short stay to explore the region with its famous Burgundy wines of Sancerre and Pouilly Fumé. The pitches are quite tight and are not suitable for larger units, but the site is ideal for those in motorcaravans or tents because of its proximity to the town.

Facilities

One modern toilet block has unisex toilets and showers. Bright and clean, they may be under pressure in high season. Baby area. Provision for disabled visitors. Laundry. Motorcaravan service point. Bar (all season) with snacks in high season. Off site: All the amenities of Nevers, including large stores. Boat launching 500m plus Golf and horse riding 5 km.

Open: 9 April - 10 October.

Directions

From Paris, take A6 (Lyon) and then A77 direction Bourges/Nevers. Take exit 37, direction Nevers. Shortly after town sign, site is on the right before the bridge. Avoid arriving between 12.00-14.00 (site closed) as there is no waiting place outside.
GPS: 46.98209, 3.16098

Charges guide

Per unit incl. 2 persons and electricity	€ 16,80 - € 20,60
extra person	€ 1,25 - € 3,00

Camping Cheques accepted.

Palinges

Camping du Lac

Le Fourneau, F-71430 Palinges (Saône-et-Loire) T: **03 85 88 14 49**. E: **camping.palinges@hotmail.fr**
alanrogers.com/FR71110

Camping du Lac is a very special campsite and it is all due to M. Labille, the owner, who thinks of the campsite as his home and every visitor as his guest. The campsite has 50 pitches in total, 16 of which have 10A electricity and 20 are fully serviced. There are six chalets to rent. The site is adjacent to a lake with a beach and safe bathing. Set in the countryside yet within easy reach of many tourist attractions, especially Cluny, the local Château Digoin and Mont St Vincent with distant views of Mont Blanc on a clear day. If you want to visit a specific place, then Monsieur knows exactly where you should go – he never recommends anything that he hasn't personally tried out. Monsieur Labille provides tables and chairs for tent campers and he freezes bottles of water for cyclists to take away (free of charge).

Facilities

The central sanitary block provides all necessary facilities including those for campers with disabilities. This site is particularly well adapted for disabled visitors. Motorcaravan services. Washing machine and fridge. Bread and croissants to order. Boules. Play area. TV room. Sports field, lake beach and swimming adjacent. Bicycle and pedalo hire in July/Aug. Off site: Bar/snack bar outside entrance (weekends only outside 1/7-31/8). Riding 200 m. Palinges is within walking distance, cycle and walking routes, museums, cruises on canals, châteaux, 'museographical' complex.

Open: 1 April - 30 October.

Directions

Palinges is midway between Montceau les Mines and Paray le Monial. From Montceau take N70, then turn left onto D92 to Palinges. Follow campsite signs. Site is also well signed from D985 Toulon-sur-Arroux to Charolles road. GPS: 46.56124, 4.22546

Charges 2010

Per unit incl. 2 persons and electricity	€ 21,80

No credit cards.

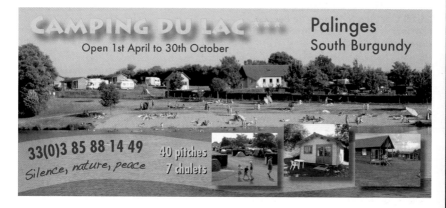

Saint Boil

Camping le Moulin de Collonge

Moulin de Collonge, F-71390 Saint Boil (Saône-et-Loire) T: **03 85 44 00 32**. E: **millofcollonge@wanadoo.fr**
alanrogers.com/FR71050

This well run, family site offers an 'away from it all' situation surrounded by sloping vineyards and golden wheat fields. It has an instant appeal for those seeking a quiet, relaxing environment. There are 61 level pitches, most with electrical hook-ups although long cables may be required. Flower arrangements are in abundance and, like the shrubs and grounds, are constantly being attended. Beyond the stream that borders the site are a swimming pool, patio and a pizzeria (also open to the public all year). A new lake, 1.8 m. deep, has been created for leisure activities.

Facilities

Well kept toilet facilities housed in a converted barn. Laundry and dishwashing sinks. Washing machine and dryer. Freezer for campers' use. Bread each morning. Basic shop (1/5-30/9). Pizzeria, snack bar (1/7-31/8). Internet café. Swimming pool covered – some walls can be opened in good weather. Playgrounds. Bouncy castle. Bicycle hire. Table tennis. Fishing. Pony trekking. WiFi (free).
Off site: Riding 4 km. Châteaux, wine route, churches. 'Voie Vert', 117 km. track for cycling or walking near the site.

Open: 1 April - 30 September.

Directions

From Chalon-sur-Saône travel 9 km. west on the N80. Turn south on D981 through Buxy (6 km). Continue south for 7 km. to Saint Boil and site is signed at south end of the village. GPS: 46.64621, 4.69479

Charges guide

Per unit incl. 2 persons and electricity	€ 18,00 - € 22,50
extra person	€ 5,50 - € 4,50
child (under 7 yrs)	€ 3,50 - € 4,50

Less 20% outside July/Aug.

Saint Honoré-les-Bains

Camping des Bains

15 avenue Jean Mermoz, F-58360 Saint Honoré-les-Bains (Nièvre) T: **03 86 30 73 44**
E: **camping-les-bains@wanadoo.fr** **alanrogers.com/FR58010**

You are assured of a warm welcome at this attractive family run site, situated within walking distance of the village, in an area of rolling countryside, woods, rivers and country villages and ideal for walking or cycling. The spacious 130 level grassed pitches (6A electricity, lond leads advised) are mostly separated by hedges with mature trees offering varying amounts of shade. Adjacent to the site there is the 'thermal spa' with opportunities to 'take the waters' for a three day session or a full blown cure of three weeks! Reception has details. There is an excellent restaurant almost opposite the campsite entrance and a casino in the village.

Facilities

Two main sanitary units have mostly British style WCs, washbasins in cabins and showers. Laundry facilities and baby bath. Facilities for disabled visitors. Bar provides food and a takeaway (1/4-30/9). Swimming pool, slide and paddling pool (15/6-15/9). Play area. Streams for children to fish. Minigolf. Games room. Entertainment for children (July/Aug). TV and DVDs. Internet access and WiFi (charged). Off site: St Honoré-les-Bains with shops, banks, bars and restaurants 800 m. Bicycle hire or riding 500 m. Fishing 5 km.

Open: 1 April - 25 October.

Directions

From Nevers, travel east on the D978. 6 km. beyond Châtillon-en-Bazois turn right onto the D985 to St Honoré-les-Bains. Site is signed on entering town. Care is needed at narrow site entrance.
GPS: 46.90671, 3.82843

Charges 2010

Per unit incl. 2 persons	€ 11,00 - € 16,00
extra person	€ 2,85 - € 4,50
electricity (6A)	€ 3,50

Camping Cheques accepted.

Saint Pereuse-en-Morvan

Castel Camping le Manoir de Bezolle

F-58110 Saint Pereuse-en-Morvan (Nièvre) T: **03 86 84 42 55**. E: **info@camping-bezolle.com**
alanrogers.com/FR58030

Manoir de Bezolle is in the heart of Burgundy, well situated to explore the Morvan Natural Park and the Nivernais area and is open all year round. It has been attractively landscaped to provide a number of different areas, some giving pleasant views over the surrounding countryside. There are 100 spacious pitches with 84 for touring, most with 10A electricity (long leads advised). One area is set out on terraces and some pitches are slightly sloping. Many have good shade from a variety of magnificent trees. There is a good children's play area and three well stocked, small lakes for anglers.

Facilities

Two main toilet blocks provide washbasins in cabins, mostly British style WCs, baths, provision for disabled visitors and a baby bath. A small unit contains two tiny family suites for rent. Facilities by the pools can be heated in winter. Laundry. Motorcaravan services. Shop. Bar and restaurant. Pizza and takeaway. Internet point and WiFi (charged). Two heated pools (1/5-15/9). Play area. Minigolf. Boules. Fishing.
Off site: Walking and cycling in the Morvan Regional Park.

Open: All year.

Directions

Site is between Nevers and Autun. Leave the D978, 13 km. east of Châtillon-en-Bazois (site signed) onto D11. Site is a few hundred metres on the right.
GPS: 47.05877, 3.81716

Charges guide

Per unit incl. 2 persons	€ 19,00 - € 23,00
extra person	€ 5,00
child (0-6 yrs)	€ 4,00

Savigny-les-Beaune

Camping les Premier Pres

Route de Bouilland, F-21420 Savigny-les-Beaune (Côte d'Or) T: **03 80 26 15 06**
E: **mairie.savigny-les-beaune@wanadoo.fr** **alanrogers.com/FR21030**

This popular site is ideally located for visiting the Burgundy vineyards, for use as a transit site or for spending time in the town of Beaune. During the high season it is full every evening, so it is best to arrive by 4 pm. The 90 level pitches are marked and numbered, with electric hook-ups and room for an awning. A former municipal site, now privately owned. Whilst the famed wine region alone attracts many visitors, Beaune, its capital, is unrivalled in its richness of art from times gone by. Narrow streets and squares are garlanded with flowers, pavement cafés are crammed with tourists and overlooking the scene is the glistening Hotel Dieu.

Facilities

Well kept sanitary facilities are housed in a modern building behind reception. Additional WCs and water points are conveniently placed towards the middle of the site. Motorcaravan service point. Ice available to purchase. Torch useful. Off site: Sunday market in the village 1 km. Beaune 7 km.

Open: 29 April - 30 September.

Directions

From A6 autoroute take exit 24 signed Beaune and Savigny-les-Beaune onto D2. Turn right towards Savigny-les-Beaune (3 km) and follow signs to site.
GPS: 47.069, 4.803

Charges guide

Per person	€ 2,30
pitch incl. electricity	€ 6,55

No credit cards.

Tazilly

Airotel Château de Chigy

Chigy, F-58170 Tazilly (Nièvre) T: **03 86 30 10 80**. E: **reception@chateaudechigy.com.fr**
alanrogers.com/FR58050

This very spacious site (20 ha. for pitches and another 50 ha. of fields, lakes and woods) lies at the southern tip of the Morvan Regional Natural Park. The château houses the reception and apartments. Most of the facilities are nearby, and behind are 54 good sized, shaded and slightly sloping pitches, many uneven, all with electricity (6A). There is a large woodland area with paths, beyond which are 100 or so less shaded pitches, some of up to 150 sq.m. Most are slightly sloping and some are on low terraces, nearly all with electricity. Most have very good views.

Facilities

Two toilet blocks with British style WCs, washbasins in cubicles, and showers, but a good distance from pitches. A Portacabin has 4 cubicles, each with toilet, washbasin and shower (can be hired in July/Aug). Facilities for disabled people and babies. Laundry facilities. Gas supplies. Shop. Bar, restaurant and takeaway (July/Aug). Two outdoor pools, (15/5-30/9). Lake swimming. Covered pool. Games rooms. Playground. Minigolf. Off site: Luzy 4 km. Riding 9 km.

Open: 26 April - 30 September.

Directions

Leave Autun on N81 south west (signed Bourbon-Lancy) through Luzy (D973, signed Bourbon-Lancy). Site is signed to the left after approx. 4 km. GPS: 46.75746, 3.94478

Charges guide

Per unit incl. 2 persons	€ 16,00 - € 20,00
extra person	€ 4,00 - € 6,50
electricity	€ 4,00

Tournus

Camping de Tournus

Rue des Canes, F-71700 Tournus (Saône-et-Loire) T: **03 85 51 16 58**. E: **info@camping-tournus.com**
alanrogers.com/FR71190

This very well-maintained, pleasant site is just a few minutes from the A6 autoroute, 200 metres from the River Saône and close to the interesting old market town of Tournus. It is ideal for a night halt but deserving of a longer stay. The surrounding area is well worth exploring with its beautiful scenery and many picturesque old towns and villages. The site has 90 fairly level grassy pitches all for touring, 70 having 6A electricity. A few trees give some pitches varying amounts of shade. Access is very easy for big units. The new owners have plans for many improvements including some hardstanding pitches.

Facilities

Two clean toilet blocks near the entrance provide all necessary facilities, including for campers with disabilities. Small café (no alcohol) also stocking some daily necessities and bread to order (all season). Small play area. Internet terminal. Bicycle hire. Motorcaravan services planned. Off site: Fishing 200 m. Tournus, Saturday market, shops, bars, cafes, banks etc. short walk/bike ride alongside river. Municipal pool next door.

Open: 1 April - 30 September.

See advertisement on page 211

Directions

From the A6 take exit 12 for Tournus and the N6 south for just over 1 km. In Tournus (opposite railway station), turn left signed camping and follow signs to site, about 1 km. GPS: 46.574321, 4.909515

Charges guide

Per unit incl. 2 persons	€ 14,30 - € 17,70
extra person	€ 2,40 - € 4,90
electricity (6A)	€ 3,50 - € 4,20

Camping Cheques accepted.

Vandenesse-en-Auxois

Sunêlia Lac de Panthier

RD977b, F-21320 Vandenesse-en-Auxois (Côte d'Or) T: **03 80 49 21 94**. E: **info@lac-de-panthier.com**
alanrogers.com/FR21000

Camping Lac de Panthier is an attractively situated lakeside site in the Burgundy countryside. It is divided into two distinct areas, the smaller section houses the reception, shop, restaurant, indoor pool and sauna. The second, larger area is 200 m. along the lakeside road is where the other site activities take place and the outdoor pools can be found. The 207 pitches (157 for touring) all have electricity and are mostly on gently sloping grass, although in parts there are shallow terraces. The restaurant and some of the pitches have panoramic views over the lake which offers many watersports. Used by tour operators.

Facilities

Each area has two adequate unisex toilet blocks including provision for babies and disabled visitors. Shop, bar and restaurant. Games and TV rooms. Swimming pool, children's pool and slide (15/5-15/9). Indoor pool, sauna and gym. Fishing. Riding. Bicycle hire (including electric bikes with trailers for children) and canoe hire. Watersports. Entertainment and activities. Off site: Boat excursions from Pouilly-en-Auxois (8 km). Riding and golf 10 km. Dijon, Autun and Beaune. Bus to Poilly-en-Auxois 300 m.

Open: 4 April - 10 October.

See advertisement on page 263

Directions

From the A6 join the A38 and exit immediately at junction 24. Take N81 south towards Arnay Le Duc, over A6, shortly turn left on D977 for 5 km. Fork left for Vandenesse-en-Auxois. Through village on D977 for 2.5 km, turn left and site is on left. GPS: 47.23661, 4.62810

Charges guide

Per unit incl. 2 persons	€ 18,00 - € 25,00
extra person	€ 2,00 - € 7,00

Camping Cheques accepted.

The Travel Service to book this site call 01580 214000 ...we'll arrange everything

Located to the south of Alsace, the historic province of Franche Comté boasts a varied landscape ranging from flat plains to dense woodland, rugged dramatic mountains and limestone valleys.

DÉPARTEMENTS: 25 DOUBS, 39 JURA, 70 HAUTE-SAÔNE, 90 TRE. DE BELFORT

MAJOR CITY: BESANÇON

Franche Comté is really made up of two regions. The high valley of the Saône is wide, gently rolling farmland with a certain rustic simplicity, while the Jura mountains are more rugged with dense forests, sheer cliffs, craggy limestone escarpments and torrents of clear, sparkling water gushing through deep gorges. It is for this thrilling scenery that Franche Comté is best known. Nature lovers can climb, bike and hike in the mountains or explore the hills honeycombed with over 4,000 caves. The streams and lakes provide world-class fishing. The spa towns of Salins les Bains and Besançon offer relaxation and a chance to 'take the waters'.

The region has a rich architectural heritage dating from many different periods, including medieval abbeys and châteaux and a poignant chapel in memory of the war. Roman remains, fortresses perched on cliff tops and elegant spa towns can all be explored at leisure. The region's position, bordering Switzerland and close to Germany, is reflected in its culture and also the great diversity of architectural style in the many fine buildings.

Places of interest

Arbois: Pasteur Family Home and Museum, Museum of Wine and Wine Growing.

Belfort: sandstone lion sculpted by Bartholdi; Memorial and Museum of the French Resistance.

Besançon: citadel with good views over the city.

Champlitte: Museum of Folk Art.

Dole: lovely old town, Louis Pasteur's birthplace.

Gray: Baron Martin Museum.

Luxeuil-les-Bains: Tour des Echevins Museu

Ornans: Gustave Courbet birthplace, museum.

Ronchamp: Chapel of Notre-Dame du Ha de Ronchamp designed by Le Corbusier.

Salins-les-Bains: Salt mines and tunnels.

Sochaux: Peugeot Museum.

Cuisine of the region

Freshwater fish such as trout, grayling, pi and perch are local specialities. The regior has a rare wine known as *vin de paille* as well as *vin jaune* (deep yellow and very d and *vin du jura*, Jura wine.

Brési: water-thin slices of dried beef; man local hams.

Gougére: hot cheese pastry based on the local *Comté* cheese.

Jésus de Morteau: fat pork sausage smok over pine and juniper.

Poulet au vin jaune: chicken, cream and *morilles* cooked in *vin jaune*.

www.franche-comte.org
info@franche-comte.org
00800 2006 2010 (free from the UK

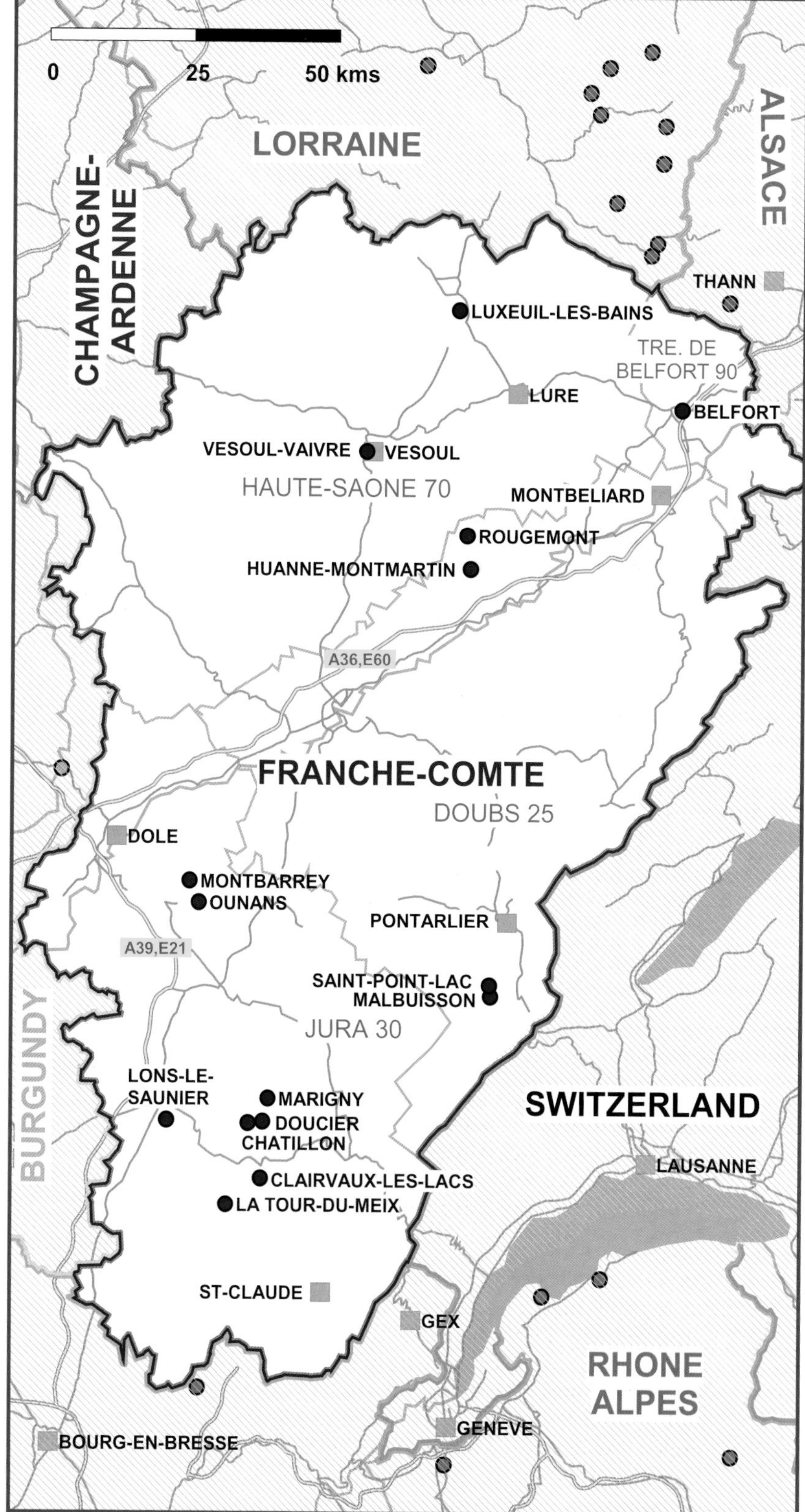
0
25
50 kms
LORRAINE
ALSACE
CHAMPAGNE-
ARDENNE
THANN
LUXEUIL-LES-BAINS
TRE. DE
BELFORT 90
LURE
BELFORT
VESOUL-VAIVRE
VESOUL
HAUTE-SAONE 70
MONTBELIARD
ROUGEMONT
HUANNE-MONTMARTIN
A36,E60
FRANCHE-COMTE
DOUBS 25
DOLE
MONTBARREY
OUNANS
PONTARLIER
A39,E21
SAINT-POINT-LAC
MALBUISSON
JURA 30
BURGUNDY
LONS-LE-
SAUNIER
MARIGNY
DOUCIER
CHATILLON
SWITZERLAND
LAUSANNE
CLAIRVAUX-LES-LACS
LA TOUR-DU-MEIX
ST-CLAUDE
GEX
RHONE
ALPES
GENEVE
BOURG-EN-BRESSE

Belfort

Camping l'Etang des Forges

11 rue Béthouart, F-90000 Belfort (Tre.-de-Belfort) T: **03 84 22 54 92**. E: **contact@camping-belfort.com**
alanrogers.com/FR90000

Belfort (known as the City of the Lion) is a historic fortified town with much history. Although 178 pitches are marked out, this very spacious site only uses 90 of them, and you should always be able to find room here. The pitches are all on level, mostly open ground divided by bushes. A few trees around one end give a little shade to some pitches and there are electricity hook-ups (6A) to all pitches and a good supply of water taps. The reception building also contains a small shop and cafe.

Facilities

A single modern sanitary building (heated in cool weather) provides washbasins in cubicles, a suite for disabled people, dishwashing and laundry sinks, a washing machine and dryer. Motorcaravan services. Outdoor swimming pool (6/6-9/9). Volleyball. Table tennis. Small playground. TV Room. Shop and café (6/6-5/9). Internet terminal. Off site: Large supermarket is on edge of town on the Mulhouse road.

Open: 7 April - 30 September.

Directions

Site is northeast of town centre towards Offemont, adjacent to the lake and sports facilities (well signed). GPS: 47.65333, 6.86443

Charges guide

Per unit incl. 2 persons and electricity	€ 18,00 - € 21,50
extra person	€ 3,50 - € 4,50
child (5-9 yrs)	€ 2,50 - € 3,50

Camping Cheques accepted.

Chatillon

Kawan Village Domaine de l'Epinette

kawan VILLAGES www.kawan-villages.com

15 rue de l'Epinette, F-39130 Chatillon (Jura) T: **03 84 25 71 44**
E: **info@domaine-epinette.com** **alanrogers.com/FR39080**

This site is set in charming wooded countryside on land sloping down to the river Ain, which is shallow and slow moving. There are 150 grassy pitches, 110 are available for touring units, some slightly sloping. These are arranged on terraces and separated by hedges and young bushes and trees, about half being shaded. Nearly all have electricity hook-ups, although some long leads are needed. Four pitches have hardstanding. There is an attractive swimming pool (heated 1/7-31/8) with a paddling pool. An activity club for children takes place in July/August. Guided canoe trips on the Ain start and finish at the campsite.

Facilities

Two modern toilet blocks. Unit for disabled visitors. Baby bath. Dishwashing and laundry sinks. Washing machine and dryer. Small shop for basics. Snack bar and takeaway (evenings). New reception, bar, TV room and shop. Swimming pool. Playground. Boules. Direct access to river for swimming and canoeing. Off site: Riding 6 km. Golf 25 km. Shops, etc. in Doucier 6 km.

Open: 9 June - 15 September.

Directions

From Lons-le-Saunier take D471 eastwards towards Champagnole. After about 8 km. fork right onto D39 towards Doucier. After 11 km. at Chatillon turn right onto D151 south towards Blye. Site is less than 2 km. on the left. GPS: 46.65887, 5.72978

Charges guide

Per unit incl. 2 persons and electricity	€ 17,00 - € 27,00
extra person	€ 3,00 - € 4,50

Camping Cheques accepted.

Clairvaux-les-Lacs

Yelloh! Village Fayolan

yelloh! VILLAGE

B.P. 52, F-39130 Clairvaux-les-Lacs (Jura) T: **04 66 73 97 39**. E: **info@yellohvillage-fayolan.com**
alanrogers.com/FR39050

This large, spacious site is modern and well equipped. Backed by wooded hills, it is situated on the shores of Le Petit Lac amid the lakes and forests of the Jure, about a mile from the town of Clairvaux-les-Lacs. It is in two parts, with 516 pitches either on terraces overlooking the lake or on the flatter area near the shore. With 456 for touring units, all have electricity (10A) and 200 are fully serviced. The pitches are separated by hedges and mature trees giving most some shade. Many activities are organised on site, some in low season. Used by tour operators (130 pitches).

Facilities

Four modern well equipped toilet units. Baby room. Washing and drying machines. Ironing facilities. Shop. Restaurant. Bar. Snack bar/pizzeria and takeaway. Swimming pool complex with indoor pool (all season), outdoor pool with toboggan (heated) and large outdoor pool and paddling pool (16/5-2/9). Fitness centre sauna, steam bath, massage (16/5-2/9). Entertainment area. Playground. Organised activities, children's club. Internet access. Fishing. Beach sports area and lake swimming. Boules. Organised walks. Off site: Bicycle hire 800 m.

Open: 30 April - 6 September.

Directions

Clairvaux-les-Lacs is on the D678 about 23 km. southeast of Lons-le-Saunier. In Clairvaux follow signs for 'Lacs Campings' and Fayolan (1.5 km southeast of town). GPS: 46.56438, 5.75621

Charges guide

Per unit incl. 2 persons and electricity	€ 15,00 - € 41,00
extra person	€ 5,00 - € 7,00
child (3-7 yrs)	free - € 5,00

Doucier

Camping Domaine de Chalain

F-39130 Doucier (Jura) T: **03 84 25 78 78**. E: **chalain@chalain.com**

alanrogers.com/FR39030

Doucier lies 25 km. east of Lons-le-Saunier among the wooded hills of the Jura and rather away from the main routes. This large, spacious site is in a parkland setting beside Lac de Chalain and is surrounded by woods and cliffs. Large areas are left for sports and recreation. The lake shelves gently but then becomes deep quite suddenly. The site also has an attractive, well equipped pool complex. There are 800 good-sized, level pitches with 462 for touring units, Most have electricity (7A) and there are varying amounts of shade. Booking is obligatory for caravans or motorcaravans over 7 m.

Facilities

Nine well equipped sanitary blocks with facilities for babies and disabled people. Shops (some high season only). Restaurant and bar (all season). Takeaway, snacks (20/6-31/8). Swimming pool complex with heated indoor pool, outdoor pools with slide, sauna and spa (one entrance per day). Many large play areas. Fishing. Pedalo and bicycle hire. Range of sports activities including rock climbing, archery, aquagym. TV room. Disco, entertainment, organised activities. Dogs not permitted on lake beach. Off site: Riding 2 km. Golf 25 km.

Open: 23 April - 21 September.

Directions

Doucier is 25 km. east of Lons-le-Saunier. In village turn left off D39, site signed, entrance in 3 km. GPS: 46.66435, 5.81315

Charges guide

Per unit incl. 3 persons acc. to location and services	€ 22,00 - € 38,00
extra person	€ 4,00 - € 6,00
child (4-15 yrs)	€ 3,00 - € 5,00
dog	€ 2,00

Doucier

Camping les Mérilles

Rue des 3 Lacs, F-39130 Doucier (Jura) T: **03 84 25 73 06**. E: **camping.lesmerilles@wanadoo.fr**

alanrogers.com/FR39170

Camping les Mérilles is a small, good quality, family run campsite 500 m. from the small town of Doucier and only 2 km. from the beautiful Lac de Chalain. It has 96 good sized, level, grass pitches separated by hedging. A variety of trees give some shade. There are 73 pitches for touring with 16 having a private bathroom. All have electricity (6/10A). This site is a quieter alternative to the much busier sites near the lake. The surrounding area is well worth exploring and is well known for its lakes, waterfalls and Caves. Owners of large outfits should phone ahead to reserve the larger pitches.

Facilities

One modern, well appointed and heated toilet block near reception, one older and very small block plus 16 private cabins to rent with certain pitches. Motorcaravan services. Basic shop and bar with TV (1/6-30/9). Takeaway (1/7-30/9). Outdoor heated pool and paddling pool (1/5-30/9). Playground. Bicycle hire. Wifi (free). Organised family activities (July/Aug). Off site: Doucier with small shops, bar and restaurant 500 m. Lac Chalain, indoor pool 2 km.

Open: 1 April - 30 September.

Directions

Doucier is 25 km. east of Lons-le-Saunier. The site is 500 m. east of Doucier on the D39 with the entrance on the right. GPS: 46.65178, 5.77491

Charges guide

Per unit incl. 2 persons and electricity	€ 15,50 - € 18,90
incl. private bathroom	€ 19,10 - € 24,95
extra person	€ 3,80 - € 3,95
child (2-7 yrs)	€ 2,00 - € 2,30

Huanne-Montmartin

Camping du Bois de Reveuge

F-25680 Huanne-Montmartin (Doubs) T: **03 81 84 38 60**. E: **info@campingduboisdereveuge.com**

alanrogers.com/FR25030

Bois de Reveuge has 340 pitches including 150 mobile homes located in woodland to one side of the site. The terraced pitches have good views across the surrounding countryside and lead down to two lakes which may be used for fishing and canoeing. 190 pitches available for tourers have water and electricity and some are extra large (150-180 sq.m). Tall trees have been left standing at the top of the hill but there is little shade in the touring areas. There is a good solar heated swimming pool which can be covered in cool weather and another pool with four water slides and paddling pool, supervised in high season.

Facilities

Four modern sanitary blocks with all necessary facilities (only two blocks open in low season). Facilities for disabled visitors, children and babies. Laundry facilities. Kiosk for basics, restaurant/pizzeria (1/5-15/9). Swimming pools. Play areas. Miniclub (high season). Video screen, music and other entertainment. Bowling alley. Shooting range. Pony club. BMX track. Aquagym. Groups may request activities such as orienteering. Package deal includes use of canoes, archery, fishing, bicycle hire and pedaloes.

Open: 23 April - 17 September.

Directions

Site is well signed from the D50. From A36 autoroute south of the site, take exit for Baume-les-Dames and head north on D50 towards Villersexel for about 7 km. to camp signs. GPS: 47.4405, 6.34335

Charges guide

Per unit incl. 2 persons and electricity	€ 19,00 - € 37,00
extra person	€ 4,00 - € 7,00
child (2-5 yrs)	€ 2,00 - € 5,00

La Tour-du-Meix

Camping de Surchauffant

Le Pont de la Pyle, F-39270 La Tour-du-Meix (Jura) T: **03 84 25 41 08**. E: **surchauffant@chalain.com**
alanrogers.com/FR39020

With only 180 pitches, this site may appeal to those who prefer a more informal atmosphere, however it can be lively in high season. It is pleasantly situated above the beaches bordering the Lac de Vouglans, which can be reached quickly on foot directly from the site. The 133 touring pitches are of a reasonable size and are informally arranged, some are fully serviced and most with electricity (5A). They are divided by hedges and there is some shade. The lake offers a variety of watersports activities, boat trips, etc. and is used for fishing and swimming (guarded in high season as it shelves steeply).

Facilities

The sanitary facilities are older in style and adequate rather than luxurious, but reasonably well maintained and clean when we visited. They include some washbasins in private cabins. Laundry. Heated swimming pool (200 sq.m), paddling pool and surround (15/6-15/9). Three playgrounds. Animation (July/Aug). Safety deposit boxes. Off site: Bicycle hire or riding 5 km. Restaurant, takeaway and shops adjacent.

Open: 24 April - 15 September.

Directions

From A39 take exit 7 and N1082 to Lons-le-Saunier. Continue south on D52 for about 20 km. to Orgelet. Site is by the D470, at La Tour-du-Meix, about 4 km. east of Orgelet. GPS: 46.5231, 5.67401

Charges guide

Per unit incl. 2 persons and electricity	€ 16,00 - € 22,00
extra person (over 4 yrs)	€ 3,30 - € 4,70
dog	€ 1,60

Lons-le-Saunier

Camping la Marjorie

640 boulevard de l'Europe, F-39000 Lons-le-Saunier (Jura) T: **03 84 24 26 94**. E: **info@camping-marjorie.com**
alanrogers.com/FR39060

La Marjorie is a spacious site set on the outskirts of the spa town of Lons-le-Saunier with a long season. Bordering one area of the site are open fields and woodlands. It has 200 level pitches, 185 for touring units and 130 with electricity (6/10A). Some are on hardstanding and 37 are fully serviced. They are separated by well trimmed hedges interspersed with tall trees which gives privacy plus some shade. There is a cycle path from the site into town (2.5 km) and a mountain bike track behind the site. This is a good site for a long or short stay.

Facilities

Three well maintained toilet blocks, two modern and heated, Baby baths, facilities for disabled people. Small shop (15/6-31/8). Small bar with takeaway meals (all 15/6-31/8). TV room. Small play area. Boules. Football field. Archery, canoeing and riding. Motorcaravan service point (charge). Bicycle hire. Off site: Swimming pool 200 m (free for min. 5 day stay). Bus stop 400 m. Restaurants 500 m. Fishing 3 km. Riding 5 km. Golf 6 km. Caves and waterfalls 17 km.

Open: 1 April - 15 October.

Directions

Site is off the N1083 Lons-le-Saunier - Besançon road, just north of Lons. Follow signs for 'camping' and 'piscine'. GPS: 46.68437, 5.56843

Charges guide

Per unit incl. 2 persons and electricity	€ 14,90 - € 19,60
extra person	€ 2,70 - € 4,50
child (under 10 yrs)	€ 1,50 - € 2,90
dog	€ 1,30

Luxeuil-les-Bains

Domaine du Chatigny

14 rue du Gramont, F-70300 Luxeuil-les-Bains (Haute-Saône) T: **03 84 93 97 97**
E: **camping.ot-luxeuil@wanadoo.fr** **alanrogers.com/FR70010**

An excellent example of a well cared for municipal site, du Chatigny is located on a hillside backing onto woods, yet is only a five-minute walk from the centre of the interesting old spa town of Luxeuil-les-Bains. As the site has only recently been opened, all facilities are of a high quality and were very clean when we visited. There are 98 good sized, level or slightly sloping, grass pitches separated by young shrubs and trees with not much shade. Of the 78 touring pitches 52 have electricity (16A) and 26 are fully serviced. Some activities are organised on site, but a wide programme of events is offered nearby.

Facilities

One modern, heated toilet block is excellent and provides all necessary facilities. Motorcaravane services. Snack bar, swimming and paddling pool (open weekends June, Sept and every day July/Aug). Games/TV room. Tennis. Internet, WiFi. Off site: Fishing and riding 2 km. Golf 10 km. Spa town of Luxeuil-les-Bains with good range shops, bars, restaurants, Casino, Saturday market and many organised events, 5 minutes walk.

Open: 1 April - 31 October.

Directions

The site is 45 km. south of Epinal. There is no access for vehicles from the centre of Luxeuil-les-Bains. Bypass Luxeuil-les-Bains on the N57 and at the supermarket (site signed) turn west into rue Ste Anne. Bear right three times to site (900 m). GPS: 47.8236, 6.381667

Charges guide

Per unit incl. 2 persons and electricity	€ 17,00 - € 20,00
incl. full services	€ 18,50 - € 22,50
extra person	€ 2,00 - € 4,00

Malbuisson

Camping les Fuvettes

F-25160 Malbuisson (Doubs) T: **03 81 69 31 50**. E: **les-fuvettes@wanadoo.fr**
alanrogers.com/FR25080

High in the Jura and close to the Swiss border, Les Fuvettes is a well established family site beside Lac Saint Point. The 320 reasonably sized grass pitches are separated by hedges and small trees with varying degrees of shade and many are slightly sloping. There are 250 for touring with 200 having electricity (4/6A). Only a few have views over the lake. The swimming pool complex is impressive with water slides and a separate children's pool. The site's bar/snack bar is housed in an attractive, steep roofed building and offers panoramic views across the lake.

Facilities

Three toilet blocks include facilities for babies and disabled people. Shop. Bar and snack bar. Swimming pool with water slides, jacuzzi and paddling pool (from June). Play area. Minigolf. Archery. Bicycle hire. Sports pitch. Fishing (permit needed). Boat and pedalo hire. Games room. TV room. Children's club in peak season. Entertainment and excursion programme (July/Aug). Mobile homes and chalets for rent. Off site: Lakeside beach. Sailing school. Tennis. Riding 1 km. Bicycle hire 3 km. Many cycling and walking trails. Malbuisson (walking distance).

Open: 1 April - 30 September.

Directions

From Besançon, head south on the N57 to just beyond Pontarlier. Take the D437 signed Lac St Point and Mouthe. The road skirts the lake and through Malbuisson. Site is on right at the end of the village. GPS: 46.79197, 6.29334

Charges guide

Per unit incl. 2 persons and electricity	€ 17,60 - € 26,10
extra person	€ 3,50 - € 5,20
child (under 7 yrs)	€ 1,80 - € 2,90

Marigny

Kawan Village la Pergola

1 rue des Vernois, F-39130 Marigny (Jura) T: **03 84 25 70 03**
E: **contact@lapergola.com** **alanrogers.com/FR39040**

Close to the Swiss border and overlooking the sparkling waters of Lac de Chalain, La Pergola is a good quality terraced site set amid the rolling hills of the Jura. Neat and tidy, it is very well appointed, with 350 pitches, 100 for touring, mainly on grass and gravel and separated by small hedges. All have electricity (6A), water and drainage and some have shade from a variety of mature trees. The bar/restaurant and terrace are next to the three swimming pools and entertainment area, with good views over the lake. This is a good family holiday base in high season and English is spoken.

Facilities

Three good quality toilet blocks provide all the necessary facilities including those for disabled visitors, and excellent provision for children. Motorcaravan services. Shop (1/6-15/9). Bar. Self service restaurant. Pizzeria/takeaway (15/5-15/9). Pool complex, two pools heated. Good play areas and children's club. Archery. Boules. Lake swimming. Fishing. Pedaloes, canoes and small boats for hire. Organised programme in high season, entertainment. Internet access and WiFi. Off site: Hang-gliding 2 km. Riding 3 km. Golf 25 km. Many marked walks and cycle trails.

Open: 15 May - 15 September.

Directions

Doucier is 25 km. east of Lons-le-Saunier. On outskirts of Doucier turn north onto D27, site signed. Site in 3 km beside Lac de Chalain. GPS: 46.6771, 5.78094

Charges guide

Per unit incl. 2 persons and electricity	€ 21,00 - € 36,00
extra person	€ 5,50 - € 7,00
child (3-7 yrs)	free - € 5,50
animal	€ 4,00

Camping Cheques accepted.

Meursault

Kawan Village la Grappe d'Or

2 route de Volnay, F-21190 Meursault (Côte d'Or) T: **03 80 21 22 48**
E: **info@camping-meursault.com** **alanrogers.com/FR21050**

Meursault, the capital of the great white wines of Burgundy, is southwest of Beaune and Camping de la Grappe d'Or offers terraced pitches overlooking acres of vineyards. Most of the 125 touring pitches are flat, of varying sizes, and some have shade from mature trees. They all have electrical connections (15A). There is an outdoor pool and flume and, during July and August, aqua gym and other water activities are organised. There is a fenced play area for youngsters and, just across the road from the entrance, there are two tennis courts for campers.

Facilities

Sanitary facilities are in three blocks with some washbasins in cabins. Child/baby room. Facilities for visitors with disabilities. Laundry fcilities. Shop. Bar, restaurant, takeaway (1/5-30/9). Swimming pool (15/6-15/9). Play area. Tennis. Bicycle hire. Off site: Golf or riding 7 km. Indoor pool 7 km. Fishing 8 km. Beaune 9 km.

Open: 1 April - 15 October.

Directions

Site is north of Meursault. Take N74 from Beaune and follow the sign for Meursault. Site is signed from town but not very clearly (tents with three arrows).
GPS: 46.98574, 4.76858

Charges 2010

Per unit incl. 2 persons	€ 17,00 - € 21,50
extra person	€ 3,00 - € 3,70

Camping Cheques accepted.

Montbarrey

Flower Camping les Trois Ours

28 rue du Pont, F-39380 Montbarrey (Jura) T: **03 84 81 50 45**
E: **contact@camping-les3ours-jura.com** **alanrogers.com/FR39150**

This is a site for those seeking a shady, quiet and pleasant location. It provides good clean, modern facilities and a good restaurant with a river terrace, and a bar with TV (which is open all season). The adjacent River Loue will be an attraction for fishermen and river bathing is also possible. There are mobile homes and chalets to rent, but there should be around 90 shady level grassy touring pitches all with 10A electricity. During peak season various activities are organised.

Facilities

A fairly modern block provides all the usual facilities. Restaurant and bar. Small adventure style playground. Boules. Small lake for fishing (free), river fishing (permit required). Off site: Golf 13 km. Riding 3 km. Bicycle hire 3 km. Shops, ATM and services in Ounans 3 km.

Open: 1 May - 30 September.

Directions

From D472 Salins-les-Bains - Dole road, turn north on D11, 3.5 km. west of Ounans. Site is 3 km. on left just after river bridge. GPS: 47.011917, 5.6305

Charges guide

Per unit incl. 2 persons and electricity	€ 13,10 - € 20,90
extra person	€ 1,90 - € 4,50

Ounans

Kawan Village la Plage Blanche

3 rue de la Plage, F-39380 Ounans (Jura) T: **03 84 37 69 63**
E: **reservation@la-plage-blanche.com** **alanrogers.com/FR39010**

Situated in open countryside, along the banks of the River Loue, this spacious site has 220 good-sized, marked grass pitches on level ground, 194 for touring units, all with 6A electricity. Trees provide varying amounts of shade. Some of the pitches are a long walk from the pool and play area near the entrance. About a kilometre of riverside provides points of access, some with a small beach area. At low water levels the river provides an ideal setting for children to swim and play safely in the gently flowing, shallow water. Inflatables are popular and there is a canoe/kayak base within a few hundred metres.

Facilities

Modern, well kept sanitary facilities in three unusual blocks. Launderette. Motorcaravan service area. No shop but bread to order. Bar/restaurant with terrace. Pizzeria and takeaway (1/5-15/9). TV room. Library. Swimming and paddling pools (1/5-30/9). Play area. River fishing and fishing lake. Canoeing. Entertainment and activities (1/7-30/8). Internet access. Off site: Shop 1.5 km. Supermarket 6 km. Bicycle hire 200 m. Riding 10 km. Golf 13 km. Paragliding and hang-gliding.

Open: 1 April - 15 October.

Directions

Ounans is 20 km. southeast of Dole. From autoroute A36, exit 6 (Dole) and take the N5 southeast to Mont-sous-Vaudrey (10 km). Bear left on D472 to Ounans (5 km). In Ounans take D71 north signed Montbarrey for 1 km. Turn left to site immediately after river. GPS: 47.00284, 5.663

Charges guide

Per unit incl. 2 persons and electricity	€ 17,00 - € 22,00
extra person	€ 3,50 - € 5,00

Camping Cheques accepted.

Rougemont

Castel Camping le Val de Bonnal

Bonnal, F-25680 Rougemont (Doubs) T: **03 81 86 90 87**. E: **val-de-bonnal@wanadoo.fr**
alanrogers.com/FR25000

This is an impressive, generally peaceful, well managed site in a large country estate, harmoniously designed in keeping with the surrounding countryside, well away from main roads and other intrusions. The site itself is very busy, with a wide range of activities and amenities. The 350 good sized, landscaped pitches (190 for touring) with electricity (5A) are separated by a mixture of trees and bushes. A newer area has pitches of 200-250 sq.m. but are less secluded. The main attraction must be the variety of watersports on the three large lakes and nearby river. The range of activities available in high season is almost inexhaustible, not to say exhausting!

Facilities

...r clean toilet blocks include washbasins in cabins, suites ...abled visitors and facilities for children and babies. ...facilities. Riverside restaurant, snack bar/takeaway, ...race, shop (all 20/5-8/9). Swimming pool ... water slides. Well equipped play areas. ...oules. Bicycle hire. Watersports. Fishing ...e. Fitness suite. Internet access. ...3.5 km. Golf 6 km. Day trips to

...r.

Directions

From Vesoul take D9 towards Villersexel. After about 20 km. turn right in Esprels signed Val-de-Bonnal. Continue for 3.5 km. to site on left. From autoroute A36, exit Baume-les-Dames; go north on D50, then D486 to Rougemont and follow site signs. GPS: 47.50698, 6.35487

Charges guide

Per unit incl. 2 persons and electricity	€ 35,00
extra person	€ 9,00
child (2-9 yrs)	€ 4,00

Less 25% outside July/Aug.

Saint Point-Lac

Camping Municipal de Saint Point-Lac

8 rue du Port, F-25160 Saint Point-Lac (Doubs) T: **03 81 69 61 64**. E: **camping-saintpointlac@wanadoo.fr**
alanrogers.com/FR25050

A good example of a municipal campsite in which the village takes a pride, this site is on the banks of a small lake with views to the distant hills. The 84 level, numbered pitches are on grass and 60 have electricity (16A). It is worth making a detour from the Pontarlier - Vallorbe road or for a longer stay. The village shop and restaurant are a 200 m. walk from the site entrance. Units over 7 m. are not accepted.

Facilities

Well maintained, older style central sanitary block (partly refurbished) has British style WCs and free hot water. Suite for disabled visitors. Laundry facilities. Hot snacks and takeaway in high season (July/Aug). Fishing.
Off site: Lakeside walk. Motorcaravan services opposite. Beach and swimming area. Pedalo hire. Bicycle hire 5 km.

Open: 1 May - 30 September.

Directions

From north, take D437 south of Pontarlier and keep on west side of the lake to the second village (Saint Point-Lac); from south exit N57 at Les Hopitaux-Neufs and turn west to lake. GPS: 46.8118, 6.3031

Charges guide

Per unit incl. 2 persons and electricity	€ 12,80 - € 14,50
extra person	€ 2,00 - € 2,50
child (4-10 yrs)	€ 1,00 - € 1,25
dog	€ 1,00

Vesoul-Vaivre

Camping International du Lac

Avenue des Rives du Lac, F-70000 Vesoul-Vaivre (Haute-Saône) T: **03 84 76 22 86**
E: **camping_dulac@yahoo.fr** **alanrogers.com/FR70020**

This is one of the better examples of a town site and is part of a leisure park around a large lake. The campsite does not have direct access to the lake as it is separated by a security fence, but access is possible at the site entrance. There are 160 good sized, level, grass pitches, all with electricity (10A). Access is from hard roads and pitches are separated by shrubs and bushes. There is a large area in the centre of the site with a play area. A 5 km. path has been created around the lake for jogging, walking and cycling.

Facilities

Three good quality toilet blocks, one heated, are well spaced around the site and provide a mix of British and Turkish style WCs, washbasins and showers. Baby room. Two superb suites for disabled visitors. Washing machines and dryers. Motorcaravan service point. Baker calls daily (July/Aug); bread ordered from reception at other times. Animation (July/Aug). Bicycle hire. TV and games room. Boules. Internet access. Fishing. Off site: Bar and restaurant adjacent. Lake beach 100 m. Sailing 2 km. Riding 4 km.

Open: 1 March - 31 October.

Directions

The site is on road D457 to west of Vesoul on the route to Besançon, well signed around the town. GPS: 47.63054, 6.12946

Charges 2010

Per person	€ 3,60
child (under 7 yrs)	€ 1,70
pitch	€ 3,50
incl. electricity	€ 5,50
vehicle	€ 2,70

**This quiet and dee
rural province is ri
the centre of Franc
the south of the to
region of the Loire Va
Unspoilt and thinly popu
it is unknown to many but by
others is considered close to
paradise.**

DÉPARTEMENTS: 19 CORRÈZE, 23 CREUSE, 87 HAUTE-VIENNE

MAJOR CITIES: LIMOGES, BRIVE-LA-GAILLARDE

On the western side of the Massif Central, this stunningly beautiful region of still lakes, fast flowing streams, gentle rolling valleys and forested mountains has been one of the best kept secrets in France. Lush green meadows are grazed by the Limousin breed of cattle, numerous ancient villages and churches dot the landscape, as well as more imposing abbey churches and fortresses. The region's moorland has made it popular with horse breeders and the Anglo-Arab horse originated from the famous studs of Pompadour.

The city of Limoges, synonymous with porcelain production, produced the finest painted enamelware of Europe in the 16th and 17th centuries and today remains the porcelain capital of France. Aubusson is renowned for its beautiful and intricate tapestries.

But Limousin's appeal is more than anything the freedom of the countryside and it has not yet been discovered except by the discerning traveller. It is said that in Limousin a discovery awaits you at the end of every path and we consider this to be a fairly accurate description.

Places of interest

Aubusson: long tradition of tapestry making, Hotel de Ville tapestry collecti

Grimel-les-Cascades: a pretty hamlet se a deep gorge.

Gueret: built around a monastery foun in the 8th century, the municipal muse houses a fine collection of porcelain.

Limoges: porcelain, enamel and faienc work, château, church of St Michel-de Lions, cathedral of St Etienne.

Noilac: abbey.

Segur-le-Château: picturesque village dominated by its fortified château, Henry IV's house.

Treignac: Rocher des Folles with a view the Vézères gorges.

Tulle: 12th-century cathedral and cloist City museum, Maison de Loyac.

Cuisine of the region

Traditional dishes include a variety of s such as pote, cassoulet, beans and por sauced dishes accompanied by chestnu rye pancajes. Limousin beef is tender a full of flavour.

Bréjaude: a soup eaten with rye bread so thick with cabbage and other veget that a spoon will stand up in it.

Clafoutis: a pancake batter poured, for example, over fruit.

Galette Corrzienne: almond cake.

Gargouillau and Milliard: clafoutis of p and cherries, respectively.

**www.tourismelimousin.com or
www.massifcentral-tourisme.com
documentation@crt-limousin.fr
(0)5 55 11 05 90**

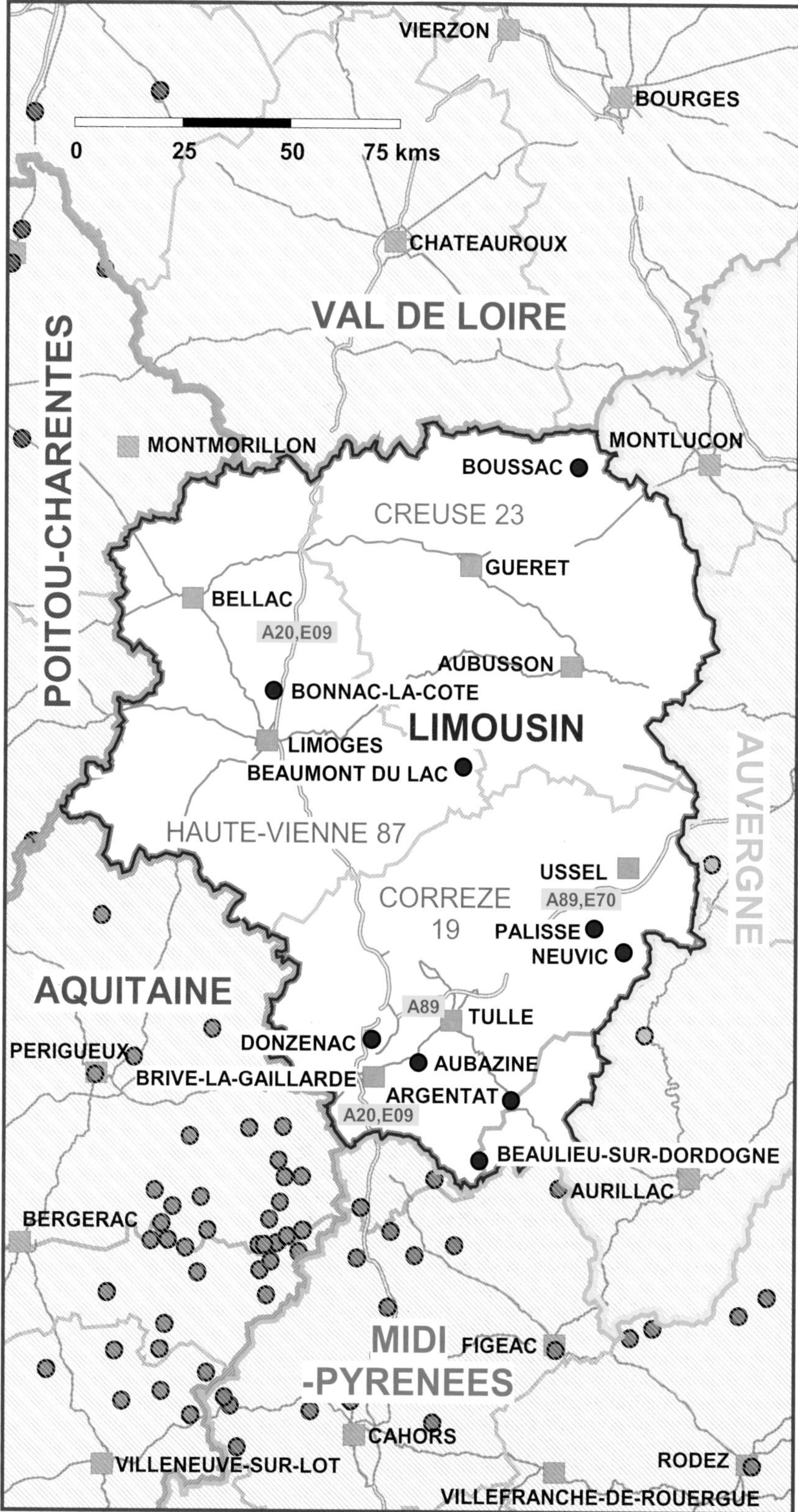
VIERZON
BOURGES
0
25
50
75 kms
CHATEAUROUX
VAL DE LOIRE
POITOU-CHARENTES
MONTMORILLON
MONTLUCON
BOUSSAC
CREUSE 23
GUERET
BELLAC
A20,E09
AUBUSSON
BONNAC-LA-COTE
LIMOUSIN
LIMOGES
BEAUMONT DU LAC
AUVERGNE
HAUTE-VIENNE 87
USSEL
CORREZE
19
A89,E70
PALISSE
NEUVIC
AQUITAINE
A89
TULLE
DONZENAC
PERIGUEUX
AUBAZINE
BRIVE-LA-GAILLARDE
ARGENTAT
A20,E09
BEAULIEU-SUR-DORDOGNE
AURILLAC
BERGERAC
MIDI
-PYRENEES
FIGEAC
CAHORS
VILLENEUVE-SUR-LOT
RODEZ
VILLEFRANCHE-DE-ROUERGUE

Argentat

Camping le Vaurette

Monceaux-sur-Dordogne, F-19400 Argentat (Corrèze) T: **05 55 28 09 67**. E: **info@vaurette.com**

alanrogers.com/FR19090

You are assured of a warm welcome at this immaculate site, beautifully situated beside the shallow river Dordogne and just a few kilometres from Argentat. There are 120 large, gently sloping grass pitches, 118 for touring. Separated by a large variety of beautiful trees and shrubs offering varying amounts of shade, all have 6A electricity and many have good views over the river Dordogne as the pitches nearest the river are slightly terraced. The owners run an active campsite for all the family whilst maintaining an air of tranquility (no radios). Excellent English is spoken. The ancient barn at the far end of the site houses the bar and a large TV room (large screen) and the terrace overlooks the good sized and attractive, heated swimming and paddling pools (all season).

Facilities

Two very clean traditional toilet blocks offer all the expected facilities, including facilities for disabled people. Further facilities are near the bar and heated pool. Motorcaravan service point. Shop and takeaway (July/Aug). Football. Gym. Badminton. Boules. Tennis. Fishing. River bathing. Accompanied canoe trips, walks and mountain bike rides. Organised activities for all the family (July/Aug) but no late night discos etc. WiFi. Off site: Argentat with shops and watersports centre 9 km. Riding 15 km.

Open: 1 May - 21 September.

Directions

From the A20 or A89 take the exit for Tulle, then the N120 to Argentat, onto the D12 towards Beaulieu. The site is on the left. GPS: 45.0464, 1.8821

Charges guide

Per unit incl. 2 persons	€ 15,50 - € 23,50
extra person (over 2 yrs)	€ 3,30 - € 5,00
electricity (6A)	€ 3,30
dog	€ 2,00 - € 3,50

Argentat

Sunêlia Au Soleil d'Oc

Monceaux-sur-Dordogne, F-19400 Argentat (Corrèze) T: **05 55 28 84 84**. E: **info@dordogne-soleil.com**

alanrogers.com/FR19100

You will be assured of a very warm welcome, throughout the long season, at this attractive family run site set amongst a variety of tall trees on the banks of the river Dordogne. The 120 large, level, grass pitches, 80 for tourists, all with 6A electricity, are mostly separated by neatly trimmed shrubs and hedges. They are set out on two levels; the lower level nearer the river, with fewer static pitches, being some distance from the toilet facilities and sports area. This site should appeal to lovers of watersports and other activities, particularly in July and August when there is plenty to do for all the family.

Facilities

Two unisex toilet blocks offer all the facilities one would expect. Baby facilities. Shop. Bar. Restaurant and takeaway (1/6-30/9). Outdoor pool (1/5-15/10). New indoor pool planned. Motorcaravan service point. Bathing in the river Dordogne. Canoe hire and organised trips. Volleyball, football, pool table and electronic games. Archery. Minigolf. Fishing. Bicycle hire. Guided walks and bike rides. Entertainment programme (July/Aug). WiFi. Off site: River Dordogne. Argentat 4 km. Riding 15 km.

Open: 1 April - 1 November.

Directions

Leave Argentat on D12 heading southwest (Beaulieu). In 3.5 km. (village of Laygue) turn left across a single track bridge spanning the river Dordogne. Immediately turn left and site is a few hundred metres on left. GPS: 45.0753, 1.91699

Charges guide

Per unit incl. 2 persons	€ 14,50 - € 20,70
extra person	€ 3,80 - € 5,80
child (2-13 yrs)	free - € 3,90
dog	free - € 3,00

Camping Cheques accepted.

Aubazine

Campéole le Coiroux

Centre Touristique du Coiroux, F-19190 Aubazine (Corrèze) T: **05 55 27 21 96**. E: **coiroux@campeole.com**
alanrogers.com/FR19140

Le Coiroux, part of the Campéole group, is set in a picturesque location in the heart of a forest on the edge of a large leisure park and lake. There are 174 large pitches, 62 for touring all with 10A electricity. They are flat and grassy with small dividing hedges and trees giving shade. The large number of mobile homes and chalets on site are separate from the camping area and not intrusive. There is everything one needs for a family holiday at this site which caters for adults and children of all ages.

Facilities

One large modern very well equipped sanitary block with all necessary facilities including those for campers with disabilities and baby room. Washing machines and tumble dryers. Motorcaravan service point. Large heated swimming pool (17/5-28/9). Poolside bar and snack bar and large shop selling groceries, fruit and vegetables (14/6-14/9). Boules. Tennis. Organised activities for children, teenagers and adults throughout the day (July/Aug). Accommodation for hire (until 3/11). Off site: Leisure park (reduced fees charged). Excellent 27-hole golf complex 800 m. Lake fishing 300 m. Tree walking adventure course. Paintball. Rocamadour and many other tourist destinations are within 1 hours drive.

Open: 2 April - 26 September.

Directions

Leave the A20 at exit 50 for Brive centre, and take the N28 towards Tulle. At the village of Gare d'Aubazine turn right to Aubazine. Continue for 6 km. through village, take road to Chastang and follow signs to Parc Touristique du Coiroux about 4 km.
GPS: 45.18633, 1.70775

Charges guide

Per unit incl. 2 persons and electricity	€ 15,10 - € 24,00
extra person	€ 4,00 - € 5,90
child (2-6 yrs)	free - € 3,90
dog	€ 2,00 - € 2,60

Beaulieu-sur-Dordogne

Flower Camping des Iles

Boulevard Rodolphe de Turenne, F-19120 Beaulieu-sur-Dordogne (Corrèze) T: **05 55 91 02 65**
E: **info@campingdesiles.fr** **alanrogers.com/FR19130**

This is a very pleasant and well equipped site in a beautiful location on a small island in the river Dordogne. Camping les Iles is a very attractive family run site only five minutes' walk away from the centre of the medieval town of Beaulieu-sur-Dordogne with its ancient streets, old churches, many shops and restaurants. This five-hectare site has 120 shady, grass pitches, 90 of which are available for touring all with 10A electricity. The added bonus of its close proximity to the centre of the village makes this an ideal site for tourers.

Facilities

Three modern, clean toilet blocks. Baby room. Facilities for campers with disabilities. Laundry room. Motorcaravan service point. Heated pool (June - Sept), poolside bar, snacks. Boules. Canoe hire. Fishing. Children's entertainment (3-12 yrs) 4 days per week. Evening soirees 2 evenings per week. No shop or bread available on site because of its close proximity to the town. Off site: Pizzeria and takeaway 200 m. Tennis 600 m. Bicycle hire 8 km. Golf or riding 18 km. Gouffre de Padirac, Rocamadour, Collonges-la-Rouge (less than 1 hour). Caves, museums, several beautiful ancient villages.

Open: 7 April - 15 October.

Directions

The site is in the centre of the Beaulieu-sur-Dordogne on the D940. From Tulle turn right or from Montal turn left. Approach site with care through the narrow streets. Enter site through narrow archway.
GPS: 44.979705, 1.840146

Charges guide

Per unit incl. 2 persons	€ 11,90 - € 19,90
with electricity	€ 14,90 - € 23,50
extra person	€ 3,90 - € 6,50
child (2-7 yrs)	free - € 3,00

Low season reductions.

Beaumont du Lac

Domaine Cévéo de Pierrefitte

Lac de Vassivière, F-87120 Beaumont du Lac (Haute-Vienne) T: **05 55 69 15 88**. E: **resa@ceveo.com**
alanrogers.com/FR87040

The pitches at this campsite are used exclusively for mobile home accommodation. For full details please see our PRL section starting on page 501.

Bonnac-la-Côte

Castel Camping le Château de Leychoisier

Domaine de Leychoisier, 1 route de Leychoisier, F-87270 Bonnac-la-Côte (Haute-Vienne) T: **05 55 39 93 43**
E: **contact@leychoisier.com** **alanrogers.com/FR87020**

You will receive a warm welcome at this beautiful, family-run 15th-century château site. It offers peace and quiet in superb surroundings. It is ideally situated for short or long stays being only 2 km. from the A20/N20 and 10 km. north of Limoges. The large, slightly sloping and grassy pitches are in a parkland setting with many magnificent mature trees offering a fair amount of shade. Of the 90 pitches, 85 are for touring, 80 have 10A electricity and many have a tap, although long leads and hoses may be necessary. Explore the grounds and walk down to the four hectare lake. The lake provides free fishing, boating, canoeing and a marked off area for swimming.

Facilities

The toilet block is very clean, but perhaps cramped at busy times. Some washbasins in cabins with good provision for disabled visitors. Washing machine. Basic food provisions. Restaurant (from 10/5). Bar, TV room and snack bar. Small swimming pool with sunbathing area (proper trunks, no shorts). Lake. Play area. Tennis and boules courts (in need of repair when we visited). Torch useful. Off site: Shop 2 km. Supermarket 5 km. Riding 7 km. Golf 20 km.

Open: 15 April - 20 September.

Directions

From A20, north of Limoges, take exit 27 (west) signed Bonnac-La-Côte. In village turn left and follow signs to site. GPS: 45.93299, 1.29006

Charges guide

Per person	€ 6,00 - € 7,50
child (under 7 yrs)	€ 4,00 - € 5,00
pitch	€ 9,00
electricity	€ 5,00
dog	€ 1,00

No credit cards.

Boussac

487

Castel Camping le Château de Poinsouze

Route de la Châtre, B.P. 12, F-23600 Boussac-Bourg (Creuse) T: **05 55 65 02 21**

E: **info@camping-de-poinsouze.com** **alanrogers.com/FR23010**

Le Château de Poinsouze is a well-established site with pitches arranged on the open, gently sloping, grassy park to one side of the Château's main drive – a beautiful plane tree avenue. It is a well designed, high quality site. The 145 touring pitches, some with lake frontage, all have electricity (6-25A), water, drainage and 66 have sewerage connections. The site has a friendly family atmosphere, there are organised activities in main season including dances, children's games and crafts, family triathlons and there are marked walks around the park and woods. All facilities are open all season. This is a top class site with a formula which should ensure a stress-free, enjoyable family holiday. Boussac (2.5 km) has a market every Thursday morning. The massive 12th-/15th-century fortress, Château de Boussac, is open daily all year. The Château (not open to the public) lies across the lake from the site. Exceptionally well restored outbuildings on the opposite side of the drive house a new restaurant serving superb cuisine, other facilities and the pool area.

Facilities

High quality, sanitary unit, washing machines, dryer, ironing, suites for disabled people. Motorcaravan services. Well stocked shop. Takeaway. Bar, internet, two satellite TVs, library. Restaurant with new mini-bar for low season. Heated swimming pool, slide, children's pool. Fenced playground. Pétanque. Bicycle hire. Free fishing in the lake, boats and lifejackets can be hired. Sports facilities. Dogs are only allowed for one overnight stay between 11/7-14/8.

Open: 15 May - 11 September.

Directions

Site entrance is 2.5 km. north of Boussac on D917 (towards La Châtre). GPS: 46.37243, 2.20268

Charges 2010

Per unit incl. 2 persons and electricity	€ 19,00 - € 34,00
extra person	€ 3,00 - € 6,00
child (2-7 yrs)	€ 2,00 - € 5,00
dog	€ 3,00

Camping Cheques accepted.

The Travel Service to book this site call 01580 214000 ...we'll arrange everything

Donzenac

Camping la Rivière

Route du Camping Louis Madrias, F-19270 Donzenac (Corrèze) T: **05 55 85 63 95**
E: **info@campingdonzenac.com** **alanrogers.com/FR19050**

The Corrèze is less well known than the Dordogne to the immediate south, but it is a beautiful area deserving more attention. Donzenac is an attractive small town with a variety of shops, restaurants, etc. This former municipal site is situated on the outskirts, just under a mile from the centre (an uphill walk). The site is small and neat with 68 fairly large pitches on level grass, the majority with electricity (10A). A variety of trees and shrubs give some shade. The site is next door to the town tennis courts and swimming pool (open for July and August, and free to campers).

Facilities

Modernised sanitary facilities are very good and include a laundry room with washing machine and microwave. Baker calls in July/Aug. Bar (July/Aug; June or Sept. on demand). Games room. Boules. Minigolf. Play area. Fishing. WiFi in bar area. Double axle caravans are not accepted. Off site: Riding 4 km. Golf 15 km.

Open: 1 April - 30 September.

Directions

At roundabout at southern end of Donzenac (D920) turn southwest onto D170 signed Ussac and La Rivière. Entrance to site is shortly on the right. GPS: 45.2187, 1.5187

Charges guide

Per unit incl. 2 persons	€ 13,50 - € 16,50
extra person	€ 2,00 - € 4,80
electricity	€ 2,90

No credit cards.

Neuvic

Camping Domaine le Mialaret

Route d'Egletons, F-19160 Neuvic (Corrèze) T: **05 55 46 02 50**. E: **info@lemialaret.com**
alanrogers.com/FR19060

Mialaret is 4 km. from the village of Neuvic and only 6 km. from the Gorges of the Dordogne. It is set in the grounds of a 19th-century château, now a hotel and restaurant with a good reputation. Most pitches are set in gently sloping parkland where 80 trees and many bushes have been planted. Some pitches are level and separated by small bushes, most have some shade and 10A electricity. Entertainment and activities are organised in high season including Djembe drum workshops, a circus school, fishing lessons and evening concerts. In low season there are cooking courses with the chefs of the hotel.

Facilities

Refurbished sanitary blocks give an adequate provision, one heated, facilities for disabled people, washing machines. Motorcaravan services. Shop with bread. Bar, snacks, takeaway. Dinner at hotel. Swimming pool with shallow area. Play areas. Tennis. Fishing. Off site: Village with shops and lake 4 km. Golf 4 km. Canoeing, cycling and riding trips organised.

Open: 1 April - 31 October.

Directions

From Clermont-Ferrand or Brives on the A89, take exit 23 for and follow signs for Neuvic (20 km). In Neuvic follow signs for La Mialaret (take first right after Ecomarché). Site is 4 km. GPS: 45.38242, 2.22910

Charges guide

Per person	€ 5,00 - € 7,50
child (2-8 yrs)	free - € 5,00
pitch incl. electricity	€ 8,50 - € 12,50
dog	free

Camping Cheques accepted.

Palisse

Camping le Vianon

F-19160 Palisse (Corrèze) T: **05 55 95 87 22**. E: **camping.vianon@wanadoo.fr**
alanrogers.com/FR19080

You will receive a very warm welcome from the Dutch owners of this spacious and peaceful site and they speak excellent English. The site is tucked away in the lesser known, very beautiful Corrèze region yet it is only a few kilometres from the river Dordogne. This region is reputed to have the purest air in France. The grassy, slightly sloping pitches are of a good size in a natural woodland setting with tall trees offering shade and all have 16A electricity. The bar, restaurant and terrace overlook the swimming pool and sunbathing area and are open all season.

Facilities

Modern toilet blocks with all the necessary facilities. Unit for disabled visitors. Bar. Restaurant, takeaway. Shop. Boules. Spacious play area. Bicycle hire. Lake fishing. Off site: Small town Neuvic with shops, restaurants 9 km. Large lake with water sports, swimming. Canoeing in the Dordogne (30 minutes). Riding and golf course at Neuvic. Marked walks and cycle rides.

Open: All year (telephone first Oct - Apr).

Directions

Leave A89 southwest of Ussel and take N89 towards Egletons. In about 7 km. just before Combressol, turn left on D47 signed Palisse and Camping le Vianon. Site entrance is on the left in 7 km.
GPS: 45.42678, 2.20583

Charges guide

Per unit incl. 2 persons and electricity	€ 20,00 - € 29,35
extra person (over 2 yrs)	€ 4,00 - € 5,50
dog	€ 1,50 - € 2,00

Set in the heart of the Massif-Central, the Auvergne was formed by a series of volcanic eruptions and is a dramatic region of awe-inspiring, non-active volcanoes, lakes, sparkling rivers, green valleys and forests.

DÉPARTEMENTS: 03 ALLIER, 15 CANTAL, 43 HAUTE-LOIRE, 63 PUY-DE-DÔME

MAJOR CITY: CLERMONT-FERRAND

The Auvergne is a wonderful destination for nature lovers, for those who enjoy active outdoor pursuits or for people would like to relax at a spa resort. The 'Parc Naturel Régional des Volcans d'Auvergne' – the Auvergne Volcano Park – is the largest national park in France and is a protected environment for exceptional flora and fauna. The mountains provide three classified downhill ski resorts and excellent cross-country skiing. A very wide range of outdoor activities is available. The ancient volcanoes have also provided ten thermal spa areas, five of which are among the leading thermal resorts in France.

For those interested in sightseeing, the region offers beautiful Romanesque churches, medieval castles, ruined fortresses and stiff black sculptures of the Madonna and child. Visit Vulcania, the European Volcano Park, and adults and children can learn about the fascinating science of volcanoes. The area was once fairly isolated and inward looking, but access is now much improved and roads are well engineered, so the region is now realising its potential as a holiday area.

Places of interest

Aurillac: old town, wax museum, archaeology museum.

Clermont-Ferrand: old city centre, 11th-12th-century Notre Dame du Port Basilica, 13th-century cathedral; known as 'ville noire' for its houses built in local black volcanic rock.

Le Mont-Doré: spa, winter sports, panoramic view.

Puy-de-Dôme: Gallo-Roman site, television tower and observatory.

Vichy: spa, natural spring park.

Volvic: lava quarry, Volvic springs.

Vulvania: 15 km from Clermont-Ferrand, a unique experience that, until now, was reserved only for volcanologists. A scientific exploration park, designed for children and adults who want to discover and understand the fascinating world of volcanoes and the Earth sciences.

Cuisine of the region

Local specialties include ham and andouille sausages, stuffed cabbage and bacon with lentil and cèpes (mushrooms). Le Puy is famed for its lentils and Vereine du Velay – yellow and green liqueurs made from over 30 mountain plants.

Aligot: purée of potatoes with Tomme de Cantal cheese, cream, garlic and butter.

Perdrix à l'Auvergnate: partridge stewed in white wine.

Potée Auvergnate: a stew of vegetables, cabbage, pork and sausage.

www.auvergne-tourisme.info.uk or
www.massifcentral-tourisme.com
documentation@crt-auvergne.fr
(0)4 73 29 49 99

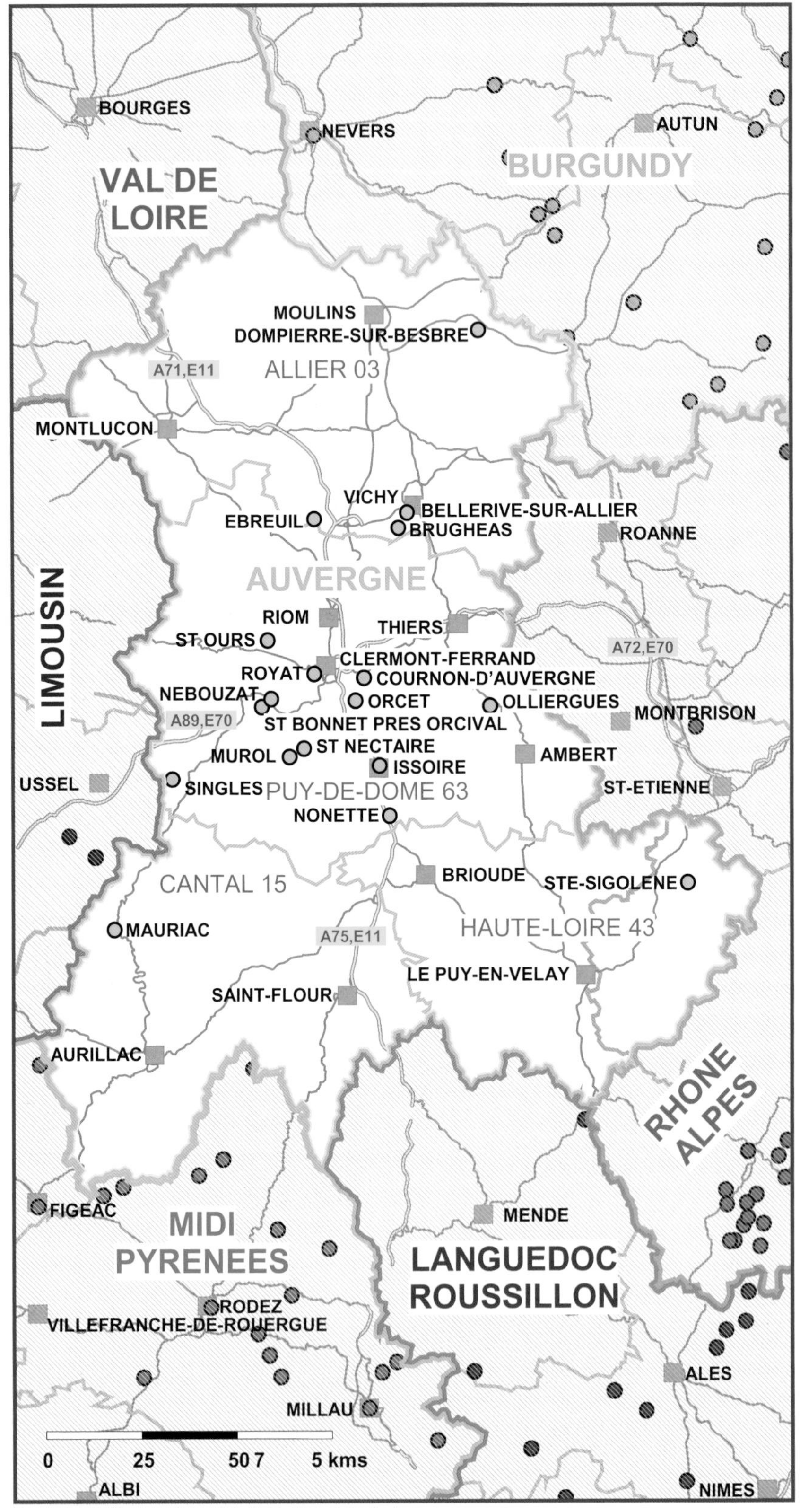
BOURGES
NEVERS
AUTUN
BURGUNDY
VAL DE LOIRE
MOULINS
DOMPIERRE-SUR-BESBRE
A71,E11
ALLIER 03
MONTLUCON
VICHY
BELLERIVE-SUR-ALLIER
EBREUIL
BRUGHEAS
ROANNE
AUVERGNE
LIMOUSIN
RIOM
THIERS
ST OURS
CLERMONT-FERRAND
A72,E70
ROYAT
COURNON-D'AUVERGNE
NEBOUZAT
ORCET
OLLIERGUES
MONTBRISON
A89,E70
ST BONNET PRES ORCIVAL
MUROL
ST NECTAIRE
AMBERT
ISSOIRE
USSEL
SINGLES
PUY-DE-DOME 63
ST-ETIENNE
NONETTE
BRIOUDE
CANTAL 15
STE-SIGOLENE
MAURIAC
A75,E11
HAUTE-LOIRE 43
LE PUY-EN-VELAY
SAINT-FLOUR
AURILLAC
RHONE ALPES
FIGEAC
MIDI PYRENEES
MENDE
LANGUEDOC ROUSSILLON
RODEZ
VILLEFRANCHE-DE-ROUERGUE
ALES
MILLAU
0
25
50 7
5 kms
ALBI
NIMES

Bellerive-sur-Allier

Camping Beau Rivage

Rue Claude Decloître, les Berges de l'Allier, F-03700 Bellerive-sur-Allier (Allier) T: **04 70 32 26 85**
E: **camping-beaurivage@wanadoo.fr** **alanrogers.com/FR03030**

This well-maintained, compact, urban site beside the River Allier is on the outskirts of the famous spa town of Vichy. It has recently been completely refurbished by the enthusiastic new owners (good English and Dutch spoken). Some of the 80 medium sized, reasonably level pitches have delightful views across the river to the beautiful Parc Napoléon beyond. They are separated by flowering shrubs and hedging; mature trees offer some shade. 10A electricity is available on all pitches and 12 are fully serviced. Almost 50% of the pitches are occupied by mobile homes and chalets to rent.

Facilities

Very clean, modern airy sanitary facilities in individual cubicles in pleasantly decorated buildings. Fully equipped, they include mostly British type toilets and a baby room. Laundry facilities. Motorcaravan service point. Small bar with snacks (March - Oct). River fishing. Play area. Bicycles and pedaloes. Minigolf. Archery. Internet including WiFi. Off site: Riding, canoeing and tennis nearby. Very close to the site are several bars and restaurants. Hypermarket complex within 1 km. Vichy 2 km.

Open: 22 March - 30 October.

Directions

Well signed in Bellerive on the west bank of the River Allier. Leave A71 at exit 12 (Vichy). After about 15 km. turn right at large roundabout with fountains and follow signs, Berges des Allier, Campings and Beaurivage. GPS: 46.09695, 3.44012

Charges guide

Per person	€ 3,80 - € 4,90
child (0-7 yrs)	€ 2,90 - € 3,80
pitch	€ 3,80 - € 6,00
electricity (10A)	€ 3,00

Camping Cheques accepted.

Brugheas

Flower Camping la Roseraie

Route de Randan, F-03700 Brugheas (Allier) T: **04 70 32 43 33**
E: **camping.laroseraie@wanadoo.Fr** **alanrogers.com/FR03120**

La Roseraie is a member of the Flower group of campsites and can be found in the volcanic region of the Auvergne with fine mountain views all around. The site is on the edge of the pretty village of Brugheas, parts of which date back to the Roman era. The attractive spa town of Vichy with its parks stretching along the banks of the Allier is very close and easily visited by cycle. There are 80 pitches here, some of which are occupied by mobile homes and chalets. The pitches, grassy and mostly shaded are large (minimum 100 sq.m), some very large (250 sq.m)and the majority have electrical connections.

Facilities

Shop. Bar. Restaurant/snack bar and takeaway. Swimming pool and new paddling pool for children for 2009. Games room. Play area. Archery. Bicycle hire. Minigolf. Activity and entertainment programme. Mobile homes for rent.
Off site: Vichy 7 km. Cycle and walking tracks. Puy de Dôme. Le Pal theme park.

Open: 1 April - 30 October.

Directions

From Vichy, cross the Allier and head south west on the D1093 and then the D117 as far as Brugheas. The site is clearly signed. GPS: 46.07961, 3.38213

Charges guide

Per unit incl. 2 persons and electricity	€ 17,80
extra person	€ 4,00 - € 6,00
child (under 7 yrs)	€ 3,00

Cournon-d'Auvergne

Camping le Pré des Laveuses

Rue des Laveuses, F-63800 Cournon-d'Auvergne (Puy-de-Dôme) T: **04 73 84 81 30**
E: **camping@cournon-auvergne.fr** **alanrogers.com/FR63230**

A well-equipped municipal site, le Pré des Laveuses is adjacent to a boating and fishing lake and its beach, alongside the River Allier, close to Cournon d'Auvergne and the A75 autoroute. This site will be busy in the high season due to its public bar/restaurant, new heated swimming pool complex, nearby activities and its proximity to Clermont Ferrand. There are 150 large, grassy, mostly level pitches with 120 for touring (all with 10A electricity, long leads advised). They are separated by neat hedges with mature trees giving some shade and many have pleasant views over the surrounding hills and the town, although hedging obscures views of the lake.

Facilities

Two modern toilet blocks with all necessary facilities (possibly stretched when the site is busy) Facilities for disabled visitors. Washing machine and dryer. Public bar/restaurant with TV (June-Sept). New heated swimming pool complex. Children's room (TV). Play area. Boules. Overnight parking and services for motorhomes outside gate. WiFi (free). Many high season sporting and family activities, children's club. Off site: Lake, bathing, boating and free fishing (adjacent). Canoeing (high season) and free fishing in River Allier. Minigolf. Tennis. Excellent play and picnic areas, walks, bike rides in adjacent park. Cournon 2 km. Clermont Ferrand 12 km. Bicycle hire 2.5 km. Riding 10 km.

Open: 1 April - 31 October.

Directions

Site is 12 km. southeast of Clermont Ferrand. Leave autoroute A75 at exit 1, taking D212 to Cournon d'Auvergne. Site is well signed to east of town, beside River Allier. Follow Zone de Loisirs.
GPS: 45.74019, 3.22266

Charges guide

Per unit incl. 2 persons	€ 14,50 - € 16,60
extra person	€ 4,20 - € 4,70
child (under 7 yrs)	€ 2,10 - € 2,60
electricity (10A)	€ 2,00 - € 3,10

Dompierre-sur-Besbre

Camping Municipal Dompierre-sur-Besbre

F-03290 Dompierre-sur-Besbre (Allier) T: **04 70 34 55 57**
alanrogers.com/FR03170

This immaculate, attractive and excellent value-for-money site has 68 level, partly shaded, individually hedged, grassy pitches, all with easy access. There are a few long stay units, leaving about 65 for tourists, all with electricity (10A) and most being fully serviced. It is located next to the municipal sports fields and is ideal for motorcaravans being within easy walking distance of the town centre and supermarket (700 m). The warden is very proud of his efficiently run site and its award-winning floral displays. Twin axle caravans are not accepted.

Facilities

Modernised, heated toilet blocks, very clean with all necessary facilities including provision for disabled visitors. Some washbasins in curtained cubicles for ladies. Washing machine. Excellent motorcaravan services. Charcoal barbecues are not permitted. Off site: The small town has shops, restaurants and a Saturday market. Vallée de la Besbre has a wealth of activities, several rivers and small lakes nearby for fishing. Cycle tracks, footpaths, equestrian centres. Le Pal theme park and zoo 8 km.

Open: 15 May - 15 September.

Directions

Dompierre is 35 km. east of Moulins. Leave N79 at eastern end of Dompierre bypass, turn southwest on N2079 towards town. Entrance to sports complex and campsite is on left beyond D55 before the river bridge and town centre. GPS: 46.51564, 3.68434

Charges guide

Per person	€ 2,20
child (5-12 yrs)	€ 1,30
pitch	€ 1,80 - € 2,10
electricity	€ 2,10
dog	free

Ebreuil

Camping de la Filature

Ile de Nieres, F-03450 Ebreuil (Allier) T: **04 70 90 72 01**. E: **camping.filature@aliceadsl.fr**

alanrogers.com/FR03010

Near the spa town of Vichy and beside a fine fly fishing river, this traditional touring and camping site makes a good base to explore the Auvergne including the nearby river gorges, châteaux, mountains and lakes. There are 80 spacious, grassy pitches, most with shade from mature trees and many directly by the river. The river is clean, shallow and pleasant to play in with a deeper swimming area 500 m. away. Most pitches have electricity (3/6A). You will receive a warm welcome from the English owners, who provide good value and very popular takeaway food. The quiet country roads are ideal for walking and cycling, especially mountain biking, and for touring by car. Bird watching and rare wild flowers are additional attractions.

Facilities

Very clean sanitary facilities are in individual cubicles. Fully equipped, they include mostly British type toilets, a bathroom and a room for disabled visitors. Laundry facilities. Small shop for essentials (1/5-30/9). Baker calls. Bar (1/6-30/9). Excellent takeaway (1/6-30/9). Barbecues and pizza nights organised in high season. River bathing and fishing. Play area. Bicycle hire. Minigolf. Off site: Riding, canoeing and tennis nearby. Ébreuil with shops and restaurants 1 km.

Open: 31 March - 1 October.

Directions

Site is well signed from exit 12 of A71 autoroute to Clermont Ferrand in the direction of Ébreuil. It is about 6 km. from the A71 and 1 km. west of Ébreuil beside the river on the D915 towards the Chouvigny gorges. GPS: 46.10877, 3.07338

Charges guide

Per unit incl. 2 persons and electricity	€ 20,50
extra person	€ 5,00
child (under 16 yrs)	€ 3,00
dog	free

Discounts in low season.

Issoire

Château Camping la Grange Fort

Les Pradeaux, F-63500 Issoire (Puy-de-Dôme) T: **04 73 71 02 43**. E: **chateau@lagrangefort.com**

alanrogers.com/FR63040

This site has good, modern facilities, yet is oozing with character. It is very popular with the Dutch. The new reception is well stocked with tourist information and an internet access point. The cosy bar still has the old stable stalls and hay racks. The 120 pitches (90 for touring units) are of average size, mostly on grass but with some crushed stone hardstandings, and they are connected by rather narrow roads with limited play space for children. Some of the smaller pitches are in sunny fields around the castle, others in bays with hedges and trees. All have 6A electricity.

Facilities

Refurbished sanitary blocks have facilities for disabled visitors and a 'hydra shower'. Laundry room. Bread. Restaurant and takeaway (1/5-15/9). Bar (15/6-15/9). Indoor pool with sliding glass doors, sauna, massage table (15/4-15/10). Outdoor pools (15/6-1/10), grass sunbathing areas. New swimming pool (24.5 x 14.5 m) with jacuzzi. Play area, games room. Internet. WiFi. Tennis, minigolf, football, boules. Organised activities in season. Torches useful. Off site: Fishing 250 m. Riding 8 km. Good touring area with magnificent scenery. The Parc des Volcans and the Vulcania exhibition are a must.

Open: 10 April - 15 October.

Directions

From A75 autoroute take exit 13 onto D996 east towards Parentignat. At first roundabout take first exit on D999 new road (St Remy, La Vernet). At next roundabout take first exit (D34) and follow campsite signs. GPS: 45.50875, 3.28488

Charges guide

Per unit incl. 2 persons	€ 17,40 - € 24,50
extra person	€ 4,75 - € 6,10
child (under 10 yrs)	€ 3,70 - € 4,90
electricity	€ 3,25
dog	€ 3,00

Mauriac

Camping Caravaning le Val Saint-Jean

F-15200 Mauriac (Cantal) T: **04 71 67 31 13**. E: **valsaintjean@mauriac.fr**

alanrogers.com/FR15030

Le Val Saint-Jean is set beside a lake in the heart of the département of Cantal. The campsite has 100 generously-sized, slightly sloping, touring pitches (with 10A electricity), many with good views. It is organised for maximum privacy and you are never far from a sanitary block. Most of the activities are situated by the lake where you can use all the facilities of the leisure club (high season) including cycling, canoeing, kayaking and pedaloes. This less well known region is well worth exploring and the local gastronomy can be experienced in the village of Mauriac with its attractive architecture typical of the area. Salers, one of the most beautiful French towns is 20 km.

Facilities

The two toilet blocks are well equipped with hot water throughout, providing some washbasins in cabins, dishwashing sinks and a laundry room. Facilities for people with disabilities. Limited shop. Bar, snack bar and restaurant (all May-Sept). Play area and playing field. Activities organised for children in July/Aug. Off site: Sandy beach. Lake fishing and swimming. Swimming pool (1/6-15/9). Golf. Guided walks. Mauriac village 1.6 km. Riding 3 km.

Open: 25 April - 27 September.

Directions

Mauriac is around 120 km. southwest of Clermont-Ferrand. Leave A89 autoroute at exit 23 (Ussel West), take D979 (Bort-les-Orgues) for 5 km. Turn right onto D982 (Mauriac) for 40 km. Follow site signs in town. GPS: 45.21867, 2.31588

Charges guide

Per unit incl. 2 persons and electricity	€ 17,10 - € 23,10
extra person	€ 4,40 - € 5,40
child (2-7 yrs)	free - € 3,30
dog	€ 1,50

Murol

Sunêlia la Ribeyre

Jassat, F-63790 Murol (Puy-de-Dôme) T: **04 73 88 64 29**. E: **laribeyre@free.fr**

alanrogers.com/FR63050

The friendly Pommier family have put much personal care into the construction of this site. There are 400 level, grassy pitches, of which 310 are for tourers and 200 of these have electricity (6/10A). Electricity, water and drainage is available for 71 pitches. A superb large indoor/outdoor water park includes slides, toboggan and lazy river and a small man-made lake at one end provides facilities for water sports. It is a great base for touring being only 1 km. from Murol, dominated by its ancient Château, 6 km. from St Nectaire and about 20 km. from le Mont Doré and Puy de Sancy, the highest peak in the area.

Facilities

Six excellent, very clean modern toilet blocks with facilities for disabled persons. Washing machines, dryers. Snack bar in peak season (1/6-31/8). Large indoor/outdoor water park (heated July/August). TV. Games room. Tennis. Fishing. Lake swimming and canoeing. Many organised activities in high season. Off site: Riding 300 m. Shops and restaurants and a large Wednesday market (high season) in Murol 1.5 km. Bicycle hire 1 km. Fishing and watersports at Lac Chambon 3 km.

Open: 1 May - 15 September.

Directions

From A75 autoroute take exit 6 signed St Nectaire. Continue to Murol, D978 then D996, several sites signed in town. Turn left up hill, D5, shortly turn right opposite car park, D618, site signed. Site is second on left. GPS: 45.56251, 2.93852

Charges 2010

Per unit incl. 2 persons and electricity	€ 24,75 - € 32,60
extra person	€ 5,60 - € 7,20
child (under 1-5 yrs)	€ 4,10 - € 5,70
dog	€ 2,50 - € 2,70

Murol

Camping le Pré Bas

Lac Chambon, F-63790 Murol (Puy-de-Dôme) T: **04 73 88 63 04**. E: **prebas@campingauvergne.com**
alanrogers.com/FR63070

Le Pré Bas is especially suitable for families and those seeking the watersports opportunities that the lake provides. Level, grassy pitches are divided up by mature hedging and trees and, with 106 mobile homes for rent, around 74 pitches are available for tourists, all with electricity (6A). A gate leads to the lakeside, where in high season there is windsurfing, pedaloes, canoes and fishing, and 50 m. away is a beach with supervised bathing and a snack bar. The site has a pool complex with heated swimming pools (one covered), a large slide and a paddling pool. A 'Family Center' was added in 2008 comprising a 300 sq.m. covered area with sauna, jacuzzi and Turkish bath. The site is in the heart of the Parc des Volcans d'Auvergne, beside the beautiful Lac Chambon with its clear, clean water, The cable car ride up to the Puy de Sancy, the highest peak in the area, provides superb views offering an excellent opportunity for trekking and mountain bike rides. Superb scenery abounds; wooded mountains rising to over 6,000 feet, flower-filled valleys and deep blue lakes.

Facilities

Refurbished toilet building with facilities for disabled guests plus four smaller units. Washing machines, dryers, ironing, baby room. Motorcaravan services. Snack bar (10/6-10/9 and some weekends in low season). Three pools of different depths (20/5-10/9, lifeguard in July/Aug). Watersports, fishing in lake. Games room, table tennis, table football, pool, TV, library. Adventure style playground, football, basketball. Organised activities. WiFi. Off site: Lakeside bars, restaurants, shops. Murol 4 km. St Nectaire famous for cheese. Puy-de-Dôme, hang gliding, Vulcania Exhibition.

Open: 1 May - 30 September.

Directions

Leave A75 autoroute at exit 6 and take D978 signed St Nectaire and Murol, then D996. Site is located on left, 3 km, west of Murol towards Mont Doré, at the far end of Lac Chambon. GPS: 45.57516, 2.91428

Charges guide

Per unit incl. 2 persons and electricity	€ 17,90 - € 26,60
extra person	€ 4,10 - € 5,80
child (0-10 yrs)	€ 2,70 - € 5,80
dog	free - € 2,00

Nébouzat

Camping les Domes

Les Quatre Routes de Nébouzat, F-63210 Nébouzat (Puy-de-Dôme) T: **04 73 87 14 06**
E: **camping.les-domes@wanadoo.fr** **alanrogers.com/FR63090**

A popular site, it is ideally situated for exploring the beautiful region around the Puy de Dôme. The site has 65 small to medium sized pitches, most for touring, 50 with 10/15A electricity, separated by trees and hedges. Some pitches have a level, paved area ideal for caravans and motorcaravans. Rock pegs are advised. The attractive reception area comprising the office, a small shop for essentials (high season only) and a meeting room has lots of local information and interesting artefacts. An added small attraction is a heated, covered swimming pool, which can be opened in good weather.

Facilities

Well appointed, clean toilet block, no special facilities for disabled visitors. Basic shop (baker calls). Breakfast, snacks. Boules, pool table, table football, table tennis, giant chess, drafts. Small play area. TV and games room. Off site: Fishing 100 m. Restaurant 200 m. Nebouzat 1.3 km. (shops etc). Riding 6 km. Hang gliding and parascending 8 km. (Puy de Dôme). New Vulcania exhibition 15 minutes' drive. Watersports 9 km. Golf 10 km. Clermond Ferrand with its interesting old town and hypermarkets (18 km). Many marked walks and cycle routes.

Open: 1 May - 30 September.

Directions

Site is 18 km. southwest of Clermont Ferrand and is well signed from the roundabout at the junction of the D2089 and the D941A. It is a few hundred metres from the roundabout along the D216 towards Orcival. GPS: 45.72562, 2.89005

Charges guide

Per unit incl. 2 persons	€ 10,00
extra person	€ 4,00 - € 6,50
electricity (10A)	€ 5,00

No credit cards.

Nonette

Camping les Loges

F-63340 Nonette (Puy-de-Dôme) T: **04 73 71 65 82**. E: **les.loges.nonette@wanadoo.fr**
alanrogers.com/FR63140

This is a pleasant, spacious, rural site bordering the River Allier and close to the A75 autoroute. There are 126 good sized, level, grassy pitches offering plenty of shade, 100 for touring and all with 6A electricity. This site would suit those seeking a quieter holiday without too many organised activities. The river is good for bathing and canoeing and there are many walks and bike rides in the area. It is also well placed to explore the beautiful Auvergne countryside, the extinct volcanoes and the many attractive old towns and villages.

Facilities

Modern toilet blocks contain all the usual facilities. Small shop (July/Aug). Bar, restaurant, takeaway (mid June-mid Sept). TV room. Heated swimming pool (June-Sept). Sauna, spa room (July/Aug). Table tennis. Play areas, play room. River fishing, bathing. Sunday evening dances in high season. Canoe trips. Off site: Walking and cycling routes. Riding 5 km. Small village of Nonette 3 km. Small range of shops at Saint Germain 5 km. Parc des Volcans.

Open: Easter - 13 October.

Directions

From A75 exit 17 (south of Issoire), turn left (D214) signed Le Breuil. Bypass Le Breuil, turn left (D123) signed Nonette. Cross river, turn left then immediately very sharp left just after roundabout - take care (site signed). Entrance is 1 km. GPS: 45.47310, 3.27223

Charges guide

Per unit incl. 2 persons	€ 12,00 - € 16,20
extra person	€ 2,40 - € 4,60
electricity (6A)	€ 3,50

Olliergues

Camping les Chelles

F-63880 Olliergues (Puy-de-Dôme) T: **04 73 95 54 34**. E: **info@camping-les-chelles.com**
alanrogers.com/FR63220

A very rural, rustic site, les Chelles is run by enthusiastic Dutch owners. It is situated in the Parc Naturel Livradois, 25 km. south of Thiers, and is ideal for nature lovers and those seeking a quiet retreat. There are many marked walks and challenging cycle routes close by. There are 60 pitches with 50 slightly sloping grassy pitches for touring, some with views over the surrounding wooded hills (15A electricity, long leads advised). The pitches are naturally laid out on woodland terraces but not ideal for those with walking difficulties or for large or underpowered units due to the hilly terrain. Some family activities are organised in high season.

Facilities

Centrally placed basic toilet block. Washing machine and dryer. Motorcaravan service point (charge). Bar/restaurant (all season) with TV. Bread to order. Small swimming and paddling pools near small play area. Tennis. Boules. Bicycle hire (high season). Small fishing lake. Some activities for younger children, bike rides (high season). WiFi (charge). Off site: Olliergues, bank, shops, restaurants, bars 5 km. Thiers, larger range of shops etc, cutlery museum 25 km. Many challenging cycle rides and walks.

Open: 1 April - 30 October.

Directions

Olliergues is on D906 25 km. south of Thiers. On entering Olliergues bear left up hill, D37. Shortly turn sharp left on D87. In 1.5 km. at church turn right and shortly left to site. Well signed from Olliergues. GPS: 45.68987, 3.63336

Charges 2010

Per unit incl. 2 persons and electricity	€ 15,80
extra person	€ 3,00
child (under 13 yrs)	€ 1,80
dog	€ 1,00

Orcet

Camping le Clos Auroy

Rue de la Narse, F-63670 Orcet (Puy-de-Dôme) T: **04 73 84 26 97**. E: **info@campingclub.info**
alanrogers.com/FR63060

You are assured a friendly welcome at Le Clos Auroy. It is a very well maintained and popular site, 300 metres from Orcet, a typical Auvergne village just south of Clermont Ferrand. Being close (3 km) to the A75, and open all year, it makes an excellent stopping off point on the journey north and south but you may be tempted to stay longer. The 90 good size pitches are on level grass, separated by very high, neatly trimmed conifer hedges, offering lots of privacy but not much shade. All have electricity (5/10A) and 25 are fully serviced. In winter only 20 pitches are available. Access is easy for large units.

Facilities

High quality, very clean toilet blocks. Washing machine, dryer. Motorcaravan services. Small shop (1/7-31/8), bar and takeaway (1/6-31/8). Heated pool, jacuzzi, large pool for children (15/5-15/9), terrace near bar (1/6-31/8). Playground. Coffee evenings. Tennis. Children's activities. Off site: Large playground nearby and riverside walk just outside gate. Village with shops and three wine 'caves' 300 m. Fishing and canoeing 500 m. Parc des Volcans.

Open: 4 January - 1 November.

Directions

From A75 take exit 4 or 5 towards Orcet and follow campsite signs. It is just before the village. GPS: 45.70018, 3.16902

Charges 2010

Per unit incl. 2 persons and electricity	€ 21,70 - € 27,70
extra person	€ 3,10 - € 5,60
dog	free - € 3,00

No credit cards.

Royat

Camping Indigo Royat

Route de Gravenoire, F-63130 Royat (Puy-de-Dôme) T: **04 73 35 97 05**

E: **royat@camping-indigo.com** **alanrogers.com/FR63120**

This is a spacious and attractive site sitting high on a hillside on the outskirts of Clermont Ferrand, but close to the beautiful Auvergne countryside. It has nearly 200 terraced pitches on part hardstanding. There are 143 available for touring units, all with 6/10A electricity (long leads may be needed). The pitches are informally arranged in groups, with each group widely separated by attractive trees and shrubs. The bar and terrace overlooks the irregularly shaped swimming pool, paddling pool, sunbathing area, tennis courts and play areas. Although very peaceful off season, the site could be busy and lively in July and August.

Facilities

Five well appointed toilet blocks, some heated. They have all the usual amenities but it could be a long walk from some pitches. Small shop. Bar, takeaway. Attractive swimming, paddling pools, sunbathing area. Tennis. Boules. Bicycle hire. Two grassy play areas. Organised entertainment in high season. Internet. Off site: Royat 20 minutes walk but bus every 30 minutes in the mornings. Clermont Ferrand, Puy-de-Dôme, Parc des Volcans, Vulcania exhibition.

Open: 2 April - 16 October.

Directions

From A75 exit 2 follow signs for Bordeaux (D799). At third roundabout exit left signed Bordeaux. Shortly take exit right then turn right, signed Ceyrat. Leaving Ceyrat, at lights take D941C signed Royat and Puy-de-Dôme. At top of hill turn left (D5) site signed. Entrance 800 m. GPS: 45.7587, 3.05509

Charges guide

Per unit incl. 2 persons	€ 18,90 - € 27,70
extra person	€ 2,60 - € 5,30

Camping Cheques accepted.

Saint Bonnet près Orcival

Camping de la Haute Sioule

Route du Camping, F-63210 Saint Bonnet près Orcival (Puy-de-Dôme) T: **04 73 65 83 32**

E: **info@chalets-auvergne.info** **alanrogers.com/FR63210**

This simple, small site is family run in a quiet, rural location in the heart of the beautiful Parc des Volcans. With good views over the surrounding hills, it is close to the Puy de Dôme and several winter and summer resorts. Developed from a farm with sheep and geese roaming freely until mid June, the site has 70 sloping, slightly uneven, grassy pitches with about 45 for touring (4-13A electricity, long leads needed). Access is not easy for motorhomes and large outfits. It would be a good base for touring the region but may be noisy in the high season due to the seasonal caravans.

Facilities

Central basic toilet block with mainly Turkish toilets. No facilities for campers with disabilities. Washing machine and dryer. Bar with TV, restaurant and snacks (all season). Play area for younger children. Minigolf. Boules. WiFi. Off site: St Bonnet 200 m. with some small shops, a restaurant and a bar. Orcival 4 km. Puy de Dôme and other extinct volcanoes. Volcania exhibition. Winter ski resorts 20 km. Lakes. Fishing 5 km. Riding 7 km.

Open: 15 March - 1 November.

Directions

A75 just south of Clermont Ferrand at exit 2, signed Bordeaux and La Bourboule. Continue on D2089 until Les Quatre Routes. Turn left at roundabout, D216. Bear left to site entrance in just over 500 m. GPS: 45.7084, 2.86087

Charges guide

Per unit incl. 2 persons	€ 12,00
extra person	€ 1,90 - € 3,90
electricity (4-13A)	€ 2,70 - € 5,90

Saint Nectaire

Camping la Vallée Verte

Route des Granges, F-63710 Saint Nectaire (Puy-de-Dôme) T: **04 73 88 52 68**. E: **lavalleeverte@libertysurf.fr**

alanrogers.com/FR63180

Vallée Verte is a very well tended, peaceful, good value campsite. Set in the heart of the beautiful Parc des Volcans d'Auvergne, it is only a short walk from the small spa town of Saint Nectaire and close to Lac Chambon with its sandy beach and some water sports. There are many other interesting towns and villages waiting to be explored. The site has 90 level grass pitches (5/8A electricity) with 74 for touring units. Separated by wooden rails or a variety of hedging, a mixture of trees gives shade to some of the pitches. Twin axle caravans are not accepted.

Facilities

Excellent new toilet block with all necessary facilities including a superb room for families and campers with disabilities. Motorcaravan services. Shop, bar and restaurant with takeaway (all season). Play areas. Boules. Organised meals and walks in high season. Off site: St Nectaire with shops, bars, restaurants. Casino. Caves. Petrified fountains 500 m. Lac Chambon with beach, windsurfing, bicycle hire, bars and restaurants 6 km. Vulcania Exhibition.

Open: 15 April - 15 September.

Directions

Leave autoroute A75 at exit 6 south of Clermont Ferrand. Take D978 then D996 to St Nectaire. On entering St Nectaire turn left, D642 (site signed). Entrance is a few hundred metres. GPS: 45.57523, 2.99981

Charges guide

Per unit incl. 2 persons	€ 9,50 - € 13,50
extra person	€ 3,00 - € 4,60
electricity (5/8A)	€ 3,00 - € 3,50

Saint Ours

Camping Bel-Air

F-63230 Saint Ours (Puy-de-Dôme) T: **04 73 88 72 14**. E: **contact@campingbelair.fr**
alanrogers.com/FR63160

This is an attractive, family-run site. In traditional style, but with modern facilities, it has a rural location lying within the Parc des Volcans. There are 60 level grass pitches, 28 with 6/10A electricity, including three with hardstanding for larger motorcaravans and three chalets. The pitches are spaced around a wooded clearing, most with varying degrees of shade. This site is ideal for those seeking a peaceful holiday in a wonderful area yearning for exploration – there are no organised activities here. Its position only 6 km. from the A89 autoroute makes it ideal for both short and long stays. Double-axle caravans are not accepted.

Facilities

Modern well equipped toilet block with baby room and facilities for disabled visitors. Washing machine and dryer. Motorcaravan service point. Small shop (bread to order). Minigolf and boules. Gas and electric barbecues only (communal barbecue provided). Play area. WiFi in reception. Off site: Pontgibaud with shops, restaurants 3 km. Puy-de-Dôme 18 km, Vulcania Exhibition 8 km. Excellent area for touring on foot, bike or by car. Medieval villages and extinct volcanoes.

Open: 1 May - 30 September.

Directions

Leave A89 west of Clermont Ferrand at exit 26. Take D941 bypassing Pontgibaud. At roundabout turn left, D943 St Ours. Site shortly on left.
GPS: 45.84436, 2.87672

Charges guide

Per person	€ 2,70 - € 4,60
pitch	€ 4,50
electricity (6/10A)	€ 3,30 - € 4,00

No credit cards.

Sainte Sigolène

Kawan Village de Vaubarlet

Vaubarlet, F-43600 Sainte Sigolène (Haute-Loire) T: **04 71 66 64 95**
E: **camping@vaubarlet.com** **alanrogers.com/FR43030**

This peacefully located, spacious riverside family site has 131 marked, level, grassy, open pitches, with those around the perimeter having shade, all having electricity (6A). With 102 pitches for tourists, the remainder are occupied by site owned tents or mobile homes. Those who really like to get away from it all can use a small 'wild camping' area on the opposite side of the river with its own very basic facilities. This area is reached either by footbridge or a separate road access. The main site is separated from the river (unfenced) by a large field used for sports activities.

Facilities

Good, clean toilet blocks, baby room, washing machine, dryer. Two family bathrooms are also suitable for disabled people. WiFi. Small shop, bread. Takeaway, bar (all season). Attractive swimming pool, children's pool. Bicycle hire. Boules. Large games area. Playground. Activities in season include camp fire, music evenings, children's canoe lessons. Trout fishing. Birdwatching. Off site: Shops in Ste. Sigolène 6 km. Riding 15 km. Walks and cycle tracks from site.

Open: 1 May - 30 September.

Directions

Site is 6 km. southwest of Ste Sigolène on the D43 signed Grazac. Keep left by river bridge, site signed. Site shortly on right. GPS: 45.2163, 4.2124

Charges guide

Per unit incl. 2 persons and electricity	€ 16,50 - € 22,00
extra person	€ 2,25 - € 4,00

Camping Cheques accepted.

Singles

Camping le Moulin de Serre

Vallée de la Burande (D73), F-63690 Singles (Puy-de-Dôme) T: **04 73 21 16 06**
E: **moulin-de-serre@wanadoo.fr** **alanrogers.com/FR63080**

Off the beaten track, this spacious and well maintained site is set in a wooded valley beside a river where one can pan for gold. It offers a good base for those seeking quiet relaxation in this lesser known area of the Auvergne. The 90 large pitches (55 for touring) are separated by a variety of trees and hedges giving good shade. Some pitches have hardstanding and all have electricity (3-10A), long leads may be necessary. Access around the site is easy but the narrow lanes leading to it are twisting which might prove difficult for larger units.

Facilities

Well appointed, clean toilet blocks, one heated with good facilities for disabled people and babies. New communal barbecue. Heated swimming pool, terrace (8/6-28/9). Takeaway (July/Aug), bar/restaurant (July/Aug). Bread (19/5-16/9). Washing machine, dryer. Motorcaravan services. Large play area. Tennis. Canoe hire in high season. Organised activities (July/Aug). Off site: Lake for fishing 2 km. Château de Val 20 km. La Bourboule 25 km.

Open: 11 April - 13 September.

Directions

Site is about 25 km. southwest of La Bourboule. Turn west off the D922 just south of Tauves at site sign. Follow site signs along the D29 and then the D73 for about 10 km. GPS: 45.54317, 2.54275

Charges guide

Per unit incl. 2 persons and electricity	€ 13,50 - € 22,55
extra adult	€ 2,30 - € 4,20
child (under 10 yrs)	€ 1,60 - € 2,90

With a rich and varied landscape, the Rhône Alpes offers a spectacular region that includes the craggy gorges and scented hills of the Rhône Valley, the deep valleys and mountain slopes of the Savoy Alps and the forbidding Dauphiné Alps, all offering spectacular scenery.

DÉPARTEMENTS: 01 AIN, 07 ARDÈCHE, 26 DRÔME, 38 ISÈRE, 42 LOIRE, 69 RHÔNE, 73 SAVOIE, 74 HAUTE-SAVOIE

MAJOR CITIES; LYON, GRENOBLE

The Rhône valley holds areas of great interest and natural beauty. From the sun-baked Drôme, with its ever-changing landscapes and the isolated mountains of the Vercors to the deep gorges and high plateaux of the Ardèche, studded with prehistoric caves and lush valleys filled with orchards; and encompassing the vineyards of the Beaujolais and the Rhône Valley. For the energetic there are cycling, horse riding and even white-water rafting opportunities, while for the more leisurely inclined, the remote areas are a haven for bird watching and walking.

Lying between the Rhône Valley and the Alpine borders with Switzerland and Italy are the old provinces of Savoie and Dauphiné. This is an area of enormous granite outcrops, deeply riven by spectacular glacier hewn valleys. One of the world's leading winter playgrounds there is also a range of outdoor activities in the summer. Despite development, great care has been taken to blend the old with the new and many traditional villages still retain their charm and historical interest. For many, it is an opportunity to escape the crowds and enjoy some clean air, unusual wildlife, stunning views and hidden lakes.

Places of interest

Aix-les-Bains: spa resort on the Lac du Bourget, boat excursions to the Royal Abbey of Hautecombe.

Annecy: canal-filled lakeside town, 12th-century château, old quarter.

Beaujolais: vineyards and golden-stone villages.

Bourg-Saint-Maurice: centre of Savoie café society.

Chambéry: old quarter, Dukes of Savoie château, Savoie museum.

Chamonix: site of first Winter Olympics in 1924, world capital of mountain climbing.

Grenoble: University city, Fort de la Bastille.

Lyon: Gallo-Roman artifacts, Renaissance quarter, historical Fabric Museum, silk museum.

Vallon-Pont d'Arc: base from which to visit Gorges de l'Ardèche.

Cuisine of the region

Bresse (Poulet, Poularde, Volaille de): the best French poultry, fed on corn and when killed bathed in milk.

Farcement (Farçon Savoyard): potatoes baked with cream, eggs, bacon, dried pears and prunes.

Gratin Dauphinois: potato dish with cream, cheese and garlic.

Gratin Savoyard: another potato dish with cheese and butter.

Tartiflette: potato, bacon, onions and Reblochon cheese.

www.rhonealpes-tourism.co.uk
info@rhonealpes-tourisme.com
(0)4 72 59 21 59

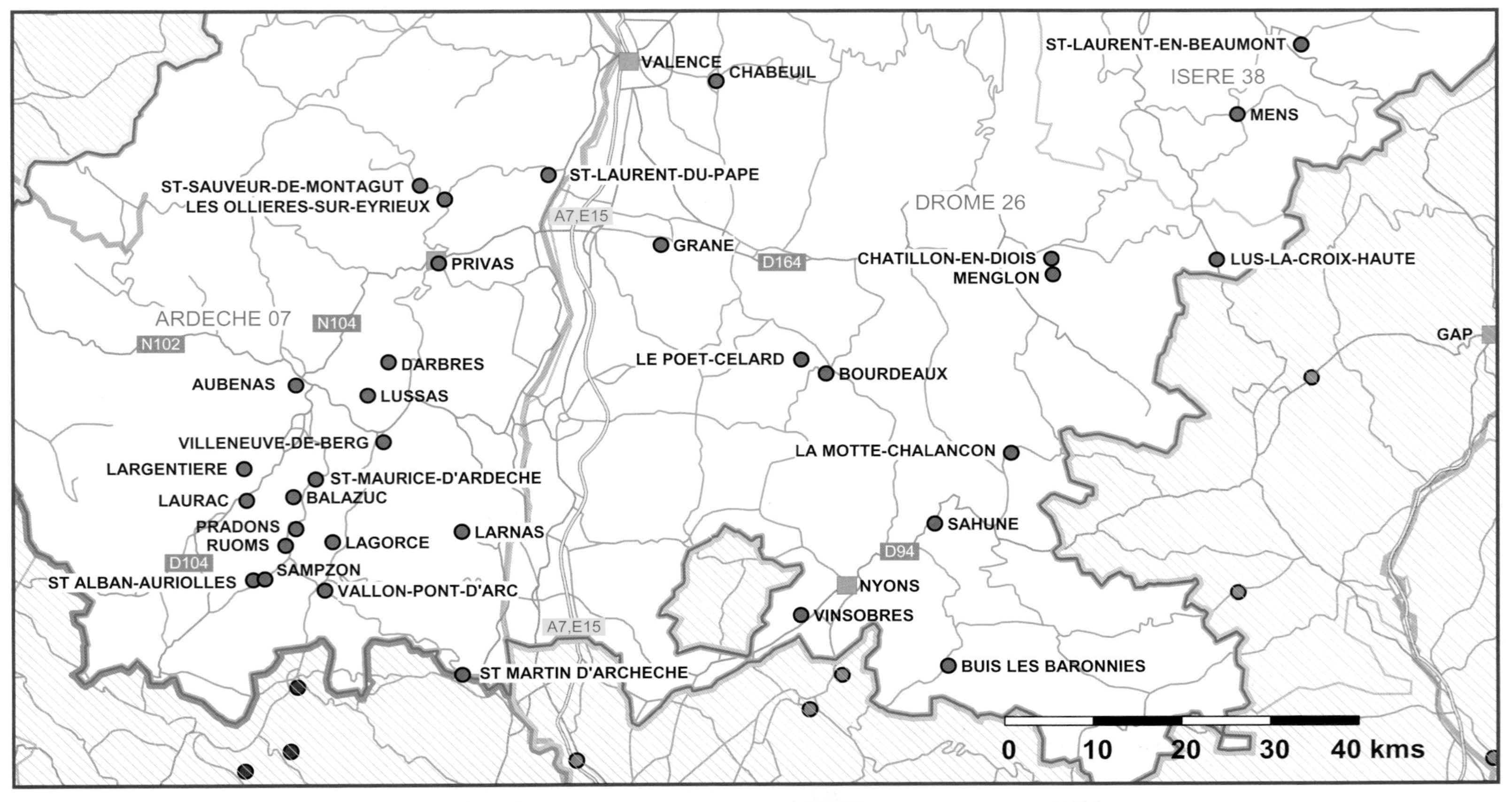
ST-LAURENT-EN-BEAUMONT
VALENCE
CHABEUIL
ISERE 38
MENS
ST-SAUVEUR-DE-MONTAGUT
LES OLLIERES-SUR-EYRIEUX
ST-LAURENT-DU-PAPE
A7,E15
DROME 26
GRANE
PRIVAS
D164
CHATILLON-EN-DIOIS
MENGLON
LUS-LA-CROIX-HAUTE
ARDECHE 07
N104
N102
GAP
DARBRES
LE POET-CELARD
BOURDEAUX
AUBENAS
LUSSAS
VILLENEUVE-DE-BERG
LA MOTTE-CHALANCON
LARGENTIERE
ST-MAURICE-D'ARDECHE
LAURAC
BALAZUC
PRADONS
RUOMS
LAGORCE
LARNAS
SAHUNE
D104
D94
SAMPZON
ST ALBAN-AURIOLLES
VALLON-PONT-D'ARC
NYONS
VINSOBRES
A7,E15
BUIS LES BARONNIES
ST MARTIN D'ARCHECHE
0
10
20
30
40 kms

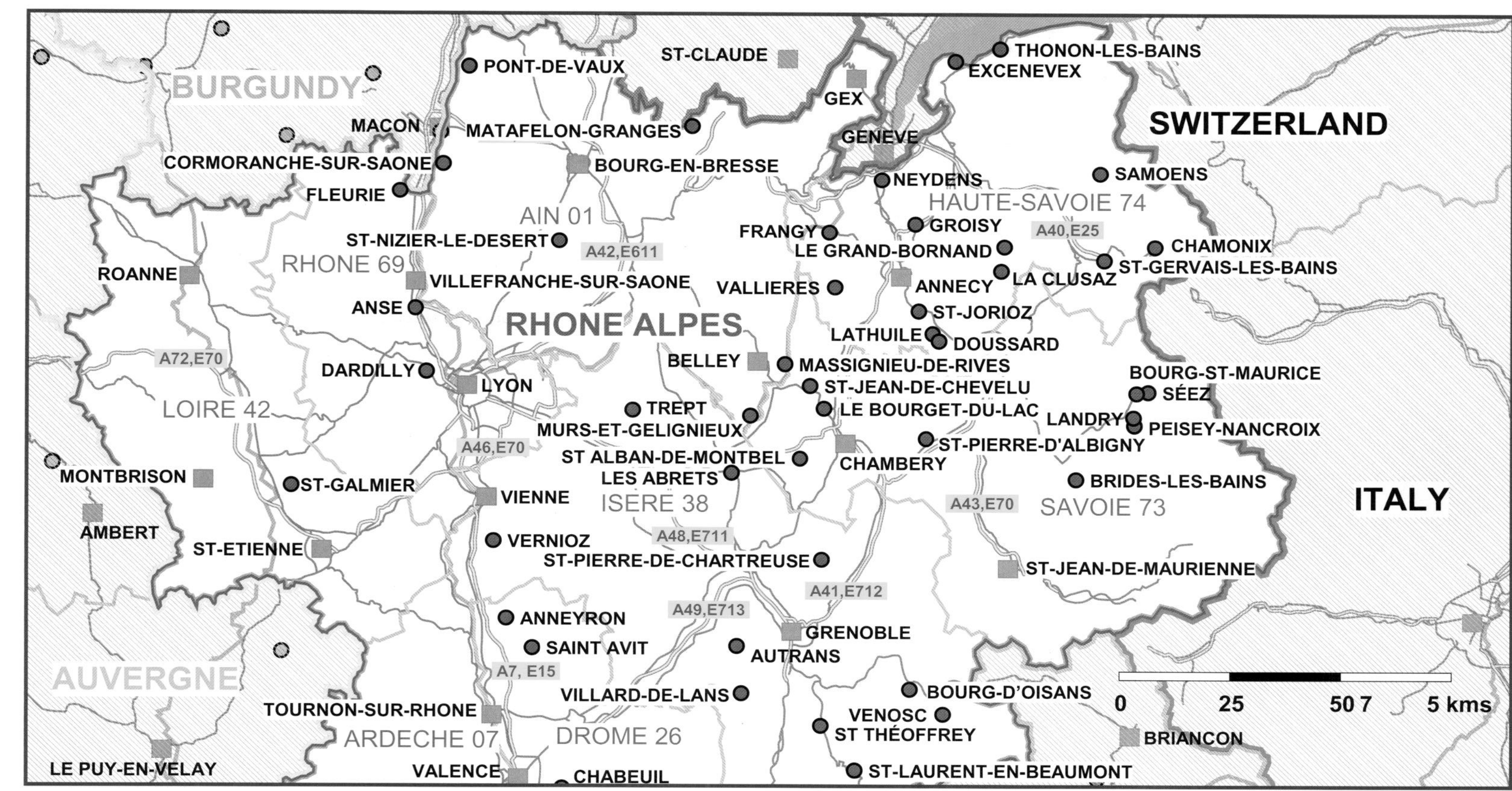

BURGUNDY
PONT-DE-VAUX
ST-CLAUDE
THONON-LES-BAINS
EXCENEVEX
GEX
MACON
MATAFELON-GRANGES
GENEVE
SWITZERLAND
CORMORANCHE-SUR-SAONE
BOURG-EN-BRESSE
NEYDENS
SAMOENS
FLEURIE
HAUTE-SAVOIE 74
AIN 01
FRANGY
GROISY
A40,E25
ST-NIZIER-LE-DESERT
A42,E611
LE GRAND-BORNAND
CHAMONIX
RHONE 69
ST-GERVAIS-LES-BAINS
ROANNE
VILLEFRANCHE-SUR-SAONE
VALLIERES
ANNECY
LA CLUSAZ
ANSE
ST-JORIOZ
RHONE ALPES
LATHUILE
DOUSSARD
A72,E70
BELLEY
MASSIGNIEU-DE-RIVES
DARDILLY
LYON
ST-JEAN-DE-CHEVELU
BOURG-ST-MAURICE
SÉEZ
LOIRE 42
TREPT
LE BOURGET-DU-LAC
LANDRY
MURS-ET-GELIGNIEUX
PEISEY-NANCROIX
A46,E70
ST-PIERRE-D'ALBIGNY
ST ALBAN-DE-MONTBEL
CHAMBERY
MONTBRISON
LES ABRETS
BRIDES-LES-BAINS
ST-GALMIER
VIENNE
ISERE 38
A43,E70
SAVOIE 73
ITALY
AMBERT
VERNIOZ
A48,E711
ST-ETIENNE
ST-PIERRE-DE-CHARTREUSE
ST-JEAN-DE-MAURIENNE
A41,E712
ANNEYRON
A49,E713
GRENOBLE
SAINT AVIT
AUTRANS
AUVERGNE
A7, E15
VILLARD-DE-LANS
BOURG-D'OISANS
TOURNON-SUR-RHONE
VENOSC
0
25
50 7
5 kms
ST THÉOFFREY
ARDECHE 07
DROME 26
BRIANCON
LE PUY-EN-VELAY
VALENCE
CHABEUIL
ST-LAURENT-EN-BEAUMONT

Anneyron

Flower Camping la Châtaigneraie

Route de Mantaille, F-26140 Anneyron (Drôme) T: **04 75 31 43 33**
E: **contact@chataigneraie.com** **alanrogers.com/FR26140**

Small and neat, La Châtaigneraie is a family run, terraced site (English spoken) tucked away in the countryside and will suit those seeking a quieter, relaxing family orientated site. It is not ideal for those with walking difficulties. There are 71 medium sized, slightly sloping, grassy pitches, 30 for touring away from the static units. They are separated by a variety of hedges and young trees provide varying degrees of shade and all have 6/10A electricity. The Drôme is a beautiful area to explore with many old towns and villages with their markets and museums. Enjoy the local produce and the wines of the Rhône valley.

Facilities

The single toilet block at the top of the site is a good, modern building kept very clean. Bar and small shop. Good restaurant/takeaway. Swimming and paddling pools (15/5-15/9). Short tennis. TV and games room. Bicycle hire. Farmers' market twice a week. Entertainment for children and adults (July/Aug). WiFi internet access near bar. Only electric barbecues can be allowed. Off site: Marked walks and cycle tracks in the hills around. Fishing and golf 3 km.

Open: 1 April - 30 September.

Directions

Leave A7 south of Lyons at exit 12 and go south on the N7 for 7 km. Turn left on D1 to Anneyron. In the village turn right on D161 signed Mantaille and in 3 km. turn right on D301, signed Albon. Site is shortly on the right, well signed. GPS: 45.2547, 4.9039

Charges guide

Per unit incl. 2 persons and electricity	€ 14,90 - € 23,50
extra person	€ 2,00 - € 5,00

Aubenas

487

Camping Domaine de Gil

Route de Vals-les-Bains, Ucel, F-07200 Aubenas (Ardèche) T: **04 75 94 63 63**. E: **info@domaine-de-gil.com**
alanrogers.com/FR07150

Under new ownership, this very attractive and well organised, smaller site in a less busy part of the Ardèche should appeal to couples and families with younger children. The 80, good sized, level pitches, 38 for touring, are surrounded by a variety of trees offering plenty of shade and all have 10A electricity. The focal point of the site is formed by the very attractive swimming pool and paddling pool which are heated to 27°C all season and their large sunbathing area. The bar, restaurant and well appointed play areas for children are all adjacent. A spacious sports area and shady picnic and play area are alongside the river Ardèche – an ideal spot to cool off on a hot day.

Facilities

Modern well appointed toilet block, washing machine and iron. Motorcaravan services. Basic shop. Bar/restaurant, takeaway (from June). Heated swimming pool, paddling pool. Two play areas. Boules, minigolf, football and tennis. Canoeing, boating and fishing. Organised activities in high season. Only gas and electric barbecues. Off site: Shops at Vals-les-Bain 1.5 km. Interesting old town of Aubenas with larger range of shops, restaurants, bars 3 km. Organised canoe trips, canyoning on river Ardèche. Bicycle hire, riding 4 km.

Open: 17 April - 19 September.

Directions

Site north of Aubenas. From southeast (N102), after tunnel, turn right, roundabout (signed Ucel), cross river into Pont d'Ucel (3.5 tonne limit). Bear right and at roundabout, last exit (signed Ucel). Shortly turn left (signed Ucel D218), then right (Ucel D578B). Site is 2 km. GPS: 44.64263, 4.37958

Charges 2010

Per unit incl. 2 persons and electricity	€ 22,00 - € 36,00
extra person	€ 2,50 - € 6,00

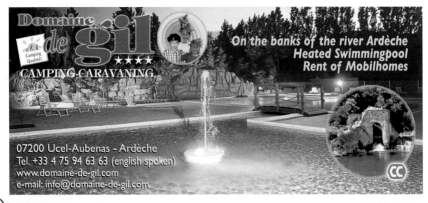

Anse

Camping les Portes du Beaujolais

Avenue Jean Vacher, F-69480 Anse (Rhône) T: **04 74 67 12 87**. E: **campingbeaujolais@wanadoo.fr**
alanrogers.com/FR69030

Situated just off the A6 motorway at Anse, this campsite would make a good overnight stop. The good public transport from Anse also means that it could be used as a base for visiting Lyon. Despite some noise from the motorway and the main line railway, this well run site has much to offer. It has good facilities with modern buildings of traditional design and materials. There are 150 formal pitches which are shady, level, numbered and marked, with neat grass and hedges, and 10A electricity. Around 40 are fully serviced. Some space is available for those who prefer to pitch in simple and open surroundings.

Facilities

Modern toilet blocks include facilities for disabled people and baby rooms. Motorcaravan services. Washing machines. Shop. Gas supplies. Bar, restaurant, takeaway (1/6-15/9). Swimming and paddling pools (1/5-30/9). Playground. Playing field. Tennis. Minigolf. Boules. Games room. Internet access and WiFi. Free loan of barbecues. Chalets, mobile homes and 3 teepees to rent. Off site: Anse 1 km. Narrow gauge railway at exit. Fishing 200 m (permits sold on site). Boat launching 500 m. Riding 1.5 km.

Open: 1 March - 31 October.

Directions

Leave the A6 at exit 32 and join the N6 to Anse. Site is signed from northern and southern ends of village. There are height limits on all approaches (3 or 3.2 m). GPS: 45.9405, 4.7268

Charges guide

Per unit incl. 2 persons	€ 17,20 - € 18,90
incl. services	€ 22,00 - € 24,00
extra person	€ 3,40 - € 4,80

Camping Cheques accepted.

The Travel Service to book this site call 01580 214000 ...we'll arrange everything

Autrans

Kawan Village Au Joyeux Réveil

Kawan VILLAGES www.kawan-villages.com

Le Château, F-38880 Autrans (Isère) T: **04 76 95 33 44**
E: **camping-au-joyeux-reveil@wanadoo.fr** **alanrogers.com/FR38080**

The superb, well organised summer and winter site is run by a very friendly family (English is spoken). It is on the outskirts of Autrans, high on a plateau (1,050 m) in the Vercors region close to a ski jump and short lift. There are 108 pitches with 78 for touring, electricity 2-6A. They are mainly on gently sloping grass, in a sunny location with fantastic views over the surrounding wooded mountains with small trees giving just a little shade. There is a new swimming pool area with two pools, one covered, a river and slide plus a separate paddling pool. Here the days can be very hot and sunny and the nights quite chilly. This site is ideally situated for many of the activities that this wonderful area has to offer – from walking, mountain biking and potholing in summer to downhill and cross-country skiing in winter, it is all there for you in magnificent scenery.

Facilities

The spotless toilet block is very well appointed, with underfloor heating and all the expected facilities. Another chalet-style building houses a bar with terrace, snack bar/takeaway (July/Aug). Two pools, one covered, toboggan for children, sunbathing area and a separate paddling pool. Small play area. TV room. Internet point and WiFi. Family entertainment in July/Aug. Off site: Autrans with a few shops 500 m. Villard de Lans, supermarket, shops, restaurants, bars, ice rink and many other activities 16 km. Short ski lift is near the site and a shuttle bus runs (in winter) to the longer runs (5 km). Fishing, bicycle hire and riding 300 m. Bus to Villard de Lans and Grenoble.

Open: 1 December - 31 March, 1 May - 30 September.

Directions

Leave A48, northwest of Grenoble, exit 13 (going south) or 3A (north). Follow N532 to Sassenage, turn west at roundabout, D531 to Lans-en-Vercors. At roundabout turn right, D106 Autrans. At roundabout in Autrans turn right (site signed) and very shortly right again. Site is on the left. This is the only route recommended for caravans and motorcaravans. GPS: 45.17517, 5.54762

Charges guide

Per unit incl. 2 persons and electricity	€ 20,50 - € 36,00
extra person	€ 3,50 - € 5,00

Camping Cheques accepted.

The Travel Service to book this site call 01580 214000 ...we'll arrange everything

Balazuc

Camping le Chamadou

Mas de Chaussy, F-07120 Balazuc (Ardèche) T: **0820 366 197**. E: **infos@camping-le-chamadou.com**

alanrogers.com/FR07620

La Chamadou is a delightful, well maintained and peaceful site run by an enthusiastic and friendly family. It is situated in the southern Ardèche, close to the medieval, perched village of Balazuc, not far from the river Ardèche. There are 86 slightly sloping grass and stone pitches with 69 for touring (electricity 10A). They are separated by hedges and flowering shrubs with a variety of trees giving some shade. There are several small very clean toilet blocks with excellent facilities. A cosy restaurant and terrace have panoramic views. The narrow approach road makes access difficult for large outfits.

Facilities

Several small, but very clean toilet blocks have all the necessary facilities including those for campers with disabilities. Bar/TV (all season). Tiny shop with necessities. Restaurant and takeaway (July/Aug and some special occasions). Swimming pool, paddling pool, toboggan. Good play area. Games room. Lake fishing. Canoe trips and bike hire organised. Only electric and gas barbecues allowed. Off site: Small village of Vogüé 3 km. Small shop 2 km. River bathing 2 km. Riding and bicycle hire 4 km.

Open: 1 April - 31 October.

Directions

Site in is in southern Ardèche south of Aubenas. Leave Aubenas on the D104, signed Alès. Shortly turn left on D579 signed Vallon-Pont-d'Arc. Bypass Vogüé, cross river and keep right. In 4.5 km. turn left at site sign along narrow lane to site in 2 km.
GPS: 44.50778, 4.40347

Charges guide

Per unit incl. 2 persons	€ 17,00 - € 22,50
extra person	€ 3,40 - € 5,10
electricity (10A)	€ 4,00 - € 4,20

Bourdeaux

488

Camping les Bois du Chatelas

Route de Dieulefit, F-26460 Bourdeaux (Drôme) T: **04 75 00 60 80**. E: **contact@chatelas.com**

alanrogers.com/FR26210

Located at the heart of the the Drôme Provencale, Les Bois du Chatelas is a smart, family run site which has undergone many recent improvements. The site is just a kilometer from the delightful village of Bourdeaux which offers a good range of shops, cafés, etc. There are 120 pitches here of which 69 are occupied by mobile homes. Although situated on a hillside, the pitches are level and of a good size. They all offer electricity, water and drainage. Les Bois du Chatelas is a particularly good choice for those seeking an active holiday. The long distance GR9 footpath passes through the site and there are very many walking and cycle routes close at hand. A popular aquagym is organised in the large outdoor pool in high season, as is a lively entertainment programme and cycling and walking excursions. A member of 'Sites et Paysages'.

Facilities

Two heated toilet blocks (on upper and lower levels) with facilities for babies and disabled people (note: the site is hilly and may be unsuitable). Shop. Bar. Restaurant/pizzeria. Indoor swimming pool. Outdoor pool with water slide, waterfall and jacuzzi. Sports pitch. Archery. Play area. Bicycle hire. Entertainment and excursion programme (July/Aug). Mobile homes for rent. Off site: Rafting and canoe trips. Riding 5 km. Fishing 1 km. Very extensive walking and cycle (mountain bike) opportunities. Vercors mountain range. Many stunning medieval villages.

Open: 7 April - 30 September.

Directions

From the north, leave A7 at exit 16 and join the eastbound D104 to Crest. Upon reaching Crest take D538 south to Bourdeaux and continue towards Dieulefit. Site is on the left 1 km. beyond Bourdeaux and is well signed. GPS: 44.57825, 5.12795

Charges guide

Per unit incl. 2 persons	€ 14,00 - € 24,00
extra person	€ 4,20 - € 5,00
child (1-7 yrs)	€ 2,70 - € 2,90
electricity (10A)	€ 4,30 - € 4,50

Bourg-d'Oisans

Camping la Cascade

Route de l'Alpe d'Huez, F-38520 Bourg-d'Oisans (Isère) T: **04 76 80 02 42**. E: **lacascade@wanadoo.fr**
alanrogers.com/FR38030

La Cascade has a long season and it is within sight and sound of the waterfall from which it takes its name. It is only 2 km. from Bourg-d'Oisans which lies in the Romanche valley 725 m. above sea level surrounded by high mountains. The area is a sun trap and gets very hot in summer. The site has 133 individual grassy pitches, 106 for touring units on mainly flat ground and of varying size. Although most are quite adequate, larger units are best near the entrance as the pitches and roads do become narrow. All have 16A electricity.

Facilities

Two heated sanitary blocks are of good quality with mainly British style toilets, washbasins in cabins and showers. Laundry facilities. Bar and snack bar (25/6-30/8). Good sized, heated and sheltered swimming pool and paddling pool (1/6-30/9) surrounded by large, enclosed sunbathing area. TV in bar. Off site: Supermarket 500 m. Fishing 500 m. Bicycle hire or riding 1 km. Bourg-d'Oisans 1 km.

Open: 20 December - 30 September.

Directions

From Grenoble take N91 to Bourg-d'Oisans, cross river bridge, after 730 m. turn left on to D211, signed Alpe d'Huez. Site is on right in 600 m.
GPS: 45.06408, 6.03903

Charges guide

Per unit incl. 2 persons and electricity	€ 21,80 - € 29,30
extra person (over 5 yrs)	€ 4,80 - € 6,50

Bourg-d'Oisans

Camping á la Rencontre du Soleil

Route de l'Alpe d'Huez, F-38520 Bourg-d'Oisans (Isère) T: **04 76 79 12 22**. E: **rencontre.soleil@wanadoo.fr**
alanrogers.com/FR38040

The Isère is an attractive and popular region with exceptional scenery. Bourg-d'Oisans lies in the Romanche valley 725 m. above sea level surrounded by high mountains. This compact site, pleasant, friendly and family run, nestles between two impressive mountain ranges, at the base of France's largest National Park, Le Parc des Ecrins. It is a real sun trap and gets very hot in summer. It is only 2 km. from the busy town of Bourg-d'Oisans. It has 73 level, hedged pitches of small to average size with mature trees offering good shade (43 for touring with 6/10A electricity). Rock pegs are advised. A 'Sites et Paysages' member.

Facilities

Heated toilet block provides all the usual amenities, but no facilities for disabled people. Washing machine and dryer. Motorcaravan services. Bread to order. Restaurant and takeaway (all season). Room with TV, children's play room. Small, sheltered swimming pool (all season). Play area. Children's club. Activities in high season include walking, mountain biking. Off site: Supermarket 1 km. Fishing 5 km. Bicycle hire, riding 2 km. Canoeing, rafting, riding, hiking, climbing. Cable car at Alpe d'Huez.

Open: 1 May - 30 September.

Directions

From Grenoble bypass Bourg-d'Oisans on the N1091 towards Briancon. At end of bypass turn left at roundabout on D211 signed Alpe-d'Huez. Site is on left beyond Camping la Piscine and just before a sharp lefthand bend - take care. GPS: 45.06547, 6.0394

Charges guide

Per unit incl. 2 persons and electricity	€ 19,00 - € 30,80
extra person	€ 3,45 - € 6,60

Camping Cheques accepted.

Bourg-d'Oisans

Camping Belledonne

Rochetaillée, F-38520 Bourg-d'Oisans (Isère) T: **04 76 80 07 18**. E: **info@rcnbelledonne.fr**
alanrogers.com/FR38100

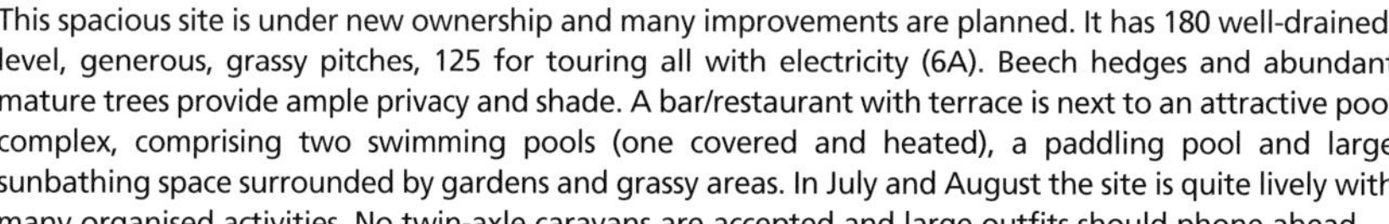

This spacious site is under new ownership and many improvements are planned. It has 180 well-drained, level, generous, grassy pitches, 125 for touring all with electricity (6A). Beech hedges and abundant mature trees provide ample privacy and shade. A bar/restaurant with terrace is next to an attractive pool complex, comprising two swimming pools (one covered and heated), a paddling pool and large sunbathing space surrounded by gardens and grassy areas. In July and August the site is quite lively with many organised activities. No twin-axle caravans are accepted and large outfits should phone ahead.

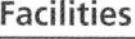

Facilities

Two well appointed sanitary blocks with baby room and facilities for disabled visitors. Shop. Bar/restaurant and takeaway (all open all season). TV/games room. Swimming and paddling pools (one covered and heated). Sauna. Tennis. Good play area, large meadow with fitness course. Bicycle hire (July/Aug). WiFi. Off site: Allemont, shops 2 km. Bourg-d'Oisans, shops, bars, restaurants and Saturday market 8 km. Fishing 4 km. Riding 1 km. Hiking, mountain biking, bungee jumping, paragliding and much more.

Open: 26 April - 26 September.

Directions

Site is 8 km. west of Bourg-d'Oisans. From Grenoble take N85 to Vizille and then N91/D1091 towards Bourg-d'Oisans. In Rochetaillée branch left (site signed) onto D526, signed Allemont. Site is 250 m. on right. GPS: 45.11423, 6.00765

Charges guide

Per unit incl. 2 persons, car and electricity	€ 16,25 - € 43,50

Special offers for long stays, children and over 50's.
Camping Cheques accepted.

Bourg-d'Oisans

Camping le Colporteur

Le Mas du Plan, F-38520 Bourg-d'Oisans (Isère) T: **04 76 79 11 44**. E: **info@camping-colporteur.com**
alanrogers.com/FR38140

The site is within a few minutes level walk of an attractive market town and ski resort, making this an ideal spot for motorcaravanners. There are 150 level grassy pitches, 120 for touring, including ten hardstandings for motorhomes. All pitches have 15A electricity and rock pegs are advised. They are mostly separated by hedging and a variety of mature trees that offer some shade. There is no pool on site but campers have free entry to the adjacent municipal pool. In July and August the attractive bar/restaurant is the focal point for evening activities. Bourg-d'Oisans is in the largest national park in France. It is at an altitude of 700 m. and is surrounded by high mountains making it a real suntrap. The days can be very hot, especially in summer. The area is revered by serious cyclists as several mountain roads close by are regularly used by the Tour de France. This is an ideal base for exploring this scenic region with its abundance of wild flowers, old villages and rushing waterfalls; by car, on foot or by bike.

Facilities

Two large, clean toilet blocks are well equipped, modern and airy with all the necessary facilities including washbasins in cabins, baby room and en-suite room for disabled campers. Restaurant, bar and takeaway (mid June-end Aug). Games room. Boules. Small play area. Organised family activities (July/Aug). Off site: Shops, bars, restaurants in town and supermarket 500 m. Ski resorts of Alpe-d'Huez (13 km) and Les Deux Alpes (19 km). Cycling, mountain biking, hiking, rafting, canoeing, climbing, riding, hang-gliding, Parc des Ecrins, cable cars (July/Aug) and many mountain passes. Bus services.

Open: 17 May - 20 September.

Directions

Site is in Bourg-d'Oisans. From Grenoble follow the N91 into town and shortly after the road bears left in the town centre and just beyond a petrol station, turn right (site signed). Follow signs to site, a few hundred metres. GPS: 45.0526, 6.0355

Charges guide

Per unit incl. 2 persons and electricity	€ 23,10 - € 29,20
extra person	€ 4,70 - € 6,50
child (5-10 yrs)	€ 2,60 - € 4,50
dog	€ 1,20 - € 1,70

Bourg-d'Oisans

Castel Camping le Château de Rochetaillée

Chemin de Bouthean, Rochetaillée, F-38520 Bourg-d'Oisans (Isère) T: **04 76 11 04 40**
E: **jcp@camping-le-chateau.com** **alanrogers.com/FR38180**

Set in the grounds of the small château, with spectacular views, this site has recently been upgraded to provide high quality amenities. The grounds are shared with chalets and tents to rent, with these in a separate area. There are 97 touring pitches, all with 6/10A electricity hook-ups on level areas (some large) separated by hedges and trees. The site has an excellent heated swimming pool, a fitness room, sauna, bar/restaurant and takeaway food together with a small shop with bread and basic groceries. The site is in the centre of an area ideal for walkers, cyclists and climbers.

Facilities

Three very good toilet blocks are colourful and very clean. Shower room with facilities for babies. Excellent, spacious facilities for disabled visitors. Small launderette with ironing. Freezer space. Shop, Bar, snacks, takeaway and separate restaurant (all 1/6-14/9). Swimming pool. Sauna, fitness room and jacuzzi. Climbing wall. Daily activities for children (July/Aug). Guided mountain walks and other activities. Fishing. Safe hire. Barbecue area. Internet and WiFi.
Off site: Mountain activities. Riding and bicycle hire 4 km.

Open: 13 May - 14 September.

Directions

Site is signed from the N91, just north of Rochetaillée. GPS: 45.11530, 6.00548

Charges 2010

Per unit incl. 2 persons and electricity	€ 21,50 - € 35,70
extra person	€ 5,20 - € 8,10
child (0-10 yrs)	€ 3,40 - € 5,10

Bourg-Saint-Maurice

Camping Caravaneige le Versoyen

Route des Arcs, F-73700 Bourg-Saint-Maurice (Savoie) T: **04 79 07 03 45**. E: **leversoyen@wanadoo.fr**
alanrogers.com/FR73020

Bourg-St-Maurice is on a small, level plain at an altitude of 830 m. on the River Isère, surrounded by mountains. Le Versoyen attracts visitors all year round (except for a short time when they close). The site's 205 unseparated, flat pitches (180 for touring) are marked by numbers on the tarmac roads and all have electrical connections (4/6/10A). Most are on grass but some are on tarmac hardstanding making them ideal for use by motorcaravans or in winter. Trees give shade in some parts, although most pitches have almost none. Duckboards are provided for snow and wet weather.

Facilities

Two acceptable toilet blocks can be heated, although the provision may be hard pressed in high season. British and Turkish style WCs. Laundry. Motorcaravan service facilities. Outdoor and covered pools (July/Aug). Heated rest room with TV. Small bar with takeaway in summer. Free shuttle in high season to funicular railway. Off site: Fishing or bicycle hire 200 m. Tennis and swimming pool 500 m. Riding 1 km.

Open: All year excl. 7/11-14/12 and 2/5-25/5.

Directions

Site is 1.5 km. east of Bourg-St -Maurice on CD119 Les Arcs road. GPS: 45.62248, 6.78475

Charges guide

Per unit incl. 2 persons and electricity	€ 16,10 - € 21,00
extra person	€ 4,00 - € 4,60
child (4-13 yrs)	€ 2,50 - € 4,40

Brides-les-Bains

Camping La Piat

Avenue du Comte Greyfie de Bellecombe, F-73570 Brides-les-Bains (Savoie) T: **04 79 55 22 74**
E: **contact@camping-brideslesbains.com** **alanrogers.com/FR73160**

La Piat is a small family run campsite nestling at an altitude of 600 m. and surrounded by beautiful mountains. It is open for a long season and is only a few minutes walk from the small, attractive spa town of Brides-les-Bains. There are 80 often irregularly shaped, grass pitches laid out on low terraces with about 60 for touring (electricity 6/10A, very long leads may be needed). On site access is good for large outfits but the final approach road is quite narrow. This site makes an ideal base for motorhomes and those seeking a peaceful and relaxing holiday as there is no on-site entertainment.

Facilities

Two good, small toilet blocks, one quite new and there are plans to refurbish the other, with all necessary facilities including those for babies and disabled visitors. Bread etc. July/Aug. Motorcaravan services. Small play area. Boules. Off site: Spa town of Brides-les-Bains 500 m, with Casino, swimming pool, tennis, bars, restaurants, disco and a range of shops. Fishing 7 km. Golf or riding 13 km. Rafting. Canyoning. Many marked walks and cycle rides. Meribel 12 km. Courcheval 18 km.

Open: 11 April - 15 October.

Directions

Leave Albertville south on N90 to Moutier. Turn right, follow D915 to centre of Brides-les-Bains. Turn right by fountain, site signed. Site on right in 550 m. Approach from other direction is difficult and not recommended. GPS: 45.45294, 6.56232

Charges guide

Per unit incl. 2 persons	€ 8,95 - € 10,40
extra person	€ 2,80 - € 3,20
child (4-12 yrs)	€ 1,45 - € 1,70
electricity (6/10A)	€ 2,70 - € 3,70

Buis-les-Baronnies

Camping Domaine de l'Ecluse

Bénivay, F-26170 Buis-les-Baronnies (Drôme) T: **04 75 28 07 32**. E: **camp.ecluse@wanadoo.fr**
alanrogers.com/FR26200

Tucked away in the beautiful Drôme Provençal region, this quiet, rural site is situated high in the hills northeast of the Roman city of Vaison-la-Romaine. There are 75 level, stony pitches of average size, with 53 for touring (6A electricity, long leads necessary). They are separated by hedges and mature poplar trees giving varying amounts of shade. Rock pegs are advised. The attractive L-shaped swimming pool has a toboggan and sunbathing area. This site would make an ideal base for those who love serious hill-walking and biking. Visitors in June will be amazed by the variety of wild flowers and butterflies.

Facilities

Two toilet blocks with all the necessary modern facilities include rooms for babies and campers with disabilities. Small shop (May-Sept). Bar and restaurant (July/Aug). Takeaway (1/5-9/8). Swimming pool (April-Sept). Games field. Simple progamme of events and some excursions (July/Aug). Gas barbecues only. Internet link via a cable. Off site: Restaurant nearby. Bicycle hire, fishing and riding 8 km. Lake bathing 8 km. Historic villages of Buis-les-Boronies 8 km. Mollans 8 km. Vaison la Romaine 14 km. Nyons with excellent market and large range of shops 20 km. Mont Ventoux.

Open: 5 April - 15 November.

Directions

Site is northeast of Vaison la Romaine. The only recommended access is via Buis-les-Baronnies. Just south of the village turn northwest on the D147 for 7 km. over the pass to Propiac. Turn right on D347 and climb to site in 2 km. At entry pull hard over to the right to take sharp left hand bend down slope. GPS: 44.28995, 5.1917

Charges guide

Per person	€ 3,50 - € 4,00
child (0-7 yrs)	€ 1,50 - € 2,00
pitch	€ 5,50 - € 7,00
electricity (6A)	€ 3,20

Chabeuil

Le Grand Lierne

B.P. 8, F-26120 Chabeuil (Drôme) T: **04 75 59 83 14**. E: **contact@grandlierne.com**
alanrogers.com/FR26030

In addition to its obvious attraction as an overnight stop, fairly convenient for the A7 autoroute, this site provides a pleasant base to explore this little known area between the Ardèche and the Vercors mountains and the Côtes du Rhône wine area. It has 198 marked, stony pitches, 61 for touring units (6/10A electricity), separated by hedges and oak trees which offer varying amounts of shade. The site has an attractive pool complex with several pools including a new covered heated pool for bathing in poor weather. They are surrounded by terraces with loungers for sunbathing. There are very good sporting facilities with many organised activities making this a lively site in July and August. English and Dutch are spoken. The site is used by tour operators (30%).

Facilities

Two sanitary blocks, one refurbished in 2008, with modern facilities including those for disabled people. Washing machines, dryers. Motorcaravan services. Shop/restaurant, terrace (1/7-31/8). Bar/takeaway (all season). Fridge rental. Four pools (all season), one covered and heated. Paddling pool, water slide, toboggans and lazy river. Playgrounds. Minigolf. Archery and extensive entertainment programme in high season. WiFi. Only gas and electric barbecues are permitted. Dogs are not accepted in high season.
Off site: Golf 3 km. Bicycle hire 4.5 km. Fishing 5 km. Riding 7 km. Canoe/kayak near. Vercors mountains. Chabeuil 5 km. Valence 11 km.

Open: 18 April - 26 September, with all services.

Directions

Site signed from Chabeuil about 11 km. east of Valence. Best approached from south side of Valence via Valence ring road. D68 to Chabeuil. Site is off D125 to Charpey, 5 km. from Chabeuil, well signed.
GPS: 44.91572, 5.065

Charges guide

Per unit incl. 2 persons and electricity	€ 21,60 - € 36,60
extra person	€ 5,00 - € 8,00
child (2-7 yrs)	€ 3,00 - € 5,00
dog	€ 5,00

Chamonix

Camping de la Mer de Glace

200 chemin de la Bagna, les Praz, F-74400 Chamonix (Haute-Savoie) T: **04 50 53 44 03**
E: **info@chamonix-camping.com** **alanrogers.com/FR74150**

This attractive site is convenient for Chamonix but is in a tranquil setting away from its hustle and bustle. The buildings are of typical regional timber construction, decorated with traditional painted flower designs. Set in a large level clearing, with a view of the Mont Blanc range, it has been kept as natural as possible without a pool, restaurant, bar or disco and is well suited to those looking for quiet and relaxation. The area is rich in trails for walking and mountain biking and many pass nearby. There are 150 pitches of varying sizes, most with shade and 75 have electricity connections (3-10A).

Facilities

Three sanitary blocks with facilities for disabled visitors. Washing machine, dryer. Motorcaravan services. Bread. Pizza van twice weekly in July/Aug. Meeting room, snack room. Small playground for young children. Free internet and WiFi access. Off site: Fishing and golf 500 m. Bicycle hire 1 km. Riding 5 km. Shops, etc. 700 m. in Les Praz or 1.5 km. in Chamonix. Indoor and outdoor swimming pools in Chamonix 1.5 km. Free bus/train pass in locality.

Open: 23 April - 3 October.

Directions

From Chamonix take N506 northeast towards Les Praz. After 1 km. site signed to right. NOTE: the first two signs direct you under a 2.4 m. high bridge. Continue to a small roundabout at entrance to Les Praz, turn right and follow signs.
GPS: 45.93805, 6.89267

Charges 2010

Per unit incl. 2 persons and electricity	€ 20,80 - € 24,60
extra person (over 3 yrs)	€ 6,10 - € 7,00

Chamonix

Camping l'Ile des Barrats

185 chemin de l'Ile des Barrats, F-74400 Chamonix (Haute-Savoie) T: **04 50 53 51 44**
E: **campingiledesbarrats74@orange.fr** **alanrogers.com/FR74160**

l'Ile des Barrats is a delightful neat, tidy, small and tranquil site. It is within easy walking distance of the beautiful town of Chamonix, although there are bus and train services close by if needed. There are 53 slightly sloping, grassy pitches all for touring mostly separated by small hedges and a variety of trees offering some shade. All have electricity (5/10A) and 32 have water and a drain. This is an ideal site for those wishing to roam the mountain trails and for those seeking a peaceful and relaxing holiday in a most superb setting. No twin-axle caravans.

Facilities

A modern, clean toilet block offers all necessary facilities, including those for disabled visitors. Covered picnic area with table and benches, ideal for those with small tents. Motorcaravan services. Store room for mountaineers. Mobile shop in July/Aug. No organised activities.
Off site: Baker 500 m. Chamonix 800 m. level walk (high class summer and winter resort with colourful Saturday market). Hang-gliding, funicular railway, cable cars and chair lifts nearby.

Open: 15 May - 1 October.

Directions

On entering Chamonix from Geneva, turn left at first roundabout after turn off for the Mont Blanc Tunnel (follow signs for Hospital). A next roundabout, turn left, site is opposite hospital. GPS: 45.9143, 6.8615

Charges guide

Per person	€ 6,40
child (0-7 yrs)	€ 4,90
pitch incl. car	€ 7,90
electricity (5/10A)	€ 3,30 - € 4,30

No credit cards.

Chatillon-en-Diois

Flower Camping Lac Bleu

Quarter la Touche, F-26410 Chatillon-en-Diois (Drôme) T: **04 75 21 85 30**
E: **info@lacbleu-diois.com** **alanrogers.com/FR26150**

This spacious and peaceful site is run by a very friendly family who have made many improvements to the site with many more in the pipeline. It lies in a beautiful valley surrounded by mountains, south of the Vercors National Park. The 90 pitches (78 for touring) are level with rough grass, slightly bumpy and separated by a variety of trees offering some shade (rock pegs advised). All have electricity (6/10A). At the centre of the site is a lake of 2.5-hectares with warm clean water fed by springs making it ideal for swimming and fishing. A good bar, restaurant and terrace overlook the lake and there is plenty of space for children to play. An evening stroll around the lake is recommended. The site is near the very small Bez river and not far from the interesting and ancient small town of Die, the home of the famous Clairette de Die – a sparkling wine mentioned in dispatches by the Romans around 40AD. It is a very good site for exploring this picturesque part of France, yet to completely unwind and enjoy the views, the beautiful sunset over the mountains and the very clean air.

Facilities

Two clean toilet blocks one new, the other refurbished, with all the necessary facilities. Baby room. Facilities for disabled campers. There are some rather uneven wooden steps to access one block. Motorcaravan service point. Small shop. Bar/restaurant. Takeaway. TV and games room. Play area bordering the lake. Large sports/play area. Bicycle hire. Footpaths around lake. Lake bathing and fishing. Pedaloes. Internet point. Only gas and electric barbecues allowed.
Off site: Medieval villages. Canoeing, canyoning, grottos.

Open: 1 April - 30 September.

Directions

Head southeast from Die on the D93, signed Gap. After about 5 km. turn left on D539 signed Châtillon-en-Diois. After 4.5 km. bear right onto D140, site signed. Follow signs to site, shortly on left.
GPS: 44.6824, 5.44795

Charges guide

Per unit incl. 2 persons	€ 9,90 - € 23,00

Cormoranche-sur-Saône

Camping la Pierre Thorion

Base de Loisirs, les Luizants, F-01290 Cormoranche-sur-Saône (Ain) T: **03 85 23 97 10**
E: **contact@lac-cormoranche.com** **alanrogers.com/FR01090**

Situated in a region famous for its wines, gastronomy and picturesque old villages, this site is part of the 42-hectare landscaped recreation park that surrounds a tree lined lake. The 117 generous pitches are level, grassed and enclosed by hedges, all with electricity and drainage. A small dam divides the lake into two areas, one for swimming, the other, larger part for fishing (also permitted at night) and boating. To the far side of the park is a TGV railway track. During the day the trains are fairly frequent, but there are no night services and the daytime noise is a moderate rumble. The reception office has a good selection of tourist information on a region lined with the wine routes of Beaujolais, Macon and Bourgogne. In addition, this is the region of Bresse chickens and fresh water fish and in the surrounding picturesque towns and villages there are many good restaurants, the most famous being that of Geoges Blanc in Vonnas.

Facilities

Modern sanitary building provides free preset showers and (a little small), washbasins in cabins. Facilities for disabled people. Laundry room with washing machine. Motorcaravan service point. Small shop (order bread for following morning). Bar and restaurant with takeaway, overlooking lake. Lake swimming with a separate area for small children. Off site: Macon, Bourg-en-Bresse and the village of Perouges.

Open: 1 April - 30 September.

Directions

Site is 5 km. south-southwest of Macon on the eastern site of the Saône. It is well signed from all directions 'Base de Loisirs'. If approaching from the west via Creches, there is a 2.6 m. height restriction. GPS: 46.25167, 4.8261

Charges guide

Per person	€ 4,10 - € 5,00
child (2-12 yrs)	€ 1,60 - € 2,50
pitch	€ 5,00 - € 7,00
incl. electricity	€ 5,80 - € 8,50

Darbres

Camping les Lavandes

Le Village, F-07170 Darbres (Ardèche) T: **04 75 94 20 65**. E: **sarl.leslavandes@online.fr**
alanrogers.com/FR07140

Situated to the northeast of Aubenas, in a quieter part of this region, Les Lavandes is surrounded by magnificent countryside, vineyards and orchards. The enthusiastic, welcoming French owners, who speak good English, run a site that appeals to all nationalities. The 70 pitches (58 for touring) are arranged on low terraces separated by a variety of trees and shrubs that give welcome shade in summer. Electricity (6/10A) is available to all. Visit at the end of May to see the campsite trees laden with luscious cherries. Organised activities include wine tasting, shows, musical evenings and children's games.

Facilities

Comprehensive and well maintained facilities, baby room and excellent facilities for disabled people. Washing machine. Small shop (1/7-31/8). Bar, terrace (1/6-31/8). Restaurant (15/6-31/8). Takeaway (15/4-31/8). Excellent swimming pool, paddling pool, sunbathing areas, all with super views. Two small play areas for younger children. Games room. Outdoor chess. Electric barbecues are not permitted. Off site: Fishing 1 km. Riding 3 km. Tennis 5 km. Bicycle hire 15 km. Canoeing, walking, cycling, riding, carting nearby. Climbing (Courpatas, Chabanne, Saint Michel de Boulogne, Lavilledieu).

Open: 15 April - 30 September.

Directions

Site is best approached from the south. From Montélimar take N102 towards Aubenas. After Villeneuve, in Lavilledieu, turn right at traffic lights on D224 to Darbres (10 km). In Darbres turn sharp left by post office (care needed) and follow site signs. GPS: 44.64788, 4.50338

Charges guide

Per unit incl. 2 persons	€ 12,50 - € 18,50
extra person	€ 1,50 - € 3,50
electricity	€ 3,50
dog	€ 1,50 - € 2,50

Dardilly

Camping Indigo Lyon

Porte de Lyon, allée du Camping, F-69570 Dardilly (Rhône) T: **04 78 35 64 55**
E: **lyon@camping-indigo.com** **alanrogers.com/FR69010**

This is a modern overnight site just off the A6 autoroute. Kept busy with overnight trade, reception and the café (in main season) open until quite late. There are 180 separate numbered plots. Many have 10A electricity, water and waste water drainage. Those for caravans are mostly on hardstandings on a slight slope, with another small grassy part, while those for tents are on a flatter area of grass. A very large commercial centre has been developed just outside the site, with eight hotels, restaurants, a supermarket, petrol station, etc. There is some road noise.

Facilities

Three sanitary blocks, one heated, have free hot water (solar heated) and washbasins in cabins. Baby changing facilities and washing machines. Motorcaravan service point. Swimming and paddling pools (1/6-15/9, supervised and free). Playground. TV room. Games room. Reading room (books and local information). Boules. Picnic and barbecue area. Off site: Riding 2 km. Golf 12 km.

Open: All year.

Directions

Travelling south, do not take A46 motorway around Lyon, continue on A6, take exit Limonest, Dardilly, Porte de Lyon. About 8 km. north of Lyon tunnel; turn left for Porte de Lyon (well signed).
GPS: 45.82035, 4.7604

Charges guide

Per unit incl. 2 persons and electricity	€ 20,40 - € 25,20
extra person	€ 4,10 - € 4,40
child (2-7 yrs)	€ 2,70 - € 3,00
dog	€ 3,00

Camping Cheques accepted.

Doussard

Camping International le Lac Bleu

Route de la Plage, F-74210 Doussard (Haute-Savoie) T: **04 50 44 30 18**. E: **contact@camping-lac-bleu.com**
alanrogers.com/FR74180

This lakeside site has its own beach and jetty and a short walk brings you to the lake ferry. The site has breathtaking views, a swimming pool and 220 pitches divided by privet and beech hedges. This site is perfect for walking, cycling or sailing and in low season provides a tranquil base for those just wishing to relax. In high season it will be busy and popular. The proximity of the public lakeside area which is often used as a festival venue could be either a source of noise or an exciting place to be depending on your point of view. When we visited the music stopped at 23.00. A nearby cycle track on a disused railway to Annecy gives a level 16 km. ride with mountains on the left and the lake to the right. In high season there is a children's club for the under eights. The bar has a thriving takeaway (roast whole chickens and pizza) and an 'al fresco' eating area.

Facilities

Three toilet blocks are of a high standard with free showers. Good provision for babies and disabled visitors. Bar (15/5-15/9) and integral small shop. Takeaway. Swimming pool (15/5-15/9). Bicycle hire. Boat launching (sailing lessons and boat hire nearby). Multisports pitch. Private beach. Off site: Small supermarket 100 m. Hypermarket 4 km. Village close with bars and restaurants. Fishing 100 m. Riding and golf 7 km.

Open: 1 April - 25 September.

Directions

Site is 16 km. south of Annecy on Route d'Albertville, well signed. GPS: 46.317367, 6.362967

Charges guide

Per unit incl. 2 persons	€ 16,00 - € 28,00
extra person	€ 4,00 - € 5,90
child	free - € 5,90
electricity (8A)	€ 3,80

Doussard

Camp de la Ravoire

Bout-du-Lac, route de la Ravoire, F-74210 Doussard (Haute-Savoie) T: **04 50 44 37 80**
E: **info@camping-la-ravoire.fr** **alanrogers.com/FR74040**

La Ravoire is a high quality site, 800 m. from Lake Annecy, noted for its neat and tidy appearance and the quietness of its location in this popular tourist region. The 112 level pitches are on well mown grass with some shade and separated by small shrubs and some hedging. The 90 pitches for touring (21 with water and drain) have electricity (5-15A). Those looking for a campsite in this attractive region without the 'animation' programmes that many French sites feel are necessary, will find this a peaceful base. Take to the back roads and explore the ancient villages and wonderful countryside. Access to the banks of the lake is a walk away (across a busy road).

Facilities

Very good toilet block, facilities for disabled people, laundry room, washing machines, dryers and irons. Bar, snack bar, takeaway. Shop. Outdoor pool, water slide and paddling pool. All open all season. Good play area. Sports areas. Off site: Fishing, boat launching, bicycle hire 1 km. Riding 6 km. Golf 8 km. Good restaurants on the lakeside, shops in Doussard and Annecy. Cycle track (20 km) almost to Annecy passes close by. Canyoning and hang-gliding close. Boat trips.

Open: 15 May - 7 September.

Directions

Site signed from N508 Annecy - Albertville road. About 13 km. south of Annecy, at traffic lights in Brédannaz, turn right (site signed) and then immediately left. Site on left in about 1 km.
GPS: 45.80256, 6.20977

Charges 2010

Per unit incl. 2 person, water and electricity (5A)	€ 30,00 - € 33,50
incl. 1 child under 10 yrs	€ 31,00 - € 34,50
extra person	€ 6,50
child (2-15 yrs)	€ 3,00 - € 4,50
electricity (10/15A)	€ 2,50 - € 3,50

Less 20% outside July/Aug.
Camping Cheques accepted.

Doussard

Campéole

Campéole la Nublière

30 allée de la Nublière, F-74210 Doussard (Haute-Savoie) T: **04 50 44 33 44**. E: **nadine.ferran@atciat.com**
alanrogers.com/FR74190

If you are looking for large pitches, shady trees, mountain views and direct access to the lakeside beach, this site is for you. There are 271 touring pitches of which 243 have electrical hook-ups (6A). This area is very popular and the site is very likely to be busy in high season. There will be some noise from the road and the public beach. La Nublière is 16 km. from old Annecy and you are spoilt for choice in how to get there. Take a ferry trip, hire a sailing boat or pedalo, or walk or cycle along the traffic free track towards the town. The local beach and sailing club are close and there is a good restaurant on the site perimeter. Across the road from the site are courts for tennis and boules. The site is perfect for walking, cycling or sailing and in low season provides a tranquil base for those just wishing to relax in natural surroundings on the edge of a nature reserve.

Facilities

Large clean sanitary blocks include free hot showers and good facilities for disabled people. Laundry. Shop (1/5-15/9). Restaurant on site perimeter (closed Mondays). Children's club (3/7-26/8) for 4-8 yrs. Gas barbecues for hire. Safe deposit. Off site: Small supermarket adjacent to site. Good watersports area within 70 m. Access to town beach from site. Fishing 100 m. Golf and riding 4 km. Bicycle hire 7 km.

Open: 28 April - 24 September.

Directions

Site is 16 km. south of Annecy on Route d'Albertville, well signed. GPS: 45.7908, 6.2197

Charges guide

Per unit incl. 2 persons	€ 13,00 - € 21,80
extra person	€ 4,50 - € 6,10
child (2-6 yrs)	free - € 3,90
electricity	€ 3,90

Excenevex

Campéole

Campéole La Pinède

F-74140 Excenevex Plage (Haute-Savoie) T: **04 50 72 85 05**. E: **nadine.ferran@atciat.com**

alanrogers.com/FR74280

La Pinède is a member of the Campéole group and has direct access to Escenevex beach, the only naturally sandy beach on Lake Geneva. The site has a pleasant woodland setting and pitches are of a good size, mostly with electrical connections. Mobile homes, chalets and fully-equipped tents are available for rent (including specially-adapted units for wheelchair users). There is a supervised bathing area on the beach, which shelves gradually, and a small harbour (suitable only for boats with a shallow draught). Other amenities include a shop and takeaway food service, as well as an entertainment marquee and children's play area. There is plenty of activity here in high season with a children's club and regular discos and karaoke evenings. Geneva is just 25 km. distant and other possible excursions include Thonon-les-Bains with its weekly market and, of course, boat trips on Lake Geneva. Dramatic mountain scenery is close at hand, notably the spectacular Dent d'Oche (2,222 m) and the Gorges du Pont du Diable.

Facilities

Lake beach. Takeaway food. Children's play area. Bouncy castle. Activities and entertainment programme. Tourist information. Mobile homes, chalets and equipped tents for rent. Off site: Geneva 25 km. Thonon-les-Bains 15 km. Hiking and cycle tracks. Riding. Golf

Open: 11 April - 11 September.

Directions

From Geneva head along the south side of the lake on the D1005 as far as Massongy and shortly beyond here take the northbound D324 to Escenevex. The site is well indicated from here. GPS: 46.34492, 6.35808

Charges 2010

Per unit incl. 2 persons and electricity	€ 17,10 - € 26,60

Fleurie

Camping Municipal la Grappe Fleurie

La Lie, F-69820 Fleurie (Rhône) T: **04 74 69 80 07**. E: **camping@fleurie.org**

alanrogers.com/FR69020

With easy access from both the A6 autoroute and the N6, this site is ideally situated for night stops or indeed for longer stays to explore the vineyards and historic attractions of the Beaujolais region. Virtually surrounded by vineyards, but within walking distance (less than 1 km) of the pretty village of Fleurie, this is an immaculate small site, with 85 separated touring pitches. All are grassed and fairly level with the benefit of individual access to water, drainage and electrical connections (10A). A baker calls 07.30-08.30. Wine tasting is arranged twice weekly in high season. Restaurants and shops are available in the village.

Facilities

Sanitary facilities in two blocks have British and Turkish style toilets and very satisfactory shower and washing facilities (showers closed 22.00-07.00). Facilities for disabled visitors. Two cold showers are provided for those wishing to cool down in summer. Washing machine and dryer. Outdoor swimming pool (15 x 7 m). Small playground. Only gas or electric barbecues are allowed. Off site: Fishing 10 km. Fleurie 600 m.

Open: Late March - end October.

Directions

From N6 at Le Maison Blanche/Romanech-Thorins, take D32 to village of Fleurie from where site is signed. GPS: 46.1879, 4.69916

Charges guide

Per unit incl. 2 persons and electricity	€ 13,50 - € 16,00
tent pitch incl. 2 persons and electricity	€ 2,90 - € 3,40
extra person	€ 4,70 - € 5,70
child (5-10 yrs)	€ 3,20 - € 3,70

Frangy

Camping le Chamaloup

Contamine Sarzin, F-74270 Frangy (Haute-Savoie) T: **04 50 77 88 28**. E: **camping@chamaloup.com**
alanrogers.com/FR74240

Le Chamaloup is a neat and tidy site run by a very friendly family. It is situated midway between the lakes of Annecy, Geneva and de Bourget and only ten minutes from the A40 autoroute making it an ideal centre for exploring this beautiful region. There are only 60 level, grass pitches which are separated by small fences. Mature trees give varying amounts of shade. The 43 pitches for touring (with 10A electricity) are well separated from authentic wooden chalets for rent. The emphasis here on quiet family holidays with occasional soirées in the high season. Although access is easy for large units, twin axle caravans are not accepted.

Facilities

Two modern toilet blocks with all necessary facilities including those for campers with disabilities. Bar, restaurant, takeaway (July/Aug). Heated swimming and paddling pools. Games/TV room. Some organised family activities (July/Aug). Internet access (WiFi). Off site: Riding 4 km. Golf, bicycle hire, lake beach, windsurfing, boat ramp 15 km. Frangy with small range of shops, bars, restaurants 4 km. Annecy 23 km. Geneva 34 km.

Open: 1 May - 15 September.

Directions

Leave A40 autoroute at exit 11, signed Frangy. Take N508 14 km. southeast, and after bypassing Frangy, site is on the left in 4 km. GPS: 46.01061, 5.97621

Charges 2010

Per unit incl. 2 persons and electricity	€ 23,50 - € 26,00
extra person	€ 4,50 - € 5,50
child (1-12 yrs)	€ 3,50
dog	€ 2,00

Grâne

Kawan Village Les Quatre Saisons

www.kawan-villages.com

Route de Roche-sur-Grâne, F-26400 Grâne (Drôme) T: **04 75 62 64 17**
E: **contact@camping-4-saisons.com** **alanrogers.com/FR26110**

This small, terraced site, open all year, nestles in the hillsides of the lower Drôme valley close to the Vercors mountains. With 82 pitches (71 for touring units), it mainly provides accommodation for overnight, but it is worth a longer stay. The pitches are level and stony, of variable size, cut out of the hillside and reached by a one-way system on tarmac roads. All pitches have electricity (6A), some with water and drain. The modern main building houses reception on the top floor, with other facilities below, and provides commanding views across the valley towards Crest and the Vercors.

Facilities

Good sanitary facilities include baby room, en-suite facilities for disabled visitors (but site is very sloping and not suitable for wheelchairs). Washing machine. Bar (1/5-30/9). TV room. Small swimming pool (1/5-15/9). Play area. Barbecues are not allowed. Trampoline. Off site: Village nearby with shops catering for most needs. Fishing 1 km. Riding 3 km. Crest. Bicycle hire 2/3 km.

Open: 1 April - 30 September.

Directions

From A7 exit 17, or the N7 at Loriol, take the D104 towards Crest. After 8 km. in Grâne take D113 south. Site is on left about 600 m. beyond the village. GPS: 44.7277, 4.9265

Charges guide

Per unit incl. 2 persons and electricity	€ 18,00 - € 26,00
extra person	€ 5,00
child (under 6 yrs)	€ 3,50
dog	free

Camping Cheques accepted.

Groisy

Camping Moulin Dollay

206 rue du Moulin Dollay, F-74570 Groisy (Haute-Savoie) T: **04 50 68 00 31**. E: **moulin.dollay@orange.fr**
alanrogers.com/FR74170

Nestling between Annecy (15 km) and Geneva (35 km), this spacious site is a gem with only 30 pitches, all for touring. The friendly and enthusiastic owner has worked hard to develop this site to a high quality. The large to very large, level, grass pitches are partially separated by hedging and a variety of trees provide some shade. All pitches have 6A electricity and rock pegs are recommended. As there are only a few activities organised for youngsters on site it is perhaps better suited to those who would appreciate a peaceful site in a parkland setting alongside a rushing stream.

Facilities

Spacious, well appointed, heated toilet block, including facilities for disabled visitors and a baby room. Washing machine, dryer. Motorcaravan services. Bar, TV corner. Large open play and sports area. Fishing and bathing in shallow river. Off site: Some shops, restaurants, bank and super-markets at Groisy 1 km. Interesting little town of Thorens-Glières with its 11th-century château 5 km. Annecy with wide range of facilities 12 km. Lake Annecy and watersports 15 km. Riding 4 km. Golf 6 km.

Open: 1 May - 30 September.

Directions

Site is north of Annecy. Heading north on N1203 Annecy - Bonneville road, turn right on D2 signed Thorens-Glières and site, then immediately right again. Site is 300 m. GPS: 46.00238, 6.19079

Charges guide

Per unit incl. 2 persons and electricity	€ 17,00 - € 20,00
extra person	€ 2,00 - € 5,00

No credit cards.

La Clusaz

Camping le Plan du Fernuy

Route des Confins, F-74220 La Clusaz (Haute-Savoie) T: **04 50 02 44 75**. E: **info@plandufernuy.com**
alanrogers.com/FR74090

This neat and open site has separate summer and winter seasons. It has 80 average sized, stony, grass pitches, 58 for tourists with electricity and 22 fully serviced. There are good mountain views but little shade, rock pegs essential. The site's crowning glory is an excellent indoor heated pool with large windows looking out on to the mountains. This is a good site for skiing in winter (with access to a ski-tow from the campsite and a free bus to other centres). In summer it is a good base for walking and cycling with other sporting opportunities nearby.

Facilities

Very good heated sanitary provision. Baby room. Facilities for disabled visitors. Washing machine and dryer. Drying room for ski clothing and boots. Motorcaravan services. Small shop and bar, snacks, takeaway. Games, TV room. Heated indoor pool and paddling pool. Skiing from site and ski excursions organised. Off site: Shops and restaurants in village 2 km. Riding 800 m. Golf, bicycle hire and fishing 1.5 km.

Open: 4 June - 4 September, 18 December - 24 April.

Directions

From Annecy take D909 to La Clusaz and at roundabout turn towards Les Confins. Site is on right after 2 km. (well signed). It is best to avoid using D909 from Flumat particularly with caravans or motorhomes. GPS: 45.90922, 6.45203

Charges guide

Per unit incl. 2 persons	€ 20,00 - € 24,00
incl. electricity (4-13A)	€ 23,50 - € 32,00
extra person	€ 5,50 - € 6,50

Lagorce

502

Castel Camping Domaine de Sévenier

F-07150 Lagorce (Ardèche) T: **04 75 88 06 63**. E: **domainedesevenier@orange.fr**
alanrogers.com/FR07660

The pitches at this campsite are used exclusively for mobile home accommodation. For full details please see our PRL section starting on page 501.

La Motte Chalancon

Camping Indigo la Ferme de Clareau

Route de Die (RD61), F-26470 La Motte Chalancon (Drôme) T: **04 75 27 26 03**
E: **fermedeclareau@camping-indigo.com** **alanrogers.com/FR26300**

La Ferme de Clareau is a recent addition to the Indigo group of campsites. It is located at the heart of La Drôme Provençale, close to the pretty village of La Motte Chalancon. There are 50 spacious pitches here, mostly with electrical connections. There are also no fewer than three toilet blocks, dispersed around the site. La Ferme de Clareau is situated within a large natural park and one side stretches along the River Oule (suitable for swimming and fishing). A new swimming pool was opened in 2008. The old farm buildings have been sensitively restored and now house the site's bar and shop (specializing in local produce including Pre Chorier naturally leavened bread).

Facilities

Shop. Bar. Snack bar (farmhouse breakfasts available). Swimming pool. Direct access to river. Bicycle hire. Play area. Entertainment and activity programme. Fully equipped tents for rent. Off site: La Motte Chalancon 1 km. Fishing (river). Maison des Vautours wildlife centre. Cycle and walking tracks.

Open: 18 April - 19 October.

Directions

La Motte Chalancon lies midway between Nyons and Gap. Approaching from the west (Nyons) use the D94 as far as Rémuzat. Then take the northbound D61 to La Motte Chalancon. Site is a short distance beyond the village. GPS: 44.48022, 5.39458

Charges guide

Per unit incl. 2 persons and electricity	€ 13,60 - € 16,60
extra person	€ 3,10 - € 4,00
child (2-7 yrs)	€ 1,70 - € 2,30

Landry

Camping Caravaneige l'Eden

F-73210 Landry (Savoie) T: **04 79 07 61 81**. E: **info@camping-eden.net**
alanrogers.com/FR73060

L'Eden is open almost all year round (it is closed for three weeks in May). Beside the Iser river and set in beautiful woodland glades, it is perfect for winter skiing and summer walking and cycling. The site is set in a valley with the Alpine peaks as a backdrop. The 132 good, spacious pitches all have 10A electrical hook-ups and individual water supplies (available when no frost is likely). The pristine, modern sanitary blocks are heated in colder weather and include a large drying room. There is a pool for summer lounging, a bar and a welcoming communal area with bar, TV and internet access.

Facilities

Two heated toilet blocks with drying rooms, good facilities for disabled visitors and for babies. Small launderette. Communal area with bar, TV and internet. Snack bar and takeaway (July/Aug). Swimming pool (13.5 x 5 m; June-Sept). Games room. Play area. Fishing. Ski passes for sale on-site. Off site: Shops and restaurants in village. Many leisure pursuits including rafting, paragliding, cycle and cross-country ski tracks. Riding 10 km. Golf 15 km.

Open: All year excl. 1-23 May.

Directions

From the RN90 take D87 towards Landry. Site is on left after 250 m. and is well signed from the RN90. GPS: 45.57652, 6.73457

Charges guide

Per unit incl. 2 persons	€ 10,70 - € 21,40
extra person	€ 2,90 - € 5,70
child (0-7 yrs)	€ 2,30 - € 4,50
electricity (10A)	€ 2,00 - € 6,00

Largentière

Kawan Village les Ranchisses

Route de Rocher, F-07110 Largentière (Ardèche) T: **04 75 88 31 97**

E: **reception@lesranchisses.fr** **alanrogers.com/FR07070**

This is a very well equipped, modern campsite in a lesser known area of the Ardèche. There are 165 good-sized, level, grass pitches, 88 for tourists with electricity (10A) including 44 which are fully serviced. There are two distinct areas, one which is well shaded and the lower part with less shade. There is traffic noise in some areas. A small river pool provides opportunities for bathing, fishing or canoeing (free life jackets) with one part of the bathing area quite safe for youngsters. Well run and with the emphasis on personal attention, this is a highly recommended site.

Facilities

Comprehensive toilet buildings include facilities for babies and disabled visitors. Laundry facilities. Motorcaravan services. Shop. Bar. Restaurant (regional specialities), takeaway/pizzeria and terrace. Two large pools, paddling pool (heated). New indoor pool complex completed in 2008. Adventure style playground. Organised amusements for children (from 1/6). Skate park. Tennis. Minigolf. Boules. Canoeing. Internet access. Off site: Canoe, kayaking arranged (mid June-Aug). Medieval village, Largentière 1.5 km. Riding 8 km. Bicycle hire 10 km.

Open: 3 April - 25 September.

Directions

Largentière is southwest of Aubenas best approached using D104. Just beyond Uzer, 16 km. From Aubenas, turn northwest on D5. After 5 km. fork left downhill signed Rocher and Valgorge. Site on left in about 1.8 km. just beyond rocky gorge. The approach from Valgorge is not recommended.
GPS: 44.56071, 4.28463

Charges 2010

Per unit incl. 2 persons	€ 19,00 - € 42,00
extra person	€ 5,00 - € 9,00

Camping Cheques accepted.

Larnas

La Domaine d'Imbours

F-07220 Larnas (Ardèche) T: **04 75 54 39 50**. E: **info@domaine-imbours.com**

alanrogers.com/FR07290

This large site is part of a holiday complex with many mobile homes (99), chalets (41), an hotel and 200 camping pitches. These are on scrub grass, not marked, with some shade from mature trees and 6A electricity (long leads may be helpful). For those looking for more or less everything organised for them in high season, this complex may suit. Out of season it is different, with not much happening. The complex is dominated by the hotel which is about 1 km. from the camping area along a descending site road. Around the hotel is a large and well designed pool complex. In high season there are evening shows and dancing, again at the hotel. Here too one can play tennis on one of four courts. To use the laundry one needs to transport washing to the hotel complex, where there are machines. There are quad bikes for hire which seem to be driven round the camping area with some speed As the complex of 270-hectares is rather remote, there is a well stocked, small supermarket and even a cash point on site.

Facilities

Good sanitary blocks with well designed showers and hot and cold water for washing (in cubicles). Facilities for children and disabled visitors. Laundry. Small but well stocked supermarket (the site is quite remote). ATM. Bar and restaurant. Takeaway (1/6-31/8). Swimming pool complex (outdoor pools heated 1/430/9, indoor pool all season). Play area on sand. Tennis. Bicycle and quad bike hire. Archery. Riding. Activity clubs for all ages and entertainment (high season). Barbecues are not permitted.

Open: 24 March - 6 October.

Directions

From N86 Bagnols - Aubenas road, exit onto the D4 at Bourg St Andeo to Remeze (a good road). Turn right at entrance to village on the D362 towards Larnas and site is on the right in Imbours. Do not attempt other routes with a caravan. GPS: 44.43681, 4.57754

Charges guide

Per person	€ 4,20 - € 7,00
child (0-7 yrs)	€ 2,30 - € 4,20
pitch (low season)	€ 4,20
pitch incl. 3 persons (high season)	€ 26,00 - € 29,00

Lathuile

Camping l'Idéal

715 route de Chaparon, F-74210 Lathuile (Haute-Savoie) T: **04 50 44 32 97**. E: **camping-ideal@wanadoo.fr**
alanrogers.com/FR74200

For panoramic views of mountains and the lake, this family run site is excellent. Trim and neat, the site is well cared for and the welcome is warm. The 300 pitches are generally large and well drained, some with small hedges but mostly open and with 6A electricity. These pitches share the site with chalets which are located at the top of the site well away from the tourers. L'Idéal is far enough from the lake to avoid the noise and crowds but close enough to take advantage of the facilities there. From the site you can cycle downhill to the Annecy cycle route.

Facilities

Three very well designed toilet blocks include excellent facilities for babies and disabled visitors. A further new block is planned. Laundry facilities. Shop (June-Sept). Bar. Restaurant, snack bar and takeaway (June-mid Aug). Two swimming pools. Tennis. Paragliding lessons. Bicycle hire. Play area. Children's club. Activities and excursions in high season. Off site: Lake 900 m. Golf and riding 5 km.

Open: 8 May - 5 September.

Directions

Lathuile is 18 km. southeast of Annecy and site is well signed in the village. GPS: 45.79514, 6.20564

Charges guide

Per unit incl. 2 persons and electricity	€ 18,70 - € 25,20
extra person	€ 3,50 - € 5,00
child (2-7 yrs)	€ 2,50 - € 4,20

Laurac

Flower Camping Saint-Amand

F-07110 Laurac (Ardèche) T: **04 75 36 84 45**. E: **st-amand@wanadoo.fr**
alanrogers.com/FR07640

Saint Amand is a member of the Flower group and can be found around 15 km. west of Vallon Pont d'Arc, close to the appropriately named village of Bellevue. There are 116 pitches, most with electrical connections and good shade. A number of pitches are occupied by mobile homes and fully equipped tents (available for rent). From the site's pool, there are some fine views across the surrounding scrubland and vineyards. Other amenities include a small restaurant, specializing in home-made pizzas and a new playing area for children. The closest shops are in the village of Laurac (2.5 km).

Facilities

Small shop. Pizzeria and snack bar. Takeaway. Swimming pool. Children's pool. Play area. Activity and entertainment programme. Mobile homes for rent. Off site: Laurac 2.5 km. Vallon Pont d'Arc 15 km. Cycle and walking tracks.

Open: 1 April - 19 September.

Directions

Approaching from the north (Privas), head southwest on the D104 to Aubenas and then continue to Bellevue. Site is clearly signed from here. GPS: 44.49964, 4.30619

Charges guide

Per unit incl. 2 persons and electricity	€ 13,90 - € 21,50
extra person	€ 2,30 - € 3,50
child (2-6 yrs)	free - € 3,00
dog	€ 1,50

Le Bourget-du-Lac

Camping International l'île aux Cygnes

501 boulevard Ernest Coudurier, F-73370 Le Bourget-du-Lac (Savoie) T: **04 79 25 01 76**
E: **camping@bourgetdulac.com** **alanrogers.com/FR73130**

This is a large municipal site in a fantastic location with wonderful views on the shores of Lake Bourget, the largest natural lake in France. The surrounding mountains create a scenic backdrop. The 235 pitches are level and a few have dividing hedges. Mature trees give some shade, but the site is mostly open. Many pitches border the lake or rivers which run along two sides of the site. Caution must be taken as there are some unfenced stretches. All pitches have easy access to electricity (10A) and there are adequate water points around the site. The lake offers many watersports.

Facilities

Four sanitary blocks with some basins in cubicles, preset showers, baby room, children's washbasins, en-suite facilities for disabled visitors. Washing machines and dryer. Motorcaravan service point. Well stocked shop. Bar, restaurant with terrace, takeaway and pizzas. Play area. TV room. Internet access. Fishing, swimming, canoes. Bicycle hire. Off site: Minigolf, archery, tennis, boat launching, sailing all within 500 m. Golf 10km.

Open: Last week of April - last week of September.

Directions

From motorway junction of A43 Lyon - Chambéry with A41 Annecy - Grenoble (exit 14 at Chambéry), head north on N201/N504 for 8 km. to Lac-du-Bourget. Then follow signs for 'Plage Municipal' and yacht club. Site is 300 m. after the yacht club. GPS: 45.6553, 5.8613

Charges guide

Per unit incl. 2 persons and electricity	€ 15,95 - € 19,50
extra person	€ 3,00 - € 4,30
child (2-12 yrs)	€ 1,35 - € 2,00
dog	€ 1,55

Le Grand-Bornand

Camping Caravaning l'Escale

Route de la Patinoire, F-74450 Le Grand-Bornand (Haute-Savoie) T: **04 50 02 20 69**
E: **contact@campinglescale.com** **alanrogers.com/FR74070**

You are assured a good welcome in English from the Baur family at this beautifully-maintained and picturesque site, situated at the foot of the Aravis mountain range. There are 149 pitches with 122 for touring. Of average size, part grass, part gravel they are separated by trees and shrubs that give a little shade. All pitches have electricity (2-10A) and 86 are fully serviced. Rock pegs are essential. A 200-year-old building houses a bar/restaurant decorated in traditional style and offering regional dishes in a delightful, warm ambience. The village is 200 m. and has all the facilities of a resort with activities for summer or winter holidays.

Facilities

Good toilet blocks (heated in winter) have all the necessary facilities. Drying room for skis, clothing and boots. Superb pool complex with interconnected indoor (all season) and outdoor pools and paddling pools (15/6-29/8), jacuzzi and water jets. Cosy bar/restaurant and takeaway (all season). Play area. Tennis. WiFi. Activities for adults and children. Discounts on organised walks and visits to Chamonix-Mont Blanc. Off site: Village (5 minutes walk), shops, bars, restaurants, archery, paragliding, golf, minigolf. 150 km. of signed walks. Activities organised for children and adults. Ice skating, snow shoes in winter. Bicycle hire 200 m. Riding and golf 3 km. Free bus for cable car (500 m) for skiing and snowboarding.

Open: 4 December - 18 April, 21 May - 26 September.

Directions

From Annecy follow the D16 and D909 towards La Clusaz. At St Jean-de-Sixt, turn left at roundabout D4 signed Grand-Bornand. Just before village fork right signed Vallée de Bouchet and camping. Site entrance is on right at roundabout in 1.2 km.
GPS: 45.94036, 6.42842

Charges 2010

Per unit incl. 2 persons and electricity	€ 19,80 - € 29,40
extra person (over 2 yrs)	€ 4,90 - € 5,70
dog	€ 2,30

Le Poët-Célard

Kawan Village le Couspeau

kawan VILLAGES
www.kawan-villages.com

F-26460 Le Poët-Célard (Drôme) T: **04 75 53 30 14**. E: **info@couspeau.com**
alanrogers.com/FR26040

As one approaches this site, a magnificent landscape of mountains and valleys unfolds. The site has 127 pitches with 83 for touring (6A electricity). Access to the older section of the site is reasonably easy and mature trees here provide some shade. The 30 fully-serviced pitches on the lower section are large and separated by small hedges with little shade. Access is via a steep road but tractor assistance is available. Rock pegs are advised. The most direct approach to the site is via a steep road and with several hairpin bends to negotiate, care is required (not advised for underpowered or large units).

Facilities

Three sanitary blocks. Washing machines, dryer. Facilities for disabled campers (the site is not ideal with steep roads and steps). Shop (15/4-14/9). Bar (20/6-14/9). Restaurant and takeaway (25/6-25/8). Swimming pool (1/6-30/8) and small, heated, covered paddling pool (14/4-14/9). Play area, organised activities. Tennis. Bicycle hire. Rafting, canoe trips (on River Drôme), riding, paragliding. Off site: Riding, fishing 5 km. Ideal area for the serious cyclist, mountain biker and hiker. Medieval towns and villages, markets and châteaux. Crest, Poët-Laval. Vercors mountains.

Open: 15 April - 14 September.

Directions

From A7, exit 16, take D104 towards Crest. At traffic lights on Crest bypass, turn right, D538 towards Bourdeaux. Before Bourdeaux turn right over bridge, D328B, signed Le Poët-Célard. Climb for 1.5 km. to T-junction, turn right. D328. Before Le Poët-Célard turn left, D328A to site. GPS: 44.59587, 5.11153

Charges guide

Per unit incl. 2 persons	€ 14,00 - € 30,00
extra person	€ 5,00
electricity (6A)	€ 3,00

Camping Cheques accepted.

Les Abrets

Kawan Village le Coin Tranquille

6 chemin des Vignes, F-38490 Les Abrets (Isère) T: **04 76 32 13 48**

E: **contact@coin-tranquille.com** **alanrogers.com/FR38010**

Kawan VILLAGES www.kawan-villages.com

Les Abrets is well placed for visits to the Savoie regions and the Alps. It is an attractive, well maintained site of 192 grass pitches (178 for tourers), all with electricity. They are separated by neat hedges of hydrangea, flowering shrubs and a range of trees to make a lovely environment doubly enhanced by the rural aspect and marvellous views across to the mountains. This is a popular, family run site with friendly staff that makes a wonderful base for exploring the area. Set in the Dauphiny countryside north of Grenoble, Le Coin Tranquille is truly a 'quiet corner', especially outside school holiday times.

Facilities

The central well appointed sanitary block is well kept, heated in low season. Facilities for children and disabled people. Two smaller blocks provide facilities in high season. Busy shop. Excellent restaurant. Swimming pool and paddling pool (15/5-30/9; no Bermuda style shorts) with sunbathing areas. Play area. TV and games in bar. Quiet reading room. Weekly entertainment for children and adults (July/Aug) including live music (not discos). Bicycle hire (limited). Off site: Riding 6 km. Fishing 8 km. Golf 25 km. Les Abrets with shops and supermarket 2 km.

Open: 1 April - 31 October.

Directions

Les Abrets is 70 km. southeast of Lyon at junction of N6 and N75. From roundabout in town take N6 towards Chambéry, turning left in just under 2 km. (signed Restaurant and Camping). Follow signs along country lane for just over 1 km. and entrance is on right. GPS: 45.54115, 5.60778

Charges 2010

Per unit incl. 2 persons	€ 18,00 - € 32,00
extra person	€ 4,00 - € 7,50
child (2-7 yrs)	€ 2,50 - € 5,00

Camping Cheques accepted.

Les Ollières-sur-Eyrieux

Kawan Village Mas de Champel

Quartier Champel, F-07360 Les Ollières-sur-Eyrieux (Ardèche) T: **04 75 66 23 23**

E: **masdechampel@wanadoo.fr** **alanrogers.com/FR07440**

Kawan VILLAGES www.kawan-villages.com

This is a simple campsite with easy access and within walking distance of a small village. It has a lively entertainment programme plus many organised activities in the high season. There are 95 unmarked, level grassy pitches, 51 for touring (electricity 6A, may need long leads) with almost no shade. A small sandy beach alongside the Eyrieux river offers lots of space for children to play in the shallow water. The bar and restaurant offer meals including breakfast and entertainment is provided in the area adjacent.

Facilities

Two small old, adequate toilet blocks with all necessary facilities. Bar, restaurant/takeaway. Swimming pool, heated paddling pool and sunbathing area. Games/TV room. Small, simple play area. Fishing. Bicycle hire. Motorcaravan services. Only gas barbecues permitted. Many organised family activities in July/Aug. Off site: Ollières-sur-Eyrieux, small shops, bar, restaurant 500 m. Riding 7 km.

Open: 11 April - 30 September.

See advertisement opposite.

Directions

Leave N86 south of Valence at Beauchastel. Turn west, D120, to Ollières sur Eyrieux (about 20 km). Site is on right at entrance to village and is signed. GPS: 44.80721, 4.61489

Charges guide

Per unit incl. 2 persons and electricity	€ 17,90 - € 28,80
extra person	€ 3,90 - € 6,90
child (2-7 yrs)	free - € 4,90

Camping Cheques accepted.

Les Ollières-sur-Eyrieux

Camping le Domaine des Plantas

F-07360 Les Ollières-sur-Eyrieux (Ardèche) T: **04 75 66 21 53**. E: **plantas.ardeche@wanadoo.fr**

alanrogers.com/FR07090

Under new ownership, this is a good quality site in a spectacular setting on the steep banks of the Eyrieux river. Old, original buildings house the reception, restaurant and bar. The terrace provides a stunning viewpoint. The 169 pitches (100 for touring) are steeply terraced and shaded with electricity (10A, long leads may be needed). Much up and down walking is required making this site unsuitable for those with walking difficulties There is a sandy beach beside the quite fast-flowing, but fairly shallow river. The 3 km. approach road is a twisting, single track and may present a problem for larger outfits.

Facilities

Two excellent well equipped toilet blocks (one heated). There are some facilities which will certainly please the very young. Washing machine. Motorcaravan services. Small shop, bar, restaurant, disco. Heated, covered and outdoor swimming pools, paddling pool and toboggans. Adventure play area. High season children's activities, discos for 14-18 year olds. Many activities and excursions. Only gas and electric barbecues. Off site: Riding 15 km.

Open: 21 April - 5 October.

Directions

Leave A7 exit 15 (Valence Sud). Turn right to Valence centre, follow signs to Montélimar via N7 for 7 km. Turn right towards Charmes-sur-Rhône to Beauchastel. Take D120 to Ollières-sur-Eyrieux. Cross river, turn left and follow site signs (3 km) along narrow track. GPS: 44.80917, 4.63581

Charges guide

Per unit incl. 2 persons	€ 19,00 - € 31,00

Lussas

Ludocamping

Route de Lavilledieu, F-07170 Lussas (Ardèche) T: **04 75 94 21 22**. E: **info@ludocamping.com**

alanrogers.com/FR07170

This is a quiet family campsite offering a really wide range of activities. From mid July - early August, only families with children under 14 yrs are accepted which allows the activities to be focused on this age group. The 160 grassy pitches, all for touring, 5-10A electricity, are in two areas. The upper area has large super pitches with wonderful views but little shade. The lower area, closer to the small river, has pitches set naturally amongst the trees and they have good shade. There is an attractive swimming pool (heated all season), good sized paddling pool and large sunbathing area.

Facilities

Clean, good quality toilet blocks offer all necessary facilities. Bar (all season), takeaway (from 1/5), terrace overlooking the valley. Play area. Recreational area next to river. Fishing. Bicycle hire. Club for over 6/7 yr olds offering a very wide range of activities. Off season club for older children. Seniors excursions in campsite coach. Only gas and electric barbecues. Off site: Lussas (few shops, restaurant, bar) 600 m. Riding 6 km. Gliding, hang-gliding, canoeing, speed boating.

Open: 1 April - 15 October.

Directions

From Montélimar take N102 west towards Aubenas, pass around Villeneuve, at traffic lights in Lavilledieu turn right onto D224 towards Lussas. Site entrance is on right just before village (about 4 km. from N102). GPS: 44.60495, 4.4712

Charges guide

Per unit incl. 2 persons	€ 11,00 - € 25,00
extra person	€ 2,00 - € 6,00
child (under 6 yrs)	€ 2,00 - € 3,00
electricity (6A)	€ 3,00

No credit cards.

Lus-la-Croix-Haute

Camping Champ la Chèvre

F-26220 Lus-la-Croix-Haute (Drôme) T: **04 92 58 50 14**. E: **info@campingchamplachevre.com**

alanrogers.com/FR26270

This is a pleasant, unpretentious site with some really magnificent views across towards the western Alps. Formerly a farm (hence its name!) and now under new management, Champ la Chèvre is undergoing a steady process of refurbishment and is attractively located just 200 m. from the village and 500 m. from the N75. There are 100 pitches, for the most part sunny and quite spacious, and many with fine mountain views. Some pitches are sloping and most pitches have 6A electrical connections. This is a good base for exploring the mountains and the owners have many ideas for excursions in the area, including downhill mountain biking, swimming in local rivers and hundreds of kilometres of walking trails. The nearby village of Lus-La-Croix-Haute is pretty and has a good range of shops and a small railway station.

Facilities

Centrally located toilet block with facilities for disabled visitors. Motorcaravan services. Play area. Minigolf. Mobile homes and chalets for rent. Heated swimming pool (15/6-31/8). Restaurant, bar. Off site: Village of Lus-La-Croix-Haute 200 m. Railway station 300 m. Tennis. Walking and cycle trails. Riding 100 m. Bicycle hire 500 m. Fishing 3 km.

Open: 24 April - 15 September.

Directions

From the north, head south from Grenoble initially on the A480 and then the A51 towards Sisteron. Then join the southbound N75 for around 35 km. to Lus-La-Croix-Haute. Drive through the village and site is well signed. GPS: 44.66440, 5.70742

Charges 2010

Per unit incl. 2 persons and electricity	€ 18,05 - € 20,85
extra person	€ 4,10 - € 5,00
child (under 10 yrs)	€ 3,00 - € 3,90

Massignieu-de-Rives

Kawan Village Lac du Lit du Roi

La Tuillière, F-01300 Massignieu-de-Rives (Ain) T: **04 79 42 12 03**

E: **info@camping-savoie.com** **alanrogers.com/FR01040**

This attractive and well cared for, family run site is ideal for those seeking an active holiday in a peaceful setting. This superb, picturesque area offers wonderful opportunities for exploration by foot, bicycle, car and boat. Take time to sample the wines and other local produce on offer. Of the 120 pitches (electricity 10A), 90 are available for touring, all being close to the lake and many having wonderful views over the lake and the wooded hills beyond. The slightly sloping, grassy pitches are set on low terraces and are partly separated by hedging and a variety of trees give some shade.

Facilities

Two modern toilet blocks offer all necessary facilities with provision for disabled visitors. Washing machines. Motorcaravan services. Small shop, bar, restaurant and terrace. Bread. Swimming pool, children's play area with water features. Tennis. Play area beside lake. Grassy beach, pedaloes, canoes, surf bikes for hire. Bicycle hire. Lake fishing. Winter caravan storage. Internet and free WiFi. Fridge and barbecue rental. Off site: Shops at Belley 8 km. Lac du Bourget (watersports, boat hire). Nature reserve. Marina, boat ramp nearby. Golf 8 km. Riding 15 km.

Open: 11 April - 4 October.

See advertisement on page 263

Directions

Site is about 8 km. east of Belley. Travelling south on N504 towards Aix-les Bains bypass Belley and at roundabout (Champion supermarket) turn east D992, signed Culoz and Seyssel. After 4 km. turn right over bridge, D37 signed Massignieu. Follow signs to site (2 km). GPS: 45.76883, 5.76942

Charges guide

Per unit incl. 2 persons	€ 22,50 - € 29,00
extra person	€ 5,00 - € 6,50
child (1-7 yrs)	€ 3,00 - € 5,00

Camping Cheques accepted.

Matafelon-Granges

Camping des Gorges de l'Oignin

Rue du Lac, F-01580 Matafelon-Granges (Ain) T: **04 74 76 80 97**

E: **camping.lesgorgesdeloignin@wanadoo.fr** **alanrogers.com/FR01050**

This family run, terraced site (English spoken) offers lovely views across the lake to the hills beyond. There are 132 good sized pitches, 102 for touring, separated by young trees and flowering shrubs and with a choice of grass or hardstanding. About half have their own water point and all have 10A electricity. Twin axle caravans are not accepted. The reception, bar/restaurant and the pool complex are at the top of the site with a steep road down to the terraces and the rest of the campsite. At the bottom of the site is a large grassy area next to the lake for sunbathing and activities.

Facilities

Two modern, well equipped and clean toilet blocks with all the usual facilities except facilities for disabled people. Bar/restaurant, takeaway and TV room (July/Aug). Swimming pool, paddling pool and new 'lazy river' (1/6-30/9). Playground and sports area. Swimming, fishing and boating on the lake (no motorboats). Off site: Golf 2 km. Riding 2 km. Matafelon 800 m. Thoirette 6 km.

Open: 1 April - 30 September.

Directions

Matafelon is 40 km. east of Bourg-en-Bresse. Leave autoroute A404 at Oyonnax, exit 11 and head west on D13 to Matafelon (10 km). On entering village and opposite the Mairie turn left, signed camping, and descend to site (800 m). GPS: 46.25535, 5.55717

Charges 2010

Per unit incl. 2 persons	€ 16,60 - € 24,00
extra person	€ 2,40 - € 5,20

Menglon

Kawan Village l'Hirondelle

Bois de Saint Ferreol, F-26410 Menglon (Drôme) T: **04 75 21 82 08**

E: **contact@campinghirondelle.com** **alanrogers.com/FR26130**

This natural, spacious and peaceful site is run by a very friendly family and you are assured a good welcome. It lies in a beautiful valley, south of the Vercors mountains and the Vercors National Park, beside the River Bez, a tributary of the River Drôme which is also close by. In natural openings in woodland, the 100 large to very large pitches all have electricity (3/6A) and are stony and slightly bumpy (rock pegs advised). There are 58 for touring units. The large pitches are separated from others by a wide variety of trees with the 1.5 km. of river bank on one side.

Facilities

Two large toilet blocks offer all the necessary facilities. Very good bar/restaurant and takeaway (all season). Small range of supplies, including bread, on sale from the bar. Excellent pool complex with small slide, paddling pool and jacuzzi (1/5-13/9). Playground. Club/TV room. Internet access. Fishing. Football, boules, volleyball, archery. Multisport court. Bicycle hire. Organised events for young children and adults. Occasional evening events. Off site: Riding 5 km.

Open: 28 April - 17 September.

Directions

From Die follow D93 southwards and after 5 km. at Pont de Quart, turn left on D539 signed Châtillon. After about 4 km. turn right on D140, signed Menglon. Site entrance is shortly on the right just after crossing a small river. GPS: 44.68142, 5.44743

Charges guide

Per unit incl. 2 persons	€ 19,90 - € 31,50
extra person	€ 5,00 - € 7,90

Camping Cheques accepted.

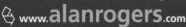

Mens

Camping le Pré Rolland

Rue de la Piscine, F-38710 Mens (Isère) T: **04 76 34 65 80**. E: **contact@camping-prerolland.fr**
alanrogers.com/FR38230

Le Pré Rolland is a small, well maintained family run site on the outskirts of the little town of Mens. It is surrounded by beautiful mountain scenery making it an ideal base for nature lovers touring this little known region of the Trièves. There are 98 mainly level, good sized grass pitches, 90 for touring and all having electricity (10A). Some are delineated by flowering shrubs and mature trees and are quite shady, others are more open and sunny. The snack bar and bar, with terrace overlooking the pool is a peaceful place to unwind after a day exploring the region. There is no on site entertainment.

Facilities

Two well maintained and clean toilet blocks with all the necessary facilities, including those for babies and campers with disabilities. Covered area with tables, small kitchen and bunk room. Bar/snack bar (all season). Adjacent municipal swimming pool, free (1/6-31/8). Day room/TV. Playground. Wifi (free). Off site: Small town of Mens with range of small shops, bar and restaurant 500 m. Fishing 1.5 km. Riding 2 km. Many marked walks and cycle rides. Rock climbing, bungee jumping.

Open: 1 May - 30 September.

Directions

From the A51 going south from Grenoble take the N75 towards Sisteron. After about 50 km, at Clelles, turn east D521 to Mens. On entering town turn right, signed site and 'piscine'. GPS: 44.814807, 5.7485

Charges guide

Per unit incl. 2 persons and electricity	€ 16,50 - € 19,00
extra person	€ 4,00 - € 6,00
child (2-7 yrs)	€ 3,00 - € 3,50

Murs-et-Gèlignieux

Flower Camping Ile de la Comtesse

Route des Abrets, F-01300 Murs-et-Gèlignieux (Ain) T: **04 79 87 23 33**
E: **camping.comtesse@wanadoo.fr** **alanrogers.com/FR01060**

A very pleasant, family run, lakeside site, there are 100 medium to large, level grassy pitches here. With 69 for touring, many are separated by low hedges and tall poplar trees offer some shade. All have 6A electricity (but very long leads may be necessary) and most have views over the lake and craggy hills beyond. High season activities are aimed mainly at younger children and the family. Fishing, sailing, canoeing and bathing are possible on the lake that borders the site. There is plenty of space around the lake for leisure activities, including marked walks and cycle trails.

Facilities

Modern and well appointed toilet block with all necessary facilities. Facilities for disabled visitors. Motorcaravan service point. Small bar/restaurant with takeaway and small shop. Large marquee used for TV and organised activities. Swimming and paddling pools. Daily programme of activities for young children and the family in high season. Bicycle hire. WiFi. Off site: Restaurant adjacent. Aost with shops, etc. 5 km. Walaibi Theme Park 10 km. Riding 10 km.

Open: 3 April - 30 September.

Directions

From the A43 (Lyon - Chambery) autoroute, take exit 10 and go north on D592 for about 10 km. After crossing the lake turn right on the D992 and site is shortly on the right. GPS: 45.63995, 5.64900

Charges guide

Per unit incl. 2 persons and electricity	€ 14,90 - € 30,50
extra person	€ 2,90 - € 7,50

Neydens

kawan VILLAGES
www.kawan-villages.com

Kawan Village la Colombière

Saint Julien-en-Genevois, F-74160 Neydens (Haute-Savoie) T: **04 50 35 13 14**
E: **la.colombiere@wanadoo.fr** **alanrogers.com/FR74060**

La Colombière, a family-owned site, is on the edge of the small village of Neydens, a few minutes from the A40 autoroute and only a short drive from Geneva. It is an attractive site with 115 pitches (93 for touring with electricity 5-15A), all reasonably level and separated by fruit trees, flowering shrubs and hedges. Neydens makes a good base for visiting Geneva and the region around the lake. It is a very pleasant, friendly site where you may drop in for a night stop – and stay for several days! The site is open all year for motorcaravans and suitable caravans. English is spoken. A 'Sites et Paysages' member.

Facilities

Good sanitary blocks (one heated) with facilities for disabled people. Motorcaravan services. Fridge hire. Gas supplies. Good bar/restaurant and terrace overlooking the pool (1/5-15/9). New heated, indoor pool, spa pool and jacuzzi (21/3-11/11). Games room. Organised visits and activities. Bicycle hire. Archery. Boules. Playground. Internet (WiFi). Off site: Fishing, riding 1 km. Golf 7 km. Lake beach and windsurfing 12 km. Switzerland 3 km.

Open: 20 March - 11 November, (all year for motorcaravans and suitable caravans).

Directions

From A40 south of Geneva take exit 13 and then N201 towards Annecy. After 2 km. turn left into village of Neydens and follow campsite signs to site in just over 1 km. GPS: 46.1201, 6.10552

Charges guide

Per unit incl. 2 persons and electricity	€ 21,00 - € 30,50
extra person	€ 3,50 - € 6,00

Camping Cheques accepted.

Peisey-Nancroix

488

Camping les Lanchettes

F-73210 Peisey-Nancroix (Savoie) T: **04 79 07 93 07**. E: **lanchettes@free.fr**
alanrogers.com/FR73030

This site is in the beautiful Vanoise National Park and at 1,470 m. is one of the highest campsites in this guide. There is a steep climb to the site but the spectacular scenery is well worth the effort. It is a natural, terraced site with 90 good size, reasonably level and well drained, grass and stone pitches, with 70 used for touring units, all having electricity (3-10A). Because of the altitude and cold winters there are no outside taps (warm bedding advised). For those who love walking and biking, the wonderful scenery, flora and fauna, this is the site for you. Underpowered units not advised.

Facilities

Well appointed heated toilet block. Motorcaravan services. Restaurant, takeaway (July/Aug. and winter). Playground. Club/TV room. Large tent/marquee used in bad weather. In winter a small bus (free) runs to all the hotels, bars, ski tows. Off site: Walks in National Park. Riding next to site. Peisey-Nancroix with restaurants, bars and shops 3 km. Les Arcs winter sports centre 6 km. Outdoor swimming pool and bicycle hire 6 km. Golf and indoor pool 8 km.

Open: 15 December - 30 April and 1 June - 15 October.

Directions

From Albertville take N90 towards Bourg-St-Maurice, through Aime. In 9 km. turn right on D87, signed Peisey-Nancroix. Follow a winding hilly road (with hairpin bends) for 10 km. Pass through Peisey-Nancroix; site on right about 1 km. beyond Nancroix. GPS: 45.53137, 6.77560

Charges guide

Per unit incl. 2 persons	€ 12,30 - € 13,80
electricity (3-10A)	€ 3,10 - € 8,20

Camping Cheques accepted.

Pont-de-Vaux

Camping les Ripettes

Chavannes-sur-Reyssouze, F-01190 Pont-de-Vaux (Ain) T: **03 85 30 66 58**. E: **info@camping-les-ripettes.com**
alanrogers.com/FR01030

A friendly welcome is assured from the owners of this spacious site situated in quiet, flat countryside near the pleasant small town of Pont-de-Vaux. The 2.5 hectare (six-acre) site has 54 large (100 sq.m. to 400 sq.m) level grassy pitches, 51 of which are available to tourists. Nearly all are separated by hedges and about half are shaded by the many trees on the site. All but two have electrical connections (10A), and there are ample water points. The site is a useful stop on the way to or from the south of France, and also serves as a centre to explore the interesting surrounding area.

Facilities

Two well appointed, small sanitary blocks contain a suite for disabled visitors. Washing machine and dryer. Limited range of food stocked and wine, ice cream, meat for barbecues at reception. Two swimming pools. Areas for ball games. Board games, books. WiFi. Communal Sunday barbecues are popular. Off site: Restaurant 1 km. Riding 2 km. Shops, etc., in Pont-de-Vaux 4 km. Fishing 4 km. Golf 15 km.

Open: 1 April - 30 September.

Directions

Leave N6 at Fleurville (14 km. south of Tournus). Go east on D933A to Pont-de-Vaux (5 km) where site is signed. Take D2 east towards St Trivier. After 3 km. turn left after water tower, left again at next junction (100 m). Site is 300 m. GPS: 46.44455, 4.98067

Charges guide

Per unit with 2 persons	€ 15,60 - € 19,00
extra person	€ 3,15 - € 3,50

Pradons

Camping les Coudoulets

Pradons, F-07120 Ruoms (Ardèche) T: **04 75 93 94 95**. E: **camping@coudoulets.com**
alanrogers.com/FR07130

For those who prefer a more intimate, peaceful campsite beside the river Ardèche, only a short distance away from the main centre, then this very well cared for site, run by a very friendly family, could be for you. There are 125 good sized, grassy and well shaded pitches, separated by trees and shrubs. There are 109 for touring, all with 10A electricity. Organised family activities take place in July/August such as barbecues and musical evenings (no discos). There is an area for bathing in the river and it is an ideal spot for canoeists. The family own a small vineyard and their wine is on sale in the bar; we fully recommend it.

Facilities

Good, clean, recently refurbished block has all the necessary facilities including excellent facilities for disabled people. Motorcaravan services. Bar, TV, terrace (May-Sept) bread, ices, drinks. Snacks (July/Aug). Butcher calls in high season. Small heated swimming pool, paddling pool. Superb new aquatic play area and pool for children (May-Sept). Fishing. WiFi. Off site: Shop 300 m. Ruoms with shops 4 km.

Open: 1 May - 10 September.

Directions

Leave Montélimar westwards on N102 towards Aubenas. After passing Villeneuve-de-Berg turn left on D103 towards Vogüé for 5 km. Turn left on D579 towards Ruoms, site on right on entering Pradons (10 km). GPS: 44.47663, 4.35857

Charges guide

Per unit incl. 2 persons	€ 14,00 - € 25,00
extra person	€ 4,50 - € 6,00
child (under 7 yrs)	€ 3,80 - € 4,80
electricity (6A)	€ 4,00

Privas

Kawan Village Ardèche

Boulevard de Paste, F-07000 Privas (Ardèche) T: **04 75 64 05 80**
E: **jcray@wanadoo.fr** **alanrogers.com/FR07180**

This spacious, family run site is on the southern outskirts of Privas and would be a good base for exploring the lesser known parts of the Ardèche. Bus and coach trips are available to explore these areas. The site has 166 large, grass, reasonably level pitches, of which 153 are for tourers. A wide variety of trees provide reasonable shade and electricity (6/10A) should now be available on most pitches. Two tour operators use the site. Recent additions include new heated swimming and paddling pools. There is a play area for children and a miniclub, but (deliberately) no provision for teenagers.

Facilities

Two toilet blocks, only one open in low season. Facilities for disabled people. Motorcaravan service point. Bar and restaurant (1/5-30/9). Boules. Play area. Miniclub. Entertainment (high season). Only gas barbecues are permitted. Tents (4) for rent. Off site: Swimming pool and tennis courts adjacent. Supermarket 100 m. Bicycle hire 2 km. Riding 5 km.

Open: 1 April - 30 September.

Directions

At traffic lights in the centre of town take D2, signed Montélimar. Descend the winding road for about 1 km. then at roundabout (near Intermarché) turn right and then shortly left, signed Espace Ouvéze. The entrance is straight on. GPS: 44.72611, 4.59845

Charges guide

Per unit incl. 2 persons	€ 14,50 - € 19,00
extra person	€ 3,50 - € 5,00
child (3-6 yrs)	€ 2,50 - € 3,00
electricity (6A)	€ 3,50

Camping Cheques accepted.

Ruoms

Yelloh! Village la Plaine

F-07120 Ruoms (Ardèche) T: **04 75 39 65 83**. E: **info@yellohvillage-la-plaine.com**
alanrogers.com/FR07250

One of the 'all singing, all dancing' type of campsite, La Plaine is quiet in low season, but in high season with all-day and evening activities for both teenagers and adults, and a miniclub each day, there is no reason to feel bored! There are 212 pitches of moderate size (77 used for their air conditioned mobile homes), of which 160 have electricity. They are protected from the sun and marked by many trees. A stage and sound equipment are in use most nights and might cause some noise problems. This is a young family site for people with lots of energy, perhaps not for a quiet holiday in high season!

Facilities

Three sanitary blocks, clean and modern provide all facilities under cover. Young children's toilet facilities. Good facilities for disabled visitors. Excellent laundry room. Fridge hire. Shop, restaurant, bar and takeaway. Heated swimming pool complex (all season). Gym. Games room and TV. Boules. Small football field. Play area (unfenced). Fitness room. Activity and entertainment programme day and evening. Miniclub (5-12 yrs). Fishing. River beach. New multisport area. Bicycle hire. Off site: Town facilities 3 km. Riding 2 km.

Open: 3 April - 12 September.

Directions

Exit Ruoms south on the D579 and at junction 2 km, south, take D111 signed St Ambroix. Site is on the left. GPS: 44.427067, 4.335617

Charges 2010

Per unit incl. 2 persons and electricity (6A)	€ 15,00 - € 41,00
extra person	€ 5,00 - € 7,00
child (3-7 yrs)	free - € 7,00
dog	€ 4,00

Ruoms

Camping le Petit Bois

87 rue du Petit Bois, F-07120 Ruoms (Ardèche) T: **04 75 39 60 72**. E: **vacances@campinglepetitbois.fr**
alanrogers.com/FR07360

Situated only 800 metres from the ancient town centre of Ruoms, and yet within an area of trees and rocky outcrops, this site offers a centre for those wishing to explore this part of the Ardèche valley. The 118 pitches are of irregular shape and size and are a mix of stone and grass (76 are used for mobile homes). There is some shade. The site is now thirty years old and at the time of our visit was in need of some restoration, which is now underway (some standpipes had coils of tubing attached – if still present, perhaps these should not be used for domestic water purposes). A 'Sites et Paysages' member.

Facilities

Three toilet blocks (only one open in low season) were in need of some maintenance when we visited. Cleaning appeared somewhat erratic. Motorcaravan service point. Bar (all season). Restaurant and takeaway (1/7-31/8). New heated swimming pool (1/4-30/6) and solarium. Playground. Games and TV rooms in season. Fishing. Entertainment organised in high season. Off site: Town with shops, etc. 300 m. Riding and bicycle hire 1 km.

Open: 1 April - 30 September.

Directions

Approaching Ruoms on the D579 from Vallon-Pont-d'Arc go straight on at first (Super U) and second roundabouts. At third roundabout turn left signed Largentier (site is signed). GPS: 44.46063, 4.3373

Charges guide

Per unit incl. 2 persons	€ 15,00 - € 28,00
with electricity (10A)	€ 19,00 - € 28,00
extra person	€ 4,80 - € 5,80
child (1-7 yrs)	€ 2,80 - € 3,80

Ruoms

Aluna Vacances

Route de Lagorce, F-07120 Ruoms (Ardèche) T: **04 75 93 93 15**. E: **alunavacances@wanadoo.fr**
alanrogers.com/FR07630

Aluna is a large holiday park close to the market town of Ruoms in the southern Ardèche, famous for its Gorges and the large range of watersports and other tourist activities. This will be a very lively site in July and August with a wide range of activities organised for all age groups, all day and into the night. There are 200 pitches mainly occupied by mobile homes and tour operators with only 40 slightly uneven and sloping pitches for touring (electricity 6A, rock pegs advised). All the main activities take place in a single area, including a magnificent aqua park.

Facilities

Facilities: Well appointed and very clean modern toilet blocks with all necessary facilities including those for campers with disabilities. Motorcaravan services. Shop, bar, restaurant, takeaway (26/4-14/9). Superb aqua park complex (all season, heated March and April). Fitness room (all season). Large play area. Miniclubs (over 5 years). Tennis. Multisport court. Boules. Underground disco (until 02.00), outdoor stage (both July/Aug). Extensive activity programme (July/Aug). Only electric barbecues on site. Off site: Bicycle hire 2 km. River bathing 2 km. Riding 5 km.

Open: Late March - 16 September.

Directions

Site is in the southern Ardèche south of Aubenas. Leave Aubenas on D104 signed Alès. Shortly turn left on D579 signed Vallon-Pont-d'Arc. Bypass Vogüé, cross river and keep right. At Ruoms turn left at roundabout on D559 signed Lagorce. In about 1 km. turn right to site on right. GPS: 44.44407, 4.36704

Charges guide

Per unit incl. 2 persons and electricity	€ 36,70 - € 41,00
extra person (over 2 yrs)	€ 8,70 - € 9,80
dog	€ 4,10

Sahune

Flower Camping les Ramières

Curnier, F-26110 Sahune (Drôme) T: **04 75 27 40 45**. E: **contact@lesramieres.com**
alanrogers.com/FR26310

This rugged area of La Drôme Provencale is quite in contrast with the gentler landscape in the northern parts of the département. The scent of lavender and reseda hangs in the air and the vibrant colours are a delight. There are 75 pitches here, mostly well shaded and with electricity (10A). A number of wooden chalets are available for rent. The site boasts a swimming pool and also access to the River Eygues. Les Ramières is under new ownership and there are plans to add a range of new amenities, including a snack bar and shop.

Facilities

Swimming pool. Direct access to river. Play area. Volleyball. Tourist information. Chalets for rent. Off site: Sahune 1.5 km. Nyons 12 km. Walking and cycle tracks. Riding. Rock climbing. Canoeing.

Open: 3 April - 26 September.

Directions

Les Ramières can be found around 12 km. east of Nyons. From there, head east on D94 and the site is between the villages of Curnier and Sahune. GPS: 44.402254, 5.253589

Charges 2010

Per unit incl. 2 persons and electricity	€ 15,50 - € 23,30

Saint Alban-Auriolles

Sunêlia le Ranc Davaine

Saint Alban-Auriolles, F-07120 Ruoms (Ardèche) T: **04 75 39 60 55**. E: **camping.ranc.davaine@wanadoo.fr**
alanrogers.com/FR07050

Le Ranc Davaine is a large, busy, family oriented site with direct access to the River Chassezac. There are 435 pitches with 87 for touring, all with electricity (10/16A) for which very long leads are required (some may cross roads). Most pitches are scattered between static caravan and tour operator pitches on fairly flat, stony ground under a variety of trees, some of which are quite low giving much needed shade. Rock pegs are advised. The site can get very busy for much of the season. A lively entertainment programme is aimed at young children and teenagers with enclosed disco four nights a week until 03.00.

Facilities

Fully equipped, very clean and modern toilet blocks include facilities for disabled visitors. Washing machines, dryers. Large shop. Internet. Bar/restaurant, pizzeria, takeaway. Swimming pool, covered pool (heated), two small square pools, slide (all facilities, all season; no shorts allowed). Large play area. Tennis. Minigolf. Fishing. Extensive activity and entertainment programme (July/Aug). Discos. Fitness hall (charged). Off site: Canoe hire nearby for excursions down the River Ardèche. Canyoning. Bicycle and quadbike hire 2 km. Riding 5 km. Karting.

Open: 4 April - 13 September.

Directions

From Ruoms go south on the D111. Just before Grospierres turn right onto D246, cross the river bridge (2.5 m. width restriction) and then left on D208 towards Chandolas and site. GPS: 44.4141, 4.2729

Charges guide

Per unit incl. 2 persons	€ 20,60 - € 36,00
incl. electricity	€ 25,75 - € 40,20
extra person	€ 6,40 - € 9,60
child (2-13 yrs)	€ 3,75 - € 9,60

Saint Alban-de-Montbel

Camping le Sougey

Lac Rive Ouest, F-73610 Saint Alban-de-Montbel (Savoie) T: **04 79 36 01 44**. E: **info@camping-sougey.com**
alanrogers.com/FR73120

In scenic surroundings, this site is only 200 m. from Lake Aiguebelette, the third largest natural lake in France. The 165 pitches (140 for touring units) all have 6/10A electricity and are set amongst many mature trees and well-manicured hedges, giving a tropical feel and plenty of shade and privacy. Most pitches are flat, but some are on a steep hillside and therefore sloping. There are adequate water points around the site and there are 30 serviced pitches are available. This is a very peaceful quality site with good views of the surrounding countryside and mountains. The owner, Philippe Kremer, is very friendly and speaks excellent English.

Facilities

Two identical sanitary blocks provide excellent facilities, washbasins in cabins, controllable showers, baby bath, 2 shower units with en-suite washbasin. Good facilities for disabled visitors. Separate laundry. Freezer. Shop (1/7-31/8). Bar and restaurant (open to public, just outside main gate). Well maintained play area. Miniclub. TV room. Chalets to rent. Off site: Fishing, boating, swimming, rafting at lake 200 m. Bicycle hire 3 km. Walks with llamas and paragliding.

Open: 1 May - 16 September.

Directions

From A43 Chambéry - Lyon motorway, take exit 12 and D921 south towards Lac d'Aiguebelette. Follow signs to Plage du Sougey. Site is on the left just before the Plage. GPS: 45.55582, 5.79081

Charges guide

Per unit incl. 2 persons	€ 12,70 - € 16,70
incl. electricity (6A)	€ 15,80 - € 19,80
with full services	€ 17,30 - € 24,10
extra person (over 5 yrs)	€ 3,60
dog	€ 1,70

Saint Avit

Domaine la Garenne

RD53, F-26330 Saint Avit (Drôme) T: **04 75 68 62 26**. E: **garenne.drome@wanadoo.fr**
alanrogers.com/FR26160

This very spacious, partly terraced rural site lies in pleasant countryside to the east of the Rhône valley. Most of the very large pitches are spread out naturally under pine trees but a lower grass area is more open and young trees give little shade at present. Although all the pitches have electricity (3/6A) very long leads are necessary. Of the 100 pitches, 25 are taken up by long stay units. The facilities are old but very clean and could entail a long walk. The small pool and its sunbathing area are next to the reception but there are few other amenities. Torches and rock pegs essential.

Facilities

Four small basic toilet blocks with washbasins in cabins. Some facilities for disabled people but the rough paths and terracing make this site unsuitable for those with walking difficulties. Washing machine. Motorcaravan services. Baker calls July/Aug. Small bar plus takeaway food (July/Aug). Kitchen area with tables under cover. Small swimming pool. Large sports area. Play area. Communal barbecue (not allowed on the pitches). Some family activities (July/Aug). WiFi at reception. Off site: Fishing 1 km. Riding 2 km. Golf 15 km. Village shops at Châteauneuf 3 km. Many marked walks and cycle routes.

Open: 1 May - 15 September.

Directions

Leave the N7 16 km. north of Tournon. Turn east on D51, signed Châteauneuf. After about 15 km. at Mureils, turn right on D363, signed St Avit. After 2 km. turn left on D53 (site signed) and site entrance is shortly on the right. GPS: 45.20205, 4.95719

Charges guide

Per unit incl. 2 persons	€ 20,00
extra person	€ 3,50 - € 5,50
electricity (3/4A)	€ 3,00 - € 5,00
animal	€ 2,50

Low season discounts.

Saint Galmier

Campéole

Campéole Val de Coise

Route de la Thiéry, F-42330 Saint Galmier (Loire) T: **04 77 54 14 82**. E: **nadine.ferran@atciat.com**

alanrogers.com/FR42040

Val de Coise is a member of the Campéole group and has an attractive location in the Massif Central, north of St Etienne. This is rugged, dramatic country – ideal for walking and mountain biking. The nearby spa town of St Galmier is home to the Badoit water plant (guided tours possible), as well as a number of art galleries. Val de Coise is an attractive site located between the River Coise and a dense forest. Pitches here are grassy and of a good size, mostly with electrical connections. Mobile homes, chalets and fully equipped tents are available for rent (short term hire possible). There is a swimming pool on site and other on-site amenities include minigolf and giant chess. There is plenty of activity here in high season with a children's club and regular discos and karaoke evenings. Off site, guided walks are organized by the local tourist office in the surrounding forests, and the Monts du Forez and Monts du Lyonnais are within easy access. Given its location, close to France's geographical centre, this site may be a good option for an en-route overnight stop.

Facilities

Swimming pool. Multisport terrain. Volleyball. Badminton. TV room. Shop. Children's play area. Giant chess. Bouncy castle. Activities and entertainment programme. Tourist information. Mobile homes, chalets and equipped tents for rent. Off site: St Galmier 2 km. Tennis 2 km. Fishing (in River Coise). Hiking and cycling. Riding. Golf. St Etienne 22 km.

Open: 15 April - 15 October.

Directions

From St Etienne head north on the A72 and leave at the Andrezieux - Bouthéon - St Galmier exit. The site is well indicated from here. GPS: 45.59272, 4.33542

Charges 2010

Per unit incl. 2 persons and electricity	€ 15,10 - € 19,10

Campéole
CAMPSITES AND RENTALS
Val de Coise***
Pitches and accommodations
of high quality,
with swimming pool.
RHÔNE-
ALPES
42330 St Galmier- Tel.: +33-477-5414-82 - www.camping-valdecoise.com / val-de-coise@campeole.com

Saint Jean-de-Chevelu

Flower Camping Lacs de Chevelu

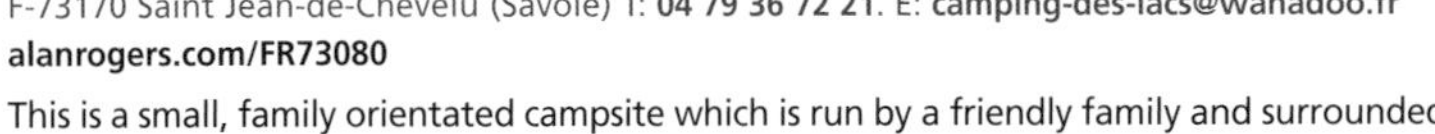

F-73170 Saint Jean-de-Chevelu (Savoie) T: **04 79 36 72 21**. E: **camping-des-lacs@wanadoo.fr**

alanrogers.com/FR73080

This is a small, family orientated campsite which is run by a friendly family and surrounded by delightful scenery, not far from Lac du Bourget. Beside the site is a small lake which is fed by springs and has a sandy beach ideal for swimming and playing around in small boats. The site has 120 average to large size, grass pitches with 110 for touring. There are 50 with 10A electricity (long leads advised). They are numbered and marked by very small trees with a few having some shade. This site ideal for families who are happy to make their own entertainment.

Facilities

Excellent newly refurbished toilet block with all necessary facilities including those for babies and campers with disabilities. Motorcaravan services. Shop. Bar (1/6-30/8). Takeaway snacks (1/6-30/8). Fishing. Lake bathing (lifeguard in high season). Organised walks and bike rides. Covered games area. Boules. TV room. Play area. Some family entertainment in high season. Off site: Riding, bicycle hire, canoeing, hang gliding 5 km. Boat ramp, tennis 7 km. Golf 10 km. Yenne with shops, bars and restaurants 5 km. Chambéry (much larger) 13 km.

Open: 1 May - 28 September.

Directions

Leave A43 at exit 13 (Chambéry) and take N504 north towards Belley. After the 'Tunnel du Chat', in Saint-Jean-de-Chevelu, turn right (site signed). Site is just over 1 km. GPS: 45.69378, 5.82491

Charges guide

Per unit incl. 2 persons	€ 12,50 - € 17,90
with electricity (10A)	€ 13,90 - € 20,90
extra person	€ 2,60 - € 3,90
child (2-7 yrs)	€ 2,10 - € 2,90

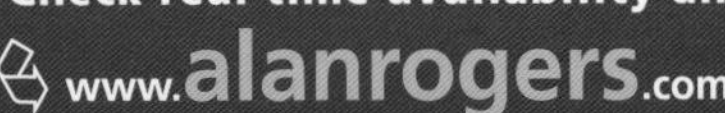

Saint Gervais-les-Bains

Camping les Dômes de Miage

197 route des Contamines, F-74170 Saint Gervais-les-Bains (Haute-Savoie) T: **04 50 93 45 96**
E: **info@camping-mont-blanc.com** **alanrogers.com/FR74140**

Saint Gervais is a pretty spa town in the picturesque Val-Monjoie valley and this site is 2 km. from its centre. It is 22 km. west of Chamonix and centrally located for discovering this marvellous mountain region. Nestled among the mountains, this sheltered, well-equipped site provides 150 flat grassy pitches of a good size. About half have shade and there are 100 with electricity points (3-10A). The remainder on terraced ground are used for tents. Third generation hosts, Stéphane and Sophie, will welcome you to the site, and their passion for this area at the foot of Mont Blanc is infectious. A number of Savoyard-style chalets to let are planned for the future. This is a good site for large motorcaravans. There is no on-site entertainment programme, but a wealth of information about the area and activities available nearby is provided at reception where they will help with your itinerary. The region is good for walking and there is a bus service into Saint Gervais, from where there is a frequent shuttle bus to its spa and a tramway to the Mont Blanc range. There is good public transport between the town and Chamonix.

Facilities

Two sanitary blocks, one heated, with a suite for disabled visitors and baby room. Washing machines and dryer. Motorcaravan services. Small basic shop. Bar/restaurant. TV room, library, ironing board. Excellent playground. Playing field. Off site: Fishing 100 m. Bicycle hire 1 km. Riding 7 km. Shops, etc. and outdoor swimming pool in St Gervais.

Open: 1 May - 12 September.

Directions

From St Gervais take D902 towards Les Contamines and site is on left after 2 km. GPS: 45.87389, 6.7199

Charges 2010

Per unit incl. 2 persons and electricity	€ 19,40 - € 25,10
extra person	€ 3,00 - € 4,10
child (2-10 yrs)	€ 2,50 - € 3,50
dog	€ 2,00

Camping Cheques accepted.

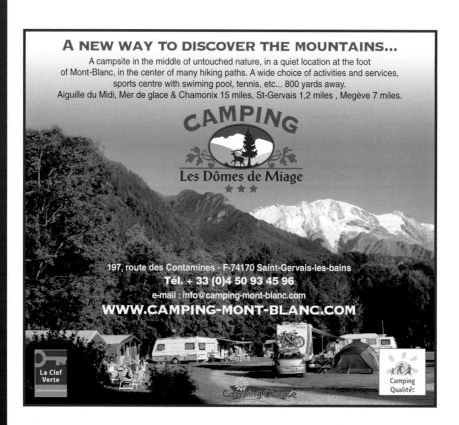

Saint Jorioz

Village Camping Europa

1444 route Albertville, F-74410 Saint Jorioz (Haute-Savoie) T: **04 50 68 51 01**. E: **info@camping-europa.com**
alanrogers.com/FR74100

You will receive a friendly welcome at this quality, family run site. The flowers, shrubs and trees are lovely and everything is kept neat and tidy. There are 210 medium to large size pitches (110 for touring) on level stony grass. Rock pegs are advised. All pitches have electricity (6A) close by and 18 have water and drainage. The static units are separated from the touring section by high hedges giving the impression that you are on a small site. There may be some noise from the adjacent main road. This is a good base from which to tour the Lake Annecy area.

Facilities

Two very good toilet blocks, recently modernised to a high standard, have all the necessary facilities including some large cubicles with both showers and washbasins. Motorcaravan service point. Good bar and restaurant (1/6-31/8). Swimming pool complex (entry bracelet € 2). Bicycle hire. Internet access. Miniclub. Some musical evenings. Off site: Fishing 300 m. Boat launching 500 m. Lakeside beach 2 km. Riding 3 km. Golf 8 km. Lakeside bike ride (40 km). St Joriz. Canyoning and hang-gliding nearby.

Open: 30 April - 20 September.

Directions

From Annecy take N508 signed Albertville. Site is well signed on the right on leaving Saint Jorioz.
GPS: 45.8246, 6.1758

Charges guide

Per unit incl. 2 persons and electricity	€ 14,50 - € 29,10
serviced pitch	€ 22,70 - € 37,30
extra person	€ 4,20 - € 6,20
dog	€ 3,00

Saint Laurent-du-Pape

Camping la Garenne

Chemin de la Garenne, F-07800 Saint Laurent-du-Pape (Ardèche) T: **04 75 62 24 62**
E: **info@lagarenne.org** **alanrogers.com/FR07100**

This spacious, family orientated site has a long season and is within easy reach of the A7/N7 south of Valence. It is only a short stroll from the village which has a range of small shops. Guests are mainly Dutch but all are made welcome and English is widely spoken. The 120 hard pitches (rock pegs advised), some terraced and some sloping, have varying degrees of shade. Some are separated by hedges and all have electricity, but only 4A (some need long leads). Visitors' pursuits have been carefully considered resulting in a variety of family activities from mid May to mid September.

Facilities

Excellent and very clean, modern toilet blocks provide all necessary facilities including those for children and disabled visitors. Small shop for basics. Bar, restaurant and takeaway (all 15/5-15/9). Swimming pool and sunbathing terrace (20/5-30/9). Paddling pool. Boules. Games room. Barbecues are not permitted. Off site: Village. Fishing 1 km. Riding 2 km. Bicycle hire 3 km. Walking, biking, canoeing, canyoning and exploring the Ardèche region.

Open: 1 March - 1 November.

Directions

Leave the N86 at Beauchastel, 20 km. south of Valence and follow the D21 to Saint Laurent-du-Pape. In the village, turn right just before the post office and the site is at the end of this road, beyond the tennis court. GPS: 44.82663, 4.76171

Charges guide

Per unit incl. 2 persons and electricity	€ 18,50 - € 30,50
extra person	€ 5,50

Saint Laurent-en-Beaumont

Camping Belvédère de l'Obiou

Les Egats, F-38350 Saint Laurent-en-Beaumont (Isère) T: **04 76 30 40 80**
E: **info@camping-obiou.com** **alanrogers.com/FR38130**

This very good, small Alpine site with just 45 pitches is in the centre of the Ecrins National Park. It is therefore ideal for walkers and cyclists looking to take advantage of the well marked trails. It has most things a good site should have, with its restaurant (high season), heated pool and sitting room with TV and library. The welcoming owners will even supply you with breakfast. The views from the terraced pitches are spectacular and there is a wealth of activities in the area ranging from bungee jumping to beaver watching by the Lac du Vallon. Bicycles are available to hire.

Facilities

Two modern toilet blocks, one part of the main building, the other Portacabin style, are immaculate and can be heated. High standard facilities for disabled visitors. Laundry. Motorcaravan services. Restaurant (May-Sept) with Savoyard menu, excellent takeaway and breakfast. Small family run shop with ice cream and soft drinks. Heated swimming pool (May-Sept). Bicycle hire. Good play area. Off site: Fishing 5 km. Walking, cycling and mountain activities.

Open: 15 April - 15 October.

Directions

From Grenoble take exit 8 onto the RN85. After 9 km. left onto D529 towards La Motte d'Aveillans and back onto the RN85 at La Mure. 7 km. south of La Mure site is clearly signed on the left.
GPS: 44.87593, 5.83741

Charges guide

Per unit incl. 2 persons	€ 13,00 - € 18,00
extra person	€ 3,00 - € 5,00
child (2-10 yrs)	€ 2,20 - € 3,50
electricity (4-10A)	€ 3,00 - € 5,50

Camping Cheques accepted.

Saint Maurice d'Ardèche

Domaine du Cros d'Auzon

Saint Maurice d'Ardèche, F-07200 Vogüé-Gare (Ardèche) T: **04 75 37 75 86**. E: **camping.auzon@wanadoo.fr**
alanrogers.com/FR07340

This site can be described with the word 'immaculate'. The 55 pitches on well cut grass, are all of a very generous size and all have water, drainage and electricity. On the banks of the Ardèche, the site is part of a holiday complex which includes a hotel and conference centre, separated by a 300 m. driveway. Out of season it is very quiet, but in July and August a newly built bar, takeaway and restaurant together with an 'animations' building, become the focal point of the evenings. There are 115 mobile homes for hire (some tour operators).

Facilities

Two excellent, modern toilet blocks of an unusual design are kept very clean. Well equipped laundry room. Fridge hire. Bar, takeaway, restaurant and shop (July/Aug). At the hotel: outdoor swimming pool (1/5-15/9) and indoor pool (all season), minigolf and tennis. Play area of generous size. Bicycle hire. Internet access. Charcoal barbecues are not permitted. Off site: Village 500 m. Golf. Riding 10 km.

Open: 4 April - 18 September.

Directions

The D579 between Ruoms and Aubenas passes through the village of Vogüé. At the only roundabout take road to the southwest. Site is signed from the roundabout (about 800 m). GPS: 44.53416, 4.40690

Charges 2010

Per unit incl. 2 persons and electricity	€ 18,00 - € 29,50

Saint Nizier-le-Désert

Camping la Nizière

F-01320 Saint Nizier-le-Désert (Ain) T: **04 74 30 35 16**. E: **laniziere@cc-chalamont.com**
alanrogers.com/FR01120

La Nizière is a spacious campsite in a woodland setting beside two lakes extending over 25 hectares. It is in a region of farmland, forests and hundreds of lakes. There are 70 pitches with most having electricity (6A), long leads advised. There is a small open grass section near the lake with good views. A larger, heavily shaded section further back has stony pitches, many occupied by seasonal caravans. There are also 8 chalets close to a lake. The lakes are well stocked with fish making the site popular with anglers. There are over 40 km. of walking and cycling tracks around the site. The surrounding area covers a large flat plain between the rivers Saône, Rhône and Ain. The nearby town of Chalamont has a range of shops, bars and restaurants and there are many interesting places to visit. Plans for 2010 include a new ecological swimming pool and new toilet blocks.

Facilities

Three clean, small basic blocks with many Turkish style WCs, facilities for disabled visitors, quite a distance from some of the pitches. Washing machine. Snack bar, restaurant and takeaway (all season). Games room/TV. Lake fishing but no bathing. Tennis. Motorcaravan services (charged). No barbecues. Some family activities in high season. Off site: Marked walking and cycling routes. Golf and riding 5 km. Chalamont 8 km. Sailing 8 km. Bird Park in Villars les Dombes 12 km. Medieval city of Pérouges 16 km. Bourg-en-Bresse with its cathedral 20 km.

Open: 3 April - 26 September.

Directions

St Paul-de-Varax is on N83 between Bourg-en-Bresse and Lyon. Leave N83 at St Paul-de-Varax, take D70b to St Nizier-le-Désert, then D90 to site (well signed from village). GPS: 46.05454, 5.15984

Charges guide

Per unit incl. 2 persons and electricity	€ 15,00
extra person	€ 3,10
child (2-12 yrs)	€ 1,90

Saint Pierre-d'Albigny

Flower Camping du Lac de Carouge

Base de Loisirs, F-73250 Saint Pierre-d'Albigny (Savoie) T: **04 79 28 58 16**

E: **campinglacdecarouge@orange.fr** **alanrogers.com/FR73090**

Camping Lac de Carouge is a well maintained and pleasant campsite next to a very clean, gently shelving, spring fed lake. This is ideal for swimming and playing around in small boats, with pedaloes for hire. There are many marked walks and cycle tracks in this beautiful regional park. The site provides 80 large, level, grass pitches with 67 for touring (electricity 6/10A), separated by hedges giving privacy and some shade. There are good views of the surrounding mountains but not of the lake. Access to the site is easy from the A41, A43 and A430 autoroutes making it ideal for a short stay but you may be tempted to stay longer.

Facilities

Two new (2007) toilet blocks with excellent facilities. A family room and suite for campers with disabilities. Large tent for bar and children's room (July/Aug). Volleyball, table tennis, boules. Off site: Lake bathing, play area, shaded picnic and play area, pedaloes 200 m. Bar/restaurant 200 m. and 500 m. Bike rides and walks around lake. Supermarket 1 km. St Pierre-d'Albigny some shops restaurants 2 km. Albertville with shops, bars and restaurants 26 km.

Open: 25 April - 15 September.

Directions

St Pierre-d'Albigny is just north of the N90/N6, mid way between Albertville and Chambéry. Site is well signed on outskirts of village. GPS: 45.55663, 6.16616

Charges 2010

Per unit incl. 2 persons and electricity	€ 16,50 - € 25,50
extra person	€ 3,40 - € 4,90
child (2-7 yrs)	€ 2,40 - € 3,90

Saint Pierre-de-Chartreuse

Camping de Martinière

Route du Col de Porte, F-38380 Saint Pierre-de-Chartreuse (Isère) T: **04 76 88 60 36**

E: **camping-de-martiniere@orange.fr** **alanrogers.com/FR38160**

Chamechaude, the 2,082 m. Eiger-like peak, presides benevolently over the 86 touring pitches at this beautiful, high alpine site open from May to September. The 86 large touring pitches, with electricity available (2-10A), have some shade and are slightly sloping. The site has a heated pool in the open air so that not a moment of the views is lost. This well run, family owned enterprise, set around a traditional Savoyard farmhouse, is a peaceful centre for walking, climbing, cycling or just soaking up the air and ambience. It is in the centre of the Chartreuse National Forest. A 'Sites et Paysages' member.

Facilities

Two heated toilet blocks, one at each end of the site provide excellent, clean facilities. Facilities for babies but not for disabled visitors. Laundry facilities. Shop (1/6-15/9). Bar (10/6-15/9) with snacks (1/7-1/9). Heated swimming and paddling pools (1/6-5/9). Play area. Indoor sitting area for poor weather. Extensive paperback library (NL, IT, FR, UK). Off site: Restaurant 50 m. from site entrance. Bicycle hire 3 km. Skiing 6 km. Walking, cycling and mountain activities.

Open: 1 May - 12 September.

Directions

From St Laurent-du-Pont (north from Voiron or south from Chambery), take D512 signed St Pierre-de-Chartreuse. Site is well signed in the village (the road south from St Pierre-d'Entremont is not recommended for towing). GPS: 45.3258, 5.7972

Charges 2010

Per unit incl. 2 persons and electricity	€ 17,00 - € 26,20
extra person	€ 2,70 - € 5,60

Camping Cheques accepted.

Saint Sauveur-de-Montagut

Camping Caravaning l'Ardéchois

Le Chambon, Gluiras, F-07190 Saint Sauveur-de-Montagut (Ardèche) T: **04 75 66 61 87**

E: **ardechois.camping@wanadoo.fr** **alanrogers.com/FR07020**

This attractive site is quite a way off the beaten track and the approach road is winding and narrow in places. However, it is worth the effort, to find it in such a spectacular setting. This site has 106 pitches (83 for touring with 10A electricity) laid out on steep terraces and many separated by trees and plants. Some are alongside the small, fast-flowing stream, while the rest (60%) are on higher, sloping ground nearer the restaurant/bar and pool. The main site access roads are tarmac but are quite steep and larger units may find access to some terraces difficult. On arrival park outside reception.

Facilities

Two very good sanitary blocks include facilities for families and people with disabilities. Laundry facilities. Motorcaravan services. Shop. Cosy restaurant. Swimming and paddling pools (heated), adjacent bar, snack bar, terrace. TV. Bicycle hire, archery, fishing. Comprehensive entertainment programme. Only gas/electric barbecues are permitted. Off site: Canyoning, climbing, river walking and canoeing trips organised.

Open: 27 April - 30 September.

Directions

From Valence take N86 south for 12 km. At La Voulte-sur-Rhône turn right onto D120 to St Sauveur-de-Montagut (site well signed), in centre turn left onto D102 towards Mézilhac for 8 km. to site. GPS: 44.82842, 4.52332

Charges guide

Per unit incl. 2 persons and electricity	€ 28,30 - € 47,50
extra person	€ 4,00 - € 8,50

Camping Cheques accepted.

Saint Théoffrey

Camping Ser Sirant

Lac de Laffrey, Petichet, F-38119 Saint Théoffrey (Isère) T: **04 76 83 91 97**. E: **info@campingsersirant.com**
alanrogers.com/FR38020

This small lakeside site, a few kilometres from La Route Napoléon, has 87 touring pitches (6A reverse polarity) and six chalets, set on a level, partly terraced, grassed area. There is a pleasant lakeside terrace just outside the bar and reception, whilst about 70 metres up the lakeside there is a sailing school for you to improve (or start) your sailboarding skills. On site there are kayaks for hire and fishing on the lake. This is a picturesque site with the minimum of extras which will appeal especially to water lovers.

Facilities

A single toilet block is at one end of the site. Equipped to basic standards it could be under pressure at peak times. Half the WCs are Turkish style. No facilities for children. Launderette. Small bar with shop for basic supplies. Takeaway at weekends in July/Aug. Kayak hire. Fishing. Chalets to rent. Off site: Shops and restaurants within 1 km. Riding and bicycle hire 5 km.

Open: 1 May - 30 September.

Directions

Petichet is on the Route Napoléon between Grenoble and La Mure. Site is well signed and easy to find by the lake. GPS: 45.00817, 5.79267

Charges 2010

Per unit incl. 2 persons and electricity	€ 19,50 - € 21,00
extra person	€ 2,50 - € 4,90

No credit cards.

Saint-Jorioz

Camping International du lac d'Annecy

1184 route d'Albertville, F-74410 Saint-Jorioz (Haute-Savoie) T: **04 50 68 67 93**
E: **contact@camping-laclannecy.com** **alanrogers.com/FR74270**

International du Lac d'Annecy is a good quality, family run campsite within 500 m. of the crystal clear water of Lac d'Annecy which in high season offers a very wide range of watersports and other leisure activities. Passing close to the site is an excellent cycle route alongside the full length of the lake. The site has 163 level, grass pitches of a good size. There are 140 for touring units, all with electricity (6/10A). The pitches are arranged in pairs separated by a few flowering shrubs with mature trees giving some shade. Access is easy for large outfits. A new swimming pool complex is planned for 2010.

Facilities

Very good toilet block with all necessary facilities including those for campers with disabilities. Bar/restaurant and takeaway (all season). Heated swimming pool (8/5-18/9). Play areas. Multisport pitch. Boules. Bicycle hire. Children's club and family entertainment (July/Aug). Wifi (charge). Off site: Fishing and bathing in lake 500 m. Beach, boat ramp, windsurfing 1 km. Golf 10 km. Riding 15 km. St Jorioz with bar/restaurants, shops 1 km. Annecy with large range of shops, bar/restaurants, museums, market and interesting old town 10 km. Cycle track (30 km).

Open: 8 May - 18 September.

Directions

From Annecy take D1580 south, signed Albertville, for 10 km. to Jorioz. Site is on the right 1 km. after traffic lights. GPS: 45.83084, 6.17842

Charges guide

Per unit incl. 2 persons	€ 16,00 - € 24,00
incl. electricity	€ 25,00 - € 31,00
extra person (over 2 yrs)	€ 3,90 - € 4,60

Saint Martin-d'Ardèche

Camping Indigo le Moulin

F-07700 Saint Martin-d'Ardèche (Ardèche) T: **04 75 04 66 20**
E: **moulin@camping-indigo.com** **alanrogers.com/FR07650**

Le Moulin is a member of the Indigo group and is located just 300 m. from the centre of St Martin-d'Ardèche. The site has its own river beach and is very well placed for canoe trips on the Ardèche. There are 200 pitches here, extending over the site's 7 hectares. The pitches are well shaded and most have electrical connections. Rental accommodation includes innovative 'wood and canvas' tents and Romany style caravans. Amenities include a pleasant snack bar and a small shop. A children's club (recré-enfants) operates in peak season, focusing on craft activities and games.

Facilities

Snack bar. Small shop. Play area. Children's activity programme. Tourist information. Direct access to the river. Canoeing. Tents and caravans for rent. Off site: St Martin 300 m. (shops, cafes and restaurants). Cycle and walking tracks. Riding. Aiguèze (pretty craft village).

Open: 3 April - 27 September.

Directions

From Pont St Esprit, take the northbound D6086, becoming D86 after crossing the river, and then D290 to St Martin-d'Ardèche. The site is clearly signed. GPS: 44.300272, 4.571171

Charges guide

Per unit incl. 2 persons and electricity	€ 17,10 - € 22,40
extra person	€ 3,10 - € 4,90
child (3-7 yrs)	€ 2,00 - € 3,50

Camping Cheques accepted.

The Travel Service to book this site call 01580 214000 ...we'll arrange everything

Samoëns

Camping Caravaneige le Giffre

La Glière, F-74340 Samoëns (Haute-Savoie) T: **04 50 34 41 92**. E: **camping.samoens@wanadoo.fr**
alanrogers.com/FR74230

Surrounded by magnificent mountains in this lesser known Alpine area, yet accessible to major ski resorts, le Giffre could be the perfect spot for those seeking an active, yet relaxing holiday. There are 300 firm, level pitches on stony grass (rock pegs advised) with 288 for touring units. Most have electricity (6/10A) but long leads may be needed. They are spaced out amongst mature trees which give varying amounts of shade and some overlook the attractive lake and leisure park. The small winter/summer resort of Samoëns is only a 15-minute level stroll away. Mr Dominach loves gardening and the site is bedecked with flowers. Make sure you do not miss the small vegetable and herb garden at the entrance. There is little in the way of on site entertainment but there are many activities available in Samoëns and the surrounding area.

Facilities

Three adequate toilet blocks, heated in winter with facilities for campers with disabilities. Games room. Play area. Boules. Fishing. Off site: Leisure park next to site – pool (entry free summer), ice skating (entry free winter), tennis (summer), archery, adventure park. Paragliding. Rafting, many walks and bike rides (summer) and ski runs (winter). Snack bar and baker (high season) 100 m. Samoëns with a good range of shops, bars, restaurants 1 km. Grand Massif Express cable car 150 m. Bicycle hire 200 m. Riding 2 km.

Open: All year.

Directions

Leave the A40 autoroute at Cluses (exit 18 or 19). Go north on D902 towards Taninges. Just before Taninges turn east on D4 to Samoëns. After crossing river, at roundabout, turn left and site is immediately on the left. Park outside the entrance.
GPS: 46.07731, 6.71851

Charges 2010

Per unit incl. 2 persons and electricity	€ 14,60 - € 25,50
extra person	€ 2,50 - € 3,80

Camping Cheques accepted.

Sampzon

Yelloh! Village Soleil Vivarais

F-07120 Sampzon (Ardèche) T: **04 75 39 67 56**. E: **info@yellohvillage-soleil-vivarais.com**
alanrogers.com/FR07030

A large, lively, high quality site bordering the River Ardèche, complete with beach, Soleil Vivarais offers much to visitors, particularly families with children. Of the 350 pitches, 110 generously sized, shady and level pitches are for tourers, all with 10A electricity. Rock pegs are advised. During the day the proximity of the swimming pools to the terraces of the bar and restaurant make it a pleasantly social area. A new section beyond the beach has a very attractive new pool complex. In the evening, the purpose-built stage, with professional lighting and sound system, provides an ideal platform for a regular family entertainment programme, mostly mimed musical shows.

Facilities

Modern, clean, well equipped toilet blocks, facilities for people with disabilities. Washing machines, dryers. Motorcaravan services. Small supermarket. Bar/restaurant, takeaways and pizzas (cooked in a wood burning oven). Heated pool (to be completely refurbished for 2010), paddling pool. Water polo. Aquarobics. Fishing. Boules. Archery. Bicycle hire. River bathing. Extensive animation programme in June, July and August. Massage and beauty parlour. Off site: Riding 800 m. Mountain biking, walking, canoeing, rafting, climbing, caving.

Open: 1 April - 12 September.

Directions

On D579, 2 km. south of Ruoms, turn left at roundabout, signed Vallon-Pont-d'Arc. Shortly turn right over river bridge, site on right.
GPS: 44.42917, 4.35531

Charges 2010

Per unit incl. 2 persons and electricity	€ 15,00 - € 43,00
extra person	€ 5,00 - € 7,00
dog	free - € 4,00

The Travel Service to book this site call 01580 214000 ...we'll arrange everything

Sampzon

RCN la Bastide en Ardèche

Route d'Alès (D111), Sampzon, F-07120 Ruoms (Ardèche) T: **04 75 39 64 72**
E: **info@rcn-labastideenardeche.fr** **alanrogers.com/FR07080**

You can be assured of a good welcome at this recently upgraded site. There are 300 good sized, level, grassy pitches marked out by trees which give plenty of shade of which 260 are touring pitches. All have electricity 6A, and 86 are fully serviced. On driving down to your pitch, it seems that there are many mobile homes, actually there are only 30 plus another 20 pitches used by a tour operator. Canoe trips are arranged down the Gorge d'Ardèche and in late June each year a large section of the river bank next to the site is cleared of boulders and sand put down. Security patrols ensure quiet nights.

Facilities

Two well equipped toilet blocks, one new and one refurbished, with baby room and facilities for disabled people. Shop, attractive restaurant, pizzeria and bar (1/4-1/10). Heated swimming pool (1/4-1/10). Play area. Tennis. Fishing. Organised activities. Recreation room in restored medieval building. Only gas barbecues are permitted. Bicycle hire. Off site: Riding 3 km. Watersports on River Ardèche, quad riding, adventure camp. Ruoms 3 km. Vallon-Pont-d'Arc 7 km. Medieval villages.

Open: 20 March - 9 October.

Directions

Going south from Ruoms on the D579, after 2.5 km. at roundabout, turn right on D111 signed Alès. After 1 km. cross river bridge and site is 200 m. on the left. GPS: 44.42292, 4.32162

Charges guide

Per unit incl. 2 persons, electricity and water	€ 19,50 - € 43,50
incl. 3-6 persons	€ 21,50 - € 56,00
dog	€ 6,00

Many discounts offered in low season.

Sampzon

Flower Camping le Riviera

F-07120 Sampzon (Ardèche) T: **04 75 39 67 57**. E: **leriviera@wanadoo.fr**
alanrogers.com/FR07400

This large, well organised, family run site is situated beside the River Ardèche not far from Vallon-Pont-d'Arc. There are 180 pitches in total with 144 of average size on grass and stone for touring (rock pegs are advised). Separated by hedges and trees, pitches have varying degrees of shade and 10A electricity connections are available. In July and August daily and evening activities are organised for all the family. The site's facilities are of a high standard and disabled visitors are well provided for. Access to some of the pitches is not ideal in some parts and may prove to be difficult for larger units.

Facilities

Two toilet blocks, one new and excellent, providing cubicles with washbasins, showers, baby room and excellent facilities for disabled visitors. Washing machines and dryer. Swimming and paddling pools and sunbathing terrace (all season, heated). Bar, restaurant with covered terrace (6/8-8/9 and weekends). Shop (July/Aug). Bicycle and canoe hire (July/Aug). Fishing. Stony river beach. Disco or karaoke every evening until midnight. Off site: Shop open all season close to entrance. Riding 1 km. Bicycle hire 3 km.

Open: 1 April - 30 September.

Directions

On D579 2 km. south of Ruoms, turn left at roundabout signed Vallon-Pont-d'Arc. Shortly turn right over river bridge. Site on left. GPS: 44.42838, 4.35527

Charges guide

Per unit incl. 2 persons and electricity (10A)	€ 16,00 - € 38,00
extra person	€ 4,50 - € 8,40
child (under 7 yrs)	free - € 7,40

Thonon-les-Bains

Camping Saint-Disdille

117 avenue de Saint Disdille, F-74200 Thonon-les-Bains (Haute-Savoie) T: **04 50 71 14 11**
E: **camping@disdille.com** **alanrogers.com/FR74220**

Saint Disdille is situated close to the beautiful Lake Geneva and the famous spa town of Thonon-les-Bains, which can be reached on a bus that passes the site. There are 600 large, level pitches on stone and rough grass (rock pegs are essential). Large trees give some shade. The 300 pitches reserved for touring (200 with 6-10A electricity) are scattered amongst mobile homes and permanent weekender caravans and can be some distance from the facilities. The site is ideally situated for the large range of watersports in the area and Switzerland is easily accessible by car, bus, train or boat. This site will be lively in the high season due to the large number of long stay units and the on-site and adjacent discos finish after midnight. Although there are no problems with large units on the site, access is not easy due to the urban location. A new bypass around Thonon makes access easier.

Facilities

Five adequate toilet blocks, 4 recently refurbished inside. Shop. Bar with TV, restaurant with takeaways (all season). Diving and rafting clubs. Play area with bouncy castle. Multisport court. Boules. Games room with pool table. WiFi (free) and internet point (fee). Twin-axle vans are not accepted. Bicycle hire. Off site: Small lakeside public beach and disco 300 m. Fishing 500 m. Large open air pool 1 km. Boat ramp, windsurfing, bicycle hire 2 km. Many other water sports in the area. Golf 5 km. Thonon-les-Bains 2 km.

Open: 1 April - 30 September.

Directions

From Annemasse take N5 to Thonon-les-Bains. In Thonon follow signs for Evian to Intermarché supermarket. At next roundabout follow signs to campsite and Parc de la Chataigneraie.
GPS: 46.39765, 6.50335

Charges 2010

Per unit incl. 2 persons and electricity	€ 17,20 - € 23,70
extra person	€ 3,40 - € 4,80
child (3-10 yrs)	€ 2,20 - € 3,40

Trept

Domaine les Trois Lacs du Soleil

La Plaine, F-38460 Trept (Isère) T: **04 74 92 92 06**. E: **info@les3lacsdusoleil.com**
alanrogers.com/FR38060

Les Trois Lacs is situated on the edge of three lakes in flat, open country in the north of Dauphine. The camping area is on one side of the largest lake with tall trees on one edge and views of distant mountains. The 200 good-size pitches, with 180 for tourists, are well spaced and separated by trees and hedges. All have 6A electricity. There is plenty of activity on offer for the whole family including fishing in one lake, swimming in the other two and, for the more energetic, roller blading. There is plenty of space around the lake for children to play. The land around the lakes has been well landscaped with grassy banks, shrubs and trees. This is a good base from which to enjoy either the countryside, the historic places of the region or the programme of leisure activities provided by the site (July/August).

Facilities

Two fully equipped toilet blocks are in the centre of the camping area. Toilets for children. Baby room. Laundry facilities. Small shop (July/Aug). Bar/restaurant. Snack bars. Outdoor pool (all June-Sept). Lakeside beach and water slide. Discos and entertainment in high season. TV and sports hall. Roller blade hire. Walking. Fishing. Gas barbecues only. Off site: Riding 500 m. Trept 2 km. Mountain bike hire 10 km.

Open: 1 May - 12 September.

Directions

From A43 take exit 7 on to D522 north. Turn left after 7 km. on to D65 then after 5 km. turn right on the D517. Site is 2 km. east of Trept with signs in village.
GPS: 45.68699, 5.35191

Charges guide

Per unit incl. 2 persons and electricity	€ 18,50 - € 31,00
extra person	€ 3,00 - € 7,00
child (0-10 yrs)	free - € 3,50
animal	€ 1,50

Séez

Camping le Reclus

F-73700 Séez (Savoie) T: **04 79 41 01 05**. E: **contact@campinglerecus.com**

alanrogers.com/FR73100

This small mountain campsite, set in the hills above Bourg-St-Maurice, is enthusiastically run by Mélanie Bonato who has great plans to offer the unexpected. The 90 pitches, some gently sloping, are set amongst mature pine trees giving plenty of shade; 80 have electricity. The site borders a fast-flowing mountain stream, which is well fenced. The site is undergoing redevelopment, with many new facilities being introduced. A new TV room was just about to open on our visit. The village of Séez is a few minutes' walk away. This site is not recommended for larger units.

Facilities

Two sanitary blocks, the central one more modern, have small shower cubicles with preset hot water; and open style basins. Laundry room with washer/dryer and indoor drying area. Restaurant and takeaway (1/7-5/9). Small play area. Bread, drinks and ice cream for sale. Bicycle hire.
Off site: Shops and bars in the village of Séez. Access to the ski resort of Les Arcs via the funicular railway in Bourg-St-Maurice 2 km. Riding 1 km. Swimming pools 2 km. Golf 15 km.

Open: All year.

Directions

From A43 Lyon - Chambéry - Grenoble motorway take A430 to Albertville and RN90 to Moutiers and Bourg-St-Maurice. Drive through town, at third roundabout follow signs for Tignes and Val d'Isère. Site is 2 km. up the hill on the right on entering village of Séez.
GPS: 45.62592, 6.79371

Charges guide

Per unit incl. 2 persons and electricity	€ 16,30 - € 17,10
extra person	€ 2,50 - € 4,20

Vallières

Camping les Charmilles

D14, F-74150 Vallières (Haute-Savoie) T: **04 50 62 10 60**. E: **les.charmilles.camping@wanadoo.fr**

alanrogers.com/FR74290

Les Charmilles is a friendly site in the village of Vallières, to the west of Annecy. There are 70 pitches, most with electricity (6/8A). A number of pitches are occupied by chalets and caravans (for rent). The site restaurant, Le Marilyn, is open to the general public and specialises in Savoyard cuisine. Takeaway meals are also possible. On-site leisure amenities include a swimming pool, paddling pool and volleyball. During peak season, various activities are organized including theme evenings, as well as a children's club specializing in craft activities and games. The village centre is around 500 m. distant and has a number of shops including a post office and a specialist cheese shop. Rumilly is a larger village, around 5 km. to the south, and has two supermarkets and a wider selection of shops, cafes and restaurants. It also has a popular market every Thursday. Annecy is, of course, a delightful town and its old quarters and lakeside promenades are highly recommended.

Facilities

Bar/restaurant. Swimming pool. Paddling pool. Play area. Tourist information. Entertainment and activity programme. Chalets and caravans for rent. Off site: Village centre 500 m. Rumilly 5 km. Vineyards. Mountain biking.

Open: 1 April - 31 October.

Directions

Approaching from then north, leave A40 autoroute at exit 11 and head south on D1508 and D1504 to Frangy. Then continue south on D910 to Vallières and then follow signs to the site. GPS: 45.90194, 5.92766

Charges guide

Per unit incl. 2 persons and electricity	€ 18,05 - € 19,00

Vallon-Pont-d'Arc

Castel Camping Nature Parc l'Ardéchois

Route touristique des Gorges, F-07150 Vallon-Pont-d'Arc (Ardèche) T: **04 75 88 06 63**
E: **ardecamp@bigfoot.com** **alanrogers.com/FR07120**

This very high quality, family run site is within walking distance of Vallon-Pont-d'Arc. It borders the River Ardèche and canoe trips are run, professionally, direct from the site. This campsite is ideal for families with younger children seeking an active holiday. The facilities are comprehensive and of an extremely high standard, particularly the central toilet block. Of the 244 pitches, there are 225 for tourers, separated by trees and individual shrubs. All have electrical connections (6/10A) and 125 have full services. Forming a focal point are the bar and restaurant (good menus), with a terrace and stage overlooking the attractive heated pool. There is also a large paddling pool and sunbathing terrace. For children, there is a well thought out play area plus plenty of other space for youngsters to play, both on the site and along the river. Activities are organised throughout the season; these are family based – no discos. Patrols at night ensure a good night's sleep. Access to the site is easy and suitable for large outfits. A member of 'Leading Campings Group'.

Facilities

Two well equipped toilet blocks, one superb with everything working automatically. Facilities are of the highest standard, very clean and catering for babies, campers with disabilities, washing up and laundry. Four private bathrooms to hire. Washing machines. Well stocked shop. Swimming pool and paddling pool (no Bermuda shorts). Tennis. Very good play area. Internet access. Organised activities, canoe trips. Only gas barbecues are permitted. Communal barbecue area. Off site: Canoeing, rafting, walking, riding, mountain biking, golf, rock climbing, bowling, wine tasting and dining. Vallon-Pont-d'Arc 800 m. Explore the real Ardèche on the minor roads and visit Labaume, Bazakuc and Largentière (market Tuesday).

Open: 1 April - 30 September.

Directions

From Vallon-Pont-d'Arc (western end of the Ardèche Gorge) at a roundabout go east on the D290. Site entrance is shortly on the right.
GPS: 44.39804, 4.39878

Charges guide

Per unit incl. 2 persons and electricity	€ 29,50 - € 44,00
extra person	€ 5,80 - € 9,30
child (2-13 yrs)	€ 4,20 - € 7,20
dog	€ 3,40 - € 7,20

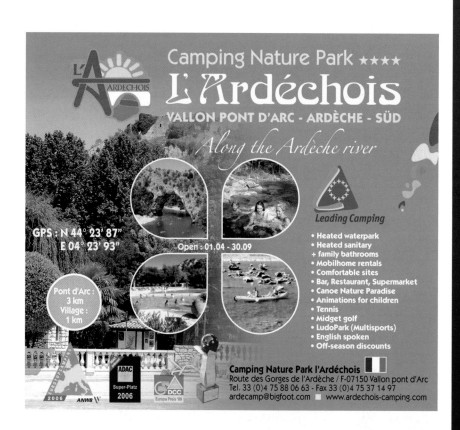

Vallon-Pont-d'Arc

Camping la Roubine

Route de Ruoms, F-07150 Vallon-Pont-d'Arc (Ardèche) T: **04 75 88 04 56**. E: **roubine.ardeche@wanadoo.fr**
alanrogers.com/FR07310

This site on the bank of the Ardèche has been in the same family ownership for some 30 years. During this time there has been constant upgrading and it must now be considered one of the best sites in the area. There are 114 touring pitches, all with electricity (10A) and quite spacious. Well tended grass, trimmed hedging and mature trees and smart tarmac roads create a calm and well kept atmosphere. The proprietors, M. Moulin and Mme. Van Eck like to welcome their guests and are available to help during the day – they are rightly proud of their well run campsite. Much attention is given to cleanliness – the toilet blocks are cleaned three times a day. A variety of sporting facilities are available on the site. The pool complex is heated when necessary throughout the season. There is a bar and restaurant of most modern design which, together with a mini-market, are open throughout the season. The campsite also caters for their young visitors with children's club in high season complete with an adventure playground and even an amphitheatre. There is an internet room for visitors.

Facilities

Several small sanitary blocks include washbasins in cubicles. The main toilet block has showers, washbasins in vanity units, a baby bathroom and facilities for disabled visitors. Laundry. Swimming pools, paddling pool and seperate childrens pool. Tennis. Boules, Fishing. Barbecues only permitted on communal sites. River beach. Off site: Bicycle hire and riding 1 km. Footpath to town 700 m. Supermarket in town.

Open: 26 April - 18 September.

Directions

From Vallon take the D579 towards Ruoms. Site is well signed on left 400 m. from town. From west (Ruoms) site signed on right near Vallon town sign. If missed proceed to roundabout at entrance to Vallon, go around and return some 400 m. (as above).
GPS: 44.40547, 4.37916

Charges guide

Per unit incl. 2 persons and electricity	€ 22,50 - € 41,00
extra person	€ 3,40 - € 8,20
child (0-13 yrs)	€ 1,50 - € 7,20
dog	free - € 4,00

Venosc

Camping le Champ du Moulin

Bourg d'Arud, F-38520 Venosc (Isère) T: **04 76 80 07 38**. E: **info@champ-du-moulin.com**
alanrogers.com/FR38110

Le Champ du Moulin is in the narrow Vénéon valley at an altitude of 960 m., so the days may be hot and the nights cool. It is open summer and winter and has 84 level stone and grass pitches, 69 used for touring. They are delineated by a variety of trees that offer some shade and all have electricity (6/10A). Rock pegs are essential. When the mountain snow melts in Spring the river beside the site changes a trickle to an impressive torrent and parents need to be especially vigilant. Large units are accepted but please book ahead.

Facilities

Heated, well equipped toilet block. Baby room. Facilities for disabled people. Motorcaravan services. Chalet restaurant and bar with home cooking. Small shop in reception selling bread. Play area. Sauna. TV room. Internet/WiFi. Boules. Fishing. Off site: Municipal heated outdoor pools and flume next door open in summer, playground, tennis, tree-top adventure park. Rafting, canoeing, paragliding, bungee jumping, hill walking and summer mountain biking available nearby. Discounted ski passes. Golf 3 km. (summer only).

Open: 15 December - 30 April, 1 June - 15 September.

Directions

From Grenoble bypass Bourg-d'Oisans on the RD1091, signed Briançon. After 3 km. turn right on D530 signed Venosc. In 8 km. pass the telecabin on left. Site on right in 400 m. GPS: 44.98695, 6.11992

Charges guide

Per unit incl. 1 or 2 persons	€ 13,60 - € 19,40
extra person	€ 2,40 - € 4,90
electricity (3/6/10A)	€ 4,20 - € 8,30

Vernioz

Kawan Village le Bontemps

5 impasse du Bontemps, F-38150 Vernioz (Isère) T: **04 74 57 83 52**
E: **info@campinglebontemps.com** **alanrogers.com/FR38120**

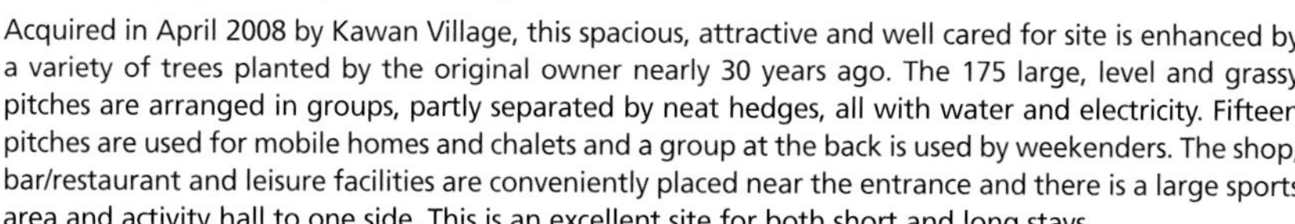

Acquired in April 2008 by Kawan Village, this spacious, attractive and well cared for site is enhanced by a variety of trees planted by the original owner nearly 30 years ago. The 175 large, level and grassy pitches are arranged in groups, partly separated by neat hedges, all with water and electricity. Fifteen pitches are used for mobile homes and chalets and a group at the back is used by weekenders. The shop, bar/restaurant and leisure facilities are conveniently placed near the entrance and there is a large sports area and activity hall to one side. This is an excellent site for both short and long stays.

Facilities

Two toilet blocks. Motorcaravan service points. Shop, bar (all season). Restaurant and takeaway (15/4-15/9). Swimming pool (all season). Several play areas. Minigolf. Tennis. Badminton. Electronic games. Fitness equipment. Extensive list of activities for all the family (high season). Small fishing lake. Off site: Small river for fishing. Vernioz 2 km. Bicycle hire 20 km. Vienne 20 km. Golf 20 km. Pilat Regional Park 15 km.

Open: 28 March - 31 October.

Directions

From the A7 south of Lyons take exit 9. Continue south for about 7 km. on N7. Just north of Auberives turn left on D37. Follow campsite signs for 7 km. Entrance is on right 4 km. beyond Vernioz.
GPS: 45.4283, 4.928233

Charges guide

Per unit incl. 2 persons	€ 21,50 - € 28,00
extra person	€ 2,50 - € 6,00

Camping Cheques accepted.

Villard-de-Lans

Camping l'Oursière

F-38250 Villard-de-Lans (Isère) T: **04 76 95 14 77**. E: **info@camping-oursiere.fr**
alanrogers.com/FR38070

This friendly, family run site is within easy walking distance of the attractive resort of Villard-de-Lans. The town provides a wide range of summer and winter activities and therefore little is organised on site. It is ideal for those who prefer a peaceful site in a more natural setting. The 186 good sized grass and stone pitches are slightly uneven but with magnificent views over the surrounding mountains. There are 146 for touring, most with electricity (6/10A). A variety of trees offer some shade. Rock pegs are essential. This is an excellent value for money site and a good base for those seeking a relaxing or active holiday.

Facilities

Clean, heated toilet blocks with all necessary facilities including those for disabled campers, ski store and drying room. Motorcaravan services. Single building houses reception, bar and snack bar (both July/Aug), cosy lounge with open fireplace, TV room, games rooms. Internet access and WiFi. Play area. Boules. Trout fishing. Off site: Bus to Autrans and Grenoble. Free bus to ski resorts (winter). Supermarket 1 km. Bicycle hire 1 km. Skiing 2 km. Riding 4 km. Golf 8 km.

Open: All year excl. 28 September - 4 December.

Directions

Northwest of Grenoble, leave A48 autoroute at exit 13 or 3A. Follow N532 to Sassenage, at roundabout take D531. In 25 km on entering Villard-de-Lans, fork left signed Villard Centre, site is shortly on left. Only route for caravans and motorcaravans.
GPS: 45.077583, 5.55616

Charges 2010

Per unit incl. 2 persons and electricity	€ 18,00 - € 22,50
extra person	€ 3,60 - € 4,85

Villeneuve-de-Berg

Domaine le Pommier

RN102, F-07170 Villeneuve-de-Berg (Ardèche) T: **04 75 94 82 81**. E: **info@campinglepommier.com**

alanrogers.com/FR07110

Domaine Le Pommier is an extremely spacious Dutch-owned site of ten hectares in 32-hectares of wooded grounds. The site is steeply terraced (a tractor is available for assistance) and has wonderful views over the Ardèche mountains and beyond. There are 423 pitches with 275 for tourists. They are grassy/stony, of good size and well spaced. Separated by young trees and hedges, some have little or no shade. All have access to electricity, and water is close by. The site is not recommended for large units. Recent developments include a mini-farm, with llamas, goats and ponies, and a pancake restaurant.

Facilities

Four excellent toilet blocks, one with underfloor heating, provide all the necessary facilities. Comprehensive shop. Bar/restaurant. Swimming pool complex with slides, paddling pools, etc. Boules. Minigolf. Activities including games in the woods, archery, water polo and tug-of-war. Bridge and water colour classes. Tennis. Soundproof disco. Very extensive programme of events on and off site. Low season excursions. Off site: Villeneuve-de-Berg 1.5 km. River Ardèche 12 km. Potholing, rock climbing, canoeing, canyoning, mountain biking, walking or riding.

Open: 30 April - 18 September.

Directions

Site is west of Montélimar on the N102. The entrance is adjacent to the roundabout at the eastern end of the Villeneuve-de-Berg bypass.
GPS: 44.57250, 4.51115

Charges guide

Per unit incl. 2 persons and electricity	€ 21,50 - € 35,50
extra person	€ 2,50 - € 7,00

Max. 6 persons per pitch.
Special offers for longer stays in low season.

Vinsobres

Camping le Sagittaire

Pont de Mirabel, F-26110 Vinsobres (Drôme) T: **04 75 27 00 00**. E: **camping.sagittaire@wanadoo.fr**

alanrogers.com/FR26100

Le Sagittaire is beautifully situated in this picturesque region with its Côtes du Rhône vineyards, lavender fields and medieval hilltop villages. It is only 2.5 km. from Vinsobres and 6 km. from Nyons, well known for its olives and its Provençal market. There are 270 level grassy pitches with 124 for touring, all with electricity (6/10A). Most are separated by hedges and there are mature trees offering some shade. The hub of the site is a water park with indoor and outdoor pools, slides and toboggans. A one-hectare lake surrounded by a sandy beach is ideal for children.

Facilities

Three excellent modern toilet blocks. Facilities for disabled campers and families. Motorcaravan services. Shop. Bar with TVs. Restaurant. Takeaway. Games room (1/4-30/9). Outdoor swimming pool, toboggan, slides, lazy river, cascades (1/5-30/8). Heated covered pool, paddling pool, jacuzzi (1/4-30/9). Small lake with sandy beach, picnic area. Excellent range of sporting facilities. Play areas. Fitness room. Extensive programme family activities in July/Aug. Fishing. Bicycle hire. Minigolf. Charcoal barbecues not allowed. Cycling is forbidden. Off site: Riding nearby. Nyons, Vaison la Romaine, Chateaux at Grignan and Suze la Rousse. Mont Ventoux for keen cyclists. Mediterranean beaches 1.5 hours away.

Open: All year.

Directions

Leave A7 at exit 19 (Bollène) and follow signs for Nyons (D94). Site is well signed on right just beyond Vinsobres (about 30 km). GPS: 44.32773, 5.07905

Charges guide

Per unit incl. 2 persons	€ 17,50 - € 31,00
extra person	€ 3,60 - € 7,50
child (under 7 yrs)	€ 2,10 - € 4,50
electricity (3/6A)	€ 3,70 - € 4,80

Long stay off season discounts.

From the endless shimmering beaches and dunes and the fragrant pine forests of the Atlantic coast to the historical and beautiful Dordogne with its gastronomic delights, it's easy to see the attraction of this popular holiday region.

DÉPARTEMENTS: 24 DORDOGNE, 33 GIRONDE, 40 LANDES, 47 LOT-ET-GARONNE, 64 PYRÉNÉES-ATLANTIQUES

MAJOR CITY: BORDEAUX

The history of Aquitaine goes back many thousands of years to when man lived in the caves of the Périgord and left cave paintings at sites such as Les Eyzies and Lascaux. The ancient dukedom of Aquitaine was ruled by the English for 300 years following the marriage of Eleanor of Aquitaine to Henry Plantagenet, the future king, in 1154. The fortified villages and castles of the area bear evidence of the resulting conflict between the French and the English for control of Aquitaine, and today add character to the countryside.

This is a diverse region of mountains and vineyards, vast beaches, fertile river valleys, rolling grasslands and dense forests. Within its boundaries are the beautiful valleys of the Dordogne and Vézère, the forests of the Landes and the beaches of the Atlantic which stretch from the Gironde estuary to the Basque Country and the rocky Pyrénées mountains on the Spanish border.

Some of the world's most famous vineyards are around Bordeaux, the capital of the region. These are especially famous for their Médoc, Sauternes and St Emilion wines and most châteaux allow visits to their cellars and wine tastings.

Places of interest

Agen: a rich agricultural area, famous for its prunes.

Bordeaux: 14,000-piece Bohemian glass chandelier in foyer of the Grand Theatre, 29-acre Esplanade des Quinconces.

Rocamadour: cliffside medieval pilgrimage site.

Saint Cirq-La Popie: medieval village perched on a cliff.

St Emilion: visit the castle ramparts or drink 'premier cru' St Emilion at pavement cafés.

St Jean-de-Luz: seaside resort and fishing village.

St Jean-Pied-de-Port: ancient city with citadel, bright Basque houses in steep streets.

Cuisine of the region

Local specialities include fish dishes: carp stuffed with foie gras, mullet in red wine and besugo (sea bream), plus cagouilles (snails from Charentes).

Cassoulet: a hearty stew of duck, sausages and beans.

Cèpes: fine, delicate mushrooms; sometimes dried.

Chorizos: spicy sausages.

Chou farci: stuffed cabbage, sometimes aux marrons (with chestnuts).

Foie Gras: specially prepared livers of geese and ducks, stuffed with truffles.

Magret de canard: duck breast fillets.

Lamproie: eel-like fish with leeks, onions and red Bordeaux wine.

www.tourisme-aquitaine.fr/en
tourisme@tourisme-aquitaine.fr
(0)5 56 01 70 00

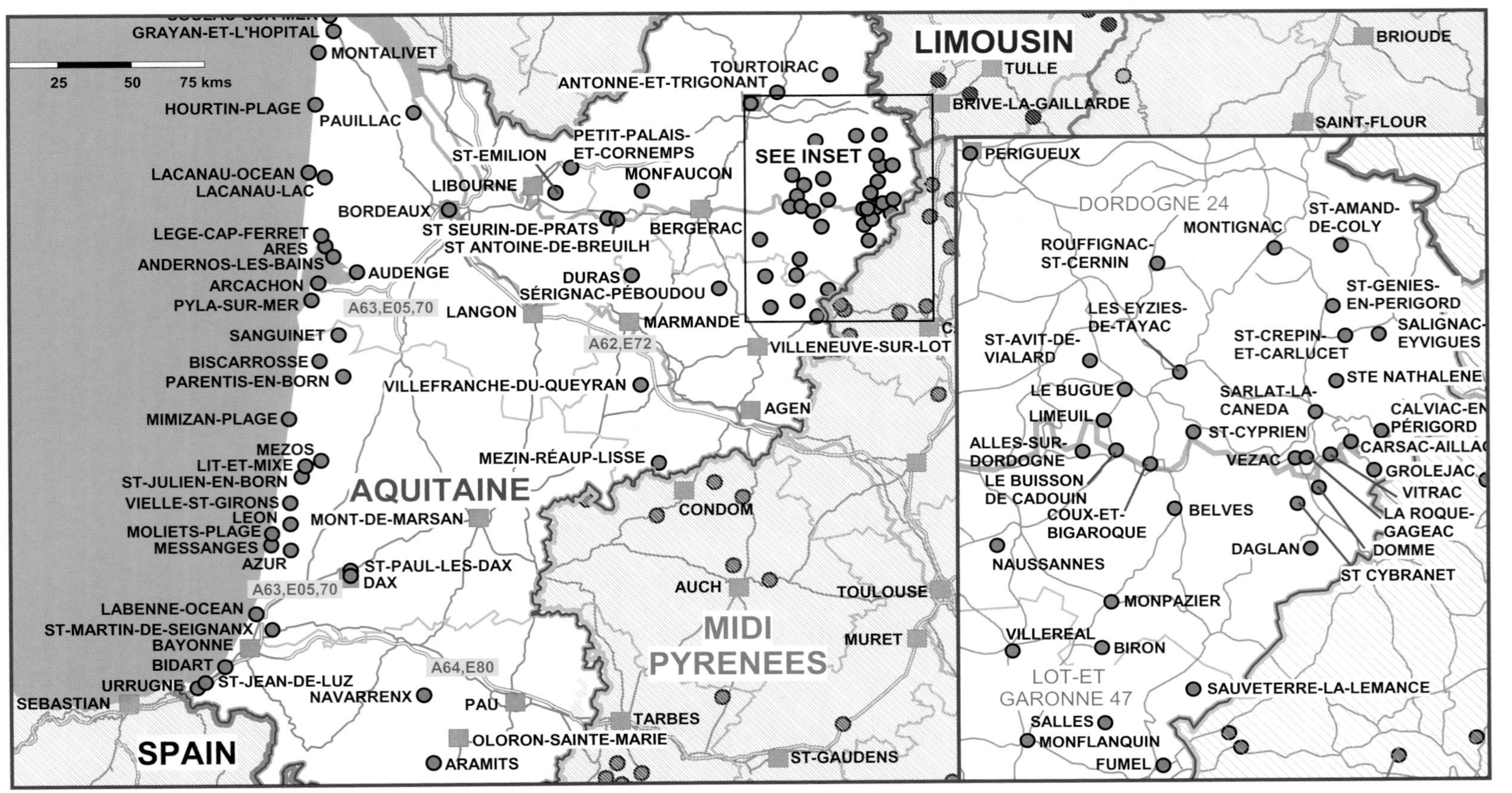

GRAYAN-ET-L'HOPITAL
MONTALIVET
25
50
75 kms
HOURTIN-PLAGE
PAUILLAC
LACANAU-OCEAN
LACANAU-LAC
BORDEAUX
LIBOURNE
ST-EMILION
PETIT-PALAIS-ET-CORNEMPS
MONFAUCON
ANTONNE-ET-TRIGONANT
TOURTOIRAC
SEE INSET
LIMOUSIN
TULLE
BRIVE-LA-GAILLARDE
BRIOUDE
SAINT-FLOUR
LEGE-CAP-FERRET
ARES
ANDERNOS-LES-BAINS
ARCACHON
PYLA-SUR-MER
AUDENGE
ST SEURIN-DE-PRATS
ST ANTOINE-DE-BREUILH
BERGERAC
DURAS
SÉRIGNAC-PÉBOUDOU
A63,E05,70
LANGON
MARMANDE
SANGUINET
A62,E72
VILLENEUVE-SUR-LOT
BISCARROSSE
PARENTIS-EN-BORN
VILLEFRANCHE-DU-QUEYRAN
MIMIZAN-PLAGE
AGEN
MEZOS
LIT-ET-MIXE
ST-JULIEN-EN-BORN
MEZIN-RÉAUP-LISSE
AQUITAINE
VIELLE-ST-GIRONS
LEON
MOLIETS-PLAGE
MESSANGES
AZUR
MONT-DE-MARSAN
CONDOM
ST-PAUL-LES-DAX
DAX
A63,E05,70
AUCH
TOULOUSE
LABENNE-OCEAN
ST-MARTIN-DE-SEIGNANX
BAYONNE
BIDART
URRUGNE
ST-JEAN-DE-LUZ
SEBASTIAN
A64,E80
NAVARRENX
PAU
MIDI PYRENEES
MURET
TARBES
OLORON-SAINTE-MARIE
ARAMITS
ST-GAUDENS
SPAIN
PERIGUEUX
DORDOGNE 24
MONTIGNAC
ST-AMAND-DE-COLY
ROUFFIGNAC-ST-CERNIN
LES EYZIES-DE-TAYAC
ST-GENIES-EN-PERIGORD
ST-AVIT-DE-VIALARD
ST-CREPIN-ET-CARLUCET
SALIGNAC-EYVIGUES
STE NATHALENE
LE BUGUE
SARLAT-LA-CANEDA
CALVIAC-EN-PÉRIGORD
LIMEUIL
ST-CYPRIEN
ALLES-SUR-DORDOGNE
CARSAC-AILLAC
VEZAC
GROLEJAC
LE BUISSON DE CADOUIN
VITRAC
COUX-ET-BIGAROQUE
BELVES
LA ROQUE-GAGEAC
DOMME
DAGLAN
NAUSSANNES
ST CYBRANET
MONPAZIER
VILLEREAL
BIRON
LOT-ET-GARONNE 47
SAUVETERRE-LA-LEMANCE
SALLES
MONFLANQUIN
FUMEL

Allés-sur-Dordogne

Camping le Port de Limeuil

F-24480 Allés-sur-Dordogne (Dordogne) T: **05 53 63 29 76**. E: **didierbonvallet@aol.com**
alanrogers.com/FR24170

At the confluence of Dordogne and Vézère rivers, opposite the picturesque village of Limeiul, this delightful family site exudes a peaceful and relaxed ambience. There are 75 marked touring pitches on grass, some spacious and all with electricity (5/10A). The buildings are in traditional Périgourdine style and surrounded by flowers and shrubs. A sports area on a large open grassy space between the river bank and the main camping area adds to the feeling of space and provides an additional recreation and picnic area (there are additional unmarked pitches for tents and camper vans along the bank here).

Facilities

Two clean, modern toilet blocks provide excellent facilities. Bar/restaurant with snacks and takeaway (all 20/5-5/9). Small shop. Swimming pool with jacuzzi, paddling pool and children's slide (1/5-30/9). Badminton, football and boules. Trampoline. Mountain bike hire. Canoe hire, launched from the site's own pebble beach. WiFi in bar area (free). Off site: The pretty medieval village of Limeuil 200 m. Riding 1 km. Golf 10 km.

Open: 1 May - 30 September.

Directions

Site is 7 km. south of Le Bugue. From the D51/D31E Le Buisson to Le Bugue road turn west towards Limeuil. Just before bridge into Limeuil, turn left (site signed), across another bridge. Site shortly on the right. GPS: 44.87977, 0.88587

Charges 2010

Per unit incl. 2 persons and electricity	€ 16,50 - € 25,40
extra person	€ 2,50 - € 6,50

Andernos-les-Bains

Camping Caravaning Fontaine-Vieille

4 boulevard du Colonel Wurtz, F-33510 Andernos-les-Bains (Gironde) T: **05 56 82 01 67**
E: **contact@fontaine-vieille.com** **alanrogers.com/FR33020**

Fontaine-Vieille is a large, traditional site that has been operating for over 50 years. The site stretches along the eastern edge of the Bassin d'Arcachon under light woodland in the residential area of the small town of Andernos. Popular with the French, it has nearly 700 individual pitches, of which 520 are touring pitches (about 400 with electricity). On flat, grassy or sandy ground, they are marked by stones in the ground or young trees. Some pitches have excellent views of the Bassin, but a premium is charged.

Facilities

Seven adequate sanitary blocks with facilities for people with disabilities and children. Shop (1/6-15/9). Bar, terrace, takeaway and restaurant (15/5-15/9). Swimming pool complex. Tennis. TV room. Play areas for little ones and adventure area for older children. Minigolf. Boats, sailboards. Sports organised (high season). Internet access. Communal barbecue areas (only gas may be used on pitches). Off site: Grocery shop and bakery 1 km. Town centre 2.5 km. Golf 3 km. Riding 5 km.

Open: 1 April - 30 September.

Directions

From A63 at exit 22, take A660 towards Arcachon. Turn off A660 at exit 2 towards Facture then take RD3 north along edge of the Bassin. Site signed to left as you enter Andernos. GPS: 44.72603, -1.08076

Charges guide

Per unit incl. 2 persons	€ 13,30 - € 20,40
incl. electricity (5A)	€ 17,10 - € 27,10
extra person	€ 2,60 - € 6,00

Camping Cheques accepted.

Antonne-et-Trigonant

Camping Caravaning le Bois du Coderc

Route des Gaunies, F-24420 Antonne-et-Trigonant (Dordogne) T: **05 53 05 99 83**
E: **coderc-camping@wanadoo.fr** **alanrogers.com/FR24410**

Located in the scenic Perigord region, 10 km. from Périgueux, le Bois du Coderc, under new ownership, has been completely renovated. It is a calm, picturesque, part wooded, riverside site, ideally situated for visiting many interesting places. The touring pitches (there are no individual marked-out pitches) and mobile homes are spaced out over a field and woodland, with electricity hook-ups (10A) and water points. This campsite has a calm, relaxing atmosphere. However, it is well placed near the historical town of Périgueux which is rich in history and culture and full of charm and character, with cobbled streets, various squares with restaurants, bars and a large selection of shops.

Facilities

One male and female sanitary block with preset showers (no charge) clean and well maintained (only one toilet and a shower are open in winter). Baby changing area. Dishwashing area. Laundry facilities. Small shop and bar (all year). Snacks and takeaway (July/Aug). Bar/games room. Small play area. The river Isle runs through the campsite and is suitable for paddling. WiFi. Heated (15/5-15/9) outdoor swimming pool.

Open: All year.

Directions

Heading north on the N21 Limoges - Périgueux road, 2.5 km. north of Antonne et Trigonant turn right at Routier Restaurant (near km. marker 49). Continue along this country road following signs. Travelling south from Limoges direction turn is on left 3 km. south of Sarliac sur L'Isle. GPS: 45.2194, 0.8636

Charges guide

Per unit incl. 2 persons and electricity	€ 14,20 - € 17,00
extra person	€ 1,50 - € 3,50

Reductions in mid and low seasons.

Aramits

Camping Barétous-Pyrénées

Quartier Ripaude, F-64570 Aramits (Pyrénées-Atlantiques) T: **05 59 34 12 21**. E: **atso64@hotmail.com**
alanrogers.com/FR64020

Located on the edge of the Pyrénées, this quiet site is well away from the tourist bustle, particularly in early or late season. It has a rural location, yet is close to the town. This is a wonderful location for exploring the region and offers a peaceful haven for those wishing to stay in quiet surroundings. The shady, grass pitches are attractive and of a good size with hedges. They offer both water and electricity (10A). The welcoming reception (English is spoken) sells local produce and organic food. The heated swimming and paddling pool area is overlooked by a small sun terrace with a café/bar.

Facilities

Two sanitary blocks, one old, one modern, offer clean facilities with unisex toilets and showers. Facilities for disabled visitors. Café/bar (July/Aug). Heated swimming and paddling pools (May-Sept). Communal room with TV, games, library and drinks. Small shop selling organic food. Boules. Small play area with sandpit. Off site: Town with supermarket and ATM 250 m. Fishing 50 m. Riding 3 km. Snow skiing 25 km.

Open: 1 March - 31 October.

Directions

From Oloron-Sainte-Marie, head southwest on the D919 to Aramits. Through village bear right on the D918. Cross river and immediately turn right at campsite sign. GPS: 43.1214, -0.732317

Charges 2010

Per unit incl. 2 persons and electricity	€ 18,30 - € 24,80

Camping Cheques accepted.

Arès

Camping la Cigale

Route de Lège, F-33740 Arès (Gironde) T: **05 56 60 22 59**. E: **campinglacigaleares@wanadoo.fr**
alanrogers.com/FR33120

La Cigale is an attractive little site with charm and ambience where the owners extend a very warm welcome. Small and beautifully maintained, it is set amid a variety of trees that give some dappled shade. M. Pallet's floral displays add colour to the 41 neatly hedged, grassy touring pitches (100 sq.m. and most with 6A electricity, ten also with water and drainage). There is a small, unheated swimming pool and a paddling pool. The bar has a terrace where drinks, meals and snacks are served under the shade of large plane trees. The six delightful chalets for rent are spacious, modern and well presented.

Facilities

The well equipped toilet block includes a family room with two showers and facilities for disabled visitors. Washing machine and dryer. Motorcaravan services. Simple shop. Bar, terrace, meals, snacks. Pizza takeaway (all 17/6-10/9). Swimming and paddling pools (25/5-12/9). Small play area. Entertainers for children and adults in July/Aug. Free donkey cart rides every Sunday in season. Off site: Site is convenient for a wide choice of beaches. Village centre 800 m. Fishing or riding 1 km.

Open: 5 May - 30 September.

Directions

Leave Bordeaux ring road at exit 10 (D213) or exit 11 (D106) and continue direct to Arès. Turn into Arès following road to church square. Turn right following signs for Lège-Cap Ferret. Site is 800 m. on left. GPS: 44.772917, -1.142233

Charges guide

Per unit incl. 2 persons	€ 19,00 - € 29,00
extra person	€ 6,00
child (0-7 yrs)	€ 3,00
electricity (4/6A)	€ 5,50

Arès

Flower Camping la Canadienne

Route de Lège, 82 rue Genéral de Gaulle, F-33740 Arès (Gironde) T: **05 56 60 24 91**
E: **info@lacanadienne.com** **alanrogers.com/FR33420**

La Canadienne is situated between Arcachon and Lège-Cap Ferret, just 7 km. from the beach and 1 km. from the centre of Arès, a pleasant little resort. There is direct access to 150 km. of cycle tracks. The campsite has 60 mobile homes for rent and 20 touring pitches, most with 15A electricity. Good shade is provided by tall oak trees. Swimming and paddling pools are centrally located, along with a shop, bar, restaurant and snack bar. In July and August dancing, musical and paella evenings are organised, together with children's clubs (3-10 yrs) and sports tournaments. Large units may have difficulty manoeuvring onto some pitches.

Facilities

Sanitary facilities are clean but in need of some updating. Shop. Bar, restaurant, snack bar and takeaway (1/7-31/8). Swimming pool (1/6-15/9). Play area. Bicycle hire. TV room. Activity and entertainment programme. Mobile homes and equipped tents for rent. Off site: Village centre 1 km. Riding 5 km. Fishing 7 km. Golf 15 km. Dune du Pyla. Cycle tracks.

Open: 1 February - 29 November.

Directions

Leave the Bordeaux ring road at exit 10 (D213) and drive to Arès. Continue to the village centre and then follow signs for Lège and Cap Ferret. Site is on this road after a further 1 km. GPS: 44.77792, -1.1428

Charges guide

Per unit incl. 2 persons and electricity	€ 17,90 - € 31,90
extra person	€ 3,00 - € 6,00

Arcachon

Camping Club Arcachon

5 allée Galaxie, B.P. 46, F-33312 Arcachon Cedex (Gironde) T: **05 56 83 24 15**

E: **info@camping-arcachon.com** **alanrogers.com/FR33030**

This campsite enjoys a position well back from the hustle and bustle, where nights are quiet and facilities are of a high standard. The 176 touring pitches are divided into areas for tents, caravans, and motorcaravans and are on neatly-formed terraces beneath tall pine trees. Most have electricity (6/10A). The site is quite hilly and the narrow roads that wind around it could possibly make it difficult for larger motorcaravans to manoeuvre and find suitable pitches. At night, wardens ensure that security and noise levels are controlled. A 1 km. walk takes you to the town of Arcachon where there are plenty of shops, bars and restaurants. However, the campsite bar, restaurant and takeaway are open at weekends from April to September (daily in July/August) if you prefer to stay on site. Watersports, paragliding, sailing, tennis tournaments, climbing the biggest sand dune in Europe and not forgetting such gastronomic delights as oysters and mussels, are readily available.

Facilities

Three sanitary blocks with the usual facilities. Motorcaravan services. Washing machine, dryers. Fridge hire. Shop (15/6-15/9). Bar, restaurant, snack bar, takeaway (April-Sept). Swimming pool (1/5-30/9). Bicycle hire. Play area. Games room. Children's club and entertainment for all age groups (1/7-31/8). Barbecues are only permitted in communal areas. Internet access and WiFi. Off site: Beach 1.8 km. Arcachon 2-3 km. Riding 1 km. Golf 2 km.

Open: All year (excl. 12 November - 12 December).

Directions

Approaching Arcachon from Bordeaux on the N250 take exit for 'Hopital Jean Hameau' (D217). Cross over bypass following signs for hospital, then signs for Abatilles. At next roundabout follow signs for 'Camping'. Take care as the route travels through suburban housing. Follow campsite signs, not satnav. GPS: 44.6513, -1.174083

Charges guide

Per unit incl. 2 persons	€ 13,00 - € 31,00
extra person	€ 4,00 - € 8,00
child (4-10 yrs)	€ 1,00
electricity	€ 3,00 - € 4,00
animal	€ 2,00 - € 4,00

The Travel Service to book this site call 01580 214000 ...we'll arrange everything

Audenge

Camping le Braou

Route de Bordeaux, F-33980 Audenge (Gironde) T: **05 56 26 90 03**. E: **info@camping-audenge.com**
alanrogers.com/FR33260

The present owners, M. and Mme. Gharbi, were the wardens of this simple, former municipal site and now lease it from the town. They have funded several developments since they took over in 2003, including a swimming pool, a snack bar, play area and new electrical hook-ups. The site is flat with easy access, and the large pitches are in avenues, separated by newly-planted small shrubs. There is little natural shade. The new electricity hook-ups (on 116 of the 148 pitches) are 10A. Outside high season this is a pleasant, reasonably priced place to stay while exploring the Bassin d'Arcachon with its bird reserve, oyster-beds, way-marked walks and cycle tracks.

Facilities

The two toilet blocks have been recently refurbished and are very adequate. Washbasins are in cubicles, showers are controllable for temperature, pushbutton operated. Shop for basics. Bar and snack bar (July/Aug). Swimming pool (1/6-31/8). Play area. Internet access. Motorcaravan service point and overnight pitches outside site. Mobile homes to rent. Off site: Town facilities 800 m. Beach and fishing 15 km. Riding 2 km. Golf 5 km.

Open: 1 April - 30 September.

Directions

From A63 take exit 22 onto A660 towards Arcachon. From A660 take exit 2 towards Facture, then the D3 through Biganos to Audenge. Site is signed 'Camping Municipal' at lights in town.
GPS: 44.6841, -1.00433

Charges guide

Per person	€ 3,00 - € 5,00
child (4-13 yrs)	€ 3,00 - € 4,50
pitch	€ 10,50 - € 17,50
electricity (10A)	€ 3,50 - € 3,50

Azur

Camping Village la Paillotte

66 route des campings, F-40140 Azur (Landes) T: **05 58 48 12 12**. E: **info@paillotte.com**
alanrogers.com/FR40040

La Paillotte, in the Landes area of southwest France, is a site with a character of its own. It lies beside the Soustons Lake only 1.5 km. from Azur village, with its own sandy beach. This is suitable for young children because the lake is shallow and slopes gradually. All 310 pitches at La Paillotte are mostly shady with shrubs and trees. The 132 pitches for touring vary in price according to size, position and whether they are serviced. La Paillotte is an unusual site with its own atmosphere which appeals to many regular clients. The campsite buildings (reception, shop, restaurant, even sanitary blocks) are all Tahitian in style. Circular in shape and constructed from local woods with the typical straw roof (and a layer of waterproof material underneath), some are now being replaced but still in character. For boating the site has a small private harbour where you can keep your own non-powered boat (of shallow draught).

Facilities

Well equipped toilet blocks. Washing machines, dryers. Motorcaravan services. Shop (1/6-1/9). Good restaurant with terrace overlooking lake, bar, takeaway (all 22/4-24/9). Swimming pool complex (22/4-24/9). Sports, games and organised activities. Miniclub. TV room, library. Fishing. Bicycle hire. Sailing, rowing boats and pedaloes for hire. Torches useful. Dogs are not accepted. Off site: Riding 5 km. Golf 10 km. Atlantic beaches 10 km.

Open: 24 April - 20 September.

Directions

Coming from the north along N10, turn west on D150 at Magescq. From south go via Soustons. In Azur turn left before church (site signed).
GPS: 43.78696, -1.3093

Charges guide

Per unit incl. 2 persons and 10A electricity	€ 15,50 - € 38,00
incl. electricity and water	€ 17,50 - € 40,00
pitch by the lake	€ 20,00 - € 46,00
extra person (over 4 yrs)	€ 3,00 - € 7,50

Belvès

Camping les Hauts de Ratebout

Saint Foy de Belvès, F-24170 Belvès (Dordogne) T: **05 53 29 02 10**. E: **camping@hauts-ratebout.fr**

alanrogers.com/FR24050

A member of the FranceLoc chain of sites, Les Hauts de Ratebout is situated in the hills of the Perigord Noir. There are stunning views of the surrounding countryside from many of the 260 terraced pitches which are mostly shady and level. They vary in size (100-240 sq.m), all with 10A electricity and some with water and drainage. There are 91 mobile homes and chalets to rent, together with four houses. A tour operator has 40 pitches for tents. Large motorhomes and twin axled caravans are accepted by prior arrangement. There is a good restaurant with an extensive menu and reasonably priced food. Ingredients are locally produced where possible. There are two swimming pools, one heated and covered in low season. There is also a pool for younger children. Slides and toboggans complement the area. There are many sporting activities on site and in high season there is a children's club and disco nights. The walled town of Belvès is well worth a visit.

Facilities

Four high standard toilet blocks offer the usual amenities including private washbasins and facilities for people with disabilities. Washing machines and dryers. Small shop (with gas) and takeaway service. Restaurant/bar and second bar and terrace. Swimming pool complex (proper trunks). Adventure playground on gravel. General room with pool and football tables and TV. Tennis. Organised activities in season. Nightly videos and sporting events. Dogs are not accepted. Off site: Fishing and bicycle hire 6 km. Riding 7 km. Golf 8 km.

Open: 13 May - 10 September.

Directions

From Belvès, take D710 southwards for 2 km. then turn east on D54. After 2 km. turn left, and after a further 500 m. left again (following campsite signs all the way). Site is 1.5 km. along on the right. GPS: 44.74175, 1.04513

Charges guide

Per unit incl. 2 persons and electricity	€ 19,00 - € 32,00
extra person	€ 5,00 - € 7,50
child (2-7 yrs)	€ 2,60 - € 6,00

Belvès

RCN le Moulin de la Pique

F-24170 Belvès (Dordogne) T: **05 53 29 01 15**. E: **info@rcn-lemoulindelapique.fr**

alanrogers.com/FR24350

This high quality campsite set in the heart of the Dordogne has fine views looking up to the fortified town of Belvès. It is a splendid rural estate where there is plenty of space and a good mixture of trees and shrubs. Set in the grounds of a former mill, the superb traditional buildings date back to the 18th century. There are 200 level pitches with 154 for touring units, all with 6A electricity, a water point and drainage. The remainder are used for mobile homes to rent. The site is ideally suited for families with young and teenage children as there is so much to do, both on site and in the surrounding area.

Facilities

Three modern sanitary blocks include facilities for disabled people. Launderette. Shop. Bar. Restaurant. Snack bar and takeaway. Swimming pools (two heated). Recreational lake. Playgrounds. Library. Fossil field. Sports field. Tennis. Minigolf. Boules. Satellite TV. Games room. Bicycle hire. Internet facilities. WiFi. Off site: Bars, restaurants and shops in the village of Belvès 2 km. Canoeing 2 km. Riding 5 km. Golf 7 km.

Open: 10 April - 2 October.

Directions

Site is 35 km. southwest of Sarlat on the D710, about 7 km. south of Siorac-en-Périgord. GPS: 44.76228, 1.01412

Charges 2010

Per unit incl. 2 persons, electricity and water	€ 7,00 - € 43,50

Camping Cheques accepted.

Belvès

Flower Camping les Nauves

Le Bos Rouge, F-24170 Belvès (Dordogne) T: **05 53 29 12 64**. E: **campinglesnauves@hotmail.com**
alanrogers.com/FR24470

Les Nauves is a pretty and well maintained site, 4 km. from the beautiful medieval village of Belvès in the Périgord Noir region of the Dordogne. The site consists of 100 pitches, 60 for touring and 40 dedicated to mobile homes, chalets and bungalow tents. There are some pitches that are separated and shaded by mature trees, while others are open with good views of the surrounding countryside. The ground on most of the pitches is soft, sandy soil and may cause some difficulty for large vehicles in wet weather. The owners are very dedicated to providing a quality site.

Facilities

The single sanitary block is clean and well maintained. Facilities for disabled visitors. Baby room (with adult shower). Laundry area with one washing machine. Good shop. Bar/restaurant with patio, and takeaway on request. Swimming pool and paddling pool. Good play area. Boules. Library (French and Dutch books). Games room. Riding. Off site: Fishing 2 km. Golf 10 km. Bicycle hire 4 km.

Open: 23 April - 25 September.

Directions

From Belvès take D53 southwest towards Monpazier. Site is 4 km. from Belvès on the left hand side. Follow signs and site is 800 m. off the main road. GPS: 44.75275, 0.98445

Charges 2010

Per unit incl. 2 persons and electricity	€ 13,95 - € 24,50
extra person	€ 2,50 - € 4,90
child (2-7 yrs)	€ 2,00 - € 3,20
dog	free - € 3,00

Bidart

Castel Camping le Ruisseau des Pyrénées

Route d'Arbonne, F-64210 Bidart (Pyrénées-Atlantiques) T: **05 59 41 94 50**
E: **francoise.dumont3@wanadoo.fr** **alanrogers.com/FR64070**

This busy site, with a large play area filled with equipment is ideal for young families. It is about 2 km. from Bidart and 2.5 km. from a sandy beach. There are two swimming pools with slides on the main site and across the road, an indoor heated pool and new spa complex (charged July/August) with outdoor fitness equipment. Pitches on the main campsite are individual, marked and of a good size, either on flat terraces or around the lake. The terrain is wooded so the great majority of them have some shade. Electrical connections are available throughout. The site has a number of steep slopes to negotiate.

Facilities

Two main blocks and some extra smaller units. Washing machines. Motorcaravan service point. Shop. Large self-service restaurant with takeaway and bar with terraces, and TV. Outdoor swimming pools, indoor pool and spa complex (all season). Sauna. Large play area. Two tennis courts (free outside July/Aug). Fitness track. TV and games rooms. Minigolf. Bicycle hire. Fishing. Internet access.
Off site: Riding and golf 3 km.

Open: 22 May - 19 September.

Directions

Site is east of Bidart on a minor road towards Arbonne. From A63 autoroute take Biarritz exit (4), turn towards St Jean-de-Luz and Bidart on N10. After Intermarché turn left at roundabout and follow signs to site. GPS: 43.4367, -1.5677

Charges guide

Per unit incl. 2 persons and electricity	€ 19,00 - € 39,00
extra person	€ 5,00 - € 7,00

Bidart

Sunêlia Berrua

Rue Berrua, F-64210 Bidart (Pyrénées-Atlantiques) T: **05 59 54 96 66**. E: **contact@berrua.com**
alanrogers.com/FR64140

Berrua is in a useful situation on the Basque coast, 10 km. from the Pyrénées, 20 km. from Spain and a five-minute drive from Biarritz. Just 1 km. from the sea, it is an ideal location for visiting the beaches in southwest France. A neat and tidy site, it has 270 level pitches (120 for touring units) set amongst trees. Most have electricity (6A) and some are fully serviced. The focal point of the site is an excellent swimming pool complex with several pools, slides and paddling pools which is surrounded by sunbeds for sunbathing. Organised activities and entertainment for both adults and children in high season, guided walks, dances, sporting competitions, bingo and karaoke. A member of the Sunêlia group.

Facilities

Toilet facilities are good (unisex) consisting of two blocks with washbasins in cabins, baby rooms, facilities for disabled visitors, washing machines. Motorcaravan services. Shop (July/Aug). Bar/restaurant and takeaway (15/4-15/9). New pool complex. Games room. Play area (3-10 yrs only). Bicycle hire. Archery. Boules. Off site: Fishing 1 km. Golf and riding 3 km. Beach 1 km.

Open: 6 April - 5 October.

Directions

From A63 exit 4, take N10 south towards Bidart. At roundabout after the Intermarché supermarket, turn left. Bear right then take next right (site signed). GPS: 43.43822, -1.58237

Charges guide

Per unit incl. 2 persons	€ 16,10 - € 30,20
electricity (6A)	€ 2,90 - € 4,90

Camping Cheques accepted.

Bidart

Camping le Pavillon Royal

Avenue du Prince de Galles, F-64210 Bidart (Pyrénées-Atlantiques) T: **05 59 23 00 54**
E: **info@pavillon-royal.com** **alanrogers.com/FR64060**

Le Pavillon Royal has an excellent situation on raised ground overlooking the sea, with good views along the coast to the south and to the north coast of Spain beyond. There is a large heated swimming pool and sunbathing area in the centre of the site. The camping area is divided up into 303 marked, level pitches, many of a good size. About 50 are reserved for tents and are only accessible on foot. The remainder are connected by asphalt roads. All have electricity and most are fully serviced. Much of the campsite is in full sun, although the area for tents is shaded. Beneath the site – and only a very short walk down – stretches a wide sandy beach where the Atlantic rollers provide ideal conditions for surfing. A central, marked-out section of the beach is supervised by lifeguards (from mid June). There is also a section with rocks and pools. Reservation in high season is advisable.

Facilities

Good quality toilet blocks with baby baths and unit for disabled people. Washing facilities are closed at night except for two single night units. Washing machines, dryers. Motorcaravan services. Shop (including gas). Restaurant and takeaway (from 1/6). Bar. Heated swimming and paddling pools. Playground. General room, TV room, games room, films. Fishing. Surf school. Dogs are not accepted. Fitness room. Off site: Golf 0.5 km. Bicycle hire 2 km. Riding 3 km. Sailing 5 km.

Open: 15 May - 30 September.

Directions

From A63 exit 4, take the N10 south towards Bidart. At roundabout after the Intermarché supermarket turn right (signed for Biarritz). After 600 m. turn left at site sign. GPS: 43.45458, -1.57649

Charges 2010

Per unit incl. 2 persons, electricity and water	€ 29,00 - € 49,00
tent pitch incl. 1 or 2 persons	€ 23,00 - € 39,00
extra person (over 4 yrs)	€ 7,50 - € 10,00

Bidart

yelloh! VILLAGE

Yelloh! Village Ilbarritz

Avenue de Biarritz, F-64210 Bidart (Pyrénées-Atlantiques) T: **04 66 73 97 39**
E: **info@yellohvillage-ilbarritz.com** **alanrogers.com/FR64150**

This is a very pleasant, reasonably priced site which will appeal greatly to couples and young families. Set on a fairly gentle hillside, the top level has reception and bar. Slightly lower are the paddling and swimming pools in a sunny location with sunbeds. Next comes the well stocked shop, tennis courts and the rest of the pitches. Some pitches are behind reception and others, lower down, some slightly sloping, are under trees and separated by hydrangea hedges. Some have electricity (10A, long leads required). There is a varied entertainment programme in July and August. The site is not suitable for American motorhomes.

Facilities

The two toilet blocks have some washbasins and showers together. Washing machines, dryers, ironing boards and facilities for disabled people. Motorcaravan services. Shop and bar open all season, restaurant (1/6-10/9) and takeaway (1/7-31/8). Pool open all season. Games room. Table tennis. Tennis (charged in July/Aug). Play area (3-8 yrs). Bicycle hire. Off site: Lake 600 m. with fishing (no licence required). Golf 1 km. Riding 1 km. Beach with lifeguard 600 m.

Open: 8 May - 20 September.

Directions

Heading south on the A63 towards Spain, take exit J4 onto the N10 towards Bidart. At the roundabout straight after Intermarche turn right towards Biarritz. The site is on the right after 1 km.
GPS: 43.4531, -1.5737

Charges guide

Per unit incl. 2 persons	€ 15,90 - € 24,50
extra person (over 2 yrs)	€ 3,30 - € 5,80
electricity	€ 3,30 - € 5,10

Camping Cheques accepted.

Biron

Camping le Moulinal

F-24540 Biron (Dordogne) T: **05 53 40 84 60**. E: **lemoulinal@perigord.com**
alanrogers.com/FR24100

A rural, lakeside site in woodland, Le Moulinal offers activities for everyone of all ages. Of the 280 grassy pitches, only around 62 are available for touring units and these are spread amongst the site's own mobile homes, chalets and a small number of British tour operator tents. All pitches are on flat grass and have 6A electricity, but vary considerably in size (75-100 sq.m). The five acre lake has a sandy beach and is suitable for boating (canoe hire is available), swimming and fishing. Ambitious, well organised animation is run throughout the season including craft activities and a children's club.

Facilities

Toilet facilities, built to harmonise with the surroundings, include facilities for disabled people and babies. Washing machines, dryers. Motorcaravan services. Excellent restaurant. Bar. Snack bar/takeaway. Large, heated swimming pool with jacuzzi and paddling pool. Rustic play area. Multisport court. Boules. Tennis. Archery. Roller skating. Mountain bike hire. All facilities are open all season. Off site: Riding and climbing 5 km. Potholing 10 km. Bastide towns of Monpazier, Villeréal and Monflanquin 15 km.

Open: 1 April - 16 September.

Directions

Site is 53 km. southeast of Bergerac. From the D104 Villeréal - Monpazier road take the D53/D150 south. Just before Lacapelle Biron turn right onto D255 towards Dévillac, (site signed). Site is 1.5 km. on the left. GPS: 44.5998, 0.8708

Charges guide

Per unit incl. 2 persons and electricity	€ 20,00 - € 43,00

Biscarrosse

488

Camping du Domaine de la Rive

Route de Bordeaux, F-40600 Biscarrosse (Landes) T: **05 58 78 12 33**. E: **info@camping-de-la-rive.fr**
alanrogers.com/FR40100

Surrounded by pine woods, La Rive has a superb beach-side location on Lac de Sanguinet. It provides mostly level, numbered and clearly defined pitches of 100 sq.m. all with electricity connections (6A). The swimming pool complex is wonderful with pools linked by water channels and bridges. There is also a jacuzzi, paddling pool and two large swimming pools all surrounded by sunbathing areas and decorated with palm trees. An indoor pool is heated and open all season. There may be some aircraft noise from a nearby army base. This is a friendly site with a good mix of nationalities. The latest addition is a super children's aquapark with various games. The beach is excellent, shelving gently to provide safe bathing for all ages. There are windsurfers and small craft can be launched from the site's slipway.

Facilities

Five good clean toilet blocks have washbasins in cabins and mainly British style toilets. Facilities for disabled visitors. Baby baths. Motorcaravan service point. Shop with gas. Restaurant. Bar serving snacks and takeaway. Swimming pool complex (supervised July/Aug). Games room. Play area. Tennis. Bicycle hire. Boules. Archery. Fishing. Waterskiing. Watersports equipment hire. Tournaments (June-Aug). Skateboard park. Trampolines. Miniclub. No charcoal barbecues on pitches. Off site: Golf 8 km. Riding 5 km.

Open: 3 April - 5 September.

Directions

Take the D652 from Sanguinet to Biscarrosse and site is signed on the right in about 6 km. Turn right and follow a tarmac road for 2 km.
GPS: 44.46052, -1.13065

Charges guide

Per unit incl. 2 persons and electricity	€ 21,50 - € 46,00
extra person	€ 3,60 - € 7,80
child (3-7 yrs)	€ 2,40 - € 6,30
dog	€ 2,10 - € 5,00

Camping Cheques accepted.

club otel
Domaine de La Rive
a Paradise for Children
www.larive.fr
Pool complex and a covered heated swimming pool

Biscarrosse

Campéole Navarrosse

712 chemin de Navarrosse, F-40600 Biscarrosse (Landes) T: **05 58 09 84 32**. E: **nadine.ferran@atciat.com**
alanrogers.com/FR40230

Navarosse is a member of the Campéole group and is located on the very large Lac de Sanguinet, just 7 km. from the Atlantic beaches. The location of this atraditional campsite is attractive, with a long sandy beach and a small harbour (ideal for mooring small boats) on one side and to the other, a small canal. Pitches are of a good size, mostly on fairly level, sandy soil with good shade. Most have 10A-electricity. Many water-based activities take place on the lake, including sailing jet skiing and windsurfing. For cyclists there are many tracks to various places. Mobile homes, chalets and fully equipped tents are available for rent.

Facilities

Two sanitary units comprising separate blocks of toilets and showers. One modern block with facilities for disabled people. Laundry facilities. Motorcaravan services. Bar, snack bar and takeaway (1/7-31/8). Tennis. Multisports pitch. Archery. Bicycle hire. Play area. Bouncy castle. Activity and entertainment programme (1/7-31/8). WiFi. Mobile homes, equipped tents and chalets for rent. Off site: Riding. Water sports. Biscarosse 3 km. Nearest beach 7 km. Golf.

Open: 3 April - 30 September.

Directions

From the north on the D652 turn right onto the D305. After about 1.5 km. turn right at campsite sign and towards lake. GPS: 44.43192, -1.16885

Charges guide

Per unit incl. 2 persons and electricity	€ 17,90 - € 30,00
extra person	€ 4,60 - € 8,90
child (2-6 yrs)	€ 2,50 - € 5,40

Biscarrosse

Camping Mayotte Vacances

368 chemin des Roseaux, F-40600 Biscarrosse (Landes) T: **05 58 78 00 00**. E: **mayotte@yellohvillage.com**
alanrogers.com/FR40240

This appealing site is set amongst pine trees on the edge of Lac de Biscarrosse. Drive down a tree- and flower-lined avenue and proceed toward the lake to shady, good sized pitches which blend well with the many tidy mobile homes that share the area. Divided by hedges, all the pitches have electricity (10A) and water taps. There may be some aircraft noise at times from a nearby army base. The pool complex is impressive, with pools, slides, chutes, jacuzzi and sauna, all surrounded by paved sunbathing areas. The excellent lakeside beach provides safe bathing for all ages with plenty of watersports available.

Facilities

Four good quality, clean toilet blocks. Good facilities for visitors with disabilities. Unusual baby/toddler bathroom. Motorcaravan services. Laundry. Supermarket. Boutique. Rental shop (July/Aug). Restaurant. Swimming pools (one heated; supervised July/Aug and weekends). Play area. Bicycle hire. Fishing. Watersports. Organised activities and entertainment (July/Aug). Clubs for toddlers and teenagers (July/Aug). Charcoal barbecues not permitted. Hairdressers (seasonal). ATM. Internet access. Off site: Golf 4 km. Riding 100 m. Beach 10 km. Town 2 km. with restaurants and bars.

Open: 30 April - 24 September.

Directions

From the north on D652 turn right on D333 (Chemin de Goubern). Pass through Goubern and Mayotte Village. Take next right (signed to site) into Chemin des Roseaux. GPS: 44.43495, -1.15505

Charges guide

Per unit incl. 2 persons	€ 17,00 - € 39,00
extra person	€ 3,50 - € 7,50
child (3-7 yrs)	free - € 3,50
dog	€ 3,00 - € 5,00

Bordeaux

Camping Bordeaux Lac

Chemin de Bretous, boulevard Jacques Chaban Delmas, F-33000 Bordeaux Lac (Gironde) T: **05 57 87 70 60**
E: **contact@camping-bordeaux.com** **alanrogers.com/FR33410**

Bordeaux is undeniably one of France's 'must see' cities and now it has a superior campsite. Adjacent to the exhibition centre and Bordeaux Lac, the site opened in 2009 and is open all year. The facilities and accommodation are of top quality. There are 119 touring pitches, some on well kept grass, others, primarily for motorcaravans, have hardstanding. All have electricity, 40 have water and drainage and 70 also have sewerage disposal. Within the 14-hectare campsite there are also 93 well-equipped chalets and mobile homes (three specifically for disabled visitors) for rent. The site is arranged around five attractive, man-made lakes and set amongst tall trees.

Facilities

Modern, heated sanitary block. Laundry. Restaurant, bar and supermarket. Swimming pool. Play area. Mobile homes and chalets for rent. WiFi. Off site: Golf and fishing (Bordeaux Lac complex). Large shopping centre. Cycle and walking tracks. Bordeaux centre 5 km.

Open: All year.

Directions

At Bordeaux, take the A630 ring road and exit 4A. Follow signs for Parc des Expositions and signs for campsite. At roundabout take second exit (right) and site is 700 m. on the right. GPS: 44.89805, -0.58194

Charges guide

Per unit incl. 2 persons and electricity	€ 20,00 - € 29,00
extra person	€ 3,00 - € 8,00

Calviac-en-Périgord

Camping Domaine des Chênes Verts

Route de Sarlat, F-24370 Calviac-en-Périgord (Dordogne) T: **05 53 59 21 07**. E: **chenes-verts@wanadoo.fr**
alanrogers.com/FR24220

This peaceful countryside family campsite is set in a beautiful area of the Dordogne valley, and is complemented by the renovated Périgourdine farm buildings which house the amenities at the centre of the site. The spacious grounds which contain many trees provide 143 pitches on either side of the main buildings, of which 63 are for touring units. Most of the good sized, grass pitches are shaded, and all are separated by hedging. There is electricity (6A) to all pitches, and water points nearby. The majority of pitches are large and level but some are gently sloping.

Facilities

Two fully equipped unisex toilet blocks include washbasins in cabins, dishwashing and laundry areas. Washing machine. Small shop (fresh bread daily), bar, snack bar and takeaway. Motorcaravan service point. Fridge hire. Gas supplies. Medium sized swimming pool with large sunbathing area (15/6-15/9), covered, heated pool (1/4-20/9) and paddling pool. Play area. Multisport court. Entertainment for children. TV and games room. Charcoal barbecues provided. Off site: Forest walks and cycle tracks lead from the site.

Open: 1 May - 28 September.

Directions

From D704 Sarlat - Gourdon road turn east on D704A towards Souillac and Calviac (this turning is about 3.5 km. from Sarlat). Site is about 5 km. along this road on the left. GPS: 44.86277, 1.29517

Charges guide

Per person	€ 3,75 - € 4,70
child (under 7 yrs)	€ 2,15 - € 2,70
pitch incl. electricity	€ 11,70 - € 13,90
dog	€ 1,75 - € 2,20

Carsac-Aillac

Village Center Aqua Viva

Route Sarlac-Souillac, Carsac-Aillac, F-24200 Sarlat-la-Canéda (Dordogne) T: **08 25 00 20 30**
E: **contact@village-center.com** **alanrogers.com/FR24110**

This shaded woodland site is ideally situated for visits to Rocamadour and Padirac, as well as exploring the Dordogne region, including the medieval town of Sarlat, only 7 km. away. The site is divided into two sections, separated by a small access road. The 179 pitches are flat, mainly on grass, divided by shrubs and they vary in size (80-150 sq.m). Many have shade from the numerous trees and all have electricity (6/10A). A wide range of organised activities, children's clubs and entertainment run throughout the season, making this site popular with families, especially those with pre-teen and younger teenage children.

Facilities

Each part of the site has a modern toilet block, with facilities for disabled people and babies. Bar, restaurant and takeaway with terrace. Good shop. Heated swimming pool, children's pool. Small fishing lake. Minigolf. Half tennis. Good play park for under 7 yrs. Floodlit boules pitch and multisport court. Bicycle hire. Off site: Aerial woodland assault course 500 m. Riding and golf 5 km.

Open: 30 April - 13 September.

Directions

Site is 6 km. from Sarlat south of the D704A road from Sarlat to Souillac. From Souillac, the access road to the site is just around a left hand bend, not easy to see. GPS: 44.86743, 1.27941

Charges guide

Per unit incl. 2 persons and electricity	€ 16,00 - € 29,00
extra person	€ 3,00 - € 5,00

Coux-et-Bigaroque

Camping les Valades

D703, F-24220 Coux-et-Bigaroque (Dordogne) T: **05 53 29 14 27**. E: **info@lesvalades.com**
alanrogers.com/FR24420

Sometimes we come across small but beautifully kept campsites which seem to have been a well kept secret, and Les Valades certainly fits the bill. Set on a hillside overlooking countryside between the Dordogne and Vezère rivers, each pitch is surrounded by variety of flowers, shrubs and trees. There are 75 pitches are flat and grassy, mostly on terraces, all with 10A electricity and most with individual water and drainage as well. Some very large pitches available for weekly hire have their own sanitary unit, dishwashing, fridge and barbecue. At the bottom of the hill, away from the main area, is a swimming pool and a good sized lake for carp fishing, swimming or canoeing (free canoes). Rustic chalets for rent occupy 50 of the largest pitches. From the moment you arrive you can see that the owners, M. and Mme. Berger, take enormous pride in the appearance of their campsite and there is an abundance of well tended flowers and shrubs everywhere you look. A convivial and family atmosphere is very much in evidence and the site is therefore ideal for families with young children. Couples both young and mature will also enjoy this site.

Facilities

Two clean modern toilet blocks, one with family shower rooms. Facilties for disabled people. Washing machine. Main reception building houses a bar, restaurant (both July/Aug) and a terrace overlooking valley. Heated swimming pool, sun terrace, paddling pool (all season). Play area near the lake and pool. Off site: Small shop, bar, restaurant in Coux-et-Bigaroque 5 km. Supermarket at Le Bugue 10 km. Riding and bicycle hire 5 km. Golf 6 km.

Open: 1 April - 15 October.

Directions

Site is signed down a turning on west side of D703 Le Bugue - Siorac-en-Perigord road, about 3.5 km. north of village of Coux-et-Bigaroque. Turn off D703 and site is 1.5 km. along on right.
GPS: 44.86056, 0.96385

Charges 2010

Per unit incl. 2 persons and electricity	€ 24,00
extra person	€ 5,80
child (0-6 yrs)	€ 4,00
dog	€ 3,00

No credit cards.

Daglan

Camping le Moulin de Paulhiac

F-24520 Daglan (Dordogne) T: **05 53 28 20 88**. E: **Francis.Armagnac@wanadoo.fr**
alanrogers.com/FR24230

You will be guaranteed a friendly welcome from the Armagnac family, who are justifiably proud of their well-kept and attractive site, built in the grounds surrounding an old mill. The facilities have been continually updated and improved over the years. The 150 shady pitches (93 for touring) are separated by hedges and shrubs, all fully serviced. Many pitches are next to a small river that runs through the site and joins the River Ceou along the far edge. A tent field slopes gently down to the river, which is quite shallow and used for swimming. This site will appeal especially to families with younger children.

Facilities

Two clean toilet blocks provide modern facilities, including those for disabled visitors. Good shop, restaurant, takeaway. Main pool, heated and covered by a sliding roof in low season, children's pool, a further small pool and a toboggan and slide. Boules. Bicycle hire. Small river with beach. Fishing. Canoe trips organised on the Dordogne. Organised evening activities. Children's club in high season. Off site: Riding 5 km. Golf 10 km.

Open: 15 May - 15 September.

Directions

Site is 17 km. south of Sarlat and is on the east side of the D57, about 5 km. north of the village of Daglan.
GPS: 44.76762, 1.17635

Charges guide

Per person	€ 7,15
child (0-10 yrs)	€ 2,70 - € 5,20
pitch	€ 9,90 - € 11,00
dog	€ 1,90

Dax

Camping les Chênes

Bois de Boulogne, F-40100 Dax (Landes) T: **05 58 90 05 53**. E: **camping-chenes@wanadoo.fr**

alanrogers.com/FR40020

Les Chênes is a well-established site, popular with the French themselves and situated on the edge of town amongst parkland (also near the river) and close to the spa for the thermal treatments. The 176 touring pitches are of two types, some large and traditional with hedges, 109 with electricity, water and drainage, and others more informal, set amongst tall pines with electricity if required. This is a reliable, well run site, with a little of something for everyone, but probably most popular for adults taking the 'treatments'. Dax is not a place that springs at once to mind as a holiday town but, as well as being a spa, it promotes a comprehensive programme of events and shows during the summer season.

Facilities

Two toilet blocks, one new and modern with heating, washbasins in cubicles, facilities for disabled people, babies and young children. The older block has been refurbished. Laundry and dishwashing facilities. Shop also providing takeaway food (3/4-30/10). Swimming and paddling pools (1/5-18/9). Play area. Field for ball games. Boules. Bicycle hire. Miniclub for children (July/Aug). Occasional special evenings for adults. Charcoal barbecues are not permitted. Off site: Restaurant opposite. Riding, fishing and golf all within 200 m. Beaches 28 km.

Open: 20 March - 6 November.

Directions

Site is west of town on south side of river, signed after main river bridge and at many junctions in town – Bois de Boulogne (1.5 km). In very wet weather the access road to the site may be flooded (but not the site).
GPS: 43.71182, -1.07329

Charges guide

Per unit incl. 2 persons and electricity (5A)	€ 12,80 - € 17,20
incl. water and drainage	€ 16,60 - € 19,40
extra person	€ 6,00
child (2-10 yrs)	€ 4,00
animal	€ 1,50

Camping Les Chênes ★★★★
Hôtel de plein air
du Bois de Boulogne
40100 DAX
Tel. 0033 558 90 05 53
Fax 0033 558 90 42 43

Domme

Camping le Bosquet

La Rivière, F-24250 Domme (Dordogne) T: **05 53 28 37 39**. E: **info@lebosquet.com**

alanrogers.com/FR24760

Located between Sarlat and Bergerac, this great little campsite is set in lovely countryside and is landscaped with flowers and shrubs, with trees to offer some shade. The site is maintained to a good standard and is kept very clean. The natural environment gives a sense of tranquillity and calm – here you can relax. M. and Mme. Vrand will do everything they can to ensure you have a great holiday. There are 60 level pitches with 10A electricity, with 40 for touring units. The remainder are used for mobile homes to rent. The Dordogne river is 300 m. away and the canoeing here is good and convenient.

Facilities

The toilet block includes facilities for disabled visitors. Washing machine and iron. Restaurant. Takeaway. Small shop. Swimming pool. Library. Entertainment (July/Aug). Play area. Pétanque. Fishing. TV. WIFI free in reception area. Off site: Golf 2 km. Riding 4 km. Bicycle hire 1 km. Tennis 2 km. Canoeing 1 km.

Open: 1 April - 30 September.

Directions

Take the D46 from Sarlat to Vitrac. Cross the river bridge in Vitrac and the site is on the right hand side 1 km. further on. Well signed.
GPS: 44.82241, 1.225319

Charges guide

Per person	€ 3,00 - € 4,00
child (under 7 yrs)	€ 2,10 - € 2,20
pitch	€ 3,30 - € 3,80
electricity	€ 2,50
dog	free - € 2,00

Duras

Le Cabri Holiday Village

Route de Savignac, F-47120 Duras (Lot-et-Garonne) T: **05 53 83 81 03**. E: **holidays@lecabri.eu.com**
alanrogers.com/FR47110

This is a good quality site set in 14-acres of beautiful countryside, on the border of the Dordogne and the Lot-et-Garonne, between the two rivers of the same name. The views are superb. Le Cabri Holiday Village is an English owned and run, small holiday complex. The new owners, Peter and Eileen Marston who are keen caravanners themselves, have developed 24 new spacious pitches (generally 150 sq.m), all with electricity (4/16A) and water. The open, level pitches are all on hardstandings surrounded by grass and separated by shrubs. Access for large motorhomes causes no problems whatsoever as they were considered when the site was planned. Open all year round, the site has excellent facilities including a swimming pool, a fishing pond and other leisure facilities. Wildlife watching is another pastime here with red deer and wild boar populating the area. Le Cabri also benefits from its own high quality restaurant which specialises in local cuisine. Open all year, it draws clientele from the local area as well as those staying on the site. Although situated in a very rural and peaceful area, the historic village of Duras is only a ten-minute walk, with its good selection of shops, restaurants, bars and the famous fortified château standing guard at the head of the village square.

Facilities

A recently refurbished sanitary block is central, heated in low season and includes three new private cabins. Separate cabin for disabled visitors. Washing machines, dryers and ironing board. Shop (all year) selling basics including bread. Restaurant (all year). Internet access. Swimming pool. Large play area. Boules. Well stocked fishing pond. Off site: Riding 1 km. Golf (international course) 10 km. Tennis 1 km. Watersports 7 km. Canoeing 8 km.

Open: All year.

Directions

In Duras, look for the D203 and follow signs for site. It is less than 1 km. away. GPS: 44.68296, 0.18615

Charges guide

Per person	€ 4,00 - € 5,00
child (under 11 yrs)	€ 2,00 - € 3,00
pitch	€ 5,00 - € 7,00
electricity (4/10A)	€ 3,00 - € 5,00

Fumel

Domaine de Guillalmes

Condat, F-47500 Fumel (Lot-et-Garonne) T: **05 53 71 01 99**. E: **info@guillalmes.com**
alanrogers.com/FR47150

Domaine de Guillalmes is a very attractive site on the banks of the River Lot and close to the village of Fumel. It was until recently exclusively for 18 chalets but the British owners have now added a ten-pitch touring caravan area all with 4/16A electricity and water. These pitches are on hardstandings divided by small hedges and small trees giving some shade. They are spacious and ideal for very large outfits and American motorhomes. All the facilities are available to tourers including the magnificent pool and bar terrace. The site is an ideal stopover but you may decide to stay longer.

Facilities

Shower and toilet available to tourers, other facilities including for campers with disabilities in the restaurant area (08.00-22.00). The owners are currently building two additional showers. Washing machine and dryer. Bar, terrace and takeaway. Restaurant. Bread to order. Swimming pool (June-Oct) with jacuzzi. Tennis. Boules. Free use of bikes and canoes. Occasional soirées. Children's activities.
Off site: Cycling and walking routes. Cahors vineyards 2 km. Fummel, Rocamadour and Cahors.

Open: All year.

Directions

Site is between Fumel and Soturac. From Fumel, take D911 signed Cahors, then follow signs to Domaine de Guillalmes. Turn right 150 m. before Soturac (site signed). GPS: 44.4831, 1.0094

Charges guide

Per unit incl. 2 persons	€ 18,00 - € 22,00
extra person	€ 3,50 - € 5,50
electricity (4/6A)	€ 5,00 - € 6,00

Groléjac-en-Perigord

Camping Caravaning les Granges

F-24250 Groléjac-en-Perigord (Dordogne) T: **05 53 28 11 15**. E: **contact@lesgranges-fr.com**

alanrogers.com/FR24020

Situated only 500 metres from the village of Groléjac, Les Granges is a lively and well maintained campsite set on sloping ground in woodland. There are 188 pitches, of which 100 are available for touring units. The pitches are marked and numbered on level terraces and most receive good shade from mature trees and shrubs. All pitches have electricity (6A) and water either on the pitch or close by. The site has a good sized swimming pool and a large shallow pool for children. A bridge connects these to a fun pool with water slides. Around 88 pitches are used by tour operators.

Facilities

The toilet blocks are of a very high standard with good facilities for disabled visitors. Bar/restaurant and snack bar also providing takeaway food (15/5-15/9). No shop, but bread and milk can be ordered. Play area. Minigolf. Climbing wall. Canoe and bicycle hire. Off site: Shops in the nearby village of Groléjac and hypermarkets of Sarlat or Gourdon are not far away. Golf and riding 6 km.

Open: 24 April - 11 September.

Directions

In centre of village of Groléjac on main D704 road. Site signed through a gravel parking area on west side of road. Drive through this area and follow road around to T-junction. Turn right, under railway bridge, and immediately left (site signed). Site is just along this road on left. GPS: 44.81593, 1.29086

Charges guide

Per unit incl. 2 persons and electricity	€ 17,55 - € 27,50
extra person (over 5 yrs)	€ 5,50 - € 7,30
dog	free - € 3,00

La Roque Gageac

Camping Beau Rivage

Gaillardou, F-24250 La Roque Gageac (Dordogne) T: **05 53 28 32 05**. E: **camping.beau.rivage@wanadoo.fr**

alanrogers.com/FR24800

Beau Rivage has an undeniably fine location, just 7 km. from Sarlat, close to La Roque Gageac, with its ancient, honey-coloured houses, sheer rock face and Dordogne river frontage. This site had new owners in 2009 and various improvements are envisaged. There are 290 pitches of which 242 are for touring units, the remainder used for mobile homes to rent. The pitches are level, well shaded and some are on the banks of the Dordogne. They are of a good size and 6A electricity is available. The site has a good range of amenities including a swimming pool, a restaurant, a well stocked shop and a bar overlooking the pool.

Facilities

Two toilet blocks include facilities for disabled people. Washing machines. Shop. Bar. Restaurant and takeaway. Swimming and paddling pools. Play area. Pétanque. Tennis. Canoeing. WIFI in bar area. Electric barbecues are not permitted. Off site: Golf 3 km. Rding 5 km. Bicycle hire 2 km.

Open: 4 April - 10 September.

Directions

From Sarlat, take the D46 to Vitrac and then the D703 towards La Roque Gageac. Site is on the left, well signed. GPS: 44.81621, 1.21488

Charges guide

Per unit incl. 2 persons	€ 12,00 - € 22,00
extra person	€ 3,00 - € 4,00
electricity	€ 2,00 - € 4,00

Hourtin-Plage

Airotel Camping de la Côte d'Argent

489

F-33990 Hourtin-Plage (Gironde) T: **05 56 09 10 25**. E: **info@camping-cote-dargent.com**
alanrogers.com/FR33110

Côte d'Argent is a large, well equipped site for leisurely family holidays. It makes an ideal base for walkers and cyclists with over 100 km. of cycle lanes in the area. Hourtin-Plage is a pleasant invigorating resort on the Atlantic coast and a popular location for watersports enthusiasts, The site's top attraction is its pool complex where wooden bridges connect the pools and islands and there are sunbathing and play areas plus an indoor heated pool. The site has 618 touring pitches, not clearly defined, arranged under trees with some on soft sand. Entertainment takes place at the bar near the entrance (until 00.30). Spread over 20-hectares of undulating sand-based terrain and in the midst of a pine forest. There are 48 hardstandings for motorcaravans outside the site, providing a cheap stopover, but with no access to site facilities. The site is well organised and ideal for children.

Facilities

Very clean sanitary blocks include provision for disabled visitors. Washing machines. Motorcaravan service points. Large supermarket, restaurant, takeaway, pizzeria bar. Four outdoor pools with slides and flumes. Indoor pool. Massage (Institut de Beauté). Tennis. Play areas. Miniclub, organised entertainment in season. Bicycle hire. Internet. ATM. Charcoal barbecues are not permitted. Hotel (12 rooms). Off site: Path to the beach 300 m. Fishing and riding. Golf 30 km.

Open: 12 May - 19 September.

Directions

Turn off D101 Hourtin-Soulac road 3 km. north of Hourtin. Then join D101E signed Hourtin-Plage. Site is 300 m. from the beach. GPS: 45.22297, -1.16465

Charges 2010

Per unit incl. 2 persons and electricity	€ 24,00 - € 52,00
extra person	€ 3,00 - € 7,50
child (3-9 yrs)	€ 2,50 - € 6,50
dog	€ 2,00 - € 5,50

Camping Cheques accepted.

Labenne-Océan

Yelloh! Village le Sylvamar

Avenue de l'Océan, F-40530 Labenne-Océan (Landes) T: **05 59 45 75 16**. E: **camping@sylvamar.fr**
alanrogers.com/FR40200

Less than a kilometre from a long sandy beach, this campsite has a good mix of tidy, well maintained chalets, mobile homes, a tree house and touring pitches. The 216 touring pitches (562 in total) are level, numbered and mostly separated by low hedges. Following development, all now have electricity (10A), water and drainage. They are set around a superb pool complex with pools of various sizes (one heated, one not) with a large one for paddling, a wild water river, toboggans and slides. In a sunny setting, all are surrounded by ample sunbathing terraces and overlooked by the excellent bar/restaurant.

Facilities

Four modern toilet blocks have washbasins in cabins. Excellent facilities for babies and disabled visitors. Laundry. Fridge hire. Shop, bar/restaurant and takeaway (all season). Play area. Games room. Cinema, TV and video room. Fitness centre. Tennis. Football pitch. Bicycle hire. Library. Extensive entertainment programme for all ages. Internet access. No charcoal barbecues. Off site: Beach 900 m. Fishing, riding 1 km. Golf 7 km.

Open: 1 April - 20 September.

Directions

Labenne is on the N10. In Labenne, head west on D126 signed Labenne-Océan and site is on right in 4 km. GPS: 43.59570, -1.45638

Charges 2010

Per unit incl. 2 persons and electricity	€ 15,00 - € 43,00
extra person	€ 5,00 - € 8,00
child (3-7 yrs)	free - € 5,00
dog	€ 4,00

A 3500 m² aquatic complex with slides and jacuzzis, covered and heated swimming pool

Club Airotel Hourtin Plage

★★★★ Camping Caravaning

de la côte d'argent

www.cca33.com

Camping Special offer (except July and August) 14 = 11 and 7 = 6

Campsite La Cote d'Argent is a very attractive 20 acre park, situated in the heart of the pine forest and on only 300m distance from the Atlantic Ocean Beach.
This characteristic park is protected for the ocean wind by the dunes and the forest. The Village Club Cote d'Argent is the perfect destination for your calm holiday in nature.

IFI - hotel - shops - restaurant bar - food - sportive animations - tennis archery - mini-club - games room - sailing (4 km) - surf (300m)

33990 Hourtin Plage
Tél : +33 (0)5.56.09.10.25 Fax : +33 (0)5.56.09.24.96
www.campingcotedargent.com www.campingcoteouest.com
www.campingaquitaine.com

Lacanau-Océan

Yelloh! Village les Grands Pins

Plage Nord, F-33680 Lacanau-Océan (Gironde) T: **04 66 73 97 39**. E: **info@yellohvillage-les-grands-pins.com**
alanrogers.com/FR33130

This Atlantic coast holiday site with direct access to a fine sandy beach, is on undulating terrain amongst tall pine trees. A large site with 600 pitches, there are 430 of varying sizes for touring units. One half of the site is a traffic free zone (except for arrival or departure day, caravans are placed on the pitch, with separate areas outside for parking). There is a good number of tent pitches, those in the centre of the site having some of the best views. This popular site has an excellent range of facilities available for the whole season.

Facilities

Four well equipped toilet blocks, one heated, with baby room and facilities for disabled people. Launderette. Motorcaravan services. Supermarket. Bar, restaurant, snack bar, takeaway. Heated swimming pool (lifeguard in July/Aug) with sunbathing surround. Fitness activities. Jacuzzi. Games room. Fitness suite. Tennis. Two playgrounds. Adventure playground. Bicycle hire. Organised activities. WiFi in the bar (on payment). Only gas barbecues are permitted. Off site: Fishing, golf, riding and bicycle hire 5 km.

Open: 26 April - 20 September.

Directions

From Bordeaux take N125/D6 west to Lacanau-Océan. At second roundabout, take second exit: Plage Nord, follow signs to 'campings'. Les Grand Pins signed to right at the far end of road.
GPS: 45.01107, -1.19337

Charges guide

Per unit incl. 2 persons and electricity	€ 15,00 - € 44,00
extra person	€ 5,00 - € 9,00
child (3-11 yrs)	free - € 5,00
dog	€ 4,00

Half-board arrangements available.

Lacanau-Lac

Camping le Tedey

Par le Moutchic, route de Longarisse, F-33680 Lacanau-Lac (Gironde) T: **05 56 03 00 15**
E: **camping@le-tedey.com** **alanrogers.com/FR33290**

With direct access to a large lake and beach, this site enjoys a beautiful tranquil position set in an area of 14-hectares amidst mature pine trees. There are 700 pitches of which 630 are for touring units with 36 mobile homes and chalets available for rent. The pitches are generally level and grassy although the site is on a slope. Dappled sunlight shines through the trees. Electricity is available to all pitches and 223 also have water and waste water drainage. The bar is close to the lake with a large indoor and outdoor seating area. The owners and staff are friendly and helpful and English is spoken. There is an open air cinema on Saturdays and Wednesdays as well as other entertainment in July and August. A children's club is also organised. The takeaway sells a variety of food and the shop next door is well stocked. This is an attractive well maintained site where you get a feeling of space and calm. There are many places of interest nearby and a short drive from Bordeaux.

Facilities

Four modern sanitary blocks with facilities for disabled visitors and babies. Laundry facilities. Bar with terrace. Crêperie. Takeaway. Bicycle hire. Boating on the lake. Pétanque. Playground. Gas barbecues only on pitches. Dogs accepted but not in July or August. Internet access. Off site: Surfing. Riding. Golf. Cycling.

Open: 28 April - 19 September.

Directions

From Lacanau take the D6 to Lacanau-Océan. Take Route de Longarisse and camping is well signed.
GPS: 44.98620, -1.13410

Charges guide

Per unit incl. 1 or 2 persons, and electricity	€ 17,00 - € 21,00
incl. water and drainage	€ 21,00 - € 25,00
extra person	€ 3,50 - € 5,50
child (2-10 yrs)	€ 2,70 - € 3,20

Lacanau-Océan

Camping Airotel de l'Océan

F-33680 Lacanau-Océan (Gironde) T: **05 56 03 24 45**. E: **airotel.lacanau@wanadoo.fr**
alanrogers.com/FR33240

Its location on the Atlantic coast, 600 m. from a lovely sandy beach makes this site extremely popular. Set in 10-hectares of heavily-wooded sand dunes, the site is quite hilly with 550 pitches (279 for touring units) set amongst pine trees with areas for peace and quiet and areas for those who want to be close to the facilities. Some pitches are quite spacious, some level and others requiring blocks. There is a large swimming pool complex, a bar and soundproofed disco. A welcoming new reception completes a pleasant entrance courtyard with shops in high season and a new sanitary block.

Facilities

Four traditional toilet blocks and one modern block provide spacious facilities including a room for disabled visitors in each block. Baby rooms. Washing machines. Motorcaravan services. Large supermarket. Various boutique shops (July/Aug). Bar, restaurant, takeaway (all 7/4-15/9). Large leisure pool complex. Fitness gym. TV, games rooms. Internet access and WiFi. Bicycle hire. Barbecue area. Off site: Beach 600 m. Shops 1 km.

Open: 7 April - 27 September.

Directions

From Bordeaux take the N215/D106 then the D3 to Lacanau-Océan. At roundabout before village turn right and site is 800 m. on the right.
GPS: 45.00852, -1.19240

Charges guide

Per unit incl. 2 persons and electricity	€ 12,50 - € 33,00
extra person	€ 3,50 - € 8,00
child (4-10 yrs)	free - € 5,00

Laruns

Camping des Gaves

Quartier Pon, F-64440 Laruns (Pyrénées-Atlantiques) T: **05 59 05 32 37**. E: **campingdesgaves@wanadoo.fr**
alanrogers.com/FR64040

Set in a secluded valley, Camping des Gaves is a clean, small and well managed site, open all year, with very friendly owners and staff. It is set high in Pyrennean walking country on one of the routes to Spain and is only 30 km. from the Spanish border. There are 99 pitches including 43 level grassed touring pitches of which 38 are fully serviced, numbered and separated (the remainder are used for seasonal units). Mature trees provide plenty of shade. The river runs alongside the site (well fenced) and fishing is possible. The busy little tourist town of Laruns is only a short walk.

Facilities

The very clean toilet block can be heated in cool weather and has modern fittings. Washbasins for ladies in curtained cubicles and one shower in ladies' suitable for showering children. Dishwashing and laundry sinks. Laundry room. No shop but baker calls daily (July/Aug). Small bar with large screen TV, pool and video games (July/Aug). Larger bar with table tennis. Small play area. Fishing. Card operated barrier (€ 20 deposit). Motorcaravan service point. Off site: Bicycle hire 500 m. Shops, restaurant and bars 1 km.

Open: All year.

Directions

Take N134 from Pau towards Olorons and branch left on D934 at Gan. Follow to Laruns and just after town, turn left following signs to site.
GPS: 42.98241, -0.41591

Charges guide

Per unit incl. 2 persons and electricity	€ 16,90 - € 23,30
extra person	€ 3,20 - € 4,30
child (4-10 yrs)	€ 2,10 - € 2,90

Le Bugue

Camping Caravaning la Linotte

F-24260 Le Bugue (Dordogne) T: **05 53 07 17 61**. E: **campinglalinotte@orange.fr**
alanrogers.com/FR24260

This is a really pleasant, good quality site which has plenty of space and fantastic views. It is located in the heart of the Périgord Noir and is conveniently placed to be able to visit many of the attractions in the area. The amenities are superb and include a heated swimming pool, a children's pool, a jacuzzi and two toboggans. There are 120 pitches, of which 80 are for mobile homes and chalets (all to rent). They are on large pitches that offer a degree of privacy. There are also 40 pitches for touring uits. These are again of a good size, level and divided by shrubs and trees. Electricity is 5A. All the pitches are well away from the site's hub and are therefore peaceful and relatively quiet, ideal for families.

Facilities

A smart sanitary unit provides a mix of British and Turkish style WCs, showers and washbasins in cubicles. Facilities for babies and disabled people. Dishwashing and laundry sinks. Bar/restaurant also providing takeaway and breakfast (1/7-30/8). Small shop with bread to order (1/7-30/8). Pool complex (15/5-15/9) main pool (unheated), water slides and splash pool, paddling pool (both heated), and jacuzzi. Small playground with trampolines. Boules. Off site: Riding 8 km.

Open: 4 April - 27 September.

Directions

From Le Bugue follow signs for Périgueux along the D710. On outskirts of Le Bugue turn right onto the D32E for Rouffignac and site. After about 1.5 km. turn right on to minor road for a further 1 km. to site entrance on right. GPS: 44.934117, 0.9371

Charges guide

Per unit incl. 2 persons and electricity	€ 18,00 - € 26,00
extra person	€ 3,00 - € 5,00

Le Bugue

Camping Brin d'Amour

Saint Cirq, F-24260 le Bugue (Dordogne) T: **05 53 07 23 73**. E: **campingbrindamour@orange.fr**

alanrogers.com/FR24660

This attractive Dordogne site is situated in the Périgord Noir with wonderful views across the undulating hills and the Vezère valley. Here there is a feeling of tranquillity, spaciousness and calm. The owners offer a welcome and outstanding customer service. With 80 pitches, 60 are for touring units, the remaining 20 for chalets and mobile homes which are all available to rent. All are level, easily accessible and mostly shaded. There is also a pond at the far end of the site. The main building is of fine traditional Périgordine quality and houses a very attractive restaurant and bar. This is a small site where you can relax in a family atmosphere. This is an ideal place from which you can explore the countryside by foot or by bicycle, take an excursion, visit the caves or canoe down the river. With a romantic history, the site's name translates as 'a piece of love'. Definitely a site not to be missed.

Facilities

Modern sanitary block with facilities for disabled visitors and babies. Washing machine. Shop (15/5-20/10). Bar (1/4-15/9). Restaurant and takeaway (1/6-15/9). Swimming and paddling pools (1/4-30/9, heated from 1/5). Tennis. Fishing. Pétanque. Play area. Children's club (July/Aug). Bicycle hire. Fridge hire. WiFi. Charcoal barbecues are not permitted. Max. 1 dog per pitch. Off site: Riding 2 km. Canoeing 5 km. Sailing, golf 10 km. Prehistoric Park. Caves.

Open: 1 April - 30 October.

Directions

Take D710 from Périgueux to Le Bugue and 500 m. after Le Bugue entry sign turn sharp left on D32e to St Cirq. Site is signed from here.
GPS: 44.944837, 0.960145

Charges guide

Per unit incl. 2 persons	€ 12,00 - € 18,00
extra person	€ 3,50 - € 5,00
child (1-10 yrs)	€ 2,50 - € 4,00
electricity	€ 3,00
dog (max. 1)	€ 2,00

Le Buisson-de-Cadouin

Camping du Pont de Vicq

F-24480 Le Buisson-de-Cadouin (Dordogne) T: **05 53 22 01 73**. E: **le.pont.de.vicq@wanadoo.fr**

alanrogers.com/FR24730

Camping du Pont de Vicq is located on the Dordogne, on the edge of the Périgord Noir. It is situated between the towns of Périgueux (50 km), Bergerac (35 km) and Sarlat (35 km) and is well located for visiting the area's many castles, caves, chasms and prehistoric sites. Set in 5.5-hectares, there are 130 pitches of which 107 are for touring units, the remainder used for mobile homes to rent. The pitches are level and separated by hedges and trees, so there is a choice of shade. Electricity is 6A. The river is one of the main attractions and there is a 680 m. beach alongside the campsite which is sectioned off from the river.

Facilities

Toilet facilities include washbasins in cabins and facilities for disabled vsitors. Motorcaravan service point. Bar, snack bar and shop (all June-Aug). River beach. Fishing. Play area. Activities and entertainment. Electric barbecues are not permitted. Mobile homes for rent. Off site: Canoeing. Hiking and cycle tracks. Bicycle hire. Riding. Medieval Sarlat 35 km.

Open: 21 March - 1 October.

Directions

Le Buisson-de-Cadouin lies to the west of Sarlat. From Bergerac follow signs to Sarlat on D660 and D29. Upon arrival at Le Buisson-de-Cadouin follow signs to Le Bugue (D51) and then to the campsite.
GPS: 44.85416, 0.91208

Charges guide

Per unit incl. 2 persons and electricity	€ 14,00 - € 17,20
extra person	€ 3,90 - € 4,95
child (2-10 yrs)	€ 2,20 - € 3,30
dog	€ 0,90 - € 1,10

Le Verdon-sur-Mer

Sunêlia la Pointe du Medoc

Route de la Pointe de Grave, F-33123 Le Verdon-sur-Mer (Gironde) T: **05 56 73 39 99**
E: **info@camping-lapointedumedoc.com** **alanrogers.com/FR33210**

Situated roughly equidistant between a sandy Atlantic beach (accessed by a pleasant walk through the forest opposite the site) and the Gironde estuary, this site has 260 pitches. There are 112 for touring units with 10A electricity, 70 with water and drainage. Heavier units will need to use those pitches with plastic runners to ensure easy access on and off the sandy ground. The pitches are generally large and most are in full sun but some smaller ones towards the rear of the site offer much more shade. Out of season this is a quiet campsite, but in July and August it becomes busy with familes enjoying the excellent facilities.

Facilities

Good clean sanitary facilities. Shop (July/Aug). Bar, restaurant and takeaway. Outdoor swimming pool (heated) with water jets, jacuzzi and paddling pool. Indoor pool. Massage. Minigolf. Multisport terrain. Bicycle hire. Communal barbecues. Organised entertainment and children's club (4-11 yrs). Small farm and children's garden. Activities for teenagers in July/Aug. Internet access and WiFi. Off site: Sea fishing 1 km. Riding 5 km.

Open: 26 April - 12 September.

Directions

Site is on the N215 (D1215) just south of Le Verdon. Approaching Le Verdon it is important to follow the signs for Royan and Point de Medoc. Site is on the right. It is possible to take the ferry from Royan, but this can be expensive. GPS: 45.54540, -1.07950

Charges guide

Per unit incl. 2 persons and electricity	€ 18,00 - € 30,00
extra person (over 4 yrs)	€ 3,00 - € 6,00

Lège-Cap-Ferret

Camping International le Truc Vert

Route du Truc-Vert, F-33950 Lège-Cap-Ferret (Gironde) T: **05 56 60 89 55**. E: **truc-vert@tiscali.fr**
alanrogers.com/FR33230

Relaxing amidst the tall pines of this 10 hectare hillside site is pleasant, but if you are looking for more activity there are many cycle ways and walks to enjoy in the lovely local countryside. The site provides over 480 pitches (280 with 6A electricity) with trees giving shade. Some pitches are level but for many you will need levelling blocks. Some site roads are a little steep so care is needed and also while travelling on the local main roads through the woods (keep to speed limits) as the occasional wild boar ventures out onto the roads. The entrance area is decked with flowers and very welcoming.

Facilities

Seven toilet blocks (not all open all season) spread well around the site offer satisfactory facilities with showers and washbasins in cubicles, facilities for disabled people (although some may find the roads on site a little steep). Motorcaravan service area. Laundry facilities. Bar/brasserie (1/5-30/9). Restaurant (1/6-30/9). Shop. Play area. TV/games room. Some evening entertainment in season. Internet access. Charcoal barbecues are not permiited.
Off site: Riding 500 m. Fishing and beach 300 m.

Open: 1 May - 30 September.

Directions

From Bordeaux take D106 towards Lège-Cap-Ferret. Continue on D106 through town and in Les Jacquets, just before village sign for Le Petit Piquey, turn right. Follow through residential area and woods for about 4 km. Site is on left. GPS: 44.71550, -1.24289

Charges guide

Per unit incl. 2 persons	€ 13,00 - € 19,70
extra person	€ 3,00 - € 4,30
child (2-10 yrs)	free - € 4,30
electricity (6A)	€ 3,50

Léon

Airotel Lou Puntaou

Au bord du Lac, F-40550 Léon (Landes) T: **05 58 48 74 20**. E: **reception@loupuntaou.com**
alanrogers.com/FR40280

Set between Lac de Léon and the nature reserve park of Huchet, this site offers plenty for young families. The level pitches are mainly grass, hedged and have electricity (15A). Trees offer reasonable shade. In July and August only, there may be some noise from the lake car park and activities. The lake is 200 m. away with watersports, fishing, restaurants and bars, plus plenty of cycle rides. In July and August a full range of activities is organised on the site with sports and clubs for children and activities and evening entertainment for adults. A number of tour operators use the site. The pool complex consists of a covered heated pool with a jacuzzi and another (unheated) with water slides and toboggan, plus a paddling pool. There is a pleasant bar/restaurant nearby.

Facilities

Three traditional style toilet blocks include facilities for disabled visitors and children. Laundry facilities. Motorcaravan service point. Simple shop at site entrance. Bar, restaurant and takeaway (all season). TV and games rooms. Tennis. ATM. Internet. Only electric barbecues are permitted (communal area available). Off site: Village 500 m. Lake 200 m. Beach 7 km. Riding 10 km.

Open: 1 April - 30 September.

Directions

From N10 take exit 12 towards Castets. Take the D142 to Léon and at island take first exit 'Centre Ville'. At T-junction turn left on D652. After 300 m. turn left at sign for site and lake. After 500 m. site is on left. GPS: 43.88469, -1.31497

Charges guide

Per person	€ 3,00 - € 6,00
pitch incl. electricity	€ 9,00 - € 27,00

Léon

Yelloh! Village Punta Lago

Avenue du Lac, F-40550 Léon (Landes) T: **05 58 49 24 40**. E: **info@yellohvillage-punta-lago.com**

alanrogers.com/FR40290

Five hundred metres from the charming village of Léon, this site offers above average size, level, grass pitches (some sandy). Most have electricity, water and drainage and they are separated by hedges. Shade is welcome from the tall oak trees. Whilst the pitches would be considered typical for the region, the buildings are a mix of old and new, the old being the sanitary block, in good order, clean and with all the usual facilities including a lovely new children's bathroom and facilities for disabled visitors. The new encompasses an indoor heated pool, a recreation room serving as a gym and a TV room.

Facilities

The single toilet block is old, but kept clean and well maintained. Facilities for children and disabled visitors. Laundry facilities. Large shop. Restaurant and takeaway. Bar. Heated indoor and outdoor pools. Bicycle hire. Play area. Fridge hire. Entertainment and activities (July/Aug). Barbecues are not permitted. Off site: Lake 300 m. with sailing, windsurfing, kayak, swimming and fishing. Léon 500 m. with market at every day (June/Sept). Beach 7 km. Golf 8 km. Riding 5 km.

Open: 20 March - 26 September.

Directions

From N10 take exit 12 towards Castets. Take D142 to Léon and at island take first exit to 'Centre Ville'. At T-junction turn left on D652 and after 300 m. turn left at sign for site and lake. After 500 m. site is on the left. GPS: 43.8842, -1.313

Charges 2010

Per unit incl. 2 persons and electricity	€ 15,00 - € 40,00
extra person	€ 3,00 - € 6,00
child (3-7 yrs)	free - € 6,00

Les Eyzies-de-Tayac

Camping le Pech Charmant

F-24620 Les Eyzies-de-Tayac (Dordogne) T: **05 53 35 97 08**. E: **info@lepech.com**

alanrogers.com/FR24370

As the name suggests, this is a charming site set on the top of a hill in the heart of the Perigord Noir, yet just 2 km. from Les Eyzies. The site is on two levels and the lower, quieter level has a superb spacious feeling with touring caravans and tents being positioned around its perimeter, leaving the centre clear. There are 80 level pitches, of which ten are used for mobile homes and two new chalets. The pitches have dappled shade and 10A electricity. Donkey renting is popular with donkeys being used to help out with walks lasting from half a day to three days and more.

Facilities

Modern sanitary block with facilities for disabled visitors. Bar. Restaurant/snack bar. Takeaway. TV, internet access and WiFi in the bar. Swimming and paddling pools. Boules. Play area. Private access to the river. Fishing. Sports field. Only gas barbecues are permitted. American type motorhomes are not accepted. Off site: Bicycle hire 2 km. Riding 3 km. Golf 13 km.

Open: 15 April - 1 October.

Directions

From Les Eyzies head south on the D706 towards Le Bugue. Turn left immediately after the Renault garage and follow road for about 2 km. Site is signed along this road. GPS: 44.92404, 1.02982

Charges guide

Per person	€ 3,00 - € 5,50
child (3-8 yrs)	€ 2,50 - € 4,15
pitch	€ 6,00 - € 9,00
electricity (10A)	€ 3,00
dog	€ 1,50

Limeuil

Camping la Ferme de Perdigat

F-24510 Limeuil (Dordogne) T: **05 53 63 31 54**. E: **accueil@perdigat.com**

alanrogers.com/FR24750

The delightful French owners, Michel and Noelle Paille, make this a happy place to stay and everyone we spoke to praised it highly. The site nestles beautifully in a very natural environment at the base of tree-lined hills which provide a wonderful scenic background. Flowers, bushes and trees give a superb sense of well being and much care and attention is given to the environment. A superb lake is 100 m. from the site where visitors staying at the farm may fish without charge. The river is also the same distance away in a different direction. There are only 64 pitches, 15 of which are used for mobile homes to rent.

Facilities

The completely refurbished shower block is bright and airy. Laundry facilities. Shop. Bar. Snack bar. Swimming and paddling pools. Games room. WiFi in the bar area. Play area. Private fishing lake and the Vezere river. Canoes and kayaks. Off site: Limeuil listed as one of the most beautiful villages in France. Supermarkets in Le Bugue 3 km.

Open: 1 March - 30 October.

Directions

From Le Bugue, take the D703 to La Borie and turn left to Limeuil. Campsite is well signed.
GPS: 44.894765, 0.912509

Charges guide

Per person	€ 3,00 - € 4,40
child (under 8 yrs)	€ 2,00 - € 2,80
pitch	€ 3,00 - € 4,70
electricity	€ 3,00 - € 3,10

Lit-et-Mixe

Village Center les Vignes

Route de la Plage du Cap de L'Homy, F-40170 Lit-et-Mixe (Landes) T: **05 58 42 85 60**
E: **contact@les-vignes.com** **alanrogers.com/FR40160**

Les Vignes is a large holiday site close to the Atlantic coast with 450 pitches, of which 285 are occupied by a mix of mobile homes, bungalows and tents, most of which are for rent. The 165 touring pitches are relatively level on a sandy base, all serviced with electricity (10A) and water, some with waste water drains. The site's amenities, including a supermarket, restaurant and bar, are located at the entrance to the site. The rather stylish swimming pool complex includes a six lane water slide.

Facilities

Four modern sanitary units. Facilities for babies and disabled people. Washing machines and dryers. Large supermarket, restaurant, bar and takeaway (all 5/6-10/9). Swimming pool complex (4/4-15/9), water complex (1/6-15/9). Tennis. Minigolf. Pétanque. Riding. Kids club and playground. Bicycle hire. Internet access and WiFi. Off site: Golf course, canoeing, kayaking, surfing, riding. Many cycle tracks.

Open: 4 April - 13 September.

Directions

Lit-et-Mixe is on the D652 20 km. south of Mimizan. Turn west on D88 1 km. south of town towards Cap de l'Homy for 1.5 km. where site entrance is on left. GPS: 44.02292, -1.27978

Charges guide

Per unit incl. 2 persons, electricity and water	€ 14,00 - € 40,00
extra person	€ 3,00 - € 6,00

Messanges

Camping les Acacias

Route d'Azur, quartier Delest, F-40660 Messanges (Landes) T: **05 58 48 01 78**. E: **lesacacias@lesacacias.com**
alanrogers.com/FR40220

Close to the Atlantic beaches of Les Landes, this small, well designed campsite is quiet and peaceful. Family run and well cared for, it is a site for couples looking for relaxation or families who want a safe environment for young children to play. There are 79 flat touring pitches, all with 5/10A electricity and separated by trees and shrubs. Mobile homes are arranged unobtrusively on two sides of the site. The pitches are easily accessed by tarmac roads, although units longer than 7 m. may have some difficulty. M. and Mme. Dourthe are constantly seeking to improve this charming campsite.

Facilities

One modern, clean and well designed toilet block with facilities for disabled people. Laundry facilities. Motorcaravan services. Fridge hire. Shop (15/6-15/9). Takeaway (1/7-31/8). Games room. Small play area. Boules. Football field. Bicycle hire. WiFi. Off site: Bus service 1 km. Beach 2 km. Fishing 3 km. Riding 1.5 km. Golf 4 km. Supermarket 2 km.

Open: 25 March - 25 October.

Directions

Approaching Messanges from the north, continue through the centre of village on the D652 (site signed). At roundabout turn left onto C3 toward Azur and site is 1.5 km. on the left.
GPS: 43.79836, -1.37550

Charges guide

Per unit incl. 2 persons and electricity	€ 13,00 - € 22,30
extra person	€ 2,00 - € 3,80

Mézin-Réaup-Lisse

Flower Camping du Lac de Lislebonne

Le Bétous, F-47170 Mézin-Réaup-Lisse (Lot-et-Garonne) T: **05 53 65 65 28**
E: **domainedelislebonne@free.fr** **alanrogers.com/FR47090**

Lac de Lislebonne can be found on the eastern edge of the vast Landes forest, in the Lot et Garonne département. This small site has just 40 pitches, some of which are occupied by attractive wooden chalets (available for rent). There are 22 touring pitches. These are of a good size and all have electricity (10A). The site lake is a pleasant spot to cool off and has a sandy beach. Various activities are organised in and around the lake, including water polo, canoeing and beach volleyball. Bicycle hire is available on site and there are over 250 km. of marked cycle tracks in the area.

Facilities

Shop. Bar. Snack bar. Takeaway. Lake swimming. Play area. Bicycle and canoe hire. Fishing. TV room. Activity and entertainment programme. Chalets for rent. Off site: Riding. Golf. Tennis. Château du Moulin 10 km. Cycle tracks.

Open: 25 April - 25 September.

Directions

Leave the A62 autoroute at exit for Agen and head southwest on the D656 to Nérac and then Mézin. Join the 149 towards Réaup-Lisse and follow signs to Base de Loisirs. GPS: 44.07335, 0.20973

Charges guide

Per unit incl. 2 persons and electricity	€ 12,90 - € 18,50

Messanges

489

Camping le Vieux Port

Plage Sud, F-40660 Messanges (Landes) T: **01 76 76 70 00**. E: **contact@levieuxport.com**

alanrogers.com/FR40180

A well established destination appealing particularly to families with teenage children, this lively site has 1,546 pitches of mixed size, most with electricity (6A) and some fully serviced. The camping area is well shaded by pines and pitches are generally of a good size, attractively grouped around the toilet blocks. There are many tour operators here and well over a third of the site is taken up with mobile homes and another 400 pitches are used for tents. The heated pool complex is exceptional boasting five outdoor pools and three large water slides. There is also a heated indoor pool. An enormous 7,000 sq.m. Aquatic Parc is now open and all the sanitary facilities are to be renovated.

Facilities

Nine well appointed, recently renovated toilet blocks with facilities for disabled people. Motorcaravan services. Good supermarket and various smaller shops in high season. Several restaurants, takeaway and three bars (all open all season). Large pool complex (no Bermuda shorts) including new covered pool and Polynesian themed bar. Tennis. Multisport pitch. Minigolf. Bicycle hire. Riding centre. Organised activities in high season including frequent discos and karaoke evenings. Only communal barbecues are allowed. Off site: Fishing 1 km. Golf 8 km.

Open: 31 March - 26 September.

Directions

Leave RN10 at Magescq exit heading for Soustons. Pass through Soustons following signs for Vieux-Boucau. Bypass this town and site is clearly signed to the left at second roundabout.

GPS: 43.79778, -1.40111

Charges 2010

Per unit incl. 2 persons and electricity	€ 19,00 - € 54,30
extra person	€ 4,50 - € 8,30
child (under 13 yrs)	€ 3,50 - € 5,70
dog	€ 3,00 - € 5,20

Camping Cheques accepted.

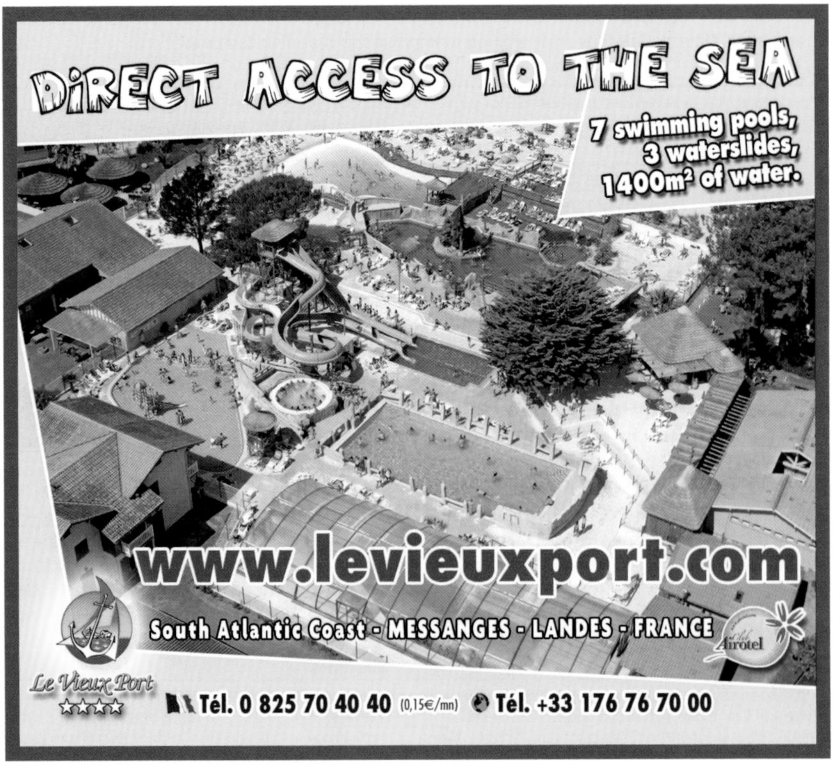

Mézos

Le Village Tropical Sen-Yan

Le Village Tropical, F-40170 Mézos (Landes) T: **05 58 42 60 05**. E: **reception@sen-yan.com**
alanrogers.com/FR40110

This exotic family site is about 12 km. from the Atlantic coast in the Landes forest area, just outside the village. There are 140 touring pitches set around a similar number of mobile homes. Pitches are marked with hedges and have electricity (6A). The reception, bar and pool area is almost tropical with the luxuriant greenery of its banana trees, palm trees, tropical flowers and its straw sunshades. The covered, heated pool, new water slide, gym with sauna and jacuzzi all add to the attractiveness. A new covered animation area provides entertainment and discos during high season.

Facilities

Three well maintained and clean toilet blocks with good quality fittings and showers, washbasins in cabins and British style WCs. The newest block is especially suitable for low season visitors with a special section for babies, plus excellent facilities for disabled people. Shop (from 15/6). Bar, restaurant and snacks (1/7-31/8). Outdoor swimming pools (1/7-15/9). Heated indoor pool (1/5-15/9). Archery. Practise golf. Bicycle hire. No charcoal barbecues.
Off site: Fishing 500 m. Riding 6 km. Beach 12 km.

Open: 1 May - 15 September,
(from 3 April for accommodation).

Directions

From N10 take exit 14 (Onesse-Laharie), then D38 Bias/Mimizan road. After 13 km. turn south to Mézos from where site is signed. GPS: 44.07208, -1.15671

Charges guide

Per unit incl. 2 persons	€ 20,00 - € 32,50
incl. 6A electricity	€ 24,50 - € 37,50
extra person	€ 5,00 - € 7,00
child (under 7 yrs)	free - € 6,00

Mimizan-Plage

Camping de la Plage

Boulevard de l'Atlantique, F-40200 Mimizan-Plage (Landes) T: **05 58 09 00 32**
E: **contact@mimizan-camping.com** **alanrogers.com/FR40380**

This municipal site is located 800 m. from the Atlantic beach at Mimizan Plage. This is a large site with 787 pitches of which around 460 are available for touring units. The rest are occupied by mobile homes and chalets (available for rent). Pitches are well shaded beneath pines and many are equipped with 10A electricity. A separate area (without electricity) is reserved for tents. Leisure amenities include a multisport terrain, two beach volleyball courts and a climbing wall. An entertainment and activity programme is organised in peak season, including a programme for children. The site operates to very strict environmental guidelines. Economy lighting, for example, is used throughout and a water economizer system is also in place. Guests of the site are required to wear a special bracelet which aids security and ensures access to all site amenities. During high season, a well stocked shop is available as well as a fast food facility (including breakfast and takeaway meals). Off site, Mimizan Plage is a lively resort development with many cafes and restaurants.

Facilities

Shop. Bar/snack bar. Games room. Multisport terrain. Climbing wall. Play area. Tourist information. Mobile homes and chalets for rent. Off site: Nearest beach 800 m. Walking and cycle tracks through the forest. Surfing. Fishing.

Open: 3 April - 27 September.

Directions

Approaching from the north, leave N10 at Labouheyre and follow signs to Mimizan on D626. Drive though the town and follow signs for Mimizan Plage. Site is clearly signed and is to the north of the river.
GPS: 44.216482, -1.285653

Charges guide

Per unit incl. 2 persons and electricity	€ 12,40 - € 20,15
extra person	€ 6,20 - € 8,25
child (3-12 yrs)	€ 4,10 - € 6,20

Mimizan

Airotel Club Marina-Landes

Rue Marina, F-40200 Mimizan (Landes) T: **05 58 09 12 66**. E: **contact@clubmarina.com**
alanrogers.com/FR40080

Well maintained and clean, with helpful staff, Club Marina-Landes would be a very good choice for a family holiday. Activities include discos, play groups for children, specially trained staff to entertain teenagers and concerts for more mature campers. There are numerous sports opportunities and a superb beach nearby. A nightly curfew ensures that all have a good night's sleep. The site has 444 touring pitches (304 with 10A electricity) and 128 mobile homes and chalets for rent. The pitches are on firm grass, most with hedges and they are large (mostly 100 sq.m. or larger). If ever a campsite could be said to have two separate identities, then Club Marina-Landes is surely the one. In early and late season it is quiet, with the pace of life in low gear – come July and until 1 September, all the facilities are open and there is fun for all the family with the chance that family members will only meet together at meal times.

Facilities

Five toilet blocks (opened as required), well maintained with showers and many washbasins in cabins. Facilities for babies, children and disabled visitors. Laundry facilities. Motorcaravan services. Fridge hire. Shop (freshly baked bread) and bar (30/4-10/9). Restaurant, snack bar, pizzas and takeaway (1/5-10/9). Covered pool and outdoor pools (30/4-13/9). Minigolf. Tennis. Bicycle hire. Play area. Internet access. Entertainment and activities (high season). Gas or electric barbecues only. Off site: Beach and fishing 7 km. Bus service 1 km. Riding 1 km. Golf 8 km. Mimizan 8 km.

Open: 30 April - 13 September.

Directions

Heading west from Mimizan centre, take the D626 passing Abbey Museum. Straight on at lights (crossing D87/D67). Next lights turn left. After 2 km. at T-junction turn left. Follow signs to site.
GPS: 44.20447, -1.29099

Charges guide

Per unit incl. 2 persons and electricity	€ 17,00 - € 44,00
extra person	€ 3,00 - € 8,00
child (3-13 yrs)	€ 3,00 - € 6,00
dog	€ 2,00 - € 4,00

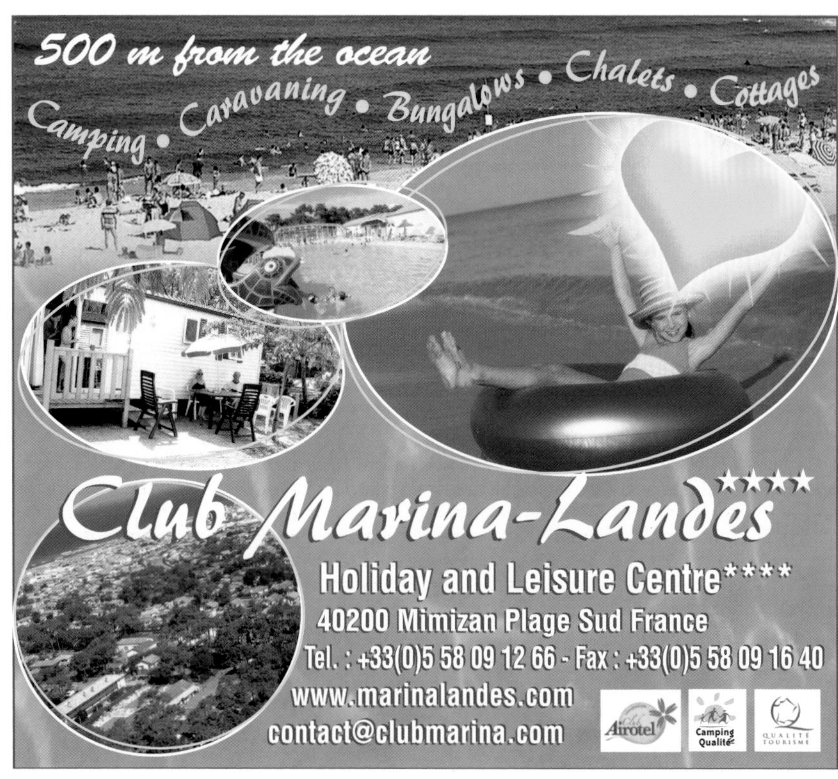

Moliets-Plage

489

Le Saint-Martin Camping

Avenue de l'Océan, F-40660 Moliets-Plage (Landes) T: **05 58 48 52 30**. E: **contact@camping-saint-martin.fr**
alanrogers.com/FR40190

A family site aimed mainly at couples and young families, St-Martin is a welcome change from most of the sites in this area in that it has only a small number of chalets (85) compared to the number of touring pitches (575). First impressions are of a neat, tidy, well cared for site and the direct access to the beach is an added bonus. The pitches are mainly typically French in style with low hedges separating them plus some shade. Electricity hook ups are 10-15A and a number of pitches also have water and drainage. Entertainment in high season is low key (with the emphasis on quiet nights) – daytime competitions and a miniclub, plus the occasional evening entertainment, well away from the pitches and with no discos or karaoke. With pleasant chalets and mobile homes to rent, and an 18-hole golf course 700 m. away (special rates negotiated), this would be an ideal destination for a golfing weekend or longer stay.

Facilities

Seven toilet blocks of a high standard and very well maintained, have washbasins in cabins, large showers, baby rooms and facilities for disabled visitors. Motorcaravan service point. Washing machines and dryers. Fridge rental. Supermarket. Bars, restaurants and takeaways. Indoor pool, jacuzzi and sauna (charged July/Aug). Outdoor pool area with jacuzzi and paddling pool (15/6-15/9). Multisport pitch. Play area. Internet access. Electric barbecues only.
Off site: Excellent area for cycling, bicycle hire 500 m. Golf and tennis 700 m. Riding 8 km.

Open: 19 March - 11 November.

Directions

From the N10 take D142 to Lèon, then D652 to Moliets-et-Mar. Follow signs to Moliets-Plage, site is well signed. GPS: 43.85242, -1.38732

Charges guide

Per unit incl. 2 persons and electricity	€ 22,00 - € 44,50
extra person	€ 6,00 - € 7,00
child (under 10 yrs)	€ 4,00 - € 5,00
dog	free - € 4,00

Prices are for reserved pitches.

Monfaucon

Domaine de l'Etang de Bazange

F-24130 Monfaucon (Dordogne) T: **05 53 24 64 79**. E: **etangdebazange@aol.fr**
alanrogers.com/FR24820

This campsite is located in the heart of the Périgord Poupre, in an area where rolling hillside vineyards give it a Tuscan air and where the Dordogne river winds gently through its sun-filled valley, with orchards and vineyards scattered along its banks. Monfaucon is between Bergerac and Saint Emilion. Set in 9-hectares of pine and oak forests, this is a peaceful site where you can relax in calm and tranquil surroundings. Most of the 50 level pitches have some shade and are terraced on a gentle slope. There are 23 mobile homes to rent. Electricity is 6A. A pleasant swimming pool with a slide and toboggan are set well away from the pitches.

Facilities

Bar. Restaurant (July/Aug). Takeaway. Swimming pool with slides and toboggan. Paddling pool. Fishing lake. Playground. Games room. Entertainment. Organised excursions. Bicycle hire. Barbecues are not permitted (communal ones around the site). Off site: Shops and supermarkets 4 km. and 10 km. Tennis 4 km. Canoeing and kayaking. Golf and riding 5 km.

Open: 1 June - 15 September (mobile homes 1 April - 31 October).

Directions

From A89 exit 12 take D708 and turn left after St Meard-de-Gurcon. The site is then well signed. GPS: 44.917471, 0.247836

Charges guide

Per unit incl. 2 persons	€ 12,00 - € 15,00
extra person	€ 4,00 - € 4,50
child (2-9 yrs)	€ 2,00 - € 3,50
electricity	€ 3,00 - € 3,50

Monpazier

Village Center Moulin de David

Gaugeac, F-24540 Monpazier (Dordogne) T: **04 99 57 21 21**. E: **contact@village-center.com**
alanrogers.com/FR24080

Set in a 14-hectare wooded valley, this site has 160 pitches split into two sections, 102 are available for touring units – 33 below the central reception complex in a shaded situation, and 69 above on partly terraced ground with varying degrees of shade. All pitches have electricity (3/6/10A). Spacing is good and there is no crowding. The site has been attractively planted with a pleasing variety of shrubs and trees and combined with the small stream that runs through the centre of the site they create a beautiful and tranquil setting.

Facilities

Three good toilet blocks, including facilities for disabled visitors and babies. New mobile home. Laundry room. Good shop. Bar/restaurant with shaded patio, takeaway. Swimming pool and paddling pool, freshwater pool with waterslide. Play area. Boules. Half-court tennis. Trampoline. Library. Bicycle hire. Events, games and canoe trips.
Off site: Small supermarket and ATM in Monpazier 2.5 km.

Open: 30 April - 12 September.

Directions

From Monpazier take the D2 Villeréal road. Take third turning left (after about 2 km), signed to Moulin de David and Gaugeac Mairie. Site is about 500 m. along this road on the left. GPS: 44.65949, 0.87898

Charges 2010

Per unit incl. 2 persons and electricity	€ 16,00 - € 24,00

Montignac

Camping le Paradis

Saint Léon-sur-Vézère, F-24290 Montignac (Dordogne) T: **05 53 50 72 64**. E: **le-paradis@perigord.com**
alanrogers.com/FR24060

Le Paradis is a well maintained riverside site, halfway between Les Eyzies and Montignac. The site is very well kept and landscaped with a variety of mature shrubs and trees. The gardens are beautifully maintained which gives a wonderful sense of tranquillity. It is very easy to relax on this ecologically friendly, site. Systems of reed based filters enhance efficient natural drainage. This is a family run site and you are guaranteed a warm and friendly welcome. There are 200 good sized pitches, with 27 for mobile homes to rent. The pitches are level and with easy access, all with 10A electricity, water and drainage. There are some special pitches for motorcaravans. An excellent restaurant offers a good menu, reasonably priced and using fresh local produce where appropriate. The terraced area outside, makes for a convivial and family atmosphere. There are many sport and leisure activities. Direct access to the Vézère river is possible at one end of the site for canoeing and swimming. Organised games, competitions and evening events are aimed at maintaining a true French flavour. English is spoken. This is a site of real quality, which we thoroughly recommend.

Facilities

High quality, well equipped, heated toilet blocks are kept very clean. Well stocked shop (with gas). Good restaurant, takeaway. Good pool complex heated in low season, paddling pool. Play area. Tennis. BMX track. Multisport court. Canoe hire. Fishing. Bicycle hire. Quad bike and horse riding excursions. WiFi throughout. Large units accepted by arrangement. Mobile homes to rent (no smoking) including one for visitors with disabilities (no dogs permitted).
Off site: Riding 3 km.

Open: 1 April - 19 October.

Directions

Site is 12 km. north of Les Eyzies and 3 km. south of St Léon-sur-Vézère, on the east side of the D706. GPS: 45.00207, 1.0711

Charges guide

Per unit incl. 2 persons and electricity	€ 21,60 - € 30,50
extra person	€ 5,40 - € 7,40
child (3-12 yrs)	€ 4,40 - € 6,40
dog	€ 2,00

Low season reductions.
10% discount for pensioners in low season.

Montalivet

Centre Helio-Marin de Montalivet

46 avenue de l'Europe, F-33930 Montalivet (Gironde) T: **05 56 73 73 73**. E: **infos@chm-montalivet.com**
alanrogers.com/FR33370

This is a large naturist village with everything that you would need without leaving the site during your holiday. It has direct access to the sea with its own beautiful golden sandy beaches with coastguard surveillance in high season. Watersports are numerous with lessons if you require. The main emphasis here is to keep the family entertained. There are a total of 2,800 pitches, of which 1,700 are for touring. Pitches are level, on grass or sand, and mature trees provide shade in some areas. Circus school, dancing classes and skate boarding are just some of the activities organised here.

Facilities

Numerous sanitary blocks with facilities for disabled visitors and children. Shops, restaurants and bars. Launderette. Motorcaravan service point. Children's clubs. Evening entertainment. Two swimming pool complexes with slides and toboggan. Playgrounds. Sports grounds. TV rooms and cinema. Large library. Wellness centre offering numerous treatments and massage as well as saunas and jacuzzis. Off site: Golf. Riding. Cycling. Sailing and fishing.

Open: All year.

See advertisement on page 473

Directions

From Royan, take the ferry to Verdon-sur-Mer and continue on N215 for 34 km. Turn right on D102 to Montalivet. Nearing the sea turn left for Hourtins and site is 1 km. on the right. GPS: 45.36348, -1.14575

Charges guide

Per unit incl. 2 persons and electricity	€ 16,30 - € 31,50
extra person	€ 3,30 - € 7,50
dog	€ 6,50 - € 7,00

Navarrenx

Camping Beau Rivage

Allée des Marronniers, F-64190 Navarrenx (Pyrénées-Atlantiques) T: **05 59 66 10 00**
E: **beaucamping@free.fr** **alanrogers.com/FR64120**

Cross the picturesque river and follow the old town walls to discover this well cared for family owned campsite (English). The site is tiered and the large, well maintained grass pitches are surrounded by mature hedges offering a peaceful and relaxed setting. The site is now well lit – torches are no longer needed. The attention to well cared for detail is carried into the two sanitary blocks. Recent projects include a heated swimming pool, low key entertainment area (wine tasting, barbecues, etc), additional chalets, hardstandings and a baby room, adding to an already impressive campsite. Richard has now trained as a pizzaiolo and can now offer fresh pizzas.

Facilities

Two very clean sanitary blocks with good separate facilities for ladies and men include provision for disabled visitors. Laundry facilities in top block. Playground for small children has recently been renewed with improved bark finish. Play field. Off site: Shop at end of road. Town is five minutes walk for further shops, bars, restaurants, ATM and bicycle hire. Fishing 200 m. Riding 15 km.

Open: 26 March - 15 October.

Directions

From the north take D936 to Navarrenx. Turn left at first roundabout on D115 into Navarrenx. Turn left at T-junction, go over bridge and follow walls of town all the way around. At next island turn right on D947 and site is signed. GPS: 43.32001, -0.761

Charges guide

Per unit incl. 2 persons and electricity	€ 17,50 - € 23,00
extra person	€ 4,00 - € 5,00

Parentis-en-Born

Camping l'Arbre d'Or

75 route du Lac, F-40160 Parentis-en-Born (Landes) T: **05 58 78 41 56**. E: **contact@arbre-dor.com**
alanrogers.com/FR40350

L'Arbre d'Or is a friendly, family site on the outskirts of Parentis-en-Born. There are 200 pitches here, all well shaded by tall pine trees and most offering electrical connections. Around 90 pitches are occupied by mobile homes and chalets. l'Arbre d'Or lies 400 m. from the large Lac de Parentis where many watersports are available. The nearest coastal beach is at Biscarosse Plage, 19 km. distant. The site boasts two swimming pools, one of which is covered in inclement weather, as well as a restaurant and an activity programme. Bicycle hire is available and there are hundreds of kilometres of cycle trails through the surrounding forest.

Facilities

Two well located toilet blocks are a good provision and are kept clean. Preset showers. Facilities for disabled visitors. Bar, restaurant and takeaway (15/5-15/9).Two heated swimming pools. Play area. Bicycle hire. Entertainment and activities in peak season. Games room. Mobile homes and chalets for rent. Off site: Shop 800 m. Golf and riding 9 km. Lac de Parentis 400 m.

Open: 1 April - 31 October.

Directions

From Bordeaux head south on the A63 and then the N10 as far as Liposthey. Then head west on the D43 to Parentis-en-Born. The site is well signed from here on the Route du Lac. GPS: 44.34622, -1.0929

Charges guide

Per unit incl. 2 persons and electricity	€ 17,20 - € 21,50

Pauillac

Camping Municipal les Gabarreys

Route de la Rivière, F-33250 Pauillac (Gironde) T: **05 56 59 10 03**. E: **camping.les.gabarreys@wanadoo.fr**
alanrogers.com/FR33150

An attractive, small site with well-tended flower beds, Les Gabarreys is surrounded by vineyards of the Médoc region. An excellent site, it has 59 pitches, most with hardstanding for caravans or motorcaravans (so pegging out awnings could be a problem), some grass pitches for tents and 6 mobile homes, all with electric hook-ups (5/10A, some may require long leads). The 'Maison du Tourisme et du Vin' should be your first port of call. The surrounding area is well supplied with wine caves, and being fairly level you could perhaps cycle to some of them.

Facilities

Two immaculate toilet blocks provide open and cubicle washbasins and excellent facilities for disabled visitors. Motorcaravan services. General room with satellite TV, fridge-freezer and a small library. New play area. Minigolf (free) and volleyball. New spa and sauna.

Open: 3 April - 9 October.

Directions

Pauillac lies NNW of Bordeaux. From Bordeaux take D1 to St Laurent, then D206 to Pauillac. At roundabout turn right to Pauillac Guais, then straight ahead at next roundabout and turn right before the Maison du Tourisme. GPS: 45.1852, -0.742567

Charges guide

Per unit incl. 2 persons	€ 12,50 - € 14,00
extra person	€ 4,00 - € 4,50
child (2-7 yrs)	€ 3,00 - € 3,50
electricity (5/10A)	€ 3,80 - € 5,20

Périgueux

490

Camping le Grand Dague

Route du Grand Dague, Atur, F-24750 Périgueux (Dordogne) T: **05 53 04 21 01**. E: **info@legranddague.fr**
alanrogers.com/FR24160

This is a beautifully situated campsite in the centre of a wooded area in an ideal location from which to discover the area of the Dordogne. The village of Atur is closest to the site and the town of Périgueux, the capital of the region, is just a few kilometres away. The site was bought by the present owners in 2009 and many changes have been made. There are now 242 pitches, 121 for mobile homes and 71 for touring units. A tour operator has 50 frame tents on the site. There is a new swimming pool complex with a lagoon style pool and a pirate ship. There is also a separate paddling pool and water slide. The restaurant and bar is also new and provides a varied menu at reasonable prices. There is plenty to do at this site and children of all ages are welcome. Besides a play area, there is also an entertainment programme for the whole family. Off site there are museums, Roman remains and a medieval town centre, or for the more adventurous, there is canoeing on the rivers Isle, Dordogne and Vezere.

Facilities

Excellent, part heated sanitary facilities include a baby room and facilities for people with disabilities. Launderette. Small shop and bar (all season). Attractive restaurant with appetising menu (May-Sept) and takeaway (June-Aug). Swimming pool, water slide and paddling pool (all season). Covered play area. Pétanque. Minigolf. Play area. Fishing. Off site: Paintball outside gate. Riding and fishing 5 km. Bicycle hire 8 km. Golf 10 km.

Open: 29 May - 26 September.

Directions

From the Bordeaux - Brive inner ring road in Périgueux take D2 south, signed Atur. Campsite signed. Turn east at roundabout just before entering Atur. Site is in 3 km. GPS: 45.14833, 0.77817

Charges guide

Per unit incl. 2 persons and electricity	€ 14,00 - € 29,00
extra person	€ 4,00 - € 6,75
child (3-11 yrs)	€ 2,50 - € 4,50
animal	€ 2,00

Petit Palais-et-Cornemps

Flower Camping le Pressoir

29 Queyrai, F-33570 Petit Palais-et-Cornemps (Gironde) T: **05 57 69 73 25**
E: **contact@campinglepressoir.com** **alanrogers.com/FR33090**

Buried in the famous wine producing countryside of the Lussac, Pomerol and St Emilion areas north of Bordeaux, Le Pressoir is surrounded by fields of vines. The 100 large pitches are arranged on either side of a gravel road leading up a slight hill. Most are shaded by attractive trees, but almost all are sloping. They are over 100 sq.m. and equipped with electricity. The old barn has been converted into a stylish bar and a really charming, separate restaurant. A quiet, family site, Le Pressoir provides a comfortable base for a holiday in this area famous for good food and wine.

Facilities

Fully equipped toilet block with facilities for disabled visitors, and washing machine. Bar and pleasant restaurant (all year). Heated swimming pool (15/5-15/9, no Bermuda shorts). Playground with timber equipment. Pétanque. Mountain bike hire. Free WiFi. Mobile homes to rent (5). Bicycle hire. Off site: Tennis nearby. Fishing 1 km. Riding 5 km.

Open: All year.

Directions

From A89 Bordeaux - Périgueux take exit 11 to Saint Médard de Guizières where you turn south towards Lussac on the D21 (site signed from Saint Médard). From Castillon-la-Bataille on D936 Libourne - Bergerac road, south of site, take D17 north towards St Médard then D21 through Petit Palais. Site signed.
GPS: 44.9971, -0.06326

Charges guide

Per unit incl. 2 persons	€ 16,50 - € 28,00
extra person	€ 2,00 - € 7,50

Pyla-sur-Mer

Yelloh! Village Panorama du Pyla

Grande Dune du Pyla, route de Biscarrosse, F-33260 Pyla-sur-Mer (Gironde) T: **04 66 73 97 39**
E: **info@yellohvillage-panorama.com** **alanrogers.com/FR33310**

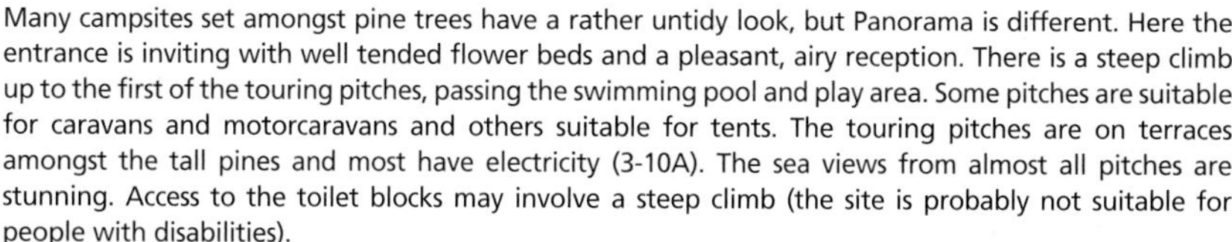

Many campsites set amongst pine trees have a rather untidy look, but Panorama is different. Here the entrance is inviting with well tended flower beds and a pleasant, airy reception. There is a steep climb up to the first of the touring pitches, passing the swimming pool and play area. Some pitches are suitable for caravans and motorcaravans and others suitable for tents. The touring pitches are on terraces amongst the tall pines and most have electricity (3-10A). The sea views from almost all pitches are stunning. Access to the toilet blocks may involve a steep climb (the site is probably not suitable for people with disabilities).

Facilities

Seven toilet blocks (only two open in low season) are clean and well maintained with baby rooms and facilities for disabled people. Fridge hire. Laundry facilities. Motorcaravan services. Restaurant with panoramic view of the ocean. Three heated swimming pools and jacuzzi. Adjacent play area. Tennis. Minigolf. Paragliding. Sub-aqua diving. Organised entertainment in high season for all ages. Library and internet access. Off site: Riding and golf 10 km.

Open: 18 April - 29 September.

Directions

From N250, just before La Teste, take D259 signed Biscarrosse and Dune du Pyla. At roundabout at end of road turn left (south) on D218 coast road signed Biscarrosse and Dune du Pyla. Site is 4 km. on right.
GPS: 44.57265, -1.22053

Charges guide

Per unit incl. 2 persons and electricity	€ 17,00 - € 40,00
extra person	€ 3,00 - € 7,00

Rouffignac-Saint Cernin

Camping BleuSoleil

Domaine Touvent, F-24580 Rouffignac-Saint Cernin (Dordogne) T: **05 53 05 48 30**
E: **infos@camping-bleusoleil.com** **alanrogers.com/FR24380**

Camping BleuSoleil is delightfully and quietly located in the countryside, with magnificent views from all areas of the site. It comprises 70 acres and, at present, has 110 pitches, 95 for touring and 15 used for wooden chalets. Electricity is avialable on every pitch. Set in an open, woody, and hilly area, some of the pitches have partial shade from well-sited trees and hedges. There is some terracing. You will receive a warm welcome at BleuSoleil and a comfortable stay. The village of Rouffignac-St Cernin-de-Reilhac, with its small bars, restaurants and other amenities is 1 km. away and within walking distance.

Facilities

Three modern unisex sanitary blocks are clean, well maintained. En-suite toilet for disabled visitors. Baby room with bath. Enclosed laundry area with two washing machines and dryer. Shop, small bar with TV, and restaurant (high season) Large 200 sq.m. swimming pool and paddling pool. New multisports area. Boules. Small play area and a pen with donkeys and goats. Off site: Village facilities 1 km. Fishing 2 km. Riding 4 km.

Open: 3 April - 30 September.

Directions

From Périgueux take N89 east for 17 km. to Thenon, then D31 south signed Balou. Continue from Balou for 3 km. to the outskirts of Rouffignac-St Cernin-de-Reilhac and look for site sign on the left. Turn off main road to site (less than 1 km). GPS: 45.05497, 0.98691

Charges guide

Per person	€ 3,20 - € 4,60
pitch	€ 5,20 - € 6,90
electricity (10A)	€ 3,90

Saint Amand-de-Coly

Yelloh! Village Lascaux Vacances

F-24290 Saint Amand-de-Coly (Dordogne) T: **04 66 73 97 39**. E: **info@yellohvillage-lascaux-vacances.com**
alanrogers.com/FR24690

Saint Amand-de-Coly can be found at the heart of the Périgord Noir, just five minutes from the world-renowned caves at Lascaux. The site, formerly known as Les Malénies, is a recent member of the Yelloh! Village group and an extensive programme of renovation and development has been carried out since its current owners took over in 2003. There are 44 pitches here, some of which are occupied by mobile homes and chalets (available for rent). The new swimming pool complex is impressive and incorporates a spa bath and sauna. Other on-site amenities include a supermarket and restaurant.

Facilities

Shop. Bar. Restaurant. Takeaway food. Swimming pools with sauna and spa bath. Play area. Bicycle hire. Riding. Activity and entertainment programme. Mobile homes and chalets for rent. Off site: Fishing. Walking and cycle tracks. Lascaux caves 2 km. Sarlat 20 km.

Open: 5 April - 30 September.

Directions

Leave the A89 (Bordeaux - Clermont Ferrand) at exit 17 (Peyrignac) and head south on the D6089 as far as Le Lardin - Saint Lazare. Here, join the southbound D62 to Coly and then follow signs to Saint Amand-de-Coly. Site is well signed from here.
GPS: 45.05494, 1.24656

Charges guide

Per unit incl. 2 persons and electricity	€ 15,00 - € 29,00
extra person	€ 5,00 - € 6,00
child (3-6 yrs)	free - € 6,00
dog	€ 4,00

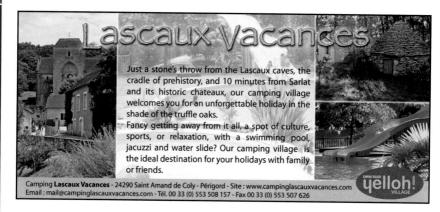

Saint Antoine-de-Breuilh

Flower Camping la Rivière Fleurie

180 rue Théophile Cart, F-24230 Saint Antoine-de-Breuilh (Dordogne) T: **05 53 24 82 80**
E: **info@la-riviere-fleurie.com** **alanrogers.com/FR24300**

This quiet and pleasant campsite is close to the vineyards of Pomerol and St Emilion and not far from the extensive shopping of St Foy la Grande and Bergerac. The 66 pitches are all spacious, divided by shrubs and maturing trees are beginning to provide shade. All pitches have electricity (4/10A) There are no tour operators, but 16 pitches are used for mobile homes to rent and there are studio apartments to let throughout the year. The site has a tranquil and peaceful ambience, suitable for anyone looking for a quiet and relaxing holiday. You will receive a warm and friendly welcome and there is a convivial, family atmosphere.

Facilities

Sanitary facilities are plentiful and modern including an excellent new block. Bar and terrace restaurant. Swimming pool (100 sq.m) and toddlers' pool. TV room. Weekly 'soirées' where the owners host an evening of French food and entertainment. Canoe trips arranged. WiFi (free).
Off site: Tennis court adjacent. Fishing 100 m. Riding 4 km. Bicycle hire 8 km. Golf 10 km. Supermarket 5 km.

Open: 1 April - 30 September.

Directions

Site is in St Aulaye, 3 km. south of D936 Bordeaux - Bergerac road. 6 km. east of Lamothe-Montravel turn south on local roads and follow signs to site 150 m. from river. GPS: 44.82905, 0.12238

Charges guide

Per unit incl. 2 persons and electricity	€ 17,00 - € 23,40
extra person	€ 4,50 - € 5,50
child (under 7 yrs)	€ 2,80 - € 3,50
dog	€ 1,80 - € 2,00

Saint Avit-de-Vialard

Camping Caravaning Saint-Avit Loisirs

Le Bugue, F-24260 Saint Avit-de-Vialard (Dordogne) T: **05 53 02 64 00**
E: **contact@saint-avit-loisirs.com** **alanrogers.com/FR24180**

Although Saint Avit Loisirs is set in the middle of rolling countryside, far from the hustle and bustle of the main tourist areas of the Dordogne the facilities are first class, providing virtually everything you could possibly want without the need to leave the site. This makes it ideal for families with children of all ages. The site is in two sections. One part is dedicated to chalets and mobile homes, whilst the main section of the site contains 199 flat and mainly grassy, good sized pitches, 99 for touring, with electricity (6A), arranged in cul-de-sacs off a main access road.

Facilities

Three modern unisex toilet blocks provide high quality facilities, but could become overstretched (particularly laundry and dishwashing sinks) in high season. Shop, bar, restaurant, cafeteria. Outdoor swimming pool, children's pool, water slide, 'crazy river', heated indoor pool with jacuzzi, fitness room. Soundproofed disco. Minigolf. Boules. BMX track. Tennis. Play area. Canoe trips on the Dordogne and other sporting activities organised. Good walks from site. Off site: Sarlat and Périgueux for markets and hypermarkets.

Open: 1 April - 27 September.

Directions

Site is 6 km. north of Le Bugue. From D710 Le Bugue - Périgueux road, turn west on narrow and bumpy C201 towards St Avit-de-Vialard. Follow road through St Avit, bearing right and site is 1.5 km.
GPS: 44.95161, 0.85042

Charges guide

Per unit incl. 2 persons and electricity	€ 19,50 - € 30,40
extra person	€ 4,00 - € 10,20
child (under 4 yrs)	free
dog	€ 2,20 - € 4,90

Saint Crépin-Carlucet

490

Camping les Peneyrals

Le Poujol, F-24590 Saint Crépin-Carlucet (Dordogne) T: **05 53 28 85 71**. E: **infos@peneyrals.com**
alanrogers.com/FR24320

Within easy reach of all the attractions of the Périgord region, M. and Mme. Havel have created an attractive and friendly family campsite at Les Peneyrals. There are 250 pitches, 111 of which are for touring. The pitches at the bottom of the hill tend to be quieter as they are further from the main facilities, but are all level and grassy (some on terraces), with electricity (5/10A) and most have some shade. An attractive bar and restaurant with terrace overlook the excellent pool complex and at the bottom of the site is a small fishing lake. The site is set on a wooded hillside, with flowers in abundance (thanks to the dedication of Mme. Havel's mother). Activities are organised over a long season, including archery, various sports tournaments, aquagym, discos and a children's club. It is used fairly unobtrusively by a UK tour operator (76 pitches).

Facilities

Two modern, unisex toilet blocks provide good quality facilities, including provision for babies and disabled visitors. Motorcaravan services. Good value shop, excellent restaurant and takeaway (whole season). Pool complex with two large pools (one heated), paddling pool and four slides with splash pool. Indoor heated pool. Bicycle hire. Minigolf. Tennis (charged). Badminton. Play area. Games room, WiFi zone, TV room and small library. Off site: Supermarkets, banks, etc. in Sarlat 11 km.

Open: 11 May - 12 September.

Directions

Site is 11 km. north of Sarlat. From D704 Sarlat - Montignac road turn east on D60 towards Salignac-Eyvigues. After 4 km. turn south on D56 towards St Crépin-Carlucet. Site is about 500 m. along this road on the right. GPS: 44.95776, 1.2729

Charges guide

Per unit incl. 2 persons and electricity	€ 19,00 - € 31,80
extra person	€ 4,90 - € 8,20
child (under 7 yrs)	free - € 6,10

Saint Cybranet

Camping Bel Ombrage

F-24250 Saint Cybranet (Dordogne) T: **05 53 28 34 14**. E: **belombrage@wanadoo.fr**
alanrogers.com/FR24140

Bel Ombrage is a quiet, well maintained site located in a pretty location by the little River Céou, with a pebble beach that is safe and clean for bathing. The site has a good pool complex, but otherwise there are few on site facilities. The 180 well shaded, good sized and flat grass pitches are marked by trees and bushes and all with electricity. The quiet and tranquil setting makes the site particularly popular with couples. Bel Ombrage is very close to Domme and Castelnaud and would make an ideal and inexpensive base for visiting the southern Dordogne area. It is a short walk to the village of St Cybranet, with bar, restaurant and a small well stocked supermarket, and a short drive takes you to the beautifully restored village of Daglan.

Facilities

Two modern toilet blocks are kept spotlessly clean, with facilities for disabled visitors and babies. Laundry facilities. Bread van. Large swimming pool with sun terrace, children's pool. Paddling pool. Play area. Games room. Fishing. Excursions can be booked at reception. Off site: Pizzeria next door. Tennis and canoeing close. Riding and bicycle hire 3 km. Golf 6 km. More shops at Cénac.

Open: 1 June - 5 September.

Directions

Site is about 14 km. south of Sarlat, on the east side of the D57 Castelnaud-la-Chapelle - St Cybranet road, about 1 km. north of the junction with the D50.
GPS: 44.79128, 1.16214

Charges guide

Per person	€ 5,30
child (under 7 yrs)	€ 3,30
pitch	€ 7,00
electricity (10A)	€ 3,80

No credit cards.

Saint Cyprien

Domaine le Cro Magnon

Le Raisse, Allas-les-Mines, F-24220 Saint Cyprien (Dordogne) T: **05 53 29 13 70**
E: **contact@domaine-cro-magnon.com** **alanrogers.com/FR24560**

Le Cro Magnon is pleasantly situated in the heart of the Dordogne valley in the Périgord Noir. The 160 spacious, mostly shady pitches are divided in two different types: tent pitches without electricity and serviced pitches (6A electricity hook up, water and waste water drainage). The site also offers various accommodation for rent. The swimming complex includes two pools (one outdoor, one indoor), one heated, water slides, a jacuzzi and a sauna. Near the entrance of the site are a snack bar, pizzeria, bar, a well stocked shop and the reception. From a viewpoint on the site there are incredible views over the Dordogne valley.

Facilities

Two toilet blocks provide the usual facilities including facilities for disabled visitors. Washing machines. Motorcaravan services. Shop. Bar with TV. Snack bar and takeaway. Swimming pools with slides, jacuzzi and sauna. Multisport court. Boules. Play area. Off site: Canoeing, walking and cycling. Fishing.

Open: 11 May - 30 September.

Directions

From the A20 (Limoges - Brive) take exit 55 for Souillac and Sarlat. In Sarlat take D57 to Vézac, then D703 to St Cyprien. In St Cyprien follow D703, then D50 (left) to Berbiguières and follow signs for site.
GPS: 44.83627, 1.06262

Charges guide

Per unit incl. 2 persons and electricity	€ 16,30 - € 30,20
extra person	€ 3,40 - € 7,40
child (0-3 yrs)	free
dog	€ 1,90 - € 3,60

Saint Emilion

Domaine de la Barbanne

Route de Montagne, D122, F-33330 Saint Emilion (Gironde) T: **05 57 24 75 80**. E: **barbanne@wanadoo.fr**
alanrogers.com/FR33080

La Barbanne is a pleasant, friendly, family-owned site in the heart of the Bordeaux wine region, only 2.5 km. from the famous town of St Emilion. With 174 pitches, most for touring, the owners have created a carefully maintained, well equipped site. The large, level and grassy pitches have dividing hedges and electricity (long leads necessary). The original parts of the site bordering the lake have mature trees, good shade and pleasant surroundings, whilst in the newer area the trees have yet to provide full shade and it can be hot in summer. Twelve pitches for motorcaravans are on tarmac surrounded by grass.

Facilities

Two modern, fully equipped toilet blocks include facilities for campers with disabilities. Motorcaravan services. Well stocked shop. Bar, terrace, takeaway, restaurant (1/6-20/9). Two swimming pools, one heated with water slide (15/4-22/9). Enclosed play area with seats for parents. Children's club (from 1/7). Tennis. Boules. Minigolf. Bicycle hire. Evening entertainment (from 1/7). Off site: St Emilion and shops 2.5 km. Riding 8 km.

Open: 1 April - 22 September.

Directions

Site is 2.5 km. north of St Emilion. Caravans and motorhomes are forbidden through the village of St Emilion and they must approach the site from Libourne on D243 or from Castillon leave D936 and take D130/D243. GPS: 44.91679, -0.14148

Charges 2010

Per unit incl. 2 persons and electricity	€ 22,00 - € 35,00
extra person	€ 3,00 - € 9,00

Camping Cheques accepted.

Saint Geniès-en-Périgord

Camping Caravaning la Bouquerie

F-24590 Saint Geniès-en-Périgord (Dordogne) T: **05 53 28 98 22**. E: **labouquerie@wanadoo.fr**
alanrogers.com/FR24310

La Bouquerie is a well maintained site, situated within easy reach of the main road network in the Dordogne, but without any associated traffic noise. The main complex is based around some beautifully restored traditional Périgordin buildings. It includes a shop and a bar and restaurant overlooking the pool complex, with a large outdoor terrace for fine weather. The excellent restaurant menu is varied and reasonably priced. Of the 180 pitches, 91 are used for touring units and these are of varying size (80-120 sq.m), flat and grassy, some with shade, and all with electrical connections (10A). The rest of the pitches are taken up by site owned mobile homes and a UK tour operator. In high season the site offers a range of tournaments and sporting activities (aqua-gym, archery, canoeing, walks etc) as well as a children's club each weekday morning. La Bouquerie is ideally situated for exploring the Périgord region, and has something to offer families with children of all ages.

Facilities

Three well maintained toilet blocks with facilities for disabled visitors and baby rooms. Washing machines and covered drying lines. Small shop (15/5-15/9), takeaway food. Bar, restaurant (both 15/5-15/9). New heated swimming pool complex including water slides, paddling pool and sunbathing areas with loungers. Carp fishing in lake on site. Bicycle hire. Riding. Off site: Shops and restaurants, etc. in the nearby village of St Geniès.

Open: 19 April - 19 September.

Directions

Site is signed on east side D704 Sarlat - Montignac, about 500 m. north of junction with D64 St Geniès road. Turn off D704 at campsite sign and take first left turn signed La Bouquerie - site is straight ahead. GPS: 44.99865, 1.24549

Charges guide

Per unit incl. 2 persons and electricity	€ 19,00 - € 25,50
extra person	€ 4,60 - € 6,50
child (under 7 yrs)	€ 3,20 - € 4,50

Saint Jean-de-Luz

Camping les Tamaris Plage

Quartier Acotz, 720 route des Plages, F-64500 Saint Jean-de-Luz (Pyrénées-Atlantiques) T: **05 59 26 55 90**
E: **tamaris1@wanadoo.fr** **alanrogers.com/FR64080**

This is a popular, small and pleasant site which is well kept. It is situated outside the town and just across the road from a sandy beach. The 35 touring pitches, all with 7/10A electricity, are of good size and separated by hedges, on slightly sloping ground with some shade. The site becomes full for July and August with families on long stays, so reservation then is essential. Mobile homes for rent occupy a further 40 pitches. A leisure centre and club provides a heated pool and various other free facilities for adults and children. A gym, Turkish bath, massage and other relaxing amenities are available at an extra charge. There is no shop, but bread is available daily across the road. Opposite the site, a popular surf school offers instruction to new and experienced surfers.

Facilities

The single toilet block of good quality and unusual design should be an ample provision. Facilities for disabled people. Washing machine. Wellness health club with free facilities: swimming pool, TV and play room and club for children (4-11 yrs) and on payment: gym, Turkish bath and other health facilities, sunbathing area, jacuzzi, adult TV lounge. Off site: Beach, fishing, surfing 30 m. Bicycle hire or golf 4 km. Riding 7 km.

Open: All year.

Directions

Proceed south on N10 and 1.5 km. after Guethary take first road on right (before access to the motorway and Carrefour centre commercial) and follow site signs. GPS: 43.41794, -1.62399

Charges 2010

Per unit incl. 2 persons and electricity	€ 17,00 - € 29,00
extra person (over 2 yrs)	€ 5,00 - € 7,00
dog	€ 6,00

Saint Julien-en-Born

Yelloh! Village Lous Seurrots

Contis Plage, F-40170 Saint Julien-en-Born (Landes) T: **05 58 42 85 82**
E: **info@yellohvillage-lous-seurrots.com** **alanrogers.com/FR40070**

Lous Seurrots is only a short 300 m. walk from the beach and parts of the site have views across the estuary. There are 610 pitches, mainly in pine woods on sandy undulating ground. They are numbered but only roughly marked out, most have good shade and all 345 touring pitches have electrical hook-ups (adaptors required). The site's pool complex (two heated) is in a superb setting of palm trees and flower beds and the paved sunbathing areas have wonderful views out to the estuary and the sea. For all its size, Lous Seurrots is a family site with the emphasis on peace and tranquillity (no discos).

Facilities

Six well kept, modern toilet blocks, baby rooms and facilities for disabled people. Washing machines. Motorcaravan services. Large shop and Bar (15/5-15/9). Restaurant (1/4-15/9) plus takeaway (1/4-30/9). Swimming pool complex (1/5-30/9) and a jacuzzi with keep fit classes (July/Aug). Tennis. Archery. Minigolf. Canoeing. Bicycle hire. Fishing. Miniclub. Evening entertainment twice weekly in high season in open air auditorium. Only gas barbecues are permitted. Internet. Off site: Riding 3 km.

Open: 31 March - 19 September.

Directions

Turn off D652 on D41 (15 km. south of Mimizan) to Contis-Plage and site is on left as you reach it. GPS: 44.08881, -1.31634

Charges guide

Per unit incl. 2 persons and electricity	€ 15,00 - € 39,00
extra person	€ 5,00 - € 7,00
child (3-7 yrs)	free - € 7,00
animal	€ 4,00

Saint Jean-de-Luz

Camping Atlantica

Quartier Acotz, F-64500 Saint Jean-de-Luz (Pyrénées-Atlantiques) T: **05 59 47 72 44**
E: **info@campingatlantica.com** **alanrogers.com/FR64250**

This is a friendly, family run site with 200 shady and well kept grass pitches set amongst many shrubs, flowers and hedges. There are 99 pitches for touring, 69 have 6A electricity and 41 have water and drainage. The excellent swimming pool area is attractively landscaped with plenty of sunbeds. With a bar, restaurant and takeaway open June to September, the beach 500 m. and the cosmopolitan town of St Jean-de-Luz only 3 km. away, this site is suitable for families and couples of all ages. If excessively wet, motor caravans are advised to call ahead to check availability. The three bright and very clean sanitary blocks are well maintained with large showers and piped music. A comprehensive fitness room includes a sauna and during July and August a trained attendant is available for advice.

Facilities

Three immaculate toilet blocks include facilities for babies and campers with disabilities. Excellent laundry. Swimming pool and fitness room (April-Sept). Bar, restaurant, shop, takeaway (all 15/6-15/9). Games Room. Multisport court. Motorcaravan services. Modern, fenced children's play area. Family entertainment (July/Aug). Off site: Bus to major town 400 m. Large supermarket 1 km. Golf 4 km.

Open: 1 April - 30 September.

Directions

Leave A63, exit 3, taking N10 toward Bayonne. Take the second left turn signed 'Acotz Campings Plages'. At T-junction turn right and follow signs. Campsite is on the right. GPS: 43.41569, -1.61646

Charges guide

Per unit incl. 2 persons and electricity	€ 17,60 - € 33,60
extra person	€ 3,20 - € 6,50
child (under 7 yrs)	€ 2,20 - € 4,00

Saint Paul-lès-Dax

Les Pins du Soleil

Route des Minieres, quartier la Pince, F-40990 Saint Paul-lès-Dax (Landes) T: **05 58 91 37 91**
E: **info@pinsoleil.com** **alanrogers.com/FR40030**

This site will appeal to families, particularly those with younger children, or those who prefer to be some way back from the coast within easy reach of shops, cultural activities, etc. and well placed for touring the area. The new young owners are keen to make improvements to what is already a very pleasant site with 145 good sized pitches. There are 62 pitches for touring units all of which have electricity and drainage. The site benefits from being developed in light woodland so there is a fair amount of shade from the many small trees.

Facilities

Sanitary facilities include washbasins, hot showers and provision for disabled visitors. Laundry. Motorcaravn services. Small supermarket (1/6-31/10). Bar. Takeaway. Attractive, medium sized swimming pool with café, new paddling pool and jacuzzi (all 2/6-15/9). Playground and children's miniclub in high season. Covered entertainmetns area. Bicycle hire. Off site: Bus to the thermal baths 1 km. Fishing 1 km. Riding 3 km.

Open: 1 April - 31 October.

Directions

From west on N124, avoid bypass, follow signs for Dax and St Paul. Almost immediately turn right at roundabout onto D459 and follow signs. Site shortly on left. It is well signed from town centre, north of river. GPS: 43.72103, -1.09354

Charges guide

Per unit incl. 2 persons	€ 8,00 - € 18,00
incl. electricity, water and drainage	€ 15,00 - € 24,00
extra person	€ 6,00
child (4-13 yrs)	€ 3,50
animal	€ 2,00

Reduced rate for stays over 21 nights.
Camping Cheques accepted.

Saint Martin-de-Seignanx

490

Camping Caravaning Lou P'tit Poun

110 avenue du Quartier Neuf, F-40390 Saint Martin-de-Seignanx (Landes) T: **05 59 56 55 79**
E: **contact@louptitpoun.com** **alanrogers.com/FR40140**

The manicured grounds surrounding Lou P'tit Poun give it a well kept appearance, a theme carried out throughout this very pleasing site which celebrated its 20th anniversary in 2009. It is only after arriving at the car park that you feel confident it is not a private estate. Beyond this point an abundance of shrubs and trees is revealed. Behind a central sloping flower bed lies the open plan reception area. The avenues around the site are wide and the 168 pitches (142 for touring) are spacious. All have 10A electricity, many also have water and drainage and some are separated by low hedges. The jovial owners not only make their guests welcome, but extend their enthusiasm to organising weekly entertainment for young and old during high season. A 'Sites et Paysages' member.

Facilities

Two unisex sanitary blocks, maintained to a high standard and kept clean, include washbasins in cabins, a baby bath and provision for disabled people. Laundry facilities with washing machine and dryer. Motorcaravan service point. Small shop (1/7-31/8). Café/restaurant (1/7-31/8). Swimming pool (1/6-15/9) Play area. Games room, TV. Half-court tennis. Off site: Bayonne 6 km. Fishing or riding 7 km. Golf 10 km. Sandy beaches of Basque coast a 10-minute drive.

Open: 2 June - 12 September.

Directions

Leave A63 at exit 6 and join D817 in the direction of Pau. Site is signed at Leclerc supermarket. Continue for 3.5 km. and site is clearly signed on right.
GPS: 43.52406, -1.41196

Charges guide

Per unit incl. 2 persons and electricity	€ 22,00 - € 33,00
extra person	€ 7,00 - € 7,50
child (under 7 yrs)	€ 5,00 - € 5,50
dog	€ 4,00 - € 5,00

Saint Seurin-de-Prats

Camping la Plage

F-24230 Saint Seurin-de-Prats (Dordogne) T: **05 53 58 61 07**. E: **info@camping-in-france.net**
alanrogers.com/FR24120

This is a beautiful site where the natural environment blends in harmony with nature. It is more like a park than a campsite with a differing array of trees and shrubs. Camping la Plage nestles gently beside the River Dordogne where there is a feeling of spaciousness, tranquillity and calm. The owners are friendly and helpful and are keen to ensure you enjoy your holiday. The 85 pitches are generous in size with some being open and some shaded, and 15A electricity is provided. They are separated by shrubs and hedges. Access for motorcaravans and large units does not cause a problem.

Facilities

Two traditional style sanitary blocks. No facilities for disabled visitors. Bar (all year) and restaurant (Apr-Oct). Takeaway. TV. Swimming pool. Pétanque. Play area. Private access to the river. Fishing. Communal barbecues only. Off site: Golf 12 km. Riding 6 km.

Open: 15 May - 15 September (gites longer).

Directions

Take the D936 from Bergerac to Bordeaux. Bypass St Foy Le Grande and a few kilometres further on is a roundabout with St Seurin-de-Prats on the left. Take that road and site is on the right, well signed.
GPS: 44.82205, 0.07501

Charges guide

Per unit incl. 2 persons	€ 15,00 - € 18,50
extra person	€ 3,00 - € 6,00
electricity (15A)	€ 4,00

Saint Pardoux

Kawan Village Chateau le Verdoyer

Kawan Villages
www.kawan-villages.com

Champs Romain, F-24470 Saint Pardoux (Dordogne) T: **05 53 56 94 64**

E: **chateau@verdoyer.fr** **alanrogers.com/FR24010**

The 26-hectare estate has three lakes, two for fishing and one with a sandy beach and safe swimming area. There are 135 good sized touring pitches, level, terraced and hedged. With a choice of wooded area or open field, all have electricity (5/10A) and most share a water supply between four pitches. There is a swimming pool complex and in high season activities are organised for children (5-13 yrs) but there is no disco. This site is well adapted for those with disabilities, with two fully adapted chalets, wheelchair access to all facilities and even a lift into the pool. Le Verdoyer has been developed in the park of a restored château and is owned by a Dutch family. We particularly like this site for its beautiful buildings and lovely surroundings. It is situated in the lesser known area of the Dordogne sometimes referred to as the Périgord Vert, with its green forests and small lakes. The courtyard area between reception and the bar is home to evening activities, and provides a pleasant place to enjoy drinks and relax. The château itself has rooms to let and its excellent lakeside restaurant is also open to the public.

Facilities

Well appointed toilet blocks include facilities for disabled people and baby baths. Serviced launderette. Motorcaravan services. Fridge rental. Shop with gas. Bar, snacks, takeaway and restaurant, both open all season. Bistro (July/Aug). Two pools the smaller covered in low season, slide, paddling pool. Play areas. Tennis. Minigolf. Bicycle hire. Small library. Off site: Riding 5 km.

Open: 26 April - 6 October.

Directions

Site is 2 km. from the Limoges (N21) - Chalus (D6bis-D85) - Nontron road, 20 km. south of Chalus and is well signed from main road. Site on D96 about 4 km. north of village of Champs Romain. GPS: 45.55035, 0.7947

Charges guide

Per unit incl. 2 persons and electricity	€ 18,00 - € 29,00
full services	€ 18,00 - € 33,50
extra person	€ 3,00 - € 6,50

Camping Cheques accepted.

The Travel Service to book this site call 01580 214000 ...we'll arrange everything

Salignac-Eyvigues

Flower Camping le Temps de Vivre

F-24590 Salignac-Eyvigues (Dordogne) T: **05 53 28 93 21**. E: **contact@temps-de-vivre.com**

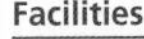
alanrogers.com/FR24460

Le Temps de Vivre is situated in the centre of the Périgord Noir, in the countryside and lies about 250 m. above sea level. The area of the campsite covers about 4.5-acres in total, with 1.5-acres in use at present. It is a small, friendly, family run site with 50 pitches, 30 of which are for touring and 20 for mobile homes. The pitches are wide and terraces separate some of them. All have electricity connections available (10A) and you will find a variety of trees and bushes often as a natural separation. This is a delightful and peaceful rural site.

Facilities

One modern unisex sanitary block, very clean, well maintained, serviced, and adequate for the number of pitches. En-suite toilet for disabled visitors. Baby room with bath. Covered laundry area. Small shop all season in the reception area. Small bar, restaurant and takeaway (July/Aug). Two swimming pools (one for children). Boules. Play area. Off site: Shops and restaurants, etc. within walking distance in the nearby village of Salignac-Eyvigues.

Open: 1 April - 1 November.

Directions

From Brive-La-Gaillarde heading south on the A20 continue for 30 km. to exit 55 signed Souillac. Take the D62/D15 northwest for 12 km. until Salignac-Eyvigues. As you drive through the town centre look for blue sign for site. Follow the sign off the main road for about 2 km. GPS: 44.96374, 1.32813

Charges guide

Per unit incl. 1 person	€ 11,00 - € 18,50
extra person	€ 2,50 - € 4,50

The Travel Service to book this site call 01580 214000 ...we'll arrange everything

Sanguinet

491

Camping les Grands Pins

1039 avenue de Losa, F-40460 Sanguinet (Landes) T: **05 58 78 61 74**. E: **info@campinglesgrandspins.com**
alanrogers.com/FR40250

Approached by a road alongside the lake, this site is set amongst tall pine trees. The gravel pitches are of average size, mostly level and shaded. Hedges divide those available for tourers and these are set amongst the many mobile homes. Large units may find manoeuvring difficult. There may be some aircraft noise at times from a nearby army base. A central pool complex includes a covered heated indoor pool, an outdoor pool, water slide and flume. In early and late season this is a very quiet site with very few facilities open. However, there are plenty of walks, cycle rides and the lake to enjoy. The poolside bar, restaurant and shops are only open in July and August when the site is busy, offering watersports, minigolf, a children's club, boat trips and organised activities. Fishing is also available. The charming small village of Sanguinet is 2 km. away with shops, bars, restaurants and an archaeological museum.

Facilities

Four toilet blocks include washbasins in cabins, showers and British style toilets (not all open in low seasons). Baby bath and provision for disabled visitors. Laundry facilities. Motorcaravan service point. Shop, bar, restaurant and takeaway (1/7-31/8). Indoor pool (all season). Outdoor pool complex (1/7-31/8). Play area. Games room and TV in bar. Tennis. Bicycle hire (July/Aug). Children's club. Pets are not accepted in July/Aug. Barbecues are not allowed (dedicated area provided). Off site: Beach 30 m. Fishing 2 km. Golf and riding 15 km. Boat launching 1 km.

Open: 1 April - 31 October.

Directions

Enter Sanguinet from the north on the D46. At one way system turn right. Do not continue on one way system but go straight on toward lake (signed) on rue de Lac. Site is 2 km. on left.
GPS: 44.48396, -1.089716

Charges guide

Per unit incl. 2 persons and electricity	€ 16,00 - € 37,00
extra person	€ 4,50 - € 6,50
child (3-7 yrs)	€ 4,00 - € 5,00

Salles

Camping des Bastides

Terre Rouge, F-47150 Salles (Lot-et-Garonne) T: **05 53 40 83 09**. E: **info@campingdesbastides.com**
alanrogers.com/FR47130

Attractive and well maintained, this 6.5-hectare site is hilly and terraced with good views from the top of the site. Although the terrain is hilly, most of the 90 medium sized touring pitches are fairly level and moderately shaded. The friendly Dutch owners of 11 years are warm and welcoming. Tight turns with narrow gravel paths and overhanging trees may cause some difficulties for larger units. Reception keeps information on a variety of local walking and cycling routes. Weekly trips are arranged to one of the wine growing châteaux in the region.

Facilities

Two modern, clean and well maintained sanitary blocks can be heated. Facilities for disabled visitors. Excellent children's facilities with baby bath and child-size facilities. Private en-suite facilities for hire. Shop for essentials (with gas). Bar/reception and snack restaurant (including takeaway). Swimming pool complex with swimming pool, pool with slides, and two paddling pools. Boules. Play area with bouncy castle. Small indoor play area with TV and small library. WiFi access. Entertainment (high season) including excursions and weekly barbecues. Off site: Fumel 8 km. Fishing 1 km. Riding and bicycle hire 10 km. Golf 25 km.

Open: 1 May - 15 September.

Directions

From Fumel, take D710 north towards Cuzorn. Before reaching Cuzorn, turn northwest on D162 and site is 6 km. on the right hand side (well signed).
GPS: 44.5525, 0.8815

Charges guide

Per unit incl. 2 persons and electricity (6A)	€ 15,00 - € 25,00
extra person	€ 4,00 - € 5,50
child (2-12 yrs)	€ 2,25 - € 2,75
dog	free - € 2,00

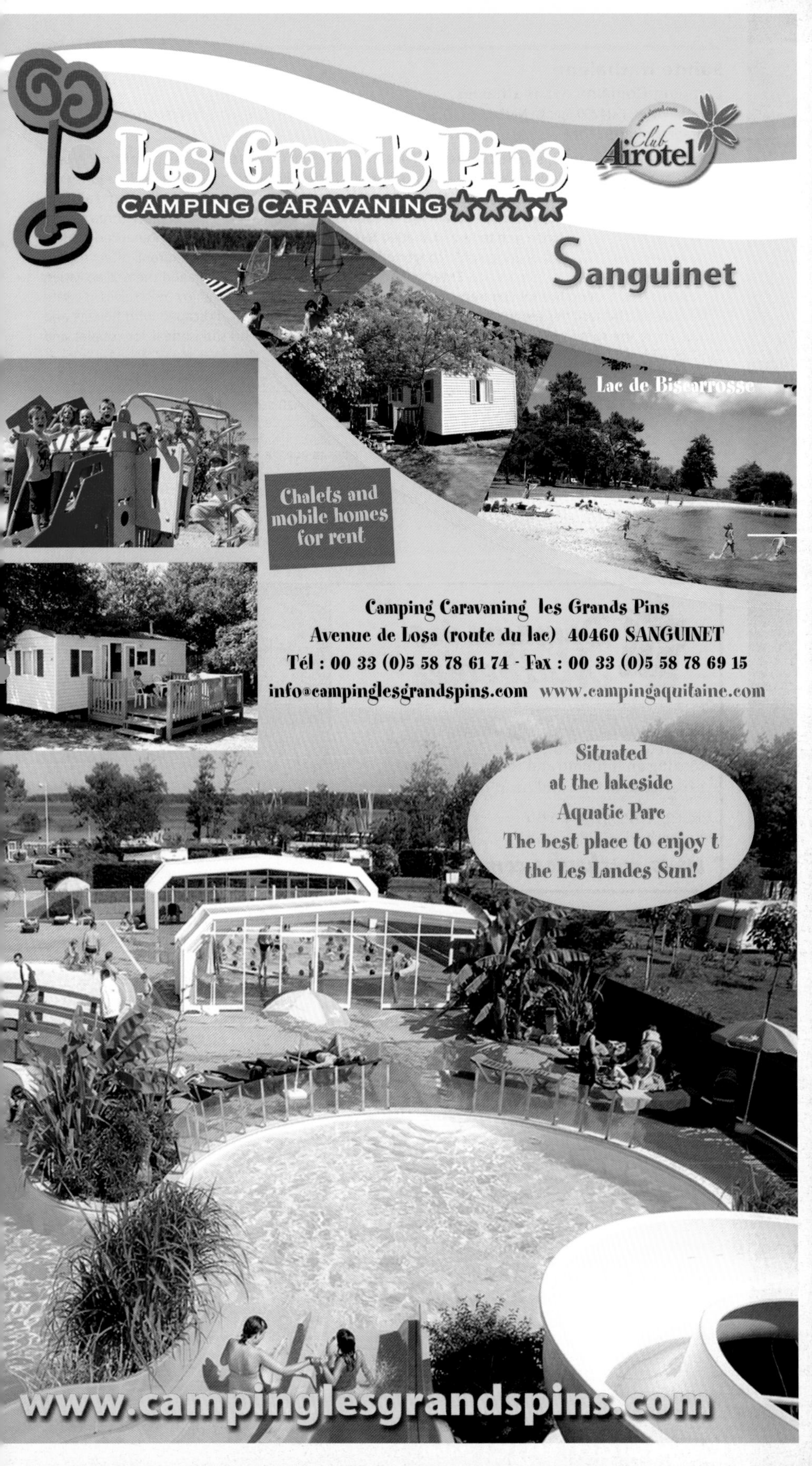
Les Grands Pins
CAMPING CARAVANING ★★★★
Club Airotel
www.airotel.com
Sanguinet
Lac de Biscarrosse
Chalets and mobile homes for rent
Camping Caravaning les Grands Pins
Avenue de Losa (route du lac) 40460 SANGUINET
Tél : 00 33 (0)5 58 78 61 74 - Fax : 00 33 (0)5 58 78 69 15
info@campinglesgrandspins.com www.campingaquitaine.com
Situated
at the lakeside
Aquatic Parc
The best place to enjoy t
the Les Landes Sun!
www.campinglesgrandspins.com

Sainte Nathalène

Camping Domaine des Mathevies

Les Mathevies, F-24200 Sainte Nathalène (Dordogne) T: **05 53 59 20 86**. E: **mathevies@mac.com**
alanrogers.com/FR24740

This site is a rustic treasure, situated in the rural heart of the Perigord. Family run, the delightful owners, Patrick and Natalie McAlpine, will give you a warm and friendly welcome. The rural location gives a wonderful feeling of a tranquillity. The 26 pitches are large and generous at 150-280 sq.m. and all have 10A electricity, five also with water and drainage. In addition, there are six wooden chalets, three mobile homes and a traditional stone gite to rent. A shaded terrace is next to the beautiful, original Perigordine building and the barn has been lovingly converted into the restaurant. The restaurant offers superb home cooked food with local produce. Entertainment includes a barbecue soirée and themed activities. Pony riding and a camp fire for children go down really well and children can enjoy themselves in a safe environment. The facilities are well maintained and the site is beautifully landscaped with flowers and shrubs There are some wonderful views over the rolling countryside. This site is ideal for couples and families with young children and all will enjoy what it has to offer.

Facilities

Sanitary facilities include provision for disabled visitors. Bar. Restaurant. Swimming and paddling pools. Tennis court. Library. Selection of games. Satelite TV. Free WiFi. Playground. Pétanque. Special interest groups catered for. Off site: Riding 2 km. Fishing and canoeing 5 km. Golf 8 km.

Open: 24 April - 26 September.

Directions

From the A20 exit 55 for Souillac follow road to Roufillac and Carlux. Continue to Sainte Nathalène and site is signed from there.
GPS: 44.918056, 1.277778

Charges guide

Per person	€ 4,50 - € 7,00
child (2-7 yrs)	€ 3,50 - € 4,50
pitch	€ 5,50 - € 7,50
electricity	€ 4,00

Sarlat

Camping les Tailladis

Marcillac-Saint Quentin, F-24200 Sarlat (Dordogne) T: **05 53 59 10 95**. E: **tailladis@wanadoo.fr**
alanrogers.com/FR24480

Les Tailladis is a well situated, mature campsite of some 17-hectares of woodland, owned by the same Dutch and French family for over 42 years. It is about 12 km. from Sarlat, Eyzies and Montignac-Lascauax, and 35 km. from Souillac. Four hectares of the total provides medium to large pitches which are grassy, terraced and partially shaded, with electricity (6A), and water points close by. There is also a small stream and pond. The access road and campsite roads/tracks are narrow and winding, which may cause some difficulties for some larger units. The hosts are welcoming and you will be greeted with a drink and warm, friendly service.

Facilities

One heated sanitary block is well sited for all pitches. En-suite toilet for disabled visitors. Baby bath and changing area. Laundry room. Motorcaravan service point. Large shop (fresh bread and milk can be ordered). Restaurant, bar. Library. Swimming pool and paddling pool. Play area with trampoline. Activities organised during high season. Internet access (charged). Off site: Riding 3 km. Bicycle hire 12 km. Golf 25 km. Boat launching 25 km.

Open: All year.

Directions

From Sarlat-la-Canéda, take D704 heading north. After 10 km, look for signs on the left for Marcillac St Quentin. Take this road heading northwest, and site is less than 3 km. after Marcillac-St Quentin on the left hand side. Access and site roads are narrow for large units. GPS: 44.97450, 1.18832

Charges guide

Per person	€ 3,21 - € 5,35
child (3-8 yrs)	€ 2,28 - € 3,80
pitch with electricity	€ 7,77 - € 10,55

Sarlat-la-Canéda

491

Camping les Grottes de Roffy

Sainte Nathalène, F-24200 Sarlat-la-Canéda (Dordogne) T: **05 53 59 15 61**. E: **roffy@perigord.com**

alanrogers.com/FR24130

About 5 km. east of Sarlat, Les Grottes de Roffy is a pleasantly laid out, family site. There are 162 clearly marked pitches, some very large, set on very well kept grass terraces. They have easy access and good views across an attractive valley. Some have plentiful shade, although others are more open, and all have electricity (6A). The reception, bar, restaurant and shop are located within converted farm buildings surrounding a semi-courtyard. The site shop is well stocked with a variety of goods and a tempting epicerie (home made on site) with plenty of ideas for the barbecue and to takeaway. In season there is something for all the family, with evening entertainment (including jazz and Latin evenings) and daily activities for children. A variety of activities and excursions for all ages includes quad biking, pottery, massage and yoga. Conveniently located for Sarlat and all other Dordogne attractions, this is a good site for families. Used by tour operators.

Facilities

Two toilet blocks with modern facilities are more than adequate. Well stocked shop. Bar and 'gastronomique' restaurant with imaginative and sensibly priced menu. Takeaway (all amenities from 6/5). Good swimming pool complex comprising two deep pools (one heated), a fountain, paddling pool and heated jacuzzi. Tennis. Games room. Play area. Entertainment and activities for all ages. Off site: Fishing 2 km. Bicycle hire 7 km. Riding 10 km. Golf 15 km.

Open: 26 April - 21 September.

Directions

Take D47 east from Sarlat to Ste Nathalène. Just before Ste Nathalène the site is signed on the right hand side of the road. Turn here, and the site is about 800 m. along the lane. GPS: 44.90404, 1.2821

Charges guide

Per person	€ 5,50 - € 7,20
child (2-7 yrs)	€ 4,00 - € 5,50
pitch	€ 7,10 - € 10,30
incl. electricity	€ 9,80 - € 13,10
with full services	€ 11,80 - € 15,10

les
Grottes
de
Roffy
camping
caravaning
Sainte-Nathalèle • 24200 Sarlat • France
E-mail contact@roffy.fr Tél. +33 (0)5 53 59 15 61 • Fax +33 (0)5 53 31 09 11

Sarlat

Camping la Palombière

Sainte Nathalène, F-24200 Sarlat (Dordogne) T: **05 53 59 42 34**. E: **la.palombiere@wanadoo.fr**

alanrogers.com/FR24570

This site is set in a gorgeous, rural part of France amongst the beauty of the Perigord countryside with its rolling green hills and ancient buildings. The restored and preserved buildings at la Palombière add to the pleasure of this delightful site. It is evident that much investment has gone into making this holiday destination a place to remember. There are 177 pitches of which 88 are for touring caravans and tents. All have electricity (10A) and some are fully serviced. Most are level and shaded from the sun, with some terracing because of the different levels. There are 89 mobile homes with 45 to rent.

Facilities

Two modern sanitary blocks include facilities for babies and disabled people. Washing machines and dryers. Well stocked shop, bar, restaurant, snack bar and takeaway, (all 1/5-11/9) Heated swimming pool complex with slide and toboggan (all season). Gymnasium. Playgrounds. Library. Sports field. Tennis. Minigolf. Boules. Satellite TV. Games room. Bicycle hire. Internet facilities. WiFi. Off site: Riding 3 km. Canoeing 3 km. Golf 10 km.

Open: 30 April - 12 September.

Directions

Take the D47 east from Sarlat to Ste Nathalène. Site is signed from village and is reached by taking a left turn just beyond it. GPS: 44.90819, 1.29252

Charges 2010

Per unit incl. 2 persons and electricity	€ 19,00 - € 29,30
extra person	€ 4,50 - € 7,70
child (1-7 yrs)	free - € 5,40
dog	€ 2,00

Sarlat

Camping le Montant

Saint André-d'Allas, F-24200 Sarlat (Dordogne) T: **05 53 59 18 50**. E: **lemontant@wanadoo.fr**
alanrogers.com/FR24610

Camping le Montant is a family run site and is located on a hillside overlooking beautiful countryside only 2 km. away from Sarlat. The 100 large touring pitches, all with electricity (up to 10A) are divided into two areas, each with its own sanitary block. A main central building, surrounded by flowers, houses the reception, bar with terrace and takeaway. One part of the site is shaded with hedges, the other area is more open with flat terraced pitches looking out over the wooded hills. The site has an excellent heated pool area on three levels with a covered jacuzzi, pool and children's pool.

Facilities

Both toilet blocks are very well equipped especially the new one with its baby room and large laundry (washing machines, dryers etc). Restaurant, takeaway and bar (1/5-20/9). Pool table, table football and some electronic games. Minigolf. Boules. Activities organised for children, teenagers and adults both during the day and evenings (July/Aug). Off site: Historic Sarlat 2 km. Riding 3 km. Fishing and golf 5 km.

Open: 1 May - 20 September.

Directions

Site is 2 km. south of Sarlat off the D57 Sarlat - Baynac road. If approaching from Sarlat, site is signed to the right. Follow this road for about 1 km.
GPS: 44.865344, 1.187704

Charges guide

Per unit incl. 2 persons and electricity	€ 13,90 - € 26,10
extra person	€ 3,50 - € 6,50
child (2-7 yrs)	€ 2,10 - € 4,50
dog	free - € 1,00

Sarlat-la-Canéda

Camping les Périères

Rue Jean Gabin, F-24203 Sarlat-la-Canéda (Dordogne) T: **05 53 59 05 84**. E: **les-perieres@wanadoo.fr**
alanrogers.com/FR24030

Les Périères is a good quality small site set on an attractive hillside within easy walking distance of the beautiful medieval town of Sarlat. The 100 pitches are arranged on wide terraces around the semi-circle of a fairly steep valley, overlooking a central leisure area that includes indoor and outdoor swimming pools and two tennis courts. The pitches are of a very good size, all equipped with electricity (6A), individual water and drainage points and many have dappled shade from the numerous walnut trees on the site (the walnuts can be bought in the campsite shop).

Facilities

Good toilet blocks with facilities for disabled visitors, baby bathroom, washing machines and dryers. Motorcaravan services. Small shop. Pleasant bar. Small snack bar/takeaway (July/Aug). Outdoor swimming pool (no shorts), paddling pool, indoor spa pool and sauna (all season). Tennis, football, fitness track. Stone cottages to rent. No electric barbecues allowed. Off site: Bicycle hire 1 km. Fishing 5 km. Riding and golf 7 km.

Open: Easter - 30 September.

Directions

Site is on the east side of Sarlat, on the D47 to Ste Nathalène (negotiating Sarlat town centre is best done outside peak hours). GPS: 44.8937, 1.22748

Charges guide

Per unit incl. 2 persons	€ 19,70 - € 26,90
incl. electricity	€ 23,50 - € 30,90
extra person	€ 6,30
child (under 7 yrs)	€ 4,30

Credit cards accepted with 2% fee.

Sarlat-la-Canéda

Castel Camping le Moulin du Roch

Route des Eyzies-Le Roch (D47), F-24200 Sarlat-la-Canéda (Dordogne) T: **05 53 59 20 27**
E: **moulin.du.roch@wanadoo.fr** **alanrogers.com/FR24040**

The site has 195 pitches, of which 124 are for touring units. They are mostly flat (some slope slightly) and grassy and all have electricity (6A). Pitches on the upper levels have plenty of shade, whilst those on the lower level near the amenities and the fishing lake are more open. Entertainment and activities are organised from June to September, with something for everyone from quizzes and sports tournaments to canoeing and riding for the more adventurous. An excellent multi-lingual children's club runs in July and August. Walking and mountain biking routes lead from the site through surrounding woodland.

Facilities

Modern, well maintained, clean toilet blocks. Washing machines, dryers. Good shop, Bar with WiFi and terrace, Takeaway, Superb restaurant, Attractive swimming pool, paddling pool, sun terrace, (all open all season) Fishing lake. Tennis. Boules. Playground. Evening entertainment throughout the high season. Pets are not accepted.
Off site: Supermarkets, banks, etc. at Sarlat 10 km. Bicycle hire and riding 10 km. Golf 15 km.

Open: 10 May - 17 September.

Directions

Site is 10 km. west of Sarlat-la-Canéda, on the south side of the D47 Sarlat - Les Eyzies road.
GPS: 44.90867, 1.1148

Charges guide

Per unit incl. 2 persons	
and electricity	€ 19,00 - € 33,00
incl. full services	€ 23,00 - € 37,00
extra person	€ 5,00 - € 9,50
child (3-7 yrs)	free - € 4,50

Camping Cheques accepted.

Sarlat-la-Canéda

Camping les Terrasses du Périgord

Pech-d'Orance, F-24200 Sarlat-la-Canéda (Dordogne) T: **05 53 59 02 25**
E: **terrasses-du-perigord@wanadoo.fr** **alanrogers.com/FR24670**

Set on a hill top on the edge of Sarlat, this site has panoramic views across the Périgord. There are 90 pitches, of which 75 are for touring units, with the remaining 15 being for chalets and mobile homes for rent. The site is sloping on different levels but the pitches are generally level. All are shady, marked and separated by trees. Electricity is 6, 10 or 16A. For those with larger units, it is essential to phone in advance for pitch availability, as not all are suitable. A warm and friendly welcome is given by the French owners. An old, fully restored farmhouse fitted out as a bar and a wine cave offers you tasting together with a bistro. A well stocked shop is next to the games room which doubles up for evening entertainment. This includes Périgordine dancing and shows. The swimming pool and children's pool have only recently been added and a large playground has a cable slide. There are many places to visit in the surrounding area. Sarlat is 2 km. away.

Facilities

One modern sanitary block divided into two provides all facilities including those for disabled visitors and babies. Washing machine and dryer. Motorcaravan services. Shop. Bar with snack bar and takeaway. Wine tastings. Swimming pool and toddler's pool. Play area with cable slide. Minigolf. Bicycle hire. Gas and electric barbecues only. Evening entertainment. Off site: Caves. Châteaux. Fishing 2 km. Canoeing 2 km. Riding 8 km.

Open: 25 April - 7 September.

Directions

From Sarlat, take D47 to Proissans. Continue on D56 to Proissans and site is 500 m. on the left. In Sarlat, follow the signs for hospital as it is nearby.
GPS: 44.9058, 1.23598

Charges 2010

Per unit incl. 2 persons	
and electricity	€ 15,60 - € 19,70
extra person	€ 3,90 - € 5,00
child (under 7 yrs)	€ 2,20 - € 2,90

No credit cards.

Sauveterre-la-Lemance

Flower Camping Kawan Village Moulin du Périé

F-47500 Sauveterre-la-Lemance (Lot-et-Garonne) T: **05 53 40 67 26**
E: **moulinduperie@wanadoo.fr** **alanrogers.com/FR47010**

Set in a quiet area and surrounded by woodlands this peaceful little site is well away from much of the tourist bustle. It has 125 reasonably sized, grassy pitches, all with 6A electricity, divided by mixed trees and bushes with most having good shade. All are extremely well kept, as indeed is the entire site. The attractive front courtyard is complemented by an equally pleasant terrace at the rear. Two small, clean swimming pools overlook a shallow, spring water lake, ideal for inflatable boats and paddling and bordering the lake, a large grass field is popular for games. The picturesque old mill buildings, adorned with flowers and creepers, now house the bar and restaurant. The food is to be recommended here, as is the owner's extensive knowledge of wine that he is pleased to share with visitors. A quiet, friendly site with regular visitors – reservation is advised for July/August. Bergerac Airport is an hour away so it may suit those choosing a mobile home or bungalow tent and wanting to travel light.

Facilities

Two clean, modern and well maintained toilet blocks include facilities for disabled visitors. Motorcaravan services. Fridge, barbecue. Basic shop. Bar/reception, restaurant and takeaway. Two small swimming pools (no Bermuda-style shorts). Boules. Outdoor chess. Playground. Small indoor play area. Bicycle hire. Organised activities in high season including canoeing, riding, wine tasting visits, sightseeing trips, barbecues, gastronomic meals. Winter caravan storage. Off site: Fishing 1 km. Riding 7 km. Small supermarket in village and larger stores in Fumel.

Open: 12 May - 18 September.

Directions

From D710, Fumel - Périgueux, turn southeast into Sauveterre-la-Lemance. Turn left (northeast) at far end on C201 signed Château Sauveterre and Loubejec (site also signed). Site is 3 km. on right.
GPS: 44.59016, 1.04761

Charges 2010

Per unit incl. 2 persons and electricity	€ 18,15 - € 27,60
extra person	€ 4,50 - € 7,00
child (2-7 yrs)	€ 1,90 - € 3,70
dog	€ 2,30 - € 4,40

Camping Cheques accepted.

Sérignac-Péboudou

Camping la Vallée de Gardeleau

F-47410 Sérignac-Péboudou (Lot-et-Garonne) T: **05 53 36 96 96**. E: **valleegardeleau@Wanadoo.fr**

alanrogers.com/FR47120

Camping La Vallée is a delightful, small, family run site established over 12 years ago. It is well hidden and private, some 9 km. from civilization and deep in the countryside of Lot-et-Garonne, very close to the border of the Dordogne and 150 km. from the Atlantic coast. It has a total of 33 pitches, 26 for touring, seven mobile homes, and four bungalow tents. The medium-sized pitches are well laid out, all with hedges and some shade, some with views. The owners Pierre and Marie-Madeleine Pécheux are very conscientious and work extremely hard to keep the site clean and well maintained.

Facilities

Two heated sanitary blocks are well sited and clean. Facilities for disabled visitors. Baby room. Washing machine. Shop with daily deliveries of fresh bread. Bar with snack bar and TV. Restaurant (high season). Swimming pool. Large boules area (need to bring own boules). Small play area. Animation for children (high season). Off site: Fishing and riding 2 km. Bicycle hire 9 km. Golf 20 km.

Open: 2 March - 31 October.

Directions

From Castillones on the N21 find the D254 to Sérignac-Péboudou and follow this. Some 10 km. along this road, look for signs to site which is on the left hand side. GPS: 44.61606, 0.51821

Charges 2010

Per unit incl. 2 persons	€ 12,70 - € 17,80
extra person	€ 1,70 - € 4,00

Soulac-sur-Mer

Camping Club Les Lacs

126 route des Lacs, F-33780 Soulac-sur-Mer (Gironde) T: **05 56 09 76 63**. E: **info@camping-les-lacs.com**

alanrogers.com/FR33400

Given its proximity to the Gironde ferry terminal at Le Verdon, many campers head south through Soulac. It is, however, a smart resort with a fine sandy beach. Camping Club Les Lacs is one of the best sites here and has 228 pitches on offer, of which 114 are available to touring units. All pitches have electrical connnections (5A). Site amenities are impressive with a large, modern complex at the entrance housing a large bar, restaurant, shop and stage for evening entertainment (high season). There is a large outdoor pool and covered pool adjacent (open for the full season). A member of 'Sites et Paysages'.

Facilities

Good quality, modern toilet blocks.with showers and washbasins in cubicles. Facilities for disabled visitors. Washing machines and dryers. Shop. Bar, restaurant and takeaway (1/6-15/9). Swimming and paddling pools (1/6-15/9). Indoor pool all season. Water slide. Minigolf. Games room. Playground. Entertainment and children's club in peak season. Off site: Nearest beach 2.5 km. Bicycle hire 2 km. Riding 12 km. Fishing 4 km.

Open: 5 April - 8 November.

Directions

Site is 1 km. south of Soulac on the D101 (Routes des Lacs) and is well signed. GPS: 45.48355, -1.11952

Charges guide

Per unit incl. 2 persons	€ 16,00 - € 26,00
extra person	€ 4,00 - € 5,00
child (3-10 yrs)	€ 2,00 - € 4,00
electricity (5A)	€ 5,00

Urrugne

Sunêlia Col d'Ibardin

F-64122 Urrugne (Pyrénées-Atlantiques) T: **05 59 54 31 21**. E: **info@col-ibardin.com**

alanrogers.com/FR64110

This family-owned site at the foot of the Basque Pyrénées is highly recommended and deserves praise. It is well run with emphasis on personal attention, the friendly family and their staff ensuring that all are made welcome. It is attractively set in the middle of an oak wood with a mountain stream cascading through it. Behind the forecourt, with its brightly coloured shrubs and modern reception area, various roadways lead to the 191 pitches. These are individual, spacious and enjoy the benefit of the shade (if preferred a more open aspect can be found). There are electricity hook-ups (4/10A) and adequate water points. A very attractive chalet 'village' has recently been added. From this site you can enjoy the mountain scenery, be on the beach in 7-10 km. or cross the border into Spain in about 14 km.

Facilities

Two toilet blocks, one rebuilt to a high specification, are kept very clean. WC for disabled people. Dishwashing and laundry facilities. Motorcaravan service point. Shop for basics and bread orders (15/6-15/9). Restaurant, takeaway service and bar (15/6-15/9). Heated swimming pool and paddling pool. Playground and club (adult supervision). Tennis. Boules. Video games. Bicycle hire. Multisport area. Not suitable for American motorhomes.
Off site: Supermarket and shopping centre 5 km. Fishing and golf 7 km. Riding 20 km.

Open: 1 April - 30 September.

Directions

Leave A63 at St Jean-de-Luz sud, exit no. 2 and join RN10 in direction of Urrugne. Turn left at roundabout (Col d'Ibardin) on D4. Site on right after 5 km. Do not turn off to the Col itself, carry on towards Ascain.
GPS: 43.33376, -1.68458

Charges guide

Per unit incl. 2 persons and electricity	€ 16,50 - € 34,00
extra person	€ 3,00 - € 6,00
child (2-7 yrs)	€ 2,00 - € 3,50
pet	€ 2,50

Tourtoirac

Camping les Tourterelles

F-24390 Tourtoirac (Dordogne) T: **05 53 51 11 17**. E: **les-tourterelles@aliceadsl.fr**

alanrogers.com/FR24250

This is a well maintained, Dutch owned site with its own equestrian centre that will appeal to lovers of the countryside, in an area that is ideal for walking or horse riding, yet is within easy reach of Pèrigueux and the better known sights of the Dordogne. There are 125 pitches in total, but the site has some chalets, bungalows and mobile homes which leaves around 88 grassy pitches for tourists. These are on several different levels most with good shade from mature trees and all have electricity hook-ups (6A). In low season the site can organise tours to local walnut farms, dairies etc. Rallies are welcome and themed programmes can be arranged.

Facilities

Three good, fully-equipped toilet blocks include facilities for disabled visitors and a baby unit. Laundry. Bread to order. Bar/restaurant serving good value meals, with takeaway. Freezer pack service. Swimming pool (20 x 10 m) and paddling pool. Riding. Tennis. Badminton. Children's club and activity and entertainment programme in main season. Off site: Shop at Tourtoirac 1 km. Supermarket at Hautefort 6 km. Fishing 1 km. Bicycle hire 6 km.

Open: 16 April - 30 September.

Directions

Site is 46 km. northeast of Périgueux. From Périgueux, take D5 east to Tourtoirac. Turn north onto D67 on entering village (site signed) and shortly fork left on D73 towards Coulaures; site is on left in 1 km. GPS: 45.28068, 1.04825

Charges guide

Per unit incl. 2 persons and electricity	€ 15,00 - € 25,00
extra person	€ 3,00 - € 4,20

Low season discounts for over 55s.
No credit cards.

Vézac

Camping les Deux Vallées

La Gare, F-24220 Vézac (Dordogne) T: **05 53 29 53 55**. E: **les2v@perigord.com**

alanrogers.com/FR24150

This site is enviably situated almost under the shadow of Beynac castle in the heart of the Dordogne. There are 96 flat marked touring pitches, most of a good size, some large, and with electricity (6/10A). There is plenty of shade and the general feel is of unspoilt but well managed woodland. There is a small fishing lake on site and it is only a short distance to the Dordogne river for bathing or canoeing. The site is being upgraded by its Dutch owners who provide a warm and friendly welcome. English is spoken.

Facilities

The modern unisex, clean toilet blocks (one heated) have facilities for disabled visitors and babies. Shop, bar/restaurant with takeaway (24/4-30/10). Good sized pool complex (24/4-30/9). Minigolf. Boules. Play area. Games room. Fishing. Entertainment including quiz nights and barbecues (July/Aug). Off site: Bicycle hire 200 m. Riding 2 km. Golf 8 km. Lake beach 450 m.

Open: All year.

Directions

Leave A20 at exit 55 and follow D804 to Sarlat. From Sarlat continue onto the D57 towards Beynac-et-Cazenac and directly after village sign for Vézac take first right turn to site. GPS: 44.83560, 1.15873

Charges guide

Per person	€ 3,20 - € 5,20
pitch	€ 4,00 - € 6,75
electricity (6A)	€ 3,50

Vielle-Saint-Girons

Sunêlia le Col-Vert

Lac de Léon, F-40560 Vielle-Saint-Girons (Landes) T: **0890 710 001**. E: **contact@colvert.com**

alanrogers.com/FR40050

This large, well maintained campsite is well laid out on the shores of Lac de Léon and offers 185 mobile homes for rent and 380 touring pitches. In low season it is a quiet site and those pitches beside the lake offer a wonderful backdrop to relaxing pastimes. During the main season it is a lively place for children of all ages. A pool complex offers a standard pool for swimming, a pool for children with water canon and fountains, plenty of sunbeds and a heated indoor pool. Swimming is also permitted in the lake alongside the many water-based activities.

Facilities

Four toilet blocks, one heated. One block for children with a Disney theme. Facilities for disabled people. Laundry facilities. Motorcaravan services. Shops, bar/restaurant, takeaway (1/4-5/9). Swimming pool complex with three pools. Spa, fitness centre and sauna. Play area. Games room. Sports areas. Boules. Tennis. Bicycle hire. Minigolf. Fishing. Riding. Sailing school (15/6-15/9). Communal barbecues. Internet access and WiFi. Off site: Walking and cycle ways in the forest. Atlantic beaches 5 km. Golf 10 km.

Open: 1 April - 19 September.

Directions

Site is off D652 Mimizan - Léon road, 4 km. south of crossroads with D42 at St Girons. The road to the lake and the site is signed at Vielle.
GPS: 43.90285, -1.3125

Charges guide

Per unit incl. 2 persons and electricity	€ 14,20 - € 53,80
extra person	€ 2,00 - € 6,50
child (3-13 yrs)	€ 1,50 - € 5,50

Vielle-Saint-Girons

Camping Club International Eurosol

Route de la Plage, F-40560 Vielle-Saint-Girons (Landes) T: **05 58 47 90 14**. E: **contact@camping-eurosol.com**
alanrogers.com/FR40060

This attractive and well maintained site is set on undulating ground amongst mature pine trees giving good shade. The 356 pitches for touring are numbered and 209 have electricity with 120 fully serviced. A family site with multilingual entertainers, many games and tournaments are organised and a beach volleyball competition is held each evening in front of the bar. A third covered pool has recently been added to the smart, landscaped pool complex. A sandy beach 700 m. from the site has supervised bathing in high season.

Facilities

Four main toilet blocks and two smaller blocks are clean, comfortable and have facilities for babies and disabled visitors. Motorcaravan services. Fridge rental. Well stocked shop and bar (all season). Restaurant, takeaway (10/6-4/9). Stage for live shows arranged in July/Aug. Outdoor swimming pool and heated covered pool (all season). Tennis. Multisport court. Bicycle hire. Internet and WiFi. Charcoal barbecues are not permitted. Off site: Riding school opposite. Fishing 700 m. Golf 18 km.

Open: 15 May - 11 September.

Directions

Turn off D652 at St Girons on D42 towards St Girons-Plage. Site is on left before coming to beach (4.5 km). GPS: 43.95166, -1.35212

Charges 2010

Per unit incl. 2 persons and electricity	€ 18,00 - € 35,00
extra person (over 4 yrs)	€ 5,00
dog	€ 4,00

Villefranche-de-Queyran

Camping Moulin de Campech

F-47160 Villefranche-de-Queyran (Lot-et-Garonne) T: **05 53 88 72 43**. E: **campech@wanadoo.fr**
alanrogers.com/FR47050

This well shaded, pretty site is run by Sue and George Thomas along with Sue's parents, Dot and Bob Dunn. At the entrance to the site, a trout lake with graceful weeping willows feeds under the restored mill house which is home to the owners as well as housing the bar and restaurant. Children will need supervision around the lake and at the pool which is on an elevated area above the mill house. The 60 large-sized pitches are mostly divided by hedges, with electricity (6A, long leads may be necessary in places, but can be borrowed free of charge).

Facilities

The single, rather ordinary toilet block has modern fittings. Washing machine and tumble dryer. Bar, restaurant. Terraced swimming pool. Open grass games area. Board games and English library. Boules. Barbecue, gourmet nights in high season. Fishing (discounted rate for campers, no permit required). Torch useful. Off site: Watersports, bicycle hire, golf or riding 10 km. Markets every day in villages and towns around the region. Numerous wine caves and Armagnac products.

Open: 1 April - 19 October.

Directions

Take A10 south to Bordeaux. Join A62 for Toulouse and take exit 6 for Damazan. Follow D8 to Mont de Marsan, at Cap du Bosc turn right onto D11 for Casteljaloux. Site is signed, 5 km. on right. GPS: 44.27179, 0.19093

Charges guide

Per person	€ 3,95 - € 5,75
child (under 7 yrs)	€ 2,90 - € 4,00
pitch with electricity	€ 11,60 - € 14,60
dog	€ 2,40

Vitrac

492

Domaine de Soleil Plage

Caudon par Montfort, Vitrac, F-24200 Sarlat-la-Canéda (Dordogne) T: **05 53 28 33 33**. E: **info@soleilplage.fr**

alanrogers.com/FR24090

This site is in one of the most attractive parts of the Dordogne valley, with a riverside location. There are 199 pitches, in three sections, with 104 for touring units. The smallest section surrounds the main reception and other facilities. There are 40 mobile homes, 20 chalets and 17 bungalow tents. The site offers river bathing from a sizeable pebble or sand bank or there is a very impressive heated pool complex. All pitches are bounded by hedges and are of adequate size. Most pitches have some shade and have electricity and many have water and a drain. If you like a holiday with lots going on, you will like this one. Various activities are organised during high season including walks and sports tournaments, and daily canoe hire is available from the site. Once a week in July and August there is a 'soirée' (charged for) usually involving a barbecue or paella, with band and lots of free wine – worth catching! The site is busy and reservation is advisable. English is spoken. The site is expensive in high season and you also pay more for a riverside pitch, but these have fine river views.

Facilities

Toilet facilities are in three modern unisex blocks. You will need to borrow a plug for the baby bath (€ 5 deposit). Washing machines and dryer. Motorcaravan service point. Well stocked shop, pleasant bar with TV and attractive, newly refurbished restaurant with terrace (all open from May 1st). Very impressive heated main pool, paddling pool, spa pool and two water slides. Tennis. Minigolf. Playground. Fishing. Canoe and kayak hire. Bicycle hire. Currency exchange. Small library. Off site: Golf 1 km. Riding 5 km.

Open: 3 April - 27 September.

Directions

Site is 6 km. south of Sarlat. From A20 take exit 55 (Souillac) towards Sarlat. Follow the D703 to Carsac and on to Montfort. At Montfort castle turn left for 2 km. down to the river.
GPS: 44.825, 1.25388

Charges guide

Per unit incl. 2 persons	€ 21,00 - € 33,50
incl. full services	€ 24,50 - € 47,00
extra person	€ 5,00 - € 7,50
child (2-8 yrs)	€ 3,00 - € 4,50

The Travel Service
to book this site call 01580 214000
...we'll arrange everything

Villeréal

Camping le Château de Fonrives

Rives, F-47210 Villeréal (Lot-et-Garonne) T: **05 53 36 63 38**. E: **chateau.de.fonrives@wanadoo.fr**

alanrogers.com/FR47030

Le Château de Fonrives is situated in Lot-en-Garonne. The site is set in pretty part-farmed, part-wooded countryside. It is a mixture of hazelnut woodland with lake and château (mostly 16th century). An attractive avenue leads to the barns adjacent to the château which have been converted. There are 200 pitches, 96 of which are for touring units, with electricity. Pitches near the woodland receive moderate shade, but elsewhere there is light shade from hedges and young trees. Former barns have been converted to provide a restaurant with covered terrace and bar with an open terrace overlooking the outdoor pool.

Facilities

One sanitary block. Shop. Restaurant, snacks and takeaway. Bar with disco area and terrace. Covered swimming pool (April-Oct), outdoor pool, water slides, paddling pool. Small play area. Small field for volleyball and football. Library. Minigolf, tennis, bicycle hire (all charged). Activities organised for children and adults in season, including excursions and walks. Caravan storage. Hairdresser (July/Aug). Off site: Riding 8 km.

Open: 4 May - 14 September.

Directions

Site is about 2 km. northwest of Villeréal, on west side of the D14/D207 Bergerac - Villaréal road.
GPS: 44.65723, 0.72847

Charges guide

Per unit incl. 2 persons and electricity	€ 15,00 - € 33,50
extra person	€ 4,00 - € 4,70
child (under 6 yrs)	€ 2,00 - € 2,70
dog	€ 3,00

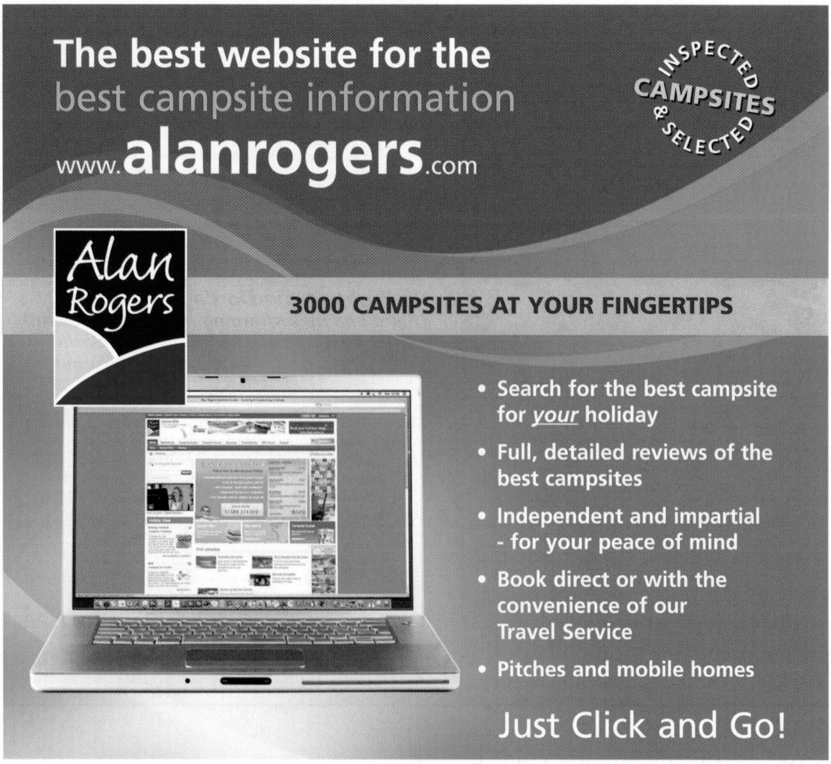

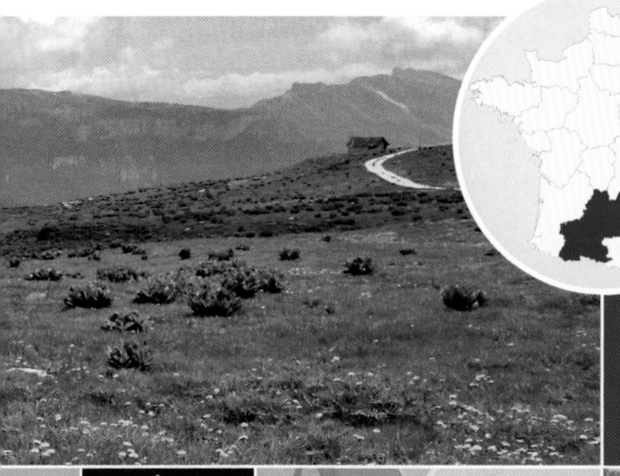

Rolling fields of yellow sunflowers, the Armagnac vineyards and crumbling, ancient stone buildings amidst the sleepy villages make this colourful region popular with those who enjoy good food, good wine and a taste of the good life.

DÉPARTEMENTS: 09 ARIÈGE, 12 AVEYRON, 31 HAUTE-GARONNE, 32 GERS, 46 LOT, 65 HAUTES-PYRÉNÉES, 81 TARN, 82 TARN-ET GARONNE.

MAJOR CITY: TOULOUSE

Home of Armagnac, rugby and the Three Muskateers, the Midi-Pyrénées is the largest region of France, extending from the Dordogne in the north to the Spanish border.

It is blessed by radiant sunshine and a fascinating range of scenery. South of the cultivated fields and Cliffside villages beside the Lot river, lie the stony lands of the Quercy Causse and the rocky gorges of the Aveyron and Tarn rivers. Centered around Millau, there are tortuous gorges and valleys, spectacular rivers, underground caves and grottoes and forested mountains.

Further south, high chalk plateaux, majestic peaks, tiny hidden valleys and small fortified sleepy villages, which seem to have changed little since the Middle Ages, contrast with the high-tech, industrial and vibrant university city of Toulouse.

Lourdes is one of the most visited pilgrimage sites in the world. Toulouse-Lautrec, the artist, was born at Albi, the capital of the département of Tarn.
In the east, the little town of Foix, is a convenient centre from which to explore the prehistoric caves at Niaux and the Aladdin's Cave of duty-free gift shops in the independent state of Andorra.

Places of interest

Albi: birthplace and Museum of Toulouse-Lautrec, imposing Ste Cécile cathedral with 15th-century fresco of 'The Last Judgement'.

Auch: capital of ancient Gascony, boasts a fine statue of d'Artágnan.

Collonges-la-Rouge: picturesque village of Medieval- and Renaissance-style mansions and manors.

Conques: 11th-century Ste Foy Romanesque church.

Foix: 11th/12th-century towers on rocky peak above town; 14th-century cathedral.

Lourdes: famous pilgrimage site where Ste Bernadette is said to have spoken to the Virgin Mary in a grotto and known for the miracles said to have been performed there.

Cuisine of the region

Food is rich and strongly seasoned, making generous use of garlic and goose fat, and there are some excellent regional wines. Seafood such as oysters, salt-water fish, or piballes from the Adour river are popular.

Cassoulet: stew of duck, sausages and beans.

Confit de Canard (d'oie): preserved duck meat.

Grattons (Graisserons): a mélange of small pieces of rendered down duck, goose and pork fat.

Magret de canard: duck breast fillets

Ouillat (Ouliat): Pyrénées soup: onions, tomatoes, goose fat and garlic.

Tourtière Landaise: a sweet of Agen prunes, apples and Armagnac.

www.tourisme-midi-pyrenees.com
information@crtmp.com
(0)5 61 13 55 48

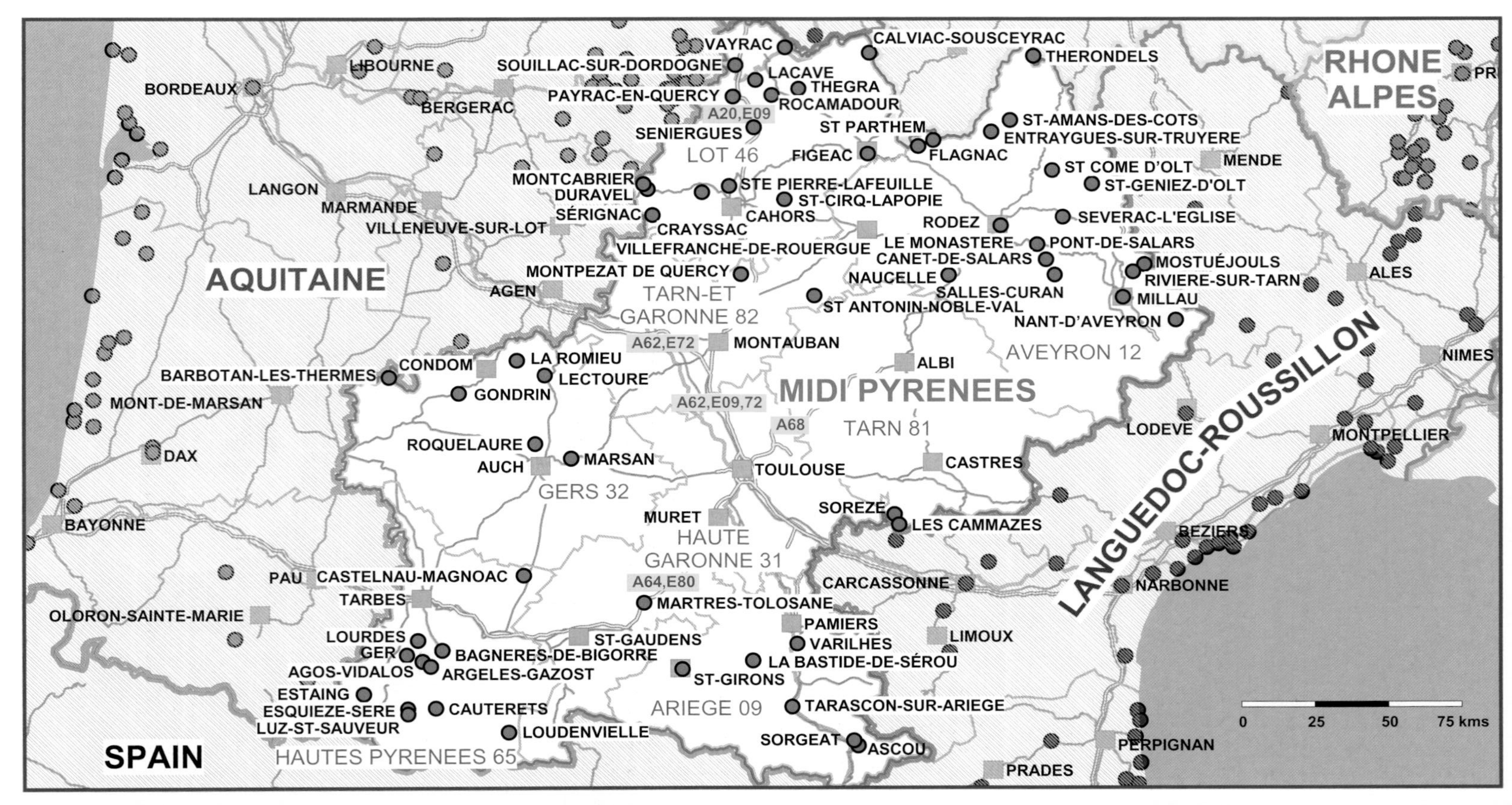

RHONE ALPES
AQUITAINE
MIDI PYRENEES
LANGUEDOC-ROUSSILLON
SPAIN
LOT 46
TARN-ET GARONNE 82
AVEYRON 12
TARN 81
GERS 32
HAUTE GARONNE 31
ARIEGE 09
HAUTES PYRENEES 65
A20,E09
A62,E72
A62,E09,72
A68
A64,E80
BORDEAUX
LIBOURNE
BERGERAC
LANGON
MARMANDE
VILLENEUVE-SUR-LOT
AGEN
VAYRAC
SOUILLAC-SUR-DORDOGNE
LACAVE
THEGRA
PAYRAC-EN-QUERCY
ROCAMADOUR
SENIERGUES
CALVIAC-SOUSCEYRAC
THERONDELS
ST PARTHEM
FIGEAC
FLAGNAC
ST-AMANS-DES-COTS
ENTRAYGUES-SUR-TRUYERE
MENDE
ST COME D'OLT
ST-GENIEZ-D'OLT
MONTCABRIER
DURAVEL
SÉRIGNAC
STE PIERRE-LAFEUILLE
ST-CIRQ-LAPOPIE
CAHORS
CRAYSSAC
VILLEFRANCHE-DE-ROUERGUE
RODEZ
SEVERAC-L'EGLISE
LE MONASTERE
PONT-DE-SALARS
CANET-DE-SALARS
MOSTUÉJOULS
RIVIERE-SUR-TARN
MONTPEZAT DE QUERCY
NAUCELLE
SALLES-CURAN
MILLAU
ST ANTONIN-NOBLE-VAL
NANT-D'AVEYRON
ALES
MONTAUBAN
ALBI
NIMES
CONDOM
LA ROMIEU
LECTOURE
BARBOTAN-LES-THERMES
GONDRIN
MONT-DE-MARSAN
DAX
ROQUELAURE
AUCH
MARSAN
TOULOUSE
CASTRES
LODEVE
MONTPELLIER
BAYONNE
MURET
SOREZE
LES CAMMAZES
BEZIERS
NARBONNE
PAU
CASTELNAU-MAGNOAC
CARCASSONNE
TARBES
MARTRES-TOLOSANE
OLORON-SAINTE-MARIE
PAMIERS
LIMOUX
LOURDES
GER
ST-GAUDENS
VARILHES
BAGNERES-DE-BIGORRE
AGOS-VIDALOS
ARGELES-GAZOST
LA BASTIDE-DE-SÉROU
ST-GIRONS
ESTAING
ESQUIEZE-SERE
CAUTERETS
TARASCON-SUR-ARIEGE
LUZ-ST-SAUVEUR
LOUDENVIELLE
SORGEAT
ASCOU
PERPIGNAN
PRADES
0
25
50
75 kms

Agos-Vidalos

Camping Soleil du Pibeste

16 avenue du Lavedan, F-65400 Agos-Vidalos (Hautes-Pyrénées) T: **05 62 97 53 23**

E: **info@campingpibeste.com** **alanrogers.com/FR65090**

Soleil du Pibeste is a quiet, rural site with well tended grass and flower beds. It has 67 pitches for touring, all having electricity (3-15A) and some shade. The Dusserm family welcomes all arrivals with a drink and they are determined to ensure that you have a good stay. There is no shop but the supermarket is only 5 km. and ordered bread is delivered to your door daily. The swimming pool is on a terrace above the pitches. It has sun beds, a paddling pool and waterfall and the most magnificent view of the mountains.

Facilities

Two heated toilet blocks. Baby room. Facilities for disabled visitors (key). Cleaning can be variable. Washing machine, dryer. Motorcaravan services. Bar, snacks, piano, internet. Room for playing cards or reading. Swimming, paddling pools. Small play area. Boules, archery, basketball, volleyball. Table tennis. Bicycle hire. Tai Chi and other relaxation classes. Off site: Fishing 800 m. Golf 10 km. Rafting 2 km. Skiing 2 km.

Open: 1 May - 30 September.

Directions

Agos Vidalos is on the N21, 5 km. south of Lourdes. Leave express-way at second exit, signed Agos Vidalos and continue to site, a short distance on the right. GPS: 43.03557, -0.07093

Charges guide

Per unit incl. 2 persons and electricity	€ 17,00 - € 32,00
extra person	€ 8,00
dog	€ 8,00

Argelès-Gazost

Sunêlia les Trois Vallées

Avenue des Pyrénées, F-65400 Argelès-Gazost (Hautes-Pyrénées) T: **05 62 90 35 47**

E: **3-vallees@wanadoo.fr** **alanrogers.com/FR65020**

This is a large, ever-expanding site on the road from Lourdes into the Pyrénées. It has an unprepossessing entrance and pitches near the road may have some background noise, but at the back, open fields allow views of surrounding mountains on all sides. Amenities include an indoor pool, two jacuzzis and an enormous play area that seems to have everything! The site has 483 flat, grassy pitches of reasonable size, 200 are for tourers, all with 3A or 6A electricity, some fully serviced. The site is popular with young people and could be quite lively at times.

Facilities

The toilet blocks are a little dated, facilities for disabled people. Cleaning can be variable and facilities could be under pressure at peak times. Bread. Bar/disco. Café, takeaway. Swimming pool complex (from 15/5), paddling pool, spa bath, large jacuzzi and two water slides. TV room. Good playground. Volleyball, football, boules, archery. Entertainment in high season. Off site: Supermarket across the road. Bicycle hire 50 m. Fishing 500 m. Riding 3 km. Nearby is 'La Voie Verte', a 17 km. traffic-free cycle path from Lourdes south to Soulom.

Open: 3 April - 2 November.

Directions

Argelès-Gazost is 13 km. south of Lourdes. From A64 take exit for Lourdes and follow the D821 towards Argelés-Gazost, then onto 'La Voie Rapide' and turn right at the first roundabout, after 300 m. right at the new roundabout and you are at the site. GPS: 43.01216, -0.09711

Charges 2010

Per unit incl. 2 persons	€ 12,00 - € 34,00
extra person	€ 5,00 - € 9,50
child (2-12 yrs)	€ 3,50 - € 8,50

Argelès-Gazost

Kawan Village du Lavedan

kawan VILLAGES www.kawan-villages.com

Lau-Balagnas, F-65400 Argelès-Gazost (Hautes-Pyrénées) T: **05 62 97 18 84**

E: **contact@lavedan.com** **alanrogers.com/FR65080**

Camping du Lavedan is an old established and very French site set in the Argelès-Gazost valley south of the Lourdes. It is beside the main road so there is some daytime road noise. The 105 touring pitches are set very close together on grass with some shade and all have electricity (2-10A). The area is fine for walking, biking, rafting and of course, in winter, skiing. There is a swimming pool which can be covered in inclement weather and a twice weekly event is organised in July/August, weekly in June.

The Travel Service to book this site call 01580 214000 ...we'll arrange everything

Facilities

Acceptable toilet block. Baby room. Facilities for disabled visitors. Washing machines and dryer in separate block heated in winter. Restaurant with takeaway and terrace (1/5-15/9). Bar, TV (all year). No shop, bread delivery (1/5-15/9). Swimming pool (with cover), paddling pool. Excellent play area. Internet (July/Aug). Boules, table tennis. Off site: Fishing or bicycle hire 1 km. Supermarket or rafting 2 km. Riding 5 km. Golf 15 km. Nearby is 'La Voie Verte', a 17 km. traffic-free cycle path from Lourdes south to Soulom.

Open: All year.

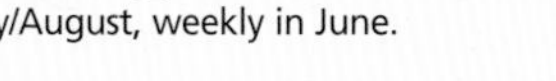

Directions

Lau-Balagnas, 15 km. south of Lourdes. From Lourdes take the N21 (Voie rapide) south, exit 3 (Argelès-Gazost). Take N2021, D921 or D21 towards Luz-St-Sauveur for 2 km. to Lau-Balagnas. Site on right, southern edge of town. GPS: 42.98822, -0.08900

Charges guide

Per unit incl. 2 persons	€ 15,00 - € 23,00
incl. 3 persons	€ 19,00 - € 29,00
electricity (10A max)	€ 1,00
extra person	€ 4,50 - € 6,50

Camping Cheques accepted.

Ascou

Camping Ascou la Forge

F-09110 Ascou (Ariège) T: **05 61 64 60 03**. E: **info@ascou-la-forge.fr**

alanrogers.com/FR09120

The Dutch owners of Ascou La Forge will give you a warm, friendly welcome at their oasis in the mountains of the Pyrenees, close to the borders of Andorra and Spain. The site is 3,500 feet above sea level but is easily accessible for motorhomes and caravans. Lying alongside the Lauze river, there are 50 pitches. In low season 44 mainly level, grass touring pitches with electricity are available, but this number reduces to 20 in July and August to allow more room for the large influx of campers with tents. There are also two chalets and one apartment available to rent.

Facilities

Modern, bright, sanitary block is fully equipped including facilities for disabled visitors which double as a family shower room with a baby bath. Shop. Bar with large screen for major sports events and films about the local flora/fauna. Play area. Maps and walking routes are available from reception. Free WiFi. Off site: Restaurant next door to site (all year). Restaurants, bars and shops in Ax-les-Thermes 7 km.

Open: All year.

Directions

From Ax-les-Thermes take D613 signed Quérigat, Quillan and Ascou-Pailhéres. After 3.6 km. turn right on D25 to site on right after 3.4 km.
GPS: 42.72444, 1.89274

Charges 2010

Per unit incl. 2 persons and electricity	€ 15,00 - € 23,00
extra person	€ 3,50 - € 5,00
child (0-7 yrs)	€ 2,50 - € 3,50

Bagnères-de-Bigorre

Camping le Monlôo

Chemin du Monlou (RD8), F-65200 Bagnères-de-Bigorre (Hautes-Pyrénées) T: **05 62 95 19 65**
E: **campingmonloo@yahoo.com** **alanrogers.com/FR65160**

A relatively small site of 120 touring pitches, Le Monlôo is set in a wide valley in the Pyrénées. The immediate surroundings of farmland, with crops growing and cows at pasture, give way to some magnificent views of the mountains towering away from the front of the site, whilst the back is right at the base of some smaller foothills. This area is a paradise for walkers and cyclists and travelling just a short distance opens up new horizons with some large waterfalls not far away. The friendly family take their job seriously and will show you a range of available pitches from the comfort of their electric car.

Facilities

Ample toilet facilities are provided in three blocks. Facilities for disabled visitors. Washing machines. Motorcaravan services. Bread to order. Open air heated pool with slide. Simple play area. Gas or electric barbecues are permitted. Off site: Spa town of Bagnères-de-Bigorre 2 km.

Open: All year.

Directions

From the A64 take exit 14 signed Bagnères-de-Bigorre. Enter town and take D8 road to the right for Ordizan. Site is just a few hundred metres along this road, well signed. GPS: 43.08180, 0.15139

Charges guide

Per unit incl. 2 persons	€ 11,00 - € 16,50
extra person	€ 3,50 - € 4,00
child (2-8 yrs)	€ 1,50 - € 2,80
electricity (2-6A)	€ 2,00 - € 5,50

Barbotan-les-Thermes

Camping du Lac de l'Uby

Barbotan-les-Thermes, F-32150 Gaubazon (Gers) T: **05 62 09 53 91**. E: **balia-vacances@wanadoo.fr**

alanrogers.com/FR32110

Camping du Lac de l'Uby is a large, mature site set alongside a lake and close to the thermal spa town of Barbotan-Les-Thermes in the Gers Gascogne region. The site is well shaded by mature trees in most areas and has 280 pitches with 240 available for tourers, the remainder taken up with mobile homes and chalets to rent. The mixture of large and average sized pitches are on level grass and gravel, all having 5/10A electricity (French sockets). Children are well catered for with a good play area and organised activities in July and August, including a circus school two days each week.

Facilities

Five well distributed sanitary blocks include facilities for disabled visitors and a separate baby bathroom. Separate laundry room. Motorcaravan service point. Shop, restaurant and bar, (1/6-30/9). Play area and covered entertainment area. Fishing. Bicycle hire. Off site: Leisure centre with pool, beach, and large play area 500 m. All weather tennis courts 400 m. Thermal spa facilities 1 km. Golf 20 km. Minigolf 50 m. Lakeside path outside entrance.

Open: 15 March - 30 November.

Directions

From Condom take D931 to Eauze then head west on N524 to Cazaubon. From Cazaubon continue on the N524 towards Barbotan-Les-Thermes, site is signed on right after 2 km. GPS: 43.94002, -0.04465

Charges guide

Per person	€ 3,50 - € 5,50
child (3-12 yrs)	€ 2,00 - € 4,00
pitch	€ 6,50 - € 13,00
electricity (6A)	€ 2,50 - € 5,50

No credit cards.

Calviac-Sousceyrac

Camping les 3 Sources

F-46190 Calviac-Sousceyrac (Lot) T: **05 65 33 03 01**. E: **info@les-trois-sources.com**

alanrogers.com/FR46220

This rural site is beautifully situated in the hilly surroundings of the Lot region, only 20 km. from the Dordogne river. The site offers 137 well maintained pitches in an attractive, wooded area. There are also 16 chalets and 20 mobile homes for rent. The 100 touring pitches are numbered and all have electricity connections (6/10A) and water points within easy reach. Following a fire in 2005 when the site's facilities burned down, and at the time of our visit, the reception and snack bar were housed in chalets on what was the terrace of the restaurant. A new restaurant, shop and reception are promised.

Facilities

Two toilet blocks provide good facilities including washbasins in cabins. Facilities for babies and disabled visitors. Laundry facilities including ironing. Snack bar (to be replaced by new bar and restaurant) plus swimming and paddling pools (all season). Games room. Trim trail on island in the lake. Fishing. Play area. Activities and entertainment including children's club. Off site: Riding 15 km. Lake beach 17 km. Golf 18 km.

Open: 1 June - 30 September.

Directions

From A20 (Chateauroux, Limoges, Brive) follow D8/D20 towards Vayrac and Bretenoux. Do not go through Martel. Follow signs for St Cère and Sousceyrac (D673) and turn left to Calviac after 6 km. (towards Lamativie). After 2 km. site is on right hand side. GPS: 44.93948, 2.05122

Charges guide

Per unit incl. 2 persons and electricity	€ 18,50 - € 24,50
extra person	€ 2,15 - € 5,50
dog	€ 2,95 - € 3,45

Canet-de-Salars

Castel Camping le Caussanel

Lac de Pareloup, F-12290 Canet-de-Salars (Aveyron) T: **05 65 46 85 19**. E: **info@lecaussanel.com**

alanrogers.com/FR12170

The site has 235 large, fairly level, grassy pitches, 105 for touring. Most have 6A electricity but very long leads may be necessary, and 37 are fully serviced. The pitches are defined by a tree or boulder in each corner and offer little privacy but many have wonderful views over the lake. Most pitches have little shade, a few having good shade. The site has swimming pools with toboggan and slides and a large paddling pool for children with small slides. The adjacent lake offers a large area, one kilometer long, for swimming and all the usual watersports. This large, extremely spacious site on the banks of Lac de Pareloup is greatly improved. It is ideal, in low season, for those seeking a tranquil holiday in a beautiful region of France or in high season, for those seeking an active holiday. One tour operator takes 20 pitches.

Facilities

Modern toilet blocks have all the necessary facilities. Motorcaravan services. Shop. Bar. Restaurant, takeaway (5/6-4/9). Swimming pool complex (10/5-4/9). Large play area. Boules. Tennis. Football. TV room, clubhouse. Organised activities (July/Aug). Fishing. Bicycle hire (July/Aug). Motor boat launching. Water sports (July/Aug). Swimming in lake. Internet access. Off site: Paths around lake (24 km). Other marked walks and cycle rides. Shops, banks, restaurants 8 km. Riding 10 km. Golf 30 km. Canoeing, rafting, paragliding caving, windsurfing.

Open: 10 May - 11 September.

Directions

From D911 Rodez - Millau road, just east of Pont de Salars, turn south on D993 signed Salles-Curan. In 6 km. at crossroads turn right on D538 signed Le Caussanel. Very shortly turn left and continue to site. GPS: 44.21462, 2.76658

Charges 2010

Per unit incl. 2 persons and electricity	€ 17,90 - € 33,00

Camping Cheques accepted.

Cauterets

Camping Cabaliros

Pont de Secours, F-65110 Cauterets (Hautes-Pyrénées) T: **05 62 92 55 36**. E: **info@camping-cabaliros.com**
alanrogers.com/FR65110

After driving up a steady incline through a sheer sided, tree lined valley, the terrain opens up just before you reach the town of Cauterets. Here you will find the delightful Camping Cabaliros where you will receive a warm and friendly welcome. With wonderful views, the site is owned by Jean and Chantal Boyrie and has been in the family since it was opened in 1959. There are four chalets for rent, 36 pitches without electricity (mainly for tents) and 60 pitches with 6A electricity (French sockets) for tourers. All of the touring pitches are on well manicured grass and those around the perimeter of the site are reasonably level with some shade provided by mature trees.

Facilities

Sanitary block near to site entrance with WCs, hot showers and washbasins in cubicles. Dishwashing and laundry sinks with cold water only. Washing machine and dryer. Motorcaravan service point. Large library (mainly French) and excellent meeting room with television. Play area for over 7s. Fishing. Off site: Restaurant (July/Aug) 50 m. Supermarket 1 km. Shops, restaurants and bars 2 km. Riding 10 km. Indoor and outdoor swimming pools 2 km. Walking. Pont d'Espagne 9 km. Route de Cascades (waterfalls) 4 km.

Open: 1 June - 30 September.

Directions

From Lourdes head south on the N21 to Argelès-Gazost then take D921 followed by the D920 to Cauterets. Site is on right 1 km. after 'SHOPI' supermarket just before Cauterets.
GPS: 42.90347, -0.10714

Charges 2010

Per unit incl. 2 persons and electricity (6A)	€ 15,80 - € 17,60

Crayssac

Campéole les Reflets du Quercy

Mas de Bastide, F-46150 Crayssac (Lot) T: **05 65 30 00 27**. E: **nadine.ferran@atciat.com**
alanrogers.com/FR46170

Set in the west of the Lot department, about 16 km. from the large town of Cahors, this site is owned by the Campéole group and is classed as a holiday village. Located on a hill with good views of the surrounding countryside, the pitches are hilly and terraced. Most are partially shaded with Quercy oak trees and some are set apart by small Crayssac stone walls. Almost half of the touring pitches are located on good, level hardstanding. At the rear of the site is a large area of independently owned mobile homes and residents here also have access to the campsite facilities. The site has a good 25 m. swimming pool overlooked by the terrace of the bar and snack bar. The site is managed by a very friendly French couple and a welcoming Campéole team.

Facilities

Three clean and well maintained sanitary blocks (not all open outside high season). Facilities for disabled visitors. Baby room with bath. Laundry facilities. Motorcaravan service point. Shop (July/Aug). Bar and snacks (July/Aug). Swimming and paddling pools (July/Aug). TV and games room. Boules. Tennis court. Play area with large bouncy castle. Animation in high season. Off site: Fishing and riding 7 km. Bicycle hire 15 km. Good shops 16 km.

Open: 5 April - 28 September.

Directions

From Cahors on the RN20, follow D911 northwest towards Puy-l'Évêque, Mercuès and Prayssac. Several kilometres after Labarthe, take D23, on the left near Crayssac. Site is well signed from Crayssac.
GPS: 44.50690, 1.32410

Charges guide

Per unit incl. 2 persons	€ 13,00 - € 18,90
extra person	€ 4,00 - € 6,10
child (2-5 yrs)	free - € 3,90
electricity (10A)	€ 3,90

Duravel

Club de Vacances Duravel

Port de Vire, F-46700 Duravel (Lot) T: **05 65 24 65 06**. E: **clubduravel@wanadoo.fr**
alanrogers.com/FR46140

This quality site is beautifully situated on the banks of the Lot River, only 35 km. from the historic town of Cahors. The site has 300 clearly defined, large pitches all with electricity. Some of these are fully serviced with water and drainage, and private sanitary facilities. The reception, bar, restaurant, snack bar and the shop are all located beside the river and from the terrace you can enjoy lovely views over the water. The pool complex offers two large pools (one is heated) with water slides and a children's pool. Duravel is a holiday destination which would suit all ages.

Facilities

Two clean toilet blocks include facilities for disabled people. Baby rooms. Laundry facilities. Serviced pitch facility provides a toilet, shower and sink (with hot water; cleaning charge € 13,50 per stay). Well stocked shop. Restaurant. Bar. Pizzeria and takeaway. Two tennis courts. Multisport area. Play area. Fishing. Boat launching. WiFi.

Open: 25 April - end September.

Directions

From Paris A10 towards Orleans and A71 towards Vierzon. Follow A20 and take exit 57 to Villeneuve sur Lot. Take the D811 to Cahors, Puy l'Evêque and the D58 to Duravel. Site is well signed.
GPS: 44.49636, 1.08176

Charges guide

Per person	€ 4,30 - € 6,35
pitch	€ 6,85 - € 10,00
incl. individual sanitary facilitiy	€ 14,75 - € 18,00
electricity	€ 3,50

Entraygues-sur-Truyère

Camping du Val de Saures

Village de Gîtes le Bastie, F-12140 Entraygues-sur-Truyère (Aveyron) T: **05 65 44 56 92**
E: **info@camping-valdesaures.com** **alanrogers.com/FR12260**

Camping Le Val de Saures is a well presented, value for money site only five minutes across a river bridge from the interesting old town of Entraygues. Situated at the confluence of the rivers Lot and Truyère, it is a good base for relaxing and exploring this beautiful area of Aveyron. There are 110 good sized level grassy pitches (6A-electricity) separated by small shrubs and trees with varying amount of shade. Many overlook the river Lot. Although the site has no shop, bar or restaurant these are all available in the town. In the area there are many wonderful medieval villages, with their narrow streets and Tudor houses with the famous grey Lauze tiles. Canoeing or rafting are possible and there are marked paths to explore on foot, on horseback or by bike.

Facilities

Three very clean and well appointed toilet blocks with all the necessary facilities including those for campers with disabilities. Motorcaravan service point. TV/games room. WiFi. Playground. River fishing but no bathing.
Off site: Fortified town of Entraygues (400 m. by footbridge) with a good range of shops, banks, bars and restaurants. Swimming pool (free), tennis courts and large playground close by. Watersports excursion 400 m. Riding 10 km.

Open: 1 May - 24 September.

Directions

Entraygues-sur-Truyère is 42 km. southeast of Aurillac on the D920. At southern end of Entraygues on the D920 turn right (site signed), over river bridge onto the D904 and immediately right again. Just past the tennis courts fork right and follow lane down to site.
GPS: 44.64243, 2.56414

Charges guide

Per unit incl. 2 persons	€ 10,00 - € 17,00
extra person	€ 2,50 - € 4,00
child (2-13 yrs)	free
electricity	€ 3,00

Esquieze-Sere

Airotel Pyrénées

46 avenue du Barége, F-65120 Esquieze-Sere (Hautes-Pyrénées) T: **05 62 92 89 18**
E: **airotel.pyrenees@wanadoo.fr** **alanrogers.com/FR65030**

It is located on the main road into the mountains, south from Argelès-Gazost and surrounded by the high peaks (some pitches will have daytime road noise). There are 163 level pitches, with 85 for touring units, all with electricity and 90 fully serviced. They are on terraced ground and separated by bushes. Lighting runs through the site and across some pitches. The layout of the pitches with the mobile homes can give a rather crowded feel. In high season a programme of activities and tournaments is arranged, from walking and mountain bike trips to rafting. There are tour operator pitches.

Facilities

Fairly modern, well appointed, toilet blocks (one heated), facilities for disabled people also doubling as a baby room. Bottled water is advised for drinking and cooking. Motorcaravan services. Small shop (1/7-31/8), bread (15/5-15/9). Outdoor pool (15/6-15/9). Indoor pool, balneotherapy pool, sauna, fitness room (1/12-30/9). Water slides. Practice climbing wall, half-court tennis and boules. Small playground. Off site: Bicycle hire and fishing 1 km. Skiing 10 km.

Open: All year, excl. 1 October - 30 November.

Directions

Take N21 (Voie rapide) south from Lourdes past Argelès-Gazost towards Luz-St-Sauveur. The site is on left at Esquièze-Sere, just before Luz-St-Sauveur. Site is on left immediately after Camping International.
GPS: 42.88115, -0.00957

Charges guide

Per unit incl. 2 persons	€ 15,50 - € 26,00
extra person	€ 3,50 - € 6,00
electricity (3-10A)	€ 3,50 - € 6,50

Estaing

Camping Pyrénées Natura

Route du Lac, F-65400 Estaing (Hautes-Pyrénées) T: **05 62 97 45 44**. E: **info@camping-pyrenees-natura.com**
alanrogers.com/FR65060

Pyrénées Natura, at an altitude of 1,000 m. on the edge of the National Park is the perfect site for lovers of nature. The 60 pitches (46 for tourists), all with electricity, are in a large, level, open and sunny field. Around 75 varieties of trees and shrubs have been planted – but they do not spoil the fantastic views. The reception and bar are in a traditional style stone building with an open staircase. The small shop in the old water mill stocks a variety of produce, it is open all day but unmanned so you pay at reception.

Facilities

First class toilet blocks include facilities for disabled visitors and babies. Washing machine and airers (no lines allowed). Motorcaravan services. Small shop, takeaway (15/5-15/9). Small bar (15/5-15/9). Lounge, library, TV (mainly used for videos of the National Park). Sauna, solarium (free between 12.00-17.00). Music room. Play area for the very young. Small 'beach' beside river. Boules. Giant chess. Weekly evening meal in May, June and Sept. Internet.
Off site: Village with two restaurants.

Open: 1 May - 20 September.

Directions

From Lourdes take N21 towards Argelès-Gazost, then exit 2, N2021/D21, into Argelès. Approaching town turn onto D918 towards Aucun. After 8 km. turn left on D13 to Bun, cross the river, then right on D103 to site (5.5 km). Narrow road, few passing places.
GPS: 42.94152, -0.17726

Charges guide

Per unit incl. 2 persons and electricity (3A)	€ 15,50 - € 24,50
extra person	€ 5,25
child (under 8 yrs)	€ 3,50

Less in low season.

Figeac

Camping les Rives du Célé

Domaine du Surgié, F-46100 Figeac (Lot) T: **05 61 64 88 54**. E: **contact@marc-montmija.com**
alanrogers.com/FR46320

Very conveniently placed, 2 km. from the town centre of Figeac, this site has a rural location. This is a campsite where activities on site and in the surrounding areas are numerous and it would therefore suit an active family including teenagers. Navigation around the park is easy for larger units due to good design. There are 163 pitches, 103 for touring units, the remaining 60 for mobile homes and gîtes, all of which are for rent. The pitches are level, with a mixture of shade and sun and all have 10A electricity. The site is split into different areas with the aquatic centre next to the camping area.

Facilities

Three fully equipped, modern sanitary blocks include facilities for babies and disabled people. Laundry. Shop, bar, restaurant and takeaway (all from 30/4). Swimming pool complex. Sports competitions and party nights with themed dining. Children's clubs. Canoeing. Fishing. Minigolf. Boules. Bicycle hire. Off site: Riding 2 km.

Open: 30 April - 30 September.

Directions

From Cahors, take the D653 to Figeac from where the site is well signed. GPS: 44.60989, 2.05015

Charges guide

Per unit incl. 2 persons and electricity	€ 14,00 - € 22,00
extra person	€ 4,00 - € 6,80
child (3-12 yrs)	€ 2,50 - € 4,00
dog	€ 1,50 - € 2,50

Flagnac

Flower Camping le Port de Lacombe

flower campings

F-12300 Flagnac (Aveyron) T: **05 65 64 10 08**. E: **accueil@campingleportdelacombe.com**

alanrogers.com/FR12290

The new managers, Patrick and Marie-Claude Comtat, have plans to improve this leased municipal site. It is well kept and is situated on the banks of the Lot river, a location ideal for walking, cycling, fishing and canoeing. The 91 grass touring pitches are level and range in size from 100-130 sq.m. A large natural swimming pool is fed by the river and provides a separate paddling area and a large slide. Using the D42, one can wind through the valley and climb to over 2,000 feet to the Plateau de la Viadene. The scenery is panoramic and picturesque.

Facilities

Two separate sanitary blocks, each with the usual facilities including provision for disabled visitors. Washing machine. Bar (all season) with restaurant and takeaway (both 15/6-15/9). TV in function room. Play area. Swimming pool fed from the river and paddling pool (1/7-31/8). Bicycle hire. Fishing in river. Entertainment (July/Aug).

Open: 1 April - 30 September.

Directions

Driving south from Brive-la-Gaillarde, take N140 to Decazeville, turning north on D963 to Flagnac. Site is well signed on the left. From Rodez take N140 to Decazeville, then as above.
GPS: 44.60915, 2.23597

Charges guide

Per unit incl. 2 persons	€ 8,00 - € 22,00
incl. electricity (6A)	€ 11,00 - € 20,00
extra person	€ 2,00 - € 4,00
child (3-6 yrs)	€ 1,50 - € 3,00

Ger

Aire Naturelle de Camping l'Arrayade

Arrayade, F-65100 Ger (Hautes-Pyrénées) T: **05 59 56 10 60**.

alanrogers.com/FR65170

This unique little campsite, situated quite high up in the Pyrénées with some amazing views down the valley, could well be near perfect for anyone seeking a relaxing, informal and friendly atmosphere. On a very small site of just 15 pitches, Mme. Pique is a gracious host who will do her best to ensure your stay is as pleasant as possible. She has prepared plenty of information on the local area, the best walks to go on and the cycle pathway that runs past the site that takes you into Lourdes centre in just 3 km. You can taste the freshness of the air up here and outdoor lovers will feel really at one with nature.

Facilities

One very modern toilet block situated in the reception area. Provision is adequate. All fittings are very new and the arrangement makes this area feel almost like a private bathroom. Washing machine and dryer. Small bar where breakfast and evening meals are served. Peaceful lounge. Sauna, jacuzzi and small gym. Internet access.
Off site: Walking, climbing cycling and fishing all on the door step. Monsieur Pique, a qualified pilot, offers flights over the Pyrénées for the ultimate sightseeing experience.

Open: 15 May - 15 September.

Directions

From Lourdes head south on the D921 signed Lugagnan. After 3 km. bear right on D13 for Ger. As you approach a few houses on your left the site entrance is on the right, set back a little in a lay-by.
GPS: 43.05771, -0.04151

Charges guide

Per unit incl. 2 persons	€ 10,00
extra person	€ 2,50
electricity	€ 2,50 - € 5,00

Gondrin

Camping le Pardaillan

27 rue Pardaillan, F-32330 Gondrin (Gers) T: **05 62 29 16 69**. E: **camplepardaillan@wanadoo.fr**

alanrogers.com/FR32090

In the heart of the Armagnac region of the Gers between Condom and Eauze make a stop at the village of Gondrin and stay at the attractive, family run campsite of Le Pardaillan. Neatly manicured and well laid out, the site has 115 pitches arranged on four separate terraced areas; 51 of these are for tourers, the remainder used for chalets (to rent all year). Level and grassy, the touring pitches are small to average in size, separated by tidy hedges and partially shaded by mature trees. Each has 6/10A electricity and 30 also have water and waste water points.

Facilities

Three toilet blocks include WCs, hot showers and washbasins in cubicles. Facilities for disabled visitors. Heated family shower room. Washing machines, dryers, and ironing board. Bar, restaurant and takeaway (mid June-mid Sept). WiFi internet access. Play area. Children's club and excursions (July/Aug). Fishing lake. Off site: Leisure centre 200 m. Shops, restaurant and bars 500 m. Golf 6 km. Riding 15 km.

Open: Easter - mid October.

Directions

From the A62 exit at Agen and take the D931 west towards Eauze. Site is in village of Gondrin (between Condom and Eauze) and is signed.
GPS: 43.8832, 0.2385

Charges guide

Per unit incl. 2 persons and electricity (6A)	€ 12,00 - € 23,50
extra person (over 3 yrs)	€ 3,20 - € 5,70
10A electricity	€ 2,50

The Travel Service to book this site call 01580 214000 ...we'll arrange everything

La Bastide-de-Sérou

492

Camping l'Arize

Lieu-dit Bourtol, F-09240 La Bastide-de-Sérou (Ariège) T: **05 61 65 81 51**. E: **camparize@aol.com**
alanrogers.com/FR09020

The site sits in a delightful, tranquil valley among the foothills of the Pyrénées and is just east of the interesting village of La Bastide-de-Sérou beside the River Arize (good trout fishing). The river is fenced for the safety of children on the site, but may be accessed just outside the gate. The 70 large pitches are neatly laid out on level grass within the spacious site. All have 3/6/A electricity and are separated into bays by hedges and young trees. An extension to the site gives 24 large, fully-serviced pitches (10A) and a small toilet block.

Facilities

Toilet block includes facilities for babies and disabled visitors. Laundry room. Motorcaravan services. Small swimming pool and sunbathing area. Entertainment in high season. Weekly barbecues and welcome drinks on Sundays. Fishing, riding and bicycle hire. WiFi. Off site: Several restaurants and shops within a few minutes' drive. The nearest restaurant is 200 m. and will deliver takeaway meals. Golf 5 km.

Open: 12 March - 10 November.

Directions

Site is southeast of the village La Bastide-de-Sérou. Take the D15 towards Nescus and site is on right after about 1 km. GPS: 43.00182, 1.44538

Charges guide

Per unit incl. 2 persons and electricity	€ 16,40 - € 24,70
extra person	€ 4,00 - € 5,40
child (0-7 yrs)	€ 3,00 - € 3,60

The Travel Service to book this site call 01580 214000 ...we'll arrange everything

La Romieu

492

Kawan Village le Camp de Florence

Route Astaffort, F-32480 La Romieu (Gers) T: **05 62 28 15 58**
E: **info@lecampdeflorence.com** **alanrogers.com/FR32010**

Camp de Florence is an attractive site on the edge of an historic village in pleasantly undulating Gers countryside. The 183 large, part terraced pitches (100 for tourers) all have electricity (10A), 14 with hardstanding and eight fully serviced. They are arranged around a large field (full of sunflowers when we visited) with rural views, giving a feeling of spaciousness. The 13th-century village of La Romieu is on the Santiago de Compostela pilgrim route. The Pyrénées are a two hour drive, the Atlantic coast a similar distance. The site has been developed by the friendly Mynsbergen family who are Dutch (although Susan is English). They have sympathetically converted the old farmhouse buildings to provide facilities for the site. The collegiate church, visible from the site, is well worth a visit (the views are magnificent from the top of the tower), as is the local arboretum, the biggest collection of trees in the Midi-Pyrénées.

Facilities

Three toilet blocks (one completely rebuilt for 2009), provide all the necessary facilities. Washing machines and dryers. Motorcaravan services. Restaurant (1/5-30/9, also open to the public). Takeaway. Bread. Swimming pool area with water slide. Jacuzzi, protected children's pool (open to public in afternoons). Adventure playground, games and pets areas. Bouncy castle, trampoline. Outdoor fitness machines. Games room. Tennis. Pétanque. Bicycle hire. Video shows, discos, picnics, musical evenings. Excursions. Internet and WiFi. Off site: Shop 500 m. in village. Fishing 5 km. Riding 10 km. Walking tours, excursions and wine tasting arranged.

Open: 1 April - 10 October.

Directions

Site signed from D931 Agen - Condom road. Small units turn left at Ligardes (signed), follow D36 for 1 km, turn right turn La Romieu (signed). Otherwise continue until outskirts of Condom and take D41 left to La Romieu, through village to site.
GPS: 43.98299, 0.50183

Charges 2010

Per unit incl. 2 persons and electricity	€ 17,50 - € 34,90
extra person	€ 3,60 - € 7,20
child (4-9 yrs)	€ 2,60 - € 5,20
dog (max. 2)	€ 1,50 - € 2,25

Special prices for groups, rallies, etc.
Camping Cheques accepted.

Lacave

Camping la Rivière

Le Bougayrou, F-46200 Lacave (Lot) T: **05 65 37 02 04**. E: **campinglariviere@free.fr**
alanrogers.com/FR46370

Camping La Riviere is situated on the banks of the Dordogne with direct access to the river and a sand and pebble beach. It is a natural rural site and in a pleasant location. The A20 motorway and the town of Souillac are just 15 km away. The welcome from the owners is warm and friendly and they place much importance on customer service and a family atmosphere is of conviviality. There are 110 pitches of which 15 are for mobile homes (all for rent). The remaining 95 pitches are for touring units. Of average size, all are level and on grass and divided by trees and shrubs which provide a good amount of shade. All have electricity (4/10A).

Facilities

Three toilet blocks include facilities for disabled visitors and babies. Laundry. Shop. Bar. Snack bar. Takeaway. Two swimming pools including a children's pool. Two games areas. Minigolf. Barbecue and picnic areas. Organised excursions. Disco and Karaoke evenings. Off site: The Caves of Padirac. Rocamadour. Sarlat and numerous theme parks. Museums. Off road cycling. Canoeing. Kayaking. Climbing. Riding. Golf. Lacave 3 km. St Sozy 4 km.

Open: 1 May - 19 September.

Directions

From Souillac take the D43 and site is very well signed. GPS: 44.86171, 1.559372

Charges guide

Per person	€ 5,00
child (under 10 yrs)	€ 3,00
pitch	€ 5,30
electricity	€ 3,00 - € 4,00

Le Monastère

503 Campéole

Campéole Domaine de Combelles

F-12000 Le Monastère (Aveyron) T: **05 65 77 30 04**. E: **nadine.ferran@atciat.com**
alanrogers.com/FR12400

The pitches at this campsite are used exclusively for mobile home accommodation. For full details please see our PRL section starting on page 501.

Lectoure

Yelloh! Village le Lac des Trois Vallées

F-32700 Lectoure (Gers) T: **04 66 73 97 39**. E: **info@yellohvillage-lac-des-3-vallees.com**

alanrogers.com/FR32060

This is a large 140-hectare site with many facilities. It is a large holiday complex and good for families with young children or teenagers. The large lake provides the opportunity for canoeing, swimming, diving and there are four water slides. There is a large safe paddling area and a separate fishing lake. The impressive heated pool complex complete with gymnasium and jacuzzi also has paved areas for sunbathing and a large paddling pool. Of the 500 pitches, over 200 are well situated for touring on shaded or open ground, all with electricity (10A). Used by tour operators (100 pitches).

Facilities

Eight modern sanitary blocks each with baby bathing facilities. Provision for disabled visitors. Laundry facilities. Motorcaravan services. Shop. Restaurants and bars. Lakeside snack bar and drinks kiosk. Heated swimming pool complex. Lake complex. Multisports pitch. BMX/skateboard area. Fishing. Tennis. Minigolf. Video games room. Disco. Cinema. Children's club. Internet access (charged). Off site: Golf 10 km. Riding 20 km. Walking and mountain bike trails. Quad bikes. Hot air balloon rides.

Open: 6 June - 6 September with all facilities.

Directions

Take N21 south from Lectoure for 2 km. Site is well signed and is a further 2 km. after turning left off the N21. GPS: 43.91250, 0.64852

Charges guide

Per unit incl. 2 persons and electricity	€ 15,00 - € 43,00
extra person	€ 5,00 - € 8,00
child (under 7 yrs)	free - € 8,00
dog	€ 4,00

Les Cammazes

Camping de la Rigole

Route de Barrage, F-81540 Les Cammazes (Tarn) T: **05 63 73 28 99**. E: **campings.occitanie@orange.fr**

alanrogers.com/FR81100

La Rigole is located high in the hills above Lac des Cammazes. Although the site slopes, of the 66 pitches, the 34 for touring are on small terraces and many have quite deep shade. All have electricity (4-13A). There is a small bar and snackbar. One evening each week in main season a regional meal is organised. Small children are well catered for with play areas for tiny tots and under-sevens. There is a delightful children's farm with animals. The site is totally unsuitable for American RVs and large units.

Facilities

Fairly modern toilet block. Baby room. Facilities for disabled campers (although the slopes might be difficult). Washing machines, dryer. Small shop. Bar. Takeaway. Swimming pool and children's pool. All open in high season. Table tennis. Badminton. Volleyball. Boules. WiFi (free). Off site: Lac des Cammazes with its dam 400 m. Lac de St Ferréol 5 km, with large sandy beach. Fishing 0.4 km. Riding 1.5 km.

Open: 15 April - 15 September.

Directions

Les Cammazes is 25 km. northeast of Castelnaudary, 10 km. southeast of Revel. From Revel take D629 to Cammazes, continue through village, after 1 km. turn left towards Barrage (site signed), site entrance 200 m. on right. GPS: 43.407867, 2.0866

Charges guide

Per unit incl. 2 persons and electricity	€ 15,85 - € 19,80
extra person	€ 3,50 - € 4,70
child (0-7 yrs)	€ 2,15 - € 2,90

Loudenvielle

Flower Camping Pène Blanche

F-65510 Loudenvielle (Hautes-Pyrénées) T: **05 62 99 68 85**. E: **info@peneblanche.com**

alanrogers.com/FR65140

La Pène Blanche is spacious and well kept, in an idyllic location standing high over Lake Loudenvielle and surrounded by high mountains. There are 120 small, pitches which are not separated, 80 are for touring (40 with 5/10A electricity). The area is ideal for walking, hiking or biking in the mountains. An outdoor swimming pool is just 200 m. away and nearby is the Balnea centre with its spa waters. The resorts of Val Louron and Peyragudes are within easy reach for skiing. For the very brave there is paragliding and hang gliding or you can relax in the park to watch them gracefully coming in to land.

Facilities

Two toilet blocks, one traditional, one modern and heated with facilities for campers with disabilities. Dishwashing and laundry room with washing machine, dryer and ironing board. Children's play area. Off site: Restaurant, snack bar, bar and local shops all within 100 m. Cinema 200 m. Motorcaravan services 300 m. Within walking distance are the Balnea Centre with its spa water baths and adjacent swimming pool with waterslide. Tennis. Minigolf. Hiking. Mountain Biking. Paragliding. Hang gliding. Skiing.

Open: All year except November.

Directions

A64 Tarbes to Toulouse, exit junction 16, on D929 follow signs to Arreau, then D618 to D25 signed Loudenvielle. GPS: 42.79531, 0.40861

Charges guide

Per unit incl. 2 persons	€ 11,50 - € 16,90
with electricity (5/10A)	€ 15,30 - € 21,90
extra person	€ 3,80 - € 5,10
child (0-7 yrs)	free - € 3,90

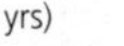

Lourdes

Camping le Moulin du Monge

Avenue Jean Moulin, No 28, F-65100 Lourdes (Hautes-Pyrénées) T: **05 62 94 28 15**
E: **camping.moulin.monge@wanadoo.fr** **alanrogers.com/FR65100**

A well-organised, family-run site with a friendly welcome, Moulin du Monge has a convenient location for visiting Lourdes, only 3 km. away. There will be some traffic noise from the nearby N21 and railway line. This attractive garden-like site has 57 grassy pitches in several different areas and on different levels. Some are in a level orchard area and are closest to the main road. A few pitches are on a little woodland knoll behind reception, with the remainder on a higher level at the back of the site. All have electrical hook-ups (2-6A).

Facilities

The heated toilet blocks have all necessary facilities, including washing machine and dryer. Facilities for disabled campers. Baby room. Motorcaravan services. Well stocked shop (15/6-20/9). Heated swimming pool, sliding cover (20/5-20/9), paddling pool. Games/TV room. Barbecue, terrace. Sauna. Boules. Playground, trampolines.
Off site: Good transport links to the city centre with its famous grotto and all shops and services. Fishing 3 km. Golf 4 km. Bicycle hire 500 m.

Open: 1 April - 10 October.

Directions

Site is just off the N21 on northern outskirts of Lourdes. From north, on N21 (2 km. south of Adé) be prepared to take slip lane in centre of road. Turn left into Ave. Jean Moulin. Site shortly on left.
GPS: 43.115516, -0.031583

Charges 2010

Per unit incl. 2 persons and electricity	€ 17,30 - € 19,30
extra person	€ 5,10
child (0-7 yrs)	€ 3,30

Luz-Saint-Sauveur

Camping International

F-65120 Luz-Saint-Sauveur (Hautes-Pyrénées) T: **05 62 92 82 02**. E: **reception@international-camping.fr**
alanrogers.com/FR65040

Located in the foothills of the Pyrénées, Camping International is an attractive, family-run site with 180 pitches, most are on the fairly level lower section. There are 146 grassy pitches for tourists all with electricity (2/6A), many divided by hedges and some with a little shade. Around 40 pitches (more for tents) are on terraces on the mountainside at back of the site, all accessed by tarmac roads and with stunning views. However some fairly steep up and down walking will be necessary. Most of the amenities are grouped around the reception area along the front of the site.

Facilities

Well equipped toilet blocks (one heated), facilities for babies and disabled campers. Shop. Snack bar, takeaway. Heated swimming pool and jacuzzi, all open (1/6-30/9). Bar (20/6-10/9). Half-court tennis. Table tennis. Boules. Minigolf. Volleyball. Badminton. Playground. Organised activities, main season. WiFi. Off site: Luz-St-Sauveur Jazz Festival in July, Internet (free). Paragliding near Barèges, cable car to the Pic du Midi observatory. Climbing, rafting, walking, winter skiing. Fishing 500 m. Bicycle hire 1 km. Riding 7 km. Golf 30 km.

Open: 1 June - 30 September.

Directions

From Lourdes take new N21 (Voie rapide) south, pass Argelès-Gazost continuing towards Luz-St-Sauveur on D921. Site is on left at Esquièze-Sere (just before Luz), proceed carefully, site entrance is well signed but congested at peak times. GPS: 42.882683, -0.013433

Charges guide

Per unit incl. 2 persons and electricity	€ 14,60 - € 25,50
extra person	€ 3,00 - € 5,00
child (0-7 yrs)	€ 3,00 - € 3,30
dog	free

Camping Cheques accepted.

Luz Saint Sauveur

Village Cévéo de Luz

Quartier Maoubèze, F-65120 Luz Saint Sauveur (Hautes-Pyrénées) T: **05 62 92 84 72**. E: **luz@ceveo.com**
alanrogers.com/FR65180

The pitches at this campsite are used exclusively for mobile home accommodation. For full details please see our PRL section starting on page 501.

Luz-Saint-Sauveur

Camping Pyrenevasion

Route de Luz-Ardiden, Sazos, F-65120 Luz-Saint-Sauveur (Hautes-Pyrénées) T: **05 62 92 91 54**
E: **camping-pyrenevasion@wanadoo.fr** **alanrogers.com/FR65130**

In the heart of the Pyrénées, Camping Pyrenevasion is at a height of 830 metres on a picturesque hillside with panoramic views of the mountains and the town of Luz-St-Sauveur in the valley below. This family run site, where you will receive a warm and friendly welcome, has 60 well laid out, tidy touring pitches. On level, grassy terraces on the hillside which are partially shaded by young trees, each pitch has electricity (French sockets) adjacent and all are reasonably close to the modern heated sanitary block. There are 12 modern, comfortable chalets for rent (all year).

Facilities

Heated sanitary block with showers, WCs, washbasins (cubicles and open area). Facilities for disabled visitors. Baby bath. Washing machine and dryer. Motorcaravan services. Bread can be ordered at reception for next morning delivery. Bar (all year). Takeaway (1/6-1/10). Heated swimming and paddling pools (15/5-1/10). Small play area (up to 6 yrs). Sports area. Off site: Shops, restaurant and bar 2 km. Fishing 200 m. Riding 10 km. Golf 30 km. Skiing 10 km. Jazz festival in Luz-St-Sauveur in early July.

Open: All year.

Directions

From Lourdes take N21 south to Pierrefit-Nestalas then the D921 to Luz-St-Sauveur. Follow signs from Luz-St-Sauveur to Luz-Ardiden (D12). Site is on right as you enter the village of Sazos. GPS: 42.88283, -0.02241

Charges guide

Per unit incl. 2 persons	€ 10,00 - € 16,00
extra person	€ 5,00
child (2-6 yrs)	€ 3,00
electricity (3-10A)	€ 3,50 - € 11,50

Marsan

Flower Camping Aramis

Quartier Gaubette, F-32270 Marsan (Gers) T: **05 62 65 60 11**. E: **piraux.sylvie@wanadoo.fr**
alanrogers.com/FR32170

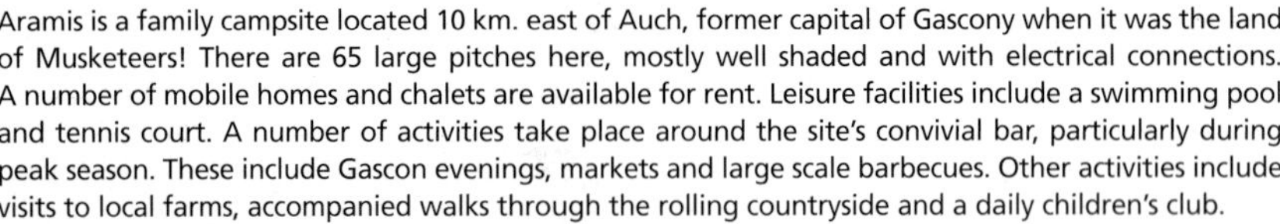

Aramis is a family campsite located 10 km. east of Auch, former capital of Gascony when it was the land of Musketeers! There are 65 large pitches here, mostly well shaded and with electrical connections. A number of mobile homes and chalets are available for rent. Leisure facilities include a swimming pool and tennis court. A number of activities take place around the site's convivial bar, particularly during peak season. These include Gascon evenings, markets and large scale barbecues. Other activities include visits to local farms, accompanied walks through the rolling countryside and a daily children's club.

Facilities

Snack bar/bar. Swimming pool. Children's pool. Tennis. Play area. Tourist information. Entertainment and activity programme. Mobile homes for rent. Off site: Auch 10 km. Walking and cycle tracks. Jazz festival at Marciac. Riding. Golf.

Open: All year.

Directions

Camping Aramis can be found around 10 km. east of Auch. From there, head east on N124 to Marsan and then follow signs to the site.
GPS: 43.658577, 0.733429

Charges 2010

Per unit incl. 2 persons and electricity	€ 15,50 - € 23,00

Martres-Tolosane

Camping le Moulin

Lieu-dit le Moulin, F-31220 Martres-Tolosane (Haute-Garonne) T: **05 61 98 86 40**
E: **info@campinglemoulin.com** **alanrogers.com/FR31000**

Set in a 12 hectare estate of woods and fields, Camping Le Moulin is a family run campsite in the foothills of the Pyrénées, close to the interesting medieval village of Martres-Tolosane and situated on the site of an old mill on the bank of the River Garonne. There are 99 pitches (60 available for tourers) all of which have electrical connections. Most pitches are level and grassy, of a good size and with shade from mature trees. A number of very large (150-200 sq.m) 'super' pitches are available and there are 24 chalets and mobile homes for rent.

Facilities

Large modern sanitary block with separate ladies and gents WC's. Communal area with showers and washbasins in cubicles. Separate heated area for disabled visitors with shower, WC and basin. Baby bath. Laundry facilities. Motorhome services. Outdoor bar with WiFi. Snackbar and takeaway (1/6-15/9). Daily baker's van (except Monday). Heated swimming and paddling pools (1/6-15/9). Fishing. Tennis. Canoeing. Archery. Walks in the countryside. BMX track. Playground. Games room. Entertainment programme and children's club (high season). Off site: Martres-Tolosane 1.5 km. Walking trails and cycle routes. Horse riding 4 km. Golf 12 km.

Open: 22 March - 30 September.

Directions

From the A64 motorway (Toulouse-Tarbes) take exit 21 (Boussens) or exit 22 (Martres-Tolosane) and follow signs to Martres-Tolosane. Site is well signed from village. GPS: 43.19048, 1.01788

Charges guide

Per unit incl. 2 persons and electricity	€ 18,50 - € 34,10
extra person	€ 4,00 - € 5,70
child (under 7 yrs)	€ 2,20 - € 3,10
dog	€ 1,50 - € 2,10

Less 20% outside July/Aug.

Millau

Camping Le Millau Plage

Rte de Millau Plage, F-12100 Millau (Aveyron) T: **05 65 60 10 97**. E: **info@campingmillauplage.com**
alanrogers.com/FR12390

This slightly old site is situated on the banks of the Tarn river 1.5 km. outside Millau. This is an historical town in its own right and a very popular place for hang-gliding and watersports, as well as for people wishing to get a view of the Millau suspension bridge further down the valley. Plenty of trees provide ample shade and the site could be a little dark on cloudy or dull days. The river will attract older children who will love to climb the trees and jump or dive into the water, but as the site is open onto the river younger children would need supervision. Everyone will enjoy the large pool that is next to the restaurant and bar area.

Facilities

Four toilet blocks along the middle of the site provide easy access from most pitches. The blocks are old and due some modernisation. Motorcaravan services. Small shop, bar with TV and snack type restaurant, takeaway (all 1/7-31/8). Large irregular shaped pool filled with river water (1/5-31/8). Limited children's club in high season along with video and non-professional entertainment for adults in the evening in high season. Off site: Historic town of Millau. Hang-gliding, fishing and canoeing and walking in the impressive Massive Central.

Open: 29 March - 30 September.

Directions

Millau is best accessed from the A75 motorway. From either north or south take the N9, following it round the town until roundabout signed for Millau Plage. Cross the river and take third exit at next roundabout. Site is on left 1.5 km. after the final roundabout and after passing two other sites. GPS: 44.11552, 3.08692

Charges 2010

Per unit incl. 2 persons and electricity	€ 15,50 - € 26,00
extra person	€ 3,50 - € 6,00
child (2-4 yrs)	€ 2,00 - € 4,00
dog	€ 2,00 - € 4,00

Millau

Camping Caravaning les Rivages

Avenue de l'Aigoual, route de Nant, F-12100 Millau (Aveyron) T: **05 65 61 01 07**
E: **campinglesrivages@wanadoo.fr** **alanrogers.com/FR12020**

Les Rivages is a large, well-established site on the outskirts of the town. It is well situated, being close to the high limestone Causses and the dramatic gorges of the Tarn and Dourbie. Smaller pitches, used for small units, abut a pleasant riverside space suitable for sunbathing, fishing or picnics. Most of the 314 pitches are large, and well shaded. A newer part of the site has less shade but larger pitches. All pitches have electricity (6A), and 282 have water and drainage. The site offers a very wide range of sporting activities close to 30 in all (see facilities).

Facilities

Four well kept modern toilet blocks have all necessary facilities. Special block for children. Small shop (1/6-15/9). Terrace, restaurant and bar overlooking swimming pool, children's pool (from 10/5). Play area. Entertainment, largely for children, child-minding, miniclub. Impressive sports centre with tennis (indoor and outdoor), squash and badminton. Boules. River activities, walking, bird watching, fishing. Off site: Rafting and canoeing arranged. Bicycle hire 1 km. Riding 10 km. Hypermarket in Millau.

Open: 1 April - 15 October.

Directions

From Millau, cross the Tarn bridge and take D991 road east towards Nant. Site is about 400 m. from the roundabout on the right, on the banks of the Dourbie river. GPS: 44.10079, 3.09605

Charges guide

Per unit incl. 2 persons and electricity	€ 18,60 - € 29,00
extra person	€ 3,50 - € 5,50
child (2-7 yrs)	€ 25,00 - € 4,00
pet	€ 1,50 - € 3,50

Millau

Camping Côté Sud

Avenue de l'Aigoual, F-12100 Millau (Aveyron) T: **05 65 61 18 83**. E: **camping-cotesud@orange.fr**
alanrogers.com/FR12350

Le Côté Sud is a family run site just 500 m. from the lively market town of Millau which lies in the valley below the imposing Millau suspension bridge. The owners speak German, Dutch and English so all will get a great welcome here. There are 160 good sized, slightly sloping grassy pitches with varying degrees of shade and good views over the wooded hills. There are 140 pitches for tourers, 6/10A electricity – long leads needed. The site has a heated swimming pool, sauna and snack bar/bar, pleasant for unwinding after a busy day touring making it ideal for long or short stays.

Facilities

Modern well equipped, clean toilet blocks with all necessary facilities including those for campers with disabilities. Snack bar/bar (July/Aug). Swimming pool, sauna (June - Sept). Small TV room. Play area. Activity and entertainment programme, mainly off site. River fishing and bathing. Off site: Millau centre 500 m. Bicycle hire 300 m. Riding 2 km. Walking and cycling in the Grands Causses park. Roquefort cheese cellars. Caves (Aven Armand and Dargilan).

Open: 1 April - 30 September.

Directions

Leave A75 autoroute at exit 45 before crossing viaduct and follow signs to Millau. On entering Millau turn left at roundabout, signed Zone Commerciale and follow signs for 'Campings'. Turn left at roundabout, cross river and shortly turn right to campsite.
GPS: 44.10240, 3.09100

Charges guide

Per unit incl. 2 persons and electricity	€ 10,00 - € 24,00
extra person	€ 3,00 - € 4,50
child (5-11 yrs)	€ 2,00 - € 3,50

Montpezat de Quercy

Camping le Faillal

F-82270 Montpezat de Quercy (Tarn-et-Garonne) T: **05 63 02 07 08**. E: **contact@revea-vacances.com**
alanrogers.com/FR82050

Le Faillal is a member of the Revea group and is located at Montpézat de Quercy, around 35 km. north of Montauban. There are 47 pitches here, all of a good size and mostly with electricity (4/6A). The site forms a part of the Parc de Loisirs de Faillal, and this comprises a large swimming pool (open to the public and free to campers), tennis, sports area and a small village of holiday cottages. The site shop stocks basics with other shops in the nearby village. Montpézat is a delightful village that is best known for its 14th-century college. There are many excellent cycle tracks through the rolling countryside of the Quercy and the site managers will be pleased to recommend routes. Cahors and its world renowned vineyards are just 25 km. distant and the Aveyron gorges are around 30 km. away. Le Faillal is open for a long season and is a tranquil spot for a holiday, particularly outside the peak holiday period.

Facilities

Small shop. Swimming pool. Play area. Tourist information. Chalets for rent. Off site: Village centre 800 m. Fishing (river) 3 km. Riding 12 km. Golf 15 km.

Open: 4 April - 10 October.

Directions

Approaching from the north, leave A20 autoroute at exit 58 and head west on D19 and then south on D820 as far as La Baraque. Then head southwest on D20 to Montpézat de Quercy and follow signs to the site. GPS: 44.243139, 1.47764

Charges guide

Per unit incl. 2 persons and electricity	€ 15,40 - € 17,80
extra person	€ 3,00 - € 3,60
child (2-7 yrs)	free - € 1,60

Montcabrier

Camping Moulin de Laborde

F-46700 Montcabrier (Lot) T: **05 65 24 62 06**. E: **moulindelaborde@wanadoo.fr**
alanrogers.com/FR46040

Based around a converted 17th-century watermill, Moulin de Laborde has been created by the van Bommel family to provide a tranquil and uncommercialised campsite for the whole family to enjoy. Bordered by woods, hills and a small river, there are 90 flat and grassy pitches, all of at least 100 sq.m. with electricity (6A). A variety of pretty shrubs and trees divide the pitches and provide a moderate amount of shade. A gate at the back of the site leads walkers onto a 'Grand Randonée' footpath which passes through the village of Montcabrier, 1 km. away.

Facilities

Well designed, clean toilet block, unit for disabled people. Washing machine, dryer. Basic shop (all season). Small bar, restaurant, takeaway. Swimming pool, sunbathing area, paddling pool (all season). Play area. Small lake, free rafts and rowing boats. Fishing. Volleyball. Badminton. Boules. Covered recreation area. Mountain bike hire. Rock climbing. Archery. Dogs are not accepted. WiFi (free). Off site: Riding 5 km. Golf 8 km. Tennis nearby and canoeing on the Lot. The Château of Bonaquil 6 km. Fumel 12 km.

Open: 4 April - 26 September.

Directions

Site is on the north side of the D673 Fumel - Gourdon road about 1 km. northeast of the turn to village of Montcabrier. GPS: 44.5475, 1.08388

Charges guide

Per unit incl. 2 persons and electricity	€ 19,68 - € 24,60
extra person	€ 5,20 - € 6,50
child (under 7 yrs)	€ 2,80 - € 3,50

Less 20% outside July/August.
No credit cards.

Mostuéjouls

Camping Saint-Pal

Route du Gorges du Tarn, F-12720 Mostuéjouls (Aveyron) T: **05 65 62 64 46**. E: **saintpal@wanadoo.fr**
alanrogers.com/FR12240

Saint-Pal is ideally situated on the approach road to the Gorges du Tarn, so access to the site is easy. This small, very neat site is run by a very friendly family and is aimed at those who prefer peace and quiet and less in the way of organised activity. Beside the Tarn river, the site is arranged in the open valley and is fairly flat. There are 74 large, level, grassy pitches, with 64 for touring. Separated by hedging, most are shaded by mature trees and 6A electricity is available. Some pitches are alongside the attractive river.

Facilities

One very clean, modern toilet block with good facilities includes a room for babies and campers with disabilities. Motorcaravan service point. Small shop (1/6-15/9). Bar/restaurant and takeaway (1/7-31/8). Small swimming pool (all season). Play area, TV/games room. River bathing, boating and fishing. Organised walks and low key entertainment in July/Aug but no musical events.
Off site: Bicycle hire 500 m. Riding 5 km. Le Rozier 1 km.

Open: 19 May - 15 September.

Directions

Leave A75 at exit 44, north of Millau. Take N9 south for 14 km. to Aquessac. Turn left on D907 and site is on right in 14 km. just before village of Le Rosier. GPS: 44.19585, 3.199717

Charges guide

Per unit incl. 2 persons and electricity	€ 14,60 - € 23,20
extra person	€ 3,30 - € 4,80
child (under 5 yrs)	€ 23,00 - € 3,50

Nant-d'Aveyron

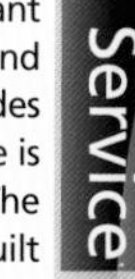

RCN Val de Cantobre

F-12230 Nant-d'Aveyron (Aveyron) T: **05 65 58 43 00**. E: **info@rcn-valdecantobre.fr**
alanrogers.com/FR12010

Imaginatively and tastefully developed by the Dupond family over the past 30 years, this very pleasant terraced site is now owned by the RCN group. Most of the 200 touring pitches (all with electricity and water) are peaceful, generous in size and blessed with views of the valley. The terrace design provides some peace and privacy, especially on the upper levels. Rock pegs are advised. An activity programme is supervised by qualified instructors in July and August and a new pleasure pool has been added. The magnificent carved features in the bar create a delightful ambience, complemented by a recently built terrace.

Facilities

The fully equipped toilet block is well appointed. Fridge hire. Small shop including many regional specialities, attractive bar, restaurant, pizzeria and takeaway (all season). There are some fairly steep up and down walking from furthest pitches to some facilities. Swimming pools (all season). Minigolf. Play area. Activity programme. All weather sports pitch. Torch useful. Off site: Fishing 4 km. Riding 15 km. Bicycle hire 25 km.

Open: 10 April - 2 October.

Directions

Site is 4 km. north of Nant, on D991 road to Millau. From Millau direction take D991 signed Gorge du Dourbie. Site is on left, just past turn to Cantobre. GPS: 44.04467, 3.30228

Charges guide

Per unit incl. 2 persons, electricity and water	€ 19,50 - € 43,50
extra person (4 yrs and over)	€ 4,00 - € 7,00

Camping Cheques accepted.

Naucelle

Flower Camping du Lac de Bonnefon

L'Etang de Bonnefon, F-12800 Naucelle (Aveyron) T: **05 65 69 33 20**
E: **email-camping-du-lac-de-bonnefon@wanadoo.fr** **alanrogers.com/FR12250**

This small family run site, popular with French campers, lies in a picturesque region waiting to be discovered, with rolling hills, deep river valleys, lakes and many old fortified villages. This site is more suitable for those seeking a quieter holiday with less in the way of entertainment. There are 112 good sized, grassy, slightly sloping pitches with 74 for touring (50 with 10A electricity). Some are separated by laurel hedging with others more open and maturing trees give a little shade. The new enthusiastic and friendly owners have recently extended the site and refurbished the facilities to a high standard.

Facilities

Two toilet blocks include some washbasins in cabins and good facilities for disabled visitors. No shop but bread to order. Bar with TV (all season). Snack bar (July/Aug, other times on demand). Swimming and paddling pools (1/6-30/9). Playground. Archery. Good lake fishing but no bathing. Activities for all the family in July/Aug.
Off site: Riding 500 m. Small village of Naucelle with a few shops and large heated pool complex 1 km.

Open: 1 April - 31 October.

Directions

Site is just off the N88 about halfway between Rodez and Albi. From Naucelle Gare take D997 towards Naucelle. In just over 1 km. turn left on D58 and follow signs to site in just under 1 km.
GPS: 44.18805, 2.34827

Charges guide

Per unit incl. 2 persons and electricity	€ 13,50 - € 22,00
extra person	€ 2,00 - € 5,00

Payrac-en-Quercy

Flower Camping les Pins

F-46350 Payrac-en-Quercy (Lot) T: **05 65 37 96 32**. E: **info@les-pins-camping.com**
alanrogers.com/FR46030

Set amongst four hectares of beautiful pine forest, Camping Les Pins is well situated for exploring the historical and natural splendours of the Dordogne region, as well as being a convenient overnight stop when heading north or south. There are 125 clearly marked, level pitches (100 sq.m), of which 55 are for touring units. The pitches are well marked and separated by small shrubs or hedges. Many have shade from the abundant pine trees and all have 10A electricity connections. There is a bar and a good value restaurant with a terrace overlooking the pool area.

Facilities

Three toilet blocks (heated April-May), well maintained and include washbasins in cabins and good baby bath facilites. Laundry facilities. Motorcaravan service point. Shop with basics (1/6-12/9). Bar with TV. Restaurant and takeaway. Heated swimming pool (1/5-12/9), three slides and smaller paddling pool. Tennis. Small library. Some entertainment in season, including weekly family discos. Walking routes starting from site. English and Dutch are spoken.
Off site: Fishing 7 km. Riding 10 km.

Open: 17 April - 12 September.

Directions

Site entrance is 16 km. from Souillac on western side of the N20 just south of the village of Payrac-en-Quercy. GPS: 44.78946, 1.47204

Charges 2010

Per unit incl. 2 persons and electricity	€ 17,50 - € 30,50

Special low season prices.

Rivière-sur-Tarn

Flower Camping Caravaning de Peyrelade

Route des Gorges du Tarn, F-12640 Rivière-sur-Tarn (Aveyron) T: **05 65 62 62 54**
E: **campingpeyrelade@orange.fr** **alanrogers.com/FR12000**

The 145 touring pitches (100-150 sq.m) are terraced, level and shady with 6A electricity hook-ups (long leads may be required for the riverside pitches). There are also 43 mobile homes. The site is ideally placed for visiting the Tarn, Jonte and Dourbie gorges, and centres for rafting and canoeing are a short drive up the river. Other nearby attractions include the Caves of Aven Armand, the Chaos de Montpellier, Roquefort (of cheese fame) and the pleasant town of Millau. Many of the roads along and between the Gorges are breathtaking for passengers, but worrying for drivers who may not like looking down!

Facilities

Two well equipped toilet blocks. Young children are catered for, also people with disabilities. Washing machines, dryer. Bar, restaurant, pizzeria, takeaway (all from 1/6). Paddling pool, attractive heated swimming pool (proper swimming trunks, no shorts). Good playground. Games room. Miniclub. Fishing. Off site: Bicycle hire 100 m. Riding 3 km. Nearby leisure centre can be booked at reception at reduced charges. Millau, hypermarket, shops, night markets.

Open: 15 May - 15 September.

Directions

Take autoroute A75 to exit 44-1 Aguessac then onto D907 (follow Gorges du Tarn signs). Site is 2 km. past Rivière-sur-Tarn, on the right - the access road is quite steep. GPS: 44.19047, 3.15638

Charges guide

Per unit incl. 2 persons and electricity	€ 19,00 - € 34,00
extra person	€ 3,50 - € 6,00
child (under 7 yrs)	€ 2,00 - € 4,00
dog	€ 2,00

Pont-de-Salars

Flower Camping les Terrasses du Lac

Route du Vibal, F-12290 Pont-de-Salars (Aveyron) T: **05 65 46 88 18**

E: **campinglesterrasses@orange.fr** **alanrogers.com/FR12050**

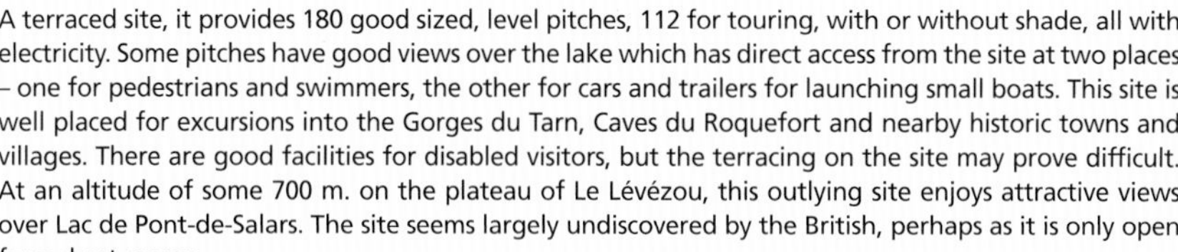

A terraced site, it provides 180 good sized, level pitches, 112 for touring, with or without shade, all with electricity. Some pitches have good views over the lake which has direct access from the site at two places – one for pedestrians and swimmers, the other for cars and trailers for launching small boats. This site is well placed for excursions into the Gorges du Tarn, Caves du Roquefort and nearby historic towns and villages. There are good facilities for disabled visitors, but the terracing on the site may prove difficult. At an altitude of some 700 m. on the plateau of Le Lévézou, this outlying site enjoys attractive views over Lac de Pont-de-Salars. The site seems largely undiscovered by the British, perhaps as it is only open for a short season.

Facilities

Four toilet blocks with adequate facilities. Fridge hire. Shop. Bar/restaurant with a lively French ambience serving full meals (high season) snacks (other times), takeaway (all 1/7-31/8). Heated swimming pool, children's pool (1/6-30/9). Solarium. Playground. Petanque. Billiards. Games and TV rooms. Activities high season. Barbecue area. Off site: Tennis 3 km. Riding 5 km. Golf 20 km.

Open: 29 March - 29 September.

Directions

Using D911 Millau - Rodez road, turn north at Pont-de-Salars towards lake on D523. Follow site signs. Ignore first site and continue, following lake until Les Terraces (about 5 km). GPS: 44.30498, 2.73556

Charges 2010

Per unit incl. 2 persons and electricity	€ 14,90 - € 26,50
extra person	€ 4,00 - € 5,50
child (2-7 yrs)	€ 3,00 - € 4,00
dog	€ 1,75

Rivière-sur-Tarn

Kawan Village les Peupliers

Route des Gorges du Tarn, F-12640 Rivière-sur-Tarn (Aveyron) T: **05 65 59 85 17**

E: **lespeupliers12640@orange.fr** **alanrogers.com/FR12160**

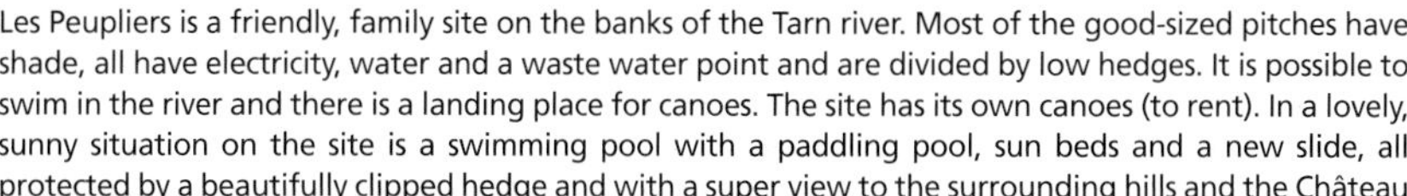

Les Peupliers is a friendly, family site on the banks of the Tarn river. Most of the good-sized pitches have shade, all have electricity, water and a waste water point and are divided by low hedges. It is possible to swim in the river and there is a landing place for canoes. The site has its own canoes (to rent). In a lovely, sunny situation on the site is a swimming pool with a paddling pool, sun beds and a new slide, all protected by a beautifully clipped hedge and with a super view to the surrounding hills and the Château du Peyrelade perched above the village.

Facilities

Large, light and airy toilet facilities, baby facilities with baths, showers and WCs, facilities for disabled visitors. Washing machines. Shop (1/6-30/9). Bar, TV. Internet. Snack bar, takeaway (1/5-30/9). Swimming pool (from 1/5). Games, competitions July/Aug. Fishing. Play area. Weekly dances July/Aug. Canoe hire. Off site: Village with shops and restaurant 300 m. Riding 500 m. Bicycle hire 2 km. Golf 25 km. Rock climbing, canyoning, cycling and walking.

Open: 1 April - 30 September.

Directions

Heading south from Clermont Ferrand to Millau on the A75 autoroute take exit 44-1 signed Aguessac/Gorges du Tarn. In Aguessac turn left and follow signs to Riviere-sur-Tarn (5 km). Site is clearly signed down a short road to the right. GPS: 44.18577, 3.13068

Charges guide

Per unit incl. 2 persons and electricity	€ 20,00 - € 32,00
extra person	€ 2,00 - € 7,00

Camping Cheques accepted.

Rocamadour

Camping les Cigales

L'Hospitalet, F-46500 Rocamadour (Lot) T: **05 65 33 64 44**. E: **camping.cigales@wanadoo.fr**

alanrogers.com/FR46380

Les Cigales has 100 pitches of which 47 are for mobile homes and bungalows which are all available to rent. The remaining 53 are used for touring caravans, motorcaravans and tents. Most are level with some shade and range in size from 80-120 sq.m; 53 have 10A electricity. The site is quite spacious with a large area for activities and, with the emphasis on conviviality in a family atmosphere, it is ideally suited to families with children of all ages. There is entertainment in high season day and evening, the latter including discos, karaoke, bingo and cinema evenings. There are also themed nights as well as bowls tournaments. The minigolf course is large and with lighting on until midnight.

Facilities

Sanitary facilities include washbasins in cabins. Facilities for disabled visitors. Motorcaravan service point. Swimming and paddling pools. Play area. Boules. Minigolf. Giant screen for films and TV. Day and evening entertainment. Off site: Golf 20 km. Riding 5 km. Bicycle hire 20 km. Monkey Park. Caves of Merveilles.

Open: 4 April - 24 October.

Directions

From the A20 take exit 55 for Souillac and take the road to Gramat. Site is signed in Rocamadour centre. GPS: 44.804981, 1.632242

Charges guide

Per unit incl. 2 persons	€ 17,00
extra person	€ 4,00 - € 6,00
electricity	€ 3,00

Roquelaure

Kawan Village le Talouch

kawan VILLAGES www.kawan-villages.com

F-32810 Roquelaure (Gers) T: **05 62 65 52 43**. E: **info@camping-talouch.com**

alanrogers.com/FR32080

Although enjoying a quiet and rural location, this neat and tidy site is only a short drive from the town of Auch with its famous legendary son, d'Artagnan. The entrance is fronted by a parking area with reception to the right and the bar and restaurant facing. Beyond this point lies the top half of the touring area with generous pitches of at least 120 sq.m. located between mature trees and divided by hedges, some with chalets. There are 100 pitches for touring, with electricity (6A). The rear half of the site has unshaded pitches in a more open aspect.

Facilities

Two toilet blocks with open style washbasins and controllable showers. Baby unit. One toilet for disabled visitors. Coin-operated washing machine and laundry sinks. Small shop (1/4-30/9). Bar, restaurant and takeaway. Two swimming pools, one heated and covered. Sauna and spa. Bicycle hire. GPS hire with pre-programmed walking routes. Play areas. Tennis and hard surface sports area. Organised entertainment in high season. Internet and WiFi in reception. Off site: Fishing and riding within 8 km.

Open: 1 April - 30 September.

Directions

Situated some 11 km. north of Auch on the D149, and 64 km. east of Toulouse the site is well signed. From the north approach via the A62 motorway, leaving at Layrac and heading towards Auch on the N21. GPS: 43.71283, 0.5645

Charges guide

Per unit incl. 2 persons and electricity	€ 17,20 - € 31,50
extra person	€ 3,85 - € 7,20

Camping Cheques accepted.

Saint Amans-des-Cots

Village Center les Tours

F-12460 Saint Amans-des-Cots (Aveyron) T: **04 99 57 21 21**. E: **resa@village-center.com**

alanrogers.com/FR12040

This impressive campsite is set in beautiful countryside close to the Truyère Gorges, Upper Lot valley and the Aubrac Plateau. Efficiently run, it is situated on the shores of the Lac de la Selves. There are 275 average sized pitches with 6A electricity, some bordering the lake, the rest terraced and hedged with views of the lake. About 100 pitches also have water points. The site has a spacious feel, enhanced by the thoughtfully planned terraced layout and it is well kept and very clean. There is some up and down walking to the facilities, especially from the upper terraces. Used by tour operators (70 pitches).

Facilities

Four well equipped toilet blocks. Attractive central complex housing the amenities. Shop (with gas). Restaurant, bar. Takeaway (high season). Swimming pools (May-Sept). Play area. Tennis. Daytime and evening activities, with miniclub, archery and tree climbing (all supervised). Lake activities include fishing, canoeing, pedaloes, windsurfing, water skiing and provision for launching small boats. Internet terminal. Off site: Riding 6 km. Golf 9 km. Bicycle hire 12 km.

Open: 30 April - 5 September.

Directions

Take D34 from Entraygues-sur-Truyère to St Amans-des-Cots (14 km). In St Amans take D97 to Colombez and then D599 to Lac de la Selves (site signed, 5 km. from St Amans). GPS: 44.66668, 2.68001

Charges 2010

Per unit incl. 2 persons and electricity	€ 16,00 - € 34,00

Saint Antonin-Noble-Val

Flower Camping les Gorges de l'Aveyron

Marsac bas, F-82140 Saint Antonin-Noble-Val (Tarn-et-Garonne) T: **05 63 30 69 76**
E: **info@camping-gorges-aveyron.com** **alanrogers.com/FR82040**

This is a friendly, family site which is undergoing a process of renovation by its new owners, Stephane and Johanna Batlo. The site has an attractive wooded location, sloping down to the River Aveyron and facing the Roc d'Anglars. Reception and the two toilet blocks are housed in traditional, converted farm buildings. There are 80 pitches of which 50 are for touring units and these all have electrical connections (3-10A). The pitches are grassy and well shaded and may become very soft in times of poor weather. Some pitches are available close to the river but we would suggest that these are unsuitable for younger children as the river is unfenced. The owners have ambitious plans for the future and are planning to add a swimming pool and third toilet block. This is a very quiet site in low season and some amenities, notably the snack bar and shop are only available in the peak season. The nearby town of St Antonin-Noble-Val dates back to the eighth century and is just 1.5 km. from the site. The town is well worth a visit and has a good range of shops and restaurants.

Facilities

Two toilet blocks with washing machines and dryers. Small shop, bar, snack bar and takeaway (June - Sept). Direct access to river. Fishing. Canoeing. Play area. Entertainment and activities in high season. Mobile homes for rent.
Off site: St Antonin-Noble-Val with a wide choice of shops, restaurants and bars 1.5 km. Cordes-sur-Ciel 35 km. Bicycle hire 1.5 km. Riding 2 km. Many paths and cycle trails.

Open: 10 April - 26 September.

Directions

From the north, take exit 59 from the A20 autoroute joining the D926 and follow signs to St Antonin. Site can be found on the D115, 1.5 km. east of the town. GPS: 44.1519, 1.7715

Charges guide

Per unit incl. 2 persons and electricity	€ 9,40 - € 16,30
extra person	€ 2,90 - € 5,00
child (under 7 yrs)	€ 1,60 - € 2,50

Camping Cheques accepted.

Saint Cirq-Lapopie

Camping la Truffière

F-46330 Saint Cirq-Lapopie (Lot) T: **05 65 30 20 22**. E: **contact@camping-truffiere.com**
alanrogers.com/FR46150

Set in four hectares of mature oak woodland, only 2.5 km. from the cliff top village of St Cirq-Lapopie, La Truffière is well suited to those seeking a peaceful countryside holiday amongst the stunning natural scenery of the 'Parc naturel régional des Causses de Quercy'. The 90 terraced touring pitches are of varying sizes and on a mixture of grass and gravel (larger units should reserve pitches in advance). All pitches have electricity (6A) and most have shade from the abundant trees. There are various walks and mountain bike trails in the area and you can hire bikes on site.

Facilities

Two well appointed, clean, modern toilet blocks (one heated) include facilities for disabled visitors. Motorcaravan services. Fridge hire. Small shop (open all season). Bar/restaurant (1/6-31/8), terrace overlooking pool and playing field. Snack bar (1/6-31/8). Swimming pool, paddling pool, sun terrace (1/5-15/9). Playing field, volleyball, basketball, football. Adventure style play area. Trampolines. Boules. English spoken. Off site: Small shop in village. Supermarkets in Cahors 25 km. Riding 3 km. Fishing (in the River Lot) 3 km.

Open: 3 April - 30 September.

Directions

From D911 Cahors - Rodez road, turn north on D42 at Concots (signed St Cirq-Lapopie). Site about 5 km. on right. Approaching from north on D42 via St Cirq-Lapopie not recommended due to extremely tight left turn in village. GPS: 44.44855, 1.67455

Charges guide

Per unit incl. 2 persons and electricity	€ 19,20 - € 21,70
extra person	€ 5,10

Camping Cheques accepted.

Saint Come-d'Olt

Camping Belle Rive

Rue du Terral, F-12500 Saint Come-d'Olt (Aveyron) T: **05 65 44 05 85**. E: **bellerive12@voila.fr**
alanrogers.com/FR12380

Small and simple, this family run campsite, beside the River Lot, is on the edge of a delightful medieval village. The region has many historic towns and villages with chateaux and ancient churches and is close to the Pilgrim route. The local produce, for example Roquefort cheese, is well worth sampling. The site is good for those seeking a tranquil spot with little in the way of on site activities. There are 71 good sized grassy pitches delineated by a variety of tall trees giving good shade on most of the pitches (6A electricity). Access to the site is not suitable for large outfits due to the many small twisting roads.

Facilities

Adequate but very clean old style central block with combined shower and washbasin cubicles. Washing machine. Facilities for disabled campers. Play area. Some family activities (high season). River bathing and fishing. Off site: Village, small shops, bank, bar/restaurants 400 m. Espalion with larger shops and market 4 km. Swimming pool 4 km. Riding 12 km. Canoeing. Ancient villages, chateaux, churches. Many walking and cycling routes. Takeaway (all season).

Open: 1 May - 30 September.

Directions

Leave A75 at exit 42, signed Sévérac le Château. Take N88 west, then D28 to Espalion. Cross river on D987 to St Côme-d'Olt (4 km). On entering village bear left, following signs to site. Do not drive through the village. GPS: 44.51376, 2.81847

Charges 2010

Per unit incl. 2 persons and electricity	€ 13,30
extra person	€ 3,10
child (under 7 yrs)	€ 1,70
dog	€ 0,70

No credit cards.

Saint Geniez-d'Olt

Campéole

Campéole la Boissière

Route de la Cascade, F-12130 Saint Geniez-d'Olt (Aveyron) T: **05 65 70 40 43**. E: **boissiere@campeole.com**
alanrogers.com/FR12090

With trout in the river and carp in the lakes, La Boissière is a fisherman's paradise. The site is a member of the Campéole group and is situated on the banks of the River Lot, surrounded by wooded hills. Walking, swimming, canoeing or cycling are alternative pursuits here. Mature trees provide plenty of shade on the generous, partly hedged, grassy pitches, all of which have electricity connections (6A) and frequently placed water points. Reception is housed in an old, converted farmhouse. The nearby old town of St Geniez-d'Olt should satisfy all shopping needs and day or longer fishing licences can be obtained there (the helpful site staff will advise). There is direct access through the site to the river, which is suitable for swimming and canoeing. La Boissière has 150 pitches, of which around 70 are used for mobile homes, chalets or fully equipped tents (available for rent) There is much of interest in the area and the Tarn gorges and Grandes Causses are both within easy access.

Facilities

Basic provisions are stocked (milk and bread in high season only). Bar with terrace. Large, heated swimming pool and paddling pool. Multisport terrain. Bouncy castle and playground. Entertainment is organised in July/Aug. Mobile homes, chalets and tents for rent. Vlakbij: St Geniez-d'Olt (500 m). Bicycle and canoe hire.

Open: 18 April - 20 September.

Directions

Site is off the D988 east of Saint Geniez-d'Olt. GPS: 44.4686, 2.9825

Charges guide

Per unit incl. 2 persons and electricity	€ 7,55 - € 12,00

Saint Geniez-d'Olt

Kawan Village Marmotel

F-12130 Saint Geniez-d'Olt (Aveyron) T: **05 65 70 46 51**. E: **info@marmotel.com**

alanrogers.com/FR12150

The road into Marmotel passes various industrial buildings and is a little off-putting – persevere, as they are soon left behind. The campsite itself is a mixture of old and new. The old part provides many pitches with lots of shade and separated by hedges. The new area is sunny until the trees grow. These pitches each have a private sanitary unit, with shower, WC, washbasin and dishwashing. New and very well designed, they are reasonably priced for such luxury. All the pitches have electricity (10A). A lovely restaurant has a wide terrace with views of the hills and overlooking the heated swimming and paddling pools. These have fountains, a toboggan and sun beds either on grass or the tiled surrounds. The Lot river runs alongside the site where you can fish or canoe.

Facilities

Good sanitary facilities include baby baths and facilities for disabled visitors. Washing machines. Bar/restaurant, takeaway. Swimming pools. Small play area. Multisports area. Entertainment July/Aug. including disco below bar, cinema, karaoke, dances, miniclub (4-12 yrs) Bicycle hire. Fishing. Canoeing. Off site: Large supermarket 500 m. Riding 10 km. Bicycle tours and canoe trips on the Lot and rafting on the Tarn are organised.

Open: 10 May - 18 September.

Directions

Heading south on autoroute 75 (free) take exit 41 and follow signs for St Geniez-d'Olt. Site is at western end of village. Site is signed onto D19 to Prades d'Aubrac, then 500 m. on left. GPS: 44.46165, 2.96318

Charges 2010

Per unit incl. 1 or 2 persons and electricity	€ 18,00 - € 27,00

Camping Cheques accepted.

Saint Girons

Parc d'Audinac les Bains

Montjoie-Audinac, F-09200 Saint Girons (Ariège) T: **05 61 66 44 50**. E: **accueil@audinac.com**

alanrogers.com/FR09100

Remnants of an old thermal springs can be found on the site at Parc d'Audinac les Bains, a tranquil haven with wonderful views of the surrounding mountains. Owned by a charming French couple, Olivia and Jérôme Barbry, you are guaranteed a friendly welcome on this site which has 60 touring pitches and 40 chalets for rent. The terraced touring pitches are mostly level, although some do have a slight slope. They are on well-drained grass and each has 10A electricity supplied (the older part of the site via French sockets). Water supplies are conveniently located for all of the pitches, as are the sanitary facilities.

Facilities

New chalets. Two small bright and modern toilet blocks (one unisex) with hot and cold water to showers and washbasins. British and Turkish style WC's. Washing machines. Motorcaravan service point. Good sized outdoor swimming pool and paddling pool with WCs, showers and changing facilities. Small shop for drinks and ice creams (July/Aug) in the old thermal spring building adjacent to the pool. Children's club (July/Aug). Tennis. Boules. Sports area. Off site: Shops, bars, restaurants and supermarket at St Girons 3 km. Many outdoor activities available in the surrounding area (the owners will advise and have arranged discounts at some).

Open: 1 May - 30 September.

Directions

From St Girons take D117 towards Foix. Turn left on D627 signed St Croix and Merigon. Site is on the right just after Audinac-les-Bains. GPS: 43.00740, 1.18260

Charges 2010

Per unit incl. 2 persons	€ 11,50 - € 16,00
extra person	€ 4,00 - € 6,00
child (0-6 yrs)	€ 3,00 - € 5,00
electricity (10A)	€ 3,50

Saint Parthem

Camping la Plaine

F-12300 Saint Parthem (Aveyron) T: **05 65 64 05 24**. E: **infos@camping-laplaine.fr**
alanrogers.com/FR12360

Strung out along the bank of the Lot river, this small, spacious, delightful site is family run. The enthusiastic and very friendly Dutch owners are making many improvements here including the addition of a new swimming pool in 2008. There are 65 grassy, fairly level pitches with 61 for touring with electricity (6A, long leads advised). The pitches are separated by maturing trees and some hedging with views over the river and the wooded gorge. Some pitches have little shade. Swimming and canoeing are possible from the small pebbly beach.

Facilities

Old style but very clean central block and small satellite block with all necessary facilities. Facilities for disabled visitors. Washing machine, ironing board. Small bar/restaurant with takeaway (all season). Bread to order. Swimming pool with patio. River fishing and bathing from pebble beach. Tennis. Boules. Off site: Small village, small shop, 500 m. Riding 8 km. Canoeing 15 km. Picturesque medieval towns and villages, e.g. Conques 14 km.

Open: 5 April - 14 September.

Directions

Site is northeast of Decazeville. Leave Decazeville on the D963 signed Aurillac. After 6 km. cross river and turn east onto D42 to St Parthem (6 km). Site is well signed. GPS: 44.6292, 2.32059

Charges guide

Per unit incl. 2 persons	€ 12,50
extra person	€ 2,00 - € 3,50
electricity (6A)	€ 3,00

No credit cards.

Sainte Pierre-Lafeuille

Camping Quercy Vacances

Mas de la Combe, F-46090 Sainte Pierre-Lafeuille (Lot) T: **05 65 36 87 15**. E: **quercy-vacances@wanadoo.fr**
alanrogers.com/FR46240

This clean, well run site is owned by a young, English-speaking, French couple who are determined to improve the facilities and ambiance. It is only 4.5 km. from the A20 and an ideal stopover site for holidaymakers travelling to and from Spain. However, it is better than just a stopover site and is worth staying a few extra days. It has 70 large unmarked touring pitches most of which have 6/10A hook-ups. The site facilities include a bar and restaurant which has hand-painted murals on the walls. The toilets and laundry are also in this split-level building with the toilets to the rear of the building on a lower level.

Facilities

Clean, modern toilet block, recently refurbished. Facilities for campers with disabilities are located in a separate building adjacent to the camping area. Small basic shop. Bar and takeaway. Restaurant serving specials like couscous and paella once a week. Large round swimming pool (20/6-15/9), unsuitable for young children, minimum depth 1.2 m. Live music, dancing (July/Aug). Small play area. Off site: Riding 5 km. Bicycle hire, fishing 10 km.

Open: 1 April - 31 October.

Directions

Leave A20 exit 57 (Cahors). Shortly turn left on N20 and then turn right on small un-named road (site signed) before reaching St Pierre-Lafeuille (about 4.5 km. from the A20). Site on right in about 600 m. GPS: 44.53136, 1.45926

Charges guide

Per person	€ 3,80 - € 5,00
pitch	€ 5,00 - € 8,80
electricity (6/10A)	€ 3,30 - € 5,50

Salles-Curan

Kawan Village les Genêts

Lac de Pareloup, F-12410 Salles-Curan (Aveyron) T: **05 65 46 35 34**
E: **contact@camping-les-genets.fr** **alanrogers.com/FR12080**

The 163 pitches include 80 grassy, mostly individual pitches for touring units. These are in two areas, one on each side of the entrance lane, and are divided by hedges, shrubs and trees. Most have electricity (6A) and many also have water and waste water drain. The site slopes gently down to the beach and lake with facilities for all watersports including water skiing. A full entertainment and activities programme is organised in high season, and there is much to see and do in this attractive corner of Aveyron. This family-run site is on the shores of Lac de Pareloup, with both family holiday and watersports facilities.

Facilities

Two sanitary units with suite for disabled people. The older unit has been refurbished. Baby room. Laundry. Well stocked shop. Bar, restaurant, snacks (main season). Swimming pool, spa pool (from 1/6; unsupervised). Playground. Minigolf. Boules. Bicycle hire. Pedaloes, windsurfers, kayaks. Fishing licences available. WiFi in bar.

Open: 31 May - 11 September.

Directions

From Salles-Curan take D577 for about 4 km. and turn right into a narrow lane immediately after a sharp right hand bend. Site is signed at junction. GPS: 44.18933, 2.76693

Charges guide

Per unit incl. 1 or 2 persons and 6A electricity	€ 13,00 - € 33,00
lakeside pitch	€ 13,00 - € 39,00
extra person	€ 4,00 - € 7,00

Camping Cheques accepted.

Séniergues

Kawan Village Domaine de la Faurie

F-46240 Séniergues (Lot) T: **05 65 21 14 36**. E: **contact@camping-lafaurie.com**

alanrogers.com/FR46190

A stunning array of tended shrubs and thoughtful flower plantings is spread throughout this very pretty site which is located on a hilltop with wide open views of the surrounding hills and valleys. Although hidden away, it is an excellent base for exploring the Lot and Dordogne regions. The site is separated into two distinct areas, an open, lightly shaded front section and a much more densely shaded area with tall pine trees all around the pitches. The pitches are large and most are at least 100 sq.m. The friendly French owners will tell you that they consider the three-hectacre site their personal garden.

Facilities

The single sanitary block is clean and well maintained. Facilities for disabled visitors. Washing machine. Motorcaravan service point. Excellent gift shop selling regional and local produce (bread available). Bar, restaurant and takeaway. Swimming pool and paddling pool. TV and games rooms. Boules. Bicycle hire. Play area. Small library. Weekly soirées in high season. Max. 1 dog per pitch. Off site: Fishing 3 km. Golf 8 km. Riding 15 km.

Open: 7 April - 30 September.

Directions

From the A20 exit on N56 and turn right towards St Germain du Bel Air. Continue for 5 km. and the site is on the right. GPS: 44.69197, 1.53461

Charges guide

Per person	€ 6,50
child (1-7 yrs)	€ 4,50
pitch	€ 9,00
electricity (6A)	€ 3,50

Camping Cheques accepted.

Sévérac-l'Eglise

Flower Camping la Grange de Monteillac

F-12310 Sévérac-l'Eglise (Aveyron) T: **05 65 70 21 00**. E: **info@la-grange-de-monteillac.com**

alanrogers.com/FR12070

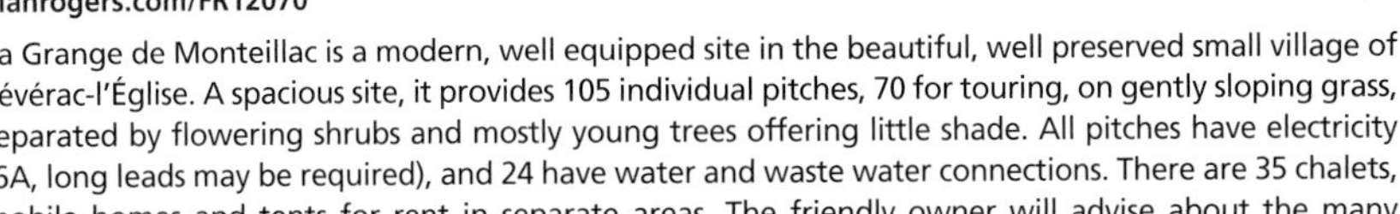

La Grange de Monteillac is a modern, well equipped site in the beautiful, well preserved small village of Sévérac-l'Église. A spacious site, it provides 105 individual pitches, 70 for touring, on gently sloping grass, separated by flowering shrubs and mostly young trees offering little shade. All pitches have electricity (6A, long leads may be required), and 24 have water and waste water connections. There are 35 chalets, mobile homes and tents for rent in separate areas. The friendly owner will advise about the many interesting activities in the region. An evening stroll around this delightful village is a must.

Facilities

Modern toilet block with facilities for babies and disabled people. Washing machine, dryer. Shop (1/7-31/8). Poolside restaurant/snack bar serving pizzas, grills etc, takeaway (1/6-15/9). Music or groups feature in the bar (July/Aug). Two swimming pools (1/6-15/9). Spacious, well equipped playground. Bicycle hire. Archery. Floodlit boules court. Organised activities. Children's club. Off site: Fishing 1 km. Shops in village 3 km. Riding 9 km. Golf 25 km. Many marked walks and bicycle rides, canoeing, rafting, canyoning, rock climbing and hang gliding.

Open: 1 May - 15 September.

Directions

Site is on the edge of Sévérac-l'Église village, just off N88 Rodez - Sévérac Le Château road. From A75 use exit 42. At Sévérac-l'Église turn south onto D28, site is signed. Site entrance is very shortly on left. GPS: 44.3652, 2.85142

Charges guide

Per unit incl. 2 persons and electricity	€ 15,50 - € 26,30
extra person	€ 2,00 - € 6,00

Less 30% outside July/Aug.

Sorèze

Camping Saint-Martin

F-81540 Sorèze (Tarn) T: **05 63 50 20 19**. E: **campings.occitanie@orange.fr**

alanrogers.com/FR81110

There are 48 individual touring pitches with 10A electricity and six wooden chalets for rent at this site. The pitches are all on grass, some divided by newly planted hedging and there are some mature trees for shade. Six pitches are reserved for motorcaravans, although these are rather compact. A small swimming pool is well fenced and gated. Reception has a small bar and snack bar and can also provide basic supplies including drinks, sweets, speciality foods and snacks. However, you are only 100 metres from the town centre shops.

Facilities

Sanitary unit is well built. Facilities for disabled visitors. Covered dishwashing and laundry sinks plus a washing machine. Small shop. Bar with TV. Snack bar. Swimming pool. WiFi (free). All amenities open 15/6-15/9. Boules. Communal barbecue. Small playground. Entertainment in high season. Off site: Municipal leisure and sports facilities including tennis courts adjacent.

Open: 15 June - 15 September.

Directions

Sorèze is on the D85 about 25 km. southwest of Castres, 5 km. east of Revel. The site is well signed within the town. GPS: 43.454517, 2.069583

Charges guide

Per unit incl. 2 persons and electricity	€ 15,05 - € 18,50
extra person	€ 3,40 - € 4,50
child (0-7 yrs)	€ 2,00 - € 2,70

Sorgeat

Camping Municipal la Prade

F-09110 Sorgeat (Ariège) T: **05 61 64 36 34**. E: **sorgeat.mainie@wanadoo.fr**
alanrogers.com/FR09050

Superbly situated high on the mountainside overlooking a valley, this site has magnificent views, with a river 300 m. and a lake 2 km. A small site, it provides just 40 pitches on terraces, some of which are occupied by long stay units, (electricity 5-10A). Well supervised, with the warden present at varying times, the site is kept very clean. A small stream tinkles through the edge of the site and the attractive hills towering above it reverberate with the sound of goat bells. A separate area has permanent brick barbecues for use by campers. A most reasonably priced campsite.

Facilities

The original, rather small sanitary block has only two showers and two WCs in each half. However, a second block has now been added and standards are very high. Facilities for disabled visiotrs are also very good with special washbasin and a very large shower suite. Washing machine. Small play area. Off site: Shop and café in village. Fishing 500 m. Riding and bicycle hire 5 km.

Open: All year.

Directions

From Ax-les-Thermes take D613 towards Quillan for 4 km. Turn onto D52 and continue for 1 km. Follow site signs. Bear left at first junction up through Sorgeat village to site. Mountain roads may be difficult for large units. GPS: 42.7329, 1.8539

Charges 2010

Per unit incl. 2 persons and electricity	€ 13,60
extra person	€ 3,30

No credit cards.

Souillac

Flower Camping les Ondines

Rue des Ondines, F-46200 Souillac (Lot) T: **05 65 37 86 44**. E: **info@camping-lesondines.com**
alanrogers.com/FR46390

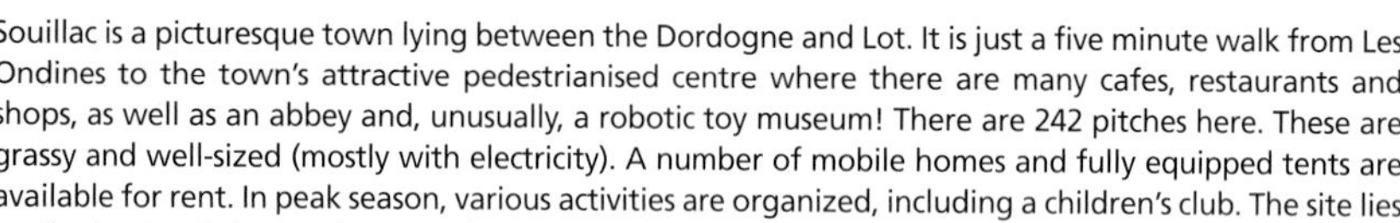

Souillac is a picturesque town lying between the Dordogne and Lot. It is just a five minute walk from Les Ondines to the town's attractive pedestrianised centre where there are many cafes, restaurants and shops, as well as an abbey and, unusually, a robotic toy museum! There are 242 pitches here. These are grassy and well-sized (mostly with electricity). A number of mobile homes and fully equipped tents are available for rent. In peak season, various activities are organized, including a children's club. The site lies on the banks of the Dordogne and canoe rental is available in the town.

Facilities

Swimming pool. Volleyball. Play area. Tourist information. Activity and entertainment programme. Mobile homes and tents for rent. Off site: Swimming pool 300 m. Souillac (cafes, shops and restaurants). Walking and cycle tracks. Riding. Canoeing. Supermarket Quercyland water park.

Open: 14 May - 30 September.

Directions

Approaching from the north, leave the A20 motorway at exit 55 and head for Souilllac. Drive through the town and, around 500 m. beyond the traffic lights, turn right following signs to Les Ondines and Quercyland. Continue to follow signs to the site. GPS: 44.888871, 1.474196

Charges guide

Per unit incl. 2 persons and electricity	€ 9,70 - € 12,20

Souillac-sur-Dordogne

Castel Camping le Domaine de la Paille Basse

F-46200 Souillac-sur-Dordogne (Lot) T: **05 65 37 85 48**. E: **paille.basse@wanadoo.fr**
alanrogers.com/FR46010

Set in a rural location some 8 km. from Souillac, this family owned site is easily accessible from the N20 and well placed to take advantage of excursions into the Dordogne. It is part of a large domain of 80 hectares, all available to campers for walks and recreation. The site is quite high up and there are excellent views over the surrounding countryside. The 262 pitches are in two main areas – one is level in cleared woodland with good shade, and the other on grass without shade. Numbered and marked, the pitches are a minimum 100 sq.m. and often considerably more. All have electricity (3/6A) with about 80 fully serviced.

Facilities

Three main toilet blocks all have modern equipment and are kept very clean. Laundry. Small shop with a large selection of wine. Restaurant, bar (open until 2 am. in high season), terrace, pizza takeaway. Crêperie. main swimming pool, a smaller one, paddling pool (unheated), water slides. Sun terrace. Sound-proofed disco (three times weekly in season). TV (with satellite). Cinema below the pool area. Tennis. Play area. Library. Off site: Golf 4 km.

Open: 15 May - 15 September.

Directions

From Souillac take D15 and then D62 roads leading northwest towards Salignac-Eyvignes and after 6 km. turn right at site sign and follow steep and narrow approach road for 2 km. GPS: 44.94728, 1.43924

Charges guide

Per person	€ 5,40 - € 7,00
pitch	€ 7,80 - € 13,00

Less 20% outside 15/6-1/9.
Camping Cheques accepted.

Tarascon-sur-Ariege

Kawan Village le Pré Lombard

F-09400 Tarascon-sur-Ariège (Ariège) T: **05 61 05 61 94**. E: **leprelombard@wanadoo.fr**

alanrogers.com/FR09060

This busy, good value site is located beside the attractive river Ariège near the town. There are 180 level, grassy, pitches with shade provided by a variety of trees (electricity 10A). At the rear of the site are 70 site-owned chalets and mobile homes. A gate in the fence provides access to the river bank for fishing. Open for a long season, it is an excellent choice for early or late breaks, or as a stop-over en-route to the winter sun destinations in Spain. This region of Ariège is in the foothills of the Pyrénées and 85 km. from Andorra. Didier Mioni, the manager here follows the town motto S'y passos, y demoros – 'if you wish to come here, you will stay here' in his aim to ensure your satisfaction on his site. At Tarascon itself you can visit the Parc Pyrénéen de l'Art Préhistorique to view prehistoric rock paintings, or the really adventurous can take to the air for paragliding, hang-gliding, or micro lighting.

Facilities

Five toilet blocks of varying age, facilities for disabled people. Laundry. Motorcaravan services. Bar and takeaway. Shop. Restaurant, entertainment, dancing (15/5-30/9). Heated swimming pool (15/5-30/9). Playgrounds for toddlers and older children. Video games machines. Boules. Multisport court. Fishing. Internet and WiFi on payment. Satellite TV. Entertainment (high season), nightclub, children's club, sports tournaments. Activity programmes for small groups. Off site: Supermarket 300 m. Town 600 m. Archery, kayaking and fishing nearby. Riding 5 km. Golf 30 km. Skiing 20 km.

Open: 27 March - 13 November.

Directions

Site is 600 m. south of town, adjacent to the river. From north, turn off main N20 into the town, site well signed. From south (Andorra) site signed at roundabout on town approach.
GPS: 42.83985, 1.61200

Charges 2010

Per unit incl. 2 persons and 10A electricity	€ 15,00 - € 32,00
extra person	€ 4,00 - € 8,00
child (2-7 yrs)	free - € 6,50
dog	free - € 2,50

Camping Cheques accepted.

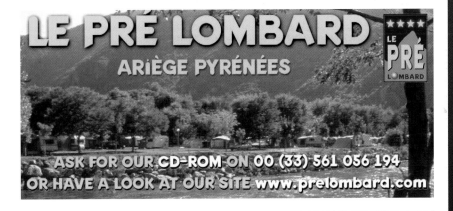

Thégra

Camping le Ventoulou

Ventoulou, F-46500 Thégra (Lot) T: **05 65 33 67 01**. E: **contact@leventoulou.com**

alanrogers.com/FR46180

Le Ventoulou is a small, well-kept and peaceful site on the Périgord 'walnut' route, at the heart of the Quercy Causses natural park. The site is based around an ancient farmhouse located between the quaint villages of Padirac and Thégra. Of just over half a hectare, the site is compact, yet because of careful spacing of pitches does not seem crowded. You will receive a warm welcome from the French owners. The Padirac Aquapark is just 3 km. away. There is a weekly soirée during the high season. Both the culture and history of the area, including local châteaux, windmills, pigeon houses and ancient bread ovens will keep you occupied during your stay. A 'Sites et Paysages' member.

Facilities

One very well equipped sanitary block is clean and well maintained. Good facilities for disabled visitors. Baby room with bath. Laundry facilities. Shop. Bar with TV. Restaurant and takeaway. Swimming pool and paddling pool. Bicycle hire. Boules. Play area with trampolines. Games room and library. Off site: Riding 2 Km. Fishing 10 km. Golf 15 km.

Open: 4 April - 28 September.

Directions

From A20 south exit 54 follow the N140 southeast to Gramat. Take the D807 northeast to Lavergne, then the D11 to Thégra and look for signs to the site which is less than 2 km. GPS: 44.8269, 1.7789

Charges guide

Per unit incl. 2 persons	€ 11,50 - € 19,50
extra person	€ 1,90 - € 6,00
electricity (10A)	€ 4,20 - € 4,20

Therondels

Flower Camping la Source

Presqu'île de Laussac, F-12600 Therondels (Aveyron) T: **05 65 66 27 10**
E: **info@camping-la-source.com** **alanrogers.com/FR12210**

This extremely spacious, steeply terraced site borders the long and narrow Lac de Sarrans with its steep wooded sides. The site is run by a very friendly family and is better suited for the younger family wanting to 'get away from it all'. All the facilities are first class, although the layout of the site means that pitches may be some distance and a steep climb away. The owners prefer to provide tractor assistance for caravans. There are 110 medium to large, slightly sloping, grassy pitches with 64 for touring, all with 6/10A electricity, water and drainage.

Facilities

Two large, well appointed and clean toilet blocks with all the necessary facilities including those for babies and campers with disabilities. Bar with TV (all season. Shop, restaurant and takeaway (26/6-27/8)). Heated swimming pool with toboggan and paddling pool (all season). Play area. TV room. Activities in high season for all the family. Lake fishing. Off site: Boat ramp 500 m. Golf 6 km. Riding and bicycle hire 15 km.

Open: 13 May - 6 September.

Directions

Leave the A75 at exit 28 or 29 (St Flour). Go through town and take D921 towards Rodez. After 12 km. turn right on D990 to Pierrefort and 3 km. after village turn left on D34, signed Laussac. Follow narrow twisting lanes down to site (about 9 km).
GPS: 44.853716, 2.77105

Charges 2010

Per unit incl. 2 persons and electricity	€ 15,50 - € 29,50
extra person	€ 3,00 - € 4,90

Camping Cheques accepted.

Vayrac

Camping les Granges

F-46110 Vayrac (Lot) T: **05 65 32 46 58**. E: **info@les-granges.com**
alanrogers.com/FR46310

Situated just over 3 km. outside Vayrac in a very rural position, this site nestles quietly beside the river in a tranquil and peaceful area. Pitches along the river frontage are popular and this should be remembered when reserving a space if that area is preferred. There is direct access to the river at one end of the site which can be useful for setting off in a canoe and enjoying the pleasures of the Dordogne river. There are 150 pitches with 116 of average size for touring units and the remaining 34 for mobile homes, the latter all available for rent. The pitches are level, mostly shaded and have 10A electricity. Entertainment is organised in high season. The owners are friendly and helpful and are keen to ensure you enjoy your holiday whilst on their family orientated site. This part of France offers many places of interest to visit with many fine châteaux and historic sites. Restaurants abound and offer a gastronomic experience with great local cuisine. Off site activities are numerous and the staff at the local tourist office in Vayrac are very helpful. In this area, the natural environment is protected and you can explore the beautiful countryside on foot or on a bicycle.

Facilities

Two modern sanitary blocks include facilities for disabled visitors. Washing machine and ironing board. Snack bar and takeaway. Swimming pool and fun pool for small children. Play area. Organised entertainment (12/7-16/8). Fishing. Only 1 dog allowed. Off site: Bicycle hire 1 km. Golf and riding 10 km.

Open: 1 May - 18 September.

Directions

From Brive, take the D20 towards Figeac. In Vayrac turn right just before the church at sign for 'Campings' and 'Stade'. Site is signed from here.
GPS: 44.93462, 1.67981

Charges 2010

Per unit incl. 2 persons and electricity	€ 16,48 - € 19,60
extra person	€ 2,80 - € 5,00

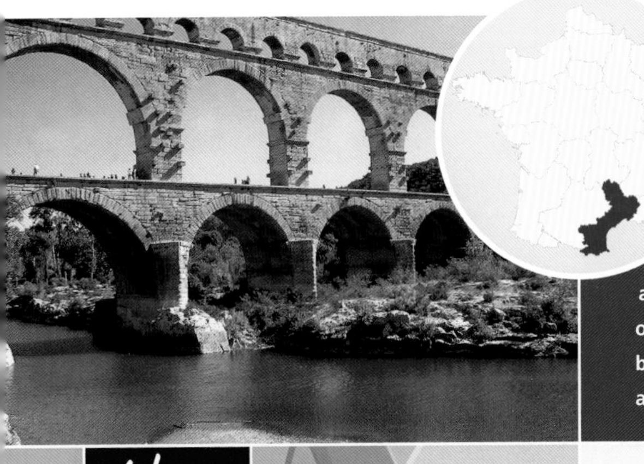

Languedoc and Roussillon form part of the Massif Central. With its huge sandy beaches the mountainous Languedoc region is renowned for its long sunshine records, and the pretty coastal villages of Roussillon are at their most beautiful at sunset, erupting in a riot of colour.

DÉPARTEMENTS: 11 AUDE, 30 GARD, 34 HÉRAULT, 48 LOZÈRE, 66 PYRÉNÉES-ORIENTALES

MAJOR CITIES: MONTPELLIER, PERPIGNAN, CARCASSONNE

Once an independent duchy, the ancient land of Languedoc combines two distinct regions: the vineyards of the Corbières and Minervois and the coastal plain stretching from the Rhône to the Spanish border. Much of the region is rugged and unspoilt, offering opportunities for walking and climbing.

There is ample evidence of the dramatic past. Ruins of the former Cathar castles can be seen throughout the region. The walled city of Carcassonne with its towers, dungeons, moats and drawbridges is one of the most impressive examples of medieval France.

Today, Languedoc and Roussillon are wine and agricultural regions. Languedoc, with considerable success, is now a producer of much of the nation's better value wines. But above all, vast hot sandy beaches and long hours of sunshine make this a paradise for beach enthusiasts. La Grande Motte, Cap d'Agde and Canet, are all being promoted as an alternative to the more famous Mediterranean stretches of the Côte d'Azur.

Places of interest

Aigues-Mortes: medieval city.

Béziers: wine capital of the region, St Nazaire cathedral, Canal du Midi.

Carcassonne: largest medieval walled city in Europe.

Limoux: medieval town, Notre Dame de Marseilla Basilica, St Martin church.

Montpellier: universities, Roman sites; Gothic cathedral.

Nîmes: Roman remains, Pont du Gard.

Perpignan: Kings Palace; Catalan characteristics, old fortress.

Villeneuve-lés-Avignon: Royal City and residence of popes in 14th century.

Cuisine of the region

Cooking is characterised by garlic and olive oil with sausages and smoked hams. Fish is popular along the coast. Wines include Corbières, Minervois, Banyuls and Muscat.

Aïgo Bouido: garlic soup.

Boles de picoulat: small balls of chopped-up beef and pork, garlic and eggs.

Bouillinade: a type of *bouillabaisse* with potatoes, oil, garlic and onions.

Boutifare: a sausage-shaped pudding of bacon and herbs.

Cargolade: snails, stewed in wine.

Ouillade: heavy soup of *boutifare* leeks, carrots, and potatoes..

Touron: a pastry of almonds, pistachio nuts and fruit.

www.sunfrance.com
contact.crtlr@sunfrance.com
(0) 4 67 20 02 20

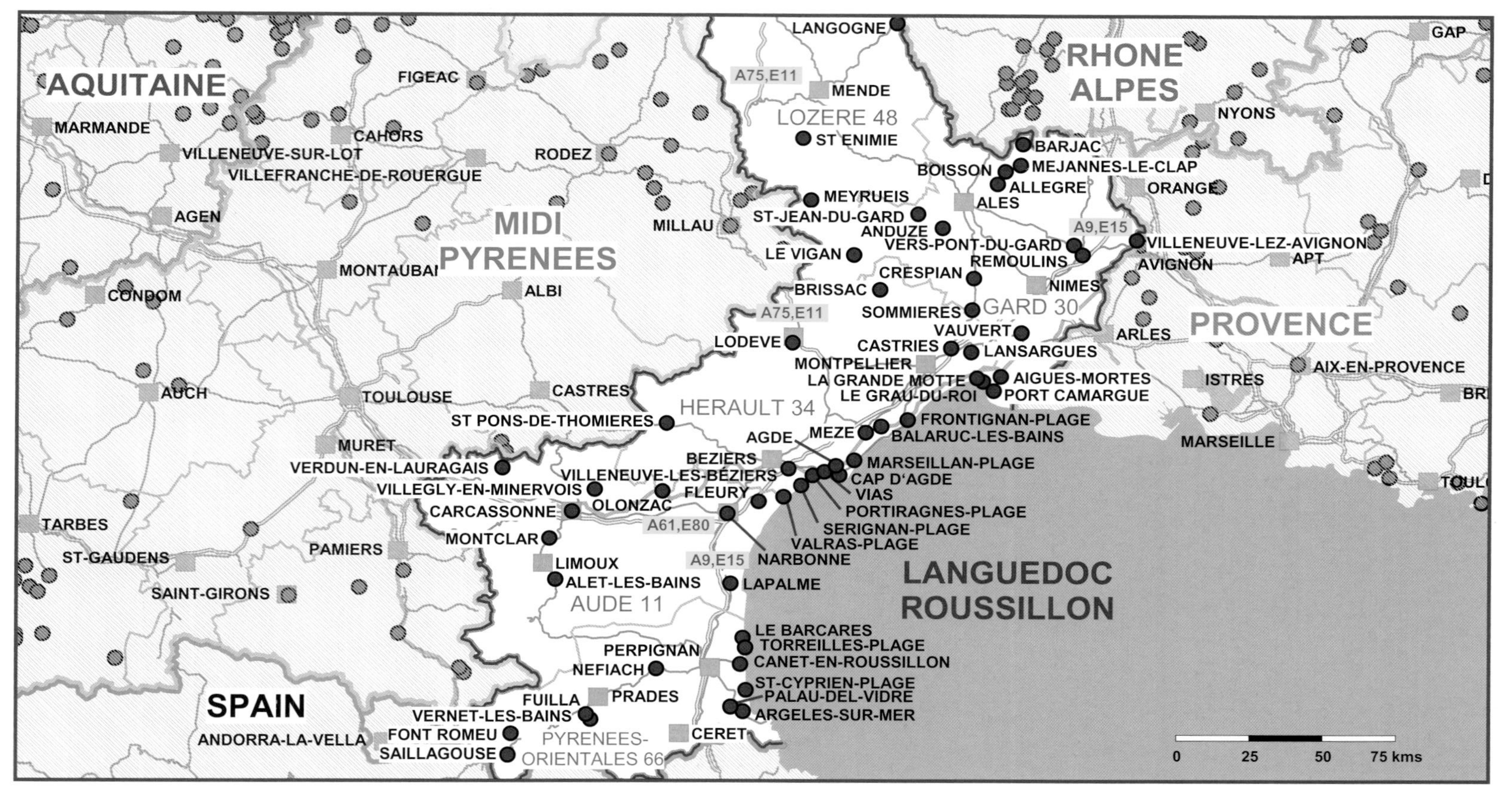
AQUITAINE
MIDI PYRENEES
RHONE ALPES
PROVENCE
LANGUEDOC ROUSSILLON
SPAIN
LOZERE 48
GARD 30
HERAULT 34
AUDE 11
PYRENEES-ORIENTALES 66
A75,E11
A9,E15
A61,E80
LANGOGNE
MENDE
ST ENIMIE
BARJAC
MEJANNES-LE-CLAP
BOISSON
ALLEGRE
ALES
MEYRUEIS
ST-JEAN-DU-GARD
ANDUZE
VERS-PONT-DU-GARD
REMOULINS
LE VIGAN
CRESPIAN
BRISSAC
SOMMIERES
VAUVERT
NIMES
LODEVE
CASTRIES
LANSARGUES
MONTPELLIER
LA GRANDE MOTTE
AIGUES-MORTES
LE GRAU-DU-ROI
PORT CAMARGUE
FRONTIGNAN-PLAGE
MEZE
BALARUC-LES-BAINS
AGDE
BEZIERS
MARSEILLAN-PLAGE
CAP D'AGDE
VIAS
VILLENEUVE-LES-BEZIERS
FLEURY
PORTIRAGNES-PLAGE
SERIGNAN-PLAGE
VALRAS-PLAGE
NARBONNE
LAPALME
ST PONS-DE-THOMIERES
VERDUN-EN-LAURAGAIS
VILLEGLY-EN-MINERVOIS
OLONZAC
CARCASSONNE
MONTCLAR
LIMOUX
ALET-LES-BAINS
LE BARCARES
TORREILLES-PLAGE
CANET-EN-ROUSSILLON
PERPIGNAN
NEFIACH
ST-CYPRIEN-PLAGE
PALAU-DEL-VIDRE
ARGELES-SUR-MER
FUILLA
PRADES
VERNET-LES-BAINS
FONT ROMEU
SAILLAGOUSE
CERET
ANDORRA-LA-VELLA
FIGEAC
MARMANDE
CAHORS
VILLENEUVE-SUR-LOT
VILLEFRANCHE-DE-ROUERGUE
RODEZ
AGEN
MILLAU
MONTAUBAI
ALBI
CONDOM
AUCH
TOULOUSE
CASTRES
MURET
TARBES
ST-GAUDENS
PAMIERS
SAINT-GIRONS
GAP
NYONS
ORANGE
VILLENEUVE-LEZ-AVIGNON
AVIGNON
APT
ARLES
AIX-EN-PROVENCE
ISTRES
MARSEILLE
0
25
50
75 kms

Agde

Kawan Village le Neptune

46 boulevard du St Christ, F-34300 Agde (Hérault) T: **04 67 94 23 94**
E: **info@campingleneptune.com** **alanrogers.com/FR34130**

Kawan VILLAGES www.kawan-villages.com

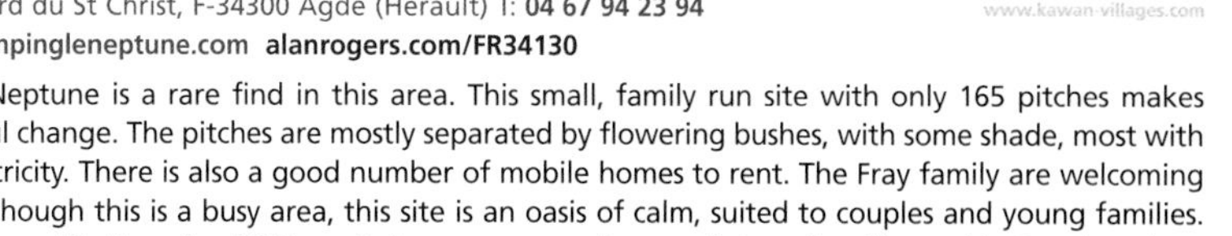

Camping Neptune is a rare find in this area. This small, family run site with only 165 pitches makes a delightful change. The pitches are mostly separated by flowering bushes, with some shade, most with 6/10A electricity. There is also a good number of mobile homes to rent. The Fray family are welcoming and even though this is a busy area, this site is an oasis of calm, suited to couples and young families. Situated alongside the splendid Herault river, one can cycle or walk into the village of le Gau d'Agde or on into the historic centre of Agde itself. The site's swimming pool is in a sunny position and is overlooked by the bar.

Facilities

Two toilet blocks provide roomy preset showers, washbasins in cabins, three cold showers for hot weather. Facilities for disabled visitors. Laundry. Small shop, bar and snack bar (all 15/5-30/9). Heated swimming pool (15/4-30/9, bracelets required). Field for sports. WiFi. Boat mooring facility on the River Hérault across the road. Only one dog allowed. Barbecues not permitted. Off site: Beach 2 km. Riding 2 km. Golf 5 km. Fishing in Herault. Canal du Midi and round lock 2 km.

Open: 1 April - 30 September.

Directions

From A9 exit 34 follow signs for (Agde, Bessau, Vias), then Cap d'Agde. Exit for Grau d'Agde. At the roundabout (with statue) left following signs for Grau d'Agde, and again at second roundabout (left). Keep straight on to fifth roundabout where left and under bridge. Site is 600 m. on left. GPS: 43.29803, 3.45628

Charges guide

Per unit incl. 2 persons	€ 17,90 - € 27,20
extra person	€ 2,90 - € 7,20

Camping Cheques accepted.

Agde

Kawan Village les Champs Blancs

Route de Rochelongue, F-34300 Agde (Hérault) T: **04 67 94 23 42**
E: **champs.blancs@wanadoo.fr** **alanrogers.com/FR34190**

Kawan VILLAGES www.kawan-villages.com

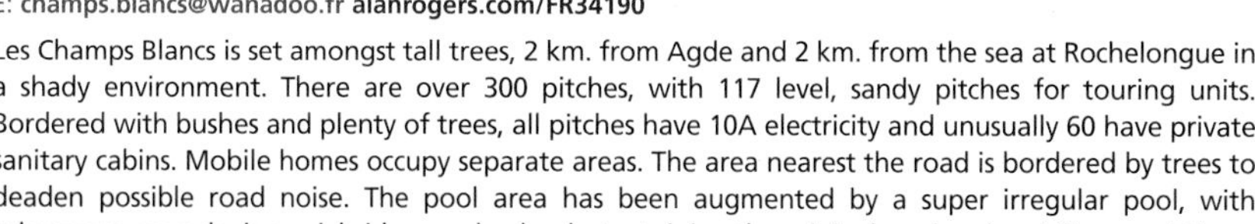

Les Champs Blancs is set amongst tall trees, 2 km. from Agde and 2 km. from the sea at Rochelongue in a shady environment. There are over 300 pitches, with 117 level, sandy pitches for touring units. Bordered with bushes and plenty of trees, all pitches have 10A electricity and unusually 60 have private sanitary cabins. Mobile homes occupy separate areas. The area nearest the road is bordered by trees to deaden possible road noise. The pool area has been augmented by a super irregular pool, with toboggans, cascade, jacuzzi, bridges and palms but retaining the original pool and paddling pool. There are tennis courts and other leisure facilities.

Facilities

Modern, fully equipped toilet blocks include 60 en-suite private cabins containing WC, shower and washbasin. Unit for disabled visitors. Washing machines and dryers. Motorcaravan services. Well stocked shop (high season, bread only in low season. Bar (from 1/6). Restaurant (20/6-15/9). Swimming complex (from 8/4 depending on weather; € 5 bracelet required). Good play area. Minigolf. Tennis. Multisport court. Off site: Riding 1 km. Golf and bicycle hire 2 km. Beach 2 km.

Open: 8 April - 30 September.

Directions

From A9 exit 34, follow N312 for Adge, joins N112 Béziers - Sète road. Cross bridge over river, take first turn signed Rochelongue, turn right at roundabout, next left, then next left (signed Adge). Site on left before another bridge back over N112. GPS: 43.29702, 3.47547

Charges guide

Per unit incl. 2 persons	€ 22,00 - € 50,00
extra person	€ 10,00

Camping Cheques accepted.

Agde

Camping les 7 Fonts

Chemin de Baldy, F-34300 Agde (Hérault) T: **04 67 94 14 62**. E: **contact@village-center.com**
alanrogers.com/FR34590

If you are seeking a less hectic option, 7 Fonts has a rural feel to it, albeit that it is situated on the edge of the town of Agde. A long time ago it was a vineyard but the traditional house with its courtyard (now reception) is the only evidence remaining. The site is now owned by the Village Center Group. It is split into two parts separated by a small road. There are 300 grass pitches, partially separated by shrubs and with good shade from tall trees. At least half are taken by mobile homes some of which are for rent.

Facilities

Two traditional style toilet blocks. Facilities for disabled visitors. Small shop. Bar, simple restaurant and takeaway. Swimming pool complex with water slides and spa bath (1/5-15/9). Hairdressing and beauty salon (1/7-31/8). Bicycle hire. Activity and entertainment programme (1/7-31/8). Mobile homes and equipped tents to rent. Free shuttle bus for beach (high season). WiFi around reception (charged). Off site: Riding, golf and fishing 4 km. Beach 4 km.

Open: 4 April - 13 September.

Directions

From the autoroute take exit 34 towards Agde and Bessan. Follow the N312 (Agde, Vias) then pick up the N112 (Agde, Sète). Pass turnings for Agde until road divides. Right is for Sete but take left for Agde and Centre commercial. Site is signed some 250 m. up this road. GPS: 43.31157, 3.49844

Charges guide

Per unit incl. 2 persons	€ 14,00 - € 34,00
extra person	€ 3,00 - € 8,00

Aigues Mortes

Camping Fleur de Camargue

D46, Saint Laurent d'Aigouse, F-30220 Aigues Mortes (Gard) T: **04 66 88 15 42**. E: **sarlaccv@aol.com**

alanrogers.com/FR30410

A green oasis in the heart of the Petite Camargue, this traditional type of site is regularly laid out with hedged, level grass pitches. Mixed trees and shrubs give shade and an almost park-like appearance. There are over 170 pitches of reasonable size which include some 60 mobile homes to let and 20 privately owned. A pleasant pool area (with toboggans) and a play area for children in one corner of the site is a very pleasant amenity. The bar/restaurant is centrally situated and open from mid-June to mid-September. The beaches and harbour of le Grau du Roi are 10 km. and the walled town of Aigues-Mortes only 5 km.

Facilities

One large traditional toilet block, plus a smaller one for high season, are fully equipped and complete with a baby bath and facilities for disabled people. Motorcaravan service point. Washing machines. Bar, restaurant and takeaway (15/6-15/9). Heated swimming pool (15/5-27/9). Playground. WiFi. Off site: Beaches 10 km. Riding 3 km. Bicycle hire 5 km. Fishing 12 km. Golf 20 km.

Open: 4 April - 26 September.

Directions

From the A9 autoroute exit 9, follow signs for Aigues-Mortes on the N313. After 19 km. turn for St Laurent d'Aigouze and follow signs through village to D979. Site is on right after 2 km. GPS: 43.61102, 4.20952

Charges guide

Per unit incl. 2 persons	€ 19,00 - € 29,00
extra person (over 4 yrs)	€ 4,00 - € 5,00

Aigues-Mortes

yelloh! VILLAGE

Yelloh! Village la Petite Camargue

B.P. 21, D62, F-30220 Aigues-Mortes (Gard) T: **04 66 53 98 98**. E: **info@yellohvillage-petite-camargue.com**

alanrogers.com/FR30020

This is a large, impressive site (553 pitches) with a huge swimming pool complex and other amenities to match, conveniently situated beside one of the main routes across the famous Camargue. The busy road is an advantage for access but could perhaps be a drawback in terms of traffic, although when we stayed overnight in season it was virtually silent. It offers a variety of good sized pitches, regularly laid out and with varying amounts of shade. There are 144 touring pitches (with 6/10A electricity) interspersed amongst more than 300 mobile homes and 145 tour operator pitches.

Facilities

Three toilet blocks provide modern facilities including many combined showers and washbasins. Laundry facilities. Motorcaravan service point. Range of shops, bar/restaurant with pizzeria and takeaway. Hairdresser and beauty centre. L-shaped swimming pool complex with jacuzzi. Play area, and children's club. Riding at adjoining large stables. Tennis. Jogging circuit. Bicycle hire. Quad bikes. Disco. Diving school. Free shuttle bus to the beach in July and August, Nightclub (over 16s). Off site: Fishing 3 km. Nearest beach 3.5 km. with free bus service July/Aug. Golf 8 km.

Open: 23 April - 19 September, with all services.

Directions

From A9, exit 26 (Gallargues), towards Le Grau-du-Roi, site 18 km. Continue past Aigues-Mortes on D62, site is 2 km. on the right, just before large roundabout for La Grand-Motte and Le Grau-du-Roi junction. GPS: 43.56307, 4.15888

Charges guide

Per unit incl. 2 persons and electricity	€ 15,00 - € 43,00
extra person	€ 4,00 - € 8,00
child (3-7 yrs)	free - € 8,00

Alet-les-Bains

Camping Val d'Aleth

F-11580 Alet-les-Bains (Aude) T: **04 68 69 90 40**. E: **camping@valdaleth.com**

alanrogers.com/FR11110

In the gateway to the upper Aude valley, open all year round, this popular small site is run by Christopher and Christine Cranmer who offer a warm welcome. The mellow medieval walls of Alet-les-Bains form one boundary of the site, while on the other and popular with anglers, is the River Aude (fenced for safety). Beyond this is the D118 and a railway which produces noise at times. The 37 mainly small, numbered pitches, around half of which are on hardstandings, all have electricity hook-ups (4-10A) and are separated by hedges and mature trees which give shade.

Facilities

New bright toilet blocks, fully equipped and heated in winter. Facilities for disabled visitors. Washing machine and dryer. New reception with small shop, drinks, wine, beer, use of freezer. Small play area. Mountain bike hire. Internet. Off site: White water sports. The area is very popular with walkers and mountain-bikers. Public transport to Carcassonne and Quillan. Some shops and restaurants in town, full range at Limoux (10 km. north). Second weekend in June 'Fete de l'eau' in village.

Open: All year.

Directions

From Carcassonne take D118 south for 32 km. Ignore first sign to Alet (to avoid narrow stone bridge) and after crossing the river, turn into town. Site is 800 m. on the left (signed). GPS: 42.99482, 2.25605

Charges 2010

Per unit incl. 2 persons and electricity	€ 17,75 - € 19,00
extra person	€ 3,75
child (under 10 yrs)	€ 2,30

Allègre

Camping Domaine des Fumades

Les Fumades, F-30500 Allègre (Gard) T: **04 66 24 80 78**. E: **domaine.des.fumades@wanadoo.fr**
alanrogers.com/FR30060

Domaine des Fumades is a pleasant, busy site with a friendly atmosphere near the thermal springs at Allègre. The entrance as a whole has a very tropical feel with its banana plants and palm trees. The 230 pitches, 80 for touring, are large and level, all with 4A electricity. A variety of trees add privacy and welcome shade. Three pleasantly landscaped swimming pools have ample sunbathing space, bridges and new jacuzzis. This is a good area for walking, cycling, riding, climbing and fishing. Used by tour operators (80 pitches). Reception at the site is a joy to behold. Set in an attractive courtyard, within the farmhouse, it has a central fountain and masses of tubs and baskets of colourful flowers.

Facilities

Well appointed sanitary blocks with facilities for disabled people are well maintained but cleaning is variable. Laundry. Shop. Bar, restaurant, snack bar, takeaway. Barbecue areas. Swimming pools and sunbathing space. Large, well equipped and fenced playground. Games room. Tennis, volleyball and boules. Well planned entertainment programme, designed to appeal to families. No barbecues. Off site: Riding 2 km.

Open: 14 May - 2 September.

Directions

From Alès take D16 through Salindres, continue towards Allègre, until signs for Fumades (and thermal springs) on the right. GPS: 44.18538, 4.22918

Charges guide

Per unit incl. 2 persons and electricity	€ 16,00 - € 30,00
extra person	€ 3,00 - € 7,00
child (under 7 yrs)	€ 2,50 - € 4,00

Anduze

Kawan Village Domaine de Gaujac

kawan VILLAGES www.kawan-villages.com

Boisset-et-Gaujac, F-30140 Anduze (Gard) T: **04 66 61 67 57**
E: **contact@domaine-de-gaujac.com** **alanrogers.com/FR30000**

The 293 level, well shaded pitches include 175 for touring with electricity (4-10A) with 22 fully serviced. Access to some areas can be difficult for larger units due to narrow winding access roads, trees and hedges. Larger units should ask for lower numbered pitches (1-148) where access is a little easier. In high season this region is dry and hot, thus grass quickly wears off many pitches leaving just a sandy base. There are 12 special hardstanding pitches for motorcaravans near the entrance. The site has a new covered entertainment area and courtyard terrace.

Facilities

Heated toilet blocks include facilities for disabled visitors. Washing machines and dryer. Motorcaravan services. Good shop (2/6-27/8). Newsagent. Takeaway/crêperie (15/4-15/9). Bar, restaurant (15/4-15/9). New heated swimming, paddling pool (all season with lifeguard 5/7-15/8) and jacuzzi. Playground, sports field. Tennis. Minigolf. Only gas and electric barbecues. Off site: Fishing 100 m. Bicycle hire 5 km. Riding, golf 8 km. Mining museum at Alès, steam trains between Anduze and St Jean-du-Gard, music museum at Anduze, number of spectacular caverns and grottoes. River beach 70 km.

Open: 1 April - 30 September.

Directions

From Alès take N110 towards Montpellier. At St Christol-les-Alès fork right on D910 towards Anduze and in Bagard, at roundabout, turn left on D246 to Boisset et Gaujac. Follow signs to site in 5 km. GPS: 44.03580, 4.02425

Charges guide

Per unit incl. 2 persons and electricity	€ 19,00 - € 25,50
extra person	€ 4,50 - € 5,70
child (0-7 yrs)	free - € 4,90

Credit cards accepted in high season only. Camping Cheques accepted.

Anduze

Camping Cévennes-Provence

Corbès-Thoiras, F-30140 Anduze (Gard) T: **04 66 61 73 10**. E: **marais@camping-cevennes-provence.com**
alanrogers.com/FR30200

Whenever a new guest arrives at this spectacular and family owned site, one of the seven members of the family takes time to drive the visitors around to enable them to choose what suits their particular needs. From a place on river bank, to the highest pitch some 330 feet higher, the emphasis is on calmness and tranquility. There are 250 pitches on the various levels, 200 with electricity (3-10A). The river is very popular for swimming and in a separate section for enjoying the rough and tumble of a small 'rapids'. There are no activities arranged on site.

Facilities

The 10 toilet blocks are excellent with modern equipment and are kept exceptionally clean and a new sanitary facility is heated. Good facilities for disabled visitors. Large and well stocked shop. Restaurant, takeaway and bar (1/5-31/8). Comprehensive play area. Minigolf. Volleyball. River bathing and fishing. Many activities off site willingly arranged at reception. Internet point including WiFi. Off site: Bicycle hire 20 km. Riding 4 km. Golf 10 km. Adventure and discovery park on opposite bank of river offering sports facilities.

Open: 20 March - 20 October.

Directions

From Anduze on the D907 take D284 alongside the river. Site is signed on right about 3 km. from the town. Take care on the approach – there is a narrow lane for 100 m, then a narrow bridge to cross, but visibility is good. GPS: 44.07763, 3.96484

Charges 2010

Per unit incl. 2 persons, vehicle and electricity	€ 17,50 - € 25,90
extra person	€ 3,50 - € 6,10
child (2-6 yrs)	€ 2,30 - € 3,40
child (7-12 yrs)	€ 3,50 - € 5,00
dog	€ 1,90 - € 2,90

Argelès-sur-Mer

Camping le Dauphin

Route de Taxo à la Mer, F-66704 Argelès-sur-Mer (Pyrénées-Orientales) T: **04 68 81 17 54**
E: **info@campingledauphin.com** **alanrogers.com/FR66110**

Near Taxo in the quieter, northern part of Argelès (a somewhat frenzied resort in season), this family owned site on flat, grassy parkland with plenty of tall trees enjoys good views of the Pyrénées from the terrace area surrounding its excellent complex of swimming pools. There are 346 level, grassy, well shaded pitches, all with 10A electricity and some with individual sanitary units. Located some 1.5 km. from the town and beach, there is a regular connecting 'road train' service to and fro throughout the day and evening until midnight.

Facilities

A central sanitary block completly renovated provides all essential facilities including washbasins en-suite. One third of the pitches have their own fully equipped individual sanitary unit. Shops, bar/restaurant, pizzeria with takeaway (all 15/5-5/9). Two large swimming pools and padding pool (all season). Two play areas. Tennis. Multisport courts. Minigolf. Games room. Full entertainment programme in high season. Torches useful in some areas. Off site: Riding 1 km. Fishing 2 km.

Open: 15 May - 18 September.

Directions

Site is on north side of Argelès. From autoroute take exit Perpignan-Nord for Argelès and follow directions for Plage-Nord and Taxo-d'Avall (similarly from the N114). GPS: 42.57229, 3.02167

Charges 2010

Per unit incl. 2 persons and electricity	€ 18,00 - € 32,20
extra person	€ 4,00 - € 6,90
child (under 5 yrs)	free - € 4,30
dog	€ 2,50 - € 3,50

Argelès-sur-Mer

Camping la Sirène

Route de Taxo à la Mer, F-66702 Argelès-sur-Mer (Pyrénées-Orientales) T: **04 68 81 04 61**
E: **contact@camping-lasirene.fr** **alanrogers.com/FR66560**

From the moment you step into the hotel-like reception area you realise that this large site offers the holiday maker everything they could want in a well managed and convenient location close to Argelès-sur-Mer and the beaches. The 740 mobile homes and chalets vary in standard but all are less than five years old, very clean, comfortable and located on neat tidy pitches. There are also some touring pitches. In the summer there are 170 staff on duty to ensure your stay is as enjoyable as they can make it. All the shops and amenities are near reception making the accommodation areas quite peaceful and relaxing.

Facilities

Restaurant, bar and takeaway. Large shop (all season). Large aqua park, paddling pools, slides, jacuzzi. Games room. Multisports field, tennis, archery, minigolf, football. Theatre, evening entertainment, discos, show time spectacular. Riding. Bicycle hire. Off site: Resort of Argelès-sur-Mer and its beaches 2 km, as is karting, 10-pin bowling, amusement park and the sites private beach club Emeraude. Interesting old town of Collioure close by. Fishing 4 km. Golf 7 km.

Open: 17 April - 26 September.

Directions

Leave A9 motorway, junction 42, take D114, towards Argelès. Leave D114, junction 10 and follow signs for Plage Nord. Site signed after first roundabout. Site on right 2 km. after last roundabout.
GPS: 42.57093, 3.02906

Charges 2010

Per unit incl. 1-3 persons and electricity	€ 26,00 - € 43,00
extra person	€ 4,00 - € 9,00

Argelès-sur-Mer

Camping l'Hippocampe

Route de Taxo à la Mer, F-66702 Argelès-sur-Mer (Pyrénées-Orientales) T: **04 68 81 04 61**
E: **contact@camping-lasirene.fr** **alanrogers.com/FR66570**

A sister site to La Sirène just opposite, this site has some touring pitches along with 170 mobile home and chalet pitches and is aimed at families with young children and adults looking for a quieter site. The mobile homes and chalets are all modern, well maintained and have space around them to provide privacy. The pool on site is dedicated to the smaller children and is a great place for them to gain confidence in the water whilst still being able to play. Entertainment, shops, bars and the full range of activities offered by La Sirène, just across the road.

Facilities

Pool and laundry. Shop, small bar (all season). All other facilities are at La Sirène just across the road. Riding. Bicycle hire. Off site: Beach, Argelès sur Mer within 2 km. Karting, 10-pin bowling, amusement park within 1 km. Fishing 4 km. Golf 7 km.

Open: 17 April - 26 September.

Directions

Leave A9 junction 42. Take D114, Argelès road. Leave D114 junction 10, follow signs for Plage Nord. Site signed after the first roundabout, on left 2 km. after last roundabout. GPS: 42.57050, 3.03065

Charges 2010

Per unit incl. 1-3 persons and electricity	€ 26,00 - € 43,00
extra person	€ 4,00 - € 9,00

Argelès-sur-Mer

Camping le Bois du Valmarie

F-66702 Argelès-sur-Mer (Pyrénées-Orientales) T: **04 68 81 09 92**. E: **contact@camping-lasirene.fr**
alanrogers.com/FR66590

The pitches at this campsite are used exclusively for mobile home accommodation.

Argelès-sur-Mer

Camping le Soleil

Route du Littoral, F-66702 Argelès-sur-Mer (Pyrénées-Orientales) T: **04 68 81 14 48**
E: **camping.lesoleil@wanadoo.fr** **alanrogers.com/FR66040**

Le Soleil is an attractive site with direct access to the sandy beach. It is a busy, popular, family owned site which over the years has developed into a small village. It has over 800 pitches of ample size, of which around 550 are used for touring units, on sandy/grassy ground and with a mixture of trees and shrubs providing plenty of shade, all with electricity (6A). Caravans sometimes needs care on the narrow access roads. The site has a wide range of amenities, including an impressive pool complex with activities and entertainment for all the family. All facilities are open when the site is open. Spain and the Pyrénées are near enough for excursions. There are over 200 pitches used by tour operators and 70 occupied by mobile homes. English is spoken and there is a comprehensive reservation system (advised for most of July and August). Le Soleil also works with the group 'Les Pieds dans l'Eau' (sites with direct access to water such as the sea, river or lake).

Facilities

Seven toilet blocks of the type with external access to individual units. Some family cabins with washbasins, showers. Washing machines. Supermarket, general shop, press, tabac. Restaurant. Takeaway. Bar with disco (July/Aug), beach bar. California type swimming pool complex and entertainment area. Adventure playground. TV room. Internet. WiFi. Tennis. Diving and riding in high season (charge). Dogs are not accepted. Off site: Fishing and mooring boats on the adjacent river. Golf 5 km.

Open: 16 May - 19 September.

Directions

Site is at north end of the beach, about 1 km. from Argelès-Plage village. GPS: 42.57552, 3.04232

Charges 2010

Per unit incl. 2 persons and electricity	€ 26,25 - € 37,50
extra person (over 5 yrs)	€ 6,51 - € 9,70

Less 30% in May, June and August.

Argelès-sur-Mer

Castel Camping les Criques de Porteils

RD114, route de Collioure, F-66701 Argelès-sur-Mer (Pyrénées-Orientales) T: **04 68 81 12 73**
E: **criquesdeporteils@wanadoo.fr** **alanrogers.com/FR66150**

This is an amazing site situated on the cliff top with views across the sea to Argelès, set against a backdrop of mountains and close to Collioure, the artists' paradise. What more could you ask? Under new ownership, the facilities are being renovated and some of the pitches being redesigned for easier access. There are around 250 of varying sizes and shapes due to the nature of the terrain, level in places up and down in others. Most have sea views and 5A electricity available. There are three small coves of grey sand accessed by steep steps (gated).

Facilities

Two renovated toilet blocks, fully equipped with super children's room, all small equipment and colourful. Laundry room with internet point. Motorcaravan service point. Shop. Bar. Restaurant with takeaway. Swimming pool. Play area. Sports field. Off site: Collioure 5 mins.

Open: 1 April - 9 September.

Directions

Exit A9 at Perpignan Sud or Le Boulou. Head for Argelès to pick up signs for 'Collioure par la Corniche'. Watch for site signs coming into a bend as you come down a hill by hotel. GPS: 42.53508, 3.06854

Charges guide

Per unit incl. 2 persons and electricity	€ 24,00 - € 39,00
extra person	€ 6,00 - € 9,00
child (0-4 yrs)	€ 4,00 - € 6,00
dog	free - € 4,00

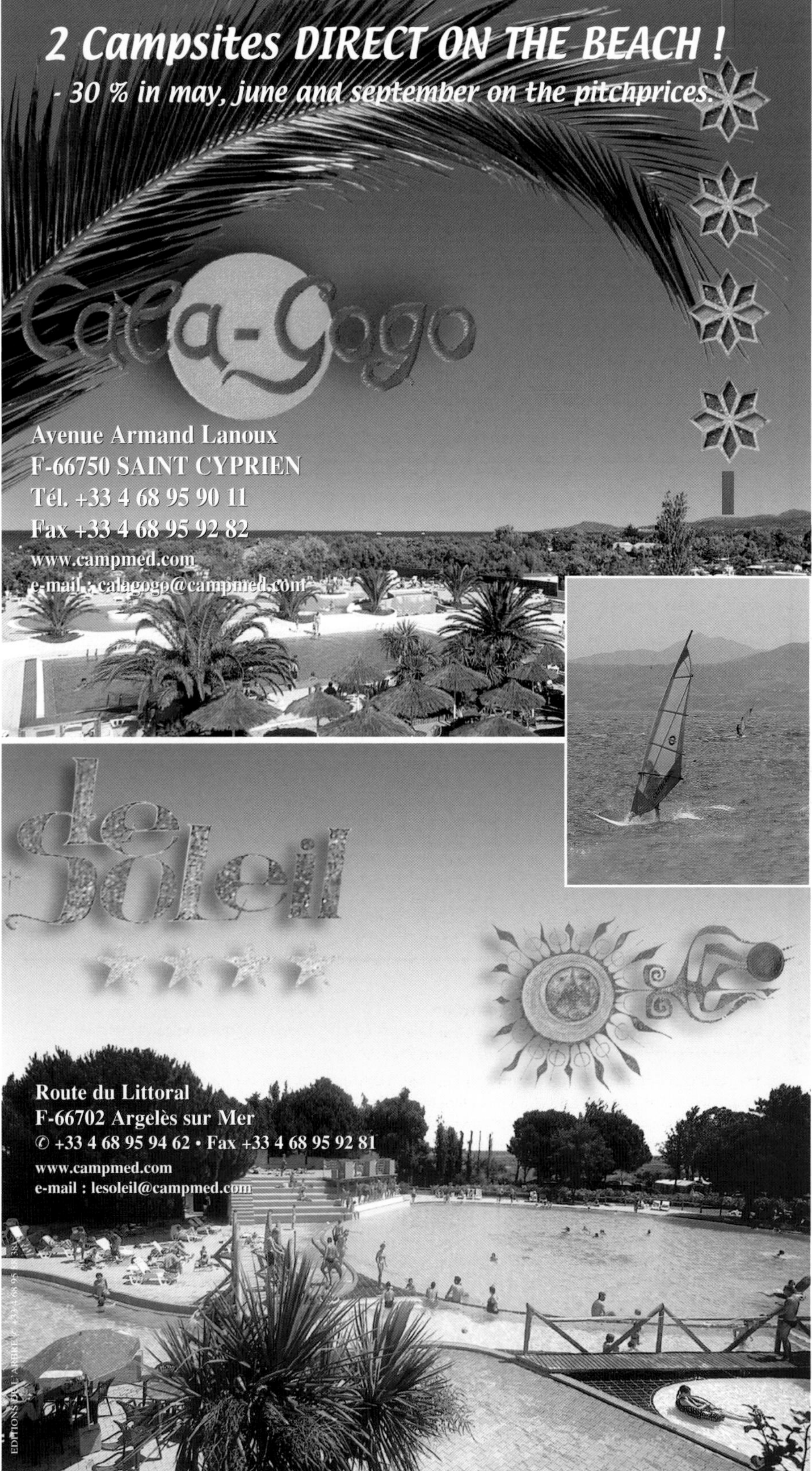

2 Campsites DIRECT ON THE BEACH !
- 30 % in may, june and september on the pitchprices.
Cala-Gogo
Avenue Armand Lanoux
F-66750 SAINT CYPRIEN
Tél. +33 4 68 95 90 11
Fax +33 4 68 95 92 82
www.campmed.com
e-mail : calagogo@campmed.com
le Soleil
Route du Littoral
F-66702 Argelès sur Mer
© +33 4 68 95 94 62 • Fax +33 4 68 95 92 81
www.campmed.com
e-mail : lesoleil@campmed.com

Argelès-sur-Mer

Camping la Massane

25 avenue Molière, F-66702 Argelès-sur-Mer (Pyrénées-Orientales) T: **04 68 81 06 85**
E: **info@camping-massane.com** **alanrogers.com/FR66260**

Set a little bit back from the seafront, La Massane is one of the traditional older sites with good views of the Canigou and a pool open for a longer season. With 184 pitches and only 26 taken by mobile homes, it could make a good, quiet and relaxing choice. In July and August it will be a little more hectic (as is the whole resort) with a bar and some family entertainment. Other amenities are within walking distance. Pitches are divided, level and semi-grassed with a mixture of shade from tall trees or shrubs. Electricity (6/10A) is available.

Facilities

Two toilet blocks, one large and modernized with a baby room and facilities for disabled visitors. A smaller, traditional block is used early in the season. Laundry room. Swimming pool (heated 15/4-30/9) with paddling pool. Shop, bar, takeaway and entertainment July/Aug only. Play area. Charcoal barbecues not permitted. WiFi free. New adult exercise/games area. Off site: Village of Argelès. Beach 1 km. Bicycle hire 1 km. Spain within driving distance.

Open: 15 March - 15 October.

Directions

From the A9 take exit 42 (Perpignan Sud) and follow N114 for Argelès to exit 10.for Pujols. At first roundabout take 'Centre Plage'. Pass school on left and site is almost immediately on left.
GPS: 42.550717, 3.031267

Charges guide

Per unit incl. 2 persons and electricity	€ 11,50 - € 30,50
extra person	€ 2,50 - € 5,50

Balaruc-les-Bains

Camping le Mas du Padre

4 chemin du Mas du Padre, F-34540 Balaruc-les-Bains (Hérault) T: **04 67 48 53 41**
E: **info@mas-du-padre.com** **alanrogers.com/FR34100**

Mas de Padre is a pleasant little site run by the Durand family and it makes a good base from which to explore the Sète area or 'take the waters' at Balaruc-les-Bains. Madame Durand speaks excellent English. On a hillside, just 2.5 km. from Balaruc-les-Bains and near the Etang de Thau (famous for oysters), this small site is unusually situated in a residential area that has obviously developed around it over the years. The secluded pitches are of varying sizes and are marked by hedges, mature trees and shrubs. Some are on a very gentle slope and hard ground. There are 112 touring pitches with 6/10A electricity and 18 mobile homes to let.

Facilities

Fully equipped toilet blocks include baby changing area, facilities for disabled campers, washing machines. Reception sells basic provisions. Swimming pool (open and heated 1/5-30/9), plus one for children. Tennis half-court, boules, mini adventure playground. Sports programme, aquarobics, entertainment for children, weekly dance (all in high season). WiFi. Off site: Fishing, bicycle hire, boat launching and riding 2 km. Seaside beach 10 km. Lake beach 2 km.

Open: 4 April - 18 October.

Directions

From A9, exit Sete, follow N800 to Balaruc le Vieux, first roundabout (D2), second roundabout both following Balaruc-les-Bains/Sete. After 50 m. right for Balaruc-les-Bains, immediately left across road, double back down it (50 m). Immediately right, follow Chemin du Mas du Padre. GPS: 43.45219, 3.69241

Charges guide

Per unit incl. 2 persons	€ 14,80 - € 37,05
extra person (over 13 yrs)	€ 3,20 - € 4,55

Boisson

Castel Camping le Château de Boisson

Boisson, F-30500 Allègre-les-Fumades (Gard) T: **04 66 24 82 21**. E: **reception@chateaudeboisson.com**
alanrogers.com/FR30070

Château de Boisson is a quiet family site within easy reach of the Cévennes, Ardèche or Provence. Reception at the entrance is new, light and cool, built from the stone in the local style. The site is hilly so the pitches are on two levels, many of which slope slightly and all have 5A electricity. Five have personal bathrooms. Rock pegs are essential. Trees provide some shade. The large attractive swimming pool with a slide and paddling pool is at the castle in a sunny location and there is also an indoor pool (all season) of excellent quality.

Facilities

Refurbished, clean and well maintained toilet blocks. Washing machines, baby room, facilities for disabled visitors. Small shop (1/5-1/9). Good restaurant, bar, snacks (all season). Play area. Indoor (all season) and outdoor pools (1/5-25/9). Bridge tournaments in low season. Painting classes. Tennis. Boules. Internet, WiFi. Entertainment in July and Aug for 4-12 yr olds, outdoor competitions for adults. Appartments to rent in the castle. Barbecues are not permitted. Dogs are not accepted (7/7-18/8)

Open: 3 April - 25 September.

Directions

From Alès take the D16 northeast towards Salindres and Auzon. After Auzon turn right across river, immediately left, signed Barjac and site. Shortly turn right, site signed. Only route for trailers and motorcaravans. Do not drive through the village of Boissons.
GPS: 44.20967, 4.25625

Charges guide

Per unit incl. 2 persons and electricity	€ 19,00 - € 34,00
extra person	€ 3,00 - € 7,00

Canet-en-Roussillon

F 493 yelloh! VILLAGE

Yelloh! Village le Brasilia

B.P. 204, F-66141 Canet-en-Roussillon (Pyrénées-Orientales) T: **04 68 80 23 82**

E: **info@yellohvillage-brasilia.com** **alanrogers.com/FR66070**

Situated across the yacht harbour from the upmarket resort of Canet-Plage, le Brasilia is an impressive, well managed family site directly beside the beach. It is pretty, neat and well kept with an amazingly wide range of facilities – indeed, it is camping at its best. There are 473 neatly hedged touring pitches, all with electricity and many with water and drainage. They vary in size from 80 to 120 sq.m. and some of the longer pitches are suitable for two families together. With a range of shade from pines and flowering shrubs, less on pitches near the beach, there are neat access roads (sometimes narrow for large units). There are also 130 pitches with mobile homes or chalets to rent (the new ones have their own gardens). The sandy beach here is busy, with a beach club (you can hire windsurfing boards) and a naturist section is on the beach to the west of the site. A completely new pool complex is planned with pools catering for all ages and hydrotherapy facilities for adults and all overlooked by its own snack bar and restaurant. The village area of the site offers a range of shops, a busy restaurant and bar, entertainment (including a nightclub) and clubs for children of all ages. In fact you do not need to stir from the site which is almost a resort in itself. It does have a nice, lively atmosphere but is orderly and well run. If you would like to visit Canet-Plage, a free tourist train runs in summer and a small ferry crosses the harbour. A member of 'Yelloh! Village' and 'Leading Campings Group'.

Facilities

Ten modern sanitary blocks are very well equipped and maintained, with British style WCs (some Turkish) and washbasins in cabins. Good facilities for children and for disabled people. Laundry room. Motorcaravan services. Range of shops. Gas supplies. Bars and restaurant. New pool complex (heated). Play areas. Sports field. Tennis. Sporting activities. Library, games and video room. Hairdresser. Internet café and WiFi. Daily entertainment programme. Bicycle hire. Fishing. ATM. Exchange facilities. Post office. Weather forecasts. Only gas or electric barbecues are allowed. Off site: Boat launchng and sailing 500 m. Riding 5 km. Golf 12 km.

Open: 26 April - 27 September.

Directions

From A9 exit 41 (Perpignan Centre, Rivesaltes) follow signs for Le Barcarès and Canet on D83 for 10 km. then for Canet (D81). At first Canet roundabout, turn fully back on yourself (Sainte-Marie) and watch for Brasilia sign almost immediately on right.
GPS: 42.70467, 3.03483

Charges guide

Per unit incl. 2 persons and electricity (6A)	€ 19,00 - € 47,50
extra person	€ 6,00 - € 8,50
child (3-6 yrs)	free - € 8,50
dog (max. 2)	€ 4,00

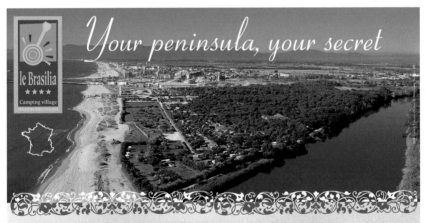

Brissac

Domaine d'Anglas

F-34190 Brissac (Hérault) T: **04 67 73 70 18**. E: **contact@camping-anglas.com**
alanrogers.com/FR34600

In the upper Hérault valley to the south of the Cévennes mountains, Domaine d'Anglas is a delightful, small site. The top part of the site is on quite stony ground with pitches divided by vines and mixed trees that provide a degree of shade. The lower part is more open, with some mature trees and pitches are not clearly divided but it makes a wonderful spot to camp. With 100 pitches in total, there are 91 for touring units. A stream runs through the site, dry when we visited, but it is quite possibly a torrent in winter time. Wooden bridges allow access to the toilet blocks on the other side.

Facilities

Two toilet blocks provide all necessary facilities. Baby bath. Facilities for disabled visitors but some up and down walking on site. Washing machine. Shop for bread and simple needs. Communal barbecue. Play field. Wine evening. Off site: Register at reception for canoeing, climbing, karting, mountain biking, walks and adventure tours through the woods and on Saturday evenings tour through the owners vineyard, taste the wines and sample the 'assiettes du terroir'.

Open: 30 April - 5 September.

Directions

From Montpellier follow the D986 north towards Ganges. After about 40 km, just before entering the village of St Bauzille de Putois turn right signed Brissac. Cross the Hérault river over a narrow bridge and pick up site signs. GPS: 43.876056, 3.716083

Charges guide

Per unit incl. 2 persons and electricity	€ 12,00 - € 21,50
extra person	€ 3,50 - € 5,50
child (under 7 yrs)	free - € 4,00

Canet-en-Roussillon

Kawan Village Caravaning Ma Prairie

kawan VILLAGES www.kawan-villages.com

1 avenue des Coteaux, F-66140 Canet-en-Roussillon (Pyrénées-Orientales)
T: **04 68 73 26 17**. E: **ma.prairie@wanadoo.fr** **alanrogers.com/FR66020**

Ma Prairie is an excellent site and its place in this guide goes back over 30 years. Then it was simply a field surrounded by vineyards. The trees planted then have now matured, more have been planted, along with colourful shrubs providing a comfortable, park-like setting with some 260 pitches, all with electricity and 35 with water and drainage. It is a peaceful haven some 3 km. back from the sea but within walking distance of Canet village itself. The Gil family still provide a warm welcome and reception boasts an impressive international collection of hats, helmets and uniform caps.

Facilities

Fully equipped toilet blocks, baby bath. Washing machines and dryers. No shop but bread can be ordered. Covered snack bar and takeaway. Air-conditioned bar and restaurant. Large adult pool, splendid children's pool. Multiplay sport area. TV. Amusement machines. Busy daily activity programme in season including dancing and live music once a week. Off site: Supermarket 400 m. Riding 600 m. Golf 6 km. Canet Village within walking distance with all amenities. Bus/tram services to the busy modern resort of Canet Plage.

Open: 5 May - 25 September.

Directions

Leave autoroute A9 at Perpignan North towards Barcarès. Site access is from the D11 Perpignan road (exit 5), close to the junction with D617 in Canet-Village. Go under bridge, right at roundabout the left to site. GPS: 42.70135, 2.99968

Charges 2010

Per unit incl. 2 persons and electricity	€ 21,50 - € 38,50
extra person	€ 4,00 - € 7,50
child (4-9 yrs)	free - € 6,00
dog	free - € 3,00

Camping Cheques accepted.

Cap d'Agde

Yelloh! Village Mer et Soleil

Chemin de Notre Dame á Saint Martin, Rochelongue, F-34300 Cap d'Agde (Hérault) T: **04 67 94 21 14**
E: **contact@camping-mer-soleil.com** **alanrogers.com/FR34290**

Close to Cap d'Agde, this popular, well-equipped site has many facilities. The pool area is particularly attractive with large palm trees, a whirlpool, slides as well as a gym and wellness centre. An upstairs restaurant overlooks this area and the entertainment stage next to it. There are 500 pitches, around half taken by mobile homes and chalets (some to let, some privately owned). The touring pitches are hedged and have good shade, all with 6A electricity. A path from the back of the site leads to a 1 km. long path leading to the white sandy beach at Rochelongue.

Facilities

One large toilet block plus three smaller ones are fully equipped. Attractive units for children with small toilets, etc. Units for disabled visitors. Motorcaravan service point. Washing machine. Shop. Bar and restaurant. Swimming pools. Gym. Tennis. Archery. Sporting activities and evening entertainment. Off site: Beach 1 km. Riding 1 km. Sports complex opposite site.

Open: 3 April - 16 October.

Directions

From A9 exit 34, follow N312 for Agde. It joins the N112 Béziers - Sète road. Cross bridge over Hérault river and turn right for Rochelongue. Turn left at next roundabout and site is a little further on the right. GPS: 43.286183, 3.478

Charges guide

Per unit incl. 2 persons and electricity	€ 36,00
extra person	€ 5,00
child (7-13 yrs)	€ 4,50
dog	€ 4,00

Carcassonne

Campéole

Campéole la Cité

Route de Saint-Hilaire, F-11000 Carcassonne (Aude) T: **04 68 25 11 77**. E: **nadine.ferran@atciat.com**
alanrogers.com/FR11100

A visit to the medieval cité of Carcassonne is a must and Campéole de la Cité is within walking distance along a shaded footpath beside a stream. The majority of pitches are very large, separated by bushes and with good shade. There are also some undefined places under trees for small tents. In total there are 200, with 143 for touring, 95 having 10A electricity and the rest used for mobile homes or chalets to hire. Because of its situation it is very popular and you need to arrive early in the high season. A swimming pool, snack bar and small shop make this a very comfortable and useful site. It is a neat and tidy site that is very well organised. A shuttle bus (charge) runs to the town centre during the season. There are also good facilities for children with activities and sports organized in July and August. The Black mountain is to the north, the Corbières to the east, the Pyrénées to the south and the beaches of the Mediterranean only 70 km. If you are there for Bastille Day (14 July), there is a magnificent fireworks display covering the citadel.

Facilities

Motorcaravan service point. Fridge hire. Shop, bar and snack bar/ Takeaway meals. TV and games room. Bread delivery. Multisport pitch. Swimming and paddling pools. Play area. Communal barbecue (only gas or electric permitted on pitches). Chalets and mobile homes to rent. Off site: Golf 2 km. Bicycle hire 2 km. Riding 3 km. Lake with beaches 6 km. Mediterranean beaches 70 km.

Open: 15 March - 15 October.

Directions

From A61 autoroute take exit 24 onto N113 following signs for city centre. Site is well signed (look carefully) from all roads into the city. GPS: 43.200315, 2.353767

Charges 2010

Per unit incl. 2 persons and electricity	€ 20,10 - € 28,40

Castries

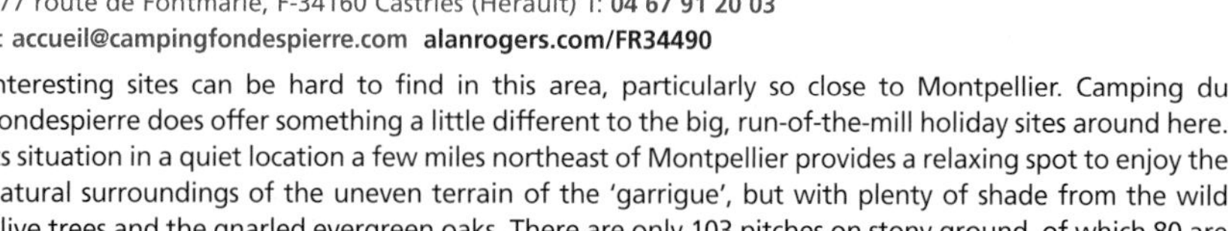

Flower Camping de Fondespierre

277 route de Fontmarie, F-34160 Castries (Hérault) T: **04 67 91 20 03**
E: **accueil@campingfondespierre.com** **alanrogers.com/FR34490**

Interesting sites can be hard to find in this area, particularly so close to Montpellier. Camping du Fondespierre does offer something a little different to the big, run-of-the-mill holiday sites around here. Its situation in a quiet location a few miles northeast of Montpellier provides a relaxing spot to enjoy the natural surroundings of the uneven terrain of the 'garrigue', but with plenty of shade from the wild olive trees and the gnarled evergreen oaks. There are only 103 pitches on stony ground, of which 80 are used for touring units, all with 10A electricity. The site is open all year round. The relaxed atmosphere dominates the site with a simple bar overlooking the pool. It is possible to walk into the village – about a kilometre away.

Facilities

The modern toilet block is fully equipped and can be heated in winter. Washing machine and dryer. Motorcaravan service point. Bar. Some emergency supplies in bar. Two swimming pools one with reverse current. Play area. Football field. Internet. Bicycle hire. Off site: Village 1 km. with shops, restaurants and bars. Riding 3 km. Golf 5 km. Lake for leisure activities and fishing 10 km. Beaches 25 km.

Open: All year.

Directions

From the A9 take exit 28 (Vendargues) towards Castries via the RN110. Pass through village following signs 'Domaine de Fondespierre'. Turn left 800 m. after the village, then second left and right at 'cross' to site. GPS: 43.6934, 3.9962

Charges guide

Per unit incl. 2 persons	€ 16,00 - € 24,00
incl. electricity (10A)	€ 20,50 - € 28,50
extra person	€ 4,00 - € 5,50

Crespian

Kawan Village le Mas de Reilhe

Chemin du Mas de Reilhe, F-30260 Crespian (Gard) T: **04 66 77 82 12**
E: **info@camping-mas-de-reilhe.fr** **alanrogers.com/FR30080**

This is a comfortable family site nestling in a valley with 95 pitches (73 for tourers), most have electricity (6/10A), some also have water and waste water and some of the upper ones may require long leads. The large lower pitches are separated by tall poplar trees and hedges, close to the main facilities but may experience some road noise. The large terraced pitches on the hillside are scattered under mature pine trees, some with good views, more suited to tents and trailer tents but with their own modern sanitary facilities. The heated swimming pool is in a sunny position and overlooked by the attractive bar/restaurant. There are no shops in the village, the nearest being at the medieval city of Sommières ten kilometres away (and well worth a visit). From here you can explore the Cevennes gorges, enjoy the Mediterranean beaches, visit the Petite Camargue or Nimes with its Roman remains from le Mas de Reilhe. The entertainment in July and August is for children with just the occasional event for adults.

Facilities

Good toilet facilities with washbasins in cabins and preset showers. Dishwashing and laundry sinks. Washing machine. Reception with limited shop (bread can be ordered) and bar, takeaway and restaurant (1/6-12/9). Small play area on grass. Pétanque. Heated swimming pool (30/4-19/9). Internet access (WiFi on each pitch on payment). Motorcaravan services. Off site: Tennis 500 m. Fishing 3 km. Riding 5 km. Bicycle hire 10 km. Golf 25 km. The sea and the gorges are about 30 km. and Nîmes 25 km.

Open: 3 April - 19 September.

Directions

From the A9 take exit Nimes-ouest signed Alès, then onto the D999 towards Le Vigan. The site is on the D6110 just north of the junction with the D999 at the southern end of the village of Crespian. GPS: 43.87931, 4.09637

Charges guide

Per unit incl. 2 persons and electricity	€ 18,40 - € 24,40
extra person	€ 3,50 - € 5,50

Camping Cheques accepted.

Fleury

Cottage Village Aux Hamacs

504

Route des Cabanes, F-11560 Fleury (Aude) T: **04 68 33 22 22**. E: **info@cottagevillage.fr**
alanrogers.com/FR11020

The pitches at this campsite are used exclusively for mobile home accommodation. For full details please see our PRL section starting on page 501.

Font-Romeu

HUTTOPIA

Huttopia Font-Romeu

Route de Mont-Louis, F-66120 Font-Romeu (Pyrénées-Orientales) T: **04 68 30 09 32**
E: **font-romeu@huttopia.com** **alanrogers.com/FR66250**

This is a large, open site of some seven hectares, nestling on the side of the mountain at the entrance to Font-Romeu. This part of the Pyrénées offer some staggering views and the famous Mont-Louis is close by. An ideal base for climbing, hiking or cycling, it would also provide a good stopover for a night or so whilst traveling between Spain and France or to or from Andorra into France. The terraced pitches are easily accessed, with those dedicated to caravans and motorcaravans at the top of the site, whilst tents go on the lower slopes. Trees provide shade to many of the pitches from the sun which can be quite hot at this altitude. Facilities on site are limited to very good toilet blocks and a very large games room and assembly hall which is used by those in tents when it rains.

Facilities

Two toilet blocks, one behind reception, the other in the centre of the tent pitches. Traditional in style, they are bright and clean with modern fittings. Toilet for children and excellent facilities for disabled visitors. Washing machines and dryers at each block. large games hall. Only gas barbecues are permitted. Off site: Opportunities for walking and climbing are close by as are golf, riding, fishing, cycling and tennis. The small town of Font-Romeu is very near with all the usual shops and banking facilities.

Open: 12 June - 19 September and 18 December - 2 April.

Directions

Font-Romeu is on the D118, some 12 km. after it branches off the N116 heading west, just after Mont-Louis. This is an interesting road with magnificent views and well worth the climb. The site is just before the town, on the left and accessed off the car park. GPS: 42.51511, 2.05183

Charges guide

Per unit incl. 2 persons and electricity	€ 18,80 - € 34,20
extra person	€ 5,00 - € 6,20
child (2-7 yrs)	€ 3,00 - € 4,20
dog	€ 4,00

Frontignan-Plage

Camping les Tamaris

140 avenue d'Ingril, F-34110 Frontignan-Plage (Hérault) T: **04 67 43 44 77**. E: **les-tamaris@wanadoo.fr**
alanrogers.com/FR34440

This is a super site, unusually situated on a strip of land that separates the sea from the étang or inland lake, and therefore Fontignan Ville from Fontignan Plage. The design of the site is unusual which adds to its attractiveness. The pitches are laid out in hexagons divided by tall hedging and colourful shrubs. In total, there are 250 pitches with 100 taken by mobile homes which are let by the site. All have 10A electricity and are on level sandy grass. Direct access to the sandy beach is possible via three gates.

Facilities

Three modern toilet blocks with en-suite showers and washbasins. Excellent facilities for children. Unit for disabled visitors. Motorcaravan service point. Shop. Bar, restaurant and takeaway (all season). Swimming pool (from 1/5). Hairdresser. Gym. Play area. Miniclub. Archery. Bicycle hire. Internet access. Entertainment for all ages. Off site: Riding 150 m. Sailing 1 km. Boat launching 2.5 km. Golf 15 km.

Open: 1 April - 22 September.

Directions

From the north on the A9 take exit 32 and follow N112 towards Sète and Frontignan. After 16 km. ignore sign for Frontignan town and continue to Frontignan-Plage following site signs along the road between the sea and étang. From the south use exit 33 and follow N300 to roundabout beside the port of Sète (11 km). Turn left on N112 and take second exit for Frontignan-Plage. GPS: 43.44970, 3.80603

Charges guide

Per unit incl. 2 persons	€ 24,00 - € 38,00
extra person	€ 4,00 - € 8,00

Camping Cheques accepted.

Frontignan-Plage

Camping Club du Soleil

60 avenue d'Ingrill, F-34110 Frontignan-Plage (Hérault) T: **04 67 43 02 02**. E: **campingdusoleil@wanadoo.fr**
alanrogers.com/FR34510

Camping Club du Soleil is a pretty and relaxed seaside site just 80 m. from the beach. An attractive little heated pool was added in 2007 and the site boasts a good bar and restaurant, also open to the public. This busy little site offering some entertainment and excursions in peak season, is interestingly situated on the strip of land between the sea and the Etang d'Ingril. There are 95 level pitches in total, half of which are used by mobile homes, some available to rent. All pitches are generally well shaded and of a reasonable size, separated by flowering shubs and trees with 6A electricity.

Facilities

Modern fully equipped toilet block. En-suite facilities for disabled visitors. Washing machine. Restaurant/snack bar. Bar. Takeaway meals. Heated swimming pool. Play area. Entertainment, activities and excursions in high season. Bicycle hire. Mobile homes and chalets for rent. WiFi in reception area. Off site: Beach 80 m. Supermarket 50 m. Other shops 100 m. Marina and boat launching 1.5 km. Sailing 2 km.

Open: 4 April - 28 September.

Directions

From the A9 autoroute take exit 32 (St Jean de Védas) and join the N112 towards Sète. After 13 km. at a roundabout take the third exit following signs for Plage les Aresquiers (D114). Site is a further 4 km. GPS: 43.44487, 3.79891

Charges guide

Per unit incl. 2 persons and electricity	€ 18,00 - € 35,00
extra person	€ 4,00 - € 6,00

Fuilla

Camping le Rotja

F-66820 Fuilla (Pyrénées-Orientales) T: **04 68 96 52 75**. E: **campinglerotja.ellenetwim@wanadoo.fr**
alanrogers.com/FR66310

La Rotja is a pretty, Dutch-owned site, set up a little valley above the fortified old town of Villefranche-de-Conflent and watched over by the impressive, snow-capped Pic de Canigou. The older part of the site is semi-wooded with wonderful silver birches, whilst the newer part further up the hill is more open and terraced. There is room for 100 fairly level pitches of which 80 have 6/10A electricity and one can chose a shaded place or not. A small pool at the top of the site is very welcome in high season. Trips are organized into the mountains, along with barbecue evenings.

Facilities

Two toilet blocks, both fully equipped. The older one beside the bar area can be heated, a larger, more modern one is in the new area. Facilities for disabled visitors and babies. Bar, outside restaurant (15/5-30/9). Swimming and paddling pools (1/5-30/9). Gas barbecues only. Bicycle hire.
Off site: Tennis 100 m. Fishing 300 m. Riding 7 km. Beach 55 km. Rafting, canyoning, hydro-speed and 'parc-aventure' possible with trained guides. Walking, VTT.

Open: 1 April - 31 October.

Directions

Follow the N116 from Perpignan (route to Andorra). After about 50 km. bypass Prades and continue to Villefranche-de-Conflent. Follow around and past it to take left turn signed Fuilla and Sahorre. After 2 km. turn right at village to site. GPS: 42.56241, 2.35942

Charges guide

per unit incl. 2 persons	€ 13,25 - € 18,25
incl. electricity	€ 15,50 - € 20,50
extra person	€ 2,75 - € 3,75
child (0-7 yrs)	€ 1,75 - € 2,75

La Grande Motte

Camping le Garden

44 place des Tamaris, F-34280 La Grande Motte (Hérault) T: **04 67 56 50 09**. E: **campinglegarden@orange.fr**
alanrogers.com/FR34020

Le Garden is a well cared for and pretty site, situated amongst tall pines and flowering shrubs, some 400 m. back from a fine sandy beach. The pitches are of a good size (100 sq.m) on sandy grass. There are 116 mobile homes to rent and 86 touring places, most with 10A electricity, water and waste water drain. An attractive pool is overlooked by the restaurant. The site also has a small 'centre commercial' with a range of shops and a bar which is next door and open to the public. Le Garden is a very comfortable and quiet site (possible road nose during the day) within pleasant walking distance of the town centre and port. La Grande Motte is a product of the sixties tourist boom when much building went on and, at the time the apartment blocks seemed very futuristic. It has now matured into a smart, upmarket seaside resort with plenty of green space. There is much to see in the area, being on the edge of the Petite Camargue and only a few kilometres from the old walled town of Aigues Mortes. A regular bus service (half hourly) runs from outside the site to Montpellier and other places.

Facilities

Three well situated toilet blocks, smartly refurbished in Mediterranean colours, include washbasins in cabins and baby bath. Laundry facilities. Unit for disabled visitors. Shops to one side of the site with groceries, cigarettes, newspapers, boutique and bar (1/3-31/10). Restaurant and takeaway on site (from 15/5). Swimming pool and paddling pool (15/5-30/9). Play area. TV room. Internet access and WiFi. Off site: Beach 400 m. Tennis, riding, bicycle hire and boat launching 500 m. Golf and fishing 2 km.

Open: 1 April - 15 October.

Directions

Entering La Grande Motte from D62 dual-carriageway, keep right following signs for 'campings' and petite Motte. Turn right at traffic lights by Office de Tourism and right again by Bar Le Garden and site is almost immediately on right. GPS: 43.56322, 4.07278

Charges guide

Per unit incl. 1-3 persons	€ 29,50
incl. electricity, water and drainage	€ 39,50
extra person	€ 9,50

Bracelet required for pool € 10.

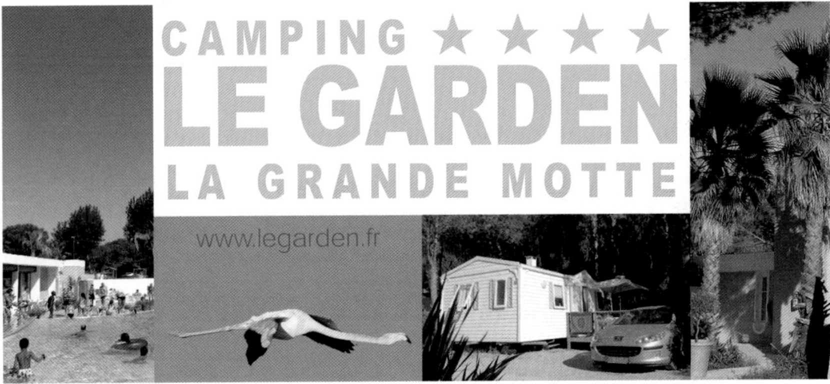

Langogne

Camping les Terrasses du Lac de Naussac

Lac de Naussac, F-48300 Langogne (Lozère) T: **04 66 69 29 62**. E: **info@naussac.com**
alanrogers.com/FR48060

With friendly, family owners, this very spacious campsite and hotel complex is on the side of a steep hill at nearly 1,000 m. altitude (nights can be cold). There are 180 good size, grassy, sloping pitches, often with part hardstanding (165 for touring). All have 6/10A electricity and many have panoramic views over the lake and surrounding hills. There are small trees on site offering a little shade. The lake offers a wide range of water based activities, notably sailing and fishing. The Lac de Naussac is the largest in the Lozère and this site has direct access to the lake.

Facilities

Three modern and well maintained, newly refurbished toilet blocks. Motorcaravan service point. Small shop (1/5-30/9). Restaurant/takeaway in hotel. Small swimming pool (1/6-30/9). Lively entertainment programme in peak season including children's club but no discos. Play area. Communal barbecue area. Gas and electric barbecues only. Internet point and WiFi. Off site: Disco 300 m. All kinds of water sports with equipment for hire on lake. Cycle ride around lake of 30 km. Langogne (shops, restaurants, Stevenson trail etc). 2 km. 9-hole golf course 3 km. Bicycle hire 3 km.

Open: 15 April - 30 September.

Directions

Leave N88 (Le Puy - Mende) just southwest of Langogne. Turn north on D26 towards Lac de Naussac and follow signs to site (2.5 km). Park beside lake and just before hotel. Reception inside hotel.
GPS: 44.73472, 3.83527

Charges guide

Per unit incl. 2 persons	€ 12,50 - € 13,50
extra person	€ 3,50
child (2-6 yrs)	€ 1,50
electricity	€ 2,50

Camping Cheques accepted.

Lansargues

Camping le Fou du Roi

Chemin des Codoniers, F-34130 Lansargues (Hérault) T: **08 74 56 00 27**. E: **campinglefouduroi@free.fr**
alanrogers.com/FR34470

Beside the mellow stone village of Lansargues on the edge of the Camargue, Le Fou du Roi was taken over by the Brunel family two years ago. They have done much to update it with a new reception/bar area complete with an attractive Tahitian style construction which can be left open or closed depending on the weather. Altogether this a lovely little site. There are 82 pitches with 30 for touring units with 10A electricity, arranged in light shade amongst the vineyards. A small pool and play area for children make it a very comfortable site with a nice long season.

Facilities

Two toilet blocks, the first modern and fully equipped, the second not open when we visited. Facilities for disabled visitors. Washing machine and dryer. Motorcaravan service point. Small shop (July/Aug). Bar, simple snacks and takeaway (fully open July/Aug). Swimming pool (1/5-15/9). Play area. Only gas barbecues are permitted (communal area provided). Off site: Fishing and riding 3 km. Golf 4 km. Tennis in village. Village within easy walking distance with restaurants and shops.

Open: 30 March - 14 October.

Directions

From A9 exit 27 follow signs for Lunel and from there pick up D24 going south. Lansargues is 7 km. Do not take 'village centre' sign but continue past and pick up site sign just past village on right.
GPS: 43.65181, 4.06635

Charges guide

Per unit incl. 2 persons	€ 13,50 - € 18,60
extra person	€ 3,00 - € 6,00
child (under 7 yrs)	free - € 3,00
electricity	€ 4,00

Le Barcarès

Camping Club le Floride et l'Embouchure

Route de Saint-Laurent, F-66423 Le Barcarès (Pyrénées-Orientales) T: **04 68 86 11 75**
E: **campingfloride@aol.com** **alanrogers.com/FR66290**

Essentially a family run enterprise, le Floride et l'Embouchure is really two sites in one – l'Embouchure the smaller one with direct access to the beach and le Floride on the opposite side of the fairly busy road into Le Barcarès village. Apart from having some unusual accommodation to rent (the 'Bungahomes') and a few pitches with their own individual sanitary facility, the sites are fairly unremarkable, albeit within a very friendly, family-centred environment, very popular with Dutch visitors. In total there are 632 pitches, all with 10A electricity. The site is relatively inexpensive, especially outside the July/August peak period. It offers a comfortable, if unpretentious, holiday opportunity with reasonably sized pitches (300 for touring units) and ample shade. In the case of l'Embouchure, there is direct access to a popular beach, but le Floride has the pool complex complete with toboggan.

Facilities

Four fully equipped toilet blocks on Le Floride and two on L'Embouchure where 50 pitches near the beach have individual facilities. Shop, bar, restaurant and takeaway (all 15/6-5/9). Three swimming pools (one heated outside July/Aug). Play area. Entertainment programme (July/Aug). Charcoal barbecues are not permitted. Off site: Fishing 1 km. Riding 1.5 km. Bicycle hire 3 km. Beach 100 m.

Open: 1 April - 30 September.

Directions

From A9 take exit 41 (Perpignan Nord) and follow signs for Canet and Le Barcarès via D83. At J9 follow D81 (Canet) then next left into Le Barcarès Village. Site is 1 km. on the left and right sides of the road.
GPS: 42.77855, 3.03010

Charges guide

Per unit incl. 2 persons	
and electricity	€ 12,50 - € 34,00
incl. individual sanitary facility	€ 16,00 - € 42,00
extra person	€ 2,60 - € 6,20
child (1-4 yrs)	free - € 3,60

Le Barcarès

Yelloh! Village le Pré Catalan

Route de Saint-Laurent, F-66420 Le Barcarès (Pyrénées-Orientales) T: **04 66 73 97 39**
E: **info@yellohvillage-pre-catalan.com** **alanrogers.com/FR66300**

The green foliage from the mixed trees and the flowering shrubs makes the site very attractive and an avenue of palms is particularly spectacular. There has been a camping site on the spot since 1960 but the present owners, the Galidie family, took over in 1982 and the site is now run by their son Francois and his English wife, Jenny. With 250 pitches in total, there are 140 taken by mobile homes and chalets, half to let and half privately owned. These are mixed amongst the 80 touring pitches which are on level, sandy ground, clearly divided by hedging and with 10A electricity. The newer part has been planted in the same way as the original areas. It has less shade but enjoys views across to the mountains. The facilities are opened all season but hours are adapted according to the number of visitors on site. An upstairs bar has a long terrace which overlooks the pool area. A footpath of just less than 1 km. leads to the sandy beach. All in all, this a pleasant and comfortable place to stay.

Facilities

Good modern facilities include small showers for children. Laundry. Small shop. Bar, restaurant and takeaway (all season). Heated swimming pool and paddling pool. Excellent play area. Tennis. Archery. Internet access. Library. Activities for children with miniclub and evening entertainment (July/Aug). Gas barbecues only.
Off site: Beach 900 m. River fishing 1 km. Riding 1.5 km. Boat launching 3 km. Nearby La Réserve Africaine de Sigean and Le Château de Salses.

Open: 8 May - 19 September.

Directions

From A9 exit 41 (Perpignan Nord), follow signs for Le Barcarès and Canet (D83). At exit 9 take D81 (Canet), then first left to Le Barcarès (D90). Site is on left after 500 m. next to Le California. Follow narrow lane to site entrance. GPS: 42.78106, 3.02282

Charges guide

Per unit incl. 2 persons and electricity	€ 17,00 - € 37,00
child (3-6 yrs)	free - € 6,00

Le Barcarès

L'Oasis Camping Club

Route de Saint-Laurent, F-66420 Le Barcarès (Pyrénées-Orientales) T: **04 68 86 12 43**
alanrogers.com/FR66630

L'Oasis has quite a park-like feel with mixed deciduous trees and grass of sorts. The 496 pitches are well spaced with 249 for touring units and some 49 used by tour operators. The remainder feature mobile homes or chalets to rent. All have 10A electricity and are most are fairly level on sandy soil and grass, with varying degrees of shade. A smart new bar/restaurant area with a stage for entertainment was just being finished adjacent to the pool area when we visited. A sandy beach is within walking distance (about 1 km) but the site also has a comfortably sized pool complex.

Facilities

Two modern toilet blocks are fully equipped and include facilities for babies and disabled people. Laundry room. Bar, restaurant, takeaway and shop (open by early July). Heated outdoor pool (14/06-13/09). Tennis. Play area.
Off site: Fishing 1 km. Riding 1 km. Minigolf 1 km. Boat launching and wind surfing 3 km.

Open: 14 June - 13 September.

Directions

From A9 autoroute exit 41, follow the D83 towards Barcarès for about 9 km. At exit 9 take D81 towards Canet. Take first left turn signed Le Barcarès village and site is on left after 500 m. past Camping California. GPS: 42.77641, 3.02494

Charges guide

Per unit incl. 2 persons and electricity	€ 12,50 - € 29,00
extra person	€ 3,50 - € 6,50
child (4-10 yrs)	€ 1,50 - € 4,60
dog	€ 1,50 - € 4,00

Camping Cheques accepted.

Le Barcarès

Camping Club las Bousigues

Avenue des Corbières, F-66423 Le Barcarès (Pyrénées-Orientales) T: **04 68 86 16 19**
E: **info@camping-barcares.com** **alanrogers.com/FR66480**

Under new ownership, Las Bousigues enjoys a quiet situation set well back from Le Barcarès amongst the vineyards. A mature site with lots of greenery, it provides a mix of mobile homes or chalets to rent and pitches for touring, some of which have individual sanitary blocks. The area in front of the pool, bar and restaurant with its plane trees is like a village square. Indeed, the site has a distinctly French ambience unlike some of the 'all singing, all dancing' sites nearer the beach. With around 200 pitches, most with 10A electricity, the site is of a comfortable size and would suit families with younger children. Le Barcarès is a popular holiday destination with long sandy beaches. It is not far from the Spanish border and the Pyrénées should the beach pall and you wish to explore the area.

Facilities

Two fully equipped toilet blocks, one with access for disabled people. Small shower and toilet for children. Individual en-suite units on some pitches. Dog shower. Laundry. Shop. Bar, restaurant and takeaway (holiday weekends and main season). Swimming pool (heated in low season) with small toboggan. Good sized play area beside communal barbecue. Internet access.

Open: 31 March - 30 September.

Directions

From the A9 take exit 40 signed Leucate. Follow D627 towards Port Leucate, then D83 towards Le Barcarès. Take exit 10 for Le Barcarès village. At first roundabout follow campsite sign to right. Site short distance on left. GPS: 42.78583, 3.01927

Charges guide

Per unit incl. 2 persons	€ 9,00 - € 25,00
incl. electricity (10A)	€ 11,00 - € 34,00
extra person	€ 4,60 - € 7,00
child (under 10 yrs)	free - € 4,50

Le Barcarès

Camping Club Village l'Europe

Route de Saint Laurent, F-66420 Le Barcarès (Pyrénées-Orientales) T: **04 68 86 15 36**
E: **reception@europe-camping.com** **alanrogers.com/FR66670**

Le Barcarès is a popular resort with a busy market and a fishing port. It has a good number of campsites but l'Europe is a little different in that it is open all year and each pitch has its own private sanitary facilities. There is a gate at the back of the site for the sandy beach which is a walk of some 600 m. However, the site has its own pool complex overlooked by the bar/restaurant and stage where nightly shows are performed in high season. In total, there are 339 pitches of a good size (100 for touring units) and with some shade from mixed trees and shrubs. The partly hedged pitches are level on sandy grass. The fact that the site is open all year round and that Perpignan airport is nearby has proved popular with visitors looking to buy their own mobile home. There are 75 mobile homes or chalets to rent and 145 privately owned. A new concept financed by the local authority has resulted in a tarmac path, the 'voie verte de l'Agly' which follows the Agly river running past the site. It is 15 km. long from le Barcarès to Rivesaltes and is used for cycling, jogging, walking or roller skating (but no cars).

Facilities

Individual sanitary facilities on every pitch including dishwashing sink. Laundry. Shop (15/4-30/9). Bar/restaurant and takeaway (high season, on demand at other times). Outdoor pool (15/4-30/9). Play area. Tennis. Evening shows and children's club (high season). Bicycle hire. WiFi at reception. Off site: Nearest beach 600 m. Supermarket. Fishing. Watersports. Le Barcarès resort with many shops, cafes, restaurants and market.

Open: All year.

Directions

From A9 take exit 41 (Perpignan Nord) and follow signs for Canet and Le Barcarès via the D83. At exit 9 follow the D81 (Canet), then next left for Le Barcarès. Site is almost immeadiately on the right. GPS: 42.774931, 3.021004

Charges guide

Per unit incl. 2 persons and electricity	€ 23,50 - € 46,50
extra person	€ 4,00 - € 8,00

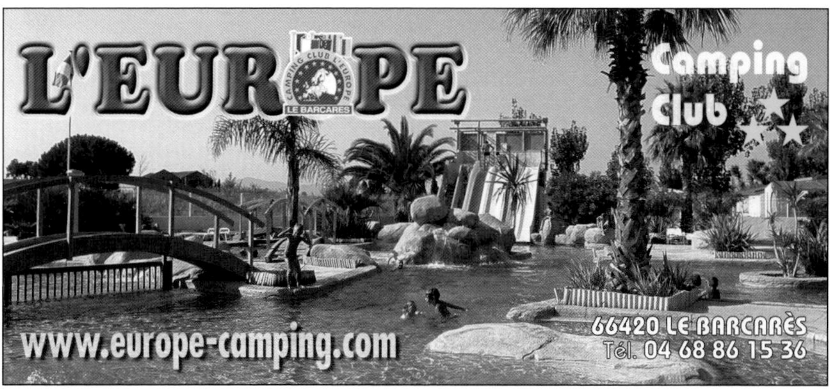

Le Grau-du-Roi

Camping Caravaning le Boucanet

B.P. 206, F-30240 Le Grau-du-Roi (Gard) T: **04 66 51 41 48**. E: **contact@campingboucanet.fr**
alanrogers.com/FR30160

Le Boucanet has a superb situation beside the beach between La Grande Motte and Le Grau-du-Roi. Many trees have been planted and are growing but as yet most are not tall enough to give much shade. As to be expected, the 458 pitches are sandy. They are on the small side, but are level and most have 6A electricity (long leads and adaptors useful). The 250 for touring are mixed amongst the mobile home and chalet pitches and are separated by small bushes. Plenty of flowers decorate the site and the pleasant restaurant (open lunchtimes and evenings) overlooks the pool area. One pool has a sliding cover and both are heated in early and late season. An excellent shopping arcade provides groceries, fruit, newspapers, a butcher and cooked meats, rotisserie and pizzas. In July and August organised events include games, competitions, gymnastics and water polo, plus musical evenings and shows.

Facilities

The fully equipped toilet blocks include facilities for disabled people. Baby rooms. Laundry facilities. Fridge hire. Motorcaravan services. Range of shops. Restaurant, bar and snacks (16/5-15/9). Takeaway (1/7-31/8). Large swimming pool, smaller covered pool, toboggans and paddling pool. Play area on sand. Miniclub (July/Aug). Tennis. Bicycle hire. Windsurfing board hire (July/Aug). Internet access and WiFi. Dogs are not accepted. Off site: Riding 1 km. Golf 2 km.

Open: 11 April - 4 October.

Directions

Site is between La Grande Motte and Le Grau-du-Roi on the D255 coastal road, on the seaward side of the road. GPS: 43.5543, 4.10706

Charges guide

Per unit incl. 2 persons and electricity	€ 22,00 - € 39,00
pitch on first row of beach, plus	€ 5,00 - € 6,00
extra person	€ 6,00 - € 9,00

Le Grau-du-Roi

Yelloh! Village Secrets de Camargue

Route de l'Espiguette, F-30240 Le Grau-du-Roi (Gard) T: **04 66 80 08 00**
E: **info@yellohvillage-secrets-de-camargue.com** **alanrogers.com/FR30380**

Les Secrets de Camargue is a recent addition to the Yelloh! Village group, best described as 'stylish and elegant'. It has the unusual feature that it is reserved for over 18s and for families with children under 3 years old. In total there are 176 pitches with 28 for touring units (with 10A electricity) on level sandy grass. The majority of pitches are for mobile homes and chalets with the unusual feature of thatched roofs. The heart of the site is the Lodge Club which faces the pool and the surrounding sand dunes. The Lodge Club houses the site's bar and restaurant and it is also here that evening entertainment is organised throughout the high season. The nearest beach, l'Espiguette, is just 1.5 km. away and is said to be one of the largest in the south of France.

Facilities

Fully equipped sanitary block includes facilities for disabled visitors. Small shop (2/4-19/9). Restaurant, bar (all season). Swimming pool. Aquagym. Activities and entertainment. Mobile homes and chalets for rent. Off site: Free use of facilities at the the nearby Camping Les Petits Camarguais. Nearest beach 1.5 km. Riding 0.8 km. Fishing 5 km. Golf 16 km. Watersports 4 km. Village of Le Grau-du-Roi 3 km. Walled town of Aigues Mortes 12 km.

Open: 26 March - 3 October.

Directions

Leave the A9 at exit for Gallargues and head for Aigues Mortes on the D979. Continue to Le Grau-du-Roi and then follow signs to Port Camargue on the D62, continuing to join the D255. Site is well signed from this point. GPS: 43.48736, 4.14202

Charges 2010

Per unit incl. 2 persons	€ 15,00 - € 44,00
extra person	€ 4,00 - € 8,00

Le Grau-du-Roi

Yelloh! Village les Petits Camarguais

Route de l'Espiguette, F-30240 Le Grau-du-Roi (Gard) T: **04 66 51 16 16**
E: **info@yellohvillage-petits-camarguais.com** **alanrogers.com/FR30390**

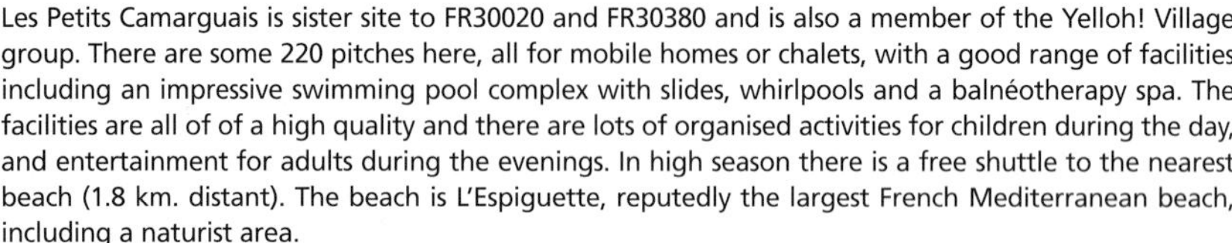

Les Petits Camarguais is sister site to FR30020 and FR30380 and is also a member of the Yelloh! Village group. There are some 220 pitches here, all for mobile homes or chalets, with a good range of facilities including an impressive swimming pool complex with slides, whirlpools and a balnéotherapy spa. The facilities are all of of a high quality and there are lots of organised activities for children during the day, and entertainment for adults during the evenings. In high season there is a free shuttle to the nearest beach (1.8 km. distant). The beach is L'Espiguette, reputedly the largest French Mediterranean beach, including a naturist area.

Facilities

Mobile homes and chalets for rent. Shop. Bar. Restaurant. Takeaway food. Swimming pool complex with slides, paddling pools, counter current swimming, water games and a balneotherapy spa. Aquagym in high season. Volleyball. Mini football. Activity and entertainment programme. Dogs are not accepted. Off site: Nearest beach 1.8 km. (free shuttle in peak season). Riding. Sea fishing. Golf. Casino. Lunapark fairground. Seaquarium park.

Open: 2 April - 19 September.

Directions

Leave the A9 autoroute at the Gallargues exit and head for Aigues Mortes on the D979. Continue to Le Grau-du-Roi and then follow signs to Port Camargue on the D62, continuing to join the D255b. The site is well signed from this point. GPS: 43.50847, 4.14554

Charges 2010

Contact the site.

Lodève

Camping Municipal les Vailhés

B.P. 62, F-34702 Lodève (Hérault) T: **04 67 44 25 98**
alanrogers.com/FR34550

Les Vailhés is a popular municipal site with a wonderful situation on the shores of the Lac du Salagou which is a haven for watersports. The views across the lake are good, and the red rocks are most unusual. In total there are 200 pitches, most with electricity; some are for mobile homes on ground sloping towards the lakeside beach. The majority are hedged and there is a fair amount of shade from various types of trees. The site is fenced off from the lake but the gates are open during the day. A sailing school is next door to the site offering a range of watersports.

Facilities

Two toilet blocks, fully equipped if a little Spartan include washing machines. Play area with small climbing wall. Lake amenities (lifeguards July/Aug) and beach café (July/Aug). Windsurfing, sailing, canoes, and pedalos. Archery.
Off site: Ancient town of Lodève 6 km. Beaches of the Mediterranean one hour's drive.

Open: 1 April - 30 September.

Directions

From the A75 take exit 54 or 55, and follow directions to Lac du Salagou. Then follow site signs to left.
GPS: 43.67026, 3.35572

Charges guide

Per person	€ 3,11
child (under 7 yrs)	€ 1,84
pitch	€ 3,44 - € 4,26
electricity	€ 2,50

Le Vigan

Camping le Val de l'Arre

Route du Pont de la Croix, F-30120 Le Vigan (Gard) T: **04 67 81 02 77**. E: **valdelarre@wanadoo.fr**
alanrogers.com/FR30230

Camping Val de l'Arre is situated along the Arre river, a tributary of the Herault river, and in the centre of the Cevennes National Park. The site is well managed by M. Triaire and his Dutch wife, who between them speak English, Dutch and Spanish, as well as French. There are 180 pitches, 156 for touring of which most have electricity (10A). On well-drained grass, there is shade from deciduous trees. There is a pleasant swimming pool with an outdoor bar. A pebble beach at the river bank provides many opportunities for play, and fishing enthusiasts will also certainly appreciate the river. There are numerous possibilities for outdoor activities such as white-water rafting, canoeing or mountain biking. Qualified guides may take you on mountain expeditions on foot or by bicycle. The nearby Les Grottes des Demoiselles, are some of France's foremost caves. There is also the opportunity to taste the great wines of the Herault region.

Facilities

Three toilet blocks are well spaced around the site. Washbasins, both open style and in cabins, and controllable showers. Facilities for babies and disabled visitors. Washing machines. Shop, open air bar with snacks and restaurant (all 1/6-31/8). Swimming and paddling pools (1/6-15/9). Boules. Play area. Guided walks organised. Off site: Bicycle hire 2.5 km. Riding 8 km.

Open: 1 April - 30 September.

Directions

Coming from the A75 (Millau - Beziers) leave at exit 48 and follow D7 and D999 to Le Vigan. From Montpellier take tD986 to Ganges, then the D999 to Le Vigan. Site is signed in the town.
GPS: 43.992067, 3.6374

Charges guide

Per unit incl. 2 persons and electricity	€ 16,00 - € 19,50
extra person	€ 3,50 - € 5,00
child (2-6 yrs)	€ 2,50 - € 3,00
dog	€ 2,00

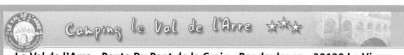

Marseillan-Plage

Yelloh! Village les Méditerranées

262 avenue des campings, F-34340 Marseillan-Plage (Hérault) T: **04 66 73 97 39**
E: **info@yellohvillage-mediterranees.com** **alanrogers.com/FR34150**

Marseillan Plage is a small, busy resort east of Cap d'Adge and it enjoys a super position immediately beside a long gently shelving sandy beach. Les Méditerranées is made up of two sites – Nouvelle Floride beside the beach and Charlemagne across the road, both with super pool complexes. Both are good quality sites set under tall trees with neat hedges separating around 500 pitches. There are about 200 for touring units on sandy soil, all with water and 6A electricity. The pitches nearer the sea have less shade. Amenities and facilities are generally of excellent quality and include a smart bar area overlooking the beach with a raised stage for entertainment.

Facilities

Very impressive toilet blocks include some en-suite showers and washbasins, facilities for disabled visitors, dog shower. Motorcaravan services. Shops. Bars, restaurants. Two swimming pool complexes, slides, Jacuzzi, paddling pools (all season). Play area. Fitness centre. Multisport court. Watersports. Weekly films, variety of organised games, competitions, dances, discos. WiFi. Miniclub in school holidays. Bicycle hire. Off site: Riding, bicycle hire 500 m. Boat launching and watersports 1 km. Golf 5 km.

Open: 3 April - 3 October.

Directions

From A9 autoroute exit 34, follow N312 to Agde then take N112 towards Sete. Watch for signs to Marseillan-Plage from where site is well signed.
GPS: 43.30870, 3.54168

Charges guide

Per unit incl. 2 persons and electricity	€ 15,00 - € 46,00
extra person	€ 6,00 - € 8,00
child (3-6 yrs)	free - € 8,00
dog	€ 20,00 - € 52,00

Marseillan-Plage

Camping la Creole

74 avenue des campings, F-34340 Marseillan-Plage (Hérault) T: **04 67 21 92 69**
E: **campinglacreole@wanadoo.fr** **alanrogers.com/FR34220**

This is a surprisingly tranquil, well cared for small campsite in the middle of this bustling resort that will appeal to those seeking a rather less frenetic ambience typical of many sites in this area. Essentially a family orientated site, it offers around 110 good-sized, level grass pitches, all with 6A electricity and mostly with shade from trees and shrubs. It also benefits from direct access to an extensive sandy beach and the fact that there is no swimming pool or bar actually contributes to the tranquillity. It may even be seen as an advantage for families with younger children. The beach will be the main attraction here no doubt, and the town's extensive range of bars, restaurants and shops are all within a couple of minutes' walk.

Facilities

Toilet facilities are housed in a traditional building, modernised inside to provide perfectly adequate, if not particularly luxurious facilities including some washbasins in private cabins, a baby room and dog shower. Small play area. In high season beach games, dances, sangria evenings etc, are organised, all aimed particularly towards families. Barbecue area. Bicycle hire. Off site: Local market day Tuesday. Riding 1 km.

Open: 1 April - 15 October.

Directions

From A9 exit 34 take N312 towards Agde, then N112 towards Sète keeping a look-out for signs to Marseillan-Plage off this road. Site is well signed in Marseillan-Plage. GPS: 43.3206, 3.5501

Charges guide

Per unit incl. 2 persons	€ 13,50 - € 27,20
extra person	€ 3,00 - € 5,00
electricity	€ 2,80
dog	€ 2,00 - € 3,00

Meyrueis

Camping Caravaning le Champ d'Ayres

Route de la Brèze, F-48150 Meyrueis (Lozère) T: **04 66 45 60 51**. E: **campinglechampdayres@wanadoo.fr**
alanrogers.com/FR48000

This is a traditional family run site, set in the heart of the Cevennes Champ d'Ayres. Neat, tidy and well kept, it is run with young families in mind (teenagers might be bored). The site is slightly sloping with 85 grass pitches, 62 for touring, the majority hedged with well trimmed bushes and most with some shade. All have electricity (6/10A) but some may require long leads. The area is surrounded by mountains and gorges and some of the roads are not for the faint-hearted or those with large and under-powered units. Being very centrally located, there are many attractions in the area.

Facilities

The excellent toilet block is kept very clean and has all the necessary facilities. Baby room. Facilities for disabled visitors. Laundry facilities. Shop, small bar and takeaway (all 1/5-15/9). New heated swimming and paddling pool (8/5-15/9). Play area. Games room. Boules. Bicycle hire. Activities arranged (July/Aug). WiFi. Off site: The small, pretty town of Meyrueis (500 m) has many good shops and restaurants. Fishing 100 m. Riding 1 km.

Open: 3 April - 18 September.

Directions

From N9 at Aquessac (5 km. north of Millau) take D907 (Gorge du Tarn). At Rozier turn right on D996 (Meyrueis and Gorges de la Jonte). In Meyrueis follow signs for Château d'Ayres and site signs. Site is 500 m. east of town. GPS: 44.18077, 3.43507

Charges 2010

Per unit incl. 2 persons	€ 10,00 - € 21,50
extra person	€ 3,00 - € 5,00
child (under 7 yrs)	€ 2,00 - € 3,00
electricity	€ 3,00

Meyrueis

Kawan Village de Capelan

F-48150 Meyrueis (Lozère) T: **04 66 45 60 50**. E: **camping.le.capelan@wanadoo.fr**

alanrogers.com/FR48020

The Lozère is one of France's least populated regions but offers some truly spectacular, rugged scenery, wonderful flora and fauna and old towns and villages. Le Capelan has 119 grassy pitches in total, 79 are for touring and are strung out alongside the river, most with some shade and all with electrical connections (6/10A). Around 40 pitches are used for mobile homes. There is direct river access from the site and trout fishing is popular. Although there are special facilities, the site is not ideal for disabled visitors. English and Dutch are spoken.

Facilities

Well maintained toilet blocks, facilities for disabled visitors (but not ideal). Three bathrooms for rent. Small shop. Bar (both from 1/6). Takeaway (from 1/7). Swimming, paddling pools, sunbathing terrace (from 1/6), access via 60 steps. Multisports terrain. Satellite TV. Play area. Leisure activities including supervised rock climbing. Fishing. Internet. Communal barbecue area, only gas and electric barbecues. Off site: Town centre with shops 1 km. Bicycle hire 1 km. Riding 3 km. Canoeing. Cévennes national park. Caves.

Open: 1 May - 15 September.

Directions

From Clermont Ferrand on the A75 take exit 44-1 Aguessac-le Rozier towards Meyrueis. The site is 1 km. west of Meyruels on the D996, the road to La Jonte. It is well signed from the centre of the town. GPS: 44.18583, 3.41988

Charges guide

Per unit incl. 2 persons	€ 13,50 - € 21,00
incl. electricity	€ 16,50 - € 24,00
extra person	€ 3,00 - € 4,70

Camping Cheques accepted.

Méze

Kawan Village Beau Rivage

RD613, F-34140 Méze (Hérault) T: **04 67 43 81 48**

E: **reception@camping-beaurivage.fr** **alanrogers.com/FR34260**

Beau Rivage is situated on the inland shore of the 4.5 km. by 19.5 km. Etang du Thau. This inland salt lake, lying parallel to the Mediterranean and separated by a very narrow strip of land, is well known for its oyster beds. It also popular for fishing, diving and watersports. The campsite, on the edge of the town, is within easy walking distance of the harbour and the shops. The site has 150 level, sandy-grass pitches all with 6A electricity available for touring units and 134 mobile homes to rent. The main features of the site are a pleasant pool and paddling pool with a bar and snack restaurant for the high season.

Facilities

One fully equipped small toilet block is open all season and a larger block for the main season. Baby bath. Facilities for disabled people. Washing machine. Motorcaravan service point. Bar providing snacks and simple takeaway food (July/Aug). Heated swimming and paddling pools (all season). Play area. Activities in July and August. Communal barbecues. Off site: Restaurant 300 m. Supermarket 200 m. Beach 500 m. Tennis and bicycle hire 1 km.

Open: 5 April - 20 September.

Directions

From the A9 take exit 33 for Sète. Follow RN113 for Poussan, Bouzigues and Mèze. Continue for 5 km. to outskirts of Mèze and site is on left just after a petrol station. The entrance is hidden between the petrol station and a pottery. GPS: 43.43051, 3.61038

Charges guide

Per unit incl. 2 persons	€ 18,00 - € 37,00
extra person	€ 4,00 - € 7,00

Camping Cheques accepted.

Montclar

yelloh! VILLAGE

Yelloh! Village Domaine d'Arnauteille

F-11250 Montclar (Aude) T: **04 68 26 84 53**. E: **info@arnauteille.com**

alanrogers.com/FR11060

Enjoying some beautiful and varied views, this site is ideal exploring the little known Aude Département and for visiting the walled city of Carcassonne. The site is set in farmland on hilly ground with the original pitches on gently sloping, lightly wooded land. Newer ones are on open ground, of good size, with water, drainage and electricity (5/10A), semi-terraced and partly hedged. Of the 198 pitches, 138 are for touring. The facilities are quite spread out with the swimming pool complex, in the style of a Roman amphitheatre, set in a hollow basin surrounded by fine views. Access, although much improved, could be difficult for large, twin-axle vans.

Facilities

Toilet blocks, one with a Roman theme. Laundry, facilities for disabled people and a baby bath. Motorcaravan services. Small shop, bar, restaurant in converted stable block and takeaway (all open 15/5-15/9). Swimming pool (25 m. 1/5-30/9), paddling pool, river with water massage and sunbathing terrace. Games court. Boules. Play area. Riding (1/7-31/8). Day trips. Library, internet, games room, TV. Off site: Fishing 3 km. Bicycle hire 8 km. Golf 10 km.

Open: 1 April - 26 September.

Directions

D118 from Carcassonne, pass Rouffiac d'Aude. Before the end of dual carriageway, turn right to Montclar up narrow road (passing places) for 2.5 km. Site signed very sharp left up hill before village.
GPS: 43.12714, 2.25953

Charges 2010

Per unit incl. 2 persons	€ 15,00 - € 36,00
extra person	€ 6,00 - € 8,00

Camping Cheques accepted.

Narbonne

Kawan Village les Mimosas

Chaussée de Mandirac, F-11100 Narbonne (Aude) T: **04 68 49 03 72**
E: **info@lesmimosas.com** **alanrogers.com/FR11070**

Six kilometres inland from the beaches of Narbonne and Gruissan, this site benefits from a less hectic situation than others by the sea. The site is lively with plenty to entertain the younger generation whilst offering facilities for the whole family. A free club card is available in July and August to use the children's club, gym, sauna, tennis, minigolf, billiards etc. There are 250 pitches, 150 for touring, many in a circular layout of very good size, most with electricity (6A). There are a few 'grand confort' serviced pitches with reasonable shade, mostly from 2 m. high hedges. There is also mobile homes and chalets to rent. This could be a very useful site offering many possibilities to meet a variety of needs, entertainment (including an evening on Cathar history), and easy access to popular beaches. Nearby Gruissan is a fascinating village with its wooden houses on stilts, beaches, ruined castle, port and salt beds. Narbonne has Roman remains and inland Cathar castles are to be found perched on rugged hilltops.

Facilities

Sanitary buildings refurbished to a high standard. Washing machines. Shop and 'Auberge' restaurant (open all season). Takeaway. Bar. Small lounge, amusements (July/Aug). Landscaped heated pool with slides and islands (open 1 May), plus the original pool and children's pool (high season). New play area. Minigolf. Mountain bike hire. Tennis. Sauna, gym. Children's activities, sports, entertainment (high season). Bicycle hire. Multisports ground. Off site: Riding. Windsurfing/sailing school 300 m. Gruissan's beach 10 minutes. Lagoon, boating fishing via footpath (200 m).

Open: 27 March - 1 November.

Directions

From A9 exit 38 (Narbonne Sud) take last exit on roundabout, back over the autoroute (site signed from here). Follow signs La Nautique and then Mandirac and site (6 km. from autoroute). Also signed from Narbonne centre. GPS: 43.13662, 3.02562

Charges 2010

Per unit incl. 2 persons and electricity	€ 17,50 - € 33,00
incl. water and waste water	€ 21,70 - € 38,00
extra person	€ 4,10 - € 10,00

Camping Cheques accepted.

Narbonne

493

Camping la Nautique

La Nautique, F-11100 Narbonne (Aude) T: **04 68 90 48 19**. E: **info@campinglanautique.com**

alanrogers.com/FR11080

Owned and run by a very welcoming Dutch family, this well established site has pitches each with individual sanitary units. It is an extremely spacious site situated on the Etang de Bages, where flat water combined with strong winds make it one of the best windsurfing areas in France. La Nautique has 390 huge, level pitches, 270 for touring, all with 10A electricity and water. Six or seven overnight pitches with electricity are in a separate area. The flowering shrubs and trees give a pleasant feel. Each pitch is separated by hedges making some quite private and providing shade. Entertainment is organised for adults and children from Easter to September (increasing in high season) and a sports club for supervised surfing, sailing, rafting, walking and canoeing (some activities are charged for). The unspoilt surrounding countryside is excellent for walking or cycling and locally there is horse riding and fishing. English is spoken in reception by the very welcoming Schutjes family. This site caters for families with children including teenagers and is fenced off from the water for the protection of children. Windsurfers can have a key for the gate (with deposit) that leads to launching points on the lake.

Facilities

Each pitch has its own fully equipped sanitary unit. Specially equipped facilities for disabled visitors. Laundry. Shop. Bar/restaurant, terrace, TV. Takeaway (all 1/5-30/9). Snack bar (1/7-31/8). Swimming pools, water slide, paddling pool. Play areas. Tennis. Minigolf. Pétanque. Miniclub (high season). Games room. Internet. Only electric barbecues are permitted. Torch useful. Off site: Large sandy beaches at Gruissan (12 km) and Narbonne Plage (20 km). Narbonne is only 4 km. Walking and cycling. Canoeing, sailing and windsurfing on the Etang.

Open: 15 February - 15 November.

Directions

From A9 take exit 38 (Narbonne Sud). Go round the roundabout to the last exit and follow signs for La Nautique and site, then further site signs to site on right in 2.5 km. GPS: 43.14696, 3.00439

Charges 2010

Per unit incl. 2 persons, water electricity and sanitary unit	€ 19,50 - € 42,00
extra person	€ 5,00 - € 8,00
child (1-6 yrs)	€ 3,00 - € 6,00
dog	€ 2,50 - € 4,00

Néfiach

Flower Camping la Garenne

RD916, F-66170 Néfiach (Pyrénées-Orientales) T: **04 68 57 15 76**

E: **camping.lagarenne.nefiach@wanadoo.fr** **alanrogers.com/FR66490**

Situated just off the N116 which runs through the foothills of the Pyrénées from Perpignan to Andorra, this site is ideally situated for hiking, climbing, cycling and canoeing. The pitches are all level with very easy access, have a degree of privacy to them, and all are close to the swimming pool and children's play area. A few mobile homes are on the site and some of these are attractively designed to look like chalets found high up in the mountains. Great views of the surrounding hills and mountains are enjoyable from all areas of the site whilst at the back there are vineyards with black grapes in abundance.

Facilities

Single toilet block in the centre of the site provides modern facilities. Baby area and facilities for disabled visitors. Washing machine. Cozy bar area and snack type restaurant with covered area for singing and dancing. Weekly paella evening. Swimming pool with sunbathing terrace and small pool for young children. Play area. Outdoor fitness machines for adults. Off site: Hiking, climbing, cycling and canoeing all nearby. Attractive town of Ile-sur-Têt 3 km.

Open: All year.

Directions

From the N116 (Perpignan - Andorra), take exit for Nefiach and head up the old road to Ile-sur-Têt and the site is on the right. GPS: 42.69067, 2.65785

Charges guide

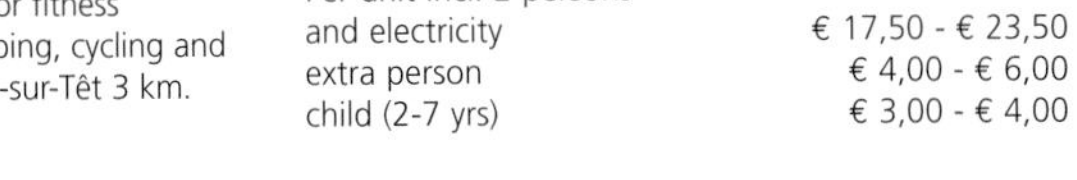

Per unit incl. 2 persons and electricity	€ 17,50 - € 23,50
extra person	€ 4,00 - € 6,00
child (2-7 yrs)	€ 3,00 - € 4,00

Palau-del-Vidre

Kawan Village le Haras

Domaine Saint Galdric, F-66690 Palau-del-Vidre (Pyrénées-Orientales)
T: **04 68 22 14 50**. E: **haras8@wanadoo.fr** **alanrogers.com/FR66050**

Situated in the mature grounds of an old hunting lodge, later developed into an arborteum, Le Haras is a rather special site. The pitches are in bays of four arranged amidst an amazing variety of trees and shrubs that provide colour and shade for 49 touring units and some 15 mobile homes to rent. All the touring pitches have 6A electricity, 18 are fully serviced. Some of the access roads are narrow. Under the same family management as Ma Prairie at Canet Village (FR66020), this is a comfortable site popular with British visitors. Rail noise is possible, although the line is screened by large trees.

Facilities

Fully equipped toilet blocks. Facilities for disabled visitors. Washing machines. Motorcaravan service point. Fridge hire. Bar. Restaurant and takeaway (15/3-30/9). Swimming and paddling pools (1/5-15/9). Play area. Archery (10/7-25/8). Only gas or electric barbecues are allowed. Internet access (charged) and WiFi (free). Off site: Beaches 10 minutes drive. Fishing 500 m. Riding 2 km. Bicycle hire 6 km. Golf 7 km.

Open: 20 March - 20 October.

Directions

From A9, exit 43 (Le Boulou) follow D618 towards Argelès for 13 km. From the bypass at St André, turn left for Palau-del-Vidre (D11). Bear right through village, on D11 towards Elne. Site on right at end of village, before railway bridge. GPS: 42.57639, 2.96444

Charges guide

Per unit incl. two persons	€ 19,00 - € 19,60
extra person	€ 3,60 - € 5,50

Camping Cheques accepted.

Port Camargue

Camping Abri de Camargue

320 route du Phare de l'Espiguette, Port Camargue, F-30240 Le Grau-du-Roi (Gard) T: **04 66 51 54 83**
E: **contact@abridecamargue.fr** **alanrogers.com/FR30030**

This pleasant site has an attractive pool area overlooked by the bar with its outdoor tables on a pleasant sheltered terrace. The larger outdoor pool has surrounds for sunbathing and the smaller indoor one is heated. With 277 level pitches, there are 57 for touring units, mainly of 100 sq.m. (there are also smaller ones). Electricity and water are available on most, and the pitches are well maintained and shaded, with trees and flowering shrubs, quite luxuriant in parts. Recent additions include an air-conditioned cinema room and a club for children in high season.

Facilities

Well appointed toilet blocks and facilities for disabled visitors. Motorcaravan services. Shop. Bar, TV, restaurant, takeaway. Heated indoor pool, outdoor pool and paddling pool. Cinema. Entertainment programme. High quality play area. Children's club. P'tanque. Music room for young people in high season. WiFi near restaurant (charged). Site access card (deposit € 15). Off site: Tennis 800 m. Riding, bicycle hire 1 km. Fishing 2 km. Golf 5 km. Nearest beach Port Camargue 900 m. L'Espiguette 4 km.

Open: 1 April - 30 September.

Directions

Site is 45 km. southwest of Nimes. From the A9 autoroute, exit 26, Gallargues to Le Grau-du-Roi. From bypass follow signs Port Camargue and Campings. Then follow Rive gauche signs towards Phare l'Espiguette. Site is on right opposite Toboggan Park. GPS: 43.5225, 4.1491

Charges guide

Per unit incl. 2 persons and electricity	€ 27,00 - € 56,00
extra person	€ 7,00

Portiragnes-Plage

Camping Caravaning les Mimosas

Port Cassafières, F-34420 Portiragnes-Plage (Hérault) T: **04 67 90 92 92**
E: **les.mimosas.portiragnes@wanadoo.fr** **alanrogers.com/FR34170**

Les Mimosas is quite a large site with 400 pitches – 200 for touring units, the remainder for mobile homes – in a rural situation. The level, grassy pitches are of average size, separated and numbered, all with 6A electricity (long leads may be required), some have good shade others have less. The pool area, a real feature of the site, includes a most impressive wave pool, various toboggans, the 'Space Hole' water slide, a large swimming pool and a super paddling pool (nine pools in all) with lots of free sun beds. This is a friendly, family-run site with families in mind with something new for each year.

Facilities

Modern toilet blocks include baby rooms, children's toilets, facilities for disabled people. En-suite facilities on payment. Washing machines and dryers. Motorcaravan services. Fridge hire. Shop. Bar, snacks all season, restaurant (from 1/6). Swimming pool complex (early June). Good play area. Miniclub (4-8 yrs). Boules. Gym with instructor and sauna. Multisport court. Bicycle hire. Games/TV room. Evening entertainment. Internet access and WiFi (charged). Communal barbecues only. Off site: Fishing and riding 1 km. Portiragnes Plage 2 km. Golf 10 km.

Open: 20 May - 5 September.

Directions

From A9 exit 35 (Béziers Est) take N112 south towards Serignan (1 km). Large roundabout follow signs for Cap d'Agde, watch carefully for D37, Portiragnes (1-2 km), follow signs for Portiragnes Plage. Site well signed before Portiragnes Plage (5 km). GPS: 43.29153, 3.37348

Charges guide

Per unit incl. 2 persons	€ 22,00 - € 37,50
extra person	€ 5,00 - € 9,00
private sanitary unit	€ 8,50 - € 9,50

Portiragnes-Plage

Camping les Sablons

Avenue des Muriers, F-34420 Portiragnes-Plage (Hérault) T: **04 67 90 90 55**. E: **contact@les-sablons.com**
alanrogers.com/FR34400

Les Sablons is an impressive and popular site with lots going on. Most of the facilities are arranged around the entrance with shops, a restaurant, bar and a large pool complex with no less than five slides, three heated pools and large stage for entertainment. There is also direct access to the white sandy beach at the back of the site close to a small lake. There is good shade on the majority of the site, although some of the newer touring pitches have less shade but are nearer the gate to the beach. On level sandy grass, all have 6A electricity. Of around 800 pitches, around half are taken by a range of mobile homes and chalets (many for hire, some by British tour operators). A wide range of sporting activities, and evening entertainment is arranged with much for children to do. In fact, this is a real holiday venue aiming to keep all the family happy.

Facilities

Well equipped, modernised toilet blocks include large showers some with washbasins. Baby baths and facilities for disabled visitors. Supermarket, bakery and newsagent. Restaurant, bar and takeaway. Swimming pool complex. Entertainment and activity programme with sports, music and cultural activities. Beach club. Tennis. Archery. Play areas. Electronic games. ATM. Internet access.
Off site: Riding 200 m. Bicycle hire 100 m.

Open: 1 April - 30 September.

Directions

From A9 exit 35 (Béziers Est) follow signs for Vias and Agde (N112). After large roundabout pass exit to Cers then take exit for Portiragnes (D37). Follow for about 5 km. and pass over Canal du Midi towards Portiragnes-Plage. Site is on left after roundabout.
GPS: 43.28003, 3.36396

Charges year

Per unit incl. 2 persons and electricity	€ 18,00 - € 46,00
extra person	€ 6,00 - € 10,00
child (5-13 yrs)	free - € 8,00
dog	€ 4,00

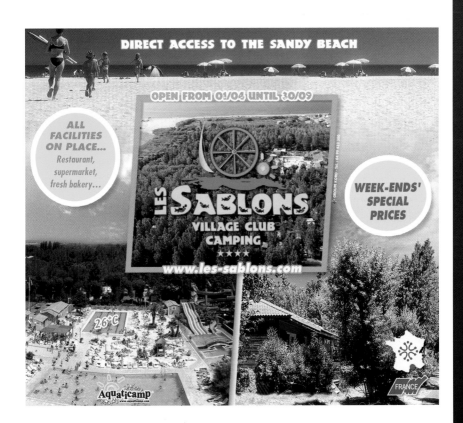

Port-La-Nouvelle

Camping Côte Vermeille

Chemin des Vignes, F-11210 Port-La-Nouvelle (Aude) T: **04 68 48 05 80**
E: **infos@camping-cote-vermeille.com** **alanrogers.com/FR11250**

Port la Nouvelle is a traditional seaside resort with a large marina and a busy commercial port. Côte Vermeille can be found a few kilometres from the resort and is some 150 m. from a long, sandy beach. It is behind the scrubland of the littoral, so the sea is not directly visible from the site. There are 286 pitches, of which around 115 are used for for touring units. These are of a reasonable size on sandy grass with some shade. Half have 6A electricity. A large pool complex is the main feature of the site with several large water slides. A railway line passes at the back of the site.

Facilities

Fully equipped toilet blocks in traditional style. Laundry. Shop. Bar and snack bar. Takeaway. Swimming pool complex with paddling pool and water slides. Play area. Sport and entertainment programme with club for children (5-12 yrs). Windsurfing off the beach. Barbecues are not permitted. Mobile homes for rent. Off site: Beach 150 m. Riding nearby. Fishing and boatlaunching 2 km. Port la Nouvelle 2 km. African safari park at Sigean 9 km. Narbonne 20 km.

Open: 4 April - 10 October.

Directions

From the north, leave the A9 at exit 39 and head east on the D6139 to Sigean and then Port la Nouvelle. Site is signed at new roundabout. Follow narrow road alongside railway line for 2 km. to site.
GPS: 42.99801, 3.04929

Charges guide

Per unit incl. 2 persons and electricity	€ 19,70 - € 32,70
extra person	€ 4,70 - € 7,00
child (2-7 yrs)	€ 2,60 - € 4,50
dog	€ 5,00

Remoulins

Camping la Soubeyranne

1110 route de Beaucaire, F-30210 Remoulins (Gard) T: **04 66 37 03 21**. E: **soubeyranne@franceloc.fr**
alanrogers.com/FR30140

Owned by the group FranceLoc, this site is well positioned for visiting the Pont du Gard, Nîmes and Uzès, famed for their Roman connections. The 200 pitches offer extremely generous amounts of shade and keeping the six hectares watered involves over 5 km. of hose pipe. The touring pitches, of which there are 79, are large, level, numbered and separated, and all have 6A electricity connections. An entertainment programme (July/August) is aimed mainly at young children (teenagers may find the site rather quiet).

Facilities

One unisex toilet block is basic but clean and give more than adequate facilities and include washbasins in cubicles. Motorcaravan service point. Fridges for hire. Small shop selling basics. Restaurant, bar and takeaway (all 4/4-27/9) – menu not extensive but adequate and moderately priced. Heated swimming pool complex (4/4-27/9) with 20 x 10 m. pool and smaller toddlers' pool (unsupervised). Play area including inflatable castle. Minigolf. Boules. Tennis. Bicycle hire. Off site: Fishing 1 km. Remoulins 1.5 km.

Open: 4 April - 27 September.

Directions

From Uzès take D981 to Remoulins, turn right at lights over river bridge, left at roundabout, then left (signed D986 Beaucaire). Site is 1.5 km. further on left.
GPS: 43.942282, 4.559669

Charges guide

Per unit incl. 2 persons and electricity	€ 19,70 - € 31,20
extra person	€ 4,70 - € 7,00
child (under 7 yrs)	€ 2,60 - € 4,50
animal	€ 5,00

Saillagouse

502

PRL Le Vedrignans

Route de Vedrignans, F-66800 Saillagouse (Pyrénées-Orientales) T: **04 68 04 04 79**
E: **contact@levedrignans.com** **alanrogers.com/FR66700**

The pitches at this campsite are used exclusively for mobile home accommodation. For full details please see our PRL section starting on page 501.

Saint Cyprien-Plage

Camping Cala Gogo

Avenue Armand Lanoux, les Capellans, F-66750 Saint Cyprien-Plage (Pyrénées-Orientales)
T: **04 68 21 07 12**. E: **camping.calagogo@wanadoo.fr** **alanrogers.com/FR66030**

This is an excellent, well-organised site and it is agreeably situated by a superb sandy beach with a beach bar and boat launching. There are 654 pitches in total with 450 average sized, level, pitches for touring, electrical connections (6A) everywhere and some shade. The site has a most impressive pool complex laid out with palm trees in ample sunbathing areas. The large bar complex becomes very busy in season and dancing or entertainment is arranged on some evenings on a large stage recently built alongside the bar. A feature of the site is the provision of special beach buggies for visitors with disabilities. The site is now part of the 'Les Pieds dans l'Eau' group (having direct access to water, either sea, river or lake). A large Aquapark, reputed to be amongst the best in southern France, is nearby. Used by tour operators (148 pitches). There are 57 chalets and mobile homes to rent.

Facilities

Fully equipped toilet blocks are of a high standard. Good supermarket and small shopping mall. Sophisticated restaurant with excellent cuisine. Self-service restaurant with simple menu. Takeaway. Bar. Small beach bar (high season). Fridge hire. Disco. TV. Three swimming pools plus one for children, water-jets, jacuzzi, waterfall. Play area. Tennis. Fishing. Diving club. Internet access and WiFi. Bicycle hire. Events, sports and entertainment organised in season. Torches useful. Off site: Golf, riding and boat launching 3 km. Boat excursions and courses in skin-diving, sailing or windsurfing nearby.

Open: 8 May - 18 September.

Directions

Using D81 (southward) avoid St Cyprien-Plage and continue towards Argelès. Turn right at roundabout signed Le Port and Aquapark and pick up site signs. Site is just past the Aquapark.
GPS: 42.59939, 3.03761

Charges 2010

Per unit incl. 2 persons and electricity	€ 25,97 - € 37,10
extra person	€ 4,50 - € 7,00
dog	free - € 3,00

See advertisement on page 375

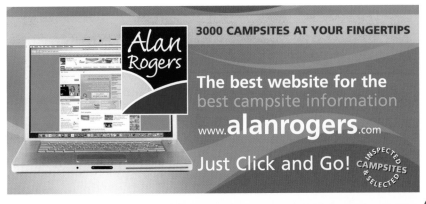

Saint Enimie

Camping Couderc

Route de Millau, F-48210 Saint Enimie (Lozère) T: **04 66 48 50 53**. E: **campingcouderc@orange.fr**
alanrogers.com/FR48080

A spacious rural site, Couderc is strung out along 1 km. of the clear shallow River Tarn, although access to the river is not easy. The beautiful Gorges du Tarn and the high plateaux are well worth exploring. Come in May and June to see the wonderful flowers and butterflies with vultures soaring overhead. There are 130 good sized, level grassy/stony pitches here, separated by vines and mature trees. With 123 for touring units, most have welcome shade and 10A electricity (long leads may be needed). Rock pegs are advised. Although the local roads are winding and narrow, access on the site is good.

Facilities

Several toilet blocks with adequate facilities including those for children. Facilities for disabled visitors (but the terrain makes it not ideal for those with walking difficulties). Bar/TV room. Breakfast (all season). Basic shop, bread to order. Swimming and paddling pools (a steep climb from pitches). Play area. Canoe hire and trips run from site. Boules. River fishing. Electric barbecues only – communal barbecues provided. Off site: Ste Enimie 1.5 km. with bank, shops, restaurants, bars. Grottos, canyoning, rock climbing, caving.

Open: 19 April - 20 September.

Directions

Leave A75 at exit 40 for La Canourgue. Take the D998 to Ste Enimie (28 km) following signs for Millau, Gorges du Tarn. Take the D907 to site on left in 1.5 km. Approach from south not recommended for large outfits. GPS: 44.353606, 3.401347

Charges 2010

Per unit incl. 2 persons and electricity	€ 14,00 - € 22,00
extra person	€ 3,00 - € 4,00
child (under 7 yrs)	€ 1,30 - € 1,60

Saint Jean-du-Gard

Camping Mas de la Cam

Route de Saint André-de-Valborgne, F-30270 Saint Jean-du-Gard (Gard) T: **04 66 85 12 02**
E: **camping@masdelacam.fr** **alanrogers.com/FR30180**

Camping Mas de la Cam is rather unusual in that all the pitches are used for touring. It is a very pleasant and spacious site with well trimmed grass and hedges and a profusion of flowers and shrubs. Lying alongside the small Gardon river, the banks have been left free of pitches giving neat grass for sunbathing and some trees for shade, whilst children can amuse themselves in the water (no good for canoes). Slightly sloping, the 200 medium to large pitches are on level terraces, some with varying amounts of shade, electricity (6A). There is no evening entertainment. Nearby one can walk in the footsteps of Robert Louis Stevenson (Travels with a Donkey), ride on a steam train, explore the deep underground caverns, visit a giant bamboo forest and explore the region by foot, on bike or by car. Entrance is via a narrow unfenced bridge, but wide enough for large outfits. Nine gîtes for rent in beautiful old farmhouse. A quiet, family site; you are assured of a good welcome (English is spoken).

Facilities

High quality toilet blocks with a baby bath and facilities for disabled visitors. Washing machines. Bar/restaurant, terrace. Small shop. Attractive large swimming (heated) and paddling pools. Huge play and sports areas, multisport court for football, volleyball and basketball. Club, used in low season for bridge, in high season as games room. Fishing. Off site: St Jean-du-Gard (3 km) with shops, market. Bus twice a day. Riding 5 km. Bicycle hire 15 km.

Open: 28 April - 20 September.

Directions

Site is 3 km. northwest of St Jean-du-Gard in direction of St André-de-Valborgne on D907, site signed, fork left, descend across a narrow unfenced bridge to site. Site entrance not accessible from north.
GPS: 44.11235, 3.8541

Charges guide

Per unit incl. 2 persons	€ 14,00 - € 23,00
incl. electricity	€ 17,00 - € 27,00
extra person	€ 3,30 - € 5,70
child (under 7 yrs)	free - € 3,80

Saint Pons-de-Thomières

Camping la Borio de Roque

Route de la Salvetat, F-34220 Saint Pons-de-Thomières (Hérault) T: **04 67 97 10 97**
E: **info@borioderoque.com** **alanrogers.com/FR34180**

La Borio de Roque is a peaceful site in a very rural location hidden in a wooded valley 4 km. from St Pons. It lies at the end of a 1.5 km. rough track but it is well worth the effort and it is set around a lovely restored farmhouse with the outbuildings made into four very attractive gîtes. The 25 large, individually shaped, terraced pitches have 10A electricity and some shade. Some are private to which the owners will escort you. When the site was developed, many different varieties of trees were planted which has created a very attractive environment.

Facilities

Toilet block, baby bath. Use of large freezer. Bread all season. Local wine, coffee and tea. Swimming pool (from 1/6). Small fishing lake. Small grassy play area. Barbecue areas. Unsuitable for American motorhomes. Off site: Bicycle hire 5 km. Golf and riding 20 km. Beach 50 km.

Open: 15 May - 15 September.

Directions

St Pons-de-Thomières is on the N112 northwest of Béziers. Site is 4.5 km. north of the town on the D907 signed Salvetat, on the right on a bend, then 1.5 km. on a rough track (signed). GPS: 43.51093, 2.74648

Charges guide

Per person	€ 3,50 - € 4,50
pitch	€ 7,75 - € 9,00
electricity	€ 3,00
vehicle	€ 2,00 - € 2,25

No credit cards.

Sérignan-Plage

Camping le Paradis

Route de Valras, F-34410 Sérignan-Plage (Hérault) T: **04 67 32 24 03**. E: **paradiscamping34@aol.com**
alanrogers.com/FR34560

Family owned and run, Le Paradis is a little haven of tranquillity set some 3 km. back from the sea. With only 129 average sized, grassy pitches, of which 22 are taken by mobile homes to rent, it is comfortable and peaceful. Even the pool is hidden behind fencing so it does not intrude. A mix of trees and shrubs give shade and all the pitches are level with 6A electricity. There is a pleasant shaded area to one corner of the pool near the bar. Entertainment is arranged on simple lines – music evenings two nights a week in July and August with darts or tennis tournaments for children.

Facilities

Fully equipped central toilet facilities. Provision for disabled visitors and a baby bath. Washing machine and drier. Small shop for essentials. Bar/restaurant (meals need to be pre-booked). Takeaway. Reasonably sized pool. Play area. Gas and electric barbecues only. Dogs are not accepted. Off site: Supermarket 200 m. Beach 2.5 km. Fishing and boat launching 2 km. Bicycle hire 1 km. Riding 3 km. Golf 15 km.

Open: 1 April - 30 September.

Directions

From A9 exit 35 (Béziers Ouest), follow signs for Valras Plage. At second roundabout beside McDonalds and Hyper U take left turn to site on right, clearly signed. GPS: 43.26926, 3.28727

Charges 2010

Per unit incl. 2 persons and electricity	€ 15,50 - € 31,50
extra person	€ 3,00 - € 5,00
child (under 7 yrs)	€ 2,00 - € 3,00

Sérignan-Plage

yelloh! VILLAGE

Yelloh! Village Aloha

F-34410 Sérignan-Plage (Hérault) T: **04 66 73 97 39**. E: **info@yellohvillage-aloha.com**
alanrogers.com/FR34390

A well run, orderly site beside the beach at Sérignan-Plage, Aloha offers a wide range of good quality facilities all open when the site is open. There are 472 pitches with over 170 mobile homes for hire in attractively landscaped settings. The 295 pitches for touring units are of good size, regularly laid out on level, sandy grass. Easily accessed from tarmac roads, all have 10A electricity. Half are on one side of the small beach road with the swimming pools and other facilities, the other half are somewhat quieter with more grass but less shade across the road.

Facilities

Seven toilet blocks, including three large ones, offer all modern facilities and are well equipped for children. Laundry. Motorcaravan service point. Supermarket including fresh produce market. Bakery, newsagent, bazaar, hairdresser. Bar, restaurant, snack bar, pizzeria, takeaway. Large heated pool and fun pools. Playground. Tennis. Multisports facility. Beach and sailing club. Bicycle hire. Range of activities. Evening entertainment. Off site: Riding 800 m. Boat launching 8 km. Golf 20 km.

Open: 25 April - 13 September.

Directions

From A9 exit 35 (Béziers Est) follow signs for Sérignan then Sérignan Plage (D64, about 10 km). Once at Sérignan-Plage continue straight. Follow the sign for Aloha to right after the pink building. GPS: 43.273333, 3.348333

Charges guide

Per unit incl. 2 persons and electricity	€ 15,00 - € 45,00
extra person	€ 5,00 - € 6,00
child (3-7 yrs)	free - € 6,00

Sérignan-Plage

Yelloh! Village le Sérignan-Plage

Le Sérignan Plage, F-34410 Sérignan-Plage (Hérault) T: **04 67 32 35 33**. E: **info@leserignanplage.com**
alanrogers.com/FR34070

With direct access onto a superb 600 m. sandy beach (including a naturist section) and with three swimming pools and another planned for next year, this is a must for a Mediterranean holiday. It is a friendly, family orientated site with perhaps the most comprehensive range of amenities we have come across. The enthusiastic owners, Jean-Guy and Catherine continually surprise us with their unique style and new developments. A collection of spa pools (balnéo) built in Romanesque style with colourful terracing and columns, overlooked by a very smart restaurant 'Le Villa' is the 'pièce de résistance'. The balnéo spa is shared with the adjoining naturist site (under the same ownership). Having recently acquired an adjacent site, there are now over 1,000 pitches with 400 available for touring units and this is now a pretty large campsite. The touring pitches vary in size and in terms of shade. They are mainly on sandy soil and all have electricity. There are over 300 mobile homes and chalets to let, plus some 400 privately owned units. The heart of the site, developed in the local Catalonian style, is some distance from reception and is a busy area with shops, another good restaurant, the Au Pas d'Oc, an indoor pool and a super roof-top bar. There is a range of entertainment for adults and children in the evenings.

Facilities

Several modern blocks of individual design with good facilities including showers with washbasin and WC. Facilities for disabled people. Baby bathroom. Launderette. Motorcaravan services. Supermarket, bakery and newsagent (all season). Other shops (1/6-15/9). ATM. Restaurants, bar and takeaway. Hairdresser. Balnéo spa. Gym. Heated indoor pool. Outdoor pools (24/4-21/9). Children's clubs. Evening entertainment. Sporting activities. Bicycle hire. Bus to Sérignan village July/Aug. Beach (lifeguards 1/6-15/9). Off site: Riding 2 km. Golf 10 km. Sailing and windsurfing school on beach (lifeguard in high season). Local markets.

Open: 29 April - 26 September.

Directions

From A9 exit 35 (Béziers Est) follow signs for Sérignan, D64 (9 km). Before Sérignan, turn left, Sérignan-Plage (4 km). At small sign (blue) turn right. At T-junction turn left over small road bridge and after left hand bend. Site is 100 m. GPS: 43.26398, 3.321

Charges 2010

Per unit incl. 2 persons and electricity	€ 15,00 - € 48,00
extra person	€ 5,00 - € 8,00
child (3-7 yrs)	free - € 8,00
dog	€ 4,00

Low season offers.

Sommieres

Castel Camping Domaine de Massereau

Les Hauteurs de Sommieres, route d'Aubais, F-30250 Sommieres (Gard) T: **04 66 53 11 20**
E: **info@massereau.fr** **alanrogers.com/FR30290**

A member of the Castels group, de Massereau was opened in August 2006 and is set within a 50-hectare vineyard dating back to 1804. There are now 120 pitches, with 75 available for touring units. Pitch sizes range from 150-250 sq.m. but the positioning of trees on some of the pitches severely limits the useable space. The large modern sanitary block is thoughtfully designed with superb facilities for disabled visitors and children. There is an attractive pool complex and a wide range of leisure facilities for all ages. The restaurant offers a reasonable range of good value cuisine and there is a well stocked shop including the vineyard's wines. Good English is spoken.

Facilities

The modern toilet block has excellent facilities for children and disabled visitors. Laundry area. Motorcaravan service point. Well stocked shop and newspapers. Restaurant. Bar. Pizzeria and outdoor grill. Takeaway. Heated swimming pool with slide. New sauna, steam bath and jacuzzi. Play area. Trampoline. Minigolf. Bicycle hire. Fitness trail. Pétanque. Short tennis. TV room. Barbecue hire. Fridge hire. Gas. WiFi. Charcoal barbecues are not allowed. Off site: Fishing 3 km. Riding 3 km. Golf 30 km. Sailing 30 km.

Open: 27 March - 15 November.

Directions

From the south on A9 take exit 27 and D12 towards Sommieres. Site is 5 km. on right. From the north, there is a width and weight restriction in Sommieres. To avoid this remain on the N110 and then take the N2110 into Sommieres, crossing the river and turn right onto the D12. Site is on left in 1 km. GPS: 43.76717, 4.09849

Charges guide

Per unit incl. 2 persons and electricity	€ 19,40 - € 38,40
extra person	€ 3,00 - € 9,30
child (under 7 yrs)	free
dog	€ 3,00 - € 5,20

Imagine – hot sunshine, blue sea, vineyards, olive and eucalyptus trees, alongside a sandy beach – what a setting for a campsite – not just any campsite either! With three pool areas, one with four toboggans surrounded by sun bathing areas, an indoor pool for baby swimmers plus a magnificent landscaped, Romanesque spa-complex with half Olympic size pool and a superb range of hydro-massage baths to let you unwind and re-charge after the stresses of work. And that 's not all – two attractive restaurants, including the atmospheric "Villa" in its romantic Roman setting beside the spa, three bars, a mini-club and entertainment for all ages, all add up to a fantastic opportunity to enjoy a genuinely unique holiday experience.

Le Sérignan Plage
The Mediterranean
The place for your holidays

34410 Sérignan Tél : +33 (0)4 67 32 35 33 Fax : +33 (0)4 67 32 68 39
info@leserignanplage.com www.leserignanplage.com

yelloh!

Torreilles-Plage

Village Camping Spa Marisol

Boulevard de la Plage, F-66440 Torreilles-Plage (Pyrénées-Orientales) T: **04 68 28 04 07**
E: **marisol@camping-marisol.com** **alanrogers.com/FR66170**

Good quality sites with direct access to the beach are hard to find and Marisol is a useful option. It is a fairly large site with 377 pitches with a significant number of mobile homes, but with 170 available for touring. These are sandy grass pitches of good size with some shade. All have electricity (10A). There is a beauty centre where you can enjoy a sauna, Turkish or spa bath. This is essentially a 'holiday' site with all the popular facilities and an extensive entertainment programme, fitness courses and children's club during the main season. The owners have renovated the pool area and plan other improvements.

Facilities

Fully equipped toilet blocks, baby bath. Washing machine. Small supermarket. Bar. TV. Restaurant. Takeaway. Heated swimming pool, water slide, children's pool. Beauty centre (including special packages). Fitness room. Play area. Tennis. Archery. Side gate with access to path across dunes to sandy beach. Watersports activities. Off site: Sea fishing, watersports on beach. Riding 500 m. Minigolf 500 m. Microlights, karting 1.5 km. Bicycle hire 2 km. Golf 10 km. Diving, water skiing 4 km.

Open: 3 April - 25 September.

Directions

From A9 take exit 41 (Perpignan Nord) towards Le Barcarès for 9 km. Then south on D81 towards Canet for 3 km. before turning to Torreilles-Plage. Site is signed. GPS: 42.78432, 3.03290

Charges 2010

Per unit incl. 2 persons and electricity	€ 15,00 - € 49,00
extra person	€ 5,50 - € 9,40

Torreilles-Plage

Camping la Palmeraie

Boulevard de la Plage, F-66440 Torreilles-Plage (Pyrénées-Orientales) T: **04 68 28 20 64**
E: **info@camping-la-palmeraie.com** **alanrogers.com/FR66160**

La Palmeraie is a very attractive, top quality campsite situated some 600 metres from the beach at Torreilles-Plage. Arguably the prettiest campsite in the area, there is an abundance of foliage, including a variety of trees and flowering shrubs which provide ample shade – unusual in a situation on the littoral and so close to the sea. The site is a credit to the owners. The 110 touring pitches (out of a total of 240 in all) are generally on the large side. All the facilities, including an attractive pool and surrounding sunbathing area, are of a good quality and lend an air of elegance to this excellent campsite.

Facilities

Three well equipped, sanitary blocks are traditional in style with modern fittings. Facilities for disabled visitors and children. Laundry facilities. Fridge hire. Shop. Bar, restaurant and takeaway (all open when site is open). Swimming and paddling pools. Play area. Games room. Multisport court. Internet access. Evening entertainment and organised sports activities in July/Aug. Children's club (6-12 yrs).
Off site: Beach 600 m. Riding 500 m. Sailing, beach club, minigolf and other activities in the local area.

Open: 27 May - 30 September.

Directions

From A9 take exit 41 and follow signs for Canet via D81 and D83. Once on D83 look for signs for Torreilles-Plage. Site is on right hand side as you approach from the roundabout on the D83.
GPS: 42.76570, 3.02740

Charges guide

Per unit incl. 2 persons	€ 15,70 - € 24,50
extra person	€ 5,00 - € 7,50
electricity (5/10A)	€ 3,50 - € 6,60

Torreilles-Plage

Sunêlia les Tropiques

Boulevard de la plage, F-66440 Torreilles-Plage (Pyrénées-Orientales) T: **04 68 28 05 09**
E: **contact@campinglestropiques.com** **alanrogers.com/FR66190**

Les Tropiques makes a pleasant holiday destination, only 400 metres from a sandy beach and also boasting two pools. It will provide families with children of all ages with an ideal seaside holiday. There are 450 pitches with 200 given over to mobile homes and chalets. Pleasant pine and palm trees with other Mediterranean vegetation give shade and provide an attractive environment. Activities are provided for all including a large range of sports, activities, caberets and shows. An identity bracelet for entry to the site is obligatory in high season (a small payment is required).

Facilities

Modern, fully equipped sanitary facilities, provision for disabled visitors. Launderette. Shop, bar (1/5-15/9). Restaurant, takeaway, pizzeria (all 1/6-15/9). Heated pool (all season) and water slides. Paddling pool. Tennis (floodlit). Multisport area (basketball, football, volleyball). Pétanque. Archery (1/7-31/8). TV, billiards room. Play area. Disco (every evening), miniclub for 6-12 ys in July/Aug. Bicycle hire (15/6-15/9). WiFi. Off site: Minigolf 300 m. Windsurf board hire, sea fishing 400 m. Riding 400 m. Microlights, karting 1.5 km. Diving, waterskiing 4 km. Golf 15 km.

Open: 3 April - 2 October.

Directions

From A9 exit Perpignan Nord, follow D83 towards Le Barcarès for 9 km. Take D81 south towards Canet for 3 km. turn left at roundabout for Torreilles-Plage. Site is the last but one on left. GPS: 42.76750, 3.02972

Charges 2010

Per unit incl. 2 persons and electricity	€ 17,50 - € 44,00
extra person	€ 3,85 - € 8,75
child (6-13 yrs)	€ 3,50 - € 6,60
child (0-6 yrs)	€ 2,55 - € 6,00

Valras-Plage

Camping Caravaning Domaine de la Yole

B.P. 23, F-34350 Valras-Plage (Hérault) T: **04 67 37 33 87**. E: **info@campinglayole.com**
alanrogers.com/FR34090

A busy happy holiday village with over 1,100 pitches could seem a little daunting. There are 590 pitches for touring. Most pitches are of a good size, all are level, hedged and have electricity, water and waste water points and, very importantly for this area, they all have shade. The extensive pool area is attractive with lots of sunbathing areas and the impressive activities are located in a central area. The beach, a long stretch of beautiful sand, is 500 m. with trampolining, paragliding and jet-skis. This is a busy site with something for all the family.

Facilities

Well maintained toilet blocks include baby rooms. Facilities for families and/or disabled visitors. Washing machines, dryers. Motorcaravan service points. Fridge hire. Shops. Good restaurant, terrace, amphitheatre for daily entertainment (in season). Two large pools, paddling pool (all season). Full- and half-size tennis courts. Multisports court. Play areas. Children's club. Boules. Internet.
Off site: Fishing or riding 2 km. Beach 500 m, path from site.

Open: 25 April - 19 September.

Directions

From A9 autoroute take Béziers Ouest exit for Valras-Plage (13-14 km) and follow Casino signs. Site is on left, just after sign for Vendres-Plage.
GPS: 43.23708, 3.26234

Charges guide

Per unit incl. 2 persons	€ 18,00 - € 37,35
extra person	€ 5,70 - € 6,30
child (7-16 yrs)	free - € 3,75
child (under 7 yrs)	free - € 1,90
dog	free - € 3,50

Valras-Plage

Camping Blue Bayou

Vendres Plage Ouest, F-34350 Valras-Plage (Hérault) T: **04 67 37 41 97**. E: **bluebayou@infonie.fr**
alanrogers.com/FR34370

A pleasant site, Blue Bayou is situated at the far end of Vendres Plage near Le Grau Vendres (the port of Vendres). It is therefore in a much quieter location than many other sites, away from the more hectic, built-up areas of Vendres and Valras-Plage The beach is 300 m. across sand dunes and there are open views from the site creating a feeling of spaciousness. There are 256 pitches, all with 10A electricity, with 74 privately owned mobile homes and 92 to let, including some chalets. The touring pitches are large, some with their own sanitary arrangements. Light shade is provided by a mixture of trees. The restaurant and bar area is very attractive, overlooking two swimming pools, one with a toboggan, joined by a bridge where lifeguards station themselves. The site is under new ownership with all the family involved and you are made to feel very welcome. The site would make a very good choice for couples and families, perhaps best visited outside the height of the season when it becomes very busy.

Facilities

Individual toilet units for about half the touring pitches. Two separate blocks are fully equipped (may come under pressure at peak times). Baby bath. Facilities for disabled visitors. Laundry. Bar, restaurant and takeaway (on demand in early season). Swimming pool (heated all season). Multisport court. Play area. Bicycle hire. Off site: Fishing, boat launching and riding 1 km. Golf 25 km.

Open: 4 April - 26 September.

Directions

From A9 exit 36 (Béziers Ouest) follow directions for Valras-Plage and Vendres Plage over four roundabouts. At fifth roundabout (Port Conchylicole) follow sign for Vendres Plage Ouest and site is 500 m. on the left past the Ranch and tourist office. The entrance is quite tight. GPS: 43.227167, 3.238167

Charges guide

Per unit incl. 2 persons	€ 19,00 - € 37,00
incl. private sanitary facility	€ 23,00 - € 45,00
extra person	€ 5,00 - € 9,00
child (0-2 yrs)	free

Valras-Plage

Siblu Camping les Sables du Midi

B.P. 29, F-34350 Valras-Plage (Hérault) T: **04 67 39 59 06**. E: **campingoccitanie@wanadoo.fr**

alanrogers.com/FR34430

Les Sables du Midi (formerly known as L'Occitanie) is a good value site, particularly for low season visits, and is within walking distance of Valras Plage. The site is virtually a straight road from the autoroute exit (12 km). On arrival, don't be put off by the entrance (it could be more inspiring). You can find a more open pitch in the higher part of the site which is lightly wooded with some views of the surrounding countryside, or choose the lower area with plenty of shade which French visitors seem to do. A right of way divides the site into two parts. The bar, restaurant and pool make a nice social area in the higher part. There are 400 pitches with 30 privately owned mobile homes and 58 for hire. All pitches have 6A electricity and are of reasonable size on level rough grass. The town is a 20 minute walk and the beach is 1 km. It is therefore a relatively peaceful location and seems to attract a mix of visitors.

Facilities

Five toilet blocks are fully equipped and opened as required. En-suite unit with ramped access for disabled visitors. Baby bath. Washing machine. Motorcaravan service point. Bar, restaurant and takeaway. Swimming and paddling pools. Play area. Minigolf. Daytime activities for children and sports for adults in high season and some evening entertainment.

Open: 31 May - 6 August.

Directions

From A9 exit 35 (Béziers Est) follow signs for Valras-Plage (12 km). Continue straight on at roundabout beside McDonalds and Hyper U and again at next one towards Valras. Then turn immediately left into site. GPS: 43.2572, 3.2847

Charges guide

Per unit incl. 2 persons and electricity	€ 17,00 - € 29,00
extra person	€ 2,00 - € 5,00
child (0-7 yrs)	free - € 3,00

Vauvert

Flower Camping Mas de Mourgues

Gallician, F-30600 Vauvert (Gard) T: **04 66 73 30 88**. E: **info@masdemourgues.com**

alanrogers.com/FR30040

John and Lynn Foster are proud of their campsite on the edge of the Petite Camargue region, a unique area of France. It can be hot here, the Mistral can blow and you may have some road noise, but having said all that, the present owners, who moved from England over ten years and live in the old Mas, have created quite a rural idyll and fit in well with the local community. There are 71 pitches with 46 for touring units (10A electricity), nine mobile homes to rent and four apartments. Originally a vineyard on stony ground (stong pegs needed), some of the vines are now used to mark the pitches, although many other varieties of trees and shrubs have been planted.

Facilities

Two small toilet blocks provide for all needs. Facilities for disabled visitors. Washing machine. Motorcaravan service point. Chips and panini to takeaway (high season). Reception keeps essentials and bottled water. Bread to order (evening before). Play area. Games for children once a week (July/Aug). Internet access and WiFi (charged). Communal barbecue but gas or electric ones are allowed. Apartments, mobile homes and tents to rent.
Off site: Fishing 2 km. (licence not required). Riding 8 km. Bicycle hire 1 km. Golf 20 km. Boat launching 25 km. Beach 26 km. Nîmes and Arles both within 30 minutes drive.

Open: 1 April - 30 September.

Directions

Leave A9 autoroute at exit 26 (Gallargues) and follow signs for Vauvert. At Vauvert take N572 towards Arles and St Gilles. Site is on left after 4 km. at crossroads for Gallician. GPS: 43.6575, 4.2943

Charges guide

Per unit incl. 2 persons and electricity	€ 13,50 - € 20,40
extra person	€ 3,00 - € 4,40
child (2-10 yrs)	€ 1,50 - € 2,20
dog	€ 1,90 - € 2,50

Verdun-en-Lauragais

Yelloh! Village le Bout du Monde

Ferme de Rhodes, Verdun-en-Lauragais, F-11400 Castelnaudary (Aude) T: **04 66 73 97 39**
E: **info@yellohvillage-leboutdumonde.com** **alanrogers.com/FR11230**

Le Bout du Monde can be found at the heart of the Montagne Noire, on the edge of the Haut Languedoc regional park. This small site is a member of the Yelloh! Village group and has 53 touring pitches with a further 27 pitches occupied by mobile homes. This is a very remote rural setting (hence the site's name!) with large, grassy pitches, a fishing lake and a stream rushing through the site. There is also a children's farm and riding stable. Farm produce is available for purchase.

Facilities

Shop. Restaurant (specialising in local cuisine). Takeaway. meals. Swimming pool. Fishing lake. Archery. Sports field. Children's farm. Bicycle hire. Riding. Entertainment and activity programme. Mobile homes for rent.
Off site: Multisports pitch. GR7 long-distance footpath. Haut Languedoc Regional Park. Sailing. Canoeing. 'Accrobranche' aerial assault course.

Open: 20 June - 14 September.

Directions

From the A61 take Castenaudary exit and proceed to Castelnaudary. Here, take the D103 towards Saissac. After passing through St Papoul, turn left to join the D803 to Verdun-en-Lauragais. Join the northbound D903 and site is well signed. GPS: 43.37671, 2.07463

Charges guide

Per unit incl. 2 persons and electricity	€ 17,00 - € 27,00
extra person (over 1 yr)	€ 4,00 - € 5,00

Vernet-les-Bains

Hotel de Plein Air l'Eau Vive

Chemin de Saint-Saturnin, F-66820 Vernet-les-Bains (Pyrénées-Orientales) T: **04 68 05 54 14**
E: **info@leau-vive.com** **alanrogers.com/FR66130**

Enjoying dramatic views of the Pic du Canigou (3,000 m), this small site is 1.5 km. from the centre of Vernet-les-Bains in the Pyrénées. It is approached via a twisting road through a residential area. The 70 tourist pitches, with electricity (4/10A) and 45 fully serviced, are on a slight slope, part hedged and some terraced, with a separate tent field. Most pitches have some shade. Although there is no swimming pool, the site has a very attractive, natural pool with water pumped from the nearby stream, with a small beach. There is a central floating safety line across the pool but parents should keep an eye on children around the pool as there is no supervision or safety fence.

Facilities

First class toilet facilities and provision for disabled people. Washing machine. Bread, main season. Bar/reception, pool table, library. Snack bar, takeaway (15/6-31/8). A 'meal of the day' can be ordered. Play area. Natural pool for children. Sports field. WiFi (free) on the terrace.
Off site: Fishing 200 m. Swimming pool, thermal centre in village 1 km. Organised rafting, canoeing, hydrospeed trips. Bicycle hire 2 km.

Open: 16 December - 25 October.

Directions

Following N116 towards Andorra. At Ville Franche, turn south, D116, for Vernet-les-Bains. After 5 km. keep right avoiding town. Turn right over bridge towards Sahorre. Immediately turn right (Ave de Saturnin) for about 1 km. beyond houses, site signed. GPS: 42.55506, 2.37779

Charges 2010

Per unit incl. 2 persons and electricity	€ 15,00 - € 22,00
extra person (over 4 yrs)	€ 2,50 - € 3,50
car on pitch	€ 3,00

Discounts for weekly stays.
Credit cards accepted 1/6-31/8 only.

Vers-Pont-du-Gard

Camping International des Gorges du Gardon

Chemin de la Barque Vieille, F-30210 Vers-Pont-du-Gard (Gard) T: **04 66 22 81 81**
E: **camping.international@wanadoo.fr** **alanrogers.com/FR30190**

Probably the main attraction in the Gardon area of France is the Pont-du-Gard, an amazing Roman aqueduct built around 50 AD. It provides 200 level, mostly good-sized pitches, 180 for touring. Many are on stony terraces in a woodland setting offering good shade while others are more open, all with electricity (10-15A). Rock pegs are essential. There is direct access to the river where swimming is permitted, although in summer the water level may be a little low. Attractive, heated swimming and paddling pools (unsupervised) provide an alternative. The owners, Joseph and Sylvie Gonzales speak a little English, and visitors will always receive a warm and friendly welcome. Joseph previously owned a restaurant and we highly recommend his site restaurant. Tourist information is in the reception (open all day) and Sylvie will share her local knowledge if you need any additional help. There are other attractions worthy of a visit, such as the medieval village of Castillon-du-Gard perched on a rocky peak with narrow cobbled streets, and Collias at the bottom of the gorge from where you can hire canoes.

Facilities

Two toilet blocks provide facilities for disabled visitors. Baby room. Washing machine, dishwashing and laundry sinks. Bar and good restaurant (table service and takeaway). Heated swimming, paddling pools (unsupervised). Play areas. Games room and TV. Organised family entertainment during July/Aug. Canoeing arranged. Off site: Many old towns and villages with colourful markets (Uzès Saturday 10 km). Historic cities of Nîmes and Avignon.

Open: 15 March - 31 October.

Directions

Exit A9 at Remoulins, then take D981 towards Uzès. About 4 km. after Remoulins, just after the junction for the Pont-du-Gard, turn left, site signed and follow signs to site (a few hundred metres).
GPS: 43.95744, 4.51503

Charges guide

Per unit incl. 2 persons	€ 12,50 - € 18,50
extra person	€ 4,00 - € 6,50
electricity	€ 3,20

Vias-Plage

Camping l'Air Marin

F-34450 Vias Plage (Hérault) T: **04 67 21 64 90**. E: **info@camping-air-marin.fr**
alanrogers.com/FR34530

A shaded haven, l'Air Marin is set back beside the Canal du Midi, away from the busy hectic centre of Vias Plage. This site exudes its own identity with distinctive sculptures and artwork all around, including decoratively tiled water points. The facilities are to one side and form the core of the site, attractively arranged overlooking the pool complex. Flowering shrubs separate the 150 pitches for chalets and mobile homes to let, while the 150 level grass places for touring units are more open among tall trees. All have 6A electricity. The site opens quite early in the season compared with some in the area, with all facilities also said to be open all season.

Facilities

Two fully equipped toilet blocks provide a baby bath and a unit for disabled people. Laundry facilities. Shop. Bar, restaurant and takeaway café. Pool complex with covered heated pool, larger outdoor one and paddling pool. Gym. Play area. Tennis (30/6-30/8). Multisport court. Playing field. Activities and entertainment in high season. Communal barbecues. Off site: Fishing (permission needed). Beach 800 m. Minigolf, riding, bicycle hire 300 m. Karting 500 m. Golf 10 km.

Open: 15 April - 15 September.

Directions

From the A9 autoroute exit 34, follow N312 towards Agde for about 9 km. Pick up the N112 direction Beziers and take next left for Vias-Plage. At tourist centre follow signs for Campings Est alongside the Canal du Midi to pick up site signs.
GPS: 43.30135, 3.42304

Charges guide

Per unit incl. 2 persons and electricity	€ 35,00
extra person	€ 7,00
child (under 4 yrs)	free

No credit cards.

Vias-Plage

Yelloh! Village le Club Farret

F-34450 Vias-Plage (Hérault) T: **04 67 21 64 45**

E: **info@yellohvillage-club-farret.com** **alanrogers.com/FR34110**

Well maintained and with welcoming, helpful staff, everywhere is neat and tidy. It is a large, busy site but the atmosphere is very relaxed. There are 710 good size, level, grassy pitches, with 340 for touring with 6A electricity. And there is some shade from many trees. The large heated pool has lots of sunbathing room. The safe beach is alongside the site so some pitches have sea views. There is a wide range of entertainments and the activities include an extensive art programme. The restaurant is high above the pool with views of the sea, everything is open all season. This superb site of excellent quality has been developed by the Giner family with love and care over the last 50 years. Activities include pottery, silk painting, mosaics and water colours. The mobile home areas are very smart and have been attractively landscaped, with African or Balinese themes. A new area for mobile homes is 'vehicle free'.

Facilities

Very clean toilet blocks, children's toilets, baby rooms, facilities for disabled visitors. Washing machines. Dog shower. Well stocked supermarket. Hairdresser. Bars with pizzas, snacks, takeaway. Restaurant. Heated swimming pool complex (now enlarged to 1000 sq.m) with lifeguard all season. Spa with sauna, jacuzzi etc. Excellent new play area. Miniclub (5-10 yrs). Teenagers' club (11-15 yrs). Tennis. Archery. Programme of games. Multisports court. Bicycle hire. Off site: Riding 1 km. Golf 10 km. Sailing and windsurfing on beach.

Open: 25 March - 25 September.

Directions

Site is south of Vias at Vias-Plage. From N112 (Béziers - Agde) take D137 signed Vias-Plage. Site is signed on the left. GPS: 43.29103, 3.41912

Charges 2010

Per unit incl. 2 persons and electricity	€ 19,00 - € 47,00
extra person	€ 6,00 - € 8,00
extra tent	€ 3,00
pet	€ 4,00

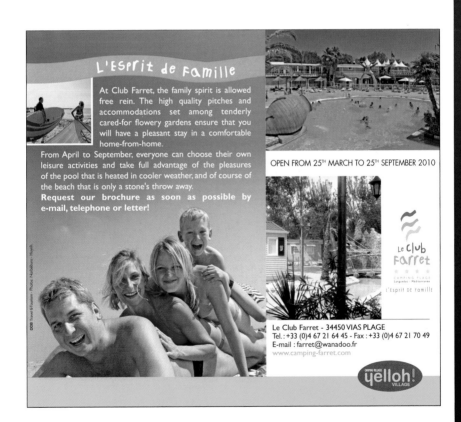

Vias-Plage

Camping les Salisses

Route de la Mer, F-34450 Vias-Plage (Hérault) T: **04 67 21 64 07**. E: **info@salisses.com**
alanrogers.com/FR34520

A traditional-style French campsite, Les Salisses is well run and managed with an impressive range of swimming pools and other facilities. The 400 plus level pitches of average size are separated by flowering shrubs and trees that provide shade – all rather pretty. There are just over 100 places for touring units with 8A electricity, the rest being taken by a range of mobile homes, some to let. Vias Plage is a busy, somewhat hectic resort and Les Salisses has its own section of beach with a bar. However, the site's own pools are also very welcoming, the indoor one reserved for naturists in the high season.

Facilities

Four fully equipped toilet blocks. Facilities for disabled visitors. Laundry. Shop. Bar and restaurant. Takeaway pizzeria (1/7-31/8). One indoor pool heated for low season used by naturists in high season, Two other pool complexes, one large pool for real swimming plus a long slide. Play area. Sports field (rugby posts). Multisport court. Tennis. Minigolf. Bicycle hire. Watersports at beach (800 m). Wide range of entertainment and activities. Off site: Riding 1 km. Golf 5 km. Bus stop for Vias town.

Open: 5 April - 13 September.

Directions

From the A9 take exit 34, then the N312 towards Vias and Agde. Join the N112 to avoid Vias town to pick up sign for Vias-Plage. Site is first on the right.
GPS: 43.29657, 3.41640

Charges guide

Per unit incl. 2 persons and electricity	€ 24,00 - € 36,00
extra person	€ 6,50 - € 8,50

Camping Cheques accepted.

Vias-sur-Mer

Camping le Méditerranée Plage

Côte Ouest, F-34450 Vias-sur-Mer (Hérault) T: **04 67 90 99 07**. E: **contact@mediterranee-plage.com**
alanrogers.com/FR34410

Set beside the beach in a quiet part of the coast, this site is somewhat different from the majority of beach sites. It has a most impressive entertainment complex situated to one side of the site with very comfortable outdoor seating facing a large stage for entertainment and a very smart bar and restaurant. The colourful furnishings and modern design reflect its Mediterranean setting. The site is very well cared for, with 410 pitches (some 185 used for touring units). Either grassy with a degree of shade or, as you get nearer the beach, more sandy with less shade, all have 6A electricity.

Facilities

Two large toilet blocks are modern, one very impressive with a special nursery unit. Two small ones are more traditional. Facilities for disabled visitors. Laundry. Motorcaravan service point. Smart restaurant and bar. Supermarket. Snack bar. Hairdressers. TV room. Play area. Games room. Tennis. Archery. Windsurfing possible from beach. Activity programme, children's entertainment, circus school, evening shows and dancing. Internet access. Off site: Riding 2 km. Canal du Midi. Luna Park at Vias.

Open: 22 March - 20 September.

Directions

From A9 exit 35 (Béziers Est) follow directions for Agde and Sète on N112. After 4.2 km. turn for Portiragnes. Pass village and continue for 2.5 km. over Canal du Midi then turn left and follow site signs.
GPS: 43.28202, 3.37105

Charges guide

Per unit incl. 2 persons and electricity	€ 16,50 - € 36,40
extra person	€ 3,00 - € 6,20

Vias-sur-Mer

Sunêlia Domaine de la Dragonnière

RN112, F-34450 Vias-sur-Mer (Hérault) T: **04 67 01 03 10**. E: **dragonniere@wanadoo.fr**
alanrogers.com/FR34450

La Dragonnière is a busy family site, located between the popular resorts of Vias and Portiragnes. There are no less than nine swimming pools here and a lively entertainment programme in high season. Many of the pitches are occupied by mobile homes and chalets but there are around 200 reasonably sized touring pitches, all offering some shade. The pitches all have electrical connections (6A) and many also offer water and drainage. La Dragonnière lies 5 km. from the nearest beach and a free shuttle operates in peak season. This is an ideal site for families with teenagers searching for a wide range of activities.

Facilities

Well maintained toilet blocks include facilities for babies and disabled people. Laundry. Supermarket. Two swimming pool complexes with children's pools. Bar and restaurant complex, with good range of meals. Play area. Sauna and gym. Tennis. Multisport pitch. Excursions reserved at reception. Sports competitions, children's club and evening entertainment in high season, including talent shows, regular discos and cabaret evenings. Mobile homes and chalets for rent. Off site: Nearest beach 5 km. (free shuttle in peak season). Fishing 4 km. Golf 12 km.

Open: 15 March - 6 October.

Directions

Take the Béziers Est exit from the A9 autoroute. Follow directions to Villenevue, Serignan and Valras-Plage. After 800 m. at the large roundabout, follow signs to Vias aéroport on the N112. After a further 7 km, the campsite can be found on the right.
GPS: 43.31300, 3.36517

Charges guide

Per unit incl. 3 persons, water, waste water and electricity	€ 19,00 - € 42,00
extra person	€ 6,00 - € 7,00

Camping Cheques accepted.

Villegly-en-Minervois

Camping le Moulin de Sainte Anne

Chemin de Sainte Anne, F-11600 Villegly-en-Minervois (Aude) T: **04 68 72 20 80**
E: **campingstanne@wanadoo.fr** **alanrogers.com/FR11210**

Just a few years ago le Moulin de Sainte Anne was a vineyard but, with much hard work by Antoine and Magali Laclive and the backing of the Mairie, there is now a flourishing campsite on the edge of the town. There are 45 level grass pitches of a good size and hedged. All have water and electricity and are terraced where necessary and landscaped with growing trees and shrubs. The facilities are modern, well kept and in keeping with the area. They include a heated pool and a very attractive entertainment area. There is close cooperation with the village and villagers are welcome to the evening entertainment. A 'Sites et Paysages' member.

Facilities

A modern toilet block is very well equipped. Shared facilities for disabled visitors and babies. Washing machine. Motorcaravan service point. Bar, snack bar with takeaway (15/6-25/8). Heated swimming and paddling pools (1/5-30/9). Games room. Play area. Communal barbecues only. Chalets to rent (15). Off site: Multisport pitch, tennis (free), fishing (licence from garage). Shops. Bus stop by bridge. Carcassonne 12 km. Golf 18 km. Bicycle hire 12 km.

Open: 1 March - 15 November.

Directions

Driving north from Carcassonne on D118 turn on D620 signed Villalier and Villegly for 7 km. Site is at entrance to village. Turn right over bridge just before the cemetery. GPS: 43.28308, 2.44152

Charges guide

Per person	€ 3,00 - € 4,40
child (under 13 yrs)	€ 1,90 - € 3,20
pitch incl. electricity	€ 6,20 - € 7,80

Villeneuve-les-Béziers

Camping les Berges du Canal

Promenade les Vernets, F-34420 Villeneuve-les-Béziers (Hérault) T: **04 67 39 36 09**
E: **contact@lesbergesducanal.com** **alanrogers.com/FR34210**

There are surprisingly few campsites which provide an opportunity to enjoy the rather special ambience for which the Canal du Midi is renowned, so we were really pleased to discover this delightful campsite right alongside the canal at Villeneuve-les-Béziers. The campsite has 75 level pitches on sandy grass of average size, mostly with 10A electricity, in a peaceful and shady situation, separated from the canal by an access road. There is a pleasant pool complex, one of the two pools being fitted with a jacuzzi-style facility, but there are no slides or toboggans thereby ensuring that it is relatively peaceful.

Facilities

A fully equipped toilet block has mainly British style WCs and some Turkish style, and some washbasins in cabins. Facilities for disabled visitors (with key) and children. Beauty therapist visits weekly. Laundry facilities. Motorcaravan service point. Two swimming pools. Bar/snack bar (serving breakfast too). Small restaurant attached to site. Evening entertainment during high season. Off site: Attractive old village centre of Villeneuve-les-Béziers. Beach at Portiragnes Plage. Riding 5 km. Canal du Midi.

Open: 15 April - 15 September.

Directions

From A9 exit 35, follow signs for Agde, at first roundabout take N112 (Béziers). First left onto the D37 signed Villeneve-les-Béziers and Valras-Plage. Pass traffic lights, left at roundabout and follow site signs (take care at junction beside bridge).
GPS: 43.31673, 3.28433

Charges guide

Per unit incl. 2 persons	€ 14,00 - € 19,00
incl. electricity	€ 16,00 - € 23,00
extra person	€ 2,50 - € 4,50

Villeneuve-lez-Avignon

Campéole Ile des Papes

Barrage de Villeneuve, F-30400 Villeneuve-lez-Avignon (Gard) T: **04 90 15 15 90**. E: **ile.papes@wanadoo.fr**
alanrogers.com/FR30120

Quite a new site, Camping Ile des Papes is large, open and very well equipped. Avignon and its Palace and museums are 8 km. away. The site has an extensive swimming pool area and a fishing lake with beautiful mature gardens. The railway is quite near but noise is not too intrusive. The 450 pitches are of a good size on level grass and all have electricity, 150 taken by mobile homes or chalets. Games and competitions for all ages are organised in high season.

Facilities

Toilet blocks of very good quality include baby rooms. Washing machines. Motorcaravan services. Well stocked shop (limited hours in low seasons). Bar and restaurant. Two large swimming pools and one for children. Play area. Lake for fishing. Archery, tennis, minigolf and basketball (all free). Bicycle hire. Off site: Riding 3 km.

Open: 25 March - 20 October.

Directions

From Avignon take N100 Nîmes road towards Bagnoles-sur-Cèze, after crossing Rhône turn right. Turn left along river bank, follow signs for Roquemaure (D980). After 6 km. turn right on D228, signed Barrage de Villeneuve, site is 1 km.
GPS: 43.97660, 4.79440

Charges guide

Per unit incl. 2 persons	€ 16,00 - € 23,00
extra person	€ 4,50 - € 6,30
electricity (6A)	€ 3,90

This is a corner of
France that evokes
dreamy images of la
afternoons amongst
sleepy village squares,
sunny vineyards and beautif
lavender fields basking under t
dazzling blue of the sky.
Alan
Rogers

DÉPARTEMENTS: 04 ALPES-DE-HAUTE-PROVENCE, 05 HAUTES-ALPES, 13 BOUCHES-DU-RHÔNE, 83 VAR, 84 VAUCLUSE

MAJOR CITY: MARSEILLES

Provence is a region of magical light, bleached landscapes, olive groves, herb-scented garrigue, vineyards and Roman and medieval antiquities. The river valleys provide natural routes through the mountain barrier. Roman monuments can be seen at Orange, and Vaison-la-Romaine, where a 2,000-year-old bridge is still in use. Avignon was the site of the papal court and the Palais des Papes at Avignon is a spectacular construction.

The Hautes-Alpes will reward with stunning vistas, peace and quiet. Briançon is the highest town in Europe and many of the high passes are not for the faint-hearted. The Vaucluse, where in the late spring the southern slopes of the Montagne du Luberon are a mass of colour with wild flowers. The extinct volcanic cone of Mont Ventoux provides dramatic views. The scents, colours and an amazing intensity of light have encouraged artists and writers to settle amidst the sleepy villages, with narrow streets and ancient dwellings topped with sun-baked terracotta tiles, where the air is fragrant with the perfume of wild herbs and lavender.

Places of interest

Avignon: ramparts, old city, Papal Palace, old palace, Calvet museum.

Mont Ventoux: near Carpentras, one of t best known stages of the classic Tour de France annual cycle race.

Orange: Roman city, gateway to the Mid Colline St Europe.

St Vaison la Romaine: Roman city, the French Pompei.

Cuisine of the region

Influenced by the Savoie area to the nort and the Côte d'Azur to the south, with emphasis on herbs and garlic, and fish. The wine region is mainly known for its fruity rosé wines: Bandol, Bellet, Palette, Cassis. Red wines include Côtes du Rhôn and Châteauneuf-du-Pape.

Aigo Bouido: garlic and sage soup with bread (or eggs and cheese).

Aïoli (ailloli): a mayonnaise sauce with ga and olive oil.

Bouillabaisse: fish soup served with rouill sauce, saffron and aioli.

Bourride: a creamy fish soup (usually ma with large white fish), thickened with aïc and flavoured with crawfish.

Pissaladière: Provencal bread dough with onions, anchovies, olives.

Pollo pépitora: Provencal chicken fricasse thickened with lemon-flavoured mayonnaise.

Ratatouille: aubergines, courgettes, onio garlic, red peppers and tomatoes in olive

www.discover-southoffrance.com
information@cft-paca.fr
(0)4 91 56 47 00

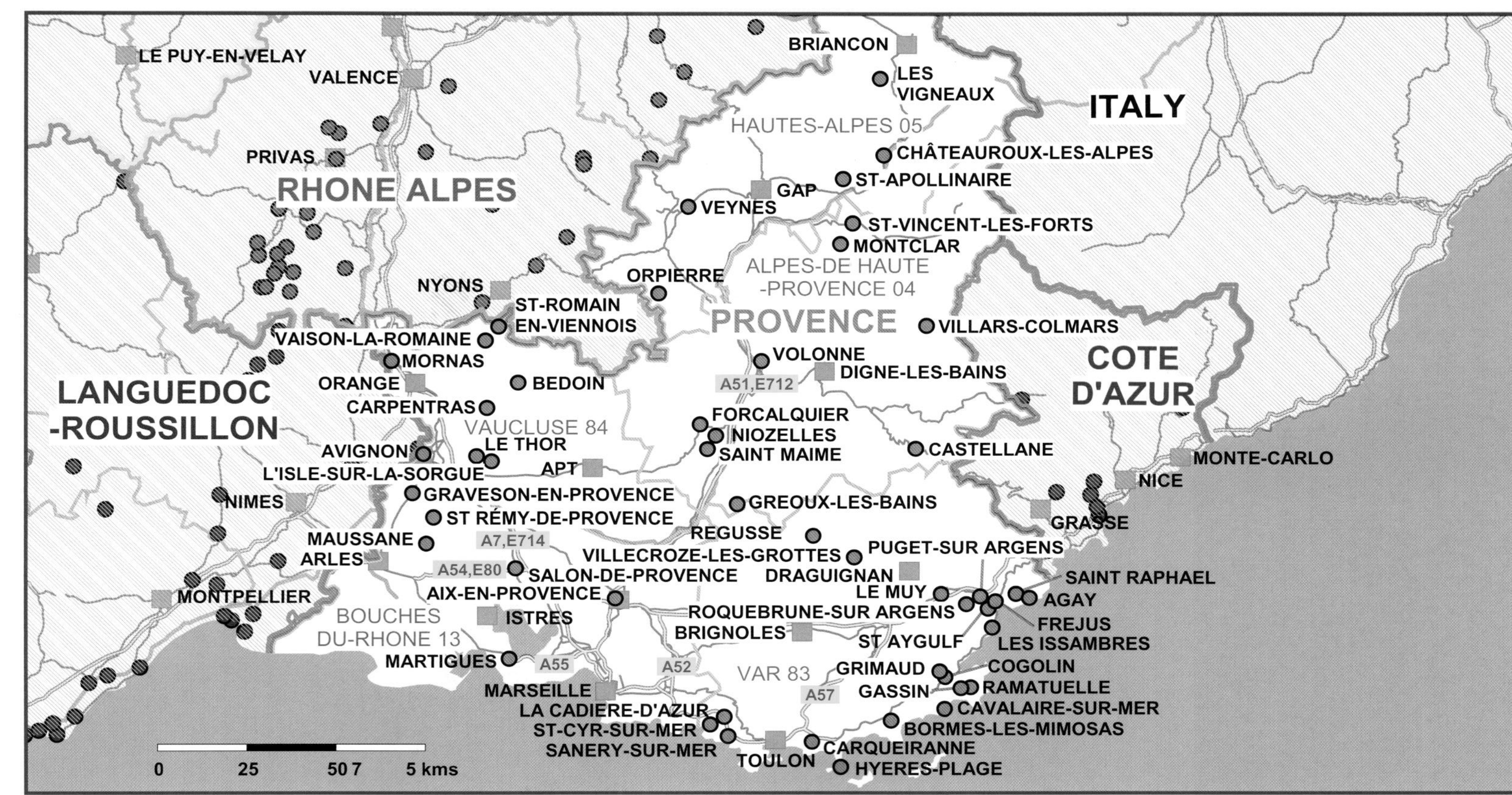
LE PUY-EN-VELAY
VALENCE
PRIVAS
RHONE ALPES
BRIANCON
LES
VIGNEAUX
ITALY
HAUTES-ALPES 05
CHÂTEAUROUX-LES-ALPES
ST-APOLLINAIRE
GAP
VEYNES
ST-VINCENT-LES-FORTS
MONTCLAR
ORPIERRE
ALPES-DE HAUTE
-PROVENCE 04
NYONS
ST-ROMAIN
EN-VIENNOIS
PROVENCE
VILLARS-COLMARS
VAISON-LA-ROMAINE
MORNAS
VOLONNE
DIGNE-LES-BAINS
COTE
D'AZUR
LANGUEDOC
-ROUSSILLON
ORANGE
BEDOIN
A51,E712
CARPENTRAS
VAUCLUSE 84
FORCALQUIER
NIOZELLES
SAINT MAIME
AVIGNON
LE THOR
CASTELLANE
MONTE-CARLO
APT
L'ISLE-SUR-LA-SORGUE
NICE
GRAVESON-EN-PROVENCE
NIMES
GREOUX-LES-BAINS
ST RÉMY-DE-PROVENCE
GRASSE
REGUSSE
MAUSSANE
A7,E714
PUGET-SUR ARGENS
VILLECROZE-LES-GROTTES
ARLES
A54,E80
SALON-DE-PROVENCE
DRAGUIGNAN
SAINT RAPHAEL
LE MUY
AIX-EN-PROVENCE
AGAY
MONTPELLIER
ROQUEBRUNE-SUR ARGENS
BOUCHES
DU-RHONE 13
ISTRES
FREJUS
BRIGNOLES
ST AYGULF
LES ISSAMBRES
MARTIGUES
A55
A52
GRIMAUD
COGOLIN
VAR 83
MARSEILLE
GASSIN
RAMATUELLE
A57
LA CADIERE-D'AZUR
CAVALAIRE-SUR-MER
ST-CYR-SUR-MER
BORMES-LES-MIMOSAS
SANERY-SUR-MER
CARQUEIRANNE
TOULON
HYERES-PLAGE
0
25
50 7
5 kms

Agay

Camping Caravaning Esterel

Avenue des Golf, Agay, F-83530 Saint Raphaël (Var) T: **04 94 82 03 28**
E: **contact@esterel-caravaning.fr** **alanrogers.com/FR83020**

Esterel is a quality caravan site east of St Raphaël, set among the hills at the back of Agay. The site is 3.5 km. from the sandy beach at Agay where parking is perhaps a little easier than at most places on this coast. It has 230 pitches for tourers, for caravans but not tents, all have electricity and water tap, 18 special ones have their own en-suite washroom adjoining. Pitches are on shallow terraces, attractively landscaped with good shade and a variety of flowers, giving a feeling of spaciousness. Some 'maxi-pitches' from 110 to 160 sq.m. are available with 10A electricity. Developed by the Laroche family for over 30 years, the site has an attractive, quiet situation with good views of the Esterel mountains. Wild boar occasionally come to the perimeter fence to be fed by visitors. This is a very good site, well run and organised in a deservedly popular area. A pleasant courtyard area contains the shop and bar, with a terrace overlooking the attractively landscaped (floodlit at night) pool complex.

Facilities

Excellent refurbished, heated toilet blocks. Individual toilet units on 18 pitches. Facilities for disabled people. Laundry room. Motorcaravan services. Shop. Gift shop. Takeaway. Bar/restaurant. Five circular swimming pools (two heated), one for adults, one for children (now covered and heated), three arranged as a waterfall (all season). Spa with sauna etc. Disco. Archery. Minigolf. Tennis. Pony rides. Pétanque. Squash. Playground. Nursery. Bicycle hire. Internet access. Organised events in season. No barbecues. Off site: Golf nearby. Trekking in Esterel forest park. Fishing, beach 3 km.

Open: 27 March - 2 October.

Directions

From A8, exit Fréjus, follow signs for Valescure, then for Agay, site on left. The road from Agay is the easiest to follow but it is possible to approach from St Raphaël via Valescure. GPS: 43.45378, 6.83275

Charges guide

Per unit incl. 2 persons and electricity	€ 18,00 - € 60,00
extra person	€ 9,00
child (1-7 yrs)	€ 7,00
dog	€ 2,00

Aix-en-Provence

Camping Chantecler

41 avenue du Val Saint André, F-13100 Aix-en-Provence (Bouches du Rhône) T: **04 42 26 12 98**
E: **info@campingchantecler.com** **alanrogers.com/FR13120**

Cézanne is amongst Aix's most famous former residents, but many just see the town as a stop on the journey south. This good, quiet campsite might change that image; on the southeast edge of the town, close to the motorway it is only minutes by the good bus service from the city centre. The site provides 240 pitches (160 for tourers) in mature woodland with good facilities. Under the new leadership of Serge Carcolse, the site is destined to change for the good whilst retaining the best that already exists. Cézanne's studio is amongst the numerous places to visit in Aix. The town has something to offer everyone, from modern pedestrian shopping to numerous museums and cultural sites and endless restaurants and bars. The Office du Tourism also arranges a variety of excursions on a weekly basis to the surrounding area, ranging from bird sanctuaries in the Camargue to Marseille and the Luberon.

Facilities

Four sanitary blocks provide ample WCs, washbasins and hot showers around the site. Facilities for disabled campers. Motorcaravan service point. Bar and restaurant (1/5-15/9). Swimming pool (1/5-15/9). Tennis. Boules. Internet access and WiFi. Barbecues are not permitted. Twin-axle units are not accepted. Mobile homes to rent. Off site: Bus service 200 m. Aix-en-Provence 2 km. Riding 2 km. Golf 5 km.

Open: All year.

Directions

Leave the A8 at exit 31 (Aix-Sud) and at roundabout turn right. At second set of lights turn left and within 300 m. at roundabout turn right to the site in 200 m. GPS: 43.51636, 5.47495

Charges guide

Per unit incl. 2 persons, electricity	€ 22,90 - € 24,20
extra person	€ 6,10 - € 6,50
child (under 7 yrs)	€ 3,60 - € 3,70

Avignon

Camping du Pont d'Avignon

10 chemin de la Barthelasse, Ile de la Barthelasse, F-84000 Avignon (Vaucluse) T: **04 90 80 63 50**
E: **info@camping-avignon.com** **alanrogers.com/FR84090**

This is a city site, yet it is in a quiet location and only a short walk or free ferry ride from the town. The well shaded and neat layout of the pitches and the very good access will ensure a pleasant stay. There are 300 level pitches, some on grass and some with hardstanding. 120 with 10A electricity. A good play area, tennis courts and volleyball pitch are in the centre of the site separating the tent pitches on one side and the electric pitches on the other. Many pitches are separated by hedges. The restaurant, bar and terrace overlook the attractive pool.

Facilities

Well maintained and clean toilet blocks, facilities for disabled visitors. Washing machines, dryer. Motorcaravan services. Well stocked shop (4/4-3/10). Bar/restaurant, takeaway (4/4-20/9). Swimming pool, paddling pool (2/5-20/9). Play area with climbing frame. Tennis (free). Bicycle hire (July/Aug). Internet access and WiFi (charged). Off site: Avignon with famous bridge and Pope's Palace. Ferry to town centre. Bicycle hire 2 km. Riding 3 km. Golf 10 km.

Open: 16 March - 1 November.

Directions

Site is on an island in River Rhône. Well signed from roads into Avignon, ring road has complex junctions. Accessed from Pont Daladier towards Villeneuve les Avignon. Just after crossing first section of river fork right, site signed, site about 1 km.
GPS: 43.95153, 4.80193

Charges guide

Per unit incl. 2 persons and electricity	€ 16,82 - € 26,72
extra person	€ 3,41 - € 4,86
child (3-12 yrs)	free - € 4,30

Camping Cheques accepted.

Carpentras

Flower Camping Lou Comtadou

881 avenue Pierre de Coubertin, F-84200 Carpentras (Vaucluse) T: **04 90 67 03 16**
E: **info@loucomtadou.com** **alanrogers.com/FR84180**

Lou Comtadou can be found 20 km. from Avignon at the foot of the Mont Ventoux. This is an area which is often considered to be the gateway to Provence. It is also a region of fine cuisine, lavender fields and wonderful sunlight, which has always attracted artists to this corner of the region. Lou Comtadou is open for a long season and has 100 pitches, some of which are occupied by mobile homes and fully equipped tents for rent. Pitches are grassy and generally well shaded. All are equipped with electricity (6A).

Facilities

Bar. Snack bar. Takeaway. Shop. TV room. Motorcaravan services. Playground. Mobile homes and equipped tents for rent. Off site: Tennis. Swimming pool. Shops, cafés and restaurants in Carpentras. Avignon 20 km. Mont Ventoux.

Open: 1 March - 31 October.

Directions

Approaching from the north, leave the A7 at exit 22 (Orange Sud) and follow signs to Carpentras on D907 and D950. Upon arrival in Carpentras follow signs to St Didier and then Complexe Sportif. The site forms part of this complex. GPS: 44.04379, 5.05363

Charges guide

Per unit incl. 2 persons and electricity	€ 17,50 - € 24,50
extra person	€ 5,50 - € 6,90
child (2-7 yrs)	€ 3,00 - € 4,00

Carqueiranne

Flower Camping le Beau Vezé

Route de la Moutonne, F-83320 Carqueiranne (Var) T: **04 94 57 65 30**
E: **info@camping-beauveze.com** **alanrogers.com/FR83130**

Le Beau Vezé is a quiet site, some way inland from the busy resort of Hyères. The owner tries to keep it as a family site with its quiet position, although the superb beaches and hectic coastal areas are within easy reach. On a steep hillside it has terraced pitches and a plateau with more pitches on the top. The 150 pitches are well shaded but some will be rather difficult to manoeuvre onto due to overhanging trees and could be a problem for motorcaravans. There is some road noise on the lower pitches.

Facilities

Reasonable standard sanitary blocks, two heated, although maintenance may be variable. Some showers with washbasin. Baby room. Washing machines. Bar/restaurant, takeaway. Bread. Medium sized pool, paddling pool. Play area. Minigolf, boules and tennis. Bicycle hire. Jet-ski hire. Walking tours, visits to vineyard. Evening entertainment in restaurant. Off site: Golf 2 km. Fishing 3 km. Riding 5 km. The lovely old town of Hyères is only 8 km.

Open: 15 May - 15 September.

Directions

From A57 take exit for Toulon Est and follow D559 between Carqueiranne and Le Pradet. Take D76 northwards signed La Moutonne and site is signed on right of D76. GPS: 43.11413, 6.05640

Charges guide

Per unit incl. 2 persons	€ 21,50 - € 27,00
extra person	€ 5,50 - € 6,30
electricity (6A)	€ 4,00

No credit cards. Camping Cheques accepted.

Bormes-les-Mimosas

Camp du Domaine

B.P. 207 La Favière, F-83230 Bormes-les-Mimosas (Var) T: **04 94 71 03 12**. E: **mail@campdudomaine.com**

alanrogers.com/FR83120

Camp du Domaine, 3 km. south of Le Lavandou, is a large, attractive beach-side site with 1,200 pitches set in 45 hectares of pinewood, although surprisingly it does not give the impression of being so big. The pitches are large (up to 200 sq.m) and most are reasonably level, 800 with 10A electricity. The most popular pitches are beside the beach, but the ones furthest away are generally larger and have more shade. Amongst the trees, many are more suitable for tents. The price for all the pitches is the same – smaller but near the beach or larger with shade. The beach is the attraction however and everyone tries to get close. American motorhomes are not accepted. Despite its size, the site does not feel too being busy, except perhaps around the supermarket. This is mainly because many pitches are hidden in the trees, the access roads are quite wide and it all covers quite a large area (some of the beach pitches are 600 m. from the entrance). Its popularity makes early reservation necessary over a long season (about mid June to mid September) as regular clients book from season to season. English is spoken.

Facilities

Ten modern, well used but clean toilet blocks. Mostly Turkish WCs. Facilities for disabled visitors (but steep steps). Baby room. Washing machines. Fridge hire. Well stocked supermarket, bars, pizzeria (all open all season). No swimming pool. Excellent play area. Boats, pedaloes for hire. Wide range of watersports. Games, competitions (July/Aug). Children's club. Tennis. Multisport courts. Barbecues are strictly forbidden. Dogs are not accepted 3/7-31/8. Off site: Bicycle hire 500 m. Riding or golf 15 km.

Open: 27 March - 31 October.

Directions

Just outside and to west of Le Lavandou, at roundabout, turn off D559 towards the sea on road signed Favière. After 2 km. turn left at site signs. GPS: 43.11779, 6.35176

Charges 2010

Per unit incl. 2 persons and electricity	€ 27,00 - € 39,00
extra person	€ 5,60 - € 8,50
child (under 7 yrs)	€ 1,00 - € 4,50

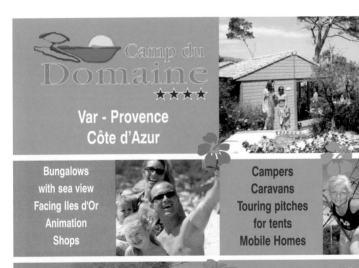

Castellane

496

Castel Camping le Domaine du Verdon

Camp du Verdon, F-04120 Castellane (Alpes-de-Haute-Provence) T: **04 92 83 61 29**
E: **contact@camp-du-verdon.com** **alanrogers.com/FR04020**

Close to the 'Route des Alpes' and the Gorges du Verdon. Two heated swimming pools and numerous on-site activities during high season help to keep non-canoeists here. Du Verdon is a large level site, part meadow, part wooded, with 500 partly shaded, rather stony pitches (390 for tourists). Numbered and separated by bushes, they vary in size, have 6A electricity, and 125 also have water and waste water. They are mostly separate from the mobile homes (60) and pitches used by tour operators (110). Some overlook the unfenced river Verdon, so watch the children. This is a very popular holiday area, the gorge, canoeing and rafting being the main attractions, ideal for active families. One can walk to Castellane without using the main road. Dances and discos in July and August suit all age groups.The latest finishing time is around 23.00, after which time patrols make sure that the site is quiet. The site is popular and very busy in July and August.

Facilities

Refurbished toilet blocks include facilities for disabled visitors. Washing machines. Motorcaravan services. Restaurant, terrace, log fire for cooler evenings. New supermarket. Pizzeria/crêperie. Takeaway. Heated swimming pools, paddling pool with 'mushroom' fountain). Organised entertainment (July/Aug). Play areas. Minigolf. Archery. Organised walks. Bicycle hire. Riding. Small fishing lake. ATM. Room for games and TV. Internet access and WiFi. Off site: Castellane and the Verdon Gorge 1 km. Riding 2 km. Boat launching 4.5 km. Golf 20 km. Water sports.

Open: 15 May - 15 September.

Directions

From Castellane take D952 westwards towards Gorges du Verdon and Moustiers. Site is 1 km. on left.
GPS: 43.83921, 6.49396

Charges guide

Per unit incl. 2 or 3 persons	€ 20,00 - € 33,00
incl. electricity	€ 25,00 - € 41,00
extra person (over 3 yrs)	€ 8,00 - € 13,00
dog	€ 3,00

Camping Cheques accepted.

Castellane

RCN les Collines de Castellane

Route de Grasse, F-04120 Castellane (Alpes-de-Haute-Provence) T: **04 92 83 68 96**
E: **info@rcn-lescollinesdecastellane.fr** **alanrogers.com/FR04040**

RCN, a Dutch company, runs a chain of good campsites in the Netherlands. They now operate six sites in France, all with Dutch managers who speak good French and English. Les Collines de Castellane is pleasantly situated in the mountainous landscape of the Alpes-de-Haute-Provence. There are 160 touring pitches spread over a series of flat terraces under umbrella pines with electric tricycles provided for transport up and down the quite steep pathways. At the top of the site, near the entrance, is a combined reception and small restaurant area. The adjoining swimming pool is quite large and offers a water slide and a paddling pool for small children.

Facilities

Tiled, modern toilet facilities include individual cabins and facilities for disabled visitors and babies. Washing machines, dryers and ironing area. Shop. Library. Small restaurant (including takeaway) with terrace. Heated swimming pool with slides and paddling pool. Tennis court. Boules. Three play areas. Organised activities (May-Sept). Off site: Golf 10 km.

Open: 22 April - 22 September.

Directions

Take the N85 (Route Napoléon) from Digné-les-Bains towards Castellane and Grasse. Site is 6 km. south of Castellane, on the right hand side of the road.
GPS: 43.82423, 6.57296

Charges guide

Per unit incl. 2 persons, electricity and water	€ 18,00 - € 45,50
incl. up to 6 persons	€ 23,40 - € 46,00
dog	€ 4,00

Castellane

Kawan Village International

www.kawan-villages.com

Route Napoléon, F-04120 Castellane (Alpes-de-Haute-Provence) T: **04 92 83 66 67**
E: **info@camping-international.fr** **alanrogers.com/FR04100**

Camping International has very friendly, English speaking owners and is a reasonably priced, less commercialised site situated in some of the most dramatic scenery in France. The 274 pitches, 130 good sized ones for touring, are clearly marked, separated by trees and small hedges, and all have electricity and water. The bar/restaurant overlooks the swimming pool with its sunbathing area set in a sunny location, and all have fantastic views. In high season English-speaking young people entertain children (3-8 years) and teenagers. Access is good for larger units.

Facilities

Small toilet blocks are of an older design. One newer block has modern facilities, including those for disabled visitors. Washing machines and dryer. Motorcaravan services. Fridge hire. Shop. Restaurant/takeaway (May-Sept). Swimming pool (1/5-30/9). Club/TV room. Children's entertainment, occasional evening entertainment (July/Aug). Play area. Boules. Internet access. Free WiFi. Off site: Riding 800 m. Castellane 1.5 km. with river, canyon and rapids, ideal for canoeing, rafting and canyoning etc.

Open: 31 March - 1 October.

Directions

Site is 1 km. north of Castellane on the N85 'Route Napoléon'. GPS: 43.85897, 6.49837

Charges guide

Per unit incl. 2 persons and electricity	€ 18,00 - € 23,50
extra person	€ 3,00 - € 4,50
dog	€ 2,00

Camping Cheques accepted.

Grimaud

Camping de la Plage

RD559, F-83310 Grimaud (Var) T: **04 94 56 31 15**. E: **campingplagegrimaud@wanadoo.fr**
alanrogers.com/FR83100

A site on the beach is always in great demand, and Camping de la Plage is no exception, consequently it becomes very crowded. With 450 pitches, the site is divided into two parts by the N98 although a dangerous crossing is avoided by an underpass. The pitches in the area away from the beach will be the more peaceful and have more shade as they are in light woodland. They are mostly of a good size. In the area over the road there is more grass. There is some traffic noise on the pitches close to the busy road. All pitches have electricity (4-10A) but long leads may be required.

Facilities

Six toilet blocks of varying quality but well equipped and clean. Baby bath. Facilities for disabled visitors. Motorcaravan services. Large supermarket (all season). Bar, restaurant, takeaway (all season). Tennis. Small play area. Bicycle hire. Fridge rental. Charcoal barbecues are not permitted. Off site: Golf and riding 3 km. Boat hire nearby.

Open: One week before Easter - 12 October.

Directions

Site is on N98 main coast road about 6 km. southwest of Ste Maxime. Take care – this road is very busy in main season. GPS: 43.2819, 6.5859

Charges guide

Per unit incl. 2 persons and electricity	€ 27,00 - € 38,50
extra person	€ 6,30 - € 7,40
child (under 7 yrs)	€ 3,10 - € 3,60

Cavalaire-sur-Mer

Kawan Village Cros de Mouton

494

B.P. 116, F-83240 Cavalaire-sur-Mer (Var) T: **04 94 64 10 87**

E: **campingcrosdemouton@wanadoo.fr** **alanrogers.com/FR83220**

Cros de Mouton is a reasonably priced campsite in a popular area. High on a steep hillside, about 2 km. from Cavalaire and its popular beaches, the site is a calm oasis away from the coast. There are stunning views of the bay but, due to the nature of the terrain, some of the site roads are very steep – the higher pitches with the best views are especially so. There are 199 large, terraced pitches (electricity 10A) under cork trees with 73 suitable only for tents with parking close by, and 80 for touring caravans. English is spoken by the welcoming and helpful owners. The terrace of the restaurant and the pool area share the wonderful view of Cavalaire and the bay. Olivier and Andre are happy to take your caravan up with their 4 x 4 Jeep if you are worried.

Facilities

Clean, well maintained toilet blocks have all the usual facilities including those for disabled customers (although site is perhaps a little steep in places for wheelchairs). Washing machine. Shop. Bar/restaurant with reasonably priced meals and takeaway. Swimming and paddling pools with many sunbeds on the terrace and small bar for snacks and cold drinks. Small play area. Games room.
Off site: Beach 1.5 km. Bicycle hire 1.5 km. Riding 3 km. Golf 15 km.

Open: 15 March - 9 November.

Directions

Take the D559 to Cavalaire-sur-Mer (not Cavalière 4 km. away). Site is about 1.5 km. north of the town, very well signed from the centre.
GPS: 43.18247, 6.5161

Charges guide

Per unit incl. 2 persons and electricity	€ 24,00 - € 29,10
extra person	€ 6,50 - € 8,20
child (under 7 yrs)	€ 4,10 - € 4,50
dog	free - € 2,00

Camping Cheques accepted.

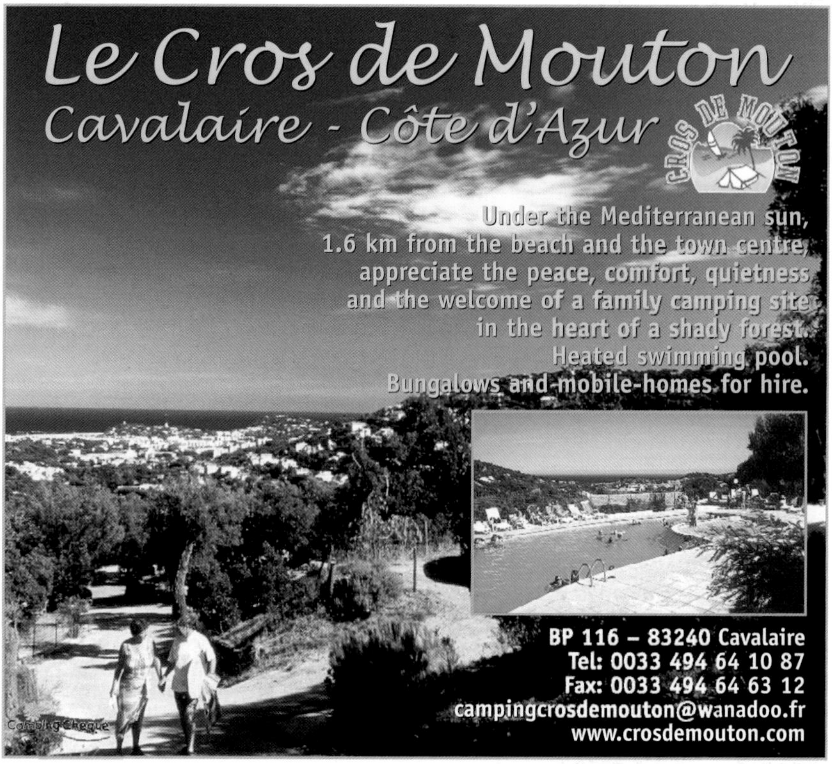

Cavalaire-sur-Mer

Camping Bonporteau

B.P. 18 (RD559), F-83240 Cavalaire-sur-Mer (Var) T: **04 94 64 03 24**. E: **contact@bonporteau.fr**

alanrogers.com/FR83340

This terraced site is situated northeast of and above the pleasant and popular holiday resort of Cavalaire where there is a harbour, restaurants and shops. A long, sandy beach runs right round the bay and there are plenty of watersport activities nearby. The site is only 200 metres from the beach, very well positioned for a family holiday, and only a short walk from a very good hypermarket. The 170 individual touring pitches are on sloping, sandy ground with terracing and good access roads, and all have electricity hook-ups (10A). The remaining 70 pitches are used for mobile homes and chalets.

Facilities

Three main toilet blocks are modern and include washbasins in cabins, Toilets are mainly British style. Launderette. Small shop. Small but attractive, restaurant (1/4-30/9). Bar. Takeaway. Entertainment with dance evenings. Swimming pool with terrace (15/3-30/9) and small paddling pool. Playground. Table tennis. TV and games room.
Off site: Beach 200 m. Bicycle hire 800 m. Riding 2 km. Golf 20 km.

Open: 15 March - 15 October.

Directions

Take D559 to Cavalaire-sur-Mer (not Cavalière, some 4 km. away). Site is signed by yellow signs from the main road before entering the town.
GPS: 43.16681, 6.51953

Charges guide

Per unit incl. 1-3 persons	€ 19,00 - € 41,50
extra person	€ 5,00 - € 9,00
child	€ 2,50 - € 4,50
dog	€ 2,70 - € 4,50

Weekly bookings only 28/6-22/8.

Châteauroux-les-Alpes

Camping les Cariamas

Fontmolines, F-05380 Châteauroux-les-Alpes (Hautes-Alpes) T: **04 92 43 22 63**. E: **p.tim@free.fr**

alanrogers.com/FR05070

Set 1,000 metres up in the stunning scenery of the Alps, Les Cariamas is at the gateway to Ecrin National Park and within easy reach of the Serre-Ponçon lake and the Rabioux-Durance river. Of the 150 pitches, 120 are for touring and all have electrical connections (6-10A), are pleasantly shaded and many offer beautiful views of the surrounding countryside. There are some mobile homes and chalets to rent. Amenities on the site include an outdoor heated swimming pool.

Facilities

Sanitary facilities include washbasins in cabins and hot showers. No failities for disabled visitors. Laundry. Small shop and takeaway (from 1/5). Communal barbecue area. Swimming pool (1/5-30/9). Play area. Mountain bike hire. Fishing. Off site: Riding 15 km. Canoeing, climbing, hiking, mountain biking and rafting. Tennis.

Open: 1 April - 31 October.

Directions

From Gap follow signs to Embrun Briançon. Take turning for Châteauroux-les-Alpes at first roundabout after Embrun. Shortly (800 m.) before the village turn right and follow signs to site.
GPS: 44.58981, 6.511294

Charges 2010

Per unit incl. 2 persons and electricity	€ 19,75
extra person	€ 5,25
child (under 6 yrs)	€ 2,50
dog	€ 3,00

Cogolin

Camping l'Argentière

Chemin de l'Argentiere (D48), F-83310 Cogolin (Var) T: **04 94 54 63 63**. E: **campinglargentiere@wanadoo.fr**
alanrogers.com/FR83310

This little jewel of a site is in a pleasant setting and the intervening wooded area seems to give it sufficient screening to make the campsite itself quite peaceful. It is only 5 km. from the beach at Gogolin or St Tropez, so its position is handy for one of the showplaces of the Riviera, but away from the hustle and bustle of the beach resorts. There are 150 good sized touring pitches (out of 238 with the others used for mobile homes to rent). All have electricity although long leads may be necessary. The site is very well maintained.

Facilities

Two of three toilet blocks are near the touring pitches and are well kept and clean. Washbasins have warm water (some in cabins). Washing machines (near site entrance). Water has to be taken from the sanitary block. Fridge hire. Shop (1/6-30/9). Bar (1/6-30/9). Restaurant (15/6-15/9) and takeaway (15/6-31/8). Large swimming pool (15/5-30/9). Play equipment. Bicycle hire. Barbecues are only permitted on a communal area. Off site: Shops close. Riding 2 km. Fishing 4 km. Golf 6 km. Beach 5 km.

Open: 1 April - 30 September.

Directions

From the A8 (Aix en Provence - Cannes) take exit 36 (Le Muy), then, D25 to Ste Maxime and the coast road N98 towards St Tropez. After Grimaud keep following signs for Cogolin. When near that village follow D48 towards St Maur-en-Collobrière, then signs to site in the suburb of L'Argentière.
GPS: 43.256083, 6.5124

Charges guide

Per unit incl. 2 persons and electricity	€ 16,00 - € 35,00
extra person	€ 3,00 - € 4,00
child (under 7 yrs)	€ 1,50 - € 2,50
dog	€ 2,00 - € 4,00

Forcalquier

Camping Indigo Forcalquier

Route de Sigonce, F-04300 Forcalquier (Alpes-de-Haute-Provence) T: **04 92 75 27 94**
E: **forcalquier@camping-indigo.com** **alanrogers.com/FR04120**

Although Camping Indigo is an urban site, there are extensive views over the surrounding countryside where there are some excellent walks. The pitches are on grass and are of good size, all with electricity, six fully serviced. The site is secure, with an electronic barrier (card deposit required) and there is no entry between 22.30 and 07.00. Local guides lead tours of the historic town and areas. This is an excellent base for visiting Forcalquier, a 15th century fortified hill town and the Monday market (the best in Haute-Provence). Since this site was acquired by new owners, an extensive modernisation programme has been put into effect.

Facilities

Two refurbished toilet blocks with washbasins in cubicles and excellent facilities for disabled visitors. They are cleaned twice daily. Bar. Snack bar and takeaway (1/7-1/9). Play area. Heated swimming and paddling pools. Off site: All shops, banks etc. in town centre 200 m.

Open: 2 April - 17 October.

Directions

From town centre, follow signs for Digne, Sisteron for 400 m, turning sharp left onto Sigonce road after Esso petrol station, then first right and site is 200 m. on the right. Well signed from town.
GPS: 43.96206, 5.78743

Charges guide

Per unit with 2 persons and electricity	€ 18,40 - € 27,40
extra person	€ 4,80 - € 5,80
child (2-7 yrs)	€ 3,10 - € 3,90
dog	€ 3,00 - € 4,00

Fréjus

Camping Caravaning les Pins Parasols

3360 rue des Combattants d'Afrique du Nord, F-83600 Fréjus (Var) T: **04 94 40 88 43**
E: **lespinsparasols@wanadoo.fr** **alanrogers.com/FR83010**

Not everyone likes very big sites and Les Pins Parasols with its 189 pitches is of a comfortable size which is quite easy to walk around. It is family owned and run. Although on very slightly undulating ground, virtually all the pitches (all have electricity) are levelled or terraced and separated by hedges or bushes with pine trees for shade. There are 48 pitches equipped with their own fully-enclosed sanitary unit, with WC, washbasin, hot shower and dishwashing sink. These pitches naturally cost more but may well be of interest to those seeking a little bit of extra comfort. The nearest beach is the once very long Fréjus-Plage (5.5 km) now reduced a little by the new marina, and adjoins St Raphaël. The site is used by tour operators (10%).

Facilities

Average quality toilet blocks (one heated) providing facilities for disabled people. Small shop with reasonable stocks, restaurant, takeaway (both 15/4-20/9). General room, TV. Swimming pool, attractive rock backdrop, separate long slide with landing pool, small paddling pool (heated). Half-court tennis. Off site: Bicycle hire or riding 2 km. Fishing 6 km. Golf 10 km. Bus from the gate into Fréjus 5 km. Beach 6 km.

Open: 3 April - 25 September.

Directions

From A8 take exit 38 for Fréjus Est. Turn right immediately on leaving pay booths on a small road which leads across to D4, then right again and under 1 km. to site. GPS: 43.46290, 6.72570

Charges guide

Per unit incl. 2 persons and electricity	€ 18,00 - € 27,30
pitch with sanitary unit	€ 22,70 - € 34,00
extra person	€ 4,50 - € 6,35
child (under 7 yrs)	€ 3,00 - € 3,85

Fréjus

La Pierre Verte Camping Village

Route de Bagnols-en-Forêt, F-83600 Fréjus (Var) T: **04 94 40 88 30**. E: **info@campinglapierreverte.com**
alanrogers.com/FR83360

This attractive, terraced site, set on a hillside under umbrella pines, has been gradually and thoughtfully developed. The genuine, friendly welcome means many families return year upon year, bringing in turn new generations. The site is divided into terraces, each with its own toilet block. The 200 generously sized pitches for touring units enjoy good shade from trees and have electricity (6A). There are 350 mobile homes in separate areas. For those seeking to 'get away from it all' in an area of outstanding natural beauty, there can be few more tranquil sites, but the many beaches, watersports and excursions the Gulf of St Tropez has to offer can also be enjoyed. For those staying on site, there are two large swimming pools (one heated), with large sunbathing areas and exciting water slides. Not far away, some exhilarating hang-gliding and parascending can be enjoyed.

Facilities

Five toilet blocks with mostly British style WCs and washbasins in cubicles are extremely clean and accessible from all levels. Baby bath. Laundry facilities. Bread available each morning. Bar with reasonably priced takeaway service. One heated (15 x 15 m) and one unheated swimming pool (25 x 15 m) and paddling pool. Play area Boules. Games room. Fridge and Bicycle hire. Entertainment and activities in high season. Barbecues are not permitted. Off site: A few shops 2 km. Nearest shopping centre Fréjus 8 km. Riding 1 km. Fishing 8 km. Golf 12 km.

Open: 3 April - 26 September.

Directions

From the A8 (Aix-en-Provence - Nice) take exit 38 onto D4 towards Bagnols-en-Forêt. Site lies along this road past a military camp. GPS: 43.48389, 6.72058

Charges guide

Per unit incl. 2 persons and electricity	€ 23,00 - € 39,00
extra person	€ 6,00 - € 8,00
child (2-6 yrs)	€ 4,00 - € 6,00
dog	€ 3,00 - € 4,00

Fréjus

Camping Resort la Baume – la Palmeraie

495

3775 rue des Combattants d'Afrique du Nord, F-83618 Fréjus (Var) T: **04 94 19 88 88**
E: **reception@labaume-lapalmeraie.com** **alanrogers.com/FR83060**

La Baume is large, busy site about 5.5 km. from the long sandy beach of Fréjus-Plage, although with its fine and varied selection of swimming pools many people do not bother to make the trip. The pools with their palm trees are remarkable for their size and variety (water slides, etc.) – the very large 'feature' pool a highlight. Aquatic play area and two indoor pools with a slide and a spa area. The site has nearly 250 adequately sized, fully serviced pitches, with some separators and most have shade. Although tents are accepted, the site concentrates mainly on caravanning. It becomes full in season. Adjoining La Baume is its sister site La Palmeraie, providing self-catering accommodation, its own landscaped pool and offering some entertainment to supplement that at La Baume. There are 500 large pitches with mains sewerage for mobile homes. La Baume's convenient location has its downside as there is some traffic noise on a few pitches from the nearby autoroute – somewhat obtrusive at first but we soon failed to notice it. It is a popular site with tour operators.

Facilities

Seven refurbished toilet blocks. Supermarket, several shops. Two bars, terrace overlooking pools, TV. Restaurant, takeaway. Six swimming pools (heated all season, two covered, plus steam room and jacuzzi). Fitness centre. Tennis. Archery (July/Aug). Skateboard park. Organised events, daytime and evening entertainment, some English. Amphitheatre. Discos all season. Children's club (all season). 2 play areas. Off site: Bus to Fréjus by gate. Riding 2 km. Fishing 3 km. Golf 5 km. Beach 5 km.

Open: 27 March - 25 September, with full services.

Directions

From west, A8, exit Fréjus, take N7 southwest (Fréjus). After 4 km, turn left on D4 and site is 3 km. From east, A8, exit 38 Fréjus and follow signs for Cais. Site is signed. GPS: 43.45998, 6.72048

Charges 2010

Per unit incl. 2 persons, water, electricity, and drainage	€ 19,00 - € 45,00
extra person	€ 5,00 - € 13,00
child (under 7 yrs)	free - € 7,00
dog	€ 4,00 - € 5,00

Min. stay for motorhomes 2 nights.
Large units should book.

Fréjus

Yelloh! Village Domaine du Colombier

Route de Bagnols-en-Forêt, 1052 rue des Combattants d'AFN, F-83600 Fréjus (Var) T: **04 66 73 97 39**
E: **info@domaine-du-colombier.com** **alanrogers.com/FR83230**

Domaine du Colombier is located between Cannes and St Tropez, alongside a main road 2 km. from the centre of Fréjus and 4 km. from the sandy beaches of Fréjus-Saint-Raphaël. There are 70 touring pitches, ranging in size from 80-150 sq.m, and all with 16A electricity. Over recent years there has been much investment in high quality facilities. An attractive pool complex includes a heated pool, a large paddling pool, water slides and Jacuzzis and is surrounded by sunloungers, a fitness area and a grill restaurant. Plenty of activities and excursions are arranged all season and the site caters principally for families.

Facilities

Three well maintained, fully equipped toilet blocks (two heated and with baby rooms). Facilities for disabled visitors. Laundry. Well stocked shop. Bar/restaurant, takeaway. Soundproofed nightclub. Large heated swimming pool with paddling pool, slides and jacuzzis (all season). Fitness facilities. Three play areas and four sports areas. Picnic area with communal barbecue. Internet access and WiFi. Fridge, safe and barbecue hire. Off site: Bus stop 50 m.

Open: 31 March - 15 October.

Directions

From A8 exit 37, follow signs for Fréjus, turning left at second lights (D4) and site is 1 km. on the right. From A8 exit 38 east (Nice) straight on at three roundabouts, then right at fourth and fifth. Site is 300 m. on right. From west (Aix) turn right at first roundabout, after 1 km. turn left and site is 1 km. on the left.
GPS: 43.44583, 6.72727

Charges guide

Per unit incl. 3 persons and electricity	€ 30,00 - € 55,00
extra person	€ 5,00 - € 8,50
child (3-7 yrs)	free - € 6,50
dog	€ 4,00

Special low season offers.

Gassin

Camping Parc Saint James-Gassin

Route de Bourrian, F-83580 Gassin (Var) T: **04 94 55 20 20**. E: **gassin@camping-parcsaintjames.com**
alanrogers.com/FR83620

A member of the Parc Saint James group, this attractive campsite was formerly known as Parc Montana and is very well positioned close to St Tropez. The majority of the pitches are occupied by individually owned mobile homes and chalets but there are also 50 touring pitches on the lower part of the site. The 30-hectare estate clings to the hillside with fragrant woodland providing good shade to the mainly terraced pitches. There is a good range of activities here; in high season, the activity and entertainment programme is popular and includes soirées on the site's attractive bar terrace.

Facilities

Five toilet blocks provide adequate facilities although rather dated. Facility for disabled visitors in one block. Laundry. Small supermarket. Swimming pools and separate children's pool. Bar and restaurant. Takeaway. Play area. Tennis. Multisports area. Games room. Children's club. Evening entertainment. Disco. Mobile homes and chalets for rent. Off site: St Tropez, Port Grimaud and Cogolin. Nearest beaches 5 km. Riding. Fishing. Walking trails.

Open: 6 January - 24 November.

See advertisement on page 435

Directions

From A8 autoroute take Le Muy exit and follow signs to St Tropez and La Croix-Valmer. Pass Sainte Maxime and continue on the N98. At large roundabout take signs to Gassin. Cross first roundabout and turn left at next traffic lights. Site is also signed as Parc Montana in places. GPS: 43.24035, 6.57345

Charges guide

Per unit incl. 2 persons and electricity	€ 18,00 - € 35,00
extra person	€ 2,50 - € 5,00

Graveson-en-Provence

Camping les Micocouliers

445 route de Cassoulen, F-13690 Graveson-en-Provence (Bouches du Rhône) T: **04 90 95 81 49**
E: **micocou@free.fr** **alanrogers.com/FR13060**

M. et Mme. Riehl started work on Les Micocouliers in 1997 and they have developed a comfortable site. On the outskirts of the town, the site is only some 10 km. from St Rémy and Avignon. Purpose-built, terracotta 'houses' in a raised position provide all the facilities at present. The 75 pitches radiate out from here with the pool and entrance to one side. The pitches are on level grass, separated by small bushes, and shade is developing well. Electricity connections are possible (4-13A). There are also a few mobile homes. Bread can be ordered, and in July and August a simple snack kiosk operates.

Facilities

Unisex facilities in one unit provide toilets and facilities for disabled visitors (by key), another has showers and washbasins in cabins and another laundry facilities. Reception and limited shop (July/Aug). Swimming pool (12 x 8 m; 5/5-15/9). Paddling pool (1/7-31/8). Play area. Off site: Fishing 5 km. Bicycle hire 1 km. Riding next door. Golf 5 km. Beach 60 km. at Ste Marie-de-la-Mer.

Open: 15 March - 15 October.

Directions

Site is southeast of Graveson. From the N570 at new roundabout take D5 towards St Rémy and Maillane and site is 500 m. on left. GPS: 43.84397, 4.78131

Charges guide

Per unit incl. 2 persons	€ 14,00 - € 18,80
extra person	€ 4,80 - € 6,20
electricity	€ 2,50 - € 6,80

Camping Cheques accepted.

Gréoux-les-Bains

yelloh! VILLAGE

Yelloh! Village Verdon Parc

Domaine de la Paludette, F-04800 Gréoux-les-Bains (Alpes-de-Haute-Provence) T: **04 66 73 97 39**
E: **info@yellohvillage-verdon-parc.com** **alanrogers.com/FR04110**

Friendly and family run, this very spacious site borders the River Ardèche and is close to the attractive spa town of Gréoux-les-Bains. The 280 medium to very large, stony or gravel pitches (150 for tourists) are in two sections. The main part of the campsite has large pitches laid out in rows separated by poplar trees. Along the river bank the larger, more natural pitches are scattered amongst the trees and are of irregular shape and size. These have very pleasant views across the river to the town beyond. Electrical connections (10A) and water taps are reasonably close to most pitches. Unfortunately river swimming is forbidden but there is a large swimming pool on site.

Facilities

Several toilet blocks (one heated in low season) are clean and to a high standard, with all the necessary facilities including those for disabled visitors. Laundry room. Motorcaravan service point. Small shop. Bar and courtyard terrace. Restaurant and takeaway (Apr-Sept). TV. Internet point. Large play area. Miniclub (high season). Organised sports. Evening entertainment. Dogs are not accepted in high season. Off site: Gréoux-les-Bains 1 km. Riding and bicycle hire 1 km. Small lakeside beach 8 km.

Open: 21 March - 29 October.

Directions

Leave A51 autoroute at Manosque and take the D907 southeast towards Gréoux-les-Bains. Turn right on D4, then left on D82 to Gréoux-les-Bains. Follow main road downhill through town to roundabout with fountain. Take second right, signed D8 St Pierre and descend for 1 km. Cross river and immediately turn left. Site is shortly on the left. GPS: 43.7602, 5.8825

Charges 2010

Per unit incl. 2 persons	€ 15,00 - € 33,00
extra person	€ 4,00 - € 5,00

Grimaud

Camping de la Plage

RD559, F-83310 Grimaud (Var) T: **04 94 56 31 15**. E: **campingplagegrimaud@wanadoo.fr**
alanrogers.com/FR83100

A site on the beach is always in great demand, and Camping de la Plage is no exception, consequently it becomes very crowded. With 450 pitches, the site is divided into two parts by the N98 although a dangerous crossing is avoided by an underpass. The pitches in the area away from the beach will be the more peaceful and have more shade as they are in light woodland. They are mostly of a good size. In the area over the road there is more grass. There is some traffic noise on the pitches close to the busy road. All pitches have electricity (4-10A) but long leads may be required.

Facilities

Six toilet blocks of varying quality but well equipped and clean. Baby bath. Facilities for disabled visitors. Motorcaravan services. Large supermarket (all season). Bar, restaurant, takeaway (all season). Tennis. Small play area. Bicycle hire. Fridge rental. Charcoal barbecues are not permitted. Off site: Golf and riding 3 km. Boat hire nearby.

Open: One week before Easter - 12 October.

Directions

Site is on N98 main coast road about 6 km. southwest of Ste Maxime. Take care – this road is very busy in the main season. GPS: 43.2819, 6.5859

Charges guide

Per unit incl. 2 persons and electricity	€ 27,00 - € 38,50
extra person	€ 6,30 - € 7,40
child (under 7 yrs)	€ 3,10 - € 3,60

Grimaud

Camping des Prairies de la Mer

Quartier Saint-Pons (RN98), les Mûres, F-83310 Grimaud (Var) T: **04 94 79 09 09**
E: **prairies@riviera-villages.com** **alanrogers.com/FR83380**

This busy site is in the pleasant and popular holiday resort of Port Grimaud where there is a luxurious harbour, restaurants and shops. A long, sandy beach runs right round the bay. The site is right on the beach and is very well equipped for a family holiday. In fact, it is a complete holiday resort, even including its own amusement park for children. There are 500 individual touring pitches on flat, sandy ground, all with electricity. A further 900 pitches are used for mobile homes and chalets. Trees have grown well to give plenty of shade and but there is no swimming pool.

Facilities

Nine modern toilet blocks with three near the touring pitches include washbasins in cabins. Toilets are all British style, Launderette. Large shopping complex. Bar. Attractive, Italian-style restaurant (all season). Good takeaway. Entertainment programme with live music evenings. Play area. Sports ground. TV room. Bicycle hire. Sailing and diving schools. Miniclub. ATM. Excursions. Beach.
Off site: Golf 3 km. Riding 2 km.

Open: 1 April - 8 October.

Directions

From the A8 (Aix-en-Provence - Cannes) exit 36 (Le Muy) take the D25 to St Maxime, then the coast road N98 towards St Tropez. Site is 6 km. on the left.
GPS: 43.277133, 6.581833

Charges guide

Per unit incl. 2 persons	€ 18,00 - € 42,00
extra person	€ 3,00 - € 7,00
child (5-13 yrs)	€ 2,00 - € 4,00
electricity	free - € 5,00

Grimaud

Domaine des Naïades

Quartier Cros d'Entassi, Saint Pons-les-Mûres, F-83310 Grimaud (Var) T: **04 94 55 67 80**
E: **info@lesnaiades.com** **alanrogers.com/FR83640**

Les Naïades is a well equipped site with an enviable setting close to the modern resort of Port Grimaud and the Gulf of St Tropez. Pitches are of a good size and well shaded. Most are equipped with electricity and some have sea views. The site boasts an Olympic sized pool and two water slides, as well as a separate children's pool. The restaurant specialises in Mediterranean cuisine and local wines such as Côteaux Varois or Côtes de Provence. Les Naïades becomes lively in high season with a full activity and entertainment programme, as well as a miniclub for children. Port Grimaud is a stylish resort, built in the 1960s in the marshy delta of the Giscle. It is modelled on Venice and is a car-free environment. Most property owners are able to moor their boats on the many canals which criss-cross the resort. Grimaud, in contrast, is a hilltop village dominated by its partially restored 11th-century castle. St Tropez needs little introduction and, although very busy in the summer months, it resumes a rather more sedate character in the low season.

Facilities

Shop. Bar. Restaurant. Swimming pool with water slides. Children's play area. Tourist information. Motorcaravan services. Mobile homes and chalets for rent. Off site: Port Grimaud. St Tropez. Fishing. Watersports. Walking and cycle routes in the Massif des Maures.

Open: 27 March - 23 October.

Directions

The site is located slightly to the north of Port Grimaud. From there head north to St Pons-les-Mûres and the site is clearly signed.
GPS: 43.285278, 6.579722

Charges guide

Per unit incl. 3 persons and electricity	€ 29,00 - € 50,00
extra person (over 7 yrs)	€ 5,00 - € 8,00
dog	€ 5,00

Grimaud

Club Holiday Marina

Le Ginestrel (RN98), F-83310 Grimaud (Var) T: **04 94 56 08 43**. E: **info@holiday-marina.com**
alanrogers.com/FR83400

Owned and operated by an English family this site is an established favourite with British families. It is located in the busy holiday area of the Gulf of St Tropez. The site has a large and well kept pool area and its own adjacent moorings for small yachts. Smaller than many sites in this area, there are 230 good sized pitches of which 49 for touring units. Each of these has its own spacious bathroom with a good shower, washbasin and WC and a shared outdoor sink. On level, rather sandy ground, with variable shade, all have 20A electricity. Cars are parked separately to reduce noise.

Facilities

Private toilet blocks include washbasin, shower and WC, heated in low seasons. Dishwashing sinks. Laundry. Two restaurants with varied and full menu (15/6-31/8). Snacks and takeaway. Separate building houses a bar and games room. TV room. Swimming and paddling pools. Miniclub for children and evening entertainment in season. Fishing in adjacent canal. Off site: Beach 850 m. Golf 4 km.

Open: 1 April - 31 October.

Directions

From the A8 (Aix-en-Provence - Cannes) take exit 36 (Le Muy) and D25 to St Maxime. Follow N98 coast road towards St Tropez and site is 10 km. after very busy roundabout at Grimaud. GPS: 43.2728, 6.5215

Charges guide

Per unit incl. 2 persons and electricity	€ 19,00 - € 49,00
family rate (2 adults, up to 3 childen)	€ 29,00 - € 59,00
extra person	€ 5,00 - € 19,00

Provence

Hyères-Plage

Camping la Presqu'île de Giens

153 route de la Madraque-Giens, F-83400 Hyères-Plage (Var) T: **04 94 58 22 86**. E: **info@camping-giens.com**

alanrogers.com/FR83190

La Presqu'île de Giens a good family campsite at the southern end of the Giens peninsula. The site is well maintained and extends over 17 acres of undulating terrain. Of the site's 460 pitches, 170 are reserved for touring. These are generally of a good size and well shaded – there is a separate area of smaller pitches reserved for tents. Electrical connections (16A) are available on all pitches. In high season this becomes a lively site with a well-run children's club (small charge) and an evening entertainment programme including discos, singers and dancers. Although there is no swimming pool, the site lies between two sandy beaches, and in July and August a free shuttle bus runs to the nearest, 800 metres away. Excursions are organised to the adjacent islands of Porquerolles, Port Cros and Le Levant. There is a beautiful walking trail set out all around the peninsula.

Facilities

Five toilet blocks, three very good new ones (heated in low season), and two refurbished with a higher proportion of Turkish style toilets. All was clean and well maintained. Facilities for disabled visitors. Washing machines and dryers. Shop. Bar, restaurant and takeaway (all season). Play area. Children's club. Evening entertainment. Sports pitch. Diving classes. Sports tournaments. Excursion programme. Only electric barbecues are permitted. Off site: Beach 800 m. Fishing 1 km. Bicycle hire 1 km. Riding 5 km. Golf 20 km. 'Golden islands' excursions.

Open: 27 March - 3 October.

Directions

From the west, leave A57 at Hyères and continue to Hyères on the A570. At Hyères follow signs to Giens - Les Iles (D97). At end of this road, after 11 km. turn right towards Madraque. Site is on the left.
GPS: 43.04071, 6.1435

Charges 2010

Per unit incl. 2 persons and electricity	€ 19,70 - € 27,90
extra person	€ 4,50 - € 7,20
child (0-5 yrs)	free
dog	€ 3,00

Camping Cheques accepted.

Isle-sur-la Sorgue

Camping Caravaning la Sorguette

Route d'Apt, F-84800 Isle-sur-la Sorgue (Vaucluse) T: **04 90 38 05 71**. E: **sorguette@wanadoo.fr**
alanrogers.com/FR84050

This popular, well organised site is well placed, 1.5 km. from Isle-sur-la-Sorgue. Arranged in groups of four, the 164 medium sized level pitches (124 for touring) all have electricity (6-10A). Each group is separated by tall hedges and most have a little shade during the day. In high season a few competitions are organised (boules or volleyball), plus some children's entertainment, but this is quite low key. Running alongside the site, the river Sorgue is only 6 km. from its source in the mountains. It is still very clear and used for canoeing, swimming or fishing.

Facilities

Well maintained toilet blocks, washing machines. Units for disabled people. Baby room. Motorcaravan services. Fridge hire. Shop, bar, snacks (1/7-25/8). Entertainment (July/Aug). Play area, half-court tennis, basketball. Canoe, bicycle hire. Internet. Indian tipis, yurts; Mongolian circular tents and Inuit-style tents with kitchens. WiFi. Off site: Indoor/outdoor swimming pools (preferential rates) 2 km. Fishing and riding 5 km. Walking and cycling circuits. Canoeing on the Sorgue river.

Open: 15 March - 15 October.

Directions

Site is 1.5 km. east of'Isle-sur-la-Sorgue on the N100 towards Apt. It is well signed from the town. GPS: 43.91488, 5.07758

Charges guide

Per unit incl. 2 persons and electricity	€ 18,50 - € 25,30
extra person	€ 5,70 - € 7,20
child (1-11 yrs)	€ 2,90 - € 3,60
dog	€ 2,30 - € 2,90

La Cadière d'Azur

Domaine de la Malissonne

F-83740 La Cadière d'Azur (Var) T: **04 94 90 10 60**. E: **info@domainemalissonne.com**
alanrogers.com/FR83440

This pleasant site is part of the FranceLoc group and is a park for caravan holiday homes with over 200 mobile homes. There are just four pitches without electricity for touring campers and these are really only for tents. Although the site is close to the A50 we heard little noise and site does provide a good base for touring the western Var and Bouche du Rhône departments. Surrounded by vineyards, this sloping site is very well maintained. It is a quiet and restful environment, yet is only minutes from the coast at Les Lecques. Jean Marc, the son of the former owners, manages the site to perfection.

Facilities

Two good sanitary blocks. Launderette. Bar. Restaurant and shop. Three swimming pools. Fitness area. Play area. Gym. Volleyball. Boules. Archery. Minigolf. Entertainment in high season. TV room and electronic games room. WiFi. Dogs are not accepted 1/7-30/8. Off site: Massif de la Sainte Baume.

Open: 1 March - 13 November.

Directions

Site is on the D66 about 2 km. west of Cadière. Leave the A50 at exit 11 and go towards the town. Then follow signs to the site which itself is close to a motorway bridge. GPS: 43.2023, 5.7382

Charges guide

Per unit incl. 2 persons	€ 20,50 - € 27,50
extra person	€ 6,10
child (under 7 yrs)	€ 4,50

Le Muy

RCN Domaine de la Noguière

Route de Fréjus, F-83490 Le Muy (Var) T: **04 94 45 13 78**. E: **info@rcn-domainedelanoguiere.fr**
alanrogers.com/FR83090

A Dutch company, RCN runs a chain of good campsites in the Netherlands. They now operate six sites in France, all with Dutch managers who speak good French and English. Domaine de la Noguière is located amongst beautiful Provençal scenery with lavender fields, yellow mimosa trees and reddish brown rocks. The Mediterranean beaches at the famous resorts of Fréjus and St Raphaël are only 16 km. There are 200 pitches all with 6A electricity, arranged on small terraces on the slightly sloping ground. At the entrance to the site there is a reception area and a restaurant serving regional specialities.

Facilities

Two new sanitary buildings have been added with family showers and children's rooms. Toilets are fully tiled with individual cabins and access for disabled visitors. Washing machines, dryers and ironing area. Bar/restaurant with terrace. Small meeting room with library and large TV. Swimming pool with large slides. Tennis. Boules. Games field.

Open: 21 March - 31 October.

Directions

From the A8, take exit 37 toward Roquebrune-sur-Argens and Puget-sur-Argens (this is the second exit towards Roquebrune, drive past exit 36). At roundabout, take first right turn toward Roquebrune and Le Muy (N7). Continue on this road for 8 km. to site on the right. GPS: 43.46832, 6.59202

Charges guide

Per unit incl. 2 persons, electricity and water	€ 21,00 - € 47,50
incl. up to 6 persons	€ 23,50 - € 63,00

Camping Cheques accepted.

The Travel Service to book this site call 01580 214000 ...we'll arrange everything

Le Thor

Domaine le Jantou

535 chemin des Coudelières, F-84250 Le Thor (Vaucluse) T: **04 90 33 90 07**. E: **accueil@lejantou.com**

alanrogers.com/FR84040

Le Jantou has been expanded over the years from an 18th-century farm and farmhouse. It is bordered by a small river said to be good for trout fishing. The 160 level, small to medium sized, fairly stony pitches (rock pegs advised) are in small groups separated by tall hedges and mature trees giving heavy shade to many. All have electricity (3-10A). About half of them are used for touring with most of them in a separate section. There is a large pool, children's pool and paddling pool surrounded by paved and grass sunbathing areas.

Facilities

Two central toilet blocks partially refurbished with all the necessary facilities, include washbasins in cabins, a baby room and facilities for disabled visitors (key access). Washing machine and dryer. Motorcaravan service point. Small bar/restaurant with takeaway (July/Aug). Small shop with basic provisions. Swimming pools. Play area. Large sports area. Fishing. Bicycle hire. Small games room. TV and internet access. Barbecues are not allowed (four communal barbecue areas). Barrier key € 15 deposit. Off site: Riding 5 km. Supermarket 1 km. Canoeing. Thor, shops, bars, restaurants, bank 2 km. Isle-sur-la-Sorgue (antiques and Provençal markets) 5 km.

Open: 1 April - 31 October.

Directions

Site is just west of Le Thor. Leave A7 autoroute at Avignon north (exit 23) onto D942 signed Carpentras. Shortly turn south on D6 and in 8 km. turn east on N100, signed Le Thor. Just before bridge turn left on D1 and shortly left again to site entrance.
GPS: 43.9294, 4.98315

Charges guide

Per unit incl. 2 persons	€ 19,00 - € 22,00
extra person	€ 4,60 - € 6,50
child (2-12 yrs)	€ 2,50 - € 4,00
electricity	€ 3,00 - € 4,70
animal	€ 4,30

Les Issambres

Au Paradis des Campeurs

La Gaillarde-Plage, F-83380 Les Issambres (Var) T: **04 94 96 93 55**

alanrogers.com/FR83080

Family owned and run, this popular site has 180 pitches, all with 6A electricity and 132 with water and drainage. The original pitches vary in size and shape but all are satisfactory and most have some shade. The newer pitches are all large and have rather less shade although trees and bushes are maturing nicely. There is no entertainment which gives peaceful nights. The gates are surveyed by CCTV (especially the beach gate) and a security man patrols all day. With direct access to a sandy beach (via an underpass) and being so well maintained, the site has become deservedly popular so it is essential to book for June, July and August.

Facilities

Excellent, refurbished, well maintained toilet blocks. Facilities for babies and children with shower at suitable height. En-suite for disabled visitors. Washing machines and dryer. Motorcaravan services. Shop, restaurant and takeaway service. TV room. Internet and WiFi. Excellent play areas with top quality safety bases, catering for the under and over 5s. Boules. Car wash area. Off site: Bicycle hire 2.5 km. Riding 3 km. Golf 6 km.

Open: 28 March - 16 October.

Directions

Site is signed from N98 coast road at La Gaillarde, 2 km. south of St Aygulf. GPS: 43.36593, 6.71230

Charges guide

Per unit incl. 2 persons	
and electricity	€ 18,00 - € 27,00
incl. water and drainage	€ 20,00 - € 31,00
extra person	€ 6,00
child (under 5 yrs)	€ 3,00

Les Vigneaux

Campéole

Campéole le Courounba

D994, F-05120 Les Vigneaux (Hautes-Alpes) T: **04 92 23 02 09**. E: **nadine.ferran@atciat.com**
alanrogers.com/FR05140

Le Couronba is a member of the Campéole group, located at the entrance to the magnificent Parc National des Ecrins. Pitches are shady and spacious, dispersed around 12 hectares of woodland. Many of the pitches have superb views of the surrounding mountain scenery. Mobile homes for rent (including specially adapted units for the disabled). There is also a good sized swimming pool with a water slide and other on-site amenities include two tennis courts and volleyball pitch. Most facilities are free of charge (including tennis). The site has a friendly bar/restaurant and also a well stocked shop (high season only). There is dramatic mountain scenery all around. Mont Brison is the highest limestone rockface in France and Mont Pelvoux, at 3,943 metres has an all-year snow cap. Le Couronba is on the banks of the River Gyronde, popular for fishing. A little further afield, Briançon is a superb town, fortified by Vauban and well worth a visit.

Facilities

Bar/snack bar. Swimming pool and water slide. Volleyball. Tennis. Bouncy castle. Shop. Children's play area. Activity and entertainment programme. Tourist information. Mobile homes for rent. Off site: Fishing. Hiking and cycle tracks. Riding. Bicycle hire. Briançon 17 km.

Open: 22 May - 26 September.

Directions

The site is close to the village of Les Vigneaux, south of Briançon. From Briançon, head south on N94 as far as Prelles and then join the D4 to Les Vigneaux. The site is well indicated from here.
GPS: 44.82483, 6.52566

Charges 2010

Per unit incl. 2 persons and electricity € 17,10 - 24,70

Les Vigneaux

Campéole

Campéole les Vaudois

F-05120 Les Vigneaux (Hautes-Alpes) T: **04 92 23 02 09**. E: **nadine.ferran@atciat.com**
alanrogers.com/FR05150

Les Vaudois is a member of the Campéole group and is located at the edge of the Parc National des Ecrins. The site stands on the banks of the river Gyronde and at the foot of Mont Brison, France's highest limestone rock face. There are very few amenities on site but guests are able to use the facilities at the sister site, Le Courounba, around 1 km. away. Amenities there include a swimming pool (with water slide) and a bar/restaurant. There are 141 touring pitches at Les Vaudois, and a further nine pitches reserved for mobile homes. Most pitches are equipped with electricity. This is, of course, excellent country for adventure sports and Les Vaudois is well located for a wide range of activities, including white-water rafting, rock climbing and mountain biking. The Parc National des Ecrins is a vast area, one of only nine French national parks, established back in 1913 as the Parc National Bérarde. There are over 700 km. of marked footpaths in the park and a great wealth of wildlife.

Facilities

Play area. Tourist information. Mobile homes for rent. Off site: Swimming pool. Bar/restaurant. Cycle and walking tracks. Tennis. Canoeing. White water sports on the river.

Open: 26 June - 28 August.

Directions

From Briançon, take N94 towards Prelles and St Martin de Queyrières, and then follow signs for l'Argentière. Take the D104A to La Batie des Vigneaux and then continue to Les Vigneaux and the campsite.
GPS: 44.8213, 6.5355

Charges 2010

Per unit incl. 2 persons and electricity € 15,10 - € 18,30

Martigues

Flower Camping Marius

Plage de la Saulce, La Couronne, F-13500 Martigues (Bouches du Rhône) T: **04 42 80 70 29**
E: **contact@camping-marius.com** **alanrogers.com/FR13140**

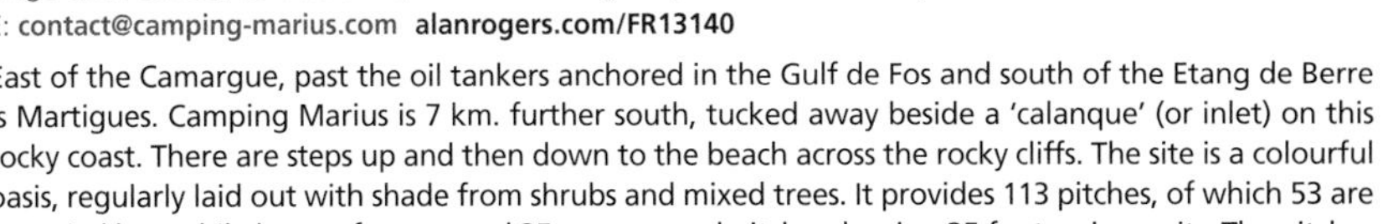

East of the Camargue, past the oil tankers anchored in the Gulf de Fos and south of the Etang de Berre is Martigues. Camping Marius is 7 km. further south, tucked away beside a 'calanque' (or inlet) on this rocky coast. There are steps up and then down to the beach across the rocky cliffs. The site is a colourful oasis, regularly laid out with shade from shrubs and mixed trees. It provides 113 pitches, of which 53 are occupied by mobile homes for rent and 35 are seasonal pitches, leaving 25 for touring units. The pitches are rather small but each has its own sink and water supply.

Facilities

A good modern toilet block is well equipped and is supplemented by a smaller one. Baby bath. Facilities for disabled visitors. Very small shop. Bar and takeaway. Play area. Bicycle hire. Canoe hire. Activity and entertainment programme. Direct access via steep steps and some rough walking to beach 200 m. Mobile homes for rent.
Off site: Nearest village is La Couronne (good range of shops and restaurants and railway station). Fishing village of Carro (3 km) with daily fish market. Riding 5 km. Snack bar 200 m.

Open: 29 March - 10 November.

Directions

Approach Martigues from the north on the D5 and cross the Canal de Caronte, continuing south on the D5, then D49 to La Couronne (7 km). At roundabout on outskirts of La Couronne, turn left for Sausset-les-Pins' and Saint Croix. Site is signed from there. Using the A55 take left turn immediately on crossing the bridge signed Fos (exit 12) and follow road back under bridge until right sign for La Couronne. On A55 from Marseille take exit for Carry-le-Rouet.
GPS: 43.3351, 5.0676

Charges guide

Per unit incl. 2 persons and electricity	€ 18,40 - € 25,40
extra person	€ 3,80 - € 6,20
child (2-7 yrs)	€ 1,90 - € 3,10
dog	free

Maussane

Camping Municipal les Romarins

Route de Saint-Remy, F-13520 Maussane (Bouches du Rhône) T: **04 90 54 33 60**
E: **camping_municipal_maussane@wanadoo.fr** **alanrogers.com/FR13010**

A well kept, neat municipal site, Les Romarins has been in the Guide for several years and remains popular with our readers. Tarmac access roads lead to 145 good sized grassy pitches separated by hedges and bushes, all with 6A electricity, some with water and a drain. The municipal swimming pool (with discounts) is near and shops and restaurants are in the pleasant little town. Les Baux and St-Remy-de-Provence are tourist attractions not to be missed, especially St-Remy's Roman ruins. Les Romarins is popular and becomes very busy from 1 July until late August.

Facilities

Three toilet blocks, two refurbished, showers (on payment). An older block opens for July and August. Facilities for disabled visitors. Baby room. Laundry facilities. Plans for refurbishment. Motorcaravan services. Municipal swimming pool (100 m. from site) free to campers 15/6-31/8. Play area. Free tennis. Reading room. Internet access.
Off site: Bus services in town. Bicycle hire or golf 1 km. Fishing or riding 3 km. Walking in les Alpilles.

Open: 15 March - 15 October.

Directions

Site is within the little town of Maussane on the eastern edge. GPS: 43.72128, 4.80967

Charges guide

Per unit incl. 2 persons	€ 17,20 - € 18,90
extra person	€ 4,00 - € 4,40
child (under 12 yrs)	€ 2,20 - € 2,80
dog	€ 2,70
electricity	€ 3,50

Less 10-20% for longer stays.

Montclar

Yelloh! Village l'Etoile des Neiges

F-04140 Montclar (Alpes-de-Haute-Provence) T: **04 66 73 97 39**. E: **info@yellohvillage-etoile-des-neiges.com**
alanrogers.com/FR04080

This attractive, family run site near the mountain village and ski resort of St Jean Montclar is open most of the year. Being at an altitude of 1,300 m. the nights can get quite cold in summer. The 130 shady terraced pitches, with 70 for touring, are separated by small shrubs and alpine trees. All pitches are close to electricity and water points. An attractive bar and restaurant overlooks the two swimming pools, with the shallow pool having a water slide ideal for children. The site has no shop but local shops are only a few minutes walk away. Although situated in the southern high Alps, the site can be reached without climbing any stiff gradients. This beautiful alpine region offers all the usual alpine activities.

Facilities

Central toilet block (heated in winter) and facilities for disabled visitors. Two washing machines. Motorcaravan services. Bar/restaurant. Swimming pool (all amenities open 15/5-9/9). Tennis. Boules. Two play areas. Rafting, walking (July/Aug). Off site: Shops in village a few minutes walk. Bicycle hire and riding in village. Fishing 1.5 km. Watersports and beach at Lac Serre Ponçon 7 km.

Open: All year excl. 26/3-29/4 and 16/9-19/12.

Directions

Site is 35 km. south of Gap via D900B. Beyond Serre Ponçon, turn right, D900 signed Selonnet, St Jean Montclar. Entering St Jean Montclar turn left, pass chalets, shops, fork right to campsite. Approach roads are steep and icy in winter. GPS: 44.39367, 6.34400

Charges guide

Per unit incl. 2 persons	€ 17,00 - € 31,00
extra person	€ 4,00 - € 5,00
child (2-5 yrs)	free - € 4,00
electricity (6A)	€ 3,00 - € 4,00

Mornas

Camping Beauregard

Route d'Uchaux, F-84550 Mornas (Vaucluse) T: **04 90 37 02 08**. E: **beauregard@wanadoo.fr**
alanrogers.com/FR84140

Just a kilometre off the D7 and near an A7 exit, this site may appeal to those needing a night stop when travelling to or from the Mediterranean coast. Although there are many mobile homes, there are 89 pitches available for tourists. The pitches are under large pine trees and are rather sandy and firm pegging might be difficult. They are of various shapes and sizes, mainly about 90 sq.m. Efforts are being made to upgrade what was an old fashioned campsite. There is a new and attractive pool complex including a covered pool (heated from April) – the pools are used by some local people. Entertainment is organised for high season evenings. A good sized shop sells the essentials.

Facilities

Two toilet blocks, one of which is heated when necessary, with washbasins in cabins. Facilities for disabled visitors (access by key). Laundry facilities. Shop (April-Oct). Bar, restaurant and takeaway (April-Sept). Swimming pools, one covered. Tennis. Play area. Boules. Quad bike hire. Fitness trail. Entertainment (high season). Barbecues are not permitted. Off site: Fishing and riding 5 km. Golf 12 km.

Open: 25 March - 4 November.

Directions

From the A7 take exit for Bollene, then the N7 towards Orange. At north end of Mornas village, turn left on D74 signed Uchaux. Site is on left after 1.7 km. GPS: 44.21540, 4.74530

Charges guide

Per unit incl. 2 persons	€ 21,00 - € 24,00
extra person	€ 4,60 - € 7,00
child (under 7 yrs)	€ 2,50 - € 4,20
electricity	€ 4,70

Niozelles

Camping le Moulin de Ventre

Niozelles, F-04300 Forcalquier (Alpes-de-Haute-Provence) T: **04 92 78 63 31**. E: **moulindeventre@aol.com**

alanrogers.com/FR04030

This is a friendly, family-run site in the heart of Haute-Provence, near Forcalquier, a bustling small French market town. Attractively located beside a small lake and 28 acres of wooded, hilly land, which is available for walking. Herbs of Provence can be found growing wild and flowers, birds and butterflies abound – a nature lovers' delight. The 124 level, grassy pitches for tourists are separated by a variety of trees and small shrubs, 114 of them with electricity (6A; long leads may be necessary). Some pitches are particularly attractive, bordering a small stream. English is spoken. The site is well situated to visit Mont Ventoux, the Luberon National Park, the Gorges du Verdon and a wide range of ancient hill villages with their markets and museums etc. A 'Sites et Paysages' member.

Facilities

Refurbished toilet block. Facilities for disabled people. Baby bath. Washing, drying machines. Fridge hire. Bread. Bar/restaurant, takeaway (all season), themed evenings (high season). Pizzeria. Swimming pools (15/5-15/9). New playground. Bouncy castle. Fishing, boules. Some activities organised in high season. No discos. Only electric or gas barbecues. Internet access. Off site: Shops, local market, doctor, tennis 2 km. Supermarket, chemist, riding, bicycle hire 5 km. Golf 20 km. Walking, cycling.

Open: 5 April - 30 September.

Directions

From A51 motorway take exit 19 (Brillanne). Turn right on N96 then turn left on N100 westwards (signed Forcalquier) for about 3 km. Site is signed on left, just after a bridge 3 km. southeast of Niozelles.
GPS: 43.93364, 5.86815

Charges guide

Per unit incl. 2 persons and electricity	€ 17,20 - € 26,70
extra person (over 4 yrs)	€ 3,50 - € 5,50
child (2-4 yrs)	€ 2,00 - € 3,00
dog	€ 1,50 - € 3,00

No credit cards.

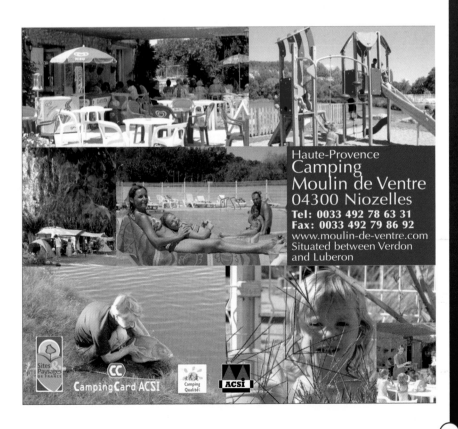

The Travel Service to book this site call 01580 214000 ...we'll arrange everything

Puget-sur-Argens

Parc Saint-James Oasis

Route de la Bouverie, F-83480 Puget-sur-Argens (Var) T: **04 98 11 85 60**
E: **oasis@camping-parcsaintjames.com** **alanrogers.com/FR83610**

The pitches at this campsite are used exclusively for mobile home and chalet accommodation.

Puget-sur-Argens

Camping Club la Bastiane

1056 chemin de Suvières, F-83480 Puget-sur-Argens (Var) T: **04 94 55 55 94**. E: **info@labastiane.com**
alanrogers.com/FR83040

With a shady woodland setting, La Bastiane is a well established site with good amenities, well located for exploring the Côte d'Azur and with easy access to nearby beaches. There are 180 pitches here of which 47 are reserved for touring. They are generally of a good size and are all supplied with electrical connections (6A). The terrain is somewhat undulating but most of the pitches are on level terraces. There is a good swimming pool and a range of amenities including a shop, bar and restaurant.

Facilities

Four toilet blocks, three of modern construction, one refurbished. Facilities for disabled visitors. Washing machines, dryers. Shop, bar and takeaway (8/4-20/10). Restaurant (17/4-12/10). Heated swimming pool (8/4-20/10). Tennis. Multisport terrain. Children's club. Play area. Games/TV room. Bicycle hire. Evening entertainment in peak season. Excursion programme. Only electric barbecues. One dog only. Mobile homes and chalets for rent. Off site: Beach 7 km. Lake beach 8 km. Riding 500 m. Fishing 3 km. Golf 9 km.

Open: 3 April - 23 October.

Directions

Leave A8 at exit 37 (Puget), take right turn at first roundabout (signed Roquebrune), join N7. Turn right, first traffic lights (200 m), then left at T-junction. Site signed from here, on the right 2.5 km. from the motorway. GPS: 43.46966, 6.67845

Charges 2010

Per unit incl. 2 persons and electricity	€ 19,90 - € 39,90

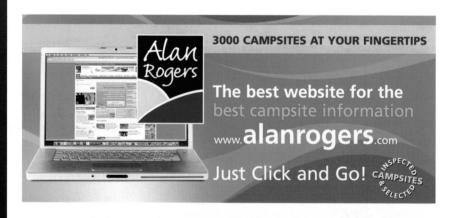

Orpierre

Camping des Princes d'Orange

F-05700 Orpierre (Hautes-Alpes) T: **04 92 66 22 53**. E: **campingorpierre@wanadoo.fr**

alanrogers.com/FR05000

This attractive, terraced site, set on a hillside above the village has been thoughtfully developed. The genuine, friendly welcome means many families return year upon year, bringing in turn new generations. Divided into five terraces, each with its own toilet block, all its 100 generously sized pitches (96 for tourists) enjoy good shade from trees and wicker canopies and have electricity connections (10A). In high season one terrace is reserved as a 1-star camping area for young people. Orpierre also has an enchanting maze of medieval streets and houses, almost like a trip back through the centuries. Whether you choose to drive, climb, walk or cycle there is plenty of wonderful scenery to discover in the immediate vicinity, whilst not far away, some exhilarating hang-gliding and parascending can be enjoyed. For those seeking to 'get away from it all' in an area of outstanding natural beauty, there can be few more tranquil sites. There can be no doubt that you will be made most welcome and will enjoy the quiet splendours the region has to offer. Renowned as a serious rock climbing venue.

Facilities

Six well equipped toilet blocks. Baby bath. Laundry facilities. Bread. Bar (1/4-31/10). Heated swimming pool, paddling pool (15/6-15/9). Play area with small trampoline with safety net. Boules. Games room. Fridge hire. Only gas barbecues are permitted. Off site: Orpierre with a few shops and bicycle hire 500 m. Fishing 7 km. Nearest shopping centre Laragne 12 km. Riding 19 km. Hang-gliding, parascending. Gorges de Guil.

Open: 1 April - 31 October.

Directions

Turn off N75 road at Eyguians onto D30 – site is signed on left at crossroads in the centre of Orpierre village. GPS: 44.31121, 5.69677

Charges guide

Per unit incl. 2 persons and electricity	€ 26,30
extra person	€ 7,00
child (under 7 yrs)	€ 3,50
dog	€ 1,50

Less 25% in low season.
No credit cards.

Ramatuelle

Yelloh! Village les Tournels

Route de Camarat, F-83350 Ramatuelle (Var) T: **04 66 73 97 39**. E: **info@yellohvillage-les-tournels.com**
alanrogers.com/FR83210

Les Tournels is a large site set on a hillside and pitches have panoramic views of the Gulf of St Tropez and Pampelonne beach. The hillside is covered in parasol pines and old olive trees. The pitches are reasonably level, shady, variable size, most with electricity (long leads). The swimming pool, play area, shop and bar maybe some distance away. Recent additions include a superb new spa centre with gym, sauna and jacuzzi, with an excellent pool alongside, all reserved for over 18s, and a new restaurant with a large terrace. Competitions and shows are organised for adults and children in July and August.

Facilities

Well equipped toilet blocks, some heated, baby baths, children's WCs, facilities for disabled visitors. Laundry facilities. Fridge hire. Bar and restaurant (1/4-15/10). Takeaway. Bar and disco well away from most pitches. Large heated swimming pool 1/4-20/10. Fitness centre and pool. Good quality play area. Boules. Archery. Miniclub (over 5 yrs). Safety deposit boxes. Only gas barbecues permitted. Off site: Shopping centre 500 m, shuttle bus service. Golf 6 km. Beach 1.5 km.

Open: 13 March - 7 January.

Directions

From A8 exit 36 take D25 to Ste Maxime, then D98 towards St Tropez. On outskirts of St Tropez, take D93 to Ramatuelle. Site is signed on left in 9 km. GPS: 43.20596, 6.65083

Charges guide

Per unit incl. 2 persons and electricity and water	€ 17,00 - € 40,00
extra person	€ 6,00 - € 8,00
child (2-7 yrs)	free - € 4,00

Régusse

Camping les Lacs du Verdon

Domaine de Roquelande, F-83630 Régusse (Var) T: **04 94 70 17 95**. E: **info@lacs-verdon.com**
alanrogers.com/FR83140

In beautiful countryside and within easy reach of the Grand Canyon du Verdon and its nearby lakes, this site is only 90 minutes from Cannes. This bustling and possible noisy campsite is ideal for active families and teenagers. The 30-acre wooded park is divided in two by a minor road. The 480 very stony, but level pitches (rock pegs advised) are marked and separated by stones and trees. 130 pitches are for tourists, many irregular in shape, but all of average size with 10A electricity (long leads may be necessary).

Facilities

Modernised toilet blocks have mainly have British style WCs and some washbasins in cubicles. Laundry and dishwashing facilities. Motorcaravan service point. Shop. Bar. Restaurant and pizzeria. Excellent swimming pool/paddling pool complex. Artificial grass tennis courts. Boules. Bicycle hire. Playground. TV and teenage games room. Entertainment programme. Discos, dances and theme nights. Only electric barbecues are permitted. Off site: Régusse 2.5 km. Aups 7 km. Riding 10 km. Fishing, beach, sailing and windsurfing at Saint Croix 15 km.

Open: 29 April - 23 September.

Directions

Leave A8 motorway at St Maximin and take the D560 northeast (Barjols). At Barjols turn left on the D71 (Montmeyan), turn right on D30 (Régusse) and follow site signs. GPS: 43.6602, 6.1511

Charges guide

Per unit incl. 1 or 2 persons	€ 18,00 - € 27,00
extra person	€ 5,00 - € 7,50
child (3-7 yrs)	€ 4,00 - € 6,00
electricity (10A)	€ 4,00
dog	€ 3,00

Roquebrune-sur-Argens

Camping Caravaning Moulin des Iscles

Chemin du Moulin des Iscles, F-83520 Roquebrune-sur-Argens (Var) T: **04 94 45 70 74**
E: **moulin.iscles@wanadoo.fr** **alanrogers.com/FR83240**

Moulin des Iscles is a small, pretty site beside the river Argens with access to the river in places for fishing, canoeing and swimming, with some sought after pitches overlooking the river. The 90 grassy, level pitches have water and electricity (6A). A nice mixture of deciduous trees provides natural shade and colour and the old mill house is near the entrance, which has the security barrier closed at night. This is a quiet site with little on-site entertainment, but with a pleasant restaurant. Visitors with disabilities are made very welcome. It is a real campsite, not a 'camping village'.

Facilities

Fully equipped toilet block, plus small block near entrance, ramped access for disabled visitors. Some Turkish style toilets. Washbasins have cold water. Baby bath and changing facilities. Washing machine. Restaurant, home cooked dish-of-the-day. Well stocked shop. Library with some English books. TV, pool table, table tennis. Play area, minigolf, boules, all outside the barrier. Internet terminal. Canoeing possible. Off site: Bicycle hire 1 km. (cycleway to St Aygulf). Riding and golf 4 km. Beach 9 km.

Open: 1 April - 30 September.

Directions

From A8, exit Le Muy, follow N7 towards Fréjus for 13 km. Cross over A8 and turn right at roundabout through Roquebrune-sur-Argens towards St Aygulf for 1 km. Site signed on left. Follow private unmade road for 500 m. GPS: 43.44513, 6.65783

Charges guide

Per unit incl. 2 persons and electricity	€ 20,10 - € 23,40
extra person	€ 2,60 - € 3,30

Camping Cheques accepted.

Roquebrune-sur-Argens

Camping Caravaning Leï Suves

Quartier du Blavet, F-83520 Roquebrune-sur-Argens (Var) T: **04 94 45 43 95**
E: **camping.lei.suves@wanadoo.fr** **alanrogers.com/FR83030**

This quiet, pretty site is a few kilometres inland from the coast, 2 km. north of the N7. Close to the unusual Roquebrune rock, it is within easy reach of St Tropez, Ste Maxime, St Raphaël and Cannes. The site entrance is appealing – wide and spacious, with a large bank of well tended flowers. Mainly on a gently sloping hillside, the 310 pitches are terraced with shade provided by the many cork trees which give the site its name. All pitches have electricity and access to water. A pleasant pool area is beside the bar/restaurant and entertainment area. It is possible to walk in the surrounding woods. There are 150 mobile homes available to rent.

Facilities

Modern, well kept toilet blocks include washing machines, facilities for disabled visitors. Shop. Good sized swimming pool, paddling pool. Bar, terrace, snack bar, takeaway (all 1/4-30/9). Outdoor stage near the bar for evening entertainment in high season. Excellent play area. Table tennis, tennis, sports area. Internet terminal. Only gas barbecues are permitted. Off site: Bus stop at site entrance. Riding 1 km. Fishing 3 km. Bicycle hire 5 km. Golf 7 km. Beach at St Aygulf 15 km.

Open: 1 April - 15 October.

Directions

Leave autoroute at Le Muy and take the N7 towards St Raphaël. Turn left at roundabout onto D7 heading north signed La Boverie (site also signed). Site on right in 2 km. GPS: 43.47793, 6.63881

Charges 2010

Per unit incl. 2 persons and electricity	€ 25,50 - € 43,00
incl. 3 persons	€ 27,50 - € 45,50
extra person	€ 5,00 - € 9,00
child (under 7 yrs)	€ 3,10 - € 6,20
dog	€ 2,00 - € 3,50

Roquebrune-sur-Argens

Camping Domaine de la Bergerie

Vallée du Fournel, route du Col-du-Bougnon, F-83520 Roquebrune-sur-Argens (Var) T: **04 98 11 45 45**
E: **info@domainelabergerie.com** **alanrogers.com/FR83170**

This excellent site near the Côte d'Azur will take you away from all the bustle of the Mediterranean to total relaxation amongst the cork, oak, pine and mimosa in its woodland setting. The 60-hectare site is quite spread out with semi-landscaped areas for mobile homes and, grassy avenues of 200 separated pitches for touring caravans and tents. All pitches average over 80 sq.m. and have electricity, with those in one area also having water and drainage. The restaurant/bar, a converted farm building, is surrounded by shady patios, whilst inside it oozes character with high beams and archways leading to intimate corners. Activities are organised daily and, in the evening, shows, cabarets, discos, cinema, karaoke and dancing at the amphitheatre prove popular (possibly until midnight). A superb new pool complex supplements the original pool adding more outdoor pools with slides and a river feature, an indoor pool and a fitness centre with jacuzzi, sauna, Turkish bath, massage, reflexology and gym.

Facilities

Four toilet blocks are kept clean and include washbasins in cubicles, facilities for disabled people and babies. Supermarket. Bar/restaurant. Takeaway. Pool complex (all season) with indoor pool and fitness centre (body building, sauna, gym, etc). Tennis courts. Archery. Roller skating. Minigolf. English speaking children's club. Mini-farm for children. Fishing. Internet access and WiFi. Only gas barbecues are permitted. Off site: Riding or golf 2 km. Bicycle hire 7 km. Beach, St Aygulf or Ste Maxime 7 km. Water skiing and rock climbing nearby.

Open: 24 April - 30 September
(mobile homes 15 February - 15 November).

Directions

Leave A8 at Le Muy exit on N7 towards Fréjus. Drive for 9 km. then right onto D7 signed St Aygulf. Continue for 8 km. and then right at roundabout on D8; site is on the right. GPS: 43.4091, 6.6747

Charges guide

Per unit incl. 2 persons and electricity (6A)	€ 19,00 - € 36,50
incl. water and drainage	€ 24,50 - € 46,50
extra person	€ 5,00 - € 9,30
child (under 7 yrs)	€ 3,70 - € 6,70
dog	free - € 5,00

Roquebrune-sur-Argens

Kawan Village les Pêcheurs

F-83520 Roquebrune-sur-Argens (Var) T: **04 94 45 71 25**
E: **info@camping-les-pecheurs.com** **alanrogers.com/FR83200**

Les Pêcheurs will appeal to families who appreciate natural surroundings together with many activities, cultural and sporting. Interspersed with mobile homes, the 150 good sized touring pitches with electricity (6/10A) are separated by trees or flowering bushes. The Provençal-style buildings are delightful, especially the bar, restaurant and games room, with its terrace down to the river and the site's own canoe station (locked gate). Across the road is a lake used exclusively for water skiing with a sandy beach, a restaurant and minigolf. Enlarged spa facilities include swimming pool, large jacuzzi, massage, steam pool and a sauna. Developed over three generations by the Simoncini family, this peaceful, friendly site is set in more than four hectares of mature, well-shaded countryside at the foot of the Roquebrune Rock, which can be climbed accompanied by a guide. We became more and more intrigued with stories about the Rock, and the Holy Hole, the Three Crosses and the Hermit all call for further exploration, which reception staff are happy to arrange, likewise trips to Monte Carlo, Ventimigua (Italy) and the Gorges du Verdon, etc. The medieval village of Roquebrune is within walking distance.

Facilities

Modern, refurbished, well designed toilet blocks, baby baths, facilities for disabled visitors. Washing machines. Shop. Bar and restaurant (all open all season). Heated outdoor swimming pool (all season), separate paddling pool (lifeguard in high season), ice cream bar. Games room. Spa facilities. Playing field. Fishing. Canoeing. Waterskiing. Rafting and diving schools. Activities for children and adults (high season), visits to local wine caves. Only gas or electric barbecues. WiFi in reception, bar/restaurant and pool area. Off site: Bicycle hire 1 km. Riding 5 km. Golf 5 km. (reduced fees).

Open: 1 April - 30 September.

Directions

From A8 take Le Muy exit, follow N7 towards Fréjus for 13 km. bypassing Le Muy. After crossing A8, turn right at roundabout towards Roquebrune-sur-Argens. Site is on left after 1 km. just before bridge over river. GPS: 43.450783, 6.6335

Charges 2010

Per unit incl. 2 persons and electricity	€ 23,00 - € 43,00
extra person	€ 4,00 - € 7,80
child (5-10 yrs)	€ 3,20 - € 6,20
dog (max. 1)	€ 3,20

Camping Cheques accepted.

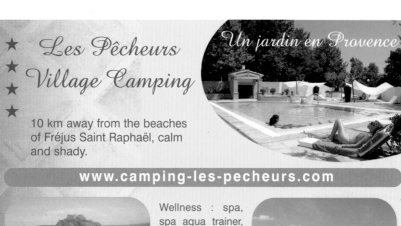

Saint Apollinaire

Campéole

Campéole le Clos du Lac

F-05160 Saint Apollinaire (Hautes-Alpes) T: **04 92 44 27 43**. E: **nadine.ferran@atciat.com**

alanrogers.com/FR05130

Le Clos du Lac is a member of the Campéole group and can be found close to the little mountain village of St Apollinaire on the southern fringe of the immense Ecrins National Park. The site has an altitude of 1,485m and has 73 pitches. Many of the pitches have fine views over the Lac de Serre Ponçon below and the mountain scenery all around. There is a smaller lake nearby, popular for its 'no kill' fly fishing, and also for swimming. This is also a great place to watch the night sky with a special astronomy week in August. The nearby Boscodon forest has been officially acknowledged as the least polluted place in France. On-site amenities include a small shop and communal barbecue area. The Lac de Serre Ponçon is popular for many water sports and the site is well located for exploring this wonderful mountain landscape. The popular Montagne aux Marmottes animal park is close at hand, along with the Cathedral of Notre Dame du Réal at Embrun. Le Clos du Lac is a good base for walking and mountain biking and the site's friendly managers will be pleased to recommend possible itineraries.

Facilities

Shop. Children's play area. Tourist information. Mobile homes for rent. Off site: St Apollinaire (shops and restaurants). Canoe hire. Fishing. Minigolf. Water sports. Hiking and mountain biking. Bicycle hire. National park of Les Ecrins.

Open: 29 May - 19 September.

Directions

St Apollinaire is on the north side of Lac de Serre Ponçon. From Gap head west on N94 towards Embrun. At Chorges join the D9 to St Apollinaire from where the site is well indicated. GPS: 44.5647, 6.3652

Charges 2010

Per unit incl. 2 persons and electricity	€ 15,10 - 18,30

Saint Aygulf

Camping de Saint Aygulf-Plage

270 avenue Salvarelli, F-83370 Saint Aygulf-Plage (Var) T: **04 94 17 62 49**. E: **info@camping-cote-azur.com**

alanrogers.com/FR83290

This is a large, well-run and self-sufficient campsite with a range of good facilities and direct access to the beach. The pitches here are well marked, flat and arranged in long rows, many with good shade from the pine trees. There are 1,100 in total, with 700 for touring units and the remainder used for mobile homes and chalets. Electricity is available on 500 touring pitches. Although there is no swimming pool on the site, direct access to the beach makes this is a fine family holidaying campsite. The beach is part of a long sandy bay which shelves gradually into the sea, suitable for children of all ages.

Facilities

Four large toilet blocks provide good, clean facilities. No facilities for disabled visitors. Laundry facilities. Supermarket. Bakery. Two restaurants. Bar with patio and stage for discos and entertainmanet. Pizzeria and takeaways. Multisports court. Play areas. Boules. First aid. Caravan storage. Beach. Only gas and electric barbecues are permitted.
Off site: Bicycle hire 100 m. Riding 1 km. Golf 6 km.

Open: 1 May - 19 September
(chalets, mobile homes 29 March - 25 October).

Directions

From A8 take exits for Puget or Fréjus and RN7 to Fréjus town. Follow signs to sea front and join the RN98. Saint Aygulf is 2 km. towards St Tropez. Site is signed and is behind Hotel Van der Valk.
GPS: 43.39229, 6.72685

Charges guide

Per unit incl. 2 persons	€ 11,50 - € 40,00
incl. electricity	€ 14,50 - € 50,00
extra person	€ 3,00 - € 8,00
child (0-7 yrs)	€ 2,00 - € 4,00
dog	€ 1,50 - € 4,00

Saint Aygulf

Caravaning l'Etoile d'Argens

F-83370 Saint Aygulf (Var) T: **04 94 81 01 41**. E: **info@etoiledargens.com**

alanrogers.com/FR83070

First impressions of l'Etoile d'Argens are of space, cleanliness and calm. This is a site run with families in mind and many of the activities are free, making it an excellent choice for a good value holiday. There are 450 level, fully-serviced grass pitches (all with 10A/16 electricity). Separated by hedges, they range in size from 100-250 sq.m. and mainly have good shade. The pool and bar area is attractively landscaped with olive and palm trees on beautifully kept grass. There are two heated pools (one for adults, one for children) both of which are designed very much with families in mind. Reception staff are very friendly and English is spoken. The exceptionally large pitches could easily take two caravans and cars or one family could have a very spacious plot with a garden like atmosphere. The river runs alongside the site with a free boat service to the beach (15/6-15/9). This is a good family site for the summer but also good in low season for a quiet stay in a superb location with excellent pitches. There are 88 mobile homes for rent. For a large site, l'Etoile d'Argens is unusually calm and peaceful, even in July.

Facilities

Over 20, well kept, small toilet blocks. Supermarket and gas supplies. Bar, restaurant, pizzeria, takeaway. Two adult pools (heated 1/4-30/6), paddling pool, jacuzzi, solarium. Floodlit tennis with coaching. Minigolf. Aerobics. Archery (July/Aug). Football and swimming lessons. Boules. Good play area. Children's entertainment (July/Aug). Activity programme with games, dances and escorted walking trips to the surrounding hills within 3 km. Off site: Golf and riding 2 km. Beach 3.5 km.

Open: 1 April - 30 September, with all services.

Directions

From A8 exit 36, take the N7 towards Le Muy, Fréjus. After 8 km. at roundabout take D7 signed Roquebrune, St Aygulf. In 9.5 km. (after roundabout) turn left signed Fréjus. Site is signed. Ignore width and height limit signs as site is before the limit (500 m). GPS: 43.41581, 6.70545

Charges guide

Per tent pitch (100 sq.m) incl. 2 persons and electricity	€ 14,00 - € 38,00
comfort pitch (130 sq.m) incl. 3 persons, water and drainage	€ 29,00 - € 62,00
luxury pitch (180 sq.m) incl. 4 persons	€ 33,00 - € 72,00
extra person	€ 6,00 - € 9,00
child (under 7 yrs)	€ 5,00 - € 7,00

Saint Cyr-sur-Mer

Camping Clos Sainte-Thérèse

Route de Bandol, F-83270 Saint Cyr-sur-Mer (Var) T: **04 94 32 12 21**. E: **camping@clos-therese.com**

alanrogers.com/FR83300

This is a very attractive, family-run campsite set in hilly terrain four kilometres from the beaches of Saint Cyr. The terraced pitches are level, some with sea views, the friendly owners offering a tractor service if required. There is a good shade from pines, olives, almonds and evergreen oaks. There are 88 pitches for touring units, all with electricity and 35 for chalets or mobile homes. Five pitches are fully serviced. The landscaped pool complex is pretty and well kept, with a small slide, jacuzzi and a separate paddling pool. This is a friendly, small site, ideal for couples or families with younger children.

Facilities

Clean, well maintained toilet facilities. Fridge hire. Shop. Bar, restaurant (15/6-15/9). Swimming pools (one heated) and paddling pool (1/4-30/9). Games room. TV room and library. Boules. Play area. Activities in high season. Off site: Golf course (9 and 18 holes, driving range) 500 m. Tennis opposite site. Bicycle hire 2 km. Beach 4 km. Fishing 4 km. Riding 8 km.

Open: 1 April - 30 September.

Directions

From A50 take D559 to Saint Cyr. Continue towards Bandol and site is 3 km. on the left. GPS: 43.15873, 5.72854

Charges guide

Per unit incl. 2 persons and electricity	€ 19,50 - € 28,60
extra person	€ 3,70 - € 5,60
child (3-7 yrs)	€ 2,30 - € 3,40
dog	€ 2,10 - € 2,40

L'Etoile d'Argens

✡✡✡✡

2010

Camping-Caravaning

www.etoiledargens.com
E-mail : info@etoiledargens.com
83370 Saint Aygulf - Tel : +33 4 94 81 01 41

Saint Aygulf

496

Camping Résidence du Campeur

B.P. 12, D7, F-83371 Saint Aygulf (Var) T: **04 94 81 01 59**. E: **info@residence-campeur.com**
alanrogers.com/FR83050

This excellent site near the Côte d'Azur will take you away from all the bustle of the Mediterranean coast. Spread out over ten hectares, there are separate areas for mobile homes and touring caravans and tents, with pitches arranged along avenues. The 67 touring pitches average 100 sq.m. in size and all have electricity connections and private sanitary facilities. The bar/restaurant is surrounded by a shady terrace, whilst friendly staff provide an excellent service. A pleasant pool complex is available for those who wish to stay on site instead of going swimming in the nearby lake or from the Mediterranean beaches. Activities are organised daily during the summer season and the site has it's own open-air cinema.

Facilities

Private toilet blocks are cleaned at regular intervals and include a washbasin, shower and WC. Laundry area with washing machines. Good supermarket. Bar/restaurant. Takeaway (all open all season). New swimming pool complex with four water slides (high season). Two tennis courts. Minigolf. Boules. Fishing. Bicycle hire. Play area. Games/TV room. Only gas or electric barbecues are permitted. Off site: Riding 1.5 km. Golf 2 km. Beach 2.5 km.

Open: 27 March - 30 September.

Directions

Leave A8 at Le Muy exit (no. 36) on N555 towards Draguignan then onto the N7 towards Fréjus. Turn right on D7 signed St Aygulf and site is on right about 2.5 km. before town. GPS: 43.40905, 6.70893

Charges guide

Per unit incl. 3 persons and electricity	€ 30,10 - € 50,15
extra person	€ 5,19 - € 8,65

Saint Aygulf

Camping les Lauriers Roses

Route de Roquebrune (D7), F-83370 Saint Aygulf (Var) T: **04 94 81 24 46**
E: **lauriersroses-camping@orange.fr** **alanrogers.com/FR83490**

Les Lauriers Roses is an attractive, small site with up-to-date facilities and the emphasis on comfort and relaxation. Steeply terraced over two hectares with views of the Mediterannean, it is owned by a friendly Dutch family who will personally site caravans on some of the more challenging areas of the site. There are 88 pitches (75 for touring units, with 6A electricity) of a good size, the majority set out on individual terraces. Units over 7.5 m. and twin-axle caravans are not accepted. Good English is spoken. A peaceful, comfortable site, there is a large, heated outdoor swimming pool with an adjoining bar and restaurant area. The restaurant offers a good selection of meals including Indonesian dishes and spare ribs. In high season limited sports, games and activities are organised for both young and old. There is a safe play area for children. The local town of Saint Aygulf is a lively resort town offering good shops, restaurants and attractions. The nearest supermarket is 250 m. away. Reception is closed 12.30-15.00 and the owners strictly observe these times.

Facilities

Two modern sanitary blocks. Good facilities for babies. Laundry and dishwashing areas. Bread to order. Bar and restaurant with terrace (19/4-29/9). TV for special sport events. Takeaway (19/4-29/9). Large heated outdoor swimming pool. Pétanque. Multisports court. Play area. Entertainment for adults and children (July/Aug). Internet access. Only gas barbecues are permitted. Caravan storage area. WiFi. Off site: Supermarket 200 m. Fishing (trout) 1 km. Boat hire 200 m. Riding 2 km. Beach 3 km. Water theme park 3 km. Golf 2 km. Tennis. Diving. Canoeing.

Open: 17 April - 25 September.

Directions

From A8 take exit 37 towards Puget-sur-Argens. Turn onto N7 (Fréjus). At first roundabout after Fréjus town sign, turn right (first exit) to Saint Aygulf at junction immediately after roundabout. Pass under railway bridge (4.5 m.) and turn right on D8. At T-junction, turn left on D7. Site is 2 km. on the right.
GPS: 43.40693, 6.70912

Charges 2010

Per unit incl. 2 persons and electricity	€ 36,00
extra person	€ 8,50

No credit cards.

Saint Maime

Flower Camping la Rivière

Lieu dit Les Côtes, F-04300 Saint Maime (Alpes-de-Haute-Provence) T: **04 92 79 54 66**
E: **info@camping-lariviere.com** **alanrogers.com/FR04220**

La Rivière is a member of the Flower group and is located on the edge of the Lubéron national park, bordering the river Largue. There are 100 pitches here. These are well shaded, of a good size and mostly with electrical connections (6A). A number of pitches are occupied by mobile homes and fully equipped tents, for rent. On-site amenities include a swimming pool, fishing lake and bar/restaurant (with takeaway food). The site becomes livelier in July and August with various activities including giant board games, dance evenings and various sports competitions.

Facilities

Small shop. Snack bar/restaurant. TV room. Volleyball. Takeaway meals (including home made pizzas). Swimming pool. Paddling pool. Fishing lake. Football. Play area. Activity and entertainment programme. Tourist information. Mobile homes and tents for rent. Off site: St Maime (shops and cafés). Cycle and walking tracks. Riding. Pierrevert (18-hole golf course).

Open: All year.

Directions

From Manosque, head north on D4096 to Voix and then head west on D13 towards St Maime. You will see the site before reaching the village.
GPS: 43.89778, 5.806376

Charges guide

Per unit incl. 2 persons and electricity	€ 16,50 - € 21,50

Saint Raphaël

Kawan Village Douce Quiétude

3435 boulevard Jacques Baudino, F-83700 Saint Raphaël (Var) T: **04 94 44 30 00**
E: **sunelia@douce-quietude.com** **alanrogers.com/FR83250**

Douce Quiétude is 5 km. from the beaches at Saint Raphaël and Agay but is quietly situated at the foot of the Estérel massif. There are 400 pitches, of which only 70 of are for touring set in pleasant pine woodland or shaded, green areas. The pitches are of a comfortable size, separated by bushes and trees. Electricity (6A), water, drainage and telephone/TV points are provided. This mature site offers a wide range of services and facilities including a pool complex. It can be busy in the main season yet is relaxed and spacious. Security is good with the wearing of identity bracelets mandatory throughout your stay.

Facilities

Fully equipped modern toilet blocks, facilities for babies and disabled visitors. Launderette. Bar, restaurant, takeaway, pizzeria (3/4-3/9). Shop. Three swimming pools (two heated), water slide, jacuzzi. Play area. Children's club, activities for teenagers (all July/Aug). Sports area. Games room. Tennis. Minigolf. Archery. Fitness centre, sauna. Evening entertainment, shows, karaoke, discos (July/Aug). Mountain bike hire. Only gas barbecues. Off site: Bus route 1 km. Golf and riding 2 km. Windsurf hire and sea fishing 5 km.

Open: 3 April - 2 October.

Directions

From A8 exit 38 (Fréjus/St Raphaël) take D100, signed Valescure then Agay. Follow site signs (round the back of Fréjus/St Raphaël). Access via N98 coast road turning north at Agay on D100. Pass Esterel Camping, then site signed. GPS: 43.44727, 6.80600

Charges guide

Per unit incl. 2 persons and electricity	€ 18,00 - € 47,50
extra person	€ 5,00 - € 9,00
child (3-13 yrs)	€ 4,00 - € 7,00
animal	€ 4,00

Camping Cheques accepted.

Saint Rémy-de-Provence

Camping Monplaisir

Chemin de Monplaisir, F-13210 Saint Rémy-de-Provence (Bouches du Rhône) T: **04 90 92 22 70**
E: **reception@camping-monplaisir.fr** **alanrogers.com/FR13040**

Only a kilometre from the centre of St Rémy, in the foothills of the Alpilles mountains, this is one of the most pleasant and well-run sites we have come across. St Rémy is a very popular town and the site was full when we visited in mid June. Everything about it is of a high standard and quality. The good impression created by the reception and shop continues through the rest of the site. In all there are 130 level grass pitches with nine taken by smart mobile homes, with 10A electricity everywhere. Flowering shrubs and greenery abounds, roads are tarmac and all is neat and tidy. There are six toilet blocks strategically placed for all areas. All are heated and one is larger, but all are unisex. The recreation area with a swimming pool (18 x 10 m), jacuzzi and paddling pool is overlooked by the bar. Open in July and August, it provides light meals and snacks and some entertainment.

Facilities

Six good quality, unisex toilet blocks are all heated in low season and have some washbasins in cabins. Family rooms and en-suite facilities for disabled people in two. Washing machines. Two motorcaravan service points. Shop with essentials (good cheese and cold meat counter), also takeaway pizzas. Bar with snacks (July/Aug). Swimming pool. Play area. Boules. Only gas or electric barbecues are permitted. Off site: St Rémy 1 km. Les Baux 5 km. Bicycle hire 1 km. Fishing 2 km. Riding 5 km. Golf 10 km.

Open: 1 March - 31 October.

Directions

From St Rémy town centre follow signs for Arles and Nîmes. At roundabout on western side of town take D5 signed Maillane and immediately left by a supermarket. Site is signed and is 500 m. on the left. GPS: 43.79695, 4.82372

Charges guide

Per unit incl. 2 persons and electricity (6A)	€ 18,10 - € 26,60
extra person	€ 4,50 - € 6,50
child (2-7 yrs)	€ 3,00 - € 5,50
dog	€ 1,80 - € 1,80

Saint Rémy-de-Provence

Camping Mas de Nicolas

Avenue Plaisance du Touch, F-13210 Saint Rémy-de-Provence (Bouches du Rhône) T: **04 90 92 27 05**
E: **camping-masdenicolas@nerim.fr** **alanrogers.com/FR13050**

The site has a very spacious feel to it, due mainly to the central area of gently sloping grass, dotted with shrubs, that is kept clear of pitches and used for leisure and sunbathing. The 140 pitches are separated by hedges and flowering shrubs, 34 for mobile homes, the remainder for touring units. The pitches all have electricity, water and drainage, and access roads are wide. Some pitches are an irregular shape and some are sloping, but many have views and they are mostly organised into groups of two and four. There is an attractive pool area with 'Balnéotherapie et Remise en form' or, as we would call it, a spa and gym.

Facilities

Good, modern toilet blocks including baby bathroom. Plans to refurbish one block. Dishwashing and laundry sinks, washing machines. Small bar (w/ends only until high season), occasional paella evenings. Swimming pool (15/5-15/9). Sauna, steam room, spa bath, gym. Play area. Bicycle hire. Internet access. Off site: Adjacent municipal gym, tennis, volleyball courts. Bicycle hire, riding 1 km. Fishing 2 km. Golf 15 km. St Rémy has a wide selection of restaurants, Wednesday market.

Open: 1 March - 31 October.

Directions

St Rémy-de-Provence is located where the D571 from Avignon connects with the D99 Tarascon - Cavaillon road. Site is signed from the village centre on the north side. Leave the A7 at Cavaillon or Avignon-Sud. GPS: 43.79622, 4.83879

Charges guide

Per unit incl. 2 persons and electricity	€ 18,00 - € 24,00
extra person	€ 5,50 - € 7,00
child (under 10 yrs)	€ 2,50 - € 5,50
animal	€ 5,50

Saint Romain-en-Viennois

Camping le Soleil de Provence

Route de Nyons, F-84110 Saint Romain-en-Viennois (Vaucluse) T: **04 90 46 46 00**
E: **info@camping-soleil-de-provence.fr** **alanrogers.com/FR84100**

The site has been developed to a high standard. The 162 average sized pitches, 150 for touring, are separated by hedges and a variety of young trees offering only a little shade (10A electricity). The excellent pool, surrounded by a sunbathing terrace, and overlooked by the bar, is an unusual shape with an island in the centre. Although there is no paddling pool one end of the pool is very shallow. There is organised entertainment in July and August but the emphasis is on a quiet, peaceful environment.

Facilities

Modern well appointed, heated toilet blocks, facilities for disabled visitors, baby room. Washing machine, dryer. Motorcaravan services. Small shop for bread, open on demand. Bar, snack bar (all season). New aqua park with waterslides and paddling pool. Small play area. Volleyball, table tennis, boules. Off site: Tennis 1 km. Vaison-la-Romaine 4 km. Rafting, hiking, cycling, mountain biking 4 km. (Mont Ventoux is a real challenge). Bicycle hire 5 km. Fishing 15 km. Medieval villages, market towns. vineyards.

Open: 15 March - 31 October.

Directions

Site is 4 km. north of Vaison-la-Romaine on the D938 road to Nyons. Turn right, signed St Romain-en-Viennois (site signed) and take first left to site. GPS: 44.26902, 5.10597

Charges guide

Per person	€ 3,50 - € 6,50
pitch	€ 3,00 - € 5,00
car	€ 3,00 - € 5,00
electricity (10A)	€ 4,00

No credit cards.

Salon-de-Provence

Camping le Nostradamus

Route d'Eyguières, F-13300 Salon-de-Provence (Bouches du Rhône) T: **04 90 56 08 36**
E: **gilles.nostra@wanadoo.fr** **alanrogers.com/FR13030**

Only some 5 km. from Salon-de-Provence, near the village of Eyguières, this is a very pleasant campsite with grassy shaded pitches thanks to the many trees which have been preserved here as a result of the imaginative irrigation scheme developed by the owners in the 18th century. The campsite edging the canal was first opened 42 years ago as a farm site but has now been developed to offer 83 hedged pitches including 10 used for mobile homes. There are 20 with full services, the rest having electricity connections (4/6/10A). This is a family site but having said that, the canal is unfenced.

Facilities

One large block with showers and toilets upstairs, and one small toilet block both provide all modern facilities including an en-suite unit for babies and children and another for disabled visitors (key). Washing machine (key). Motorcaravan service point. Shop (basic essentials) and bar. Takeaway/restaurant (15/5-30/9). Swimming and paddling pools (15/5-30/9). Play area outside entrance. Pétanque. Fishing. WiFi (charged). Off site: Regular bus service on the main road, timetables in reception. Riding 5 km. Golf 12 km.

Open: 1 March - end October.

Directions

From A7 exit 26 (Senas) follow N538 south for 5 km. Then take D175 west and pick up the D17 going south to Salon. Site is at junction of the D17 and CD72 with the entrance off the CD72. From A54 exit 13 go north towards Eyguières and take first right on CD72 (site signed). Entrance is just before the T-junction with the D17. GPS: 43.67772, 5.06476

Charges guide

Per unit incl. 2 persons	€ 16,85 - € 22,90
extra person	€ 5,60

Camping Cheques accepted.

Sanary-sur-Mer

Campasun Parc Mogador

167 chemin de Beaucours, F-83110 Sanary-sur-Mer (Var) T: **04 94 74 53 16**
E: **mogador@campasun.com / campasun@free.fr** **alanrogers.com/FR83320**

This site in the Mediterranean countryside is very much geared for family holidays with children. Some 20 minutes on foot from the beach, the site has a very large and well kept pool area and a stage for entertainment. Somewhat smaller than other sites of this type, there are 180 good sized pitches (160 for touring units). The ground is mainly level, if rather stony and sandy. Variable shade is available and all pitches have 10A electricity. There are plans to enlarge some of the smaller, 80 sq.m. pitches. The attractive pool, is surrounded by ample paved sunbathing areas.

Facilities

Two large, super deluxe toilet blocks, one including washbasins and showers in cabins. Laundry. Motorcaravan services. Restaurant with varied and full menu (1/4-5/11), also snacks, pizzas and takeaway. Swimming pool and paddling pool, solarium. Boules. Separate, building houses a TV room also used for entertainment shows, cabarets, etc. Miniclub for children and evening entertainment in season. Dogs are not accepted. Off site: Beach 800 m. Golf 6 km.

Open: 15 March - 5 November.

Directions

Take Bandol exit 12 from A50 and head for Six Fours on the N 559. Arriving at Sanary-sur-Mer turn left towards Beaucours and site is on left after 100 m. GPS: 43.1488, 5.7732

Charges guide

Per unit incl. 2 persons	€ 18,00 - € 36,00
with individual sanitary facility	€ 22,00 - € 42,00
extra person	€ 5,00 - € 7,00

Camping Cheques accepted.

Saint Vincent-les-Forts

Campéole le Lac

Le Fein, F-04340 Saint Vincent-les-Forts (Alpes-de-Haute-Provence) T: **04 92 85 51 57**
E: **nadine.ferran@atciat.com** **alanrogers.com/FR04210**

Le Lac is a member of the Campéole group and enjoys a fine location in the mountains of Haute Provence. The site can be found at an altitude of 800 m. on the banks of the large Lac de Serre Ponçon and many of the pitches have fine views of the lake and the surrounding mountains. The waters of the lake have an alluring blue-green hue and shelve gradually from the site's beach. There is also an ecological swimming pool, using natural water, consistent with this stunning natural setting. Other on-site amenities include a shop, restaurant and various sports facilities, notably volleyball and tennis. A number of pitches have lakeside positions and are particularly popular with fishermen. Water sports are popular and a hire service is offered, including canoes, electric boats and wakeboards. This is a great area for hiking and mountain biking, with many excellent routes passing very close to the campsite.

Facilities

Bar and snack bar. Shop. 'Eco' swimming pool. Fishing. Volleyball. Tennis. Children's play area. Canoes and boat hire. Activity and entertainment programme. Tourist information. Mobile homes, chalets and equipped tents for rent. Off site: Hiking and cycle tracks. Montagne aux Marmottes (animal park). Riding. Serre Ponçon dam.

Open: 1 May - 30 September.

Directions

The site is close to the village of St Vincent-les-Forts. From Gap, head south on N85 and then join the D900b following signs to Barcelonnette. Continue on this road along the valley of the Durance passing the massive Barrage (dam) de Serre Ponçon and continue towards St Vincent-les-Forts. The site is well indicated from here. GPS: 44.45682, 6.36529

Charges 2010

Per unit incl. 2 persons and electricity	€ 17.10 - 26.60

Vaison-la-Romaine

Camping Club International Carpe Diem

Route de Saint-Marcellin, B.P. 68, F-84110 Vaison-la-Romaine (Vaucluse) T: **04 90 36 02 02**
E: **contact@camping-carpe-diem.com** **alanrogers.com/FR84070**

Carpe Diem is a new site, attractively themed with Greek statues and an amphitheatre surround to its main pool. This is a good site for active families seeking all day entertainment and the situation is quite impressive with magnificent views over one of the most beautiful parts of France, yet only 800 m. from the fascinating town of Vaison-la-Romaine. There are 232 pitches with 119 small to medium sized, grass touring pitches, all with electricity and many with some degree of shade. A new terraced area has mobile homes, chalets and unshaded touring pitches. The main pool is impressive with its tiered seating, plants, etc. It is used as a theatre for evening entertainment. A simple pool with grass surrounds is near the play area. Organised activities off site include canoeing, riding, climbing, walking and mountain biking.

Facilities

Central toilet block with fountain and super children's facilities. Washing machine. Motorcaravan services. Reception, small shop (25/3-1/11). Bar (3/6-2/9), pizzeria (14/4-30/9). TV. Swimming pools including slides and flumes, one new, covered and heated. Play area. Minigolf, archery, volleyball, football, basketball. Mountain bike hire. Miniclub. Entertainment programme. Barbecues for hire. Off site: Fishing 1 km. Riding 2 km. Golf 20 km. Organised canoeing, riding, climbing, walking, mountain biking. Vaison-la-Romaine (800 m), with magnificent Roman ruins.

Open: 25 March - 1 November.

Directions

Leave Vaison-la-Romaine on D938 heading south towards Carpentras. 1 km. beyond the 'Super U' roundabout turn left on D151, signed St Marcellin. Site entrance is on the left immediately after the junction. GPS: 44.23431, 5.08964

Charges guide

Per unit incl. 2 persons	€ 16,00 - € 29,00
extra person	€ 4,60 - € 7,00
electricity (6/10A)	€ 3,70 - € 4,70

Veynes

Camping Solaire

F-05400 Veynes (Hautes-Alpes) T: **04 92 58 12 34**. E: **info@camping-solaire.com**

alanrogers.com/FR05080

An attractive, well-kept site surrounded by mountains and scenes of pastural beauty, the owners have developed Le Solaire to offer a wide range of facilities including a large jacuzzi heated to 30ºC. The swimming pools for adults and youngsters are supervised by a lifeguard, who also gives swimming lessons. The owners are particularly proud of their grasslands and of the 167 large pitches. There are 73 for touring in a separate area, many with good shade and all having 6A electricity with water close by. You can use the site's website to view and select your pitch. The site is well placed to explore the area around Gap and the surrounding countryside. The village of Veynes is ancient and attractive and has a range of shops and facilities.

Facilities

Modern, clean and heated toilet blocks with facilities for campers with disabilities. Bar (1/6-30/9). Shop, snacks, takeaway. (1/7-30/9). Swimming pools (1/6-30/9). Jacuzzi (1/7-30/9). Large games room/TV. Football. Bicycle hire. Off site: Fishing 100 m. Lake, beach, swimming, boating, 300 m. Rafting, hang gliding, Rock climbing, many bike rides and hiking tracks. Veynes with range of shops and facilities 2 km. Old market towns with museums and ancient houses.

Open: All year.

Directions

From Grenoble on N75, in town of Aspres-sur-Buëch, take D994a to join D994 travelling northeast towards Veynes. Site is signed on right 1 km. before village. After 300 m. take next right, entrance on right within 50 m. GPS: 44.52161, 5.80341

Charges guide

Per unit incl. 2 persons	€ 10,00 - € 17,00
extra person	€ 4,00 - € 6,90
child (2-9 yrs)	€ 1,85 - € 3,50
electricity (5A)	€ 3,00

Villars-Colmars

Camping Caravaning le Haut-Verdon

RD908, F-04370 Villars-Colmars (Alpes-de-Haute-Provence) T: **04 92 83 40 09**
E: **campinglehautverdon@wanadoo.fr** **alanrogers.com/FR04060**

For those seeking a quiet, family site set in most spectacular scenery, Camping le Haut-Verdon is ideal. It is on the banks of the Verdon, an excellent trout river, which flows through the spectacular gorge. Surrounded by the majestic peaks of the Alpes-de-Haute-Provence, it is on the doorstep of the Mercantour National Park. Set amongst the pines, the 109 pitches are mostly on the large size but are rather stony. With 73 for touring units, all have electricity (6/10A) but some require long leads. There is a small village nearby and the town of St André is 23 km. away.

Facilities

Refurbished, heated toilet block. Washing machines. Freezer for ice packs. Room for tenters for inclement weather. Motorcaravan services. Small shop. Bar/restaurant, takeaway. Heated swimming, paddling pools (from 1/6). Small play area. Giant chess. Boules. Skittle alley. Tennis. TV room. Organised games and competitions. Fishing. Barbecue areas (portable ones banned). Off site: Riding 1 km. Bicycle hire 3 km.

Open: 5 May - 16 September.

Directions

Follow D955 north from St André les Alpes towards Colmar. After 11 km. road number changes to D908. Site on right at southern edge of Villars-Colmars. Caravans not advised to use the D908 from Annot or Col d'Allos from Barcelonnette.
GPS: 44.1601, 6.60625

Charges guide

Per unit incl. 2 persons	€ 13,00 - € 25,00
extra person	€ 3,00 - € 5,00
child (2-7 yrs)	€ 2,00 - € 3,00
dog	free - € 2,00
electricity (6/10A)	€ 3,00 - € 4,00

Villecroze-les-Grottes

Camping Club le Ruou

Les Esparrus 309, RD 560, F-83690 Villecroze-les-Grottes (Var) T: **04 94 70 67 70**. E: **info@leruou.com**
alanrogers.com/FR83410

This is a family-oriented site in the Provençal countryside, very much geared for family holidays with children. Some 45 minutes by car from the coast at Fréjus, the site has a large and well kept pool area and a mobile stage for entertainment. Smaller than some other sites of this type, there are 100 good sized pitches (26 for touring units). On mainly terraced, rather stony, ground with good shade, all have 6/10A electricity. Some of the pitches for caravans are along a steep path but there is a 4 x 4 available to assist. The heated pool complex with three slides is surrounded by a sunbathing area and some shade.

Facilities

One new super de-luxe toilet block includes washbasins in cabins. Facilities for babies and disabled visitors. Laundry facilities. Snacks and takeaway (15/6-31/8). The main building houses a bar and entertainment room with TV. Area for shows, cabarets, etc. with mobile stage. Two swimming pools. Tennis. Boules. Play area. Miniclub for children and evening entertainment in season. Charcoal barbecues are not permitted. Off site: Beach 35 km. Fishing, riding and bicycle hire 5 km. Golf 25 km.

Open: 1 April - 30 October.

Directions

Villecroze-les-Grottes is northwest of Fréjus. From the A8 (Toulon - Mandelieu-la-Napoule) take exit 13 onto the N7 towards Le Muy. At Les Arcs turn left on D555 (Draguignan), then onto D557 to Villecroze. Site is on the left side of this road. GPS: 43.55345, 6.297983

Charges guide

Per unit incl. 2 persons and electricity	€ 18,20 - € 30,20
extra person	€ 3,80 - € 6,20
child (2-7 yrs)	€ 2,20 - € 5,00
dog	€ 1,40 - € 2,80

Camping Cheques accepted.

Volonne

Sunêlia Hippocampe

Route de Napoléon, F-04290 Volonne (Alpes-de-Haute-Provence) T: **04 92 33 50 00**
E: **camping@l-hippocampe.com** **alanrogers.com/FR04010**

Hippocampe is a friendly, family-run, 'all-action' lakeside site, with families in mind, situated in a beautiful area of France. The perfumes of thyme, lavender and wild herbs are everywhere and the higher hills of Haute Provence are not too far away. There are 447 level, numbered pitches (221 for touring units), medium to very large (130 sq.m) in size. All have electricity (10A) and 243 have water and drainage, most are separated by bushes and cherry trees. Some of the best pitches border the lake. The restaurant, bar, takeaway and shop have all been completely renewed. Games, aerobics, competitions, entertainment and shows, plus a daily club for younger family members are organised in July/August. A soundproof underground disco is set well away from the pitches and is very popular with teenage customers. Staff tour the site at night ensuring a good night's sleep. The site is, however, much quieter in low season and, with its good discounts, is the time for those who do not want or need entertaining. The Gorges du Verdon is a sight not to be missed and rafting, paragliding or canoe trips can be booked from the site's own tourist information office. Being on the lower slopes of the hills of Haute-Provence, the surrounding area is good for both walking and mountain biking. All in all, this is a very good site for an active or restful holiday and is suitable for outfits of all sizes. English is spoken.

Facilities

Toilet blocks vary from old to modern, all with good clean facilities that include washbasins in cabins. Washing machines. Motorcaravan service point. Bread available (from 26/4). Shop, bar, restaurant and pizzeria (26/4-7/9). Large, heated pool complex (24/4-30/9) with five new waterslides, (second pool 13/6-30/9). Tennis. Fishing. Canoeing. Boules. Several sports facilities (some with free instruction). Charcoal barbecues are not permitted. Off site: Village of Volonne 600 m. Bicycle hire 1 km. Riding 12 km. Various sporting opportunities.

Open: 3 April - 30 September.

Directions

Approaching from the north turn off N85 across river bridge to Volonne, then right to site. From the south right on D4, 1 km. before Château Arnoux.
GPS: 44.10462, 6.01688

Charges 2010

Per unit incl. 2 persons and electricity	€ 16,00 - € 32,00
extra person (over 4 yrs)	€ 3,00 - € 6,50
dog	€ 2,00 - € 4,00

Special low season offers.
Camping Cheques accepted.

Bathed in sunshine from early spring to late autumn, surrounded by stunning scenery, cosmopolitan towns and superb sandy beaches, no wonder this is one of France's most sought-after destinations.

DÉPARTEMENT: 06 ALPES-MARITIME

MAJOR CITIES: NICE, CANNES, MONTE CARLO (MONACO)

The glittering Côte d'Azur, perhaps better known as the French Riviera, is a beautiful stretch of coast studded with sophisticated towns such as the famous Monte Carlo, Nice, and Cannes, not forgetting the other famous and arguably the most glamorous resort of St Tropez. With its vast expanses of golden sandy beaches and long lazy hours of sunshine, this is a paradise for sun worshippers and beach enthusiasts.

It's a spectacular coast of rugged coves, sweeping beaches and warm seas. The quaint harbours and fishing villages have become chic destinations, now full of pleasure yachts, harbour-side cafés and crowded summertime beaches. Further up in the hills are quieter tiny medieval villages with winding streets and white-walled houses with terracotta roofs, which have attracted artists for many years. In St Paul-de-Vence visitors browse through shops and galleries set on narrow winding cobblestone streets and inland Grasse is the perfume capital of the world, surrounded by the Provençal lavender fields and shady olive groves which pervade the air with a magical scent at certain times of the year.

Places of interest

Antibes: old city with 17th-century ramparts, 12th-century castle.

Cannes: popular for conventions and festivals, Cannes film festival, la Croisette, old city.

Grasse: capital of the perfume industry.

Menton: warmest of coastal cities, year round resort.

Nice: Promenade des Anglais, fine arts museum, Matisse museum.

Roquebrune: château, Ste Marguerite church.

Saint Paul-de-Vence: medieval village, Maeght Foundation.

Cuisine of the region

Aigo Bouido: garlic and sage soup.

Bouillabaisse: fish soup.

Rouille: an orange coloured sauce with peppers, garlic and saffron.

Bourride: a creamy fish soup.

Pissaladière: Provençal bread dough with onions, anchovies and olives.

Pistou (Soupe au): vegetable soup bound with *pommade*.

Pommade: a thick paste of garlic, basil, cheese and olive oil.

Ratatouille: aubergines, courgettes, onions, garlic, red peppers and tomatoes in olive oil.

www.guideriviera.com
info@guideriviera.com
(0)4 93 37 78 78

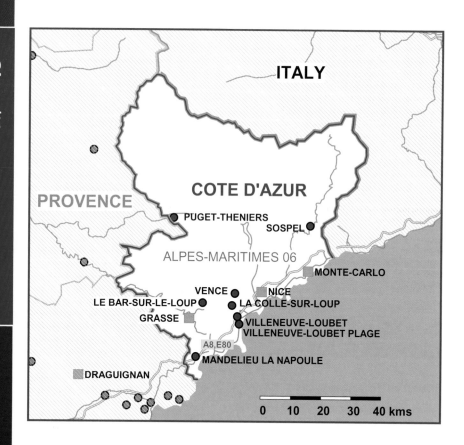

ITALY
COTE D'AZUR
PROVENCE
PUGET-THENIERS
SOSPEL
ALPES-MARITIMES 06
MONTE-CARLO
VENCE
NICE
LE BAR-SUR-LE-LOUP
LA COLLE-SUR-LOUP
GRASSE
VILLENEUVE-LOUBET
VILLENEUVE-LOUBET PLAGE
A8,E80
MANDELIEU LA NAPOULE
DRAGUIGNAN
0 10 20 30 40 kms

La Colle-sur-Loup

Camping les Pinèdes

Route du Pont de Pierre, F-06480 La Colle-sur-Loup (Alpes-Maritimes) T: **04 93 32 98 94**
E: **camplespinedes06@aol.com** **alanrogers.com/FR06100**

Les Pinèdes is 7 km. inland from the busy coast, at the centre of all the attractions of the Côte d'Azur, yet far enough away to be a peaceful retreat at the end of a busy day. Run by the third generation of family owners, the site is terraced on a wooded hillside where olives and vines used to grow. All the level pitches have electricity (3-10A), most also with water and they are separated by low bushes. There are plans for 12 new pitches at the top of the site and also a small children's pool. The restaurant at the site entrance has an excellent reputation. A 'Sites et Paysages' member.

Facilities

Two excellent new toilet blocks. One block has facilities for disabled visitors. Baby room. Shop, bakery. Bar, restaurant, takeaway. Swimming pool. Play area. Field for volleyball, basketball, football, archery, boules. Entertainment (July/Aug). Weekly walks in the hills (June-Sept., light breakfast carried by the donkeys). New mobile homes to rent. WiFi. Off site: River fishing 50 m. Village 1 km. (tennis, riding, leisure park, keep fit course, antiques quarter). St Paul-de-Vence is 15 minutes away.

Open: 15 March - 30 September.

Directions

From A8 take D2 towards Vence. At Colle-sur-Loup roundabout take D6 signed Grasse, site on right in 3 km. at large sign after the restaurant entrance. GPS: 43.6817, 7.08335

Charges 2010

Per unit incl. 2 persons and electricity	€ 18,70 - € 36,50
extra person	€ 4,10 - € 5,50
child (under 6 yrs)	€ 2,20 - € 3,50
dog	€ 2,10 - € 3,20

Le Bar-sur-Loup

Camping Caravaning les Gorges du Loup

965 chemin des Vergers, F-06620 Le Bar-sur-Loup (Alpes-Maritimes) T: **04 93 42 45 06**

E: **info@lesgorgesduloup.com** **alanrogers.com/FR06090**

Les Gorges du Loup is situated on a steep hillside above Grasse. The one kilometre lane which leads to the site is narrow with passing places. The 70 pitches are on level terraces, all with electricity and many have stupendous views. Some pitches are only suitable for tents and the site roads are quite steep. A quiet family site, there is no organised entertainment. Grasseis surrounded by fields of lavender, mimosa and jasmine and has been famous for the manufacture of perfume since the 16th century. The friendly and enthusiastic owners provide 4 x 4 assistance and there is a new parking area at the entrance.

Facilities

Clean toilet blocks with washbasins and hot showers, dishwashing and laundry sinks have only a single hot tap. Washing machine and iron. Reception, small shop, bread. Small bar/restaurant with terrace, takeaway (all 3/6-8/9). Swimming pool, small slide, diving board, but no pool for small children. Boules. Skittles. TV room. Children's climbing frame, slide. No charcoal barbecues. Chalets, mobile homes for hire. Off site: Bar-sur-Loup with its few shops, restaurants is only a 500 m. walk. Grasse 9 km.

Open: 3 April - 25 September.

Directions

From Grasse on the D2085 Nice road. D3 briefly to Châteauneuf Pré du Lac. D2210 to Pont-de-Loup, Vence. Site signed on right. Pass village of Bar-sur-Loup on left, after sharp right turn, follow narrow access road 750 m. (passing places).
GPS: 43.7017, 6.9948

Charges guide

Per unit incl. 2 persons	€ 18,50 - € 25,00
extra person	€ 4,58

No credit cards.

Mandelieu-la-Napoule

497

Camping Caravaning les Cigales

505 avenue de la Mer, F-06210 Mandelieu-la-Napoule (Alpes-Maritimes) T: **04 93 49 23 53**

E: **campingcigales@wanadoo.fr** **alanrogers.com/FR06080**

It is hard to imagine that such a quiet, peaceful site could be in the middle of such a busy town and so near Cannes. The entrance (easily missed) has large electronic gates that ensure that the site is very secure. There are only 115 pitches (42 mobile homes) so this is quite a small, personal site. There are three pitch sizes, from small ones for tents to pitches for larger units and all have electricity (6A), some fully serviced. All are level with much needed shade in summer, although the sun will get through in winter when it is needed. The site is alongside the Canal de Siagne and for a fee, small boats can be launched at La Napoule, then moored outside the campsite's side gate. Les Cigales is open all year so it is useful for the Monte Carlo Rally, the Cannes Film Festival and the Mimosa Festival, all held out of the main season. English is spoken.

Facilities

Well appointed, clean, heated toilet blocks. Facilities for babies and disabled visitors. New laundry area. Motorcaravan services. Restaurant and takeaway (May-Oct). Heated swimming pool and large sunbathing area (April-Oct). New play area. Two games machines. Canal fishing. Off site: Beach 800 m. The town is an easy walk. Two golf courses within 1 km. Railway station 1 km. for trains to Cannes, Nice, Antibes, Monte Carlo. Hypermarket 2 km. Bus stop 10 minutes.

Open: All year.

Directions

From A8, exit 40, bear right. Remain in right hand lane, continue right signed Plages-Ports, Creche-Campings. Casino supermarket on right. Continue under motorway to T-junction. Turn left, site is 60 m. on left opposite Chinese restaurant.
GPS: 43.5391, 6.94275

Charges 2010

Per unit incl. 2 persons and electricity	€ 39,00 - € 51,50
extra person	€ 8,00
child	€ 4,00
dog	€ 1,50

Sospel

Camping Domaine Sainte Madeleine

Route de Moulinet, F-06380 Sospel (Alpes-Maritimes) T: **04 93 04 10 48**
E: **camp@camping-sainte-madeleine.com** **alanrogers.com/FR06010**

Domaine Sainte Madeleine is an attractive, peaceful site, with swimming pool, in spectacular mountain scenery. It is about 20 km. inland from Menton, and very near the Italian border. The approach to this site involves a 17 km. climb with hairpin bends and then a choice of going through the pass or an 800 m. long tunnel (3.5 m. high, 3 m. wide). Situated on a terraced hillside with mountain views towards Italy, manoeuvring within the site presents no problem as the pitches are on level, well drained grass. The lower ones have shade but those higher up have none. Electricity is available to 60 of the 66 pitches.

Facilities

Good quality toilet block with hot showers (token required). Hot water (often only warm) for dishwashing and laundry sinks drawn from single tap. Washing machines. Motorcaravan services. Gas supplies. Bread can be ordered. Swimming pool (140 sq.m. and heated in spring and autumn). Off site: The attractive small town of Sospel is 4 km. with many restaurants, bars, cafés and shops. Tennis, riding and a centre for mountain biking. Fishing 1 km.

Open: 31 March - 30 September.

Directions

From A8 take Menton exit towards Sospel from where you turn onto the D2566 (route de Moulinet). Site is 4 km. north of Sospel on the left.
GPS: 43.89702, 7.41685

Charges guide

Per unit incl. 2 persons	€ 19,00
extra person	€ 4,20
child (under 6 yrs)	€ 2,40
electricity (10A)	€ 2,90
animal	€ 1,40

Less 15% outside July/Aug. No credit cards.

Vence

Camping Caravaning Domaine de la Bergerie

1330 chemin de la Sine, F-06140 Vence (Alpes-Maritimes) T: **04 93 58 09 36**
E: **info@camping-domainedelabergerie.com** **alanrogers.com/FR06030**

La Bergerie is a quiet, family owned site, situated in the hills 3 km. from Vence and 10 km. from the sea at Cagnes-sur-Mer. With no mobile homes or chalets, this extensive, natural, lightly wooded site is in a secluded position about 300 m. above sea level. Most of the pitches are shaded and all are of a good size. There are 450 pitches, 224 with electricity (2/5A), water and drainage. Because of the nature of this site, some pitches are a little distance from the toilet blocks. With the aim of keeping this a quiet and tranquil place to stay, there are no organised activities and definitely no groups allowed. It is a large site but because it is so extensive it does not give that impression.

Facilities

Refurbished toilet blocks, excellent provision for disabled people (pitches near the block are reserved for disabled people). Good shop. Small bar/restaurant, takeaway (all 1/5-30/9). Large swimming pool, paddling pool, spacious sunbathing area (1/5-30/9). Playground. Bicycle hire. Tennis. 12 shaded boules pitches (lit at night) with competitions in season. No barbecues. Off site: Riding and fishing 10 km. Golf 18 km. Hourly bus service (excl. Sundays) from site to Vence.

Open: 25 March - 15 October.

Directions

From A8 exit 47 take Cagnes-sur-Mer road towards Vence. Site west of Vence – follow 'toutes directions' around town, join D2210 Grasse road. In 2 km. at roundabout, turn left, follow site signs, 1.5 km. Site is on right in light woodland. GPS: 43.71174, 7.0905

Charges guide

Per unit incl. 2 persons and electricity	€ 19,00 - € 26,00

Less 10-15% for longer stays.
Camping Cheques accepted.

Villeneuve-Loubet

Parc Saint-James le Sourire

Route de Grasse, F-06270 Villeneuve-Loubet (Alpes-Maritimes) T: **04 93 20 96 11**
E: **info@camping-parcsaintjames.com** **alanrogers.com/FR06190**

Le Sourire is a member of the Parc Saint James group. There are 411 pitches here and many are occupied by mobile homes and chalets. There are however 241 touring pitches dispersed throughout the wooded terrain. The site is close to the impressive La Vanade sports complex which has a massive range of activities including no fewer than 55 tennis courts, a riding centre and a nine-hole golf course. There is a good range of activities on site too, including a large swimming pool with a regular programme of aqua gym, water polo and other activities. Le Sourire is a good base for exploring the area and lies close to the Provençal village of Villeneuve Loubet, midway between Cannes and Nice. The nearest beach is just 4 km. Children are well catered for here with an active children's club and a good play area. There is a lively activity programme including excursions and entertainment is arranged regularly during the peak season. Mobile homes and chalets for rent.

Facilities

Laundry. Supermarket. Swimming pool and separate children's pool. Bar and restaurant. Takeaway. Play area. TV room. Gym. Games room. Sports competitions. Children's club. Evening entertainment. Disco. Off site: Cannes and Nice. Nearest beaches 4 km. Marineland water park. Leisure park at La Vanade.

Open: 15 May - 15 September.

Directions

Take the Villeneuve-Loubet exit from the A8 autoroute and follow signs to Grasse joining the D2085. The site can be found on the left, 2 km. from Villeneuve Loubet. GPS: 43.6603, 7.10429

Charges guide

Per unit incl. 2 persons and electricity	€ 17,00 - € 28,00
extra person	€ 2,50 - € 4,50
child (under 10 yrs)	€ 1,50 - € 4,00

Parc Saint-James
Villages Club
Parc Saint-James LE SOURIRE
Route de Grasse 06270 Villeneuve-Loubet
Tél : 00 33 4 93 20 96 11 - Fax : 00 33 4 93 22 07 52
Enjoy the pleasure of spending your holidays outdoors in our village-club where everything has been designed for your leisure and well-being. Everyone is catered for young and old alike; you can do everything of nothing. So come and discover your future holidays at Le Sourire. Choose your kingdom, well look after the rest.
www.camping-parcsaintjames.com

Villeneuve-Loubet-Plage

Castel Camping la Vieille Ferme

296 boulevard des Groules, F-06270 Villeneuve-Loubet-Plage (Alpes-Maritimes) T: **04 93 33 41 44**
E: **info@vieilleferme.com** **alanrogers.com/FR06050**

In a popular resort area and open all year, La Vieille Ferme is a family owned site with good facilities. It has 113 level gravel-based touring pitches, 95 fully serviced and the majority separated by hedges. Some are only small, simple pitches for little tents. There is also a fully serviced pitch on tarmac for motorhomes. There are special winter rates for long stays with quite a few long stay units on site. The entrance to the site is very colourful with well tended flower beds. English is spoken at reception and the whole place has a very friendly feel to it.

Facilities

Modern, heated, well kept toilet blocks, children's toilets, baby room, facilities for disabled people. Motorcaravan services. Washing machines, dryer. Shop (Easter-Sept). Machine with drinks, sweets, ices in TV room. Gas, bread, milk to order. Refrigerator hire. Swimming pool, children's pool, heated and covered for winter use (closed mid Nov-mid Dec). Jacuzzi. Internet. Boules. Games, competitions organised in July/Aug. Off site: Bus from outside site. Beach 1 km. Fishing 1 km. Golf and bicycle hire 2 km. Riding 6 km. Marineland water park.

Open: All year.

Directions

From west, A8, exit 44 Antibes, D35, 3.5 km. Left towards Nice, N7. After 3.5 km. turn left for site between Marine Land and Parc de Vaugrenier. Site is 150 m. on right. Avoid N98 Route du Bord de Mer. GPS: 43.62002, 7.12586

Charges guide

Per unit incl. 2 persons	€ 13,50 - € 31,00
extra person	€ 3,90 - € 5,00
child (under 5 yrs)	€ 2,50 - € 3,00
electricity (2-10A)	€ 2,50 - € 6,00
dog	€ 1,50

The island of Corsica both dramatic and beautiful. The scene is spectacular with b of white sand lapped the clear blue waters of Mediterranean. At certain ti of the year the entire island is ablaze with exotic flowers, aide Corsica's excellent sunshine rec

DÉPARTEMENTS: 2A CORSE-SUD; 2B HAUTE-CORSE

MAJOR CITIES: AJACCIO AND BASTIA

Corsica is regarded by some as the jewel of the Mediterranean islands and is made up of two départements: Haute Corse (upper Corsica) and Corse du Sud (southern Corsica). The island has endured a bloody history, having being much disputed by the Greeks, Romans and Lombards. Five hundred years of Italian rule has influenced the look of the island with Italian-style hilltop hamlets and villages developed alongside mountain springs. Many of the villages feature rustic, unadorned churches and also a few Romanesque examples too.

The variety of scenery is spectacular. Across much of the island one can discover dramatic gorges, glacial lakes, gushing mountain torrents and magnificent pine and chestnut forests.You'll also experience the celebrated perfume of the Corsican maquis: a tangled undergrowth of fragrant herbs, flowers and bushes that fills the warm spring and summer air. The highest mountains lie to the west, while the gentler ranges, weathered to strange and often bizarre shapes, lie to the south and a continuous barrier forms the island's backbone.

Places of interest

Ajaccio: a dazzling white city full of Napoleonic memorabilia.

Bastia: historic citadel towering over the headland. The old town has preserved its streets in the form of steps connected by vaulted passages, converging on the Vieu port (the old port). The new port is the re commercial port of the island.

Cuisine of the region

Brocchui: sheeps' milk cheese is used muc in cooking in both its soft form (savoury c sweet) or more mature and ripened.

Capone: local eels, cut up and grilled on a spit over a charcoal fire.

Dziminu: fish soup, like bouillabaise but much hotter. Made with peppers and pimentos.

Figatelli: a sausage made of dried and spiced pork with liver. Favourite between-meal snack.

Pibronata: a highly spiced local sauce.

Prizzutu: a peppered smoked ham; resembles the Italian prosciutto, but with chestnut flavour added.

www.visit-corsica.com
info@visit-corsica.com
(0)4 95 51 00 00

SAINT FLORENT
BASTIA
N197
CALVI
HAUTE-CORSE 2B
SAN-NICOLAO
CORTE
BRAVONE
ALERIA
CORSICA
SAGONE
GHISONACCIA
N198
AJACCIO
CORSE-DU-SUD 2A
STE LUCIE-DE-PORTO-VECCHIO
PORTO-VECCHIO
BONIFACIO
0 25 50 75 kms

Bonifacio

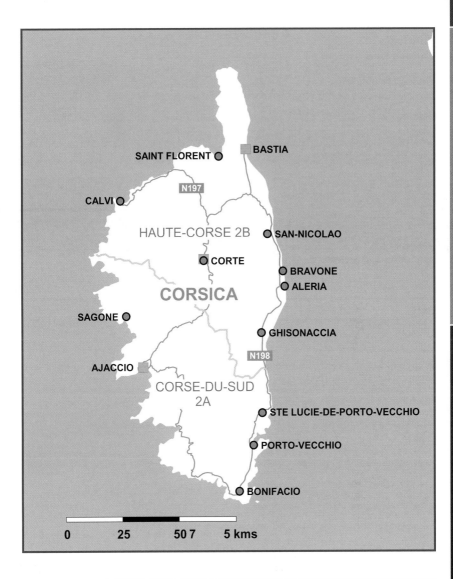

Camping U-Farniente de Pertamina Village

RN198, F-20169 Bonifacio (Corse-du-Sud) T: **04 95 73 05 47**. E: **pertamina@wanadoo.fr**

alanrogers.com/FR20000

Whether or not you are using the ferry to Sardinia, Bonifacio deserves a visit and this is a convenient site for a night stop or longer stay. The 120 pitches, many in delightful settings, have electricity (3A), are partially terraced and are hedged with trees and bushes, providing shade. They are fairly flat and vary in size, many being well over 100 sq.m. A central feature of the site is the large attractive swimming pool, surrounded by terraces. The bar, restaurant, pizzeria/grill and crêperie are on a series of terraces above the pool and patios.

Facilities

Two toilet blocks include washbasins in semi-private cubicles, British and Turkish style WCs, washing machines plus drying and ironing facilities. Motorcaravan service point at entrance (public). Shop. Takeaway. Bar, restaurant, pizzeria/grill serving set meals and à la carte menu at reasonable prices (shorter opening hours in May, June and Oct). Swimming pool. Tennis. Play area. TV room. Excellent gym. Off site: Bonifacio 4 km.

Open: Easter - 15 October.

Directions

Site is on the RN198 road, 4 km. north of Bonifacio to the east. Well signed as Pertamina Village.
GPS: 41.41790, 9.17990

Charges guide

Per unit incl. 2 persons and electricity	€ 19,50 - € 30,00
extra person	€ 6,50 - € 9,50
child (under 8 yrs)	free - € 5,80

Camping Cheques accepted.

Bonifacio

Camping Rondinara

Suartone, F-20169 Bonifacio (Corse-du-Sud) T: **04 95 70 43 15**. E: **reception@rondinara.fr**
alanrogers.com/FR20240

The views from every pitch in this site are stunning, either coastal or the rolling hills and cliffs inland. The 'great outdoors' describes this campsite which is away from the any tourist over-development and is at one with nature. The natural and informal pitches sit on the hillside above a superb bay with sheltered water, fine silver sand and safe swimming. Most pitches have shade but most tree foliage is relatively low as yet. Large boulders make natural divisions and some pitches need long leads for the 6A electricity. The beach is a 400 m. walk down a rough track through the maquis.

Facilities

Three excellent, modern toilet blocks are very clean and offer hot water throughout, hot showers and single sex British style toilets. Motorcaravan service point. Shop. Pizza restaurant. Bar. Swimming pool. Play area. Games room. Electronic games. Entertainment and family activities. Torches are essential here. Off site: Beach, boat launching and fishing 400 m. Golf, riding and sailing 15 km.

Open: 15 May - 30 September.

Directions

Site is mid-way between Bonifacio and Porto-Vecchio off the RN 198. Take the D158 to Baie de la Rondinara for 7 km. (site is well signed). The road is rough and narrow but large units will have no trouble negotiating it. GPS: 41.47323, 9.26316

Charges guide

Per unit incl. 2 persons and electricity	€ 21,40 - € 26,80
extra person	€ 5,90 - € 7,60

Calvi

Camping Paduella

Route de Bastia, F-20260 Calvi (Haute-Corse) T: **04 95 65 06 16**. E: **campingpaduella@wanadoo.fr**
alanrogers.com/FR20170

Camping Paduella is a beautifully maintained, simple site which has been run by the friendly Peretti family for 40 years. As it is a popular site, it is best to book ahead for high season. There is a wide choice of pleasant pitches, some shaded under pines, others grassed and hedged with less shade. All are well maintained on level terraces with good access. The lovely white sand beach is 300 m. away and the picturesque town of Calvi is a delightful 30 minute walk. There is a fairly busy road and light railway to cross to get to the beach but most of the walk is through the shaded beach parkland.

Facilities

Two centrally located spotless modern sanitary blocks (British style WCs). Well equipped showers. New baby bathroom. Laundry with washing machines, ironing board. Small shop with basic supplies and fresh bread. Pizzeria and bar. Internet access. Play area. Sports ground. Fridge hire can be arranged. Off site: Supermarket and ATM 200 m. Adventure activities 200 m. Riding and bicycle hire 700 m. Boat launching and marina 1 km. Scuba diving, rowing and sailing nearby.

Open: 1 May - 15 October.

Directions

From the north, site is just before the town of Calvi. It is directly off the RN197 on the left and is well signed. GPS: 42.55210, 8.76410

Charges guide

Per unit incl. 2 persons and electricity	€ 21,70 - € 25,50
extra person	€ 6,30 - € 7,70
child (-7)	€ 3,15 - € 3,75

No credit cards.

Calvi

Camping la Pinède

Route de la Pinède, F-20260 Calvi (Haute-Corse) T: **04 95 65 17 80**. E: **info@camping-calvi.com**
alanrogers.com/FR20180

Camping La Pinède is a well ordered, family site of 185 touring pitches, all with 4-16A electricity. The pitches are marked and level (although the pine roots are a nuisance in places). There is access for large units in some areas. Water points are spread around the site and everything is kept tidy and clean. Under the mature pines it can be quite dark but there are plenty of alternatives in the light. The site is divided into areas of accommodation – pitches for tour operators, mobile homes and tourers. Unusually all facilities are in separate buildings.

Facilities

Three well maintained and well placed concrete sanitary buildings offer hot showers and facilities for disabled campers. Washing machines. Clean and fresh, these blocks are better than most on the west coast. Motorcaravan service point. Shop (June-Sept). Bar. Restaurant (May-Sept). Swimming pool (no lifeguard). Internet access. Play area. Tennis. Overnight parking for late arrivals. Off site: Beach 200 m. Fishing 200 m. Riding 500 m. Boat launching 2 km. Bicycle hire 2 km. Golf 22 km.

Open: 1 April - 31 October.

Directions

Site is north of Calvi off the RN197, just south of the D251 road to the airport. Look for signs off the roundabout here and take care along a narrow road with leaning fir trees. GPS: 42.55320, 8.76860

Charges guide

Per person	€ 6,50 - € 8,50
child (under 7 yrs)	€ 3,50 - € 4,50

Corte

Camping Restonica

Faubourg Saint Antoine, F-20250 Corte (Haute-Corse) T: **04 95 46 11 59**. E: **vero.camp@worldonline.fr**
alanrogers.com/FR20110

Tucked away alongside the pretty Restonica river and near the Pont Neuf leading into the stunning mountainside old city of Corte, Camping Restonica is ideally placed for tourists wanting to visit Corte or travel on the popular inland mountain railway (the station is only a few hundred metres from the site). This is a small, simple site catering for those who want to enjoy the many delights of Corte. The entrance is steep but manageable for all but very large units, there are flat pitches for campers and caravans in the middle of the site, and many beautiful terraced pitches for tents dotted along the shady riverbank.

Facilities

Single, central toilet block is unisex and somewhat dated, although very clean. Toilet for disabled visitors but site not really suitable. Washing machine. Bread to order. Bar and snack bar. River fishing. Off site: Sightseeing. Famous train journeys across Corsica. Museum. Only university in Corsica (politically significant).

Open: 15 April - 30 September.

Directions

Approaching Corte, turn left at first roundabout onto Ave du 9 Septembre. Site is 300 m. on the right. It is signed from the roundabout and at the top of the steep, narrow access road. GPS: 42.30150, 9.15200

Charges guide

Per person	€ 6,50
pitch	€ 5,00 - € 7,50

No credit cards.

Ghisonaccia

Camping Arinella Bianca

Route de la Mer, F-20240 Ghisonaccia (Haute-Corse) T: **04 95 56 04 78**. E: **arinella@arinellabianca.com**
alanrogers.com/FR20010

Arinella is a lively, family-oriented site on Corsica's east coast. The 415 level, grassy, good size, irregular shape pitches (198 for touring units) have a variety of trees and shrubs providing ample shade and 6A electricity (long leads needed). Some pitches overlook attractive lakes which have fountains and are lit at night. The site has direct acess to a long beach of soft sand. The brilliantly designed resort-style pools and paddling pool, overlooked by an attractive large restaurant, terraced bar and entertainment area, form the hub of Arinella Bianca. When we visited the area was buzzing with activity at night and appeared to delight everyone with its excellent family entertainment. The extremely active children's club with an information point, boutique and supermarket complete the area. A huge range of sport and leisure facilities is also available. Evening entertainment starts at 21.00 and a local disco can continue until the early hours. This site is a tribute to its owner's design and development skills, appearing to be in natural glades when, in fact, they were created from former marshland with a freshwater lake.

Facilities

Four open plan sanitary blocks provide showers, (some with dressing area), washbasins in cabins, mainly British style WCs. Laundry. Motorcaravan services. Shop, bar, terrace, restaurant, amphitheatre, snack bar (all 10/5-15/9). Swimming pool (from 1/5). Windsurfing. Canoeing. Fishing. Tennis. Riding. Bicycle hire. Miniclub. Play area. Disco. Good entertainment programme in the main season. Communal barbecue area. WiFi. Off site: Sailing 300 m. Boat launching 2 km.

Open: Mid April - 30 September.

Directions

Site is 4 km. east of Ghisonaccia. From N198 in Ghisonaccia look for sign 'La Plage, Li Mare'. Turn east on D144 at roundabout just south of town. Continue for 3.5 km. to further roundabout where site is signed to right. Site is 500 m. Watch for speed bumps on approach road and on site. GPS: 41.99840, 9.44200

Charges guide

Per unit incl. 2 persons	€ 22,00 - € 38,00
extra person	€ 8,00 - € 10,50
electricity (6A)	€ 5,50

Camping Cheques accepted.

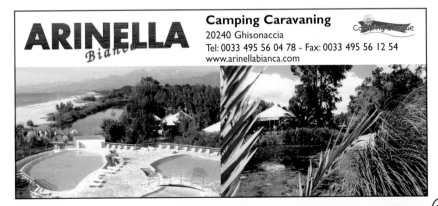

Porto-Vecchio

Camping la Vetta

Route de Bastia, la Trinité, F-20137 Porto-Vecchio (Corse-du-Sud) T: **04 95 70 09 86**
E: **info@campinglavetta.com** **alanrogers.com/FR20060**

This is a site not to be missed in Corsica, the English/French owners Nick and Marieline Long having created a very friendly and peaceful country park setting for their campsite to the north of La Trinité village. The 8.5 hectares of well maintained campsite are part sloping, part terraced with an informal pitch allocation system. It seems to stretch endlessly. The abundance of tree varieties including many cork oaks give shade to 111 pitches which all have 10A electricity. The site has a brilliant new lagoon-style pool, all landscaped and serviced by its own snack bar and crêperie.

Facilities

Spotless, traditional style toilet facilities have plenty of hot water. Laundry facilities. Shop (July/Aug), gas supplies. Excellent restaurant, patio, bar (July/Aug). Swimming pool, paddling pool and water play area. Snooker table. Play area. TV. Entertainment in high season. Off site: Beach 1.5 km. Supermarket 2 km. Fishing, watersports and boat launching 1.5 km. Riding 4 km. Bicycle hire 5 km. Golf 7 km. Public transport 800 m.

Open: 1 June - 1 October.

Directions

Site is in La Trinité village, off the RN198 (east side), north of Porto-Vecchio. GPS: 41.63160, 9.29290

Charges guide

Per unit incl. 2 persons and electricity	€ 21,50 - € 26,10
extra person	€ 6,50 - € 7,80
child (under 7 yrs)	€ 3,00 - € 4,00

Sagone

Camping le Sagone

Route de Vico, F-20118 Sagone (Corse-du-Sud) T: **04 95 28 04 15**. E: **sagone.camping@wanadoo.fr**
alanrogers.com/FR20230

Situated outside the bustling seaside resort of Sagone, surrounded by protective hills, this campsite which used to be a fruit farm is in an ideal location for exploring Corsica's wild and rocky west coast or its mountainous interior. The large site borders a pleasant river and has 300 marked, shaded pitches, 250 with electricity (6A). There are 105 bungalows offered for rent, which are generally separated. The restaurant/bar and games room overlook the pool and they are the focal point of this well managed site. Entertainment takes place in the central area by the pool during the high season.

Facilities

Clean, fully equipped toilet blocks with washbasins in cubicles. Facilities for disabled people. Baby baths. Washing machines, dryers. Motorcaravan services. Large supermarket (all year). Restaurant, pizzeria, bar, games room. Swimming pool (June-Sept). Half-court tennis. Play area. Sub-aqua experience in pool. Communal barbecues. Satellite TV. Internet. Car wash. New putting and golf practice area. Off site: Riding 500 m. Diving, windsurfing, mountain biking, fishing, bicycle hire, climbing nearby. Tours to local places of interest.

Open: 1 May - 30 September.

Directions

From Ajaccio take the RD81 in direction of Cergése and Calvilby (by coast road). In Sagone take RD70 in direction of Vico, Sagone can be found on left after 1.5 km. next to supermarket. GPS: 42.13040, 8.70550

Charges guide

Per unit incl. 2 persons	€ 14,50 - € 23,00
extra person	€ 4,50 - € 7,70
child (under 12 yrs)	€ 2,25 - € 3,90
electricity	€ 3,0

Camping Cheques accepted.

Saint Florent

Camping d'Olzo

L.D. Strutta, F-20217 Saint Florent (Haute-Corse) T: **04 95 37 03 34**. E: **info@campingolzo.com**
alanrogers.com/FR20150

The friendly Barenghi family who own this site are delightful. They are pleased to welcome you to their compact site and Dutch, Italian and English are spoken. The site is flat and very peaceful with a wide variety of trees, including gums and olives, which offer shade to most of the informal pitches. There is ample room to manoeuvre for large units. All 60 pitches have electricity (10A) and are not far from the central sanitary block or the facilities which are grouped near reception. The site is a short walk from the beach. A swimming pool was added in 2008.

Facilities

Single central block has unisex toilets (Turkish and British style) and single sex hot showers. Water at the sinks is cold. Everything is kept very clean and smart. Washing machines. Motorcaravan service point. Facilities for disabled campers. Small shop supplies most essentials (July/Aug), bread to order. Restaurant/pizzeria and bar. Swimming pool planned. Internet access. Play area. Communal barbecue area. Mobile homes for hire. Off site: Town of St Florent with usual facilities. Bus from gate. Riding 500 m. Bicycle hire 2 km. Boat launching 2 km. Sailing 2 km. Fishing 500 m.

Open: 1 April - 30 September.

Directions

From Bastia take the D81 west to St Florent. After some 30 minutes the site is well signed as you enter the village on the right. GPS: 42.69360, 9.32650

Charges 2010

Per unit incl. 2 persons and electricity	€ 22,00 - € 26,50
extra person	€ 3,30 - € 6,00
child (under 10 yrs)	€ 1,65 - € 3,00
dog	€ 1,20 - € 1,50

Sainte Lucie-de-Porto-Vecchio

Camping Caravaning Santa Lucia

Lieu-dit Mulindinu, F-20144 Sainte Lucie-de-Porto-Vecchio (Corse-du-Sud) T: **04 95 71 45 28**
E: **information@campingsantalucia.com** **alanrogers.com/FR20070**

Camping Santa Lucia is a very small, friendly, family run site in a delightful southern Corsican setting, where little English is spoken. Behind the little reception hut is an unsophisticated restaurant and bar which have terraces overlooking the pool. It is very pleasant in the evenings when ornamental lamps light up the area. There are 160 pitches, 60 with 6A electrical connections and 18 serviced pitches. Some of the pitches are in enclosed bays created from huge boulders, making them very private. This site is only minutes by car from Porto Vecchio and with very reasonable prices, will suit many.

Facilities

Two clean and pleasant toilet blocks include British style toilets, some washbasins in cubicles, dishwashing and laundry sinks, and a washing machine. Facilities for disabled visitors. Bread to order. Bar (15/6-15/9). Restaurant and takeaway (1/7-31/8). Swimming and paddling pools. Play area and high season miniclub for children. Minigolf. Communal barbecues. Satellite TV. WiFi. Off site: Beach, fishing and watersports 5 km. Golf 20 km. Supermarket opposite site entrance and services such as a doctor, chemist, grocers and newsagent in village.

Open: 15 May - 10 October.

Directions

Site is at south end of Sainte-Lucie-de-Porto-Vecchio village, off N198 and well signed.
GPS: 41.69660, 9.34340

Charges guide

Per person	€ 5,00 - € 7,00
child (2-10 yrs)	free - € 3,30
pitch	€ 3,20 - € 4,75
incl. electricity	€ 5,00 - € 7,50

San-Nicolao

Camping Merendella

Moriani-Plage, F-20230 San-Nicolao (Haute-Corse) T: **04 95 38 53 47**. E: **merendel@club-internet.fr**
alanrogers.com/FR20030

This attractive family run site has the advantage of direct access to a pleasant, long sandy beach. It is peacefully situated on level grass with many well tended trees and shrubs providing shade and colour. Level green sites such as this are unusual in Corsica and are ideal for families or those with mobility problems. There are 196 pitches, all with electricity (2/5A, long leads required) and a minimum of 100 sq.m. There is a dedicated night parking area if you arrive late. An excellent bar, restaurant/pizzeria is close to the site entrance (takeaway pizzas are available).

Facilities

Modern blocks, two individual cabin units near the beach. Washbasins in private cubicles. British and Turkish style WCs. Facilities for disabled campers. Laundry facilities. Motorcaravan services. Shop. Bar/restaurant, pizzeria. TV room. Games room. Late arrival area. Diving centre. Play area. Torches essential. No pets. Off site: Restaurant outside gate. All watersports 200 m. along beach from site. Bus 800 m. from gate. Town 800 m. with usual amenities. Bicycle hire 800 m. Tennis and riding 2 km.

Open: 15 May - 30 September.

Directions

Site is to seaward side of the RN198, 800 m. south of Moriani Plage. GPS: 42.3631, 9.5298

Charges guide

Per person	€ 6,35 - € 7,50
caravan and car	€ 6,15 - € 6,95
motorcaravan	€ 5,95 - € 7,10
electricity (2/5A)	€ 3,30 - € 4,30

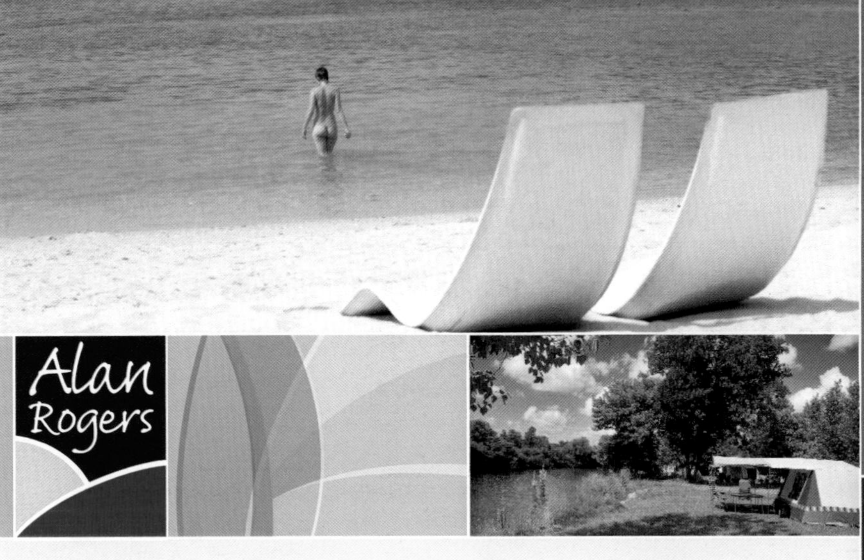

Today there are many more people that enjoy naturist campsites than one would at first think. Some are dedicated naturists who practise their way of life wherever they may and who in the UK may well belong to clubs of like-minded people. For others, especially those who have enjoyed sunbathing on one of the many designated naturist areas on European beaches and feel comfortable with it, the logical next step is to try a holiday in a naturist village or campsite.

This growing number of 'holiday naturists' clearly enjoy the relaxed atmosphere prevailing on naturist sites. If they are not members of British Naturism they can pick up a naturist card on the first site they visit. The rules are simple: respect for the environment and for other visitors. You are encouraged to strip off but, in reality, it is up to you, except in and around the swimming pool where there is always a 'no clothes' rule. Clothes do tend to label people and without them there is a relaxed informality and sense of equality often missing in today's 'designer society'.

We feature some 23 naturist campsites in this guide and have been impressed by the friendly welcome and cultural aspects of their entertainment and range of activities – classical music beside the pool, walking trails to discover local wildlife or book-binding classes, for example. Most campsites make an effort to provide good entertainment and to make your holiday memorable; on the naturist sites in particular this is usually achieved quite elegantly without the frenzy that sometimes pervades more commercially-minded sites.

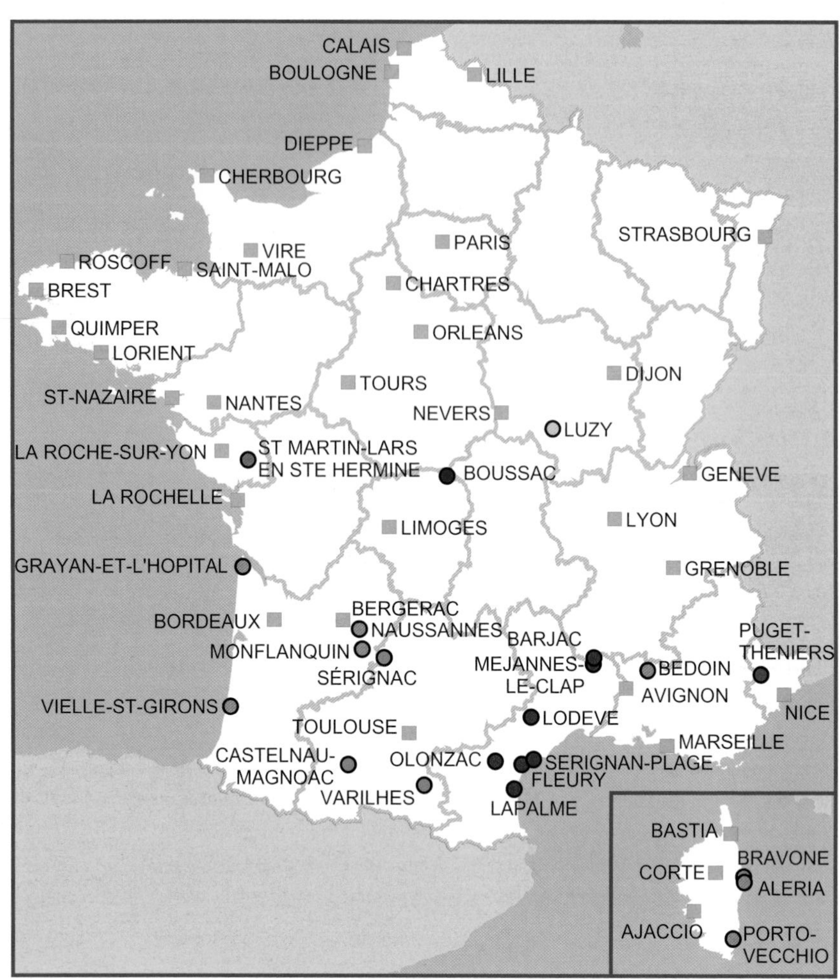

Saint Martin-Lars en Sainte Hermine

Camping Naturiste le Colombier

Le Colombier, F-85210 Saint Martin-Lars en Sainte Hermine (Vendée) T: **02 51 27 83 84**
E: **lecolombier.nat@wanadoo.fr** **alanrogers.com/FR85140**

A countryside site for naturists near La Roche sur Yon, just right for those seeking a peaceful holiday. It provides around 160 pitches in seven very natural fields on different levels linked by informal tracks. There are level, terraced areas for caravans and a feeling of spaciousness with pitches around the edges of fields, unmarked and with electricity (6/10A, some may require long leads). The bar/restaurant is in a converted barn. The site's 125 acres provide many walks throughout the attractive, wooded valley and around the lake.

Facilities

Fully equipped toilet blocks are good, providing some showers in cubicles. Motorcaravan service point. Grocer/baker calls daily. Bar/restaurant with à la carte and full menus (order before 13.00), home baked bread and pizzas. Heated swimming pool. Fishing. Volleyball, boules and table tennis. Playground. Pony-and-trap rides and one day a week children can make their own bread. Plans for a sauna and aquagym. Off site: Shop 1 km.

Open: 1 April - 30 October.

Directions

From N148, La Roche-sur-Yon - Niort road, at Sainte Hermine, turn onto D8 eastward for 4 km. Turn left on D10 to Saint Martin-Lars. Site is signed.
GPS: 46.59795, -0.96936

Charges guide

Per unit incl. 2 persons and electricity	€ 18,50 - € 21,50
child (3-9 yrs)	€ 3,40 - € 3,50
child (10-16 yrs)	€ 4,70 - € 4,80

Luzy

Domaine Naturiste de la Gagère

F-58170 Luzy (Nièvre, Burgundy) T: **03 86 30 48 11**. E: **info@la-gagere.com**

alanrogers.com/FR58060

At this secluded and attractive campsite, you will receive a really good welcome from the enthusiastic founders of Naturocamp. The site is spacious and well equipped with 120 good sized level grassy pitches, some shaded, some open, of which 100 are available for tourers. Many are arranged in groups around three sides of rectangles between hedges. Electricity (4-10A) is supplied to 84 pitches, six of which are fully serviced, but some require leads of up to 40 m. There are plenty of water points. In high season there are organised activities and entertainment and a children's club meets twice per week.

Facilities

Three modern unisex toilet blocks, one heated, contain British style WCs, washbasins and preset showers. Facilities for disabled people. Baby changing. Motorcaravan services. Laundry facilities. Shop (31/5-15/9). Bar (all season). Restaurant with snack bar and takeaway (1/5-15/9). Satellite TV. Two heated swimming pools (one all season, the other 15/5-15/9). Sauna and health suite. Playgrounds. Boules. Bicycle hire. Only gas barbecues permitted (available for hire). Off site: Luzy 10 km. Fishing 10 km. Riding 20 km.

Open: 1 April - 1 October.

Directions

Leave Autun, N81, south-west towards Bourbon-Lancy. In 27 km. turn left (signed Gagère) down a narrow lane. Site is approx. 3 km.
GPS: 46.81692, 4.05636

Charges 2010

Per unit incl. 2 persons and electricity	€ 30,75 - € 34,00
extra person	€ 6,50

Admin fee for stays of 3 nights or less (€ 5).

Boussac

Creuse Nature Naturisme

Route de Bétête (D15), F-23600 Boussac (Creuse, Limousin) T: **05 55 65 18 01**

E: **creuse.nature@wanadoo.fr** **alanrogers.com/FR23030**

This is a very spacious and well maintained naturist site set in the beautiful Limousin region in the centre of France. The 100 large grassy pitches, some slightly sloping, are laid out in an open wooded parkland setting. The 80 touring pitches all have electricity (10A) and are mainly positioned around the perimeter of the site or the small fishing lake. A central feature is the swimming pool, bar and restaurant complex. Various activities are organised for all the family and there are many footpaths to enjoy around the borders of the site.

Facilities

Four modern, very clean toilet blocks with the usual facilities (open plan, so little privacy). Facilities for disabled visitors. Dishwashing and laundry facilities. Small shop (baker calls). Indoor (heated) and outdoor pools. Paddling pool. Sauna. Bar. Restaurant (July/Aug). Archery (high season). Boules. Bicycle hire. Lake fishing. Internet access. Gas barbecues only. Accommodation for hire. Off site: Boussac 5 km.

Open: 1 April - 31 October.

Directions

Boussac lies 35 km. west of Montluçon, midway between the A20 and A71 autoroutes. In Boussac, site is well signed. Take D15 west for about 3 km. Site is on right. GPS: 46.34902, 2.18691

Charges 2010

Per unit incl. 2 persons and electricity	€ 21,50 - € 29,50
extra person	€ 4,00 - € 7,00

Grayan et l'Hôpital

Espace Naturiste Euronat

F-33590 Grayan et l'Hôpital (Gironde, Aquitaine) T: **05 56 09 33 33**. E: **info@euronat.fr**

alanrogers.com/FR33160

Euronat is really a large naturist town with extensive facilities, direct access to 1.5 km. of sandy beach and a thalassotherapy centre. The caravan and camping sites are in two areas separate from the chalets and mobile homes. A variety of good sized, fairly flat and sandy pitches, includes some suitable for large motorhomes. All pitches have 10A electricity and some also have water and drainage. The 'town centre' is superb with two supermarkets, an organic supermarket, cashpoint, butcher, fish shop, bakery where freshly squeezed orange juice is available, restaurants including fish, brasserie, pizzeria/crêperie, and a takeaway with hot and cold dishes and desserts which you can eat in the 'square' at picnic tables.

Facilities

Sanitary blocks are well maintained with some heated (not all open in low season). Facilities for people with disabilities. Launderette. Motorcaravan services. Shops, restaurants. Swimming pool, flumes, children's pool. Swimming lessons. Activities and workshops, archery, pony club, riding, tennis, pétanque. Children's activities and day care. TV rooms, video/games centre. Library. Multi-purpose hall for dances, film nights, music evenings, sports activities. Supervised beach. No barbecues (communal areas provided). Torch may be useful. Off site: Long distance cycle path passes site.

Open: 23 March - 3 November.

Directions

From Bordeaux ring road take exit 7, then D1215 to Lesparre and Vensac, then follow (large) signed route.
GPS: 45.41627, -1.13178

Charges guide

Per unit incl. 2 persons, electricity, water and drainage	€ 23,00 - € 43,50
extra person	€ 4,00 - € 7,00

Camping Cheques accepted.

Monflanquin

Camping Naturiste Domaine Laborde

Paulhiac, F-47150 Monflanquin (Lot-et-Garonne, Aquitaine) T: **05 53 63 14 88**
E: **domainelaborde@wanadoo.fr** **alanrogers.com/FR47140**

Ideally situated on the border of Lot-et-Garonne and Dordogne, Domain Laborde is a naturist site of outstanding quality, with sweeping views from many of the higher pitches. This hilly and terraced site has 120 well maintained touring pitches, many shaded, some partially shaded and all surrounded by woodland. Electricity (3/6/10A) is available. There are also 30 chalets for rent. The site has something for everyone and even in low season it is very popular. If you are new to naturist sites, then this is a must. The ambience is good and you will make new friends. A 'Sites et Paysages' member.

Facilities

New wash block as well as three sanitary blocks are well sited and clean. Washing machines and dryer. Shop with daily deliveries of fresh bread and milk. Bar with TV. Snack bar serving pizzas. Restaurant. Large swimming pool, whirlpool, sauna, children's pool and indoor heated pool. Massage. Trampoline. Two play areas. Boules. Giant chess board. Communal barbecue. Entertainment for children (high season). Various excursions and other activities for adults and children are organised. Off site: Riding 2 km. Golf 30 km.

Open: 1 April - 1 October.

Directions

From Monflanquin take D272 towards Monpazier. About 10 km. along the road look for the signs to site. It is very well signed at regular intervals and will read 'Domaine Laborde' GPS: 44.613889, 0.835556

Charges 2010

Per unit incl. 2 persons and electricity	€ 23,00 - € 29,50
extra person	€ 5,00 - € 6,00
child (under 6 yrs)	€ 4,00 - € 4,50
dog	€ 3,50

Vielle-Saint-Girons

Domaine Naturiste Arnaoutchot

F-40560 Vielle-Saint-Girons (Landes, Aquitaine) T: **05 58 49 11 11**. E: **contact@arna.com**
alanrogers.com/FR40120

'Arna' is a large naturist site with extensive facilities and direct access to the beach. Even with 500 pitches, its layout in the form of a number of sections, each with its own character, makes it quite relaxing and very natural. These sections amongst the trees and bushes of the Landes provide a variety of reasonably sized pitches, most with electricity (3/6A), although the hilly terrain means that only a limited number are flat enough for motorcaravans. The centrally located amenities are extensive and of excellent quality. We suggest that new visitors telephone before arrival as the site can require them to be proposed by a family who have stayed at the campsite for at least three years.

Facilities

Heated sanitary facilities include the usual naturist site type of blocks with communal hot showers and also a number of tiny blocks. Motorcaravan services. Supermarket, other shops. Bar/restaurant, pizzeria and tapita (fish) bar. Heated indoor swimming pool with solarium, whirlpool and slide. Outdoor pool, sunbathing area. New paddling pool. Spa, sauna, steam, whirlpool, massages. TV, games rooms. Cinema. Library. Internet point. Bicycle hire. Fishing. Torches useful. Gas and electric barbecues permitted. American motorhomes not accepted. Off site: Riding or golf 5 km.

Open: 4 April - 27 September.

Directions

Site is signed off the D652 road at Vielle-Saint-Girons. Follow D328 for 3-4 km. GPS: 43.9075, -1.361683

Charges guide

Per unit incl. 2 persons	€ 11,90 - € 36,50
extra person (over 3 yrs)	€ 2,00 - € 7,50
electricity (3/6A)	€ 4,00 - € 5,60
animal	€ 1,40 - € 3,30

Special offers available.
Camping Cheques accepted.

Naussannes

Centre Naturiste le Couderc

Le Couderc, F-24440 Naussannes (Dordogne, Aquitaine) T: **05 53 22 40 40**. E: **info@lecouderc.com**
alanrogers.com/FR24190

This is one of the most beautiful camping sites in the Dordogne and probably the best naturist site that we have seen. Set in 28 hectares of open countryside, there is a feeling of spaciousness, calm and tranquillity. The family go the extra mile to ensure visitors enjoy their visit. There are 188 pitches of which 170 are for touring units and the remainder being chalets which are available for rent. One is adapted for disabled visitors. The site is on different levels with undulating slopes but the generous pitches are level and easily accessible. Generally open but mature trees all around offer some shade. There is a very attractive restaurant and bar housed in a fine old Perigordine style building. A dining terrace outside adds to the ambiance on a summer evening. The swimming pool is solar heated as is the pool for toddlers. A jacuzzi and sauna are in the same area. Children will enjoy a well equipped play area in plenty of space together with a children's club in July and August. Music evenings and sporting competitions are also organised.

Facilities

Five very clean modern toilet blocks with facilities for children and disabled visitors. Washing machines. Dryer. Superb restaurant and bar. Takeaway. Terrace. Shop. Heated swimming pools. Jacuzzi. Sauna. Bicycle Hire. Two ponds, one for fishing the other with cable slide. Children's club with sculpture and circus lessons. Play area. Entertainment. Walking tracks. Caravan storage. Off site: Caves. Châteaux. Market towns. Walking. Riding 10 km. Golf 20 km.

Open: 1 April - 1 October.

Directions

From Bergerac take N21. Turn left on D25 to Issigeac. Continue towards Naussannes for 8 km. Turn left at signpost indicating Naussannes 2 km. Le Couderc is 350 m. on the right. GPS: 44.75602, 0.70212

Charges guide

Per person	€ 4,20 - € 7,00
child (under 12 yrs)	€ 2,75 - € 4,65
pitch	€ 8,35 - € 13,90
electricity	€ 4,50
dog	€ 2,75 - € 4,65

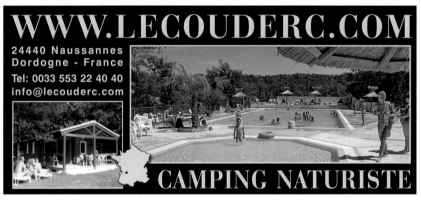

Castelnau-Magnoac

Domaine Naturiste l'Eglantière

Aries-Espenan, F-65230 Castelnau-Magnoac (Hautes-Pyrénées) T: **05 62 39 88 00**. E: **info@leglantiere.com**
alanrogers.com/FR65010

Alongside a small, fast flowing river, in woods it comprises 12 hectares for camping and caravanning, with a further 32 for walking and relaxing. The river is suitable for swimming and canoeing, with fishing nearby. The 83 traditional, varying size, grassy, level pitches have 10A electricity (long leads). The older secluded ones are separated by a variety of tall trees and bushes, the newer ones more open. There is a tenting area across the river. The site has a medium sized swimming pool with sunbathing areas and a children's pool, overlooked by the clubhouse and terrace.

Facilities

Two toilet blocks in typically naturist style, providing under cover, open plan, facilities. Small block has individual cubicles. Shop (July/Aug). Clubhouse, bar, small restaurant (June-Sept), pizzeria, takeaway (July/Aug), internet. Soundproofed activities/disco area, play room for younger children. Swimming pool. Play area, children's entertainment in season. Volleyball, badminton, table tennis, pétanque, archery. River activities. Canoe, mountain bike hire. Trekking, cross-country cycling. No barbecues. Torches useful. Off site: Restaurants in the nearby village.

Open: Easter - October.

Directions

From Auch take D929 south towards Lannemezan. After Castelnau-Magnoac continue past aerodrome and turn onto the D9 towards Monleon-Magnoac. Take the first left towards Ariès-Espénan and follow site signs. GPS: 43.26466, 0.52119

Charges guide

Per unit incl. 2 persons	€ 9,50 - € 32,90
extra person	free - € 5,90
child (3-8 yrs)	free - € 3,80
electricity (10A)	€ 4,90

Camping Cheques accepted.

Sérignac

Camping Naturiste le Clos Barrat

Mauroux, F-46700 Sérignac (Lot, Midi-Pyrénées) T: **05 65 31 97 93**. E: **thierry.schmutz@orange.fr**
alanrogers.com/FR46300

This site is southwest of Cahors in ten hectares of forest and pasture amongst the rich countryside of the Lot/Quercy area. This is a family run naturist site where you will receive a warm and friendly welcome which is extended throughout your stay. It offers spaciousness and tranquillity with 90 generous pitches (over 120 sq.m), all with 6/10A electricity. There are also six mobile homes, chalets or apartments to rent. The site is on a gentle rolling slope and this is reflected in some of the pitches although most are mainly level, and access for larger units is not a problem.

Facilities

Three traditional style sanitary blocks with two offering facilities for disabled visitors. Bar and restaurant. Small shop. Swimming pool and paddling pool. Play area. Trampoline. Tennis. Archery. Organised activities. Library. Barbecues are not permitted. Mobile homes, chalets and apartments for rent. Off site: Many cycle and walking trails. Fishing 6 km. Riding 6 km. Golf 20 km.

Open: 29 April - 31 December.

Directions

From Cahors take the D653 to Villesque. Join the D656 towards Tournon d'Argenais and at St Matre follow signs to Serignac on the D4. Site is signed from there. GPS: 44.43080, 1.06850

Charges guide

Per person	€ 5,00 - € 6,50
child (3-18 yrs)	€ 1,00 - € 2,00
pitch	€ 4,80 - € 6,50
incl. electricity	€ 7,70 - € 9,50

Varilhes

Naturiste Camping Millefleurs

Le Tuilier Gudas, F-09120 Varilhes (Ariège, Midi-Pyrénées) T: **05 61 60 77 56**. E: **simone.groot@orange.fr**
alanrogers.com/FR09090

Millefleurs is a quiet site in a secluded location for naturists. It is peaceful with some 70 acres of woods and meadows providing guided naturist walks in total privacy. The site has 40 large, flat, mostly terraced pitches (34 with 6-10A electricity), and long leads are required if pitching off the terraces. There are also very secluded pitches in wooded areas with shade, or you can pitch a tent in the meadows if you prefer. There are few of the normal camping leisure facilities here and the site is definitely aimed at the more mature naturist camper.

Facilities

An excellent toilet block with facilities for disabled campers. Bread available to order in high season. Guests dine together in the 'salle de réunion' within the farmhouse two nights a week or just meet friends for a drink. Refrigerator with drinks. Pétanque. Guide book for walks and cycle rides. Torches essential. Pick ups from airports and stations arranged. Off site: The coast is 1.5 hours.

Open: 1 April - 1 November.

Directions

From Varilhes, 8 km. south of Pamiers on D624 (parallel to N20). Take D13 for Dalou and Gudas cross railway and N20. The site is 2 km. past Gudas, on right. GPS: 42.9927, 1.6788

Charges guide

Per unit incl. 2 persons	€ 19,00 - € 19,50
extra person	€ 5,25
child (4-12)	€ 2,50 - € 3,00

No credit cards.

Barjac

Camping Naturiste de la Sablière

Domaine de la Sablière, Saint Privat-de-Champclos, F-30430 Barjac (Gard, Languedoc-Roussillon)
T: **04 66 24 51 16**. E: **contact@villagesabliere.com** **alanrogers.com/FR30100**

Spectacularly situated in the Cèze Gorges, this naturist site with a surprising 497 pitches, 240 for touring, tucked away within its wild terrain offers a wide variety of facilities, all within a really peaceful, wooded and dramatic setting. The pitches themselves are mainly on flat stony terraces, attractively situated among a variety of trees and shrubs (some with a low overhang). Many are of a good size and have electricity (6/10A), very long leads may be needed. Nudity is only obligatory around the pool complex. You must expect some fairly steep walking between the pitches and facilities.

Facilities

Six good unisex sanitary blocks have excellent free hot showers in typical open plan, naturist style, washbasins (cold water), baby baths and facilities for people with disabilities. Laundry. Good supermarket. Bar (1/4-22/9). Excellent open air, covered restaurant and takeaway (1/4-22/9). Small café/crêperie. Swimming pool complex. Fitness room. TV room and disco. Tennis. Minigolf. Fitness trail. Archery. Activity and entertainment programme. Torch useful. Barbecues are not permitted. Off site: Walking and cycling. Bicycle hire 8 km. Riding 10 km. Golf 12 km.

Open: 1 April - 1 October.

Directions

From Barjac take D901 east for 3 km. Turn right at site sign just before St Privat-de-Champclos and follow site signs along winding country lane to site entrance in 4 km. GPS: 44.26685, 4.35202

Charges guide

Per unit incl. 2 persons	€ 19,00 - € 37,00
extra person	€ 5,00 - € 7,00
child (4-8 yrs)	free - € 1,80
dog	free - € 2,50

Camping Cheques accepted.

Fleury

Domaine Naturiste la Grande Cosse

Saint Pierre-la-Mer, F-11560 Fleury (Aude, Languedoc-Roussillon) T: **04 68 33 61 87**
E: **contact@grandecosse.com** **alanrogers.com/FR11190**

Any slight difficulty in finding this secluded naturist site is compensated for immediately you arrive. The abundance of flowers, shrubs and the generally peaceful ambience makes this a delightful place for a relaxing naturist holiday, and the extensive facilities mean you only need to leave the site for sightseeing rather than for necessities. In total there are a total of 480 pitches, of which about 146 are for mobile homes, and the mainly large touring pitches, all with 8A electrical connections, are informally and very attractively arranged in a variety of different areas. Naturism here is pretty relaxed – the only area where clothing is not permitted is in the swimming pools.

Facilities

Five sanitary blocks are opened progressively throughout the season. Fully equipped modern facilities, including a choice of private or communal showers, and some washbasins in cabins. Laundry facilities. Motorcaravan service point. Gas. Well stocked shop, bar, restaurant and takeaway (all 26/3-2/10). Three swimming pools, two for adults and a smaller one for children, (26/3-2/10). Play area. Tennis. Archery. Playing field. Internet access. Communal barbecues. Off site: Boat launching 5 km. Riding 2 km.

Open: 26 March - 2 October.

Directions

From the A9 take exit 36 to Vendres. Pass through town, continue to Lespignan, then Fleury. At roundabout turn left signed Cabanes-de-Fleury. Follow for 4 km. to site sign to left. Continue for 2 km. and site signed to right. GPS: 43.20582, 3.21099

Charges guide

Per unit incl. 2 persons and electricitry	€ 18,00 - € 40,00
extra person	€ 5,00 - € 7,00

Lodève

Domaine Naturiste de Lambeyran

Hameau de Lambeyran, F-34700 Lodève (Hérault, Languedoc-Roussillon) T: **04 67 44 13 99**
E: **lambeyran@wanadoo.fr** **alanrogers.com/FR34540**

A wooded valley covering 340 hectares allows Domaine de Lambeyran a place in the Guinness Book of Records for having the largest area available for naturists in the world. It is a wonderful natural area with amazing views across to Lodève. Naturists can enjoy the marked trails around the valley or the welcome pool whilst choosing from 160 huge (200 sq.m) pitches. Where necessary the pitches have been levelled with local stone which has also been used to create short stairways in the terrain. Electricity (3/6A) is available on 110 pitches. Many pitches are quite private and hidden away amongst wild shrubs.

Facilities

Two large tiled toilet blocks and a smaller one are fully equipped and give good coverage for the various areas. Washing machine. Small shop. Bar and simple restaurant (in the evenings from 7/7). Swimming pool with sunbathing terrace. Some play equipment for children and indoor area for older children. Walking/hiking trails from 5-30 km. Mountain biking. Dancing, films and organised trips such as canoeing down the Orb Gorges. Communal barbecue area. Dogs are only allowed in one area. Off site: Tennis and riding 4 km. Beaches at Lac du Salagou 16 km.

Open: 1 May - 20 September.

Directions

From A75 take exit for Lodève and follow signs for town centre. Cross town following signs for Lunas (D35) picking up site signs. Ignore right turn for les Plans and take next right and follow up hill for 3 km. to site. The road is good but is single file in parts. GPS: 43.73615, 3.26654

Charges guide

Per person	€ 4,20 - € 6,20
pitch	€ 7,60 - € 12,80
electricity (3/6A)	€ 4,20

No credit cards. Naturist access per day € 0,50.

Lapalme

Camping Naturiste le Clapotis

Lieu-dit Pech-Redon, F-11480 Lapalme (Aude, Languedoc-Roussillon) T: **04 68 48 15 40**
E: **info@leclapotis.com** **alanrogers.com/FR11090**

Le Clapotis is a small and tranquil naturist site, situated between Narbonne and Perpignan in a secluded pine wood beside the Etang de Lapalme (a large sea lagoon). There is direct access to the lagoon, which is popular with those in pursuit of the ideal conditions provided for windsurfing. The site comprises 173 touring pitches, all have electricity (4A) and are of a good size on stony or sandy ground. Pitches in the older part have excellent shade from the pine trees, and in the newer area shade will be provided as the hedges grow. There is a relaxed feeling of harmony and freedom about this site.

Facilities

Two large and one small sanitary block, fairly basic but fully equipped. Showers are both open and in cabins. Facilities for babies and disabled campers. Washing machines. Well stocked shop (end May-mid Sept). Bar and restaurant (from 15/6). Swimming pool (15/6-15/9). Pétanque. Windsurfing. Fishing. Internet and WiFi. Off site: Sandy beach 5 km. Riding 10 km. Bicycle hire 9 km. Golf 10 km.

Open: 15 March - 15 October.

Directions

From N9 exit 40 (Port Leucate), at roundabout take N9 north for 3 km. to next roundabout. Turn right (Port-la-Nouvelle). Site sign in 500 m. on right. Follow narrow, poorly made up road for 2 km. bearing left up hill to site. GPS: 42.958, 2.99586

Charges guide

Per unit incl. 2 persons	€ 22,00 - € 26,00
extra person	€ 4,00

Méjannes-le-Clap

Camping Naturiste la Genèse

Route de la Genèse, F-30430 Méjannes-le-Clap (Gard, Languedoc-Roussillon) T: **04 66 24 51 82**
E: **info@lagenese.com** **alanrogers.com/FR30400**

La Genèse is a well equipped naturist site close on the banks of the River Cèze on the northern edge of the Cévennes national park. This is a large site with 483 well shaded pitches. These are divided into 'sauvage' (without electricity) and 'prairie' (with electricity 6A). A number of chalets and mobile homes are also available for rent. A wide variety of activities are on offer here, including art and craft workshops, bridge evenings and a cinema. Sports amenities include a large swimming pool with a daily aquagym session in high season, separate children's pool, tennis and archery. Canoeing is excellent here and canoe hire is available. This is also wonderful walking country and accompanied walks are arranged in peak season. 'Les Petits Malins' is a daily children's club for four to 12 year olds. Activities are also organised for teenagers, including regular discos in peak season. There is much to see in the area, including the Ardèche gorges and Roman city of Orange, as well as the Cévennes National park.

Facilities

Shop. Bar. Restaurant. Swimming pool and children's pool. Sauna. Archery. Games room. Art and craft workshops. Cinema. Canoe hire. Play area. Activity and entertainment programme. Direct access to river. Mobile homes and chalets for rent. Off site: Cycle and walking tracks in the Cévennes national park. Méjannes-le-Clap (shops and restaurants). Orange 50 km.

Open: 29 March - 30 September.

Directions

Approaching from the west (Pont St Esprit) use the D901 to Barjac and then the D979 to Rochegude. Shortly beyond Rochegude, join the D176 to Méjannes-le-Clap and follow signs to the site. GPS: 44.26772, 4.37013

Charges guide

Per unit incl. 2 persons and electricity	€ 19,00 - € 26,00
extra person	€ 4,00 - € 6,00
child (4-17 yrs)	€ 3,00 - € 4,00
dog	free - € 4,00

Olonzac

Camping Naturiste le Mas de Lignière

Cesseras-en-Minervois, F-34210 Olonzac (Hérault, Languedoc-Roussillon) T: **04 68 91 24 86**
E: **lemas1@tiscali.fr** **alanrogers.com/FR34050**

A naturist site hidden in the hills of the Minervois, only 3 km. from the medieval town of Minerve. There are marvellous views to the Pyrénées, the Corbières and the coast at Narbonne. The owners Jeanne and Gilles, offer a warm welcome and promote an enjoyable family atmosphere. The site has 50 large pitches (electricity 6/10A), and 25 super pitches. Mainly on level grass, separated by mature hedges giving considerable privacy. Some smaller pitches are available for tents, with cars parked elsewhere. There is natural shade and a variety of flora and fauna including four types of orchid.

Facilities

Clean toilet block has open washbasins and showers, facilities for disabled visitors. Washing machine. Simple shop. Bread (15/6-15/9). Bar (15/7-15/8). Swimming pool, sliding cover for use when cold. Paddling pool. Room for general use with TV, library, separate provision for young people. Playground. Tennis, volleyball, boules. Torch useful. Only gas barbecues. Off site: Sailing, riding and canoeing nearby – Lac de Jouarres. Canal du Midi.

Open: 1 May - 2 October.

Directions

From A61 take exit for Lézignan-Corbières, D611 to Homps, then D910 to Olonzac. Through village following signs to Minerve (D10). Continue. 4 km. Turn left to Cesseras (D168). At Cesseras follow signs Fauzan for 4 km. (site signed) on right, narrow, winding road. GPS: 43.34092, 2.70648

Charges guide

Per unit incl. 2 persons, electricity (6A), water and drainage	€ 22,00 - € 25,00
smaller pitch excl. electricity	€ 19,00
extra person	€ 4,00
child (2-7 yrs)	€ 3,00
dog	€ 1,50

Reductions for longer stays.

Sérignan-Plage

Camping le Sérignan-Plage Nature

L'Orpellière, F-34410 Sérignan (Hérault, Languedoc-Roussillon) T: **04 67 32 09 61**
E: **info@leserignannature.com** **alanrogers.com/FR34080**

Sérignam Plage Nature benefits from the same 600 m. of white, sandy beach as its sister site next door. Being a naturist site, it actually abuts the naturist section of the beach with direct access to it. It also has the use of the Sérignan-Plage balnéo pool in the mornings. The site has 286 good sized pitches on level sandy grass of which 94 are used for touring (6A electricity). There is plenty of shade except on the pitches beside the beach. Many mobile homes and chalets are available to rent. A friendly bar and shop serve the site although visitors may use the facilities at Le Sérignan-Plage.

Facilities

Two toilet blocks of differing designs (one refurbished to a very modern design) offer modern facilities with some washbasins in cabins. All clean and well maintained. Washing machines. Supermarket, fresh fruit and vegetables, newsagent/souvenir shop and ice cream kiosk. Small bar/café. Evening entertainment. Play area, miniclub and disco for children. Facilities and pools at Serignan Plage. Off site: Riding 1.5 km.

Open: 29 April - 26 September.

Directions

From A9 exit 35 (Béziers Est) towards Sérignan, D64 (9 km). Before Sérignan, take road to Sérignan-Plage. At small sign (blue) turn right for 500 m. At T-junction turn left over bridge, site is 75 m. just after left hand bend (the second naturist site).
GPS: 43.26403, 3.3203

Charges 2010

Per unit incl. 2 persons and electricity	€ 16,00 - € 48,00
extra person	€ 6,00 - € 8,00

Camping Cheques accepted.

Bédoin

497

Domaine Naturiste de Bélézy

F-84410 Bedoin (Vaucluse, Provence) T: **04 90 65 60 18**. E: **info@belezy.com**
alanrogers.com/FR84020

At the foot of Mt Ventoux, surrounded by beautiful scenery, Bélézy is an excellent naturist site with many amenities and activities and the ambience is relaxed and comfortable. The 248 marked pitches are set amongst many varieties of trees and shrubs. Electricity points (12A) are plentiful but long leads are necessary. So far as naturism is concerned, the emphasis is on personal choice, the only stipulation being the requirement for complete nudity in the pools and pool area. An area of natural parkland with an orchard, fishpond and woodland (complete with red squirrels), has a good range of sports facilities.

Facilities

Sanitary blocks differ – newer ones are excellent, with showers and washbasins in cubicles, others have hot showers in the open air, screened by stone dividers. Shop (3/4-19/9). Excellent restaurant and takeaway. Two swimming pools. Sauna. Tennis. Adventure play area. Activities in low season. Archery. Guided walks. Children's club. Hydrotherapy centre (1/4-30/9). Barbecues are prohibited. Pets are not accepted. Off site: Bédoin 1.5 km.

Open: 23 March - 2 October.

Directions

From A7 autoroute or RN7 at Orange, take D950 southeast to Carpentras, then northeast via D974 to Bédoin. Site is signed in Bédoin, being about 1.5 km. northeast of the village. GPS: 44.13352, 5.18745

Charges 2010

Per unit incl. 2 persons and electricity	€ 14,50 - € 39,00
extra person	€ 5,50 - € 9,30

Camping Cheques accepted.

Puget-Theniers

Domaine Naturiste Club Origan

F-06260 Puget-Theniers (Alpes-Maritimes, Côte d'Azur)) T: **04 93 05 06 00**. E: **origan@wanadoo.fr**
alanrogers.com/FR06070

Origan is a naturist site set in the mountains behind Nice, at a height of 500 m. The access road is single track and winding with a few passing places, so arrival is not recommended until late afternoon. The site's terrain is fairly wild and the roads stony and it is not suitable for caravans longer than six metres due to the steep slopes, although the site will assist with a 4 x 4 vehicle if requested. The 100 touring pitches, in three areas, are of irregular size and shape with good views. Electricity connection (6A) is possible on most pitches (by long cable). A member of 'France 4 Naturisme'.

Facilities

Sanitary facilities, are clean and of a standard and type associated with most good naturist sites – mostly open-plan hot showers. Laundry facilities. Shop (1/6-30/8). Takeaway. Bar/restaurant. Heated swimming pools. Jacuzzi and sauna. Disco. Tennis. Fishing. Bicycle hire. Organised activities for all (high season). Only gas or electric barbecues are permitted. Torches advised. Off site: Puget-Theniers with bars, cafés, shops, etc. Steam train. Eco-museum of the Roudoule.

Open: 15 April - 30 September.

Directions

Heading west on the N202, just past the town of Puget-Theniers, turn right at campsite sign at level crossing; site is 1 km. GPS: 43.957633, 6.860883

Charges guide

Per unit incl. 2 persons and electricity	€ 29,00 - € 36,00
extra person	€ 4,00 - € 8,00
incl. electricity	€ 29,50 - € 36,50

Camping Cheques accepted.

Alèria

Riva Bella Nature Resort & Spa

498

B.P. 21, F-20270 Alèria (Haute-Corse, Corsica) T: **04 95 38 81 10**. E: **riva-bella@wanadoo.fr**
alanrogers.com/FR20040

This is a relaxed, informal, spacious site alongside an extremely long and beautiful beach. Riva Bella is naturist from 15 May to 20 September only. It offers a variety of pitches, situated in beautiful countryside and seaside. The site is divided into several areas with 200 pitches and bungalows, some alongside the sandy beach with little shade, others in a wooded glade with ample shade. The huge fish-laden lakes are a fine feature of this site. Although electricity is available in most parts, a long cable may be needed. The ground is fairly flat with terracing for tents.

Facilities

High standard toilet facilities. Provision for disabled people, children and babies. Laundry. Large shop (15/5-15/10). Fridge hire. Restaurant with lake views (all season) with reasonable prices. Excellent beach/snack bar. Bar. Watersports, sailing school, fishing, sub-aqua. Balnéotherapy centre. Sauna. Aerobics. Giant draughts. Archery. Fishing. Riding. Mountain bike hire. Half-court tennis. Walk with llamas. Internet. WiFi. Professional evening entertainment programme.

Open: 30 March - 2 November.

Directions

Site is 12 km. north of Aleria on N198 (Bastia) road. Watch for large signs and unmade road to site and follow for 4 km. GPS: 42.16151, 9.55269

Charges guide

Per unit incl. 2 persons and electricity	€ 15,00 - € 38,00
extra person	€ 5,00 - € 9,00
child (3-8 yrs)	€ 2,00 - € 6,00

Special offers and half-board arrangements available. Camping Cheques accepted.

Bravone

Camping Bagheera Naturisme

Route 198, F-20230 Bravone (Haute-Corse, Corsica) T: **04 95 38 80 30**. E: **bagheera@bagheera.fr**
alanrogers.com/FR20080

An extremely long private road leads you to this naturist site which is alongside a 3 km. fine sand beach and has been run by the same family for 30 years. There are 190 pitches which are separated from the numerous bungalows. Well shaded under huge eucalyptus trees, all have 10A electricity (long leads may be necessary). Some beach-side pitches have sea views but most others are further back from the sea. All pitches are on sandy grass and are kept clean and neat. Large units will have no problems with access here. The restaurant and beach bar have superb panoramic views of the sea.

Facilities

Four sanitary blocks (one new in 2008) offer hot water throughout. Washing machines. Excellent restaurant (Corsican menu, children's menu). Bar. Comprehensive beach snack bar and bar. Pizzeria. Shop. All amenities 1/6-30/10. Swimming pool. New play area. Gym. Massage. Sauna. Pedaloes. Pétanque. Sub-aqua diving. Beach umbrella rental. Refrigerated lockers for hire. Tennis. Bicycle hire. Fishing. Entertainment programme all season. TV. Internet. Off site: Riding. Boat launching 15 km. Town 11 km.

Open: 1 April - 30 October (bungalows all year).

Directions

Site is between Bastia and Aleria near Bravone, 7 km. north of Aleria on the N198. It is well signed off the N198. Follow site road 4 km. east to beach. GPS: 42.21940, 9.55410

Charges guide

Per unit incl. 2 persons	€ 16,00 - € 22,40
extra person	€ 3,60 - € 5,80
child (3-15 yrs)	€ 1,60 - € 3,25

Porto-Vecchio

Village Naturiste la Chiappa

498

Route de Palombaggia, F-20137 Porto-Vecchio (Corse-du-Sud, Corsica) T: **04 95 70 00 31**
E: **chiappa@wanadoo.fr** **alanrogers.com/FR20050**

This is a large naturist campsite on the Chiappa peninsula with 220 pitches for tourers and tents, plus 250 bungalows. A few touring pitches have sea views and are taken first in high season. The pitches are informally marked and have a variety of shapes and sizes, some with difficult slopes and access, especially for large units. (75-125 sq.m). Cars are parked separately. Very long electricity leads are necessary here for most pitches (10A) electricity. The beaches are between long rocky outcrops and it is generally safe to swim, or alternatively enjoy the swimming pool by the main beach.

Facilities

The sanitary facilities were tired and in need of refurbishment when we visited. Washing machines. Motorcaravan service point. Well stocked shop. Two bars and restaurants with snacks. Baby sitting service. Swimming pool. Play area for children. Riding. Tennis. Minigolf. Fishing. Diving, windsurfing and sailing schools. Keep fit, yoga, sauna (extra cost). Bistro. Satellite TV. Internet access. Torches essential. Off site: Excursions. Car rental. Bus to La Chiappa once a week (10 persons).

Open: 9 May - 10 October.

Directions

From Bastia, N198 heading south, take Porto-Vecchio bypass (signed Bonofaccio). At southern end, take first left signed Pont de la Chiappa, unclassified road. After 8 km. site signed. Turn left and follow rough track for 2 km. to site. GPS: 41.59387, 9.35713

Charges guide

Per unit incl. 2 persons and electricity	€ 27,00 - € 35,00
extra person	€ 8,00 - € 10,00
child (5-13 yrs)	€ 4,00 - € 5,00

Accommodation

Over recent years many of the campsites featured in this guide have added large numbers of high quality mobile homes and chalets. Many site owners believe that some former caravanners and motorcaravanners have been enticed by the extra comfort they can now provide, and that maybe this is the ideal solution to combine the freedom of camping with all the comforts of home.

Quality is consistently high and, although the exact size and inventory may vary from site to site, if you choose any of the sites detailed here, you can be sure that you're staying in some of the best quality and best value mobile homes available.

Home comforts are provided and typically these include a fridge with freezer compartment, gas hob, proper shower – often a microwave and radio/cassette hi-fi too but do check for details. All mobile homes and chalets come fully equipped with a good range of kitchen utensils, pots and pans, crockery, cutlery and outdoor furniture. Some even have an attractive wooden sundeck or paved terrace – a perfect spot for outdoors eating or relaxing with a book and watching the world go by.

Regardless of model, colourful soft furnishings are the norm and a generally breezy décor helps to provide a real holiday feel.

Although some sites may have a large number of different accommodation types, we have restricted our choice to one or two of the most popular accommodation units (either mobile homes or chalets) for each of the sites listed.

The mobile homes here will be of modern design, and recent innovations, for example, often include pitched roofs which substantially improve their appearance.

Design will invariably include clever use of space and fittings/furniture to provide for comfortable holidays – usually light and airy, with big windows and patio-style doors, fully equipped kitchen areas, a shower room with shower, washbasin and WC, cleverly designed bedrooms and a comfortable lounge/dining area (often incorporating a sofa bed).

In general, modern campsite chalets incorporate all the best features of mobile homes in a more traditional structure, sometimes with the advantage of an upper mezzanine floor for an additional bedroom.

Our selected campsites offer a massive range of different types of mobile home and chalet, and it would be impractical to inspect every single accommodation unit. Our selection criteria, therefore, primarily takes account of the quality standards of the campsite itself.

However, there are a couple of important ground rules:

- FEATURED MOBILE HOMES MUST BE NO MORE THAN 5 YEARS OLD
- CHALETS NO MORE THAN 10 YEARS OLD
- ALL LISTED ACCOMMODATION MUST, OF COURSE, FULLY CONFORM WITH ALL APPLICABLE LOCAL, NATIONAL AND EUROPEAN SAFETY LEGISLATION.

For each campsite we given details of the type, or types, of accommodation available to rent, but these details are necessarily quite brief. Sometimes internal layouts can differ quite substantially, particularly with regard to sleeping arrangements, where these include the flexible provision for 'extra persons' on sofa beds located in the living area. These arrangements may vary from accommodation to accommodation, and if you're planning a holiday which includes more people than are catered for by the main bedrooms you should check exactly how the extra sleeping arrangements are to be provided!

Charges

An indication of the tariff for each type of accommodation featured is also included, indicating the variance between the low and high season tariffs. However, given that many campsites have a large and often complex range of pricing options, incorporating special deals and various discounts, the charges we mention should be taken to be just an indication. We strongly recommend therefore that you confirm the actual cost when making a booking.

We also strongly recommend that you check with the campsite, when booking, what (if anything) will be provided by way of bed linen, blankets, pillows etc. Again, in our experience, this can vary widely from site to site.

On every campsite a fully refundable deposit (usually between 150 and 300 euros) is payable on arrival. There may also be an optional cleaning service for which a further charge is made. Other options may include sheet hire (typically 30 euros per unit) or baby pack hire (cot and high chair).

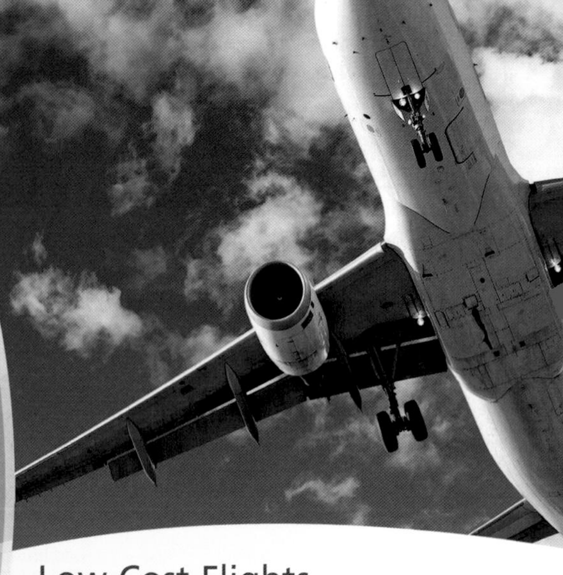

Low Cost Flights

An Inexpensive Way To Arrive At Your Campsite

Many campsites are conveniently served by a wide choice of low cost airlines. Cheap flights can be very easy to find and travellers increasingly find the regional airports often used to be smaller, quieter and generally a calmer, more pleasurable experience.

Low cost flights can make campsites in more distant regions a much more attractive option: quicker to reach, inexpensive flights, and simply more convenient.

Many campsites are seeing increased visitors using the low cost flights and are adapting their services to suit this clientele. An airport shuttle service is not uncommon, meaning you can take advantage of that cheap flight knowing you will be met at the other end and whisked to your campsite. No taxi queues or multiple drop-offs.

Obviously, these low cost flights are impractical when taking all your own camping gear but they do make a holiday in campsite owned accommodation much more straightforward. The low cost airline option makes mobile home holidays especially attractive: pack a suitcase and use bed linen and towels provided (which you will generally need to pre-book).

Pricing Tips

- Low cost airlines promote cheap flights but only a small percentage of seats are priced at the cheapest price. Book early for the best prices (and of course you also get a better choice of campsite or mobile home)
- Child seats are usually the same costs as adults
- Full payment is required at the time of booking
- Changes and amendments can be costly with low cost airlines
- Peak dates can be expensive compared to other carriers

Car Hire

For maximum flexibility you will probably hire a car from a car rental agency. Car hire provides convenience but also will allow you access to off-site shops, beaches and tourist sights.

FR29180 Camping les Embruns

see report page 35

Rue du Philosophe Alain, le Pouldu, F-29360 Clohars-Carnoêt (Brittany)

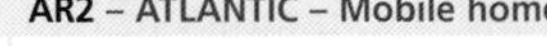

AR1 – OCEANE – Mobile home

Sleeping: 2 bedrooms, sleeps 4: 1 double, 2 singles

Living: living/kitchen area, heating, shower, WC

Eating: fitted kitchen with hobs, oven, coffee maker, fridge

Outside: table & chairs

Pets: accepted (with supplement)

AR2 – ATLANTIC – Mobile home

Sleeping: 3 bedrooms, sleeps 6: 1 double, 2 singles, bunk bed

Living: living/kitchen area, heating, shower, WC

Eating: fitted kitchen with hobs, oven, coffee maker, fridge

Outside: table & chairs

Pets: accepted (with supplement)

Other (AR1 and AR2): cot, highchair to hire

Open: 1 April - 18 September

Weekly Charge	AR1	AR2
Low Season *(from)*	€ 290	€ 395
High Season *(from)*	€ 660	€ 840

FR29010 Castel Camping le Ty-Nadan

see report page 37

Route d'Arzano, F-29310 Locunolé (Brittany)

AR1 – IRM – Mobile home

Sleeping: 2 bedrooms, sleeps 6: 1 double, 2 singles, sofa bed, pillows and blankets provided

Living: living/kitchen area, heating, shower, WC

Eating: fitted kitchen with hobs, oven, fridge

Outside: table & chairs, parasol, 2 sun loungers

Pets: accepted

AR2 – CHALET – Chalet

Sleeping: 2 bedrooms, sleeps 6: 1 double, 2 singles, sofa bed, pillows and blankets provided

Living: living/kitchen area, heating, shower, WC

Eating: fitted kitchen with hobs, oven, fridge

Outside: table & chairs, parasol, 2 sun loungers

Pets: accepted

Other (AR1 and AR2): bed linen, cot, highchair to hire

Open: 27 March - 2 September

Weekly Charge	AR1	AR2
Low Season *(from)*	€ 312	€ 414
High Season *(from)*	€ 910	€ 1176

FR29090 Camping le Raguenès-Plage

see report page 39

19 rue des Iles, F-29920 Névez (Brittany)

AR1 – VARIANTE – Mobile home

Sleeping: 2 bedrooms, sleeps 5: 1 double, 2 singles, sofa bed, pillows and blankets provided

Living: living/kitchen area, heating, air conditioning, shower, separate WC

Eating: fitted kitchen with hobs, oven, microwave, coffee maker, fridge, freezer

Outside: table & chairs, parasol, 2 sun loungers, barbecue

Pets: accepted (with supplement)

AR2 – OHARA COTTAGE – Mobile home

Sleeping: 2 bedrooms, sleeps 4: 1 double, 2 singles, sofa bed, pillows and blankets provided

Living: living/kitchen area, heating, air conditioning, shower, separate WC

Eating: fitted kitchen with hobs, microwave, coffee maker, fridge, freezer

Outside: table & chairs, parasol, 2 sun loungers, barbecue

Pets: accepted (with supplement)

Other (AR1 and AR2): bed linen to hire

Open: 1 April - 30 September

Weekly Charge	AR1	AR2
Low Season *(from)*	€ 320	€ 340
High Season *(from)*	€ 699	€ 745

FR29050 Castel Camping l'Orangerie de Lanniron

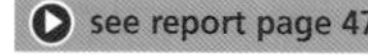
see report page 47

Château de Lanniron, F-29336 Quimper (Britany)

AR1 – ZEN – Mobile home	AR2 – CONFORT – Mobile home
Sleeping: 3 bedrooms, sleeps 6: 1 double, 3 singles, bunk bed, pillows and blankets provided	**Sleeping:** 2 bedrooms, sleeps 5: 1 double, 2 singles, sofa bed, pillows and blankets provided
Living: living/kitchen area, heating, air conditioning, shower, separate WC	**Living:** living/kitchen area, heating, shower, separate WC
Eating: fitted kitchen with hobs, microwave, coffee maker, fridge, freezer	**Eating:** fitted kitchen with hobs, microwave, coffee maker, fridge, freezer
Outside: table & chairs, parasol, 2 sun loungers, barbecue	**Outside:** table & chairs, parasol, 2 sun loungers, barbecue
Pets: not accepted	**Pets:** not accepted

Other (AR1 and AR2): bed linen, cot, highchair to hire

Open: 1 April - 31 October

Weekly Charge	AR1	AR2
Low Season *(from)*	€ 476	€ 385
High Season *(from)*	€ 994	€ 896

FR29080 Camping le Panoramic

see report page 54

Route de la Plage-Penker, F-29560 Telgruc-sur-Mer (Brittany)

AR1 – TRIGANO ELEGANTE 33 m² – Mobile home	AR2 – TRIGANO ELEGANTE 25 m² – Mobile home
Sleeping: 3 bedrooms, sleeps 6: 1 double, 4 singles, pillows and blankets provided	**Sleeping:** 2 bedrooms, sleeps 4: 1 double, 2 singles, sofa bed, pillows and blankets provided
Living: living/kitchen area, heating, shower, WC	**Living:** living/kitchen area, heating, shower, WC
Eating: fitted kitchen with hobs, fridge, freezer	**Eating:** fitted kitchen with hobs, fridge
Outside: table & chairs, parasol, 2 sun loungers, barbecue	**Outside:** table & chairs, parasol, 2 sun loungers, barbecue
Pets: accepted (with supplement)	**Pets:** accepted (with supplement)

Open: 1 May - 15 September

Weekly Charge	AR1	AR2
Low Season *(from)*	€ 300	€ 280
High Season *(from)*	€ 660	€ 850

FR27070 Camping de l'Ile des Trois Rois

see report page 59

1 rue Gilles Nicolle, F-27700 Andelys (Normandy)

AR1 – MOBILE HOME – Mobile home	AR2 – MOBILE HOME – Mobile home
Sleeping: 2 bedrooms, sleeps 4: 1 double, 2 singles	**Sleeping:** 3 bedrooms, sleeps 6: 1 double, 4 singles
Living: living/kitchen area, heating, shower, WC	**Living:** living/kitchen area, heating, shower, WC, separate WC
Eating: fitted kitchen with hobs, fridge	**Eating:** fitted kitchen with hobs, fridge
Outside: table & chairs, barbecue	**Outside:** table & chairs, barbecue
Pets: not accepted	**Pets:** not accepted

Open: 13 March - 15 November

Weekly Charge	AR1	AR2
Low Season *(from)*	€ 320	€ 380
High Season *(from)*	€ 520	€ 620

FR80060 Camping le Val de Trie

see report page 87

Rue des Sources, Bouillancourt-sous-Miannay, F-80870 Moyenneville (Picardy)

AR1 – MOREVA – Mobile home	AR2 – PRIVILEGE ZEN – Mobile home
Sleeping: 2 bedrooms, sleeps 6: 1 double, 2 singles, sofa bed, pillows and blankets provided	**Sleeping:** 3 bedrooms, sleeps 6: 1 double, bunk bed, pillows and blankets provided
Living: living/kitchen area, heating, shower, separate WC	**Living:** living/kitchen area, heating, shower, separate WC
Eating: fitted kitchen with hobs, microwave, coffee maker, fridge, freezer	**Eating:** fitted kitchen with hobs, microwave, dishwasher, coffee maker, fridge, freezer
Outside: table & chairs, parasol, barbecue	**Outside:** table & chairs, parasol, barbecue
Pets: not accepted	**Pets:** not accepted

Other (AR1 and AR2): bed linen, cot, highchair to hire

Open: 1 April - 15 October

Weekly Charge	AR1	AR2
Low Season *(from)*	€ 299	€ 385
High Season *(from)*	€ 595	€ 693

FR80070 Kawan Village la Ferme des Aulnes

see report page 88

1 rue du Marais, Fresne-sur-Authie, F-80120 Nampont-Saint Martin (Picardy)

AR1 – CONFORT – Mobile home	AR2 – PRIVILEGE – Mobile home
Sleeping: 2 bedrooms, sleeps 5: 1 double, 2 singles, sofa bed, pillows and blankets provided	**Sleeping:** 3 bedrooms, sleeps 6: 1 double, 2 singles, bunk bed, pillows and blankets provided
Living: living/kitchen area, heating, TV, shower, separate WC	**Living:** living/kitchen area, heating, TV, shower, separate WC
Eating: fitted kitchen with hobs, microwave, coffee maker, fridge, freezer	**Eating:** fitted kitchen with hobs, microwave, coffee maker, fridge, freezer
Outside: table & chairs, parasol, barbecue	**Outside:** table & chairs, parasol, barbecue
Pets: accepted (with supplement)	**Pets:** accepted (with supplement)

Other (AR1 and AR2): bed linen, cot, highchair to hire

Open: 1 April - 1 November

Weekly Charge	AR1	AR2
Low Season *(from)*	€ 490	€ 590
High Season *(from)*	€ 690	€ 790

FR80150 Camping Airotel Le Walric

see report page 90

Route d'Eu, F-80230 Saint Valery-sur-Somme (Picardy)

AR1 – COTTAGE 4 COUCHAGES – Mobile home	AR2 – COTTAGE 6 COUCHAGES – Mobile home
Sleeping: 2 bedrooms, sleeps 4: 1 double, 2 singles, pillows and blankets provided	**Sleeping:** 3 bedrooms, sleeps 6: 1 double, 4 singles, pillows and blankets provided
Living: living/kitchen area, heating, TV, shower, WC, separate WC	**Living:** living/kitchen area, heating, TV, shower, WC, separate WC
Eating: fitted kitchen with hobs, microwave, coffee maker, fridge, freezer	**Eating:** fitted kitchen with hobs, microwave, coffee maker, fridge, freezer
Outside: table & chairs, parasol, barbecue	**Outside:** table & chairs, parasol, barbecue
Pets: accepted	**Pets:** accepted

Other (AR1 and AR2): cot, highchair to hire

Open: 1 April - 1 November

Weekly Charge	AR1	AR2
Low Season *(from)*	€ 290	€ 390
High Season *(from)*	€ 595	€ 690

FR77020 Camping le Chêne Gris

see report page 97

24 place de la Gare de Faremoutiers, F-77515 Pommeuse (Paris/Ile de France)

AR1 – BALI – Mobile home	AR2 – TAHITI – Mobile home
Sleeping: 2 bedrooms, sleeps 6: 1 double, 2 singles, bunk bed, sofa bed, pillows and blankets provided	**Sleeping:** 2 bedrooms, sleeps 5: 1 double, 2 singles, bunk bed, pillows and blankets provided
Living: living/kitchen area, heating, air conditioning, shower, separate WC	**Living:** living/kitchen area, heating, air conditioning, shower, WC
Eating: fitted kitchen with hobs, microwave, coffee maker, fridge, freezer	**Eating:** fitted kitchen with hobs, coffee maker, fridge, freezer
Outside: table & chairs, parasol, 2 sun loungers	**Outside:** table & chairs, parasol
Pets: not accepted	**Pets:** not accepted

Other (AR1 and AR2): bed linen, cot, highchair to hire

Open: 1 April - 31 October

Weekly Charge	AR1	AR2
Low Season *(from)*	€ 413	€ 441
High Season *(from)*	€ 763	€ 798

FR88040 Kawan Village Lac de Bouzey

see report page 115

19 rue du Lac, F-88390 Sanchey (Lorraine-Vosges)

AR1 – FLORES – Mobile home	AR2 – ZEN – Mobile home
Sleeping: 2 bedrooms, sleeps 5: 1 double, 2 singles, sofa bed	**Sleeping:** 3 bedrooms, sleeps 6: 1 double, 4 singles
Living: living/kitchen area, shower, WC	**Living:** living/kitchen area, shower, WC
Eating: fitted kitchen with hobs, microwave, fridge, freezer	**Eating:** fitted kitchen with hobs, microwave, fridge, freezer
Outside: table & chairs, parasol, 2 sun loungers, barbecue	**Outside:** table & chairs, parasol, 2 sun loungers, barbecue
Pets: accepted	**Pets:** accepted

Other (AR1 and AR2): cot to hire

Open: All year

Weekly Charge	AR1	AR2
Low Season *(from)*	€ 490	€ 560
High Season *(from)*	€ 770	€ 840

FR88130 Kawan Village Vanne de Pierre

see report page 114

5 rue du camping, F-88100 Saint Dié-des-Vosges (Lorraine-Vosges)

AR1 – COUNTRY LODGE – Chalet	AR2 – ZEN – Cottage
Sleeping: 2 bedrooms, sleeps 5: 1 double, 2 singles, sofa bed	**Sleeping:** 3 bedrooms, sleeps 6: 1 double, 4 singles
Living: living/kitchen area, heating, shower, separate WC	**Living:** living/kitchen area, heating, shower, separate WC
Eating: fitted kitchen with hobs, microwave, fridge	**Eating:** fitted kitchen with hobs, microwave, fridge
Outside: table & chairs, parasol, 2 sun loungers	**Outside:** table & chairs, parasol, 2 sun loungers
Pets: accepted	**Pets:** accepted

Open: All year

Weekly Charge	AR1	AR2
Low Season *(from)*	€ 560	€ 490
High Season *(from)*	€ 840	€ 770

FR41070 Kawan Village la Grande Tortue

see report page 126

3 route de Pontlevoy, F-41120 Candé-sur-Beuvron (Val de Loire)

AR1 – IRM SUPER MERCURE – Mobile home	AR2 – LOUISIANE – Mobile home
Sleeping: 2 bedrooms, sleeps 5: 1 double, 2 singles, bunk bed, pillows and blankets provided	**Sleeping:** 3 bedrooms, sleeps 6: 1 double, 4 singles, pillows and blankets provided
Living: living/kitchen area, heating, shower, separate WC	**Living:** living/kitchen area, heating, shower, separate WC
Eating: fitted kitchen with hobs, microwave, coffee maker, fridge	**Eating:** fitted kitchen with hobs, microwave, coffee maker, fridge
Outside: table & chairs, 2 sun loungers	**Outside:** table & chairs, 2 sun loungers
Pets: accepted (with supplement)	**Pets:** accepted (with supplement)

Other (AR1 and AR2): bed linen, cot, highchair to hire

Open: 5 April - 20 September

Weekly Charge	AR1	AR2
Low Season *(from)*	€ 300	€ 420
High Season *(from)*	€ 665	€ 728

FR37060 Kawan Village l'Arada Parc

see report page 135

Rue de la Baratière, F-37360 Sonzay

AR1 – SAMIBOIS – Chalet	AR2 – OHARA – Mobile home
Sleeping: 3 bedrooms, sleeps 6: 2 doubles, bunk bed, pillows and blankets provided	**Sleeping:** 2 bedrooms, sleeps 5: 1 double, 2 singles, sofa bed, pillows and blankets provided
Living: living/kitchen area, heating, shower, separate WC	**Living:** living/kitchen area, heating, shower, separate WC
Eating: fitted kitchen with hobs, microwave, coffee maker, fridge, freezer	**Eating:** fitted kitchen with hobs, microwave, coffee maker, fridge
Outside: table & chairs, barbecue	**Outside:** table & chairs, barbecue
Pets: accepted (with supplement)	**Pets:** accepted (with supplement)

Other (AR1 and AR2): bed linen, cot, highchair to hire

Open: 28 March - 30 October

Weekly Charge	AR1	AR2
Low Season *(from)*	€ 345	€ 295
High Season *(from)*	€ 645	€ 595

FR41020 Castel Camping Château de la Grenouillère

see report page 135

RN 152, F-41500 Suèvres (Val de Loire)

AR1 – COTTAGE 6 PERS PREMIUM – Mobile home	AR2 – CHALET 6 PERS – Chalet
Sleeping: 3 bedrooms, sleeps 6: 1 double, 4 singles, pillows and blankets provided	**Sleeping:** 3 bedrooms, sleeps 6: 2 doubles, bunk bed, pillows and blankets provided
Living: living/kitchen area, heating, shower, separate WC	**Living:** living/kitchen area, heating, shower, separate WC
Eating: fitted kitchen with hobs, microwave	**Eating:** fitted kitchen with hobs, microwave
Outside: table & chairs, parasol, 2 sun loungers, barbecue	**Outside:** table & chairs, parasol, 2 sun loungers, barbecue
Pets: not accepted	**Pets:** not accepted

Other (AR1 and AR2): bed linen, cot, highchair to hire

Open: 17 March - 11 September

Weekly Charge	AR1	AR2
Low Season *(from)*	€ 420	€ 350
High Season *(from)*	€ 920	€ 850

FR44220 Camping Parc de Léveno

see report page 143

Route de Sandun, F-44350 Guérande (Pays de la Loire)

AR1 – COTTAGE CONFORT – Mobile home	AR2 – COTTAGE CONFORT – Mobile home
Sleeping: 2 bedrooms, sleeps 6: 1 double, 2 singles, sofa bed, pillows and blankets provided	**Sleeping:** 3 bedrooms, sleeps 6: 1 double, 4 singles, pillows and blankets provided
Living: living/kitchen area, heating, shower, separate WC	**Living:** living/kitchen area, shower, separate WC
Eating: fitted kitchen with hobs, fridge	**Eating:** fitted kitchen with hobs, fridge
Outside: table & chairs, parasol	**Outside:** table & chairs, parasol
Pets: accepted (with supplement)	**Pets:** accepted (with supplement)

Other (AR1 and AR2): bed linen, cot, highchair to hire

Open: 5 April - 30 September

Weekly Charge	AR1	AR2
Low Season *(from)*	€ 330	€ 350
High Season *(from)*	€ 900	€ 1000

FR44210 Camping de l'Océan

see report page 148

15, route de la Maison Rouge, F-44490 Le Croisic (Pays de la Loire)

AR1 – COTTAGE OCEAN ESPACE – Mobile home	AR2 – OCEAN GRAND CONFORT FAMILLE – Mobile home
Sleeping: 2 bedrooms, sleeps 5: 1 double, 2 singles, sofa bed, pillows and blankets provided	**Sleeping:** 3 bedrooms, sleeps 6: 1 double, 4 singles, pillows and blankets provided
Living: living/kitchen area, heating, shower, WC	**Living:** living/kitchen area, shower, WC
Eating: fitted kitchen with hobs, fridge	**Eating:** fitted kitchen with hobs, fridge
Outside: table & chairs, parasol	**Outside:** table & chairs, parasol
Pets: accepted (with supplement)	**Pets:** accepted (with supplement)

Other (AR1 and AR2): bed linen, cot, highchair to hire

Open: 4 April - 30 September

Weekly Charge	AR1	AR2
Low Season *(from)*	€ 390	€ 435
High Season *(from)*	€ 875	€ 1150

FR44070 Camping Parc du Guibel

see report page 153

Route de Kerdrien, F-44420 Piriac-sur-Mer (Pays de la Loire)

AR1 – GALION – Chalet	AR2 – CHALET TYPE 2 – Chalet
Sleeping: 2 bedrooms, sleeps 5: 1 double, 1 single, sofa bed, pillows and blankets provided	**Sleeping:** 3 bedrooms, sleeps 7: 1 double, 1 single, bunk bed, sofa bed, pillows and blankets provided
Living: living/kitchen area, heating, shower, separate WC	**Living:** living/kitchen area, heating, shower, separate WC
Eating: fitted kitchen with hobs, oven, grill, coffee maker, fridge, freezer	**Eating:** fitted kitchen with hobs, oven, grill, coffee maker, fridge, freezer
Outside: table & chairs, 2 sun loungers	**Outside:** table & chairs, 2 sun loungers
Pets: accepted (with supplement)	**Pets:** accepted (with supplement)

Other (AR1 and AR2): bed linen, cot, highchair to hire

Open: 1 April - 30 September

Weekly Charge	AR1	AR2
Low Season *(from)*	€ 322	€ 371
High Season *(from)*	€ 721	€ 805

FR44180 Camping de la Boutinardière

see report page 154

Rue de la Plage de la Boutinardière 23, F-44210 Pornic (Pays de la Loire)

AR1 – MOBILE HOME 5 PERS. – Mobile home	AR2 – MOBILE HOME 6 PERS. – Mobile home
Sleeping: 2 bedrooms, sleeps 5: 1 double, 2 singles, sofa bed, pillows and blankets provided	**Sleeping:** 3 bedrooms, sleeps 6: 1 double, 4 singles, pillows and blankets provided
Living: living/kitchen area, heating, shower, WC	**Living:** living/kitchen area, heating, shower, WC
Eating: fitted kitchen with hobs, fridge	**Eating:** fitted kitchen with hobs, fridge
Outside: table & chairs, parasol	**Outside:** table & chairs, parasol
Pets: accepted (with supplement)	**Pets:** accepted (with supplement)

Other (AR1 and AR2): bed linen, cot, highchair to hire

Open: 5 April - 4 October

Weekly Charge	AR1	AR2
Low Season *(from)*	€ 370	€ 330
High Season *(from)*	€ 830	€ 900

FR44190 Camping le Fief

see report page 155

57 chemin du Fief, F-44250 Saint Brévin-les-Pins (Pays de la Loire)

AR1 – COTTAGE – Mobile home	AR2 – COTTAGE – Mobile home
Sleeping: 3 bedrooms, sleeps 6: 1 double, 4 singles	**Sleeping:** 2 bedrooms, sleeps 4: 1 double, 2 singles
Living: living/kitchen area, shower, WC	**Living:** living/kitchen area, shower, WC
Eating: fitted kitchen with hobs, microwave, fridge	**Eating:** fitted kitchen with hobs, microwave, fridge
Outside: table & chairs	**Outside:** table & chairs
Pets: accepted (with supplement)	**Pets:** accepted (with supplement)

Other (AR1 and AR2): bed linen, cot, highchair to hire

Open: 22 March - 5 October

Weekly Charge	AR1	AR2
Low Season *(from)*	€ 434	€ 364
High Season *(from)*	€ 1043	€ 994

FR44090 Kawan Village du Deffay

see report page 156

B.P. 18 Le Deffay, Sainte Reine-de-Bretagne, F-44160 Pontchâteau (Pays de la Loire)

AR1 – MOBILE HOME 5 – Mobile home	AR2 – CHALET 4/6 – Chalet
Sleeping: 2 bedrooms, sleeps 5: 1 double, 1 single, bunk bed, pillows and blankets provided	**Sleeping:** 2 bedrooms, sleeps 6: 1 double, bunk bed, sofa bed, pillows and blankets provided
Living: living/kitchen area, heating, shower, separate WC	**Living:** living/kitchen area, heating, shower, WC
Eating: fitted kitchen with hobs, microwave, coffee maker, fridge, freezer	**Eating:** fitted kitchen with hobs, microwave, grill, dishwasher, coffee maker, fridge, freezer
Outside: table & chairs, parasol, 2 sun loungers, barbecue	**Outside:** table & chairs, parasol, 2 sun loungers, barbecue
Pets: not accepted	**Pets:** not accepted

Other (AR1 and AR2): bed linen, cot, highchair to hire

Open: 1 April - 31 October

Weekly Charge	AR1	AR2
Low Season *(from)*	€ 219	€ 249
High Season *(from)*	€ 669	€ 719

FR85150 Camping la Yole

see report page 175

Chemin des Bosses, Orouet, F-85160 Saint Jean-de-Monts (Vendée)

AR1 – LOUISIANE FLORES – Mobile home	AR2 – LOUISIANE FLORES 2 – Mobile home
Sleeping: 3 bedrooms, sleeps 6: 1 double, 4 singles, pillows and blankets provided	**Sleeping:** 2 bedrooms, sleeps 6: 1 double, 2 singles, sofa bed, pillows and blankets provided
Living: living/kitchen area, heating, shower, WC	**Living:** living/kitchen area, heating, shower, WC
Eating: fitted kitchen with hobs, microwave, fridge, freezer	**Eating:** fitted kitchen with hobs, microwave, fridge, freezer
Outside: table & chairs, parasol, 2 sun loungers	**Outside:** table & chairs, parasol, 2 sun loungers
Pets: not accepted	**Pets:** not accepted

Other (AR1 and AR2): bed linen, cot, highchair to hire

Open: 5 April - 26 September

Weekly Charge	AR1	AR2
Low Season *(from)*	€ 430	€ 395
High Season *(from)*	€ 825	€ 780

FR17280 Camping la Grainetière

see report page 190

Route de Saint-Martin, F-17630 La Flotte-en-Ré (Poitou-Charentes)

AR1 – CONFORT – Mobile home	AR2 – LUXE – Mobile home
Sleeping: 2 bedrooms, sleeps 5: 1 double, 2 singles, sofa bed, pillows and blankets provided	**Sleeping:** 2 bedrooms, sleeps 5: 1 double, 2 singles, sofa bed, pillows and blankets provided
Living: living/kitchen area, shower, separate WC	**Living:** living/kitchen area, shower, separate WC
Eating: fitted kitchen with hobs, microwave, coffee maker, fridge	**Eating:** fitted kitchen with hobs, microwave, coffee maker, fridge
Outside: table & chairs, parasol	**Outside:** table & chairs, parasol
Pets: accepted (with supplement)	**Pets:** accepted (with supplement)

Other (AR1 and AR2): highchair to hire

Open: 4 April - 30 September

Weekly Charge	AR1	AR2
Low Season *(from)*	€ 230	€ 255
High Season *(from)*	€ 760	€ 790

FR17010 Camping Bois Soleil

see report page 200

2 avenue de Suzac, F-17110 Saint Georges-de-Didonne (Poitou-Charentes)

AR1 – COTTAGE DE CHARME – Mobile home	AR2 – COTTAGE BOIS – Mobile home
Sleeping: 2 bedrooms, sleeps 4: 1 double, 2 singles, pillows and blankets provided	**Sleeping:** 2 bedrooms, sleeps 4: 1 double, 2 singles, pillows and blankets provided
Living: living/kitchen area, heating, shower, WC	**Living:** living/kitchen area, heating, shower, WC
Eating: fitted kitchen with hobs, microwave, fridge	**Eating:** fitted kitchen with hobs, microwave, fridge
Outside: table & chairs, parasol	**Outside:** table & chairs, parasol
Pets: not accepted	**Pets:** not accepted

Open: 4 April - 2 November

Weekly Charge	AR1	AR2
Low Season *(from)*	€ 500	€ 300
High Season *(from)*	€ 1080	€ 940

FR71070 Kawan Village Château de l'Epervière

see report page 210

F-71240 Gigny-sur-Saône (Burgundy)

AR1 – LOUISIANE ZEN – Mobile home

Sleeping: 3 bedrooms, sleeps 6: 1 double, 2 singles, bunk bed, pillows and blankets provided

Living: living/kitchen area, heating, TV, shower, separate WC

Eating: fitted kitchen with hobs, microwave, coffee maker, fridge, freezer

Outside: table & chairs, parasol, 2 sun loungers

Pets: not accepted

Other: bed linen, cot, highchair to hire

Open: 1 April - 30 September

Weekly Charge	AR1
Low Season *(from)*	€ 399
High Season *(from)*	€ 799

FR23010 Castel Camping le Château de Poinsouze

see report page 229

Route de la Châtre, B.P. 12, F-23600 Boussac-Bourg (Limousin)

AR1 – IRM SUPER MERCURE – Mobile home

Sleeping: 2 bedrooms, sleeps 6: 1 double, 2 singles, sofa bed

Living: living/kitchen area, shower, separate WC

Eating: fitted kitchen with hobs, fridge, freezer

Outside: table & chairs, parasol, 2 sun loungers, barbecue

Pets: not accepted

AR2 – COUNTRY LODGE – Chalet

Sleeping: 2 bedrooms, sleeps 5: 1 double, 2 singles, sofa bed

Living: living/kitchen area, shower, separate WC

Eating: fitted kitchen with hobs, microwave, coffee maker, fridge, freezer

Outside: table & chairs, parasol, 2 sun loungers, barbecue

Pets: not accepted

Other (AR1 and AR2): bed linen, cot, highchair to hire

Open: 11 May - 11 September

Weekly Charge	AR1	AR2
Low Season *(from)*	€ 280	€ 330
High Season *(from)*	€ 570	€ 640

FR07150 Camping Domaine de Gil

see report page 244

Route de Vals-les-Bains, Ucel, F-07200 Aubenas (Rhône Alpes)

AR1 – CONFORT – Mobile home

Sleeping: 2 bedrooms, sleeps 4: 1 double, 2 singles, pillows and blankets provided

Living: living/kitchen area, heating, shower, WC

Eating: fitted kitchen with hobs, coffee maker, fridge

Outside: table & chairs, parasol, 1 sun lounger

Pets: not accepted

AR2 – GRAND LUXE – Mobile home

Sleeping: 3 bedrooms, sleeps 6: 1 double, 4 singles, pillows and blankets provided

Living: living/kitchen area, heating, shower, separate WC

Eating: fitted kitchen with hobs, microwave, coffee maker, fridge

Outside: table & chairs, parasol, 1 sun lounger

Pets: not accepted

Other (AR1 and AR2): bed linen, cot to hire

Open: 17 April - 19 September

Weekly Charge	AR1	AR2
Low Season *(from)*	€ 231	€ 315
High Season *(from)*	€ 630	€ 798

FR26210 Camping les Bois du Chatelas

see report page 246

Route de Dieulefit, F-26460 Bourdeaux (Rhône Alpes)

AR1 – GOELAND – Bungalow

Sleeping: 2 bedrooms, sleeps 6: 2 doubles, 1 single, sofa bed, pillows and blankets provided

Living: living/kitchen area, heating, shower, separate WC

Eating: fitted kitchen with hobs, microwave, coffee maker, fridge, freezer

Outside: table & chairs

Pets: accepted

AR2 – TEXAS WATIPI – Bungalow

Sleeping: 3 bedrooms, sleeps 7: 1 double, 4 singles, sofa bed, pillows and blankets provided

Living: living/kitchen area, heating, shower, separate WC

Eating: fitted kitchen with hobs, microwave, coffee maker, fridge, freezer

Outside: table & chairs

Pets: accepted

Other (AR1 and AR2): bed linen, cot, highchair to hire

Open: 21 April - 28 October

Weekly Charge	AR1	AR2
Low Season *(from)*	€ 343	€ 329
High Season *(from)*	€ 798	€ 749

FR73030 Camping les Lanchettes

see report page 267

F-73210 Peisey-Nancroix (Rhône Alpes)

AR1 – CHALET VANOISE – Chalet

Sleeping: 2 bedrooms, sleeps 5: 1 double, 3 singles

Living: living/kitchen area, shower, WC

Eating: fitted kitchen with hobs, oven, dishwasher, fridge

Outside: table & chairs, parasol

Pets: accepted (with supplement)

AR2 – CHARLEY BELLECÔTE – Mobile home

Sleeping: 2 bedrooms, sleeps 5: 1 double, 4 singles

Living: living/kitchen area, shower, separate WC

Eating: fitted kitchen with hobs, oven, fridge

Outside: table & chairs, parasol

Pets: accepted (with supplement)

Open: 15 December - 30 September

Weekly Charge	AR1	AR2
Low Season *(from)*	€ 285	€ 285
High Season *(from)*	€ 600	€ 600

FR40100 Camping du Domaine de la Rive

see report page 294

Route de Bordeaux, F-40600 Biscarrosse (Aquitaine)

AR1 – SAVANNAH – Mobile home

Sleeping: 2 bedrooms, sleeps 6: 1 double, 2 singles, sofa bed, pillows and blankets provided

Living: living/kitchen area, heating, shower, WC

Eating: fitted kitchen with hobs, microwave, fridge, freezer

Outside: table & chairs, parasol, 2 sun loungers

Pets: not accepted

AR2 – COTTAGE 3 – Mobile home

Sleeping: 3 bedrooms, sleeps 6: 1 double, 4 singles, pillows and blankets provided

Living: living/kitchen area, shower, WC

Eating: fitted kitchen with hobs, microwave, fridge, freezer

Outside: table & chairs, parasol

Pets: not accepted

Other (AR1 and AR2): bed linen, cot, highchair to hire

Open: 3 April - 5 September

Weekly Charge	AR1	AR2
Low Season *(from)*	€ 455	€ 462
High Season *(from)*	€ 1057	€ 1071

FR33110 Airotel Camping de la Côte d'Argent

see report page 302

F-33990 Hourtin-Plage (Aquitaine)

AR1 – SAVANNAH – Mobile home

Sleeping: 2 bedrooms, sleeps 5: 1 double, 2 singles, sofa bed, pillows and blankets provided

Living: living/kitchen area, shower, WC

Eating: fitted kitchen with hobs, microwave, coffee maker, fridge, freezer

Outside: table & chairs, parasol

Pets: not accepted

AR2 – SUPER FAMILY – Mobile home

Sleeping: 3 bedrooms, sleeps 6: 1 double, 4 singles, pillows and blankets provided

Living: living/kitchen area, shower, WC

Eating: fitted kitchen with hobs, microwave, coffee maker, fridge, freezer

Outside: table & chairs, parasol, 2 sun loungers

Pets: not accepted

Open: 17 May - 14 September

Weekly Charge	AR1	AR2
Low Season *(from)*	€ 240	€ 256
High Season *(from)*	€ 945	€ 1043

FR40180 Camping le Vieux Port

see report page 310

Plage Sud, F-40660 Messanges (Aquitaine)

AR1 – MOBILE HOME STANDARD – Mobile home

Sleeping: 2 bedrooms, sleeps 4: 1 double, 2 singles, pillows and blankets provided

Living: living/kitchen area, heating, shower, WC

Eating: fitted kitchen with hobs, fridge

Outside: table & chairs, parasol

Pets: not accepted

AR2 – CHALET 4/5 – Chalet

Sleeping: 2 bedrooms, sleeps 5: 1 double, 3 singles, pillows and blankets provided

Living: living/kitchen area, heating, shower, WC

Eating: fitted kitchen with hobs, fridge, freezer

Outside: table & chairs, parasol, 2 sun loungers

Pets: not accepted

Other (AR1 and AR2): cot, highchair to hire

Open: 31 March - 26 September

Weekly Charge	AR1	AR2
Low Season *(from)*	€ 455	€ 595
High Season *(from)*	€ 840	€ 1239

FR40190 Le Saint-Martin Camping

see report page 313

Avenue de lÔOcéan, F-40660 Moliets-Plage (Aquitaine)

AR1 – DUO – Mobile home

Sleeping: 1 bedroom, sleeps 3: 2 singles, pillows and blankets provided

Living: living/kitchen area, heating, shower, separate WC

Eating: fitted kitchen with hobs, microwave, coffee maker, fridge, freezer

Outside: table & chairs

Pets: accepted (with supplement)

AR2 – ZEPHYR – Chalet

Sleeping: 2 bedrooms, sleeps 5: 1 double, 2 singles, sofa bed, pillows and blankets provided

Living: living/kitchen area, heating, shower, separate WC

Eating: fitted kitchen with hobs, microwave, coffee maker, fridge, freezer

Outside: table & chairs

Pets: accepted (with supplement)

Other (AR1 and AR2): cot to hire

Open: 31 March - 11 November

Weekly Charge	AR1	AR2
Low Season *(from)*	€ 190	€ 460
High Season *(from)*	€ 600	€ 1300

FR24160 Camping le Grand Dague

see report page 316

Route du Grand Dague, Atur, F-24750 Périgueux (Aquitaine)

AR1 – BALI – Mobile home

Sleeping: 2 bedrooms, sleeps 6: 1 double, 2 singles, bunk bed, sofa bed, pillows and blankets provided

Living: living/kitchen area, heating, shower, separate WC

Eating: fitted kitchen with hobs, microwave, fridge, freezer

Outside: table & chairs, parasol, 2 sun loungers

Pets: not accepted

AR2 – WAIKIKI – Cottage

Sleeping: 3 bedrooms, sleeps 6: 1 double, 4 singles, sofa bed, pillows and blankets provided

Living: living/kitchen area, heating, shower, separate WC

Eating: fitted kitchen with hobs, microwave, fridge, freezer

Outside: table & chairs, parasol, 2 sun loungers

Pets: not accepted

Other (AR1 and AR2): bed linen, cot, highchair to hire

Open: 29 April - 26 September

Weekly Charge	AR1	AR2
Low Season *(from)*	€ 180	€ 264
High Season *(from)*	€ 651	€ 805

FR24320 Camping les Peneyrals

see report page 319

Le Poujol, F-24590 Saint Crépin-Carlucet (Aquitaine)

AR1 – MERCURE – Mobile home

Sleeping: 2 bedrooms, sleeps 5: 1 double, 2 singles, sofa bed, pillows and blankets provided

Living: living/kitchen area, heating, shower, separate WC

Eating: fitted kitchen with hobs, microwave, coffee maker, fridge

Outside: table & chairs, parasol, 2 sun loungers, barbecue

Pets: accepted (with supplement)

AR2 – EQUINOXE – Chalet

Sleeping: 3 bedrooms, sleeps 7: 1 double, 4 singles, sofa bed, pillows and blankets provided

Living: living/kitchen area, heating, TV, shower, separate WC

Eating: fitted kitchen with hobs, microwave, coffee maker, fridge

Outside: table & chairs, parasol, 2 sun loungers, barbecue

Pets: accepted (with supplement)

Other (AR1 and AR2): bed linen to hire

Open: 14 May - 15 September

Weekly Charge	AR1	AR2
Low Season *(from)*	€ 300	€ 490
High Season *(from)*	€ 840	€ 995

FR40140 Camping Caravaning Lou P'tit Poun

see report page 324

110 avenue du Quartier Neuf, F-40390 Saint Martin-de-Seignanx (Aquitaine)

AR1 – FABRE REVE – Chalet

Sleeping: 2 bedrooms, sleeps 5: 1 double, 3 singles

Living: living/kitchen area, shower, WC

Eating: fitted kitchen with fridge

Outside: table & chairs, 2 sun loungers

Pets: not accepted

AR2 – IRM MEROURE – Mobile home

Sleeping: sleeps 5: 1 double, 2 singles, sofa bed

Living: living/kitchen area, shower, WC

Eating: fitted kitchen with fridge

Outside: table & chairs, 2 sun loungers

Pets: not accepted

Open: 1 June - 11 September

Weekly Charge	AR1	AR2
Low Season *(from)*	€ 460	€ 430
High Season *(from)*	€ 750	€ 730

FR40250 Camping les Grands Pins

see report page 326

1039 avenue de Losa, F-40460 Sanguinet (Aquitaine)

AR1 – OHARA OCEANE – Mobile home

Sleeping: 3 bedrooms, sleeps 6: 1 double, 4 singles, pillows and blankets provided

Living: living/kitchen area, heating, shower, separate WC

Eating: fitted kitchen with hobs, microwave, coffee maker, fridge, freezer

Outside: table & chairs, parasol, 2 sun loungers

Pets: not accepted

AR2 – GITOTEL FABRE – Chalet

Sleeping: 2 bedrooms, sleeps 4: 1 double, 2 singles, pillows and blankets provided

Living: living/kitchen area, heating, shower, WC

Eating: fitted kitchen with hobs, microwave, fridge

Outside: table & chairs

Pets: not accepted

Open: 3 April - 26 September

Weekly Charge	AR1	AR2
Low Season *(from)*	€ 420	€ 399
High Season *(from)*	€ 945	€ 924

FR24130 Camping les Grottes de Roffy

see report page 329

Sainte Nathalène, F-24200 Sarlat-la-Canéda (Aquitaine)

AR1 – OHARA – Mobile home

Sleeping: 2 bedrooms, sleeps 6: 1 double, 2 singles, bunk bed, sofa bed, pillows and blankets provided

Living: living/kitchen area, shower, separate WC

Eating: fitted kitchen with hobs, microwave, coffee maker, fridge, freezer

Outside: table & chairs, parasol, 2 sun loungers, barbecue

Pets: accepted

AR2 – OHARA 3 BEDROOMS – Mobile home

Sleeping: 3 bedrooms, sleeps 6: 1 double, 4 singles, sofa bed, pillows and blankets provided

Living: living/kitchen area, heating, shower, separate WC

Eating: fitted kitchen with hobs, microwave, coffee maker, fridge, freezer

Outside: table & chairs, parasol, 2 sun loungers, barbecue

Pets: accepted

Other (AR1 and AR2): bed linen, cot to hire

Open: 18 April - 19 September

Weekly Charge	AR1	AR2
Low Season *(from)*	€ 270	€ 280
High Season *(from)*	€ 833	€ 903

FR47010 Kawan Village Moulin du Périé

see report page 332

F-47500 Sauveterre-la-Lemance (Aquitaine)

AR1 – IRM SUPER MERCURE – Mobile home

Sleeping: 2 bedrooms, sleeps 5: 1 double, 2 singles, pillows and blankets provided

Living: living/kitchen area, heating, shower, WC

Eating: fitted kitchen with hobs, fridge

Outside: table & chairs, parasol

Pets: not accepted

AR2 – FABRE REVE – Chalet

Sleeping: 2 bedrooms, sleeps 7: 1 double, 2 singles, pillows and blankets provided

Living: living/kitchen area, heating, shower, WC

Eating: fitted kitchen with hobs, fridge

Outside: table & chairs, parasol

Pets: not accepted

Other (AR1 and AR2): bed linen, cot, highchair to hire

Open: 12 May - 18 September

Weekly Charge	AR1	AR2
Low Season *(from)*	€ 336	€ 392
High Season *(from)*	€ 658	€ 742

FR24090 Domaine de Soleil Plage

see report page 337

Caudon par Montfort, Vitrac, F-24200 Sarlat-la-Canéda (Aquitaine)

AR1 – CHALET PRESTIGE – Chalet

Sleeping: 3 bedrooms, sleeps 7: 1 double, 4 singles, sofa bed, pillows and blankets provided

Living: living/kitchen area, heating, TV, shower, WC, separate WC

Eating: fitted kitchen with hobs, microwave, grill, coffee maker, fridge, freezer

Outside: table & chairs, parasol, 2 sun loungers, barbecue

Pets: accepted (with supplement)

AR2 – MOBILE HOME 3 CHAMBRES – Mobile home

Sleeping: 3 bedrooms, sleeps 7: 1 double, 4 singles, sofa bed, pillows and blankets provided

Living: living/kitchen area, heating, shower, separate WC

Eating: fitted kitchen with hobs, microwave, coffee maker

Outside: table & chairs, parasol, 2 sun loungers, barbecue

Pets: accepted (with supplement)

Other (AR1 and AR2): bed linen, cot, highchair to hire

Open: 2 April - 11 November

Weekly Charge	AR1	AR2
Low Season *(from)*	€ 450	€ 380
High Season *(from)*	€ 840	€ 720

FR09020 Camping l'Arize

see report page 348

Lieu-dit Bourtol, F-09240 La Bastide-de-Sérou (Midi-Pyrénées)

AR1 – LOUISIANE FLORES CONFORT PLUS – Mobile home

Sleeping: 2 bedrooms, sleeps 7: 1 double, 2 singles, bunk bed, sofa bed, pillows and blankets provided

Living: living/kitchen area, heating, shower, separate WC

Eating: fitted kitchen with hobs, microwave, grill, fridge, freezer

Outside: table & chairs, parasol, barbecue

Pets: accepted (with supplement)

AR2 – CHALET 3 BEDROOMS – Chalet

Sleeping: 3 bedrooms, sleeps 8: 1 double, 3 singles, bunk bed, sofa bed, pillows and blankets provided

Living: living/kitchen area, heating, shower, separate WC

Eating: fitted kitchen with hobs, microwave, grill, fridge, freezer

Outside: table & chairs, parasol, barbecue

Pets: accepted (with supplement)

Open: 30 January - 30 November

Weekly Charge	AR1	AR2
Low Season *(from)*	€ 392	€ 455
High Season *(from)*	€ 749	€ 749

FR32010 Kawan Village le Camp de Florence

see report page 348

Route Astaffort, F-32480 La Romieu (Midi-Pyrénées)

AR1 – LOUISIANE ZEN – Mobile home

Sleeping: 3 bedrooms, sleeps 6: 1 double, 2 singles, bunk bed, pillows and blankets provided

Living: living/kitchen area, heating, shower, separate WC

Eating: fitted kitchen with microwave, fridge, freezer

Outside: table & chairs, 2 sun loungers

Pets: accepted

AR2 – IRM DELUXE – Mobile home

Sleeping: 2 bedrooms, sleeps 6: 1 double, 2 singles, sofa bed, pillows and blankets provided

Living: living/kitchen area, heating, shower, separate WC

Eating: fitted kitchen with microwave, fridge, freezer

Outside: table & chairs, 2 sun loungers

Pets: accepted

Open: 1 April - 11 October

Weekly Charge	AR1	AR2
Low Season *(from)*	€ 392	€ 522
High Season *(from)*	€ 882	€ 826

FR66070 Yelloh! Village le Brasilia

see report page 377

B.P. 204, F-66141 Canet-en-Roussillon (Languedoc-Roussillon)

AR1 – OKAVANGO – Mobile home

Sleeping: 2 bedrooms, sleeps 6: 1 double, 2 singles, bunk bed, pillows and blankets provided

Living: living/kitchen area, heating, shower, WC

Eating: fitted kitchen with hobs, microwave, grill, coffee maker, fridge, freezer

Outside: table & chairs, parasol, 2 sun loungers

Pets: accepted (with supplement)

AR2 – PINÈDE – Bungalow

Sleeping: 2 bedrooms, sleeps 4: 1 double, 2 singles, bunk bed, pillows and blankets provided

Living: living/kitchen area, heating, TV, shower, WC

Eating: fitted kitchen with hobs, microwave, grill, coffee maker, fridge, freezer

Outside: table & chairs, 2 sun loungers

Pets: accepted (with supplement)

Other (AR1 and AR2): bed linen, cot, highchair to hire

Open: 25 April - 26 September

Weekly Charge	AR1	AR2
Low Season *(from)*	€ 273	€ 273
High Season *(from)*	€ 1043	€ 1043

FR11070 Kawan Village les Mimosas

see report page 392

Chaussée de Mandirac, F-11100 Narbonne (Languedoc-Roussillon)

AR1 – MOBILE HOME PLANCHA – Mobile home

Sleeping: 2 bedrooms, sleeps 4: 1 double, 2 singles, pillows and blankets provided

Living: living/kitchen area, TV, shower, WC

Eating: fitted kitchen with hobs, microwave, coffee maker, fridge, freezer

Outside: table & chairs, 2 sun loungers, barbecue

Pets: not accepted

AR2 – FLORÈS – Mobile home

Sleeping: 3 bedrooms, sleeps 6: 1 double, 4 singles, pillows and blankets provided

Living: living/kitchen area, heating, air conditioning, shower, WC

Eating: fitted kitchen with hobs, microwave, coffee maker, fridge, freezer

Outside: table & chairs, 2 sun loungers

Pets: not accepted

Other (AR1 and AR2): bed linen, cot, highchair to hire

Open: 27 March - 1 November

Weekly Charge	AR1	AR2
Low Season *(from)*	€ 273	€ 343
High Season *(from)*	€ 658	€ 854

FR11080 Camping la Nautique

see report page 393

La Nautique, F-11100 Narbonne (Languedoc-Roussillon)

AR1 – TYPE IV – Mobile home

Sleeping: 2 bedrooms, sleeps 6: 1 double, 2 singles, sofa bed, pillows and blankets provided

Living: living/kitchen area, heating, shower, separate WC

Eating: oven, coffee maker, fridge

Outside: table & chairs, parasol, 2 sun loungers

Pets: not accepted

AR2 – TYPE X – Mobile home

Sleeping: 2 bedrooms, sleeps 6: 1 double, 2 singles, sofa bed, pillows and blankets provided

Living: living/kitchen area, heating, shower, separate WC

Eating: oven, coffee maker, fridge, freezer

Outside: table & chairs, parasol, 2 sun loungers

Pets: not accepted

Other (AR1 and AR2): bed linen, cot, highchair to hire

Open: 15 February - 15 November

Weekly Charge	AR1	AR2
Low Season *(from)*	€ 294	€ 350
High Season *(from)*	€ 707	€ 910

FR34070 Yelloh! Village le Sérignan Plage

see report page 400

Le Sérignan Plage, F-34410 Sérignan (Languedoc-Roussillon)

AR1 – COTTAGE VIP – Mobile home	AR2 – COTTAGE CABANE – Mobile home
Sleeping: 2 bedrooms, sleeps 4: 1 double, 2 singles, pillows and blankets provided	**Sleeping:** 3 bedrooms, sleeps 6: 1 double, 2 singles, bunk bed, pillows and blankets provided
Living: living/kitchen area, heating, shower, separate WC	**Living:** living/kitchen area, heating, TV, air conditioning, shower, separate WC
Eating: fitted kitchen with hobs, microwave, coffee maker, fridge, freezer	**Eating:** fitted kitchen with hobs, microwave, dishwasher, coffee maker, fridge, freezer
Outside: table & chairs, 2 sun loungers	**Outside:** table & chairs, 2 sun loungers
Pets: not accepted	**Pets:** not accepted

Other (AR1 and AR2): bed linen, cot, highchair to hire

Open: 23 April - 27 September

Weekly Charge	AR1	AR2
Low Season *(from)*	€ 273	€ 413
High Season *(from)*	€ 1162	€ 1876

FR34110 Yelloh! Village le Club Farret

see report page 407

F-34450 Vias-Plage (Languedoc-Roussillon)

AR1 – BALI – Mobile home	AR2 – AFRICA – Mobile home
Sleeping: 3 bedrooms, sleeps 6: 1 double, 4 singles, pillows and blankets provided	**Sleeping:** 2 bedrooms, sleeps 5: 1 double, 2 singles, sofa bed, pillows and blankets provided
Living: living/kitchen area, heating, air conditioning, shower, separate WC	**Living:** living/kitchen area, heating, shower, separate WC
Eating: fitted kitchen with hobs, microwave, coffee maker, fridge, freezer	**Eating:** fitted kitchen with hobs, microwave, coffee maker, fridge, freezer
Outside: table & chairs, parasol, 2 sun loungers	**Outside:** table & chairs, parasol, 2 sun loungers
Pets: not accepted	**Pets:** not accepted

Other (AR1 and AR2): bed linen, cot, highchair to hire

Open: 25 March - 25 September

Weekly Charge	AR1	AR2
Low Season *(from)*	€ 315	€ 273
High Season *(from)*	€ 1274	€ 1057

FR83220 Kawan Village Cros de Mouton

see report page 418

B.P. 116, F-83240 Cavalaire-sur-Mer (Provence)

AR1 – PRESTIGE – Mobile home	AR2 – TEXAS – Mobile home
Sleeping: 2 bedrooms, sleeps 5: 1 double, 2 singles, sofa bed, pillows and blankets provided	**Sleeping:** 3 bedrooms, sleeps 6: 1 double, 4 singles, pillows and blankets provided
Living: living/kitchen area, heating, air conditioning, shower, separate WC	**Living:** living/kitchen area, heating, air conditioning, shower, separate WC
Eating: fitted kitchen with hobs, microwave, coffee maker, fridge, freezer	**Eating:** fitted kitchen with hobs, microwave, coffee maker, fridge, freezer
Outside: table & chairs, parasol, 2 sun loungers	**Outside:** table & chairs, parasol, 2 sun loungers
Pets: accepted	**Pets:** accepted

Other (AR1 and AR2): bed linen, cot, highchair to hire

Open: 15 March - 4 November

Weekly Charge	AR1	AR2
Low Season *(from)*	€ 455	€ 530
High Season *(from)*	€ 830	€ 930

FR83060 Camping Resort la Baume – la Palmeraie

see report page 422

3775 rue des Combattants d'Afrique du Nord, F-83618 Fréjus (Provence)

AR1 – BASTIDON – Bungalow

Sleeping: 3 bedrooms, sleeps 7: 1 double, 4 singles, sofa bed

Living: living/kitchen area, shower, WC

Eating: fitted kitchen with hobs, microwave, fridge, freezer

Outside: table & chairs, 2 sun loungers

Pets: accepted

AR2 – PHOENIX – Mobile home

Sleeping: 3 bedrooms, sleeps 6: 1 double, 4 singles, sofa bed

Living: living/kitchen area, shower, WC

Eating: fitted kitchen with hobs, microwave, fridge, freezer

Outside: table & chairs, 2 sun loungers

Pets: accepted

Other (AR1 and AR2): bed linen, cot, highchair to hire

Open: 27 March - 25 September

Weekly Charge	AR1	AR2
Low Season *(from)*	€ 469	€ 336
High Season *(from)*	€ 1386	€ 970

FR83030 Camping Caravaning Leï Suves

see report page 438

Quartier du Blavet, F-83520 Roquebrune-sur-Argens (Provence)

AR1 – TYPE D – Mobile home

Sleeping: 2 bedrooms, sleeps 6: 1 double, 2 singles, sofa bed

Living: living/kitchen area, shower, WC

Eating: fitted kitchen with hobs, oven, fridge

Outside: table & chairs

Pets: not accepted

AR2 – LUXE – Mobile home

Sleeping: 2 bedrooms, sleeps 5: 1 double, 2 singles, sofa bed

Living: living/kitchen area, shower, WC

Eating: fitted kitchen with hobs, oven, fridge

Outside: table & chairs

Pets: not accepted

Open: 3 April - 15 October

Weekly Charge	AR1	AR2
Low Season *(from)*	€ 365	€ 420
High Season *(from)*	€ 760	€ 850

FR83200 Kawan Village les Pêcheurs

see report page 440

F-83520 Roquebrune-sur-Argens (Provence)

AR1 – SHELBOX PARADIS – Mobile home

Sleeping: 2 bedrooms, sleeps 6: 1 double, 3 singles, sofa bed, pillows and blankets provided

Living: living/kitchen area, heating, shower, separate WC

Eating: fitted kitchen with hobs, microwave, coffee maker, fridge, freezer

Outside: table & chairs, parasol, 2 sun loungers

Pets: accepted (with supplement)

AR2 – OHARA OPHEA – Mobile home

Sleeping: 2 bedrooms, sleeps 6: 1 double, 2 singles, sofa bed, pillows and blankets provided

Living: living/kitchen area, heating, shower, separate WC

Eating: fitted kitchen with hobs, microwave, coffee maker, fridge, freezer

Outside: table & chairs, parasol, 2 sun loungers

Pets: accepted (with supplement)

Other (AR1 and AR2): bed linen, cot, highchair to hire

Open: 1 April - 30 September

Weekly Charge	AR1	AR2
Low Season *(from)*	€ 330	€ 400
High Season *(from)*	€ 805	€ 895

FR83050 Camping Résidence du Campeur

see report page 444

B.P. 12, D7, F-83371 Saint Aygulf (Provence)

AR1 – MOBIL HOME 4/5 PERSONS JUNIOR – Mobile home

Sleeping: 2 bedrooms, sleeps 5: 1 double, 2 singles, sofa bed, pillows and blankets provided

Living: living/kitchen area, heating, shower, separate WC

Eating: fitted kitchen with hobs, oven, microwave, grill, coffee maker, fridge, freezer

Outside: table & chairs, 2 sun loungers

Pets: accepted

AR2 – GRAND CONFORT 6 PERSONS – Mobile home

Sleeping: 2 bedrooms, sleeps 5: 1 double, 2 singles, sofa bed, pillows and blankets provided

Living: living/kitchen area, heating, shower, separate WC

Eating: fitted kitchen with hobs, oven, microwave, grill, coffee maker, fridge, freezer

Outside: table & chairs, 2 sun loungers

Pets: accepted

Other (AR1 and AR2): bed linen, cot, highchair to hire

Open: 27 March - 30 September

Weekly Charge	AR1	AR2
Low Season *(from)*	€ 290	€ 430
High Season *(from)*	€ 790	€ 990

FR04010 Sunêlia Hippocampe

see report page 451

Route de Napoléon, F-04290 Volonne (Provence)

AR1 – SUNELIA FAMILY – Mobile home

Sleeping: 3 bedrooms, sleeps 6: 1 double, 4 singles, pillows and blankets provided

Living: living/kitchen area, heating, air conditioning, shower, WC

Eating: fitted kitchen with hobs, microwave, fridge, freezer

Outside: table & chairs, parasol, 2 sun loungers

Pets: accepted

AR2 – SUNELIA GRAND CONFORT – Mobile home

Sleeping: 2 bedrooms, sleeps 6: 1 double, 2 singles, pillows and blankets provided

Living: living/kitchen area, heating, shower, WC

Eating: fitted kitchen with hobs, fridge

Outside: table & chairs, parasol, 2 sun loungers

Pets: accepted

Other (AR1 and AR2): cot, highchair to hire

Open: 3 March - 30 September

Weekly Charge	AR1	AR2
Low Season *(from)*	€ 336	€ 336
High Season *(from)*	€ 987	€ 987

FR04020 Castel Camping le Domaine du Verdon

see report page 416

Camp du Verdon, F-04120 Castellane (Provence)

AR1 – WATIPI – Mobile home

Sleeping: 2 bedrooms, sleeps 4: 1 double, 2 singles, pillows and blankets provided

Living: living/kitchen area, shower, WC

Eating: fitted kitchen with hobs, fridge

Outside: table & chairs, 2 sun loungers

Pets: accepted

AR2 – TITOM – Mobile home

Sleeping: 2 bedrooms, sleeps 4: 1 double, 2 singles, bunk bed, pillows and blankets provided

Living: living/kitchen area, shower, WC

Eating: fitted kitchen with hobs, fridge

Outside: table & chairs, 2 sun loungers

Pets: accepted

Other (AR1 and AR2): bed linen, cot, highchair to hire

Open: 15 May - 15 September

Weekly Charge	AR1	AR2
Low Season *(from)*	€ 322	€ 364
High Season *(from)*	€ 714	€ 763

FR06080 Camping Caravaning les Cigales

505 avenue de la Mer, F-06210 Mandelieu-la-Napoule (Côte d'Azur)

AR1 – COTTAGE – Cottage

Sleeping: 2 bedrooms, sleeps 6: 1 double, 2 singles, sofa bed, pillows and blankets provided

Living: living/kitchen area, heating, shower, WC

Eating: fitted kitchen with hobs, fridge

Outside: table & chairs, parasol

Pets: accepted (with supplement)

AR2 – OPTIMA – Mobile home

Sleeping: 2 bedrooms, sleeps 6: 1 double, 2 singles, sofa bed, pillows and blankets provided

Living: living/kitchen area, shower, WC

Eating: fitted kitchen with hobs, fridge

Outside: table & chairs, parasol

Pets: accepted (with supplement)

Other (AR1 and AR2): bed linen to hire

Open: All Year

Weekly Charge	AR1	AR2
Low Season *(from)*	€ 405	€ 405
High Season *(from)*	€ 810	€ 810

FR84020 Domaine Naturiste de Bélézy

see report page 474

F-84410 Bedoin (Provence)

AR1 – NAUTILHOME – Bungalow

Sleeping: 2 bedrooms, sleeps 5: 1 double, 2 singles, sofa bed, pillows and blankets provided

Living: living/kitchen area, shower, separate WC

Eating: fitted kitchen with hobs, microwave, coffee maker, fridge, freezer

Outside: table & chairs, 2 sun loungers

Pets: not accepted

AR2 – BOIS – Bungalow

Sleeping: 2 bedrooms, sleeps 5: 1 double, 2 singles, sofa bed, pillows and blankets provided

Living: living/kitchen area, shower, separate WC

Eating: fitted kitchen with hobs, microwave, dishwasher, coffee maker, fridge, freezer

Outside: table & chairs, 2 sun loungers

Pets: not accepted

Other (AR1 and AR2): bed linen, cot, highchair to hire

Open: 23 March - 2 October

Weekly Charge	AR1	AR2
Low Season *(from)*	€ 350	€ 350
High Season *(from)*	€ 966	€ 868

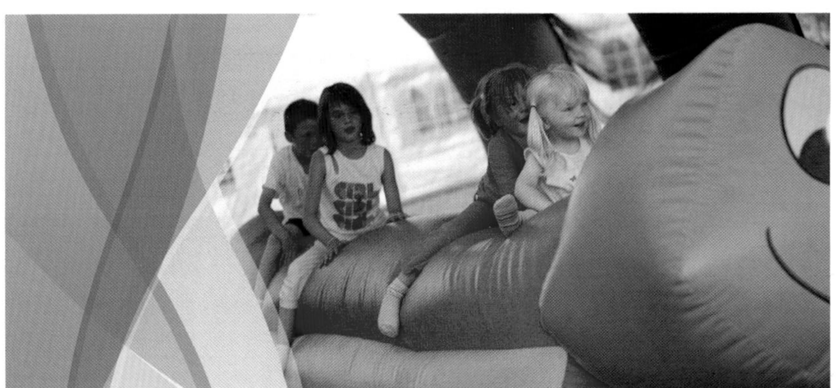

FR20040 Riva Bella Nature Resort & Spa

see report page 475

B.P. 21, F-20270 Alèria (Corsica)

AR1 – CHALET 4 – Chalet	AR2 – CHALET TYPE 2 – Chalet
Sleeping: 2 bedrooms, sleeps 5: 1 double, 2 singles, pillows and blankets provided	**Sleeping:** 2 bedrooms, sleeps 4: 1 double, bunk bed, pillows and blankets provided
Living: living/kitchen area, heating, shower, WC	**Living:** living/kitchen area, heating, shower, WC
Eating: fitted kitchen with hobs, fridge	**Eating:** fitted kitchen with hobs, fridge
Outside: table & chairs, parasol, 2 sun loungers	**Outside:** table & chairs, parasol, 2 sun loungers
Pets: accepted (with supplement)	**Pets:** accepted (with supplement)

Open: 15 May - 20 September

Weekly Charge	AR1	AR2
Low Season *(from)*	€ 798	€ 623
High Season *(from)*	€ 1169	€ 791

FR20050 Village Naturiste la Chiappa

see report page 475

Route de Palombaggia, F-20137 Porto-Vecchio (Corsica)

AR1 – TYPE C – Bungalow	AR2 – TYPE B – Bungalow
Sleeping: 2 bedrooms, sleeps 4: 4 singles, pillows and blankets provided	**Sleeping:** 1 bedroom, sleeps 2: 2 singles
Living: living/kitchen area, shower, WC	**Living:** living/kitchen area, shower, WC
Eating: fitted kitchen with hobs, fridge	**Eating:** fitted kitchen with fridge
Outside: table & chairs	**Outside:** table & chairs
Pets: accepted	**Pets:** accepted

Other (AR1 and AR2): bed linen, cot, highchair to hire

Open: 15 May - 9 October

Weekly Charge	AR1	AR2
Low Season *(from)*	€ 630	€ 420
High Season *(from)*	€ 1050	€ 700

Parcs Résidentiels de Loisirs

Recent years have seen a significant increase in the number of Parcs Résidentiels de Loisirs in France. In many ways, these parks resemble good campsites but with the important distinction that they do not have any touring pitches!

Amenities at the parks are invariably very impressive, often with top quality swimming pool complexes and fine restaurant facilities. However, all the pitches on these sites are occupied by either mobile homes or chalets, many of which are available for let.

These parks have been developed by their owners often with the expectation that their clients may be former campers or caravanners, or possibly those travelling from afar, with the common desire to combine the freedom of camping and caravanning with a high standard of home comforts.

We have chosen to include a small selection of the best Parcs Résidentiels, all of which are attractively located in popular regions of France. In every case, there will be a good choice of accommodation available for rent. We are, however, featuring 2 types of accommodation and give full details of what is provided in terms of living and sleeping accommodation, as well as an indication of the park's tariffs.

FR27060 Domaine de Marcilly

see report page 66

Route de Saint-Andre-de-l'Eure, F-27810 Marcilly-sur-Eure (Eure)
T: **02 37 48 45 42**. E: **domainedemarcilly@wanadoo.fr** **alanrogers.com/FR27060**

Just between Ile de France and Normandy, less than an hour's drive from Paris, Domaine de Marcilly is beautifully located in a 15 hectare park, surrounded by pine, oak and birch trees. Although most pitches are dedicated to mobile homes, this park also welcomes motorcaravans and each pitch has a picnic table. Leisure facilities include a swimming pool and two tennis courts. There are paths and cycle routes through the parkland and surrounding countryside, as well as riding and fishing. The site is well located for exploring the northern Loire Valley and both Chartres and Paris are within easy reach.

Facilities

Motorcaravan service point. Heated swimming pool (1/6-30/9). Boules. Tennis. Internet point. TV room. Animation and entertainment during high season.
Off site: Local shops 900 m. Riding 3 km. Golf 10 km.

Directions

From Paris A13, A12 exit onto N12 for Houdan, take exit Goussainville, Havelu, Bu, then Marcilly. Site is on the D52 in the direction of St Andre.
GPS: 48.8252, 1.3237

AR1 – OPHEA – Mobile home

- **Sleeping:** 2 bedrooms, sleeps 5: 1 double, 2 singles, sofa bed, pillows and blankets provided
- **Living:** living/kitchen area, heating, shower, WC
- **Eating:** fitted kitchen with hobs, oven, microwave, fridge
- **Outside:** table & chairs, barbecue
- **Pets:** accepted

AR2 – OPHEA – Mobile home

- **Sleeping:** 3 bedrooms, sleeps 6: 1 double, 2 singles, sofa bed, pillows and blankets provided
- **Living:** living/kitchen area, heating, shower, WC
- **Eating:** fitted kitchen with hobs, oven, microwave, fridge
- **Outside:** table & chairs, barbecue
- **Pets:** accepted

Open: 1 April - 29 October

Weekly Charge	AR1	AR2
Low Season *(from)*	€ 300	€ 400
High Season *(from)*	€ 590	€ 660

FR57090 Parc Résidentiel de la Tensch

see report page 112

F-57670 Francaltroff (Moselle) T: **03 87 01 79 04**. E: **tensch@tensch.com**
alanrogers.com/FR57090

La Tensch is a large leisure park located south of St Avold in the Moselle département. The park has been developed around three lakes and fishing is understandably very popular here, although many watersports are also possible, including windsurfing, canoeing and jet skiing. Although there are a few touring pitches, this is primarily a 'parc résidentiel' with a large number of mobile homes and chalets for rent, as well as residential units. Many footpaths lead around the lakes passing picnic areas and well designed playgrounds. There are two swimming pools, one especially for children with a water slide.

Facilities

Shop. Bar/restaurant. Takeaway. Swimming pool. Children's pool. Pedaloes. Canoe hire. Bicycle hire. Tennis. Trampolines. Play area. Games room. Activity and entertainment programme. Mobile homes and chalets for rent.
Off site: Riding. Fishing. Cycle and walking tracks. St Avold.

Directions

Leave the A4 autoroute at exit 39 for St Avold and head south on D633 to St Avold. Continue south on D22 to Francaltroff and the site is clearly signed.
GPS: 48.96083, 6.77444

AR1 – CHALET – Chalet

- **Sleeping:** 2 bedrooms, sleeps 5: 1 double, 2 singles, sofa bed, pillows and blankets provided
- **Living:** living/kitchen area, heating, TV, shower, separate WC
- **Eating:** fitted kitchen with hobs, oven, microwave, coffee maker, fridge, freezer
- **Outside:** table & chairs
- **Pets:** accepted (with supplement)

Other (AR1 and AR2): bed linen, cot to hire

Open: 6 May - 18 December

Weekly Charge	AR1
Low Season *(from)*	€ 340
High Season *(from)*	€ 460

FR07660 Castel Camping Domaine de Sévenier

F-07150 Lagorce (Ardèche) T: **04 75 88 06 63**. E: **domainedesevenier@orange.fr**
alanrogers.com/FR07660

Le Domaine de Sévenier is a new chalet site located 4 km. from Vallon Pont d'Arc and 800 m. from the pretty village of Lagorce. The site has been developed by the same owners as FR07120. The domaine is an old winery which has been sensitively converted into a high quality holiday village. The owners suggest that the site has a 'zen' ambience, in contrast to the busier sites at nearby Vallon Pont d'Arc. Sévenier enjoys a hilltop location with fine panoramic views over the surrounding garrigue, a unique mix of oak trees, juniper, rosemary and thyme.

Facilities

Restaurant. Bar. Shop. Swimming pool. Children's pool. Activity programme. Play area. Minigolf. Tourist information. Fully equipped chalets for rent. Off site: Lagorce 800 m. (shops and cafés). Cycle and walking tracks. Riding. Vallon Pont d'Arc 5 km.

Directions

Head north from Vallon Pont d'Arc (at western end of the Ardèche gorges) on D1 and upon reaching Lagorce, follow signs to the site.
GPS: 44.434151, 4.410989

AR1 – CHENE BLANC – Chalet	AR2 – CHENE VERT – Chalet
Sleeping: 2 bedrooms, sleeps 5: 1 double, 2 singles, bunk bed, sofa bed, pillows and blankets provided	**Sleeping:** 3 bedrooms, sleeps 6: 1 double, 4 singles, bunk bed, sofa bed, pillows and blankets provided
Living: living/kitchen area, heating, TV, air conditioning, shower, separate WC	**Living:** living/kitchen area, heating, TV, air conditioning, shower, separate WC
Eating: fitted kitchen with cooker, microwave, dishwasher, coffee maker, fridge/freezer	**Eating:** fitted kitchen with cooker, microwave, dishwasher, coffee maker, fridge/freezer
Outside: table & chairs, 1 sun lounger	**Outside:** table & chairs, 1 sun lounger
Pets: accepted (with supplement)	**Pets:** accepted (with supplement)

Other (AR1 and AR2): bed linen, cot and highchair to hire

Open: 13 March - 13 November

Weekly Charge	AR1	AR2
Low Season *(from)*	€ 448	€ 637
High Season *(from)*	€ 1169	€ 1673

FR66700 PRL Le Vedrignans

Route de Vedrignans, F-66800 Saillagouse (Pyrénées-Orientales)
T: **04 68 04 04 79**. E: **contact@levedrignans.com** **alanrogers.com/FR66700**

Le Verdrignans can be found deep in the Catalan Pyrénées Regional Park. It enjoys a spectacular natural setting, overlooked by towering mountains but with a very pleasant Mediterranean climate. This is a parc résidentiel de loisirs and there are no touring pitches here. Instead, accommodation is provided in a range of attractive wooden chalets. These range from the smaller 'Genets' model, which can sleep up to 4, to the larger 'Edelweiss' chalets which can accommodate up to 8 people.

Facilities

Play area. Games room. Tourist information. Chalets to rent. Off site: Village centre 300 m. Le train jaune. Ski resorts. Walking and cycling tracks. Covered swimming pool. Tennis.

Directions

Saillagouse lies around 90 km. west of Perpignan. From there head west on N116 to Prades and Mont Louis. Continue on this road to Saillagouse and the site is clearly indicated. GPS: 42.457712, 2.039638

AR1 – GENET – Chalet	AR2 – EDELWEISS – Chalet
Sleeping: 2 bedrooms, sleeps 4: 2 singles, bunk bed, pillows and blankets provided	**Sleeping:** 4 bedrooms, sleeps 8: 3 doubles, 2 singles, pillows and blankets provided
Living: living/kitchen area, heating, TV, shower, separate WC	**Living:** living/kitchen area, heating, TV, shower, separate WC
Eating: fitted kitchen with hobs, microwave, grill, coffee maker, fridge, freezer	**Eating:** fitted kitchen with hobs, oven, microwave, grill, dishwasher, coffee maker, fridge, freezer
Outside: table & chairs, parasol, 2 sun loungers, barbecue	**Outside:** table & chairs, parasol, 4 sun loungers, barbecue
Pets: accepted (with supplement)	**Pets:** accepted (with supplement)

Other (AR1 and AR2): bed linen, cot, highchair to hire

Open: All year

Weekly Charge	AR1	AR2
Low Season *(from)*	€ 330	€ 630
High Season *(from)*	€ 480	€ 900

FR12400 Campéole Domaine de Combelles

Campéole

F-12000 Le Monastère (Aveyron) T: **05 65 77 30 04**. E: **nadine.ferran@atciat.com**

alanrogers.com/FR12400

Domaine de Combelles is well equipped parc résidentiel which can be found at the heart of the Aveyron, quite close to the village of Le Monastère. Please note that there are no touring pitches here, but a range of attractive chalets and mobile homes are available for rent. This site is also unusual in that it also incorporates an excellent riding centre, with opportunities for beginners as well as seasoned riders. Vehicle circulation is not allowed within the site – a large car park is available at the site entrance. This is a spacious site and most facilities are located some distance from the accommodation units, ensuring their tranquility. On-site amenities include a bar and snack bar, and leisure facilities include a swimming pool and tennis court. Most leisure facilities (including tennis) are free of charge. Bicycle hire and riding are available for a small charge. There are plenty of activities and a lively entertainment programme in the peak season, including children's club as well as discos and karaoke. The surrounding country is ideal for walking and cycling and the site managers will be please to recommend possible routes.

Facilities

Bar/restaurant. Swimming pool. Riding centre. Bicycle hire. Volleyball. Bouncy castle. Children's play area. Activities and entertainment programme. Tourist information. Mobile homes and chalets for rent (there are no touring pitches). Off site: Le Monastère (attractive village with shops and restaurants). Walking and cycle tracks. Fishing. Rodez (cathedral city) 5 km. Tarn gorges.

Open: 1 May - 31 October.

Directions

From Albi head north on N88 towards Rodez via Luc la Primaube and Flavin. From here follow signs to the site which is well indicated. GPS: 44.3301, 2.5901

Charges

For full details of charges and accommodation available, please contact the site.

FR11020 Cottage Village Aux Hamacs

Route des Cabanes, F-11560 Fleury (Aude) T: **04 68 33 22 22**
E: **info@cottagevillage.fr** **alanrogers.com/FR11020**

If you are looking for sun, sea and sand, Aux Hamacs is a good location and there is a wide choice of mobile homes (no touring pitches). It is situated adjacent to the Aude river in the Parc Naturel de la Nabonnaise, 2 km. from the sea and sandy beach at Cabanas de Fleury. The attractive main village of Fleury is some 6 km. inland. Quietly situated amongst nature, the site is well away from the frenzy and rush associated with some of the resorts in this region, yet has all the amenities for an enjoyable stay. As yet there is not much shade. There is a pool complex complete with toboggans, an interesting range of sporting activities for children and evening entertainment.

Facilities

Shop, bar, simple restaurant and takeaway (all fully open 27/6-15/9). Swimming pool complex with three slides and paddling pool (27/6-15/9). Play areas. Activities and entertainment (high season). TV room. Games room. Internet access and WiFi. Fishing (no permit). Dogs and other animals are not accepted. Off site: Beach 2 km. Boat launching 2 km. Riding 5 km.

Open: 1 April - 30 September.

Directions

From the A9 exit 36 (Beziers Ouest) follow directions for Vendres Plage and Port Vendres (Grau de Vendres) on the D64, then the D37E9. On reaching the port turn right along a small poorly surfaced road following the river Aude for 3 km. Turn left over the bridge, then right to site 400 m. on right.
GPS: 43.22237, 3.21682

AR1 – TYPE 1 – Mobile home	**AR2 – TYPE 2 – Mobile home**
Sleeping: 2 bedrooms, sleeps 4: 1 double, 2 singles	**Sleeping:** 3 bedrooms, sleeps 6: 1 double, 4 singles
Living: living/kitchen area, heating, shower, separate WC	**Living:** living/kitchen area, heating, shower, separate WC
Eating: fitted kitchen with hobs, microwave, coffee maker, fridge, freezer	**Eating:** fitted kitchen with hobs, microwave, coffee maker, fridge, freezer
Outside: table & chairs, parasol, 2 sun loungers	**Outside:** table & chairs, parasol, 2 sun loungers
Pets: not accepted	**Pets:** not accepted

Open: 1 April - 30 September

Weekly Charge	AR1	AR2
Low Season *(from)*	€ 308	€ 413
High Season *(from)*	€ 903	€ 987

Open All Year

The following sites are understood to accept caravanners and campers all year round. It is always wise to phone the site to check as the facilities available, for example, may be reduced.

Brittany

FR56150 Haras

Normandy

FR27060 Marcilly
FR76090 Mun. Etennemare

Nord/Pas-de-Calais

FR62120 Eté Indien

Paris-Ile de France

FR91010 Beau Village
FR75020 Bois de Boulogne
FR77110 Parc de Paris

Lorraine

FR88050 Champé
FR88040 Lac de Bouzey
FR88090 Lac de la Moselotte
FR88130 Vanne de Pierre

Alsace

FR68030 Masevaux

Val de Loire

FR45040 Jardin de Sully

Pays de la Loire

FR53020 Malidor
FR49150 Thouet

Vendée

FR85930 Forges
FR85890 Rouge-Gorge

Poitou-Charentes

FR86120 Dienné
FR86040 Futuriste
FR17070 Gros Joncs

Burgundy

FR21090 Arquebuse
FR58030 Manoir de Bezolle

Limousin

FR19080 Vianon

Rhône Alpes

FR74230 Giffre
FR69010 Lyon
FR73100 Reclus
FR26100 Sagittaire

Aquitaine

FR24410 Bois du Coderc
FR33410 Bordeaux Lac
FR47110 Cabri
FR24150 Deux Vallées
FR64040 Gaves
FR47150 Guillalmes
FR33370 Montalivet
FR33090 Pressoir
FR24480 Tailladis
FR64080 Tamaris Plage

Midi-Pyrénées

FR32170 Aramis
FR09120 Ascou la Forge
FR65080 Lavedan
FR65160 Monlôo
FR09050 Prade
FR65130 Pyrenevasion

Languedoc-Roussillon

FR66670 Europe
FR34490 Fondespierre
FR66490 Garenne
FR11110 Val d'Aleth
FR66700 Vedrignans

Provence

FR13120 Chantecler
FR04220 Rivière
FR05080 Solaire

Côte d'Azur

FR06080 Cigales
FR06050 Vieille Ferme

Quick Reference - Open All Year

Dogs

Since the introduction in 2000 of the Passports for Pets scheme many British campers and caravanners have been encouraged to take their pets with them on holiday. However, Pet Travel conditions are understandably strict, the procedure is quite lengthy and complicated so we would advise you to check the current situation before travelling. The Passports for Pets official website is: www.defra.gov.uk/animalh/quarantine/pets/

For the benefit of those who want to take their dogs to France, we list here the sites which have indicated to us that they do not accept dogs or have certain restrictions. If you are planning to take your dog we do advise you to phone the site first to check – there may be limits on numbers, breeds, or times of the year when they are excluded.

Sites that do not accept dogs

Normandy
FR14090 Brévedent

Alsace
FR68080 Clair Vacances

Vendée
FR85210 Ecureuils
FR85020 Jard

Poitou-Charentes
FR17010 Bois Soleil
FR16020 Gorges du Chambon

Aquitaine
FR24050 Hauts de Ratebout
FR24040 Moulin du Roch
FR40040 Paillotte
FR64060 Pavillon Royal

Midi-Pyrénées
FR46040 Moulin de Laborde

Languedoc-Roussillon
FR30160 Boucanet
FR11020 Hamacs
FR34560 Paradis
FR30390 Petits Camarguais
FR66040 Soleil

Provence
FR83320 Mogador

Corsica
FR20030 Merendella

Naturist
FR84020 Bélézy (Naturiste)

Sites that accept dogs but with certain restrictions:

Brittany
FR29000 Mouettes
FR29380 Port de Plaisance

Val de Loire
FR37140 Rillé
FR28140 Senonches

Pays de la Loire
FR72040 Molières

Vendée
FR85870 Baie d'Aunis
FR85440 Brunelles
FR85770 Ferme du Latois
FR85030 Loubine
FR85720 Noirmoutier
FR85270 Oceano d'Or
FR85000 Petit Rocher
FR85280 Places Dorées
FR85450 Roses
FR85310 Trévillière
FR85150 Yole

Poitou-Charentes
FR17170 Charmilles
FR17580 Indigo Oléron
FR17210 Interlude
FR17290 Peupliers

Limousin
FR23010 Château Poinsouze

Auvergne
FR63070 Pré Bas
FR63120 Royat

Rhône Alpes
FR07630 Aluna
FR07080 Bastide
FR38100 Belledonne
FR74060 Colombière
FR26200 Ecluse
FR26030 Grand Lierne
FR07650 Indigo Moulin

Aquitaine
FR33080 Barbanne
FR40250 Grands Pins
FR24100 Moulinal
FR33210 Pointe du Medoc
FR33290 Tedey

Midi-Pyrénées
FR12170 Caussanel
FR82050 Faillal
FR46190 Faurie
FR46310 Granges
FR12040 Tours

Languedoc-Roussillon
FR30070 Boisson
FR66290 Floride l'Embouchure
FR66250 Font-Romeu
FR66490 Garenne
FR66170 Mar I Sol
FR34130 Neptune

Provence
FR83040 Bastiane
FR83120 Domaine
FR04120 Forcalquier
FR83440 Malissonne
FR04110 Verdon Parc

Golf

We understand that the following sites have facilities for playing golf. Where facilities are within easy reach and we have been given details, we have included this information in the individual site reports. However, we recommend that you contact the site to check that they meet your requirements.

FR29050 Orangerie Lanniron
FR29470 Deux Fontaines
FR35020 Ormes
FR41030 Alicourts

Travelling

When taking your car (and caravan, tent or trailer tent) or motorcaravan to the continent you do need to plan in advance and to find out as much as possible about driving in the countries you plan to visit. Whilst European harmonisation has eliminated many of the differences between one country and another, it is well worth reading the short notes we provide in the introduction to each country in this guide in addition to this more general summary.

Of course, the main difference from driving in the UK is that in mainland Europe you will need to drive on the right. Without taking extra time and care, especially at busy junctions and conversely when roads are empty, it is easy to forget to drive on the right. Remember that traffic approaching from the right usually has priority unless otherwise indicated by road markings and signs. Harmonisation also means that most (but not all) common road signs are the same in all countries.

Your vehicle

Book your vehicle in for a good service well before your intended departure date. This will lessen the chance of an expensive breakdown. Make sure your brakes are working efficiently and that your tyres have plenty of tread (3 mm. is recommended, particularly if you are undertaking a long journey).

Also make sure that your caravan or trailer is roadworthy and that its tyres are in good order and correctly inflated. Plan your packing and be careful not to overload your vehicle, caravan or trailer – this is unsafe and may well invalidate your insurance cover (it must not be more fully loaded than the kerb weight of the insured vehicle).

CHECK ALL THE FOLLOWING:

- **GB sticker.** If you do not display a sticker, you may risk an on-the-spot fine as this identifier is compulsory in all countries. Euro-plates are an acceptable alternative within the EU (but not outside). Remember to attach another sticker (or Euro-plate) to caravans or trailers. Only GB stickers (not England, Scotland, Wales or N. Ireland) stickers are valid in the EU.

- **Headlights.** As you will be driving on the right you must adjust your headlights so that the dipped beam does not dazzle oncoming drivers. Converter kits are readily available for most vehicle, although if your car is fitted with high intensity headlights, you should check with your motor dealer. Check that any planned extra loading does not affect the beam height.

- **Seatbelts.** Rules for the fitting and wearing of seatbelts throughout Europe are similar to those in the UK, but it is worth checking before you go. Rules for carrying children in the front of vehicles vary from country to country. It is best to plan not to do this if possible.

- **Door/wing mirrors.** To help with driving on the right, if your vehicle is not fitted with a mirror on the left hand side, we recommend you have one fitted.

- **Fuel.** Leaded and Lead Replacement petrol is increasingly difficult to find in Northern Europe.

Compulsory additional equipment

The driving laws of the countries of Europe still vary in what you are required to carry in your vehicle, although the consequences of not carrying a required piece of equipment are almost always an on-the-spot fine.

To meet these requirements we suggest that you carry the following:

- FIRE EXTINGUISHER
- BASIC TOOL KIT
- FIRST AID KIT
- SPARE BULBS
- TWO WARNING TRIANGLES – two are required in some countries at all times, and are compulsory in most countries when towing.
- HIGH VISIBILITY VEST – now compulsory in France, Spain, Italy and Austria (and likely to become compulsory throughout the EU) in case you need to walk on a motorway.

Insurance and Motoring Documents

Vehicle insurance

Contact your insurer well before you depart to check that your car insurance policy covers driving outside the UK. Most do, but many policies only provide minimum cover (so if you have an accident your insurance may only cover the cost of damage to the other person's property, with no cover for fire and theft).

To maintain the same level of cover abroad as you enjoy at home you need to tell your vehicle insurer. Some will automatically cover you abroad with no extra cost and no extra paperwork. Some will say you need a Green Card (which is neither green nor on card) but won't charge for it. Some will charge extra for the Green Card. Ideally you should contact your vehicle insurer 3-4 weeks before you set off, and confirm your conversation with them in writing.

Breakdown insurance

Arrange breakdown cover for your trip in good time so that if your vehicle breaks down or is involved in an accident it (and your caravan or trailer) can be repaired or returned to this country. This cover can usually be arranged as part of your travel insurance policy (see below).

Documents you must take with you

You may be asked to show your documents at any time so make sure that they are in order, up-to-date and easily accessible while you travel. These are what you need to take:

- **Passports** (you may also need a visa in some countries if you hold either a UK passport not issued in the UK or a passport that was issued outside the EU).
- **Motor Insurance Certificate**, including Green Card (or Continental Cover clause)
- **DVLC Vehicle Registration Document** plus, if not your own vehicle, the owner's written authority to drive.
- **A full valid Driving Licence** (not provisional). The new photo style licence is now mandatory in most European countries).

Personal Holiday insurance

Even though you are just travelling within Europe you must take out travel insurance. Few EU countries pay the full cost of medical treatment even under reciprocal health service arrangements. The first part of a holiday insurance policy covers people. It will include the cost of doctor, ambulance and hospital treatment if needed. If needed the better companies will even pay for English language speaking doctors and nurses and will bring a sick or injured holidaymaker home by air ambulance.

An important part of the insurance, often ignored, is cancellation (and curtailment) cover. Few things are as heartbreaking as having to cancel a holiday because a member of the family falls ill. Cancellation insurance can't take away the disappointment, but it makes sure you don't suffer financially as well. For this reason you should arrange your holiday insurance at least eight weeks before you set off.

Whichever insurance you choose we would advise reading very carefully the policies sold by the High Street travel trade. Whilst they may be good, they may not cover the specific needs of campers, caravanners and motorcaravanners.

Telephone **0870 405 4059** for a quote for our European Camping Holiday Insurance with cover arranged through Green Flag Motoring Assistance and Inter Group Assistance Services, one of the UK's largest assistance companies. Alternatively visit our website at **www.insure4campers.com.**

Travelling continued

European Health Insurance Card (EHIC)

Make sure you apply for your EHIC before travelling in Europe. Eligible travellers from the UK are entitled to receive free or reduced-cost medical care in many European countries on production of an EHIC. This free card is available by completing a form in the booklet 'Health Advice for Travellers' from local Post Offices. One should be completed for each family member. Alternatively visit **www.dh.gov.uk/travellers** and apply on-line. Please allow time to send your application off and have the EHIC returned to you.

The EHIC is valid in all European Community countries plus Iceland, Liechtenstein, Switzerland and Norway. If you or any of your dependants are suddenly taken ill or have an accident during a visit to any of these countries, free or reduced-cost emergency treatment is available - in most cases on production of a valid EHIC.

Only state-provided emergency treatment is covered, and you will receive treatment on the same terms as nationals of the country you are visiting. Private treatment is generally not covered, and state-provided treatment may not cover all of the things that you would expect to receive free of charge from the NHS.

Remember an EHIC does not cover you for all the medical costs that you can incur or for repatriation - it is not an alternative to travel insurance. You will still need appropriate insurance to ensure you are fully covered for all eventualities.

Travelling with children

Most countries in Europe are enforcing strict guidelines when you are travelling with children who are not your own. A minor (under the age of 18) must be accompanied by a parent or legal guardian or must carry a letter of authorisation from a parent or guardian. The letter should name the adult responsible for the minor during his or her stay. Similarily, a minor travelling with just one of his/her parents, must have a letter of authority to leave their home country from the parent staying behind. Full information is available at **www.fco.gov.uk**

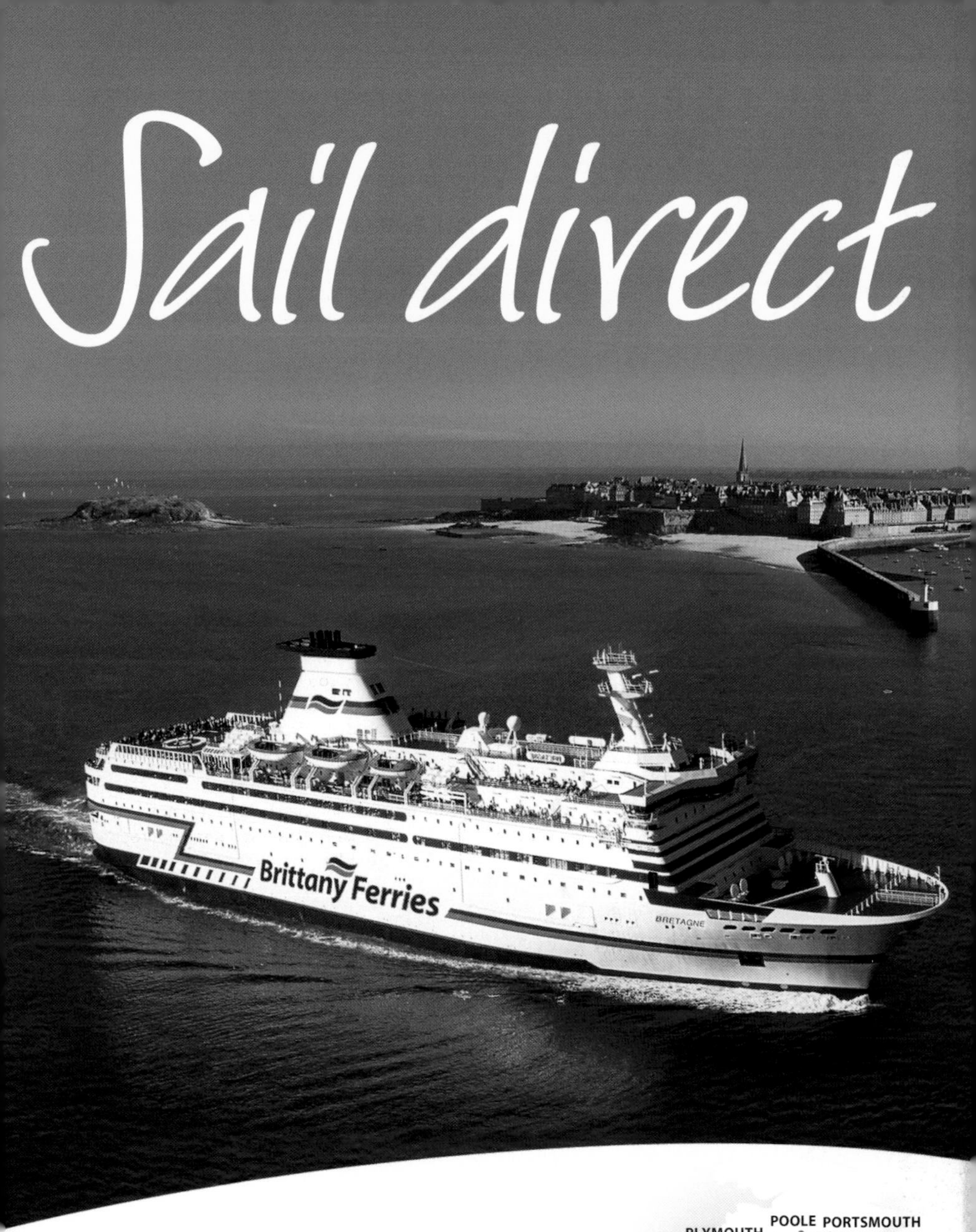
Sail direct
Brittany Ferries

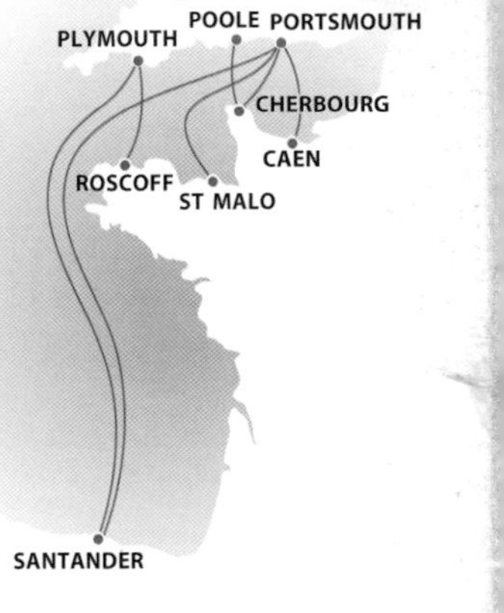
PLYMOUTH
POOLE
PORTSMOUTH
CHERBOURG
CAEN
ROSCOFF
ST MALO
SANTANDER

LES CASTELS

Superb 4-star touring sites in exceptional settings across France

Camping★★★★ • Caravaning • Chalets • Mobil-homes • Gîtes

come to Les Castels where the grounds of nning castles, beautiful manors and charming ntry houses provide unique natural settings for e of the finest touring sites in France, all created by owners with a passion for the simpler things in life. You will be assured of a warm and courteous welcome, tranquil surroundings, great services and a taste of authentic French "art de vivre".

- urtesy, conviviality & hospitality
- oice, comfort and 4-star quality
- perb touring pitches
- cellent services & facilities

ntact us for a brochure and discover astels site that matches your idea of a fect holiday destination.

DISCOVER OUR LOYALTY PROGRAMME, THE CASTELLISME CARD!

Enjoy Castellissime Card advantages, all year round! Earn points during your stay in any of Les Castels campsites, then redeem them for up to 15%* price reductions on your next stay!

**Season-based, from 2% to 15% (view the GSC on www les-castels.com)*

ok on line on:

ww.les-castels.com

4 STARS ★ AND A SOUL

Les Castels - Manoir de Terre Rouge - 35270 Bonnemain - France
Tel. +33 (0)2 23 16 03 20 / Fax +33 (0)2 23 16 03 23

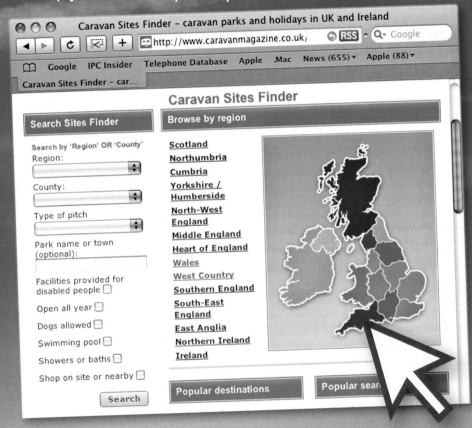

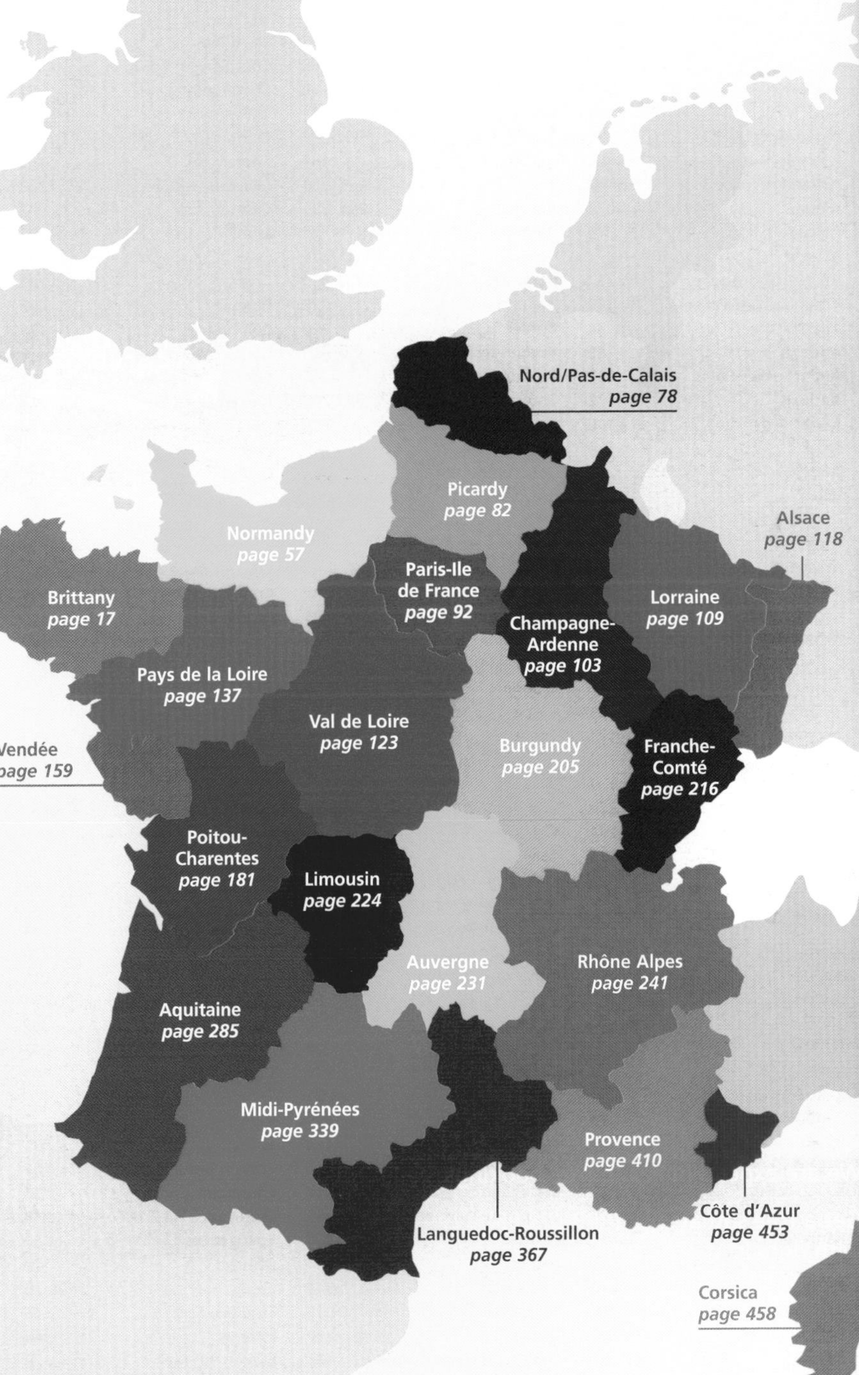
Nord/Pas-de-Calais
page 78
Picardy
page 82
Alsace
page 118
Normandy
page 57
Paris-Ile
de France
page 92
Brittany
page 17
Lorraine
page 109
Champagne-
Ardenne
page 103
Pays de la Loire
page 137
Val de Loire
page 123
Burgundy
page 205
Franche-
Comté
page 216
Vendée
page 159
Poitou-
Charentes
page 181
Limousin
page 224
Auvergne
page 231
Rhône Alpes
page 241
Aquitaine
page 285
Midi-Pyrénées
page 339
Provence
page 410
Côte d'Azur
page 453
Languedoc-Roussillon
page 367
Corsica
page 458

Town and Village Index

Index by Campsite Number

FR01030 - FR09120

FR10010 - FR19140

Index by Campsite Number continued

Index by Campsite Number continued

FR60020 - FR69030

Index by Campsite Number continued

Index by Campsite Region and Name

Index by Campsite Region and Name continued

Picardy

Paris-Ile de France

Champagne-Ardenne

Lorraine

Alsace

Val de Loire

Pays de la Loire

Vendée

Poitou-Charentes

Burgundy

Index by Campsite Region and Name continued

Aquitaine

Index by Campsite Region and Name continued

Languedoc-Roussillon

Provence